The
AMERICAN
FAMILY
COOKBOOK

The AMERICAN FAMILY COOKBOOK

Edited by Melanie De Proft

Revised by
the Staff of the Culinary Arts Institute

Culinary Arts Institute
Chicago

Acknowledgments

The generous support and cooperation of many private organizations within the food industry have helped make this book a success. The publishers wish to acknowledge their contributions and thank them for furnishing the color photographs: American Dairy Association (*opposite pages 65 — top, 576, and 577, and the endpapers*); Brussels Sprout Marketing Program; Brussels Sprout Shippers of California (*opposite page 321*); California Strawberry Advisory Board (*opposite pages 64 and 512*); Filbert/Hazelnut Commission (*opposite page 256*); General Foods Kitchen (*opposite page 416*); International Shrimp Council (*opposite page 352*); Japan External Trade Organization (*opposite page 353*); National Cherry Growers and Industries Foundation (*opposite page 417*); National Kraut Packers Association (*opposite page 320*); Pickle Packers International, Inc. (*opposite page 257*); Poultry & Egg National Board (*opposite page 513*); 7-Up (*opposite page 65 — bottom, and 193*); Spanish Green Olive Commission (*opposite page 192*).

CULINARY ARTS INSTITUTE STAFF
Sherrill Corley • Bertha Gehrke • Helen Geist
Ingeborg Karlowicz • Ivanka Simatic

Designed by Jeanne Pearson

Illustrated by Luciana Peters

The American family has a rich culinary heritage which has been derived from the many groups living within the United States. No other country produces such a tremendous variety of foods to satisfy the taste preferences of each group within it.

In the early days, the availability of the foodstuffs, rather than the settlers' tastes, was the main factor in shaping the American menu. The colonists had to learn to live on whatever was readily available in their new surroundings, even if such foods as beechnuts, squash, corn, red squirrels, and raccoon meat were strange to their tastes.

As living conditions in the New World improved, people were guided by their traditions in the choice of grains and vegetables they planted, and the fruits and livestock they raised. Corn bread, succotash, baked beans, and pumpkin pie, once accepted out of sheer necessity, have now become lasting favorites of the American people.

Thus, from the beginning, the spirit of American cooking has been one of discovery. It has remained so through the years. As new lands were colonized, regional specialties such as the Maryland crab, Virginia oyster, Louisiana shrimp, and Florida orange were discovered by the pioneers, who soon incorporated them into their daily fare. This rich variety of foods alone would have made the American cuisine unique. But our culinary horizon was further expanded by the arrival in this country of immigrants from the "four corners of the earth." Each group of newcomers brought its recipes for special dishes and its favored spices and delicacies. Many of these ethnic specialties were shared with neighbors who found them to their liking. Improved transportation, the advent of refrigeration and freezing, and progress in food processing and marketing further increased the variety of foods available to the American family.

Our culinary curiosity continues unabated. The recent increase in the number of Americans traveling abroad and their exposure to new eating experiences have resulted in many exotic dishes gaining wide acceptance in this country.

THE AMERICAN FAMILY COOKBOOK reflects this universality of our tastes, the stupendous wealth of our land, and the diverse styles of life in this country. It is a cookbook for the beginner as well as the experienced homemaker, designed to meet the needs of today's American families.

Melanie De Proft

Contents

Culinary Know-How

Presented here are basic information for food preparation and reference material. Before you begin to cook, read especially Use Correct Techniques, Culinary Terms, and How To Do It. Become familiar with the other information given and refer to it as needed.

EQUIPPING YOUR KITCHEN

Your choice of equipment often depends upon the amount of cupboard and other storage space available. With a minimum of space one must choose essential items wisely, making sure that a bulky item such as a large saucepot or skillet can serve more than one purpose. The following list should help in making a wise choice of equipment.

For food preparation:

Set of measuring spoons—¼ teaspoon, ½ teaspoon, 1 teaspoon, 1 tablespoon
Set (or nest) of measuring cups—¼ cup, ⅓ cup, ½ cup, 1 cup
Glass measuring cups for liquids—1 cup, 2 cups (1 pint), 4 cups (1 quart)
Mixing bowls—1 pint, 1 quart, 3 quarts
Knives—butcher knife, serrated bread knife, slicing knife (with long, thin blade), chopping knife (French), paring knives, grapefruit knife
Forks—long-handled fork, two-tined fork, two or three small forks, blending fork
Spoons—three wooden spoons of various sizes and lengths, slotted metal spoon, slotted

wooden spoon, two metal tablespoons, three metal teaspoons
Spatulas—small, medium
Rubber scrapers—two plate and bowl scrapers (wide), one bottle and jar scraper (narrow)
Beater—hand rotary type
Strainers—small, medium
Colander
Cookie cutters—assorted sizes and shapes
Juicer or reamer
Vegetable parer
Vegetable brush (stiff)
Kitchen shears
Apple corer
Graters—small hand grater, set of larger graters for fine and coarse grating and shredding
Cutting board
Wire cooling racks—

two or three
Pancake turner
Pastry blender
Rolling pin (stockinette cover)
Pastry brush
Pastry canvas
Flour sifter

For baking and top-of-range cooking:

Custard cups—six (6 ounce)
Muffin (or cupcake) pans—two sets of six (one set 1¾ x 1 inch, one set 2½ x 1¼ inch)
Casseroles with covers—1½, 2, and 3 quarts
Individual casseroles or ramekins—six
Pie pans—8 inch, 9 inch
Cake pan (square)—8 inch, 9 inch
Cake pans (round)—two or three 8 or 9 inch
Cake pan (tubed)—9 or 10 inch
Baking pan—11 x 7 x 1½ inch

Miscellaneous items (handy to have):

Food mill
Garlic press
Meat grinder
Timer
Wooden chopping bowl and chopper
Potato masher or ricer

Flour shaker
Salt and pepper shakers
Can opener (wall-type or electric)
Funnels
Ladle
Tongs

Loaf pan—9 x 5 x 3 inch
Open roasting pan—13 x 9 x 2 inch
Double boiler—1½ quarts
Saucepans with tight-fitting covers—1, 2, and 3 quarts
Dutch oven—3 quarts
Coffee maker—4 or 6 cups
Teakettle
Teapot—6 cups
Toaster
Skillets with tight-fitting covers—two (one small 6 or 8 inch, one large deep 10 inch)
Molds—two or three, including a ring mold

Melon ball cutter
Steam cooker
Ice cream scoop
Corkscrew and bottle opener
Knife sharpener—wall-type or electric

Tea ball
Thermometers—meat, candy, deep frying, portable oven thermometer (if oven is unreliable)
Sink strainer
Juice can opener
Biscuit and bun warmer
Jars with screw-top covers (for storing foods in refrigerator and on cupboard shelves)
Canister set

Hot pads, tiles, or stands (for hot dishes)
Pot holders
Garbage can
Freezer storage containers and moisture-vaporproof bags
Refrigerator storage dishes with covers
Aluminum foil
Paper baking cups
Waxed paper
Paper towels

Nice-to-have appliances:
Coffee maker
Waffle baker
Blender

Electric mixer—table-type or portable
Electric skillet

USE CORRECT TECHNIQUES

Read recipe carefully.

Assemble all ingredients and utensils.

Select pans of proper kind and size. Measure pans inside, from rim to rim.

Use standard measuring cups and spoons. Use liquid measuring cups (rim above 1-cup line) for liquids. Use nested or dry measuring cups (1-cup line even with top) for dry ingredients. When measuring with a tablespoon, use a standard one which holds 1/16 of a cup.

Check liquid measurements at eye level.

Level dry measurements with a straight-edged knife or spatula. Fill the cup, spoon, or other measure to overflowing before passing spatula or knife over top. *To measure flour*, fill cup lightly; do not dip measuring cup into container with flour. *To measure regular brown sugar*, pack into measuring cup so that sugar will hold the shape of cup when turned out.

Level fats with a spatula or straight edge of knife after pressing fat firmly into nested-type measuring cup. To measure amounts of fat less than 1 cup, use individual cups (¼, ⅓, or ½), or measure in tablespoons. The water-displacement method may be used if the water that clings to the fat will not affect the product. To measure ¼ cup fat, for example, pour ¾ cup cold water into a standard measuring cup for liquids. Then add the fat to water until the water level rises to the 1-cup mark in the cup. (Be sure water entirely covers the fat.) Drain off the water thoroughly.

Sift regular all-purpose flour before measuring if you so desire. Milling processes have improved considerably through the years until today's all-purpose flour is of such high quality that sifting is not always necessary. Follow miller's directions on the package, if available. Spoon, without sifting, the whole-grained types of flour (whole wheat, buckwheat, etc.) into measuring cup.

Beat whole eggs until thick and piled softly when recipe calls for well-beaten eggs.

Beat egg whites as follows: *Frothy*—entire mass forms bubbles; *Rounded peaks*—peaks turn over slightly when beater is slowly lifted upright; *Stiff peaks*—peaks remain standing when beater is slowly lifted upright.

Beat egg yolks until very thick when recipe calls for well-beaten egg yolks.

Place oven rack so top of product will be almost at center of oven. Stagger pans so no pan is directly over another and they do not touch each other or the walls of oven. Place single pan so that center of product is near center of oven.

Covering foods to be stored in the refrigerator will depend upon the type of refrigerator used.

MEASUREMENTS & EQUIVALENTS

Dash, speck, or few grains . less than ⅛ teaspoon
60 drops . . . . 1 teaspoon
3 teaspoons (½ fluid ounce) . . . . . . 1 tablespoon
⅛ cup (1 fluid ounce) . . . . 2 tablespoons
¼ cup (2 fluid ounces) . . . . 4 tablespoons
⅓ cup . . . . 5 tablespoons plus 1 teaspoon
½ cup (4 fluid ounces) . . . . 8 tablespoons
⅔ cup . . . . 10 tablespoons plus 2 teaspoons
¾ cup (6 fluid ounces) . . . . 12 tablespoons
1 cup (8 fluid ounces) . . . . 16 tablespoons
2 cups (16 fluid ounces) . . . . 1 pint
4 cups (32 fluid ounces) . . . . 1 quart
2 pints . . . . 1 quart
2 quarts . . . . ½ gallon
4 quarts (liquid) . . . . 1 gallon
8 quarts (dry) . . . . 1 peck
4 pecks . . . . 1 bushel
16 ounces (dry measure) . . . . 1 pound
1 ounce . . . . 28.35 grams
1 pound . . . . 453.59 grams

Additional Equivalents & Substitutions

Baking powder, 1 teaspoon . . . 1 teaspoon cream of tartar plus ¼ teaspoon baking soda
Baking powder, double-acting . . . 1 teaspoon will leaven 1 cup flour

Baking soda .... ½ teaspoon with 1 cup fully soured milk will neutralize the acid in that amount of milk and leaven 1 cup flour
Bread, 1 to 2 slices (soft) .... 1 cup crumbs
    1 pound loaf ...... 10 cups small bread cubes
Butter, 1 cup .. ⅞ to 1 cup vegetable shortening or lard plus ½ teaspoon salt
Butter or margarine, 2 tablespoons .... 1 ounce
    ½ cup (4 ounces) .... 1 stick
Chocolate, unsweetened, 1 square ..... 1 ounce
    1 square .... 3 to 4 tablespoons cocoa plus 1 tablespoon shortening
Cornstarch, 1 tablespoon ..... 2 tablespoons all-purpose flour
Cream, light (20%), 1 cup ...... ⅞ cup milk plus 3 tablespoons butter
Cream, heavy (40%), 1 cup .... ¾ cup milk plus ⅓ cup butter
    1 cup .... 2 cups whipped
Eggs, whole, 4 to 6 .... 1 cup
    whites, 8 to 10 .... 1 cup
    yolks, 10 to 14 .... 1 cup
Flour, cake, 1 cup sifted .... ⅞ cup (or 1 cup minus 2 tablespoons) all-purpose flour
Garlic, 1 clove ...... ¼ teaspoon garlic powder
Marshmallows, 10 miniature .... 1 large
    16 large .... ¼ pound (4 ounces)
Onion, ¼ cup chopped ..... 1 tablespoon instant minced onion or 1 teaspoon onion powder
Sugar, granulated, 2¼ cups .... 1 pound
    superfine, 2⅓ cups .... 1 pound
    brown, about 2¼ cups firmly packed . 1 pound
    granulated brown, about 3⅛ cups ... 1 pound
    confectioners', 3½ cups .... 1 pound
Syrup, corn, about 1½ cups .... 1 pound
    maple, about 1½ cups .... 1 pound

INGREDIENTS

Baking powder—double-acting type.

Bread crumbs—two slices fresh bread equals about 1 cup soft bread crumbs or ¼-inch cubes. One slice dry or toasted bread equals about ½ cup dry cubes or ¼ to ⅓ cup fine dry crumbs. *Buttered crumbs* are soft or dry bread or cracker crumbs tossed in melted butter or margarine. Use 1 to 2 tablespoons butter or margarine for 1 cup soft crumbs and 2 to 4 tablespoons butter or margarine for 1 cup dry crumbs.

Catsup—See *Ketchup.*

Chocolate—the term chocolate refers to *unsweetened* chocolate. *Sweet chocolate* is chocolate with sugar added. It may also contain cocoa butter and flavorings. It is used for dipping candies and other confections. *Semisweet chocolate* is small pieces or 1-ounce squares formed from slightly sweetened chocolate and used for candymaking or baked products, or eaten as a confection. (Also available in the form of bars.) *Cocoa* is a powdered chocolate product from which some of the cocoa butter has been removed. The fat content varies from 10% to 22%. *Breakfast cocoa* is a high-fat cocoa which contains at least 22% cocoa fat. *Dutch process cocoa* can be either "cocoa" or "breakfast cocoa" which is processed with one or more alkaline materials as permitted under government regulations. *Instant cocoa* is a mixture of cocoa, sugar, and an emulsifier. It can be prepared for use by dissolving in hot liquid with no cooking necessary.

Cornstarch—thickening agent. 1 tablespoon has the thickening power of 2 tablespoons flour.

Fats and Oils—Butter is fat from sour or sweet cream gathered in a mass, sometimes salted and colored. It contains not less than 80% by weight of milk fat. *Unsalted butter* is butter made from sweet cream. Also called sweet butter. *Whipped butter* is butter into which air has been whipped. *Cooking or salad oils* include: corn oil, refined from the dried, crushed corn germ; cottonseed oil, refined from the crushed seed of the cotton plant; peanut oil, the oil extracted from peanuts, a by-product of peanut butter; safflower oil, the oil extracted from the seed of the safflower plant, used for cooking purposes and also used commercially for the manufacture of safflower margarine. *Cracklings* are the residue from rendered fat of meat. *Hard fats* are coconut or palm oils in solid form used mostly in candymaking. *Lard* is fat rendered from the fatty tissues of the hog. *Margarine* is made by the emulsification of various oils with cultured milk and further processing to produce a consistency similar to that of butter; contains 80% fat; usually colored; may or may not have salt added. Soft-type and whipped margarine are also available. *Olive oil* is oil from the flesh of ripe olives. Virgin olive oil is that which is first extracted and is better in flavor and appearance than the oil produced by the second or third pressing. Use olive oil when specified in a recipe. *Poultry fat* is a cooking fat made commercially by rendering the leaf fat removed from the body cavities of chickens and turkeys and sometimes from the fat that is skimmed from vats of poultry being cooked for canning. *Shortening* is a general term used for cooking fats. May be meat fats or vegetable oils. Or, may be a blend of animal fats; or a blend of vegetable oils; or a blend of animal and vegetable. *Suet* is the clear, white fat of beef and mutton.

Flour—the term flour when used in recipes with no other qualifications as to special purpose or preparation (bread, cake, self-rising flour) usually refers to all-purpose or general-purpose flour. *Bread flour* is milled from blends of spring and winter hard wheats or from either type alone. It has a fairly high protein content and is slightly granular to the touch. It may be bleached or unbleached and is milled mostly for commercial bakers. *All-purpose flour* is a blend of hard or soft wheat flours which are lower in protein content than bread flour, but higher than cake flour. It can usually be used with good results for most home-baked products. Blends are prepared to satisfy the demands of different areas. In the South, for instance, a softer blend is available to make satisfactory quick breads, while in the North a harder blend is marketed for use in making yeast breads and rolls. *Instant-blending flour* is an all-purpose flour which some associate with the term "instantized" to indicate that the flour dissolves readily in liquids without forming lumps. *Self-rising flour* is flour to which leavening agents and salt have been added in proper proportions for home-baking. The leavening agent most often used, with soda, is calcium phosphate. *Whole-wheat flour* (also graham flour) is flour milled so that the natural constituents of the wheat kernel remain unaltered. *Pastry flour* is made of either hard or soft wheats, but usually the latter. It is fairly low in protein and finely milled though not as fine as cake flour. It is used chiefly by bakers and biscuit manufacturers. *Cake flour* is milled from soft wheats. The protein content is low and the granulation so fine that the flour feels soft and satiny.

Fruit pectin—a substance in fruit which, when used in the right proportions with sugar and acid, forms a jelly. *Liquid or bottled pectin* is refined from apple juice. *Powdered pectin* is made from citrus or apple pectin, then dried and packaged.

Gelatin—a granulated animal product used to thicken salads, desserts, and some soups. Available unflavored or in packaged form with sugar, color, and flavoring.

Grated peel—whole citrus fruit peel finely grated through colored part only (white is bitter).

Herb bouquet (bouquet garni)—a bunch of aromatic herbs (such as a piece of celery with leaves, a sprig of thyme, 3 or 4 sprigs of parsley, and sometimes a bay leaf) tied neatly together and used to flavor soups, stews, braised dishes, and sauces. Enclose fine, dry herbs in a cheesecloth bag.

Julienne strips—vegetables, meats, poultry, or cheese, cut into narrow strips.

Ketchup—a smooth, well-seasoned tomato relish.

Milk and Milk Products—*Fresh fluid milk* contains not less than 3.25% milk fat and not less than 8.25% milk solids other than fat. *Vitamin D milk* is whole or skim milk in which the vitamin D content has been increased. *Homogenized milk* is fresh milk in which the size of the fat globules is reduced so that the cream does not rise to the top. *Evaporated milk* is sterilized homogenized milk containing about 60% less water than whole milk. When diluted with an equal amount of water, it is used as fresh whole milk. It is also used, undiluted, as cream. *Sweetened condensed milk* is milk from which about half the water has been removed. It contains a large amount of added sugar which acts as a preservative. *Skim milk* is milk from which most of the fat has been removed thereby reducing its vitamin A content. Some skim milks are fortified by adding a water-soluble vitamin A and D concentrate. *Sour milk*, see *To sour milk, page 20*. *Buttermilk* as sold in retail markets is usually a cultured (fermented) product made of fresh skim milk. (It is also the by-product from churning cream into butter.) The bacterial culture used converts the milk sugar into lactic acid. Cultured buttermilk may also be made from fresh fluid whole milk, concentrated fluid milk, or reconstituted nonfat dry milk. *Dry milk (whole) and dry milk (nonfat)* are made from fresh whole milk and skim milk respectively. After most of the water has been removed from them they are dried until a fine-textured powder results. The process has no appreciable effect on the nutritive value and when mixed with water these products have the original composition of pasteurized milk. *Yogurt* is a cultured product (with a consistency resembling custard) usually made from fresh partially skimmed milk enriched with added milk solids other than fats. Fermentation is accomplished by a mixed bacterial culture. *Half and half* is a mixture of milk and cream, usually 10% to 12% fat. *Light cream*, sometimes referred to as table or coffee cream, contains 18% to 20% fat. *Heavy (or whipping) cream* contains between 30% and 36% fat. *Dairy sour cream* is a cultured product sold commercially and made by adding bacterial cultures to pasteurized and homogenized cream. (See *To sour cream, page 20*.)

Monosodium glutamate (Accent, MSG, and others)—a basic seasoning produced from natural sources and added to foods to enhance their characteristic flavors without adding a flavor of its own.

Packaged mixes—flour combined with other ingredients such as shortening, baking powder or other leavening agent, sugar, and dry milk; marketed in packages. They require only the addition of liquid and sometimes eggs to prepare a batter from them.

Sugars and Syrups—*Granulated sugar* is a highly refined white sugar composed of almost pure sucrose which is found in large quantities in sugar cane and sugar beets. *Superfine granulated sugar* is a specially screened, uniformly fine-grained sugar used in cakes and in mixing drinks. *Confectioners' (powdered) sugar* is granulated sugar crushed and screened to desired fineness. A small amount of cornstarch is added to prevent caking. Confectioners' sugar is used in frostings and icings and for dusting doughnuts, pastries, etc. *Brown sugar* is unrefined cane sugar which varies in color from very light to very dark. It contains various amounts of molasses, some non-sugars (ash) naturally present in molasses, and moisture. *Granulated brown sugar* is a specially processed brown sugar which does not harden and can be poured from the package. To substitute for regular brown sugar, see manufacturer's equivalents table. *Maple sugar* is a solid product obtained by evaporating maple sap or maple syrup to the point where crystallization occurs. *Molasses* is the liquor remaining after the crystallization of raw sugar from the concentrated sap of the sugar cane. Sometimes a second and third crystallization is made, resulting in two grades of molasses known as "light" and "dark" molasses. When a large proportion of the sugar has been removed, the resulting product has a strong flavor and is called "black strap." It is used for fermentation purposes. *Sorghum (or sorgo)* is a syrup somewhat resembling molasses produced from a cane-like grass. It has a mild flavor appealing to many people especially in the Southwest where the grass is grown. *Corn syrup* is a product resulting from the partial hydrolysis of cornstarch with coloring and flavoring usually added to the syrup. Light and dark corn syrups are marketed. Many table syrups contain some corn syrup combined with such sweeteners as sorghum, cane syrup, or honey and butterscotch or vanilla for flavoring. *Honey* is defined as "the nectar and saccharine exudations of plants gathered, modified, and stored by the honey bee." Honey must contain not more than 25% water. The flavor and color of honey depends upon the source of the nectar. Orange blossoms, clover, buckwheat, and basswood are common sources. *Maple syrup* comes from the sap of the maple tree collected in early spring and concentrated to the desired consistency. Pure maple syrup contains not over 35% water. *Sugar substitutes* are non-caloric sweetening agents. *Sugar syrup* is a solution of sugar and water used to sweeten beverages, see *page 610*.

Tenderizer, Instant Meat—powdered product, seasoned and unseasoned, used on less tender cuts of meat; follow label directions.

Vinegar—usually refers to cider vinegar when the type of vinegar is not specified in recipe.

CULINARY TERMS

Bake—To cook in a container (covered or uncovered) in an oven or oven-type appliance. Usually called roasting when applied to meats, see *Roast, page 15*.

Barbecue—To roast or broil on a rack over hot coals or on a revolving spit in front of or over heat source.

Baste—To spoon liquid (or use baster) over cooking food to add moisture and flavor.

Beat—To make a mixture smooth by introducing air with a brisk motion that lifts the mixture over and over, or with a rotary motion as with a hand rotary beater or electric mixer.

Blanch—To preheat or precook in boiling water or steam. This process is used to inactivate enzymes and shrink food for canning, freezing, and drying. The blanching process is also used to aid in the removal of skins from nuts, see *page 19*, fruits, and vegetables.

Blend—To mix two or more ingredients so that each loses its identity.

Boil—To cook in liquid in which bubbles rise continually and break on the surface. Boiling temperature of water at sea level is 212°F.

Braise—To cook slowly in a covered utensil in a small amount of liquid or in steam. (Meat may or may not be browned in small amount of fat before braising.)

Bread—To coat with bread crumbs alone or to coat with bread crumbs, then with diluted slightly beaten egg or evaporated milk, and again with crumbs.

Broil—To cook by direct heat.

Candy—To cook fruit (also citrus fruit peel and ginger) in a heavy syrup until plump and transparent, then drain and dry. Candied product is also known as crystallized fruit, peel, or ginger. Term also applies to vegetables cooked in a syrup or sugar and fat mixture (i.e. candied sweet potatoes or carrots). Candy is synonymous with glaze (*i.e.* glazed or candied cherries).

Caramelize—To heat dry sugar or foods containing sugar until a brown color and characteristic flavor develop.

Chop—To cut into pieces with a knife or other sharp tool. (Also see *Mince, below.*)

Coddle—To cook slowly just below the boiling point (as applied to eggs and fruit).

Combine—To mix ingredients.

Cream—To mix one or more foods together until soft and creamy. Usually applied to shortening and sugar.

Cube—See *Dice, below.*

Cut in—To distribute solid fat in dry ingredients by chopping with pastry blender or knives until finely divided.

Devil—To mix with hot seasoning as pepper, mustard.

Dice—To cut into small cubes.

Dissolve—To cause a liquid and a dry substance to pass into solution.

Dredge—To coat or sprinkle with flour or other fine substance.

Flake fish (freshly cooked or canned)—Gently separating the fish into flakes, using a fork. Remove the bony tissue from crab meat while flaking it. (Bones of salmon are edible and need not be removed.)

Fold—To combine by using two motions, one which cuts vertically through the mixture (using a flexible metal or rubber spatula or wire whisk) and the other which turns the mixture over by sliding the implement across the bottom of the mixing bowl.

Fricassee—To cook by braising (usually applied to poultry, rabbit, and veal).

Fry—To cook in fat; called *sauté* or *panfry* when cooking with a small amount of fat; called *deep-fat frying* when cooking in a deep layer of fat.

Glacé—To coat with a thin sugar syrup cooked to the crack stage. When used for pies and certain types of bread the mixture may contain a thickening, but it is not cooked to such a concentrated form as for a glacé; or it may be uncooked.

Grate—To reduce to small particles by rubbing on anything rough and indented. Use a rotary-type grater with hand-operated crank for grating chocolate and nuts, following manufacturer's directions. Grated chocolate and nuts should be fine and light.

Grind—To reduce food to particles by cutting, crushing (electric blender may be used), or by forcing through a food chopper.

Knead—To manipulate with a pressing motion plus folding and stretching. (To knead bread, see *page 61.*)

Lard—To insert matchlike strips of fat, called lardoons, into gashes in side of uncooked lean meat by means of a larding needle or skewer; or to place on top of meat.

Marinate—To allow food to stand in liquid (usually a seasoned oil and acid mixture) to impart additional flavor.

Mask—To cover completely; usually applied to the use of mayonnaise or other thick sauce but may refer to forcemeat or jelly.

Mince—To cut or chop into small, fine pieces.

Mix—To combine ingredients in any way that effects a distribution.

Panbroil—To cook uncovered on a hot surface, usually in a skillet. (For meat, see *page 155.*)

Parboil—To boil uncooked food until partially cooked. The cooking is usually completed by another method.

Parch—To brown by means of dry heat. Applied to grains.

Pare—To cut off the outside covering. Applied to potatoes, apples, etc.

Pasteurize—To preserve food by heating to a temperature (140° to 180°F) which will destroy certain microorganisms and arrest fermentation. Applied to milk and fruit juices.

Peel—To strip off the outer covering. Applied to oranges, grapefruit, etc.

Poach—To cook in a hot liquid using precautions to retain shape. The temperature used varies with the food.

Purée—To force through a fine sieve or food mill or to blend in an electric blender until a smooth thick mixture is obtained.

Reconstitute—To restore concentrated foods to their normal state, usually by adding water. Applied to such foods as nonfat dry milk or frozen fruit juices.

Reduce liquid—To continue cooking the liquid until the amount is sufficiently decreased, thus concentrating flavor and sometimes thickening the original liquid. Simmer when wine is used; boil rapidly for other liquids.

Render—To remove fat from connective tissue over low heat.

Rice—To force food through ricer, sieve, or food mill.

Roast—To cook by dry heat, usually in an oven.

Scald milk—To heat in top of a double boiler over simmering water or in a heavy saucepan over direct heat just until a thin film appears. The term scald is also used when simmering certain foods in boiling water for a few seconds, see *Blanch, page 13.*

Scallop—To bake food, usually with sauce or other liquid. The top may be covered with crumbs. The food and sauce may be mixed in the baking dish or arranged in alternate layers with or without crumbs.

Score—To make cuts in the surface of meat before roasting, usually making a diamond pattern (example roast ham).

Sear—To brown meat quickly with intense heat.

Sieve—To force through a sieve.

Simmer—To cook in a liquid just below boiling point; bubbles form slowly and break below surface.

Steam—To cook in steam with or without pressure. The steam may be applied directly to food (*i.e.*, pressure cooker).

Steep—To allow a substance to stand in liquid below the boiling point for the purpose of extracting flavor, color, or other qualities.

Sterilize—To destroy microorganisms. For culinary purposes this is usually done at a high temperature with steam, dry heat, or by boiling in a liquid.

Stew—To cook slowly in a small amount of liquid.

Stir—To mix food ingredients with a circular motion in order to blend them.

Truss—To fasten the cavity of stuffed poultry or meat with skewers and/or cord.

Whip—To beat rapidly to produce expansion due to incorporation of air as applied to eggs, gelatin mixtures, and cream, see *To whip cream, page 20.*

PURCHASING CANNED PRODUCTS

A smart homemaker will become familiar with the sizes of canned (also packaged) goods available to her. She should also demand a certain standard in the contents. Keeping a record is helpful, grading the products as she uses them as good or poor, thus enabling her to select the best quality for the money. The common container sizes for canned foods are given below along with the Industry term which is sometimes given in recipes instead of the weight of the can.

Approximate Net Weight	Industry Term	Approximate Cups	Contents
8 oz.	8 oz.	1	Fruits, vegetables, some specialties
10½ to 12 oz.	Picnic	1¼	Condensed soups, fish, seafood, some fruits and vegetables, boned meats and poultry
12 oz.	12 oz. (vacuum)	1½	Corn (whole kernel)
14 to 16 oz.	No. 300	1¾	Pork and beans, cranberry sauce, meat products, blueberries, some specialties
16 to 17 oz.	No. 303	2	Fruits, vegetables, meat products, some specialties

Approximate Net Weight	Industry Term	Approximate Cups	Contents
1 lb. 4 oz. (20 oz.)	No. 2	2½	Few vegetables and fruits, some ready-to-serve foods
1 pt. 2 fl. oz. (18 fl. oz.)			Vegetable and fruit juices
1 lb. 13 oz. (29 oz.)	No. 2½	3½	Fruits, some vegetables (pumpkin, sauerkraut, spinach and other greens, tomatoes)
3 lbs. 3 oz. or 1 qt. 14 fl. oz. (46 oz.)	No. 3 (cylinder)	5¾	Fruit and vegetable juices, pork and beans, condensed soups, or some vegetables for institutional use
6 lbs. 8 oz. to 7 lbs. 5 oz.	No. 10	12 to 13	Fruits and vegetables for restaurant and institutional use
14 oz.		1¼	Sweetened condensed milk
6 oz.		⅔	Evaporated milk
14½ oz.		1⅔	Evaporated milk

NOTE: While the size of the can is standardized, there is a variation in weights of cans used by different canneries. This difference in weight is probably due to a more solid pack or a greater density in the syrup content used in the heavier cans. Homemakers, however can read on the label of the can not only the weight to expect, but often the number of servings.

Sizes-and-Servings of Canned and Frozen Vegetables

Canned and frozen vegetables are packed by net weight rather than volume. Therefore, deciding which can or package to buy is often difficult.

The size of an individual serving of cooked vegetables commonly used for an adult is one-half cup. However, a light eater, also a child, often finds one-fourth or one-third cup sufficient.

The number of cups obtained from a certain size container varies somewhat. The following chart shows an approximate amount of cooked vegetables obtained from average container sizes. It should help you to determine how many cans or packages you will need for your family and whether smaller or larger sizes are best for you.

Vegetable	Cans (drained)		Frozen	
	Can size	Cups	Package size	Cups
Asparagus, cut	14 oz.	1⅓	10 oz.	1¼
Beans, green or wax, cut	15½ oz.	1¾	9 oz.	1⅔
Beans, lima	16 oz.	1¾	10 oz.	1⅔
Beets, sliced, diced, whole	16 oz.	1¾		
Broccoli, cut			10 oz.	1½
Carrots, diced, sliced	16 oz.	1¾	10 oz.	1⅔
Cauliflower			10 oz.	1½
Corn, whole kernel	16 oz.	1⅔	10 oz.	1½
Kale	15 oz.	1⅓	10 oz.	1⅛
Okra	15½ oz.	1¾	10 oz.	1¼
Peas	16 oz.	1¾	10 oz.	1⅔
Potatoes, French fried			9 oz.	1⅔
Spinach	15 oz.	1⅓	10 oz.	1¼
Squash, summer, sliced			10 oz.	1⅓
Tomatoes (undrained)	16 oz.	1⅞		

OVEN TEMPERATURES

Very slow . . . . 250° to 275°F
Slow . . . . 300° to 325°F
Moderate . . . . 350° to 375°F
Hot . . . . 400° to 425°F
Very hot . . . . 450° to 475°F
Extremely hot* . . . . 500° to 525°F

*When you broil, set regulator at *Broil*. Distance from top of food to source of heat determines the intensity of heat upon food.
NOTE: Use a portable oven thermometer for double checking oven temperatures. When baking in glass, decrease oven temperature by about 25°F.

TIMETABLE FOR BAKING*

Food	Oven Temperature	Approx. Baking Time (Minutes, except as noted)
Yeast Breads		
Loaves	400°F	35 to 55
Dinner rolls	400°–425°F	15 to 25
Sweet rolls	375°–400°F	20 to 30
Quick Breads		
Fruit and nut loaves	350°–375°F	1 to 1¼ hours
Cornbreads	400°–425°F	25 to 40
Biscuits	425°–450°F	10 to 15
Muffins	400°–425°F	20 to 25
Popovers	375°F	1 hour
Cakes		
Layers, round or square	350°–375°F	25 to 40
Rectangular	350°–375°F	35 to 50
Loaf	350°F	45 to 75
Pound	300°–325°F	1 to 1½ hours
Fruitcakes	275°–300°F	2 to 4 hours
Angel food and sponge	350°–375°F	30 to 60
Cupcakes, standard size	350°–375°F	15 to 25
Pies and Pie Shells		
Custard-type pies in unbaked shell	400°–425°F	30 to 45
Two-crust pies, uncooked filling	400°–425°F	45 to 60
cooked filling	400°–450°F	30 to 45
Pie and tart shells	450°F	10 to 15
Crumb crusts	350°–375°F	8 to 10
Cookies		
Bar	350°–375°F	25 to 30
Drop	350°–400°F	8 to 15
Rolled or molded	375°–400°F	7 to 12
Miscellaneous		
Custard, baked in pan of hot water	325°–350°F	45 to 60
Macaroni and cheese	350°F	25 to 30
Rice pudding (uncooked rice)	300°F	2 to 3 hours
Scalloped potatoes	350°F	1 to 2 hours
Soufflés, baked in pan of hot water	325°–350°F	50 to 60

*When baking products from packaged mixes, follow manufacturer's directions.

HOW TO STORE FOODS

The proper treatment and storage of foods after purchasing is an important part of good homemaking. Foods stored correctly keep fresh longer, they offer more in both flavor and food values, and are more appetizing in appearance than those given little or no attention.

Some foods are best stored at room temperature, some need dry, cool storage, some should be stored in the refrigerator, and of course frozen foods need below zero storage. Refer to specific chapters for direction on proper storage of foods.

HIGH ALTITUDE COOKING

The homemaker who lives in a high-altitude region, or moves to one, soon realizes that changes must be made in many of her recipes. These changes usually involve a slight adjustment in cooking temperatures and, in the case of some baked goods, an adjustment in ingredients. Most basic recipes are adaptable without changes in areas where the altitude is not more than 3000 feet above sea level. The difference in atmospheric pressure (it decreases at higher altitude) makes it necessary to cook vegetables longer than at sea level, to use a lower final temperature when cooking candy mixtures and cake frosting, and to make adjustments in recipes for cakes and other baked products.

Water—As altitude increases and the atmospheric pressure decreases, water boils at a lower temperature because the pressure of resistance of the water surface is less. At sea level, water boils at 212°F, but for each additional 500 feet of altitude the boiling point lowers one degree. At 5000 feet the boiling point is 202°F—a decrease of 10° from the boiling point of water at sea level.

Vegetables—As altitude increases and the boiling point of water decreases, the cooking period will increase. Thus, when boiling vegetables this extra cooking time will range from 2 to 10 minutes except for beets, beans, turnips, and onions, which require considerably more time.

Frozen vegetables—Most frozen vegetables need very little additional time when cooked at a high altitude. Vegetables such as broccoli, green and wax beans, and mixed vegetables may require up to 12 minutes extra time.

Baked vegetables—The time required for baked potatoes, squash, etc., at high altitude is about the same as for low altitude.

Deep Frying—Foods such as French-fried potatoes, doughnuts, and croquettes may be prepared as easily at a high altitude as at low. Suitable temperatures for deep frying are from 350° to 375°F. Avoid much higher temperatures as the product fried is apt to be over-brown. For the best results with doughnuts modify a "sea-level recipe" by reducing the leavening agent and fat in the recipe. A recipe calling for a very rich mixture might be modified by reducing the sugar or using a proportion of hard wheat flour with the regular flour.

Liquid—The liquid content may be increased from 1 to 4 tablespoons per cup in direct proportion to the altitude above 2500 feet.

Baking Temperatures—In general, 360° to 370°F gives the best results for layer cakes and cupcakes. When paper cups are used, the oven temperature should be increased 15° to 25°F. Above 5000 feet the oven temperature might need to be increased 3° to 4° for every 1000 feet.

Candy and Cake Frostings—See *Candies & Confections, page 599.*

Yeast Breads—see *page 62.*

How to Modify Baking Recipes

	ALTITUDE		
	2500-4000 ft.	4000-6000 ft.	over 6000 ft.
Reduce baking powder: for each teaspoon use	⅞ teaspoon	¾ teaspoon	½ teaspoon
Reduce double-acting baking powder: for each teaspoon use	¾ teaspoon	½ teaspoon	¼ teaspoon
Reduce sugar: for each cup use	no change	⅞ cup	¾ cup
Increase liquid: for each cup add	no change	3-6 teaspoons	6-12 teaspoons

For more information about adjustments required in using sea-level baking recipes at high altitudes, write to the home economics department of your state university or college.

Cake Baking

In general, cake recipes which call for half as much shortening as sugar and half as much sugar as flour are best for high altitude cake baking. Recipes with these proportions may be more easily adjusted to high altitudes, and frequently require little if any modification up to 5000 feet except in the leavening agent. Sponge cake and angel food cake recipes require less modification than do some butter cakes.

Sugar—As a general rule, recipes that call for a maximum amount of sugar at sea level should be decreased approximately ½ tablespoon per cup for every 1000 feet above 3000 feet.

Leavening agent—At elevations above 3000 feet, it may be necessary to decrease the leavening agent. There can be no set rule for adjusting the amount of baking powder as the modification depends upon the type of baking powder, the number of eggs, and the amount of flour. In recipes calling for a maximum amount of baking powder, it may be decreased as much as half a teaspoon at 5000 feet. In soda and sour milk recipes, the soda must remain in proportion to the sour milk and other acid ingredients. (½ teaspoon soda will neutralize 1 cup sour milk.)

Flour—In some recipes at high altitudes an increase of one level tablespoon for each cup of flour improves the texture of the cake. This modification is easier and produces the same result as decreasing the shortening.

Shortening—For best results, the shortening should not exceed one quarter of the flour. Above 5000 feet, a decrease of about ½ teaspoon per 1000 feet may improve some recipes.

Eggs—The addition of an egg may prevent a too-rich cake from falling. Eggs also increase the capacity of the batter to hold liquid.

HOW TO DO IT

To blanch nuts—Cover nuts with rapidly boiling water and allow them to remain in the water only until the skins are loosened. Drain off the water immediately and spread nuts on absorbent paper to dry. Remove the skins by squeezing the nuts between the thumb and index finger. Dry nuts thoroughly by spreading them on absorbent paper. Avoid loss of flavor in nuts by blanching only about ½ cup at a time and allowing them to stand in the water the shortest time possible.

To deep-fat fry—About 20 minutes before ready to deep fry, fill a deep saucepan one-half to three-fourths full with vegetable shortening, all-purpose shortening, lard, or cooking oil for deep frying.

Heat slowly to temperature given in recipe. A deep frying thermometer is an accurate guide for deep frying temperatures.

If thermometer is not available, the following bread cube method may be used: A 1-inch cube of bread will brown in 60 seconds at 350° to 375°F. If using an electric deep fryer, follow manufacturer's directions for fat and timing.

To clarify fats—Strain slightly cooled fat such as lard and vegetable shortening which have been used for deep frying through several thicknesses of cheesecloth to remove foreign material. Then add several slices of pared raw potato to cooled fat in a heavy saucepot and heat slowly until potato will absorb any foreign flavors in the fat and also attract some of the sediment floating in the fat.

To make butter balls—Scald, then chill butter paddles in a bowl of ice and water. Measure butter by tablespoonfuls (for uniformity) and drop into the icy water. For each ball, place a portion of butter on the grooved side of one paddle. Using the second paddle, grooved side down, work paddles lightly in a rolling motion until a ball is formed. Drop into icy water. Later pile into a serving dish and refrigerate until ready to use.

To make butter curls—Lightly draw a special butter curler (available at most department stores) across a quarter-pound print of butter. Drop each curl into a bowl of ice and water to chill. Allow several curls for each serving.

To clean mushrooms—Wash mushrooms quickly under running cold water, spread on absorbent paper, dry completely, and cut off the tips of stems. Leave caps whole, or slice mushrooms lengthwise through stems and caps, or chop, as directed in recipe.

To cut marshmallows or dried fruits (uncooked)—Use scissors dipped frequently in water to avoid stickiness.

To melt chocolate—Melt unsweetened chocolate over simmering water or over very low heat in a heavy saucepan; sweet or semisweet over hot (not simmering) water.

To plump raisins—Place raisins in a strainer over simmering water for a few minutes, or pour boiling water over them and let stand a few minutes before draining. Then spread raisins on absorbent paper to remove excess moisture before using.

To cook wild rice—Put ½ cup wild rice into a colander or sieve and wash thoroughly with running cold water. Bring 3 cups water and 1 teaspoon salt to boiling in a large saucepan. Gradually add the rice. Cook, uncovered, 25 minutes, or until rice is tender when a kernel is pressed between fingers; drain. (1½ cups cooked rice)

To prepare crumbs—Place cookies, crackers, zwieback, or the like on a long length of heavy waxed paper. Loosely fold paper around material to be crushed, tucking under open ends. With a rolling pin, gently crush to make fine crumbs. Or place crackers in a plastic bag and crush.

To use an electric blender—Cover blender container before starting and stopping motor to avoid splashing. To aid in even mixing, frequently scrape down sides of container with a rubber spatula, first stopping motor.

To grind, put in blender container enough food at one time to cover blades. Cover; turn on motor and grind until very fine. Turning motor off and on helps to throw food back on blades. Empty container and grind next batch of food.

If using the electric blender for preparing crumbs, break 5 or 6 crackers, cookies, pieces of dry bread, or the like into blender container. Cover container. Blend as directed by manufacturer until crumbs are medium fine. Empty container and repeat blending until desired amount of crumbs is obtained.

To prepare garlic—Separate desired number of cloves from garlic root and remove outer (thin, papery) skin from cloves.

To prepare quick broth—Dissolve 1 chicken bouillon cube in 1 cup boiling water for quick chicken broth or 1 beef bouillon cube or ½ teaspoon concentrated meat extract for quick meat broth. Instant bouillon granules are also available for preparing quick broth.

To roast chestnuts—Wash chestnuts and make a slit in both sides of each shell. Turn chestnuts into a shallow pan and mix in cooking oil (about 1 tablespoon per pound). Roast in a 450°F oven 20 minutes. Cool. Remove shells and all inner skins with a sharp knife.

To toast nuts—Spread nuts in a shallow baking dish or pie pan and heat in a 350°F oven until delicately browned; move and turn nuts occasionally. Or, if desired, nuts may be browned lightly in a heavy skillet in a small amount of butter, margarine, or cooking oil over medium heat, moving nuts constantly while browning.

To salt nuts—Sprinkle salt over hot toasted nuts (brushed lightly with butter or margarine before or after toasting).

To sour milk—Add 2 tablespoons vinegar or lemon juice to each 1 pint milk. Allow to stand at room temperature 30 minutes, then return to refrigerator. To sour evaporated milk (after it has been diluted with water) follow directions for fresh milk.

To sour cream—Add 1 tablespoon vinegar or lemon juice to 1 cup cream or 1 cup undiluted evaporated milk.

To whip cream (for use as topping or filling or as an ingredient in a cake)—Pour chilled heavy (whipping) cream into a chilled bowl and beat (on medium speed at first, then on high, if using electric mixer) until soft peaks are formed when beater is slowly lifted upright. If whipped cream is to be incorporated into a frozen or refrigerator dessert or salad, beat until of medium consistency (piles softly).

The maximum amount of cream that should be whipped at one time is 1½ cups. If recipe calls for more than 1½ cups, whip 1 cup at a time. Heavy cream doubles in volume when whipped.

To whip evaporated milk—Chill undiluted evaporated milk before whipping. To chill the milk, pour the amount called for in recipe into a dry refrigerator tray. Place in freezer until ice crystals form around edges. Then turn into a chilled bowl and beat with electric beater on medium speed until stiff peaks are formed. Use immediately. If whipped milk is to be refrigerated for several hours before using, stabilize it with lemon juice in this manner: Whip the milk as directed, then add 1 tablespoon lemon juice for each cup of milk (measured before whipping). Continue beating until thoroughly blended.

HELPFUL HINTS FOR THE COOK

• To keep bacon from curling while broiling or panfrying, snip edges with shears before cooking.

• To make a smooth mixture of flour (or cornstarch) and water to be used to thicken a sauce or gravy, combine ingredients in a glass jar, cover tightly, and shake well. Sauces thickened with flour or cornstarch must be cooked rapidly and thoroughly to overcome the raw starch taste.

• When adding whole eggs or egg yolks to a sauce, always stir a little of the hot sauce into the slightly beaten eggs; immediately blend into the remaining hot sauce. Cook 3 to 5 minutes, stirring to keep the mixture cooking evenly.

- To keep cornmeal from lumping, moisten it thoroughly with cold water before pouring in the boiling water.
- To make poached fish firm and white, add a little lemon juice to the cooking liquid.
- To make applesauce with an extra-fine flavor, do not pare or core the apples. Wash and quarter them, removing stems and blossom ends. Put apples into a deep saucepan with several tablespoons of water to start the cooking. Cover and cook until apples are soft, but not mushy. Force through a colander or food mill; add sugar and spices as desired. Heat only until sugar is dissolved.
- To make a flavorful gravy from pot roast drippings, add canned consommé (instead of water) to the meat during cooking.
- To keep a mixing bowl from slipping on working surface, place a folded moist towel under it.
- To test the heat of a griddle, sprinkle several drops of water on the surface and if water "dances" in small beads the griddle is hot enough to brown the food.
- To keep a metal skillet or saucepan from warping (becoming rounded on bottom), avoid pouring cold water into the utensil while hot. The sudden change of temperature causes the warping.
- To remove fish odors from utensils, add 2 tablespoons baking soda to the dishwashing water.
- To avoid "boilovers" while cooking macaroni, spaghetti, or rice, add 1 tablespoon cooking oil or shortening to the cooking liquid.

FOREIGN WORDS & PHRASES

Ala, au, aux—Dressed in a certain style.

A la mode—In the style of.

Al dente—A term used to refer to not-quite tender pasta. In Italian it means "to the tooth."

Artichaut—Artichoke.

Asperge—Asparagus.

Aspic—Any jellied dish or a jellied glaze.

Au gratin—Baked with a topping of crumbs, and often with grated or shredded cheese.

Au jus—Served with natural juice or gravy.

Au naturel—Plainly cooked.

Beurre—Butter; *beurre fondu*, melted butter; *beurre noir*, butter browned until almost black.

Bisque—A thick soup, usually made from shellfish; or an ice cream containing ground or pulverized nuts or macaroons.

Blanquette—White meat in cream sauce that has been thickened with egg yolks.

Bombe glacée—A mold of ice cream filled with a different kind of ice cream or a water ice.

Bouchées—Small pastry shells or pepper cases filled with creamed meat or fish. The French word means "a mouthful."

Bouquet garni—See *Herb bouquet, page 12.*

Café noir—Black coffee.

Canapé—A small piece of bread, toasted or fried, spread with some highly flavored mixture and served as an appetizer.

Canard—Duck.

Cannelon—Meat stuffed, rolled up, and roasted or braised.

Cassoulet—A hearty white bean and meat mixture often with goose or duckling. The dish originated in Languedoc, France.

Caviar—The salted roe of the sturgeon.

Champignons—Mushrooms.

Chaud-froid—Literally "hot-cold." In cooking, a jellied sauce.

Chiffonade—Designates any dish served with shredded vegetables.

Chou—Cabbage.

Chou-fleur—Cauliflower.

Compote—A stew; often applied to fruits stewed in syrup.

Court bouillon—Liquid used for poaching fish.

Crème—Cream.

Croustade—Case for creamed meat, fish, poultry, and other mixtures, made of bread, rice, or pastry.

Croutons—Small cubes of fried or toasted bread served with soup or tossed with salads.

De, d'—Of.

Demitasse—Literally "half a cup." Used to signify a small cup of black coffee generally served at the close of a luncheon or dinner.

Diable—Deviled.

Dragées (silver)—Tiny edible, round silver-colored candies.

Duchesse—Whipped potatoes mixed with egg and forced through a pastry tube.

Éclair—An oblong choux pastry filled with whipped cream or custard; usually chocolate glazed.

En brochette—Impaled on a skewer.

En coquilles—In the shell.

En gelée—In jelly.

En papillote—Baked in an oiled paper case.

Entrée—The main dish of an informal meal or a subordinate dish served between main courses.

Farce—Forcemeat. A well-seasoned stuffing with chopped meat, fish, poultry or nuts.

Farci—Stuffed.

Fillets—Long, thin pieces of boneless meat or fish.

Fines herbes—Minced parsley, chives, chervil, etc. (See also *Bouquet garni, page 21,* or *Herb bouquet, page 12.*)

Flambé—A food served with lighted spirits poured over.

Fondant—A sugar and water mixture cooked to the softball stage (234°F), cooled, and kneaded.

Fondue—Literally "melted"; usually applied to cheese, eggs, and crumbs.

Fraises—Strawberries.

Frappé—Iced or semifrozen.

Fricassée—Braised meats or poultry.

Fromage—Cheese.

Gâteau—Cake.

Gelée—Jelly.

Glacé—Frozen dessert (ice or ice cream); also glazed (see *Candy* and *Glacé, page 14*).

Goulash—A thick Hungarian meat stew.

Haricots verts—Small green beans.

Huîtres—Oysters.

Jambon—Ham.

Jardinière—Mixed vegetables served in their own sauce.

Laitue—Lettuce.

Légumes—Vegetables.

Lyonnaise—Cooked with onions.

Macédoine—A mixture; usually vegetables, with or without meat. Sometimes fruit mixtures.

Marrons—Chestnuts.

Marzipan—A paste of almonds and sugar molded in various forms (realistic colors and shapes).

Meringue—Whites of eggs whipped with sugar to the stiff peak stage.

Mousse—A light appetizer, main dish, or dessert mixture containing whipped cream, flavorings or seasonings, sugar (if dessert), gelatin, and other ingredients. It is usually turned into a mold and then chilled or frozen.

Noir—Black.

Oeufs—Eggs.

Pain—Bread.

Pâté—a) Seasoned ground cooked meat including liver, poultry or fish mixture chilled before serving; b) meat mixture baked in a covered pan or casserole set in a larger pan of boiling water, cooled thoroughly, and sliced (also called *terrine*); c) meat, fish, or vegetable filling baked in a pastry case.

Pâté de foie gras—A paste of goose livers.

Pâtisserie—Pastry.

Pêche—Peach.

Petits pois—Small green peas.

Pièce de résistance—The main dish in a meal; usually the roasted meat, but also poultry or game served with sauces and stuffing.

Pois—Peas.

Polonaise, À la—Served with a topping of bread crumbs browned in butter and sieved hard-cooked egg yolk.

Pommes—Apples.

Pommes de terre—Potatoes. Literally, "apples of the earth."

Potage—Soup.

Poulet—Chicken.

Purée—Mashed or sieved food.

Ragoût—A thick, highly seasoned stew.

Ratatouille—A mixed vegetable stew that usually includes eggplant and tomatoes cooked in olive oil and is typical of the cooking in southern France.

Réchauffé—Reheated or warmed-over.

Ris de veau—Sweetbreads.

Rissoles—Minced fish or meat rolled in thin pastry and fried.

Rôti—Roast.

Roux—A mixture of butter and flour used for thickening soups or sauces.

Sauté—Fried lightly in a little fat.

Sorbet—Frozen punch. This name is often given to water-ice when several kinds of fruit are used.

Soufflé—Literally "puffed up." A delicate baked custard which may contain fruit, cheese, flaked fish, minced poultry, meat, or vegetables.

Tarte—Tart.

Tartelette—A little tart.

Timbale—An unsweetened custard, usually seasoned with fish, meat, or vegetables, baked in a mold or molds.

Timbale case—A small case of deep-fried batter in which creamed mixtures and desserts are served.

Tourte—A tart; a pie.

Truffles—A species of fungi, similar to mushrooms, growing in clusters some inches below ground. Used in seasoning and for a garnish.

Tutti-frutti—Mixed fruits.

Vapeur, À la—Steamed.

Velouté—Velvety; smooth.

Vichyssoise—A cream soup of puréed potatoes, chicken stock, and leeks. Best served icy cold.

Vinaigrette—A marinade or salad sauce of oil, vinegar, pepper, and herbs.

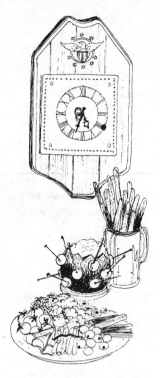

Chapter 1

APPETIZERS—Hot & Cold

Appetizers are dainty, attractive contrivances served for the purpose of putting party guests in a company mood and to *arouse* the appetite—not *satisfy* it. These morsels are usually so delicious and eye-appealing in their artful variety that it is sometimes difficult for hostess and guests alike to remember to use restraint where they are concerned.

The occasion sets the stage for the kind of appetizers offered to guests. For "stand-up" occasions when served in the living room or patio, they are usually of one- or two-bite size. They should be distinctive in flavor, zesty, and nippy, to put a sharp edge on the appetite. They should be easy to eat, not too fragile, not too "drippy."

For "sit-down" occasions, when appetizers are served at the table, generally for the first course of a meal, they may be larger in size and are eaten with a fork.

PLANNING APPETIZERS

There is no limit to the kinds of meat, poultry, fish, cheese, vegetables, and fruits that can be used. Though imagination and ingenuity are the only limiting factors in selecting appetizers, there is one rule that should be followed—*avoid repeating any food in the main part of the meal that has been used in the appetizers.* Remember that they are a part of the whole menu; select them to harmonize with the rest of the meal. Choose them for complementary flavors, for contrast of texture and color and variety of shape. Picture the serving dishes, trays, and other appointments as you plan the menu.

Avoid a last-minute rush by wise selection (do not include too many appetizers that require last-minute doing), by careful buying, and beforehand preparation. Take cues from assembly-line production techniques for organizing your work. For example, use large sandwich loaves, cut in lengthwise slices, for canapé bases and finger sandwiches; stack several slices together and cut several identi-

cal shapes at one time; spread canapé bases all at one time.

Hors d'Oeuvres—Hot or cold, simple or elaborate, hors d'oeuvres are savory tidbits about one bite in size and are eaten with the fingers from wooden or plastic picks. Almost anything that can be presented in an interesting manner can be offered. Many good leftovers can be transformed into culinary gems. They may be single items such as marinated shrimp or a combination of foods. Every nation has specialties, but all are intended to stimulate the appetite.

Hors d'oeuvres are usually served to a gathering of people at a cocktail party or before dinner. A continental custom is to serve the hors d'oeuvres at the table as the first course of a luncheon or dinner. Here the use of a fork is acceptable.

For successful hors d'oeuvres remember and practice the general suggestions and the rule given in Planning, *above.* The *Appetite Teasers, page 25,* will give a helpful start. Look also at *raw vegetable relishes, page 350,* for the pick-ups. Don't forget the many dips and dunks and the snacks such as *Crunchy Nibblers, page 40,* nuts, and potato chips.

Fill miniature shells made from puff paste or choux paste or spread waffle squares, thin griddlecakes, or crêpes with piquant mixtures—delectable!

Holders for pick-type hors d'oeuvres are available in housewares departments or can be made from a molded cheese (such as Edam), grapefruit, oranges, apples, a small head of red or green cabbage, a melon, eggplant, cucumbers, or a cauliflower. If necessary, level base by removing a thin slice from the underside. Put hors d'oeuvres on wooden or plastic picks and insert into the holder.

Canapés—Finger foods too, canapés are thin slices of fancy-cut bread or toast, or some other "base" spread with a flavored butter, then topped with a well-seasoned food (meat, fish, or vegetable) or a piquant mixture, not sweet in flavor. They are dainty "bites," fresh in appearance and easy to handle.

Bases for canapés are the many breads, used plain, toasted, or deep-fried, along with the packaged commercial products such as crackers, Melba toast, and potato chips. Brown breads, nut breads, rye, wheat, white, and pumpernickel bread give variety to canapés. The bread slices, never more than ¼ inch thick, can be cut into many shapes—rounds, squares, diamonds, ovals, rectangles, and crescents.

Spread canapé bases with butter or margarine, seasoned with herbs, prepared horseradish, or prepared mustard, if desired, then with the filling or "spread," and finally topped with a garnish. Garnishes should be scaled to the dainty size of the canapés and should be as good to eat as they are to behold.

Canapés may be sealed with a clear aspic to hold the garnishes in place, to add a gloss, and to prolong their freshness.

Take time to arrange canapés in an attractive design on the serving tray—the effect will be gratifying. Prepare enough to replenish the tray, re-creating the original arrangement.

Garnishes for Canapés:

Anchovies—fillets or rolled

Bacon (crisp cooked)—crumbled or small pieces

Carrots—thin notched rounds

Caviar (black or red)

Cheese (sharp) shredded

Chives—minced or chopped

Cream cheese—softened, plain or tinted and forced through pastry bag and decorating tubes to form rosettes, designs, or borders

Cucumbers—notched slices, half slices, or thin unpared slices

Eggs (hard-cooked)—rings, slices, sieved egg yolk, or egg-white cutouts

Green pepper—cutouts or narrow strips

Lobster—pieces of clawmeat

Mint—sprigs or chopped

Mushrooms (slices)—cooked in butter

Nuts (plain, toasted, or salted)—chopped, ground, or whole

Olives (green or ripe)—slivered, chopped, rings of pitted olives, or sliced pimiento-stuffed olives

Parsley-sprigs or snipped

Paprika

Pickles—chopped or slices

Pimiento—strips or chopped

Radishes—thin slices

Shrimp (cooked, fresh)—whole

Tomato—cutouts

Watercress-sprigs or snipped

Garnishes for the Canapé Tray: Carved vegetable flowers; fresh flowers; *Frosted Grapes, page 350;* kumquats with peel drawn back in petal shapes; parsley bouquets; *Radish Roses, page 351;* watercress.

Cocktails—The seafood or fruit (one or more kinds of fruit) cocktail is served as the first course of a meal at the table. Vegetable or fruit juices are served either at the table or in the living room before the meal.

Seafood cocktails are usually served with peppy sauce that has ketchup, chili sauce, French dressing, or mayonnaise as a base.

Fruit cocktails should be tart, though sometimes made with sweetened fruits. Frequently they are sprinkled with rum, kirsch, or a liqueur that harmonizes in flavor with the fruit.

Add seasonings such as Worcestershire sauce, Tabasco, or lemon juice to spark the flavor of vegetable juices.

Float a small scoop of fruit-flavored ice or sherbet on small servings of chilled fruit juice—a refreshing shrub.

All cocktails should be fresh, colorful, and appetizing in appearance and tantalizing in flavor. Thoroughly chill all ingredients and serving dishes. Fruit and seafood cocktails often are kept cold in beds of crushed ice. Seafood and fruit cocktails are served in stemmed or footed cocktail glasses while the juices and shrubs are served in small glasses or punch cups. Some juice cocktails are served hot; be sure they are steaming hot and served in cups or glasses that are comfortable for guests to hold.

APPETITE TEASERS

Prepare an attractive array selected from these simple recipes. All are delightful bits of finger food, though some may be easier to serve if they have stems of wooden or plastic picks.

BACON-WRAPPED OLIVES: Wrap *pimiento-* or *almond-stuffed olives* in *bacon*. Fasten with wooden picks. Put into a baking dish. Bake or broil until bacon is done.

PICKLES ON PICKS: Spread thin slices of partially cooked *bacon* (lightly browned but not crisp) with a mixture of *crunchy peanut butter* and finely chopped *chutney*. Halve each slice of bacon and top with a tiny *sweet gherkin*. Roll bacon around pickle and secure with a wooden pick. Place under broiler, turning so that bacon is crisp on all sides.

CHEESE SNACKS: Prepare *Cheese Pastry, page 457,* and roll out ⅛ inch thick. Cut into desired shapes such as rings, circles, or sticks. Prick pastry with fork; place on an ungreased baking sheet. Brush lightly with melted *butter* or *margarine, cream,* or beaten *egg yolk*. If desired, sprinkle with seeds or herbs such as *sesame seed, celery seed,* or *dill weed*. Bake according to package directions for temperature until golden.

PINEAPPLE DELIGHTS: Wrap drained *pineapple chunks* each in one third of a slice of *bacon*; secure with a *whole clove* or wooden pick. Arrange in shallow baking dish and broil until bacon is done.

MEAT 'N' CHEESE WEDGES: With a round cutter, cut 2½ to 3-inch rounds from slices of *ham, canned luncheon meat, ready-to-serve meat, bologna,* or other *sausage*. Repeat the process with thin slices of *Swiss* or *Cheddar cheese*. Alternately stack the meat and cheese rounds, using five in all. Wrap in waxed paper and chill in refrigerator until time to serve. Cut stacks into small wedges. Insert picks.

BISCUIT BITES: Dot *toasted bite-size shredded wheat biscuits* with *peanut butter*. Thread on picks alternately with thin slices of *sweet pickle*.

CHEESE POPCORN: Sprinkle *salt* and ½ *cup grated sharp Cheddar* or *Parmesan cheese* over *1 quart hot buttered popcorn*. Toss lightly.

ONION POPCORN: Combine ⅓ to ½ *cup dry onion soup mix* with ½ *cup melted butter or margarine*. Pour over *warm popcorn* (about 3 quarts) and toss gently until kernels are coated.

BRAUNSCHWEIGER SPECIALITY: Whip *braunschweiger* (smoked liver sausage) until fluffy. If necessary, blend in a small amount of *mayonnaise* or *cream* until of desired consistency. Mix in the desired amount of grated *onion, capers,* and coarsely chopped *salted pistachio nuts*. Fill speciality shaped *snacks*.

PECAN SANDWICHES: Lightly brush large *pecan halves* with *butter* and spread one layer deep on baking sheet. Toast at 350°F about 20 minutes, or until delicately browned. Finely shred *Swiss cheese*; blend in *cream* to spreading consistency. Spread one side of one pecan half with cheese mixture and top with a second half. Press gently together.

CHERRY TOMATOES GOLDENROD: Beat *cream cheese* with *milk* until fluffy. Mix in chopped *ripe olives* and *salted almonds*. Spoon onto *cherry tomato halves* seasoned with *monosodium glutamate*. Sprinkle tops with sieved *hard-cooked egg yolk*. Garnish each half with a *whole almond*.

SMOKED CHEESE BLOSSOMS: Soften *smoked cheese* and mix with chopped *pimiento, sweet pickle,* and crisp crumbled *bacon*. Roll into small balls and chill in refrigerator. Or pack mixture into a small pan, chill and cut into squares. Insert picks.

CAVIAR WITH EGG: Cut *hard-cooked eggs* into halves lengthwise or cut forming saw-tooth edges. Remove yolks and set aside for use in other food preparation. Fill whites with chilled *black* or *red caviar*. Garnish with small piece of *lemon*.

DRIED BEEF TASTERS: Flavor *cream cheese* with a small amount of *prepared horseradish*. Roll into small balls. Then roll and press balls in minced *dried beef*. Insert picks.

OLIVE TEASERS: Coat large *pimiento-stuffed olives* with softened *cream cheese*. Roll in finely chopped *nuts*. Chill in refrigerator; insert picks.

STUFFED CELERY SPEARS: Blend together softened *cream cheese* and *milk*. Mix in a *few grains celery salt, few drops Worcestershire sauce,* and very finely chopped *radish* and *green pepper* or *pimiento* and *parsley*. Stuff cleaned *celery* with the cheese mixture.

APPLE SANDWICHES: Wash and core but do not pare small *apples*. Cut crosswise into thin slices, forming rings. Dip in *lemon, orange,* or *pineapple juice* to prevent darkening. Spread *peanut butter* or a *cheese spread* on one ring; top with a second ring. Cut into thirds.

FRUIT AND HAM "KABOBS": Alternate cubes of *cooked ham* or *canned luncheon meat* on picks with *seedless grapes* or cubes of *melon* or *pineapple*.

STUFFED PRUNES OR DATES: Pit and dry plump soaked *prunes* and pit *dates*. Stuff with a tangy *cheese spread* mixed with chopped *nuts*.

HOT APPETIZERS

FONTAINEBLEAU HORS D'OEUVRE PIE

This unique anchovy-latticed pie is served at the Fontainebleau Hotel in Miami Beach, Florida.

2 cups peeled, diced ripe tomatoes	2 tablespoons butter
1 tablespoon olive oil	1 unbaked 9-in. pastry shell (pastry rolled about ¼ in. thick)
½ teaspoon rosemary	
½ teaspoon oregano	⅓ cup shredded Parmesan cheese
⅛ teaspoon garlic powder	
	2 cans (2 oz. each) anchovies, drained
⅛ teaspoon pepper	
¼ cup sliced pitted ripe olives	9 pimiento-stuffed olives
1½ cups thinly sliced onions	Olive oil

1. Mix tomatoes with olive oil, rosemary, oregano, garlic powder, pepper, and ripe olives in a large skillet; cook uncovered over medium heat about 10 minutes, or until sauce is thickened.
2. Meanwhile, in a separate pan, cook onions with butter until tender and golden; cool in pan.
3. Sprinkle bottom of pastry with half of the cheese; cover with cooled onion-butter mixture. Spread thickened tomato mixture over onions and sprinkle with remaining cheese.
4. Arrange anchovies over top, lattice fashion, making crisscross strips about 1 inch apart. Cut each olive in 3 slices and place one slice in each lattice square; brush olives lightly with olive oil.
5. Bake at 350°F 30 to 40 minutes, or until crust is well browned. Serve warm.   6 OR 12 SERVINGS

AVOCADO TOAST FINGERS

Mississippi belle Mary McKay parlayed a second-hand cookstove and a deft way with fine food into Vicksburg's now famous Old Southern Tea Room. These hot appetizers are one of her claims to fame.

1 very ripe avocado	½ teaspoon salt
1 teaspoon lemon juice	6 slices white bread, toasted and crusts removed
1 teaspoon grated onion	
1 teaspoon paprika	Bacon slices

1. Peel avocado; mash pulp with a fork. Then beat in lemon juice, onion, paprika, and salt. Beat until smooth.

2. Spread mixture over toast slices. Cut each slice into 3×1-inch strips. Place narrow strips of bacon on each toast finger.
3. Put on a baking sheet and broil until bacon is crisp. Serve immediately.   18 APPETIZERS

TERIYAKI

An oriental appetizer of Japanese origin.

1 teaspoon ground ginger	3 tablespoons cooking or salad oil
⅓ cup soy sauce	1 tablespoon cornstarch
¼ cup honey	
1 clove garlic, minced	½ cup water
1 teaspoon grated onion	⅛ teaspoon red food coloring
1 lb. beef sirloin tip, cut in 2x½x¼-in. strips	

1. Blend ginger, soy sauce, honey, garlic, and onion in a bowl. Add meat; marinate about 1 hour.
2. Remove meat, reserving marinade, and brown quickly on all sides in the hot oil in a skillet.
3. Stir a blend of cornstarch, water, and food coloring into the reserved marinade in a saucepan. Bring rapidly to boiling and cook 2 to 3 minutes, stirring constantly.
4. Add meat to thickened marinade to glaze; remove and drain on wire rack.
5. Insert a frilled wooden pick into each meat strip and serve with the sauce.

ABOUT 24 APPETIZERS

EXOTIC APPETIZER BALLS

There's a mysterious flavor in these little appetizer balls . . . coffee, perhaps?

1 lb. lean ground beef	4 teaspoons instant minced onion softened in 4 teaspoons water
1 egg, fork beaten	
½ teaspoon Worcestershire sauce	
8 drops Tabasco	½ to ¾ cup chopped water chestnuts
1 tablespoon instant coffee	
	Fine cracker crumbs
1 teaspoon salt	Butter or margarine
⅛ teaspoon pepper	

1. Lightly mix the meat with the egg, Worcester-

shire sauce, and Tabasco. Blend with a mixture of the coffee, salt, and pepper. Add the softened onion and water chestnuts; mix lightly.

2. Form mixture into 1-inch balls. Roll in crumbs.

3. Brown meatballs in hot butter in a large heavy skillet over medium heat; shake frequently to obtain even browning and round balls.

4. Spear with fancy wooden picks and serve hot. If desired, serve from a chafing dish.

ABOUT 5½ DOZEN BALLS

BLINI

Of Russian origin and for elegant entertaining, is this appetizer creation—silver dollar-sized griddle-cakes accompanied by caviar, sour cream, chopped onion, and sieved hard-cooked egg.

½ teaspoon active dry yeast	½ cup milk, scalded
1 tablespoon warm water	¼ cup buckwheat flour
¾ teaspoon sugar	6 tablespoons all-purpose flour
⅛ teaspoon salt	1 egg yolk, beaten
	1 egg white

1. Soften yeast in the warm water.

2. Combine sugar and salt in a bowl; add scalded milk and blend thoroughly. Cool to warm, then thoroughly blend in a mixture of the buckwheat flour and 2 tablespoons of the all-purpose flour.

3. Add the softened yeast and mix well. Cover bowl with waxed paper and a towel; let rise in a warm place 1½ hours, or until light.

4. Beat in remaining flour until mixture is smooth. Blend in the egg yolk.

5. Beat egg white until rounded peaks are formed and gently fold into the batter. Cover the bowl and let rise again about 20 minutes.

6. Meanwhile, heat a griddle or skillet. Lightly grease as manufacturer's instructions direct.

7. Spoon batter (use about 2 teaspoonfuls for each Blini) onto hot griddle forming pools about 1 inch in diameter and leaving at least 1 inch between each; spread batter out slightly. Turn Blini as they become puffy and full of bubbles; brown other side. Turn only once. Transfer to a warm platter and set in a 250°F oven until all are done.

8. Serve immediately, accompanied by bowls of *dairy sour cream, caviar,* finely chopped *onion,* chopped *hard-cooked egg white,* and sieved *hard-cooked egg yolk.* Arrange platter and bowls so each guest may serve himself as desired.

ABOUT 2 DOZEN BLINI

FLASH UN KAS

These melt-in-your-mouth morsels of flaky filled pastry claim a Pennsylvania Dutch heritage.

1 cup butter, softened	Filling: goose liver pâté or ground ham, *below*
8 oz. cream cheese, softened	
2 cups sifted all-purpose flour	

1. Cream butter and cream cheese together until well blended. Add the flour and mix until smooth. Chill pastry thoroughly (overnight if possible).

2. Using a small portion of pastry at a time, roll pastry about ⅛ inch thick on a lightly floured surface; cut out rounds with a 2-inch cookie cutter.

3. Spoon a rounded one-fourth teaspoonful of filling onto half of each round. Fold dough over filling and press edges together with a fork. Transfer to baking sheets.

4. Bake at 400°F 8 to 10 minutes, or until lightly browned. Serve hot.   ABOUT 9 DOZEN APPETIZERS

FILLING: Mix thoroughly *2 ounces goose liver pâté, 1 teaspoon Worcestershire sauce,* and *1 teaspoon steak sauce;* or mix *2 ounces ground country-style ham, 1 teaspoon steak sauce,* and *1 teaspoon ketchup.* (Each filling is enough for about 4½ dozen appetizers.)

NOTE: This pastry will keep for several weeks if wrapped tightly in moisture-vaporproof material and stored in the refrigerator.

SWISS CHEESE PASTRY MORSELS

2 cups finely shredded Swiss cheese	1 to 1¼ cup sifted all-purpose flour
½ cup butter or margarine, softened	Liverwurst spread
	Deviled ham
	Cocktail onions

1. Mix cheese and butter; blend in flour.

2. For each pastry morsel shape 1 teaspoon of the dough into a ball; set balls 1 inch apart on a baking sheet.

3. For liverwurst or deviled ham appetizers, make an indentation in center of each ball before baking and fill with ½ teaspoon of the spread or ham.

4. For onion appetizers, mold 1 teaspoon of the pastry dough around a cocktail onion covering it completely.

5. Bake at 400°F 15 minutes, or until golden. Serve warm.   4 DOZEN APPETIZERS

BROILED BACON-CHEESE CANAPÉS

4 oz. sharp Cheddar cheese, cut in pieces
3 slices bacon
¼ medium-sized green pepper
2 teaspoons grated onion
2 teaspoons mayonnaise
2 doz. 2-in. bread rounds

1. Put cheese, bacon, and green pepper through the coarse blade of a food chopper. Blend in the onion and mayonnaise.
2. Arrange bread rounds on a baking sheet or broiler rack. Toast on one side. Spread the topping on untoasted side. Broil 3 inches from source of heat until topping is bubbly and light golden.

2 DOZEN CANAPÉS

CHEDDAR PUFFS

¼ cup butter or margarine, softened
8 oz. shredded sharp Cheddar cheese (about 2 cups)
1¼ cups sifted all-purpose flour
¾ teaspoon paprika
¼ teaspoon dry mustard
⅛ teaspoon cayenne pepper

1. Blend butter and cheese until smooth. Mix in a blend of the flour, paprika, dry mustard, and cayenne pepper.
2. Shape dough into rolls about 1¼ inches in diameter. Wrap in waxed paper and chill.
3. Cut into ¼ inch slices. Place about 1 inch apart on lightly greased baking sheets.
4. Bake at 400°F about 8 minutes. Serve hot.

ABOUT 4 DOZEN PUFFS

RUMAKI

Succulent morsels to enhance an appetizer tray.

½ lb. chicken livers
1½ tablespoons honey
1 tablespoons soy sauce
2 tablespoons cooking oil
½ clove garlic, minced
1 can (5 oz.) water chestnuts, drained and cut in quarters or slices
Bacon slices, halved

1. Rinse chicken livers with running cold water and drain on absorbent paper; cut into halves and put into a bowl.
2. Pour a mixture of the honey, soy sauce, oil, and garlic over the liver pieces. Cover and let stand about 30 minutes, turning pieces occasionally. Remove from marinade and drain.

3. Wrap a piece of bacon around a twosome of liver and water chestnut pieces, threading each onto a wooden pick or small skewer.
4. Put appetizers on rack in broiler pan and broil with top about 3 inches from source of heat about 5 minutes. Turn with tongs and broil until bacon is browned. Serve hot. ABOUT 1½ DOZEN APPETIZERS

ON-THE-WING APPETIZERS

30 chicken wing-drums (2½ to 3½ lbs.)
½ teaspoon salt
¼ cup soy sauce
¼ cup spiced peach syrup
2 tablespoons sugar
¼ teaspoon monosodium glutamate
½ teaspoon ground ginger
1 tablespoon lemon juice
5 drops Tabasco
1 clove garlic, crushed

1. Disjoint the wings; use thickest wing portions for appetizers and remaining wing portions for chicken broth.
2. Place the wing-drums on rack on a foil-lined baking sheet or broiler pan; sprinkle with salt.
3. Mix remaining ingredients thoroughly; brush marinade generously on wing-drums.
4. Place in 350°F oven about 1 hour, or until wing-drums are golden brown and tender, brushing frequently with the marinade. ABOUT 10 SERVINGS

HOT CRAB MEAT CANAPÉS

3½ tablespoons mayonnaise
1 tablespoon prepared mustard
1 tablespoon lemon juice
¼ teaspoon salt
⅛ teaspoon freshly ground black pepper
1 egg yolk, well beaten
1⅓ cups (6½-oz. can) crab meat, drained and bony tissue removed
5 slices white bread, crusts removed
Softened butter or margarine
¼ cup shredded Parmesan cheese

1. Combine mayonnaise, mustard, lemon juice, salt, and pepper; blend in the egg yolk. Lightly mix in the crab meat.
2. Toast bread on one side; cut each slice into four strips; spread untoasted sides with butter.
3. Spread crab meat mixture on each bread finger; sprinkle about ½ teaspoon cheese over top of each; arrange on a baking sheet.

4.   Broil about 3 inches from source of heat 4 to 5 minutes. Serve hot.   ABOUT 20 CANAPÉS

BROILED DATE APPETIZERS

2 cups (1 lb.) pitted fresh dates	¼ teaspoon ground nutmeg
½ cup water	½ cup lightly packed brown sugar
½ cup orange juice	
3 tablespoons wine vinegar	⅛ teaspoon salt
	Bacon slices, cut in thirds
½ teaspoon ground cinnamon	

1.   Put dates into a bowl. Blend water, orange juice, vinegar, cinnamon, nutmeg, brown sugar, and salt in a saucepan. Bring to boiling, reduce heat and simmer 5 minutes.

2.   Pour mixture over dates; cover and let stand until cool. Refrigerate at least 24 hours to allow flavors to blend.

3.   Wrap 2 dates in one-third slice of bacon and skewer with a pick; repeat, using all dates.

4.   Broil 6 inches from source of heat 6 to 8 minutes, or until bacon is crisp, turning once.

ABOUT 2 DOZEN APPETIZERS

SAUCY COCKTAIL FRANKS

1 jar (10 oz.) currant jelly	1 lb. frankfurters, cut diagonally in 1-in. pieces
⅓ cup prepared mustard	

1.   Melt jelly and blend in mustard; heat thoroughly.

2.   Stir in the frankfurters, coating each piece; simmer about 30 minutes, stirring occasionally.

3.   Serve with wooden picks.   8 TO 12 SERVINGS

HAM NIBBLES

2 cups ground cooked ham	2 cups cheese cracker crumbs
1 can (12 oz.) vacuum packed whole kernel corn, drained	¼ cup mayonnaise
	2 eggs, well beaten
	Fat for deep frying heated to 365°F

1.   Mix in a bowl the ham, corn, 1 cup of the crumbs, mayonnaise, and eggs.

2.   Shape mixture into ¾ to 1-inch balls. Roll in remaining crumbs. Set aside about 30 minutes.

3.   Fry uncrowded in hot fat 2 minutes, or until browned. Remove to drain on absorbent paper.

4.   Serve on a heated platter.

ABOUT 7 DOZEN APPETIZERS

HAM-CHEESE PIZZAS

Pie crust mix for a 2-crust pie	⅛ teaspoon dill weed
	1 tablespoon prepared horseradish
½ cup finely chopped walnuts	
½ cup ketchup	18 squares (2 in. each) sliced cooked ham
1 teaspoon prepared mustard	18 squares (2 in. each) sliced sharp process cheese
1 tablespoon chopped parsley	
⅛ teaspoon oregano	Paprika

1.   Blend pie crust mix and walnuts in a bowl; mix according to package directions.

2.   Roll the pastry ⅛ inch thick on a lightly floured surface. Cut into eighteen 3-inch rounds. Place on an ungreased baking sheet. Prick pastry.

3.   Bake at 450°F 10 minutes, or until lightly browned.

4.   Meanwhile, combine ketchup, mustard, parsley, oregano, dill weed, and horseradish. Spread about 1 tablespoon of the ketchup mixture over the baked pastry, then place a square of ham and a square of cheese on each. Sprinkle with paprika and heat under broiler until cheese is melted. Serve immediately.   EIGHTEEN 3-INCH PIZZAS

HAM-CHEESE PUFFS

6 to 9 slices bread, toasted	½ cup Thick White Sauce, page 342
1 cup firmly packed ground cooked ham	3 oz. cream cheese, softened
3 tablespoons finely chopped green pepper	1 egg yolk
1 tablespoon prepared mustard	1 teaspoon grated onion
¼ teaspoon Worcestershire sauce	¼ teaspoon baking powder

1.   Cut eighteen 2-inch rounds from the toast.

2.   Combine ham with green pepper, mustard, and Worcestershire sauce; mix well and stir in the white sauce.

3.   Beat the cream cheese with remaining ingredients until thoroughly blended.

4. Spread toast rounds generously with ham mixture and top with cheese mixture.

5. Place under broiler about 5 inches from source of heat and broil until cheese topping is golden brown. Serve immediately.   1½ DOZEN PUFFS

SI SI PASTRIES
A south-of-the-border appetizer.

1 can (4½ oz.) deviled ham	¼ cup chopped celery
¼ cup tomato sauce	½ teaspoon chili powder
¼ cup chopped green pepper	Pastry for a 1-crust pie Yellow cornmeal

1. Blend the deviled ham, tomato sauce, green pepper, celery, and chili powder. Cover and chill.
2. Prepare pastry and roll very thin, using cornmeal instead of flour for rolling. Cut the pastry into twenty 3-inch rounds.
3. Spoon about 1 tablespoon of the chilled deviled ham mixture onto each round. Moisten half the edge of each round with water. Fold pastry in half and press edges together with a fork to seal. Place on an ungreased baking sheet.
4. Bake at 425°F 10 to 12 minutes, or until golden brown. Serve immediately.   20 PASTRIES

HOT MUSHROOM APPETIZERS

1 lb. large fresh mushrooms	1 cup crushed wheat wafers
½ teaspoon fresh onion juice	1 chicken bouillon cube
½ lb. chicken livers	½ cup boiling water
3 tablespoons butter or margarine	½ teaspoon salt
	⅛ teaspoon tarragon leaves, crushed
	Garlic butter

1. Wash mushrooms; remove stems and set caps aside.
2. Chop stems and combine with onion juice and chicken livers. Cook in heated butter in a skillet 10 minutes, stirring occasionally to cook evenly. Remove livers and chop.
3. Return chopped livers to skillet with crumbs, bouillon cube dissolved in water, the salt, and tarragon. Blend thoroughly.
4. Generously brush mushroom caps, inside and out, with garlic butter; fill with the chicken liver mixture. Place in a shallow baking pan.

5. Bake at 375°F about 20 minutes. Garnish with *sieved hard-cooked egg yolk.* Serve hot.
    ABOUT 2 DOZEN APPETIZERS

BROILED OYSTERS COLLEGE INN
Ye Old College Inn in Houston, Texas, serves these delightful morsels.

24 large oysters	1 tablespoon Worcestershire sauce
3 tablespoons butter	
2 teaspoons lemon juice	3 tablespoons sherry or Madeira
2 tablespoons steak sauce	

1. Season the oysters with *salt* and *pepper* to taste and dredge them in *flour.*
2. Melt the butter in a saucepan; stir in remaining ingredients and heat before serving.
3. Cook the oysters on lightly buttered griddle until crisp and browned on both sides.
4. Dress the oysters with the hot sauce, spear each with a frilled wooden pick and serve on a heated plate.   24 APPETIZERS

SARDINE FINGER CANAPÉS

7 slices white bread	1 can (3¾ oz.) Norwegian sardines
Herbed Mayonnaise, *page 39*	½ cup shredded Parmesan cheese

1. Toast bread slices on one side. Remove crusts and cut each slice into 3 strips. Spread untoasted sides generously with Herbed Mayonnaise.
2. Coat sardines with shredded cheese. Place 1 sardine on each toast strip.
3. Broil 3 inches from source of heat until lightly browned. Garnish each canapé with a tiny sprig of *parsley* at each end. Serve hot.   21 CANAPÉS

OLIVE BITES

25 pitted ripe olives	4 oz. sharp Cheddar cheese, shredded (about 1 cup)
2 to 3 tablespoons minced green onion	
½ cup all-purpose flour	3 tablespoons butter or margarine, melted
¼ teaspoon salt	1 teaspoon milk
⅛ teaspoon dry mustard	1 or 2 drops Tabasco

1. Stuff olives with the onion and set aside.

2.   Combine flour, salt, and mustard in a bowl. Mix in the cheese and a blend of the remaining ingredients.

3.   Using about 1 teaspoonful of dough for each, shape dough around olives and place on a baking sheet.

4.   Bake at 400°F 10 to 12 minutes. Serve at once.   25 OLIVE BITES

SOUTH AMERICAN APPETIZER TARTLETS

1¾ cups sifted all-purpose flour	1 cup milk
½ teaspoon salt	2 egg yolks, fork beaten
⅔ cup butter or margarine	¼ cup shredded Parmesan cheese
3 egg yolks, fork beaten	1 teaspoon grated onion
1 tablespoon butter or margarine	1 cup finely chopped, deveined, and peeled shrimp
1 tablespoon flour	¼ cup chopped pitted ripe olives
½ teaspoon salt	1 egg yolk, fork beaten
Few grains garlic salt	
Few grains cayenne pepper	

1.   Combine 1¾ cups flour and ½ teaspoon salt in a bowl. Cut in the ⅔ cup butter with pastry blender or two knives. Add 3 egg yolks and mix lightly with a fork until blended. Shape into a ball and cut into 36 approximately equal portions. Refrigerate 18 portions. With remaining dough, line eighteen 1¾-inch muffin-pan wells, pressing one portion of dough into each well to form a tart shell. Set aside.

2.   Heat the 1 tablespoon butter over direct heat in top of a double boiler. Stir in a mixture of 1 tablespoon flour, salt, garlic salt, and cayenne pepper; heat until bubbly. Add the milk, stirring until mixture comes to boiling; cook 1 to 2 minutes. Set over boiling water.

3.   Immediately stir about 3 tablespoons of the hot mixture into the 2 egg yolks and return to hot mixture. Cook over boiling water 3 to 5 minutes, stirring constantly. Remove from heat and stir in the cheese, onion, shrimp, and olives.

4.   Fill tart shells with the mixture. Roll remaining pastry portions on a lightly floured surface. Place each over a filled tart shell and press edges together to seal. Brush tops with the remaining egg yolk.

5.   Bake at 350°F 15 to 20 minutes, or until golden brown.   18 APPETIZERS

BACON-WRAPPED SHRIMP APPETIZERS

Chili Dip, *below*	1½ teaspoons chili powder
16 cooked shrimp	1 clove garlic, minced
½ cup butter or margarine, melted	8 bacon slices

1.   Prepare Chili Dip; chill.

2.   Meanwhile, dip shrimp into a mixture of melted butter, chili powder, and garlic. Wrap shrimp in half slices of bacon and fasten with small skewers or wooden picks.

3.   Place on rack in broiler pan and broil 3 inches from source of heat about 5 minutes. Brush with butter sauce and continue broiling about 5 minutes. Serve with chilled dip.   16 APPETIZERS

CHILI DIP: *Mix ¾ cup mayonnaise, 3 tablespoons chopped sweet pickle, 1 tablespoon chopped pimiento-stuffed olives, 1½ teaspoons grated onion, 1 tablespoon chili powder, and 1 hard-cooked egg, chopped, in a bowl. Turn dip into a chilled serving bowl and serve with the shrimp.* ABOUT 1 CUP DIP

TOSTADITAS
Use these fried tortilla quarters as dippers.

Dry *tortillas* (fresh, frozen, or canned) at room temperature about 2 hours. Cut into quarters with scissors. Heat ½ inch *lard* to 375°F in a skillet. Fry tortilla quarters 1½ to 2 minutes, or until crisp. Remove and drain on absorbent paper.

CHALUPITAS: Spread each *Tostadita* with *1 tablespoon Mexican Beans (Frijoles), page 307.* Sprinkle with *1 to 2 tablespoons shredded Cheddar cheese* and broil about 3 inches from source of heat just until cheese melts, about 1 minute. Top with a dollop of *Guacamole I, page 33*; serve hot.

"VEAL-LETS" PARMIGIANA

Cut *1 small loaf French bread* into ½-inch slices. Lightly brown slices in *¼ cup olive or other cooking oil* heated with *1 halved garlic clove* in a skillet. Drain on absorbent paper. Brown *2 veal cutlets* (pounded flat) in hot oil remaining in skillet. Drain off excess oil. Cover; cook 8 minutes, turning once or twice. Cut veal in small pieces and put on bread slices. Top each with *tomato sauce*, a square of sliced *mozzarella cheese*, a strip of *pimiento*, and a sprinkling of *seasoned pepper*, *oregano*, or *Italian seasoning*. Broil until cheese is melted.

COLD APPETIZERS

Dip-Its

CHILI AND BEAN DIP

1 cup pork and beans with tomato sauce	1 tablespoon chili powder
¼ cup mayonnaise	1 wedge onion
2 tablespoons dry onion soup mix	Dairy sour cream

1. Put all ingredients except sour cream into an electric blender container. Cover and blend.
2. Transfer mixture to a serving dish and stir in sour cream to taste, about ½ cup.
3. Serve *potato chips* and *corn chips* as dippers.

ABOUT 2 CUPS DIP

BLUE CHEESE DIP WITH MUSHROOMS

½ cup crumbled blue cheese	½ teaspoon salt
½ cup dairy sour cream	2 drops Tabasco
½ cup mayonnaise	Mushrooms, fresh or canned
½ cup finely chopped celery	

1. Mix cheese, sour cream, mayonnaise, celery, salt, and Tabasco in a bowl. Chill thoroughly.
2. Spear mushrooms with cocktail picks and use as dippers.

ABOUT 1 ½ CUPS DIP

MULTI-CHEESE BLENDIP

2 oz. Cheddar cheese, shredded	¼ cup butter, cut in pieces
2 oz. blue cheese, crumbled	½ cup dairy sour cream
2 oz. Port du Salut (Trappist cheese), cut in pieces	⅛ teaspoon salt
	1 tablespoon sherry
	¼ teaspoon Tabasco
2 oz. cream cheese, cut in pieces	⅛ teaspoon Worcestershire sauce
	1 small clove garlic, minced

1. Using an electric mixer or blender, blend all ingredients together until light and creamy; chill thoroughly.
2. Serve with a tray of assorted *crackers*.

ABOUT 2¼ CUPS DIP

TOMATO-CHEESE DIP

8 oz. cream cheese, softened	¾ teaspoon salt
1 medium-sized ripe tomato, peeled and cut in small pieces	1 teaspoon grated onion
	1 or 2 drops Tabasco

With a fork, thoroughly blend cream cheese with tomato. Mix in remaining ingredients and chill.

ABOUT 2 CUPS DIP

TUNA SENSATION

8 oz. cream cheese, softened	½ teaspoon salt
2 tablespoons minced onion	Few grains black pepper
½ clove garlic, minced	⅛ teaspoon crushed chervil
1 tablespoon prepared horseradish	½ cup dairy sour cream
1 teaspoon Worcestershire sauce	1 can (6½ or 7 oz.) tuna, drained and flaked

1. Mix into cream cheese the onion, garlic, horseradish, Worcestershire sauce, salt, pepper, and chervil. Blend in sour cream. Add tuna and mix thoroughly.
2. Turn dip into a serving bowl and ring with finely snipped *parsley*. Serve with a tray of *crackers*.

ABOUT 1⅔ CUPS DIP

CANTONESE APPETIZER SAUCES

One of the Far East specialties which imparts subtle, exciting flavor to appetizers or hors d'oeuvres is the versatile sweet-sour fruit sauce. Another, usually offered at the same time, is a very hot mustard sauce. Crisp, flavorful egg rolls, an authentic Chinese hors d'oeuvre (available in frozen form), are usually accompanied by these sauces.

SWEET-SOUR SAUCE

Garlic-Flavored Vinegar, *page 33*	½ cup honey
1 can (17 oz.) apricots	½ cup lightly packed brown sugar
½ cup crushed pineapple	½ teaspoon salt
	Few grains white pepper

1. Have ready Garlic-Flavored Vinegar.
2. Force apricots through a sieve or food mill into

a 1-quart saucepan. Stir in remaining ingredients.
3. Cook and stir over high heat until brown sugar is dissolved and mixture boils; reduce heat and cook slowly 10 minutes, stirring frequently to prevent sticking.
4. Remove from heat and stir in 2 tablespoons Garlic-Flavored Vinegar. Cool; cover sauce and chill. ABOUT 2½ CUPS SAUCE

Garlic-Flavored Vinegar: Measure ½ *cup cider vinegar* into a jar. Add ½ *clove garlic.* Cover jar tightly and refrigerate 3 days.

HOT MUSTARD SAUCE

⅓ to ½ cup dry mustard	1 tablespoon butter, melted
1 teaspoon sugar	1 teaspoon cider vinegar
¼ teaspoon salt	

Mix the mustard, sugar, and salt thoroughly in a bowl. Stir in butter, vinegar, and enough *boiling water* to make a thick sauce. ABOUT ½ CUP SAUCE

MUSTARD DIPPING SAUCE

⅔ cup mayonnaise	¼ cup bottled steak sauce
½ cup prepared mustard	Juice of 1 lemon
	10 drops Tabasco

1. Mix all ingredients well in a chilled bowl.
2. Use as a dip for chilled *lobster* or *crab meat*; crisp *raw vegetables;* or hot appetizers, such as *Vienna sausages* or *cocktail sausages,* bitesized pieces of cooked *frankfurters* or *luncheon meat* served on cocktail picks. ABOUT 1⅓ CUPS SAUCE

Spreads

GUACAMOLE I

1 chilled large ripe avocado	¾ teaspoon salt
1 chilled large ripe tomato, peeled and chopped	4 teaspoons wine vinegar
¼ cup finely chopped onion	1 tablespoon lemon juice
	½ teaspoon finely chopped hot chili pepper

1. Peel avocado; cut in pieces. Crush avocado with a fork. Add remaining ingredients; mix well.

2. Serve with *crisp crackers, potato chips, corn chips,* or *Tostaditas, page 31.* ABOUT 2 CUPS

GUACAMOLE II

1½ cups mashed ripe avocado	3 tablespoons minced onion
2 to 3 teaspoons lemon juice	⅓ cup finely chopped, peeled, and seeded ripe tomato (optional)
½ teaspoon salt	

Mix all ingredients thoroughly. Cover tightly and chill until ready to serve. ABOUT 2 CUPS

BRAUNSCHWEIGER CANAPÉ SPREAD

½ cup Braunschweiger (smoked liver sausage)	1 to 2 teaspoons grated onion

1. Beat Braunschweiger with a fork until soft; mix in onion.
2. Spread on *buttered toast rounds.* Garnish with *caviar* and *sieved hard-cooked egg yolk.*
ABOUT ½ CUP

NUT-COATED CHEESE LOG

8 oz. cream cheese, softened	1 tablespoon Worcestershire sauce
4 oz. Roquefort cheese	1 tablespoon grated onion
1 jar (5 oz.) pasteurized process sharp Cheddar cheese spread	½ teaspoon salt
	¼ cup minced parsley
	¼ cup chopped pecans

1. Thoroughly blend cheeses, Worcestershire sauce, onion, and salt. Chill several hours.
2. Shape cheese mixture into a log or mound; coat evenly with the parsley and pecans. Chill until ready to serve with *crisp crackers.* ABOUT 2 CUPS

PLANTATION CHEESE LOG

1 cup pecans	⅛ teaspoon Worcestershire sauce
2 cloves garlic	⅛ teaspoon soy sauce
6 oz. cream cheese, softened	4 drops Tabasco
⅛ teaspoon salt	1½ teaspoons chili powder

1. Put pecans and garlic through medium blade of a food chopper.

2. Blend the remaining ingredients except chili powder in a bowl; mix in the pecan-garlic mixture.
3. Shape into a roll about 1½ inches in diameter. Sprinkle chili powder evenly over a sheet of waxed paper and roll log in the powder to coat evenly.
4. Wrap tightly in moisture-vaporproof material. Chill cheese log at least 4 hours.
5. Slice before serving. If necessary, allow log to stand at room temperature to soften slightly. Serve with assorted *crisp crackers*.

1 CHEESE LOG (ABOUT 20 SLICES)

HOMEMADE POT CHEESE

1 "Baby" Gouda cheese (remove wax coating), finely shredded	2 tablespoons red wine vinegar
3 oz. blue cheese	½ cup dairy sour cream
¼ cup butter or margarine, softened	1½ tablespoons chopped chives
	Few grains cayenne pepper

1. Mix cheeses with butter in a heavy saucepan. Add remaining ingredients; blend thoroughly.
2. Cook over low heat, stirring vigorously, until cheese is melted. Cool slightly.
3. Spoon into small pots and store in refrigerator.

ABOUT 2½ CUPS

CHEESE BALL
Prepare this cheese ball well ahead of serving time.

2 pkgs. (8 oz. each) cream cheese	½ teaspoon seasoned salt
½ lb. sharp Cheddar cheese, shredded	¼ teaspoon salt
2 teaspoons grated onion	1 can (2¼ oz.) deviled ham
2 teaspoons Worcestershire sauce	2 tablespoons finely chopped parsley
1 teaspoon lemon juice	2 tablespoons finely chopped pimiento, thoroughly drained
1 teaspoon dry mustard	
½ teaspoon paprika	Finely chopped pecans (about ⅔ cup)

1. Soften the cream cheese in a small mixer bowl, beating with electric beater. Beat in the Cheddar cheese, onion, Worcestershire sauce, lemon juice, dry mustard, paprika, seasoned salt, salt, and deviled ham until mixture is creamy.
2. Stir in the parsley and pimiento. Cover and refrigerate several hours, or until cheese mixture is firm enough to handle.

3. Shape into a ball and coat evenly with the chopped pecans. Wrap in moisture-vaporproof material and refrigerate until ready to serve. Or blend nuts with snipped *parsley* or snipped slices of *dried smoked beef* before coating. Serve with assorted *crackers* and small thin *cocktail rye-bread slices*.

1 CHEESE BALL (ABOUT 3 CUPS)

CAMEMBERT MOUSSE
This delicate mousse provides a pleasant contrast to an assortment of highly seasoned appetizers.

1 env. unflavored gelatin	2 tablespoons minced parsley
½ cup cold milk	½ teaspoon paprika
8 oz. Camembert cheese, forced through a fine sieve	1 egg white, beaten to stiff, not dry, peaks
2 tablespoons sieved pimiento	½ cup chilled heavy cream, whipped

1. Soften gelatin in milk in a heavy saucepan. Stir over low heat until gelatin is dissolved. Add the cheese and stir until melted.
2. Remove from heat and mix in pimiento, parsley, and paprika. Turn into bowl, cover, and refrigerate until cool.
3. Fold egg white and cream into the cooled cheese mixture. Turn into a 2-cup fancy mold; chill several hours, or until firm.
4. Unmold onto a large serving dish or tray. Surround with assorted crisp relishes such as *celery curls*, *carrot* and *zucchini sticks*, *radish roses*, *green pepper strips*, *cucumber slices*, *green onions*, and *green* and *ripe olives*. Serve with a tray of assorted *crackers*.

ONE 2-CUP MOLD

CHICKEN LIVERS FINE CHAMPAGNE QUEEN ELIZABETH
Fine champagne, a brandy produced in the vicinity of Cognac, France, enhances this well-flavored pâté, a canapé spread served at the Queen Elizabeth Hotel in Montreal, Canada.

½ lb. chicken livers	1 stalk celery, diced
¼ cup rendered chicken fat	1 hard-cooked egg, chopped
2 tablespoons brandy	1 onion, minced

1. Sauté livers in hot chicken fat in a skillet until tender. Pour on brandy and "blaze" it.
2. Remove livers to a chopping board and finely chop them. Mix with celery, egg, and onion.

3. Add enough chicken fat to make a smooth paste. Season to taste with *salt* and *pepper*.

ABOUT 2 CUPS PÂTÉ

LIVER PÂTÉ EXCEPTIONALE

This excellent and quite different recipe from Charlie's Café Exceptionale in Minneapolis, Minnesota, is large enough to serve a crowd.

Pâté:
1 lb. onions, sliced
1 clove garlic, finely
  minced
¼ cup rendered chicken
  fat
1 lb. chicken livers,
  coarsely diced
1 teaspoon salt
Few grains freshly
  ground black pepper
Sauce:
1¼ cups olive oil

¾ cup horseradish
  mustard
¼ cup vinegar
½ cup finely diced
  celery
½ cup finely diced
  onion
¼ cup snipped parsley
1 tablespoon paprika
1 teaspoon salt
½ teaspoon freshly
  ground black pepper

1. For pâté, add the onions and garlic to hot chicken fat in a skillet. Cook, stirring occasionally, until onion is golden.
2. Add chicken livers, salt, and pepper. Cook the livers until cooked through, but not browned.
3. Put the onion-liver mixture through a food chopper; turn into a bowl and whip to a smooth paste with rotary beater. If pâté is too thick, add *chicken broth* until of desired consistency.
4. For sauce, combine the olive oil in a bowl with the remaining ingredients; mix well. Serve with the liver pâté.

2 CUPS PÂTÉ AND 3 CUPS SAUCE

Canapés & Hors d'Oeuvres

GLAZED CANAPÉS

The glaze on these canapés serves three purposes: it is the mark of a professional, it helps retain the freshness of the canapés, and it adds eye-appeal.

CLEAR GLAZE: Soften *1 envelope unflavored gelatin* in ⅔ *cup cold water* in a bowl. Pour *1 cup boiling water* over softened gelatin and stir until gelatin is dissolved. Chill until slightly thickened. **To glaze canapés:** Place canapés on wire racks over a large shallow pan. Working quickly, spoon about 2 teaspoons of slightly thickened gelatin over each canapé. (Have ready a bowl of ice and water and a bowl

of hot water. The gelatin may have to be set over one or the other during glazing to maintain the proper consistency.) The gelatin should cling slightly to canapés when spooned over them. Any drips may be scooped up and reused.

WHIPPED BUTTER: Whip chilled firm *butter* using electric mixer at high speed just until butter is fluffy and of spreading consistency.

ANCHOVY

Spread *toasted bread triangles* with *whipped unsalted butter*. Cover surface with *anchovy fillets* and top each canapé with half of a *pimiento-stuffed olive* and a small piece of *pickled cauliflower*. Glaze and chill. Just before serving, pipe a ribbon of *cooked salad dressing* over the olive.

DANISH HAM

Whip together ½ *cup whipped butter* and *2 tablespoons finely chopped pickled walnuts*. Spread on *toasted bread triangles*. Top with a thin slice of *Danish ham*, a *white asparagus tip*, a *tarragon leaf*, and a *pimiento-stuffed olive slice*. Glaze and chill.

PROSCIUTTO

Whip ¼ *cup spiced peach syrup* and *2 tablespoons sieved spiced peach* into ½ *cup whipped butter*. Spread peach butter onto *toasted bread diamonds*. Top with thin slices of *prosciutto* (Italian ham) and garnish with a *pimiento-stuffed olive slice*, sprinkled with *minced parsley*. Glaze and chill.

ROAST BEEF-OYSTER

Whip ½ *cup whipped butter*, *2 teaspoons crushed tarragon leaves*, and ¼ *teaspoon freshly ground black pepper* until just blended. Spread onto *toasted bread squares*. Top with a thin slice of *roast beef*. Place a *pimento-stuffed olive slice* at one corner, sieved *hard-cooked egg yolk* at the opposite corner, and a slice of *smoked oyster* in the middle of each canapé. Glaze and chill.

SMOKED SALMON

Mix together *6 sieved hard-cooked eggs*, ¼ *cup cooked salad dressing*, *1 tablespoon tomato paste*, 1½ *teaspoons lemon juice*, and *1 teaspoon salt*. Spread onto *toasted bread ovals*. Top with a thin strip of *smoked salmon*, rolled and sprinkled with minced *parsley*, and a *pimiento-stuffed olive slice* topped with sieved *hard-cooked egg white*. Glaze and chill.

WINE-CHEESE

Whip together ½ *cup whipped unsalted butter* and *4 teaspoons Roquefort cheese*. Spread onto *toasted bread rounds*. Whip *2 packages (3 ounces each) cream cheese* with *2 tablespoons sauterne*. Pipe a swirl of the mixture onto each canapé. Roll edges in minced *parsley*. Top with *pimiento-stuffed olive slice*; sprinkle with *paprika*. Glaze and chill.

CARCIOFI ALLA GRECA GEORGE'S

These Greek-style artichokes are included on the menu at George's on Via Marche in Rome.

6 artichokes	½ cup dry white
4 oz. fresh mushrooms,	wine
sliced	Juice of 1 lemon
⅔ cup coarsely	30 fennel seeds
chopped onion	¼ teaspoon coriander
½ cup olive oil	Salt and pepper
	to taste

1. Rinse artichokes and discard the hard outer leaves. Quarter artichokes, remove and discard "choke" or fuzzy part, and arrange the pieces in a large baking pan or shallow heatproof casserole having a cover. Allow plenty of space for the artichokes.
2. Cover artichoke pieces with the mushrooms and onion. Then pour over them a mixture of the remaining ingredients.
3. Cover and place over medium heat. Bring to a rapid boil and cook about 1 minute.
4. Transfer the pan to a 350°F oven for about 30 minutes, or until artichokes are tender.
5. Remove from oven; cool at room temperature, then refrigerate to chill thoroughly. Serve cold.

ABOUT 8 SERVINGS

CHEESY SESAME-STUFFED CELERY

3 oz. cream cheese,	2 teaspoons butter
softened	¼ cup sesame seed
1 tablespoon milk	2 tablespoons shredded
1 teaspoon grated	Parmesan cheese
onion	Celery stalks

1. Beat cream cheese, milk, and onion together until fluffy; chill in refrigerator.
2. Melt butter in a skillet over medium heat. Add sesame seed and stir constantly until delicately browned. Remove from heat and stir in the Parmesan cheese; cool.

3. To serve, fill crisp celery stalks with cheese mixture; sprinkle sesame-seed mixture generously over top. Cut crosswise into 2-inch lengths.

DANISH BLUE CHEESE PIE WITH GRAPES

From the pumpernickel crumb pie shell to the luscious green grape, blue cheese gelatin filling, this attractive and unusual pie is truly an epicurean delight.

2 env. unflavored	1 cup heavy cream,
gelatin	whipped
½ cup cold water	Baked Pumpernickel
½ lb. Danish blue	Crumb Crust, *below*
cheese	1 lb. seedless green
	grapes

1. Soften gelatin in cold water and dissolve over low heat.
2. Mash the blue cheese well and stir in gelatin; mix until blended.
3. Fold whipped cream gently into cheese mixture. Turn into prepared crust. Cover thickly with green grapes, placed upright. (Or use red Tokay or black Ribier grapes in season; cut them in half and remove seeds.) Chill until set. ONE 9-INCH PIE

DANISH BLUE CHEESE BALLS: Follow recipe for Danish Blue Cheese Pie with Grapes, preparing one half recipe of filling only; refrigerate if necessary for ease in handling. Dry and crush *4 slices pumpernickel* according to directions in recipe for Pumpernickel Crumb Crust. Form cheese mixture into 1-inch balls, roll in crumbs, and chill. Place a whole *seedless grape* on a wooden pick for each cheese ball. ABOUT 4 DOZEN CHEESE BALLS

PUMPERNICKEL CRUMB CRUST

1 loaf (11 oz.) thin-	½ cup butter,
sliced square dark	melted
pumpernickel bread,	¼ cup sugar
dried and crushed*	

1. Blend the crumbs, butter, and sugar and press firmly against the bottom and sides of a 9-inch pie plate.
2. Bake at 350°F 15 minutes. Cool before filling.

ONE 9-INCH PIE SHELL

*Put bread slices into a shallow pan and set in a 275°F oven until bread is quite dry. Remove from oven. Break bread into small pieces and crush to fine crumbs (in an electric blender if available).

MINIATURE CHEESE PUFFS

1 cup water	½ cup shredded
½ cup butter	Parmesan cheese
½ teaspoon salt	Crab Meat Salad Filling,
1 cup all-purpose flour	or Chicken Salad
4 eggs	Filling, *below*

1. Bring water, butter, and salt to a rolling boil in a heavy saucepan.
2. Add the flour all at once and cook over low heat, beating vigorously with a wooden spoon until mixture leaves the sides of pan and forms a compact ball. Remove from heat.
3. Beat in eggs, one at a time. Continue beating until mixture is smooth and has a satin sheen. Mix in the Parmesan cheese.
4. Force dough through a pastry bag and tube, or drop by slightly rounded measuring teaspoonfuls 1 inch apart onto a lightly greased baking sheet.
5. Bake at 375°F 20 minutes, or until golden. Remove the puffs to wire rack and cool.
6. When cool, cut off tops of puffs, fill as desired, and replace tops. ABOUT 5 DOZEN MINIATURE PUFFS

CRAB MEAT SALAD FILLING

1⅓ cups (6½-oz. can) crab meat, drained, bony tissue removed, and meat finely chopped	¼ cup diced celery ¼ cup chopped ripe olives ⅓ cup mayonnaise Few grains pepper

Toss all ingredients lightly together in a bowl to mix thoroughly; chill. ABOUT 1½ CUPS FILLING

CHICKEN SALAD FILLING

2 cups finely chopped cooked chicken	2 teaspoons capers, drained and chopped
1 env. Italian salad dressing mix, prepared following directions	¼ cup mayonnaise 1½ teaspoons lemon juice
¼ cup toasted blanched almonds, finely chopped	½ teaspoon salt ⅛ teaspoon black pepper
¼ cup finely chopped celery	

1. Marinate the chicken in the prepared dressing about 1 hour; drain chicken thoroughly.
2. Combine marinated chicken, the almonds, celery, and capers in a bowl. Add a mixture of the remaining ingredients. Toss lightly until thoroughly mixed; chill.
3. When ready to serve, spoon filling into the miniature cheese puffs. ABOUT 2 CUPS FILLING

CUCUMBER-CHICKEN CANAPÉS

1 cup finely chopped cooked chicken	½ cup mayonnaise Thinly sliced white
⅔ cup chopped salted pecans	bread (crusts removed), cut in
⅓ cup chopped seeded pared cucumber	1½-in. rounds Whipped butter or
1 teaspoon monosodium glutamate	margarine Unpared cucumber
Few grains white pepper	slices

1. Combine chicken with pecans, chopped cucumber, monosodium glutamate, pepper, and mayonnaise. Chill the mixture thoroughly.
2. When ready to make canapés, spread bread with whipped butter. Cover with cucumber slice and spread chicken mixture over cucumber, leaving green edge showing.
3. Cut thin slices of cucumber in half and remove seeds. Sprinkle with *paprika*. Twist cucumber and set on canapé. Place *pimiento-stuffed olive slices* or sprigs of *parsley* along side of cucumber. ABOUT 2½ DOZEN CANAPÉS

CRAB-AVOCADO CANAPÉS

1 pkg. (6 oz.) frozen crab meat, thawed, drained, and flaked	1 teaspoon capers Mayonnaise
Italian salad dressing	Avocado Spread, *below* Thinly sliced bread
¼ cup diced celery	(crusts removed), cut
1½ teaspoons diced pimiento	in fancy shapes

1. Toss crab meat with a small amount of the salad dressing. Chill well.
2. When ready to make canapés, combine crab meat with celery, pimiento, and capers; mix well. Blend with enough mayonnaise to just moisten.
3. Spread avocado mixture over bread and cover with crab mixture. Garnish each canapé with sprigs of *watercress*. ABOUT 1½ DOZEN CANAPES

AVOCADO SPREAD: Scoop out the pulp from *1 medium-sized avocado* and mash. Blend in *1 teaspoon Italian salad dressing mix, 1 teaspoon lemon juice,* and only enough *dairy sour cream* to make of

good spreading consistency. Chill until ready to use.
ABOUT ½ CUP SPREAD

SAVORY MINIATURE CROUSTADES

Miniature Croustades,
   page 116
1 can (2¼ oz.) deviled
   ham
3 tablespoons finely
   crumbled blue cheese
1 cup dairy sour cream

1. Mix the deviled ham with blue cheese and gently blend in sour cream.
2. Shortly before serving, fill Miniature Croustades with sour cream mixture. Garnish with tiny *parsley sprigs* or *pimiento pieces*.
ABOUT 4 DOZEN APPETIZERS

DEVILED HAM CANAPÉS

1 can (4½ oz.) deviled
   ham
¼ cup dairy sour cream
¼ teaspoon dill weed
3 tablespoons chopped
   cucumber pickle
¼ cup butter or
   margarine
2 teaspoons lemon
   juice

1. Mix deviled ham, sour cream, dill weed, and pickle. Chill thoroughly.
2. Cream the butter with the lemon juice until fluffy. Spread on toast rounds. Cover with deviled ham spread and garnish with slices of *pimiento-stuffed olives*.
ABOUT ¾ CUP SPREAD

LOBSTER APPETIZER TIDBITS

6 frozen South African
   rock lobster tails
   (about 5 oz. each)
1 cup mayonnaise
1 teaspoon curry
   powder
1 teaspoon prepared
   mustard
½ teaspoon onion salt
½ teaspoon paprika
1 teaspoon Angostura
   bitters

1. Drop frozen lobster tails into boiling *salted water*; cover, bring to boiling, lower heat and simmer only until lobster meat turns white (6 to 8 minutes). Drain and rinse with cold water.
2. Using scissors, remove thin membrane on underside of each tail, cutting close to shell; insert fingers under meat and remove from shell in one piece; chill thoroughly.
3. Blend mayonnaise with the remaining ingredients; chill.

4. At serving time, cut lobster into bite-size pieces, insert a wooden pick into each piece, and arrange on a platter with chilled dip in center.
APPETIZERS FOR 12

BUTTER TARTS WITH MUSHROOM CREAM
A prize-winning recipe truly worthy of its blue ribbon.

Butter Pastry for Tarts,
   page 457
2 beef bouillon cubes
⅓ cup boiling water
½ cup butter or
   margarine
½ lb. fresh mushrooms,
   chopped
¼ cup minced onion
2 tablespoons flour
1 cup heavy cream,
   whipped

1. Prepare tart shells. Cool.
2. Meanwhile, dissolve bouillon cubes in the boiling water; set aside to cool.
3. Heat butter in a skillet; add the mushrooms and onion and cook, stirring occasionally, until mushrooms are tender, about 8 minutes.
4. Put flour into a small saucepan. Add the cooled broth gradually, stirring constantly. Continue to stir and bring to boiling; boil 1 minute. Blend sauce with the mushrooms; set aside to cool.
5. When ready to serve, blend whipped cream with mushroom mixture. Spoon mushroom cream into tart shells. Garnish with sprigs of *watercress*.
ABOUT 2 DOZEN TARTS

SARDINE CARTWHEEL
The enchanting fjord city of Stavanger, Norway, is noted not only for its beauty and friendly people, but for its world-famous sardines. The catch is held in nets in the cool waters of the fjords for three days before being prepared for smoking, drenching with pure olive oil, and packing into cans.

1 slice pumpernickel
   or rye bread cut
   from a round loaf
   (bread slice about
   8 in. in diameter
   and ¼ in. thick)
Herbed Mayonnaise,
   page 39
1 chilled hard-cooked
   egg
½ teaspoon grated
   lemon peel
⅛ teaspoon salt
1 to 3 cans (3¾ oz.
   each) Norwegian
   sardines, about 22

1. For a perfect round, invert an 8-inch bowl over bread slice and cut with pointed knife around edge to remove crust. Spread bread generously with Herbed Mayonnaise.

2. Separate yolk from white of egg; finely chop white and sprinkle over mayonnaise. Sieve yolk; toss with lemon peel and salt; sprinkle lightly over white, reserving about 1 teaspoon for garnish.

3. Arrange sardines spoke-fashion over egg with large ends of sardines placed about ½ inch from outer edge of bread and tails toward the center. Turn sardines once, so a little egg yolk will adhere. Spoon reserved egg yolk in center.

4. Break wooden picks into various lengths; thread *1, 2, or 3 cocktail onions* onto each pick, depending upon length of pick. Insert picks into center of canapé in a cluster.

5. Arrange *watercress leaves* around outer edge of sardines on canapé to make a ½-inch border.

6. Using a broad spatula or turner, transfer cart-wheel to serving plate. Squeeze a few drops of *lemon juice* over each sardine.

7. To serve, cut into pie-shaped wedges with a whole sardine on each wedge. 20 TO 22 CANAPÉS

HERBED MAYONNAISE: Blend *½ cup mayonnaise, 1 teaspoon grated onion, ¼ teaspoon dill weed, ½ teaspoon crushed tarragon,* and *2 teaspoons finely snipped parsley* thoroughly. Cover and chill.

Antipasto

In Italy a dinner is likely to start with the antipasto, or "before the meal" course. This may vary from a duet of prosciutto and melon to an elaborate tray of appetizers, often including fish, meat, eggs, cheese, and raw or marinated vegetables.

MARINATED PIMIENTO PICCANTE

2 to 3 tablespoons red wine vinegar	2 jars or cans (7 oz. each) whole pimientos, drained and torn in half or in large pieces
2 cloves garlic, minced	
1 bay leaf	
½ teaspoon salt	
½ teaspoon pepper	
2 tablespoons olive or other cooking oil	1 can anchovy fillets
2 tablespoons chili sauce	¼ cup slivered ripe olives
	1 tablespoon lemon juice

1. Put the vinegar, garlic, bay leaf, salt, and pepper into a saucepan; simmer 5 minutes.

2. Blend in oil and chili sauce; pour over pimientos. Let stand about 3 hours.

3. To serve, drain pimientos and garnish with anchovy fillets and ripe olives. Drizzle lemon juice over all. 6 SERVINGS

ANTIPASTO-RELISH TRAY

Arrange the Zucchini Vinaigrette, icy-cold slices of cantaloupe, cornucopias of prosciutto, celery, and carrot curls, and anise, or finocchio pieces on a chilled serving tray. Serve with crisp crackers.

ZUCCHINI VINAIGRETTE

5 or 6 medium-sized zucchini	2 tablespoons finely chopped green pepper
1 pkg. Italian salad dressing mix	2 tablespoons finely chopped parsley
¼ cup white wine vinegar	¼ cup finely chopped green onion
½ cup salad oil	3 tablespoons sweet pickle relish

1. Cut ends from each zucchini and slice lengthwise into 6 pieces. Cook in a small amount of boiling *salted water* about 3 minutes, or until crisp-tender. Drain if necessary and cool; put into a shallow dish.

2. While zucchini is cooling, combine the remaining ingredients in a jar with a tight-fitting lid. Cover and shake vigorously to mix well.

3. Pour vinaigrette sauce over zucchini. Chill 4 hours or overnight. Serve on antipasto tray.

Nibblers

COCONUT CHIPS

1 medium-sized fresh coconut	Salt

1. With an ice pick, force holes through indentations of the coconut; drain off liquid. Put the coconut into a baking dish and heat in a 350°F oven 30 minutes.

2. Remove from oven and break the shell by tapping sharply with a hammer. Remove meat from the shell and pare off brown skin.

3. Form chips by pulling the coconut meat across a slicer, or use a vegetable parer. Spread the chips in a single layer on baking sheets. Sprinkle lightly with salt.

4. Heat in a 375°F oven 8 to 10 minutes, or until chips are lightly browned.

CRUNCHY NIBBLERS

2 cups puffed rice cereal	1 cup butter or
2 cups puffed wheat	margarine, melted
cereal	¾ teaspoon salt
1 lb. mixed salted nuts	¾ teaspoon curry
1 can (4 oz.) shoestring	powder
potatoes	¾ teaspoon onion salt
4 oz. small pretzel rings	½ teaspoon garlic salt
or sticks	

1. Stir the cereals, nuts, potatoes, and pretzels together in a large shallow baking pan. Blend the remaining ingredients and pour over cereal mixture. Toss lightly with a fork.
2. Heat at 300°F about 30 minutes, stirring sever-al times. Serve warm or cool. Store in tightly covered container in cool dry place.

ABOUT 3 QUARTS

PIQUANT PECANS
These make fine go-alongs with cold drinks.

¼ cup butter or	4 teaspoons Worces-
margarine	tershire sauce
2 teaspoons garlic salt	4 cups pecan halves
½ teaspoon Tabasco	

1. Heat butter in a skillet. Add garlic salt, Tabasco, and Worcestershire sauce; stir well. Add pecan halves and stir until coated.
2. Spread pecans in a single layer in a large shallow baking pan.
3. Heat in a 350°F oven about 25 minutes, or until deep brown and crisp, stirring occasionally. Drain on absorbent paper. 4 CUPS PIQUANT PECANS

SIT-DOWN APPETIZERS

OYSTERS ROCKEFELLER
This delectable appetizer originated at Antoine's restaurant in New Orleans where a patron tasted it and exclaimed, "Why, this is as rich as Rockefeller!"

1 egg, well beaten	1 tablespoon minced
2 cups Medium White	parsley
Sauce, *page 342*	½ teaspoon Worces-
2 doz. shell oysters	tershire sauce
2 tablespoons sherry	6 drops Tabasco
2 tablespoons butter	¼ teaspoon salt
or margarine	Few grains ground
1 tablespoon finely	nutmeg
chopped onion	¼ cup shredded
1 lb. fresh spinach,	Parmesan cheese
cooked, drained,	
and finely chopped	

1. Stir the egg into white sauce; set aside.
2. Pour *coarse salt* into a 15x10x1-inch jelly roll pan to a ¼-inch depth. Open oysters and arrange the oysters-in-the-shells on the salt; sprinkle ¼ teaspoon sherry over each.
3. Heat the butter in a heavy skillet. Add the onion and cook until partially tender. Add the chopped spinach, 2 tablespoons of the white sauce, parsley, Worcestershire sauce, and Tabasco to the skillet along with a mixture of the salt and nutmeg; mix thoroughly. Heat 2 to 3 minutes.
4. Spoon spinach mixture over all of the oysters. Spoon remaining white sauce over spinach. Sprinkle each oyster with cheese.
5. Bake at 375°F 15 to 20 minutes, or until tops are lightly browned. 4 TO 6 SERVINGS

SHRIMP COCKTAIL, SEVICHE STYLE
Seviche is a popular marinated raw fish dish served as an appetizer south of the border.

1½ lbs. cooked shrimp,	½ cup lime juice
shelled, deveined,	1½ teaspoons salt
and chilled	½ teaspoon mono-
1 firm ripe tomato,	sodium glutamate
peeled and diced	2 to 3 teaspoons soy
¼ cup thinly sliced green	sauce
onions with tops	¼ teaspoon Worces-
¼ cup thinly sliced	tershire sauce
celery	½ clove garlic, minced

1. Dice the chilled shrimp into a bowl and combine with remaining ingredients; toss lightly to mix well. Chill in refrigerator, covered, about 8 hours.
2. Serve very cold on cocktail sea shells lined with *leaf lettuce*. Or, if desired, spoon cocktail mix-

ture into ripe *avocado halves* brushed with *lime juice.* 6 SERVINGS

ROSY SAUCE
(Salsa Rosata)
From Antico Martini, a famous restaurant on St. Mark's Square in Venice, Italy, comes this delightfully smooth and piquant dressing for seafood.

¾ cup ketchup	1½ teaspoons Worcestershire sauce
½ cup mayonnaise	1 teaspoon prepared horseradish
½ cup heavy cream	4 drops Tabasco
2 tablespoons cognac	

1. Mix all ingredients; chill thoroughly.
2. Arrange chilled *seafood* on *lettuce*, drizzle with *lemon juice* and spoon on sauce.
ABOUT 1½ CUPS SAUCE

SHRIMP REMOULADE
Here is a best-liked Creole cocktail sauce to enhance shrimp or crab meat.

2 cups mayonnaise	1 teaspoon finely crushed chervil
1 tablespoon prepared mustard	1 teaspoon tarragon leaves, finely crushed
1 tablespoon finely chopped sweet pickle	½ teaspoon anchovy paste
1 tablespoon chopped capers	1 to 2 drops Tabasco
1 tablespoon minced parsley	Deveined cooked shrimp, chilled

1. Blend all ingredients except shrimp. Refrigerate until thoroughly chilled.
2. Allowing 4 or 5 shrimp for each appetizer, spoon onto crisp *lettuce* with sauce over all.
6 TO 8 SERVINGS

SHRIMP WITH PEPPY COCKTAIL SAUCE

1 cup ketchup	1 tablespoon sugar
1 tablespoon lemon juice	½ teaspoon salt
1 tablespoon prepared horseradish	¼ teaspoon monosodium glutamate
1 teaspoon onion juice	1½ lbs. fresh shrimp with shells, cooked, peeled, deveined, and chilled
¼ teaspoon Worcestershire sauce	
Few drops Tabasco	

1. Mix thoroughly in a small bowl all ingredients

except the shrimp; refrigerate until ready to serve.
2. To prepare cocktail, line 6 chilled sherbet glasses with chilled *lettuce* or *curly endive*. Arrange about 5 shrimp in each glass and top with cocktail sauce. 6 SERVINGS

LOMI LOMI SALMON
There are several versions of this fish preparation, some of them using smoked or salted salmon.

1 lb. raw salmon steaks	2 tablespoons lemon juice
½ cup cider vinegar	1 tablespoon soy sauce
¾ cup finely sliced green onions	1 tablespoon peanut oil
3 large ripe tomatoes, peeled and diced	1 teaspoon salt

1. Remove bones and skin from salmon and cut into small pieces (about 2 cups). Marinate in the vinegar about 2 hours.
2. Drain salmon and mix with the green onions and tomatoes.
3. Blend remaining ingredients. Pour over salmon and vegetables; toss lightly to mix. Chill mixture thoroughly before serving. ABOUT 6 SERVINGS

SNAILS BURGUNDY
(Escargots à la Bourguignonne)
These garlic-flavored snails, served in their shells, are a French specialty.

½ cup butter, softened	1 clove garlic, minced
1 tablespoon minced parsley	½ teaspoon white wine
1 teaspoon minced onion	¼ teaspoon Worcestershire sauce
	1 can (2 oz.) snails

1. Cream butter with parsley, onion, garlic, wine, and Worcestershire sauce until thoroughly blended. Refrigerate until ready to use.
2. Fill a large shallow baking dish with *coarse salt* to a depth of ¼ inch.
3. Drain the snails, reserving liquid. Spoon ⅛ teaspoon liquid into each shell. Spoon in ¼ teaspoon butter, put in a snail, and fill with remaining butter.
4. Place shells, open side up, in baking dish, pushing shells into the salt to keep them upright.
5. Bake at 375°F 5 to 7 minutes, or until snails are thoroughly heated. Serve immediately.
2 DOZEN SNAILS
NOTE: Snails usually come packed with shells.

SIP-ITS

SHRUBS

Fill 4- to 6-ounce glasses about ⅔ full with icy cold *fruit juice* (or a mixture of juices). If desired, spark with a dash of *sparkling water*. Float a small scoopful of *sherbet* on each serving.

ORANGE DUO: *Orange juice* with *orange sherbet*.
PINEAPPLE: *Pineapple juice* with *lime sherbet*.
APRICOT: *Apricot nectar* with *lemon sherbet*.

CRANBERRY SPRITZER

Combine equal parts of chilled *cranberry juice cocktail* and chilled *sparkling white grape juice* (or three parts chilled cranberry juice cocktail and two parts chilled sparkling white grape juice) in a tall pitcher. Mix lightly. Add a *few drops red food coloring* to tint desired shade.

SUNSHINE COCKTAIL

1 cup water	1 slice lemon with peel
½ cup orange juice	1 tablespoon plus 2
1 tablespoon lime juice	teaspoons sugar
½ cup chopped carrots	½ teaspoon seasoned
4-in. piece celery,	salt
chopped	⅛ teaspoon salt
¼ cup chopped cucumber	

1. Combine all ingredients in an electric blender container and blend until liquefied.
2. Serve chilled with *lime wedges*.

ABOUT 6 SERVINGS

LIME FIZZ

1 can (6 oz.) frozen	2½ cups chilled quinine
limeade concentrate,	water
thawed	Green food coloring
½ cup chilled bottled	
green maraschino	
cherry syrup	

1. Just before serving, combine the limeade concentrate, cherry syrup, and quinine water in a pitcher. Add enough food coloring to tint the desired shade of green. Mix; serve over crushed ice.
2. Accompany with a bowl of *Sugar-Frosted Candied Cranberries, below.* Use as floats.

ABOUT 1 QUART

SUGAR-FROSTED CANDIED CRANBERRIES: Prick *2 cups fresh cranberries* several times with a needle; set aside. Combine *2 cups sugar* and *2 cups water* in a saucepan. Bring to boiling, stirring constantly until sugar is dissolved. Set candy thermometer in place and cook, without stirring, until thermometer registers 234°F. Add cranberries, cover loosely, and continue cooking until thermometer registers 250°F. Remove from heat, remove thermometer, and lift berries out of syrup with a slotted spoon. Spread out on waxed paper or aluminum foil and cool completely. Roll each cranberry in *sugar* and let dry. Roll again in sugar.

ABOUT 1 CUP

CUCUMBER-PINEAPPLE COCKTAIL

2¼ cups chilled	1 medium-sized
unsweetened	cucumber, pared,
pineapple juice	seeded, and cut
¾ teaspoon seasoned	in pieces
salt	

1. Put all ingredients into an electric blender container. Cover and blend until liquefied.
2. Serve over ice in low 4- to 6-ounce glasses. Float a watercress-decorated slice of cucumber in each glass. (Score and thinly slice *cucumber*. Pull the stem end of a small sprig of *watercress* through the center of each slice.) ABOUT 3 CUPS

HERB-BUTTERED HOT TOMATO JUICE

1½ qts. tomato juice	¼ teaspoon oregano,
1 teaspoon Worces-	crushed
tershire sauce	4 whole cloves
½ teaspoon salt	¼ to ⅓ cup butter
¼ teaspoon marjoram,	or margarine
crushed	

Combine all ingredients in a saucepan. Set over low heat until butter is melted, stirring to blend (do not boil). Remove cloves and serve at once.

ABOUT 6 CUPS

BEEF FIZZ

2 cans (10½ oz. each) con-	1 cup chilled ginger ale
densed beef broth	2 tablespoons lemon
	juice

Combine all ingredients and pour over ice cubes in glasses. 6 TO 8 SERVINGS

Chapter 2

SOUPS—Hot & Cold

Gone is the fire-blackened iron soup kettle of yesteryear that bubbled on the kitchen stove the livelong day. But its legacy remains, and soup is still a national favorite—a fine test of a homemaker's skill in striking a harmonious balance of flavors.

Soups may be roughly divided into two groups. In the first group belong the soups made from meat stock. These are the various modifications of the brown and white stocks, the bouillons, consommés, and broths. In the second group belong the soups that may be made either with or without meat stock. These are the various modifications of cream soups, purées and bisques, of chowders and stews, and of vegetable soups.

An unthickened clear soup (bouillon, consommé, broth) is appropriately served at the beginning of a hearty meal while a cream soup may well begin a light meal. Soups may be main-dish fare, too. Here the hearty, thick varieties are appropriate—chowders, bisques, stews, and some fruit soups.

With the perfecting of modern commercial processing of soups, more time-consuming methods of preparing soup stock at home have become less common. Available to homemakers today are not only soups in cans, but also variety in packaged soup mixes. Convenience, quality, and flavor are appealing factors built into both types. Bouillon cubes also belong to the convenience group.

HELPFUL HINTS ABOUT SOUPS

• When preparing cream soups, a thorough blending of fat and flour and cooking with the milk or cream (see recipe for white sauce) help prevent a film of fat appearing on the surface of the soup. This film often forms when the soup is too thin.
• To avoid curdling of cream of tomato soup, thicken the sieved tomatoes before adding (hot) to the cold milk, stirring constantly.
• Cream soups usually have the consistency of a thin sauce. The vegetable used will determine the amount of flour needed to thicken the soup. At least ¼ cup chopped or ⅓ cup sieved vegetable per cup of thin white sauce will give a most satisfactory soup; 2 to 3 tablespoons sieved spinach per cup is a desirable proportion for cream of spinach soup. Add a little hot milk or cream if the soup is too thick, or thicken with a flour-water mixture if the soup is too thin.
• Instructions for clarifying soups are given in *Consommé*, page 47.
• The electric blender is the modern way to quick-and-easy blending of everything and anything into savory soups. Remember, when using it, to pour the liquid into container first, usually ½ to 1 cup, then gradually add the other ingredients.
• Cool soups to lukewarm before storing in covered container in the refrigerator; keep several days only. Store in freezer for longer periods.

SOUP GARNISHES
Garnishes are to soup as jewels are to the costume—a glamorous accent. They need not be elaborate. The normally stocked refrigerator will usually yield the wherewithal for many of the garnishes suggested on page 44.

Apples (red or golden) — unpared and diced
Bacon — crisp and crumbled; prepared baconlike pieces
Croutons — plain; buttered; herbed
Eggs, hard-cooked — chopped; chopped or sieved whites; sieved yolks; combined with bacon
Lemons — thinly sliced and notched or cut in fancy shapes; shredded lemon peel
Nuts (walnuts, peanuts, pecans, cashews, filberts, and pistachios) — toasted and salted or dry roasted, finely or coarsely chopped; (toasted almonds) unsalted, salted or dry roasted and slivered or coarsely chopped
Olives — sliced pimiento-stuffed olives; quartered (or wedges) ripe olives
Vegetables (fresh) — thinly sliced notched carrots; thinly sliced scored cucumbers; snipped chives; snipped parsley; snipped green onion tops; sprigs of watercress; slivered or chopped green or red peppers
Whipped Cream — unsalted, salted, seasoned or herbed; topped with caviar, sieved pimiento or hard-cooked egg yolk, black pepper, nutmeg, or shredded cheese

EGGBALLS

2 hard-cooked egg yolks, mashed	1 egg
¼ teaspoon salt	2 or 3 tablespoons fine dry bread crumbs
⅛ teaspoon pepper	Fat for deep frying heated to 365°F
⅛ teaspoon ground nutmeg	

1. Mix mashed egg yolks with salt, pepper, nutmeg, and egg, adding enough bread crumbs to hold mixture together. Form into ½-inch balls; roll in additional crumbs.
2. Fry in hot fat until golden. Serve immediately in clear broth soup. ABOUT 1 DOZEN EGGBALLS

FARFEL

2 eggs, fork beaten	1½ cups all-purpose flour
¼ teaspoon salt	

1. Mix eggs and salt; add to flour. Mix and knead with fingertips until all flour is incorporated and a very stiff ball of dough is formed. (More flour may be needed.) Let ball stand about 1 hour, or until dough is hard enough to grate.
2. Grate or very finely chop dough into small pieces about the size of barley. Toss to separate and spread thinly on a platter or cloth. Dry completely before storing in jars or plastic bags.
3. When ready to use, drop into boiling *salted water* or *soup*. Cook 15 minutes. Serve in soup.
ABOUT 2 CUPS FARFEL

MINIATURES FLORENTINE

Float these vivid green cutouts on individual servings of hot bouillon or consommé.

1 egg, well beaten	¼ clove garlic, minced
¼ cup finely chopped fresh spinach	⅛ teaspoon salt
1 tablespoon finely chopped unblanched almonds	Few grains black pepper

1. Mix all ingredients thoroughly in a bowl.
2. Meanwhile, heat a griddle or heavy skillet until moderately hot.
3. Lightly butter the griddle. Spoon the batter onto it, spreading to make a round about 7 inches in diameter. Bake until lightly browned, about 3 minutes; turn and brown second side.
4. Using hors d'oeuvre cutters (½ inch in diameter), cut out shapes from the griddlecake. Serve a spoonful in each serving of soup.

POSATELLI AND BROTH
(Posatelli in Brodo)

A recipe from Albergo Restaurant in Cervia, Italy.

1⅓ cups fine dry bread crumbs	⅛ teaspoon grated nutmeg
1 cup grated Parmesan cheese	¼ cup butter, softened
¼ teaspoon salt	3 eggs, slightly beaten
	6 cups broth (chicken or meat)

1. In a heavy saucepan, combine crumbs, cheese, salt, and nutmeg; blend in butter. Mix in eggs, forming a soft dough. Heat until warm.
2. Heat broth to simmering and force dough through ricer into broth. Simmer 1 minute. Serve immediately. 6 SERVINGS

CROUTONS

2 to 3 tablespoons butter or margarine	2 to 3 slices bread, toasted

Heat butter in a large skillet over low heat. Trim crusts from toast, if desired. Cut toast into ¼- to ½-inch cubes. Toss cubes in butter in skillet until all sides are coated and browned.   ABOUT 1½ CUPS

CHEESE-GARLIC CROUTONS: Follow directions for Croutons. Heat *1 clove garlic*, crushed, with butter. Toss browned croutons with *1 tablespoon grated Parmesan cheese*.

EGG DROPS

At The Milk Pail in Dundee, Illinois, these egg drops are served in pheasant broth.

3 eggs	3 drops yellow food coloring
¾ cup all-purpose flour	
1 teaspoon salt	

1. Beat eggs lightly. Add flour, salt, and food coloring; beat until smooth.
2. Press through colander into boiling water and cook 3 minutes, or until egg drops are set. Skim out of water and add to desired broth.

QUICK SOUPS TO SERVE HOT

BEEF BOUILLON WITH BROILED ORANGE

Vermont House, located in Newbury, Vermont, serves hot beef bouillon with a flair.

Thick orange slices	3 tablespoons sherry
2 tablespoons melted butter	Beef bouillon

1. Brush tops of orange slices with a mixture of butter and sherry. Broil with tops 2 to 3 inches from source of heat about 8 minutes, brushing occasionally with butter mixture.
2. To serve, place an orange slice in bottom of each soup dish. Pour hot beef bouillon over orange slices. Serve immediately.

SPICY TOMATO BOUILLON

1 can (18 oz.) tomato juice	1 can (10½ oz.) condensed beef consommé
¼ cup chopped onion	¼ teaspoon curry powder
1 tablespoon mixed pickling spices	½ cup heavy cream, whipped

1. Heat together tomato juice, onion, and pickling spices; simmer, uncovered, 20 minutes; strain.
2. Combine tomato mixture with consommé; heat thoroughly.
3. Beat curry powder into whipped cream with final few strokes of beating.
4. To serve, pour tomato-consommé into bowls and top with curry whipped cream.

ABOUT 6 SERVINGS

HOT MADRILÉNE

¼ cup butter	1 bay leaf
¼ cup chopped onion	Grated Parmesan cheese
2 cans (18 oz. each) tomato juice	Parsley (about ½ cup snipped)
2 cans (10½ oz. each) condensed beef broth	

1. Heat butter in a large saucepan. Add onion and cook until tender.
2. Blend in tomato juice and beef broth. Add the bay leaf. Heat just to boiling; reduce heat and simmer 5 minutes. Remove bay leaf.
3. Ladle into a tureen. Serve with the cheese and parsley.   ABOUT 1¾ QUARTS SOUP

DUTCH-STYLE CHOWDER

4 slices bacon, diced	1 soup can milk
⅓ cup chopped onion	1 soup can water
1 can (10½ oz.) condensed cream of chicken soup	1 cup drained canned whole kernel corn
1 can (10½ oz.) condensed chicken-vegetable soup	2 tablespoons snipped parsley

1. Cook bacon in a saucepan until crisp. Remove from pan to absorbent paper.
2. Pour off all except 1 tablespoon fat from pan. Add onion and cook until tender and lightly browned, stirring occasionally.
3. Stir in the soups, milk, water, and corn. Heat thoroughly, stirring frequently.

4. Garnish chowder with bacon and parsley.

ABOUT 6 SERVINGS

CARROT-PEA CREAM SOUP

1 can (10½ oz.) con-
densed cream of
chicken soup
1 can (11¼ oz.) con-
densed green pea
soup
1½ cups milk
1 cup heavy cream

½ cup cooked sliced
carrots
½ teaspoon grated
onion
¼ teaspoon freshly
ground black pepper
¼ teaspoon ground
thyme

1. Blend the soups and gradually add the milk and cream, stirring until well blended.
2. Add the remaining ingredients and cook over medium heat, stirring occasionally, until thoroughly heated.

4 TO 6 SERVINGS

FRANKFURTER-CHICKEN CREAM SOUP

2 tablespoons butter
1 medium-sized onion,
cut in ¼-in. slices
5 frankfurters, cut in
¼-in. slices
1 can (10½ oz.) con-
densed cream of
chicken soup

1 soup can water
1 soup can milk
2 chicken bouillon
cubes
¼ teaspoon ground
mace
½ teaspoon grated
lemon peel

1. Heat butter in a saucepan. Add onion and frankfurter slices. Cook until onion is transparent, occasionally moving and turning with a spoon.

2. Stir in the soup, then the water and milk, blending thoroughly after each addition.
3. Add bouillon cubes, stirring occasionally until completely dissolved. Stir in the mace and lemon peel and heat thoroughly (do not boil). Garnish with *minced parsley.*

ABOUT 6 SERVINGS

ONION SOUP LES HALLES

In this quickly prepared version of the onion soup made famous by Les Halles (former Paris market), canned vegetable juice and consommé are substituted for the long-cooking meat and vegetable stock used in the traditional recipe.

2 tablespoons butter
2 large onions, coarsely
chopped
1 clove garlic, finely
chopped
½ teaspoon salt
⅛ teaspoon black pepper
⅛ teaspoon thyme
1 large sprig parsley,
snipped

2 teaspoons tarragon
vinegar
1 can (10½ oz.) con-
densed beef
consommé
1⅓ cups water
1 can (12 oz.) cocktail
vegetable juice

1. Heat butter in a saucepan; add onions and garlic and cook about 5 minutes.
2. Stir in salt, pepper, thyme, parsley, vinegar, consommé, water, and vegetable juice. Simmer about 10 minutes.
3. Serve piping hot, floating a *buttered toast round,* topped with *shredded Parmesan cheese,* in each bowl of soup.

ABOUT 1 QUART SOUP

SOUPS TO SERVE HOT

PLANTATION SOUP

3 cups beef broth
2 carrots, pared and
chopped
2 stalks celery, chopped
2 small onions, chopped
3 tablespoons flour

6 tablespoons butter or
margarine
3 cups milk
½ cup finely shredded
Cheddar cheese

1. Combine beef broth, carrots, celery, and onions in a saucepan. Bring to boiling; reduce heat and simmer, covered, 30 minutes, or until vegetables are very tender. Strain; set the broth aside.
2. Blend the flour into hot butter in a saucepan.

Cook until bubbly, stirring constantly. Remove from heat. Gradually add the milk, stirring constantly. Bring rapidly to boiling and boil 1 to 2 minutes, continuing to stir.
3. Combine the strained broth with white sauce. Simmer, covered, about 20 minutes. When ready to serve, stir the cheese into hot soup.

6 TO 8 SERVINGS

BEEF STOCK

The simmering soup pot . . . pot-au-feu in French . . . that bubbled on the old cook stove the livelong day, is part of French-American cooking tradition and the source of many eating pleasures. Even today modern cooks continue to simmer the broth for hours to obtain flavorful and rich stock.

3 lbs. lean beef (chuck or plate), cut in 1-in. pieces	5 carrots, pared and cut in large pieces
1 soup bone, cracked	2 turnips, pared and cut in large pieces
3 qts. cold water	3 stalks celery with leaves, sliced
1½ tablespoons salt	
2 large onions	4 leeks, sliced
2 whole cloves	Herb bouquet, *page 12*

1.   Put meat and soup bone into a large saucepot; add water and salt. Cover and bring to boiling. Remove foam. Cover saucepot and simmer about 4 hours, removing foam as necessary.
2.   Slice 1 onion; insert the cloves into second onion. Add onions, remaining vegetables, and herb bouquet to saucepot. Cover and bring to boiling. Reduce heat and simmer about 1½ hours.
3.   Remove from heat; remove soup bone and strain stock through a fine sieve. Allow to cool. (The meat and vegetables strained from stock may be served as desired.)
4.   Remove fat that rises to surface (reserve for use in other food preparation). Store stock in a covered container in refrigerator for future use, or reheat and serve with slices of crisp *toast*.

ABOUT 2½ QUARTS STOCK

BROWN STOCK: Follow recipe for Beef Stock. Cut any meat from soup bone and brown the meat along with beef pieces in ¼ *cup fat* in saucepot before cooking. Proceed as in Beef Stock.

WHITE STOCK: Follow recipe for Beef Stock. Substitute *veal shank and breast* for beef. Add one half of a disjointed ready-to-cook *stewing chicken*.

CONSOMMÉ: Follow recipe for White Stock. Cool stock and stir in *2 egg whites*, slightly beaten, *crushed shells of the eggs*, and *4 teaspoons water*. Heat slowly to boiling, stirring constantly. Remove from heat and let stand 25 minutes. Strain through two thicknesses of cheesecloth.

BOUILLON: Follow recipe for Consommé. Substitute Brown Stock for White Stock.

BROWN FLOUR SOUP
(Braune Mehlsuppe)

This version of a Pennsylvania Dutch soup is similar in flavor to one popular in Switzerland.

¼ cup butter	5 cups beef broth
½ cup all-purpose flour	(dissolve 5 beef bouillon cubes in 5 cups boiling water)
⅛ teaspoon pepper	
	Finely shredded Cheddar cheese

1.   Heat the butter in a large saucepan. Blend in the flour and pepper. Heat until bubbly. Add the cooled broth gradually, stirring constantly. Bring to boiling; cook covered, over low heat at least 20 minutes.
2.   Just before serving, sprinkle cheese over top.

ABOUT 1¼ QUARTS SOUP

BLENDER ALMOND SOUP

The toasted almonds in this soup give it an unusual and pleasant flavor.

1 cup water	½ teaspoon sugar
1 cup salted blanched almonds	½ teaspoon monosodium glutamate
4 egg yolks	2 cups water
3 chicken bouillon cubes	1 cup cream
½ slice onion	

1.   Put all ingredients except 2 cups water and cream into an electric blender container and blend until almonds are finely ground.
2.   Pour into a saucepan and stir in the 2 cups water. Cook over low heat 10 to 15 minutes, or until thickened, stirring constantly (do not boil).
3.   Stir in the cream and heat thoroughly without boiling. Serve immediately. Garnish with *finely shredded orange peel.*   5 OR 6 SERVINGS

BORSCH

1 can (16 oz.) whole beets	5 tablespoons lemon juice
¼ cup sugar	1 egg, well beaten
¾ teaspoon salt	

1.   Drain contents of can of beets, reserving liquid in a 1-quart measuring cup. Put beets through food mill (or finely chop beets in an electric blender, adding about ½ cup of the reserved liquid to the blender container).

2. Add beet pulp to liquid in measuring cup and add water to make 1 quart.

3. Heat beet-water mixture, sugar, salt, and lemon juice to boiling in a saucepan, stirring occasionally.

4. Remove from heat and gradually add ¾ cup of the hot mixture to beaten egg, stirring constantly; stir into beet mixture in saucepan. Return to heat; cook, stirring, until simmering (do not boil).

5. Serve hot or cold, garnishing each serving with a dollop of *dairy sour cream*.   ABOUT 1 QUART SOUP

BEEF SOUP

This hearty soup is a favorite recipe from Mrs. Hubert Humphrey, wife of the former Vice President.

1½ lbs. beef for stew	½ cup chopped onion
1 soup bone	1 can (15 oz.) Italian-
1½ to 2 teaspoons salt	style tomatoes
½ teaspoon pepper	1 tablespoon Worcester-
2 bay leaves	shire sauce
4 medium-sized carrots,	1 beef bouillon cube
pared and sliced	Pinch oregano (or other
1 cup chopped cabbage	herb desired)
1 cup chopped celery	

1. Put meat and soup bone in a heavy 3-quart kettle; cover with cold water (about 4 cups). Add salt, pepper, and bay leaves. Bring rapidly to boiling. Reduce heat. Add carrots, cabbage, celery, and onion; cover and simmer until meat is tender, about 2½ hours.

2. Remove and discard bone and bay leaves. Cut meat into bite-size pieces and return to soup. Mix in tomatoes, Worcestershire sauce, bouillon cube, and oregano. Cover and simmer 30 minutes.

6 SERVINGS

FRENCH COTTAGE SPROUT SOUP

2 pkgs. (10 oz. each)	½ teaspoon pepper
frozen Brussels	4 cups chicken broth
sprouts	(dissolve 4 chicken
½ cup butter or	bouillon cubes in 4
margarine	cups boiling water)
¼ cup flour	½ lb. fresh mushrooms
1 teaspoon salt	2 cups light cream

1. Cook Brussels sprouts according to package directions, using ½ teaspoon salt to 1 cup water; drain, if necessary.

2. Meanwhile, heat butter in a large heavy saucepan. Blend in a mixture of the flour, salt, and pepper; cook until bubbly. Gradually add the broth, stirring to blend. Bring to boiling; stir and boil 1 minute. Remove from heat.

3. Finely chop mushrooms in an electric blender. Mix mushrooms into hot sauce; cover and simmer 20 minutes.

4. In the blender, purée one half of the sprouts with 1 cup cream. Pour into cooked mushroom sauce. Repeat with remaining Brussels sprouts and cream.

5. Heat the soup, stirring occasionally, until of serving temperature. Garnish with *parsley*.

ABOUT 2½ QUARTS SOUP

CUBAN BLACK BEAN SOUP

This soup is a specialty created by Executive Chef Robert Halberg and was featured in the Salon Reál of the Executive House's Condado Beach Hotel in San Juan, Puerto Rico.

1 lb. black beans, washed	10 tablespoons olive oil
2 quarts boiling water	½ lb. onions, peeled,
2 tablespoons salt	trimmed, and chopped
5 cloves garlic	½ lb. green peppers,
1½ teaspoons cumin	peeled, trimmed, and
1½ teaspoons oregano	chopped
2 tablespoons white	
vinegar	

1. Put beans into a large heavy saucepot or Dutch oven and add boiling water; boil rapidly 2 minutes. Cover tightly, remove from heat, and set aside 1 hour. Add salt to beans and liquid; bring to boiling and simmer, covered, until beans are soft.

2. Put the garlic, cumin, oregano, and vinegar into a mortar and crush to a paste.

3. Heat olive oil in a large skillet. Mix in onion and green pepper and fry until onion is browned, stirring occasionally. Thoroughly blend in the paste, then stir the skillet mixture into the beans. Cook over low heat until ready to serve.

4. Meanwhile, mix a small portion of *cooked rice, minced onion, olive oil,* and *vinegar* in a bowl, set aside to marinate. Add a soup spoon of rice mixture to each serving of soup.   ABOUT 2 QUARTS SOUP
NOTE: For a combination soup and salad course served before the entrée, set out chilled ripe *avocado halves* and spoon the piping hot bean soup into the cavities. (The blend of flavors is subtle, elegant, and distinctive.)

CHINESE CABBAGE SOUP

1 chicken breast (¾ lb.), cooked	1 teaspoon soy sauce
7 cups chicken broth	1¼ teaspoons salt
6 cups sliced Chinese cabbage (celery cabbage)	¼ teaspoon black pepper

1.   Cut chicken into strips about ⅛ inch wide and 1½ to 2 inches long. Combine with chicken broth and heat only until hot. Add Chinese cabbage and cook 3 to 4 minutes (only until cabbage is crisp-tender; do not overcook).

2.   Stir in the soy sauce and a mixture of the salt and pepper. Serve hot.   6 SERVINGS

NOTE: If desired, *lettuce* may be substituted for the cabbage. Reduce cooking time to 1 minute.

CABBAGE SOUP

A satisfying soup prepared frequently in the kitchen of a Jewish homemaker.

1 lb. cross-cut beef shanks	3 tablespoons salt
2 or 3 marrow bones	3 tablespoons sugar
1 cup chopped onion	½ cup lemon juice
2 qts. water	1 tablespoon rendered chicken fat
1 small head cabbage, shredded	2 tablespoons flour
	Snipped parsley

1.   Put meat, bones, and onion into a large heavy saucepot. Add water and bring to boiling; remove foam. Cover and simmer about 1½ hours, or until meat is tender. Remove bones and cut meat into small pieces; return meat to soup.

2.   Meanwhile, sprinkle cabbage with salt and let stand while soup is cooking. Pour boiling water over cabbage and drain thoroughly.

3.   Add drained cabbage to soup when meat is tender. Cook, uncovered, over low heat about 45 minutes. Add sugar and lemon juice; cook 15 minutes longer.

4.   Meanwhile, melt fat in a skillet; add flour. Stir over medium heat until flour becomes a deep brown. Gradually add some of the soup, stirring until smooth. Bring to boiling; cook 2 minutes, stirring constantly. Slowly pour flour mixture into soup, stirring constantly to prevent lumping.

5.   Add more salt or sugar to taste, if desired. Pour into individual serving bowls; sprinkle with parsley.   ABOUT 3 QUARTS SOUP

OLD DROVERS INN CHEESE SOUP

The inn where this delicious soup originated is located in Dover Plains, New York.

4 tablespoons butter	1 qt. well-seasoned chicken stock
½ cup diced carrot	6 oz. mild Cheddar cheese, finely shredded
½ cup diced green pepper	
½ cup minced onion	6 oz. sharp Cheddar cheese, finely shredded
½ cup diced celery	
2 tablespoons flour	

1.   Heat butter in the top of a double boiler over direct heat. Add the carrot, green pepper, onion, and celery; cook until tender but not brown. Blend in the flour; cook and stir 1 minute.

2.   Pour in the stock, cooking and stirring until thickened.

3.   Set over boiling water. Add the cheeses and stir until melted. Thin to cream consistency with *milk*.

4.   Strain the soup and season to taste with *salt* and *pepper*. Serve hot or chilled.

ABOUT 2 QUARTS SOUP

CREAM OF CORN SOUP

2 cans (17 oz. each) cream-style corn	5 tablespoons butter
1 qt. milk	¼ cup flour
1 large onion, grated	1 teaspoon salt
¼ cup chopped celery	¼ teaspoon pepper
¼ cup chopped carrot	½ teaspoon monosodium glutamate
1 sprig parsley	

1.   Force the corn through a sieve and set aside.

2.   Combine milk, onion, celery, carrot, and parsley in top of a double boiler. Scald over simmering water.

3.   Heat butter in a heavy 2-quart saucepan over low heat; blend in flour and remaining ingredients. Stirring constantly, heat until mixture bubbles.

4.   Strain the scalded milk mixture and add it gradually to butter-flour mixture, stirring constantly; cook and stir until mixture is thickened.

5.   Stir in the sieved corn; heat to serving temperature over very low heat (do not boil).   8 SERVINGS

SOUP MEXICANA

1 chicken breast	2 cups chopped zucchini
6 cups chicken broth	1 cup drained canned
2 onions, chopped	whole kernel corn
1 teaspoon monosodium	⅓ cup tomato purée
glutamate	2 oz. cream cheese, cut
1 tablespoon butter or	in small cubes
margarine	2 avocados, sliced
1½ teaspoons grated	
onion	

1. Cook chicken breast 30 minutes, or until tender, in the broth with the chopped onion and monosodium glutamate. Remove chicken; dice and set aside. Reserve broth.
2. Heat butter and grated onion in a large saucepan; blend in zucchini and corn. Cook about 5 minutes, stirring occasionally. Mix in the broth and tomato purée. Cover and simmer about 20 minutes.
3. Just before serving, mix in diced chicken, cream cheese, and avocados.   6 TO 8 SERVINGS
NOTE: Any remaining soup may be stored, covered, in the refrigerator.

CUCUMBER SOUP

A featured treat served at the Copper Kettle in Aspen, Colorado.

1 tablespoon butter	½ teaspoon tarragon
½ cup chopped onion	leaves, crushed
½ cup sliced carrot	6 cups chicken broth
4 cups chopped celery	2 eggs, slightly beaten
(with leaves)	1 cup heavy cream
3 cucumbers, pared and	2 tablespoons dry sherry
diced	1 teaspoon lemon juice
¼ teaspoon thyme	

1. In a kettle, cook onion, carrot, and celery with butter until vegetables are soft, about 5 minutes.
2. Add cucumber, thyme, tarragon, and chicken broth; cover and cook 10 minutes. Cool slightly.
3. Pour half of mixture into an electric blender container; blend until smooth. Repeat with remaining half. Pour purée back into kettle; heat thoroughly.
4. Blend beaten eggs with cream. Slowly stir in about ½ cup of hot purée, then stir into remaining hot purée. Heat 5 minutes, stirring constantly. Blend in sherry and lemon juice. Serve sprinkled with *paprika* and *toasted sesame seed.*

ABOUT 2 QUARTS SOUP

CREAMY CARROT SOUP

¼ to ½ cup chopped	1 teaspoon salt
onion	3 chicken bouillon
6 tablespoons butter or	cubes
margarine	3 cups boiling water
2 cups thinly sliced	¼ cup uncooked rice
pared carrots	2 cups milk

1. Lightly brown the onion in heated butter in a saucepan. Add carrots and salt; toss to coat with butter. Cook, tightly covered, over low heat for 20 minutes, stirring occasionally.
2. Add bouillon cubes, water, and rice. Cover and simmer 1 hour, stirring occasionally.
3. Pour the mixture into an electric blender container and blend until smooth. Turn into saucepan; stir in the milk and heat thoroughly. Serve hot.

ABOUT 1¼ QUARTS SOUP

SOUP KETTLE SUPPER

¼ lb. sliced bacon,	1 can (17 oz.) whole
cut in pieces	kernel corn
2 cups diced cooked	1 can (16 oz.) green
ham	beans
1 can (10½ oz.) con-	1 can (16 oz.) tomatoes
densed beef broth	1 to 2 teaspoons salt
2 cups water	⅛ teaspoon pepper
1⅓ cups packaged pre-	1 tablespoon finely
cooked rice	chopped parsley

1. Fry bacon in a kettle or Dutch oven until crisp. Remove bacon and drain on absorbent paper.
2. Pour off all but 2 tablespoons of the drippings. Fry ham in the hot bacon drippings in kettle until slightly browned.
3. Add bacon and remaining ingredients except parsley. Bring to boiling; cover and remove from heat; let stand 5 minutes.
4. Sprinkle rice mixture with parsley and serve.

ABOUT 8 SERVINGS

GREEK LEMON SOUP

1 lemon	4 egg yolks, fork beaten
6 chicken bouillon cubes	1 cup heavy cream
½ teaspoon salt	2 to 3 tablespoons
2 qts. boiling water	butter or margarine
½ cup uncooked	
long grain rice	

1. Pare thin narrow strips of lemon peel. Juice the lemon and measure 4 to 6 teaspoons; set aside.

2. Add the lemon peel, bouillon cubes, and salt to the boiling water in a large saucepot. Stir the rice into the boiling mixture; cover and cook over low heat 20 to 25 minutes, or until rice is soft.

3. Blend the egg yolks, cream, and ½ cup hot broth; stir into soup. Cook and stir over medium heat about 5 minutes. Remove from heat; stir in the reserved lemon juice.

4. Before serving, put the butter into a hot tureen and pour in the soup. Or put butter (about a quarter pat for each) into individual soup bowls before ladling the soup. Grind *black pepper* over surface.

ABOUT 3 QUARTS SOUP

PEANUT BUTTER SOUP

¼ cup finely chopped onion

⅓ cup finely chopped celery

2 tablespoons butter or margarine

1 tablespoon flour

2 cups milk

¾ cup chicken broth (dissolve 1 chicken bouillon cube in ¾ cup boiling water)

½ cup smooth peanut butter

¼ teaspoon salt

1. Cook the onion and celery in hot butter in a saucepan about 5 minutes, stirring occasionally. Blend in the flour and heat until mixture bubbles, stirring constantly.

2. Add milk and broth gradually, stirring constantly. Bring rapidly to boiling, stirring constantly. Cook 1 to 2 minutes.

3. Gradually stir white sauce into peanut butter until mixture is smooth. Return to saucepan. Stir in the salt and heat thoroughly. Serve garnished with crumbled *crisp-fried bacon.* ABOUT 3 CUPS SOUP

CREAMY MUSHROOM SOUP

¼ cup butter or margarine

1 lb. fresh mushrooms, coarsely chopped

4 green onions with tops, sliced (reserve one half of green tops)

¼ cup flour

2 teaspoons salt

4½ cups milk

1 cup beef broth (dissolve 1 beef bouillon cube in 1 cup boiling water)

1. Heat butter in a saucepan. Stir in the mushrooms and green onions; cook about 5 minutes, or until just tender. With a slotted spoon, remove vegetables to a bowl; set aside.

2. Blend a mixture of the flour and salt into the butter in saucepan; heat until mixture bubbles. Gradually add the milk and broth, stirring constantly. Bring to boiling and cook until thickened.

3. Remove from heat and stir in the vegetables.

4. Garnish each serving with a spoonful of *dairy sour cream* and the reserved green onion tops.

6 TO 8 SERVINGS

ESSENCE OF BLACK MUSHROOM SOUP AU CHABLIS

A recipe from the Pump Room of the Hotel Ambassador East in Chicago, Illinois.

3 tablespoons rendered chicken fat

1 stalk celery, coarsely chopped

1 onion, coarsely chopped

½ carrot, coarsely chopped

1 leek, coarsely chopped

1 fresh ham hock

1 bay leaf

1 clove garlic

3 whole cloves

Pinch freshly ground black pepper

¼ lb. dried black mushrooms, very finely chopped

3 qts. chicken stock

3 tablespoons arrowroot

Few drops Maggi seasoning

Salt

¼ cup Chablis

1. Heat chicken fat in a Dutch oven and add celery, onion, carrot, leek, ham hock, bay leaf, garlic, cloves, and pepper. Cook until onion is lightly browned.

2. Add mushrooms; cover and cook 10 minutes. Add chicken stock and cook slowly for 2 hours.

3. Skim the fat. Blend arrowroot with a small amount of cooled stock; stir into the soup. Bring to boiling and cook 3 minutes.

4. Strain soup through a fine sieve lined with cheesecloth. Add Maggi seasoning, salt to taste, and wine. Reheat soup before serving.

ABOUT 8 SERVINGS

TOMATO CREAM

A recipe from the Jockey Club in Madrid, Spain.

2 tablespoons butter

2 leeks, chopped (about 2½ cups)

2 carrots, diced (about 1 cup)

2 tablespoons flour

2½ cups beef broth

1 to 2 teaspoons sugar

¼ teaspoon salt

4 large ripe tomatoes (2 lbs.), cut in pieces

1. Heat butter in a saucepan. Add leeks and carrots; cook, stirring occasionally, until lightly browned. Stir in the flour and heat until bubbly.

2. Blend in the broth; bring to boiling, stirring constantly, and cook for 3 minutes.

3. Stir in sugar, salt, and tomatoes; simmer 1 hour.

4. Force mixture through a coarse sieve or food mill. Serve very hot.   4 SERVINGS

YELLOW PEA SOUP WITH PORK
(Ärter med Fläsk)
It is said that every Thursday pea soup is served throughout Sweden, from fisher's cottage to Royal Palace.

¾ lb. (about 1⅔ cups) yellow peas, rinsed	¾ cup coarsely chopped onion
2½ qts. cold water	1 teaspoon salt
1 lb. smoked shoulder butt	½ teaspoon monosodium glutamate
3 qts. water	¼ teaspoon sugar
	1 teaspoon leaf thyme

1. Cover the peas with the cold water in a large saucepan; let stand overnight.

2. Put smoked shoulder butt into a large saucepot with the 3 quarts water and onion. Simmer 1½ to 2 hours, or until meat is tender.

3. Remove meat and set aside. Skim fat from liquid, leaving about 2 tablespoons. Drain the peas and add to the broth with the remaining ingredients. Cook slowly until peas are tender.

4. Serve soup with thin slices of the smoked butt.
          ABOUT 2½ QUARTS SOUP

PEA SOUP À LA FRANÇAISE
Lettuce, leek, and chervil are cooked with green peas to give this delectable soup a French flair.

1 small head lettuce, shredded (about 5 cups)	2 tablespoons butter
	2 teaspoons chervil
	1 teaspoon sugar
2 cups shelled fresh green peas, or one 10-oz. pkg. frozen green peas	1 teaspoon salt
	¼ teaspoon black pepper
	1 can (10½ oz.) condensed beef broth
1 cup water	¾ cup water
½ cup chopped leek (white and green)	2 cups light cream

1. Put the lettuce, peas, 1 cup water, leek, butter, chervil, sugar, salt, and pepper into a large saucepan; stir and bring to boiling. Cover and cook until peas are tender.

2. Press mixture through a coarse sieve or food mill and return to saucepan. Stir in beef broth and ¾ cup water.

3. Just before serving, stir cream into mixture and heat thoroughly.   6 SERVINGS

CREAMY TUNA 'N' BROCCOLI SOUP

¼ cup butter or margarine	¼ teaspoon white pepper
3 tablespoons minced onion	Few grains cayenne pepper
3 tablespoons flour	1 qt. milk
1¼ teaspoons salt	1 pkg. (10 oz.) frozen chopped broccoli
½ teaspoon celery salt	1 can (6½ or 7 oz.) tuna, drained and cut in pieces
½ teaspoon ground sage	

1. Melt the butter in a large heavy saucepan over low heat. Add the onion and cook until tender. Blend in flour, salt, celery salt, sage, and the peppers. Heat until mixture bubbles.

2. Gradually add the milk, stirring constantly. Bring to boiling. Stir in broccoli. Cook over low heat, stirring occasionally, 10 to 12 minutes, or until broccoli is tender when pierced with a fork.

3. Mix in tuna and heat about 3 minutes.

4. Spoon into soup bowls and serve at once.
          ABOUT 6 SERVINGS

CREAM OF TURKEY SOUP

½ cup butter	3 cups turkey or chicken broth
6 tablespoons flour	
½ teaspoon salt	¾ cup coarsely chopped cooked turkey
Few grains black pepper	
2 cups cream	

1. Heat butter in a saucepan. Blend in a mixture of the flour, salt, and pepper. Heat until mixture bubbles.

2. Gradually add the cream and 1 cup of the broth, stirring constantly. Bring to boiling; cook and stir 1 to 2 minutes.

3. Blend in remaining broth and turkey. Heat thoroughly (do not boil). Garnish with slivers of *carrot*.   ABOUT 6 SERVINGS

VEGETABLE SOUP ITALIENNE

2 tablespoons butter
2 tablespoons cooking
  or salad oil
1 cup thinly sliced
  carrots
1 cup thinly sliced
  zucchini
1 cup thinly sliced
  celery

1 cup finely shredded
  cabbage
2 beef bouillon cubes
8 cups boiling water
2 teaspoons salt
2 medium-sized
  tomatoes, cut in
  pieces
½ cup uncooked broken
  spaghetti
½ teaspoon thyme

1. Heat the butter and oil in a saucepot. Add the carrots, zucchini, celery, and cabbage. Cook, uncovered, about 10 minutes, stirring occasionally.
2. Add the bouillon cubes, water, and salt. Bring to boiling; reduce heat and simmer, uncovered, 30 minutes.
3. Stir in tomatoes, spaghetti, and thyme; cook 20 minutes longer.
4. Serve hot from a tureen with *shredded Parmesan cheese* sprinkled over the top of each serving.
ABOUT 6 SERVINGS

HARVEST SOUP

There's a delightful blending of flavors in this hearty creamy soup for a crowd.

8 slices bacon, cut in
  1-to 2-in. pieces
2 cloves garlic, minced
5 cups chicken broth
  (dissolve 7 chicken
  bouillon cubes in 5
  cups boiling water)
6 cups milk
¾ cup uncooked rice
1 teaspoon oregano,
  crushed
2 teaspoons salt

½ teaspoon black
  pepper
1 pkg. (10 oz.) frozen
  peas and carrots
2 cups water
4 pkgs. (10 oz. each)
  frozen Brussels
  sprouts, partially
  thawed and quartered
¾ cup shredded
  Parmesan cheese

1. Fry bacon with garlic in a large saucepot or Dutch oven until bacon is partially cooked.
2. Add 3 cups of the broth, the milk, rice, and a mixture of the oregano, 1 teaspoon salt, and pepper. Bring to boiling, reduce heat and simmer, covered, 15 minutes.
3. Add peas and carrots; bring to boiling, reduce heat and simmer about 10 minutes, or until tender.
4. Meanwhile, combine remaining broth, salt, and water in a saucepan. Bring to boiling and add Brus-

sels sprouts. Return to boiling and simmer, uncovered, 10 minutes, or until tender.
5. Add Brussels sprouts with their cooking liquid to rice mixture. Stir in cheese. ABOUT 20 SERVINGS

Chowders & Fish Soups

BRENNAN'S GUMBO À LA CREOLE
Brennan's in New Orleans, Louisiana includes this taste-tempter among their popular dishes.

4 small onions, chopped
⅔ cup butter
¼ cup flour
2 qts. rich chicken
  stock
2½ cups cooked
  tomatoes
½ lb. okra

Bouquet garni, *page 21*
Salt
Pepper
Cayenne pepper
6 hard-shelled crabs
24 large peeled shrimp
24 oysters

1. Sauté the onions until lightly browned in heated butter in a large saucepan. Add flour and cook 5 minutes, stirring constantly.
2. Gradually add chicken stock, tomatoes, okra, bouquet garni, salt, and peppers to taste; add crabs. Simmer 1 hour.
3. Add shrimp and oysters and cook slowly 5 minutes.
4. Put a spoonful of *cooked rice* into each soup bowl and ladle in hot gumbo. ABOUT 8 SERVINGS

NEW ENGLAND CLAM CHOWDER

2 tablespoons butter or
  margarine
½ cup finely diced
  celery
¼ cup thinly sliced
  leek (white part only)
¼ cup minced onion
¼ cup minced green
  pepper
1¾ cups milk
1 cup cream
3 tablespoons flour
½ cup finely diced
  potato

12 large hard-shelled
  clams (to prepare,
  see note), or 2 cans
  (7½ oz. each) minced
  clams, drained
  (reserve liquid)
½ teaspoon Worcester-
  shire sauce
½ teaspoon salt
⅛ teaspoon thyme
3 drops Tabasco
Few grains white pepper
Finely chopped parsley

1. In a heavy 3-quart saucepan melt butter over low heat. Add the celery, leek, onion, and green

pepper; stirring occasionally, cook 6 to 8 minutes, or until partially tender.

2. Meanwhile, combine milk and cream and scald.

3. Blend flour into the vegetable-butter mixture; heat until mixture bubbles. Gradually add the scalded milk and cream, stirring constantly. Bring to boiling, stirring constantly; cook 1 to 2 minutes.

4. Stir in the potato, reserved clam liquid, salt, thyme, Tabasco, and pepper. Bring to boiling and simmer 25 to 35 minutes, stirring frequently. Add minced clams and Worcestershire sauce. Reheat.

5. Pour soup into a tureen or individual soup bowls. Garnish with parsley. Serve with *chowder biscuits* or *crackers*.   4 TO 6 SERVINGS

NOTE: To prepare clams and broth, rinse clams thoroughly under cold running water. Place clams in a saucepan and add *3 cups water.* Cook over medium heat until shells open completely. Drain the clams, reserving 2 cups of broth for chowder. Remove clams from shells. Cut off the hard outsides (combs) and chop clams into small, fine pieces. Decrease milk in chowder to 1 cup.

ZUPPA DI PESCE: ROYAL DANIELI
This fish soup recipe is from the Danieli Royal Excelsior, a hotel in Venice, Italy.

3 lbs. skinned and boned fish (haddock, trout, cod, salmon, and red snapper)	1 bay leaf, crumbled
	1 teaspoon basil
	½ teaspoon thyme
	2 tablespoons minced parsley
1-lb. lobster	½ to 1 cup dry white wine
1 lb. shrimp with shells	
½ cup coarsely cut onion	½ cup chopped peeled tomatoes
1 stalk celery with leaves, coarsely cut	8 shreds saffron
	1 teaspoon salt
2 tablespoons cider vinegar	½ teaspoon freshly ground black pepper
2 teaspoons salt	6 slices French bread
¼ cup olive oil	¼ cup olive oil
2 garlic cloves, minced	

1. Reserve heads and tails of fish. Cut fish into bite-size pieces.

2. In covered saucepot, simmer lobster and shrimp 5 minutes in 1 quart water with onion, celery, vinegar, and 2 teaspoons salt.

3. Remove and shell lobster and shrimp; devein shrimp. Cut lobster into bite-size pieces. Set lobster and shrimp aside.

4. Return shells to the broth and add heads and tails of fish. Simmer 20 minutes.

5. Strain broth, pour into saucepot and set aside.

6. Sauté all of the fish in ¼ cup oil with garlic, bay leaf, basil, thyme, and parsley 5 minutes, stirring constantly.

7. Add to reserved broth along with wine, tomatoes, saffron, 1 teaspoon salt, and the pepper. Bring to boiling; cover and simmer 10 minutes, stirring occasionally.

8. Serve with slices of bread sautéed in the remaining ¼ cup olive oil.   ABOUT 2½ QUARTS SOUP

GREEN SHUTTERS INN FISH CHOWDER
A Nova Scotia specialty from Lunenburg County.

2½ lbs. fresh or frozen halibut, cod, or haddock steaks	2 teaspoons salt
	⅛ teaspoon freshly ground black pepper
2 oz. fat salt pork, cubed	1 qt. cream or milk
	2 tablespoons butter
1 large onion, sliced	6 large soda crackers, finely crushed
2 medium-sized potatoes, pared and cubed	

1. Cook fish in a covered saucepot in a small amount of water until fish begins to separate from bones. Break up any larger pieces of fish.

2. Strain and reserve the fish stock.

3. Brown salt pork in a large kettle until cubes are a delicate brown. Add onion, potatoes, reserved fish stock, salt, and pepper. Cover and cook until potatoes are fork-tender.

4. Add fish (all bones removed) and cream; heat thoroughly (do not boil).

5. Just before serving add butter and crackers.
                6 TO 8 SERVINGS

OYSTER STEW

2 cups milk	2 teaspoons salt
2 cups cream	¼ teaspoon monosodium glutamate
¼ cup butter or margarine	⅛ teaspoon pepper
1 pt. oysters	

1. Scald the milk and cream.

2. Meanwhile, heat butter in a saucepan. Add oysters and liquor. Simmer 3 minutes, or until oysters are plump and edges begin to curl.

3. Mix contents of saucepan with the scalded

milk and cream, salt, monosodium glutamate, and pepper.

4. Serve at once with *oyster crackers*.

6 SERVINGS

SHELLFISH CHOWDER
Tradition has it that French fishermen returning to port would toss some of their catch into a huge copper pot, "la chaudière," to be used later as part of a community feast of thanksgiving for their safe return. When the custom reached New England "la chaudière" became "chowder."

1 pt. oysters	3 egg yolks
1 cup shucked clams	¾ cup cream or milk
½ lb. scallops, diced	½ teaspoon monoso-
3 cups cold chicken	dium glutamate
broth	¼ teaspoon celery salt
3 tablespoons quick-	⅛ teaspoon salt
cooking tapioca	⅛ teaspoon pepper

1. Heat oysters with liquor, clams, and scallops in a saucepan 5 minutes; drain, reserving liquid. Mix broth and tapioca; let stand 5 minutes.
2. Pour reserved liquid and chicken broth with tapioca into saucepan. Bring to boiling, stirring constantly, and cook until soup is thickened.
3. Beat egg yolks in a bowl and gradually beat in cream. Quickly stir about 3 tablespoons hot soup into egg yolk mixture. Immediately stir into soup. Stir constantly about 5 minutes (do not boil).
4. Add the oysters, clams, scallops, monosodium glutamate, celery salt, salt, and pepper. Heat thoroughly.

ABOUT 6 SERVINGS

BONGO BONGO
At Trader Vic's restaurant in San Francisco this oyster soup is served frequently.

2 cups milk	1½ teaspoons mono-
1 cup heavy cream	sodium glutamate
1 cup puréed fresh	1 teaspoon bottled
oysters	steak sauce
¼ cup puréed cooked	Few grains garlic salt
spinach	2 tablespoons butter

1. Combine the milk and cream in a heavy saucepan. Set over low heat and bring to simmering.
2. Remove from heat and blend in the oysters and spinach, then the remaining ingredients. Bring to simmering (do not boil).
3. Pour soup into heat-resistant soup cups and top each with a dollop of *whipped cream*. Set the cups under the broiler with tops about 3 inches from source of heat to brown lightly.

ABOUT 1 QUART SOUP

OYSTER BISQUE ANTOINE'S
No visit to Antoine's in New Orleans is complete without a bowl of this famous soup.

2 tablespoons minced	1 qt. milk, scalded
celery	2 cups oysters
2 tablespoons butter	¾ cup heavy cream,
3 tablespoons flour	scalded
¾ teaspoon salt	2 tablespoons sherry
⅛ teaspoon white	
pepper	

1. In a heavy saucepan, cook the celery in butter until yellow in color. Stir in the flour, salt, and pepper; cook until bubbly. Blend in the scalded milk, cooking and stirring until thickened and smooth.
2. Heat the oysters in their liquor until the edges curl. Drain and reserve the liquor. Finely chop the oysters and rub them through a fine sieve or purée oysters in a blender.
3. Add the oysters to the white sauce alternately with the cream. Add sherry. (If bisque seems too thick, thin it with some of the oyster liquor.)

ABOUT 1½ QUARTS SOUP

SALMON CHOWDER

3 tablespoons butter	1½ cups diced pared
½ cup chopped onion	potatoes, cooked
2 tablespoons chopped	1 cup diced pared
green pepper	carrots, cooked
1 can (10½ oz.) con-	1 can (16 oz.) tomatoes,
densed cream of	drained
celery soup	1 teaspoon salt
3 cups milk	½ teaspoon monoso-
1 can (16 oz.) pink	dium glutamate
salmon, drained, skin	¼ teaspoon pepper
and bones discarded,	
and meat separated in	
chunks	

1. Heat butter in a large saucepan. Add onion and green pepper; cook until tender.
2. Stir in soup and milk. Mix in salmon and remaining ingredients. Heat thoroughly, stirring occasionally (do not boil).
3. Ladle chowder into heated soup bowls and serve immediately.

8 TO 10 SERVINGS

SOUPS TO SERVE COLD

JELLIED CONSOMMÉ MADRILÈNE

3 cups tomato juice	1 teaspoon sugar
1 cup strong chicken broth (dissolve 2 chicken bouillon cubes in 1 cup boiling water)	2 env. unflavored gelatin
	¾ cup cold water
	2 teaspoons lemon juice
½ cup chopped green pepper	2 teaspoons Angostura bitters

1. Blend in a saucepan the tomato juice, chicken broth, green pepper, and sugar. Cover and simmer 6 to 8 minutes, or until green pepper is tender.
2. Soften gelatin in the cold water in a bowl.
3. Strain tomato juice mixture into bowl with gelatin and stir until dissolved. Blend in the lemon juice and bitters. Cool. Chill until firm.
4. Just before serving, stir mixture lightly with a fork. Spoon into chilled bowls. Garnish servings with notched slices of *lemon*, if desired.

4 TO 6 SERVINGS

AVOCADO SOUP

4 fully ripe avocados, peeled and pitted	½ teaspoon salt
3 cups cold chicken broth	⅛ teaspoon garlic powder
2 teaspoons lime juice	2 cups chilled cream

1. Put all ingredients except cream into an electric blender container. Cover and blend until smooth. Mix with the cream and chill thoroughly.
2. Serve with *lemon slices* or garnish as desired.

6 SERVINGS

JELLIED BORSCH

1 can (10½ oz.) condensed consommé	⅛ teaspoon cayenne pepper
1 soup can water	1 jar (16 oz.) pickled sliced beets, drained (reserve liquid)
½ clove garlic	
2 stalks celery, cut in pieces	
1 tablespoon brown sugar	1½ env. unflavored gelatin
¼ teaspoon ground ginger	¼ cup lemon juice
	1 cup dairy sour cream

1. Heat consommé and water to boiling in a saucepan. Stir in garlic, celery, brown sugar, ginger, and cayenne pepper. Remove from heat, cover, and let stand 30 minutes.
2. Meanwhile, soften gelatin in reserved beet liquid in a saucepan. Stir over low heat until gelatin is completely dissolved.
3. Strain the consommé; stir in dissolved gelatin. Chill until the consistency of unbeaten egg white, stirring occasionally.
4. Put beets and lemon juice into an electric blender container. Cover and blend thoroughly. Add to gelatin mixture along with the sour cream; blend thoroughly.
5. Pour into a shallow 3-quart dish; depth of mixture will be about ¾ inch. Chill until firm.
6. To serve, cut into cubes. Spoon into bouillon cups and garnish each with *dairy sour cream*.

ABOUT 1½ QUARTS SOUP

CRÈME SENEGALESE
The curry flavor typifies West African cuisine.

2 tablespoons butter or margarine	2 qts. chicken broth, cooled
2 stalks celery, finely chopped	½ cup finely cut fresh pineapple
2 tablespoons grated onion	1 canned pineapple slice, finely cut
1 to 2 tablespoons curry powder	1½ cups finely diced cooked chicken
2 tablespoons flour	2 cups cream

1. Heat butter in a large saucepan. Add celery and onion; cover and cook until celery is tender, stirring occasionally; remove from heat.
2. Blend curry powder and flour in a bowl; slowly add 1 cup of the chicken broth, stirring until smooth after each addition.
3. Adding gradually and stirring constantly, pour into mixture in saucepan. Bring to boiling; continue cooking 5 minutes, stirring constantly.
4. Continue stirring and gradually add remaining broth; simmer, uncovered, 30 minutes, stirring occasionally.
5. Remove from heat; sieve mixture. Stir in the fresh and canned pineapple and the diced chicken. Cool soup.
6. Blend cream into cooled soup; chill thoroughly.
7. Top each serving of chilled soup with *whipped cream*.

ABOUT 2 QUARTS SOUP

CUCUMBER SOUP, DANISH STYLE

2 medium cucumbers, pared	3 cups chicken broth
2 tablespoons butter	1 medium cucumber, pared and grated (discard seeds)
1 medium leek, sliced	
2 bay leaves	1 cup chilled light cream
1 tablespoon flour	
1 teaspoon salt	Juice of ½ lemon

1.   Slice 2 cucumbers; cook slowly in butter with the leek and bay leaves until tender but not brown. Stir in flour and salt. Heat until bubbly.

2.   Stir in the broth. Simmer 20 to 30 minutes. Press mixture through a sieve and chill.

3.   Add grated cucumber, cream, lemon juice, and a bit of *chopped fresh dill*. Correct seasoning.

4.   Serve in chilled cups with a dollop of *dairy sour cream* on top of each.   6 SERVINGS

CREAMY GARLIC SOUP

8 cloves garlic, crushed in a garlic press or minced	¼ teaspoon basil, crushed
	⅛ teaspoon salt
6 tablespoons butter or margarine	⅛ teaspoon black pepper
6 tablespoons flour	6 cups beef broth
	1¼ cups boiling water

1.   Cook garlic in hot butter in a heavy saucepan until golden, stirring occasionally. Stir in a mixture of flour, basil, salt, and pepper; heat until bubbly. Gradually add broth and water, stirring constantly. Bring rapidly to boiling and cook 2 minutes.

2.   Remove from heat; cool. Chill thoroughly.

3.   Serve soup in chilled bowls with generous dollops of *dairy sour cream*. Garnish each serving with *chopped chives* and *sieved hard-cooked egg*.
          ABOUT 1½ QUARTS SOUP

EMERALD SOUP

1 lb. fresh spinach (or one 10-oz. pkg. frozen spinach, cooked)	1 soup can water
	1 teaspoon chervil
	1 clove garlic, minced
1 can (10½ oz.) condensed cream of chicken soup	Dash Tabasco
	Dairy sour cream

1.   Wash the spinach and cook in a kettle having a tight cover; add no water.

2.   When spinach is tender, finely chop it and put through a food mill or purée in an electric blender.

3.   Blend soup and water. Mix with spinach, chervil, garlic, and Tabasco. Chill thoroughly.

4.   Serve with sour cream on top, covering generously with *freshly ground black pepper*.
          ABOUT 1 QUART SOUP

JOHN F. KENNEDY'S ICED TOMATO SOUP

6 large ripe tomatoes, coarsely chopped	2 tablespoons flour
	2 cups chicken broth (dissolve 2 chicken bouillon cubes in 2 cups boiling water)
1 onion, chopped	
¼ cup water	
½ teaspoon salt	
Dash freshly ground black pepper	1 cup chilled heavy cream
2 tablespoons tomato paste	

1.   Combine chopped tomatoes, onion, water, salt, and pepper in a saucepan. Cook over medium heat 5 minutes.

2.   Stir in a blend of tomato paste and flour, then the chicken broth. Stirring constantly, bring to boiling and cook 1 to 2 minutes.

3.   Force mixture through a fine sieve. Chill several hours.

4.   Before serving, blend in cream. Garnish each serving with a slice of peeled *tomato*.
          1¾ QUARTS SOUP

VICHYSSOISE

From the quaint, colonial Lord Jeffery Inn at Amherst, Massachusetts, comes this version of leek and potato soup.

4 to 6 leeks	1 cup light cream
3 medium-sized (1 lb.) potatoes, thinly sliced	1 cup chilled heavy cream
4 cups chicken broth (dissolve 6 chicken bouillon cubes in 4 cups boiling water)	Snipped chives

1.   Finely slice the white part and about an inch of the green part of each leek to measure about 1 cup.

2.   Cover; simmer the leeks and potatoes in broth until very soft, about 40 minutes.

3.   Sieve the cooked vegetables or blend until smooth in electric blender. Mix in the light cream; chill thoroughly.

4.   Just before serving, stir in heavy cream. Garnish with chives.   ABOUT 2 QUARTS SOUP

GAZPACHO ANDALUZ
This recipe comes from Botin's Restaurant in Madrid, Spain.

3½ cups peeled, chopped ripe tomatoes	4 cups water
1⅓ cups pared, chopped cucumber	3 tablespoons cider vinegar
1 cup chopped green pepper	2 teaspoons salt
2⅔ cups finely crumbled bread	1 tablespoon paprika
4 tablespoons olive oil	⅛ teaspoon ground cumin
	2 cloves garlic, crushed
	4 to 6 ice cubes

1. Combine tomatoes, cucumber, green pepper, bread, olive oil, and water; cover and refrigerate 1 hour.
2. Turn mixture into an electric blender container and blend. Sieve mixture and add remaining ingredients; chill thoroughly.
3. Serve in chilled soup plates. Pass a platter of garnish: mounds of *crumbled bread* and *diced green pepper*, *ripe tomato*, and *cucumber*. 8 SERVINGS

Fruit Soups

CHERRY SOUP
A Hungarian specialty.

1 qt. water	½ cup cold water
2 to 2½ lbs. frozen sweetened tart red cherries, slightly thawed	¼ cup flour
	3 egg yolks, slightly beaten
½ teaspoon salt	1 cup dairy sour cream

1. Bring the water to boiling in a large saucepan. Add cherries and salt; bring to boiling; simmer, covered, 10 minutes.
2. Pour the cold water into a 1-pint screw-top jar. Add flour; cover jar tightly; shake until blended.
3. Stirring constantly, slowly pour flour mixture into hot cherry mixture; bring to boiling, and cook 2 to 3 minutes.
4. Remove from heat; gradually add ⅓ cup hot soup to the egg yolks, stirring vigorously; blend into soup. Stirring constantly, cook over low heat 3 to 5 minutes (do not boil). Remove from heat.
5. Gradually add 1 cup hot soup to the sour cream, stirring vigorously; then blend into remaining soup. Chill and serve cold, or serve hot, if desired. 8 TO 10 SERVINGS

CHILLED PURPLE PLUM SOUP
If a frozen dessert is desired, allow about ¼ cup sugar per cup of plum soup; stir in; freeze.

2 lbs. purple prune plums	1 stick cinnamon, broken
3 cups cold water	1 teaspoon whole cloves
¼ cup honey	2 teaspoons cornstarch
1 tablespoon lemon juice	2 tablespoons cold water
2 tablespoons sugar	½ teaspoon almond extract
½ teaspoon salt	2 cups heavy cream

1. Quarter and pit plums; put into a large saucepot with water, honey, lemon juice, sugar, and salt. Tie cinnamon and cloves in a small square of cheesecloth; add the spice bag to saucepot. Bring to boiling. Reduce heat; simmer until plums are tender, 10 to 15 minutes.
2. Stir 2 tablespoons water into cornstarch to blend; pour into soup. Stirring constantly, bring to boiling; cook 2 to 3 minutes until slightly thickened.
3. Remove from heat and discard spice bag. Stir in extract. Cool completely.
4. Add cream, stirring constantly until blended. Chill. Stir again before serving.
 ABOUT 1½ QUARTS SOUP

SWEDISH FRUIT SOUP
(Fruktsoppa)

1 cup dried apricots	3 tablespoons quick-cooking tapioca
¾ cup dried apples	1 piece (3 in.) stick cinnamon
½ cup dried peaches	
½ cup prunes	1 teaspoon grated orange peel
½ cup dark seedless raisins	1 cup red raspberry fruit syrup
2 qts. water	
¼ cup sugar	

1. Rinse dried fruits with cold water; remove pits from prunes. Place fruits in a large kettle with the water; cover and allow to soak 2 to 3 hours.
2. Add the sugar, tapioca, cinnamon, and orange peel to fruits; let stand 5 minutes. Boil, cover, and simmer 1 hour, or until fruit is tender.
3. Stir in syrup; cool, then chill thoroughly.
4. Serve with *whipped cream* and *slivered blanched almonds*. ABOUT 3 QUARTS SOUP

Chapter 3

BREADS—Yeast, Quick & the Kind You Buy

Bread and life, home, and hospitality are inextricably associated in the human imagination and experience. As old as history, breadmaking was one of the first culinary arts practiced—and at a time when home itself was little more than a few flat stones arranged round a fire. Now most of the peoples of the earth have breads characteristically their own.

In our country we have no single traditional bread. We have, instead, welcomed the traditions of all the peoples who have come here and made them our own.

Made with or without leavening, bread appears in a hundred different delightful guises—as soft loaves and crusty loaves, holiday breads and coffee cakes, waffles, griddlecakes, popovers, muffins and doughnuts, and in other forms too numerous to mention.

HELPFUL HINTS ABOUT BREADS

• To glaze tops of fancy breads and rolls brush before baking with slightly beaten egg white mixed with 1 tablespoon milk or water; or egg yolk slightly beaten with a little milk or water.
• To slice newly baked bread, cut with a hot knife.
• To make a large croustade see *Croustade Basket, page 116.*
• To butter bread for thin sandwiches, spread end of loaf with softened butter, then cut off a slice as thin as possible. Repeat buttering and slicing.
• To freshen rolls, place them in a heavy paper bag. Twist top of bag and place in a 400°F oven 10 to 15 minutes. (Or wrap securely in aluminum foil.)
• Use a 1-quart glass measuring cup for mixing pancake and waffle batters, muffin and quick-bread batters. Start by measuring the liquid ingredients into the cup; mix well and beat in the combined dry ingredients. Now the batter is in a "pouring" container ready to pour onto waffle baker, griddle, or into a baking pan.
• When making baking powder biscuits, roll dough or pat to ¼-inch thickness; then fold one half of dough over the other half. Then cut out biscuit rounds. (The hot baked biscuits will split open easily for spreading with butter or margarine.)
• To prepare crumbs from dry bread, force through the fine blade of food chopper or place dry bread in a small plastic bag and crush with a rolling pin. Crush in an electric blender, if available. If using the food chopper, tie a paper bag onto end of food chopper to keep crumbs from scattering.
• Use a slotted pancake turner to transfer uncooked cut doughnuts from pastry canvas to hot fat. Fry only as many doughnuts at one time as will float uncrowded one layer deep in the fat. Drain over fat a few seconds on turner, or use a long-handled two-tined fork; put onto absorbent paper.

STORAGE

Store bread in a cool dry place. If a loaf is not consumed in several days, keep it fresh by placing in a moisture-vaporproof bag and storing it in the refrigerator. If you bake or purchase more than one loaf at a time, keep one loaf in the refrigerator and wrap the other loaf in freezer wrap and place it in the freezer. If loaf has been sliced before freezing, remove only the number of slices required for a single meal and thaw at room temperature. Baked rolls and biscuits are stored in a similar manner.

YEAST BREADS

Breadmaking methods through the years have been so improved that today no special talent is required for a homemaker to make a fine loaf of bread. Improved flour-milling processes and yeast with "speeded-up" action have also contributed to simplifying breadbaking. Gone are the times when it took several days to turn out a batch of bread. Today's homemaker can make good yeast bread in several hours.

INGREDIENTS

Yeast — Yeast is a living plant which is the leaven used in bread and rolls to make them light. *Active dry yeast* and *compressed* (fresh active) *yeast* are used for breadmaking. Dry yeast is obtainable in individual airtight packets or in jars and may be stored on cool, dry pantry shelves for months. Active dry yeast when used in conventional breadmaking recipes may be softened (dissolved) in warm water (105° to 115°F) before it is added to the other ingredients. However, this modern dry yeast is a finer product than formerly and it can be quickly mixed with the dry ingredients, thus eliminating the step of softening the yeast in water. Today's yeast also has a tolerance to higher temperatures. By mixing it with some of the dry ingredients before adding the heated liquid, the chance of "killing" the yeast is lessened and temperatures as high as 120° to 130°F may be used. A drop of the heated liquid on the wrist should feel very warm.)

Compressed yeast is perishable and must be stored in the refrigerator. It is grayish tan in color but it may be slightly browned at the edges of the cake. When fresh it breaks with a clean edge and crumbles easily between the fingers. Compressed yeast is softened in lukewarm water (80° to 100°F) before using. Or a small amount of sugar may be added to the yeast to liquefy it. The yeasts may be used interchangeably, 1 packet dry yeast (or 1 scant tablespoon from a jar) being equivalent to 1 cake of yeast ⅗ or ⅝ ounce.

Flour — *All-purpose flour* is used for making bread in the home. It contains a protein substance called gluten which becomes elastic as the batter is beaten and the dough kneaded. This elasticity accommodates the gas bubbles formed in the dough by the yeast. Other flours, such as *whole wheat*, *rye*, and *buckwheat*, are also used in yeast breads. However, they are combined with all-purpose flour. Used alone they produce heavy, compact breads which usually do not appeal to American tastes. Cereals, such as *rolled oats*, *cornmeal*, and *bran*, are used in bread, but, again, in small enough quantities to avoid a heavy loaf.

Liquid — *Milk* and *water* are the usual liquids used in bread doughs. Sometimes water in which potatoes have been cooked is used. Fluid milk, evaporated milk, or reconstituted dry milk all give satisfactory results and should be warmed before using. Unpasteurized milk must be scalded and cooled before using. If a crisp crust is desired, use water. For a less crisp, softer crust, use milk.

Sugar — Sugar is needed with yeast to produce the tiny bubbles of carbon dioxide gas which cause dough to rise. Sugar also adds flavor and helps to produce a brown crust. *Granulated white sugar* is commonly used, but *brown sugar, molasses*, or *honey* may also be used in specific recipes.

Salt — Salt adds flavor to the bread and also controls the action of the yeast, slowing down the rate that the gas bubbles form in the dough. When salt-free bread is made, the dough will rise very rapidly and must be watched carefully.

Fat — *Butter, margarine, cooking oils, vegetable or all-purpose shortenings*, or *lard* are used to give bread a soft, tender texture and a satiny crust.

Eggs — Eggs add food value, color, and flavor, and help to produce a tender crust.

REFRIGERATOR DOUGHS

Refrigerator doughs are richer and sweeter than plain bread doughs and can be successfully kept in the refrigerator (45° to 50°F) three to four days. Refrigerate immediately after mixing and kneading or after the first rising period. (Do not allow dough to rise too much.) If rising occurs during refrigeration, punch down dough occasionally. Grease the dough and cover well to keep the surface moist and elastic. When ready to bake, remove dough from refrigerator, shape, allow to rise until light and doubled before baking. For longer periods of storage, yeast doughs may be frozen. Generally, baking the bread or rolls before freezing is recommended.

BAKING PANS

Use the pan size designated in the recipe. Too small a pan causes bread to slide over sides of pan, resulting in an unattractive and poorly baked loaf. Too large a pan will result in poor volume. When using glass baking pans it is recommended that temperatures be reduced 25°.

METHODS OF MAKING YEAST BREADS

Sponge—This is one of the oldest ways of making bread. First a sponge is made by combining the softened yeast with part of the sugar, lukewarm liquid, and flour. The mixture is beaten well, covered, and set in a warm place until it is bubbly and spongelike. The salt, melted shortening, and enough remaining flour are then beaten in to make a dough which can be kneaded until smooth and satiny.

Conventional or Straight Dough—This method until recently has been most commonly used. All ingredients are beaten together to make a dough which is kneaded to satiny smoothness. Then it is given one or two risings in a warm place (80° to 100°F) before shaping. After shaping, the dough is left to rise again in baking pans.

Batter—This is a quick and easy method of making bread. As the name implies, this mixture is the consistency of a batter rather than a dough and requires no kneading or shaping. The batter is quickly mixed and allowed to rise in the mixing bowl. The consistency of batter may be quite thin or fairly thick depending upon the recipe. So-called casserole breads are prepared using the batter method of mixing.

CoolRise—This method utilizes the refrigerator rather than the "warm, draft-free place" usually chosen when yeast dough is set aside to rise. The controlled rising in the refrigerator does away with careful watching and waiting. It also makes possible the complete preparation of the dough in one operation which requires only about 45 minutes. After shaped loaves are put into loaf pans they are refrigerated (38° to 41°F) for 2 to 24 hours, no watching being necessary. When fresh bread is desired, a loaf may be removed from refrigerator and allowed to remain at room temperature about 10 minutes, or while oven is being preheated.

Instant Blend and Rapid Mix—These methods do not require the softening (dissolving) of the active dry yeast in warm water. Instead, the yeast is mixed with the dry ingredients in a mixing bowl and the liquid (with butter, margarine, or other shortening added) is heated only until the mixture is warm and the shortening is softened. Then the electric mixer takes over to blend all the ingredients with no chance of lumps. The final amount of flour is beaten in using a wooden spoon. The resulting dough is light and delicate to the touch. A second Rapid Mix technique involves the use of only one bowl and is similar to the first except that the shortening is placed on top of the dry ingredients in a large mixing bowl. Then very hot water from the tap is added before the mixer takes over.

TECHNIQUES FOR MAKING YEAST BREADS

Beating—Done with an electric mixer or vigorously by hand with a mixing spoon. Thorough beating of the batter speeds up the development of the gluten in the flour. Vigorous beating is important when making batter or casserole bread because kneading is not necessary. Batter bread has usually been beaten enough when the mixture leaves the sides of the bowl.

Stirring down—This technique appears in recipes for batter bread or when using the sponge method for mixing. With large mixing spoon, stir the raised batter or dough until it has been reduced to almost its original volume.

Kneading—Knead dough after it rests 5 to 10 minutes on a lightly floured surface or pastry canvas. All the flour needed to keep the dough from sticking to the surface should be added during this process. Do not add more flour after the dough has risen and doubled in volume as this could result in a coarsely textured loaf of bread with dark streaks through it. To knead, dust hands with a little flour and form dough into a ball on the lightly floured surface. With your fingers fold the dough toward you, then with the heel of the hand push dough away using a rolling motion and give the dough a one-quarter turn. Again, fold over dough, push away, and give it a quarter turn. Repeat (using as little flour as necessary on the kneading surface and on hands) until dough is satiny smooth, elastic, and shows small blisters directly under its surface. Place dough in a lightly greased bowl; turn to bring greased surface to top. Cover bowl.

Rising—Dough that is prepared using the conventional method requires a temperature of 80° to 85°F for rising. Place bowl in a draft-free place. (Dough that is prepared using the Cool-Rise method requires a refrigerator temperature of 38° to 41°F. Cover the bowl lightly enough to allow space between the refrigerator shelves.) Be sure the wrappings are not tucked under the bowl when placed in the refrigerator. Also allow space between the refrigerator shelves. When the dough looks double its original size, test by gently pressing two fingers lightly into dough; if dent remains, dough is light.

Punching down—With fist, punch down dough, pull edges to center, and turn dough completely over in the bowl. Let rise again until doubled, or shape it, following recipe directions.

Shaping—Follow recipe directions for shaping rolls or unusual shapes. To shape two loaves of bread, divide the dough by cutting it in half with a knife. Roll each half into a 12x8-inch rectangle of uniform thickness. Beginning with upper 8-inch side, roll dough toward you. Seal with thumbs or heel of hand, sealing ends well and folding them under. Avoid tearing dough. Place loaves in greased loaf pans; round loaves, fancy shapes, or rolls as directed. Cover; let rise until doubled.

Testing for lightness—Test loaves by pressing lightly with finger near edge. If dent remains, bread is ready to bake. In the CoolRise method dough does not always double.

Baking—Put loaves into a preheated oven on shelf placed so top of product is at center of oven. When baking two loaves, place them two inches apart to allow heat to circulate. Stagger four loaves in the oven on two shelves.

Applying baking test—When minimum baking time is up, remove one loaf from oven and tap the sides and bottom. Yeast breads are done when they sound hollow and are golden brown.

Removing loaves and rolls—Take from pans as they come from the oven unless otherwise directed. Place on wire racks to cool. *For a soft crust* brush immediately with butter or margarine. *For a crisp crust* brush before baking with milk or a mixture of egg yolk and water.

Adjusting for high altitudes—Altitudes increase the leavening power of yeast so rising time may be reduced. At altitudes over 5,000 feet, one packet of yeast is often used if recipe calls for two. Watch rising of dough carefully. Punch it down even if it hasn't quite doubled. Bake bread when dough is light, but probably not quite doubled. For additional information, see *page 18*.

Yeast Loaves

WHITE BREAD
(CoolRise Method)

2 pkgs. active dry yeast	3 tablespoons
½ cup warm water	margarine
1¾ cups warm milk	5½ to 6½ cups all-
2 tablespoons sugar	purpose flour
1 tablespoon salt	Cooking or salad oil

1. Soften yeast in the warm water in a large bowl. Add warm milk, sugar, salt, margarine, and 2 cups flour; beat with hand rotary or electric beater until smooth, about 1 minute. Add 1 cup flour and beat vigorously with a wooden spoon (150 strokes). Add enough of the remaining flour to make a soft dough.
2. Turn onto a lightly floured surface and knead until smooth and elastic. Cover with plastic wrap, then a towel, and let rest 20 minutes.
3. Punch down dough and divide into halves. Shape into loaves. Place, seam side down, in 2 greased 8x4x2-inch loaf pans. Brush with oil, then cover loaves loosely with oiled waxed paper and plastic wrap. (Be sure these layers are not tucked under the pans, as they must be loose enough to allow dough to rise.) Refrigerate 2 to 24 hours.
4. When ready to bake, remove from refrigerator, uncover, and let stand at room temperature 10 minutes. Prick any gas bubbles with an oiled wooden pick or metal skewer.
5. Bake at 400°F 30 to 40 minutes. Remove from pans, brush loaves with *melted butter or margarine*. Cool on wire racks.   2 LOAVES BREAD

NOTE: If self-rising flour is used, omit the salt.

WHITE BREAD
(Straight Dough Method)

1 pkg. active dry yeast	1 tablespoon salt
¼ cup warm water	¾ cup cold water
1 cup milk, scalded	6 cups (about) all-
2 tablespoons sugar	purpose flour
2 tablespoons shortening	

1. Soften yeast in the warm water.
2. In a large bowl combine the scalded milk, sugar, shortening, and salt. Add the cold water and cool until lukewarm. Blend in the yeast.
3. Beat in about 3 cups of the flour gradually until

batter is smooth. Then stir in enough remaining flour to form a dough stiff enough to form into a ball. Turn dough onto a lightly floured surface and let rest 5 to 10 minutes.

4.   Knead until dough is smooth and satiny, 5 to 10 minutes. Put into a greased deep bowl; turn dough to bring greased surface to top. Cover; let rise in a warm place until doubled, 45 to 60 minutes.

5.   Turn onto a lightly floured surface and divide dough into halves. Form each into a smooth ball; cover and let rest 5 to 10 minutes.

6.   Shape into loaves and place in 2 greased 9x5x3-inch loaf pans. Cover; let rise again until doubled, 45 to 60 minutes.

7.   Bake at 400°F 45 to 50 minutes.   2 LOAVES BREAD

OLD-FASHIONED HERB BREAD

Sage gives this bread its distinctive flavor.

1 pkg. active dry yeast	3 to 3½ cups all-purpose
¼ cup warm water	flour
¾ cup milk, scalded	1 egg, beaten
3 tablespoons butter	¼ teaspoon ground
3 tablespoons sugar	nutmeg
1½ teaspoons salt	2 to 3 teaspoons
	crushed sage

1.   Soften yeast in the warm water.
2.   Blend milk, butter, sugar, and salt thoroughly in a large bowl; cool to warm. Add 1 cup flour and beat thoroughly. Beat in egg, nutmeg, and sage, then the yeast. Mix in enough remaining flour to make a soft (but not sticky) dough.
3.   Turn onto a lightly floured surface and knead until smooth and elastic. Put into a greased deep bowl; turn dough to bring greased surface to top. Cover; let rise in a warm place until doubled, 1 hour.
4.   Punch down dough and let rest about 10 minutes.
5.   Shape dough into a round loaf. Place in a greased 9-inch pie pan and let rise again until doubled, about 45 minutes.
6.   Brush lightly with slightly beaten *egg white.* Sprinkle with *caraway seed.*
7.   Bake at 400°F 10 minutes; reduce oven temperature to 375°F and bake 20 to 25 minutes, or until bread is well browned.

ONE 9-INCH ROUND LOAF BREAD

NOTE: If desired, add *1 teaspoon caraway seed* to the dough and top loaf with additional seed.

POTATO BREAD

1 medium-sized potato, washed, pared, and cut in pieces	2 tablespoons shortening
2½ cups water	2 tablespoons sugar
1 pkg. active dry yeast	1 tablespoon salt
	6 cups all-purpose flour

1.   Cook the potato in the water until tender. Reserve ¼ cup liquid; cool to warm.
2.   Mash the potato in the remaining liquid; add water to make 2¼ cups liquid.
3.   Soften yeast in the reserved ¼ cup liquid.
4.   Add the potato liquid to shortening, sugar, and salt in a bowl; stir until smooth. Beat in about half of flour. Stir in the yeast. Add the remaining flour gradually, mixing well.
5.   Turn dough onto a lightly floured surface and knead until smooth and elastic. Put into a greased deep bowl and grease top of dough. Cover; let rise in a warm place until doubled, about 1 hour.
6.   Punch down dough and divide into halves. Shape into loaves. Place in 2 greased 8x4x2-inch loaf pans. Cover; let rise again until doubled, about 30 minutes.
7.   Bake at 375°F about 40 minutes.

2 LOAVES BREAD

ANADAMA BREAD

½ cup yellow cornmeal	1½ teaspoons salt
2 cups boiling water	1 pkg. active dry yeast
2 tablespoons shortening	½ cup warm water
½ cup molasses	6 cups all-purpose flour

1.   Stirring constantly, add the cornmeal to the boiling water in a large bowl. Stir in the shortening, molasses, and salt. Set aside to cool to lukewarm.
2.   Meanwhile, soften yeast in the warm water.
3.   Blend 1 cup of the flour into lukewarm cornmeal mixture; beat until very smooth. Mix in yeast. Add about half of the remaining flour and beat until very smooth. Then mix in enough of the remaining flour to make a soft dough.
4.   Turn onto a lightly floured surface. Cover and let rest 5 to 10 minutes.
5.   Knead dough until satiny and smooth. Form into a ball and put into a greased deep bowl. Turn dough to bring greased surface to top. Cover; let rise in a warm place until doubled, about 1 hour.
6.   Punch down dough and turn onto a lightly floured surface. Divide into halves and form into

smooth balls. Shape into loaves. Place in 2 greased 9x5x3-inch loaf pans. Cover; let rise again until doubled, about 1 hour.

7.   Bake at 375°F 40 to 45 minutes, or until bread tests done. Remove from pans, brush tops with *melted butter or margarine* and cool on wire racks.

2 LOAVES BREAD

GRANNY'S TEXAS BRAN BREAD

1½ cups boiling water	2 teaspoons salt
3 tablespoons shortening	1 cup whole bran
3 tablespoons brown sugar	1 pkg. active dry yeast
2 tablespoons molasses	½ cup warm water
	5 to 5½ cups all-purpose flour

1.   Pour boiling water over shortening, brown sugar, molasses, salt, and bran in a large bowl. Blend well and set aside to cool to lukewarm.

2.   Soften yeast in the warm water.

3.   Beat 1 cup flour into bran mixture. Stir yeast into batter until thoroughly blended. Continue beating while gradually adding about half of the remaining flour. Beat vigorously, then mix in enough remaining flour to make a soft (not sticky) dough.

4.   Lightly grease top of dough. Cover; let rise in a warm place until doubled, about 2 hours.

5.   Turn onto a lightly floured surface and divide into halves. Knead gently until dough is smooth and "springy."

6.   Shape dough into loaves. Place in 2 greased 8x4x2-inch loaf pans. Cover; let rise again until almost doubled, about 45 minutes.

7.   Bake in a 325°F oven (*not preheated*) 50 to 55 minutes. Remove from oven; turn out of pans onto wire rack and lightly brush loaves with *melted butter.*

2 LOAVES BREAD

OATMEAL-RAISIN BREAD

1½ cups boiling water	2 pkgs. active dry yeast
1 cup rolled oats	½ cup warm water
½ cup dark molasses	2 eggs
⅓ cup shortening	5 cups all-purpose flour
2 tablespoons sugar	1 cup seedless raisins, plumped
1 tablespoon salt	

1.   Put boiling water, oats, molasses, shortening, sugar, and salt into a large bowl; stir to blend. Cool to lukewarm.

2.   Soften yeast in the warm water. Add to lukewarm mixture in bowl. Add the eggs, one at a time, beating well after each addition.

3.   Add about half of the flour, ½ cup at a time, beating vigorously after each addition. Beat in the raisins and remaining flour. (Dough will be quite soft.)

4.   Turn dough into a greased deep bowl and grease top of dough. Cover; let rise in a warm place until doubled.

5.   Beat down dough with spoon and divide into halves. Spread each half evenly in a greased 9x5x3-inch loaf pan. Cover; let rise again until doubled, about 1 hour.

6.   Bake at 350°F about 40 minutes. Remove pans to wire racks, brush tops with *melted butter*, and cool 10 minutes in pans before removing to racks.

2 LOAVES BREAD

RAISIN BREAD

2 pkgs. active dry yeast	2 cups milk, scalded
1 cup warm water	8¼ cups (about) all-purpose flour
½ cup butter or margarine	2 eggs, slightly beaten
¼ cup sugar	1½ cups dark seedless raisins
2½ teaspoons salt	

1.   Soften yeast in the warm water.

2.   Put butter, sugar, and salt into a large bowl; pour the scalded milk over all and stir until butter is melted. Beat in about 1 cup of the flour. Stir in yeast.

3.   Gradually add about one half the flour, beating until smooth. Beat in eggs. Mix in raisins.

4.   Gradually add enough remaining flour to make a stiff dough, beating until smooth and dough comes away from sides of bowl.

5.   Turn onto a lightly floured surface and let rest about 10 minutes.

6.   Knead, adding more flour if dough seems too sticky, until satiny smooth and small blisters appear under the surface of dough. Form dough into a ball and put into a greased deep bowl. Turn dough to bring greased surface to top. Cover; let rise in a warm place until doubled.

7.   Punch down dough; turn onto a lightly floured surface. Divide dough into halves and roll each into a 14x9-inch rectangle. Beginning at a 9-inch end, roll up each rectangle, shaping into a loaf. Place each in a greased 9x5x3-inch loaf pan and lightly grease top. Cover; let rise again until doubled.

Sally Lunn with Strawberries

8. Bake at 375°F about 45 minutes. Remove from pans to wire rack. 2 LOAVES BREAD

RAISIN-FILLED BREAD: Follow recipe for Raisin Bread. Omit raisins in dough. After rolling out dough on a lightly floured surface, brush with *egg yolk glaze* (1 egg yolk blended with 1 teaspoon water). Then spoon *Raisin Filling, below,* over dough almost to edges and tightly roll up, beginning at a 9-inch end. Pinch to seal the underside; place, sealed side down, in greased 9x5x3-inch loaf pans. Proceed as for Raisin Bread.

Raisin Filling: Mix in a bowl *2/3 cup fine dry bread crumbs, 1/3 cup sugar, 4 teaspoons grated orange peel,* and *2 to 3 teaspoons ground cardamom.* Cut in *1/2 cup butter or margarine* until pieces are about the size of small peas. Mix in *2 1/2 cups dark seedless raisins,* snipped.

SWEDISH RYE BREAD
(Limpa)

Anise seed, orange peel, molasses, brown sugar, and rye flour all contribute to the exceptional flavor of this bread.

2 pkgs. active dry yeast	4 teaspoons grated
1/2 cup warm water	orange peel
1/2 cup packed dark brown	3/4 teaspoon anise seed
sugar	1 1/2 cups hot water
1/3 cup molasses	2 1/2 cups medium rye
2 tablespoons butter or	flour
margarine	3 1/2 to 4 cups all-purpose
1 tablespoon salt	flour

1. Soften yeast in the warm water.
2. Combine the brown sugar, molasses, butter, salt, orange peel, and anise in a large bowl. Add the hot water and blend. Cool to lukewarm.
3. Beat in 1 cup of the rye flour until smooth. Stir in yeast. Gradually add all of the rye flour, beating vigorously. Mix in enough of the all-purpose flour (2 1/2 to 3 cups) to make a soft dough, beating until the dough comes away from the sides of bowl.
4. Turn onto a lightly floured surface and let rest about 10 minutes.
5. Knead in enough remaining flour to make a smooth elastic dough which does not stick to kneading surface. Form into a ball and put into a greased deep bowl. Turn dough to bring greased surface to top. Cover; let rise in a warm place until doubled.
6. Punch down dough; pull edges into center and turn dough completely over in bowl. Cover; let rise again until almost doubled.
7. Punch down again and turn onto a lightly floured surface. Divide dough into halves and shape into smooth balls. Place on a greased baking sheet sprinkled with cornmeal. Cover; let rise again until doubled, about 30 minutes.
8. Bake at 375°F 25 to 30 minutes. Remove to a wire rack and immediately brush lightly with *milk.* Cool. 2 LOAVES BREAD

NOTE: *2 teaspoons caraway seed* may be substituted for orange peel. Decrease anise to 1/2 teaspoon.

WHOLE WHEAT BREAD
(Rapid Mix)

3 cups whole wheat	2 pkgs. active dry yeast
flour	1 1/2 cups water
3 1/3 cups (about) all-	3/4 cup milk
purpose flour	1/3 cup molasses
3 tablespoons sugar	1/3 cup margarine or
4 teaspoons salt	other shortening

1. Combine the flours, blending thoroughly. Into a large bowl measure 2 1/2 cups of the flour mixture. Add sugar, salt, and undissolved yeast; mix well.
2. Combine the remaining ingredients in a saucepan and place over low heat until liquids are warm (fat need not be melted).
3. Add liquids gradually to dry ingredients, beating 2 minutes at medium speed of electric mixer; scrape sides of bowl occasionally. Add 1/2 cup flour mixture or enough to make a thick batter. Beat at high speed 2 minutes, scraping sides of bowl when necessary.
4. Stir in enough additional flour to make a soft dough. (If more flour is needed, add all-purpose flour to obtain desired dough.)
5. Turn onto a lightly floured surface and knead until smooth and elastic, about 8 minutes.
6. Put into a greased deep bowl; turn dough to bring greased surface to top. Cover; let rise in warm place until doubled, about 1 hour.
7. Punch down dough; turn onto a lightly floured surface. Divide into halves and shape into loaves. Put into 2 greased 8x4x2-inch loaf pans. Cover; let rise again until doubled, about 1 hour.
8. Bake at 400°F about 30 minutes, or until done. Remove from pans to wire racks; brush loaves lightly with *melted shortening,* if desired. Cool thoroughly before storing. 2 LOAVES BREAD

TOP: *Filled Holiday Coffee Cake*
BOTTOM: *Croustade Basket filled with Scrambled Eggs and served with Mushroom-Caraway Sauce*

SALLY LUNN

This bread, named after an eighteenth century pastry cook, has many variations, some made with yeast and others with baking powder. It can be baked in a loaf or cake pan or in muffin pans and is served warm from the oven with plenty of butter.

1 pkg. active dry yeast	2 tablespoons sugar
¼ cup warm water	¾ teaspoon salt
½ cup milk, scalded	2 cups all-purpose flour
⅔ cup butter or	2 eggs, well beaten
margarine, softened	

1. Soften yeast in the warm water.
2. Pour scalded milk over butter, sugar, and salt in a large bowl; cool to lukewarm. Add about ½ cup flour and beat until smooth.
3. Stir the yeast into the batter; mix well. Add about half of the remaining flour and beat until very smooth. Add eggs; beat until smooth. Blend in the remaining flour; beat thoroughly at least 5 minutes. Scrape down from sides of bowl. Cover; let rise in a warm place until doubled, about 45 minutes.
4. When doubled, beat again at least 5 minutes.
5. Turn into a greased 1½-quart ring mold or Turk's-head mold. Cover; let rise again until doubled, about 45 minutes.
6. Bake at 350°F 25 to 30 minutes, or until golden brown. Run knife around edge of mold to loosen the loaf and gently remove to wire rack. Serve warm.

1 RING LOAF

SALLY LUNN WITH STRAWBERRIES

1 cup milk, scalded	3 eggs, beaten
½ cup sugar	5 cups all-purpose flour
2 teaspoons salt	½ teaspoon ground
½ cup butter or	nutmeg
margarine, melted	3 pts. fresh
1 pkg. active dry yeast	strawberries, sliced
½ cup warm water	and sweetened

1. Combine milk, ¼ cup of the sugar, salt, and butter; cool to lukewarm.
2. Soften yeast in the warm water in a large bowl. Blend with the milk mixture and eggs.
3. Gradually beat in the flour until smooth. Cover; let rise in a warm place until doubled, about 1 hour.
4. Stir dough down and turn into a greased and sugared 10-inch tubed pan. Cover; let rise again until doubled, about 30 minutes.
5. Mix remaining ¼ cup sugar with the nutmeg and sprinkle over top of dough.

6. Bake at 400°F about 40 minutes. Remove from oven and cool 5 minutes. Turn out Sally Lunn and serve warm or cooled with the strawberries mounded in the center of the ring. Accompany with a bowl of *whipped cream* or a pitcher of *cream.*

ONE 10-INCH RING LOAF

NOTE: If desired, the strawberries may be left whole and unhulled to be dipped into the cream as they are eaten.

EASTER EGG BREAD

Shaped in the form of a wreath and decorated with colorful Easter eggs, this bread is probably of Italian origin. However, other countries which celebrate Easter also prepare it to add a festive touch to the Easter breakfast or dinner.

2 pkgs. active dry yeast	1½ tablespoons lemon
½ cup warm water	juice
1 cup all-purpose flour	¾ cup sugar
⅓ cup water	1 teaspoon salt
¾ cup butter or	2 eggs, well beaten
margarine	3¾ to 4¼ cups all-
1 tablespoon grated	purpose flour
lemon peel	6 colored eggs
	(uncooked)

1. Soften yeast in the warm water in a bowl. Mix in the 1 cup flour, then the ⅓ cup water. Beat until smooth. Cover; let rise in a warm place until doubled, about 1 hour.
2. Cream butter with lemon peel and juice. Add sugar and salt gradually, beating until fluffy. Add eggs in halves, beating thoroughly after each addition.
3. Add yeast mixture and beat until blended. Add about half of the remaining flour and beat thoroughly. Beat in enough flour to make a soft dough.
4. Knead on floured surface until smooth. Put into a greased deep bowl; turn dough to bring greased surface to top. Cover; let rise in a warm place until doubled.
5. Punch down dough; divide into thirds. Cover; let rest about 10 minutes.
6. With hands, roll and stretch each piece into a roll about 26 inches long and ¾ inch thick. Loosely braid rolls together. On a lightly greased baking sheet or jelly roll pan shape into a ring, pressing ends together. At even intervals, gently spread dough apart and tuck in a colored egg. Cover; let rise again until doubled.

7. Bake at 375°F about 30 minutes. During baking check bread for browning, and when sufficiently browned, cover loosely with aluminum foil.

8. Transfer coffee cake to a wire rack. If desired, spread a *confectioners' sugar icing* over top of warm bread. 1 LARGE WREATH

  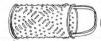

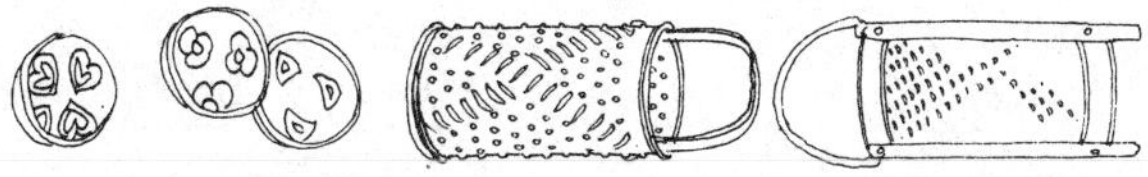

GOLDEN BRAID

1 pkg. active dry yeast	1½ teaspoons salt
1¼ cups warm water	2 tablespoons butter or
⅛ teaspoon saffron,	margarine, melted
crushed and blended	2 eggs, slightly beaten
with 1 teaspoon water	4 to 4½ cups all-purpose
½ cup all-purpose flour	flour
1 tablespoon sugar	

1. Soften yeast in the warm water in a large bowl. Mix in the saffron, ½ cup flour, sugar, and salt, then the butter and eggs.

2. Gradually add 3½ cups of the flour, beating until smooth. Add enough remaining flour to make a soft dough, beating until smooth and dough comes away from bowl.

3. Turn dough onto a lightly floured surface and let rest about 10 minutes.

4. Knead, adding more flour if dough seems too sticky, until satiny smooth and small blisters appear under the surface of dough.

5. Form into a ball and put into a greased deep bowl. Turn dough to bring greased surface to top. Cover; let rise in a warm place until doubled.

6. Punch down dough; pull edges into center and turn dough completely over in bowl. Cover; let rise again until almost doubled.

7. Punch down again and turn onto a lightly floured surface. Divide dough into thirds. Using lightly floured hands, roll each piece into a rope about 15 inches long. Place the 3 pieces, side by side, on a greased baking sheet. Begin the braiding from center toward both ends. Tuck ends under. Cover; let rise about 1 hour, or until doubled.

8. Brush with glaze (*1 egg yolk* blended with *1 teaspoon water*). Sprinkle with *poppy seed* or *sesame seed*, if desired.

9. Bake at 375°F 30 to 35 minutes. 1 LARGE BRAID

Yeast Sweet Breads & Coffee Cakes

COFFEE BRAID

Yeast Rolls, *page 73*	½ cup raisins
1 teaspoon grated	Confectioners' Sugar
lemon peel	Icing I, *below*
¼ teaspoon ground mace	

1. Follow recipe for Yeast Rolls, mixing grated lemon peel, mace, and raisins into dough before last flour addition. Proceed as directed.

2. After second rising, divide dough into thirds. Roll each into a strip about 14 inches long. Braid strips together, tucking open ends under. Cover; let rise in a warm place until doubled, about 45 minutes.

3. Bake at 350°F 35 to 40 minutes. While warm, spread with icing. Top with *candied cherries*, *pecan halves*, and bits of *candied citron*. 1 BRAID

CONFECTIONERS' SUGAR ICING I: Blend until smooth *½ cup plus 2 tablespoons confectioners' sugar*, *2 teaspoons water*, and *¼ teaspoon vanilla extract*.

COFFEE RINGS

1 pkg. active dry yeast	¼ cup milk, scalded and
¼ cup warm water	cooled to lukewarm
¾ cup butter	1 cup dairy sour cream
¾ cup sugar	¼ cup melted butter
1 teaspoon salt	1 cup sugar
3 eggs, well beaten	1 tablespoon ground
5¾ to 6 cups all-purpose	cinnamon
flour	1 cup raisins

1. Soften yeast in the warm water.

2. Beat the butter with the ¾ cup sugar and salt until thoroughly blended. Add the eggs, beating constantly until light and fluffy. Beat in 2 cups of the flour until smooth. Blend in yeast and milk, then sour cream. Beat in enough of the remaining flour to make a soft dough.

3. Turn onto a lightly floured surface and knead until smooth and elastic. Form into a ball and put into a greased deep bowl; turn dough to bring greased surface to top. Cover with moisture-vapor-proof material; place in refrigerator overnight. (Dough will not rise.)

4. When ready to roll out, divide dough into

halves. On a lightly floured surface, roll each to an 18x12-inch rectangle. Brush with half of the melted butter; sprinkle evenly with a mixture of the sugar, cinnamon, and raisins. Roll lengthwise as for a jelly roll.

5. Put each roll, seam edge down, onto an ungreased baking sheet or jelly roll pan, form into a ring and press ends together to seal. (Or each ring may be placed in a 10-inch tubed springform pan.) Cover lightly; let rise in a warm place until doubled, about 1½ hours.

6. Bake at 375°F 30 minutes, or until well browned. Remove from oven and cool slightly on wire rack. If desired, rings may be drizzled with *Glaze, below.* Serve warm.   2 COFFEE RINGS

GLAZE: Combine ¾ *cup confectioners' sugar* and ½ *teaspoon vanilla extract.* Stir in *1 to 1½ tablespoons milk or cream* until of spreading consistency.

TEA RINGS: Follow recipe for Coffee Rings. After shaping into rings, snip each ring at 2-inch intervals almost to center and turn each section on its side.

DANISH PASTRY COFFEE CAKE

1 pkg. active dry yeast	1 teaspoon vanilla
¼ cup warm water	extract
1 cup butter or	2¼ cups all-purpose
margarine	flour
2 tablespoons sugar	3 egg whites
3 egg yolks, well	¾ cup sugar
beaten	1 teaspoon ground
1½ teaspoons grated	cinnamon
orange peel	1 cup finely chopped
	nuts

1. Soften yeast in the warm water.

2. Cream butter with 2 tablespoons sugar. Beat in the yeast, beaten egg yolks, grated peel, and extract. Continue beating until well blended.

3. Add the flour, about a fourth at a time, beating until blended after each addition. Divide the dough into thirds; wrap separately in moisture-vaporproof material and refrigerate several hours or overnight.

4. When ready to roll out the pastry, prepare the filling. Beat egg whites until frothy; add a mixture of the sugar and cinnamon, 2 tablespoons at a time, beating well after each addition. Continue beating until stiff peaks are formed. Fold in the nuts.

5. Removing one portion of pastry from refrigerator at a time, roll out on floured surface into a 16x12-inch rectangle. Spread a third of the filling

evenly over rectangle, then roll up starting with long side.

6. Repeat twice using remaining pastry and place rolls several inches apart in a jelly roll pan or on a baking sheet. Cover lightly and set aside at room temperature 1 hour. (Dough will rise only slightly.)

7. Bake at 350°F 25 to 30 minutes, or until lightly browned. Let cool in pan on wire rack. While still warm, glaze with a *confectioners' sugar icing,* if desired.   3 COFFEE CAKES

MAMMOTH PECAN BRAID

1 pkg. active dry yeast	1 egg, well beaten
¼ cup warm water	Vanilla-Butter Filling,
1 cup milk, scalded	page 69
½ cup sugar	1½ cups pecans,
½ cup butter, softened	finely chopped
½ teaspoon salt	Orange Snow Icing,
4 to 5 cups all-purpose	page 69
flour	

1. Soften yeast in the warm water.

2. Pour scalded milk over the sugar, butter, and salt in a large bowl. Stir until butter is melted. Cool to lukewarm.

3. Blend in 1 cup flour, beating until smooth. Stir in yeast. Add about half of the remaining flour to yeast mixture and beat until very smooth. Beat in the egg. Beat in enough of the remaining flour to make a soft dough.

4. Turn dough onto a lightly floured surface; cover and let rest 5 to 10 minutes.

5. Knead until dough is smooth and does not stick to the surface. Form into a ball and put into a greased deep bowl; turn dough to bring greased surface to top. Cover; let rise in a warm place until doubled, about 2 hours.

6. Punch down dough. Turn onto a lightly floured surface; cover and let rest 5 to 10 minutes.

7. Roll into an 18-inch square. Cut into 6 even strips, 18x3 inches each. Spread Vanilla-Butter Filling over the 6 strips, then sprinkle with 1 cup pecans. Starting with long side, roll up each strip; seal edges well. Braid strips together in threes, then shape braids into a large wreath, pressing slightly to seal ends. Or shape each braid into a wreath.

8. Place on a lightly greased baking sheet. Cover; let rise again 30 minutes, or until doubled.

9. Bake at 350°F 20 to 25 minutes, or until golden

brown. Cool partially on wire rack. When still slightly warm, drizzle with Orange Snow Icing and sprinkle with remaining pecans.

1 LARGE OR 2 SMALL COFFEE CAKES

VANILLA-BUTTER FILLING: Cream *¾ cup butter;* add *1½ cups sifted confectioners' sugar* gradually, beating until light and fluffy. Blend in *1 teaspoon vanilla extract.*

ORANGE SNOW ICING: Blend *2 tablespoons orange juice* and *½ teaspoon vanilla extract* into *1 cup confectioners' sugar.*

CANDIED FRUIT WREATH: Follow recipe for Mammoth Pecan Braid. Omit Vanilla-Butter Filling and pecans. Add *1⅓ cups (8-ounce pkg.) diced assorted candied fruits,* finely chopped, with the second addition of flour. Proceed as directed through step 5. When the dough is risen, roll out onto a lightly floured surface into a 19x15-inch rectangle. Brush dough with *2 tablespoons melted butter* and sprinkle with *3 tablespoons red sugar.* Roll up from wider side and seal edge well; put on a baking sheet and form into a ring. Snip at 1½-inch intervals almost to center. Alternately turn sections toward the center and toward the outside of the ring with cut sides up. Brush each section with melted butter and sprinkle with red sugar. Let rise in a warm place until doubled, about 30 minutes. Bake at 350°F 35 to 40 minutes, or until golden brown. Remove to wire rack and partially cool, then drizzle with Orange Snow Icing. 1 COFFEE CAKE

HONEY BUN COFFEE RING

½ recipe for Yeast Rolls, *page 73*	½ cup honey
½ cup melted butter or margarine	1 tablespoon melted butter or margarine
½ cup finely chopped nuts	¼ cup firmly packed brown sugar
6 tablespoons seedless raisins	2 tablespoons flour
	1 teaspoon ground cinnamon

1. Follow recipe for Yeast Rolls to shaping process.
2. Divide into small pieces about the size of walnuts and shape into balls. First coat with the ½ cup melted butter, then roll in nuts. Place one layer of balls about ¼ inch apart in well-greased 9-inch tubed pan. Sprinkle with 3 tablespoons of the raisins. Arrange second layer on top of first. Sprinkle with remaining raisins. Press down slightly.

3. Combine honey and 1 tablespoon melted butter with remaining ingredients; spoon over dough.
4. Cover; let rise in a warm place 45 to 60 minutes, or until doubled.
5. Bake at 375°F 35 to 40 minutes. Allow to stand in pan 5 minutes before removing. Cover with a wire rack. Invert and remove pan. Turn right-side up immediately. ONE 9-INCH TUBED COFFEE CAKE

MORAVIAN SUGAR CAKE
A butter rich Pennsylvania Dutch favorite.

2 pkgs. active dry yeast	5 to 6 cups all-purpose flour
1 cup warm water	
1 cup sugar	1 cup packed light brown sugar
1 teaspoon salt	
2 eggs, well beaten	3 teaspoons ground cinnamon
1 cup butter, melted	
1 cup hot mashed potato	½ cup butter, melted

1. Soften yeast in the warm water.
2. Mix the sugar, salt, eggs, and 1 cup butter in a large bowl. Add the mashed potato gradually, beating well. Add 1 cup of the flour; beat until smooth.
3. Stir in yeast, then beat in enough remaining flour to form a light, soft dough. Cover; let rise in a warm place until doubled, about 2 hours.
4. Divide dough into thirds and press evenly into 3 greased 9-inch square pans. Cover; let rise again until doubled.
5. Meanwhile, blend brown sugar and cinnamon.
6. Make indentations about 1 inch apart in dough in each pan and spoon some of sugar mixture into each depression. Drizzle remaining ½ cup melted butter over sugar mixture.
7. Bake at 350°F about 20 minutes, or until cakes are golden brown. THREE 9-INCH SQUARE CAKES

FILLED HOLIDAY COFFEE CAKE

2 pkgs. active dry yeast	1 teaspoon vanilla extract
1 cup milk, scalded and cooled to warm	Vanilla-Butter Filling, *above*
4 cups all-purpose flour	
½ cup sugar	1 cup chopped nuts
1 teaspoon salt	Confectioners' Sugar Icing II, *page 70*
1 cup firm butter	
2 eggs, beaten	

1. Soften yeast in the cooled milk.

2. Mix flour, sugar, and salt in a large bowl. Cut in the butter with a pastry blender until particles are the size of rice kernels. Mixing well after each addition, add the yeast, then a mixture of eggs and extract.

3. Cover bowl with moisture-vaporproof material. Chill several hours or overnight.

4. Before removing dough from refrigerator, prepare Vanilla-Butter Filling. Spread 2 tablespoons filling over bottom and sides of each of two 9x5x3-inch loaf pans.

5. Divide dough into halves. On a lightly floured surface, roll each portion into an 18x10-inch rectangle. Spread each with half of remaining filling and sprinkle with half of nuts. Cut rectangle into three 10x6-inch strips. Starting with long side, roll up each strip and twist slightly. Braid three rolls together and place one braid in each pan, being sure to tuck ends under. Brush tops with *melted butter.*

6. Cover; let rise in a warm place until doubled, about 1½ hours.

7. Bake at 350°F 45 to 50 minutes. Immediately remove from pans and cool on wire racks.

8. Spread coffee cakes with Confectioners' Sugar Icing II. Before icing is set, decorate top with *marzipan fruit, glazed dried apricots,* and *preserved kumquats.* 2 FILLED COFFEE CAKES

CONFECTIONERS' SUGAR ICING II: Blend *1 cup confectioners' sugar, 1 tablespoon softened butter, 1 teaspoon light corn syrup,* and *1 tablespoon hot water.*

HOLLY WREATH COFFEE CAKE

1 pkg. active dry yeast	2 teaspoons vanilla
¼ cup milk, scalded and cooled to warm	extract
	2 cups filberts, finely ground
3¾ cups all-purpose flour	¼ cup red candied cherry pieces
½ teaspoon salt	½ cup sugar
6 tablespoons sugar	½ cup heavy cream
2 eggs, well beaten	1 egg, fork beaten
½ cup butter or margarine, melted and cooled	⅓ cup apricot preserves
½ cup warm milk	

1. Soften yeast in the cooled milk.

2. Blend 2 cups of the flour, the salt, and 6 tablespoons sugar in a large bowl. Beat in a mixture of the beaten eggs, melted butter, warm milk, and extract until batter is smooth. Beat in the yeast and then the remaining flour.

3. Turn dough onto a lightly floured surface and knead until smooth and elastic. Put into a greased deep bowl and turn dough to bring greased surface to top. Cover; let rise in a warm place until doubled.

4. For filling, mix filberts, cherries, ½ cup sugar, cream, and two thirds of the egg. Cover remaining egg and set aside.

5. Roll out dough into a 25x21-inch rectangle; cut into three 25x7-inch strips. Spread each with preserves and the nut filling. Turn edges of dough about one half over filling and press to seal. Starting with a long edge, roll up each portion; seal.

6. Gently braid the three long rolls. Form a wreath and press ends together. Carefully fit into a greased 9-inch tubed pan. Cover; let rise again until doubled. Brush top with the reserved egg.

7. Place in a 400°F oven; reduce oven temperature to 350°F, and bake about 30 minutes. Check cake for browning. If top is sufficiently browned, cover loosely with a piece of aluminum foil. Continue baking 15 to 20 minutes. Remove from oven; cool 5 to 10 minutes in pan on wire rack.

8. Using a holly-leaf pattern, cut shapes from *green candied pineapple slices* (thin crosswise slices).

9. Blend ¼ *cup confectioners' sugar* and *1 teaspoon water.* Spread over top of warm coffee cake. Press leaf shapes and red-candied cherry pieces on glaze at intervals to resemble a holly wreath.

ONE 9-INCH TUBED COFFEE CAKE

NORWEGIAN CHRISTMAS BREAD
(Julekake)

1 cup milk, scalded	½ cup mixed candied fruit
½ cup butter, softened	
½ cup sugar	1 tablespoon flour
1 teaspoon salt	4½ to 5 cups all-purpose flour
1 teaspoon ground cardamom	
2 pkgs. active dry yeast	1 egg, beaten
½ cup warm water	1 tablespoon sugar
½ cup currants	⅛ teaspoon ground cinnamon
½ cup coarsely chopped almonds	

1. Pour scalded milk over butter, ½ cup sugar, salt, and cardamom in a bowl. Stir until butter is melted. Cool to lukewarm.

2. Soften yeast in the warm water.

3. Toss currants, almonds, and mixed fruit with the 1 tablespoon flour; set aside.

4. Add about 2 cups of the flour to milk mixture and beat until smooth. Stir in yeast, egg, and then the fruit-nut mixture. Beat in enough of the remaining flour to make a soft dough.

5. Turn onto a lightly floured surface. Knead dough until smooth and elastic, 5 to 8 minutes. Form into a ball and place in a greased deep bowl. Turn dough to bring greased surface to top. Cover; let rise in a warm place until doubled, about 1½ hours.

6. Punch down dough and turn onto a lightly floured surface. Divide dough into halves and shape each into a round loaf. Place on a greased baking sheet. Cover; let rise again until doubled, about 1 hour.

7. Bake at 350°F 25 minutes. Brush tops with *softened butter* and sprinkle with a mixture of the sugar and cinnamon. Remove to wire racks to cool.

2 LOAVES BREAD

KULICH

This traditional Russian Easter bread is baked in mushroom or mosque-like shapes.

1 pkg. active dry yeast	¼ teaspoon ground
¼ cup warm water	cardamom
¼ cup butter or	¼ cup chopped candied
margarine, softened	red cherries
¼ cup sugar	¼ cup chopped candied
1 teaspoon salt	green cherries
¼ cup milk, scalded	2 tablespoons chopped
2¼ cups all-purpose	toasted almonds
flour	¾ cup confectioners'
1 egg, slightly beaten	sugar
½ teaspoon vanilla	4 teaspoons milk
extract	

1. Soften yeast in the warm water.

2. Put butter, sugar, and salt into a bowl; add the scalded milk and stir until butter is melted. Cool to lukewarm.

3. Beat ½ cup of the flour into milk mixture. Stir in the yeast, then beat in egg, extract, and cardamom. Add remaining flour gradually, beating thoroughly after each addition. Cover; let rise in a warm place until doubled, 1½ to 2 hours.

4. Punch down dough; let rise again until almost doubled, 30 to 45 minutes.

5. Turn dough onto a lightly floured surface. Dis-

tribute cherries and almonds evenly over dough; knead about 15 times. Shape dough into a ball and put into a well-greased 1-pound coffee can. Cover; let rise again until doubled, 30 to 40 minutes. Place can on a baking sheet, if desired.

6. Bake at 350°F 45 minutes, or until bread is well browned. Cool in can 10 to 15 minutes, then turn out onto a wire rack to cool completely.

7. Blend the confectioners' sugar and milk until smooth. Spoon icing over Kulich and allow it to drip down sides. Garnish top with a whole *candied red cherry.*

1 LOAF KULICH

FRUIT BREAD, MILAN STYLE
(Panettone)

The traditional Christmas bread of Italy.

1 pkg. active dry yeast	4 egg yolks
¼ cup warm water	3½ cups all-purpose
1 cup butter, melted	flour
1 cup sugar	1 cup dark seedless
1 teaspoon salt	raisins
2 cups sifted all-	¾ cup chopped citron
purpose flour	½ cup all-purpose flour
½ cup milk, scalded	1 egg, slightly beaten
and cooled to warm	1 tablespoon water
2 eggs	

1. Soften yeast in the warm water.

2. Pour melted butter into large bowl of electric mixer. Add the sugar and salt gradually, beating constantly.

3. Beating thoroughly after each addition, alternately add the 2 cups flour in thirds and lukewarm milk in halves to the butter mixture. Add yeast and beat well.

4. Combine eggs and egg yolks and beat until thick and piled softly. Add the beaten eggs all at one time to yeast mixture and beat well. Beating thoroughly after each addition, gradually add the 3½ cups flour. Stir in raisins and citron.

5. Sift half of the remaining flour over a pastry canvas or board. Turn dough onto floured surface; cover and let rest 10 minutes.

6. Sift remaining flour over dough. Pull dough from edges toward center until flour is worked in. (It will be sticky.) Put dough into a greased deep bowl and grease top of dough. Cover; let rise in a warm place, about 2½ hours.

7. Punch down dough and pull edges of dough in to center. Let rise again about 1 hour.

8. Divide dough into halves and shape each into a round loaf. Put each loaf into a well-greased 8-inch layer cake pan. Brush surfaces generously with a mixture of slightly beaten egg and water. Cover; let rise again, about 1 hour.

9. Bake at 350°F 40 to 45 minutes, or until golden brown. Remove to wire racks to cool.   2 PANETTONI

PLUM COFFEE CAKE
(Pflaumenkuchen)

¼ cup milk, scalded	2 eggs
½ cup butter or margarine	1 teaspoon grated lemon peel
¼ cup sugar	25 (about 1¼ lbs.)
½ teaspoon salt	small Italian plums,
1 pkg. active dry yeast	rinsed, halved, and
¼ cup warm water	pitted
3 cups all-purpose flour	

1. Pour scalded milk over the butter, sugar, and salt in a bowl; set aside.
2. Soften yeast in the warm water.
3. Add about ½ cup flour to milk mixture and beat until smooth. Stir in yeast. Add about half of the remaining flour and beat until very smooth.
4. Beat eggs with lemon peel until thick; blend into mixture. Mix in enough of the remaining flour to make a soft dough.
5. Turn onto a lightly floured surface. Cover and let rest 5 to 10 minutes.
6. Knead dough until smooth and satiny. Form into a ball and put into a greased deep bowl. Turn dough to bring greased surface to top. Cover; let rise in a warm place until doubled, about 1 hour.
7. Punch down dough and turn onto a lightly floured surface. Divide dough into halves. Press each evenly into a lightly greased (bottom only) 9-inch layer cake pan. Brush dough with *melted butter or margarine.*
8. Arrange plums, cut side up, on dough to 1 inch from edges of pans. Sprinkle with a mixture of *1½ to 2 cups sugar, 2 tablespoons flour,* and *2 teaspoons ground cinnamon.* Dot with *softened butter or margarine* (about ½ cup). Cover; let rise again until almost doubled, about 45 minutes.
9. Bake at 375°F 15 minutes. Beat together *4 egg yolks, 2 tablespoons sugar,* and *¼ cup cream;* then pour over the plums. Continue baking 15 to 20 minutes, or until custard is set. Serve slightly warm.   TWO 9-INCH ROUND COFFEE CAKES

STOLLEN

A German sweet bread shaped in long loaves, this recipe is rich with almonds, candied citron, raisins, and currants.

1⅓ cups toasted blanched almonds, chopped	2 teaspoons salt
	1 cup all-purpose flour
	1 teaspoon ground nutmeg
1 cup golden raisins	6 to 7 cups all-purpose flour
½ cup currants	
1 cup (about 7 oz.) chopped citron	3 eggs, well beaten
	Melted butter
1 tablespoon grated lemon peel	1½ cups confectioners' sugar
2 pkgs. active dry yeast	¾ teaspoon vanilla extract
½ cup warm water	
1 cup milk, scalded	2 to 3 tablespoons milk or cream
1 cup sugar	
1 cup butter, softened	

1. Reserve ⅓ cup of the almonds for topping. Mix the remaining 1 cup almonds with the raisins, currants, citron, and lemon peel; set aside.
2. Soften yeast in the warm water.
3. Pour scalded milk over sugar, butter, and salt in a large bowl. Stir until butter is melted. Cool to lukewarm.
4. Blend in a mixture of the 1 cup flour and the nutmeg; beat until smooth. Stir in yeast.
5. Add about half of the remaining flour and beat until very smooth. Add beaten eggs in thirds, beating well after each addition. Mix in the reserved fruit-nut mixture. Mix in enough of the remaining flour to make a soft dough.
6. Turn dough onto a lightly floured surface; cover and let rest 5 to 10 minutes.
7. Knead until smooth and elastic. Form into a ball and put into a greased deep bowl; turn dough to bring greased surface to top. Cover; let rise in a warm place until doubled, about 2½ hours.
8. Punch down dough; pull edges to center and turn dough completely over in bowl. Cover; let rise again until nearly doubled, about 1½ hours.
9. Punch down dough and turn onto a lightly floured surface. Divide into halves and shape into smooth balls. Shape each ball into an oval 13 inches long and about 1 inch thick. With rolling pin, flatten and press one lengthwise half of oval about ½ inch thick. Turn unflattened half of dough over flattened half; lightly press edges together. Press the fold down firmly with palm of hand; this helps to prevent dough from springing open during rising.

10. Place each stollen on a lightly greased baking sheet. Brush tops with melted butter. Cover; let rise in a warm place until doubled, about 1½ hours.

11. Bake at 325°F about 30 minutes, or until light golden brown.

12. Meanwhile, blend confectioners' sugar, extract, and enough milk to make a thin frosting.

13. Remove Stollen to wire racks. Immediately spread frosting over tops and sprinkle with reserved almonds.   2 LARGE STOLLEN

Yeast Dinner Rolls

YEAST ROLLS

2 pkgs. active dry yeast	2 teaspoons salt
½ cup warm water	6 to 7 cups all-purpose
2 cups milk, scalded	flour
½ cup sugar	2 eggs, well beaten
6 tablespoons	Melted butter or
shortening	margarine

1. Soften yeast in the warm water.

2. Pour hot milk over sugar, shortening, and salt in a large bowl. Cool to lukewarm.

3. Blend in 1 cup flour and beat until smooth. Stir in yeast. Add about half of remaining flour and beat until very smooth. Beat in the eggs. Beat in enough remaining flour to make a soft dough.

4. Turn dough onto a lightly floured surface; cover and let rest 5 to 10 minutes.

5. Knead dough until smooth and elastic. Form into a ball and put into a greased deep bowl; turn dough to bring greased surface to top. Cover; let rise in warm place until doubled, about 1 hour.

6. Punch down dough; pull edges to center and turn completely over in bowl. Cover; let rise again until almost doubled, about 45 minutes.

7. Again punch down the dough and turn onto a lightly floured surface.

8. Follow suggestions for shaping rolls, using amount needed for a single baking. Place rolls about 1 inch apart on lightly greased baking sheets or as directed. Brush tops with melted butter. Cover; let rise again until rolls are light, 15 to 25 minutes.

9. Bake at 425°F 15 to 20 minutes.
          ABOUT 5 DOZEN ROLLS

NOTE: This dough may be kept 3 days in the refrigerator. Grease top of dough and cover. Punch down occasionally as it rises. Remove amount needed for a single baking and return remainder to refrigerator. When ready to use, shape rolls and let stand at room temperature for 1 hour, or until light.

Suggestions for Shaping Rolls

Crescents: Roll dough into 8-inch rounds about ¼ inch thick. Brush with melted butter or margarine. Cut into wedges. Roll wedge from wide end. Place on greased baking sheet. Curve ends.

Snails: Roll dough into rectangle ¼ inch thick. Cut off strips ½ inch wide and 4 to 5 inches long. With hands, roll and stretch dough into longer strips. Coil each strip into a closed spiral, tucking the end under.

Eights: See Snails for shaping strips of dough. Twist each strip into a figure eight, pinching ends together at the center. Place 1 inch apart on greased baking sheets.

Bowknots: Roll dough to ¼-inch thickness. Cut off strips ½ inch wide and 4 to 5 inches long. With hands, roll and stretch into longer strips. Twist dough strips and tie into single or double knots.

Parker House Rolls: Roll dough ¼ inch thick. Brush with melted butter or margarine. Cut with lightly floured 2½-inch round cutter. Make a crease not quite in center of round with handle of knife or wooden spoon. Fold top (larger half of round) over bottom. Press edges together at each end of crease.

Curlicues: Roll dough into a rectangle ¼ inch thick. Cut into 5x¾-inch strips. With hands, roll and stretch into longer strips. Hold index finger on center of strip on greased baking sheet and coil one half of the strip up to finger; repeat for other half of strip, reversing direction.

Butterflies: Roll dough into a rectangle 6 inches wide and ¼ inch thick. Brush with melted butter or margarine. Roll dough, starting with long side. Cut into 2-inch pieces. Press knife handle across center of rolls.

Fantans: Roll dough into rectangle ¼ inch thick. Brush with melted butter or margarine. Cut into 1-inch strips. Stack six or seven strips. Cut stacks into 1½-inch sections. Place on end, in wells of greased muffin pans.

Cloverleaf Rolls: With hands, shape dough into 1-inch rolls. Cut off bits and form into balls about 1 inch in diameter. Place three balls in each muffin-pan well (grease bottoms only).

BUTTERY YEAST ROLLS

¾ cup butter or
   margarine, softened
1 cup boiling water
2 teaspoons salt
½ cup sugar
2 pkgs. active dry yeast

½ cup warm water
2 eggs, beaten
¾ cup icy cold water
6½ to 7½ cups all-
   purpose flour

1. Mix butter, boiling water, salt, and sugar in a large bowl until thoroughly blended. Cool to warm.
2. Soften yeast in the warm water. Blend in the eggs and cold water. Beat into warm mixture in large bowl. Add 3 cups flour, ½ cup at a time, beating vigorously after each addition until batter is smooth. Mix in enough remaining flour to make a soft dough that does not stick to sides of bowl.
3. Turn dough onto a lightly floured surface; let rest 5 to 10 minutes.
4. Knead until satiny and smooth. Form into a ball and put into a greased deep bowl; turn dough to bring greased surface to top. Cover tightly and refrigerate overnight or for several days.
5. Remove dough and punch down. Brush top with *oil.* Cover; let rise in a warm place until doubled. (This can take from 1 to 2½ hours.)
6. Shape as desired. Place rolls on greased baking sheets and let rise again until light.

7. Bake at 425° to 450°F 12 to 18 minutes. (Temperature and timing depend on the size of rolls.)   5 TO 6 DOZEN ROLLS

YEAST ROLLS DISTINCTIVE
Cooked potato and orange juice are the ingredients of "distinction" in these delightful rolls.

¾ cup milk, scalded
⅓ cup butter or
   margarine
⅓ cup sugar
1 teaspoon salt
1 cup sieved cooked
   potatoes
½ cup orange juice
1 tablespoon grated
   lemon peel

1 pkg. active dry yeast
¼ cup warm water
4½ to 5½ cups all-
   purpose flour
2 eggs, fork beaten
Butter or margarine,
   melted

1. Mix scalded milk, butter, sugar, and salt in a large bowl; stir in potatoes, orange juice, and lemon peel. Set aside and cool to lukewarm.
2. Meanwhile, soften yeast in the warm water.
3. Add 1 cup of the flour to the cooled milk mixture and beat until smooth. Stir in yeast.
4. Add about half of the remaining flour and beat vigorously. Add eggs and beat until smooth. Beat in

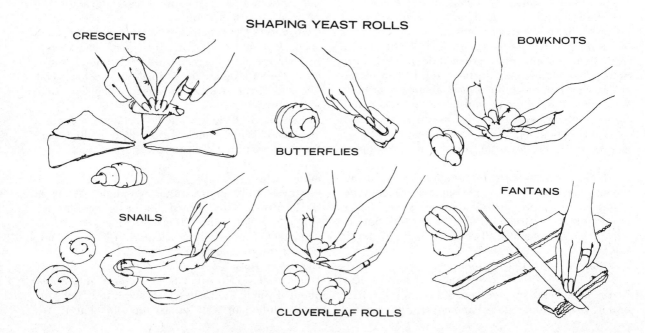

SHAPING YEAST ROLLS

CRESCENTS

BOWKNOTS

BUTTERFLIES

SNAILS

FANTANS

CLOVERLEAF ROLLS

enough of the remaining flour to make a soft, smooth dough. Cover; let rise in a warm place until dough is doubled, about 1 hour.

5. Stir dough down and let rise again until doubled, about 45 minutes.

6. Turn onto a lightly floured surface. Divide dough into thirds. Roll each third into a 9-inch round, ¼ inch thick. Brush with melted butter. Cut into 8 wedges. Roll up each wedge starting from the wide end.

7. Place rolls, points down, on greased baking sheets. Curve to form crescents. Brush with melted butter. Let rise again until doubled, about 30 minutes.

8. Bake at 375°F about 18 minutes, or until rolls are delicately browned. Remove from oven and brush with melted butter. Serve piping hot.

2 DOZEN ROLLS

CRESCENT ROLLS
(Croissants)

These flaky morsels will be recognized by any traveler to France as the traditional breakfast roll served with coffee — a duo familiarly known as the continental breakfast.

1 pkg. active dry yeast	1 cup milk, scalded
¼ cup warm water	2½ cups all-purpose
1 tablespoon sugar	flour
¾ teaspoon salt	1 cup butter

1. Soften yeast in the warm water.
2. Combine the sugar, salt, and scalded milk in a large bowl; stir until sugar is dissolved. Cool to lukewarm.
3. Beat in ½ cup of the flour. Stir in the yeast, then beat in remaining flour. Turn dough onto a lightly floured surface and let rest 5 to 10 minutes.
4. Knead until dough is smooth and elastic. Form into a ball and put into a greased deep bowl. Turn dough to bring greased surface to top. Cover; let rise in a warm place until doubled, about 1 hour.
5. When doubled, chill dough 2 hours.
6. Cream butter until softened. Turn chilled dough onto a lightly floured surface; roll into a ¼ inch thick rectangle. Spread surface with ¼ cup creamed butter and fold dough from each end over center, making three layers. Turn a quarter of the way around. Repeat rolling, spreading with butter, folding and turning three more times. Chill dough 2 hours or longer.
7. Divide dough into halves. Roll each half on a lightly floured surface into a round, ¼ inch thick. Cut each round into 12 wedge-shaped pieces. Roll up each piece beginning at outer edge. Place with points underneath on baking sheets covered with brown paper. Curve into crescents. Chill 20 minutes. Brush tops lightly with *cream.*
8. Bake at 400°F 15 minutes; reduce oven temperature to 350°F and continue baking 15 minutes longer, or until golden brown.

2 DOZEN ROLLS

BRIOCHE

A version of a famous French roll shaped like a muffin and topped with a fluffy "knob."

½ cup butter	1 egg yolk
⅓ cup sugar	2 eggs
½ teaspoon salt	3¼ cups all-purpose
½ cup undiluted	flour
evaporated milk	1 egg white, unbeaten
1 pkg. active dry yeast	1 tablespoon sugar
¼ cup warm water	

1. Cream the butter with the ⅓ cup sugar and salt in a large bowl. Beat in the evaporated milk.
2. Soften yeast in the warm water.
3. Beat egg yolk with the 2 eggs until thick and piled softly. Gradually add to the creamed mixture, beating constantly until fluffy. Blend in the yeast.
4. Add the flour, about ½ cup at a time, beating thoroughly after each addition. Cover; let rise in a warm place until doubled, about 2 hours.
5. Stir down and beat thoroughly. Cover tightly with moisture-vaporproof material and refrigerate overnight.
6. Remove from refrigerator and stir down the dough. Turn onto a lightly floured surface and divide into two portions, one using about three fourths of the dough, the other about one fourth.
7. Cut each portion into 16 equal pieces. Roll each piece into a smooth ball. Place each large ball in a well-greased muffin-pan well (2¾x1¼ inches). Make a deep indentation with finger in center of each large ball; then moisten each depression slightly with cold water. Press a small ball into each depression.
8. Cover; let rise again until more than doubled, about 1 hour.
9. Brush tops of rolls with a mixture of the egg white and 1 tablespoon sugar.
10. Bake at 375°F about 15 minutes, or until golden brown.

16 BRIOCHES

SOUR CREAM CRESCENTS

2 pkgs. active dry yeast	½ cup sugar
⅓ cup warm water	½ teaspoon salt
1 cup dairy sour cream	4 cups all-purpose flour
1 cup butter or margarine, melted	2 eggs

1. Soften yeast in the warm water.
2. Put sour cream, butter, sugar, and salt into a large bowl; beat thoroughly.
3. Blend 1 cup of flour into sour cream mixture, beating until smooth. Mix in yeast. Add 1 cup of remaining flour and beat until smooth.
4. Thoroughly beat in eggs, one at a time, then beat in the remaining flour. Cover bowl with moisture-vaporproof material and refrigerate 6 hours, or overnight.
5. Divide dough into fourths. On a lightly floured surface, roll each portion into a round, ¼ inch thick. Cut each round into 12 wedge-shaped pieces. Roll up, beginning at wide end.
6. Place rolls with points underneath on lightly greased baking sheets. Curve rolls into crescents. Cover; let rise in a warm place until light, about 1 hour.
7. Bake at 375°F 15 minutes.   4 DOZEN ROLLS

BUTTER SEMMELS

1 pkg. active dry yeast	1½ teaspoons salt
¼ cup warm water	2 cups milk, scalded
½ cup mashed potato (unseasoned)	8 to 8½ cups all-purpose flour
½ cup sugar	2 eggs
½ cup butter	Melted butter
½ cup sugar	Sesame or poppy seed

1. Soften yeast in the warm water. Mix in the mashed potato and ½ cup sugar. Cover; let rise in a warm place until doubled, about 1½ hours.
2. Put butter, ½ cup sugar, and the salt into a bowl. Add scalded milk and stir until butter is melted; cool.
3. Add 1 cup of the flour and beat until smooth. Beat in the eggs, one at a time, then the yeast mixture. Add remaining flour gradually, beating in enough to form a soft dough.
4. Turn onto a lightly floured surface and knead until smooth. Put into a greased deep bowl; turn dough to bring greased surface to top. Cover; let rise in a warm place until doubled, about 1½ hours.

5. Punch down dough. Using about a fourth of the dough at a time, put onto a lightly floured surface and shape as desired into braids, snails, crescents, or twists. (To shape into braids, roll a portion of dough ¼ inch thick; cut into 3x¾-inch strips. With hands, roll and stretch each strip; braid three strips together, tuck ends under, and place on greased baking sheet.)
6. Brush with melted butter and sprinkle with sesame or poppy seed. Cover; let rise again until doubled, about 1 hour.
7. Bake at 400°F 8 minutes, or until delicately browned.   ABOUT 6 DOZEN ROLLS

HERBED PARMESAN ROLLS

2 pkgs. active dry yeast	2 eggs, slightly beaten
1 cup warm water	1 cup grated Parmesan cheese
½ cup butter or margarine	½ teaspoon marjoram, crushed
¼ cup sugar	½ teaspoon oregano, crushed
2½ teaspoons salt	
2 cups milk, scalded	½ teaspoon rosemary, crushed
7 to 7½ cups all-purpose flour	

1. Soften yeast in the warm water.
2. Put butter, sugar, and salt into a large bowl; pour the scalded milk over all and stir until butter is melted. Beat in about 1 cup of the flour. Stir in yeast.
3. Gradually add about one half of the remaining flour, beating until smooth. Beat in eggs. Mix in a blend of cheese, marjoram, oregano, and rosemary.
4. Gradually add enough remaining flour to make a stiff dough, beating until smooth and dough comes away from sides of bowl.
5. Turn dough onto a lightly floured surface and let rest about 10 minutes.
6. Knead, adding more flour if dough seems too sticky, until satiny smooth and small blisters appear under the surface of dough. Form into a ball and put into a greased deep bowl. Turn dough to bring greased surface to top. Cover; let rise in a warm place until doubled.
7. Punch down dough; turn onto a lightly floured surface. Shape as desired (see *Suggestions for Shaping Rolls, page 73*). Cover; let rise again until doubled.
8. Bake at 425°F 10 to 12 minutes. Remove to wire racks, brush tops lightly with *melted butter or*

margarine, and cool.　　　ABOUT 5 DOZEN ROLLS

NOTE: The dough may be divided to yield both rolls and 9x5x3-inch loaves of bread. Bake bread at 375°F 30 to 40 minutes.

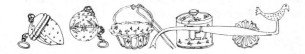

ONION ROLLS

2 pkgs. active dry yeast	1 cup dairy sour cream
½ cup warm water	5 to 5½ cups all-purpose
½ cup butter	flour
⅓ cup sugar	2 eggs
1 tablespoon salt	Onion Filling, *below*

1.　Soften yeast in the warm water.
2.　Cream butter; add sugar and salt gradually, beating constantly until thoroughly creamed. Blend in sour cream.
3.　Beat in 1 cup of the flour. Add eggs, one at a time, beating vigorously after each addition. Mix in yeast. Using a spoon, beat in enough of the remaining flour to make dough easy to handle.
4.　Turn dough out onto a lightly floured surface and knead until satiny and smooth. Form into a ball and put into a greased deep bowl. Turn dough to bring greased surface to top. Cover; let rise in a warm place until doubled, about 1½ hours.
5.　Punch down dough and shape into twenty-four 2-inch balls. Place about 2 inches apart on greased baking sheets. Flatten each ball slightly; make a large indentation in center and spoon in about 1 tablespoon of the filling. Brush with remaining beaten egg (from filling) and sprinkle with *poppy or sesame seed*. Cover and let rise again until doubled, about 45 minutes.
6.　Bake at 400°F 10 minutes, or until golden brown. Remove from baking sheets and serve hot.
　　　　　　　　　　2 DOZEN ROLLS

ONION FILLING

2 cups finely chopped onion	2 tablespoons fork beaten egg (reserve remaining egg)
¼ cup butter	
2 tablespoons light cream	¼ teaspoon salt

Cook onion until golden in butter in a skillet; cool slightly. Blend in cream, egg, and salt. Cool.

BREAD STICKS

1 pkg. active dry yeast	4½ to 5 cups all-purpose
¼ cup warm water	flour
1¾ cups warm water	1 egg, slightly beaten
2 teaspoons salt	1 teaspoon milk

1.　Soften yeast in ¼ cup warm water.
2.　Put the 1¾ cups warm water and salt into a large bowl. Blend in 3 cups of the flour. Stir in yeast.
3.　Add about half the remaining flour to the yeast mixture and beat until very smooth. Mix in enough of the remaining flour to make a soft, smooth dough.
4.　Turn onto a lightly floured surface. Cover and let rest 5 to 10 minutes.
5.　Knead dough until smooth and elastic, about 5 minutes. Form into a smooth ball and put into a greased deep bowl. Turn dough to bring greased surface to top. Cover; let rise in a warm place until doubled, about 2 hours.
6.　Punch down dough and knead on a lightly floured surface about 2 minutes. Divide into halves. Shape into smooth balls. Lightly roll each ball into a rectangle ¼ inch thick and about 6 inches wide. Cut dough crosswise with floured knife into strips 1 inch wide. Using palms of hands, roll strips to pencil thickness, stretching to about 7-inch lengths.
7.　Place strips 1 inch apart on greased baking sheets. Brush lightly with a mixture of the egg and milk. Let rise again until doubled, about 1 hour.
8.　Brush again with egg mixture and, if desired, sprinkle with *coarse salt*.
9.　Bake at 400°F 18 to 20 minutes, or until sticks are browned.　　ABOUT 4 DOZEN BREAD STICKS

Yeast Sweet Rolls & Doughnuts

SWEET-TOOTH BREAKFAST ROLLS

Follow recipe for *Yeast Rolls, page 73*. Use all of dough or divide as needed. Try any of the given sweet fillings or toppings in one of the following ways: 1) Spread a filling on buttered crescents before rolling up. 2) Brush snails or large rolls with melted butter or margarine and spread with topping before baking. 3) Glaze or frost plain baked rolls and top with nuts. 4) Put a spoonful of filling in center of 4-inch squares of ½-inch thick dough. Then fold in corners, press together and brush tops with melted butter or margarine. 5) Into bottom of greased muffin-pan well put ½ teaspoon butter or margarine and cover with filling and unbaked roll. Bake at 350°F 25 to 30 minutes. After baking, invert and allow to stand 5 minutes. Lift off pan.

Fillings

The amount of spread or filling needed will depend upon variation used and the number of rolls prepared.

Pineapple Spread: Mix in a saucepan ¼ *cup packed brown sugar, 1 tablespoon cornstarch,* and ¼ *teaspoon salt.* Blend in *1 can (8½ ounces) crushed pineapple* and syrup. Bring rapidly to boiling, stirring constantly, and cook 2 minutes, or until thickened. Blend in *1 teaspoon butter or margarine.* Cool before spreading on unbaked rolls.   1 CUP SPREAD

Orange Cube: Into each unbaked roll press a small *sugar cube* which has been dipped in *orange or lemon juice.* Sprinkle with *grated peel.*

Marmalade Spread: Spread *marmalade or jam* on baked or unbaked rolls.

Apricot Spread: Put through a sieve or food mill *1 cup drained cooked apricots.* Add ¼ *cup sugar* and ¼ *teaspoon ground nutmeg;* mix well.

1 CUP SPREAD

Almond Filling: Blend ⅔ *cup finely chopped blanched almonds,* ¼ *cup confectioners' sugar,* and *1 slightly beaten egg white.* Spread on unbaked dough and roll as for a jelly roll.

1 CUP FILLING

GERMAN-STYLE BUNS
(Buchteln)

1 pkg. active dry yeast	1 teaspoon grated
¼ cup warm water	lemon peel
1 cup milk, scalded	4 cups all-purpose flour
½ cup butter, softened	2 eggs, well beaten
¼ cup sugar	Fruit preserves
1 teaspoon salt	Melted butter or
	margarine

1. Soften yeast in the warm water.
2. Pour scalded milk over butter, sugar, salt, and lemon peel in a bowl. Stir until butter is melted. Cool to lukewarm.
3. Beat in 1 cup flour until smooth. Stir in yeast. Add about half the remaining flour and beat until very smooth. Beat in eggs. Then mix in enough

remaining flour to make a soft dough. Turn onto a lightly floured surface; cover and let rest 5 to 10 minutes.

4. Knead dough until smooth and elastic. Form into a ball and put into a greased deep bowl; turn dough to bring greased surface to top. Cover; let rise in a warm place until doubled.

5. Punch down dough and turn onto a lightly floured surface. Roll dough to ½-inch thickness. Using a sharp knife, cut dough into twenty-four 3x2-inch rectangles.

6. Spread rectangles almost to edges with fruit preserves. Starting with shorter side, roll up rectangles. Place rolls side by side in 2 greased 11x7x1½-inch baking pans. Brush rolls generously with melted butter. Cover; let rise again until almost doubled.

7. Bake at 350°F 25 to 30 minutes, or until rolls are lightly browned.

8. Remove rolls from pans to wire racks; cool slightly. Drizzle with a *confectioners' sugar glaze.*

2 DOZEN BUNS

DANISH PASTRY

"Practice makes perfect" is a good adage to remember when preparing Danish pastry. Unrivaled as accompaniments for morning or afternoon coffee, Danish pastries—flaky, rich, and delicious— well worth the time spent in perfecting one's techniques.

1½ pkgs. (1½ table-spoons) active dry yeast	½ teaspoon salt
	4 cups all-purpose flour
½ cup warm water	1⅓ cups firm butter
¾ cup milk, scalded and cooled to lukewarm	⅓ cup all-purpose flour
	Vanilla Cream Filling, *page 79*
2 eggs, beaten	Almond Paste Filling, *page 79*
¼ cup sugar	

1. Soften yeast in the warm water in a large bowl.
2. Stir the milk, eggs, sugar, and salt into the yeast. Add the 4 cups flour in fourths, beating until batter is smooth after each addition.
3. Using a pastry blender, cut butter into the ⅓ cup flour until mixture is well blended; set aside.
4. Turn dough onto a lightly floured surface; roll into a 14-inch square. Spread butter-flour mixture evenly over half of dough, leaving a 2-inch border.
5. Fold dough in half and roll about ¼-inch thick. Fold in thirds and roll out; repeat this procedure 3

times. Wrap in moisture-vaporproof material and refrigerate for 30 minutes.

6. Meanwhile, prepare desired filling.

7. Remove dough from refrigerator; working quickly, roll out dough into a 20-inch square. Shape as desired (see *Shapes, below*).

8. Place on ungreased baking sheets and let rise in a warm place about 15 minutes. Brush plain tops with *beaten egg*.

9. Bake at 450°F 6 to 10 minutes, or until golden brown. Immediately remove from baking sheets to wire racks. Serve warm.   20 TO 28 FILLED PASTRIES

VANILLA CREAM FILLING: Beat *2 egg yolks* slightly in the top of a double boiler. Stir in *1 cup milk* and a mixture of *2 tablespoons flour* and *2 tablespoons sugar*. Cook over simmering water, stirring constantly until thick. Cool, stirring occasionally. Blend in *1 tablespoon vanilla extract*.

ALMOND PASTE FILLING: Combine *⅓ pound ground almonds* and *½ cup sugar*. Gradually add *1 slightly beaten egg*, mixing until smooth.

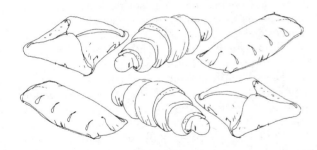

Shapes

Combs: Cut dough into 4 equal strips. On each of the strips, place about a fourth of the filling lengthwise down the center. Bring sides together at center. Coat each 20-inch strip on both sides with a mixture of 6 tablespoons finely chopped almonds and 2 tablespoons sugar. Cut each strip into five 4-inch pieces and make 4 cuts on one side of each piece about a third of the way across. Place, folded side down, on baking sheet.

Crescents: Cut dough into 4 equal strips. Cut each of the strips into 7 triangles. Spread some filling on each triangle, roll up beginning at base, curve ends slightly, and place on baking sheet with point underneath.

Envelopes: Cut dough into 4-inch squares. Spread center of each with about 1 tablespoon filling. Fold corners toward center and press edges to seal.

SEMLOR

A Shrove Tuesday Scandinavian specialty, there will be demands from your family to make these delicious almond buns at any time of the year.

1 pkg. active dry yeast	1 egg
¼ cup warm water	3 to 3¼ cups all-purpose
½ cup butter	flour
¼ teaspoon almond	¾ teaspoon salt
extract	½ cup heavy cream
½ teaspoon vanilla	¼ cup water
extract	½ cup (4 oz.) almond
¼ cup sugar	paste
2 tablespoons ground	1 tablespoon heavy
blanched almonds	cream

1. Soften yeast in the warm water.

2. Cream butter with the extracts until softened; add the sugar and almonds and beat thoroughly. Add the egg and beat until fluffy.

3. Blend in 1 cup of the flour and the salt, then the ½ cup cream and the water; beat vigorously until smooth.

4. Stir the yeast into the batter. Beat in enough remaining flour to make a soft (not sticky) dough.

5. Turn dough onto a lightly floured surface; cover and let rest 5 to 10 minutes.

6. Knead until satiny and elastic. Form into a ball and put into a greased bowl; turn dough to bring greased surface to top. Cover; let rise in a warm place until doubled, about 1 hour.

7. Meanwhile, mix almond paste with 1 tablespoon cream and blend until paste is slightly softened; set aside.

8. Punch down dough. Turn out and divide into 12 equal portions (or 18 portions for medium-sized buns). Shape each into a ball and flatten slightly. Place 1 very generous teaspoonful of the almond paste in center (slightly less for smaller buns), bring dough up over filling and seal in filling.

9. Place balls 2 inches apart on greased baking sheet. Cover; let rise again until light, 35 to 45 minutes.

10. Brush tops of buns lightly with *beaten egg*.

11. Bake at 400°F 12 to 15 minutes. Serve warm or cooled.   1 DOZEN LARGE (OR 1½ DOZEN MEDIUM-SIZED) SEMLOR

HOT CROSS BUNS: Follow recipe for Semlor, preparing the dough only. Omit the extracts and almonds. Cream ¼ *teaspoon ground cinnamon* and a *few grains ground mace* with the butter. Mix ½ *cup currants* and, if desired, *2 tablespoons finely*

chopped candied citron into dough before the final addition of flour. Proceed as directed. Shape dough into 20 buns. With lightly greased sharp knife or scissors, cut a *deep* cross in top of each bun. Bake. Prepare *Confectioners' Sugar Icing I, page 67,* and drizzle into crosses on warm buns.   20 BUNS

MINIATURE ORANGE SWEET ROLLS

1 pkg. active dry yeast	2 eggs
¼ cup warm water	2 tablespoons butter,
1 cup milk, scalded	melted
⅓ cup sugar	½ cup sugar
¾ teaspoon salt	3 tablespoons grated
⅓ cup butter or	orange peel
margarine	Orange Glaze, *below*
4 to 4½ cups all-purpose	Confectioners' Sugar
flour	Icing I, *page 67*

1. Soften yeast in the warm water.
2. Pour hot milk over sugar, salt, and butter in a large bowl and stir until butter is melted; add 1 cup flour and beat thoroughly. Stir in yeast.
3. Add the eggs, one at a time, beating vigorously after each addition.
4. Mix in enough flour to form a soft dough. Turn onto a lightly floured surface; let rest 5 to 10 minutes.
5. Knead dough until satiny and smooth. Put into a greased deep bowl; turn dough to bring greased surface to top. Cover; let rise in a warm place until doubled.
6. Using one half of dough at a time, roll each half on a lightly floured surface into a rectangle ¼ inch thick. Brush 1 tablespoon of the melted butter over dough.
7. Blend the ½ cup sugar and grated peel; sprinkle half of mixture evenly over dough.
8. Beginning with longer side, roll up dough and press edges together; cut into 1-inch slices.
9. Place, cut side up, in greased muffin-pan wells; brush lightly with melted butter. Let rise again until doubled, about 30 minutes.
10. Bake at 375°F for 12 to 15 minutes. Remove rolls to wire racks. While warm, drizzle with Orange Glaze, then with Confectioners' Sugar Icing I.   ABOUT 5 DOZEN ROLLS

ORANGE GLAZE: Stir together in a saucepan ½ *cup sugar,* ¼ *cup light corn syrup,* ¼ *cup hot water,* and *1 tablespoon grated orange peel.* Bring to boiling and cook 2 minutes, stirring occasionally.

SCHNECKEN

Rich with spice, nuts, and sugar, this is a German version of the ever-popular caramel pecan roll.

1 pkg. active dry yeast	⅔ cup butter or
¼ cup warm water	margarine, melted
1 cup milk or cream,	1 cup pecan pieces,
scalded	coarsely chopped
½ cup sugar	1 cup packed brown
1 teaspoon salt	sugar
5 cups all-purpose flour	¼ cup currants
2 eggs, well beaten	1 tablespoon ground
½ cup butter or	cinnamon
margarine, softened	1 cup small pecan
	halves

1. Soften yeast in the warm water.
2. Pour the scalded milk over sugar and salt in a large bowl; stir until sugar is dissolved. Cool to lukewarm.
3. Blend in 1 cup of the flour and beat until smooth. Stir in yeast. Add about half the remaining flour and beat until very smooth. Beat in the eggs. Vigorously beat in the ½ cup softened butter, 2 to 3 tablespoons at a time. Beat in enough remaining flour to make a soft dough.
4. Turn dough onto a lightly floured surface. Cover and let rest 10 minutes.
5. Knead until smooth and elastic. Form into a ball and put into a greased deep bowl; turn dough to bring greased surface to top. Cover; let rise in a warm place until doubled, about 1 hour.
6. Punch dough down; pull edges of dough in to center and turn over completely in bowl. Cover; let rise again until nearly doubled, about 45 minutes.
7. Lightly grease twenty-four 2½-inch muffin-pan wells. Put about 1 teaspoon of the melted butter into each well; reserve remaining butter. Mix the chopped nuts, brown sugar, currants, and cinnamon. Spoon 2 teaspoons into each well and gently press 3 or 4 pecan halves onto mixture.
8. Again punch dough down; form into 2 balls. Roll ball into a rectangle ¼ to ⅓ inch thick, 6 to 8 inches wide, and 12 inches long. Brush top surface of dough with half the remaining melted butter and sprinkle evenly with half the remaining brown sugar mixture. Beginning with longer side, roll dough tightly into a long roll. Cut roll into 12 slices. Place a slice, cut side down, in each well. Repeat with second ball. Cover; let rise again until doubled, about 45 minutes.
9. Bake at 375°F 15 to 20 minutes. Invert muffin

pans on wire racks, set on waxed paper or aluminum foil, leaving pans over Schnecken 5 minutes. Remove from pans and cool on racks, glazed side up. To store, wrap tightly in foil. Reheat just before serving.   2 DOZEN SCHNECKEN

CHERRY-CHOCOLATE DESSERT ROLLS

1 cup butter or margarine	5 cups all-purpose flour
½ cup all-purpose shortening	1 cup walnuts, ground or finely chopped
1 pkg. active dry yeast	6 oz. semisweet chocolate pieces
¼ cup warm water	½ cup maraschino cherries, cut in quarters and well drained
1 can (14½ oz.) evaporated milk	
3 egg yolks, slightly beaten	
2 tablespoons sugar	½ cup sugar
2 teaspoons salt	2 teaspoons ground cinnamon
¼ teaspoon vanilla extract	

1. Melt butter with shortening over low heat.
2. Soften yeast in the warm water.
3. Mix ⅓ cup of the evaporated milk, the egg yolks, sugar, salt, and extract in a large bowl; stir in the melted shortening.
4. Blend in 1 cup of the flour, beating until smooth; stir in yeast. Beating well after each addition, alternately add the remaining flour in fourths and the remaining evaporated milk in thirds to yeast mixture; beat until smooth.
5. Knead in the bowl until dough pulls away from sides of bowl. Cover; refrigerate 2 to 3 hours or overnight.
6. Mix walnuts, chocolate pieces, and cherries.
7. Mix the ½ cup sugar and cinnamon; use instead of flour for rolling out dough. Sprinkle mixture evenly over a board. Divide dough into halves; roll each half into a 15-inch round.
8. Cut each round into 16 wedge-shaped pieces. Put 1 teaspoon of the filling on each wedge; roll up beginning at wide end. Place rolls on greased baking sheet with points underneath. Cover; let rise in a warm place about 1 hour.

9. Bake at 350°F 20 to 25 minutes, or until lightly browned.   32 ROLLS

TEA KIPFEL

These yeast rolls, a German favorite, are usually filled with chopped nuts, dried or candied fruit, jam, or other fillings.

1 pkg. active dry yeast	2 to 2¼ cups all-purpose flour
¼ cup warm water	2 egg whites
¼ cup scalded milk, cooled to lukewarm	1 cup chopped dark seedless raisins
¼ cup plus 2 teaspoons sugar	¾ cup finely chopped almonds
½ teaspoon salt	⅓ cup chopped candied pineapple
2 egg yolks	
¼ cup butter, softened	

1. Soften the yeast in the warm water in a large bowl.
2. Mixing until smooth, blend in the scalded milk, sugar, salt, egg yolks, butter, and half of the flour. Mix in enough of the remaining flour to make a soft dough. Turn onto a lightly floured surface.
3. Knead until smooth and elastic, using additional flour if necessary. Put into a greased deep bowl; turn dough to bring greased surface to top. Cover; let rise in a warm place until doubled, about 1 hour.
4. Punch down; roll out dough into a rectangle ¼ inch thick. Beat egg whites until stiff, not dry, peaks are formed. Spread half on dough surface (reserve remaining half for topping). Sprinkle with a mixture of the raisins, ½ cup of the almonds, and the pineapple. Cut into 2½-inch squares, then cut each square diagonally in half. Bring triangle corners to center; pinch to seal and place on greased baking sheets.
5. Top with a mixture of the reserved egg white and almonds. Cover; let rise again until very light, about 45 minutes.
6. Bake at 375°F 10 minutes, or until lightly browned.   ABOUT 4 DOZEN KIPFEL

TEA CRESCENTS: Follow recipe for Tea Kipfel. Divide dough into thirds. Roll out each piece into an 8-inch round. Spread with a portion of the beaten egg white and filling mixture. Cut round into 12 wedges. Starting at wider edge, roll up and place with pointed edge down, 2 inches apart, on a greased baking sheet. Top and bake as directed. If desired, spread with a *confectioners' sugar glaze.*
          ABOUT 3 DOZEN CRESCENTS

PUMPKIN ROLLS

Here's a unique way and a rewarding one, too, for using a little leftover canned pumpkin.

¾ cup milk, scalded	¼ teaspoon ground
¼ cup shortening	nutmeg
¼ cup sugar	⅛ teaspoon ground
¾ teaspoon salt	allspice
¾ cup canned pumpkin	⅛ teaspoon ground
1 pkg. active dry yeast	cloves
½ cup warm water	⅛ teaspoon ground
3½ to 4½ cups all-purpose	ginger
flour	1 egg
½ teaspoon ground	
cinnamon	

1. Combine scalded milk, shortening, sugar, and salt in a large mixer bowl; stir in the pumpkin. Cool to lukewarm.
2. Soften yeast in the warm water.
3. Blend 1 cup of the flour and the spices thoroughly; add to cooled milk mixture and beat until smooth. Stir in yeast.
4. Beating constantly, add another cup of flour and the egg. Beat until smooth, then mix in enough remaining flour to make a soft, smooth dough. Cover; let rise in a warm place until doubled, about 1 hour.
5. Stir dough down and let rise until doubled.
6. Turn onto a lightly floured surface. Shape dough into 2-inch balls; brush with *melted butter or margarine*. Place 1 ball in each greased 2½-inch muffin-pan well. Cover; let rise again until doubled, about 30 minutes.
7. Bake at 375°F 20 minutes.   2 DOZEN ROLLS

VIRGINIA LEMON-RAISIN BUNS

1 pkg. active dry yeast	3½ to 4 cups all-purpose
¼ cup warm water	flour
1 cup milk, scalded	⅔ cup dark seedless
6 tablespoons butter	raisins, chopped
or margarine	1 teaspoon lemon
¼ cup sugar	extract
1 teaspoon salt	

1. Soften yeast in the warm water.
2. Pour scalded milk over butter, sugar, and salt in a large bowl; stir until blended. Cool to lukewarm.
3. Beat in 1 cup flour until smooth. Stir in yeast. Add about half the remaining flour and beat until

very smooth. Beat in raisins and extract. Then mix in enough of remaining flour to make a soft dough.
4. Turn dough onto a lightly floured surface; cover and let rest 5 to 10 minutes.
5. Knead until smooth and elastic. Form into a ball and put into a greased deep bowl; turn dough to bring greased surface to top. Cover; let rise in a warm place until doubled, about 1½ hours.
6. Punch down dough, pull edges in to center and turn completely over in bowl. Cover; let rise again until almost doubled, about 1 hour.
7. Again punch down dough. Turn onto a lightly floured surface and divide into halves. Roll half of dough at a time to ½-inch thickness. Cut with a lightly floured 2-inch round cutter. Place rounds about 1 inch apart on lightly greased baking sheets. Brush with melted butter. Cover; let rise again until light, about 45 minutes.
8. Bake at 375°F about 15 minutes.

ABOUT 2½ DOZEN ROLLS

CREOLE DOUGHNUTS
(Beignets)

Here's one of many versions of those famous melt-in-your-mouth morsels served freshly fried in the French quarter of New Orleans, where tourists and natives alike flock each day to enjoy them with cups of New Orleans coffee.

1 pkg. active dry yeast	2 cups milk, scalded
¼ cup warm water	6½ to 7 cups all-purpose
½ cup sugar	flour
½ cup cooking or	2 eggs, well beaten
salad oil	Fat for deep frying
1½ teaspoons salt	heated to 365°F

1. Soften yeast in the warm water.
2. Put sugar, oil, and salt into a large bowl. Immediately pour scalded milk over ingredients in bowl; stir until sugar is dissolved. Cool to lukewarm.
3. Blend in 1 cup flour, beating until smooth. Stir in yeast. Add about half of the remaining flour to yeast mixture and beat until very smooth. Beat in the eggs.
4. Beat in enough of the remaining flour to make a soft dough. Turn dough onto a lightly floured surface; cover and let rest 5 to 10 minutes.
5. Knead until dough is smooth and does not stick to the surface, about 5 minutes. Form into a ball and put into a lightly greased deep bowl; turn dough to bring greased surface to top. Cover; let rise in a warm place until doubled, about 2 hours.

6. Punch down dough. Turn onto a lightly floured surface and roll about ¼ inch thick. Cut into 2-inch diamonds or squares. Place on a lightly floured surface, cover with waxed paper, and let rise again until doubled.
7. About 20 minutes before frying, heat fat.
8. Fry pieces in heated fat 2 to 3 minutes, or until lightly browned. Fry only as many at one time as will float uncrowded one layer deep in fat. Turn as they rise to surface and several times during frying. Remove doughnuts with slotted spoon; drain over fat for a few seconds, then put on absorbent paper.
9. Shake 2 or 3 doughnuts at one time in a bag containing *confectioners' sugar.*

ABOUT 6 DOZEN DOUGHNUTS

FILLED BERLIN DOUGHNUTS
(Bismarcks)
A hint of orange and rum extract flavors these puffy Bismarcks. Fill them with your favorite jelly.

1 pkg. active dry yeast	2 teaspoons rum extract
¼ cup warm water	1 cup milk, scalded
½ cup sugar	3½ to 4 cups all-purpose flour
1 teaspoon salt	2 eggs, well beaten
⅓ cup butter	Fat for deep frying heated to 375°F
1 tablespoon orange juice	

1. Soften yeast in the warm water.
2. Put ½ cup sugar, the salt, butter, orange juice, and rum extract into a large bowl. Pour scalded milk over ingredients in bowl. Stir until butter is melted. Cool to lukewarm.
3. Blend in 1 cup of the flour and beat until smooth. Stir in yeast. Add about half of the remaining flour and beat until smooth. Beat in the eggs. Then beat in enough of the remaining flour to make a soft dough.
4. Turn dough onto a lightly floured surface and let rest 5 to 10 minutes.
5. Knead until smooth and elastic. Form into a ball and put into a greased deep bowl; turn dough to bring greased surface to top. Cover; let rise in a warm place until doubled.
6. Punch down dough. Turn dough onto a lightly floured surface and roll ½ inch thick. Cut dough into rounds with a 3-inch cutter. Cover with waxed paper and let rise on rolling surface, away from drafts and direct heat, until doubled, 30 to 45 minutes.

7. About 20 minutes before deep frying, heat fat.
8. Fry doughnuts in heated fat; fry only as many doughnuts at one time as will float uncrowded one layer deep in the fat. Fry 2 to 3 minutes, or until lightly browned; turn doughnuts with a fork or tongs when they rise to the surface and several times during cooking (do not pierce). Lift from fat; drain over fat for a few seconds before removing to absorbent paper. Cool.
9. Cut a slit through to the center in the side of each doughnut. Force about ½ *teaspoon jam or jelly* into center and press lightly to close slit. (A pastry bag and tube may be used to force jelly or jam into slit.) Shake 2 to 3 Bismarcks at one time in bag containing *sugar.*

ABOUT 2 DOZEN DOUGHNUTS

SUGARED ORANGE DOUGHNUTS

1 large potato, pared	3 tablespoons grated orange peel
3¾ to 4¼ cups all-purpose flour	¼ cup butter
2 pkgs. active dry yeast	1 egg
¾ cup sugar	Fat for deep frying heated to 375°F
1 teaspoon salt	

1. Put potato into *boiling water* in a saucepan; cover and cook until potato is tender. Drain, reserving 1 cup potato water. Mash enough potato to measure ½ cup. Set aside.
2. Mix thoroughly in a large bowl 1½ cups of the flour, yeast, sugar, salt, and orange peel.
3. Combine potato water and butter in a saucepan and heat until liquid is warm. Gradually add to dry ingredients, beating 2 minutes at medium speed of electric mixer, scraping bowl occasionally.
4. Add potato, egg, and ½ cup flour or enough flour to make a thick batter. Beat at high speed 2 minutes, scraping bowl occasionally. Stir in enough remaining flour to make a soft dough.
5. Turn dough onto lightly floured surface, knead until smooth and elastic, and form into a ball. Put into a greased deep bowl; turn to bring greased surface to top. Cover; let rise until doubled.
6. Punch down dough, turn onto lightly floured surface, and roll ½ inch thick. Cut with a 3-inch doughnut cutter. Place on greased baking sheets. Cover; let rise until doubled.
7. Fry in hot fat until golden brown on both sides. Drain on absorbent paper. Coat generously with *granulated or confectioners' sugar.*

ABOUT 2 DOZEN DOUGHNUTS

QUICK BREADS

Quick breads get their name from the relatively short time of preparation as compared with yeast breads. The leavening of quick breads is usually achieved by the use of baking powder or baking soda. Popovers are an exception with steam causing them to rise.

Sometimes the term "quick bread" is used in a broad sense so that it includes all baked products made from batters or doughs even though they are not always true breads. Thus, one method of classifying a quick bread is according to the thickness of the batter or dough before baking.

Pour Batter (popovers, timbales, waffles, griddlecakes)—Pour batters are fluid enough to pour.

Drop Batter (muffins, drop biscuits, drop cookies, cream puffs, fruit and nut loaf breads)—Drop batters are thicker than pour batters and break from the spoon instead of pouring in a stream.

Soft Dough (rolled biscuits, doughnuts)—Soft doughs feel soft but not sticky to the touch and can be handled on a lightly floured surface.

Stiff Dough (pastry, rolled cookies)—No true breads fall in this category as stiff doughs are firm and lack the resiliency of soft doughs.

An important reminder—do not overmix a quick bread. This is especially important when all-purpose flour (rather than cake flour) is used in preparing the batter or dough. Too much beating or mixing causes the gluten in flour to become elastic, a development which is desirable in making good yeast bread but should be avoided in quick breads.

TECHNIQUES FOR MAKING QUICK BREADS

(Read also *Use Correct Techniques*, page 10.)

Have all ingredients at room temperature unless recipe specifies otherwise.

Preheat oven at required temperature.

Place oven rack so top of product will be almost at center of oven. Stagger pans (when more than one rack is needed) so no pan is directly over another and they do not touch each other or the walls of the oven. Place a single pan so that the top of product is as near center of oven as possible.

Prepare pans as directed in recipe.

Sift all-purpose flour, or not, as desired. (To measure, see *page 10.*)

Cream shortening (alone or with flavoring and spices) by stirring, rubbing, or beating with spoon or electric beater until softened. Add sugar in small amounts, creaming thoroughly after each addition. Thorough creaming helps to insure a fine-grained product.

Cut in shortening—Mix cold shortening with dry ingredients using a pastry blender, two knives, or tines of fork until the mixture resembles coarse crumbs. Work gently and do not overmix. (Method is used for mixing baking powder biscuits and some loaf breads.)

Beat eggs—See *page 10.*

Fill pans one-half to two-thirds full.

Apply baking tests when minimum baking time is up. For coffee cakes and quick loaf breads, insert a cake tester or wooden pick in center; if it comes out clean, cake or bread is done.

Remove quick loaf breads and coffee cakes from pans as they come from the oven, unless otherwise directed. Set on wire racks to cool.

Wrap cooled quick loaf breads in aluminum foil or other moisture-vaporproof material.

Quick Tea Breads & Coffee Cakes

APRICOT BREAD
Served at Johnny Cake Inn, Ivoryton, Connecticut.

½ cup hot water	¼ cup butter or
1 cup dried apricots,	margarine, melted
cut fine	1 cup orange juice
2 cups sugar	4 cups sifted all-
2 eggs	purpose flour
	1 teaspoon baking soda

1.   Add hot water to apricots in a bowl; beat in the sugar thoroughly. Add eggs, one at a time, beating well after each addition. Beat in the melted butter, then the orange juice.

2.   Sift flour and baking soda together and add about ½ cup at a time to apricot mixture, mixing only until blended after each addition. Turn into 4 greased 7x4x2-inch loaf pans and spread evenly.

3.   Bake at 350°F about 30 minutes.

4.   Cool bread 10 minutes in pans on wire rack;

remove from pans and cool completely. To store, wrap and refrigerate. 4 SMALL LOAVES BREAD

APRICOT NUT BREAD

1½ cups (½ lb.) dried apricots	½ teaspoon baking soda
1 cup water	1 teaspoon salt
2½ cups sifted all-purpose flour	¾ cup coarsely chopped nuts
¾ cup sugar	1 egg, well beaten
4 teaspoons baking powder	1 cup buttermilk
	3 tablespoons butter or margarine, melted

1. Rinse, drain, and coarsely chop apricots. Add to water in a heavy saucepan. Bring to boiling; simmer, uncovered, 10 minutes, or until water is absorbed. Set the apricots aside to cool.
2. Sift flour with sugar, baking powder, baking soda, and salt into a bowl; mix in the nuts.
3. Mix the egg, buttermilk, and butter with the apricots. Make a well in the center of dry ingredients and add the liquid apricot mixture; stir only enough to moisten dry ingredients. Turn into a greased 9x5x3-inch loaf pan and spread evenly.
4. Bake at 350°F about 1 hour, or until bread tests done.
5. Cool bread 10 minutes in pan on wire rack; remove from pan and cool completely before slicing or storing. 1 LOAF BREAD

CORIANDER-BANANA NUT BREAD

1⅔ cups sifted all-purpose flour	1 large egg, well beaten
¾ cup sugar	1¼ cups mashed ripe bananas (3 to 4 medium-sized)
3 teaspoons baking powder	
½ teaspoon baking soda	⅓ cup melted shortening, cooled
½ teaspoon salt	
2 teaspoons ground coriander	¼ cup buttermilk
1½ cups (about 8 oz.) unblanched almonds, chopped (¾ cup finely chopped and ¾ cup coarsely chopped)	1 teaspoon vanilla extract

1. Sift flour with sugar, baking powder, baking soda, salt, and coriander into a large bowl; mix in the almonds and set aside.

2. Combine the egg with remaining ingredients and blend thoroughly. Add to dry mixture and stir only enough to moisten dry ingredients. Turn into 2 greased 7x4x2-inch loaf pans and spread evenly.
3. Bake at 350°F 45 to 50 minutes, or until bread tests done.
4. Cool bread 10 minutes in pans on wire racks; remove from pans and cool completely. Wrap in moisture-vaporproof material and store overnight for easier slicing. 2 SMALL LOAVES BREAD
NOTE: To serve, slice bread thinly using a serrated knife. Spread each slice generously with a mixture of *whipped unsalted butter* and *snipped watercress*. Top with second slice of bread. Cut each sandwich into halves or thirds.

PECAN BANANA BREAD: Follow recipe for Coriander-Banana Nut Bread. Increase flour to 2 cups, decrease baking soda to ¼ teaspoon and omit coriander. Omit almonds; mix *1 cup chopped pecans* with dry ingredients. Increase mashed banana to 1½ cups. Turn batter into a 9x5x3-inch loaf pan. Bake at 350°F about 1 hour.

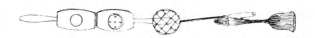

OAT FLAKE BANANA BREAD

1¼ cups sifted all-purpose flour	⅓ cup butter or margarine, melted and cooled
⅔ cup lightly packed brown sugar	1 teaspoon vanilla extract
2½ teaspoons baking powder	⅔ cup water
½ teaspoon salt	1 tablespoon orange-flavored instant drink granules
1 large egg	
1 cup mashed banana (2 to 3 bananas with brown-flecked peel)	2 cups ready-to-eat oat flakes
	½ cup chopped nuts

1. Mix the flour, brown sugar, baking powder, and salt together in a bowl; set aside.
2. Beat egg until thick and piled softly. Mix in banana, cooled butter, extract, and then a mixture of the water and drink granules.
3. Add liquid ingredients all at one time to the dry ingredients. Stir just enough to moisten flour. Mix in oat flakes and nuts. Turn into a greased 8x4x2-inch loaf pan and spread evenly.

4. Bake at 350°F 55 minutes, or until bread tests done.

5. Cool in pan on wire rack 10 minutes. Remove from pan and cool completely on rack. 1 LOAF BREAD

BANANA BREAD

A favorite of former President Lyndon B. Johnson.

½ cup butter	2 cups all-purpose flour
1 cup sugar	1 teaspoon baking soda
2 eggs, well beaten	¼ teaspoon salt
3 medium-sized ripe bananas with brown-flecked peel, mashed	1 cup sour milk

1. Cream butter and sugar together thoroughly. Add the eggs and beat well. Mix in bananas.

2. Sift flour, baking soda, and salt together. Add alternately with sour milk to banana mixture. Turn into a greased 9x5x3-inch loaf pan and spread evenly.

3. Bake at 350°F about 1 hour, or until bread tests done. 1 LOAF BANANA BREAD

CHEESE-CRANBERRY BREAD

1½ cups cranberries, cut in halves	2 teaspoons grated orange peel
½ cup sugar	1½ cups finely shredded sharp Cheddar cheese
2¼ cups sifted all-purpose flour	1 egg, slightly beaten
¾ cup sugar	1 cup milk
3 teaspoons baking powder	¼ cup butter, melted and cooled
½ teaspoon salt	
½ cup coarsely chopped walnuts	

1. Mix cranberries and ½ cup sugar well.

2. Sift flour, sugar, baking powder, and salt together into a large bowl. Mix in the sugared cranberries, walnuts, orange peel, and cheese.

3. Beat the egg, milk, and butter together. Add to mixture in bowl; stir just until dry ingredients are moistened. Turn into a greased 9x5x3-inch loaf pan and spread evenly.

4. Bake at 350°F about 1 hour, or until bread tests done.

5. Cool bread 10 minutes in pan on wire rack; remove from pan and cool completely before slicing. To store, wrap and refrigerate. 1 LOAF BREAD

DATE NUT BREAD

3 tablespoons butter, softened	1 cup whole wheat flour
½ cup firmly packed dark brown sugar	3½ teaspoons baking powder
½ cup sugar	1 teaspoon salt
1 egg	1 teaspoon ground ginger
1 cup undiluted evaporated milk	¾ cup coarsely chopped walnuts
½ cup water	1 cup chopped dates
1⅔ cups sifted all-purpose flour	

1. Beat butter, sugars, and egg in a large bowl. Add evaporated milk and water, mixing thoroughly.

2. Reserve ¼ cup all-purpose flour; blend remaining flour with the whole wheat flour, baking powder, salt, and ginger.

3. Toss the walnuts and dates with the ¼ cup flour until well coated; set aside.

4. Add the flour mixture to the beaten egg mixture and stir until blended. Add the dates and nuts and mix just until blended. Turn into a greased 9x5x3-inch loaf pan and spread evenly.

5. Bake at 350°F 1 hour, or until bread tests done.

6. Cool 5 minutes in pan on wire rack; remove from pan and cool on wire rack. 1 LOAF BREAD

GOLDEN FIG BREAD

¾ cup sifted all-purpose flour	1½ cups chopped dried figs (stems removed)
¾ cup sugar	2 eggs
3½ teaspoons baking powder	1 cup milk
¾ teaspoon salt	¼ cup cooking or salad oil
3 cups graham cracker crumbs	1 teaspoon vanilla extract
1½ cups finely chopped walnuts	

1. Grease a 9x5x3-inch loaf pan; line bottom with waxed paper; grease waxed paper.

2. Combine the flour, sugar, baking powder, salt, and graham cracker crumbs in a bowl. Mix in the walnuts and figs.

3. Thoroughly blend eggs, milk, oil, and extract. Add to dry ingredients; stir only enough to moisten dry ingredients. Turn into pan and spread evenly.

4. Bake at 350°F about 45 minutes, or until bread tests done.

5. Cool 10 minutes in pan on wire rack. Remove from pan, immediately peel off waxed paper, and turn topside up. Cool completely. To store, wrap tightly in moisture-vaporproof material.

1 LOAF BREAD

CALIFORNIA FRUIT NUT BREAD

2½ cups sifted all-purpose flour	1 cup (about 7 oz.) pitted dates
3 teaspoons baking powder	½ cup walnuts
¾ cup sugar	Buttermilk
½ teaspoon baking soda	1 egg, well beaten
1 teaspoon salt	3 tablespoons shortening, melted and cooled
1 medium-sized orange	

1. Sift flour, baking powder, sugar, baking soda, and salt together into a large bowl.
2. Cut the orange into pieces; discard any seeds. Force through the medium blade of a food chopper with dates and nuts. Reserve orange juice in a measuring cup; add enough buttermilk to make 1 cup liquid. Combine with egg and shortening.
3. Add the liquid ingredients and orange-date mixture to dry ingredients; mix only until blended. Turn into a well greased 9x5x3-inch loaf pan and spread evenly.
4. Bake at 350°F about 1¼ hours, or until bread tests done.
5. Cool 10 minutes on wire rack. Remove loaf from pan; cool completely. To store, wrap tightly in aluminum foil or moisture-vaporproof material.

1 LOAF BREAD

BISHOP'S BREAD

1½ cups sifted all-purpose flour	1 cup (about 8 oz.) maraschino cherries, drained and sliced
1 teaspoon baking powder	2 cups walnuts, coarsely chopped
½ teaspoon salt	6 oz. semisweet chocolate pieces
3 eggs	
¾ cup sugar	
1 cup (about 7 oz.) small date pieces	

1. Lightly grease a 9x5x3-inch loaf pan. Line bottom and sides with baking parchment cut to fit pan. Lightly grease paper.
2. Sift the flour, baking powder, and salt together.
3. Beat the eggs and sugar together until mixture is thick and piled softly.

4. Add dry ingredients in thirds to egg mixture beating only until blended after each addition. Stir in the fruits, nuts, and chocolate pieces. Turn into the prepared pan and spread evenly.
5. Bake at 300°F 1 hour 45 minutes, or until bread tests done.
6. Cool 10 minutes in pan on wire rack. Loosen from pan, invert on rack, peel off paper and cool right side up. Wrap; store overnight before slicing.

1 LOAF BREAD

LEMON NUT BREAD

2½ cups sifted all-purpose flour	1 egg
1 cup sugar	2 teaspoons grated lemon peel
3 teaspoons baking powder	¾ cup undiluted evaporated milk
½ teaspoon salt	½ cup water
1 cup chopped nuts	¼ cup butter, melted

1. Sift flour, sugar, baking powder, and salt together. Mix in the nuts; set aside.
2. Thoroughly beat egg with lemon peel, then beat in the remaining ingredients in order.
3. Add the liquid mixture all at one time to the dry ingredients and stir just until the dry ingredients are moistened. Turn into 2 greased 7x4x2-inch loaf pans or one 9x5x3-inch loaf pan and spread evenly.
4. Bake at 375°F about 40 minutes, or until bread tests done.
5. Cool 10 minutes in pans on wire rack; remove from pans and cool completely.

2 LOAVES BREAD

ORANGE BRAN BREAD

2¼ cups all-purpose flour	½ cup raisins, plumped and chopped
½ cup whole bran cereal	1 medium-sized orange, pared (remove white membrane) and pulp diced
4 teaspoons baking powder	
½ teaspoon baking soda	
1 teaspoon salt	1 teaspoon grated lemon peel
1¼ cups firmly packed light brown sugar	1 tablespoon lemon juice
¼ cup honey	1 cup milk
3 tablespoons butter or margarine	1 egg, beaten

1. Mix flour, cereal, baking powder, baking soda, and salt thoroughly; set aside.

2. Combine the brown sugar, honey, and butter in a large saucepan. Bring to boiling; boil 1 to 2 minutes to dissolve the sugar, stirring constantly. Remove from heat and cool slightly. Stir in the raisins, orange pieces, lemon peel and juice, milk, and egg.

3. Add dry ingredients to the fruit mixture all at one time and stir only enough to moisten dry ingredients. Turn into 2 greased 8x4x2-inch loaf pans and spread evenly.

4. Bake at 350°F about 30 minutes, or until bread tests done.

5. Remove bread to wire racks and cool 10 minutes in pans. Remove from pans to racks and cool completely.   2 MEDIUM LOAVES BREAD

PINEAPPLE-COCONUT BREAD

1¾ cups sifted all-
  purpose flour
2 teaspoons baking
  powder
¼ teaspoon baking soda
½ teaspoon salt
¼ cup butter or
  margarine
¾ cup lightly packed
  light brown sugar
1 egg

1 can (8½ or 8¾ oz.)
  crushed pineapple
½ cup coarsely chopped
  pecans
½ cup flaked coconut
¼ cup semisweet
  chocolate pieces
2 tablespoons sugar
½ teaspoon ground
  cinnamon
2 tablespoons flaked
  coconut

1. Sift flour, baking powder, baking soda, and salt together; set aside.

2. Cream butter; gradually add the brown sugar, creaming until thoroughly blended. Add egg and beat until light and fluffy.

3. Mixing until blended after each addition, alternately add dry ingredients and undrained pineapple. Stir in pecans, the ½ cup coconut, and chocolate pieces. Turn into a greased 8x4x2-inch loaf pan and spread evenly. Spoon a mixture of sugar, cinnamon, and remaining coconut evenly over top.

4. Bake at 350°F 55 to 60 minutes, or until bread tests done.

5. Cool on wire rack 5 minutes before removing bread from pan. Serve warm.   1 LOAF BREAD

SWISS WHIPPED CREAM-NUT LOAF

1 cup heavy cream
1 egg
1 cup sugar
1 teaspoon grated
  lemon peel
1 cup chopped walnuts

1 cup golden raisins,
  plumped
1¾ cups sifted all-
  purpose flour
1½ teaspoons baking
  powder
¼ teaspoon salt

1. Beat cream until very soft peaks are formed; beat in egg and sugar until thoroughly blended. Mix in the lemon peel, walnuts, and raisins.

2. Sift the flour, baking powder, and salt together; fold into the cream-sugar mixture. Turn into a greased 9x5x3-inch loaf pan and spread evenly.

3. Bake at 325°F 70 minutes, or until bread tests done.

4. Cool bread 15 minutes in pan on wire rack; remove from pan and cool completely. 1 LOAF BREAD

IRISH SODA BREAD WITH CURRANTS

4 cups sifted all-
  purpose flour
2 tablespoons sugar
2 teaspoons baking
  soda
1½ teaspoons salt

¼ cup butter or
  margarine
⅔ cup dried currants,
  plumped
½ cup white vinegar
1 cup milk

1. Mix flour, sugar, baking soda, and salt in a bowl. Cut in the butter with pastry blender or two knives until particles resemble rice kernels. Lightly mix in currants.

2. Mix vinegar and milk. Add half of the liquid to dry ingredients; blend quickly. Add remaining liquid and stir only until blended.

3. Turn dough onto floured surface. Lightly knead dough about 10 times and shape into a round loaf. Place on greased baking sheet.

4. Bake at 375°F 35 to 40 minutes.

                    1 LARGE LOAF SODA BREAD

STEAMED BOSTON BROWN BREAD

1 cup rye flour
1 cup whole wheat flour
1 cup yellow cornmeal
1½ teaspoons baking
  powder
¾ teaspoon baking soda

1 teaspoon salt
2 cups buttermilk or
  sour milk
¾ cup molasses
1 cup dark seedless
  raisins

1. Mix the flours, cornmeal, baking powder, bak-

ing soda, and salt in a large bowl. Add a mixture of the buttermilk, molasses, and raisins; stir only enough to moisten the flour.

2. Pour an equal amount of batter into 3 well greased cans (18 to 20 ounces each). Fill not more than ⅔ full. Cover cans tightly with aluminum foil or baking parchment tied securely with string.

3. Steam (see *page 510*) 3 hours.

4. Remove cans from kettle; run a knife around inside of cans to loosen loaves and unmold onto wire rack. Serve warm, or store the cooled loaves (wrapped in moisture-vaporproof material) in a cool place. Resteam (see *page 510*) to serve.

THREE 1-POUND LOAVES

DUTCH APPLE CAKE

2 cups sifted all-purpose flour	3 medium-sized apples, washed, quartered, cored and pared
3 tablespoons sugar	
3 teaspoons baking powder	¼ cup sugar
1 teaspoon salt	½ teaspoon ground cinnamon
1 cup chilled heavy cream	2 tablespoons butter or margarine, melted

1. Sift flour, 3 tablespoons sugar, baking powder, and salt together into a bowl.

2. Beat cream until it piles softly. With a fork, lightly blend whipped cream into dry ingredients. Turn into a greased 9x9x2-inch baking pan and spread evenly.

3. Cut each apple quarter into 3 slices. Arrange slices in parallel rows on batter; press into batter. Combine ¼ cup sugar and cinnamon and sprinkle evenly over apples. Pour melted butter over top.

4. Bake at 400°F about 25 minutes, or until cake tests done. Cut into squares.   9 SERVINGS

QUICK COFFEE CAKE
(Blitzkuchen)

1⅓ cups sifted all-purpose flour	1 teaspoon vanilla extract
1½ teaspoons baking powder	⅔ cup sugar
¼ teaspoon salt	2 eggs, beaten
¼ cup butter	½ cup milk
	Topping, *below*

1. Mix flour, baking powder, and salt thoroughly and set aside.

2. Cream the butter with extract; gradually add

the sugar, creaming until fluffy. Add the eggs in thirds, beating thoroughly after each addition.

3. Alternately add dry ingredients in thirds and milk in halves to creamed mixture, mixing until blended after each addition. Turn into a well greased 9x9x2-inch pan. Sprinkle with Topping.

4. Bake at 350°F about 25 minutes.

ONE 9-INCH SQUARE COFFEE CAKE

TOPPING: Mix ¼ *cup sugar*, ½ *teaspoon ground cinnamon*, and ¼ *cup chopped walnuts*.

TENA'S COFFEE CAKE

½ cup nuts, chopped	½ teaspoon baking soda
¼ cup sugar	½ cup butter
3 teaspoons ground cinnamon	3 teaspoons vanilla extract
1½ cups sifted all-purpose flour	1 cup sugar
	2 eggs
1 teaspoon baking powder	1 cup dairy sour cream

1. Mix nuts, ¼ cup sugar, and cinnamon.

2. Blend flour, baking powder, and baking soda.

3. Cream butter with extract. Add the 1 cup sugar gradually, beating constantly until thoroughly blended. Add eggs, one at a time, beating until light and fluffy after each addition.

4. Alternately add dry ingredients and sour cream, beating only until smooth after each addition. Turn half of the batter into a greased 9x9x2-inch baking pan. Sprinkle evenly with half of the nut mixture. Repeat.

5. Bake at 375°F 30 minutes, or until coffee cake tests done.   ONE 9-INCH SQUARE COFFEE CAKE

BLUEBERRY COFFEE CAKE

2 cups sifted all-purpose flour	4 egg yolks (½ cup)
2 teaspoons baking powder	1 cup mashed potato, cooled to room temperature
1 cup butter or margarine	4 egg whites (⅔ cup)
2 teaspoons orange extract	¾ teaspoon salt
1 teaspoon grated orange peel	2 cups blueberries, fresh or thawed frozen
2 cups sugar	Orange Cream Icing, *page 90*

1. Blend the flour and baking powder; set aside.

2.   Cream butter, extract, and orange peel. Add sugar gradually, beating vigorously. Add egg yolks, one at a time, beating until light and fluffy after each addition. Mix in mashed potato.

3.   Add dry ingredients in thirds, beating only until blended after each addition.

4.   Beat egg whites and salt until stiff, not dry, peaks are formed. Gently fold into the batter.

5.   Rinse (if fresh) and thoroughly drain blueberries on absorbent paper; dredge with about 2 tablespoons flour. Using as few strokes as possible, fold berries into batter. Turn into greased and floured 3-quart (13x8-inch) shallow baking dish.

6.   Bake at 350°F 35 to 40 minutes, or until cake tests done.

7.   Cool in baking dish on wire rack. Spread with Orange Cream Icing. To serve, cut cake into squares, rectangles, or diamond-shaped pieces.

ONE 13x8-INCH COFFEE CAKE

ORANGE CREAM ICING: Combine *1 cup confectioners' sugar, 1 teaspoon butter, softened, 1 teaspoon grated orange peel, 1 teaspoon light corn syrup,* and *2 tablespoons dairy sour cream.* Beat until smooth.   ABOUT ½ CUP ICING

QUICK CHERRY BRAID

2 cups sifted all-purpose flour	⅓ cup butter
⅓ cup sugar	1 egg, beaten
3 teaspoons baking powder	⅓ to ½ cup undiluted evaporated milk
½ teaspoon salt	Cherry Filling, *below*

1.   Mix flour, sugar, baking powder, and salt in a bowl. Cut in butter with a pastry blender or two knives until mixture has a fine, even crumb.

2.   Stir in egg and enough milk to make a soft dough. Turn onto a lightly floured surface and knead with fingertips 30 seconds.

3.   Put dough on a greased baking sheet and pat or roll out into a 15x10-inch rectangle.

4.   Spoon filling onto center of dough in a 2-inch wide, lengthwise strip. Cut dough with a knife or a pastry wheel into 1-inch strips starting at the edge of a long side and cutting to within ½ inch of the filling. Repeat on second side. Braid the strips over filling by lifting one strip from each side and crossing diagonally in center. Brush top with a mixture of *1 slightly beaten egg yolk* and *1 tablespoon undiluted evaporated milk.*

5.   Bake at 375°F 20 to 25 minutes, or until lightly browned.   1 COFFEE CAKE BRAID

CHERRY FILLING: Gently stir *1 cup drained pitted tart red cherries* into a mixture of *⅓ cup packed brown sugar, 2 tablespoons flour,* and *2 tablespoons melted butter* until coated.

TOASTED FILBERT COFFEE CAKE

2 cups sifted all-purpose flour	1 teaspoon vanilla extract
2 teaspoons baking powder	1 cup sugar
½ teaspoon baking soda	2 eggs
½ teaspoon salt	1 cup dairy sour cream
½ cup butter or margarine	Toasted Filbert Topping, *below*

1.   Blend the flour, baking powder, baking soda, and salt; set aside.

2.   Cream the butter and extract. Add sugar gradually, beating constantly until thoroughly creamed. Add the eggs, one at a time, beating until light and fluffy after each addition.

3.   Alternately add dry ingredients in thirds and sour cream in halves, mixing only until blended after each addition.

4.   Spoon half of the batter into a greased and floured 9x9x2-inch baking pan; evenly sprinkle half of the filbert topping over batter. Spoon on remaining batter and top with filbert mixture.

5.   Bake at 325°F about 40 minutes, or until coffee cake tests done. Set pan on wire rack to cool.

ONE 9 INCH SQUARE COFFEE CAKE

TOASTED FILBERT TOPPING: Mix *1 cup finely chopped toasted filberts, ⅓ cup packed brown sugar, ¼ cup sugar,* and *1 teaspoon ground cinnamon.*
NOTE: To toast filberts, see *To toast nuts, page 20.*

Cornbreads

The name "johnny cake" goes back into Colonial days when a trip from one settlement to another was really a "journey." Then the traveler's good wife would make little cornmeal "journey cakes" to fit into his knapsack so he could break his fast along the way. Over the years the name has been contracted into "johnny cake" with some New Englanders having dropped the "h" along the way.

JOHNNYCAKE I

1 cup sifted all-purpose flour	¾ cup firmly packed light brown sugar
1 cup yellow cornmeal	1 egg, well beaten
½ teaspoon baking soda	½ cup buttermilk or sour milk
¼ to ½ teaspoon salt	⅓ cup dairy sour cream

1. Blend flour, cornmeal, baking soda, and salt in a bowl. Mix in brown sugar.
2. Add a mixture of egg, buttermilk, and sour cream all at one time to dry ingredients. Beat with a rotary beater until *just* smooth. Turn into a greased 11x7x1 ½-inch baking pan; spread evenly.
3. Bake at 425°F about 20 minutes.
4. Break or cut johnnycake into squares. Serve hot with *butter* and warm *maple syrup*.

ONE 11x7 INCH JOHNNYCAKE

JOHNNYCAKE II

1 cup sifted all-purpose flour	¾ teaspoon salt
1 cup yellow cornmeal	1 egg, well beaten
¼ cup sugar	1 cup buttermilk
1 teaspoon baking powder	¼ cup butter or margarine, melted
½ teaspoon baking soda	2 tablespoons molasses

1. Combine flour, cornmeal, sugar, baking powder, baking soda, and salt in a bowl; mix well.
2. Add a mixture of egg, buttermilk, butter, and molasses all at one time to dry ingredients. Beat with a rotary beater until just smooth, being careful not to overmix. Turn into a greased 8x8x2-inch baking pan and spread evenly.
3. Bake at 425°F about 20 minutes.
4. Break or cut into 2-inch squares. Serve hot with *butter* and warm *maple syrup*, if desired.

ONE 8-INCH SQUARE JOHNNYCAKE

HERMITAGE SPOON BREAD

Spoon bread was a favorite of Andrew Jackson whose Tennessee home was called the Hermitage.

1 cup white hominy grits, or water-ground white cornmeal	2 cups hot milk
	2 eggs, beaten
1½ teaspoons salt	3 tablespoons butter or margarine
1 cup cold water	

1. Combine hominy grits with the salt and cold water in a heavy saucepan. Stir until smooth, then stir in the hot milk. Cook and stir over low heat until mixture begins to thicken.
2. Remove from heat; add eggs and butter. Beat until well blended. Turn into a well greased 1-quart casserole.
3. Bake at 350°F 45 minutes, or until center is "set." Serve hot with plenty of *butter*.

ABOUT 6 SERVINGS

SOUTHWEST SOUFFLÉ

1 qt. milk	6 eggs
1½ cups yellow cornmeal	2 tablespoons sugar
¼ cup butter or margarine	2 tablespoons baking powder
2 cans (2 oz. each) grated American cheese food	1 cup chopped pimiento-stuffed olives

1. Heat 2 cups of the milk. Blend cornmeal and the remaining 2 cups milk; stir into hot milk. Cook and stir over medium heat until thickened and smooth, about 5 minutes. Remove from heat.
2. Add butter and cheese food; stir until cheese food is melted. Cool 10 minutes.
3. Meanwhile, beat eggs and a blend of the sugar and baking powder until thick and piled softly. Fold into cooled cornmeal mixture. Mix in olives. Turn into 2 greased 1½-quart baking dishes.
4. Bake at 350°F 50 minutes, or until a knife inserted about halfway between center and edge comes out clean.

ABOUT 12 SERVINGS

SOUTHERN BATTER BREAD

½ cup cornmeal	1 tablespoon melted lard
1 teaspoon salt	2 eggs, well beaten
1 cup water	
½ cup milk	

1. Mix the cornmeal and salt in a saucepan; blend in the water. Bring rapidly to boiling. Stirring constantly, boil 5 minutes (mixture will be very thick). Blend in the milk and lard. Vigorously beat into well beaten eggs.
2. Thoroughly grease a 1½-quart casserole and heat 2 to 3 minutes in oven. Turn batter into hot casserole.
3. Bake at 400°F 45 to 50 minutes, or until bread tests done. Serve immediately with *butter*, *gravy*, or *butter* and *syrup or honey*.

4 SERVINGS

CORN POCKET ROLLS

1½ cups all-purpose flour
2 tablespoons sugar
2½ teaspoons baking powder
¼ teaspoon baking soda
½ teaspoon salt
½ cup yellow cornmeal
1 egg, well beaten
¾ cup dairy sour cream
Melted butter

1.   Mix the flour, sugar, baking powder, baking soda, and salt in a bowl; stir in the cornmeal.
2.   Blend beaten egg and sour cream; stir into dry ingredients. Turn dough onto a lightly floured surface and roll about ⅛ inch thick. Brush dough with melted butter and cut with a lightly floured 2½-inch round cutter.
3.   Using the handle of a wooden spoon, make a slightly off-center crease on each round of dough; fold top (larger half) over bottom. Press edges together at each end of crease.
4.   Place rolls about 1 inch apart on lightly greased baking sheets.
5.   Bake at 425°F about 12 minutes, or until light golden brown.   ABOUT 2 DOZEN ROLLS

BACON-NUT CORN STICKS

1 cup sifted all-purpose flour
1 cup yellow cornmeal
¼ cup sugar
1 teaspoon baking powder
½ teaspoon baking soda
½ teaspoon salt
⅓ cup coarsely chopped pecans
6 to 8 slices crisply fried bacon, drained on absorbent paper and crumbled
1 egg, well beaten
1 cup buttermilk
5 tablespoons melted shortening

1.   Combine the flour, cornmeal, sugar, baking powder, baking soda, and salt in a bowl, mix well and stir in the pecans and bacon.
2.   Add a mixture of the remaining ingredients and stir only until flour is moistened. Spoon mixture into 12 preheated greased corn-stick pan sections (5½x1½ inches).
3.   Bake at 425°F 10 to 15 minutes.

1 DOZEN CORN STICKS

CORN-CHEESE TWISTS

½ cup sifted all-purpose flour
¼ cup yellow cornmeal
½ teaspoon salt
¼ to ⅓ cup (about ½ 5-oz. jar) pasteurized process sharp Cheddar cheese spread
2 tablespoons shortening
2 tablespoons cold water

1.   Mix flour, cornmeal, and salt in a bowl. Cut in the cheese spread and shortening with a pastry blender or two knives until pieces resemble coarse crumbs.
2.   Gradually add the water, stirring with a fork until mixture forms a ball and leaves sides of bowl.
3.   Roll between two sheets of waxed paper to ⅛-inch thickness. Using a pastry wheel, cut dough into 3x½-inch strips. Twist each strip by holding both ends and turning in opposite directions; press ends onto ungreased baking sheets.
4.   Bake at 425°F about 5 minutes, or until golden brown. Cool the twists on wire racks.

ABOUT 5 DOZEN TWISTS

CORNMEAL CRISPS

¼ cup cornmeal
⅛ teaspoon seasoned salt
¼ cup boiling water
1 tablespoon butter or margarine

1.   Mix cornmeal and salt in a bowl. Stir in water and butter until smooth.
2.   Drop by teaspoonfuls on a well greased baking sheet and flatten.
3.   Bake at 350°F about 20 minutes, or until browned and crisp.   ABOUT 1 DOZEN CRISPS

CORNMEAL WAFERS

1 cup sifted all-purpose flour
½ cup yellow cornmeal
1 teaspoon seasoned salt
½ cup shortening
¼ cup pasteurized process pimiento cheese spread
2 tablespoons milk
¼ cup dry onion soup mix, crushed slightly

1.   Thoroughly mix the flour, cornmeal, and salt in a bowl. Cut in shortening and cheese spread with pastry blender until blended.
2.   Add milk and stir until mixture is just moist-

ened. Form into a ball and knead gently with finger-tips a few seconds on a lightly floured surface.

3. Roll dough ⅛ inch thick. Sprinkle with dry soup mix and press lightly with rolling pin. Cut with floured 1½- or 2-inch cutter. Place on ungreased baking sheets.

4. Bake at 375°F 10 to 12 minutes.

5. Serve as an accompaniment to soup. Leftover wafers may be stored in covered containers in the refrigerator or they may be frozen; reheat before serving.   3 TO 4 DOZEN WAFERS

NOTE: If desired, substitute *2 tablespoons caraway seed or dill weed* for onion soup mix.

Biscuits & Muffins

BUTTERMILK BISCUITS

2 cups sifted all-purpose flour	1 teaspoon salt
2½ teaspoons baking powder	⅓ cup lard or vegetable shortening
¼ teaspoon baking soda	¾ cup buttermilk

1. Blend flour, baking powder, baking soda, and salt in a bowl. Cut in lard with a pastry blender or two knives until particles are the size of rice kernels. Add buttermilk and stir with a fork only until dough follows fork.

2. Gently form dough into a ball and put on a lightly floured surface. Knead lightly with fingertips 10 to 15 times. Gently roll dough ½ inch thick.

3. Cut with a floured biscuit cutter or knife, using an even pressure to keep sides of biscuits straight. Place on ungreased baking sheet, close together for soft-sided biscuits or 1 inch apart for crusty ones. Brush tops lightly with *buttermilk*.

4. Bake at 450°F 10 to 15 minutes, or until biscuits are golden brown.   ABOUT 1 DOZEN BISCUITS

BAKING POWDER BISCUITS: Follow recipe for Buttermilk Biscuits. Omit the baking soda, increase baking powder to 3 teaspoons, and substitute ¾ *cup milk* for buttermilk.

ORANGE ROLLS: Follow recipe for Buttermilk Biscuits. Roll dough into a rectangle about ¼ inch thick. Brush with *2 tablespoons softened butter or margarine*. Sprinkle dough with mixture of ½ *cup sugar* and ¼ *cup finely shredded orange peel* (reserve 1 tablespoon peel for glaze). Beginning with long side, roll up and press edges together.

Cut into 1-inch slices. Do not brush tops with milk. Place slices flat on greased baking sheet or in muffin-pan wells, and brush with some of the *Orange Glaze, below*. Bake at 425°F about 15 minutes. Spoon remaining Orange Glaze over the hot rolls.
                                              12 TO 15 ROLLS

Orange Glaze: Combine in saucepan ½ *cup sugar*, ¼ *cup light corn syrup*, *2 tablespoons hot water*, and the reserved orange peel. Bring to boiling and boil 2 minutes, stirring once or twice.

CINNAMON OR APPLE ROLLS: Follow recipe for Buttermilk Biscuits. Roll dough into a rectangle about ¼ inch thick. Brush dough with *2 tablespoons softened butter or margarine*. Sprinkle with a mixture of ¼ *cup firmly packed light brown sugar*, ¼ *cup finely chopped nuts*, and *1 teaspoon ground cinnamon*. Or, spread dough with a mixture of *1½ cups* (about 2 medium-sized) *finely chopped apples*, ½ *cup sugar*, and *1 teaspoon ground cinnamon*. Beginning with long side, roll up and press edges together to seal. Cut into 1-inch slices. Do not brush tops with milk. Place flat on greased baking sheet and bake as directed.   12 TO 15 ROLLS

COCONUT TWISTS: Follow recipe for Buttermilk Biscuits. Divide dough into halves. Roll each half ¼ inch thick into a 13x5-inch rectangle. Using half of each of the following ingredients for each portion of dough, brush with *2 tablespoons melted butter* and sprinkle one lengthwise half with ⅓ *cup firmly packed brown sugar* and then with ⅔ *cup flaked coconut*. Cover with waxed paper and lightly press mixture into dough with rolling pin; remove paper. Fold buttered half over other half; press long edges together to seal. Cut dough crosswise into ½-inch strips. Twist strips; place about 1 inch apart on baking sheets lined with heavy-duty aluminum foil; press ends to seal. Bake at 425°F about 10 minutes, or until golden brown. Spread with *Glossy Orange Frosting, page 571*, if desired.
                                          ABOUT 4 DOZEN TWISTS

TALBOTT INN BUTTERMILK BISCUITS
These biscuits appear for every meal at Talbott Tavern, an historic old inn in Bardstown, Kentucky.

3 cups sifted all-purpose flour	½ teaspoon salt
3 teaspoons baking powder	½ cup lard
½ teaspoon baking soda	1 to 1¼ cups buttermilk

1. Sift flour, baking powder, baking soda, and salt

together into a bowl; cut in the lard with a pastry blender or two knives.

2. Add enough buttermilk to form a soft dough, using as few strokes as necessary. Turn dough onto a lightly floured surface; pat or roll about ¾ inch thick.

3. Cut into rounds using a lightly floured biscuit cutter. Place close together in a baking pan.

4. Bake at 450°F 10 to 15 minutes, or until biscuits are lightly browned.

ABOUT 2 DOZEN MEDIUM-SIZED BISCUITS

BEATEN BISCUITS

A Southern favorite from 'way back, these are the only biscuits that are properly served cold. Recipes and methods of beating vary from kitchen to kitchen, but the cook who can still turn out good beaten biscuits may be justly proud.

4 cups sifted all- purpose flour	1 teaspoon salt
1 teaspoon sugar	½ cup lard
	1 cup milk

1. Mix flour, sugar, and salt thoroughly in a bowl. Cut in the lard with a pastry blender or two knives until particles are the size of rice kernels.

2. Add the milk and stir to make a stiff dough. Turn dough onto a lightly floured surface and knead until smooth, about 3 minutes.

3. Beat vigorously with a wooden mallet, turning occasionally and beating on reverse side. Beat about 30 minutes, or until dough blisters and has a satiny surface.

4. Roll about ½ inch thick and cut with a floured 1- or 1½-inch round cutter. Transfer to ungreased baking sheets and prick biscuits uniformly, using a small pointed skewer.

5. Bake at 350°F about 30 minutes, or until very delicately browned.   4 TO 6 DOZEN BISCUITS

IRISH SCONES

1¾ cups sifted all- purpose flour	½ teaspoon baking soda
1 tablespoon sugar	½ teaspoon salt
1½ teaspoons baking powder	½ cup shortening
	½ cup buttermilk

1. Mix flour, sugar, baking powder, baking soda, and salt in a bowl. Cut in shortening with a pastry blender or two knives until particles are the size of rice kernels.

2. Add the buttermilk and stir with a fork until dough follows fork and forms a ball.

3. Turn dough onto a floured surface and knead lightly with fingertips about 8 times. Divide dough in half and shape each into a round about ½ inch thick. Cut each round into 6 wedge-shaped pieces. Place on an ungreased baking sheet.

4. Bake at 450°F 8 to 10 minutes. Serve warm.

1 DOZEN SCONES

FAT RASCALS

Recipe from the favorite cookbook of Edith Roosevelt, wife of President Theodore Roosevelt.

2 cups sifted all- purpose flour	½ teaspoon salt
2 tablespoons sugar	¾ cup butter or margarine
2 teaspoons baking powder	½ lb. dried currants
	½ cup milk (about)

1. Thoroughly mix the flour, sugar, baking powder, and salt in a bowl. Cut in butter with a pastry blender or two knives until particles are the size of rice kernels. Stir in currants.

2. Add the milk and stir with a fork only until a soft dough is formed.

3. Shape dough lightly into a ball and roll out ½ inch thick on a lightly floured surface. Cut into rounds with a 2-inch cutter. Place on ungreased baking sheet.

4. Bake at 450°F 12 to 15 minutes.

ABOUT 1½ DOZEN BISCUITS

CHEESE FANS

2 cups sifted all- purpose flour	¾ cup milk
3 teaspoons baking powder	Softened butter
1 teaspoon salt	1 cup shredded sharp Cheddar cheese
½ cup lard or vege- table shortening	Melted butter

1. Mix the flour, baking powder, and salt in a bowl. Cut in lard with a pastry blender or two knives until particles resemble rice kernels.

2. Add the milk and stir with a fork only until dough follows fork.

3. Gently form dough into a ball and put on a lightly floured surface. Knead lightly with fingertips 10 to 15 times. Gently roll into a 12x10-inch rectangle about ¼ inch thick. Cut into 5 strips.

4. Spread with softened butter and sprinkle 4

strips with cheese. Stack the 4 strips and top with the last strip. Cut into 12 equal portions. Place on end in greased muffin pan wells. Brush tops with melted butter.

5.   Bake at 450°F 10 to 15 minutes, or until biscuits are golden brown. Serve hot with *butter.*

1 DOZEN CHEESE FANS

CHEESE BISCUITS: Follow recipe for Cheese Fans. Decrease cheese to ¾ cup and add with the shortening. Roll dough ½ inch thick, keeping thickness uniform. Cut with a floured biscuit cutter, using an even pressure to keep sides of biscuits straight. Place on a greased baking sheet, close together for soft-sided biscuits, or 1 inch apart for crusty ones.

BACON-BRAN MUFFINS

1 cup whole bran cereal	¼ cup sugar
¾ cup milk	2½ teaspoons baking
5 slices bacon, diced	powder
and fried (reserve	½ teaspoon salt
¼ cup drippings)	1 egg, well beaten
1 cup sifted all-	
purpose flour	

1.   Mix bran and milk; let stand until milk is absorbed, about 10 minutes.
2.   Blend flour, sugar, baking powder, and salt in a bowl. Mix in the bacon pieces.
3.   Stir reserved bacon drippings into bran mixture. Mix in egg until blended.
4.   Turn the bran mixture over dry ingredients; stir quickly and lightly only enough to moisten ingredients. Spoon batter equally into greased 2½-inch muffin-pan wells.
5.   Bake at 400°F about 20 minutes.   10 MUFFINS

APRICOT-BRAN MUFFINS

⅔ cup all-purpose flour	¼ cup chopped walnuts
¼ cup sugar	1 egg, well beaten
2½ teaspoons baking	¾ cup milk
powder	3 tablespoons shorten-
1 teaspoon ground	ing, melted and
cinnamon	cooled
¼ teaspoon salt	1½ cups bran flakes
½ cup chopped dried	
apricots	

1.   Sift the flour, sugar, baking powder, cinnamon, and salt together into a bowl.

2.   Add the apricots and nuts but do not mix in.
3.   Beat egg and milk until blended; mix in the shortening. Add all at one time to the dry ingredients and mix just enough to moisten. Quickly and lightly stir in bran flakes until just blended.
4.   Divide batter equally among 12 greased 2½-inch muffin-pan wells.
5.   Bake at 425°F 15 to 20 minutes, or until done.
6.   Loosen muffins and tip slightly Keep warm.

1 DOZEN MUFFINS

ORANGE-BRAN MUFFINS

½ cup whole bran cereal	½ teaspoon salt
½ cup orange juice	½ cup sugar
1¾ cups sifted all-	½ cup soft shortening
purpose flour	1 egg
2 teaspoons baking	¼ cup milk
powder	½ cup drained crushed
¼ teaspoon baking soda	pineapple

1.   Mix bran and orange juice; set aside.
2.   Blend flour, baking powder, baking soda, and salt in a bowl; set aside.
3.   Gradually add sugar to shortening, beating well after each addition. Add egg and beat until light and fluffy.
4.   Add the dry ingredients alternately with the milk and bran-orange juice mixture, mixing only until blended after each addition. Mix in crushed pineapple.
5.   Spoon batter equally into greased 2½-inch muffin-pan wells.
6.   Bake at 400°F about 20 minutes.

1 DOZEN MUFFINS

GINGER-DATE MUFFINS

2 cups sifted all-	2 tablespoons finely
purpose flour	slivered, preserved
⅓ cup sugar	ginger
3 teaspoons baking	Spiced sugar (use 2
powder	tablespoons sugar
½ teaspoon salt	mixed with ⅛ tea-
1 egg, well beaten	spoon each ground
1 cup milk	cinnamon, ground
¼ cup butter, melted	ginger, and nutmeg)
½ cup sliced fresh	
dates	

1.   Mix flour, sugar, baking powder, and salt in a bowl. Add a mixture of beaten egg, milk, and melted butter. Quickly and lightly stir until dry ingredi-

ents are barely moistened, adding the dates and ginger with the last few strokes.

2. Spoon batter into greased 2½-inch muffin-pan wells. Sprinkle spiced sugar over batter.

3. Bake at 425°F about 15 minutes.   15 MUFFINS

MUFFINS: Follow recipe for Ginger-Date Muffins. Omit dates, ginger, and spiced sugar. Bake 20 to 25 minutes.   1 DOZEN MUFFINS

BLUEBERRY MUFFINS: Follow recipe for Muffins. With a final few strokes, gently mix *1 cup rinsed and drained fresh blueberries* into batter.

DOUBLE GINGER-PUMPKIN MUFFINS

2 cups sifted all-purpose flour	1 cup packed brown sugar
3 teaspoons baking powder	½ cup sugar
¼ teaspoon baking soda	2 eggs
1 teaspoon salt	1 cup canned pumpkin
¼ teaspoon ground ginger	½ cup buttermilk
¼ teaspoon ground mace	⅓ cup chopped walnuts
½ cup lard	¼ cup finely chopped crystallized ginger

1. Blend flour, baking powder, baking soda, salt, ginger, and mace; set aside.

2. Cream lard with the sugars, beating until fluffy. Add eggs, one at a time, beating thoroughly after each addition. Mix in pumpkin.

3. Alternately add dry ingredients and buttermilk to the creamed mixture beating only until smooth after each addition. Mix in nuts and crystallized ginger with last few strokes. Spoon batter equally into greased 2½-inch muffin-pan wells.

4. Bake at 375°F 20 minutes.   2 DOZEN MUFFINS

STOUFFER'S PUMPKIN MUFFINS
A favorite from the Stouffer Restaurant chain.

1½ cups all-purpose flour	½ teaspoon ground nutmeg
½ cup sugar	¼ cup butter
2 teaspoons baking powder	½ cup seeded raisins
¾ teaspoon salt	1 egg, beaten
½ teaspoon ground cinnamon	½ cup milk
	½ cup canned pumpkin
	1 tablespoon sugar

1. Sift the flour, ½ cup sugar, baking powder, salt, cinnamon, and nutmeg together. Cut in butter until particles are the size of rice kernels. Mix in raisins and set aside.

2. Blend egg, milk, and pumpkin; add to dry ingredients and lightly stir until dry ingredients are barely moistened (batter will be lumpy).

3. Spoon batter into greased muffin-pan wells, filling each about ⅔ full. Sprinkle ¼ teaspoon sugar over each.

4. Bake at 400°F 18 to 20 minutes. Serve at once.   1 DOZEN MUFFINS

SALLY LUNN MUFFINS
A favorite with the diners at Beaumont Inn, Harrodsburg, Kentucky.

½ cup butter, softened	1½ cups sifted all-purpose flour
⅓ cup sugar	3 teaspoons baking powder
1 egg	
¾ cup milk	

1. Cream butter with sugar until thoroughly blended. Beat in egg until mixture is light and fluffy.

2. Beating until blended after each addition, alternately add creamed mixture and milk to a blend of flour and baking powder. Spoon batter equally into greased 2½-inch muffin-pan wells.

3. Bake at 400°F 20 minutes, or until muffins are golden brown.   1 DOZEN MUFFINS

Popovers & Other Novelty Breads

PARMESAN POPOVERS

3 eggs, slightly beaten	1 cup sifted all-purpose flour
1 cup milk	½ cup shredded Parmesan cheese
2 tablespoons cooking or salad oil	
½ teaspoon salt	

1. Beat eggs, milk, oil, and salt together in a small bowl until blended.

2. Add flour gradually to liquid ingredients, beating until batter is smooth. Stir in the cheese.

3. Divide the batter evenly among 8 greased, preheated 5-ounce heat-resistant glass custard cups or wells of iron popover pan.

4. Bake at 400°F 35 to 40 minutes, or until popovers are a deep golden brown. Serve hot with *butter or margarine.*   8 POPOVERS

HERB-GARLIC-FLAVORED POPOVERS: Follow recipe for Parmesan Popovers. Omit oil and cheese. Combine *2 tablespoons melted butter, 1 large clove garlic*, minced, *½ teaspoon thyme*, and *2 teaspoons finely snipped parsley*; add to the egg mixture.

WHOLE WHEAT POPOVERS

⅔ cup all-purpose flour	1 cup milk
⅓ cup whole wheat flour	1 tablespoon melted
¼ teaspoon salt	shortening
2 eggs (about ½ cup)	

1. Mix the flours and salt in a bowl. Add a mixture of eggs, milk, and melted shortening; beat until thoroughly blended.
2. Pour batter into ungreased 5-ounce heat-resistant glass custard cups until each is half full.
3. Bake at 450°F 15 minutes; reduce oven temperature to 350°F and bake 35 minutes. Serve hot.

6 POPOVERS

PIZZA STICKS

1 cup all-purpose flour	¼ cup butter or
¼ teaspoon salt	margarine
1 teaspoon oregano	8 oz. pizza flavored
Pinch garlic powder	cheese, shredded

1. Mix the flour, salt, oregano, and garlic powder in a bowl. Cut in butter and cheese with pastry blender or two knives. In the bowl knead mixture with fingertips and form into a ball.
2. Break off bits of dough, about one teaspoonful each; roll between palms of hands to form sticks, 2½ inches long. Put onto an ungreased baking sheet.
3. Bake at 350°F about 15 minutes, or until lightly browned on top. Serve at once.

ABOUT 3 DOZEN STICKS

PARTY PARMESAN SPIRALS

1 cup sifted all-purpose flour	⅓ cup vegetable shortening, all-purpose
½ teaspoon salt	shortening, or lard
¼ cup shredded Parmesan cheese	3 to 3½ tablespoons cold water

1. Combine the flour, salt, and cheese in a large bowl; mix well. Cut in the shortening with a pastry blender or two knives until pieces are the size of small peas.
2. Sprinkle the water gradually over mixture, a teaspoonful at a time. Mix lightly with a fork after each addition. Add only enough water to hold pastry together. Work quickly. Shape into a ball.
3. Flatten pastry ball on a lightly floured surface and roll it into a 10x8-inch rectangle. Using a pastry wheel, cut pastry in half lengthwise. Cutting crosswise, cut ten 1-inch strips from each half. Twist each strip several times, place on ungreased baking sheet, and press ends to baking sheet.
4. Bake at 450°F about 8 minutes, or until delicately browned.
5. Remove spirals to wire rack and immediately sprinkle with *paprika*. Serve warm.

20 CHEESE STICKS

CHEESE STRAWS
These melt-in-your-mouth tidbits are another favorite at the Beaumont Inn in Harrodsburg, Kentucky.

2 cups all-purpose flour	½ cup butter or
1 teaspoon dry mustard	margarine
½ teaspoon baking powder	½ lb. sharp Cheddar cheese, shredded
¼ to ½ teaspoon salt	(about 2½ cups)
Few grains cayenne pepper	

1. Combine the flour, dry mustard, baking powder, salt, and cayenne pepper in a bowl. Cut in the butter and cheese with a pastry blender or two knives until thoroughly mixed.
2. Form into a ball and turn onto a lightly floured surface. Roll out about ⅛ inch thick. Cut into 6x1-inch strips using pastry wheel, if desired. Place on ungreased baking sheet.
3. Bake at 400°F 8 to 10 minutes, or until lightly browned.

3 TO 4 DOZEN CHEESE STRAWS

NOTE: If dough cannot be shaped into a ball, add several teaspoons *cold water* while mixing.

CHAPATTIES
This bread baked on a hot griddle typifies some of the unleavened breads served in the Middle East.

1 cup sifted all-purpose flour	2 tablespoons butter, melted
1 cup whole wheat flour	½ cup water
½ teaspoon salt	

1. Combine the flours and salt in a bowl; mix well and stir in butter and water to make a stiff dough; cover and let rest 1 hour.

2. Turn dough onto a lightly floured surface and knead until elastic. Break off into 1-inch balls and roll out into very thin rounds. (It will be necessary to exert great pressure to roll thin.)

3. Bake on a hot, lightly greased griddle, over low heat, turning frequently, until lightly browned, 3 to 4 minutes. To serve, accompany with *dairy sour cream* or *butter*.   16 CHAPATTIES

Pancakes & Waffles

PANCAKES

The popularity of pancakes and syrup has spread from America's lumber camps to any place where people eat hearty breakfasts.

1½ cups sifted all-purpose flour	2 egg yolks, beaten
1 tablespoon sugar	1⅓ cups milk
1½ teaspoons baking powder	2 tablespoons butter, melted
¼ teaspoon salt	2 egg whites

1. Combine the flour, sugar, baking powder, and salt in a bowl. Add a mixture of egg yolks and milk; beat until well blended and smooth. Beat in the melted butter.

2. Beat egg whites until stiff, not dry, peaks are formed. Spread over batter and fold together.

3. Lightly grease a preheated griddle (or skillet) only if manufacturer so directs. Pour batter onto griddle from a pitcher or end of a large spoon, in small amounts about 4 inches in diameter, leaving at least 1 inch between cakes. Turn pancakes as they become puffy and full of bubbles. Turn only once.

4. Serve immediately with *butter* and warm *maple syrup*.   ABOUT 1 DOZEN GRIDDLECAKES

NOTE: For thinner pancakes add more milk.

BLUEBERRY PANCAKES: Follow recipe for Pancakes. Gently fold *2 cups rinsed and drained fresh blueberries* into batter after folding in beaten egg whites. (If desired, frozen thawed blueberries may be used. Drain them thoroughly after thawing.)

CORNMEAL PANCAKES: Follow recipe for Pancakes. Decrease flour to ¾ cup. Mix *¾ cup yellow cornmeal* with dry ingredients.

BUTTERMILK PANCAKES: Follow recipe for Pancakes. Substitute *½ teaspoon baking soda* for the baking powder and *1⅓ cups buttermilk or sour milk, page 20*, for the milk. Do not separate eggs. Beat the eggs and the buttermilk together.

RYE PANCAKES: Follow recipe for Buttermilk Pancakes. Decrease flour to ¾ cup and mix in *¾ cup rye flour*. Blend *3 tablespoons molasses* into the buttermilk-egg mixture.

HONEY BUTTER PANCAKE TOPPING

Thoroughly blend *⅓ cup honey, ¼ cup softened butter*, and *2 tablespoons coffee beverage*. Mix in *½ cup chopped nuts*. Arrange pancakes side by side on a baking sheet. Spoon about 2 tablespoons of the nut mixture onto each pancake. Place under broiler with topping about 3 inches from source of heat. Broil 2 to 3 minutes, or until topping is lightly browned and bubbly. Serve immediately.

SOUTH-OF-THE-BORDER PANCAKES

2 cups pancake mix	1½ cups milk
1 teaspoon ground cumin	1 cup (8½-oz. can) cream-style corn
½ teaspoon chili powder	½ cup finely chopped olives
1 egg, well beaten	

1. Mix the pancake mix, cumin, and chili powder in a bowl. Add a mixture of egg and milk and beat only until well blended. Add the corn and olives.

2. Pour batter onto heated griddle or into a skillet in small pools about 1½ inches in diameter and at least 1 inch apart. Turn pancakes as they become puffy and full of bubbles. Turn and cook until browned on second side.

3. Brush lightly with *butter or margarine*.
          ABOUT SIXTY-FOUR 1½-INCH PANCAKES

PETITE PANCAKE PUFFS

1½ cups all-purpose flour	1 teaspoon vanilla extract
2 tablespoons sugar	3 tablespoons butter or margarine, melted and cooled completely
1 teaspoon baking powder	
1 teaspoon baking soda	1 cup dark seedless or golden raisins, plumped
1 teaspoon salt	
1¾ cups buttermilk	
3 egg yolks	3 egg whites

1. Blend the flour, sugar, baking powder, baking soda, and salt in a large bowl; set aside.

2. Beat the buttermilk, egg yolks, extract, and butter until well mixed. Add to dry ingredients all at one time; beat thoroughly. Stir in the raisins.

3. Beat the egg whites until stiff, not dry, peaks are formed. Fold into the batter.

4. For each pancake, spoon 1 tablespoon batter onto a heated griddle or skillet and spread into a 3-inch round. Turn each pancake as it becomes full of bubbles; continue baking until lightly browned.

5. Transfer pancakes to a heated platter and immediately brush with *melted butter;* keep warm. Sprinkle pancakes with *confectioners' sugar.* Serve with heated *maple-blended syrup.*

3 DOZEN PANCAKES

CORN GRIDDLECAKES

1 egg, well beaten
½ cup milk
1 teaspoon sugar
¾ teaspoon salt
1 can (17 oz.) cream-style corn
½ cup mashed potato

3 tablespoons butter or margarine, melted
1 tablespoon finely chopped celery
1 tablespoon chopped onion
1½ cups pancake mix

1. Beat the egg, milk, sugar, and salt together until well blended. Stir in a mixture of the corn, potato, butter, celery, and onion. Add all at one time to the pancake mix and beat only until blended.

2. Pour batter onto preheated griddle (greased, if necessary), forming 5-inch rounds. Bake until browned on second side.

3. Serve the griddlecakes hot with *butter or margarine* and with *maple-blended syrup.*

ABOUT 15 GRIDDLECAKES

SMOKIE LINKS 'N' RICE PANCAKES

⅔ cup packaged precooked rice
⅔ cup water
2 egg yolks, fork beaten
¾ cup milk

1 tablespoon cooking or salad oil
1 cup pancake mix
2 egg whites
Little smokie link sausages, halved lengthwise

1. Mix rice and water; set aside.

2. Combine egg yolks, milk, and oil in a bowl. Add pancake mix and stir only until moistened. (Mixture will be lumpy.) Stir in rice.

3. Beat the egg whites until stiff, not dry, peaks are formed. Fold into the batter.

4. For each pancake, pour about ¼ cup batter onto a heated griddle or skillet and spread out the batter slightly. (Lightly grease griddle if so directed by manufacturer.) Arrange 4 to 6 sausage halves, spoke-fashion, in the batter and bake until browned on one side; turn and brown pancake on other side.

5. Stack and keep pancakes warm until ready to serve. Serve with warm *buttered maple-blended syrup* and *grated orange peel.*

ABOUT 1 DOZEN PANCAKES

NOTE: If desired, omit sausages and sprinkle *crisp crumbled bacon* or *shredded Cheddar cheese* over batter before turning pancake to brown second side.

EGG-AND-NUT-FILLED CRÊPES

6 tablespoons mayonnaise
¾ teaspoon salt
½ teaspoon ground coriander
⅛ teaspoon white pepper
Few grains paprika

3 hard-cooked eggs, chopped
½ cup filberts, finely chopped
½ cup diced celery
Crêpes, *below*
Cheese Sauce, *page 100*

1. Blend mayonnaise with a mixture of the salt, coriander, pepper, and paprika; mix in the eggs, filberts, and celery.

2. Spoon about 3 tablespoons of the filling onto each crêpe; roll up. Place crêpes in a shallow baking dish. Cover with the Cheese Sauce.

3. Heat in a 375°F oven about 20 minutes, or until sauce is bubbly.

4 OR 5 SERVINGS

CRÊPES

3 eggs
¼ cup milk
2 tablespoons flour

½ teaspoon salt
Butter

1. Beat eggs slightly in a bowl. Add the milk, flour, and salt; beat until smooth.

2. Lightly butter a 6-inch skillet. Heat to moderately hot. Spoon about 2 tablespoons batter into the skillet and tilt skillet back and forth to spread batter thinly and evenly. Cook each crêpe until lightly browned on one side only. (The crêpes are not turned.)

3. Carefully remove from skillet and place on absorbent paper. Repeat procedure for remaining batter. It should not be necessary to grease skillet for each crêpe.   8 TO 10 CRÊPES

CHEESE SAUCE

1 tablespoon flour	2 tablespoons butter or
½ teaspoon paprika	margarine
½ teaspoon dry mustard	2 cups milk
¼ teaspoon salt	4 oz. sharp Cheddar
½ teaspoon mono-	cheese, finely
sodium glutamate	shredded
Few grains cayenne	
pepper	

1. Blend the flour, paprika, dry mustard, salt, monosodium glutamate, and cayenne pepper into hot butter in a saucepan. Heat until bubbly. Add the milk gradually, stirring constantly. Cook 1 to 2 minutes.
2. Remove from heat; add the cheese and stir until sauce is smooth.   ABOUT 2 CUPS SAUCE

CHEESE BLINTZES

1 lb. cottage cheese	1 cup all-purpose flour
2 eggs	½ cup milk
4 teaspoons sugar	1 tablespoon butter,
1 teaspoon salt	melted
8 saltines, crushed	

1. Mash cottage cheese well or force through a sieve. Beat in 1 egg until mixture is light. Blend in 2 teaspoons sugar and ½ teaspoon salt. Stir in saltines until thoroughly blended; set aside.
2. Combine flour, remaining 2 teaspoons sugar, and ½ teaspoon salt. Beat remaining egg until thick and piled softly; add flour mixture and mix well. Stir in milk and melted butter.
3. Drop 1 tablespoonful batter onto a hot buttered 6- or 7-inch skillet. Fry until brown on one side. Turn out onto a paper towel, fried side up. Repeat process until all batter is used.
4. Place a heaping tablespoon of the cottage cheese mixture in the center of each pancake. Roll up and fry in buttered skillet until browned; or bake in a 350°F oven in a buttered baking dish until browned.
5. Serve hot with *jelly, dairy sour cream,* or sprinkle with *cinnamon* and *sugar.*

                    ABOUT 1½ DOZEN BLINTZES

WAFFLES

2 cups sifted all-	½ teaspoon salt
purpose flour	3 eggs, well beaten
1 tablespoon sugar	2 cups milk
3 teaspoons baking	½ cup butter or
powder	margarine, melted

1. Mix flour, sugar, baking powder, and salt in a large bowl.
2. Beat the eggs and milk together until blended; add along with the melted butter to the dry ingredients and beat only until batter is smooth.
3. Bake in a waffle baker (following manufacturer's directions).   ABOUT 8 SERVINGS

BUTTERMILK WAFFLES: Follow recipe for Waffles. Substitute *2 cups buttermilk* for milk. Decrease baking powder to 2 teaspoons; add *1 teaspoon baking soda* and blend with dry ingredients.

CHEESE WAFFLES: Follow recipe for Waffles. When batter is smooth, blend in *½ cup shredded cheese.*

MAIN-DISH WAFFLES: Follow recipe for Waffles. Sprinkle *2 tablespoons shredded cooked ham* over batter before closing waffle baker.

CHOCOLATE WAFFLES: Follow recipe for Waffles. Generously sprinkle *semisweet chocolate pieces* over batter before closing waffle baker.

RICE WAFFLES

1½ cups sifted all-	2 cups milk
purpose flour	½ cup butter or
1 tablespoon sugar	margarine, melted
3 teaspoons baking	1 cup cooked rice,
powder	cooled
½ teaspoon salt	3 egg whites
3 egg yolks	Maple Whip, *below*

1. Sift flour, sugar, baking powder, and salt together into a large bowl; set aside.
2. Beat egg yolks until thick. Gradually add the milk, mixing well. Blend in melted butter and cooled rice. Add to dry ingredients and mix only until batter is blended.
3. Beat the egg whites until stiff, not dry, peaks are formed. Gently fold into batter.
4. Bake in a waffle baker (following manufacturer's directions).
5. Serve with Maple Whip.   ABOUT 8 SERVINGS

MAPLE WHIP: Using equal parts of *whipped butter or margarine* and *maple-blended syrup,* whip syrup into butter 1 tablespoon at a time; continue to whip just until blended after each addition.

SOUR CREAM WAFFLES

1 cup all-purpose flour	¼ cup butter or margarine, melted and cooled
2 tablespoons sugar	
1 teaspoon baking soda	
1 teaspoon ground cardamom	1 cup dairy sour cream
	1 cup buttermilk
½ teaspoon salt	2 egg yolks, beaten
	2 egg whites

1.   Blend the flour, sugar, baking soda, cardamom, and salt in a large bowl; set aside.
2.   Add the melted butter, sour cream, and buttermilk gradually to the beaten egg yolks; beat until well blended. Add all at one time to the dry ingredients and beat only until smooth.
3.   Beat egg whites until stiff, not dry, peaks are formed. Fold into the batter.
4.   Bake in a waffle baker (following manufacturer's directions).
5.   If desired, blend sifted *confectioners' sugar* and *ground cardamom* to taste and sprinkle lightly over waffles.   4 TO 6 WAFFLES

SPECIALTY WAFFLES

2 cups sifted cake flour	2 eggs, separated
	1¼ cups milk
2 tablespoons sugar	5 tablespoons melted butter or margarine, cooled
1 tablespoon baking powder	
½ teaspoon salt	

1.   Combine the flour, sugar, baking powder, and salt; mix well and set aside.
2.   Beat egg yolks until thick; beat in the milk and melted butter. Add to dry ingredients and stir only until blended.
3.   Beat egg whites until stiff, not dry, peaks are formed. Gently fold into the batter. (Turn batter into a pitcher for easy pouring.)
4.   Bake in a waffle baker (following manufacturer's directions).
5.   Serve waffles immediately with *butter or margarine.*   ABOUT 8 WAFFLE SECTIONS

CORNMEAL WAFFLES: Follow recipe for Specialty Waffles. Decrease flour to 1 cup and combine ¾ *cup yellow cornmeal* with dry ingredients.

BANANA WAFFLES: Follow recipe for Specialty Waffles. Fold *1½ cups diced ripe banana* into batter before folding in the beaten egg whites.

WHIPPED CREAM WAFFLES

A Sunday breakfast or brunch will become a gala occasion when these extra rich waffles appear.

1½ cups all-purpose flour	¼ cup butter, melted
	4 egg yolks, well beaten
½ cup sugar	
3 teaspoons baking powder	1 cup heavy cream, whipped
½ teaspoon salt	4 egg whites

1.   Combine flour, sugar, baking powder, and salt in a bowl; mix well.
2.   Blend butter into beaten egg yolks, then fold whipped cream into egg yolk mixture. Add to dry ingredients and stir only until blended.
3.   Beat egg whites until stiff, not dry, peaks are formed. Gently fold into batter.
4.   Bake in a waffle baker (following manufacturer's directions).
5.   Serve immediately with *butter or margarine* and warm *maple syrup;* or sprinkle waffles with *confectioners' sugar* and top with *peach slices.*
ABOUT 4 LARGE WAFFLES

Deep-Fried Quick Breads

FUNNEL CAKES

1¼ cups all-purpose flour	¼ teaspoon salt
	1 egg, beaten
2 tablespoons sugar	⅔ cup milk
1 teaspoon baking powder	Fat for deep frying heated to 375°F

1.   Mix the flour, sugar, baking powder, and salt in a bowl. Add a mixture of egg and milk, beating until batter is smooth.
2.   Holding finger over bottom of a funnel having a ⅜- to ½-inch hole, fill funnel with batter. Hold funnel as near surface of heated fat as possible; remove finger and drop batter into hot fat, using a circular movement from center outward to form a spiral cake about 3 inches in diameter. Immediately replace finger on bottom of funnel; then form other cakes (as many as will float uncrowded).
3.   Fry until cakes are puffy and golden brown,

turning once. Lift from fat with a slotted spoon and drain for a few seconds before removing to absorbent paper.

4. Sift *confectioners' sugar* lightly over cakes and serve warm. 2 TO 2½ DOZEN CAKES

NOTE: A candy patty funnel with its regulating stick is very helpful to use when making funnel cakes.

RYE CAKES

3 cups rye flour	2 eggs, beaten
1 teaspoon baking soda	¼ cup molasses
1 teaspoon salt	Fat for deep frying
1½ cups sour milk or buttermilk	heated to 365°F

1. Mix the rye flour, baking soda, and salt together in a bowl. Blend sour milk, eggs, and molasses. Add to dry ingredients and beat until blended.

2. Drop batter by teaspoonfuls into hot fat and fry until browned, about 3 minutes; turn during frying. Drain on absorbent paper. Serve warm.

ABOUT 5 DOZEN CAKES

ROSETTES

1 cup all-purpose flour	1 cup milk
2 teaspoons sugar	Fat for deep frying
½ teaspoon salt	heated to 365°F
2 eggs slightly beaten	

1. Combine the flour, sugar, and salt in a bowl; mix well and add a mixture of eggs and milk. Beat with a wire whisk or wooden spoon until very smooth. If necessary, strain batter through a fine sieve to remove any lumps and allow batter to stand until it is free from air bubbles.

2. Heat rosette iron in hot fat about 1 minute and drain well. Dip hot iron into batter so that batter comes about two thirds to three fourths up side of mold. Quickly immerse in hot fat and fry until batter clinging to iron mold has set but has not browned. Immediately remove rosette from mold with a fork. Repeat process until there is one uncrowded layer of rosettes in the fat.

3. Fry 1 to 2 minutes, or until rosettes are golden brown, turning with a fork to brown evenly. Remove from fat with slotted spoon. Drain over fat before transferring to absorbent paper.

4. Repeat steps 2 and 3 until all batter is used. Make sure that rosette iron is hot before dipping into batter. Batter will not cling to a cool iron.

5. Serve rosettes for dessert sprinkled with *Vanilla Confectioners' Sugar, page 558.*

ABOUT 3 DOZEN ROSETTES

TIMBALE CASES: Follow recipe for Rosettes, using a timbale iron instead of rosette iron. Fry cases one at a time; drain upside down over fat, remove to absorbent paper and gently remove case from mold with fork. Fill with creamed meat or vegetables.

PILLOW CAKES
A favorite south-of-the-border recipe.

4 cups all-purpose flour	¼ teaspoon vanilla
4 teaspoons baking powder	extract
	¾ cup sugar
Few grains salt	4 eggs (about 1 cup)
⅔ cup vegetable shortening	Fat for deep frying heated to 365°F

1. Combine the flour, baking powder, and salt; mix well and set aside.

2. Cream the shortening with extract and sugar until thoroughly blended. Add eggs, one at a time, beating until fluffy after each addition. Add flour gradually, mixing only until thoroughly blended.

3. Using half of the dough at a time, roll on a lightly floured surface into a 15-inch square about ⅛ inch thick. Cut into 3-inch squares.

4. Fry uncrowded in the hot fat for 1 to 2 minutes, or until lightly browned, turning twice. Lift from fat with slotted spoon and drain a few seconds before removing to absorbent paper. While still warm, sift *confectioners' sugar* over cakes.

ABOUT 4 DOZEN CAKES

HUSH PUPPIES
These morsels, according to Southern colonial folklore, were originally made at fish-fries and on hunting trips to feed to the hungry, howling hounds to quiet them—hence "hush puppy."

2 cups yellow cornmeal	1¼ cups buttermilk
1 tablespoon flour	¾ teaspoon Angostura
1 tablespoon sugar	bitters
1 teaspoon baking powder	1 egg, well beaten
	Fat for deep frying
¾ teaspoon baking soda	heated to 375°F
¼ cup finely chopped onion	

1. Mix the cornmeal, flour, sugar, baking powder, and baking soda in a bowl. Add the onion and a

mixture of the buttermilk, bitters, and egg; mix until well blended. Using about a heaping tablespoon for each, form into small cakes.

2. Put into the hot fat only as many cakes at one time as will float uncrowded one layer deep. Fry 3 to 4 minutes, or until well browned. Turn cakes with tongs or a fork as they rise to the surface and several times during cooking (do not pierce). Lift cakes from fat with slotted spoon and drain before removing to absorbent paper. Serve hot.

ABOUT 1½ DOZEN HUSH PUPPIES

APPLE FRITTERS
This recipe is from the Ox Yoke Inn, Amana, Iowa.

1 cup all-purpose flour	6 large ripe apples,
2 tablespoons sugar	pared and cored
¼ teaspoon salt	3 tablespoons lemon
⅔ cup milk	juice
2 eggs, separated	Fat for deep frying
2 tablespoons butter,	heated to 365°F
melted	

1. Combine flour, sugar, and salt in a bowl; mix well. Add a mixture of milk, egg yolks, and melted butter; beat with electric or hand rotary beater until smooth.
2. Beat egg whites until stiff, not dry, peaks are formed and fold into batter.
3. Cut apples into ½-inch slices; toss with the lemon juice. Coat each slice with batter.
4. Fry in heated fat until nicely browned. Drain and sprinkle generously with *confectioners' sugar*.

ABOUT 8 SERVINGS

STRAWBERRY FRITTERS
These petite fritters are a very special treat served at breakfast or brunch.

1 jar (12 oz.) apricot	2 cups ground or grated
preserves	filberts or walnuts
2 pts. fresh straw-	2 eggs, slightly beaten
berries (whole and	2 cups finely crushed
unhulled), rinsed and	saltines
completely dried	Fat for deep frying
	heated to 365°F

1. Force the preserves through a sieve.
2. Gently but firmly grasp each berry by the hull; dip in preserves. Using a fork to help coat, cover berry up to hull with the preserves. Allow excess to drip through tines of fork.
3. Coat with nuts, still holding hull. Shake gently. Dip in beaten egg, smoothing off excess, and then coat with cracker crumbs up to hull. Place on wire racks and chill 30 minutes to set coating.
4. Fry berries, 6 or 8 at a time, in the hot fat until golden brown (less than 1 minute). Be sure that temperature of fat is heated to 365°F after each frying. Carefully remove with slotted spoon. Drain on paper towel-lined rack.
5. Serve warm with *confectioners' sugar*, a small individual bowl for each serving, if desired.

6 TO 8 SERVINGS

BREADS FROM MIXES

Hot Roll Mix

FRUIT-FILLED COFFEE RING

1 pkg. hot roll mix	⅓ cup chopped dried
1½ teaspoons grated	apricots
lemon peel	⅓ cup chopped prunes
¼ cup butter or	½ cup chopped walnuts
margarine, melted	Melted butter or
3 tablespoons sugar	margarine
1 cup golden raisins	Orange Glaze, *page 104*

1. Prepare hot roll mix according to package directions; add lemon peel with the dry mix. Let dough rise according to directions.

2. Mix butter with the sugar, raisins, apricots, prunes, and walnuts; set aside.
3. When dough is doubled, punch down and turn onto a lightly floured surface; roll into a 16x12-inch rectangle. Top dough evenly with fruit filling; roll up, starting with long edge. Snip off both ends on a diagonal; reserve end pieces for center.
4. Cut the roll diagonally into 12 slices; arrange slices in a circle on a large greased baking sheet with pointed ends out and each slice overlapping slightly. Place reserved ends in center; brush top with melted butter. Cover; let rise in a warm place until doubled.
5. Bake at 350°F about 30 minutes, or until golden brown. While still warm, spread with Orange Glaze

and, if desired, sprinkle with *grated orange peel*.

1 LARGE COFFEE RING

ORANGE GLAZE: Blend *1 cup confectioners' sugar* with *2 tablespoons orange juice* until smooth.

PETITE ORANGE-CURRANT LOAVES

1 pkg. hot roll mix	⅓ cup dried currants
⅔ cup chopped candied orange peel	Melted butter or margarine

1. Prepare hot roll mix according to package directions adding orange peel and currants with the dry mix. Let dough rise according to directions.
2. When dough is doubled, punch down, turn onto a lightly floured surface and divide into 4 equal portions.
3. Roll each portion into a 7x4-inch rectangle; beginning with shorter side, roll up dough; pinch edges and ends to seal. Place sealed-edge down in 4 greased 5x3x2-inch loaf pans; brush tops with *melted butter*. Cover; let rise in a warm place until doubled.
4. Bake at 375°F 20 to 25 minutes, or until golden brown. Remove loaves from pans to wire racks; turn right side up. While still hot, spread tops with desired *glaze*.   4 SMALL LOAVES

DEVILISH DANISH

¾ cup firm butter or margarine	3 cans (2¼ oz. each) deviled ham
1 pkg. hot roll mix	8 teaspoons orange marmalade
½ cup warm water	
1 egg, slightly beaten	

1. Cut the butter into ¼ cup of the hot roll mix flour mixture. Chill thoroughly, about 1 hour.
2. Soften yeast in the warm water. Add with the egg to the remaining flour mixture. Blend well, forming a stiff dough. Roll out on a lightly floured surface into a 12-inch square.
3. Roll the chilled butter-flour mixture between 2 pieces of waxed paper into a 10x4-inch rectangle. Remove top piece of paper and invert onto half the dough. Remove paper. Fold remaining half of dough over butter, press edges to seal and roll into a 12-inch square. Repeat folding and rolling 3 times. Fold again and chill dough about 1 hour.
4. Roll dough into a 16-inch square and cut into 4-inch squares. Spoon about 2 teaspoons deviled ham

and ½ teaspoon orange marmalade in the center of each. Bring opposite corners together, pressing edges to seal. Place about 2 inches apart on ungreased baking sheets. Brush with *cream* and top with a few *slivered almonds*. Cover; let rise in a warm place 30 minutes.
5. Bake at 375°F 18 to 22 minutes, or until pastries are golden brown.   16 PASTRIES

SUGARED DOUGHNUT SURPRISES

1 pkg. hot roll mix	Walnut-stuffed dates or semisweet chocolate pieces
1 tablespoon sugar	
½ teaspoon grated lemon peel	Fat for deep frying heated to 375°F

1. Prepare hot roll mix according to package directions, adding sugar and lemon peel to yeast mixture.
2. When dough has doubled, punch down and shape into 1-inch balls by molding dough around a date or about 10 semisweet-chocolate pieces. If necessary, lightly flour hands to prevent dough from sticking.
3. Place balls on lightly floured baking sheets. Cover; let rise in a warm place until doubled, about 30 minutes.
4. Fry uncrowded in hot fat 5 minutes, or until browned, turning once. Remove with a slotted spoon, drain over fat, and place on absorbent paper. Drizzle with *Confectioners' Sugar Icing III, page 585*, and serve warm.

ABOUT 2 DOZEN DOUGHNUTS

MINIATURE BUTTER CREAM LOAVES

Serve individual loaves on small bread boards with knives for morning coffee or a special brunch.

1 pkg. hot roll mix	1 cup chopped nuts
Butter Cream Filling, page 105	

1. Follow hot roll mix directions on package through first rising.
2. Meanwhile, prepare Butter Cream Filling and spread about 1 tablespoon of the filling over bottom and sides of each of four 5x3x2-inch loaf pans. Cover remaining filling; set aside.
3. When dough is doubled, punch down, turn onto a lightly floured surface and divide into 4 equal portions. Roll each portion into an 8x4-inch rectangle.

4. Reserve ¼ cup filling for topping. Spread one fourth of remaining filling over each dough rectangle and sprinkle with one fourth of the nuts. Beginning with a shorter side, tightly roll up dough; pinch edges and ends to seal.

5. Place sealed edge down in prepared pans. Brush tops with *melted butter or margarine*. Cover; let rise in a warm place until doubled.

6. Bake at 375°F 20 to 25 minutes, or until golden brown.

7. Immediately remove loaves from pans and set on wire racks. Spread reserved filling over hot loaves. 4 SMALL LOAVES

BUTTER CREAM FILLING: Prepare 1 *package vanilla- or chocolate-flavored butter cream frosting mix* according to package directions adding an additional *2 tablespoons butter* and *½ teaspoon vanilla extract* with the butter.

Biscuit Mix

FROSTED BROWN SUGAR BUBBLE LOAF

4 cups biscuit mix	2 tablespoons grated
¼ cup firmly packed	lemon peel
brown sugar	1 cup milk
1 teaspoon ground	1 egg, well beaten
cinnamon	½ cup butter or
½ teaspoon ground mace	margarine, melted
Few grains salt	½ teaspoon vanilla
¼ cup coarsely chopped	extract
toasted almonds	Coffee Glaze, *below*
¼ cup firmly packed	
brown sugar	

1. Mix biscuit mix with ¼ cup brown sugar, cinnamon, mace, and salt thoroughly; set aside.

2. Combine almonds, remaining ¼ cup brown sugar, and lemon peel; mix well.

3. Blend milk, egg, ¼ cup melted butter, and the extract. Make a well in the center of the dry ingredients and add the liquid. Stir with a fork until dough follows fork. Gently form dough into a ball and turn onto a lightly floured surface. Knead lightly 10 to 15 times.

4. Shape dough into 52 small balls, about 1 inch in diameter. Form three layers of balls, 18 in each of the first two and 12 in the third, in a greased 9x5x3-inch loaf pan, brushing each layer with some of remaining melted butter and sprinkling with a third

of the nut mixture. Place 4 balls down the center and brush with any remaining butter.

5. Bake at 350°F about 45 minutes, or until loaf is golden brown.

6. Remove from pan and drizzle with Coffee Glaze. Serve hot; pull apart with two forks. ONE 9x5-INCH LOAF

COFFEE GLAZE: Stir about *2½ teaspoons double or triple strength coffee* into *¾ cup confectioners' sugar* until smooth and of desired consistency.

BUTTER BATTER BREAD

2 eggs, well beaten	2 cups biscuit mix
1 can (10½ oz.) condensed cream of mushroom soup	¼ cup butter or margarine
	¼ cup shredded
2 tablespoons cooking or salad oil	Parmesan cheese
	Celery or sesame seed
1 teaspoon instant minced onion	

1. Combine eggs, soup, and oil; mix well.

2. Stir instant onion into biscuit mix in a bowl and make a well in the center. Add the soup mixture and stir until just blended.

3. Heat butter in a heavy 8-inch skillet with heat-resistant handle. Spoon in the batter and top with cheese and celery seed.

4. Bake at 400°F about 25 minutes. Serve hot, cut in wedge-shaped pieces. ABOUT 6 SERVINGS

KUMQUAT COFFEE CAKE

¼ cup biscuit mix	2 tablespoons kumquat
¼ cup sugar	syrup
½ teaspoon ground	1 teaspoon orange
cinnamon	extract
½ teaspoon ground	1 teaspoon lemon
nutmeg	extract
2 tablespoons butter	¼ cup milk
2 cups biscuit mix	¼ cup finely chopped
¾ cup sugar	preserved kumquats
¼ cup butter, softened	(remove seeds)
1 egg	⅓ cup finely chopped
½ cup milk	pecans

1. Mix the ¼ cup biscuit mix, ¼ cup sugar, cinnamon, and nutmeg in a bowl. Using a pastry blender or two knives, cut in the 2 tablespoons butter until mixture is crumbly; set aside for topping.

2. Combine the 2 cups biscuit mix and ¾ cup sugar in a bowl. Mix in ¼ cup butter, egg, and ½ cup milk. Beat vigorously 1 minute.

3. Beat kumquat syrup, the extracts, and ¼ cup milk into the batter, beating about ½ minute. Mix in kumquats and pecans. Turn mixture into a greased and floured 8x8x2-inch baking pan. Sprinkle topping evenly over batter.

4. Bake at 350°F 40 to 45 minutes, or until cake tests done.

5. Remove from oven; cool on rack 10 to 15 minutes. While cake is still warm, drizzle with *Speedy Orange Icing, below,* and cut into squares.

ONE 8-INCH COFFEE CAKE

SPEEDY ORANGE ICING: Put *⅔ cup confectioners' sugar* into a bowl. Blend in a mixture of *1 tablespoon milk* and *¾ teaspoon orange extract.*

QUICK 'N' EASY JAM BRAID

2 cups biscuit mix
¼ cup butter, cut in small pieces
3 oz. cream cheese, cut in small pieces
¼ cup milk
⅔ cup whole strawberry preserves

1. Put biscuit mix into a bowl; using a pastry blender, cut in butter and cheese until pieces are the size of peas.

2. Gradually add milk, blending with a fork. (Mixture will be lumpy and crumbly.) Turn dough onto a lightly greased baking sheet and roll into a 14x8-inch rectangle.

3. Evenly spread strawberry preserves through center of rectangle in a 2-inch wide, lengthwise strip. Cut dough with a knife into 1-inch strips from the outside edges to the filling. Braid the strips over filling by lifting one strip from each side and crossing diagonally in center.

4. Bake at 425°F about 15 minutes, or until lightly browned. Serve warm.   6 SERVINGS

PARMESAN QUICK BREAD

3 cups biscuit mix
¾ cup yellow cornmeal
¼ cup sugar
¾ cup shredded Parmesan cheese
1¼ cups buttermilk
2 eggs, beaten

1. Combine biscuit mix, cornmeal, sugar, and cheese in a large bowl.

2. Mix buttermilk and eggs; add to dry ingredients and stir only until blended. Turn into a buttered 9x5x3-inch loaf pan; spread evenly to edges.

3. Bake at 350°F 40 to 50 minutes, or until bread tests done.

4. Remove from pan set on a wire rack to cool completely.   1 LOAF BREAD

CHEDDAR CHEESE QUICK BREAD: Follow recipe for Parmesan Quick Bread. Increase biscuit mix to 3¾ cups. Substitute *1½ cups shredded sharp Cheddar cheese* for Parmesan. Cook *6 slices bacon* until crisp. Drain and crumble. Add bacon to the bowl with dry ingredients.

SPICY PICKLE PINWHEEL BREAD

2 cups biscuit mix
½ cup drained sweet pickle relish
8 oz. cream cheese, softened
2 tablespoons milk
¼ teaspoon salt
⅛ teaspoon black pepper
½ cup grated carrot
⅓ cup finely chopped green pepper
⅓ cup chopped scallions including tops

1. Prepare biscuit mix as directed on package for rolled biscuits.

2. Roll into a 14x11-inch rectangle. Spread with relish, then roll as for jelly roll, and set on a greased baking sheet.

3. Bake at 450°F about 15 minutes, or until lightly browned.

4. Meanwhile, blend cream cheese, 2 tablespoons milk, salt, and pepper. Stir in vegetables. Set aside.

5. Remove bread from oven to wire rack and cool on baking sheet about 10 minutes. Cut into ¾-inch crosswise slices. Spread slices with the cream cheese-vegetable mixture. Serve immediately.

12 TO 16 SLICES

SALT STICKS

1 pkg. active dry yeast
¾ cup warm water
2½ cups biscuit mix
1 egg yolk, fork beaten
Coarse salt (about 1 tablespoon)
Caraway or sesame seed (about 2 tablespoons)

1. Soften yeast in the warm water in a bowl. Add biscuit mix and beat vigorously.

2. Turn dough onto a lightly floured surface; knead until smooth (about 20 times). Shape into a ball; cover and let rest 5 to 10 minutes.

3.   Using half of dough at a time, roll each half into a rectangle about 16x12-inches; cut into 4-inch squares.

4.   Start at a corner and roll up each square diagonally to opposite corner. Place on a lightly greased baking sheet. Brush with egg yolk; sprinkle with coarse salt and caraway seed. Let rise in a warm place until doubled, about 1 hour.

5.   Bake at 400°F about 15 minutes.

2 DOZEN SALT STICKS

NEW MOON YEAST ROLLS

1 pkg. active dry yeast	2 tablespoons butter,
⅔ cup warm water	softened
3 cups biscuit mix	4 oz. (about ½ cup)
2 tablespoons sugar	almond paste
1 egg, beaten	

1.   Soften yeast in the warm water in a large bowl. Add biscuit mix, sugar, and egg; beat vigorously until well mixed.

2.   Turn dough onto a lightly floured surface and knead until smooth (about 20 times). Roll dough into a 10-inch square and spread softened butter over half of dough. Fold unbuttered half over buttered portion; press edges to seal.

3.   Roll dough into a 12-inch round and crumble almond paste evenly over surface. Cut dough into 16 wedge-shaped pieces. Beginning at wide end, roll toward point.

4.   Place each on a greased baking sheet with point underneath; curve into a crescent. Cover; let rise in a warm place until doubled, about 1 hour.

5.   Bake at 375°F 12 to 15 minutes, or until golden brown. If desired, brush with *melted butter* immediately after removing from oven. Serve warm.

16 ROLLS

CRESCENT CHEESE ROLLS: Follow recipe for New Moon Yeast Rolls. Add ¼ *to* ½ *cup finely shredded Cheddar cheese* with the biscuit mix.

ROSEMARY ROLLS

1 pkg. active dry yeast	¼ cup shredded
¾ cup warm water	Parmesan cheese
2½ cups biscuit mix	1¼ teaspoons crushed
	rosemary

1.   Soften yeast in the warm water in a bowl. Blend in biscuit mix, cheese, and rosemary; beat vigorously.

2.   Turn dough onto a lightly floured surface and shape into a ball. Cover and let rest 5 minutes. Form into a roll about 12 inches long. Cut into 12 equal pieces and shape each piece into a smooth ball.

3.   Place each in a greased 2¾-inch muffin-pan well. Cover; let rise in a warm place until doubled, about 1 hour.

4.   Bake at 400°F about 15 minutes.   1 DOZEN ROLLS

SESAME SEED TWISTS

2 cups biscuit mix	Melted butter
¼ cup butter, chilled	2 tablespoons toasted
	sesame seed

1.   Prepare biscuit mix as directed on package for rolled biscuits. Roll on lightly floured surface into a 12-inch square about ⅛ inch thick.

2.   Thinly slice and quickly place about 3 tablespoons of the chilled butter onto half of dough; fold other half over it. With rolling pin gently press down and seal the open edges. Repeat procedure using remaining chilled butter; fold other half over forming a 6-inch square. Chill about 1 hour.

3.   Roll dough into a 12-inch square. Divide into halves and set one half in refrigerator.

4.   Brush surface with melted butter. Sprinkle with some of the sesame seed. Cut into twelve 6x1-inch strips. Twist each strip and place on an ungreased baking sheet, pressing ends. Brush with a mixture of *1 egg yolk* and *1 teaspoon milk.* Sprinkle with sesame seed. Repeat.

5.   Bake at 425°F about 10 minutes.

2 DOZEN TWISTS

PARMESAN-NUT STICKS

½ cup milk	½ cup shredded Parme-
2 tablespoons cooking	san cheese
or salad oil	¼ cup chopped salted
2 cups biscuit mix	peanuts
	1 teaspoon garlic salt

1.   Add milk and oil to biscuit mix. Stir with a fork until dry ingredients are moistened.

2.   On a floured surface, roll dough into an 8-inch square. Cut into sixteen 4x1-inch strips. Roll strips in a mixture of the cheese and peanuts. Place on a greased baking sheet. Sprinkle with garlic salt.

3.   Bake at 425°F 10 to 12 minutes, or until golden.

16 CHEESE STICKS

PARMESAN CHEESE FANS

⅓ cup butter, softened
½ cup shredded Parme-
san cheese

1 tablespoon minced
parsley
2 cups biscuit mix
Melted butter

1.   Mix the butter, cheese, and parsley thoroughly. Set aside.
2.   Prepare biscuit mix according to directions on package for rolled biscuits. Roll dough into a 12x10-inch rectangle about ¼ inch thick. Cut into 5 strips. Spread evenly with the butter mixture.
3.   Stack the strips. Cut into 12 sections. Place, cut side up, in greased 2½-inch muffin-pan wells. Brush tops with melted butter.
4.   Bake at 450°F 10 to 15 minutes, or until golden brown.   1 DOZEN CHEESE FANS

HOT CROSS FRUIT MUFFINS

These quick-to-mix muffins resemble the traditional hot cross buns in flavor and appearance.

2 cups biscuit mix
3 tablespoons sugar
½ to ¾ teaspoon ground
cardamom
½ cup dark or golden
raisins
¼ cup chopped citron

1 egg, well beaten
⅔ cup milk
2 tablespoons melted
shortening, or
cooking or salad oil
Frosting, *below*

1.   Mix the biscuit mix, sugar, and cardamom in a bowl; stir in the raisins and citron.
2.   Blend the egg, milk, and shortening thoroughly. Add to dry ingredients; stir quickly and lightly until dry ingredients are barely moistened. Spoon batter into greased 2½-inch muffin-pan wells.
3.   Bake at 400°F about 15 minutes.
4.   Meanwhile, prepare Frosting.
5.   Remove muffins from pan to wire rack; cool slightly. Then form a cross on each muffin, using the frosting.   1 DOZEN MUFFINS
FROSTING: Beat together until smooth ½ *cup plus 2 tablespoons confectioners' sugar, 2 teaspoons water, ¼ teaspoon vanilla extract, and 1 tablespoon almond paste.*

DEVILED HAM MUFFINS PETITE

½ cup tomato sauce
½ teaspoon instant
minced onion
½ cup shredded sharp
Cheddar cheese
1 can (2¼ oz.)
deviled ham

1 egg, slightly beaten
2 cups biscuit mix
2 tablespoons sugar
1 egg, well beaten
⅔ cup milk

1.   Combine tomato sauce and onion in a saucepan and bring to boiling over low heat. Stir in cheese and ham; heat until cheese is melted and mixture is well blended.
2.   Stir some of the mixture into slightly beaten egg and return to saucepan, stirring vigorously. Cook over low heat, stirring constantly, about 3 minutes. Set aside to cool.
3.   Combine biscuit mix and sugar in a bowl. Add a mixture of remaining egg and milk to dry ingredients; stir with spoon until blended.
4.   Spoon 1 teaspoon of batter into each greased 2-inch muffin-pan well. Add 1 teaspoon of deviled ham mixture. Fill wells about ¾ full with batter.
5.   Bake at 400°F 15 to 18 minutes, or until lightly browned.   ABOUT 2 DOZEN SMALL MUFFINS

PRUNE TWISTS

2 cups biscuit mix
¼ cup firmly packed
brown sugar
¼ teaspoon ground
cinnamon
6 tablespoons butter

½ cup finely cut prunes
½ cup finely shredded
sharp Cheddar cheese
½ cup cream (about)
1 cup chopped walnuts

1.   Mix biscuit mix, brown sugar, and cinnamon in a bowl. Cut in butter with a pastry blender or two knives until particles are the size of rice kernels. Mix in prunes and cheese. Pour in the cream; stir with a fork until dough follows fork.
2.   Gently form dough into a ball and place on a lightly floured surface. Roll into a 12x6-inch rectangle. Cut into twelve 6x1-inch strips. With hands, roll each strip to make it about 8 inches long. Brush with *milk*; roll in the chopped walnuts.
3.   On greased baking sheet, shape each strip into a "figure 8," overlapping ends at center. Press a *candied cherry* onto center of each; sprinkle with *sugar.*
4.   Bake at 400°F about 10 minutes. Serve warm.
                                    1 DOZEN TWISTS

PEACHY RICH BREAKFAST SLICES

3 cups biscuit mix
1 cup flour or biscuit
   mix
1 cup lightly packed
   dark brown sugar
¾ cup butter or
   margarine
1 can (29 oz.) cling
   peach slices, drained
6 egg yolks
3 tablespoons sugar
6 tablespoons cream

1.   Prepare biscuit mix for biscuit dough as direct-ed on the package. Spread dough evenly over bot-tom and slightly up sides of a lightly greased 15x10x1-inch jelly roll pan.
2.   With fork, mix flour with brown sugar and cut in butter. Spoon evenly over dough in pan. Arrange peach slices in rows over crumb mixture.
3.   Bake at 375°F about 20 minutes, or until lightly browned around edge.
4.   Meanwhile, beat together the egg yolks, sugar, and cream. Pour evenly over peaches and continue baking about 10 minutes, or until custard is set. Serve warm, cut into slices.   ABOUT 24 SLICES

OLIVE-SHRIMP PIZZA

This pizza uses ingredients different from those usually found in packages.

Sauce, *below*
1 can (8 oz.) sliced
   mushrooms, drained
Pizza Dough, *below*
1 can (16 oz.) pitted
   ripe olives, drained
   and halved
½ lb. cooked deveined
   shrimp
1 teaspoon oregano,
   crushed
2½ cups shredded
   Cheddar cheese

1.   Mix mushrooms into sauce. Spread one quarter of the sauce over each dough round. Arrange over each, one quarter of the olives and shrimp. Sprin-kle tops evenly with oregano and cheese.
2.   Bake at 425°F 15 to 20 minutes, or until crust is browned.   FOUR 8-INCH PIZZAS
SAUCE: Mix in a saucepan *2 cans (8 ounces each) tomato sauce, 1 onion, chopped, 1 clove garlic, minced, ¼ teaspoon salt, ⅛ teaspoon seasoned pepper, ¼ teaspoon crushed oregano, and 1 bay leaf.* Bring to boiling, reduce heat, and simmer 5 minutes. Discard bay leaf.
PIZZA DOUGH: Sprinkle *1 package active dry yeast* over *⅔ cup warm water* in a bowl and stir until dis-solved. Add *2½ cups biscuit mix;* beat until well mixed. Turn onto a surface lightly sprinkled with

biscuit mix. Knead until smooth (about 20 times). Divide dough into fourths; roll each into an 8-inch round. Put rounds onto ungreased large baking sheets. Shape edges by pressing dough between thumb and forefinger.

CHEESY SAUSAGE PIZZA

1 pkg. active dry yeast
¾ cup warm water
2½ cups biscuit mix
1 can (28 oz.) Italian-
   style tomatoes,
   drained and sieved
1 can (6 oz.) tomato
   paste
8 oz. mozzarella cheese,
   thinly sliced
½ cup olive oil
¼ cup shredded
   Parmesan cheese
2 teaspoons oregano
1 teaspoon salt
½ teaspoon black
   pepper
2 lbs. hot Italian
   sausage

1.   Soften yeast in the warm water in a bowl. Add biscuit mix; beat until well mixed. Turn onto a lightly floured surface. Knead until smooth (about 20 times).
2.   Divide dough into halves. Roll each half into a 15-inch round. Put each round of dough onto an ungreased large baking sheet; shape edge by press-ing dough between thumb and forefinger to make ridge.
3.   Combine sieved tomatoes and tomato paste. Spread ½ of mixture over each round of dough; top each with ½ of the Mozzarella cheese. Sprinkle ½ of olive oil, Parmesan cheese, oregano, salt, and pepper over each round. Remove sausage from cas-ing and crumble over tops of pizzas.
4.   Bake at 425°F 15 to 20 minutes, or until crust is browned. To serve, cut into wedges.   2 LARGE PIZZAS
MUSHROOM PIZZA: Follow recipe for Cheesy Sau-sage Pizza. Omit sausage. Before baking, top each pizza with *1 cup (8-ounce can) drained mushrooms.*

Other Mixes

BACON UPSIDE-DOWN CORNBREAD

4 slices bacon, cut in
   thirds
1 pkg. corn muffin or
   cornbread mix

1.   Arrange bacon pieces on bottom of an 8x8x2-inch baking pan.
2.   Prepare mix according to directions on pack-

age. Spoon batter into the pan over the bacon and carefully spread to corners.

3. Bake as directed on package for cornbread.

4. Remove from oven; cool 2 minutes on wire rack. Loosen cornbread from pan and invert on a baking sheet. Set under broiler about 4 inches from source of heat and broil about 1 minute, or until bacon is crisp.   ONE 8-INCH SQUARE CORNBREAD

BANANA CORNBREAD

1 pkg. corn muffin or cornbread mix
⅓ cup sugar
⅛ teaspoon baking powder
2 medium-sized bananas having brown-flecked peel, peeled and mashed (about 1¾ cups)

2⅔ tablespoons lukewarm water
1 egg, well beaten
¼ teaspoon vanilla extract

1. Combine mix, sugar, baking powder, and a *few grains salt* in a bowl. Mix well and stir in remaining ingredients. Turn into a greased 8x8x2-inch baking pan and spread evenly.

2. Bake at 425°F about 20 minutes.

ONE 8-INCH SQUARE CORNBREAD

BANANA CORN MUFFINS: Follow recipe for Banana Cornbread. Spoon batter into greased 2½-inch muffin pan wells; fill each ¾ full. Bake at 425°F 15 to 18 minutes.   ABOUT 1 DOZEN MUFFINS

CHERRY CORN MUFFINS

1 cup corn muffin mix
½ cup biscuit mix
¼ cup finely chopped maraschino cherries, well drained

1 egg, well beaten
⅔ cup undiluted evaporated milk
2 tablespoons cooking or salad oil

1. Combine the mixes and cherries in a bowl; set aside.

2. Blend the beaten egg thoroughly with the evaporated milk and oil. Add to dry ingredients; stir quickly and lightly until dry ingredients are barely moistened.

3. Spoon batter into greased 2½-inch muffin-pan wells.

4. Bake at 400°F about 17 minutes, or until golden brown   14 MUFFINS

BLUEBERRY-BANANA NUT BREAD

2 cups pancake mix
½ cup sugar
½ teaspoon baking powder
½ cup chopped pecans
1 egg, slightly beaten
¼ cup drained canned blueberries

1 cup mashed bananas (about 2 medium-sized with all yellow or brown-flecked peel)
2 tablespoons milk
¼ cup melted shortening

1. Mix pancake mix, sugar, baking powder, and pecans in a bowl; set aside.

2. Combine egg, blueberries, bananas, milk, and shortening. Add to dry ingredients; stir only enough to moisten dry ingredients. Turn into a greased 9x5x3-inch loaf pan and spread evenly.

3. Bake at 350°F about 35 minutes, or until bread tests done.

4. Cool 10 minutes in pan on wire rack. Remove from pan and cool completely.   1 LOAF NUT BREAD

FRANKFURTER QUICK BREAD

⅓ cup sugar
¼ cup cooking or salad oil
⅓ cup orange juice
1 teaspoon prepared mustard

2 cups pancake mix
¼ cup cooking or salad oil
1 egg, slightly beaten
½ cup milk
3 or 4 frankfurters

1. Combine sugar, ¼ cup oil, orange juice, and mustard in a saucepan. Bring mixture to boiling; simmer 2 minutes. Spoon about 1 tablespoon into the bottom of each of 12 greased muffin-pan wells.

2. In a bowl combine the pancake mix with ¼ cup oil, egg, and milk. Mix only until blended and gently form dough into a ball. Turn onto a lightly floured surface; knead gently with fingertips 10 to 15 times.

3. Roll dough into a 16x9-inch rectangle ¼ inch thick. Place frankfurters end to end on longer side and roll up as for a jelly roll; press edge to seal.

4. Cut into 12 slices. Place one slice, cut side down, over orange mixture in each muffin-pan well.

5. Bake at 450°F about 20 minutes.

6. Invert muffin pan on a wire rack; allow to stand a few minutes before lifting off pan. Serve warm.

1 DOZEN ROLLS

CHEESE TWISTS
A new "twist" with pie crust mix.

Pie crust mix for a 2-crust pie	2 tablespoons cold water
½ cup shredded sharp Cheddar cheese	2 tablespoons butter, chilled

1. Blend pie crust mix and cheese in a bowl; add the cold water according to the package directions.
2. Roll the dough on a lightly floured surface into a rectangle, about 16x10 inches.
3. Using 1½ tablespoons of the butter, place thin slices evenly over half of the dough; fold the other half over it. Using a rolling pin, press the open edges to seal. Repeat procedure using remaining butter; fold dough and seal edges. Chill thoroughly, about 1 hour.
4. Roll the chilled dough on a lightly floured surface into a 12x6-inch rectangle. Cut into 4x½-inch strips. Twist each strip by holding both ends and turning in opposite directions; press ends onto ungreased baking sheets.
5. Bake at 425°F about 10 minutes, or until twists are golden brown.   3 DOZEN TWISTS

Things to do with
REFRIGERATED DOUGHS & BAKERS' BREADS

Refrigerated Doughs

CORNMEAL-KIST BISCUITS

1 pkg. (8 oz.) refrigerated fresh dough for biscuits	Yellow cornmeal

Separate biscuits and coat each with cornmeal. Place about 2 inches apart on an ungreased baking sheet. Bake as directed on package.

10 BISCUITS

MACE 'N' CHEESE BISCUITS

1 pkg. (8 oz.) refrigerated fresh dough for biscuits	2 tablespoons butter, softened
12 thin 1¾-inch squares sharp Cheddar cheese	½ teaspoon ground mace
	¼ teaspoon dry mustard

1. Separate biscuits into halves; put bottom halves on ungreased baking sheet. Top each biscuit half with a square of cheese.
2. Blend the butter, mace, and dry mustard; spread on both sides of the remaining biscuit halves and place onto cheese squares. Sprinkle tops with *poppy seed.*
3. Bake at 400°F about 8 minutes, or until biscuits are lightly browned.   10 OR 12 BISCUITS

WATERCRESS BISCUITS: Follow recipe for Mace 'n' Cheese biscuits. Omit mace and dry mustard. Blend thoroughly the butter, ⅛ *teaspoon ground allspice,* and ¼ *teaspoon chervil.* Mix in ⅓ *cup finely chopped watercress.* Spread underside of biscuit tops with the seasoned butter; place, butter side down, onto cheese squares. Brush biscuit tops with *melted butter* and sprinkle with *poppy seed.*

BISCUIT SURPRISES

2 pkgs. (8 oz. each) refrigerated fresh dough for biscuits	20 pimiento-stuffed olives, well drained

1. Separate the dough for biscuits. Flatten each round and shape around an olive, sealing edges.
2. Place in an 8- or 9-inch round layer-cake pan, forming a ring. Brush tops of biscuits with *melted butter,* then sprinkle with *parsley.*
3. Bake at 425°F about 15 minutes, or until browned.   20 BISCUITS

PAN O' ROLLS

¼ cup butter or margarine	2 pkgs. (8 oz. each) refrigerated fresh dough for biscuits
1 clove garlic, minced	½ cup shredded Parmesan cheese
2 tablespoons finely snipped parsley	

1. Heat butter and garlic in a small skillet; stir in parsley. Remove from heat.
2. Separate biscuits; dip each in the garlic butter

to coat. Overlap 15 biscuits around the outer edge of a 9-inch round layer-cake pan; form an inner circle by overlapping remaining biscuits.

3. Drizzle any remaining butter over top of biscuits and sprinkle evenly with Parmesan cheese.

4. Bake at 425°F 15 to 20 minutes, or until golden brown. Serve hot.   20 ROLLS

HERBED BISCUIT RING

¼ cup butter or margarine	Few grains salt
½ teaspoon lemon juice	Few grains paprika
½ teaspoon celery seed	1 pkg. (8 oz.)
½ teaspoon sage	refrigerated fresh
¼ teaspoon thyme	dough for biscuits

1. Cream butter; mix in the lemon juice, celery seed, sage, thyme, salt, and paprika. Cover and chill at least 1 hour to allow flavors to blend.

2. Separate biscuits and spread each with the herb butter. Arrange, slightly overlapping, to form a ring in a shallow baking pan.

3. Bake at 400°F 15 minutes, or until golden brown.   10 BISCUITS

DOUBLE ONION BISCUITS

1 pkg. (8 oz) refrigerated fresh dough for biscuits	2 tablespoons snipped parsley
¼ cup butter or margarine, softened	1½ tablespoons dry onion salad dressing mix

1. Separate and slightly flatten biscuits. Spread half of them with a mixture of the remaining ingredients. Top with remaining biscuits.

2. Cut center from each double biscuit with a doughnut cutter. Gently stretch and twist each ring into a figure eight and place on a baking sheet.

3. Bake at 425°F 10 minutes.   10 BISCUITS

BISCUIT BLOSSOMS

1 pkg. (8 oz.) refrigerated fresh dough for biscuits	½ cup confectioners' sugar
Fat for deep frying heated to 375°F	1 tablespoon instant coffee

1. Separate biscuits. With scissors, make five

cuts at regular intervals almost to center of each biscuit.

2. For each frying, drop enough cut biscuits into hot fat to form a layer. Fry 2 to 3 minutes, or until golden brown, turning several times. Drain biscuits over fat a few seconds before removing to absorbent paper.

3. While biscuits are still warm coat with a mixture of the confectioners' sugar and instant coffee.
                                          10 BISCUITS

BISCUIT TRUFFLES: Follow recipe for Biscuit Blossoms. Cut each biscuit into 4 pieces. After frying, coat with a mixture of *½ cup sugar* and *1 to 2 tablespoons ground cinnamon*. Roll in *Dutch process cocoa.*

PINEAPPLE-PECAN COFFEE CAKE

¼ cup firmly packed brown sugar	1 teaspoon grated orange peel
3 tablespoons butter	2 pkgs. (8 oz. each)
¼ cup light corn syrup	refrigerated fresh
20 pecan halves	dough for biscuits
1 can (8¾ oz.) crushed pineapple, well drained	¼ cup butter, melted

1. Mix in a 9-inch layer cake pan the brown sugar, butter, and corn syrup. Arrange pecan halves, flat side up, in the pan. Spoon a mixture of crushed pineapple and orange peel over pecans.

2. Set pan in a 425°F oven for 10 minutes.

3. Dip each biscuit in the melted butter. Overlap 15 of the biscuits around the outer edge of the pan; form an inner circle by overlapping remaining biscuits.

4. Return to oven and bake at 425°F 20 minutes.

5. Remove from oven. Cover with a serving plate and invert; allow pan to remain over cake 1 to 2 minutes. Lift off pan. Serve warm.

ONE 9-INCH COFFEE CAKE

SPINACH CRESCENTS

1 pkg. (8 oz.) refrigerated dough for crescent rolls	1 cup finely snipped spinach
Italian salad dressing (from a mix or bottled)	1½ tablespoons prepared bacon-like pieces (a soy protein product)

1. Divide rolls into triangles; cut each in half

lengthwise. Brush with salad dressing and sprinkle with *grated Parmesan-Romano cheese.*

2. Mix spinach and bacon-like pieces; press into dough. Roll up and place on a baking sheet.

3. Bake at 375°F 10 to 15 minutes. 16 CRESCENTS

FLAKY CHEESE-FILLED ROLLS

1 pkg. refrigerated fresh dough for fantan rolls	½ teaspoon Worcestershire sauce
2 slices (about 2 oz.) pasteurized process Cheddar cheese, cut in 1½-in. squares	¼ teaspoon paprika
	Few grains ground cinnamon
1 tablespoon prepared mustard	Few grains cayenne pepper

1. Remove roll dough from package and divide into 36 rounds, each round consisting of 2 layers of dough. Place a square of cheese on half the rounds.

2. Combine remaining ingredients; mix well. Spread a thin coating of the mixture over cheese. Cover with remaining rounds of dough and press edges together lightly to seal in the filling. Transfer to ungreased baking sheet.

3. Bake at 400°F about 10 minutes.
1½ DOZEN ROLLS

ORANGE STICKY BUNS

Here's a modern version of the sticky buns reputed to have been served fresh every day at breakfast, teatime, and dinner in 19th century Philadelphia.

1 medium-sized orange	1 pkg. refrigerated fresh dough for fantan rolls
1 cup sugar	

1. Put orange peel and pulp through fine blade of food chopper. Mix orange with sugar in a saucepan and bring to boiling; boil 5 minutes.

2. Spoon about 2 teaspoons of orange-sugar mixture into each of 12 greased small muffin-pan wells.

3. Separate roll dough into 12 pieces and put one in each well. Pull sections of each roll apart slightly and drizzle remaining orange-sugar mixture between the sections.

4. Bake rolls as directed on package.

5. Remove from oven and turn pan upside down on wire rack; let cool 1 to 2 minutes; remove pan. If desired, frost with a *confectioners' sugar icing* while warm. 12 SMALL BUNS

Bakers' Breads

FRENCH TOAST

2 eggs, slightly beaten	3 to 4 tablespoons butter or margarine
⅔ cup milk or cream	8 slices bread, white or whole wheat
1 tablespoon sugar	
½ teaspoon salt	

1. Combine eggs with milk, sugar, and salt in a shallow dish or pie pan.

2. Dip bread slices one at a time into egg mixture, coating each side well. Transfer to a skillet which has been preheated with some of the butter. Brown slices over medium heat, turning once. Add butter as needed to keep slices from sticking.

3. Serve with *butter, maple syrup, honey, jam, or confectioners' sugar.* 8 SLICES FRENCH TOAST

NOTE: To brown French toast in the oven, place bread slices on a well greased baking sheet. Place in a 450°F oven; allow about 10 minutes for each side.

OAHU TOAST: Drain contents of *1 can (8½ ounces) pineapple slices;* reserve syrup. Follow recipe for French Toast. Omit sugar and substitute for milk pineapple syrup and *water* to make ⅔ cup liquid. Lightly brown pineapple slices in *2 to 3 tablespoons butter or margarine.* Serve half of a pineapple slice with each slice of toast.

CINNAMON-ORANGE FRENCH TOAST: Follow recipe for French Toast. Substitute ⅔ *cup orange juice* for milk and add ½ *teaspoon ground cinnamon.* Or, add *2 teaspoons grated orange peel* and ½ *teaspoon ground cinnamon* to egg mixture.

STRAWBERRY-BUTTERED FRENCH TOAST

1 pkg. (10 oz.) frozen sliced strawberries, thawed	½ teaspoon vanilla extract
	⅓ cup cream
Strawberry Butter, *page 114*	4 slices white bread, halved
3 eggs, slightly beaten	4 teaspoons butter or margarine
2 teaspoons sugar	
2 teaspoons grated lemon peel	

1. Drain strawberries; measure ⅓ cup syrup.

2. Prepare Strawberry Butter, using the berries and any remaining syrup.

3.   Combine in a shallow bowl the eggs, sugar, lemon peel, and extract. Mix well and stir in the cream and the ⅓ cup strawberry syrup.

4.   Put bread slices into egg mixture and let stand until thoroughly moistened, turning slices once.

5.   Heat the butter in a large heavy skillet. When skillet is hot, add bread slices and brown on one side; turn and brown on the other side. Add butter as needed to keep slices from sticking.

6.   Serve immediately with Strawberry Butter.

4 SERVINGS

STRAWBERRY BUTTER: Cut *½ cup firm unsalted butter or margarine* into a bowl. Beat with electric mixer on high speed just until whipped. Add *2 tablespoons confectioners' sugar* gradually, beating thoroughly. Add reserved strawberries and syrup, 1 tablespoon at a time, beating thoroughly. Chill until ready to use.   ABOUT 1¼ CUPS SAUCE

ORANGE TOAST "BLINTZES"

You'll appreciate this modern approach to preparing the ever-popular Jewish blintze. Thin slices of bread are used instead of the thin pancakes to hold the cottage cheese filling. Not exactly a traditional blintze, but a very tasty brunch or luncheon dish.

12 thin slices white bread	1 tablespoon grated orange peel
⅓ cup milk	Few grains salt
1 egg, slightly beaten	3 tablespoons butter or margarine, melted
¾ cup small curd creamed cottage cheese	2 tablespoons sugar
1 tablespoon sugar	1 teaspoon ground cinnamon

1.   Trim crusts from bread; brush tops and sides of bread with milk.

2.   Combine the egg, cottage cheese, 1 tablespoon sugar, orange peel, and salt; mix well.

3.   Spread 2 tablespoons of the mixture evenly over each of 6 bread slices. Place remaining slices, milk-side down, on filling. Press edges together.

4.   Brush tops with melted butter and sprinkle with a mixture of sugar and cinnamon. Place "blintzes" on a greased baking sheet.

5.   Toast in a 400°F oven 10 minutes.   6 SERVINGS

FRENCH TOAST STRIPS

Orange Kirsch Sugar, *below*	1 tablespoon grated orange peel
2 eggs	12 thin slices white bread, crusts trimmed if desired
¾ cup milk	
1 tablespoon sugar	
Pinch salt	Butter or margarine (about 2 tablespoons)

1.   Prepare Orange Kirsch Sugar; set aside.

2.   Slightly beat the eggs with milk, sugar, and salt in a shallow bowl. Mix in orange peel.

3.   Cut each bread slice into 3 strips. Dip each strip into egg mixture, coating all sides and allowing excess to drain off before frying.

4.   Brown strips in hot butter in a skillet; add butter as necessary to prevent sticking.

5.   Serve hot with Orange Kirsch Sugar. 6 SERVINGS

ORANGE KIRSCH SUGAR: Mix *½ cup sugar, ¼ cup grated orange peel*, and a small amount of *kirsch*.

CHEESE-BROILED FRENCH BREAD

1 roll (6 oz.) natural cheese food	1 egg white
2 tablespoons mayonnaise	1 loaf French bread
	Paprika

1.   Cut cheese food into small pieces and put into a bowl. Add the mayonnaise and egg white; beat until fluffy.

2.   Cut loaf of bread diagonally into slices ¾ inch thick. Toast slices on one side under broiler.

3.   Turn and spread untoasted sides with the cheese mixture; sprinkle lightly with paprika. Broil 3 inches from source of heat about 3 minutes, or until cheese is bubbly and lightly browned.

1 LOAF CHEESE-BROILED FRENCH BREAD

GARLIC FRENCH BREAD

1 loaf French bread	2 tablespoons milk
2 pkgs. (3 oz. each) cream cheese, softened	2 teaspoons garlic salt
	1 tablespoon prepared horseradish

1.   Cut loaf of bread diagonally into 1½ inch slices almost through to bottom of loaf.

2.   Combine remaining ingredients. Spread mixture over the cut surfaces of the bread.

3.   Wrap loaf in aluminum foil and heat in a 350°F oven about 15 minutes. 1 LOAF GARLIC FRENCH BREAD

BUTTERED FRENCH BREAD

Cut *1 loaf French bread* on the diagonal into ¾-inch slices almost through to the bottom. Place in center of a piece of aluminum foil large enough to cover loaf. Generously spread desired *Seasoned Butter, below,* onto cut surfaces and over top of loaf. If desired, sprinkle with *paprika.* Twist ends of foil securely, leaving top partially open so steam can escape. Set in a 400°F oven 15 to 20 minutes.

SEASONED BUTTERS: Into *½ cup softened butter* blend one of the following—

⅓ cup finely chopped pimiento-stuffed olives and ¼ teaspoon oregano	2 tablespoons finely chopped parsley, 1 minced clove garlic,
1 teaspoon lemon or lime juice, and 1 tablespoon minced chives	¼ teaspoon ground coriander, ⅛ teaspoon ground ginger, and ½ teaspoon celery seed

DILLED FRENCH BREAD

1 loaf French bread	1 tablespoon prepared horseradish
½ cup softened butter	
3 tablespoons chopped parsley	¾ teaspoon prepared mustard
	1½ teaspoons dill seed

1. Cut loaf of bread into ¾-inch slices. Toast slices on one side under broiler.
2. Turn and spread untoasted sides with a mixture of the remaining ingredients.
3. Place under broiler, with tops 3 to 4 inches from source of heat, until bubbly and toasted around the edges.   1 LOAF DILLED FRENCH BREAD

SESAME SEED BREAD

1 loaf French bread	½ cup butter or margarine, melted
½ cup sesame seed	
1 tablespoon butter	½ teaspoon seasoned salt

1. Cut loaf of bread into ¾-inch slices.
2. Lightly brown the sesame seed in the 1 tablespoon butter.
3. Lightly brush one side of bread slices with a mixture of the melted butter and seasoned salt.
4. Put slices buttered side down on a baking sheet. Mix toasted sesame seed with remaining butter and brush generously on bread.
5. Set in a 325°F oven about 20 minutes, then under broiler with top about 3 inches from source of heat 1 to 2 minutes, or until lightly browned.
    1 LOAF SESAME SEED BREAD

KETCHUP BREAD

1 long narrow crusty loaf bread	Crushed basil
	⅓ cup snipped parsley
¼ cup softened butter or margarine	2 cups (8 oz.) shredded sharp Cheddar cheese
⅔ cup ketchup	

1. Slice loaf of bread lengthwise into halves. Spread cut surfaces with butter. Toast under broiler until golden brown.
2. Spread ketchup over toasted bread. Sprinkle with desired amount of basil, then the parsley and the cheese.
3. Place under broiler with top about 3 inches from source of heat until cheese is melted and lightly browned. Cut each half diagonally into slices.   1 LOAF KETCHUP BREAD

HERB-BUTTERED CRUSTY ROLLS

12 hard rolls (about 5 in. long)	1 teaspoon prepared mustard
1 cup softened butter	½ teaspoon Worcestershire sauce
2 teaspoons lemon juice	1 teaspoon basil
	⅛ teaspoon garlic salt

1. Slice rolls twice diagonally almost to bottom.
2. Mix remaining ingredients together. Spread cut surfaces of rolls with mixture. Place each roll on a piece of aluminum foil and bring sides of foil up around each roll.
3. Set in a 350°F oven about 15 minutes, or until rolls are thoroughly heated.   12 ROLLS

PARSLIED PARMESAN LOAF

1 cup butter or margarine, softened	4 tablespoons chopped parsley
½ cup shredded Parmesan cheese	½ teaspoon celery seed
	1 loaf Vienna bread

1. Blend the cheese, parsley, and celery seed into butter in a bowl.

2. Cut loaf lengthwise through center and criss-cross at 1½-inch intervals almost to bottom.

3. Spread cut surfaces and top of loaf with butter mixture. Wrap loaf in aluminum foil, leaving top of package open so steam will escape.

4. Heat in a 400°F oven 25 minutes, or until hot and crisp.　　　　　　　　　　ABOUT 8 SERVINGS

TOASTIES

RINGLET SHELLS: To serve four persons, use *12 bread slices*, about ½ inch thick. Trim off crusts and cut all slices into large squares, rectangles, or rounds (making all 12 slices the same shape). Use a biscuit or cookie cutter for cutting the rounds. Set aside four shapes. With a sharp pointed knife or cookie cutter, cut out centers from the 8 remaining shapes to make rings at least ½ inch wide. Thoroughly brush tops of uncut shapes and both sides or rings with *milk.* Stack 2 rings on each uncut shape. Brush inside and outside with *melted butter or margarine.* Place on a baking sheet and toast in a 325°F oven 12 to 20 minutes, or until golden brown and crisp.

TOAST CUPS: Cut crusts from thin *bread slices.* Lightly brush both sides with *melted butter or margarine* and press each slice into a muffin-pan well, corners pointing up. Toast in a 325°F oven 12 to 20 minutes, or until crisp and lightly browned.

TOAST POINTS: Trim crusts from *bread slices.* Toast and spread with *butter or margarine.* Cut each slice diagonally in half.

TOAST FINGERS: Trim crusts from *bread slices.* Toast and spread with *butter or margarine.* Cut slices into fingers about 1 inch wide.

CROUSTADE BASKET

1 loaf unsliced bread　　　⅓ cup melted butter or
　　　　　　　　　　　　　　　margarine

1. Neatly trim the crusts from top and sides of loaf. Using a sharp pointed knife, hollow out center, leaving 1-inch sides and bottom.

2. Brush inside and out with melted butter. Place on a baking sheet.

3. Toast in a 400°F oven 10 to 15 minutes, or until golden brown and crisp. Fill with *Scrambled Eggs* (double recipe), *page 130,* and serve with *Mushroom-Caraway Sauce, page 345.*

MINIATURE CROUSTADES: Trim crusts from top and sides of loaf of unsliced bread; cut into cubes slightly larger than 1 inch. Using a serrated knife, hollow out centers. Brush cases inside and out with a mixture of ½ *cup butter* and ¼ *teaspoon garlic salt.* Set on a baking sheet. Toast in a 350°F oven 15 to 20 minutes, turning occasionally, until golden brown and crisp. Cool. Use as cases for appetizers.

RINGLET CROUSTADES

12 slices day-old bread, about ¾ in. thick	¼ cup butter or margarine, melted
	2 tablespoons grated Parmesan cheese

1. Using a scalloped-edge cookie cutter, cut bread slices into rounds. Set 6 rounds aside.

2. With a sharp, pointed knife or cookie cutter, cut out center of the 6 remaining shapes to make rings at least ¾-inch wide.

3. Lightly brush rounds (for bases), rings, and centers with melted butter. Arrange on a baking sheet, buttered-side down.

4. Mix cheese with remaining butter. Brush sides and tops of bases, rings, and centers with butter-cheese mixture.

5. Toast in a 325°F oven 15 to 20 minutes, or until golden brown and crisp.

6. For each ringlet shell, place a ring on a base. Fill with a creamed mixture and top with a center round.　　　　　　　　　　　　　6 SERVINGS

ALMOND RINGLET CROUSTADES: Follow recipe for Ringlet Croustades. Substitute ½ *cup finely chopped, toasted blanched almonds* for the Parmesan cheese. Generously brush bases, rings, and centers with the melted butter and sprinkle each piece with the almonds.

SESAME RINGLET CROUSTADES: Follow recipe for Ringlet Croustades. Omit cheese. Lightly brown *2 to 3 tablespoons sesame seed* in 2 tablespoons of the melted butter. Mix ½ *teaspoon onion salt* with remaining 2 tablespoons melted butter. Brush bottoms of bases, rings, and centers with the butter and tops with toasted sesame seed.

Chapter 4
SANDWICHES &
SANDWICH FILLINGS

The Earl of Sandwich had only hunger and speedy service in mind when he called for his meat to be placed between two slices of bread. Little did he know what he started. In exploring his beguiling creation, homemakers have found that practically every food on earth is in some form suitable and indeed delectable as a sandwich filling.

Name a time, an occasion, or a meal—there is an appropriate sandwich for each of them. The sandwich travels with the lunch carrier or picnicker. It accompanies soup or salad for luncheon. A hearty one is a main course for supper. The sandwich bar, where guests create their own, stars at late evening meals. The sandwich dons "fancy clothes" for parties, receptions, and teas. It can be toasted or grilled. It can be made with as many slices of bread as desired: one for the open-faced; the usual two; three for the club or decker; four or more for the super-stack. Even breakfast has its sandwich— Eggs Benedict. The variety is endless.

Bread—Fresh bread is desirable for a good sandwich. However, some types of home-baked quick breads, such as nut or fruit loaves, slice easier if stored for 24 hours. Achieve interest and appeal by using a variety of breads. Bake or buy enriched white, square sandwich, French, Italian, Vienna, potato, pumpernickel, raisin, rye, whole or cracked wheat, nut or fruit bread, hard rolls, frankfurter rolls, or hamburger buns.

Ready-sliced bread is a great help for the sandwich maker. Always use adjacent slices so that sandwiches will be uniform and easy to cut when assembled. For party sandwiches, such as the loaf- and mosaic-types, the unsliced loaf is best because it can be cut into lengthwise slices. To prevent rolled sandwiches from breaking, lightly roll soft bread slices with a rolling pin.

Picture-Puzzle or Mosaic Sandwiches—Cut shapes (rabbits, chickens, dogs) or small geometric designs (crescents, rounds, diamonds, stars) from centers of an equal number of dark and white bread slices. Fit dark bread cutouts into cutouts of white bread and white cutouts into cutouts of dark bread. Bottom slice is a whole piece; if desired use contrasting breads.

Fillings and Butters—Spread softened butter or margarine or seasoned butters evenly to the edges of the bread slice. This keeps the bread moist and the filling from soaking into the bread. Cream cheese and peanut butter also give protection.

The filling should not be skimpy. Neither should it be *too* generous; use just enough for appetizing, attractive sandwiches. Be sure the filling, either mixture or sliced food, extends to the edges.

In Choosing and Making Fillings Think About:
Who is going to eat the sandwich—school child, afternoon tea guest, man-of-the-house.
What part of the menu the sandwich will be—main course, accompaniment, accessory.
Where the sandwich will be eaten—picnic grounds, living room, kitchen.
When the sandwich will be eaten—immediately, later in the day, in two or three weeks.
How the sandwich will be eaten—with a fork, from the fingers, from the hand.

Crisp lettuce leaves and tomato slices should be added to the sandwiches just before serving or wrapped separately when part of the carried lunch. Fillings that make the bread limp or soggy are not for the traveling sandwich. Several thin slices of meat, poultry, or cheese in a sandwich are better tasting and easier eating than one thick slice.

Warning About Sandwiches That Are Prepared a Few Hours Before They Will Be Eaten—Some fillings, such as meat, fish, poultry, eggs, soft cheeses, and mayonnaise require special care to prevent growth of food-poisoning bacteria. The addition to sandwich fillings of an acid ingredient, such as pickles, lemon juice, or green olives, helps to retain their keeping qualities.

Sandwiches made with jelly, peanut butter, hard or semihard cheese, and raw vegetables usually are safe for summertime packed lunches when the heat might damage more perishable fillings.

Preparation—A hardwood cutting board, portable or built into the kitchen counter, is an excellent surface on which to prepare sandwiches. A short, flexible spatula with a blade 1½ inches wide and long enough to reach across a slice of bread is a useful tool. Be sure all knives are sharp.

Begin sandwich preparation by preparing fillings and by softening the spreads. Be systematic when assembling sandwiches—do one job all at one time. Use utensils and equipment, handling the sandwich as little as possible.

Line up adjacent slices of bread in pairs and evenly spread bread to the edges with the softened spread. Spread fillings evenly or place sliced food to edges of one slice of each pair. If desired, place lettuce leaves, slices of tomato, or pickles over filling. Top filling with matching bread slices and cut into halves, quarters, wedges, or other interesting shapes and sizes.

Sandwich loaves, club sandwiches, or sandwich stacks are assembled in a similar manner. Use matched slices of bread for each sandwich; spread both sides of inner slices with softened butter or margarine or seasoned butters.

Wrapping—Wrap one whole sandwich or each section, securely and separately, in waxed paper, aluminum foil, or other moisture-vaporproof material. Cover previously wrapped sandwiches with a clean dry towel, if desired, but *never* with a damp cloth. The added moisture will encourage growth of some bacteria.

BUTTERS

Cream butter until softened. If lemon juice is called for, blend in a small amount at a time. Mix in remaining ingredients.

CURRY
½ cup butter or margarine
2 teaspoons lemon juice
1 teaspoon curry powder

HORSERADISH
½ cup butter or margarine
1 tablespoon lemon juice
2 teaspoons prepared horseradish
¾ teaspoon prepared mustard
¼ teaspoon salt

ROQUEFORT
½ cup butter or margarine
2 teaspoons lemon juice

¼ cup crumbled Roquefort cheese
2 tablespoons chopped parsley
1 tablespoon prepared horseradish

SMOKED BEEF
½ cup butter or margarine
1 cup chopped smoked sliced beef
2 tablespoons ketchup
1 teaspoon prepared mustard
½ teaspoon Worcestershire sauce

MUSTARD
½ cup butter or margarine
4 teaspoons prepared mustard

FILLINGS FOR COLD SANDWICHES

Blend ingredients thoroughly before preparing sandwiches; use *bread* spread with *butter or margarine*. Each filling is enough for 4 sandwiches. Serve cut in attractive shapes.

AVOCADO
1 ripe avocado, peeled and mashed
3 tablespoons minced parsley
4 slices bacon, diced and fried, or ⅓ cup finely chopped luncheon meat
1 tablespoon mayonnaise
1 teaspoon lime juice
⅛ teaspoon salt
Few grains cayenne pepper

BOLOGNA
¾ cup ground bologna
1 hard-cooked egg, finely chopped

2 to 3 tablespoons chili sauce
2 tablespoons salad dressing
1 teaspoon prepared horseradish
¼ teaspoon salt

CHEDDAR CHEESE
¾ cup finely shredded Cheddar cheese
½ cup finely chopped corned beef
2 tablespoons chopped sweet pickle
1 tablespoon chopped pimiento
1 teaspoon prepared mustard
¼ teaspoon onion salt

CITRUS SPECIAL

½ cup peanut butter
¼ cup orange juice
1 teaspoon grated
   orange peel
⅓ cup shredded
   coconut

CHEESE-BACON

3 oz. cream cheese,
   softened
2 tablespoons well-
   drained pickle relish
1 tablespoon salad
   dressing
1 teaspoon minced
   onion
3 drops Worcester-
   shire sauce
6 slices bacon, diced
   and fried crisp

DRIED BEEF

1 cup chopped dried
   beef
2 tablespoons chopped
   onion
1 tablespoon chopped
   green pepper
¼ cup mayonnaise
1 tablespoon ketchup
2 tablespoons
   prepared mustard
2 teaspoons Worcester-
   shire sauce
¼ teaspoon ground
   allspice
¼ teaspoon ground
   nutmeg

CHICKEN-MUSHROOM

1 cup minced cooked
   chicken
½ cup chopped
   mushrooms
¼ cup salted toasted
   almonds, chopped
2 tablespoons chopped
   green olives
3 tablespoons salad
   dressing
¼ teaspoon salt
¼ teaspoon mono-
   sodium glutamate
⅛ teaspoon paprika

EGG-ALMOND

4 hard-cooked eggs,
   finely chopped
3 tablespoons finely
   chopped, toasted,
   blanched almonds
¼ cup mayonnaise
1 teaspoon prepared
   mustard
1 teaspoon grated
   onion
½ teaspoon salt
⅛ teaspoon pepper

HAM-PINEAPPLE

½ cup ground cooked
   ham
½ cup well-drained
   crushed pineapple
3 tablespoons salad
   dressing
2 teaspoons brown
   sugar

BAKED BEAN

1 cup drained canned
   baked beans in tomato
   sauce
⅓ cup chopped sweet
   pickle
2 tablespoons ketchup
   or chili sauce
1 tablespoon minced
   onion

FAVORITE FISH

¾ cup cooked fish
   (salmon, tuna, crab
   meat, or shrimp),
   flaked or finely
   chopped
½ cup finely chopped
   cabbage
3 tablespoons chopped
   ripe olives
3 tablespoons salad
   dressing
1 tablespoon olive
   liquid (from can)
¼ teaspoon mono-
   sodium glutamate
¼ teaspoon paprika
2 or 3 drops Tabasco

DEVILED HAM-RAISIN

1 can (4¼ oz.) deviled
   ham
½ cup chopped celery
¼ cup chopped
   pecans
¼ cup chopped raisins
2 tablespoons
   mayonnaise

EGG SALAD

4 hard-cooked eggs,
   chopped
2 tablespoons chopped
   pimiento-stuffed
   olives
2 tablespoons
   mayonnaise
½ teaspoon dry
   mustard
½ teaspoon salt
Few grains pepper

LIVER SAUSAGE

6 oz. Braunschweiger
   (smoked liver
   sausage)
¼ cup drained pickle
   relish
2 tablespoons grated
   onion

SARDINE DE LUXE

Spread on *unbuttered
bread.*

1 can (3¾ oz.)
   Norwegian sardines,
   drained and mashed
2 hard-cooked eggs,
   finely chopped
1 tablespoon capers,
   drained
3 tablespoons butter or
   margarine, softened
1 tablespoon garlic
   French dressing
1 teaspoon lemon juice
¼ teaspoon salt
¼ teaspoon paprika

COLD SANDWICHES

HAM SANDWICHES DE LUXE

Whipped Cream
   Dressing, *page 120*
2 firm ripe medium-
   sized tomatoes,
   peeled and cut in
   3 slices each

3 slices white bread,
   toasted and buttered
3 large crisp lettuce
   leaves
3 slices cooked ham
3 slices Swiss cheese

1.   Prepare dressing and refrigerate.

2.   Sprinkle tomato slices with *salt* and *pepper*.
3.   To make each sandwich, put 1 slice of toast, buttered side up, on an individual salad plate. Cover toast with 1 lettuce leaf, 1 slice ham, 1 slice cheese, and 2 tomato slices. Top with one third of the dressing.
4.   To complete an attractive luncheon plate, put a whole *spiced apple or peach* and *potato chips* on the plate. Garnish with *watercress*.   3 SANDWICHES

WHIPPED CREAM DRESSING

2 tablespoons mayonnaise	2 teaspoons minced chives
1 tablespoon chili sauce	½ cup chilled heavy cream, whipped
1 tablespoon chopped ripe olives	

Mix the mayonnaise, chili sauce, olives, and chives. Blend with the whipped cream. Refrigerate until ready to use.

CRUSTY ROLL TEMPTERS

6 crusty rolls	¼ cup pimiento strips, well-drained
1 cup chopped cooked ham	¼ cup chopped salted peanuts
1 cup very finely shredded cabbage	2 tablespoons chopped pickled onion
2 hard-cooked eggs, chopped	¼ cup mayonnaise
¼ cup chopped green pepper	¾ teaspoon salt
	¼ teaspoon black pepper

1. Cut rolls lengthwise through center; scoop out insides to within ¼ inch of crust. Butter inside, if desired. Set aside.
2. Mix the remaining ingredients thoroughly. Fill the lower halves of the rolls generously with the ham mixture. If desired, sliced *pimiento-stuffed olives* may be layered in cavities before filling is added. Place scooped-out upper section of rolls over filling, cut into halves, and serve.

6 FILLED ROLLS

EGG SALAD SENSATIONS

Attractive open-faced sandwiches garnished with zesty avocado slices.

¼ cup butter	½ teaspoon salt
1½ teaspoons prepared mustard	¼ teaspoon black pepper
4 hard-cooked eggs, chopped	Slices of ripe avocado
¼ cup very finely chopped cooked ham	Lemon juice
¼ cup dairy sour cream	Seasoned salt
¾ teaspoon dry mustard	Slices of white bread
	Thin slices of large tomatoes

1. Whip butter until softened; blend in the prepared mustard. Set aside.

2. Combine the eggs, ham, and sour cream; thoroughly blend in a mixture of the dry mustard, salt, and pepper. Set aside in refrigerator.
3. Just before serving, prepare avocado slices and dip immediately in lemon juice; sprinkle with seasoned salt.
4. To assemble sandwiches, spread mustard-butter over bread slices; put tomato slices on mustard-butter; spoon egg mixture over slices. Cut each sandwich into fourths and arrange an avocado slice on each fourth.   4 TO 6 OPEN-FACED SANDWICHES

PAUL BUNYAN-SIZED TUNA HOBOS

1 loaf Italian bread (about 15 in. long), cut in half lengthwise	Tuna Salad, *below*
	Sliced tomato
	Sliced sweet onion
Horseradish Butter, or Smoked Beef Butter, *page 118*	½ lb. assorted luncheon meat
	¼ lb. sliced process American cheese
Lettuce leaves	

1. On cut surface of each bread half spread desired butter. Cover with the lettuce. Top with Tuna Salad, tomato, onion, luncheon meat, and then the cheese.
2. Spear *cherry tomatoes* and *pimiento-stuffed olives* with wooden picks and use to garnish sandwiches.   8 SERVINGS

TUNA SALAD: Mix *2 cans (6½ or 7 ounces each) tuna*, drained and flaked, *¼ cup sweet pickle relish*, and *6 tablespoons mayonnaise.*

ROQUEFORT-TONGUE SANDWICHES

Roquefort Butter, *page 118*	Sliced cooked tongue, ¼ in. thick
16 slices rye bread	⅓ cup butter or margarine
Lettuce	

1. Spread Roquefort Butter generously over 8 slices of bread. Place lettuce over each, then sliced tongue.
2. Whip ⅓ cup butter until softened and spread over remaining 8 slices of bread. Complete sandwiches with bread, buttered side down.

8 SANDWICHES

NOTE: *Sliced cooked turkey may be substituted for the tongue. If desired, increase ⅓ cup butter to ½ cup and whip with ¼ to ½ teaspoon curry powder and 2 teaspoons lemon juice.*

HOT SANDWICHES

SAUCY BEEF 'N' BUNS

2 tablespoons fat	¼ teaspoon black
½ cup chopped onion	pepper
1 lb. ground beef	¾ cup chopped celery
1 teaspoon salt	¾ cup chopped green
½ teaspoon mono-	pepper
sodium glutamate	1 cup chili sauce
	1 cup ketchup

1.   Heat the fat in a large skillet. Add the onion and cook until soft, stirring occasionally. Add the meat and a mixture of salt, monosodium glutamate, and pepper; cook until meat is lightly browned, separating it into pieces with a fork or spoon.
2.   Blend in the remaining ingredients. Simmer, uncovered, about 25 minutes; stir frequently.
3.   Serve on *buttered, toasted hamburger buns.* Accompany with *corn chips* and *dill pickle strips.*
ABOUT 6 SERVINGS

KRAUT 'N' DOGS IN THE ROUND
Tangy sauerkraut in a crusty roll partially encircled with a hot dog adds a new twist to America's national sandwich.

3 cups drained	1 tablespoon prepared
sauerkraut	horseradish
½ cup chili sauce	⅛ teaspoon dry
2 tablespoons capers	mustard
1 tablespoon light	6 (about ½ lb.)
brown sugar	frankfurters
¼ cup soft butter	6 poppy seed hard rolls
or margarine	

1.   Combine sauerkraut, chili sauce, capers, and brown sugar in a saucepan; heat before using.
2.   Cream butter, horseradish, and dry mustard together until of spreading consistency; set aside.
3.   Cut 10 deep slits in each frankfurter without cutting all the way through. Cover with boiling water in a saucepan. Let stand tightly covered about 8 minutes.
4.   Meanwhile, cut a slice off top of each roll; cut out centers (reserve centers for making bread crumbs). Lightly toast rolls under broiler heat. Spread with the horseradish butter.
5.   Place frankfurters in rolls and fill centers with sauerkraut mixture; cover with roll tops. Serve with *Cream of Corn Soup, page 49.*   6 SERVINGS

MUSHROOM-SAUCED SANDWICHES

3 tablespoons butter	6 slices bread
or margarine	1 tablespoon prepared
2 tablespoons flour	mustard
1 can (10½ oz.) con-	1 can (12 oz.) chopped
densed cream of	ham
mushroom soup	1 can (14½ oz.)
¼ cup water	asparagus spears,
½ teaspoon Worces-	drained
tershire sauce	

1.   Melt 2 tablespoons of butter in a saucepan. Blend in flour. Heat until mixture bubbles, stirring constantly. Remove from heat and blend in soup, water, and Worcestershire sauce. Cook until thoroughly heated, stirring constantly.
2.   Toast one side only of bread slices. Trim crusts from bread and spread untoasted sides with remaining butter and the mustard. Cut ham into 6 equal slices. Place one ham slice over each bread slice. Arrange 3 asparagus spears on each sandwich. Using a wide spatula, carefully transfer to individual plates.
3.   Pour the hot mushroom sauce over each sandwich. Garnish with *pimiento-stuffed olive slices* and *parsley sprigs.*   6 SERVINGS

"YARD LONG" SANDWICH SNACK

1 loaf French bread	¾ lb. canned luncheon
12 oz. cream cheese,	meat or smokie link
softened	sausages, thinly
¼ cup prepared	sliced
horseradish	1 cup finely chopped
2 tablespoons grated	ripe olives
onion	Sliced dill pickles
½ teaspoon seasoned	Cherry tomatoes, cut
salt	in halves

1.   Split bread lengthwise and hollow each half by tearing out most of the soft center (may be used in other food preparation); set aside.
2.   Mix cream cheese, horseradish, onion, and seasoned salt; spread on interior surfaces of bread.
3.   Brown sliced luncheon meat in *butter or margarine.* Arrange on bread. Sprinkle with chopped olives. Tuck in pickle slices and tomato halves sprinkled with *seasoned pepper* and *crushed basil* or *dill weed.*

4. Place on an ungreased baking sheet and set in a 400°F oven 10 minutes. Slice crosswise into large sandwiches. Garnish with *sweet onion rings* and *parsley sprigs*.　　　　6 TO 8 SERVINGS

CHEESY TOASTED SANDWICHES

5 hard-cooked eggs, chopped	¼ teaspoon pepper
½ cup finely chopped cooked ham	½ cup dairy sour cream
2 tablespoons chopped green pepper	Softened butter (about 5 tablespoons)
¾ teaspoon dry mustard	10 slices white bread, toasted
½ teaspoon salt	1 jar (5 oz.) process sharp cheese spread, softened

1. Mix together eggs, ham, and green pepper; set aside.
2. Blend the dry mustard, salt, and pepper into the sour cream. Add to egg mixture; toss lightly to mix well.
3. Butter one side of each toast slice. Spread egg mixture evenly on buttered side of 5 slices. Top with remaining toast, buttered side down. Spread sandwich tops with cheese spread.
4. Place on broiler rack. Broil with tops of sandwiches about 4 inches from source of heat about 3 minutes, or until cheese is bubbly.　5 SANDWICHES

CHICKEN FIESTA BUNS

⅓ cup finely chopped green pepper	½ teaspoon chili powder
⅓ cup finely chopped celery	½ teaspoon salt
⅓ cup finely chopped onion	½ teaspoon mono-sodium glutamate
1 clove garlic, minced	¼ teaspoon seasoned pepper
3 tablespoons butter or margarine	1½ cups chopped cooked chicken or turkey
½ cup tomato paste	
2 tablespoons Worces-tershire sauce	¼ cup chopped pimiento-stuffed olives
2 tablespoons cider vinegar	8 split frankfurter buns, heated
1 tablespoon brown sugar	

1. Cook green pepper, celery, onion, and garlic in hot butter about 3 minutes.

2. Stir in a mixture of tomato paste, Worcestershire sauce, vinegar, brown sugar, chili powder, salt, monosodium glutamate, and seasoned pepper; then chicken and olives. Simmer about 10 minutes to blend flavors, stirring occasionally.
3. Spoon mixture into buns; serve immediately.
　　　　8 SERVINGS

SARDINE PIZZA SANDWICHES

1 can (6 oz.) tomato paste	4 small English muffins, split and toasted
½ teaspoon seasoned salt	¾ cup shredded sharp Cheddar cheese
⅛ teaspoon garlic powder	1 can (3¾ oz.) sardines, drained (reserve oil)
1 teaspoon oregano, crushed	Green pepper strips
	Pimiento strips

1. Blend the tomato paste with the seasoned salt, garlic powder, and oregano. Spread about 1½ tablespoons on each toasted muffin half.
2. Sprinkle cheese over the tomato spread and arrange about 3 sardines on each muffin half. Place two green pepper strips crossing the sardines and place a pimiento strip between them. Brush top with some of the reserved oil.
3. Broil 3 to 4 inches from source of heat about 3 minutes, or until cheese is melted. Serve hot.
　　　　8 SANDWICHES

SCRUMPTIOUS TUNABURGERS

2 eggs, beaten	1½ cups soft bread crumbs
¼ cup ketchup	
1 tablespoon lemon juice	3 cans (6½ or 7 oz. each) tuna, drained and flaked
2 tablespoons capers	
2 teaspoons instant minced onion	2 tablespoons butter or margarine
¾ teaspoon lemon pepper marinade	6 hamburger buns, halved, buttered, and toasted

1. In a bowl, beat together eggs, ketchup, lemon juice, capers, onion, lemon pepper, and bread crumbs; mix thoroughly with the flaked tuna. Shape into 6 patties (mixture will not be smooth).
2. Meanwhile, heat butter in a large skillet. Put patties in hot butter as each is shaped. Cook over medium heat until browned. Using a large spatula, carefully turn patties to brown other side. Immediately transfer to toasted buns.　6 SERVINGS

PARTYTIME SANDWICHES

AVOCADO-ALMOND PINWHEELS

Avocado-Almond Spread, ¼ cup butter or
 below   margarine, softened
1 loaf unsliced
sandwich bread

1.   Prepare Avocado-Almond Spread.
2.   Trim crusts from bread. Cut 3 lengthwise slices about ½ inch thick. (Reserve remainder of loaf for other use.) Flatten each slice slightly with a rolling pin. Spread each slice with butter. Then spread to edges with Avocado-Almond Spread.
3.   Starting at one of narrow edges, roll up each slice tightly, being careful to keep ends of roll even. Secure with wooden picks. Wrap rolls individually in aluminum foil or other moisture-vapor-proof material. Chill several hours before serving.
4.   When ready to serve, remove wooden picks and cut the rolls crosswise into ½-inch slices.

ABOUT 2 DOZEN PINWHEELS

AVOCADO-ALMOND SPREAD: Peel and sieve *3 small ripe avocados.* Blend with *3 tablespoons lemon juice, 2 teaspoons Worcestershire sauce, 1 teaspoon onion juice, ½ teaspoon curry powder, ½ teaspoon salt,* and a *few grains cayenne pepper.* Cover and chill. Just before using, mix in *½ cup blanched almonds,* toasted and chopped, and *6 slices panbroiled diced bacon.*

ABOUT 2⅓ CUPS SPREAD

CURRANT CHECKERBOARDS

1 cup firm butter or 6 slices white bread
 margarine   6 slices whole wheat
2½ tablespoons   bread
 currant jelly

1.   Whip the butter using an electric mixer. Add the jelly and beat until blended. Set aside.
2.   Trim crusts from bread, trimming so that slices are square. Reserve 3 slices of white bread. Spread one side of remaining slices with currant butter.
3.   Stack 2 whole wheat slices and 1 white slice, buttered side up, beginning and ending with whole wheat slices. Repeat to form 2 more stacks. Top each stack with one of the reserved white bread slices.
4.   Using a sharp knife, cut each stack into 4 slices. Set 4 slices aside. Spread one side of all

remaining slices with currant butter. (Each slice will consist of 4 bread strips that are alternately whole wheat and white bread.) Stack two of the slices, buttered side up, so that the white strips of 1 slice are beneath the whole wheat strips of the next slice. Repeat to form 3 more stacks. Top each stack with a slice not spread with the currant butter.
5.   Wrap each stack in aluminum foil; chill.
6.   When ready to serve, using a sharp knife, cut each stack into ½-inch slices. Each slice will show a checkerboard pattern.

ABOUT 2½ DOZEN CHECKERBOARDS

DEVILED HAM OPEN-FACED SANDWICHES

1 can (4½ oz.) deviled ¼ cup butter or
 ham   margarine
¼ cup dairy sour cream 2 teaspoons lemon juice
¼ teaspoon dill weed
3 tablespoons chopped
 cucumber pickle

1.   Combine deviled ham, sour cream, dill weed, and pickle. Chill thoroughly.
2.   Cream the butter with the lemon juice until fluffy. Spread on *bread* which has been trimmed and cut into assorted shapes. Spread about 1 teaspoon of the filling on each buttered piece of bread.
3.   Garnish each sandwich with a top slice of a small, *fresh strawberry* with hull.

ABOUT 4 DOZEN SANDWICHES

HAM-PEANUT SALAD PINWHEELS

1 cup ground cooked 1 tablespoon chopped
 ham   salted peanuts
½ cup finely chopped 12 slices white bread,
 chutney   crusts removed
1 tablespoon grated
 onion

1.   Combine ham with chutney, onion, and peanuts. Blend in enough *dairy sour cream* to just moisten.
2.   Flatten bread slices lightly with a rolling pin. Spread with ham mixture and roll up jelly-roll fashion. Secure with wooden picks, wrap and chill.
3.   When ready to serve, slice rolls crosswise into fourths. Garnish with tiny sprigs of *parsley.*

ABOUT 4 DOZEN PINWHEELS

BONNET SANDWICHES

1 can (4½ oz.) deviled ham	¼ cup mayonnaise
1 cup chopped cooked chicken	8 oz. cream cheese
¼ cup chopped celery	12 slices white bread
¼ cup toasted slivered almonds	12 thin slices white bread

1. Mix the deviled ham, chicken, celery, almonds, and mayonnaise thoroughly; set aside.
2. Beat cream cheese with enough *milk* until of spreading consistency. Divide into portions and tint each with a *few drops food coloring*; set aside.
3. Using 1½-inch cookie cutter, cut rounds for hat crowns from the regular-sliced bread. Using a larger cookie cutter, cut rounds for hat brims from the thinly sliced bread.
4. Spoon 2 tablespoons of the chicken mixture on center of each large round of bread. Top with the small round. Frost each hat with the cream cheese. Decorate as desired.   1 DOZEN SANDWICHES

GOLDEN FROSTED SANDWICH LOAF

1 loaf (2 lb.) sandwich bread, unsliced	Sliced Tomato Filling, *below*
6 tablespoons butter or margarine, whipped	Chicken-Almond Filling, *below*
Creamy Ham Filling, *below*	Sharp Cheese Frosting, *below*

1. Remove crusts from bread; cut lengthwise into 4 equal slices. Spread one side of bottom and third slice with butter. Place bottom slice, buttered side up, on a large piece of heavy-duty aluminum foil.
2. Spread Creamy Ham Filling over bottom slice.
3. Spread second slice of bread with cheese-onion dip mixture; place over ham layer. Top with bacon, then tomato slices and chopped olives. Cover with third slice, buttered side up.
4. Spread Chicken-Almond Filling over third slice of bread and cover with fourth slice. Wrap loaf in the foil and set in refrigerator.
5. About 20 minutes before serving, unwrap loaf and place on a baking sheet. Frost sides and top with Sharp Cheese Frosting. Garnish with *3 thin tomato slices* and *sliced filberts or almonds*.
6. Heat in a 450°F oven 5 minutes, or until lightly browned. Serve at once.   12 TO 14 SERVINGS

CREAMY HAM FILLING: Blend thoroughly *1¼ cups ground ham, 3 tablespoons chopped pimiento-stuffed olives, 1½ teaspoons finely chopped onion, 5 tablespoons mayonnaise,* and *1½ tablespoons prepared horseradish*; cover; refrigerate.

SLICED TOMATO FILLING: Whip *3 ounces cream cheese* with *½ package (1 tablespoon) dry onion dip mix.* Cover; set aside. Prepare *3 slices diced, pan-broiled bacon, six ¼ inch tomato slices,* and *3 tablespoons chopped ripe olives*; cover; refrigerate.

CHICKEN-ALMOND FILLING: Toss together *1¼ cups chopped cooked chicken, 5 tablespoons chopped salted blanched almonds, 3 tablespoons grated coconut,* and *1½ tablespoons capers.* Blend *½ cup mayonnaise, 1½ teaspoons red wine vinegar,* and *½ teaspoon Italian salad dressing mix.* Blend thoroughly with chicken mixture; cover; refrigerate.

SHARP CHEESE FROSTING: Whip together until fluffy *2 jars (5 ounces each) sharp process cheese spread* and *2 packages (3 ounces each) cream cheese.* Set aside.

SUPER SANDWICH LOAF

1 loaf (1 lb.) French bread	1 teaspoon prepared horseradish
½ cup butter	8 slices salami
1 cup shredded sharp Cheddar cheese	8 slices mozzarella cheese
½ teaspoon dry mustard	8 thin lengthwise slices dill pickle
2 tablespoons ketchup	8 thin green pepper rings
¼ cup chopped onion	8 thin slices baked ham
2 tablespoons chopped parsley	

1. Cut loaf into 1½ inch slices almost through to bottom. Using a sharp-pointed knife, cut out alternate slices, leaving ¼ inch of the crust at bottom.
2. Blend butter and cheese; mix in the dry mustard, ketchup, onion, parsley, and horseradish.
3. Place loaf on a large piece of aluminum foil or a baking sheet. Spread cheese mixture generously over the surface of each cutout section.
4. Arrange vertically in each cavity: 1 slice of salami, folded in half, 1 slice of mozzarella cheese, 1 slice of pickle, 1 green pepper ring, and 1 slice of ham, folded in thirds.
5. Set loaf in a 400°F oven and heat about 10 minutes, or until cheese mixture begins to melt.
6. With a sharp knife divide slices in half, cutting through bottom crust to separate.   8 SERVINGS

Chapter 5

EGG & CHEESE DISHES

ABOUT EGGS The perfection of an egg is one of nature's miracles, for here is an object lovely in form, filled with nourishment, and so versatile that few foods can match it. Served alone or in combination with other foods, eggs are equally appealing in the morning, at noon, and at night.

Grading—Graded eggs in cartons kept in a clean, cold refrigerator by the dealer are safe buys.

Eggs may be graded according to federal, state, or private standards. U.S. grades refer to interior quality; sizes refer to weight per dozen.

Grade AA and A eggs are top quality. They have a large amount of thick white and a high, firm yolk. Good for all uses, they are the best choice for poaching, frying, or cooking in the shell. Grade B and C eggs have thinner whites and somewhat flatter yolks which may break easily. Offering the same food values as top-grade eggs, these less expensive eggs are a practical buy for scrambling, thickening sauces, making salad dressings, and combining with other foods. Quality of eggs should be checked before using by breaking each egg in a small dish.

Whether the color of the egg shell is brown or white makes no difference in the quality or food value of the egg, though in some localities it does influence price. Eggs with brown shells sometimes have yolks of deeper yellow color than those with white shells.

Most eggs are grouped according to these sizes: jumbo, extra large, large, medium, and small—with a minimum weight per dozen of 30, 27, 24, 21, and 18 ounces respectively. Small eggs were at one time more plentiful in late summer and fall and at that time were likely to be a good buy. However, this marketing pattern is changing to reflect the growing tendency to year-round baby chick production. Nowadays egg production is geared so that young pullets (less than a year old) come into their laying period throughout the entire year.

Their first eggs are small, increasing in size as the hen grows to maturity. Weight for weight the nutritive value and cooking performance of small eggs equal those of large eggs of the same quality grade. Only because of their smaller size is the price per dozen less than that of large eggs.

Nutrients—Eggs are an important food for children and adults alike because they contain many important nutrients—complete protein, vitamins A and D, the B vitamins, iron, and phosphorous.

Storing—As soon as possible after purchasing, store eggs in the refrigerator in their own egg container to keep them upright, or store on the egg shelf of the refrigerator door, small ends down. Remove only as many eggs as needed at one time.

Do not buy cracked or soiled eggs. If some eggs have been cracked bringing them from the market, cook those as soon as possible. If ever necessary to remove soil from eggs, wipe them with a damp cloth before storing them or wash them just before using. Washing them before storing removes the film or "bloom" which seals the pores of the shell and keeps out bacteria and odors.

Food Preparation—The fundamental rule in egg cookery is: *Cook eggs with low to medium, even heat.* This applies to all methods of cooking eggs. Too high a temperature and overcooking toughen the protein in eggs and egg dishes, making them leathery and/or curdled.

In combining hot mixtures with whole eggs or egg yolks, always *slowly* add the hot mixture (3 or 4 spoonfuls or entire amount) to the beaten egg, stirring or beating constantly.

Separating egg yolks from egg whites is quicker

and easier if done soon after eggs are removed from refrigerator. However, eggs at room temperature, especially egg whites, beat to a greater volume than eggs taken directly from the refrigerator. (For stages of beating eggs, see *page 10*.)

Leftover egg whites may be refrigerated (in covered containers) about one week. For longer periods they should be frozen. Uses for egg whites: angel food or white cake, seven-minute frosting, meringue. Store leftover egg yolks in refrigerator; use within 2 or 3 days. Freeze them for longer storage periods.

HELPFUL HINTS ABOUT EGGS

• To divide a raw egg, beat well before measuring with a tablespoon.
• To hard-cook egg yolks, use only unbroken yolks and slip them gently into simmering water. Keep below boiling point until yolks are firm. Remove with a slotted spoon.
• To slice hard-cooked eggs without breaking the yolk, dip knife into water before slicing.

SOFT-COOKED EGGS

Put eggs into a saucepan and cover with cold or warm water. Cover. Bring water rapidly to boiling. Turn off heat. If necessary to prevent further boiling, remove saucepan from heat source. Let stand, covered, 2 to 4 minutes, depending upon firmness desired. Cool eggs promptly in cold water for several seconds to prevent further cooking. Serve hot. NOTE: When cooking more than four eggs, do not turn off heat but reduce heat to keep water below simmering. (Eggs are a protein food and therefore should never be boiled.) Hold 4 to 6 minutes.

HARD-COOKED EGGS: Follow method for Soft-Cooked Eggs. After bringing water to boiling, let eggs stand, covered, 20 to 22 minutes. Cool cooked eggs promptly under running cold water and crackle the shells. Roll eggs between hands to loosen shell, then start peeling at large end.

ABOUT CHEESE

For the fullest enjoyment of most cheeses, remove them from the refrigerator at least 1 hour before serving; the interior of Camembert and Brie should be almost runny. Serve Neufchâtel, cottage, and cream cheeses chilled.

The joy of cheese is in the tasting. An English gourmet once said that "the only way to learn about cheese is to eat it," and for some 4,000 years of recorded history people have been doing just that.

No one knows just how or when cheese was discovered. The ancient Greeks esteemed it so highly that they believed it to be a gift of the gods. Legend has it that it was discovered quite by accident when an Arab traveler carried as part of his food supply on a journey across the desert some milk in a crude container fashioned from a sheep's stomach. By some happy chance the heat of the day and the rennet still remaining in the container caused the milk to separate into curds and whey. The whey satisfied the traveler's thirst and the curd his appetite —and so cheese was born.

Few foods equal cheese for nutritive value and variety of flavor and texture. More than 350 different cheeses have been catalogued and described, oftentimes in accents of rapture. Cheese is produced and prized around the world. It serves more purposes than can be listed here. It can be used as an appetizer, entrée, or dessert, and the magic of its flavor—its many flavors—combines enchantingly with many other foods. Cooking with cheese is a fascinating and rewarding adventure. Success is certain if two simple rules are kept in mind. Cheese requires a low temperature, since it is a protein food and it must not be overcooked.

In different parts of the world, different kinds of milk and different methods of handling cheese have produced many different and distinctive types. As people of many lands came to the United States, they brought the knowledge of and the taste for native cheeses with them. As a result, many kinds of cheese which originated abroad are today being produced in this country, and a good many of them are also imported from their native lands and made available to American homemakers.

A few, such as Roquefort or blue, Swiss, Parmesan, and most of all, Cheddar, have become so thoroughly domesticated here that almost everyone knows them and has used them at some time. But others, which also offer a great deal of eating pleasure, are not as widely known.

These cheese varieties are *natural cheeses*, made directly from milk, with or without aging and "ripening" by bacterial action or molds. Natural cheese is purchased in cuts made from the big "wheels" and other forms; it is also available precut into slices, wedges, and convenient-shaped pieces and prewrapped in airtight packages. Natural cheeses made domestically are often made in loaves or bricks which would not be recognized in the native lands of the cheeses.

There are four types of natural cheeses: Soft, semisoft, hard, and very hard. The *soft cheeses* include the unripened cream and cottage cheese as well as the ripened Camemberts and Bries (both table rather than cooking cheeses). The *semisoft cheeses* are Roquefort and other blue-veined cheeses which are often used in dressings and spreads. The *hard cheeses* include Swiss and Cheddar and these are the most commonly used cooking cheeses. *Very hard cheeses* like Parmesan and Romano are generally grated and used as toppings for cooked foods.

In the United States various other forms of cheese have been developed through the years,

such as: *Process cheese*—Produced from natural cheeses blended for uniformity of flavor, texture, and cooking quality. The cheeses are ground together, melted, pasteurized, and poured into molds lined with moisture-vaporproof packaging material; the packages are sealed and the cheese, virtually sterilized, is cooled in the packages. Process cheese has typically a perfectly smooth consistency and good keeping quality.

Cheese food—May either be process, made like process cheese but with certain dairy products added; or cold-pack, with the same additions but not pasteurized. The process type is perfectly smooth; the cold-pack type is somewhat granular and crumbly because it is not homogenized.

Process cheese spreads—Cheese foods of a slightly higher moisture content to produce a more spreadable consistency at room temperature.

CHEESE CHART

Name	Flavor, Texture, Color, Usage	Origin
Soft		
Bel Paese	Creamy with a firm rind and moderately sharp flavor. A pleasing addition to the cheese tray.	Italy
Boursin	Extremely delicate yet rich cream-style frequently mixed with herbs; usually served with white wine.	France
Brie	Made from whole or partly skimmed milk. A surface ripened cheese with a distinctive flavor.	France
Camembert	Very soft, almost runny, with a pungent flavor. Bring it to room temperature before serving; eat the rind with the cheese. Serve with crackers and fruit as dessert; delicious on apple slices or in a hot appetizer.	France
Cottage	Uncured; usually made from skimmed milk. It is always eaten fresh. (Covered tightly, it can be kept 2 or 3 days in the refrigerator, but not longer.) A versatile cheese, it is used in salads, with fruits, in certain cooked or baked dishes, such as the cheese cakes.	Unknown
Coulommiers	A rennet cheese somewhat like Brie.	France
Cream	Uncured; made from cream or a mixture of milk and cream. Very mild in flavor, must be eaten fresh, may be eaten alone as a rich spread on crackers or blended with more flavorful foods. Often used, softened and sweetened, as cake topping. It is also useful in cooking.	United States
Liederkranz	Surface ripened; creamy-white; mildly pungent. Fine with crackers or rye bread, on the cheese tray, and served with beer.	United States
Limburger	A rennet cheese. Resembles Liederkranz in texture, but with a much stronger flavor and aroma.	Belgium

Name	Flavor, Texture, Color, Usage	Origin
Liptauer	Made from the milk of the sheep that browse the Carpathian mountains. In its native country it is often mixed with sharp seasonings and eaten on dark bread as an appetizer.	Hungary
Livarot	Made from partially skimmed milk. Somewhat like Brie with a strong piquant flavor.	France
Neufchâtel	Similar in flavor and texture to cream cheese, but with a lower fat content. Used in the same ways. A popular dessert cheese.	France
Ricotta	Mild. Usually used in cooking. It is marketed either fresh and moist (like a smooth cottage cheese) or dry, suitable for grating.	Italy

Semisoft

Name	Flavor, Texture, Color, Usage	Origin
Appetitost	Made from sour buttermilk; nutty-flavored. Serve as an appetizer.	Denmark
Blue	Similar to Roquefort; made from cows' milk as a domestic variety. Semisoft to hard; sharp, salty flavor. (Spelled "bleu" on imported.)	United States
Brick	Mild to sharp flavor. Creamy-yellow with small holes. A popular sandwich cheese.	United States
Danish Blue	Slightly off-white with a sharp distinctive flavor. It has a creamy consistency and a blue-green mold. Very popular in salad dressing.	Denmark
Edam	Usually made in a cannonball shape; semisoft to hard; mild, salty flavor. A bright red rind is characteristic. The rind of imported Edam is colored and the cheese is then wrapped in transparent film; domestic Edams are usually covered in red paraffin or a tightly adhering red plastic film. Usually served on a cheese tray with the top cut off so the interior may be scooped out and spread on crisp crackers.	Netherlands
Gammelost	Made from skimmed sour milk; sharp, strong flavor; brownish-yellow color.	Norway
Gorgonzola	A rennet cheese with streaks of mold. Similar to Roquefort and Blue.	Italy
Gouda	Very similar to Edam; usually shaped like a flattened ball. Though Goudas may weigh as much as 50 pounds, "Baby" Goudas weighing about 1 pound are more familiar in this country. The rind is usually (but not invariably) red. A popular dessert cheese.	Netherlands
Mozzarella	Fresh, unsalted, white, and moist; delicate flavor. It may be eaten sliced or used in baked dishes. Imported Mozzarella cheeses are sometimes spherical in shape.	Italy
Muenster	Made of whole milk with caraway seed sometimes added; semisoft to hard; pungent flavor. It is used for appetizers and sandwiches.	Germany
Pont l'Évêque	Made from cows' milk; strong flavor, stronger than Camembert.	France
Port du Salut	Whole milk cheese first made by the Trappist monks. Mellow in flavor with a characteristic odor; a brownish crust seals its creamy yellow inside. Served usually with fruit and in making fondue. Also known as Oka or Trappist.	France

Name	Flavor, Texture, Color, Usage	Origin
Roquefort	The original blue-veined cheese. Only cheese made from ewe's milk in the Roquefort area of France, and cured in the caves of that district, may be called Roquefort; therefore all Roquefort is imported. Sharp and slightly peppery; firm but crumbly, with blue-green veins of mold throughout. Delicious for salads, appetizers, and dessert.	France
Scamorze	Similar to Mozzarella. Either of these cheeses may be used for pizza.	Italy
Stilton	Similar to Roquefort or blue, having a green or blue mold in a white paste; wrinkled or ridged skin or rind.	England

Hard

Caciocavallo	Spindle-shaped; piquant in flavor; similar to Provolone. May be used in the same manner as Provolone.	Italy
Cheddar	Firm; flavorful. It is reputed to have originated in the village of Cheddar, England, but it has become so Americanized that it is often known as American cheese. About 75 percent of all the cheese made in this country is Cheddar, varying in flavor from very mild to very sharp, depending on length of aging and ripening process. Used for sandwiches, in cooked dishes, on cheese trays, and often for dessert.	England
Gjetost	Made from goats' milk whey, or more commonly from whey obtained when cheese is made from a mixture of goats' and cows' milk. Mild with a sweetish flavor; firm, buttery consistency; golden brown. Most typically used for smorgasbord, almost always with dark breads.	Norway
Gruyère	Similar to Swiss cheese with smaller holes and sharper flavor.	Switzerland
Herkimer	A sharp, aged Cheddar produced in New York State; it originated in Herkimer county. Pale creamy-yellow; dry and crumbly; sharp in flavor. Excellent for cooking, sandwiches, dessert, the cheese tray.	United States
Leyden	A rennet cheese resembling Gouda. Cloves and cumin seed and sometimes color added.	Netherlands
Mysost	Similar to Gjetost, but made from cows' milk.	Norway
Parmesan (Reggiano)	Yellow-white with sharp flavor. Made from partly skimmed milk. Sold in wedges, also grated or shredded. Used as a seasoning.	Italy
Provolone	Firm, smooth, pear-shaped, usually smoked. A table cheese when partially cured; suitable for grating when fully cured and dried. Generally made from cows' milk.	Italy
Romano	Well-cured, hard; sharp flavor. It is grated for seasoning.	Italy
Samsoe	Rich, golden, resembling Swiss cheese.	Denmark
Sapsago	Very hard; colored green by the addition of powdered dried clover leaves. Suitable for grating; when grated it is used in cooking.	Switzerland
Swiss (Emmenthaler)	Almost white with elastic body, immediately recognizable by large eyes (gas holes) up to 1 inch in diameter, which develop in the curd as the cheese ripens. Mild and nut-like; imported Swiss has more pronounced flavor due to longer ripening. A favorite for sandwiches; it toasts well, is delicious in cooked dishes and adds eye appeal and flavor to the cheese tray. Slice rather thick to compensate for holes.	Switzerland

EGG DISHES

Poached Eggs

POACHED EGGS

Grease bottom of a skillet. Pour in *water* to a depth of 2 inches. Bring water to boiling; reduce heat to keep water at simmering point. Break each *egg* into a saucer or small dish and quickly slip into water, holding the saucer close to the surface of the water. Cook 3 to 5 minutes, depending upon firmness desired. Carefully remove egg with a slotted spoon or pancake turner. Drain by holding spoon on absorbent paper for a few seconds. Season with *salt* and *pepper.* Serve immediately.

EGGS AU GRATIN
(Oeufs Gratines Laperouse)
A recipe from Restaurant Laperouse in Paris.

1 cup finely chopped mushrooms	8 poached eggs, *above*
2 tablespoons butter	1 cup Hollandaise Sauce, *page 344*
1 to 1½ cups Béchamel Sauce, *page 342*	¼ cup grated Parmesan cheese

1. Cook mushrooms in butter until very dry.
2. Mix in the desired amount of Béchamel Sauce.
3. Spread the mushroom sauce in 4 ovenproof ramekins. Put 2 poached eggs in each dish and cover with Hollandaise Sauce. Sprinkle with Parmesan cheese and brown under the broiler.
4 SERVINGS

POACHED EGGS "DUCHESSE ANNE"
A breakfast or luncheon treat from the Grand Hotel de la Place in Dinan, France.

3 large tomatoes, cut in halves	½ cup strong beef broth
2 cups chopped mushrooms	¼ cup port wine
¼ cup chopped onion	6 bread rounds, 4 in. each
3 tablespoons butter	3 tablespoons butter, softened
⅓ cup chopped parsley	6 poached eggs, *above*
¼ cup soft bread crumbs	12 slices bacon, fried

1. Scoop out seeds from tomato halves. Put tomatoes into a shallow baking pan; set aside.

2. Add mushrooms and onion to 3 tablespoons hot butter in a skillet; cook until just tender. Mix in parsley and bread crumbs; heat 2 minutes.
3. Season tomato halves with *salt* and *pepper;* spoon in mushroom mixture.
4. Bake at 350°F about 20 minutes, or until tomatoes are just tender.
5. Meanwhile, simmer broth to reduce by one half; mix in the wine; simmer 5 minutes.
6. Spread the butter on both sides of the bread rounds; heat rounds in skillet until golden brown.
7. Arrange toast rounds on preheated platter. Place a tomato half on each round and drizzle with wine sauce. Top each with a poached egg and 2 bacon strips.
6 SERVINGS

EGGS BENEDICT

4 English muffin halves, buttered and toasted	4 poached eggs, *above* Hollandaise Sauce, *page 344*
4 thin slices cooked ham, heated	

Top each toasted English muffin with a ham slice. Place one poached egg on each ham slice. Season with *salt* and *pepper.* Spoon Hollandaise Sauce over each serving.
4 SERVINGS

Scrambled Eggs

SCRAMBLED EGGS

6 eggs	¾ teaspoon salt
6 tablespoons milk, cream, or undiluted evaporated milk	⅛ teaspoon pepper
	3 tablespoons butter or margarine

1. Beat the eggs, milk, salt, and pepper together until blended.
2. Heat an 8- or 10-inch skillet until hot enough to sizzle a drop of water. Melt butter in skillet.
3. Pour egg mixture into skillet and cook over low heat. With a spatula, lift mixture from bottom and sides of skillet as it thickens, allowing uncooked portion to flow to bottom. Cook until eggs are thick and creamy.
4 SERVINGS

SCRAMBLED EGGS DE LUXE: Follow recipe for

Scrambled Eggs. Add *½ teaspoon Worcestershire sauce* and *¼ cup finely shredded Cheddar cheese* to egg mixture in skillet. Cook as directed. Before removing from heat, gently stir in *1 medium-sized firm ripe tomato*, cut in small cubes, and *1 cup croutons, ¼ to ½ inch.*   4 TO 6 SERVINGS

PARTY SCRAMBLED EGGS

9 eggs	¼ teaspoon pepper
1 can (14½ oz.) evaporated milk	2 tablespoons snipped chives
1 teaspoon Worcestershire sauce	2 tablespoons butter or margarine
Few drops Tabasco	3 oz. cream cheese, cubed
¾ teaspoon salt	

1.   To the eggs in a bowl, add evaporated milk, Worcestershire sauce, Tabasco, salt, and pepper. Beat until light and foamy. Stir in the snipped chives.
2.   Pour boiling water to a depth of about 1 inch into the outer pan of a 1½-quart chafing dish; set over heat. Heat butter in the blazer (inner pan) over the hot water until completely melted.
3.   Pour in egg mixture; cover and cook for 15 minutes without stirring. Then stir once and continue cooking, covered, 15 minutes.
4.   Mix cream cheese cubes into the cooked eggs; cover and heat until cheese begins to melt, about 1 minute.   6 TO 8 SERVINGS

BACON AND CREAM CHEESE SCRAMBLE

6 tablespoons milk, cream, or undiluted evaporated milk	¼ teaspoon salt
	⅛ teaspoon black pepper
3 oz. cream cheese, cubed	3 tablespoons butter or margarine
2 tablespoons butter or margarine	½ cup diced cooked bacon
6 eggs	

1.   Put the milk, cream cheese, and 2 tablespoons butter into top of a double boiler. Heat over simmering water until cheese is softened. Stir to blend.
2.   Beat the eggs, salt, and pepper until blended. Stir into the cheese mixture.
3.   Heat a skillet until hot enough to sizzle a drop of water. Melt the 3 tablespoons butter. Add a mixture of eggs and cooked bacon. Cook over low heat.

With a spatula, lift mixture from bottom and sides of skillet as it thickens, allowing uncooked portion to flow to bottom. Cook until thick and creamy.   4 SERVINGS

HAM AND CREAM CHEESE SCRAMBLE: Follow recipe for Bacon and Cream Cheese Scramble. Substitute *½ cup diced cooked ham* for bacon.

SCRAMBLED EGGS WITH CHEESE
After a busy day Jerry Lewis finds that eggs with cheese hit the spot, so he heads for the kitchen and takes matters into his own hands.

4 eggs	¼ cup grated American cheese
¼ teaspoon salt	
Few grains pepper	1½ tablespoons butter

1.   Break eggs, one at a time, into a cup; then turn each into a medium bowl before adding the next.
2.   Add salt, pepper, and cheese, then beat with a fork just enough to blend.
3.   Melt butter in an 8-inch skillet, tilting it so bottom and sides are covered. When butter is hot, pour in egg mixture.
4.   Cook over low heat, scraping gently as eggs set, so they will cook uniformly. Cook until done, but still moist — eggs will continue to cook in the hot pan on the way to the plate. Serve immediately.   ABOUT 2 SERVINGS

FRANKFURTER-EGG SCRAMBLE

1 slice bacon, diced	3 eggs
½ cup finely chopped onion	1 tablespoon milk
	⅛ teaspoon salt
½ lb. frankfurters, sliced	Few grains black pepper
1 green pepper, cut in strips	⅛ teaspoon Worcestershire sauce
¼ cup chili sauce	

1.   Cook bacon in a large heavy skillet. Add onion and cook 3 minutes. Add frankfurter slices and green pepper strips; cook until strips are just tender. Stir in the chili sauce.
2.   Beat eggs and remaining ingredients together until blended; pour over mixture in skillet. Cook over low heat; with a spatula lift mixture from bottom and sides as it thickens, allowing uncooked portion to flow to bottom. Cook until eggs are set, but are still moist.   ABOUT 4 SERVINGS

PISTO À LA "EL CHICO"

A favorite main-dish egg scramble from Señor Benito Collada, impresario of New York City's smart El Chico Spanish Restaurant.

1 large clove garlic	⅓ cup (2 oz.) diced
1 cup thinly sliced onion	cooked ham
1 cup slivered green	2 cups small cubes
pepper	yellow summer squash
½ cup olive oil	2 cups peeled, finely
1 cup thin raw potato	cut, ripe tomatoes
strips	2 teaspoons salt
1 tablespoon chopped	1 teaspoon sugar
parsley	⅛ teaspoon pepper
	6 eggs, beaten

1. Add garlic, onion, and green pepper to heated olive oil in a large skillet; cook until softened, then remove garlic.
2. Add remaining ingredients except eggs to skillet; cook over medium heat, stirring frequently, about 10 minutes, or until squash is just tender.
3. Pour beaten eggs into vegetables and cook as for *Scrambled Eggs, page 130.*   6 SERVINGS

ANCHOVY SCRAMBLED EGGS

8 eggs	1 teaspoon lemon juice
½ to ¾ cup milk	1 teaspoon grated
½ teaspoon salt	onion
⅛ teaspoon pepper	¼ teaspoon paprika
2 tablespoons butter	2 tablespoons snipped
or margarine	parsley
1 can (2 oz.) anchovy	6 toast rounds,
fillets, drained and	buttered
rubbed to a smooth	
paste	

1. Beat the eggs, milk, salt, and pepper together until blended.
2. Pour the egg mixture into hot butter in a skillet over low heat. With a spatula, lift mixture from bottom and sides of skillet as it thickens, allowing uncooked portion to flow to bottom. Cook until eggs are slightly thickened.
3. Meanwhile, thoroughly blend the anchovies, lemon juice, onion, and paprika.
4. Gently fold about 2 teaspoons of the anchovy paste and the parsley into the slightly thickened eggs. Continue cooking until the eggs are thick and creamy.
5. Spread remaining anchovy paste over warm buttered toast rounds. Spoon egg mixture over toast and serve with crisp *bacon.*

ABOUT 6 SERVINGS

AVOCADO AND DEVILED HAM SCRAMBLE: Follow recipe for Anchovy Scrambled Eggs. Substitute *1 can (2¼ ounces) deviled ham* for the seasoned anchovy paste and parsley. Before serving, fold in *1 medium-sized ripe avocado* which has been diced, tossed with *1 teaspoon lemon juice*, and sprinkled lightly with *salt.*

Omelets

FRENCH OMELET

6 eggs	⅛ teaspoon black
6 tablespoons milk or	pepper
water	3 tablespoons butter
¾ teaspoon salt	or margarine

1. Beat the eggs, milk, salt, and pepper together until blended.
2. Heat an 8- to 10-inch skillet until just hot enough to sizzle a drop of water; melt butter in the skillet.
3. Pour egg mixture into skillet. As edges of omelet begin to thicken, draw cooked portions toward center with spoon or fork to allow uncooked mixture to flow to bottom of skillet, tilting skillet as necessary; do not stir.
4. When eggs are thickened but surface is still moist, increase heat to quickly brown the bottom of omelet. Loosen edges carefully and fold in half; slide onto a warm serving platter. If desired, garnish with sprigs of *watercress.*   4 TO 6 SERVINGS

CITRUS OMELET: Follow recipe for French Omelet. Substitute *3 tablespoons lemon or orange juice* and *3 tablespoons water* for liquid.

CHICKEN LIVER OMELET: Follow recipe for French Omelet. Just before serving, enclose in omelet *¼ pound chicken livers* which have been coated with *seasoned flour* and browned in *butter or margarine* with *minced onion.*

BACON OMELET: Unwrap *½ pound sliced bacon*, do not separate, and cut crosswise into fine thin strips. Put into an unheated 8- to 10-inch skillet and fry until crisp. Drain bacon fat from skillet and return about 2 tablespoons fat to skillet. Follow recipe for French Omelet. Decrease salt to *½ teaspoon*, omit butter, and pour egg mixture over bacon in skillet.

ROQUEFORT OMELET

At the Fleur de Lis Restaurant in San Francisco, California, Roquefort Omelet is a featured dish. Follow recipe for French Omelet. Substitute ¼ *cup heavy cream and 1 tablespoon melted butter* for the milk, decrease salt to ¼ teaspoon, omit pepper, and add a *few grains cayenne pepper*. Before browning bottom of omelet, sprinkle with about ¼ *pound crumbled Roquefort cheese* (reserve a little for garnish). Top the omelet with the cheese and snipped *parsley*.

SAUCY HAM OMELET

1 can (12 oz.) chopped ham, cut in sticks	2 tablespoons milk
2 tablespoons butter or margarine	1 tablespoon flour
	⅛ teaspoon salt
4 eggs	Apple Sauce, *below*

1. Brown ham sticks in a skillet.
2. Add butter to skillet, then a blend of the eggs, milk, flour, and salt. Arrange ham sticks spoke-fashion; cook until egg mixture is set.
3. Cut into wedges and serve with warm Apple Sauce. ABOUT 4 SERVINGS

APPLE SAUCE: Heat *1 can (12 ounce) apple juice* in a saucepan until hot. Stir in a mixture of *2 tablespoons brown sugar, 1 tablespoon cornstarch, ¼ teaspoon ground cinnamon,* and *2 tablespoons lemon juice*. Bring to boiling, stirring constantly; simmer about 10 minutes, or until slightly thickened. Remove from heat and stir in *1 tablespoon butter or margarine* until melted.

ABOUT 1¼ CUPS SAUCE

MUSHROOM OMELET

¾ lb. fresh mushrooms, sliced lengthwise	⅛ teaspoon pepper
½ cup butter or margarine	1 cup milk
¼ cup flour	3 eggs, slightly beaten
½ teaspoon salt	4 teaspoons butter or margarine

1. Cook mushrooms in ¼ cup hot butter in a large skillet until lightly browned and tender. Reserve 8 slices for garnish. Put remaining mushrooms into a bowl; cover and set aside in a warm place.
2. Blend flour, salt, and pepper into the remaining ¼ cup butter heated in a saucepan. Heat until bubbly. Gradually add the milk, stirring constantly.

3. Remove from heat and vigorously stir about ⅓ cup hot mixture into the beaten eggs. Blend into remaining hot mixture. Cover and set aside.
4. Heat an 8-inch skillet until hot enough to sizzle a drop of water; melt 1 teaspoon butter. Pour about a fourth of the egg mixture into the skillet and cook until lightly browned on bottom and firm but slightly moist on top. Loosen edges carefully with spatula and slide omelet layer into a shallow round baking dish.
5. Spoon a third of mushrooms over omelet layer. Repeat process with remaining egg mixture, alternating omelet and mushroom layers. Top the last omelet layer with reserved mushroom slices.
6. Bake at 350°F 10 to 15 minutes, or until thoroughly heated. Cut into wedges and garnish with *parsley*. 4 SERVINGS

EGG FOO YONG

These omelet-type pancakes are served in just about every restaurant where Chinese food is featured.

1 cup finely diced cooked ham, roast pork, or chicken	¼ to ½ teaspoon salt (smaller amount with ham)
1 cup drained canned bean sprouts	6 eggs, slightly beaten
¾ cup chopped onion	Fat or cooking oil (about ¼ cup or enough to form an ⅛-in. layer)
1 tablespoon soy sauce	
½ teaspoon monosodium glutamate	Sauce, *below*

1. Mix the ham, bean sprouts, onion, soy sauce, monosodium glutamate, and salt. Stir in the eggs.
2. Heat the fat in a large heavy skillet. Drop ¼-cup portions of the mixture into the hot fat to form patties. Cook about 5 minutes, or until browned on one side; turn and brown other side.
3. Lift from skillet with a pancake turner or slotted spoon; drain over fat for a few seconds. Transfer to a warm heat-resistant platter; keep warm in a 200°F oven while cooking remaining patties.
4. Pour hot sauce over the patties on the platter. Serve with fluffy *cooked rice* and additional soy sauce. 5 OR 6 SERVINGS

SAUCE: Blend *2 teaspoons cornstarch, 1 tablespoon cold water, 2 teaspoons soy sauce,* and *1 teaspoon bead molasses* in a small saucepan. Stir in *1 cup chicken broth*. Bring to boiling, stirring constantly. Boil 3 minutes, or until sauce is thickened. Keep hot. ¾ CUP SAUCE

ZUCCHINI OMELET

4 small zucchini
¼ cup butter or
  margarine
¾ teaspoon salt
Few grains pepper

½ cup shredded
  Parmesan cheese
½ teaspoon marjoram
4 eggs, beaten

1. Wash zucchini and trim off ends. Cut crosswise into ⅛-inch slices.
2. Heat the butter in a skillet over low heat; add zucchini and sprinkle with a mixture of the salt and pepper. Cook slowly, turning slices occasionally, until lightly browned.
3. Blend Parmesan cheese and marjoram into eggs. Pour mixture over zucchini in skillet and cook until egg mixture is set.
4. Remove skillet from heat and set under broiler about 4 inches from source of heat for 2 minutes, or until top is lightly browned. Serve cut in wedges.

4 SERVINGS

Shirred Eggs

SHIRRED EGGS WITH SAUSAGE AND CHEESE

Salami or bologna,
  thinly sliced
2 tablespoons butter
  or margarine

Swiss or Cheddar
  cheese, thinly sliced
6 eggs

1. Brown salami lightly in the butter in a skillet; reserve drippings in skillet.
2. Line a 9-inch pie plate with salami and add an even layer of cheese.
3. Break and slip eggs, one at a time, onto the cheese. Pour drippings over all. Season with *salt* and *pepper* and drizzle with *Worcestershire sauce*.
4. Bake at 325°F about 22 minutes, depending on doneness desired. Serve immediately with *parsley-buttered toast*.

6 SERVINGS

SHIRRED EGGS WITH CANADIAN-STYLE BACON

12 slices Canadian-style
  bacon, lightly
  browned
¼ cup cream
4 eggs

1. Butter 4 individual ramekins. Arrange 3 slices bacon in each. Add 1 tablespoon cream to each.

2. Break and slip an egg onto the bacon in each ramekin. Season eggs with *salt* and *pepper*.
3. Bake at 350°F 10 to 15 minutes, depending on doneness desired. Garnish with *fresh dill weed* and serve immediately.

4 SERVINGS

Hard-Cooked-Egg Dishes

EGGS STUFFED WITH CHICKEN LIVER PASTE

¼ lb. chicken livers
5 hard-cooked eggs
4 slices bacon, diced
  and fried until crisp
1 tablespoon chopped
  parsley
1½ teaspoons minced
  chives
½ teaspoon onion salt

¼ teaspoon tarragon
  leaves, crushed
¼ teaspoon salt
¼ teaspoon pepper
Few grains cayenne
  pepper
1½ to 2 tablespoons
  mayonnaise

1. Rinse chicken livers with cold water and drain; put livers into a saucepan and add enough hot water to barely cover. Cover saucepan and simmer 10 to 15 minutes, or until livers are tender when pierced with a fork; drain and set aside to cool.
2. Cut each hard-cooked egg into halves; remove egg yolks to a bowl and mash with a fork. Sieve the chicken livers into the bowl. Mix in bacon and remaining ingredients.
3. Fill egg whites with liver mixture and sprinkle with *paprika*. Chill thoroughly.
4. To serve, cut into halves and spear each on a frilly pick.

20 STUFFED EGG QUARTERS

CRAB-STUFFED EGGS

12 hard-cooked eggs,
  cut in halves
  lengthwise
1 can (6½ oz.) crab
  meat, drained and
  flaked
2 tablespoons melted
  butter
¼ cup dairy sour cream

2 to 3 tablespoons
  mayonnaise
4 drops Tabasco
4 teaspoons grated
  onion
½ teaspoon Worcester-
  shire sauce
½ teaspoon salt
⅛ teaspoon white
  pepper

1. Remove egg yolks from whites. Sieve yolks; toss with crab meat.

2. Blend in a mixture of the remaining ingredients. Stuff egg whites. Garnish each with *pimiento* or *parsley*.   24 STUFFED EGG HALVES

STUFFED EGGS SOPHISTICATE

12 hard-cooked eggs	2 tablespoons melted
3 oz. cream cheese,	butter
softened	¼ teaspoon Tabasco
½ cup dairy sour cream	¾ to 1 teaspoon salt
	¼ teaspoon dry mustard

1. Cut eggs lengthwise into quarters and remove egg yolks, leaving egg whites intact. Put egg yolks through a sieve. Set aside.
2. Beat cream cheese until fluffy; blend in sour cream, butter, Tabasco, and a mixture of the salt and dry mustard. Add egg yolks; mix lightly.
3. Fill egg whites by piping the mixture through a pastry bag and tube. Sprinkle with *paprika*.
4 DOZEN STUFFED EGG QUARTERS

CURRY-ALMOND-STUFFED EGGS: Follow recipe for Stuffed Eggs Sophisticate. Mix ½ *teaspoon curry powder* with salt and dry mustard. Blend ½ *cup toasted blanched almonds*, finely chopped, into the egg yolk mixture.

DILLY BACON-STUFFED EGGS: Follow recipe for Stuffed Eggs Sophisticate. Omit Tabasco and dry mustard. Blend into the cream cheese ½ *teaspoon dill weed, 1 tablespoon chopped capers,* and *2 teaspoons caper liquid.* Mix in *6 slices diced cooked bacon.*

PERKY STUFFED EGGS

12 hard-cooked eggs	2 tablespoons
⅓ cup finely chopped	mayonnaise
green pepper	2 tablespoons dairy
¼ cup chopped pimien-	sour cream
to-stuffed olives	2 teaspoons lemon
3 tablespoons finely	juice
chopped onion	6 drops Tabasco
2 tablespoons finely	¼ teaspoon salt
chopped parsley	Few grains pepper
¼ cup tomato sauce	½ teaspoon dry mustard

1. Using a sharp-pointed knife, cut a saw-toothed line lengthwise around each egg. Gently pull halves apart and remove egg yolks. Set whites aside.
2. Sieve egg yolks or mash them with a fork. Add the green pepper, olives, onion, parsley, and a mix-

ture of the remaining ingredients; mix well. Fill the egg whites with egg yolk mixture. Cover; chill thoroughly.   24 STUFFED EGG HALVES

EGGS EPICUREAN

¼ cup finely chopped	4 tablespoons butter
onion	or margarine
1 clove garlic, minced	9 hard-cooked eggs
1 tablespoon minced	¼ cup shredded
parsley	Cheddar cheese
⅛ teaspoon tarragon	2 tablespoons ketchup
⅛ teaspoon chervil	1 tablespoon dairy
½ lb. fresh mushrooms,	sour cream
finely chopped	Sauce, *below*

1. In a skillet or saucepan, cook the onion, garlic, parsley, tarragon, chervil, and mushrooms in hot butter 5 minutes, stirring occasionally.
2. Cut eggs lengthwise into halves; remove the yolks and set the whites aside. Sieve egg yolks, reserving 2 to 3 tablespoons for garnish. Add cheese, ketchup, sour cream, and mushroom mixture; blend well.
3. Spoon egg yolk mixture into reserved egg whites, rounding tops. Arrange in a buttered shallow baking dish. Cover with the sauce.
4. Heat in a 350°F oven about 15 minutes.
5. Sprinkle with reserved sieved egg yolk. Serve on buttered, toasted *English muffins.*
6 TO 8 SERVINGS

SAUCE

¼ cup finely chopped	2 cups chicken broth
onion	(dissolve 3 chicken
6 tablespoons butter	bouillon cubes in 2
or margarine	cups boiling water)
6 tablespoons flour	1½ cups cream
¾ teaspoon celery salt	¼ cup shredded sharp
½ teaspoon mono-	Cheddar cheese
sodium glutamate	2 tablespoons dairy
¼ teaspoon white	sour cream
pepper	

1. Cook onion in hot butter in a saucepan until soft. Blend in a mixture of the flour, celery salt, monosodium glutamate, and pepper; heat until bubbly.
2. Add chicken broth gradually, stirring constantly. Bring to boiling; stir and cook 2 minutes.
3. Remove from heat. Stir in cream, cheese, and sour cream until well blended.   4 CUPS SAUCE

EGG CURRY

½ cup finely chopped onion	½ teaspoon salt
3 tablespoons butter or margarine	⅛ teaspoon pepper
	1 teaspoon curry powder
2½ tablespoons flour	2 cups milk
2 teaspoons sugar	8 hard-cooked eggs

1. In a saucepan cook onion in hot butter until tender. Stir in a mixture of flour, sugar, salt, pepper, and curry powder. Add milk gradually, stirring until blended. Bring to boiling, stirring constantly, and boil 2 minutes.
2. Cut an "X" into small end of each hard-cooked egg.
3. Line a shallow serving bowl with hot fluffy *rice*, put eggs upright in rice, and spoon the hot sauce around them. Serve immediately.   4 SERVINGS

EGGS FARCI

In this casserole stuffed eggs and sausages are topped with a rich mushroom and ripe olive sauce, creating a tempting dish to offer guests.

8 hard-cooked eggs, cut in halves	4 teaspoons instant minced onion softened in 4 to 6 teaspoons water
1 cup cream	
½ cup all-purpose flour	
1 can (13¾ oz.) clear chicken broth	1 teaspoon Worcestershire sauce
2 cans (6 oz. each) chopped or sliced broiled-in-butter mushrooms, drained (reserve liquid)	1 cup pitted ripe olives, quartered lengthwise
	1 lb. pork sausage links or smokie link sausages, browned
	1 large tomato, cut in thin wedges*

1. Fill the egg white halves with a deviled mixture of *mayonnaise*, sieved egg yolks, *Worcestershire sauce*, *dry mustard*, *salt*, and *pepper* to taste. Arrange deviled egg halves in an ungreased 2-quart shallow baking dish; set aside.
2. Meanwhile, blend enough cream with flour in a saucepan to make a paste. Set over heat. Stirring constantly to keep mixture smooth, gradually add remaining cream, then chicken broth and reserved mushroom liquid. Stir occasionally until mixture begins to thicken, then stir constantly until it bubbles; continue to cook 2 to 3 minutes.
3. Blend in the onion, Worcestershire sauce,

mushrooms, and olives. Heat thoroughly and pour over stuffed eggs in the baking dish.
4. Alternate browned sausage links and tomato wedges over top, brush tomatoes with *oil*, and sprinkle with *monosodium glutamate* and *seasoned pepper*. Spoon coarse *buttered bread crumbs* (about ½ cup crumbs mixed with 1 tablespoon melted butter or margarine) over all.
5. Set under broiler about 5 inches from source of heat until crumbs are browned. Garnish with snipped *parsley*.   8 TO 10 SERVINGS
*If desired, use drained canned sliced tomatoes or tomato wedges.
NOTE: *Celery*, thinly sliced on the diagonal, may be cooked until crisp-tender in a small amount of the chicken broth and mixed into the sauce.

BACON 'N' EGG CROQUETTES

2 tablespoons chopped onion	6 hard-cooked eggs, coarsely chopped
3 tablespoons butter or margarine	8 slices bacon, cooked and finely crumbled
3 tablespoons flour	1 egg, fork beaten
½ teaspoon salt	2 tablespoons water
⅛ teaspoon black pepper	⅓ cup fine dry crumbs
¾ teaspoon dry mustard	Fat for deep frying heated to 385°F
¾ cup milk	

1. Add onion to hot butter in a saucepan and cook about 2 minutes, or until tender. Stir in a mixture of the flour, salt, pepper, and dry mustard. Heat until bubbly. Add milk gradually, stirring constantly. Cook and stir until mixture forms a ball.
2. Remove from heat and stir in chopped eggs and crumbled bacon. Refrigerate about 1 hour, or until chilled.
3. Divide mixture into 8 equal portions and shape into croquettes (balls or cones). Mix the egg with water. Roll croquettes in crumbs, dip into egg, and roll again in crumbs.
4. Fry uncrowded in the hot fat 2 minutes, or until golden. Remove croquettes with slotted spoon; drain over fat; put onto absorbent paper.
     8 CROQUETTES
HERBED EGG CROQUETTES: Follow recipe for Bacon 'n' Egg Croquettes. Decrease mustard to ¼ teaspoon and bacon to 4 slices. Add *½ teaspoon summer savory*, crushed, with mustard and *4 teaspoons snipped parsley* with chopped egg.

CHEESE DISHES

CHEESE CASSEROLE ROYALE

1 cup dairy sour cream	4 egg whites (½ cup)
⅔ cup shredded Swiss cheese	¾ teaspoon seasoned salt
4 egg yolks, well beaten	½ to ¾ cup ground walnuts
1 cup browned buttered soft bread crumbs	

1. Blend sour cream and cheese into beaten egg yolks. Turn into a greased 1½-quart shallow baking dish that has been sprinkled with the crumbs.
2. Set dish in a pan in a 375°F oven. Pour boiling water into pan to a depth of 1 inch. Bake 20 minutes, or until a knife inserted near center comes out clean.
3. Meanwhile, beat egg whites with salt until stiff, not dry, peaks are formed. Fold in walnuts.
4. Remove baking dish from oven and top with meringue. Return to oven and bake 8 minutes, or until meringue is browned.   ABOUT 6 SERVINGS

PIMIENTO-CRAB MEAT STRATA SUPREME

You'll be proud to serve this elegant dish as a colorful addition to a holiday buffet supper.

1 can (7½ oz.) Alaska king crab meat, drained and flaked	Butter or margarine, softened
½ cup finely chopped celery	3 jars or cans (4 oz. each) whole pimientos, each pimiento cut in 2 or 3 large pieces
¼ cup finely chopped onion	1 lb. Swiss cheese, shredded
¾ cup mayonnaise	5 eggs
Few grains cayenne pepper	3 cups milk
12 slices white bread, crusts removed	1 teaspoon salt
	⅛ teaspoon pepper
	¼ teaspoon dry mustard

1. Mix crab meat, celery, and onion. Blend in a mixture of the mayonnaise and cayenne pepper. Set aside.
2. Spread both sides of the bread slices with butter. Place half of the bread in one layer in a greased 3-quart shallow baking dish; reserve remainder.
3. Arrange half of the pimiento pieces over the bread, half of the crab mixture, and a third of the shredded cheese. Repeat layering using remainder of crab mixture, pimiento, and second third of the cheese. Cover with reserved bread and sprinkle with the remaining cheese.
4. Beat remaining ingredients together until frothy and blended. Pour over all. Let stand 1 hour.
5. Bake at 325°F 1 hour, or until puffed and browned.
6. Garnish top with three well-drained whole *pimientos* arranged in a bell cluster with *green pepper strips* between the bells. Nestle a small *parsley bouquet* at center.   6 TO 8 SERVINGS

DUTCH CHEESE CROQUETTES

1 cup milk	¾ lb. Gouda cheese, finely shredded
½ cup chopped carrot	1½ teaspoons lemon juice
⅓ cup chopped onion	
1 teaspoon salt	½ teaspoon ground nutmeg
¼ teaspoon thyme	
3 sprigs parsley	⅛ teaspoon black pepper
3 peppercorns	
1 bay leaf	1 cup fine dry bread crumbs
1½ teaspoons unflavored gelatin	1 egg, slightly beaten
¼ cup cold water	Fat for deep frying heated to 375°F
4½ tablespoons flour	
2 tablespoons butter	
1 egg yolk, slightly beaten	

1. Mix milk, carrot, onion, salt, thyme, parsley, peppercorns, and bay leaf in top of double boiler; heat 20 minutes over boiling water. Strain the mixture, reserving milk for sauce.
2. Soften gelatin in cold water and dissolve over hot water; set aside.
3. Blend flour into hot butter in a heavy saucepan; heat until bubbly. Add reserved milk gradually, stirring constantly. Bring to boiling; stir and cook 1 to 2 minutes.
4. Vigorously stir about 3 tablespoons hot mixture into egg yolk; immediately blend into mixture in saucepan. Cook and stir over low heat 2 minutes. Stir in cheese and heat just until melted.
5. Remove from heat. Stir in dissolved gelatin, then lemon juice, nutmeg, and pepper. Pour mixture into a shallow pan and chill about 4 hours.

6. Shape chilled mixture into balls, cones, or cylinders. Roll in bread crumbs, then dip into egg and again roll in bread crumbs, shaking off loose crumbs.

7. Deep fry in the hot fat, turning often to brown evenly. Remove with slotted spoon to absorbent paper. Serve hot. ABOUT 6 SERVINGS

Gnocchi

FORUM'S GNOCCHI

A recipe for Italian-style dumplings from New York City's The Forum of the Twelve Caesars.

1 cup water	3 eggs
2 tablespoons butter	1 cup shredded Swiss
½ teaspoon salt	cheese
¼ teaspoon cayenne	½ teaspoon dry mustard
pepper	¼ teaspoon salt
1½ cups sifted all-	Sauce, *below*
purpose flour	1 tablespoon butter

1. Bring water, butter, salt, and cayenne pepper to a rolling boil in a saucepan. Add the flour all at one time and beat vigorously with a wooden spoon until mixture leaves sides of saucepan and forms a smooth ball. Remove from heat.

2. Quickly beat in the eggs, one at a time, beating until smooth after each addition. Stir in ¼ cup of the Swiss cheese, the dry mustard, and salt.

3. Put the dough into a pastry bag fitted with a large plain tube. Squeeze dough in long pieces into gently boiling *salted water* in a saucepan.

4. Cook the gnocchi over low heat until they rise to the surface. Drain them and cut into ½-inch pieces. Turn gnocchi into a shallow baking dish.

5. Pour the sauce over the gnocchi, sprinkle evenly with the remaining ¾ cup cheese, and dot with the remaining butter. Place gnocchi under the broiler for about 3 minutes, or until golden.

4 SERVINGS

SAUCE: Stir *3 tablespoons flour* and *½ teaspoon dry mustard* into *2 tablespoons hot butter* in a saucepan. Add *1 cup milk* gradually, stirring constantly Cook and stir until bubbly. Blend in *½ cup cream* and *¼ cup shredded Swiss cheese*; cook 5 minutes. Stir a small amount of the hot sauce into a mixture of *1 egg yolk* and *¼ cup milk*. Blend egg yolk mixture into sauce; cook and stir over low heat until slightly thickened. ABOUT 1¾ CUPS SAUCE

CHEESE-SPINACH GNOCCHI

An interesting and highly nutritious meatless dish to keep in mind when balancing the food budget.

1½ cups milk	1 tablespoon chopped
1 tablespoon butter or	onion, lightly browned
margarine	in 1 teaspoon butter
¼ teaspoon salt	or margarine
Few grains ground	1½ cups shredded
nutmeg	Swiss cheese
¼ cup uncooked farina	2 eggs, well beaten
½ cup well-drained	¾ cup milk
cooked chopped	1 tablespoon flour
spinach	1 teaspoon salt
1 egg, well beaten	Few grains ground
	nutmeg

1. Bring milk, butter, salt, and nutmeg to boiling in a saucepan. Add farina gradually, stirring constantly over low heat until mixture thickens.

2. Stir in spinach, egg, onion, and 1 cup shredded cheese; mix well. Remove from heat and set aside to cool slightly.

3. Drop mixture by tablespoonfuls close together in a well-greased 9-inch shallow baking pan or casserole. Sprinkle mounds with remaining cheese.

4. Combine remaining ingredients and pour over spinach mounds.

5. Bake at 350°F 35 to 40 minutes, or until topping is golden brown. ABOUT 6 SERVINGS

GNOCCHI WESTPHALIENNE

A favorite dish from Grand Hotel National in Lucerne, Switzerland.

2 cups milk	¾ cup chopped
⅔ cup butter	Westphalian ham
2½ cups all-purpose	1 cup Béchamel Sauce,
flour	*page 342*
8 eggs	Shredded Swiss or
	Cheddar cheese

1. Bring milk, *salt* and *nutmeg* to taste, and butter to a boil in a heavy saucepan. Add flour all at once; beat vigorously with a wooden spoon until mixture is a smooth paste and leaves sides of saucepan.

2. Remove from heat and add eggs, one at a time, beating vigorously with spoon or electric beater after each addition. Stir in chopped ham.

3. Spoon the dough into a pastry bag fitted with a large plain tube. Force dough through the bag in ½-inch pieces into a saucepan of boiling *salted water*.

Gently boil the gnocchi 5 to 8 minutes, or until they are firm. Drain well and arrange in a baking dish.

4. Cover the gnocchi with Béchamel Sauce, sprinkle top with shredded cheese and dot with *butter*.

5. Place in a 400°F oven until golden brown on surface. ABOUT 6 SERVINGS

GNOCCHI ALLA SEMOLINO

1 qt. milk	¼ cup butter or
1 teaspoon salt	margarine
⅛ teaspoon freshly	3 eggs, well beaten
ground nutmeg	½ cup shredded
1 cup uncooked farina	Parmesan cheese

1. Bring the milk, salt, and nutmeg to boiling in a heavy saucepan. Add the farina gradually, stirring constantly to prevent lumping. Cook and stir over low heat 10 minutes, or until very thick. Remove from heat.

2. Beat in butter, eggs, and cheese. Spread mixture about ½ inch thick on a greased baking sheet. Chill thoroughly.

3. When ready to bake, top with bits of *butter or margarine* and generously sprinkle with *Parmesan cheese*. Heat in a 425°F oven until top is browned. (If melted butter tends to run off sides of baking sheet during baking, place a sheet of aluminum foil on rack below.) Serve cut in squares.

ABOUT 8 SERVINGS

NOTE: This recipe omits the cutting of the dough into shapes with a cookie cutter before baking.

Quiches, Pies & Tarts

QUICHE LORRAINE

Andre Pittet, Chef at the Hotel Saskatchewan of the Canadian Pacific Railway, contributed this recipe.

½ cup diced bacon	2 eggs, slightly
1 cup chopped onion	beaten
½ cup diced mushrooms	1 cup milk
1 unbaked 10-in. pastry	½ teaspoon salt
shell	⅛ teaspoon pepper
3 cups shredded white	¼ teaspoon nutmeg
Cheddar cheese	

1. Fry the bacon for 5 minutes in a skillet and pour off about half of the fat. Add onion and mushrooms and cook until onion is soft.

2. Turn contents of skillet into the pastry shell and sprinkle with cheese. Pour a mixture of eggs, milk, salt, pepper, and nutmeg over cheese.

3. Bake at 350°F 30 to 35 minutes, or until lightly browned.

4. Serve hot as an appetizer or main dish.

ONE 10-INCH PIE

PARTY PIZZA

2 cups cheese-cracker	1 tablespoon sugar
crumbs (about 44	¼ teaspoon salt
round crackers)	Few grains black
¼ cup butter or	pepper
margarine, softened	1¼ teaspoons oregano
3 tablespoons water	1 bay leaf
1 can (8 oz.) tomato	6 oz. mozzarella
sauce	cheese, thinly sliced
1 can (6 oz.) tomato	1 tablespoon olive oil
paste	

1. Turn cracker crumbs into a bowl. Using a fork, mix in the butter and water. Press crumb mixture firmly into an even layer on bottom and sides of a 9-inch pie pan. Level edges; set aside.

2. Mix in a saucepan the tomato sauce, tomato paste, sugar, salt, pepper, ¼ teaspoon oregano, and bay leaf. Simmer 5 minutes, stirring occasionally.

3. Remove from heat and discard bay leaf. Spread sauce over crust. Sprinkle evenly with 1 teaspoon oregano. Arrange cheese in a layer over sauce. Drizzle with oil.

4. Bake at 400°F 20 minutes, or until cheese is melted and lightly browned. ABOUT 6 SERVINGS

SWISS AND TUNA PIE

3 eggs	1 unbaked 9-in. pastry
½ teaspoon salt	shell, chilled
½ teaspoon dry mustard	2 cans (6½ or 7 oz.
Few grains cayenne	each) tuna, drained
pepper	and flaked
1 cup heavy cream	8 oz. Swiss cheese,
½ cup ale	shredded
	1 tablespoon flour

1. Beat eggs, salt, dry mustard, and cayenne pepper together until foamy. Beat in cream and ale.

2. Cover bottom of pastry shell with a layer of tuna. Sprinkle half of the cheese over the tuna. Repeat layering. Sprinkle flour over cheese. Pour egg mixture over all.

3. Bake at 425°F 15 minutes. Reduce oven temperature to 300°F and bake 25 minutes, or until a knife inserted halfway between center and edge of filling comes out clean. 4 TO 6 SERVINGS

OLIVE-CHEESE TART

1½ cups sliced leek or onion	½ cup shredded Parmesan cheese
2 tablespoons butter or margarine	4 teaspoons flour
1 cup sliced pimiento-stuffed olives	3 eggs (about ¾ cup)
1 9-in. unbaked pastry shell, chilled	⅛ teaspoon white pepper
½ cup shredded Swiss cheese	⅛ teaspoon ground nutmeg
	1½ cups light cream

1. Cook leek until tender in hot butter. Mix in olives and turn into the chilled pastry shell, distributing mixture evenly. Blend cheeses and flour; sprinkle over leek mixture.
2. Beat eggs, pepper, and nutmeg together. Beat in cream; pour over cheese mixture in pastry shell.
3. Bake at 425°F 15 minutes. Reduce oven temperature to 300°F and bake 20 minutes, or until a knife comes out clean when inserted halfway between center and edge of filling. Let stand 10 minutes before serving.
4. Garnish center with slices of *pimiento-stuffed olives*. Serve hot as an appetizer cut in small wedges or as a main dish cut in large wedges.
ONE 9-INCH TART

SWISS CHEESE-BACON PIE

1½ cups all-purpose flour	4 eggs, slightly beaten
½ teaspoon garlic salt	1 teaspoon Worcestershire sauce
½ teaspoon seasoned salt	2 cups light cream
½ teaspoon paprika	1 tablespoon butter, melted
⅔ cup vegetable shortening	1½ tablespoons flour
¼ cup cold water	½ teaspoon dry mustard
6 to 8 oz. sliced Swiss cheese	½ teaspoon celery salt
9 slices bacon, diced and fried until crisp	¼ teaspoon basil
	1 tablespoon butter
	½ cup chopped onion
	1 teaspoon poppy seed

1. Blend flour, garlic salt, seasoned salt, and paprika in a bowl. Using a pastry blender or two knives, cut in shortening until pieces are size of small peas. Sprinkle water over mixture, a small amount at a time; mix lightly with a fork after each addition. Add only enough water to hold pastry together. Roll out pastry and fit into a 9-inch pie pan; flute edge.
2. Cover pastry with overlapping slices of Swiss cheese and sprinkle evenly with bacon.
3. Combine in a bowl the eggs, Worcestershire sauce, cream, melted butter, and a mixture of the flour, mustard, celery salt, and basil; beat slightly to blend thoroughly. Pour over bacon and cheese.
4. Bake at 350°F 45 minutes, or until custard is set and top is lightly browned. Remove from oven.
5. Meanwhile, heat 1 tablespoon butter in a small skillet; add onion and cook until soft.
6. Top custard evenly with onion and poppy seed. Cut into wedge-shaped pieces and serve at once.
6 TO 8 SERVINGS

Fondues & Rabbits

BAKED CHEESE FONDUE

3 cups soft bread cubes	3 tablespoons grated onion
1 tablespoon melted butter or margarine	½ teaspoon salt
1 teaspoon poppy seed	¼ teaspoon pepper
2 cups milk	½ teaspoon dry mustard
1 or 2 drops Tabasco	¼ teaspoon paprika
12 oz. sharp Cheddar cheese, shredded	4 egg yolks, well beaten
	4 egg whites

1. Lightly toss 1 cup of the bread cubes with the melted butter and poppy seed. Set aside.
2. Scald milk and pour into a large bowl. Mix in Tabasco. Add remaining bread cubes, the shredded cheese, onion, and a mixture of salt, pepper, dry mustard, and paprika. Mix lightly but thoroughly until cheese is melted. Add beaten egg yolks gradually, stirring constantly.
3. Beat egg whites until stiff, not dry, peaks are formed. Gently fold with cheese mixture.
4. Turn into a lightly buttered 2-quart casserole. Top with poppy seed-coated bread cubes.
5. Set casserole in a pan in a 325°F oven. Pour boiling water into pan to a depth of 1 inch. Bake 50 to 60 minutes, or until a knife inserted halfway between center and edge comes out clean.
ABOUT 6 SERVINGS

BAKED SWISS CHEESE FONDUE

2 tablespoons flour	1 cup ¼-in. soft bread
½ teaspoon salt	cubes
Pinch black pepper	2 teaspoons grated
2 tablespoons butter	onion
or margarine	½ clove garlic, minced
1 cup milk	¼ cup snipped parsley
4 egg yolks, fork beaten	4 egg whites
8 oz. Swiss cheese,	Ground nutmeg
finely shredded	

1.   Blend a mixture of flour, salt, and pepper into hot butter in a saucepan. Heat until bubbly. Add milk gradually, stirring constantly. Bring to boiling; boil 1 to 2 minutes. Remove from heat.
2.   Blend a small amount of sauce into egg yolks; stir into remaining sauce. Mix in the cheese. Add bread cubes, onion, garlic, and parsley; mix thoroughly.
3.   Beat egg whites until stiff, not dry, peaks are formed. Gently fold with cheese mixture.
4.   Turn into a buttered 1½-quart shallow baking dish. Sprinkle top with nutmeg.
5.   Bake at 325°F 40 to 45 minutes, or until top is golden brown.   ABOUT 6 SERVINGS

SWISS CHEESE FONDUE

Fondue is more than a gourmet's delight; it is a food tradition, one of the few foods that must be prepared and served just so to be truly itself. It is a dish for friends dining intimately, for all must eat literally from the same pot. No harsh metal must ever come in contact with a fondue. It is a recipe for a chafing dish with an earthenware pan and a little cheerful flame to keep the fondue barely bubbling. When the time comes for eating the fondue, all must be prepared to dunk—for here dunking is smiled upon. Do it with cubes of French bread or hard French rolls, cut so each cube has crust on at least one side. Spear the bread cubes from the soft side, and be sure your fork penetrates the sturdy opposite crust securely, for he whose bread first falls off into the fondue traditionally pays the reckoning by purchasing a bottle of wine. Only ladies are free of this ruling. They must forfeit a kiss for every piece of bread they lose. (Special long-tined forks make the process easier.) When you dip into the pot, stir the fondue gently, thus helping to keep it well blended as well as accumulating more of the delectable cheese mixture on your bread cube. Lift it out with a twirling motion and eat—quickly! As the meal progresses, some of the cheese will form a brown crust on the bottom of the pan—this is a special delicacy which should be lifted out and divided among the company.

1 loaf (1 lb.) French	2 cups Neuchâtel or
bread	other dry white wine
1 tablespoon	1 lb. natural Swiss
corn starch	cheese, shredded
2 tablespoons kirsch	Freshly ground black
1 clove garlic, halved	pepper to taste
	Ground nutmeg to taste

1.   Cut bread into bite-size pieces each having at least one crusty side; set aside.
2.   Mix cornstarch and kirsch in a small bowl; set aside.
3.   Rub the inside of a 2-quart flame-resistant casserole or porcelain-finished saucepan with cut surface of garlic. Pour in wine; place over medium heat until wine is about to simmer (*do not boil*).
4.   Add the shredded cheese in small amounts to the hot wine, stirring constantly until cheese is melted. Heat cheese-wine mixture until bubbly.
5.   Blend in the cornstarch mixture and continue stirring while cooking 5 minutes, or until fondue begins to bubble; add seasoning.
6.   Spear bread with forks to use for dipping. Keep the fondue gently bubbling throughout serving time.   ABOUT 10 SERVINGS
NOTE: If desired, a hibachi or grill (with charcoal for fuel) may be used to cook the fondue.

CREAMY CORN DIP

Thin slices of rye bread (about 2 inches in diameter) buttered and crisply toasted, or crusty French-bread cubes make perfect "dippers." If using bread cubes, spear with a fork, dunk, and twirl in the dip.

2 tablespoons butter	1½ cups chicken broth
or margarine	(dissolve 1 chicken
2 tablespoons finely	bouillon cube in 1½
chopped green pepper	cups boiling water)
¼ cup flour	1 cup shredded Swiss
¼ teaspoon salt	cheese
⅛ teaspoon cayenne	1 cup (8-oz. can)
pepper	cream-style corn
	4 drops Tabasco

1.   Heat butter in the top of a double boiler or chafing-dish blazer over direct heat. Add green

pepper and cook until just tender, occasionally moving and turning with a spoon. Blend in the flour, salt, and cayenne pepper. Heat until mixture bubbles, stirring constantly.

2. Blend in the chicken broth, cooking and stirring until sauce thickens.

3. Remove from heat. Add the cheese all at one time, stirring until cheese is melted. Stir in the corn and Tabasco. Keep warm over hot water.

ABOUT 6 SERVINGS

WELSH RABBIT IN CHAFING DISH

¼ cup butter
2 lbs. sharp Cheddar cheese, shredded (about 8 cups)
2 teaspoons Worcestershire sauce

1 teaspoon dry mustard
Few grains cayenne pepper
4 eggs, slightly beaten
1 cup light cream or half and half

1. In a chafing dish blazer over simmering water, melt butter. Add cheese and heat, stirring occasionally, until cheese is melted. Mix in Worcestershire sauce, dry mustard, and cayenne pepper.

2. Blend eggs and cream; strain. Mix into melted cheese. Cook until thick, stirring frequently.

3. Garnish with *parsley sprigs*. Serve over toasted *English muffin halves*. 6 CUPS WELSH RABBIT

NOTE: When reheating mixture, thin with desired amount of *sherry*, *other white wine*, or *milk*.

WELSH RABBIT WITH EAST INDIAN FLAVOR

1 tablespoon butter
1 lb. sharp Cheddar cheese, shredded (about 4 cups)
½ teaspoon Worcestershire sauce

½ teaspoon dry mustard
Few grains cayenne pepper
⅔ cup milk
2 tablespoons chutney
6 slices bread, toasted

1. Heat butter in top of a double boiler over simmering water. Add cheese all at one time and stir occasionally until cheese begins to melt. Blend in the Worcestershire sauce, dry mustard, and cayenne pepper. Add milk gradually, stirring constantly until mixture is smooth and cheese is melted.

2. Spread a teaspoon of chutney over each slice of toast. Top with cheese mixture. Serve immediately. Top each serving with a *poached egg*, if desired. 6 SERVINGS

SOUFFLÉS

CHEESE SOUFFLÉ

¼ cup flour
¾ teaspoon salt
¾ teaspoon monosodium glutamate
½ teaspoon dry mustard
⅛ teaspoon paprika
1⅔ cups (14½-oz. can) evaporated milk

¼ teaspoon Tabasco
8 oz. sharp Cheddar cheese, coarsely shredded
6 egg yolks, well beaten
6 egg whites

1. Blend the flour, salt, monosodium glutamate, dry mustard, and paprika in a heavy saucepan. Add the evaporated milk gradually, then the Tabasco, stirring until smooth. Bring to boiling; stir and cook 1 to 2 minutes.

2. Add cheese all at one time and stir until cheese is melted. Remove from heat.

3. Pour sauce slowly into beaten egg yolks, beating constantly.

4. Beat egg whites until stiff, not dry, peaks are formed. Spoon the sauce over egg whites and fold

together until just blended. Turn into an ungreased 2-quart soufflé dish (deep casserole with straight sides). About 1½ inches from edge of dish, draw a circle by inserting the tip of a spoon 1 inch into the mixture to form a "top hat."

5. Bake at 300°F 55 to 60 minutes, or until a knife inserted halfway between center and edge of soufflé comes out clean. ABOUT 6 SERVINGS

DEVILED HAM SOUFFLÉ ROLL

This delicate egg roll, enhanced with a rich deviled ham and mushroom filling, is superb party food.

½ cup all-purpose flour
½ teaspoon salt
¼ cup butter or margarine
2 cups milk

4 egg yolks
4 egg whites
Deviled Ham 'n' Mushroom Filling, *page 143*

1. Grease and flour a 15x10x1-inch jelly roll pan; set aside.

2. Blend flour and salt into hot butter in a saucepan. Add milk gradually, stirring constantly until smooth. Continue to stir and bring to boiling; boil 1 to 2 minutes. Remove from heat.

3. Beat egg yolks until thick and lemon colored. Add sauce, a small amount at a time, stirring vigorously after each addition. Set aside to cool.

4. Beat egg whites until stiff, not dry, peaks are formed.

5. Gently spread egg yolk mixture over the beaten egg whites. Carefully fold together until just blended. Turn the mixture into pan and spread evenly.

6. Bake at 325°F 50 to 55 minutes, or until golden brown.

7. Loosen edges of soufflé and invert onto a sheet of foil on a large wire rack. Spread with Deviled Ham 'n' Mushroom Filling. Gently roll lengthwise, wrap in aluminum foil, and allow to stand about 10 minutes to set.

8. To serve, remove roll from foil, place on a warm serving platter, and surround with *watercress*.

ABOUT 12 SERVINGS

DEVILED HAM 'N' MUSHROOM FILLING

2 cans (4 oz. each) mushroom stems and pieces, drained	½ cup dairy sour cream
1 tablespoon butter or margarine	2 tablespoons lemon juice
2 cans (4½ oz. each) deviled ham	¼ cup chopped chives or scallions

1. Add the mushrooms to hot butter in a skillet and cook 5 minutes, or until mushrooms are lightly browned; stir occasionally.

2. Blend a mixture of the deviled ham and remaining ingredients with the mushrooms.

2 CUPS FILLING

SWISS CHEESE SOUFFLÉ

¼ cup butter or margarine	1 cup milk
¼ cup flour	6 oz. natural Swiss cheese, finely shredded (about 1½ cups)
¼ teaspoon salt	
Few grains black pepper	4 egg yolks, well beaten
⅛ teaspoon ground nutmeg	4 egg whites

1. Heat butter in a saucepan. Blend in a mixture of flour, salt, pepper, and nutmeg; heat until bubbly. Add milk gradually, stirring constantly. Bring to boiling; stir and cook 1 to 2 minutes. Remove from heat.

2. Stir in the cheese all at one time. Pour sauce slowly into beaten egg yolks, beating constantly.

3. Beat egg whites until stiff, not dry, peaks are formed. Spoon cheese mixture over egg whites; fold until just blended. Turn into an ungreased 1½-quart soufflé dish (deep casserole with straight sides).

4. Bake at 325°F about 50 minutes, or until a knife inserted halfway between center and edge of soufflé comes out clean. 6 SERVINGS

TOMATO-BACON SOUFFLÉ

2 medium-sized tomatoes, peeled, chopped, and drained	3 tablespoons butter
	6 tablespoons flour
	½ teaspoon salt
3 tablespoons finely chopped onion	⅛ teaspoon white pepper
¼ teaspoon seasoned salt	¾ teaspoon dry mustard
	⅛ teaspoon paprika
2 tablespoons butter	1½ cups milk
1 clove garlic, minced	8 oz. sharp Cheddar cheese, shredded
1¼ cups rye bread cubes	
8 slices bacon, diced and fried (reserve 3 tablespoons drippings)	6 egg yolks, well beaten
	6 egg whites

1. Mix tomatoes, onion, and seasoned salt in a bowl; set aside.

2. Heat the 2 tablespoons butter and garlic together in a skillet. Add bread cubes and brown lightly on all sides; set aside.

3. Heat the reserved bacon drippings and the 3 tablespoons butter together in a saucepan. Blend in a mixture of the flour, salt, white pepper, dry mustard, and paprika; heat until bubbly.

4. Add milk gradually, stirring until blended. Bring to boiling, stirring constantly; boil 1 to 2 minutes. Remove from heat. Add cheese and stir until melted.

5. Pour cheese sauce slowly into beaten egg yolks, beating constantly. Add bacon pieces.

6. Beat egg whites until stiff, not dry, peaks are formed. Spread over cheese mixture and gently fold together.

7. Toss toasted bread cubes with tomato mixture.

Turn into a 13x9x2-inch baking pan and top with the soufflé mixture.

8. Bake at 300°F about 1 hour, or until knife inserted halfway between center and edge of soufflé comes out clean. Cut into squares.

ABOUT 12 SERVINGS

HARVEST SOUFFLÉ

Provolone and Cheddar cheese and corn all add flavor-enhancement to this impressive soufflé.

¼ cup flour	1½ cups (about 6 oz.)
¼ teaspoon salt	shredded sharp Ched-
⅛ teaspoon garlic salt	dar cheese
¼ cup butter	½ cup (about 2 oz.)
1 can (17 oz.) cream-	shredded provolone
style corn	cheese
⅓ cup milk	6 egg yolks, well
½ teaspoon Worcester-	beaten
shire sauce	6 egg whites

1. Blend a mixture of the flour, salt, and garlic salt into hot butter in a saucepan. Heat until bubbly; remove from heat. Blend in the corn, milk, and Worcestershire sauce. Stirring constantly, bring mixture to boiling; stir and cook 1 to 2 minutes. Remove from heat.

2. Add cheeses all at one time and stir rapidly until melted.

3. Spoon sauce into beaten egg yolks, beating thoroughly after each addition.

4. Beat egg whites until stiff, not dry, peaks are formed. Gently spread egg yolk mixture over egg whites. Carefully fold together until just blended. Gently turn the mixture into an ungreased 2-quart soufflé dish (deep casserole with straight sides).

5. Bake at 350°F about 40 minutes, or until a knife inserted halfway between center and edge of soufflé comes out clean. ABOUT 6 SERVINGS

TOP HAT SHRIMP SOUFFLÉ

1 can (about 10 oz.)	¼ teaspoon dry mustard
condensed cream of	Few grains white pepper
shrimp soup	6 oz. sharp Cheddar
¼ cup dried parsley	cheese, shredded
flakes	(about 1½ cups)
2 tablespoons grated	6 egg yolks, well
onion	beaten
1 tablespoon flour	6 egg whites

1. Set out a 2-quart soufflé dish (deep casserole with straight sides); do not grease. Fold a 24-inch piece of aluminum foil lengthwise in half. Place around dish, cut side down, overlapping the ends; tie with a string to secure around dish.

2. Turn soup into a saucepan. Blend in the parsley flakes, onion, and a mixture of flour, dry mustard, and white pepper. Heat until bubbly, stirring constantly; cook 3 minutes. Remove from heat.

3. Add the cheese all at one time and stir until cheese is melted.

4. Spoon sauce into beaten egg yolks, stirring vigorously until blended.

5. Beat egg whites until stiff, not dry, peaks are formed. Spoon the egg yolk mixture over the egg whites. Gently fold together until just blended. Turn into the dish. About 1½ inches from edge of dish, draw a circle by inserting the tip of a spoon 1 inch into the mixture to form a "top hat."

6. Bake at 325°F 50 minutes, or until a knife inserted halfway between center and edge comes out clean. ABOUT 6 SERVINGS

LIGHT-AS-A-CLOUD SOUFFLÉ

A soufflé of extrafine texture and superior flavor.

2 cups milk	1 tablespoon grated
8 oz. cream cheese,	onion
softened	½ teaspoon crushed
¾ teaspoon salt	rosemary
3 cups ½-in. soft	4 egg yolks, well beaten
bread cubes	4 egg whites
1 tablespoon snipped	2 tablespoons butter
parsley	or margarine

1. Blend milk into cream cheese and salt in a heavy saucepan. Stir over low heat until mixture is creamy and smooth. Set aside to cool.

2. Toss bread cubes, parsley, onion, and rosemary together in a large bowl. Add cream cheese mixture; toss lightly and thoroughly. Blend in the beaten egg yolks.

3. Beat egg whites until stiff, not dry, peaks are formed. Fold gently into cheese-bread mixture until thoroughly blended.

4. Turn into an ungreased 1½-quart soufflé dish (deep casserole with straight sides). Dot top with small portions of butter (about 12 pieces).

5. Set dish in a pan in a 350°F oven. Pour boiling water into pan to a depth of 1 inch. Bake about 1 hour, or until a knife inserted halfway between center and edge comes out clean. 6 TO 8 SERVINGS

Meat is king of the dinner table—the food that holds the center spot in the menu and the hub around which most meals are planned. Prized for its flavor and food value, meat satisfies the appetite as no other food can—not only when it is eaten but for a longer time thereafter.

America is almost unique in the world in the abundance of its meat supply and the manner in which this abundance is taken for granted. Historically there are good reasons why this came to be. The early colonists found an almost untouched supply of game in the American wilderness. As the pioneers pushed west-

ward they encountered even more abundance. Where fruits, grains, and vegetables might be scarce because the land was not yet cultivated, there was no end to the amount of meat to be had for the shooting. No doubt, the high meat diet of the pioneers had much to do with the heartiness, toughness, and spirit which settled our country.

Meat is an excellent source, perhaps the best, of the "complete" proteins used to build and repair body tissue. It is rich in vitamins and minerals and aids in the formation of nitrogen-containing substances which are essential to enzymes, certain hormones, and to other body functions. It can also be a source of energy.

Protein for performing these body functions can also be obtained from milk, cheese, eggs, poultry, and fish, all sources which provide amino acids essential to body growth. Legumes (dry beans, peas, nuts) are another source but are called "incomplete" proteins because the necessary amino acids are present in unfavorable proportions. It is recommended that these proteins be supplemented in the same meal with meat or other animal protein.

SELECTION

Pioneer homemakers had little choice in the matter of their meat; they cooked what the hunter brought home. The modern homemaker, on the other hand, sees a vast array of meats spread out before her whenever she visits her favorite market. Her skill as a cook starts with her ability to select not only the right cut of meat for the method of preparation she plans to use, but to select meat of good quality, for the quality of the meat itself determines to a large extent the quality of the cooked food. An experienced family meat buyer learns to recognize the characteristics of meat at a glance; she is aided by a knowledge of meat inspection and grading stamps.

Inspection Stamp—All meats processed by packers who ship their products across state lines must pass Federal inspection. The round purple Federal inspection stamp ("U.S. INSP'D & P'S'D") guarantees that the meat is from healthy animals slaughtered under sanitary conditions and that it is wholesome. Meats handled by packers who market locally must pass city and state inspections. These inspections guarantee wholesomeness, not quality.

Grade Stamp—Quality grading is a separate operation and may be done according to government grade standards or according to packers' own standards, which are usually closely in line with government grades. Grade and brand names are stamped on the meat with a roller stamp which leaves its mark along the full length of the carcass. The purple ink used for both inspection and grading stamps is a harmless vegetable dye which need not be cut away before cooking.

Official U.S. Quality Grades — "Prime" is the top Federal grade of meat and sometimes is seen or available in the retail market; "Choice" often is the highest Federal grade available for home use; "Good," "Commercial," and "Utility" are lesser grades. These grades are applied to beef, veal, and (with the exception of "Commercial" grade) to lamb. Pork is not offically graded, except by the packer. Where grade stamps are in evidence, the homemaker can rely on them as indexes to quality. But in many cases, as in selecting precut and prepackaged meats, her own knowledge of the appearance of quality is a valuable guide.

What To Look For In Beef — Beef of good to prime quality, whatever the cut, is thick-fleshed and compact, implying a plump, stocky animal; in lower grades the flesh is thinner, indicating that the animal was rangy and angular. There is a good covering of fat, which becomes thinner and patchier in lower grades, and a generous marbling or flecking of fat through the lean (almost absent in lower grades). Color in all grades varies from light to dark red. Bones of young beef are red and porous; as the animal matures they become harder and white.

What To Look For In Veal — Veal, which always comes from a young animal (calves three months to a year old), is very different in appearance from beef. The lean is a light grayish-pink in color, has no marbling, and very little covering fat. The bones are red and porous; in the youngest veal the ends may still be pliable. Veal is fine-grained and less firm than beef of comparable grade; because the animal is young, veal is likely to be tender.

What To Look For In Lamb — Ninety-three percent of all sheep in this country are marketed as lambs and yearlings; only seven percent as mutton (lamb more than one year old). The bones, fat, and color of the lean are all indications of the age of lamb. Young lamb has red bones, which become white as the animal matures. The lean is light to dark pink in lambs, darkening to light red in yearlings, and light to dark red in mutton. Lamb fat is rather soft and creamy or pinkish in color; with maturity it become white and much harder.

What To Look For In Pork — Pork usually comes from animals under one year old and is almost always tender; the quality of American pork is quite uniform, with fewer grades than other meats. The color of young pork is grayish pink, which becomes pinker in older animals. The flesh is firm, fine in grain, well marbled (flecked) with fat, and covered with a layer of firm white fat.

Variety Meats — Variety meats include brains, heart, kidneys, liver, sweetbreads, tongue, tripe, and others. *Brains* (beef, veal, pork, lamb) and *sweetbreads* (beef, veal, lamb) are much alike in tenderness and texture. *Heart* and *kidneys* from beef, veal, pork, and lamb are available. Veal (calf's), lamb, and pork *livers* are more tender than beef liver. Beef and veal *tongues* are more often available in uncooked form, whereas pork and lamb tongues are available ready to serve.

Prepackaged Meats — In recent years it has become possible to buy meats on a self-service basis in many supermarkets. The meats are cut, weighed, packaged, and priced by the meat dealers, and are placed in refrigerated open cases for selection by the homemaker. Because they are wrapped in a transparent material, she can see exactly what she is buying.

STORAGE

The ideal temperature for storing unfrozen meats and meat products to be used in a day or two is as low as possible without actually freezing them.

Fresh Meats (beef, veal, pork, and lamb cuts; hamburger; variety meats such as liver, heart, and tongue) — Prepackaged fresh meat purchased in self-service markets may be refrigerated in the original wrapping providing the meat is to be used within one or two days. If kept longer, the wrapper should be loosened at the ends. Meat not prepackaged should be removed from the market wrapping paper and stored unwrapped or loosely covered with waxed paper or aluminum foil.

Frozen Meats — Meats purchased in retail markets and held more than three days should be wrapped in special freezer material using the "drugstore wrap" and stored in the freezer section of refrigerator. If fresh meat is to be frozen and stored longer than a week it should be done only in a freezer which can maintain a 0°F (or lower) temperature throughout the storage period. Meat purchased frozen must be kept frozen until used, and should be stored in freezer-storage compartment for not more than two weeks. The ice cube compartment of a home refrigerator usually does not maintain a temperature as low as a freezer storage compartment. Individual servings of fresh meat (chops and

Round Steak

Outside (Bottom) Round
Steak or Pot Roast

Standing Rump Roast

BEEF CUTS

Top Round Steak

Heel of Round

Standing Rib Roast

Blade Pot Roast
or Steak

Eye of Round

Sirloin Tip Roast

Rib Steak

Arm Pot Roast
or Steak

Club Steak

T-Bone Steak

Pin Bone Sirloin Steak

Delmonico (Rib Eye)
Roast or Steak

English (Boston) Roast

Porterhouse Steak

Flat Bone Sirloin Steak

Filet Mignon or
Tenderloin Steak

Corned Brisket

Flank Steak

Skirt Steak Fillets

Short Ribs

Chuck Short Ribs

Cube Steak

Rolled Plate

Plate Beef

Shank Cross Cuts

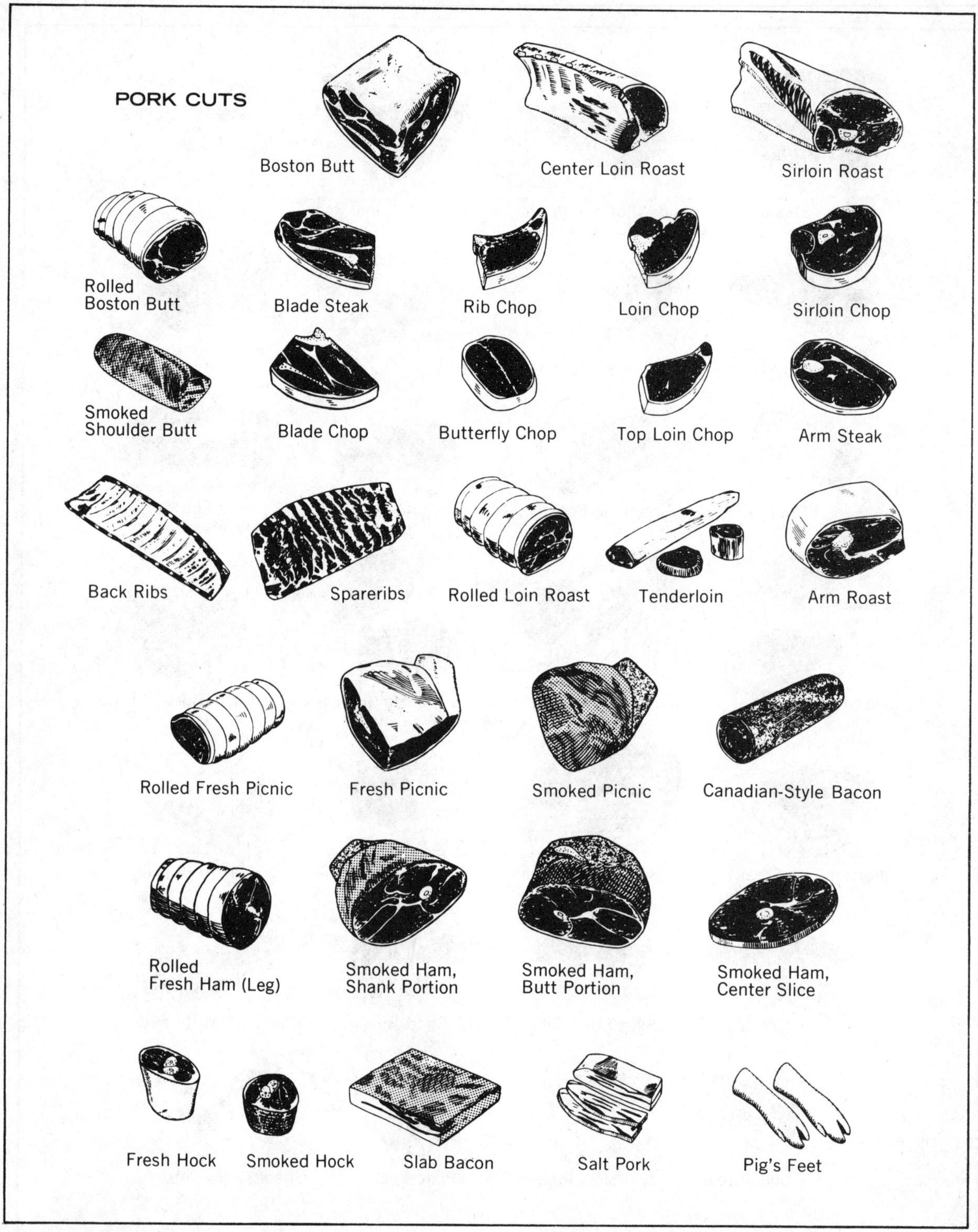

PORK CUTS

Boston Butt

Center Loin Roast

Sirloin Roast

Rolled Boston Butt

Blade Steak

Rib Chop

Loin Chop

Sirloin Chop

Smoked Shoulder Butt

Blade Chop

Butterfly Chop

Top Loin Chop

Arm Steak

Back Ribs

Spareribs

Rolled Loin Roast

Tenderloin

Arm Roast

Rolled Fresh Picnic

Fresh Picnic

Smoked Picnic

Canadian-Style Bacon

Rolled Fresh Ham (Leg)

Smoked Ham, Shank Portion

Smoked Ham, Butt Portion

Smoked Ham, Center Slice

Fresh Hock

Smoked Hock

Slab Bacon

Salt Pork

Pig's Feet

LAMB CUTS

Leg, Sirloin On

Leg, Sirloin Off

Rib Roast

Sirloin Half of Leg

Shank Half of Leg

Crown Roast

Loin Roast

Sirloin Roast

Leg Chop (Steak)

Rib Chops

English Chop

Sirloin Chop

Rolled Leg

Frenched Rib Chops

Loin Chops

Square Shoulder

Arm Chop

Breast

Rolled Breast

Rolled Shoulder

Blade Chop

Riblets

Ribs for Barbecue

Cushion Shoulder

Saratoga Chops

Fore Shank

Hind Shank

Neck Slices

VEAL CUTS

Arm Roast

Rib Roast

Loin Roast

Blade Roast

Arm Steak

Rib Chop

Loin Chop

Blade Steak

Rolled Shoulder Roast

Frenched Rib Chop

Kidney Chop

Standing Rump Roast

Shank Half of Leg

Sirloin Roast

Sirloin Steak

Rolled Leg

Center Leg

Neck

Breast

Boneless Cutlets

Round Steak

Riblets

Brisket Rolls

Rolled Cutlets (Birds)

Heel of Round

Fore Shank

Rolled Cube Steaks (Birds)

Meat-Cut Charts courtesy National Live Stock and Meat Board

ground meat patties) to be frozen should be separated by several layers of moisture-vaporproof material before overwrapping into larger packages. This facilitates easy separation of each serving before cooking.

Cooked Meats or Leftover Meats — Cool cooked leftover meats quickly, then cover and place in the refrigerator. Meat cooked for future use should be cooled, uncovered, in the refrigerator or in a cool place with good air circulation. Divide large quantities of meat dishes such as stews into smaller amounts for faster cooling.

Cured Meats (ham, bacon, etc.) **and Ready-to-Serve Meats** (luncheon meat, frankfurters, etc.) — Store in the fresh food compartment of the refrigerator, not in the freezing compartment. Freezing is not advisable for longer than one month as the salt present in these meats favors the development of rancidity when meats are frozen. Store these meat products in their original wrappers.

Canned Hams (and other perishable canned meats) — Store these meats in the unopened can in the fresh food compartment of the refrigerator unless otherwise indicated on label. Do not freeze.

STORAGE TIME CHART

	Refrigerator (38° to 40°F)*	Freezer (0°F or lower)
Meat		
Beef (fresh)	2 to 4 days	6 to 12 months
Veal (fresh)	2 to 4 days	6 to 9 months
Pork (fresh)	2 to 4 days	3 to 6 months
Lamb (fresh)	2 to 4 days	6 to 9 months
Ground beef, veal, and lamb	1 to 2 days	3 to 4 months
Ground pork	1 to 2 days	1 to 3 months
Variety meats	1 to 2 days	3 to 4 months
Luncheon meats	1 week	
Sausage, fresh pork	1 week	2 months
Sausage, smoked	3 to 7 days	
Sausage, dry and semi-dry (unsliced)	2 to 3 weeks	
Frankfurters	4 to 5 days	
Bacon	5 to 7 days	
Ham, smoked, whole	1 week	2 months
slices	3 to 4 days	
Beef, corned	1 week	2 weeks
Leftover cooked meat	4 to 5 days	2 to 3 months
Frozen Combination Foods		
Meat pies (cooked)		3 months
Swiss steak (cooked)		3 months
Stews (cooked)		3 to 4 months
Prepared meat dinners		2 to 6 months

*The range in time reflects recommendations for *maximum* storage time from several authorities. For top quality, fresh meats should be used in 2 or 3 days, ground meat and variety meats should be used in 24 hours.

METHODS OF COOKING

Since the first cave family discovered that meat tasted better when cooked, only two ways of cooking meat have ever been devised: by dry heat and by moist heat. There are several methods of cooking by dry heat: roasting, broiling, panbroiling, frying, and rotisserie cooking. There are two methods of cooking by moist heat: braising and cooking in liquid. Most of these methods have been used for thousands of years, from cave days to the present, but in the comparatively few years since the experimental method was first applied to cooking, more has been learned about the techniques that give cooked meat the best appearance, texture, and flavor than in all the millennia that went before.

In general, dry-heat methods are used for the more tender cuts of meat with little connective tissue. Exceptions to this rule are the smaller cuts (steaks, chops, and cutlets) of veal, though it is classed as a tender meat. Veal needs longer cooking to develop its flavor and to soften its connective tissue. Long cooking by dry heat tends to dry veal out; therefore a moist-heat method, braising, is the method of choice for veal cuts other than roasts.

During broiling, panbroiling, or frying, when meat is to be turned, if using a fork, insert it into fat rather than the lean portion thus avoiding loss of juices from the lean.

Roasting — To roast, in modern usage, is to cook in an oven, uncovered, and without the addition of any liquid. Thousands of laboratory tests on all kinds of roasts have revealed many facts about roasting methods which today can be stated as rules. These rules have as their objective the desired degree of doneness combined with maximum palatability and juiciness, the most appetizing appearance, and minimum shrinkage.

Rules worth noting

• A constant low temperature should be maintained throughout the cooking period.

It has been proved in test after test that searing a roast at a high temperature for a short period and then reducing heat to complete the cooking does not help "seal in" the juices. Using a constant (low) temperature cooks the meat more uniformly with less shrinkage and loss of juices and fat. In addition, this method has these advantages: It results in more palatable meat with surface fat which is not charred; it involves less work for the homemaker since there is less spattering of the fat on roasting pan and oven racks and walls; it requires less watching during cooking; it makes the final clean-up job easier.

We should add that using a high temperature at the beginning of roasting does result in more pan drippings which are a richer brown and therefore make a richer, more flavorful gravy.

• The only accurate test for doneness is the internal temperature as registered by a meat thermometer. Even though time-weight relationship tables are followed carefully and a constant temperature is used for cooking meat, it is difficult to predict accurately when any particular piece of meat will be cooked done. The shape of the roast, the proportion of lean to fat, the amount of bone, the aging of the meat—all affect the time that will be required to produce the desired degree of doneness. Timetables are useful in estimating about how much total time will be required, but only a meat thermometer will register the temperature at the center of the roast, thus indicating the degree of doneness. To use a meat thermometer, insert the thermometer so the tip is slightly beyond the center of the largest muscle. (It should not contact fat or bone.)

• Cooked fat side up the roast will be self-basting.

• Covering the roast or adding water produces moist-heat cooking and is not done in roasting.

• Seasoning may be added before or after cooking; penetration is to a depth of only ¼ to ½ inch.

• If the roast is allowed to set 20 minutes after removal from the oven, carving will be easier. The roast must be removed from the oven when the thermometer registers 5° to 10° lower than the desired doneness.

TIMETABLE FOR ROASTING

Cut	Average Weight (Pounds)	Oven Temperature Constant	Internal Temperature of Meat	Approx. Time (Min. per Pound)
Beef				
Standing rib*	6 to 8	300°-325°F	140°F (rare)	23 to 25
			160°F (med.)	27 to 30
			170°F (well)	32 to 35
	4 to 6	300°F-325°F	140°F (rare)	26 to 32
			160°F (med.)	34 to 38
			170°F (well)	40 to 42
Rolled rib	5 to 7	300°F-325°F	140°F (rare)	32
			160°F (med.)	38
			170°F (well)	48
Delmonico (rib eye)	4 to 6	350°F	140°F (rare)	18 to 20
			160°F (med.)	20 to 22
			170°F (well)	22 to 24
Tenderloin, whole	4 to 6	425°F	140°F (rare)	45 to 60**
half	2 to 3	425°F	140°F (rare)	45 to 50**
Rolled rump (high quality)	4 to 6	300°-325°F	150°-170°F	25 to 30
Sirloin tip	3½ to 4	300°-325°F	140°-170°F	35 to 40
(high quality)	4 to 6	300°F-325°F	140°-170°F	30 to 35

Veal

Leg	5 to 8	300°-325°F	170°F	25 to 35
Loin	4 to 6	300°-325°F	170°F	30 to 35
Rib (rack)	3 to 5	300°-325°F	170°F	35 to 40
Rolled shoulder	4 to 6	300°-325°F	170°F	40 to 45

Pork, Fresh

Loin, center	3 to 5	325°-350°F	170°F	30 to 35
half	5 to 7	325°F-350°F	170°F	35 to 40
blade or sirloin	3 to 4	325°F-350°F	170°F	40 to 45
rolled	3 to 5	325°F-350°F	170°F	35 to 45
Picnic shoulder	5 to 8	325°F-350°F	170°F	30 to 35
rolled	3 to 5	325°-350°F	170°F	35 to 40
cushion style	3 to 5	325°-350°F	170°F	30 to 35
Boston shoulder	4 to 6	325°-350°F	170°F	40 to 45
Leg (fresh ham)				
whole, bone in	12 to 16	325°-350°F	170°F	22 to 26
rolled	10 to 14	325°-350°F	170°F	24 to 28
half, bone in	5 to 8	325°-350°F	170°F	35 to 40
Spareribs		325°-350°F	well done	1½ to 2½ hours**

Pork, Smoked

Ham (cook before eating)				
whole	10 to 14	300°F-325°F	160°F	18 to 20
half	5 to 7	300°F-325°F	160°F	22 to 25
shank or butt	3 to 4	300°F-325°F	160°F	35 to 40
Ham (fully cooked)***				
half	5 to 7	325°F	130°F	18 to 24
Picnic shoulder	5 to 8	300°-325°F	170°F	35
Shoulder roll	2 to 3	300°-325°F	170°F	35 to 40
Canadian-style bacon	2 to 4	325°F	160°F	35 to 40

Lamb

Leg	5 to 8	300°F-325°F	175°-180°F	30 to 35
Shoulder	4 to 6	300°F-325°F	175°-180°F	30 to 35
rolled	3 to 5	300°F-325°F	175°-180°F	40 to 45
cushion	3 to 5	300°F-325°F	175°-180°F	30 to 35
rib	1½ to 3	375°F	170°-180°F	35 to 45

*Ribs which measure 6 to 7 inches from chine bone to tip of rib. *Courtesy National Live Stock and Meat Board*
**Total roasting time.
***Allow approximately 15 minutes per pound for heating whole ham.

Broiling—To broil is to cook by direct heat. It may be done with a gas flame, an electric unit, or over hot coals. The regulator is set for broiling. The broiler and broiler pan may or may not be pre-heated. The meat is placed on the rack in broiler pan, then placed in oven or broiler oven at a distance so that a moderate broiler temperature can be maintained at the surface of meat. The distance the meat is placed from the heat is determined by the thickness of the cut and the equipment being used. A 1-inch cut is placed 2 to 3 inches from the heat and a 2-inch cut 3 to 5 inches.

When browned on one side, season the meat, turn, and broil to the desired degree of doneness. Season the second side when cooking is completed. As when roasting, timetables are only a guide to broiling, so, for more accuracy, a thermometer designed especially for broiling may be inserted in the meat before cooking. A roast meat thermometer may be used to test doneness by inserting it in the steak or chop shortly before the end of the estimated total broiling time. Without the thermometer it is easy to check on doneness by cutting into the meat next to the bone and observing the color.

Broiling as a cooking method is reserved for tender steaks and chops of beef, pork, and lamb. Veal, although tender, is not usually broiled for the reasons already explained.

TIMETABLE FOR BROILING*

Cut	Approx. Total Cooking Time (Minutes)		
	Rare	Medium	Well
Beef			
Chuck steak (high quality)			
1 in., 1½ to 2½ lbs.	24	30	
1½ in., 2 to 4 lbs.	40	45	
Rib steak			
1 in., 1 to 1½ lbs.	15	20	
1½ in., 1½ to 2 lbs.	25	30	
2 in., 2 to 2½ lbs.	35	45	
Rib eye steak			
1 in., 8 to 10 oz.	15	20	
1½ in., 12 to 14 oz.	25	30	
2 in., 1 to 1¼ lbs.	35	45	
Club steak			
1 in., 1 to 1½ lbs.	15	20	
1½ in., 1½ to 2 lbs.	25	30	
2 in., 2 to 2½ lbs.	35	45	
Sirloin steak			
1 in., 1½ to 3 lbs.	20	25	
1½ in., 2¼ to 4 lbs.	30	35	
2 in., 3 to 5 lbs.	40	45	
Porterhouse steak			
1 in., 1¼ to 2 lbs.	20	25	
1½ in., 2 to 3 lbs.	30	35	

Cut	Approx. Total Cooking Time (Minutes)		
	Rare	Medium	Well
2 in., 2½ to 3½ lbs.	40	45	
Filet mignon			
1 in., 4 to 6 oz.	15	20	
1½ in., 6 to 8 oz.	18	22	
Ground beef patties			
1 in. thick by 3 in., 4 oz.	15	25	
Pork, Fresh			
Rib or loin chops			
¾ to 1 in.			20 to 25
Shoulder steaks			
½ to ¾ in.			20 to 22
Pork, Smoked			
Ham slice (tendered)			
½ in., ¾ to 1 lb.			10 to 12
1 in., 1½ to 2 lbs.			16 to 20
Loin chops			
¾ to 1 in.			15 to 20
Canadian-style bacon			
¼ in. slices			6 to 8
½ in. slices			8 to 10
Bacon**			4 to 5
Lamb			
Shoulder chops			
1 in., 5 to 8 oz.		12	
1½ in., 8 to 10 oz.		18	
2 in., 10 to 16 oz.		22	
Rib chops			
1 in., 3 to 5 oz.		12	
1½ in., 4 to 7 oz.		18	
2 in., 6 to 10 oz.		22	
Loin chops			
1 in., 4 to 7 oz.		12	
1½ in., 6 to 10 oz.		18	
2 in., 8 to 14 oz.		22	
Ground lamb patties			
1 in. thick by 3 in., 4 oz.		18	

*This timetable is based on broiling at a moderate temperature at the surface of the meat. Rare steaks are broiled to an internal temperature of 140°F; medium to 160°F; well done to 170°F. Lamb chops are broiled from 170° to 175°F. Ham is cooked to 160°F.

**The time for broiling bacon is influenced by personal preference as to crispness.

Courtesy National Live Stock and Meat Board

Rotisserie Roasting—Poultry and the tender cuts of meat are used for this type of cooking by dry heat. A spit is inserted through the piece of meat or the bird to be cooked, then it is roasted over an open fire, usually out-of-doors, or under broiler heat in an oven. A rotisserie motor is used to turn the spit slowly during the cooking process. Follow the rotisserie manufacturer's directions for regulating temperature and cooking time.

Panbroiling—To panbroil is to cook by heat transmitted through the hot metal of a skillet, but without added fat or liquid. Panbroiling is used for the same cuts as is broiling. Fat should be poured off as it collects, to insure even cooking; the pan should not be covered. To test for doneness, cut a small gash close to the bone and note the color of the meat at the center. If necessary, return to heat until done.

Frying—To fry is to cook in fat, whether in a large amount (deep frying) or a small amount (panfrying). Meats most often fried are thin steaks, chops, and liver. They are usually floured or breaded to produce a brown, flavorful crust. In panfrying the meat is browned in a small amount of fat and than cooked at moderate temperature until done, turning frequently. If the skillet is covered or water is added, the procedure becomes braising rather then true frying.

Braising—To braise meat is to brown it slowly on all sides in hot fat (meat coated with flour before browning, if desired), then to simmer it gently either in its own juices (by covering the skillet) or in a small amount of added liquid, which may be water, milk, cream, meat stock, vegetable juice, or other liquid. The cooking done after browning (braising) may be done either on top of the range or in the oven.

This method is used in cooking pot roasts, veal and pork chops and steaks. These are all either less tender cuts of meat, such as round or flank steak, or small cuts of veal which lack fat. Chops and steaks are also braised for variety.

TIMETABLE FOR BRAISING

Cut	Average Weight or Thickness	Approx. Total Cooking Time
Beef		
Pot roast, arm or blade	3 to 4 pounds	2½ to 3½ hours
boneless	3 to 5 pounds	3 to 4 hours
Swiss steak	1½ to 2½ inches	2 to 3 hours
Fricassee	2-inch cubes	1½ to 2½ hours
Beef birds	½x2x4 inches	1½ to 2½ hours
Short ribs	2x2x4-inch pieces	1½ to 2½ hours
Round steak	¾ inch	1 to 1½ hours
Stuffed steak	½ to ¾ inch	1½ hours
Pork		
Chops	¾ to 1½ inches	45 to 60 minutes
Spareribs	2 to 3 pounds	1½ hours
Tenderloin, whole	¾ to 1 pound	45 to 60 minutes
fillets	½ inch	30 minutes
Shoulder steaks	¾ inch	45 to 60 minutes
Lamb		
Breast, stuffed	2 to 3 pounds	1½ to 2 hours
rolled	1½ to 2 pounds	1½ to 2 hours
Riblets		1½ to 2½ hours
Neck slices	¾ inch	1 hour
Shanks	¾ to 1 pound each	1 to 1½ hours
Shoulder chops	¾ to 1 inch	45 to 60 minutes

TIMETABLE FOR BRAISING (Cont.)

Cut	Average Weight or Thickness	Approx. Total Cooking Time
Veal		
Breast, stuffed	3 to 4 pounds	1½ to 2½ hours
rolled	2 to 3 pounds	1½ to 2½ hours
Riblets		2 to 3 hours
Veal birds	½x2x4 inches	45 to 60 minutes
Chops	½ to ¾ inch	45 to 60 minutes
Steaks or cutlets	½ to ¾ inch	45 to 60 minutes
Shoulder chops	½ to ¾ inch	45 to 60 minutes
cubes	1 to 2 inches	45 to 60 minutes

Courtesy National Live Stock and Meat Board

Cooking in Liquid—Large, less tender cuts of meat for stews are tenderized by cooking them in liquid. This method is also used for cooking meats for soups and such variety meats as heart and tongue which are much exercised muscles.

Cover meat entirely with either hot or cold liquid. To develop flavor and increase color, brown meat slowly on all sides before adding liquid. (Do not brown corned beef or cured or smoked pork.) Add desired seasonings, cover kettle and cook slowly (do not boil) until meat is tender. If served cold, cool it, then chill in refrigerator in cooking stock. This results in more flavorful, juicy meat with very little shrinkage. If vegetables are to be served with the meat, add them just long enough before meat is tender to cook them. For preparing stews, cut the meat into 1- to 2-inch pieces, cubes, rectangles, or long narrow strips. For added flavor and color, pieces may be coated with flour and browned in hot fat before liquid is added. No fat is necessary if flour is not used. Add just enough hot or cold liquid (water, vegetable juices, or stock) to cover meat. Add seasonings; cook slowly (do not boil) until meat is tender.

To thicken cooking liquid—Pour ½ cup cold water into a screw-top jar; sprinkle ¼ cup flour onto the water (or use amounts specified in recipe). Cover jar tightly and shake until well blended. Slowly pour one half of mixture into cooking liquid, stirring constantly. Bring to boiling. Gradually add only what is needed of remaining mixture for consistency desired. Bring to boiling after each addition. After final addition cook 3 to 5 minutes, stirring occasionally.

TIMETABLE FOR COOKING IN LIQUID

Cut	Average Weight (Pounds)	Approx. Time (Min. per Pound)	Approx. Total Cooking Time
Meat			
Smoked ham (old style and country cured), whole	12 to 16	20	
half	5 to 8	30	
Smoked ham (tendered, shank or but half	5 to 8	20 to 25	
Smoked picnic shoulder	5 to 8	45	
Fresh or corned beef	4 to 6	40 to 50	
Beef for stew			2½ to 3½ hours
Veal for stew			2 to 3 hours
Lamb for stew			1½ to 2 hours

Courtesy National Live Stock and Meat Board

TIMETABLE FOR COOKING VARIETY MEATS

Kind	Broiling	Braising*	Cooking in Liquid
Liver			
Beef, 3- to 4-pound piece		2 to 2½ hrs.	
sliced		20 to 25 min.	
Veal (calf), sliced	8 to 10 min.		
Pork, 3 to 3½ pounds		1½ to 2 hrs.	
sliced		20 to 25 min.	
Lamb, sliced	8 to 10 min.		
Kidney			
Beef		1½ to 2 hrs.	1 to 1½ hrs.
Veal (calf)	10 to 12 min.	1 to 1½ hrs.	¾ to 1 hr.
Pork	10 to 12 min.	1 to 1½ hrs.	¾ to 1 hr.
Lamb	10 to 12 min.	¾ to 1 hr.	¾ to 1 hr.
Heart			
Beef, whole		3 to 4 hrs.	3 to 4 hrs.
sliced		1½ to 2 hrs.	
Veal (calf), whole		2½ to 3 hrs.	2½ to 3 hrs.
Pork		2½ to 3 hrs.	2½ to 3 hrs.
Lamb		2½ to 3 hrs.	2½ to 3 hrs.
Tongue			
Beef			3 to 4 hrs.
Veal (calf)			2 to 3 hrs.
Pork } usually sold			
Lamb } ready-to-serve			
Tripe (Beef)	10 to 15 min.**		1 to 1½ hrs.
Sweetbreads	10 to 15 min.**	20 to 25 min.	15 to 20 min.
Brains	10 to 15 min.**	20 to 25 min.	15 to 20 min.

*On top of range, or in a 300° to 325° oven.
**Time required after precooking in water.

Courtesy National Live Stock and Meat Board

COOKING FROZEN MEATS

Frozen meats which have been defrosted before cooking may be cooked in exactly the same way and by the same methods as meats which have not been frozen. Meat that is cooked before defrosting may be cooked by the same methods also, but a longer cooking time is required.

The second timetable on page 158 lists the cooking time required for various cuts when they are still frozen. In some cases the minutes per pound are given and for some the total cooking time is given.

It is especially important to use a roast meat thermometer when cooking frozen meat. Roast unthawed meat about one hour before attempting to insert the thermometer.

TIMETABLE FOR THAWING FROZEN MEATS

Cut	40°-50°F (Refrigerator)	70°-75°F (Room Temperature)
Steaks, 1 inch	12 hours	2 to 3 hours
Roasts, small	3 to 4 hours per pound	1 to 2 hours per pound
large	4 to 6 hours per pound	2 to 3 hours per pound
Ground meat patties, 2½ inches		1½ to 2 hours

Courtesy Cornell Extension Bulletin 906

TIMETABLE FOR COOKING FROZEN MEATS

Cut	Minutes per Pound		
	Rare	Medium	Well
Beef	47	55	63
Standing rib (roast at 300°F)			
Rolled rib (roast at 300°F)	53	56	65
Rump (braise)			50
Porterhouse steak (broil)			
1 inch, 1¼ to 2 pounds	21	33	
1½ inches, 2 to 3 pounds	23	38	
2 inches, 2½ to 3½ pounds	33	43	
Lamb			
Leg (roast at 300°F)			40 to 45
Boneless shoulder (roast at 300°F)			50
Pork			
Center cut (roast at 350°F)			50 to 55
Rib or loin end (roast at 350°F)			70 to 75

	Total Cooking Time
Beef	
Club steak (broil)	
¾ inch	24 to 28 minutes
1 inch	30 minutes
Ground beef patties (panbroil)	
1 inch	16 to 18 minutes
Lamb	
Loin and rib chops (panbroil)	
¾ inch	15 minutes
1½ inches	25 minutes
Shoulder chops (braise)	
½ inch	20 minutes
Pork	
Chops (braise)	
¾ inch	55 minutes

Courtesy Cornell Extension Bulletin 906

BEEF

STANDING RIB ROAST OF BEEF

3-rib (6 to 8 lbs.) standing rib roast of beef (have meat dealer saw across ribs near backbone so it can be removed to make carving easier)	1½ teaspoons salt 1 teaspoon monosodium glutamate ⅛ teaspoon pepper

1. Place roast, fat side up, in a shallow roasting pan. Season with a blend of salt, monosodium glutamate, and pepper. Insert meat thermometer so tip is slightly beyond center of thickest part of lean; be sure tip does not rest on bone or in fat.
2. Roast at 300° to 325°F, allowing 23 to 25 minutes per pound for rare; 27 to 30 minutes per pound for medium; and 32 to 35 minutes per pound for well done meat. Roast is also done when meat thermometer registers 140°F for rare; 160°F for medium; and 170°F for well done.
3. Place roast on a warm serving platter. Remove thermometer.
4. Meat drippings may be used for *Brown Gravy, page 348.* For a special treat, serve with *Yorkshire Pudding, below.* 8 TO 10 SERVINGS

NOTE: A rib roast of beef may be one of three cuts. From the short loin end of the rib section, a first-rib roast is cut. This is mostly choice, tender "rib eye" meat. From the center rib section, the center-rib roast is cut. It has less "rib eye" meat than the first-rib roast and is usually somewhat less expensive. From the shoulder end of the rib section, the sixth-and-seventh rib roast is cut. It has the least "rib eye" meat and is likely to be least tender of the three. It usually is the least expensive. When purchasing a rib roast, buy not less than two ribs for a standing roast; for a rolled rib roast, buy a 4-pound roast.

ROLLED RIB ROAST OF BEEF: Follow recipe for Standing Rib Roast of Beef. Substitute *rolled beef rib roast* (5 to 7 pounds) for the standing rib roast. Roast at 300° to 325°F, allowing 32 minutes per pound for rare; 38 minutes per pound for medium; and 48 minutes per pound for well done meat.

YORKSHIRE PUDDING: Pour ¼ cup hot drippings from roast beef into an 11x7x1½-inch baking dish and keep hot. Add *1 cup milk, 1 cup sifted all-purpose flour,* and *½ teaspoon salt* to *2 well-beaten eggs.* Beat with hand rotary or electric beater until smooth. Pour into baking pan over hot drippings. Bake at 400°F 30 to 40 minutes, or until puffed and golden. Cut into squares and serve immediately.
ABOUT 8 SERVINGS

BEEF WELLINGTON

Beef Wellington, juicy rare tenderloin spread with liver pâté and encased in flaky pastry, is symbolic of the finest in elegant dining.

3½- to 4-lb. beef tenderloin 1 can (2 to 3 oz.) liver pâté or spread	Pastry (prepared from pie crust mix or Buttery Pastry, *below*) 1 egg yolk, fork beaten 1 teaspoon water

1. Set beef on a rack in a shallow roasting pan. Roast at 425°F 25 minutes (medium rare). Remove from oven and cool completely.
2. Discard any fat on roast. Sprinkle with *salt* and *pepper* and spread with liver pâté.
3. Meanwhile, prepare pastry (enough for the equivalent of three 9-inch pie shells).
4. On a lightly floured surface, roll out pastry large enough to wrap around the roast.
5. Place meat on one edge of pastry and bring other edge over meat to cover completely; reserve extra pastry for decorations. Moisten edges with water and pinch together firmly. Place on a baking sheet. Cut out a few small holes on top to allow steam to escape.
6. Cut out decorative shapes from reserved pastry. Moisten underside of each with water and place on top. Brush entire surface of pastry with a mixture of egg yolk and water.
7. Bake at 425°F 30 to 35 minutes, or until pastry is golden brown.
8. Let stand 5 to 10 minutes before carving into thick slices. 6 TO 8 SERVINGS

For Buttery Pastry: Prepare pastry as directed in step 3, roll out on a lightly floured surface into an 18-inch square, and dot the center portion with slivers of *butter* (6 tablespoons). Fold so the two sides meet in center and seal by pressing edges with fingers. Fold ends to center and seal. Wrap and chill 20 minutes. Roll out as directed in step 4.

STEAK AU POIVRE SHELBOURNE

Flaming this pepper steak just before serving with both cognac and sherry imparts to the meat an unforgettable flavor. It's a favorite at El Paseo, a Mexico City restaurant.

4 beef tenderloin steaks (about 8 oz. each)	3 tablespoons butter
	¼ cup cognac, heated
1½ tablespoons peppercorns	1 tablespoon sherry
	½ cup Brown or Espagnole Sauce, *page 342*

1. Sprinkle meat lightly with *salt*. Crush peppercorns with a rolling pin. Using the back of a spoon, firmly press the pepper onto both sides of steaks.
2. Heat butter in a chafing dish blazer over direct heat and sauté steaks quickly on both sides. This takes about 2 minutes on each side for rare, about 5 minutes for medium.
3. Pour warm cognac over steaks and set the spirit blazing. When flame has burned out, add the sherry and Brown Sauce and simmer a few minutes. Serve immediately.   4 SERVINGS

FILET MIGNON STANLEY

Filet mignon and sautéed bananas enhanced with a piquant horseradish-flavored sauce could be the pièce de résistance of a special dinner—a feature at Brennan's in New Orleans, Louisiana.

2 beef tenderloin steaks (about ¾ lb. each)	1 cup milk
	½ cup prepared horseradish
2 bananas	
2 tablespoons butter	1½ teaspoons salt
½ cup butter	2 drops Worcestershire sauce
1 tablespoon flour	

1. Broil steaks on both sides until well browned. Season to taste with *salt* and *pepper*.
2. Meanwhile, peel bananas and halve lengthwise. Sauté on both sides in the 2 tablespoons butter in a skillet (do not overcook). Lift bananas from skillet; keep warm.
3. Melt the ½ cup butter in the skillet; stir in the flour. Pour in milk, cooking and stirring until sauce comes to boiling.
4. Reduce heat and add horseradish, salt, *pepper* to taste, and Worcestershire sauce. Cook sauce 1 minute longer.
5. Arrange broiled steaks on a platter, surround with bananas, and pour sauce over them.
                2 SERVINGS

PRIME BEEF TOURNEDOS ORLANDO

At La Rue, a well-known Los Angeles restaurant, tournedos are marinated and charcoal broiled to perfection.

4 beef tenderloin steaks (tournedos)	Pepper
	1 teaspoon chopped shallots
Olive oil	
Lemon juice	1 teaspoon chopped chives
Salt	

1. Marinate steaks 1 hour in a mixture of remaining ingredients, using proportions to taste.
2. Remove from marinade and charcoal broil to desired doneness.
3. Serve each filet on a broiled *eggplant* slice. Top with *Bordelaise Sauce, page 342*.   4 SERVINGS
NOTE: Tournedos are slices from the smaller half of a beef tenderloin and usually cut ½ to ¾ inch thick, weighing 3 to 5 ounces.

OYSTERS UP

Hollywood personality Martha Hyer serves this easy-to-prepare, perfectly delicious steak-oyster "bake" as one of her specialties.

1 beef sirloin steak, cut 1¾ in. thick	Freshly ground black pepper
2 tablespoons butter	1 pt. oysters, drained and picked over
Salt	

1. Broil steak 5 minutes on each side; remove to heatproof platter.
2. Spread steak with 1 tablespoon butter and sprinkle with mixture of ½ teaspoon salt and ⅛ teaspoon pepper. Cover steak with oysters; season oysters with ½ teaspoon salt and ⅛ teaspoon pepper and dot with remaining butter.
3. Leaving steak on platter, bake at 425°F 20 minutes, or until oysters are plump with edges curled (do not overcook).   4 TO 6 SERVINGS

STEAK DIANE

¼ cup butter or margarine, softened	Freshly ground black pepper
1 clove garlic, crushed	½ teaspoon Worcestershire sauce
8 thin slices (1 lb.) beef tenderloin	½ lemon
Salt	

1. Blend butter and garlic; set aside 20 minutes.

2.   Heat about 1 tablespoon of the garlic butter in a large heavy skillet. When very hot, add as many steaks at a time as will fit uncrowded in bottom; brown quickly on both sides.

3.   Transfer steaks to a hot serving platter and season on both sides with salt and pepper.

4.   Add remaining butter and Worcestershire sauce to pan; heat until bubbly and lightly browned.

5.   Holding the cut lemon over the pan, squeeze in some juice. Insert the tines of a fork through the peel and use to quickly blend in the juice (rubbing sides and bottom of pan with cut side).

6.   Immediately pour hot sauce over steak and sprinkle with *snipped chives.*   4 SERVINGS

GARLIC-FRIED STEAK

Beefsteaks such as T-bone, sirloin, or club, cut ¾ to 1 in. thick (allow ⅓ to ½ lb. meat per serving)	2 teaspoons Worcestershire sauce
	2 teaspoons salt
	1 teaspoon black pepper
2 cups dairy sour cream	1½ teaspoons celery salt
4 cloves garlic, crushed	1 teaspoon paprika
2 tablespoons lemon juice	Shortening for frying
	Biscuit mix

1.   Put steaks into a large shallow dish. Pour a mixture of the sour cream, garlic, lemon juice, Worcestershire sauce, salt, pepper, celery salt, and paprika over steaks. Cover; refrigerate 8 hours.

2.   Heat shortening in a large heavy skillet. Coat steaks with biscuit mix. Brown on both sides in skillet; cook to desired degree of doneness.

ABOUT 6 SERVINGS

SIRLOIN WITH BLUE RIBBON SAUCE

2 lbs. beef sirloin steak, cut about 1½ in. thick	2 tablespoons prepared mustard
	1 cup chili sauce
2 cups thinly sliced onion	1 tablespoon Worcestershire sauce
1 lemon, thinly sliced	1 teaspoon chili powder
¼ to ½ cup butter or margarine	1 can (6 oz.) cocktail vegetable juice

1.   Brown steak on both sides in a small amount of *fat* in a large skillet with a heat-resistant handle. Remove from heat. Season with *salt.*

2.   Arrange onion and lemon slices to cover meat.

3.   Cream butter and mustard together; blend in the chili sauce, Worcestershire sauce, and chili powder. Spread mixture over onion and lemon. Pour cocktail vegetable juice into skillet.

4.   Bake at 350°F 20 to 30 minutes, or until meat is medium rare or well done.   ABOUT 6 SERVINGS

STEAK À LA BARBARA STANWYCK

Extremely simple in its preparation, yet quite sophisticated in flavor, this is movie-actress Barbara Stanwyck's favorite way with steak.

½ cup soy sauce	1 club steak or small Porterhouse steak, about ¾ in. thick
1 teaspoon brown sugar	
¼ teaspoon freshly ground black pepper	
	2 tablespoons butter
1 teaspoon olive oil	

1.   Mix soy sauce with brown sugar, pepper, and olive oil; pour into shallow pan.

2.   Put steak into sauce and spoon a little sauce over top; marinate 30 minutes; turn several times.

3.   Heat a large heavy skillet; add butter and when very hot, add the steak to skillet. Cook over high heat until charred on one side; turn and cook quickly until charred on other side. (The result will be steaks charred on the outside, but pink in the middle.) Serve immediately on a well heated platter.   1 OR 2 SERVINGS

BEEF À LA FONDUE

This recipe has earned Glynis Johns, stage and screen star, such a reputation that friends call ahead to request it as part of her dinner menu.

2 teaspoons butter	1½ lbs. beef top sirloin steak, cut in bite-size pieces
1 tablespoon flour	
½ cup dry white wine	
½ lb. Swiss cheese, shredded	Cooking oil for deep frying heated to 375°F

1.   Melt butter in top of double boiler over boiling water. Remove from heat; add flour and part of wine, mixing to a smooth paste. Add remaining wine; heat over water until thickened. Add cheese; heat until melted. Keep fondue warm.

2.   At serving time, heat cooking oil. Provide guests with long-handled forks. Each guest cooks a cube of beef on the fork and dips it into the fondue

and then into other sauces and side dishes, including *horseradish sauce* (sour cream and horseradish), *tartar sauce*, *mustard sauce*, *chopped chives*, *chutney*, and the like. These accompaniments should be in small individual dishes clustered around each place setting.   4 SERVINGS

FONDUE BOURGUIGNONNE

Sauces (3 or more),
  below
Cooking oil to half-
  fill a fondue pot,
  heated to 375°F

Beef tenderloin or
  sirloin, cut in 1-in.
  pieces (allow ⅓ to ½
  lb. per person)

1. The hot oil in a copper pot (narrower at the top) is set over canned heat or an alcohol burner on a metal tray. This type of beef-fondue cooker and two-pronged forks with long handles are usually available from specialty shops or the housewares section of department stores. (Plates with dividers for the individual sauces are also available and convenient, but not necessary for this service.) One cooker is ample for four persons.
2. Dishes piled with the raw meat are set on the table between guests or at convenient intervals. Pieces of meat are speared with the forks, then plunged into the hot oil and cooked one to two minutes, or to the desired degree of doneness. Meat is transferred to the plate and eaten with a table fork, thus allowing for meat to be cooking at all times.
3. The meat is finally dipped into the sauces which have been spooned into the plate sections. Chilled crisp relishes such as *radishes*, *celery* and *carrot sticks*, and slices of *buttered dark rye bread*, along with cups of steaming hot *coffee*, complete the menu.

Jiffy Sauces for Fondue Bourguignonne

ONION-CHILI: Combine ½ *envelope (about ¾ ounce) dry onion soup mix* and ¾ *cup boiling water* in a saucepan. Cover partially and cook 10 minutes. Adding gradually, mix in 1½ *tablespoons flour* and ¼ *cup water*. Bring to boiling, stirring constantly; cook until thickened. Remove from heat; mix in 2 *tablespoons chili sauce*.

ONION-HORSERADISH: Blend ½ *envelope (about ¾ ounce) dry onion soup mix*, 1 *tablespoon milk*, 2 *teaspoons prepared horseradish*, and desired amount of *snipped parsley* into 1 *cup dairy sour cream*.

HORSERADISH: Blend 3 *tablespoons prepared horseradish*, 1 *teaspoon grated onion*, and ½ *teaspoon lemon juice* with 1 *cup mayonnaise*.

CURRY: Blend 1 *tablespoon curry powder*, 1 *teaspoon grated onion*, and ½ *teaspoon lemon juice* with 1 *cup mayonnaise*.

MUSTARD: Blend 1 *tablespoon cream* with 1 *cup mayonnaise* and stir in *prepared mustard* to taste.

CAPER: Mix 1 *tablespoon chopped capers* and 1 *cup bottled tartar sauce*; blend in 1 *tablespoon cream*.

BÉARNAISE: Blend 1 *tablespoon parsley flakes*, ½ *teaspoon grated onion*, ¼ *teaspoon crushed tarragon*, and 1 *teaspoon tarragon vinegar* into *hollandaise sauce* prepared from a mix according to package directions, or *Hollandaise Sauce, page 344*.

PAPRIKA: Prepare 1 *cup medium white sauce*. Blend in 1 *teaspoon minced onion*, *few grains ground nutmeg*, and 2 *to 3 teaspoons paprika*.

BARBECUE: Blend *prepared horseradish* to taste with a *bottled barbecue sauce*.

VELVET LEMON SAUCE

2 eggs
½ teaspoon salt
2 tablespoons lemon
  juice
½ cup soft butter

Few grains white
  pepper
½ slice onion
½ cup hot water

1. Put eggs, salt, lemon juice, butter, pepper, and onion into an electric blender container. Blend until smooth. Add hot water, a little at a time, while blending.
2. Turn into top of double boiler. Cook over simmering water, stirring constantly until thickened, about 10 minutes.   ABOUT 1¼ CUPS SAUCE

RÉMOULADE SAUCE

1 cup mayonnaise
1½ teaspoons prepared
  mustard
¼ teaspoon anchovy
  paste
2 tablespoons finely
  chopped sour pickles

1 tablespoon chopped
  capers
1½ teaspoons minced
  parsley
½ teaspoon finely
  crushed chervil
½ teaspoon crushed
  tarragon

Blend all ingredients in a small bowl. Cover; chill thoroughly.   ABOUT 1 CUP SAUCE

BEEF TENDERLOIN BOURGUIGNONNE

A princely dish, reflecting the racy traditions of an ancient French Duchy.

2 lbs. beef tenderloin	¼ teaspoon black
¼ cup cooking oil	pepper
3 tablespoons finely	⅛ teaspoon thyme
chopped onion	2 bay leaves
3 tablespoons flour	1 cup sieved tomatoes
1 teaspoon finely	½ cup red Burgundy
chopped garlic	12 small whole onions,
4 cups beef broth	cooked
¼ cup tomato paste	12 fresh mushrooms,
1 teaspoon Worcester-	sliced lengthwise
shire sauce	3 tablespoons butter
½ teaspoon mono-	or margarine
sodium glutamate	

1. Remove outer membrane of tenderloin and all connective tissue. Thinly slice tenderloin.
2. Brown slices on both sides in hot oil in a large skillet. As meat browns remove and keep hot.
3. Cook the onion 1 to 2 minutes in the skillet, stirring constantly. Blend in flour and garlic, then the broth, tomato paste, Worcestershire sauce, monosodium glutamate, pepper, thyme, and bay leaves, then the meat. Simmer 5 minutes; stir occasionally.
4. Stir in tomatoes and wine. Cover and simmer gently 25 to 30 minutes.
5. Meanwhile, lightly brown whole onions and mushrooms in hot butter in a skillet, stirring occasionally. Add to the meat mixture and spoon into a hot serving dish. Sprinkle with finely snipped *parsley*. Serve with hot buttered *wide noodles*.

6 SERVINGS

TENDERLOIN EN BROCHETTE

From Ernie's Restaurant in San Francisco, California, comes this specialty—broiled beef kabobs accompanied by a wine-flavored mushroom sauce.

Sauce Chasseur, *below*	2 green peppers, cut
2 lbs. beef tenderloin,	in squares
1 in. thick, well	½ lb. bacon, cut in
trimmed and cut in	2-in. pieces
2-in. squares	

1. Prepare the sauce.
2. Thread the meat, green pepper, and bacon pieces alternately on skewers. Season to taste with *salt* and *pepper*; brush with *cooking oil*.
3. Place kabobs under broiler with tops about 3 inches from source of heat and broil to desired doneness. Serve with the sauce. 4 SERVINGS

SAUCE CHASSEUR

½ lb. fresh mushrooms,	1 glass white wine
sliced	2 cups Brown or Espag-
1 tablespoon butter	nole Sauce, *page 342*
1 tablespoon olive oil	1 cup beef consommé
1 tablespoon chopped	½ cup chopped
shallots	tomatoes
1 large clove garlic,	1 bay leaf
chopped	1 tablespoon chopped
1 glass Marsala or	fresh parsley
port wine	

1. Sauté mushrooms in butter and oil in large saucepan. Add shallots and garlic and continue cooking until mushrooms are lightly browned.
2. Add wines and continue cooking to reduce. Add Brown Sauce, consommé, tomatoes, bay leaf, and *salt* and *pepper* to taste. Cook 20 to 25 minutes. When ready to serve sauce, blend in the chopped parsley.

CALYPSO STEAK STICKS

2 lbs. boneless beef	2 cloves garlic, minced
(tenderloin, sirloin,	¼ cup finely chopped
or rib), cut 1¼ in.	crystallized ginger
thick	2 firm bananas with
1 cup soy sauce	all-yellow peel
⅓ cup honey	¼ cup flaked coconut

1. Slice meat across grain into ¼-inch strips.
2. Combine the soy sauce, honey, garlic, and ginger; mix well and pour over the meat strips in a large shallow dish. Refrigerate about 30 minutes, turning meat once.
3. Remove meat from marinade, reserving marinade. Thread meat onto twelve 8-inch skewers, allowing space at end of each skewer for banana pieces.
4. Peel bananas and cut into ¾-inch pieces; dip pieces into marinade, roll in coconut, and drizzle with *lime juice*.
5. Put 1 or 2 pieces of banana on end of each skewer; brush meat and banana pieces with marinade.
6. Broil 3 inches from source of heat about 3 minutes, turning once and brushing with marinade. (Meat should be rare.) 6 SERVINGS

BEEF STROGANOFF

2 lbs. boneless beef
  (tenderloin, sirloin,
  or rib), cut in
  2x¼x¼-in. strips
½ cup flour
1 teaspoon salt
½ teaspoon mono-
  sodium glutamate
⅛ teaspoon black
  pepper
⅓ cup butter or
  margarine
½ cup finely chopped
  onion
2 cups beef broth
3 tablespoons butter
  or margarine
½ lb. fresh mushrooms,
  sliced lengthwise
1 cup dairy sour cream
3 tablespoons tomato
  paste
1 teaspoon Worcester-
  shire sauce

1. Coat meat strips evenly with a mixture of the flour, salt, monosodium glutamate, and pepper.
2. Heat ⅓ cup butter in a large heavy skillet. Add meat strips and onion. Brown on all sides over medium heat, turning occasionally. Add the broth; cover and simmer about 20 minutes.
3. Heat 3 tablespoons butter in a skillet over medium heat. Add mushrooms and cook until lightly browned and tender. Add mushrooms to the meat and remove skillet from heat.
4. Blending well after each addition, add a mixture of the sour cream, tomato paste, and Worcestershire sauce in small amounts. Return to heat. Continue cooking over low heat, stirring constantly, until thoroughly heated (do not boil).

ABOUT 6 SERVINGS

CAN-CAN STROGANOFF

2 lbs. boneless beef
  (sirloin)
⅓ cup flour
½ teaspoon mono-
  sodium glutamate
¼ teaspoon salt
⅛ teaspoon black
  pepper
⅓ cup butter or
  margarine
1 can (10½ oz.) con-
  densed beef broth
1 can (10½ oz.) con-
  densed onion soup
1 can (3 oz.) sliced
  broiled mushrooms,
  drained (reserve
  liquid)
1 cup dairy sour cream
5 drops Tabasco

1. Cut meat into 2x½x½-inch strips. Coat with a mixture of the flour, monosodium glutamate, salt, and pepper.
2. Heat butter in a large heavy skillet over low heat; add the meat and brown slowly and evenly on all sides.
3. Add the beef broth, onion soup, and reserved mushroom liquid; cook and stir until boiling. Reduce heat, cover, and simmer 20 to 25 minutes, or until meat is tender.
4. Stir in the mushrooms and heat thoroughly; remove skillet from heat.
5. Combine the sour cream and Tabasco and add in small amounts to the meat in skillet, stirring vigorously after each addition.
6. Return to heat; cook and stir over low heat until thoroughly heated. Turn into a warm serving dish. Serve immediately with *cooked buttered wide noodles*.

ABOUT 8 SERVINGS

SUKIYAKI

A delectable Japanese specialty usually cooked quickly at the table before the guests.

½ cup Japanese soy
  sauce (shoyu)
¼ cup sake
⅓ cup sugar
3 oz. beef suet, cut
  in small pieces
1½ lbs. beef tender-
  loin, sliced 1/16 in.
  thick and cut in pieces
  about 2½x1½ in.
12 scallions (including
  tops), cut in 2-in.
  lengths
½ head Chinese cabbage
  (cut lengthwise),
  cut in 1-in. pieces
½ lb. spinach leaves,
  cut in 1-in. strips
2 cups drained shira-
  taki (or cold cooked
  very thin long egg
  noodles)
12 large mushrooms,
  sliced lengthwise
12 cubes tofu (soybean
  curd)
1 can (8½ oz.) whole
  bamboo shoots,
  drained and cut in
  large pieces

1. Mix the soy sauce, sake, and sugar to make the sauce; set aside.
2. To prepare Sukiyaki in the traditional Japanese manner at the table, use a large skillet on a hibachi. (A hot plate or an electric skillet makes a good substitute.) Arrange all ingredients artistically on a large platter or tray and bring to the table. Prepare two servings at a time.
3. Heat beef suet in a skillet until sufficient fat is melted. Remove remaining suet. Add enough sauce to cover bottom of the skillet.
4. Add the beef and cook over high heat, turning once, just until pink color disappears; remove and set aside. Arrange all other ingredients in individual mounds in skillet. Top with beef.
5. Cook until vegetables are just tender. Do not stir. Serve immediately with bowls of *hot cooked rice*.

4 SERVINGS

NECTARINE SUKIYAKI

2 lbs. boneless beef
sirloin steak, cut
1½ in. thick, sliced
1/16 in. thick, and
cut into about 2½-in.
pieces
2 large onions, cut in
thin wedges
8 green onions
(including tops),
cut in 2-in. pieces

5 oz. fresh mushrooms,
sliced lengthwise
1 can (5 oz.) bamboo
shoots, drained and
sliced
2 cups unpared sliced
fresh nectarines
1 tablespoon fat
½ cup soy sauce
½ cup canned con-
densed beef broth
2 tablespoons sugar

1. Arrange the meat and vegetables artistically on a large platter. Prepare nectarines; set aside.
2. Heat fat in a large heavy skillet on a hibachi. Add meat and brown quickly over high heat; remove meat and set aside.
3. Arrange reserved ingredients in mounds in skillet, top with the beef. Pour a mixture of the soy sauce, beef broth, and sugar over all. Simmer 3 to 5 minutes, or until onions are just tender.
4. Serve immediately over *hot fluffy rice*.

6 TO 8 SERVINGS

BEEF CHOW MEIN

¼ cup butter or
margarine
1 lb. beef tenderloin
or sirloin steak, cut
in 3x½x⅛-in. strips
3 tablespoons butter
or margarine
½ lb. fresh mushrooms,
sliced lengthwise
2 cups sliced celery
2 green onions, sliced
½ in. thick
½ green pepper, cut in
narrow strips
1½ cups boiling water

1 teaspoon salt
½ teaspoon mono-
sodium glutamate
⅛ teaspoon pepper
2 tablespoons cold
water
2 tablespoons
cornstarch
2 teaspoons soy sauce
1 teaspoon sugar
1 can (16 oz.) Chinese
mixed vegetables,
drained
2 tablespoons coarsely
chopped pimiento

1. Heat ¼ cup butter in a large skillet. Add beef and brown evenly. Remove meat; set aside.
2. Heat 3 tablespoons butter in skillet. Stir in mushrooms, celery, green onions, and green pepper; cook and stir 1 minute. Reduce heat and blend in boiling water, salt, monosodium glutamate, and pepper. Bring to boiling; cover and simmer 2 minutes. Remove vegetables; keep warm.

3. Bring liquid in skillet to boiling and stir in a blend of cold water, cornstarch, soy sauce, and sugar. Cook and stir 2 to 3 minutes. Reduce heat; mix in meat and Chinese vegetables and pimiento. Heat thoroughly.
4. Serve piping hot with *chow mein noodles*.

4 TO 6 SERVINGS

BEEF CHUNKS POLYNESIAN

1½ teaspoons garlic
salt
1 teaspoon paprika
1 teaspoon ground
ginger
2½ lbs. beef sirloin tip,
cut in 1½-in. cubes
1 large clove garlic,
minced
2 to 3 tablespoons
cooking oil
1 can (13½ oz.) pine-
apple chunks, drained
(reserve ½ cup syrup)
1 can (10½ oz.)
condensed beef broth

½ cup garlic-flavored
wine vinegar
½ cup sliced celery
2 onions, quartered
2 large tomatoes, cut
in wedges
3 tablespoons brown
sugar
2 tablespoons
cornstarch
¼ cup water
2 tablespoons soy
sauce
½ cup sliced green
pepper

1. Mix the garlic salt, paprika, and ginger and toss mixture with meat cubes to coat.
2. Brown meat and garlic in heated oil in a heavy skillet. Stir in the pineapple syrup, beef broth, and one half of the vinegar. Cover and simmer until meat is tender, about 2 hours.
3. Stir in the celery, onions, tomatoes, and pineapple chunks, reserving a few tomato wedges and pineapple chunks. Cook, covered, 10 minutes.
4. Stir in a mixture of the brown sugar, cornstarch, water, soy sauce, and remaining vinegar. Add the green pepper. Bring to boiling and cook 3 minutes, stirring gently.
5. Stir in reserved tomato and pineapple just before serving. ABOUT 8 SERVINGS

LONDON BROIL

2½ lbs. flank steak,
scored on both sides
3 tablespoons butter
or margarine

2 teaspoons bottled
exotic sauce

1. Place flank steak on broiler rack and broil about 3 inches from source of heat 2 to 3 minutes

on each side. Season with *salt* and *pepper* before turning.

2. Meanwhile, brown butter in a skillet and add exotic sauce. Blend thoroughly.

3. Brush both sides with sauce; place on heated platter. Cut steak diagonally across grain into very thin slices. Serve with *herb-buttered noodles*.

6 TO 8 SERVINGS

CHINESE BEEF AND PEA PODS

1½ lbs. flank steak (1 or 2), thinly sliced diagonally across grain
1 to 2 tablespoons cooking oil
1 bunch green onions, chopped
1 or 2 pkgs. (7 oz. each) frozen Chinese pea pods, partially thawed to separate
1 can (10½ oz.) condensed beef consommé
3 tablespoons soy sauce
¼ teaspoon ground ginger
2 tablespoons cornstarch
2 tablespoons cold water
1 can (16 oz.) bean sprouts, drained and rinsed

1. Brown meat in hot oil in a large heavy skillet. Remove and keep warm.

2. Put the green onions and pea pods into skillet. Stir in a mixture of consommé, soy sauce, and ginger. Bring to boiling and cook, covered, about 2 minutes.

3. Mix a blend of cornstarch and water into boiling liquid in skillet. Stirring constantly, boil 2 to 3 minutes. Mix in the meat and bean sprouts; heat thoroughly.

4. Serve over *cooked rice*.   6 SERVINGS

SPICY STUFFED FLANK STEAK

⅓ cup cornmeal (about 1 cup cooked)
1 tablespoon olive oil
½ cup chopped green onion
1 clove garlic, minced
1½ teaspoons chili powder
⅛ teaspoon oregano
¼ cup snipped parsley
½ lb. sweet Italian sausage
2 flank steaks, 1 lb. each
1 teaspoon seasoned instant meat tenderizer
Bacon

1. Cook the cornmeal according to directions on package for cornmeal mush. Cool.

2. Meanwhile, heat olive oil in a skillet. Add onion and garlic and fry until lightly browned, about 3 minutes, stirring occasionally. Remove from heat. Blend in chili powder, oregano, and parsley.

3. Separate the sausage into small pieces and add to the skillet along with the cooked cornmeal; mix thoroughly. Set aside.

4. Fasten the two flank steaks together, overlapping long sides and threading skewers through both pieces. Prepare the meat as follows: Moisten each side of meat with water and sprinkle evenly with the meat tenderizer. Pierce deeply with a two-tined fork at approximately ½-inch intervals.

5. Spread cornmeal stuffing evenly on meat; roll up lengthwise as for jelly roll and secure with skewers. Place half slices of bacon crosswise on meat; tie with cord.

6. Place steak, bacon side up, on rack in a shallow roasting pan. Roast, uncovered, at 425°F 1 hour 15 minutes, or until of desired degree of doneness.

7. Remove cord, bacon, and skewers; slice.

6 TO 8 SERVINGS

GREEN PEPPER STEAK

2 lbs. flank steak
2 tablespoons olive oil
1 teaspoon garlic salt
⅛ teaspoon black pepper
¼ teaspoon ground ginger
¼ cup soy sauce
½ teaspoon sugar
2 tomatoes, peeled and quartered
2 green peppers, cut in 1-in. pieces
1 can (16 oz.) bean sprouts, drained
1 tablespoon cornstarch
6 tablespoons cold water

1. Cut flank steak into thin strips across the grain.

2. Heat olive oil in a large heavy skillet. Add meat and a mixture of the garlic salt, pepper, and ginger; brown quickly over high heat.

3. Blend in soy sauce and sugar; cover tightly and cook slowly 5 minutes. Add tomato, green pepper, and bean sprouts; bring to boiling, cover, and cook rapidly 5 minutes.

4. Stirring constantly, blend in a mixture of the cornstarch and water. Bring to boiling and cook 2 to 3 minutes, or until sauce thickens.

5. Serve with *hot fluffy rice*.   ABOUT 6 SERVINGS

STUFFED STEAK ROLLS

6 beef cube steaks	2 teaspoons ground
½ cup soy sauce	ginger
⅓ cup lemon juice	1 clove garlic, minced
⅓ cup water	Stuffing, *below*
⅓ cup sugar	2 tablespoons butter
	or margarine

1. Put cube steaks into a large, shallow dish. Pour a mixture of soy sauce, lemon juice, water, sugar, ginger, and garlic over them; marinate 30 minutes.
2. Drain steaks well, reserving marinade. Put a large spoonful of stuffing at end of each cube steak. Roll up as for a jelly roll and secure with metal or wooden picks.
3. Heat butter in a large skillet. Add the steak rolls and brown well on all sides, brushing frequently with marinade. Cover skillet and cook about 5 minutes, or until meat is tender. 6 SERVINGS

STUFFING

12 slices white bread,	¼ teaspoon crushed
toasted	rosemary
½ cup butter or	3 tablespoons snipped
margarine, melted	parsley
¼ cup milk	3 tablespoons minced
1 teaspoon salt	onion
⅛ teaspoon pepper	

Soak bread in cold water, squeeze out as much of the water as possible, and pull into fluffy pieces. Pour butter, milk, salt, pepper, and rosemary over the bread. Add parsley and onion; toss lightly.

4 CUPS STUFFING

CREOLE POT ROAST

3- to 4-lb. beef pot	2 onions, halved and
roast	sliced
3 slices salt pork or	¼ cup butter or
bacon, cut crosswise	margarine
in thin strips	3 carrots, finely
1 onion, finely chopped	chopped
1 clove garlic, minced	1 turnip, finely chopped
1 teaspoon salt	2 tablespoons snipped
¼ teaspoon pepper	parsley
¼ teaspoon cayenne	1 bay leaf, crushed
pepper	½ cup sherry or
¼ teaspoon thyme,	Madeira
crushed	

1. Cut slits several inches apart all over surface of pot roast. Insert salt pork into slits, also a mixture of chopped onion, garlic, salt, peppers, and thyme.
2. In a Dutch oven, lightly brown the onions in heated butter. Push to one side; brown meat on both sides. While second side is browning add carrots, turnip, parsley, and bay leaf; cook, turning vegetables several times.
3. When meat is browned, add wine. Cover tightly and simmer 3 hours, or until meat is tender, adding more wine or water if needed.
4. Remove meat to a heated platter.

6 TO 8 SERVINGS

SAVORY POT ROAST

3- to 4-lb. beef pot roast	⅛ teaspoon black
2 tablespoons flour	pepper
2 tablespoons paprika	3 tablespoons fat
2 teaspoons salt	4 onions, thinly sliced

1. Coat meat with a mixture of the flour, paprika, salt, and pepper. Brown meat on all sides in hot fat in a large skillet or Dutch oven.
2. Lift out meat and put about one third of the onions in a layer in bottom of skillet or Dutch oven. Return meat and cover with remaining onions.
3. Cover tightly and cook over low heat about 3 hours, or until meat is tender. 6 TO 8 SERVINGS

BEEF POT ROAST À LA PROVINCE

3 lbs. beef bottom	1 can (10½ oz.) con-
round or blade pot	densed beef
roast	consommé
¼ cup butter or	1 cup dairy sour cream
margarine	½ cup dry red wine
3 carrots, chopped	1 tablespoon drained
4 stalks celery,	capers
chopped	1 teaspoon salt
1 onion, chopped	½ teaspoon paprika
1 clove garlic, minced	⅛ teaspoon black
1 can (6 oz.) sliced	pepper
mushrooms (undrained)	

1. Brown beef on all sides in heated butter in a heavy skillet having a tight-fitting cover. Add the carrots, celery, onion, and garlic; cook until onion is golden, stirring occasionally. Add mushrooms.
2. Blend thoroughly the consommé and remaining ingredients; pour into skillet. Cover and simmer 2 to 3 hours, or until meat is tender. Remove meat to heated serving platter and keep hot.

3. Skim any excess fat from gravy. If desired, thicken gravy with flour. Serve with the roast. Garnish plate with *cauliflowerets* and *parsley.*

ABOUT 6 SERVINGS

NOTE: If desired, omit red wine and add a mixture of *1/3 cup red wine vinegar, 2 tablespoons water,* and *2 tablespoons brown sugar.*

POT ROAST PIQUANTE

3- to 4-lb. beef pot roast	1 can (16 oz.) tomatoes
1/4 cup flour	2 onions, halved and sliced
2 teaspoons salt	1/2 cup sliced pitted ripe olives
1/4 teaspoon black pepper	1/2 teaspoon chili powder
2 tablespoons cooking oil	1 ripe avocado, sliced
	Lemon juice

1. Coat meat with a mixture of flour, salt, and pepper.
2. Brown meat on both sides in hot oil in a large heavy skillet.
3. Mix in the tomatoes, onions, olives, and chili powder. Cover and simmer until meat is tender, about 3 hours.
4. Remove meat to warm serving platter and pour gravy over meat. Arrange avocado slices (drizzled with lemon juice to prevent discoloration) on top of pot roast and garnish with thin *lemon cartwheels.*

ABOUT 8 SERVINGS

SAUERBRATEN

Potato dumplings and Sauerbraten are a famous German duo.

3- to 4-lb. beef blade pot roast	2 cups water
1 clove garlic, halved	2 onions, sliced
2 teaspoons salt	2 bay leaves
1/4 teaspoon pepper	1 teaspoon peppercorns
2 cups cider vinegar	1/4 cup sugar
	2 tablespoons lard

1. Rub meat with cut surface of garlic, then with salt and pepper. Put meat and garlic into a deep casserole having a cover.
2. Heat the vinegar, water, onions, bay leaves, peppercorns, and sugar just until boiling; pour over meat and allow to cool. Cover and refrigerate 4 days, turning meat each day.
3. Remove meat; strain and reserve liquid for cooking the meat.

4. Brown meat in heated lard in a Dutch oven, turning to brown evenly. Add half of the reserved liquid; cover and simmer 2 to 3 hours, or until meat is tender, adding additional liquid as needed. Slice meat; serve with *Potato Dumplings, below* and, if desired, *Gingersnap Gravy.*   6 TO 8 SERVINGS

GINGERSNAP GRAVY: Stir *3/4 cup crushed gingersnaps* and *1 tablespoon sugar* into cooking liquid in Dutch oven. Simmer 10 minutes; stir occasionally.

POTATO DUMPLINGS
(Kartoffelklösse)

1 to 2 slices bread, cut in 1/2-in. cubes	1 teaspoon salt
1 to 1 1/2 tablespoons butter or margarine	1/8 teaspoon white pepper
1 egg, well beaten	1/4 cup cornstarch
6 potatoes, mashed or riced and cooled	2/3 to 3/4 cup all-purpose flour

1. Brown bread cubes lightly on all sides in heated butter in a large skillet; set aside.
2. Whip egg into cooled mashed potatoes until fluffy. Stir in salt, pepper, and cornstarch. Mix in enough flour to make a soft dough.
3. Break off pieces of dough and shape into 1-inch balls. Poke one of the bread cubes into the center of each ball.
4. Drop dumplings into boiling *salted water* (2 quarts water and 2 teaspoons salt) only as many as will lie uncrowded one layer deep. Cook about 5 minutes, or until dumplings rise to surface. Using a slotted spoon, remove dumplings; drain over water a few seconds. Put into a heated serving dish. Serve with *melted butter.* Dumplings may be served with sauerkraut, other meat, or poultry.

ABOUT 18 DUMPLINGS

EPICUREAN BEEF À LA FAR EAST

3- to 4-lb. beef pot roast, cut in 6 large chunks for individual servings	1 1/4 cups warm milk
	1/2 cup flaked coconut
	2 teaspoons cornstarch
3 tablespoons fat	1 teaspoon curry powder
3 onions, halved and sliced	3 cups hot cooked rice
	1/2 cup chutney
1/2 cup hot water	1/2 cup golden raisins, plumped
1/4 cup soy sauce	

1. Brown meat evenly on all sides in hot fat in a Dutch oven or saucepot. Mix in onions, hot water,

and soy sauce. Cover and simmer 2½ hours, or until meat is just tender.

2. Meanwhile, pour warm milk over coconut in a bowl; let stand about 1 hour or longer.

3. Remove meat and keep warm. If necessary, skim and discard fat from cooking liquid.

4. Drain coconut and reserve; add to coconut milk a mixture of cornstarch and curry powder and blend thoroughly. Stir into boiling liquid in Dutch oven. Cook and stir 2 to 3 minutes.

5. Lightly toss chutney, coconut, and raisins with hot rice. Serve gravy and meat on rice. If desired, accompany with *chutney* and *preserved kumquats*.

6 SERVINGS

SWEDISH POT ROAST

2 tablespoons butter or margarine	2 teaspoons salt
4- to 5-lb. boneless beef pot roast	½ teaspoon pepper
1 cup beef bouillon	2 onions, cut in ¼-in. slices
¼ cup apple cider	½ teaspoon whole allspice
2 tablespoons molasses	¼ teaspoon whole peppercorns
3 Swedish anchovy fillets, drained and mashed (reserve 1 tablespoon anchovy liquid)	2 bay leaves
	½ cup water
	3 tablespoons flour
	1 cup cream

1. Heat butter in a Dutch oven or heavy saucepot and brown roast on all sides. Add bouillon, cider, molasses, and anchovies; season meat with salt and pepper, cover with onions, and add allspice, peppercorns, and bay leaves. Cover tightly and simmer gently, basting occasionally until meat is tender, about 3½ hours.

2. Remove meat to a hot platter and keep warm while preparing gravy.

3. Strain the cooking liquid, pressing out as much of the liquid as possible; return to the Dutch oven. Bring to boiling; stir in a blend of the water and flour. Cook and stir 1 to 2 minutes. Add cream gradually, stirring constantly, and heat thoroughly. Stir in reserved anchovy liquid.

4. To serve, slice roast and overlap slices in a shallow baking dish; pour gravy over meat. Cover and set in a 350°F oven until thoroughly heated. Accompany with *boiled potatoes* coated with a mixture of *butter or margarine* and *dill weed*.

6 TO 8 SERVINGS

NOTE: *Anchovy paste*, about ¼ teaspoon each for the roast and gravy, may be substituted for the anchovy fillets and liquid.

BEEF BRISKET WITH HORSERADISH SAUCE

6- to 7-lb. fresh beef brisket	½ cup chili sauce
4½ teaspoons seasoned salt	½ cup ketchup
	1 jar (5 oz.) prepared horseradish
4 to 5 tablespoons flour	1 cup boiling water

1. Sprinkle the beef with seasoned salt; coat evenly with flour. Set on a rack in a roasting pan. Roast at 450°F 30 minutes.

2. Combine the chili sauce, ketchup, and horseradish; mix well and spoon over meat.

3. Pour boiling water into bottom of pan; cover. Reduce oven temperature to 350°F and return meat to oven. Continue roasting about 3 hours, or until meat is tender.

4. If desired, thicken cooking liquid for gravy.

10 TO 12 SERVINGS

MEAL-IN-A-KETTLE

4- to 5-lb. fresh beef brisket	1 teaspoon monosodium glutamate
2 soup bones	1 tablespoon sugar
4 white turnips, pared and diced	4 lbs. chicken pieces (breasts and legs)
1 cup chopped celery	½ cup barley
1 cup chopped onion	1 can (16 oz.) whole tomatoes
½ cup chopped parsley	
2 cloves garlic, quartered	1 lb. small white onions, peeled
1 large bay leaf	1 pkg. (10 oz.) frozen corn
½ teaspoon thyme, crushed	1 pkg. (9 oz.) frozen cut green beans
2½ tablespoons salt	
6 peppercorns	

1. Put beef and bones into a large kettle. Cover with cold water. Bring to boiling. Remove foam.

2. Add turnips, celery, chopped onion, parsley, garlic, bay leaf, thyme, salt, peppercorns, monosodium glutamate, and sugar. Return to boiling, cover, and simmer 4 hours.

3. Add chicken and continue cooking 1 hour, or until chicken and beef are tender.

4. Remove chicken and beef; set aside and keep

warm. Remove and discard bones, bay leaf, and peppercorns. Skim off fat and bring broth to boiling.

5.   Stir in barley; cover, and cook 30 minutes. Cut tomatoes in pieces and add with the tomato liquid and onions; cook, covered, 15 minutes. Mix in corn and beans, cover, and continue cooking until vegetables are just tender, about 15 minutes.

6.   Meanwhile, cut chicken and beef in serving-sized pieces, discarding chicken bones and skin and removing fat from beef. Return meat to kettle just before serving. Ladle into soup plates.

ABOUT 10 SERVINGS

BARBECUED BRISKET OF BEEF

6-lb. fresh beef brisket	¼ cup Worcester-
1 large onion,	shire sauce
quartered and sliced	2 tablespoons brown
1 bay leaf	sugar
16 whole cloves	2 tablespoons dry
1 clove garlic, halved	mustard
2 cups ketchup	

1.   Put meat into a large saucepot; cover with water. Add the onion, bay leaf, cloves, and garlic; cover and simmer 4 hours, or until meat is tender.

2.   Cool in liquid; drain. Trim off excess fat. Refrigerate several hours or overnight.

3.   Cut meat across the grain into very thin slices. Place meat slices together and stand them on edge in a large shallow baking pan. Pour a mixture of the remaining ingredients over the meat.

4.   Heat in a 350°F oven about 40 minutes, basting occasionally with sauce in bottom of pan.

ABOUT 12 SERVINGS

TOMATO-SMOTHERED STEAK

3 tablespoons fat	1½ teaspoons chili
1½ lbs. beef arm or	powder
blade steak, cut	1 teaspoon celery salt
1½ in. thick	1 large onion, sliced
¼ cup flour	¼ cup finely chopped
2½ teaspoons salt	green pepper
¼ teaspoon black	1 can (16 oz.) tomatoes
pepper	3 drops Tabasco

1.   Heat fat in large heavy skillet or in a Dutch oven over medium heat.

2.   Coat meat with a mixture of the flour, salt, pepper, chili powder, and celery salt. Brown meat on both sides in hot fat.

3.   Add onion, green pepper, tomatoes, and Tabas-

co. Bring liquid rapidly to boiling; reduce heat, cover tightly, and cook slowly over direct heat or in a 300°F oven about 2 hours, or until meat is tender.

ABOUT 6 SERVINGS

SWISS STEAK IN VEGETABLE SAUCE

¼ cup flour	1 can (10½ oz.) con-
½ teaspoon mono-	densed beef broth
sodium glutamate	½ to ¾ cup hot water
¼ teaspoon salt	½ bay leaf
Few grains pepper	⅛ teaspoon ground
1½ lbs. beef round,	cinnamon
blade, or arm steak,	1 can (10¾ oz.) con-
cut 1¼ in. thick	densed vegetable
2 tablespoons butter	soup
or margarine	⅓ cup ketchup

1.   Mix the flour, monosodium glutamate, salt, and pepper and pound into the meat with a meat hammer, using one half of mixture for each side.

2.   Heat butter in a Dutch oven or heavy saucepot; add steak and brown evenly on both sides.

3.   Add broth, hot water, bay leaf, and cinnamon. Cover pot and bring liquid rapidly to boiling; reduce heat and simmer until steak is tender, 60 to 75 minutes.

4.   Remove meat to a platter and keep warm.

5.   Pour the vegetable soup and ketchup into the pot; heat thoroughly, stirring to blend in brown residue on bottom. Remove bay leaf; pour sauce over meat and serve immediately.   ABOUT 6 SERVINGS

ESTERHAZY STEAK

A dressed-up round steak dating from the days of Hungarian nobility—named in honor of one of the oldest and most prominent families.

2 lbs. beef round steak,	1 stalk celery, chopped
cut 1 in. thick	1 teaspoon capers
¾ cup all-purpose flour	1 tablespoon fat
2 teaspoons salt	1 tablespoon flour
½ teaspoon pepper	¼ teaspoon salt
⅓ cup fat	Few grains pepper
3 carrots, thinly sliced	1 cup beef broth
2 onions, thinly sliced	¼ cup dry white wine
1 parsnip, thinly	1 cup dairy sour cream
sliced	1 teaspoon paprika

1.   Pound meat thoroughly on one side with meat hammer, pounding in ¼ cup of the flour. (Pounding increases tenderness.) Turn meat over and repeat

process, using ¼ cup flour. Cut into serving-sized pieces and coat with a mixture of ¼ cup of the flour, salt, and pepper.

2. Brown meat on both sides in ⅓ cup hot fat in a large skillet. As meat browns remove to a 2-quart shallow baking dish; set aside and keep hot.

3. Cook vegetables in the skillet 10 minutes, stirring occasionally. Spoon vegetables and capers over steak.

4. Heat 1 tablespoon fat in the skillet. Blend in 1 tablespoon flour and remaining seasonings; heat until bubbly and lightly browned, stirring constantly. Mix in beef broth. Bring rapidly to boiling, stirring constantly. Remove from heat and blend in wine. Pour over vegetables and meat. Tightly cover baking dish with aluminum foil.

5. Bake at 350°F 1¼ hours. Remove foil and spread a mixture of sour cream and paprika over vegetables. Return to oven and continue baking, uncovered, about 15 minutes, or until meat is tender. ABOUT 6 SERVINGS

BEEF SAIGON

1½ lbs. thinly sliced beef rump roast	1½ teaspoons curry powder
Unseasoned meat tenderizer	½ teaspoon ginger
3 tablespoons butter or margarine	1 tablespoon chili sauce
1 tablespoon chopped scallions	2 teaspoons soy sauce
1 tablespoon chopped onion	¾ cup tomato sauce or canned tomatoes
¼ teaspoon garlic salt	2 teaspoons sugar
	1 tablespoon lemon juice
	½ cup canned beef gravy

1. Cut beef into 3-inch squares. Treat with meat tenderizer as directed on label of jar.

2. Heat butter in a large skillet; add meat and brown pieces quickly on both sides; transfer meat to a hot platter.

3. Add scallions, onion, and garlic salt to drippings in skillet; cook gently a few minutes. Stir in remaining ingredients.

4. Heat to boiling; place meat in sauce, cover, and cook over low heat until tender, about 30 minutes.

5. To serve, place a mound of *hot cooked rice* (preferably wild rice) on a heated large platter. Cover rice with meat slices and pour gravy over all.

6. Surround meat and rice with alternating mounds of *drained bean sprouts*, heated with *2 tablespoons butter*, and a mixture of *1 cup sliced water chestnuts* and *1 cup canned sliced mushrooms*, which have been heated separately with *2 tablespoons butter*. 4 TO 6 SERVINGS

BEEF ROLL-UPS

3 tablespoons butter or margarine	2 tablespoons butter or margarine
½ lb. fresh mushrooms, chopped	1 cup coarsely chopped onion
½ lb. coarsely chopped, fully-cooked smoked ham	1 cup finely diced carrot
¼ cup chopped parsley	½ cup chopped celery with leaves
½ cup soft bread crumbs	1 teaspoon thyme
1 clove garlic, minced	4 whole cloves
½ teaspoon salt	1 small bay leaf
⅛ teaspoon pepper	1 cup strong beef broth (dissolve 2 beef bouillon cubes in 1 cup boiling water)
8 pieces (4x6-in. each) beef round steak, ½ in. thick	2 tablespoons snipped parsley

1. Heat the 3 tablespoons butter in a large heavy skillet. Add mushrooms and ham and cook over medium heat, stirring occasionally, until mushrooms are lightly browned. Remove from heat and stir in chopped parsley, crumbs, garlic, salt, and pepper.

2. On a wooden board, pound each piece of meat with a meat hammer. Place a heaping tablespoonful of the dressing on each piece; beginning with longer side, roll and tie securely. Coat with *seasoned flour*.

3. Heat the 2 tablespoons butter in skillet over medium heat; add roll-ups and brown on all sides; remove. Add to skillet a mixture of onion, carrot, celery, thyme, cloves, and bay leaf. Place roll-ups over vegetables, cover tightly, and cook until steam appears around cover, about 10 minutes.

4. Pour broth over meat, cover, and reduce heat. Simmer until tender, about 1¼ hours.

5. Remove meat from skillet and cut off cord. Place roll-ups on heated serving platter.

6. Meanwhile, cook vegetable mixture, uncovered, about 3 minutes, or until slightly thicker; remove bay leaf and cloves. Spoon mixture over roll-ups; sprinkle with remaining parsley and serve at once. 8 SERVINGS

BEEF AND BROCCOLI SKILLET

2 lbs. broccoli
¼ cup olive oil
2 cloves garlic, minced
2 lbs. boneless beef
(round or chuck),
sliced very thin and
cut diagonally in
4x½-in. strips

3 cups hot chicken
broth
4 teaspoons cornstarch
¼ cup cold water
3 tablespoons soy
sauce
1 teaspoon salt
2 cans (16 oz. each)
bean sprouts

1. Cut broccoli into pieces about 2½ inches long and ¼ inch thick; set aside.
2. Heat 2 tablespoons of the olive oil with garlic in a large skillet; add beef pieces and cook until evenly browned. Remove beef from skillet; set aside.
3. Pour remaining oil into skillet. Add broccoli; cook over high heat ½ minute, tossing constantly. Pour broth slowly into skillet; cover and cook 3 minutes. Remove broccoli; keep warm.
4. Blend in a mixture of cornstarch, cold water, soy sauce, and salt. Bring to boiling, stirring constantly, and cook until mixture thickens. Add bean sprouts, broccoli, and beef; toss to mix, then heat thoroughly. Serve with *hot fluffy rice*.   8 SERVINGS

BEEF, BURGUNDY STYLE
(Boeuf Bourguignon)

Among many interpretations of this famous French beef stew is actor David Janssen's version.

2 lbs. beef round
steak, cut in 1½-in.
cubes
2 tablespoons flour
1½ teaspoons salt
½ teaspoon freshly
ground black pepper
1 tablespoon butter or
margarine

1 cup chopped onion
½ cup chopped carrot
1 clove garlic, minced
2 tablespoons cognac
3 sprigs parsley,
chopped
1 bay leaf
¼ teaspoon marjoram
2 cups dry red wine

1. Coat meat with a mixture of flour, salt, and pepper. Brown meat quickly on all sides in heated butter in a large skillet. Then remove to a 2½-quart casserole.
2. Brown onion, carrot, and garlic in butter remaining in skillet.
3. Heat cognac; ignite and pour over beef. When flame has expired, stir in vegetables and remaining ingredients. Cover casserole and bake at 350°F about 2½ hours.   4 TO 6 SERVINGS

RAGOUT WITH PIQUANT SAUCE

½ to ¾ lb. sliced
Canadian-style bacon,
cut in strips
1½ lbs. beef round
steak, cut in 3x¼-
in. strips
3 onions, thinly sliced
4 potatoes, pared and
sliced

6 to 8 carrots, pared
and sliced
1 cup mayonnaise
1 clove garlic, minced
1 tablespoon lemon
juice
Few grains cayenne
pepper

1. Arrange bacon strips in an even layer on the bottom of a Dutch oven. Cover with the beef strips. Season to taste with *salt, pepper,* and *monosodium glutamate.* Cover with a layer of onions, potatoes, and carrots, adding more seasoning after each layer. Cover tightly and cook slowly 2 hours, or until vegetables are tender.
2. Meanwhile, blend the remaining ingredients in a bowl. Cover and chill.
3. To serve, arrange each layer separately on a large deep platter. Pour the cooking juices over all. Serve with the mayonnaise sauce.

ABOUT 6 SERVINGS

STICKY MEAT
This dish, contributed by movie actress Susan Hayward, is easy to prepare, tasty, and hearty.

3 lbs. beef top round
steak, cut 3 in.
thick
2 pieces (2 in. each)
beef suet
1 tablespoon butter

3 large yellow onions,
chopped (about 2
cups)
1 tablespoon salt
Boiling water

1. Cut the round steak into 3-inch cubes.
2. Heat suet and butter in a large deep skillet or Dutch oven. Add chopped onions and cook until tender and browned. Remove from skillet and set aside.
3. Put meat into hot skillet and brown thoroughly on all sides. Be sure not to turn the meat until it sticks to the skillet.
4. Return the onions to skillet; sprinkle with salt. Add only enough boiling water to almost cover the meat. Cover and bring to boiling; immediately lower heat and simmer 1 hour, or until meat is very tender. Remove meat to a hot platter.
5. Make a gravy by thickening the pan liquid with a mixture of flour and water. Add seasoning, if needed. Pour gravy over meat.   10 to 12 SERVINGS

RAGOUT OF BEEF HUNSTMAN

Chuck full of flavor, this beef-vegetable stew is truly a culinary accomplishment — a specialty of Ho-Ho-Kus Inn, Ho-Ho-Kus, New Jersey.

1 lb. dried red kidney beans, washed	4 medium-sized potatoes, pared and cubed
2 lbs. beef chuck, cubed	1 bunch carrots, pared and sliced
2 tablespoons shortening	3 cups water
4 onions, sliced	2 cups canned tomatoes with liquid
1 teaspoon paprika	2 cups cooked julienne green beans
1 teaspoon chili powder	3 tablespoons flour
3 cups red wine	2 cups dairy sour cream, chilled
½ yellow turnip (rutabaga), cubed	

1. Bring *6 cups water* to boiling in a Dutch oven. Add kidney beans and boil 2 minutes. Cover, remove from heat, and let stand 1 hour.
2. Simmer beans in soaking liquid 2 hours, or until tender, adding *2 teaspoons salt*.
3. Meanwhile season beef with *salt* and *pepper*. Brown on all sides in shortening in a saucepot.
4. Add onions and sprinkle with paprika and chili powder. Cook onions until lightly browned, stirring occasionally. Add wine, cover, and simmer 2 hours.
5. Add the raw vegetables and water. Simmer, covered, until tender, about 45 minutes.
6. Add tomatoes, kidney beans, and green beans. Heat thoroughly. Thicken gravy with the flour (mixed with cold water to form a smooth paste). Serve with sour cream sprinkled with *paprika*.

6 SERVINGS

BEEF WITH ONIONS
(Stifado)

This superbly flavored dish is popular at Smokey Joe's Grecian Terrace in St. Louis.

2 lbs. lean beef or pork, cut in 1½-in. pieces	4 firm ripe tomatoes, quartered
2 tablespoons butter	2 to 3 cloves garlic, minced
2 tablespoons olive oil	2 to 3 tablespoons wine vinegar
4 lbs. small white onions	2 to 3 bay leaves

1. Brown meat on all sides in hot butter and oil in a large heavy saucepot.
2. Add remaining ingredients and then enough water to half cover ingredients in the pot. Season to taste with *salt* and *pepper*.
3. Bring to boiling, cover and simmer 1½ hours, or until meat is tender and liquid is reduced to a flavorful gravy.

4 TO 6 SERVINGS

CHILI CON CARNE

This unusual chili is a favorite recipe of Tom C. Clark, former Associate Justice of the United States Supreme Court.

2 lbs. boneless lean beef for stew	1 teaspoon oregano
½ cup beef suet	4 large Mexican dried chili peppers
1 tablespoon chili powder	1 large onion, finely chopped
2 tablespoons ground comino (cumin)	3 large cloves garlic
	1 tablespoon salt

1. Cut the beef into ½-inch cubes, trimming off all fat, rind, and gristle. *Do not grind.* Cut the suet into ½-inch cubes. Put the suet into a heavy iron pot or kettle and heat over low heat until there are 1 to 2 tablespoons of fat. Remove and discard suet.
2. Put the beef into the kettle, increase heat and cook until meat is browned, stirring frequently. Add the chili powder, 1 tablespoon comino, oregano, and enough water to well cover the meat. Simmer over very low heat 2 hours, adding a little water as necessary. Stir well every 30 minutes.
3. Meanwhile, prepare the chili peppers as follows: Open the pods, remove all seeds, fibers, and stems; place in a saucepan, cover with water, and cook over medium heat about 15 minutes. Remove from pan, reserving the cooking water. Carefully strip off the thin, tough membrane that covers the peppers. (Do this while peppers are still warm.) Put the pulp into a blender container with the cooking water and blend about 1 minute. Or put pulp through a sieve, then mix with the cooking water.
4. At the end of the first hour of cooking, uncover the meat and add the pepper pulp with cooking water and the onion. Return to heat, cover and cook very slowly over an asbestos pad 2 hours.
5. Meanwhile, chop the garlic and crush it with the salt (using a pestle) until it makes a paste. Add the paste and the remaining comino to the chili and continue cooking 15 minutes or more. If the liquid is too thin, add *1 to 2 tablespoons flour* (shaken with a little cold water in a tightly covered jar); bring to boiling, stirring constantly.

6. Serve very hot, with *kidney beans*, if desired. (Never cook the beans with the chili.)

ABOUT 8 SERVINGS

GOULASH, GYPSY STYLE

¾ cup butter or
  margarine
2 teaspoons marjoram,
  crushed
1 teaspoon caraway
  seed, crushed
1 teaspoon grated
  lemon peel
1 clove garlic, crushed
1 teaspoon tomato paste
2 lbs. onions, sliced
1 tablespoon paprika

3 lbs. boneless lean
  beef for stew, cut
  in 1-in. cubes
2 teaspoons salt
⅛ teaspoon pepper
½ teaspoon mono-
  sodium glutamate
1 cup water
1 green pepper, cut in
  short strips (about
  1½ cups)

1. Heat the butter in a kettle. Combine marjoram, caraway seed, lemon peel, and garlic; add, with tomato paste, to kettle. Mix in the onions and cook, stirring occasionally until soft. Sprinkle the paprika over all and blend in well.
2. Add the beef, a mixture of the salt, pepper, and monosodium glutamate, and the water; stir. Cover and simmer until meat is tender, 1½ to 2 hours.
3. Just before serving, mix in green pepper and cook, uncovered, about 5 minutes, or until crisp-tender. Serve over *hot buttered noodles*.

6 TO 8 SERVINGS

BELGIAN-STYLE BEEF STEW
(Carbonnades de Boeuf)

2 cups thinly sliced
  onion
¼ cup cooking oil
2 lbs. boneless lean
  beef for stew, sliced
  ¼ in. thick across
  grain
1½ teaspoons salt
¼ teaspoon black
  pepper

¼ cup flour
1 teaspoon sugar
⅛ teaspoon crushed
  thyme
⅛ teaspoon ground
  nutmeg
2 cups beer
1 bay leaf
1 large sprig parsley

1. Lightly brown the onion in 2 tablespoons oil in a large heavy skillet over medium heat. Using a slotted spoon, remove onion and set aside.
2. Add remaining oil to skillet. Brown meat, a few slices at a time, on both sides in heated oil. Season with salt and pepper before turning slices to brown second side.

3. Arrange beef and onions in alternate layers in a 1½-quart casserole and keep hot.
4. Pour enough *oil* into skillet to make 2 tablespoons. Stir in a mixture of the flour, sugar, thyme, and nutmeg. Heat until bubbly. Blend in beer. Bring to boiling. Cook and stir 1 to 2 minutes. Add bay leaf and parsley. Pour into casserole over meat and onions; cover.
5. Bake at 325°F 1½ hours, or until tender.
6. Discard parsley sprig and bay leaf. Stir in *1 teaspoon cider vinegar.*

4 TO 6 SERVINGS

BURGOO

Burgoo—a stew traditionally served on Derby Day at Churchill Downs—gave its name to a colt, Burgoo King, who went on to win the Derby in 1932. Relished by Southerners any time, Burgoo is often served at sporting and political events.

1 lb. boneless beef
  (chuck or rump), cut
  in pieces
¼ lb. boneless lamb
  shoulder, cut in
  pieces
1 beef soup bone,
  cracked
1 lb. chicken breasts,
  thighs, or legs
4 teaspoons salt
¾ teaspoon black
  pepper
¼ teaspoon cayenne
  pepper

2 qts. water
1½ cups whole kernel
  corn
1⅓ cups lima beans
1 cup diced potato
1 cup chopped onion
½ cup chopped green
  pepper
½ cup diced carrot
1 cup sliced okra
2½ cups canned
  tomatoes with liquid
1 clove garlic,
  crushed or minced
½ cup chopped parsley

1. Put the meat, soup bone, chicken, salt, peppers, and water into a saucepot; cover and bring to boiling. Reduce heat and simmer about 2 hours, skimming off foam during first part of cooking.
2. Add corn, lima beans, potato, onion, green pepper, and carrot; cover and simmer 1 hour. Remove cover and cook 1 hour longer, stirring occasionally to prevent sticking on bottom of pot.
3. Add the okra, tomatoes, and garlic; cover and simmer 1 to 1½ hours longer. About 10 minutes before end of cooking period, remove bones and any pieces of fat, then stir constantly for remaining time. (Stew will thicken rapidly and may scorch if not carefully watched at this point.)
4. Remove from heat and stir in the parsley.

ABOUT 3 QUARTS BURGOO

SPICED SHORT RIBS WITH CABBAGE

Short ribs with vegetables reach gourmet heights in this piquantly-flavored dish.

3 lbs. lean beef short ribs	⅛ teaspoon crushed sage
2 tablespoons shortening	1 bay leaf
1 tablespoon dry mustard	½ cup sliced onion
2 teaspoons salt	¼ cup sliced celery
¼ teaspoon pepper	1 cup water
½ teaspoon crushed oregano	½ cup cider vinegar
	½ head cabbage, cut in 4 wedges

1. Add short ribs to heated shortening in a heavy skillet having a tight-fitting cover; brown meat well on all sides. Pour off excess fat.
2. Add a mixture of dry mustard, salt, pepper, oregano, and sage, then bay leaf, onion, celery, and a mixture of water and vinegar. Cover and cook slowly about 1½ hours, or until meat is almost tender.
3. Add cabbage wedges, cover, and cook about 25 minutes, or until tender. Add more liquid if necessary during cooking.
4. Serve ribs on a heated platter and surround with wedges of cabbage. 4 SERVINGS

"BOILED" DINNER

4 lbs. corned beef brisket	6 medium-sized potatoes, pared and quartered
⅓ to ½ cup (about 1½ oz.) dry onion soup mix	6 medium-sized carrots, pared and cut in 1½-in. pieces
4 peppercorns	½ cup celery, cut in 1-in. pieces
1 clove garlic, minced	1 medium-sized head young green cabbage, cut in wedges
1 bay leaf	
¼ teaspoon rosemary, crushed	
3 cups water	

1. Put meat into a deep saucepot or Dutch oven having a tight-fitting cover. Add soup mix, peppercorns, garlic, bay leaf, rosemary, and water. Cover, bring to boiling, and simmer 3½ hours.
2. Add vegetables, placing cabbage on top of meat. Cover and cook 1 hour, or until tender.
3. Remove vegetables and meat to a large heated serving platter. If desired, thicken liquid in saucepot and serve in a gravy boat. 6 TO 8 SERVINGS

COOKED CORNED BEEF BRISKET

5 lbs. corned beef brisket	8 peppercorns
1 onion, halved	2 bay leaves
1 clove garlic, halved	4 stalks celery, cut in pieces
6 whole cloves	

1. Put corned beef into a large kettle; cover with cold water. Add remaining ingredients and bring to boiling. Cover and simmer 3½ to 4 hours, or until the beef is tender.
2. Remove beef from liquid. Slice and serve hot with *English Mustard Sauce, page 345*.

8 TO 10 SERVINGS

OXTAIL STEW, GERMAN STYLE
(Ochsenschwanz-Eintopf)

3 oxtails (about 1 lb. each), disjointed	1½ cups hot water
½ cup all-purpose flour	4 potatoes, washed and pared
1 teaspoon salt	6 carrots, pared
¼ teaspoon pepper	2 lbs. fresh peas, shelled
3 tablespoons butter or margarine	1 tablespoon paprika
1½ cups chopped onions	1 teaspoon salt
1 can (28 oz.) tomatoes, drained (reserve liquid)	¼ teaspoon pepper
	¼ cup cold water
	2 tablespoons flour

1. Coat oxtail pieces evenly with a mixture of ½ cup flour, 1 teaspoon salt, and ¼ teaspoon pepper.
2. Heat the butter in a 3-quart Dutch oven over low heat. Add onions and cook until tender, stirring occasionally. Remove onions with a slotted spoon and set aside. Add meat and brown on all sides.
3. Return onions to Dutch oven; add reserved tomato liquid and the hot water; cover and simmer 2½ to 3 hours, or until meat is nearly tender.
4. Meanwhile, using a ball-shaped cutter, cut the potatoes and carrots into small balls; cut the tomatoes into pieces.
5. When meat is almost tender, add potatoes, carrots, peas, paprika, and remaining salt and pepper. Cover and simmer 20 minutes, or until vegetables are tender. Add tomatoes and cook 10 minutes longer, or until meat and vegetables are tender. Remove meat and vegetables; keep hot.
6. Bring cooking liquid to boiling and stir in a mixture of the cold water and 2 tablespoons flour; cook and stir 1 to 2 minutes. Return meat and vegetables and heat thoroughly. 6 TO 8 SERVINGS

PORK

FIESTA ROAST PORK

4-lb. pork loin roast	½ cup thinly sliced
1 clove garlic, crushed	olives
1 teaspoon rubbed sage	½ cup chopped green
1 teaspoon oregano	pepper
2 teaspoons salt	½ cup dark seedless
⅓ cup flour	raisins
2 cups tomato purée	1 cup sliced fresh
1 teaspoon chili powder	mushrooms
1 cup water	

1. Rub pork with a mixture of the garlic, sage, oregano, and salt. Place pork, fat side up, in a roasting pan. Insert meat thermometer so tip is slightly beyond center of thickest part of meat, being sure the tip does not rest in fat or on bone.
2. Roast, uncovered, at 325° to 350°F 2 to 2½ hours. (Allow 30 to 35 minutes per pound.) Meat is done when internal temperature reaches 170°F. Remove meat and pour off drippings; return ¼ cup drippings to pan. Reduce oven temperature to 250°F.
3. Blend the flour into drippings in pan. Stirring constantly, heat until mixture bubbles. Remove from heat. Add gradually a mixture of the tomato purée, chili powder, and water, stirring constantly. Return to heat and bring to boiling; continue stirring and cook until sauce thickens; cook 1 to 2 minutes. (Scrape pan to blend in brown residue.) Stir in remaining ingredients and cook 10 minutes.
4. Return pork roast to pan. Basting occasionally with sauce, heat in 250°F oven about 30 minutes. Serve hot.   6 TO 8 SERVINGS

PRUNE-STUFFED PORK ROAST

15 to 20 prunes	Few grains black
3- to 4-lb. pork loin	pepper
roast	1½ teaspoons ground
¾ to 1 teaspoon salt	ginger
	Prune Gravy, *below*

1. Rinse prunes, cut into halves, and remove and discard pits.
2. Rub fat side of meat with a mixture of the salt, pepper, and ginger. Lightly mark the fat side at about ½-inch intervals to indicate slices. Cut 2 or 3 pockets along each line and insert prunes so they

are completely embedded in meat. (Some prunes come to the top of the meat by the end of the roasting period.)
3. Insert meat thermometer so that tip is slightly beyond center of thickest part of meat, not in fat or on bone. Place roast, fat side up, on a rack in a shallow roasting pan.
4. Roast, uncovered, at 325° to 350°F until internal temperature registers 170°F, about 1½ to 2 hours. (Allow 30 to 35 minutes per pound.)
5. Transfer roast to heated serving platter and keep warm while preparing gravy. Pour off all but ¼ cup of drippings (to be used for gravy). Drizzle some of remaining drippings over roast.
6. To serve, carve roast so that prune design will appear to cut surface on each slice.

ABOUT 6 SERVINGS

PRUNE GRAVY: Add about *2 cups hot water* to the ¼ cup drippings in roasting pan; bring to boiling, stirring constantly to loosen brown residue. Stir in a mixture of *½ cup cold water* and *¼ cup flour*. Season with about *¾ teaspoon salt*. Bring to boiling and boil 1 to 2 minutes, stirring constantly. Stir in *½ cup chopped prunes*; heat thoroughly. Serve with the pork roast and *Franconia Potatoes, page 326*.

CARDAMOM PORK ROAST

2 tablespoons instant	2 teaspoons ground
minced onion	cardamom
2 tablespoons water	1 teaspoon salt
1 small clove garlic,	1 cup hot water
crushed	4-lb. pork loin roast
2 tablespoons cooking	Gravy, *page 177*
oil	

1. Soften onion in the 2 tablespoons water in a small custard cup.
2. Cook onion and garlic in a small skillet in hot oil about 2 minutes, stirring occasionally. Blend in cardamom, salt, and the hot water.
3. Place meat in shallow roasting pan; brush generously with the marinade. Set aside 1 hour, brushing meat occasionally.
4. Drain off marinade and reserve for basting the meat. Turn meat, fat side up, and insert a meat thermometer so tip is slightly beyond center of thickest part of roast, making sure tip does not rest

on bone. (No rack is necessary under roast as bone of loin forms a natural rack for roasting.)

5. Roast at 325° to 350°F about 2½ hours (meat thermometer registers 170°F). Without a thermometer, allow 30 to 35 minutes per pound. Baste roast occasionally with the marinade.

6. Remove thermometer and transfer roast to heated platter; keep roast warm. Prepare gravy and serve with roast. ABOUT 6 SERVINGS

GRAVY: Pour off all but 3 tablespoons drippings from roasting pan. Blend in about *3 tablespoons flour*, stirring to loosen brown residue. Slowly add about *3 cups water* (or milk), stirring constantly. Bring to boiling; cook and continue to stir 1 to 2 minutes longer. ABOUT 3 CUPS GRAVY

PORK ROAST WITH OLIVES AND RICE

7-lb. pork loin roast	¼ teaspoon pepper
3 cloves garlic, slivered	¾ cup sliced pimiento-stuffed olives
1½ cups chicken broth	Special Gravy, *below*
¾ cup dry vermouth	Saffron Rice, *below*
½ teaspoon ground sage	

1. Score fat side of pork roast; insert garlic in slits. Place, fat side up, in a shallow roasting pan. Insert a meat thermometer in roast so that tip rests in thickest part of the meat.

2. Combine broth, vermouth, sage, and pepper; pour over meat.

3. Roast at 325°F until meat thermometer registers 170°F, basting occasionally. Total cooking time will be about 2½ hours. The last hour of cooking time, add ½ cup of the sliced olives to liquid in pan.

4. Transfer roast to a heated platter; keep warm.

5. Remove olives; reserve to add to rice along with remaining olives. Use liquid for the gravy.

6. Spoon the Saffron Rice onto platter around the roast. Accompany with the gravy.

ABOUT 12 SERVINGS

SPECIAL GRAVY: Skim excess fat from reserved liquid. Measure liquid and add enough water to make 1¾ cups. Return liquid to pan or pour into a saucepan and bring to boiling. Stir a blend of *2 tablespoons cornstarch* and *¼ cup water* into boiling liquid; boil 1 to 2 minutes, stirring constantly. Pour into a gravy boat. ABOUT 2 CUPS GRAVY

SAFFRON RICE: In a large saucepan, combine *1 quart chicken broth, 2 cups uncooked white rice, 2 tablespoons butter or margarine, ½ teaspoon salt,* and *¼ teaspoon crushed saffron*. Bring to boiling, stirring with a fork. Cook, covered, over low heat 15 to 20 minutes, or until rice is tender. Toss reserved olives with rice.

ABOUT 8 CUPS

ROAST PORK, PENNSYLVANIA DUTCH STYLE

6-lb. pork loin roast	¼ teaspoon pepper
¼ cup flour	1 cup hot water
1¼ teaspoons salt	2 onions, thinly sliced
1 teaspoon ground ginger	2 tablespoons flour
	1½ cups water

1. Have meat dealer loosen chine bone. Rub meat with a mixture of the flour, salt, ginger, and pepper. Place roast, fat side up, in a shallow pan. Insert meat thermometer so tip is slightly beyond center of largest muscle, being sure the tip does not rest in fat or on bone.

2. Roast, uncovered, at 400°F 45 minutes. Turn oven temperature to 350°F and continue roasting about 1¾ hours. After the first hour, add the hot water and sliced onions; baste every 15 minutes. Meat is done when internal temperature reaches 170°F.

3. Place roast on a hot serving platter; remove thermometer and keep roast hot.

4. Stir the remaining flour into drippings in pan. Stirring constantly, add the 1½ cups water, bring rapidly to boiling and cook 1 to 2 minutes. Serve with the roast. 8 TO 12 SERVINGS

PORK TENDERLOIN STUFFED WITH PRUNES

1½ lbs. pork tenderloin, trimmed	1 teaspoon salt
12 prunes, pitted	3 tablespoons flour
2 to 3 tablespoons butter or margarine	¼ teaspoon salt
	⅛ teaspoon pepper
	1½ cups milk

1. Cut meat lengthwise about two-thirds through. Arrange prunes in the "pocket" and fasten with skewers.

2. Brown meat on all sides in heated butter in a large skillet. Sprinkle with 1 teaspoon salt. Cover and cook slowly about 1½ hours, or until meat is tender. During cooking, add a small amount of water. Remove meat to a hot platter, remove skewers and keep hot.

3. Leaving brown residue in skillet, pour drippings into a bowl. Allow fat to rise to surface; skim off fat, put 3 tablespoons of the fat into skillet, and reserve ½ cup of the drippings. Blend in flour, ¼ teaspoon salt, and pepper. Heat until bubbly, stirring constantly. Stir in milk and reserved drippings. Cook and stir 1 to 2 minutes.   4 SERVINGS

ROAST FRESH LEG OF PORK

Score rind of a *12- to 14-lb. fresh leg of pork (ham)*, spacing slits ½ inch apart, and rub with a mixture of *1 tablespoon coarse salt* and *4 teaspoons ground ginger*. Put *bay leaves* in several of the slits. Insert a meat thermometer so tip is slightly beyond center of thickest part of meat, being sure that tip does not rest in fat or on bone. Place on a rack in a shallow roasting pan. Roast, uncovered, at 325° to 350°F until internal temperature registers 170°F. (Allow 22 to 26 minutes per pound.) Remove thermometer and transfer roast to carving board or heated serving platter. For easier carving, allow roast to set 15 to 20 minutes after removing from oven.

16 TO 20 SERVINGS

FRESH LEG OF PORK WITH EXOTIC STUFFING

6- to 8-lb. boned fresh leg of pork (ham) or lean shoulder	1 can (13½ oz.) pineapple tidbits, drained (reserve syrup)
¼ cup butter or margarine	½ cup seedless raisins
1 cup uncooked rice	½ to 1 teaspoon curry powder
2 large onions, chopped (about 1½ cups)	½ teaspoon garlic powder
1 can (10½ oz.) condensed beef broth	½ teaspoon marjoram
1 teaspoon salt	1 teaspoon seasoned salt
2 cups chopped celery	1 teaspoon salt
3 cups small bread cubes	¼ teaspoon pepper
	2 teaspoons ground ginger

1. Have meat dealer bone the leg or shoulder of pork. (If leg is used, have it cut almost through to bottom so it will lie flat.) Have wooden skewers available.
2. Heat butter in a large skillet. Add rice and onion and cook over medium heat, stirring occasionally, until rice is light brown. Stir in broth and 1 teaspoon salt; cover tightly and simmer over very low heat 15 minutes.
3. Combine rice mixture with celery, bread cubes, pineapple, raisins, and a mixture of curry powder, garlic powder, marjoram, and seasoned salt; blend thoroughly by tossing lightly with a fork.
4. Rub inside surface of flattened leg or shoulder with a mixture of 1 teaspoon salt and the pepper. Spread dressing over meat; roll lengthwise, secure firmly with skewers, and lace tightly. (Any leftover stuffing may be baked in a greased casserole; place in oven about 1 hour before meat is done.)
5. Rub meat with the ginger, then place on rack in a large shallow roasting pan. Roast at 325° to 350°F 3¾ to 5 hours (allow 22 to 26 minutes per pound), or until meat thermometer registers 170°F. (Insert thermometer into meat and not into stuffing.) During last 30 minutes of roasting, occasionally spoon reserved pineapple syrup over roast.
6. Remove from oven and let stand at least 20 minutes before slicing. Place on a warm platter and garnish with *pineapple rings* and *spiced crab apples*. If desired, make pan gravy with drippings in roasting pan.   12 TO 16 SERVINGS

PORK TENDERLOIN AU CRÈME
Morsels of succulent pork are bacon-wrapped and oven-roasted before simmering gently in cream.

¾ lb. pork tenderloin, trimmed and cut in 1½-in. cubes	¼ lb. sliced bacon, partially cooked (lightly browned but still soft)
1 teaspoon paprika	1 cup heavy cream
¼ teaspoon salt	

1. Season meat with paprika and salt. Roll a slice of bacon around each tenderloin cube. Put into a 1½-quart shallow baking dish. Sprinkle lightly with paprika.
2. Roast at 350°F 25 to 30 minutes, or until tender.
3. Pour cream over all and return to oven until thoroughly heated. Serve with *hot fluffy rice* or *hot buttered noodles*.   ABOUT 4 SERVINGS
NOTE: For a thicker sauce, reduce cream to ¾ cup.

RACK OF PORK FORUM

The Forum of the Twelve Caesars, famous New York restaurant, serves this epicurean pork chop dish.

6 thick pork chops	1 tablespoon butter
½ cup packed brown sugar	¼ cup dry white wine
½ cup crème de cassis	½ cup pistachio nuts
2 red apples, cored (not pared)	½ cup chopped preserved ginger

1. Flatten the chops to ¾-inch thickness. Place in a shallow baking dish and set in a 400°F oven until browned on one side.
2. Meanwhile, in a small skillet heat brown sugar until melted, stirring frequently. Stir in crème de cassis and continue to cook until mixture is red.
3. Reduce oven temperature to 350°F. Turn chops and season with *salt*. Spoon syrup over them. Bake chops 20 minutes, or until tender.
4. Meanwhile, cut apples into thick slices. Cook slices until just tender in the butter and wine heated in a saucepan.
5. Arrange the chops in a row overlapping on a hot platter and sprinkle with nuts. Arrange the apple slices at one side and fill centers with preserved ginger.   6 SERVINGS

PORK CHOPS GOURMET

This recipe came from an amateur chef who won accolades from his fellow-gourmet-club diners for whom he originated the dish.

Fat for browning	Prepared mustard
8 pork chops, cut ½ in. thick	Dill pickles, thinly sliced
1 teaspoon salt	2 tablespoons dill pickle liquid
½ teaspoon black pepper	¼ cup dry vermouth

1. Heat the fat, add chops and brown well on both sides. Sprinkle with a mixture of salt and pepper. Spread each chop generously with mustard.
2. Arrange one layer of pork chops in a saucepot and cover with dill pickle slices. Repeat layering with chops and pickles.
3. Add pickle liquid; cover and cook over low heat 1 hour; add vermouth 20 minutes before end of cooking time.
4. Remove from heat and place chops on heated serving platter. If desired, drizzle additional vermouth over pickles and chops.   4 SERVINGS

SAUCED PORK CHOPS

Sauce, *below*	1½ cups finely crushed round buttery crackers
6 pork chops, cut 1 in. thick	
¼ cup flour	1 tablespoon butter or margarine
1¼ teaspoons salt	
¼ teaspoon pepper	2 onions, finely chopped
1 egg, slightly beaten	
2 tablespoons water	1 clove garlic, minced

1. Prepare Sauce.
2. Meanwhile, coat chops with a mixture of flour, salt, and pepper; dip both sides of each chop in a blend of egg and water, and finally coat with cracker crumbs.
3. Brown chops on both sides in hot butter in a large heavy skillet. Remove browned chops; keep warm.
4. Add onion and garlic to fat remaining in skillet. Cook, stirring occasionally, until onion is soft.
5. Return chops to skillet. Pour sauce over all. Cover and cook over low heat about 50 minutes, or until meat is tender, basting occasionally.
6. Remove chops to a warm platter. Pour sauce into a gravy boat and pass at the table.   6 SERVINGS

SAUCE: Mix *½ cup lightly packed brown sugar* and *2 teaspoons dry mustard* in a saucepan. Stir in *1 cup water, 2 tablespoons cider vinegar,* and a blend of *1 cup ketchup* and *3 ounces cream cheese.* Add *3 lemon slices* and *1 tablespoon butter or margarine.* Heat thoroughly, stirring occasionally. When ready to use, remove from heat and mix in *1 tablespoon bottled brown bouquet sauce.*

SKILLET ORANGE PORK CHOPS

1 cup orange juice	¼ teaspoon thyme, crushed
3 tablespoons instant minced onion	
2 teaspoons grated orange peel	4 pork chops, cut about 1 in. thick
1 tablespoon brown sugar	½ teaspoon salt
	½ teaspoon mono-sodium glutamate
½ teaspoon marjoram, crushed	⅛ teaspoon pepper
	Cooking oil

1. Combine orange juice, onion, orange peel, brown sugar, marjoram, and thyme; set aside.
2. Season pork chops with a mixture of the salt, monosodium glutamate, and pepper. Brown chops well on both sides in a small amount of oil in a

heavy skillet. Drain drippings from pan; add orange juice mixture.

3. Cook, covered, over low heat about 45 minutes, or until chops are very tender. If desired, thicken the sauce slightly with a cornstarch-water mixture.

4. Add sectioned pared *oranges* and heat about 5 minutes.   4 SERVINGS

STUFFED PORK CHOPS

2 teaspoons lemon juice	½ cup chopped onion
1 apple, quartered, cored, pared, and diced	¼ cup butter or margarine
2 cups soft bread crumbs	¼ cup apple cider
1 teaspoon salt	8 pork chops, cut 1 to 1¼ in. thick (have meat dealer cut a pocket for stuffing)
1 teaspoon celery seed	
⅛ teaspoon black pepper	2 teaspoons fat

1. Sprinkle lemon juice over apple in a bowl. Mix with bread crumbs, salt, celery seed, and pepper.

2. Cook onion in hot butter in a large skillet until soft. Turn the contents of the skillet into apple mixture; toss lightly with enough of the apple cider to just barely moisten. Fill pockets of each chop with the stuffing.

3. Brown chops on both sides in hot fat in the skillet. Remove to a large shallow baking dish. Cover tightly with aluminum foil.

4. Bake at 350°F 1 hour, or until chops are tender and thoroughly cooked.   8 SERVINGS

GREEN BEAN-PORK CHOP SUPPER

2 teaspoons fat	1 can (8 oz.) tomato sauce
6 pork chops, cut ½ to ¾ in. thick	1 tablespoon finely chopped onion
2 cans (16 oz. each) cut blue lake green beans, drained (reserve 2 table-spoons liquid)	1 teaspoon salt
	¼ teaspoon black pepper
1 can (12 oz.) whole kernel corn	¼ teaspoon chervil, crushed
1 tablespoon cornstarch	1 teaspoon Worcester-shire sauce

1. Heat fat in a large heavy skillet. Add chops and brown on all sides.

2. Mix beans and corn in a 2½-quart casserole.

3. Blend the reserved bean liquid with cornstarch; stir in the remaining ingredients. Pour sauce over vegetables and toss until well coated. Arrange chops on top of vegetable mixture.

4. Bake, covered, at 350°F 1 hour, or until pork chops are tender. Uncover and bake 10 minutes longer.   6 SERVINGS

PORK CHOPS TOLEDO

Reflecting Spain in color and flavor, this flamboyant pork chop dish is a distinctive creation.

2 tablespoons olive oil	½ cup Malaga wine
4 boned pork chops, about ¾ in. thick	Center Garnish, *below*
	Seasoned Rice, *below*
1 teaspoon salt	4 medium-sized tomatoes, broiled
⅛ teaspoon black pepper	6 large fresh mushrooms, quartered and cooked in butter
2 cups pimiento-stuffed olives	
1 medium-sized sweet red or green pepper, quartered	2 teaspoons cornstarch
	2 tablespoons water

1. Heat oil in a large skillet; add pork chops and brown evenly on both sides. Drain off drippings. Season chops, then add olives, peppers and wine; cover and cook over low heat about 45 minutes, or until meat is tender, turning chops once.

2. About 25 minutes before end of cooking time, prepare Center Garnish and Seasoned Rice. At serving time, turn rice into a shallow serving dish and spread evenly. Set the garnish in center of rice.

3. Remove chops to rice. Use one-half of olives and all pepper quarters for garnishing chops. Set broiled tomatoes between chops. Spoon mushrooms and remaining olives between chops and tomatoes, forming a wreath on rice.

4. Blend a mixture of the cornstarch and water into liquid in skillet. Bring to boiling and boil 1 to 2 minutes, stirring constantly. Pour over meat.

4 SERVINGS

CENTER GARNISH: Thread *romaine leaves, 2 green peppers*, and *1 sweet red pepper* onto a large skewer and insert it in an *orange*.

SEASONED RICE: Heat *2 tablespoons olive oil* in a large saucepan. Add *2 tablespoons chopped onion* and cook until onion is transparent. Stir in *3 cups hot chicken broth, ½ teaspoon rosemary*, and *1¼ cups uncooked rice*. Cover tightly and cook the mixture over low heat 25 minutes, or until rice is tender and liquid is completely absorbed.

PEACH 'N' PORK CHOP BARBECUE

6 pork chops, cut 1 in. thick
1 tablespoon fat
¼ cup lightly packed brown sugar
1 teaspoon ground cinnamon
½ teaspoon ground cloves

1 can (8 oz.) tomato sauce
6 canned cling peach halves, drained (reserve ¼ cup syrup)
¼ cup cider vinegar
¾ teaspoon salt
½ teaspoon mono-sodium glutamate
¼ teaspoon pepper

1. Brown chops on both sides in hot fat in a large heavy skillet.
2. Meanwhile, blend a mixture of brown sugar, cinnamon, and cloves with the tomato sauce, reserved peach syrup, and vinegar.
3. Pour off excess fat from skillet. Sprinkle chops with a mixture of salt, monosodium glutamate, and pepper. Place a peach half on each chop. Pour sauce over all. Cover skillet and simmer about 30 minutes, or until pork is tender; baste occasionally with the sauce. 6 SERVINGS

PORK 'N' PINEAPPLE IN GINGER SAUCE

6 thick pork chops, fat trimmed
1 can (20½ oz.) pineapple chunks
1 can (15½ oz.) crushed pineapple
½ cup chopped onion
1 cup honey
⅔ cup red wine vinegar
2 tablespoons soy sauce
6 large cloves garlic, minced

1½ to 2 tablespoons ground ginger
1 tablespoon ground coriander
2 teaspoons cornstarch
1 teaspoon salt
2 pkgs. (9 oz. each) frozen Italian-style green beans, thawed slightly to separate
2 cups matchstick carrot strips

1. Brown chops on both sides in a skillet.
2. Meanwhile, combine in a large shallow baking dish, the pineapple, onion, honey, vinegar, soy sauce, and garlic, and a mixture of ginger, coriander, cornstarch, and salt.
3. Arrange chops in the baking dish and spoon sauce over them. Cover tightly with aluminum foil.

4. Bake at 325°F 45 minutes.
5. Turn chops over, put beans and carrots over top, and spoon sauce over all. Continue baking until meat and vegetables are tender, about 35 minutes. 6 SERVINGS

FRESH PEAR AND PORK CHOP SKILLET

6 pork chops, cut ¾ to 1 in. thick
½ teaspoon salt
⅛ teaspoon pepper
6 thin lemon slices
12 thin onion slices
3 Anjou pears, halved and cored

¾ cup lightly packed brown sugar
½ cup lemon juice
½ cup water
⅓ cup soy sauce
½ teaspoon ground ginger

1. Brown chops on both sides. Drain off any fat.
2. Season chops with salt and pepper. Put a lemon slice and two onion slices on each chop. Place pear halves cut-side down in skillet around chops.
3. Combine brown sugar with the lemon juice, water, soy sauce, and ginger and pour over all. Cover; basting frequently with sauce, cook over low heat about 20 minutes; then turn pears cut-side up and cook 20 minutes longer, or until pork is tender. 6 SERVINGS

PARTY PORK CHOPS

6 pork chops, cut about 1 in. thick
2 tablespoons flour
2 tablespoons fat
1½ teaspoons salt
⅛ teaspoon pepper
¾ teaspoon dry mustard
½ teaspoon ground cinnamon

¼ teaspoon ground cloves
⅛ teaspoon ground allspice
¼ cup cider vinegar
¼ cup raspberry jam
½ cup hot water
3 large onions, cut in ½-in. slices

1. Coat pork chops with flour. Brown on both sides in heated fat in a large heavy skillet. Transfer browned chops to a shallow baking dish.
2. Mix salt, pepper, dry mustard, cinnamon, cloves, and allspice with the vinegar. Blend in jam and hot water; pour mixture over chops; cover. Bake at 350°F 40 minutes.
3. Arrange onion slices around chops. Cover and continue baking 25 minutes, or until meat is tender.
4. Remove chops and onions to warm platter. If desired, thicken drippings for gravy. 6 SERVINGS

BAKED KRAUT UN CHOPS WITH APPLES

There is a Pennsylvania Dutch legend that goes something like this—when you eat sauerkraut, pork, and apples at the beginning of the new year, good luck will be with you throughout the year.

6 loin pork chops, cut about 1 in. thick	½ cup seedless raisins, plumped
1 teaspoon salt	12 small whole canned onions
¼ teaspoon pepper	
1 to 2 tablespoons brown sugar	2 unpared apples, cored and cut in wedges
2 cups (16 oz.) undrained sauerkraut	

1.   Brown the chops on both sides in a large skillet. Season chops with half of the salt and pepper.
2.   Meanwhile, toss a mixture of brown sugar and the remaining salt and pepper with the sauerkraut. Mix in raisins, onions, and apples.
3.   Turn sauerkraut mixture into a shallow baking dish. Top with chops, slightly overlapping.
4.   Bake, covered, at 350°F about 1 hour, or until the meat is tender.   6 SERVINGS

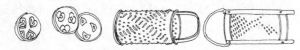

EENYHOW

Hawaiian-born James Shigeta, Hollywood actor, gives this dish a touch of the Orient with the use of soy sauce.

6 loin pork chops	3 medium-sized firm tomatoes, chopped in very small pieces
2 bunches watercress, broken in small pieces	½ to ¾ cup soy sauce
1 cup finely chopped green onions	

1.   Trim all fat from chops and cut chops in small pieces. Brown in heavy skillet with several pieces of fat to prevent sticking. When meat starts to brown, sprinkle with *soy sauce*, *salt*, and *pepper* and continue browning.
2.   Meanwhile, in a large bowl combine the watercress, green onions, and tomatoes. When the pork is thoroughly cooked, toss it with the vegetables and soy sauce like a salad. Serve over *cooked rice*.
                                        6 SERVINGS

PORK MANDARIN

3 tablespoons cooking oil	1 can (12 oz.) apricot nectar
1½ lbs. boneless pork, cut in 2x¼-in. strips	½ cup cider vinegar
2 teaspoons salt	¾ cup lightly packed brown sugar
¼ cup cornstarch	1 cup diced celery
½ cup cold water	1 large green pepper, cut in strips
2 tablespoons soy sauce	
1 can (13½ oz.) pineapple chunks, drained (reserve syrup)	1 can (16 oz.) whole tomatoes, drained and quartered
1 can (11 oz.) mandarin oranges, drained (reserve syrup)	12 blanched almonds, toasted

1.   Heat oil in a large heavy skillet. Add pork and brown well on all sides. Season with salt; cover and cook until pork is done, 10 to 15 minutes.
2.   Blend cornstarch and water in a saucepan; stir in soy sauce, reserved syrup from fruits, apricot nectar, vinegar, and brown sugar. Bring mixture to boiling, stirring constantly; cook 3 minutes.
3.   Add celery and pineapple chunks to meat. Add the sauce and cook over low heat about 5 minutes.
4.   Stir in green pepper and tomato pieces and heat about 5 minutes longer.
5.   Before serving, add mandarin oranges to mixture. Remove to heated serving dish and top with almonds. Serve with fluffy *cooked rice*.
                                        ABOUT 6 SERVINGS

PORK 'N' RICE CASSEROLE

1½ lbs. boneless pork, cut in strips	½ cup uncooked rice
⅓ cup flour	2 cans (8 oz. each) tomato sauce
¼ cup butter or margarine	2 tablespoons soy sauce
1 clove garlic, minced	1 tablespoon sugar
1 onion, coarsely chopped	½ teaspoon seasoned salt
1 green pepper, cut in strips	½ teaspoon oregano, crushed
1 cup diagonally sliced celery	¼ teaspoon pepper
2 cans (5 oz. each) water chestnuts, drained and sliced	1 env. (about 2 oz.) dry chicken noodle soup mix
	2½ cups boiling water

1.   Coat pork strips with the flour. Heat 2 table-

spoons butter in a large skillet. Add one half of pork and brown well on all sides; transfer to a 2½-quart casserole. Add 1 tablespoon butter to skillet and brown remaining meat; transfer the meat to the casserole.

2. Heat the remaining 1 tablespoon butter; add garlic, onion, green pepper, and celery. Cook 3 minutes, tossing lightly to mix.

3. Add the vegetables, water chestnuts, rice, tomato sauce, soy sauce, and a mixture of the sugar, seasoned salt, oregano, and pepper to the casserole. Add the soup mix and boiling water; mix thoroughly. Cover tightly.

4. Bake at 350°F about 45 minutes.

5. Remove from oven and stir mixture with a fork.

8 TO 10 SERVINGS

BAHMIE GORENG

This Indonesian dish was created during the days of Dutch control. The food of Aruba, Netherlands Antilles, shows the influence of Indonesian cookery. This dish is featured at Executive House's Aruba Caribbean Hotel-Casino, and the recipe was adapted for American use by Executive Chef Monsieur Robert Machax and Mr. Maurice Filleul, Director of Foods and Beverages.

½ lb. thin egg noodles	Celery (heart portion only), diced
¼ cup butter, or 3 tablespoons cooking oil	½ or 1 medium-sized cabbage, diced
1 medium-sized onion, diced	8 leeks, trimmed and diced
2 cloves garlic, minced	1 can (16 oz.) bean sprouts, drained
½ teaspoon ground ginger	Cooked shrimp (about 1 lb.)
1 lb. pork loin, diced	1 omelet (2 eggs)

1. Cook noodles following package directions. Rinse with cold water; drain.

2. Heat butter in a large saucepot or skillet. Mix in onion and garlic and sauté until browned; transfer to a small bowl. Stir the ginger into fat in skillet, and mix in the pork. Brown on all sides.

3. Mix in the vegetables, bean sprouts, onion, and garlic; cook 15 minutes, stirring occasionally. Stir while adding the drained noodles and shrimp; heat thoroughly.

4. Meanwhile, prepare the omelet. Roll up omelet and slice into thin strips for topping.

5. Turn the bahmie onto a large platter. Top with omelet strips. Serve with "sambals" such as *salted peanuts, flaked coconut, mustards,* and *ketchup.*

4 TO 6 SERVINGS

CHINATOWN CHOP SUEY

1¼ lbs. boneless pork	3 tablespoons cornstarch
1 lb. boneless beef	¼ cup water
¾ lb. boneless veal	¼ cup soy sauce
3 tablespoons cooking oil	¼ cup bead molasses
1 cup water	1 can (16 oz.) bean sprouts, drained and rinsed
3 cups diagonally sliced celery	2 cans (5 oz. each) water chestnuts, drained and sliced
2 cups coarsely chopped onion	

1. Cut meat into 1-inch cubes. Heat the oil in a large heavy skillet or saucepot. Cooking one layer of meat at a time, brown pieces on all sides. Return browned meat to skillet; cover and cook over low heat 30 minutes.

2. Mix in 1 cup water, celery, and onions. Bring to boiling and simmer, covered, 20 minutes.

3. Blend cornstarch, the ¼ cup water, soy sauce, and molasses. Stir into meat mixture. Bring to boiling and cook 2 minutes, stirring constantly. Mix in bean sprouts and water chestnuts; heat. Serve on fluffy *cooked rice.*

8 SERVINGS

SZEKELY GOULASH

A Hungarian specialty.

1½ lbs. boneless pork shoulder, cut in 1½-in. cubes	2 tablespoons finely chopped onion
2 tablespoons flour	1 can (27 oz.) sauerkraut, drained
2 teaspoons paprika	½ teaspoon caraway seed
1½ teaspoons salt	1½ cups dairy sour cream
2 tablespoons fat	

1. Coat meat evenly with a mixture of flour, paprika, and salt.

2. Heat fat in a Dutch oven or saucepot. Add onion and cook until soft, stirring occasionally.

3. Brown meat evenly on all sides in the hot fat; add *3 tablespoons hot water.* Cover and simmer 1 hour, stirring occasionally; add small amounts of water as needed during cooking.

4. Mix sauerkraut and caraway seed with the

meat; add *2 cups hot water.* Cover and simmer 30 minutes, or until meat is tender.

5. Gradually add about 1½ cups of the cooking liquid to sour cream, blending well. Stir into mixture in Dutch oven. Stirring constantly, heat (do not boil) about 5 minutes. Serve in small bowls; accompany with *boiled new potatoes.* 6 TO 8 SERVINGS

BARBECUED SPARERIBS

3 lbs. spareribs, cracked through center	3 tablespoons butter or margarine
1 tablespoon salt	½ cup cider vinegar
1 teaspoon black pepper	¼ cup ketchup
⅔ cup finely chopped green pepper	¼ cup brown sugar
	1 tablespoon Worcestershire sauce
⅓ cup finely chopped onion	½ teaspoon dry mustard
¼ cup chopped celery	½ teaspoon chili powder
	2 lemon slices

1. Cut ribs into serving-sized pieces, season with salt and pepper, and place, meaty side up, in a shallow roasting pan. Bake at 350°F 30 minutes, turning once.

2. Cook vegetables in heated butter in a saucepan until onion is tender, stirring occasionally. Blend in a mixture of the vinegar, ketchup, brown sugar, Worcestershire sauce, dry mustard, and chili powder, then lemon slices. Simmer 5 to 10 minutes, stirring frequently. Remove from heat; set aside.

3. After ribs have baked for 30 minutes, remove from oven. Pour off excess fat. Spoon one half of the sauce over ribs; cover and continue baking, basting frequently, 1 to 1½ hours, or until meat is tender. Uncover pan the last 15 to 20 minutes.

6 SERVINGS

SPARERIBS WITH TANGY PLUM SAUCE

3 lbs. spareribs, cracked through center	½ cup thawed frozen orange juice concentrate
2 teaspoons salt	½ teaspoon Worcestershire sauce
1 can (17 oz.) purple plums, drained (reserve ½ cup syrup)	

1. Cut spareribs into serving-sized pieces; put on a rack in shallow roasting pan, meaty side up. Sprinkle with salt. Roast at 350°F 1 hour.

2. Meanwhile, force plums through a sieve. Mix in plum syrup, orange juice concentrate, and Worcestershire sauce.

3. Pour off drippings from roasting pan and remove rack. Spoon one-half of plum sauce over ribs. Roast 20 minutes. Turn ribs and spoon on remaining sauce. Roast 25 minutes longer, or until meat is tender. ABOUT 8 SERVINGS

SAUCY RIBS

6 lbs. meaty spareribs or back ribs, cut across ribs and in 3-in. lengths	2 cups ketchup
	2 cups water
	6 tablespoons lemon juice
¼ cup lightly packed dark brown sugar	6 tablespoons Worcestershire sauce
2 teaspoons dry mustard	¼ cup cider vinegar
2 tablespoons seasoned salt	½ cup instant minced onion
½ teaspoon seasoned pepper	2 teaspoons prepared horseradish
	6 drops Tabasco

1. Brown ribs on both sides in Dutch oven, heavy skillets, or saucepots, pouring off fat.

2. Meanwhile, in a saucepan prepare the sauce: Blend brown sugar, dry mustard, seasoned salt, and seasoned pepper; stir in remaining ingredients. Bring to boiling, cover, and simmer 10 minutes.

3. Pour hot sauce over ribs. Bring to boiling and cover. Simmer and steam 1 to 1½ hours, or until tender, basting and turning ribs frequently.

4. Put a toasted buttered sesame or poppy seed *hamburger bun* half on each plate. Top with ribs and spoon some of the sauce over all. Serve with *potato chips* and *pickles.* ABOUT 6 SERVINGS

APPLE-KRAUT STUFFED SPARERIBS

¼ cup butter or margarine	2 cups sauerkraut
	1 teaspoon caraway seed
¼ cup chopped onion	
4 cups soft ½-in. bread cubes	2 sections spareribs, about 1 lb. each
1 cup diced pared apple	

1. Heat butter in a skillet; add onion and cook until onion is transparent. Toss lightly with bread cubes, apple, sauerkraut, and caraway seed.

2. Sprinkle both sides of sparerib sections with

salt and *pepper*; place one sparerib section on rack of a shallow roasting pan. Spread stuffing over it; cover with second section. Fasten the sections together with skewers.

3. Roast at 350°F for 1½ hours, or until meat is tender when pierced with a fork. Remove skewers; cut spareribs into serving-sized pieces and serve with the stuffing.   4 SERVINGS

NOTE: If desired, occasionally brush spareribs with *soy sauce* during roasting.

BARBECUED RIBS WITH PINEAPPLE

4 lbs. spareribs, cracked through center and cut in serving-sized pieces	⅓ cup thawed frozen orange juice concentrate
2 tablespoons cornstarch	2 tablespoons cider vinegar
6 tablespoons brown sugar	2 large cloves garlic, minced
⅔ cup light or dark corn syrup	6 tablespoons finely chopped crystallized ginger
⅔ cup Hawaiian barbecue sauce (a sweet-tart bottled sauce)	1 lemon, thinly sliced and slices quartered
	1 can (8½ oz.) crushed pineapple

1. Put spareribs into a heavy saucepot. Add *water* to cover and bring to boiling; cover and reduce heat. Simmer 1 hour, or until almost tender; drain.
2. Meanwhile, prepare sauce. In a large bowl, mix the cornstarch and brown sugar. Blend in the corn syrup, Hawaiian barbecue sauce, orange juice concentrate, and vinegar. Stir in the garlic, ginger, lemon, and pineapple with syrup.
3. Add the drained cooked ribs to sauce, turn to coat, and marinate at least ½ hour.
4. Put spareribs in a single layer in a large shallow pan or jelly roll pan and place under broiler with tops of ribs about 5 inches from source of heat. Broil 5 to 10 minutes, or until richly browned, turning and brushing several times with the sauce.
5. Arrange ribs on a heated serving platter and accompany with hot *cooked rice* and remaining sauce.   6 TO 8 SERVINGS

ZESTY SAUSAGE LOAF

2 lbs. lean bulk pork sausage	2 tablespoons grated lemon peel
4 cups soft bread crumbs	¼ to ½ teaspoon salt
1 egg	½ teaspoon paprika
	6 bacon slices
	1 cup dairy sour cream

1. Combine sausage, bread crumbs, egg, lemon peel, salt, and paprika in a bowl; mix thoroughly.
2. Shape mixture into a loaf and place in a 11x7x1½-inch baking pan. Lay the bacon slices crosswise on top of loaf. Pour about 1½ cups hot water in the bottom of the pan. Cover pan tightly with aluminum foil.
3. Bake at 350°F 1 hour. Uncover; bake 15 minutes longer. Pour off liquid. Spoon sour cream over top of loaf and bake 15 minutes longer.
4. Remove to a warm serving platter.
ABOUT 6 SERVINGS

GLAZED PORK SAUSAGE PATTIES

1 lb. bulk pork sausage, shaped in patties about ½ in. thick	½ teaspoon basil
½ cup packed dark brown sugar	4 teaspoons cider vinegar
	½ teaspoon grated onion

1. Put sausage patties into large heavy skillet; add *1 to 2 tablespoons water*, cover, and cook slowly for 5 minutes.
2. Remove cover; pour off liquid. Add a mixture of the remaining ingredients and cook, turning patties frequently, until browned and glazed. Serve immediately.   6 TO 8 SERVINGS

HALF-HOUR MEAL

1 pkg. (10 oz.) frozen lima beans	¼ teaspoon marjoram
1 lb. bulk pork sausage	2 tablespoons water
3 tablespoons finely chopped onion	1 tablespoon flour
¼ cup water	1 can (4 oz.) sliced ripe olives, drained
¼ teaspoon ground nutmeg	1 cup dairy sour cream

1. Cook lima beans following package directions; drain, if necessary.
2. Meanwhile, put sausage into a cold skillet and separate into pieces. Add onion and ¼ cup water;

cover, bring to boiling and simmer 10 minutes.

3. Drain off the drippings. Then stir nutmeg and marjoram into skillet mixture. Stir in a blend of *2 tablespoons water* and the flour; bring to boiling and cook 1 to 2 minutes, stirring constantly.

4. Mix in the lima beans and olives. Blend in the sour cream, a small amount at a time. Heat thoroughly (do not boil). Serve at once.

ABOUT 4 SERVINGS

SAUSAGE SCRAPPLE

Scrapple or ponhaws is a dish probably of Pennsylvania Dutch origin.

Prepare *cornmeal mush* according to package directions. Fry *1 pound bulk pork sausage* until thoroughly cooked; drain and stir into the mush. Turn into a loaf pan. Cool, cover, and chill thoroughly. Cut into ½-inch slices. Fry slowly in a greased skillet until golden brown on each side.

ABOUT 6 SERVINGS

PORK SAUSAGE LINKS

Cut *link sausages* apart. Place in a cold skillet. Add a small amount of *water*; cover and cook over low heat 5 minutes. Remove cover and pour off fat. Cook, turning to brown on all sides.

POLENTA

1 lb. Italian sausage, casing removed and sausage crumbled	1 teaspoon salt
	¼ teaspoon pepper
	3 cups water
1 lb. fresh mushrooms, sliced lengthwise	1½ teaspoons salt
	1 cup yellow cornmeal
2 tablespoons olive oil	1 cup cold water
2½ cups canned tomatoes	

1. Cook sausage and mushrooms in hot oil in a large heavy skillet until lightly browned. Stir in tomatoes, 1 teaspoon salt, and the pepper. Simmer 20 to 30 minutes.

2. Meanwhile, bring water and remaining salt to boiling in a saucepan. Gradually add a mixture of the cornmeal and cold water stirring constantly; continue boiling until mixture thickens. Cover, lower heat, and cook slowly 10 minutes or longer.

3. Transfer cornmeal to a warm platter and top with the sauce. Sprinkle with *shredded Parmesan*.

6 TO 8 SERVINGS

CANADIAN-STYLE BACON WITH MUSTARD SAUCE

1½ lbs. Canadian-style bacon (in one piece)	2 tablespoons prepared mustard
8 to 10 whole cloves	3 tablespoons cider vinegar
1 cup firmly packed brown sugar	1 tablespoon butter or margarine

1. Remove casing from bacon. Place bacon, fat side up, on a rack in a shallow roasting pan. Insert whole cloves. Insert a meat thermometer.

2. Roast, uncovered, at 300° to 325°F about 1 hour, or until internal temperature reaches 160°F.

3. Combine remaining ingredients in a saucepan. Stir over low heat until sugar is dissolved and mixture is heated. Serve hot with the bacon.

ABOUT 6 SERVINGS

SMOKED SHOULDER ROLL WITH MUSTARD SAUCE

1½-lb. cooked smoked pork shoulder roll (butt), *page 187*	2 egg yolks, slightly beaten
⅓ cup packed brown sugar	1 tablespoon butter or margarine
2 teaspoons flour	1 pkg. (10 oz.) frozen broccoli spears
1 teaspoon prepared mustard	1 pkg. (10 oz.) frozen cauliflower
½ cup water	½ cup shredded sharp Cheddar cheese
3 tablespoons cider vinegar	

1. Slice cooked shoulder butt.

2. Combine brown sugar and flour in top of double boiler. Stir in mustard, then water and vinegar. Continue stirring and bring to boiling over direct heat and cook 3 minutes.

3. Remove from heat and vigorously stir about 3 tablespoons of hot mixture into beaten egg yolks; immediately blend into mixture in double boiler.

4. Cook over hot water 3 to 5 minutes; stir slowly. Remove from heat and stir in the butter.

5. Cook broccoli and cauliflower according to directions on package; drain, if necessary.

6. Arrange shoulder butt slices in a shallow baking dish. Arrange broccoli spears and cauliflower over meat. Spoon mustard sauce over all and top evenly with cheese.

7. Set in a 350°F oven about 15 minutes, or until thoroughly heated.

4 SERVINGS

SMOKED SHOULDER ROLL: Put smoked shoulder roll (butt) into a large heavy saucepot. Add enough *hot water* to cover meat. Add *1 teaspoon monosodium glutamate, 5 whole cloves, 3 peppercorns,* and *1 clove garlic.* Bring liquid to boiling; reduce heat, cover and simmer (do not boil) about 1 hour, or until meat is tender.

SCHNITZ UN KNEPP
(Apples and Buttons)

Schnitz means "cut" and to the Pennsylvania Dutch the word has come to mean cut dried apples, which when soaked and cooked, are used as stewed fruit, for pie fillings, or in this meat dish.

1 qt. dried apples (about an 8 oz. pkg.)	4 teaspoons baking powder
3-lb. smoked shoulder roll (butt)	1 teaspoon salt
2 tablespoons brown sugar	¼ teaspoon pepper
	1 egg, well beaten
2 cups sifted all-purpose flour	3 tablespoons butter, melted
	½ cup milk

1. Cover the dried apples with *water;* soak overnight.
2. Next day, cover smoked shoulder roll with water in a large Dutch oven or kettle, cover loosely, and simmer about 30 minutes. Add the apples and water in which they have been soaked and continue to simmer about 1 hour. Stir in the brown sugar.
3. To prepare the dumplings, sift the flour, baking powder, salt, and pepper together into a bowl. Add all at one time a mixture of the beaten egg, melted butter, and milk; mix only until dry ingredients are moistened. Drop by tablespoonfuls onto simmering mixture. Tightly cover the Dutch oven and cook 20 minutes; do not remove cover during cooking.

8 TO 10 SERVINGS

SMOKED SHOULDER ROLL AND BEANS
(Speck un Bona)

Another dish of Pennsylvania Dutch origin.

3-lb. smoked shoulder roll (butt)	6 potatoes, washed, pared and quartered
1 qt. green beans, washed and broken into 1-in. pieces	1 to 2 teaspoons salt
	¼ teaspoon black pepper

1. Cover smoked shoulder roll with *water* and simmer 2½ hours.
2. Add the beans and cook about 10 minutes.
3. Add the potatoes and cook about 25 minutes, or until beans and potatoes are tender.
4. Serve on a heated platter. Accompany with *cider vinegar* for a piquant flavor. 6 SERVINGS

HAM

Glazes for Ham

Remove ham from oven 30 to 40 minutes before time indicated for heating through and spread generously with the desired glaze. Return to oven and continue heating, basting frequently with pan drippings. (If using canned ham, slice it and tie into shape with cord. Remove cord before serving.)

CIDER: Combine and mix thoroughly *¾ cup packed brown sugar, ½ teaspoon dry mustard,* and *2 tablespoons maple syrup.* Spread glaze over ham. Occasionally baste ham with about *¾ cup apple cider.*

APRICOT (using apricot jam): Combine *¾ cup apricot jam, ¾ cup honey,* and *2 tablespoons lemon juice or cider vinegar.* Spread glaze over ham.

APRICOT (using dried apricots): Pour *1⅓ cups apple cider* over *8 ounces dried apricots* in a bowl. Cover and refrigerate overnight. Purée apricot mixture in an electric blender or force through a food mill. Stir in a mixture of *6 tablespoons brown sugar, ½ teaspoon ground cinnamon, ½ teaspoon ground allspice,* and *¼ teaspoon ground cloves.* Spread ham generously with mixture before heating. Heat remaining sauce and serve as an accompaniment to the ham.

MUSTARD GLAZE: Mix thoroughly in a small bowl *1 cup packed brown sugar, 1 tablespoon flour,* and *1 teaspoon dry mustard.* Stir in *2 tablespoons cider vinegar* to form a smooth paste.

JELLY OR JAM: Dilute *1 cup quince or elderberry jelly, jam, or orange marmalade* with *⅓ cup very hot water.*

BROWN SUGAR: Heat together in a saucepan, stirring until sugar is dissolved, *1 cup packed brown sugar* and *⅔ cup light corn syrup.* If desired, *⅔ cup spiced fruit juice or ginger ale* may be substituted for the corn syrup.

GLAZED ROAST HAM

1. Place a *10-lb. whole smoked ham* on a rack in a shallow roasting pan. Roast at 300° to 325°F about 2 hours; remove from oven.
2. Cut off rind (if any) and score fat. Insert a *whole clove* in the center of each diamond.
3. Spread with *one of Glazes for Ham, page 187*, and continue roasting about 1 hour, or until internal temperature reaches 160°F. Serve with *Amber Raisin Sauce, page 334*.

ABOUT 20 SERVINGS

FOIL-BAKED FLAVOR-GLAZED HAM

Ham (see Timetable for Baking Ham in Aluminum Foil, *below*)

Flavor Blends, *below*
Cloves
Sauces, *below*

1. Arrange a large sheet of heavy-duty aluminum foil in a shallow roasting pan; place ham in center.
2. Pour one-half of the desired Flavor Blend over ham and brush it in. Bring foil up, covering ham loosely. Bake according to the timetable.
3. About 30 minutes before baking is finished, open and turn back foil. Spoon out melted fat; remove rind (skin). Score ham in diamond pattern.

4. Stud with cloves. Pour remaining Flavor Blend over ham. Insert meat thermometer and continue baking with foil open, basting with drippings, until browned.
5. Slip a foil frill on bone end of ham after transferring ham to serving platter. Accompany with a fruit or wine sauce.

Flavor Blends for Foil-Baked Ham

ORANGE: Combine one-half of *1 can (6 ounces) frozen orange juice concentrate*, thawed, *1 cup firmly packed brown sugar*, and *½ cup bottled steak sauce*.
PINEAPPLE: Combine *¾ cup unsweetened pineapple juice* with *1 cup firmly packed brown sugar*. Decorate ham with *pineapple slices*.
SHERRY OR MADEIRA: Pour *1 cup wine* over ham before baking. To brown and glaze, sprinkle lightly with *brown sugar* and baste with *1 cup wine*.

Sauces for Foil-Baked Ham

ORANGE: Blend remaining half of orange juice concentrate with *1 cup fruit juice or water*.
PINEAPPLE: Use *1 cup unsweetened pineapple juice*.
WINE: Use *1 cup water*. Stir in any one of the above liquids, blending with the juices and drippings in pan. To thicken, add a mixture of *cornstarch* and *liquid* (about 1 tablespoon per cup of liquid). Bring to boiling, stirring constantly, and cook 1 to 2 minutes.

TIMETABLE FOR BAKING HAM IN ALUMINUM FOIL
(Oven temperature 350°F)

Kind	Average Weight (Pounds)	Approx. Total Baking Time (Hours)	Internal Temperature of Meat
Fully Cooked			
whole, bone in	8 to 12	3	130°F
half	4 to 6	1½	130°F
whole, partially boned	7 to 11	3	130°F
half	3½ to 5½	1½	130°F
rolled, whole	6 to 10	2½ to 2¾	130°F
half	3 to 5	1 to 1½	130°F
Canned			
small	3 to 6	1	130°F
large	6 to 10	1½ to 1¾	130°F
Cook Before Eating			
whole, bone in	8 to 12	3½ to 4	160°F
half	4 to 6	1¾ to 2	160°F

BAKED HAM SLICE WITH CURRIED FRUIT

1 smoked ham slice, cut 1 in. thick	3 tablespoons water
½ cup lightly packed light brown sugar	Pepper
1 cup fine, dry bread crumbs	2 teaspoons prepared mustard

1. Cut fat from ham. Chop fat and mix with remaining ingredients. Place ham in baking pan. Cover with crumb mixture.
2. Bake at 375°F about 50 minutes. Serve with *Curried Fruit, below.*   6 SERVINGS

CURRIED FRUIT: Use halves of drained canned *apricots, pears*, and *pineapple spears or slices*. Use as many pieces as will fill a deep casserole or approximately 4 pieces fruit per serving. Pour over fruit a mixture of *½ cup butter*, melted, *1 cup lightly packed brown sugar*, and *1 tablespoon curry powder*. Bake 40 minutes in same oven with ham.

HAM STEAK ORIENTAL

¼ cup chili sauce	1 green pepper, seeded and cut in 1-in. squares
¼ cup soy sauce	
¼ cup light corn syrup	
¼ cup lemon juice	1 banana, sliced diagonally in 1-in. pieces
1 smoked ham slice, cut 1 in. thick (about 1½ lbs.)	

1. Mix chili sauce, soy sauce, corn syrup, and lemon juice together in a bowl.
2. Place ham slice in a shallow baking dish and pour soy mixture over it. Let stand at room temperature about 1 hour, spooning the marinade over ham occasionally.
3. Top ham slice with green pepper squares and spoon the sauce evenly over all.
4. Bake at 325°F about 25 minutes, basting occasionally. Add banana chunks and baste again. Bake 5 minutes longer.
5. Remove ham from dish and cut into serving-sized portions. Serve topped with green pepper, banana, and sauce.   4 SERVINGS

NOTE: If desired, cut ham in 2½-inch strips; let stand in soy mixture 1 hour. Turn into a large skillet with green pepper; heat thoroughly. Mix in banana; cook until slightly soft. Serve with *saffron-seasoned rice*.

HAM SLICE IN ORANGE SAUCE

1 smoked ham slice, cut 1½ in. thick (about 2 lbs.)	2 teaspoons grated orange peel
2 tablespoons brown sugar	1 teaspoon grated lemon peel
½ teaspoon dry mustard	1½ cups orange juice
	1 teaspoon cornstarch

1. Put ham slice into a baking dish. Insert *whole cloves* in ham slice at 1-inch intervals. Sprinkle a mixture of the brown sugar, dry mustard, and orange and lemon peels over the surface of the ham. Pour 1 cup of the orange juice over ham.
2. Bake at 300°F about 45 minutes, or until thoroughly heated, spooning the liquid over ham slice occasionally during baking.
3. Blend the remaining orange juice with the cornstarch. Remove ham from oven; pour orange juice mixture into baking dish. Return to oven for about 20 minutes, or until liquid is thickened and clear.
4. Remove cloves from ham slice before serving. Garnish with *lemon slices* and *parsley*.

4 TO 6 SERVINGS

"FRIED" HAM WITH RED GRAVY

A ham slice "fried" in this manner is really pan broiled and produces just enough drippings to make the flavorful "red" gravy dear to all Southerners. To give the palate a real surprise, try using hot coffee instead of water, as some cooks do down South.

Rub a heated large heavy skillet with a piece of *fat* trimmed from a *smoked ham slice*, cut ¼ inch thick (allow ⅓ to ½ pound meat per serving). Place ham slice in skillet and cook over medium heat. Maintain a temperature which allows juices to evaporate rather than collect in skillet. (With too low heat, meat will simmer in its own juices and become dry and less tender when cooked.) Turn meat occasionally for even browning. Remove ham slice to a hot plate; keep hot. Add *½ cup hot water* to skillet and bring to boiling, stirring and scraping bottom of skillet to loosen all drippings. Simmer until some of the water evaporates. Pour gravy over ham or serve with the ham.

HAM À LA CRANBERRY

2 cups sugar	2 teaspoons grated
¼ teaspoon salt	lemon peel
2 cups water	6 cups cubed cooked
1 lb. (about 4 cups)	smoked ham or
cranberries, washed	luncheon meat
and sorted	½ cup seedless raisins
	(optional)

1.   Combine sugar, salt, and water in a saucepan and heat to boiling; boil, uncovered, 5 minutes. Add cranberries and continue to boil, uncovered, without stirring, about 5 minutes, or until skins pop.

2.   Turn cranberry sauce into chafing dish blazer. Blend in the lemon peel, ham, and raisins, if desired. Cook over direct heat until mixture starts to bubble; stir occasionally.

3.   Place blazer over simmering water to keep mixture hot. Serve over *toast triangles, patty shells,* or *hot biscuits.*   8 TO 10 SERVINGS

MUSHROOM-HAM CASSEROLE

¼ cup butter	3 cups julienne strips
1 lb. fresh mushrooms,	cooked ham
sliced lengthwise	2 pkgs. (9 oz. each)
1 tablespoon minced	frozen cut green
onion	beans, cooked follow-
3 tablespoons flour	ing pkg. directions
1 teaspoon salt	and drained
¼ teaspoon dry mustard	¼ cup pimiento strips
1 can (14½ oz.)	½ lb. sharp Cheddar
evaporated milk	cheese, shredded
⅓ cup water	

1.   Heat butter in a large skillet; add mushrooms and onion and cook over medium heat, stirring occasionally, until mushrooms are lightly browned. Remove mushrooms from skillet and set aside.

2.   Blend a mixture of flour, salt, and dry mustard into the skillet. Heat until mixture bubbles, stirring constantly. Remove from heat. Continue stirring, gradually add evaporated milk and water; bring rapidly to boiling; cook 1 to 2 minutes.

3.   Add ham, beans, pimiento, and mushrooms; mix well. Turn into a lightly greased, shallow 2-quart baking dish. Top with half of the cheese.

4.   Set in a 350°F oven about 20 minutes, or until thoroughly heated and cheese is golden brown. Remove from oven and immediately sprinkle with remaining cheese. Garnish with *mushroom caps* browned in butter, *a ham slice,* and *parsley.*
          6 TO 8 SERVINGS

SAUERKRAUT BALLS

1 onion, finely chopped	1 tablespoon snipped
3 tablespoons butter	parsley
or margarine	½ cup beef broth
1 cup finely chopped	1 egg, fork beaten
cooked ham	2 cups milk
1 cup finely chopped	Fine dry bread crumbs
corned beef	Fat for deep frying
½ clove garlic, minced	heated to 375°F
2 cups thoroughly	
drained sauerkraut,	
ground in food	
chopper	

1.   Fry onion in hot butter in a saucepan, stirring occasionally. Add the ham, corned beef, and garlic; heat thoroughly. Stir in *6 tablespoons flour* and continue cooking and stirring until well blended.

2.   Add the sauerkraut, parsley, and beef broth. Cook and stir until mixture forms a thick paste. Spread out in a shallow pan to cool. Cover and chill.

3.   Shape the mixture into 1-inch balls. Dip them into a batter made by beating *2½ cups all-purpose flour* with the egg and milk in a bowl until smooth.

4.   Roll the balls in bread crumbs, then fry in hot fat until well browned.   ABOUT 5 DOZEN BALLS

HAM-OLIVE CRÊPES

⅓ cup butter or	¼ teaspoon oregano,
margarine	crushed
5 oz. fresh mushrooms,	1 cup (about 6 oz.)
coarsely chopped	thin 1½-in. strips
2 tablespoons grated	cooked ham
onion	⅓ cup chopped
2 tablespoons butter	pimiento-stuffed olives
or margarine	8 Crêpes, *page 99*
3 tablespoons flour	¼ cup grated Parmesan
2 cups cream	cheese
⅛ teaspoon pepper	

1.   Heat ⅓ cup butter in a large skillet; add mushrooms and onion. Cook over medium heat 5 minutes, stirring occasionally. Using a slotted spoon, remove mushrooms; set aside.

2.   Add 2 tablespoons butter to skillet; blend in flour and cook until bubbly. Remove from heat and

gradually add cream, stirring constantly. Continue to stir and bring mixture to boiling; cook 1 to 2 minutes.

3. Add 1 cup of the sauce to a mixture of the mushrooms, pepper, oregano, ham, and olives. Toss lightly until well mixed.

4. Lightly butter a shallow baking dish. Spoon enough cream sauce over bottom of baking dish to make a thin layer.

5. Spoon 2 to 3 tablespoons of the filling onto the center of each crêpe. Fold one edge of crêpe over filling and roll up. Place filled crêpes in baking dish with open edges down. Spoon remaining sauce over crêpes; sprinkle with Parmesan cheese.

6. Heat, covered, in a 350°F oven for 15 minutes. Remove the dish from oven and uncover.

7. Place baking dish under broiler with top of crêpes 3 to 4 inches from source of heat. Broil 3 to 4 minutes, or until cheese is lightly browned.

8 SERVINGS

SCRUMPTIOUS HAM-PINEAPPLE CRÊPES

Tender crêpes with a rich, tantalizing ham-pineapple sauce make an ideal party dish.

1 can (20½ oz.) pineapple chunks, drained	½ cup finely chopped celery
1½ cups chopped cooked ham	½ cup all-purpose flour
	2 cups light cream
½ cup butter or margarine	1 cup chicken broth
	2 teaspoons lemon juice
¼ cup finely chopped green onion with tops	¾ cup shredded Parmesan cheese
	8 Crêpes, *page 99*

1. Reserve ½ cup pineapple chunks for garnish. Heat remaining pineapple chunks and ham 2 to 3 minutes in 2 tablespoons hot butter in a heavy saucepan, stirring occasionally. Remove from pan and set aside.

2. Cook onion and celery in remaining 6 tablespoons hot butter in the saucepan until soft, stirring occasionally.

3. Blend in flour and heat until bubbly. Remove from heat; stir in cream and broth. Return to heat and bring rapidly to boiling, stirring constantly. Cook 1 to 2 minutes.

4. Remove from heat and mix in lemon juice, ½ cup of the cheese, and the pineapple-ham mixture.

5. Prepare crêpes. Spoon some of hot sauce along center of each baked crêpe. Roll up and place in a shallow baking dish. Spoon remaining sauce around filled crêpes. Top with reserved pineapple chunks and remaining ¼ cup cheese.

6. Heat in a 375°F oven about 20 minutes, or until sauce is bubbly. ABOUT 8 SERVINGS

HAM-ASPARAGUS ROLL-UPS

3 pkgs. (10 oz. each) frozen asparagus spears, cooked following pkg. directions	Few grains white pepper
	⅔ cup chicken broth
	⅓ cup milk
8 slices baked ham, cut about ⅛ in. thick	2 egg yolks, fork beaten
2 tablespoons butter or margarine	¼ cup shredded sharp Cheddar cheese
2 tablespoons flour	1 tablespoon lemon juice
¼ teaspoon salt	

1. Place 4 or 5 asparagus spears in the center of each ham slice. Fold slice around asparagus to form a roll; secure with a wooden pick. Place roll-ups on a baking sheet.

2. Heat in a 325°F oven 10 to 15 minutes, or until ham is thoroughly heated.

3. Meanwhile, melt butter in a heavy saucepan and blend in flour, salt, and pepper; heat until bubbly. Stir in broth and milk. Bring rapidly to boiling, stirring constantly, and cook 1 to 2 minutes. Stir about 3 tablespoons of the hot mixture into egg yolks and immediately blend into hot mixture. Cook and stir 3 to 5 minutes. Remove from heat and add cheese; stir until cheese is melted. Blend in lemon juice.

4. Transfer roll-ups to a hot platter; remove picks. Spoon sauce over roll-ups. Sprinkle with *paprika* and garnish with *parsley*. Serve immediately.

8 SERVINGS

HAM 'N' YAMS IN RAISIN-CARAMEL SAUCE

3 tablespoons butter or margarine	6 smoked ham slices (about ½ lb.), cut in halves
1 cup lightly packed light brown sugar	6 canned yams or sweet potatoes, cut lengthwise
½ cup golden raisins	
½ cup cream	

1. Heat butter in a large skillet. Add brown sugar and raisins; heat, stirring constantly, 10 minutes.

2. Remove from heat; add cream slowly, stirring until blended. Cook 1 minute.

3. Add ham and yams; spoon sauce over all. Heat

thoroughly. Thin the sauce with additional cream, if necessary. 6 SERVINGS

DANISH HAM ROLLS IN SAMSOE CHEESE SAUCE

Leeks, a popular vegetable in Denmark, are featured in this delicious luncheon dish for a party.

6 leeks	4 oz. Samsoe cheese,
3 tablespoons butter	grated
2 tablespoons flour	6 slices Danish ham
½ teaspoon salt	1 tablespoon bread
1¼ cups milk	crumbs
	¾ teaspoon paprika

1. Cut off and discard the upper green tops of the leeks. Rinse several times in cold water to remove all sand. Place in a saucepan; sprinkle with salt and add *boiling water* to cover. Simmer, covered, for 10 minutes. Drain thoroughly.
2. Meanwhile, melt butter; stir in flour and salt. Add milk gradually, stirring constantly. Bring to boiling; cook and stir 1 to 2 minutes. Add one half of cheese, stirring until blended.
3. Spread ham slices with *mustard.* Wrap a slice around drained leek. Place in a shallow baking dish (open edge down). Pour on sauce.

4. Spoon over a topping mixture of remaining cheese, bread crumbs, and paprika. Dot with *butter* (about 2 tablespoons). Broil with top of dish about 4 inches from source of heat 4 to 5 minutes.
6 SERVINGS

FANOE CABBAGE

Another favorite recipe from Denmark.

1 lb. Danish canned	¾ teaspoon salt
bacon, diced	¼ teaspoon black
1 cup chopped onion	pepper
1 medium-sized head	¾ lb. Danish canned
cabbage, coarsely	ham, sliced about ¼
chopped	in. thick

1. Fry bacon in a large skillet until well browned. Set one half aside for topping.
2. Add the onion and cabbage to the skillet and toss until coated. Cook, uncovered, over low heat until cabbage is slightly tender, about 25 minutes, stirring occasionally. Mix in salt and pepper.
3. Place ham slices over top of cabbage mixture and heat thoroughly, about 20 minutes; occasionally spoon cooking liquid over ham to keep it moist.
4. Serve in a large shallow bowl, arranging ham slices on top. Spoon reserved bacon pieces over all. ABOUT 6 SERVINGS

LAMB

ROAST LEG OF LAMB, FRENCH STYLE

5- to 6-lb. leg of lamb	Garlic cloves, cut in
(do not remove fell)	slivers
2 teaspoons salt	Melted butter or
¼ teaspoon pepper	margarine

1. Rub lamb with a mixture of the salt and pepper. Cut several small slits in surface of meat and insert a sliver of garlic in each.
2. Place lamb, skin side down, on rack in a roasting pan. Insert meat thermometer so tip is slightly beyond center of thickest part of meat; be sure that it does not rest in fat or on bone.
3. Roast, uncovered, at 325°F 2½ to 3½ hours, allowing 30 to 35 minutes per pound. Brush meat frequently with melted butter during roasting. Meat is medium done when thermometer registers 175°F and is well done at 180°F.
4. Remove meat to a warm serving platter and

garnish with *mint* or *parsley sprigs*, if desired.
ABOUT 10 SERVINGS

ROAST LAMB WITH SOUR CREAM SAUCE AU CLARET

This roast with its superb sauce could be the pièce de résistance of an elegant dinner.

4 onions, sliced	6- to 7-lb. leg of lamb
(2 cups)	2 teaspoons salt
4 carrots, sliced	¼ teaspoon black
(2 cups)	pepper
2 cups sliced celery	Sour Cream Sauce au
3 bay leaves, crumbled	Claret, *page 193*
1 cup water	

1. Toss the vegetables and bay leaves together in bottom of a shallow roasting pan; pour water over the vegetables and place lamb, rounded side down, on vegetable mixture. Roast at 500°F 25 minutes.

Roast Pork with Olives and Rice

2.   Remove meat from oven and reduce oven temperature to 300°F. Turn meat, rounded side up; sprinkle with a mixture of the salt and pepper. Insert meat thermometer so tip is slightly beyond center of thickest part of meat, being careful that it does not rest on bone or in fat.

3.   Return to oven and continue roasting until thermometer registers 180°F, about 3 hours. Remove thermometer.

4.   Transfer roast to a heated platter and keep it warm. Strain liquid from roasting pan and skim off excess fat; reserve about 1 cup liquid for sauce.

5.   Garnish platter with *spiced crab apples* and *parsley.* Accompany with the sauce.

ABOUT 12 SERVINGS

SOUR CREAM SAUCE AU CLARET

1½ cups red currant jelly	1½ cups claret
6 tablespoons butter	3 cups dairy sour cream
½ cup all-purpose flour	

1.   Melt jelly in the top of a large double boiler over simmering water.

2.   Meanwhile, heat butter in a skillet. Blend in the flour. Remove from heat and add the reserved liquid (from meat and vegetables) gradually, blending well. Cook until bubbly, stirring constantly.

3.   Mix contents of skillet into the melted jelly. Stir in the wine. Add the sour cream gradually, blending well after each addition. Heat thoroughly over simmering water, stirring occasionally.

6 CUPS SAUCE

GLAZED ROLLED LEG OF LAMB

5½- to 6-lb. leg of lamb, boned and rolled	2 medium-sized oranges, quartered, seeded, and ground
2 teaspoons salt	
¼ teaspoon pepper	1 cup strong vegetable broth (dissolve 2 vegetable bouillon cubes in 1 cup boiling water)
1 cup whole cranberry sauce	
1 cup orange juice	
½ teaspoon ground ginger	

1.   Rub lamb with the salt and pepper. Place lamb on rack in a shallow roasting pan.

2.   Combine in a saucepan the cranberry sauce (reserving some berries for garnish), orange juice, and ginger; stir in ground orange. Simmer over low heat 5 to 8 minutes, stirring occasionally during cooking. Spoon one half of the sauce over lamb.

3.   Roast at 325°F 3½ to 4 hours, allowing 40 to 45 minutes per pound. (A meat thermometer should register 175°F for medium-done lamb.) Baste lamb with broth after each 30 minutes of roasting time. About 20 minutes before lamb is done, baste the meat with remaining orange-cranberry sauce.

4.   Transfer roast to a heated platter and garnish with *notched orange slices,* reserved cranberries, and *curly endive.*

8 TO 10 SERVINGS

STUFFED LAMB SHOULDER ROAST WITH HONEY CHUTNEY GLAZE

4- to 5-lb. boned lamb shoulder roast	1 clove garlic, slivered
1 teaspoon salt	¼ cup honey
¼ teaspoon pepper	¼ cup water
⅓ cup chutney	3 tablespoons flour
2 medium-sized onions, sliced	

1.   Rub the lamb with a mixture of the salt and pepper. Spread the inside surface of the lamb with about 3 tablespoons chutney. Arrange onion and garlic over chutney and roll meat as for a jelly roll. Secure with cord.

2.   Place roast, seam side down, on a rack in a shallow roasting pan. Insert meat thermometer so tip is slightly beyond center of thickest part of meat; be sure that tip does not rest in fat or in stuffing.

3.   Roast, uncovered, at 325°F, allowing 35 to 40 minutes per pound. When meat has roasted about 1¾ hours, pour off fat drippings and reserve.

4.   Mix the honey, water, and remaining chutney; spoon over roast. Continue roasting until meat has reached the desired degree of doneness, basting occasionally. (Meat is medium done when thermometer registers 175°F and well done at 180°F.) Remove thermometer.

5.   Transfer meat to a serving platter; keep hot.

6.   Leaving the brown residue in pan, pour honey-chutney mixture into a bowl and allow fat to rise to surface. Skim off fat and return 3 tablespoonfuls to the roasting pan (use reserved drippings, if needed). Blend in the flour until smooth. Stirring constantly, heat until mixture bubbles. Remove from heat and stir in the honey mixture with enough water to make 2 cups liquid. Return to heat, bring to boiling, and boil 1 to 2 minutes, scraping bottom and sides of pan to blend in brown residue. Season to taste with *salt* and *pepper.*

6 TO 8 SERVINGS

Sauce-Crowned Meat Ring

LAMB CROWN ROAST WITH STUFFING

4- to 6-lb. crown roast
of lamb

Rice-Raisin Stuffing,
below

1. Sprinkle meat with *seasoned salt* and *pepper*; place rib-ends down on a rack in a shallow roasting pan. Roast at 325°F about 1 hour.
2. Remove from oven and turn roast rib-ends up. Insert a meat thermometer in center of the thickest part of meat. Return to oven and roast 1½ to 2½ hours, or until thermometer registers 175°F.
3. About 1 hour before end of roasting time, spoon half of the rice stuffing into center of roast. Cover with aluminum foil and return to oven. Spoon remaining stuffing into a 1-quart casserole; set in oven with the stuffed roast. Cook, uncovered, stirring occasionally with a fork.
4. Transfer roast to a serving platter. Garnish with *parsley*, and if desired, surround with rosy *apple rings* or *spiced crab apples*.   6 TO 8 SERVINGS

RICE-RAISIN STUFFING

1 pkg. (6 oz.) curry-
seasoned rice, cooked
following pkg.
directions and using
only 2¼ cups water
1 lb. ground lamb,
browned and drained
½ cup diced green
pepper

⅓ cup golden raisins
½ cup chicken broth
2 tablespoons lemon
juice
½ teaspoon seasoned
salt
½ teaspoon salt
⅛ teaspoon pepper

1. Lightly mix all ingredients.
2. Use one half as stuffing for lamb crown roast and remaining half for an accompanying casserole.

LAMB BREAST WITH CARROT STUFFING

2½ cups soft 1-in.
bread cubes
3 tablespoons butter
or margarine, melted
¾ cup finely shredded
carrots
½ cup finely chopped
onion
1 tablespoon finely
chopped parsley

1 egg, beaten
½ teaspoon salt
¼ teaspoon crushed
marjoram
2 tablespoons hot beef
bouillon
3-lb. lamb breast
(have meat dealer cut
a pocket and crack
bones)

1. Lightly toss bread cubes, butter, carrots, onion, parsley, egg, salt, and marjoram together, blending in bouillon last. Spoon into pocket of breast.
2. Place meat, rib side down, on rack in shallow roasting pan. Roast, uncovered, at 300°F about 2 hours, or until meat is tender.   ABOUT 4 SERVINGS

LAMB CHOPS EN BROCHETTE

8 loin lamb chops, cut
¾ to 1 in. thick
(allow 2 chops per
serving)
8 green pepper squares
(about 1½ in.)
4 small onions
¼ cup olive oil

4 teaspoons grated
onion
1 teaspoon thyme,
crushed
1 teaspoon salt
¼ teaspoon black
pepper
4 cherry tomatoes

1. Thread 2 lamb chops onto each of four 15-inch skewers. Alternately thread 2 green pepper squares and 1 onion onto the end of each skewer.
2. Brush chops and vegetables with a mixture of the oil, grated onion, thyme, salt, and pepper.
3. Place skewers on broiler rack and broil 3 inches from source of heat for about 12 minutes, or until chops are evenly browned on both sides; turn and brush frequently. Near end of broiling period, thread 1 cherry tomato onto the tip of each skewer.
4. Arrange the four skewers artistically on a serving platter. Spoon remaining heated marinade onto chops and sprinkle lightly with *lemon juice*.

4 SERVINGS

LAMB CHOPS PIQUANT

2 tablespoons butter
5 lamb shoulder chops,
cut ¾ in. thick
½ cup sweet pickle
liquid
½ cup tarragon vinegar
¼ cup water
4 teaspoons sugar

2 teaspoons dry
mustard
1 teaspoon salt
½ teaspoon black
pepper
2 tablespoons drained
capers (reserve 6
tablespoons liquid)
6 tablespoons water

1. Heat butter in a large heavy skillet. Add the lamb chops and brown on both sides.
2. Blend the pickle liquid, vinegar, ¼ cup water, and a mixture of the sugar, dry mustard, salt, and pepper. Pour over lamb chops in the skillet.
3. Cover and cook over low heat about 40 minutes, or until lamb is tender. Baste chops occasionally, adding a little hot water if necessary.

4. When meat is tender, pour off excess liquid. Mix capers, caper liquid, and 6 tablespoons water; pour over chops in the skillet. Heat thoroughly and serve immediately.   5 SERVINGS

STUFFED RIB LAMB CHOPS

6 double-rib lamb chops, about 2 in. thick	Few grains pepper
	3 tablespoons butter or margarine, melted
½ cup fine dry bread crumbs	¼ cup finely chopped fresh mushrooms, browned in a small amount of butter or margarine
½ teaspoon crushed basil	
¼ teaspoon salt	

1. Using a sharp knife, make a slit between rib bones into center of meat on each lamb chop; form a pocket. Set aside while preparing the stuffing.
2. Mix the bread crumbs, basil, salt, and pepper; blend in the melted butter. Toss with the mushrooms. Stuff each chop with some of the bread crumb mixture; fasten securely with skewers if necessary.
3. Broil with top of chops about 5 inches from source of heat about 15 minutes on first side. Sprinkle with *salt* and *pepper*, turn, and broil second side. Season.   6 SERVINGS

SPICY LAMB SUPERB

¼ teaspoon ground ginger	1 bay leaf
¼ teaspoon ground allspice	1 can (8 oz.) tomato sauce
¼ teaspoon ground cinnamon	¾ cup unsweetened pineapple juice
¼ teaspoon oregano	6 lamb shoulder chops, cut ½ in. thick
⅛ teaspoon curry powder	

1. Mix the ginger, allspice, cinnamon, oregano, curry powder, and bay leaf in a saucepan. Blend in the tomato sauce and pineapple juice. Bring mixture to boiling; simmer, uncovered, 5 minutes. Cool; remove bay leaf.
2. Arrange chops in a large shallow dish. Pour sauce over chops. Refrigerate about 8 hours.
3. Broil chops 3 inches from source of heat about 15 minutes on each side, brushing with marinade.
6 SERVINGS

BARBECUED LAMB SHANKS

4 lamb shanks, about 1 lb. each	½ cup water
¼ cup flour	¼ cup wine vinegar
1 teaspoon salt	4 teaspoons Worcestershire sauce
¼ teaspoon pepper	5 drops Tabasco
¼ cup fat	2 teaspoons sugar
1 cup chopped onion	2 teaspoons paprika
2 cloves garlic, minced	1 teaspoon dry mustard
1 cup ketchup	1 teaspoon salt
	½ teaspoon pepper

1. Coat the lamb shanks evenly with a mixture of the flour, 1 teaspoon salt, and ¼ teaspoon pepper.
2. Heat fat in a large heavy skillet over medium heat. Add shanks and brown well on all sides. Remove meat to a large shallow baking dish.
3. Meanwhile, combine the onion, garlic, ketchup, water, vinegar, Worcestershire sauce, and Tabasco in a saucepan. Stir in a mixture of sugar, paprika, dry mustard, salt, and pepper and heat to boiling. Pour sauce over lamb.
4. Bake, covered, at 300°F 1½ to 2 hours, or until meat is tender; turn shanks and baste frequently with the sauce.   ABOUT 4 SERVINGS

SPICY LAMB SHANKS

4 lamb shanks, about 1 lb. each	1 cup water
¼ cup flour	3 tablespoons cider vinegar
1 teaspoon salt	½ cup sugar
¼ teaspoon pepper	½ teaspoon ground allspice
¼ cup fat	
½ cup water	½ teaspoon ground cinnamon
1⅔ cups cooked dried apricots, drained	¼ teaspoon ground cloves
1 cup stewed prunes, drained and pitted	¼ teaspoon salt

1. Coat lamb shanks evenly with a mixture of the flour, salt, and pepper.
2. Heat fat in a large heavy skillet. Add shanks and brown well on all sides.
3. Remove shanks to a large shallow baking dish; add the ½ cup water. Bake, covered, at 350°F about 1½ hours, or until meat is almost tender when pierced with a fork.
4. Put cooked fruits into a saucepan and add remaining ingredients; bring rapidly to boiling and simmer 5 minutes.

5. Drain fat from meat; add the cooked fruit. Cover and return to oven 30 minutes.　　4 SERVINGS

DEVILED LAMB SPARERIBS

2½ cups lemon juice	2 teaspoons ground
1 tablespoon grated	cumin
onion	1 teaspoon thyme,
8 cloves garlic, sliced	crushed
4 teaspoons salt	½ teaspoon seasoned
4 teaspoons dry	pepper
mustard	9 to 10 lbs. lamb
4 teaspoons chili	spareribs
powder	Paprika

1. Mix lemon juice, grated onion, garlic, and a mixture of salt, dry mustard, chili powder, cumin, thyme, and seasoned pepper. Pour over lamb in a large shallow dish or pan. Cover and marinate in refrigerator 6 to 8 hours, or overnight; turn occasionally.
2. Remove spareribs from marinade and place on rack in shallow roasting pan. Roast at 325°F 1½ hours, basting occasionally with marinade.
3. Sprinkle spareribs with paprika; roast ½ hour longer, or until tender.
4. Place ribs in a serving dish and garnish with *parsley sprigs*.　　ABOUT 12 SERVINGS

GRILLED LAMB SPARERIBS: Marinate spareribs as directed in recipe for Deviled Lamb Spareribs. Remove from marinade and arrange on skewers; sprinkle with paprika. Grill 6 or 7 inches from source of heat 20 minutes on each side, or to desired degree of doneness, basting occasionally with marinade.

FRUITED LAMB SPARERIBS

3 lbs. lamb spareribs	⅓ cup finely chopped
1 teaspoon salt	celery
¼ teaspoon black	¼ cup chopped parsley
pepper	1 orange, cut in ¼-in.
1 teaspoon curry	slices
powder	1 medium-sized lemon,
1 cup orange juice	cut in ¼-in. slices
1 teaspoon grated	10 canned pineapple
lemon peel	slices

1. Put spareribs into a large heavy skillet. Combine salt, pepper, and curry powder; blend in the orange juice, lemon peel, celery, and parsley. Pour over spareribs. Top with orange, lemon, and pineapple slices.
2. Cook, covered, over low heat about 1½ hours, or until meat is tender.
3. Remove spareribs and fruit to a warm serving dish.　　4 TO 6 SERVINGS

BRAISED LAMB NECKS WITH BRUSSELS SPROUTS

2 tablespoons butter	⅛ teaspoon pepper
or margarine	1 bay leaf
6 lamb neck slices,	1½ cups strong beef
about ¾ in. thick	broth
6 whole white onions	2 pkgs. (10 oz. each)
1 teaspoon paprika	frozen Brussels
¾ teaspoon oregano	sprouts
¼ teaspoon thyme	1 pimiento, sliced
½ teaspoon salt	1½ tablespoons flour

1. Heat butter in a skillet; add lamb and brown on both sides. Add onions, seasonings, and broth. Cook, covered, over low heat 20 minutes.
2. Add frozen Brussels sprouts and pimiento. Cover and cook over low heat about 10 minutes, or until sprouts are just tender.
3. Remove lamb and vegetables to hot serving platter and keep warm.
4. Blend flour with a small amount of water; stir into liquid in skillet. Stirring constantly, bring to boiling; cook 2 to 3 minutes until thickened.
5. Serve lamb and Brussels sprouts on hot fluffy *rice*. Accompany with gravy in a sauce boat.
　　6 SERVINGS

LAMB-ON-A-STICK

¾ cup finely chopped	½ teaspoon curry
onion	powder
¾ cup finely chopped	½ teaspoon parsley
green pepper	flakes
3 tablespoons olive oil	½ teaspoon onion
1 tablespoon lemon	powder
juice	¼ teaspoon dry mustard
1 tablespoon water	⅛ teaspoon ground
1 teaspoon salt	oregano
½ teaspoon black	2 lbs. boneless lamb
pepper	(leg), cut in 1½-in.
	cubes

1. Combine the onion and green pepper. Blend the olive oil, lemon juice, and water thoroughly.

Mix together the salt, pepper, curry powder, parsley flakes, onion powder, dry mustard, and oregano.

2. Coat bottom of a shallow dish with about 1 tablespoon of the olive oil marinade; cover with one-third of the onion mixture. Sprinkle one-third of the seasonings over all. Cover with one-half of the lamb cubes. Drizzle with one-half of remaining marinade and layer with one-half of onion mixture and seasonings. Cover with remaining lamb cubes. Repeat layering with remaining ingredients. Cover and refrigerate at least 8 hours, or overnight.

3. When ready to broil, thread three lamb cubes onto each of six 6-inch wooden skewers and brush with marinade. Place kabobs on broiler rack; broil 3 inches from source of heat 10 to 15 minutes, turning meat several times and brushing with marinade. Test doneness of meat by cutting a slit in cube and noting color of meat.   ABOUT 6 SERVINGS

LAMB-PINEAPPLE KABOBS

1½ lbs. boneless lamb shoulder or leg, cut in 1½-in. cubes	¼ cup lemon juice
	2 cloves garlic, minced
1 can (13½ oz.) pineapple chunks, drained (reserve ½ cup syrup)	½ teaspoon pepper
	Orange Barbecue Sauce, *page 346*
½ cup soy sauce	

1. Put lamb cubes into a large shallow dish and pour over them a mixture of ½ cup pineapple syrup and remaining ingredients, reserving pineapple chunks. Refrigerate to marinate several hours or overnight; turn occasionally.

2. Remove meat from marinade and drain; reserve marinade for basting kabobs during cooking.

3. Alternately arrange meat pieces and the reserved pineapple chunks on four 8-inch skewers; brush with marinade.

4. Arrange kabobs on broiler rack; broil with tops of kabobs about 3 inches from source of heat 15 to 20 minutes, turning several times and brushing frequently with marinade; test for doneness by cutting a slit in meat cubes and noting color of meat.

5. Serve kabobs on fluffy *cooked rice* with Orange Barbecue Sauce.   4 SERVINGS

CURRY SUPERBE

¼ cup cooking oil	1 teaspoon sugar
1 medium-sized onion, chopped	1½ lbs. boneless lamb shoulder, cut in 1-in. cubes
1 clove garlic, minced	
¼ cup flour	1 medium-sized apple, sliced
1 tablespoon curry powder	⅓ cup seedless raisins
2 teaspoons salt	¼ cup chutney
2 cups beef broth	¼ cup slivered almonds
2 tablespoons lemon juice	

1. Heat the oil in a heavy saucepan. Add the onion and garlic and cook until onion is almost tender, about 5 minutes. Blend in a mixture of the flour, curry powder, and salt; heat until bubbly. Stir in the broth and lemon juice and cook until thickened, stirring constantly.

2. Sprinkle sugar over lamb and cook in a large heavy skillet until browned on all sides. Add apple slices; cover and cook 5 minutes.

3. Add the curry sauce to skillet and stir in the raisins, chutney, and almonds. Cover; cook 1 hour.

4. Serve over hot *cooked rice* with accompaniments such as *pimiento-stuffed olives, chutney, kumquats, sieved egg yolks, sliced green pepper,* and *toasted flaked coconut.*   6 SERVINGS

LAMB AND COCONUT CURRY

¼ cup butter or margarine	½ teaspoon ground ginger
1 lb. boneless lamb shoulder, cut in 1-in. cubes	1½ cups strong chicken broth
	⅓ cup maraschino cherry syrup
1 medium-sized onion, sliced	¼ cup lemon juice
¼ cup flour	⅓ cup flaked coconut
1 teaspoon salt	⅓ cup golden raisins
1½ tablespoons curry powder	8 oz. fine noodles, cooked and drained

1. Heat butter in a large heavy skillet. Add lamb and onion and cook over medium heat until lamb is browned on all sides. Remove meat and onion with a slotted spoon and set aside.

2. Add to the skillet a mixture of the flour, salt, curry powder, and ginger and blend well; allow mixture to bubble. Remove from heat. Add broth, cherry syrup, and lemon juice gradually, stirring

constantly. Return to heat and bring rapidly to boiling, stirring constantly; cook 1 to 2 minutes.

3. Return meat and onion to the skillet; stir in coconut and raisins. Cover and cook over low heat, stirring occasionally, about 40 minutes, or until meat is tender.

4. Serve in a bowl with cooked noodles. Accompany with *Maraschino Cherry Chutney, page 386, toasted coconut*, and chopped *mint leaves*.

4 SERVINGS

LAMB STEW PICASSO
An adaptation of an authentic Spanish recipe.

2 lbs. lamb stew meat, cut in 2-in. pieces	3 cloves garlic, minced
¼ cup flour	1 lb. potatoes, pared and sliced
1 teaspoon salt	
¼ teaspoon pepper	2 onions, sliced
¼ cup olive oil	1 cup chopped celery
1 cup beef broth	2 tomatoes, cut in wedges
2 green peppers, chopped	
½ teaspoon marjoram	1 cup pimiento-stuffed olives

1. Coat lamb pieces with a mixture of flour, salt, and pepper.
2. Heat olive oil in a large skillet; add lamb and brown evenly on all sides. Add beef broth slowly, then stir in the green pepper, marjoram, and garlic. Cover and cook over low heat 30 minutes.
3. Add potatoes, onions, and celery; cook, covered, 10 minutes, or until potatoes are tender. Mix in the tomatoes and olives; heat thoroughly.

ABOUT 6 SERVINGS

HUNTER-STYLE LAMB STEW

2 lbs. boneless lean lamb shoulder, cut in 1½-in. cubes	1 clove garlic, minced
	4 anchovies, chopped
¾ to 1 teaspoon salt	1 teaspoon basil leaves, crushed
¼ to ½ teaspoon pepper	
2 tablespoons butter or margarine	1 teaspoon rosemary leaves, crushed
	¼ teaspoon sage leaves, crushed
2 tablespoons olive oil	
1 green pepper, cut in pieces	½ cup red wine vinegar
	2 teaspoons flour

1. Season lamb with salt and pepper. Brown on all sides in heated butter and oil in a large heavy skillet.
2. Meanwhile, cook green pepper, garlic, and anchovies about 5 minutes in a small amount of *oil* in a small saucepan. Add basil, rosemary, sage, and vinegar. Cook and stir until boiling.

3. Remove lamb from skillet using a slotted spoon; set aside. Add enough *chicken broth* to the drippings in skillet to make ¾ cup liquid. Add the vinegar-herb mixture; bring to boiling, stirring to blend well. Return lamb to skillet, cover tightly and simmer until tender.

4. Combine flour with enough cooled broth to make a smooth paste. Add to liquid in skillet; cook and stir 1 to 2 minutes until thickened and smooth.

5. Serve on heated serving platter surrounded with *fettuccine* (or noodles) tossed with *shredded Parmesan cheese*. Sprinkle *parsley* over all.

5 OR 6 SERVINGS

FAVORITE LAMB STEW WITH RICE DUMPLINGS

2 lbs. boneless lean lamb shoulder, cut in 1-in. cubes	¼ teaspoon thyme leaves, crushed
	1½ cups hot water
¼ cup flour	1 can (6 oz.) tomato paste
1 tablespoon salt	
½ teaspoon pepper	2½ cups hot water
1 teaspoon paprika	12 small white onions
2 tablespoons fat	1 pkg. (10 oz.) frozen Fordhook lima beans, partially thawed
1 clove garlic, minced	
1 teaspoon dill weed, crushed	
	1 lb. carrots, cut in pieces
¼ teaspoon marjoram leaves, crushed	Rice Dumplings, *below*

1. Coat lamb with a mixture of the flour, salt, pepper, and paprika; reserve any remaining flour.
2. Brown meat evenly on all sides in the hot fat in a Dutch oven. Sprinkle remaining flour mixture over meat. Add the garlic, dill, marjoram, thyme, and 1½ cups water. Cover; simmer 1 hour.
3. Blend in a mixture of tomato paste and 2½ cups water; mix in the vegetables. Simmer, covered, about 20 minutes.
4. Drop Rice Dumpling batter onto meat and vegetables in boiling liquid. Cover tightly and cook 15 minutes; do not uncover during cooking. Serve immediately.

ABOUT 6 SERVINGS

RICE DUMPLINGS: Sift *1½ cups sifted all-purpose flour, 2½ teaspoons baking powder*, and *1 teaspoon salt* together into a bowl; mix thoroughly. Blend *1 beaten egg, ½ cup milk*, and *1 tablespoon butter or margarine*, melted. Add all at one time to dry ingredients and stir until just moistened. With last few strokes, mix in *1 cup cooked rice*. Drop by heaping tablespoonfuls onto meat and vegetables.

6 DUMPLINGS

PERSIAN STEW
The allure of the Middle East is in this hearty dish.

1½ lbs. boneless lean lamb shoulder, cut in 1- to 1½-in. pieces	⅛ teaspoon coarsely ground pepper
1 tablespoon cooking oil	½ teaspoon oregano leaves, crushed
½ cup chopped onion	½ teaspoon thyme leaves, crushed
2 cans (8 oz. each) tomato sauce	½ teaspoon ground turmeric
¼ cup water	¼ teaspoon ground cinnamon
1 tablespoon lemon juice	1¼ cups canned white beans (such as Great Northern)
1 bay leaf	
½ teaspoon salt	

1. In a large heavy skillet, brown lamb on all sides in hot oil. Add onion and cook until tender, stirring occasionally.
2. Mix tomato sauce, water, lemon juice, bay leaf, salt, pepper, oregano, thyme, turmeric, and cinnamon. Pour over meat. Bring to boiling, cover, and simmer 1½ to 2 hours, until meat is tender. Stir in beans during the last half hour of cooking.
3. Remove bay leaf. Ladle into bowls.

4 SERVINGS

FRUITED LAMB STEW DE LUXE

1½ lbs. boneless lean lamb, cut in 1½-in. pieces	3 onions, coarsely chopped
½ cup all-purpose flour	¾ cup dried apricots
4 teaspoons salt	½ cup pitted dried prunes
¼ teaspoon black pepper	4 lemon slices, cut in quarters
½ teaspoon ground allspice	3 pkgs. (10 oz. each) frozen Brussels sprouts, partially thawed to separate sprouts
2 tablespoons butter or margarine	
3 cups beef broth	
1 tablespoon brown sugar	Noodle Ring, *below*

1. Coat lamb with a mixture of flour, salt, pepper, and allspice; set remaining flour aside.
2. Brown the meat on all sides in heated butter in a large saucepot. Add 2½ cups of the broth, the brown sugar, onions, apricots, prunes, and lemon slices. Cover and bring to boiling. Reduce heat and simmer about 1 hour.
3. Add Brussels sprouts and continue cooking 15 to 20 minutes, or until sprouts are just tender.
4. Blend remaining ½ cup broth and reserved seasoned flour. Stir into boiling stew. Boil and stir 1 to 2 minutes. Serve in Noodle Ring.

6 TO 8 SERVINGS

NOODLE RING: Add *2 tablespoons salt to 4 to 6 quarts rapidly boiling water*; gradually add *1 pound medium egg noodles* so boiling does not stop. Cook, uncovered, stirring occasionally, until noodles are tender; drain. Turn into a greased 9-inch ring mold, pressing gently with a spoon. Let stand 5 minutes before unmolding onto a serving plate.

OVEN LAMB STEW
A treat for St. Patrick's Day.

2 lbs. boneless lean lamb shoulder, cut in 2-in. cubes	¼ small head cabbage, shredded
1¾ teaspoons salt	2 leeks, thinly sliced
¼ teaspoon thyme, crushed	2 medium-sized onions, sliced
1 bay leaf	1 cup sliced raw potatoes
4 whole allspice	8 small whole onions
2 tablespoons chopped parsley	4 carrots, cut in 2-in. pieces
1 clove garlic, minced	2 white turnips, quartered

1. Put the lamb into a Dutch oven. Add salt, thyme, bay leaf, allspice, parsley, garlic, cabbage, leeks, sliced onions, potatoes, and *about 4 cups water*. Cover tightly and bring rapidly to boiling.
2. Set in a 350°F oven and bake about 1½ hours, or until meat is tender.
3. About 30 minutes before baking time is ended, cook the remaining vegetables separately in boiling *salted water* until tender. Drain.
4. Turn contents of Dutch oven into a food mill set over a large bowl. Return meat to the Dutch oven and add the cooked onions, carrots, and turnips. Discarding bay leaf and allspice, force the vegetables through food mill into the bowl containing cooking liquid (or purée vegetables in an electric blender). Pour into Dutch oven. Heat stew thoroughly.

6 TO 8 SERVINGS

VEAL

STUFFED BREAST OF VEAL

½ cup butter	1 egg, slightly beaten
⅓ cup finely chopped onion	1 teaspoon salt
⅓ cup diced celery	¼ teaspoon pepper
6 slices bread, toasted and cubed	½ teaspoon poultry seasoning
½ cup water	3½-lb. breast of veal, boned and rolled
½ cup chopped cooked prunes	(about 2¼ lbs.)
1 cup diced unpared apple	½ teaspoon salt
	¼ cup butter
	½ cup water

1. Heat ½ cup butter in a skillet. Add onion and celery; cook about 5 minutes; stir occasionally.
2. Put bread cubes into a large bowl; add ½ cup water, the vegetable mixture, prunes, apple, and egg, and a mixture of the 1 teaspoon salt, pepper, and poultry seasoning; mix lightly and thoroughly.
3. Unroll veal and spread the stuffing to within 1 inch of the edge of the meat. Reroll jelly-roll fashion and tie. If necessary, secure ends with skewers. Rub meat with the ½ teaspoon salt.
4. Heat the ¼ cup butter in a roasting pan. Add the meat and brown well on all sides.
5. Set meat on a rack; slowly add the ½ cup water. Cover pan; roast at 325°F about 2 hours, or until meat is tender.
6. Transfer meat to a platter and keep warm. Prepare *Gingersnap or Ginger gravy, page 348.*

ABOUT 6 SERVINGS

VEAL FLORENTINE "21"

A popular veal dish from Jack and Charlie's "21" restaurant in New York City.

3½- to 5-lb. breast of veal with pocket (have meat dealer cut meat away from ribs to form a pocket)	3 tablespoons minced onion
	3 cups finely chopped cooked spinach
	1 cup bread crumbs
	4 eggs, fork beaten
½ lb. bulk pork sausage	1½ to 2 teaspoons salt
2 tablespoons water	¼ teaspoon black pepper

1. Rub veal outside and inside the pocket with *salt* and *pepper*; set aside.
2. Put pork sausage into a cold large skillet, cut-ting sausage apart with a spoon. Add water; cover and cook slowly 8 to 10 minutes. Remove cover; pour off liquid. Add onion and brown over medium heat, stirring occasionally.
3. Put sausage into a large bowl along with the remaining ingredients; mix well. Lightly spoon stuffing into pocket. Skewer or sew to keep stuffing in place. Put roast, rib side down, on rack in a shallow roasting pan.
4. Roast at 325°F 45 to 50 minutes, or until meat is tender. Transfer roast to a hot serving platter and remove skewers. Garnish with *parsley.*

ABOUT 8 SERVINGS

JACK AND CHARLIE'S MEDALLIONS OF VEAL
Another "21" restaurant veal recipe.

About 1 lb. medallions of veal (scallops)	2 tablespoons butter
	¼ cup Madeira
¼ cup butter	1 tablespoon butter
12 fresh mushroom caps	

1. Sauté medallions quickly in the ¼ cup butter until they are lightly browned on both sides.
2. In a saucepan, cook mushroom caps in the 2 tablespoons butter and season them lightly with *salt* and *pepper.*
3. Arrange the medallions in a warm serving dish; put the mushroom caps on top of them.
4. To the pan in which the veal was sautéed, add the wine and stir over low heat 1 minute. Add the 1 tablespoon butter, swirl the pan over heat until the butter is melted, and pour the sauce over the medallions. Serve at once.

ABOUT 4 SERVINGS

BREADED VEAL CUTLETS
(Wiener Schnitzel)

2 lbs. veal round steak (cutlet), cut ½ in. thick	¼ teaspoon pepper
	3 eggs, slightly beaten
⅓ cup flour	1½ cups French bread crumbs or sour French bread crumbs
1½ teaspoons salt	
1 teaspoon mono-sodium glutamate	Lard for deep frying heated to 375°F

1. Pound meat on one side with meat hammer. Turn and repeat process until meat is about ¼ inch

thick. Cut into 6 serving-size pieces. Coat with a mixture of the flour, salt, monosodium glutamate, and pepper. Dip veal into eggs, then lightly coat with crumbs. Let stand 5 to 10 minutes to "seal."

2. Deep fry only as many pieces at one time as will lie uncrowded one layer deep in the hot lard. Fry until brown on both sides, 3 or 4 minutes; turn slices several times during cooking (do not pierce). Remove meat with tongs and drain over fat for a few seconds before removing to absorbent paper. Serve with *lemon wedges*.   6 SERVINGS

Scaloppine (also spelled scaloppini) is a popular Italian dish made of thin slices of veal—called scaloppine in Italian, escalope in French, scalop in English—sautéed or broiled and served with a well-seasoned sauce containing wine or tomato. Here are various interpretations of this popular dish as it is served in well-known Continental and American restaurants, each recipe exemplifying Italian culinary creativity at its best.

SCALOPPINI EL PRESIDENTE
A recipe from La Scala Restaurant in Beverly Hills, California.

¼ cup flour	1 zucchini, pared and
1 teaspoon salt	cut in ½-in. slices
1 teaspoon pepper	1 egg, slightly beaten
12 small ¼-in. thick	2 to 3 tablespoons milk
slices veal steak	3 tablespoons butter
(about 2 lbs.)	or margarine
2 tablespoons clarified	¼ cup white wine
butter, *see page 19*	Finely chopped parsley

1. Combine flour, salt, and pepper; toss the veal slices in the seasoned flour to coat lightly.
2. Brown veal on both sides in hot clarified butter in a large heavy skillet over medium heat.
3. Meanwhile, coat zucchini slices with flour; dip in a mixture of the beaten egg and milk.
4. Heat butter in a heavy skillet; add zucchini slices and brown quickly on both sides. Drain on absorbent paper.
5. Place scaloppini on a heated serving platter and overlap with zucchini slices; pour the butter left in skillet over them. Set aside in a warm place.
6. Add the wine to the skillet in which the zucchini was cooked; heat, stirring in all the brown bits. Pour the sauce over meat and zucchini and sprinkle with parsley.   4 SERVINGS

SCALOPPINE ALLA MARSALA
A recipe from Rosellini's in Seattle, Washington.

1½ lbs. leg of veal	4 tablespoons olive oil
(have meat dealer	2 cups thinly sliced
cut meat into slices	fresh mushrooms
less than ½ in.	Juice of 1 lemon
thick)	½ cup Marsala or
4 tablespoons butter	sherry

1. Flatten each veal slice with a wooden mallet or the side of a cleaver. Dip the slices in *seasoned flour*.
2. Brown veal slices on both sides in hot butter and oil in a skillet. Add mushrooms; cook 10 minutes.
3. Add the lemon juice and wine; simmer 5 minutes. Serve immediately.   4 SERVINGS

VEAL SCALOPPINE LA RUE
A recipe from La Rue, a Los Angeles, California, restaurant.

2 lbs. boned veal loin,	2 eggs, well beaten
sliced	2 tablespoons flour
½ lb. butter	½ lb. fresh new peas,
½ wine glass Marsala	cooked and buttered
6 oz. fresh mushrooms	2 cups fresh tomato
4 medium zucchini,	sauce
sliced ¼ in. thick	

1. Pound veal slices until thin. Sprinkle on both sides with *salt*, *pepper*, and *flour*.
2. Heat a large skillet and cook some of the butter to a light brown. Add the scaloppine and brown on both sides. Drizzle with Marsala and turn several times.
3. Meanwhile, sauté the mushrooms in some of the butter for 10 minutes in a heavy saucepan or skillet. Season to taste with *salt* and *pepper* and add a few drops of *lemon juice*.
4. Coat zucchini slices with *flour*, then dip them in a batter made by beating eggs with the 2 tablespoons flour until smooth.
5. Sauté slices in remaining butter in a skillet until golden brown on both sides.
6. Arrange scaloppine and zucchini alternately around edge of casserole. Spoon buttered peas into center and surround peas with mushrooms. Surround mushrooms with tomato sauce. Pour browned butter and wine left in skillet over whole dish before serving. Serve very hot.   6 SERVINGS

VEAL SCALOPPINE EDOARDO

A recipe from Edoardo's of Zurich, Switzerland.

8 small veal scallops (about 1 lb.)	¼ lb. fresh mushrooms, thinly sliced
4 tablespoons butter	2 tablespoons butter
½ cup Madeira	1 cup white sauce
1 teaspoon prepared meat glaze	4 croutons (toast triangles or squares)

1. Pound scallops until thin. Sauté in 4 tablespoons butter 5 minutes. Add the wine and meat glaze; cook a few minutes until thoroughly cooked.
2. Sauté the mushrooms in the 2 tablespoons butter 5 minutes, or until lightly browned. Add the white sauce and cook 1 minute.
3. Arrange the veal slices in the center of a hot heat-resistant platter. Arrange the croutons around the veal and pour the mushrooms over the croutons. Sprinkle the mushrooms with *grated Parmesan cheese* and cover the veal with *slivered Swiss cheese.*
4. Put the platter under broiler until cheeses are melted. Serve with *green noodles.*   4 SERVINGS

VEAL SCALOPPINE WITH BURGUNDY

Here is an Americanized version, with the mellow flavor of Burgundy giving it a Gallic touch.

2 lbs. thin veal round steak	1 clove garlic, crushed
3 cups sieved tomatoes (28 oz. can)	½ cup flour
	1 teaspoon salt
2 teaspoons salt	¼ teaspoon pepper
¼ teaspoon pepper	½ cup butter or margarine
½ teaspoon oregano, crushed	1 lb. fresh mushrooms, sliced lengthwise
1 tablespoon snipped parsley	2 medium-sized onions, chopped
6 tablespoons olive oil	½ cup red Burgundy

1. Pound veal until very thin. Cut into 2-inch pieces; set aside.
2. Combine the tomatoes, salt, pepper, oregano, and parsley in a large saucepan. Bring to boiling and simmer, uncovered, 15 minutes, stirring occasionally. Remove from heat.
3. Meanwhile, heat the oil with garlic in a large skillet. Pour off all but 2 tablespoons of the garlic-flavored oil and reserve. Coat veal pieces with a mixture of flour, salt, and pepper. Add as many pieces to the hot skillet as will fit uncrowded;

brown meat quickly on both sides. Using a slotted spoon, transfer the meat to the tomato sauce. Continue frying meat, using the reserved oil as needed, and transferring the meat to the sauce.
4. Heat the butter in a large skillet. Add mushrooms and onions; cook about 5 minutes, turning occasionally. Add to the meat and sauce along with the Burgundy; mix well.
5. Transfer to a chafing dish for buffet service. Garnish with a border of finely snipped *parsley.* Or, if prepared a day or two in advance of serving, cool, cover tightly, and store in refrigerator.

ABOUT 8 SERVINGS

PAPRIKA CREAM SCHNITZEL

1½ lbs. veal round steak (cutlet), cut about ½ in. thick	1½ teaspoons salt
	1 teaspoon paprika
	1 cup dairy sour cream
4 slices bacon, diced	½ cup tomato sauce
2 tablespoons chopped onion	Shupp Noodles, *page 293*

1. Cut meat into serving-sized pieces; set aside.
2. Cook bacon until crisp in a large heavy skillet. With slotted spoon, remove bacon to a small dish, leaving the fat in skillet.
3. Put meat and onion into skillet; brown meat on both sides. Sprinkle with a mixture of the salt and paprika. Spoon a blend of the sour cream and tomato sauce over meat. Cover skillet. Cook over low heat about 20 minutes (do not boil).
4. Turn noodles onto a heated serving platter and put sauced meat on noodles. Top with reserved bacon pieces.   4 TO 6 SERVINGS

DON QUIXOTE HORCHER

A favorite at Horcher's famous Madrid restaurant.

½ teaspoon salt	⅓ cup flour
¼ teaspoon pepper	Butter
4 veal scallops, trimmed (about 1¾ lbs.)	4 bananas
	Cream Sauce, *page 203*
	Grapes or orange sections
2 eggs, fork beaten	

1. Sprinkle salt and pepper over meat. Dip each veal scallop in egg, then coat with flour.
2. Sauté each scallop quickly in 1 tablespoon hot butter in skillet until golden brown on both sides. Remove to heated platter and keep warm.
3. Peel and halve each banana lengthwise. Sauté

quickly in 1 tablespoon butter in the skillet until lightly browned on both sides.

4. Prepare Cream Sauce and add grapes.

5. To serve, place 2 banana halves on each veal scallop. Serve the sauce separately. Accompany with *saffron rice*.   4 SERVINGS

CREAM SAUCE: Blend *¼ cup flour* into *½ cup butter or margarine*, heated, in a heavy saucepan. Cook and stir until bubbly. Mix in *2 cups chicken broth* and bring rapidly to boiling, stirring constantly; cook 1 to 2 minutes. Vigorously stir about 3 tablespoons of the hot sauce into *4 fork-beaten egg yolks*. Immediately blend into mixture in saucepan. Cook over low heat 3 to 5 minutes, stirring constantly. Blend in *¼ cup butter or margarine*.

ABOUT 2 CUPS SAUCE

VEAL PAPRIKA

8 slices bacon, diced	½ teaspoon mono-
½ cup chopped onion	sodium glutamate
¼ cup chopped green	⅓ cup hot water
pepper	Spaetzle I, *below*
1½ teaspoons paprika	1 tablespoon fat
1½ lbs. boneless veal	1 tablespoon flour
shoulder, cut in	1½ to 2 teaspoons
1-in. cubes	paprika
¼ cup flour	½ cup milk
1 teaspoon salt	1 cup dairy sour cream

1. Put the bacon, onion, green pepper, and paprika into a large heavy skillet. Cook slowly until bacon and onion are lightly browned, stirring occasionally.

2. Meanwhile, coat meat evenly with a mixture of the ¼ cup flour, salt, and monosodium glutamate.

3. With a slotted spoon, remove bacon mixture to a small dish; set aside. Put meat into the skillet and brown on all sides in the hot bacon drippings. Return bacon mixture to skillet. Stir in the hot water. Cover and simmer 45 to 60 minutes, or until meat is tender, turning meat occasionally and adding small amounts of hot water as needed.

4. While veal is cooking, prepare Spaetzle I.

5. Shortly before veal is tender, heat the fat in a small saucepan. Blend in the 1 tablespoon flour and paprika. Heat until bubbly. Stir in milk. Bring rapidly to boiling, stirring constantly, cook 1 to 2 minutes. Remove from heat. Stirring vigorously with a wire whip, add sour cream in very small amounts.

6. When veal is tender, pour sauce into skillet. Cook mixture over low heat, stirring constantly, 3

to 5 minutes, or until thoroughly heated (do not boil). Serve with the hot Spaetzle.   4 TO 6 SERVINGS

SPAETZLE I

Spaetzle are small tender "drop" noodles often served with veal dishes.

1 egg, slightly beaten	1 teaspoon salt
1 cup water	¼ cup butter or
2 to 2¼ cups all-purpose	margarine, melted
flour	

1. Mix egg and water in a bowl. Gradually add a mixture of the flour and salt, beating until smooth. (Batter should be very thick and break from a spoon instead of pouring in a continuous stream.)

2. Spoon batter into boiling *salted water* (2 quarts water and 2 teaspoons salt) by ½ teaspoonfuls, dipping spoon into water each time. Cook only one layer of noodles at one time; do not crowd.

3. After noodles rise to the surface, boil gently 5 to 8 minutes, or until soft when pressed against sides of pan with spoon. Remove from water with a slotted spoon, draining over water for a second and place in a hot bowl.

4. Toss noodles lightly with the melted butter.

4 TO 6 SERVINGS

VEAL VIENNESE WITH SOUR CREAM

2 slices (about 1½ lbs.)	¼ cup butter or
veal round steak	margarine
¼ cup flour	2 cups soft bread
1 teaspoon salt	crumbs
1 teaspoon paprika	½ cup grated Parmesan
½ teaspoon poultry	cheese
seasoning	½ cup water
¼ teaspoon pepper	1 can (10½ oz.) con-
¼ cup fat	densed cream of
1 can (16 oz.) small	chicken soup
whole onions,	1 cup dairy sour cream
drained	¼ teaspoon seasoned
2 tablespoons sesame	salt
seed	

1. Coat meat with a mixture of the flour, salt, paprika, poultry seasoning, and pepper. Pound meat on one side with a meat hammer. Turn and repeat process until flour mixture is well pounded in and meat is about ¼ inch thick.

2. Brown meat on both sides in hot fat in a large skillet. Transfer meat to a 1½-quart shallow baking dish. Put onions into dish; set aside.

3. Lightly brown sesame seed in the hot butter in the skillet, stirring frequently. Add bread crumbs and stir until well coated. Remove from heat and add cheese; toss until well mixed. Spoon over the meat. Pour in water.

4. Bake at 350°F 1 hour, or until meat is tender. If necessary, add more water during baking.

5. When meat is almost tender, heat the soup to boiling in a saucepan. Stirring constantly, gradually add the sour cream. Mix in seasoned salt. Heat (do not boil). Serve with the veal.   5 OR 6 SERVINGS

EMBASSY VEAL GLACÉ

1½ teaspoons dry tarragon leaves	3 tablespoons butter or margarine
1 cup dry white wine	½ teaspoon salt
1½ lbs. veal round steak, about ¼ in. thick	⅛ teaspoon pepper
	½ cup condensed consommé
	½ cup dry vermouth

1. Stir tarragon into white wine; cover and set aside several hours, stirring occasionally.

2. Cut meat into pieces about 3x2 inches. Heat butter in skillet until lightly browned. Add meat and lightly brown on both sides; season with salt and pepper.

3. Reduce heat and pour in tarragon-wine mixture with the consommé and vermouth. Simmer, uncovered, about 10 minutes, or until veal is tender.

4. Remove veal to a heated chafing dish and cover.

5. Increase heat under skillet and cook sauce until it is reduced to a thin glaze, stirring occasionally. Pour over meat, turning meat once.

6. Serve at once.   ABOUT 6 SERVINGS

VEAL BIRDS WITH MUSHROOM STUFFING

2 lbs. veal round steak, about ½ in. thick	1 tablespoon chopped onion
1 teaspoon salt	1 cup soft bread crumbs
¼ teaspoon pepper	¼ cup milk
2 slices bacon, diced	2 tablespoons fat
1 cup chopped fresh mushrooms	½ cup water

1. Pound meat on both sides on a flat working surface with meat hammer; cut into 6 serving-size pieces. Season with a mixture of salt and pepper.

2. Cook bacon in skillet until lightly browned; remove with slotted spoon.

3. Add mushrooms and onion to bacon fat in skillet and cook about 5 minutes.

4. Lightly toss mushrooms, onion, and bacon with bread crumbs; add milk and mix lightly.

5. Spoon some of stuffing onto each piece of veal; roll meat around stuffing and fasten securely with skewer or wooden picks.

6. Heat fat in a large heavy skillet; add the veal rolls and brown on all sides. Transfer rolls to a 2-quart casserole; add the water; cover.

7. Bake at 350°F about 1 hour, or until meat is tender when pierced with a fork. If desired, thicken drippings for gravy.   6 SERVINGS

VEAL OR LAMB IN DILL

Scandia, a Hollywood, California, restaurant, serves this family-style dish with Scandinavian overtones.

2 lbs. boneless lean veal (or boneless lamb for stew)	3 tablespoons flour
1 teaspoon salt	2 to 3 tablespoons white vinegar
1 carrot	2 to 3 tablespoons sugar
1 onion	Pinch salt
1 sprig fresh dill, chopped	2 egg yolks
2 bay leaves	½ cup light cream
1½ tablespoons butter or margarine	Chopped fresh dill (or dried dill weed)

1. Add enough water to just cover meat in a heavy saucepot. Add salt, carrot, onion, dill, and bay leaves. Bring to boiling; skim off foam. Cover, reduce heat and simmer until meat is just tender. Remove meat with slotted spoon and keep hot. Strain liquid and set aside for the gravy.

2. Heat butter in the saucepan. Blend in flour and heat until bubbly, stirring constantly. Stir in enough of the strained broth to make a gravy. Cook and stir about 8 minutes. Season to taste with the vinegar, sugar, and salt.

3. Combine egg yolks with cream and blend thoroughly. Stir in about 3 tablespoons of the hot mixture and add to mixture in saucepan. Cook and stir several minutes longer. Add chopped dill and meat and heat thoroughly.

4. Serve with *boiled potatoes.*   ABOUT 6 SERVINGS

VEAL TARRAGON

1½ lbs. veal steak, cut ¼ in. thick	½ lb. fresh mushrooms, sliced
½ cup all-purpose flour	½ cup chopped onion
1½ teaspoons salt	1 cup water
½ teaspoon black pepper	1 can (14½ oz.) evaporated milk
1 teaspoon crushed tarragon leaves	¼ cup snipped parsley
6 tablespoons butter	12 oz. green noodles, cooked and buttered

1. Trim bone and excess fat from veal and discard. Cut veal into 1½-inch-square pieces. Coat pieces with a mixture of the flour, salt, pepper, and tarragon. Reserve remaining flour mixture.
2. Heat butter in a large skillet; add mushrooms and cook over medium heat until lightly browned, turning occasionally. Remove mushrooms and set aside.
3. Add veal and onion to skillet; cook over medium heat until onion is soft and meat is lightly browned. Add water, cover, and reduce heat; simmer for 30 minutes, or until meat is tender.
4. Stir reserved flour into skillet; heat until mixture bubbles. Remove from heat and add evaporated milk gradually, stirring constantly. Cook over low heat, stirring occasionally, until thickened. Add mushrooms and heat well. Stir in parsley.
5. Serve over the cooked noodles and accompany with *Glazed Oranges, page 386.* 4 TO 6 SERVINGS

MANICARETTI ALLA LUCREZIA BORGIA

These ham and asparagus stuffed veal rolls are from "Al Doro" Bar Restaurant, Tavola Calda, Ferrara, Italy.

6 slices (1½ lbs.) boneless veal cutlet	2 tablespoons butter
1 teaspoon salt	⅓ cup finely chopped parsley
¼ teaspoon black pepper	2 cloves garlic, crushed
6 slices prosciutto	3½ oz. dried mushrooms, hydrated (soaked in water)
6 slices Emmenthaler cheese	
6 white asparagus spears, 4 in. long	¼ cup beef gravy
¼ cup butter	3 cups cream
½ cup port wine	1 teaspoon salt

1. Pound veal cutlets until thin. Season with salt and pepper.
2. Place a slice of prosciutto, then a slice of cheese and an asparagus spear over each veal slice. Roll into fingers; skewer or secure with twine.
3. Melt the ¼ cup butter in a large heavy skillet. Add veal rolls; brown on all sides. Add port wine; cover and simmer about 10 minutes.
4. Meanwhile, melt the 2 tablespoons butter in a saucepan. Add and lightly brown the parsley and garlic. Mix in the mushrooms, beef gravy, and cream; simmer 5 minutes. Pour sauce over veal rolls; correct seasoning, using the remaining 1 teaspoon salt. Cover and simmer until meat is tender.
6 SERVINGS

ONE-COOK CASSEROLE
A favorite from down under — Adelaide, Australia.

2 lbs. veal cutlets	1 teaspoon brown sugar
1½ tablespoons flour	½ teaspoon paprika
½ teaspoon salt	½ teaspoon salt
3 tablespoons butter	⅛ teaspoon pepper
4 teaspoons flour	½ clove garlic, crushed
1¼ cups chicken broth	2 tablespoons sherry
½ teaspoon mustard	1 cup chopped onion
1½ teaspoons grated lemon peel	4 medium potatoes, pared and sliced wafer-thin
1 teaspoon meat extract	

1. Rub cutlets with a mixture of 1½ tablespoons flour and salt.
2. Heat 2 tablespoons of the butter in a skillet; add cutlets and brown on both sides; place in a 2-quart casserole; keep warm.
3. In the skillet, heat the remaining 1 tablespoon butter; stir in the 4 teaspoons flour; heat until flour is browned. Add broth and cook over medium heat, stirring constantly until thickened and smooth. Stir in mustard, lemon peel, meat extract, brown sugar, paprika, salt, pepper, garlic, and sherry.
4. Sprinkle chopped onions over veal cutlets in casserole; cover with layer of thinly sliced potatoes; pour prepared gravy over potatoes.
5. Cover and bake at 300°F 1½ to 2 hours.
6. Serve with *baked tomato halves* sprinkled with *chopped chives or parsley.* 4 SERVINGS

VEAL EPICUREAN

1 tablespoon olive oil
1 tablespoon butter or
  margarine
2 lbs. veal steak
  (cutlets), cut in
  2x½-in. strips
2 tablespoons flour
¾ teaspoon salt
⅛ teaspoon pepper
1 cup chicken broth

1 cup dry white wine
1 lb. small white
  onions, peeled
12 sprigs parsley,
  chopped
1 bay leaf
½ lb. small fresh
  mushrooms
3 tablespoons butter
  or margarine

1.   Heat olive oil and butter in a heavy skillet. Add meat and brown on all sides. Remove from skillet to a 1¼-quart casserole having a cover; set aside.
2.   Stir a mixture of flour, salt, and pepper into drippings in skillet. Add the broth gradually, blending thoroughly. Bring rapidly to boiling, stirring constantly; cook 1 to 2 minutes; remove from heat.
3.   Blend in wine, onions, and parsley. Pour over veal in casserole; add bay leaf.
4.   Cover and bake at 325°F about 1 hour, or until meat is tender.
5.   Cook mushrooms in the 3 tablespoons butter about 5 minutes. Add to casserole and bake about 15 minutes longer.
6.   Serve with fluffy *cooked rice* garnished with *chopped green onion*.   6 TO 8 SERVINGS

VARIETY MEATS

LIVER AND ONIONS, ITALIAN STYLE

1½ lbs. beef liver,
  sliced about ¼ to ½
  in. thick
½ cup flour
1 teaspoon salt

½ teaspoon mono-
  sodium glutamate
⅛ teaspoon pepper
2 onions, thinly sliced
⅓ cup olive oil
½ cup Marsala

1.   If necessary, remove tubes and membrane from liver; cut liver into serving-sized pieces.
2.   Coat liver with a mixture of flour, salt, monosodium glutamate, and pepper; set aside.
3.   Cook onions until tender in hot oil in a large skillet. Remove onions and add liver. Brown on both sides over medium heat.
4.   Return onions to skillet; add the wine. Bring to boiling and cook 1 minute. Serve at once.

4 OR 5 SERVINGS

LIVER IN WINE SAUCE

1 lb. liver (veal or
  calf's)
⅓ cup flour
1 teaspoon salt
½ teaspoon paprika
Few grains pepper

3 tablespoons butter
  or margarine
1 small clove garlic,
  minced
½ cup sherry or
  sauterne
¾ cup dairy sour cream

1.   If necessary, remove tubes and membrane from liver. Cut liver into strips about ½ inch wide. Coat with a mixture of the flour, salt, paprika, and pepper.
2.   Heat butter and garlic in a large skillet; cook liver until browned on all sides, about 3 minutes. Remove liver to a heated platter and keep hot.
3.   Add wine to skillet and stir until wine dissolves all pan residue. Remove from heat. With a French whip, whisk beater, or fork, vigorously stir sour cream, a small amount at a time, into hot mixture. Heat thoroughly (do not boil).
4.   Return strips to sauce and toss lightly; serve at once. If desired, garnish with chopped *parsley* and serve with *noodles*.   4 SERVINGS

LIVER ON SKEWERS
(Leberspiessli)

A favorite recipe from Gusti Egli's Columna-Treu Restaurant in Zurich, Switzerland.

1 lb. calf's liver (cut
  into strips 1½ in.
  long and ¼ in. thick)
½ teaspoon crushed
  black pepper

1 tablespoon crushed
  dried sage leaves
½ lb. bacon (about 12
  slices)

1.   Season liver strips with pepper and sage.
2.   Cut bacon slices into halves or thirds. Wrap a piece of bacon around each piece of liver. Thread onto two or three 6-inch skewers, using 5 or 6 bacon-wrapped pieces of liver for each skewer.
3.   Brown skewers on all sides in a generous amount of *butter* in a skillet. Sprinkle with *salt* to taste. Serve immediately.   2 OR 3 SERVINGS
NOTE: Liver pieces on skewers may be brushed

with *melted butter*, if desired, and broiled, turning occasionally to brown evenly.

CALF'S LIVER ON SKEWERS, ZURICH STYLE
(Brochette de Foie de Veau Zurichoise)
Veltliner - Keller, another famous Swiss restaurant in Zurich, serves this version of liver on skewers.

Season chunks of *calf's liver* with *salt* and *pepper*, place sprigs of *fresh sage* on each piece and roll a strip of *bacon* around each. Spear 6 or 7 pieces on each skewer, brush the pieces with *melted butter*, and grill under a broiler or over an open fire. Serve these on a plate with *cooked green beans, new potatoes with parsley*, and garnish with *lemon slices* and *watercress*. Serve with *red wine*, if desired.

STUFFED CALF'S LIVER DE LUXE

1 calf's liver (2 to 3 lbs.)	½ teaspoon black pepper
Stuffing, *below*	3 strips salt pork
½ cup flour	(about 8 oz.)
½ teaspoon salt	½ cup water

1.   Rinse the liver quickly in cold water; drain thoroughly on absorbent paper. Remove membrane.
2.   Make a horizontal incision in the thickest side; lightly fill with Stuffing; fasten with skewers.
3.   Coat liver with a mixture of the flour, salt, and pepper. Place on rack in a roasting pan and arrange strips of salt pork on top. Pour water into the pan.
4.   Bake at 350°F 1½ to 2 hours. Remove to heated serving platter and serve immediately.

ABOUT 12 SERVINGS

STUFFING: Soak *4 slices white bread* in *cold water* and squeeze out all excess moisture. Using a fork, fluff bread and drizzle *2 tablespoons melted butter* over bread. Blend into *1 slightly beaten egg*, a mixture of *1 teaspoon salt*, *⅛ teaspoon black pepper*, and *¼ teaspoon poultry seasoning*, then *1 teaspoon chopped parsley* and *1 teaspoon grated onion*. Add egg mixture to bread mixture and toss lightly until thoroughly mixed.

CALF'S LIVER MATIUS
A popular dish served at the famous Forum of the Twelve Caesars, New York City.

1 onion, minced	2 lbs. calf's liver,
1 clove garlic, minced	cut in 2½-inch strips
¼ teaspoon tarragon	2 tablespoons butter
1 cup dry white wine	⅓ cup applejack (apple
1 cup Brown Sauce Espagnole, *below*	brandy)

1.   Mix onion, garlic, and tarragon with the wine in a saucepan. Cook the mixture until the liquid is reduced to about half its original volume. Stir in the Brown Sauce Espagnole and heat thoroughly.
2.   In a skillet or chafing dish, sauté the liver strips in heated butter about 3 minutes, turning occasionally. The liver should be well browned outside but still pink inside.
3.   Warm the applejack, ignite it and pour over the liver strips. When the flame dies, pour the sauce over the liver. Accompany the liver with *Forum's Gnocchi, page 138.*

ABOUT 8 SERVINGS

BROWN SAUCE ESPAGNOLE

½ cup beef, veal, or pork drippings	1 stalk celery
	3 sprigs parsley
1 small carrot, coarsely chopped	1 clove garlic, crushed
2 onions, coarsely chopped	1 small bay leaf
	1 pinch thyme
½ cup all-purpose flour	¼ cup tomato purée or
8 cups hot Beef Stock, *page 46*	tomato sauce

1.   Put drippings in a heavy saucepot; add carrot and onion and cook until onion starts to turn golden, shaking the pan to insure even cooking. Blend in the flour; cook and stir until flour and vegetables are a rich brown.
2.   Add 3 cups beef stock gradually, stirring constantly; add celery, parsley, garlic, bay leaf, and thyme. Cook and stir until sauce thickens.
3.   Add 3 cups stock and simmer slowly 1 to 1½ hours, or until sauce is reduced to 3 cups; stir occasionally. Skim off fat as it rises to surface.
4.   Add tomato purée, cook several minutes longer and strain through a fine sieve.
5.   Add 2 more cups of stock and cook slowly 1 hour longer, skimming the surface occasionally. Continue cooking until reduced to about 4 cups.
6.   Cool sauce, stirring occasionally. Store in a

covered container in refrigerator. If not used within a few days, store in freezer. 1 QUART SAUCE

LIVER À LA MADAME BEGUE

1 lb. calf's liver, cut in 1-in. cubes	2 small onions, thinly sliced
1 teaspoon salt	3 large sprigs parsley
Few grains pepper	Fat for deep frying heated to 390°F

1. Sprinkle liver with salt and pepper. Put into a bowl; cover with onion and parsley. Cover and refrigerate 2 hours.
2. Fry in the heated fat 40 to 60 seconds. Drain over fat for a few seconds before removing. Serve immediately garnished with *lemon wedges* and *parsley*, if desired. 4 SERVINGS

PICKLED FRESH TONGUE

1 fresh beef tongue, 3 to 4 lbs.	1 tablespoon salt
2 tablespoons cider vinegar	4 whole cloves
	3 bay leaves

1. Wash tongue thoroughly and place in a large kettle. Add water to cover and remaining ingredients. Simmer, covered, 3 to 4 hours, or until tender.
2. Slit skin on underside of tongue and peel it off. Cut away roots and gristle. Return to liquid and cool completely. Drain and refrigerate until ready to slice and serve. ABOUT 12 SERVINGS

BEEF TONGUE WITH TOMATO SAUCE

1 fresh beef tongue, 3 to 4 lbs.	2 cans (6 oz. each) tomato paste
1 tablespoon salt	1 can (10¾ oz.) condensed tomato soup
2 or 3 bay leaves	½ to ¾ cup water
1 stalk celery with leaves, cut in pieces	¼ to ½ teaspoon thyme
1 small onion	1 pkg. (8 oz.) noodles, cooked and drained
1 teaspoon peppercorns	

1. Wash tongue and put into a 4-quart kettle. Add water to cover, salt, bay leaves, celery, onion, and peppercorns. Cover and simmer about 1 hour per pound, or until tongue is tender.
2. Place tongue on a platter. When cool enough to handle, remove skin; cut away roots, gristle, and

small bone at thick end. Diagonally cut tongue into ¼-inch slices. Put slices into a large heavy skillet and set aside.
3. Combine tomato paste, soup, water, and thyme; mix thoroughly and pour over tongue. Cover and heat about 20 minutes.
4. Serve tongue and sauce with noodles.
ABOUT 12 SERVINGS

TONGUE AND GREENS

1 fresh veal or beef tongue	½ cup heavy cream
4 slices bacon, pan-broiled (reserve 2 teaspoons drippings)	1 tablespoon prepared horseradish
¼ cup finely chopped onion	Few grains pepper
2 lbs. greens (spinach, chard, or beet tops), cooked and chopped	½ cup buttered bread crumbs
	½ teaspoon grated lemon peel

1. Wash tongue and cook about 2 hours (see *Beef Tongue with Tomato Sauce, above*).
2. When tongue is cool enough to handle, slit skin on underside and peel it off. Cut away roots and gristle. Slice tongue diagonally. Line bottom and sides of a greased 1½-quart casserole with tongue slices; set aside.
3. Put the reserved bacon drippings into a large skillet. Add onion and cook until tender, stirring occasionally. Crumble bacon and combine with onion, greens, cream, horseradish, and pepper. Lightly pile into tongue-lined casserole. Sprinkle a mixture of bread crumbs and lemon peel over top.
4. Heat in a 350°F oven 25 minutes, or until crumbs are browned. 6 SERVINGS

SWEETBREADS AUX CAPRES
A specialty de la maison of the Mill on the Floss, a 172-year old American inn with a French accent located in New Ashford, Massachusetts.

5 lbs. sweetbreads, rinsed in cold water	1 medium-sized onion, quartered
2 cups dry white wine	2 stalks celery
1 to 2 tablespoons mixed pickling spices	1 tablespoon salt
	1 heaping teaspoon capers

1. Put sweetbreads into a heavy casserole. Cover with water. Add wine, pickling spices, onion, cel-

ery, and salt. Poach gently until quite firm, about 1½ hours. Chill.

2.   Separate sweetbreads into bite-size pieces, dust with *flour*, *salt*, and *pepper*, and sauté in *butter* until golden brown and a little crisp. Remove from pan to a warm plate.

3.   Add capers and a *few drops lemon juice* to butter in pan. Pour sauce over sweetbreads. Garnish with fresh *watercress*.   10 TO 15 SERVINGS

NOTE: The strained broth makes excellent stock for lima bean, mushroom, or barley soup.

CREAMED HAM AND SWEETBREADS
When planning a bridal shower luncheon for 20 to 24 people, consider this for the main course.

2 lbs. sweetbreads, rinsed with cold water	6 cups strong chicken broth
2 qts. water	2 cups cream
4 teaspoons lemon juice	4 cups cubed cooked ham
2 teaspoons salt	1 ripe avocado, peeled and cut in cubes
1 lb. fresh mushrooms, sliced	1 cup quartered ripe olives
¼ cup chopped onion	½ cup snipped parsley
1 cup butter or margarine	2 pimientos, cut in strips
¾ cup flour	2 tablespoons drained capers
1 teaspoon celery salt	Baked puff pastry patty shells
1 teaspoon savory, crushed	
⅛ teaspoon cayenne pepper	

1.   Put the sweetbreads, water, lemon juice, and salt into a large saucepot. Cover, bring to boiling, reduce heat, and simmer 20 minutes.

2.   Drain and cover with cold water. Change water repeatedly until sweetbreads are cool. Drain. Remove tubes and membranes. Cut sweetbreads into bite-size pieces and refrigerate until ready to use. (Sweetbreads should be cooked as soon as possible after purchase.)

3.   Cook mushrooms and onion in hot butter or margarine in a large heavy saucepot or Dutch oven, stirring frequently until onion is soft and mushrooms are tender, about 5 minutes. With a slotted spoon, remove mushrooms, allowing butter to drain back into pan. Set mushrooms aside.

4.   Blend a mixture of flour, celery salt, savory, and cayenne pepper into hot butter in the sauce pot; heat until bubbly. Gradually add the chicken broth, stirring constantly; bring rapidly to boiling. Cook 2 minutes longer, stirring constantly.

5.   Stir in the cream, sweetbreads, mushrooms, ham, avocado, olives, parsley, pimientos, and capers. Heat the mixture thoroughly, stirring occasionally.

6.   Spoon sauce into warm patty shells. Replace top of shell and top with a sprig of *watercress*.

20 TO 24 SERVINGS

SWEETBREADS WESTOBER
Epicureans will appreciate this delightful dish—a favorite of Philip Ober, Hollywood personality.

2 lbs. sweetbreads	¼ lb. fresh mushrooms, rinsed and chopped
1 cup dry white wine (or 1 tablespoon vinegar)	1 tablespoon flour
3 tablespoons butter	½ cup hot water
1 green pepper, finely chopped	½ cup dry white wine
2 stalks celery, finely chopped	1 teaspoon salt
1 onion, finely chopped	½ teaspoon monosodium glutamate
1 small carrot, finely chopped	½ teaspoon fresh or dried crumbled marjoram
	¼ cup chopped pimiento

1.   Rinse sweetbreads; place in saucepan with a small amount of water and 1 cup wine. *Salt* the liquid slightly. Cover and simmer 15 minutes.

2.   Drain sweetbreads; cool. Remove membrane and tubes; separate into small pieces.

3.   Heat 1 tablespoon of the butter in a skillet; add green pepper, celery, onion, and carrot; cook over low heat until vegetables are tender; remove from skillet and set aside.

4.   Heat 1 tablespoon butter in the skillet; add mushrooms and cook slowly until tender.

5.   In a heavy saucepan, heat remaining butter; blend in flour and heat until bubbly. Remove from heat. Stirring constantly, add the hot water and ½ cup wine. Cook over medium heat until sauce thickens; cook and stir 1 minute longer.

6.   Pour sauce into top of double boiler; stir in salt, monosodium glutamate, marjoram, sweetbreads, vegetables, mushrooms, and pimiento. Place double boiler top over simmering water; heat thoroughly.   4 TO 6 SERVINGS

NOTE: For extra tenderness and delicate flavor, purchase veal sweetbreads when available.

CREAMED SWEETBREADS

1 qt. water
1 tablespoon lemon
  juice
1 teaspoon salt
1 lb. sweetbreads
½ lb. fresh mushrooms,
  sliced lengthwise
¼ cup butter
1 tablespoon chopped
  onion
⅓ cup butter
½ cup flour
¾ teaspoon salt

½ teaspoon savory
½ teaspoon celery salt
Few grains white
  pepper
1 cup chicken broth,
  cooled
2 cups milk
1 cup cream
1 cup cooked chicken
  pieces
1 pkg. (9 oz.) frozen
  green beans, cooked
  and drained

1. In a large saucepan, combine water, lemon juice, and salt. Add sweetbreads, cover and bring to boiling; lower heat and simmer 20 minutes. Drain, cool and remove membrane; cut sweetbreads into pieces and refrigerate.
2. Lightly brown the mushrooms in ¼ cup butter in a heavy skillet; set aside.
3. Cook onion about 5 minutes in ⅓ cup butter in a saucepan over low heat. Stir in a mixture of the flour, salt, savory, celery salt, and white pepper; heat until mixture bubbles. Gradually add chicken broth, milk, and cream, stirring constantly. Bring rapidly to boiling, stirring constantly; cook 1 to 2 minutes longer.
4. Gently mix in the sweetbreads, chicken, green beans, and mushrooms. Continue cooking over low heat until thoroughly heated; stir occasionally.
5. Turn into chafing dish and keep hot over the pan of simmering water.   6 TO 8 SERVINGS

HERBED LAMB KIDNEYS IN RICE RING

¾ cup butter or
  margarine
1 clove garlic,
  crushed
½ lb. fresh mushrooms,
  sliced lengthwise
1 large onion, sliced
¼ teaspoon salt
⅛ teaspoon pepper

3 to 4 tablespoons
  lemon juice
1 tablespoon crushed
  rosemary
12 lamb kidneys, cut
  in half lengthwise
  and trimmed
Parsley Rice Ring,
  below

1. Heat butter in a large skillet. Add garlic, mushrooms, onion, salt, and pepper; cook until mushrooms and onion are lightly browned, stirring occasionally. Remove vegetables; keep warm.

2. Mix lemon juice and rosemary into butter remaining in skillet. Add kidneys and cook about 10 minutes, or until kidneys are tender but still slightly pink in center; turn frequently.
3. Return vegetables to the skillet and mix lightly with the kidneys. Spoon into center of rice ring. Serve remaining sauce in a gravy boat.
6 TO 8 SERVINGS

PARSLEY RICE RING: Bring *4 cups chicken broth* to boiling; add *2 cups uncooked rice* and *2 teaspoons salt.* Cover and cook over low heat for about 25 minutes, or until rice is tender and liquid is absorbed. Stir *¼ cup butter* and *½ cup snipped parsley* into the cooked rice until well blended. Pack into a lightly buttered 5½-cup ring mold. Let stand 10 minutes; unmold onto a warm serving plate.

BEEF AND KIDNEY PIE

1 beef kidney
½ cup French dressing
1 lb. boneless lean
  beef for stew, cut
  in 1-in. pieces
⅔ cup all-purpose flour
1½ teaspoons salt
¼ teaspoon pepper
¼ teaspoon paprika
¼ cup chopped onion
3 tablespoons fat
2 cans (10¾ oz. each)
  condensed tomato soup
1 cup hot water

1 tablespoon Worcester-
  shire sauce
¼ teaspoon basil,
  crushed
1 bay leaf
1 pkg. (10 oz.) frozen
  green peas
Pastry for a 1-crust
  pie
1 can (8 oz.) mush-
  rooms, drained
3 tablespoons butter
  or margarine

1. Remove membrane from kidney and cut kidney lengthwise through center. Remove skin, white tubes, and fat. Thoroughly rinse kidney with cold water. Cut into ¾- to 1-inch cubes. Put cubes into a bowl and pour dressing over all. Turn each piece to coat. Cover and marinate at least 1 hour, turning pieces occasionally.
2. Meanwhile, coat beef pieces with a mixture of the flour, salt, pepper, and paprika.
3. Drain kidney pieces and add along with beef and onion to hot fat in a top-of-range casserole. Brown meat on all sides.
4. Stir in soup, water, Worcestershire sauce, and basil. Add more hot water if needed to cover meat. Add bay leaf. Cover; simmer 45 minutes.
5. Mix in the frozen peas and continue simmering 15 to 45 minutes, or until meat is tender.

6. Prepare pastry and roll into a round about ⅛ inch thick and larger than overall size of casserole top. Fold in quarters; with a knife make slits near center to allow steam to escape; set aside.

7. Heat mushrooms about 5 minutes in hot butter in a small saucepan, stirring constantly.

8. When meat is tender, remove bay leaf. Stir in mushrooms. If necessary, thicken liquid.

9. Moisten rim of casserole with cold water. Lift pastry gently and unfold over hot mixture in casserole. Fold extra pastry under at edge and gently press to rim of casserole to seal. Flute edge.

10. Bake at 425°F 15 to 20 minutes, or until pastry is lightly browned. 6 SERVINGS

KIDNEY IN PORT WINE

Here's a specialty of Var (Provence), a part of France memorable for its fine cooking, from Madam Hirsch, "La Paillote," Bandol, France.

1 veal kidney, about 1 lb.	¼ teaspoon salt
	Few grains pepper
2 tablespoons finely chopped onion	1 tablespoon port wine
	Buttered toast squares
1 tablespoon finely chopped parsley	(use 1 slice bread, crusts removed, for
½ teaspoon flour	4 toast squares)

1. Remove the membrane and hard parts from the kidney; cut kidney into small pieces. Put into a pan with onion and parsley; cook 10 minutes, stirring constantly.

2. Blend flour, salt, and pepper; add to kidney mixture; stir in the wine. Serve on toast squares. 1 OR 2 SERVINGS

LAMB 'N' KIDNEY GRILL

1. For lamb kidneys, remove membrane and split *kidneys* through centers. Using scissors, remove cores and tubes. Marinate kidneys 1 hour in *French dressing* or brush with *melted butter.* Broil about 5 minutes on each side, or until evenly browned. Season with *salt* and *pepper.*

2. For bacon curls, panbroil *bacon slices* until evenly browned. Remove one slice at a time from skillet and, using a fork, immediately roll into a curl; drain on absorbent paper.

3. For lamb chops, purchase *lamb chops* cut ¾ to 1 inch thick. Broil or panbroil to desired degree of doneness; season with *salt* and *pepper.*

4. To serve, arrange kidneys, bacon curls, and lamb chops in a shallow decorative baking dish and place dish over a warmer. Garnish with *broiled cherry tomatoes.*

TRIPE CREOLE

2 lbs. fresh tripe	6 tomatoes, peeled and coarsely chopped
2 onions, thinly sliced	
1 large clove garlic, minced	1 green pepper, thinly sliced
4 tablespoons butter or margarine	½ teaspoon thyme
	2 small bay leaves
¼ cup finely chopped lean ham	Few grains cayenne pepper

1. Wash the tripe thoroughly in cold water; drain. Put into a saucepan and add *salted water* to cover (1 teaspoon salt per 1 quart water). Bring to boiling, reduce heat and simmer, covered, about 5 hours, or until tender.

2. Drain tripe and cut into 2x½-inch strips.

3. Cook onion and garlic until golden in heated butter in a saucepan. Add remaining ingredients and season to taste. Bring to boiling and cook 10 minutes, stirring occasionally. Add tripe. Bring to boiling, cover and cook 30 minutes. 6 TO 8 SERVINGS

MIXED FRY
(Fritto Misto)

½ lb. brains	2 cups all-purpose flour
2 cups water	1 teaspoon salt
1½ teaspoons cider vinegar	¼ teaspoon pepper
½ teaspoon salt	6 canned-in-water artichoke hearts
½ lb. liver, cut about ½ in. thick	2 zucchini, cut crosswise in 1-in. slices
1½ cups milk	3 stalks celery, cut in 3 in. pieces
3 eggs, well beaten	Fat for deep frying
2 tablespoons melted shortening	heated to 360°F

1. Rinse brains in cold water. Simmer 20 minutes in a mixture of the water, vinegar, and salt in a saucepan. Drain brains, then cover with cold water. Drain again and remove membranes. Separate into small pieces and set aside.

2. Meanwhile, prepare liver and coat with flour mixture (see *Liver and Onions, Italian Style, page 206*). Cut liver into serving-size pieces; set aside.

3. Combine milk, eggs, and melted shortening in a bowl. Sift flour, salt, and pepper together and gradually add to milk mixture, beating until smooth. Dip vegetables and meat into batter.

4. Deep fry as many vegetables or pieces of meat as will float uncrowded one layer deep in the heated fat. Fry 5 minutes, or until golden, turning occasionally. Drain over fat before removing to absorbent paper. Serve on a hot platter.   6 SERVINGS

GLAZED STUFFED BEEF HEART

3- to 3½-lb. beef heart	3 tablespoons fat
¼ cup butter or margarine	1 cup finely chopped onion
¼ cup finely chopped onion	3 cups hot water
1 qt. soft bread crumbs	3 cups beef broth
1 tablespoon minced parsley	2 teaspoons salt
1 teaspoon poultry seasoning	¼ teaspoon pepper
¼ teaspoon salt	1 teaspoon celery salt
Few grains pepper	1 teaspoon marjoram
	½ cup red currant jelly
	1 tablespoon water
	Gravy, *below*

1. Cut arteries, veins, and any hard parts from beef heart; wash and set aside to drain.

2. Heat ¼ cup butter in a skillet; add ¼ cup chopped onion and cook until soft.

3. Turn contents of skillet into a large bowl containing a mixture of the bread crumbs, parsley, poultry seasoning, ¼ teaspoon salt, and few grains pepper; mix lightly. Stuff heart with the mixture and fasten with skewers; set aside.

4. Heat fat in a Dutch oven. Add 1 cup onion and cook until onion is soft; remove onion and set aside.

5. Put beef heart into the Dutch oven; brown lightly on all sides. Add water, beef broth, salt, pepper, celery salt, and cooked onion to Dutch oven. Bring liquid rapidly to boiling; reduce heat, cover and simmer 2½ to 3 hours, or until heart is tender. Mix in marjoram 15 minutes before end of cooking.

6. Heat jelly and water together over very low heat until jelly is melted, stirring occasionally.

7. Remove heart from liquid. Strain and reserve cooking liquid for gravy.

8. Brush beef heart with the jelly to glaze; serve with Gravy.   ABOUT 8 SERVINGS

GRAVY: Measure 3 cups of the reserved cooking liquid. Heat ⅓ *cup butter or margarine* in the Dutch oven. Blend in ⅓ *cup flour*. Heat until mixture bubbles and flour is lightly browned. Remove from heat and stir in the reserved cooking liquid and *2 teaspoons lemon juice*. Return to heat. Bring rapidly to boiling, stirring constantly, and cook until mixture thickens; cook 1 to 2 minutes longer.

HEART WITH APPLE-RAISIN DRESSING

2 lbs. heart	½ chopped onion
½ cup flour	½ cup packed brown sugar
2 teaspoons salt	½ cup seedless raisins
1 teaspoon monosodium glutamate	2 tablespoons water
½ teaspoon pepper	¼ cup fat or bacon drippings
3 tablespoons fat	1 qt. bread cubes
1 lemon, sliced	½ cup milk
8 whole cloves	2 tablespoons butter or margarine, melted
1 bay leaf	½ teaspoon salt
1 cup hot water	
3 tart apples, quartered, cored, pared, and diced	

1. Cut arteries, veins, and any hard parts from the heart. Wash and drain on absorbent paper. Cut heart into 1-inch cubes. Coat with a mixture of flour, salt, monosodium glutamate, and pepper.

2. Brown meat on all sides in 3 tablespoons hot fat in a 2-quart top-of-range casserole. Add lemon, cloves, bay leaf, and water; cover and simmer 1½ to 2½ hours, or until meat is tender. If necessary, add hot water during cooking. Drain meat; discard lemon, cloves, and bay leaf.

3. Meanwhile, mix apples, onion, brown sugar, raisins, and water into ¼ cup hot fat in a large skillet; cover and simmer 5 minutes, stirring once or twice.

4. Lightly toss together bread cubes, milk, butter, and salt. Add meat cubes and apple mixture; toss until mixed. Turn into the casserole.

5. Heat in a 350°F oven 15 to 20 minutes, or until browned.   ABOUT 6 SERVINGS

CANNED & READY-TO-EAT MEATS

CORNED BEEF-STUFFED CABBAGE

1 medium-sized head cabbage	1 teaspoon onion salt
1 can (12 oz.) corned beef	2 teaspoons cider vinegar
¾ cup cooked rice	3 or 4 drops Tabasco
3 tablespoons tomato sauce	2 whole cloves
	2 peppercorns
3 tablespoons chopped celery	1 bay leaf

1. Cut a ½-inch slice from the top of cabbage; reserve slice. Using a sharp knife and a spoon, cut and scoop out center of cabbage, leaving outer shell about ¾ inch thick. (Discard core; reserve cabbage pieces for use in other food preparation.)
2. Finely chop corned beef and put into a bowl. Lightly mix in the rice, tomato sauce, celery, onion salt, vinegar, and Tabasco. Press mixture into cabbage and place reserved slice on top.
3. Cut a square of cheesecloth (double thickness) large enough to wrap entire stuffed cabbage; tie the four corners securely.
4. Put into a large deep kettle. Add boiling water to just cover cabbage. Add *salt* (1 teaspoon per 1 quart water) and remaining ingredients. Cook 15 to 20 minutes, or until cabbage is tender. (Additional boiling water may be added to keep cabbage covered during cooking period.)
5. Remove cabbage from water and remove cheesecloth. Cut cabbage into serving-sized wedges and serve immediately.   6 SERVINGS

McGINTY'S CORNED BEEF LOAF

2 cans (12 oz. each) corned beef	2 teaspoons prepared mustard
¼ cup fine dry bread crumbs	¾ teaspoon garlic powder
1 can (6 oz.) evaporated milk	1 egg, beaten
2 tablespoons prepared horseradish	½ cup chopped pimiento-stuffed olives
	½ cup chopped celery

1. Finely chop corned beef; set aside.
2. Soften bread crumbs in evaporated milk. Blend in horseradish, mustard, and garlic powder. Add corned beef and remaining ingredients; mix lightly

but thoroughly. Pack into a 9x5x3-inch loaf pan.
3. Set in a 350°F oven about 40 minutes, or until thoroughly heated.
4. Unmold onto a warm serving platter.
                                            ABOUT 6 SERVINGS

HASH DISTINCTIVE

Add a few trimmings and corned beef hash is ready for a party.

1 can (about 16 oz.) corned beef hash, cut in 4 equal slices	1 tomato, cut in 4 slices
	½ teaspoon salt
4 teaspoons butter or margarine, melted	Few grains black pepper
2 teaspoons prepared horseradish	2 oz. sharp Cheddar cheese, shredded

1. Place hash slices on broiler rack; brush tops with one half of the melted butter.
2. Broil with top of meat 3 inches from source of heat 3 to 5 minutes, or until browned. Turn and spread tops thinly with horseradish; place 1 tomato slice on each.
3. Brush with remaining melted butter. Sprinkle with salt, pepper, and cheese. Broil about 5 minutes longer.   4 SERVINGS

CHEESE-TOPPED PEAS WITH HASH

1 can (about 16 oz.) corned beef hash	2 tablespoons flour
	¼ teaspoon salt
1 can (12 oz.) corned beef	⅛ teaspoon pepper
	1½ cups milk
½ cup shredded sharp Cheddar cheese	¼ cup instant minced onion
1 tablespoon prepared horseradish mustard	1 pkg. (10 oz.) frozen green peas
2 tablespoons butter or margarine	1 cup shredded sharp Cheddar cheese

1. Put corned beef hash and corned beef into a bowl; separate into pieces. Add the ½ cup cheese and the horseradish; mix lightly. Pile mixture diagonally across a baking dish; set aside.
2. Melt butter in a saucepan. Blend in a mixture of flour, salt, and pepper. Heat until bubbly, stirring constantly. Blend in milk and bring to boiling. Stir and cook 1 to 2 minutes. Mix in onion.

3.   Meanwhile, cook the peas following package directions. Add peas to sauce and spoon on either side of the corned beef mixture. Sprinkle 1 cup cheese evenly over the peas; mix lightly.

4.   Heat in a 325°F oven 20 minutes, or until corned beef mixture is lightly browned and cheese is melted. Garnish with *parsley*.   4 SERVINGS

BAKED LUNCHEON MEAT PATTIES

1 can (12 oz.) luncheon meat	¼ teaspoon paprika
½ cup soft bread crumbs	4 slices canned pineapple, drained (reserve ⅓ cup syrup)
¼ cup chopped nuts	
1 egg, fork beaten	2 tablespoons lemon juice
2 teaspoons brown sugar	
1 teaspoon dry mustard	2 tablespoons brown sugar

1.   Grind the luncheon meat and combine with the bread crumbs, nuts, egg, and a blend of 2 teaspoons brown sugar, dry mustard, and paprika.

2.   Lay the pineapple slices on the bottom of an 8-inch square baking dish. Shape meat mixture into 4 patties the same size as the pineapple slices. Put a patty on each slice. Mix pineapple syrup and remaining ingredients; spoon over patties.

3.   Bake at 350°F 35 to 40 minutes, basting patties with syrup several times during baking.   4 SERVINGS

LUNCHEON CUSTARD

¼ cup butter or margarine	6 oz. canned luncheon meat, ground
5 slices bread, toasted and cut in 1-in. cubes	2 eggs, slightly beaten
	1 tablespoon prepared mustard
1½ cups shredded Cheddar cheese	1 teaspoon Worcestershire sauce
	2 cups milk, scalded

1.   Melt the butter in a skillet. Add bread cubes and stir until cubes are coated on all sides. Remove from heat.

2.   Arrange a layer of cubes in the bottom of a greased 1½-quart casserole. Alternate layers of shredded cheese and remaining cubes. Top with the ground meat. Set aside.

3.   Mix eggs, mustard, and Worcestershire sauce. Gradually add the scalded milk, stirring until mix-

ture is blended. Pour over ingredients in casserole.

4.   Bake at 300°F 40 minutes, or until a metal knife comes out clean when inserted near center.

4 OR 5 SERVINGS

SKILLET LUNCHEON MEAT SURPRISE

1 can (8 oz.) tomato sauce	½ teaspoon Worcestershire sauce
1 can (about 16 oz.) sliced peaches, drained (reserve ¼ cup syrup)	¼ cup packed brown sugar
	1 teaspoon dry mustard
	½ teaspoon salt
2 tablespoons lemon juice	1 can (12 oz.) luncheon meat, cut in ¼-in. slices
1 to 2 tablespoons prepared horseradish	¼ cup thin sweet pickle slices

1.   In a large skillet combine the tomato sauce, peach syrup, lemon juice, horseradish, Worcestershire sauce, brown sugar, dry mustard, and salt. Bring to boiling. Cover and simmer 5 minutes.

2.   Add meat, peaches, and pickles to mixture in skillet; spoon sauce over all.

3.   Cover and simmer until thoroughly heated.

ABOUT 4 SERVINGS

BOLOGNA STEW

¾ lb. bologna	1 can (about 16 oz.) kidney beans, drained and rinsed
½ cup chopped onion	
½ clove garlic, minced	
3 tablespoons olive oil	1 can (about 16 oz.) whole kernel corn
¾ cup coarsely chopped pitted ripe olives	
	1 cup shredded Cheddar cheese
1 cup tomato juice	
1 teaspoon Worcestershire sauce	6 slices French bread
	¼ cup butter or margarine, softened
½ teaspoon celery salt	

1.   Cut bologna into ½-inch cubes and set aside.

2.   Cook onion and garlic until tender in hot oil in a saucepan, stirring occasionally. Mix in bologna, olives, tomato juice, seasonings, and vegetables.

3.   Increase heat and bring to boiling, stirring frequently. Remove from heat; add cheese and stir until melted. Divide mixture into 6 ramekins.

4.   Spread each slice of bread with about 2 teaspoons of the softened butter. Top each serving of stew with one of the slices.

5.   Set in a 350°F oven 20 to 25 minutes, or until bread is lightly browned.   6 SERVINGS

SPICY ORANGE-BOLOGNA ROLL

¼ cup packed brown
  sugar
¼ cup instant minced
  onion
¼ teaspoon dry mustard
⅛ teaspoon ground
  cloves
1 can (8 oz.) tomato
  sauce

1½ teaspoons grated
  orange peel
½ cup orange juice
½ cup water
¼ teaspoon Worcester-
  shire sauce
1½-lb. bologna roll

1.   In a heavy saucepan, mix the brown sugar, onion, dry mustard, and cloves. Add the tomato
sauce, orange peel and juice, water, and Worcestershire sauce; blend well. Bring to boiling, stirring
until sugar is dissolved; simmer, uncovered, about
15 minutes; stir occasionally.
2.   Meanwhile, score surface of bologna roll by
making diagonal cuts to form diamond pattern.
Place bologna in a shallow baking dish and pour
the hot sauce over it.
3.   Set in a 350°F oven 45 minutes, or until thoroughly heated, basting occasionally with sauce.

ABOUT 6 SERVINGS

APRICOT-GLAZED BOLOGNA

1 can (8¾ oz.) apricot
  halves
¼ cup crushed
  pineapple, drained
  (reserve syrup)
¼ cup honey
¼ cup packed light
  brown sugar
¼ teaspoon salt

Few grains white
  pepper
1 tablespoon cider
  vinegar
1 large clove garlic,
  quartered
1 piece (2½ lbs.)
  bologna roll (4¼ in.
  diameter)

1.   Purée apricots. Add enough reserved pineapple syrup to purée to make 1 cup. Pour into a
saucepan; stir in a mixture of the pineapple, honey,
brown sugar, salt, white pepper, and vinegar. Add
garlic pieces, speared on picks.
2.   Bring mixture rapidly to boiling, reduce heat to
medium and cook for 10 minutes, stirring occasionally. Remove garlic.
3.   Meanwhile, cut bologna diagonally into ¾-inch
slices, about one-half through the roll. Set on rack
in a shallow pan. Spoon about half of the apricot
sauce over bologna.
4.   Bake at 350°F about 45 minutes, or until bologna roll is heated through; spoon remaining sauce
over roll after about 25 minutes. ABOUT 10 SERVINGS

BOLOGNA CUPS

2 cups hot cooked rice
½ cup shredded sharp
  Cheddar cheese
½ cup condensed cream
  of celery soup
⅓ cup water

½ teaspoon grated
  onion
2 drops Tabasco
6 slices bologna, ⅛ in.
  thick

1.   Combine the rice, cheese, soup, water, onion,
and Tabasco in a bowl.
2.   Arrange bologna slices in a shallow baking
dish. (Edges of meat may touch, but should not
overlap.) Put about ⅓ cup of rice mixture in the
center of each bologna slice. Top each with a pimiento-stuffed olive slice.
3.   Place under broiler about 4 inches from source
of heat. Broil about 5 minutes, or until bologna
slices curl around filling. Serve immediately.

6 SERVINGS

SWEET-SOUR SAUSAGE

8 bratwurst or thu-
  ringer sausage links
1 medium-sized onion,
  chopped
2 tablespoons sausage
  drippings or other
  fat
2 tablespoons flour

1 cup hot water
2 tablespoons cider
  vinegar
2 tablespoons brown
  sugar
¼ teaspoon salt
⅛ teaspoon pepper

1.   Brown sausage and remove from skillet. Set
aside to keep warm.
2.   Cook onion in the sausage drippings until tender. Blend in flour. Heat until bubbly.
3.   Gradually add a mixture of remaining ingredients, stirring constantly. Bring to boiling; cook 1 to
2 minutes. Put sausages into the sauce and cook
over low heat 10 minutes, or until thoroughly
heated.   4 SERVINGS

SWEET 'N' HOT FRANKS

½ cup chopped onion
2 tablespoons butter
  or margarine
1 cup bottled barbecue
  sauce
¼ cup unsweetened
  pineapple juice

¼ cup chopped dill
  pickle
¼ cup sliced pimiento-
  stuffed olives
½ cup currant or rasp-
  berry jelly
1 lb. frankfurters

1.   Brown onion lightly in butter in a skillet. Mix

with remaining ingredients, except frankfurters.

2. Slash top of each frankfurter diagonally at 1-inch intervals. Place in sauce in a skillet. Simmer about 25 minutes, basting occasionally.

3. Split, butter, and toast *frankfurter buns*; place a frankfurter on each and top with sauce.

8 SERVINGS

KRAUT AND FRANKFURTER PLANK DINNER

The use of a plank is an attractive and convenient way to present a complete entrée with vegetable accompaniments. Select any meat or fish and surround with potatoes and other vegetables.

Sweet-Tart Kraut, *below*
8 frankfurters, slit diagonally 3 times about half-way through
Mashed potatoes for 4 servings

1. Prepare Sweet-Tart Kraut and keep it warm. Cook *carrots* or other desired vegetable.

2. Heap kraut mixture in center of a large seasoned plank.* Brush franks with *melted butter or margarine* and arrange, slit side down, at two opposite corners of plank. Pile the carrots and mashed potatoes to side of kraut at opposite corners. Drizzle melted butter or margarine over potatoes.

3. Set under broiler with top 6 to 8 inches from heat until franks are browned. Turn franks and continue broiling until franks and potatoes are lightly browned. Serve on the plank. 4 SERVINGS

SWEET-TART KRAUT

3 tablespoons butter or margarine
½ cup chopped onion
1 clove garlic, minced
2 cups drained sauerkraut, snipped
3 tablespoons sugar
¼ teaspoon salt
Few grains pepper
1 can or jar (4 oz.) whole pimientos, drained and diced

1. Heat the butter in a large skillet. Mix in the onion and garlic and cook until tender, stirring occasionally.

2. Add sauerkraut, a blend of sugar, salt, and pepper, and the pimiento; toss until well mixed. Heat thoroughly, stirring occasionally. Serve hot.

4 SERVINGS

*Plank Facts

To season a new hardwood plank: Rub well with cooking or salad oil. Heat in a 250° to 275°F oven 1 hour. Remove; wipe off excess oil. Use or cool and store, wrapped, in a cool, dry place.

To use the plank: Always put it into the cold oven and preheat together; then remove from oven, oil thoroughly, and arrange food on it.

To clean the plank: Scrape thoroughly and wipe with a paper towel. If washing is a must, wash very quickly (never soak) in hot soapy water; rinse and dry well.

PASTRY-WRAPPED STUFFED FRANKS

¼ lb. sharp Cheddar cheese, cut up
3 slices bacon, cut up
1 small onion, cut up
1 teaspoon mayonnaise
½ teaspoon dry mustard
¼ teaspoon Worcestershire sauce
16 frankfurters, slit lengthwise
1 pkg. refrigerated fresh dough for crescent rolls

1. Put cheese, bacon, and onion through medium blade of food chopper. Blend in mayonnaise, dry mustard, and Worcestershire sauce. Stuff each frankfurter with about 1 tablespoon of the mixture.

2. Separate the crescent roll dough into the triangles; cut each in half forming two long pieces. Wrap a piece of dough spiral fashion around each frankfurter. Place on baking sheet.

3. Bake at 425°F 10 minutes, or until rolls are golden.

4. Garnish each frankfurter with a *sweet gherkin* on a frilled wooden pick. Serve with *Piquant Pepper-Cabbage Slaw, page 352.* ABOUT 8 SERVINGS

HOT DOG-CHEESE SKILLET

2 tablespoons butter or margarine
1 lb. frankfurters, cut in ½-in. slices
2 tablespoons butter or margarine
5 tablespoons flour
2 cups milk
½ to 1 teaspoon salt
1 tablespoon Worcestershire sauce
Few drops Tabasco
2 oz. Cheddar cheese, finely shredded
1 pkg. (9 oz.) frozen green beans, cooked and drained

1. Heat 2 tablespoons butter in a skillet. Add frankfurters; stirring occasionally, cook until lightly browned. Remove from skillet and set aside.

2. Add the remaining 2 tablespoons butter to the skillet. Blend in the flour; stirring constantly, heat

until mixture bubbles. Remove from heat, continue stirring, and gradually add milk. Return to heat and bring to boiling, stirring constantly; cook 1 to 2 minutes.

3.   Add salt, Worcestershire sauce, Tabasco, and cheese; stir until well blended. Stir in the frankfurters and cooked beans; blend to coat well. Heat thoroughly.

4.   Spoon over *toasted buns* or *toast*.   4 SERVINGS

IRON-POT BARBECUED FRANKS

¾ cup butter	1½ cups chili sauce
1 cup minced onion	1½ cups water
½ cup flour	½ cup cider vinegar
1½ teaspoons sugar	¼ cup Worcester-
1 teaspoon dry mustard	shire sauce
½ teaspoon garlic	24 frankfurters
powder	24 frankfurter buns

1.   Heat butter in a large saucepan; add onion and cook until lightly browned, stirring occasionally.
2.   Blend in a mixture of the flour, sugar, dry mustard, and garlic powder. Stir in the chili sauce, water, vinegar, and Worcestershire sauce. Bring to boiling; boil 1 to 2 minutes, stirring constantly.
3.   Add frankfurters to sauce; cover and simmer until frankfurters are thoroughly heated.
4.   Brush buns with some of the sauce; toast under broiler or on grill. Serve frankfurters in buns and, if desired, spoon on additional sauce.   24 SERVINGS

FRANKS IN WRAPS WITH MINI BEAN POTS

3 cans (14 to 17 oz. each) pork and beans in tomato sauce, or beans with pork and molasses sauce	8 slices raisin bread
	½ cup hot dog relish (or a blend of ⅓ cup pickle relish and 2 tablespoons prepared mustard)
16 slices bacon	
8 frankfurters	

1.   Fill mini bean pots, allowing ½ can beans per individual pot; set aside.
2.   Arrange bacon in a shallow baking pan. Set in a 375°F oven 5 minutes, or until bacon is partially cooked. Remove from oven (leave oven on) and drain bacon on absorbent paper.
3.   Meanwhile, pour *boiling water* to cover over frankfurters; let stand 5 minutes; drain.

4.   Spread bread with the relish. Place a frankfurter lengthwise on each slice, bring sides of bread up around frankfurter, wrap with two bacon strips, and fasten with small metal skewers. Arrange on a rack in a shallow baking pan. If desired, brush lightly with *melted butter*.
5.   Set in a 375°F oven with the filled bean pots. Heat about 15 minutes, turning sandwiches once.
6.   Thread onto skewers *pickle fans*, *pitted ripe olives*, sandwiches, and *tomato wedges*. Remove small metal skewers from the sandwiches. Take bean pots from oven and serve with the filled skewers.   4 TO 6 SERVINGS

HOT DOGS IN SOUBISE SAUCE

2 tablespoons butter or margarine	1 cup chicken broth
	1 teaspoon honey
4 small onions, sliced	2 tablespoons butter or margarine
3 tablespoons butter or margarine	¼ cup cream
¾ cup minced onion	4 hard-cooked eggs, sliced
2 tablespoons flour	4 frankfurters, cut in ½-in. pieces
¼ teaspoon salt	
¼ teaspoon mono- sodium glutamate	4 medium-sized pota- toes, cooked, peeled,
¼ teaspoon oregano	and thinly sliced
Few grains pepper	

1.   Heat 2 tablespoons butter in a skillet. Add onion and cook until onion is transparent. Arrange onions in a greased 8-inch square baking dish.
2.   For sauce, heat the 3 tablespoons butter in skillet. Add minced onion and cook until onion is transparent. Blend in a mixture of the flour, salt, monosodium glutamate, oregano, and pepper. Add chicken broth and honey gradually, stirring constantly. Heat until mixture bubbles and continue to cook for 5 minutes, stirring constantly.
3.   Remove sauce from heat. Add the remaining butter and the cream, stirring until mixture is blended.
4.   Arrange layers of eggs, frankfurters, and half the potatoes over the onion slices. Pour some of the sauce evenly over mixture. Repeat with remaining potatoes and sauce.
5.   Bake at 350°F about 20 minutes. Remove from oven. Sprinkle with *paprika*.
6.   Put baking dish on broiler rack about 4 inches from source of heat. Broil about 2 minutes, or until top is lightly browned.   ABOUT 6 SERVINGS

HOT DOG—IT'S BEANS

3 slices bacon, pan-
broiled and crumbled
(reserve drippings)
¾ cup chopped green
pepper
½ cup chopped onion
1 lb. frankfurters,
cut in pieces

2 cans (14 to 17 oz.
each) baked beans in
tomato sauce
1 cup ketchup
2 tablespoons brown
sugar
2 tablespoons Worces-
tershire sauce

1. Add green pepper and onion to bacon drippings in skillet. Cook until onion is transparent and
green pepper is just tender, occasionally turning
with a spoon.
2. Put frankfurters into a greased 1½-quart casserole. Add the beans and crumbled bacon. Add
ketchup, brown sugar, and Worcestershire sauce
to onion and green pepper; blend thoroughly. Pour
over beans; mix lightly but thoroughly.
3. Cover and bake at 350°F 1 hour.

ABOUT 8 SERVINGS

FRANK-BEEF ROULADES

Instant mashed potatoes
(1 cup cooked)
8 frankfurters
8 slices dried beef

1 egg, beaten
1 cup (about 4 oz.)
shredded sharp
Cheddar cheese

1. Prepare mashed potatoes according to directions on package.
2. Make a lengthwise slit almost through each
frankfurter. Open slit frankfurters and fill each
with 2 tablespoons of the mashed potatoes.
3. Place each frankfurter on a slice of dried beef;
roll up and secure with wooden picks. Dip each in
beaten egg, coating completely, and roll in shredded cheese.
4. Arrange frankfurters on broiler rack with tops
3 to 4 inches from source of heat; broil 3 minutes,
or until cheese is melted, turning once.

8 FRANK-BEEF ROULADES

FRANK-LY, CURRY IN A HURRY

¼ cup butter or
margarine
½ cup chopped onion
1 lb. frankfurters,
cut in ½-in. pieces
3 tablespoons flour
1 teaspoon curry
powder
1 can (10½ oz.) con-
densed beef consommé

¼ cup currant jelly
1 tablespoon butter or
margarine
½ cup slivered
blanched almonds
¼ teaspoon salt
1 teaspoon curry
powder
Hot cooked rice

1. Heat ¼ cup butter in a large heavy skillet. Add
onion and cook over medium heat until transparent, turning occasionally with a spoon. Stir in the
frankfurter pieces. Blend in a mixture of the flour
and 1 teaspoon curry powder.
2. Add the consommé and jelly gradually, blending thoroughly. Simmer, uncovered, 20 minutes,
stirring occasionally.
3. Heat 1 tablespoon butter in a small skillet. Add
almonds and heat until lightly browned, constantly
moving and turning with a spoon. Stir in the salt
and 1 teaspoon curry powder, blending thoroughly.
Remove from heat.
4. Arrange rice around edge of serving platter.
Heap curried frankfurters in center. Sprinkle with
almonds. Serve immediately.   ABOUT 6 SERVINGS

GROUND MEAT COOKERY

Ground meats have a versatility all their own.
They are adaptable to the skillet, the casserole,
the oven, the open fire. They can be combined
deliciously with pastry, with cereal, with fruits
and vegetables; piled into molds or broiled on a
plank or a skewer; shaped into loaves or balls
or patties; add nutrition and flavor to soup.
Purchase ground beef that has been *freshly*
ground, either regular (contains not more than
25% fat) or lean (contains not more than 12%
fat). Or buy a cut of beef such as chuck,
round, flank, plate, brisket, shank, or neck
meat and have it ground. If the cut is quite
lean, have 2 ounces of suet per pound of beef
ground with the cut. A coarse grind helps to
insure extra-juicy patties.
Purchase pork that has been *freshly* ground or
have pork shoulder meat ground.
Purchase lamb that has been *freshly* ground or
have lamb shoulder meat ground.
Store ground meat uncovered or lightly covered
in refrigerator. Partial drying on the surface of

meat increases its keeping quality. Use within two days of purchase.

Store frozen ground meat in the freezing compartment of the refrigerator or in a freezer, wrapped in freezer wrapping material.

Break ground meat block apart with a wooden spoon when meat is added to skillet. Brown over medium heat. For small pieces, move and turn with a wooden spoon at beginning of browning process. For larger pieces, brown slightly before moving and turning meat.

Shape balls, burgers, and loaves with a light touch. (Excessive handling results in a compact and less juicy product.)

Always cook pork until well done.

Unmold meat loaves. For easier slicing, let meat loaves stand in pan 5 to 10 minutes after removing from oven. With spatula, gently loosen meat from sides of pan. Pour off excess juices; invert onto a platter and remove pan. For meat loaves with topping, pour off excess juices and lift loaf onto platter with two wide spatulas.

Ground Beef

SAUCY GROUND MEAT TOWERS

2 lbs. lean ground beef	½ teaspoon mono-
2 tablespoons instant	sodium glutamate
minced onion	½ teaspoon garlic salt
2 eggs, beaten	¼ cup fat
1 teaspoon Worcester-	Herbed Tomato Sauce,
shire sauce	*below*
1½ teaspoons salt	½ pkg. (4 oz.) stuffing
¼ teaspoon pepper	mix

1. Lightly mix the ground beef, onion, eggs, Worcestershire sauce, salt, pepper, monosodium glutamate, and garlic salt. Shape into 12 patties, making 6 of them slightly smaller in diameter.
2. Brown patties on both sides in heated fat in a heavy skillet. Remove to absorbent paper.
3. Prepare Herbed Tomato Sauce.
4. Prepare stuffing mix according to directions on package for moist stuffing. Shape into 6 patties, using about ⅓ cup stuffing for each.
5. Arrange the larger meat patties in skillet; put a stuffing patty on each, and top with smaller patties.
6. Pour sauce over and around the "towers"; heat thoroughly, basting occasionally. 6 SERVINGS

HERBED TOMATO SAUCE: Combine in a saucepan *2 cans (8 ounces each) tomato sauce* and *1 can (4 ounce) mushroom stems and pieces, 4 whole cloves, 1 bay leaf, ½ teaspoon salt, ⅛ teaspoon black pepper,* and *¼ teaspoon thyme.* Cover; simmer 10 minutes. Remove cloves and bay leaf.

SAUCE-CROWNED MEAT RING

¾ cup coarse dry bread	1 cup chopped onion
crumbs	1 clove garlic,
1 bottle (7 oz.) lemon-	crushed
lime carbonated	2 teaspoons salt
beverage	1½ teaspoons dill weed
2 lbs. lean ground beef	⅓ cup Worcester-
2 eggs, slightly beaten	shire sauce

1. Soak bread crumbs in lemon-lime carbonated beverage. Add ground beef, eggs, onion, garlic, salt, and dill; mix lightly, but thoroughly.
2. Pack lightly into a deep 1½-quart ring mold. Turn out onto a jelly roll pan or baking sheet. Brush the meat ring with the Worcestershire sauce.
3. Bake at 350°F 45 minutes; baste occasionally.
4. Spoon *Topping, below,* over meat. Bake 15 minutes longer. ABOUT 6 SERVINGS

TOPPING: Thoroughly blend *½ cup chili sauce* and *1 teaspoon Worcestershire sauce.*

SAUCY MINIATURE MEAT LOAVES

¾ lb. cooked ham	1¼ cups milk
2 hard-cooked eggs	¾ cup quick-cooking
1 green pepper	rolled oats
1 small onion	2 teaspoons salt
1 lb. lean ground beef	½ teaspoon dry mustard
½ lb. bulk pork	⅛ teaspoon sage
sausage	Barbecue sauce
1 egg, beaten	

1. Cut ham, hard-cooked eggs, green pepper, and onion into pieces and put through medium blade of food chopper. Combine ground mixture with the ground beef and sausage, blending evenly with a fork. Add the egg, milk, and a mixture of the oats, salt, mustard, and sage; mix lightly but thoroughly.
2. Shape mixture into 8 individual loaves. Place in a large shallow baking pan and pour barbecue sauce over each loaf.
3. Bake at 350°F 1 hour, or until meat is done.
8 INDIVIDUAL LOAVES

ITALIAN MEAT PATTIES

1 lb. lean ground beef
1 egg, fork beaten
3 tablespoons dry
    bread crumbs
2 teaspoons minced
    parsley
1 teaspoon grated
    lemon peel

1 clove garlic, minced
¾ teaspoon salt
⅛ teaspoon black
    pepper
⅛ teaspoon ground
    nutmeg

1. Lightly but thoroughly mix all ingredients in a bowl. Shape into 4 patties.
2. Brown patties on both sides in heated *olive oil* in a large skillet, cooking until of desired degree of doneness. 4 SERVINGS

GARLIC CHEESEBURGERS

Flavorful Tomato
    Sauce, *page 345*
1½ lbs. lean ground
    beef
1 egg, beaten
2 cloves garlic,
    crushed

1½ teaspoons seasoned
    salt
¼ teaspoon pepper
1 tablespoon butter or
    margarine
6 slices sharp Cheddar
    cheese

1. Prepare the tomato sauce and keep hot.
2. Lightly mix the ground beef, egg, garlic, seasoned salt, and pepper. Shape mixture into 6 patties about ¾ inch thick.
3. Brown patties on both sides in heated butter in a skillet, allowing about 10 minutes.
4. Cover each patty with a slice of cheese. Cook about 3 minutes longer, or until cheese is slightly melted.
5. Pour hot tomato sauce into a warm serving dish and arrange cheeseburgers in the sauce. 6 SERVINGS

SAUERKRAUT-PEANUT BUTTER BURGERS

¼ cup crunchy peanut
    butter
¼ cup dairy sour cream
1 egg, fork beaten
½ teaspoon salt

Few grains black
    pepper
1 cup sauerkraut,
    thoroughly drained
    and finely chopped
1 lb. lean ground beef

1. Beat the peanut butter, sour cream, egg, salt, and pepper together until blended. Mix in the sauerkraut, then lightly mix in the ground beef.

2. Shape mixture into 6 patties about ¾ inch thick.
3. Broil about 3 inches from source of heat 4 to 5 minutes. When patties are browned on one side, turn and broil second side about 3 minutes, or until desired degree of doneness. 6 SERVINGS

BEEF LINDSTROM

This meat patty, the Scandinavian counterpart of an American hamburger, is usually served with fried eggs and a green salad for lunch.

1½ lbs. lean beef,
    ground twice
2 egg yolks, beaten
¼ cup cream
2 tablespoons chopped
    onion
1 tablespoon capers
1 teaspoon salt

½ teaspoon mono-
    sodium glutamate
¼ teaspoon pepper
3 medium-sized cooked
    potatoes, diced
½ cup finely diced
    pickled beets
3 tablespoons butter
    or margarine

1. Lightly toss the ground beef, egg yolks, cream, onion, capers, salt, monosodium glutamate, and pepper in a bowl. Add potatoes and beets and mix well. Refrigerate 1 to 2 hours.
2. Shape the mixture into patties about ¾ inch thick. Brown on both sides in heated butter in a heavy skillet. Serve immediately. 6 TO 8 SERVINGS

FINNISH MEATBALLS

1½ lbs. ground round
    steak
1 egg, slightly beaten
2 teaspoons salt
½ teaspoon pepper
½ teaspoon dill weed
2 cups grated raw
    potato
½ cup finely chopped
    onion

½ cup finely chopped
    green pepper
1 to 2 tablespoons
    butter
1 can (8 oz.) tomato
    sauce
⅓ cup cold water
1 tablespoon flour
1 cup dairy sour cream

1. Combine in a bowl the ground meat, egg, and a mixture of the salt, pepper, and dill, then the vegetables; toss to mix. Lightly shape into 1-inch balls.
2. Brown meatballs evenly on all sides in hot butter in a large skillet. When thoroughly cooked, remove meatballs to a warm serving dish; keep hot.
3. Add tomato sauce to the drippings in skillet and stir in a blend of water and flour. Bring rapidly

to boiling, stirring mixture constantly; cook 1 to 2 minutes.

4. Reduce heat. Stirring gravy vigorously with a French whip or spoon, add sour cream in very small amounts. Heat thoroughly, about 3 minutes (do not boil). Pour gravy over meatballs and serve. ABOUT 6 DOZEN MEATBALLS

ORIENTAL MEATBALLS

1 slice bread	2 tablespoons finely
½ cup water	chopped onion
1 lb. lean ground beef	1 teaspoon salt
¼ cup chopped pre-	1 teaspoon mono-
served kumquats	sodium glutamate
¼ cup chopped water	⅛ teaspoon pepper
chestnuts	Cooked, drained, well-
¼ cup finely chopped	seasoned green beans
green pepper	Pineapple Glaze, *below*

1. Soak bread in water. Combine bread with the ground beef, kumquats, water chestnuts, green pepper, onion, salt, monosodium glutamate, and pepper; mix lightly but thoroughly.

2. Divide mixture into 10 or 12 portions and shape into balls. Place ½ inch apart in a shallow baking dish. Set, uncovered, in a 375°F oven 20 minutes.

3. Remove meatballs with a slotted spoon. Arrange a layer of the hot green beans in bottom of baking dish and return the meatballs.

4. Pour hot Pineapple Glaze over meatballs, arranging pineapple chunks in center; return to oven about 15 minutes, or until thoroughly heated.

5 OR 6 SERVINGS

PINEAPPLE GLAZE

Unsweetened pineapple	¼ cup white vinegar
juice	1 cinnamon stick
1⅔ cups canned pine-	5 whole cloves
apple chunks, drained	1 tablespoon corn-
(reserve syrup)	starch
½ cup syrup drained	5 or 6 drops mint
from sweet pickles	extract

1. Add enough pineapple juice to reserved pineapple syrup to make 1½ cups liquid. Combine with the pickle juice, vinegar, cinnamon stick, and cloves in a saucepan. Blend well and simmer, uncovered, 10 minutes.

2. Mix cornstarch with enough cold water to make a paste and blend into mixture in saucepan. Cook and stir until boiling; reduce heat and cook 2

or 3 minutes. Remove cinnamon stick and cloves; mix in the extract and pineapple chunks.

ABOUT 2 CUPS

LEMON-OLIVE MEATBALLS

1 lb. lean ground beef	¼ green pepper, finely
3 tablespoons lemon	chopped
juice	1 cup soft bread
1 teaspoon salt	crumbs
4 oz. sharp Cheddar	½ cup milk
cheese, shredded	1 egg, beaten
12 pimiento-stuffed	12 slices bacon,
olives, finely	partially cooked
chopped	

1. Mix ground beef with lemon juice and salt. Add remaining ingredients except bacon; mix lightly.

2. Shape into 12 balls; wrap a bacon slice around each ball and fasten with a wooden pick. Arrange meatballs in baking dish.

3. Bake at 350°F 40 minutes. 4 SERVINGS

GERMAN MEATBALLS
(Koenigsberger Klops)

1 cup soft bread	3 cups water
crumbs	2 tablespoons
¼ cup milk	chopped onion
½ cup chopped onion	1 bay leaf
2 tablespoons butter	1 whole clove
or margarine	2 peppercorns
1 lb. ground beef	¼ teaspoon salt
¼ lb. ground veal	2 tablespoons butter
4 anchovy fillets,	or margarine
mashed	2 tablespoons flour
1 egg, fork beaten	2 tablespoons lemon
1 teaspoon salt	juice
½ teaspoon mono-	1 tablespoon chopped
sodium glutamate	capers
¼ teaspoon pepper	

1. Put bread crumbs and milk into a large bowl.

2. Cook ½ cup onion in 2 tablespoons hot butter in a skillet until golden, stirring occasionally.

3. Add the contents of the skillet, the ground meat, anchovies, egg, 1 teaspoon salt, monosodium glutamate, and pepper to the bread crumb mixture; mix lightly. Shape meat mixture into 2-inch balls.

4. Bring water, 2 tablespoons chopped onion, bay leaf, clove, peppercorns, and ¼ teaspoon salt to boiling in a saucepan. Put meatballs into boiling liq-

uid. Return to boiling and simmer 20 minutes. Remove meatballs with a slotted spoon; keep hot. Strain cooking liquid and reserve 2 cups.

5. Heat remaining butter in the saucepan. Mix in flour and heat until bubbly. Stir in reserved liquid, lemon juice, and capers. Bring rapidly to boiling, stirring constantly. Cook and stir 1 to 2 minutes.

6. Return meatballs to gravy and heat thoroughly.

6 TO 8 SERVINGS

HORSERADISH MEATBALLS

1 lb. ground beef	¼ teaspoon ground
¼ lb. ground pork	cinnamon
¼ lb. ground veal	3 cups soft bread
1 egg, fork beaten	crumbs
½ cup milk	2 tablespoons cooking
¼ cup prepared	oil
horseradish	1 cup applesauce
2 teaspoons salt	¼ cup prepared
1 teaspoon crushed	horseradish
basil	2 teaspoons brown
	sugar

1. Lightly mix the ground meats and a blend of the egg, milk, ¼ cup horseradish, salt, basil, cinnamon, and bread crumbs; shape into 24 balls.

2. Brown the meatballs evenly on all sides in the hot oil in a large skillet. Mix applesauce, ¼ cup horseradish, and sugar; spread evenly over balls.

3. Cover and cook over low heat 20 minutes.

6 SERVINGS

NORWEGIAN MEATBALLS

2 tablespoons butter	½ teaspoon ground
or margarine	nutmeg
⅓ cup chopped onion	¼ teaspoon ground
1 lb. lean ground beef	allspice
¼ lb. lean ground pork	2 tablespoons butter
½ cup soft bread	or margarine
crumbs	3 tablespoons flour
½ cup milk	1 teaspoon sugar
1 egg, beaten	½ teaspoon salt
2 teaspoons sugar	¼ teaspoon black
1¼ teaspoons salt	pepper
¾ teaspoon mono-	2 cups liquid (light
sodium glutamate	cream and water)

1. Heat 2 tablespoons butter in a large heavy skillet; add onion and cook until transparent.

2. Toss together lightly the ground meats, cooked onion, bread crumbs, milk and a blend of egg, 2

teaspoons sugar, 1¼ teaspoons salt, monosodium glutamate, nutmeg, and allspice. Lightly shape into 1-inch balls.

3. Heat remaining butter in the skillet; add meatballs and brown evenly. Remove and keep warm.

4. Blend flour, 1 teaspoon sugar, ½ teaspoon salt, and pepper into the fat in skillet; heat until bubbly. Gradually add liquid, stirring constantly; bring to boiling. Cook 1 to 2 minutes. Pour over meat.

6 SERVINGS

SWEDISH MEATBALLS

1 lb. ground round	½ teaspoon brown sugar
steak	¼ teaspoon ground
½ lb. ground pork	allspice
½ cup instant mashed	¼ teaspoon ground
potatoes	nutmeg
½ cup fine dry bread	⅛ teaspoon ground
crumbs	cloves
1 egg, beaten	⅛ teaspoon ground
1 teaspoon salt	ginger
½ teaspoon mono-	½ cup fine dry bread
sodium glutamate	crumbs
¼ teaspoon pepper	3 tablespoons butter
	or margarine

1. Lightly mix in a large bowl the ground meats, potatoes, ½ cup crumbs, egg, and a mixture of the salt, monosodium glutamate, pepper, brown sugar, allspice, nutmeg, cloves, and ginger.

2. Shape mixture lightly into 1-inch balls. Roll balls in remaining crumbs.

3. Heat the butter in a large heavy skillet. Add the meatballs and brown on all sides; shake pan frequently to brown evenly and to keep balls round. Cook, covered, about 15 minutes, or until meatballs are thoroughly cooked. 3 DOZEN MEATBALLS

STUFFED SWEDISH MEATBALLS
A popular dish with ventriloquist Edgar Bergen and his family.

2 slices dry bread	1 egg, slightly beaten
½ cup milk	1 teaspoon salt
1½ lbs. lean ground	Pepper
beef	1 small jar pimiento-
1 large onion, diced	stuffed olives,
3 tablespoons snipped	drained
parsley	¼ cup peanut oil

1. Soak broken pieces of bread in milk.

2.   Mix ground beef with onion, parsley, egg, salt, and pepper. Add bread and mix well but lightly.
3.   Shape into tiny balls with a stuffed olive in the center of each.
4.   Brown meatballs in medium hot peanut oil in heavy cast iron pan or Dutch oven. When evenly browned, cover and cook over low heat 1 hour.
5.   Serve from a casserole as main dish or spear with cocktail picks and serve as appetizers.

4 SERVINGS

tomato and move meatballs through mixture; heat thoroughly.
5.   To serve, spoon onto warm platter. Garnish with the soy walnuts, reserving enough to top rice. Spoon rice into heated cups. Serve immediately.

4 TO 6 SERVINGS

TOASTED SOY WALNUTS: Blend *1 teaspoon butter or margarine* and *1 teaspoon soy sauce* in small skillet and heat. Stir in *½ cup walnut halves*, turning occasionally until nuts are toasted.

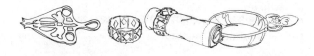

SAUCED WALNUT BEEF BALLS ORIENTALE

1 lb. lean ground beef
⅓ cup milk
½ teaspoon salt
¼ teaspoon seasoned pepper
½ cup fine soft bread crumbs
½ cup finely chopped walnuts
¼ cup finely chopped onion
1 egg, beaten
¼ cup flour
⅓ cup cooking oil
1 can (8¾ oz.) pineapple tidbits, drained (reserve syrup)
½ cup strong beef broth
3 tablespoons cider vinegar
1 tablespoon soy sauce
¼ cup sugar
2 tablespoons cornstarch
½ cup water
1 green pepper, cut in strips
1 firm ripe large tomato, cut in wedges
Toasted Soy Walnuts, *below*
Packaged precooked rice, cooked and kept warm

1.   Lightly mix the ground beef and a blend of the milk, salt, seasoned pepper, and crumbs, then mix in the walnuts and onion. Shape into 12 balls.
2.   Beat egg with flour. Coat balls with mixture. Drain on wire rack.
3.   Brown meatballs evenly on all sides in hot oil in a large (about 10-inch) heavy skillet. Remove all but 1 tablespoon of the oil and push balls to one side of skillet.
4.   Pour in the reserved pineapple syrup, beef broth, vinegar, soy sauce, and sugar, and a mixture of cornstarch and water. Stir until blended. Mix in pineapple and green pepper. Bring rapidly to boiling, stirring constantly; cook 3 minutes. Stir in

KRAUT AND BEEF PASTIES

2½ cups undrained sauerkraut
1 lb. ground round steak
½ lb. lean ground pork
½ lb. ground veal
2 to 2½ teaspoons salt
1 teaspoon monosodium glutamate
½ teaspoon marjoram leaves, crushed
¼ teaspoon black pepper
1 tablespoon cooking oil
½ cup chopped onion
½ cup Italian-style seasoned bread crumbs
2 cups sifted all-purpose flour
½ teaspoon salt
¼ teaspoon black pepper
⅔ cup vegetable shortening

1.   Drain sauerkraut thoroughly, reserving 2 tablespoons liquid; set aside.
2.   Prepare meat filling. Have beef, pork, and veal ground together at the meat market. Put meat into a large bowl and mix with a blend of salt, monosodium glutamate, marjoram, and pepper.
3.   Heat oil in a large skillet; add onion and cook until crisp-tender. Turn into bowl and blend with meat mixture.
4.   Put meat into hot skillet and, stirring occasionally, cook until meat is no longer pink. Remove from heat and stir in seasoned bread crumbs; cool.
5.   Prepare pastry. Sift together flour, salt, and pepper. Using a pastry blender, cut shortening into flour until pieces are the size of small peas.
6.   Chop the sauerkraut or snip into short lengths. Add to flour mixture. Toss with a fork until mixed. Adding gradually, drizzle reserved sauerkraut liquid over all while continuing to toss mixture until moistened. Turn onto waxed paper and press together to form a ball.
7.   Divide dough into 12 equal pieces. On a well-floured surface, roll out each to a 6-inch round. Put about ⅓ cup meat mixture (slightly off center) onto

each pastry round. Overlapping pastry, seal edges (flute, if desired), and prick tops with a fork.

8. Place on ungreased baking sheets; bake at 375°F 35 to 40 minutes, or until lightly browned. Serve hot or cold.   12 MEAT PASTIES

ZESTY KRAUT PASTRY SNACKS: Prepare pastry for Kraut and Beef Pasties. Divide dough into 4 portions for rolling. On a well-floured surface roll each fourth as thin as possible and cut into squares. Transfer to ungreased sheets; brush tops lightly with *butter or margarine* and sprinkle with any of the following: *sesame, caraway, or poppy seeds; garlic or onion salt; grated Parmesan or Cheddar cheese; instant minced onion, dill weed, chili powder, oregano, or curry powder;* or *finely chopped dried beef.* Bake at 425°F 13 minutes. Serve hot.   ABOUT 4 DOZEN SNACKS

BEEF 'N' SAUSAGE TARTS

Pie crust mix (enough for 3 pie shells)	2 tablespoons milk
¼ cup chopped onion	½ cup instant mashed potato flakes
1 tablespoon cooking oil	1 egg, fork beaten
1½ lbs. lean ground beef	½ cup undiluted evaporated milk
½ lb. bulk pork sausage	¼ cup chili sauce
1½ teaspoons salt	2 cans or jars (4 oz. each) whole pimientos, drained
1 teaspoon monosodium glutamate	2 tablespoons chopped green pepper
¼ teaspoon seasoned pepper	3 slices process Cheddar cheese, cut in 12 triangles
¼ teaspoon chili powder	3 mushrooms, halved
⅓ cup boiling water	

1. Prepare pie crust mix according to package directions; divide into 6 equal balls and roll out each 1-inch larger than inverted tart plate or pan. Line six 6-inch tart plates or pans with the pastry; flute edges (press points firmly over edge of plates) and prick bottom and sides with fork. Bake as directed. Remove from oven and set aside on wire rack. Reduce oven temperature to 350°F.
2. Cook onion in hot oil in a large skillet until transparent. Add ground beef and sausage and cook over medium heat, cutting apart with a fork or spoon, and pouring off fat as it collects. Remove from heat. Sprinkle meat with salt, monosodium glutamate, seasoned pepper, and chili powder.

3. Combine boiling water and milk; stir in potato flakes and continue stirring until soft. Lightly mix potatoes into meat.
4. Stir in a blend of egg, evaporated milk, and chili sauce. Mince 2 pimientos and mix in with the green pepper. Cut remaining pimientos into 12 triangles. Lightly spoon meat mixture into baked shells.
5. Cover tops of tarts with alternating triangles of pimiento and cheese; place a mushroom half in center of each tart. Brush tops generously with *cooking oil.*
6. Set in 350°F oven 8 to 10 minutes, or until mixture is thoroughly heated.   6 SERVINGS

DEEP-FRIED BEEF PIES

Pastry for Little Pies and Tarts, *page 454*	¼ cup finely chopped celery
¾ lb. lean ground beef	¼ cup finely chopped onion
2 tablespoons shortening	¼ cup finely chopped green onion
1½ teaspoons olive oil	1 tablespoon chopped hot red pepper
1 teaspoon salt	1 tablespoon snipped parsley
¼ teaspoon black pepper	1 tablespoon snipped seedless raisins
⅛ teaspoon cayenne pepper	1 tablespoon chopped pitted green olives
1 ripe tomato, peeled and cut in pieces	1 tablespoon capers
⅓ cup finely chopped green pepper	¼ cup water
¼ cup finely chopped carrot	Fat for deep frying heated to 375°F

1. Prepare pastry; shape into a ball and wrap in waxed paper; chill.
2. Cook ground beef in hot shortening and oil in a large skillet, separating meat with a spoon. Remove from heat and drain off fat. Mix in remaining ingredients except fat. Cover and simmer 30 minutes.
3. Working with ½ the chilled pastry at a time, roll out ⅛ inch thick on a lightly floured surface. Using a lightly floured 4-inch cutter, cut into rounds. Place 1 tablespoon filling on each round. Moisten edges with cold water, fold pastry over, press edges together and tightly seal.
4. Fry one layer at a time in the heated fat until lightly browned on both sides, about 3 minutes. Drain on absorbent paper.   ABOUT 16 PIES

BEEF TACOS

Lard
1 cup finely chopped
  onion
1 clove garlic, minced
1 lb. lean ground beef
1 teaspoon salt
2 teaspoons chili
  powder
Pinch ground cumin

12 canned or frozen
  tortillas, dried at
  room temperature
  about 2 hrs.
Finely shredded lettuce
Finely chopped onion
Shredded Cheddar
  cheese

1. Heat 3 tablespoons lard in a large heavy skillet. Add onion and garlic and cook until tender. Blend in ground beef and a mixture of salt, chili powder, and cumin; brown meat lightly.
2. Fry tortillas, one at a time, in ½ inch of lard heated to 375°F in a heavy skillet. When tortilla becomes limp, fold in half with tongs and hold edges apart while frying to allow for filling. Fry 1½ to 2 minutes, or until crisp and golden. Drain on absorbent paper.
3. To serve, spoon 3 to 4 tablespoons of beef mixture into each tortilla; top with lettuce, onion, and cheese. If desired, serve with a *salsa picante* (a Mexican hot sauce). 12 TACOS

BEEF YORKSHIRE PIE
Reminiscent of old-fashioned Yorkshire pudding (usually baked in a roasting pan along with a beef roast), this unique pie stands alone as an excellent main dish.

1½ lbs. lean ground
  beef
½ cup finely chopped
  onion
1 teaspoon salt
¼ teaspoon pepper
½ teaspoon ground
  coriander

⅛ teaspoon ground
  cumin
⅛ teaspoon garlic
  powder
1½ cups all-purpose
  flour
½ teaspoon salt
3 eggs, beaten
1½ cups milk

1. Cook ground beef and onion in hot skillet, cutting meat apart with fork. Remove from heat, drain off fat. Mix in 1 teaspoon salt, pepper, coriander, cumin, and garlic powder; set aside.
2. Place a well-greased 10-inch skillet (heat-resistant handle) in a 400°F oven until very hot.
3. Blend flour and the remaining salt in bowl. Add mixture of eggs and milk; beat until smooth.
4. Pour half of the batter into the hot skillet; cover with the beef mixture and top with remaining batter.
5. Bake at 400°F 40 minutes, or until puffed and golden. Cut into wedges and serve from skillet.
ABOUT 6 SERVINGS

TEEN-AGE DELIGHT

6 slices bread, crusts
  removed
3 tablespoons butter,
  softened
½ lb. ground beef
¼ cup chopped onion
2 tablespoons chopped
  celery

1 tablespoon prepared
  mustard
1 cup (about 4 oz.)
  shredded process
  American cheese
2 eggs, slightly beaten
1 cup milk

1. Spread both sides of bread slices with butter. Cut diagonally into halves. Arrange on bottom of a 13x9x2-inch baking dish. Toast at 350°F about 15 minutes.
2. Put ground beef, onion, celery, and mustard into a skillet. Cook over medium heat until lightly browned, breaking meat into pieces with a fork.
3. Spread meat mixture over bread slices. Sprinkle evenly with the cheese.
4. Beat together the eggs and milk. Pour over mixture in baking dish.
5. Bake at 350°F 35 minutes. Serve immediately.
6 SERVINGS

CHILI AND BEANS
Walt Disney's home and heart were in the Southwest as evidenced by one of his favorite recipes.

2 lbs. dry chili beans
  (pink or red)
2 medium onions,
  sliced (about 1½ cups)
2 to 3 teaspoons salt
½ cup cooking oil
2 cloves garlic,
  crushed
2 lbs. coarsely ground
  beef

1 can (28 oz.) whole
  red tomatoes
1 cup chopped celery
1 teaspoon chili powder
  (depending upon
  taste)
1 teaspoon paprika
1 teaspoon dry mustard
Salt to taste

1. Soak beans overnight in cold water.
2. Drain off water; put beans, onions, and salt into a large kettle; add water to come 2-inches over beans. Simmer about 4 hours, or until tender; add hot water if necessary, to maintain liquid level.
3. Meanwhile, prepare sauce. Heat oil in a large deep skillet or Dutch oven; add garlic and ground

beef; cook slowly until meat is lightly browned. Add remaining ingredients; simmer 1 hour.

4.   When beans are tender, add sauce to them and simmer 30 minutes.   3 TO 3½ QUARTS CHILI

NOTE: For a very spicy chili, add a pinch of *chili seeds, coriander seeds, cumin seeds, fennel seeds, cinnamon, cloves, ginger, turmeric,* and *1 small yellow Mexican chili pepper.*

CHILI CON CARNE

⅓ cup butter, margarine, or salad oil	3 cans (16 oz. each) kidney beans
6 onions, sliced	½ teaspoon Tabasco
3 lbs. lean ground beef	2 to 4 tablespoons chili powder
2 cans (6 oz. each) tomato paste	1 tablespoon salt
3 cans (16 oz. each) tomatoes	2 teaspoons monosodium glutamate

1.   Heat butter in a large saucepot; add onion and cook until soft. Add the ground beef and cook over medium heat until lightly browned, breaking into small pieces with a spoon.

2.   Mix in the tomato paste, tomatoes, kidney beans, Tabasco, and a blend of the chili powder, salt, and monosodium glutamate.

3.   Cover and simmer about 1 hour, stirring occasionally.   12 SERVINGS

BEEF POLYNESIAN

2 tablespoons butter	1 teaspoon curry powder
1 lb. lean ground beef	1 tablespoon soy sauce
1 can (4 oz.) mushrooms, drained	1 orange, sliced
½ cup golden raisins	½ cup salted cashew nuts
1 pkg. (10 oz.) frozen green peas	Fried Rice, *below*
½ cup beef broth	

1.   Heat butter in a large heavy skillet. Add ground beef and separate into small pieces; cook until lightly browned.

2.   Add mushrooms, raisins, peas, broth, curry powder, and soy sauce. Break block of peas apart and gently toss mixture to blend.

3.   Arrange orange slices over top. Cover loosely and cook over low heat 15 minutes.

4.   Mix in the cashews and serve with Fried Rice.   ABOUT 4 SERVINGS

FRIED RICE: Cook *½ cup chopped onion* in *2 tablespoons butter* until light golden. Mix in *2 cups cooked rice* and *2 tablespoons soy sauce.* Cook over low heat, stirring occasionally, 5 minutes. Stir in *1 slightly beaten egg* and cook until set.

BARLEY BEEF STEW

3 lbs. lean ground beef	1 cup chopped celery
3 to 3½ teaspoons salt	2 tablespoons chili powder
¼ teaspoon pepper	2 qts. tomato juice
2 tablespoons cooking oil	2 cups hot water
6 onions, chopped (about 2¼ cups)	1 cup barley

1.   Mix the ground beef with salt and pepper. Heat the oil in a large heavy saucepot. Add the beef and onions, separating the meat into pieces; cook about 5 minutes, stirring occasionally.

2.   Stir in the celery, chili powder, tomato juice, and water. Simmer, covered, about 2 hours. Skim off any excess fat, if desired.

3.   Stir in the barley and cook, covered, 1½ hours. Serve in soup plates or over *toasted buns.*

         3½ QUARTS STEW

BEEF-EGGPLANT PATTIES IN CASSEROLE

1 medium-sized eggplant, pared and cut in ½-in. cubes	3 tablespoons water
	4 eggs, beaten
1 lb. lean ground beef	6 tablespoons olive oil
½ cup soft bread crumbs	1 clove garlic
¼ cup shredded Parmesan cheese	1 can (28 oz.) Italian-style tomatoes, sieved
2 tablespoons chopped parsley	1 tablespoon chopped parsley
1 clove garlic, minced	1 teaspoon oregano
¾ teaspoon salt	¾ teaspoon basil
¼ teaspoon black pepper	¾ teaspoon salt
	⅛ teaspoon black pepper

1.   Put eggplant into a heavy saucepan with just enough boiling *salted water* to cover bottom of pan; cover tightly and cook until just tender, about 3 minutes. Drain thoroughly in a colander, discarding the liquid.

2.   Lightly but thoroughly mix ground beef with the bread crumbs, cheese, 2 tablespoons parsley,

minced garlic, and a mixture of ¾ teaspoon salt and ¼ teaspoon pepper. Mix in the water, eggs, and the eggplant. Shape mixture into 8 patties.

3.   Heat olive oil in a heavy skillet; add patties and brown on both sides over medium heat. Transfer patties to a shallow baking dish; set aside.

4.   Add garlic to oil in skillet and heat 1 minute. Remove garlic and stir in a mixture of the remaining ingredients. Simmer about 10 minutes.

5.   Pour sauce over patties in baking dish and set in a 375°F oven 15 minutes, or until thoroughly heated.   6 TO 8 SERVINGS

GROUND BEEF-EGGPLANT CASSEROLE

1 large or 2 small eggplant, pared and cut in ½-in. slices
1½ lbs. lean ground beef
¾ teaspoon salt
½ teaspoon monosodium glutamate
⅛ teaspoon black pepper
¼ cup chopped onion
1 clove garlic, minced
½ cup chopped green pepper
2 cans beef gravy-sauce with tomato
¾ teaspoon crushed basil
¼ lb. thinly sliced mozzarella cheese
¼ cup fine dry bread crumbs
1 tablespoon butter or margarine

1.   Brown eggplant slices in a small amount of hot *cooking oil* in a large skillet. Remove from skillet and set aside.

2.   Mix the ground beef with salt, monosodium glutamate, and pepper; set aside.

3.   Add about 2 tablespoons oil to the skillet. Add onion, garlic, and green pepper to hot oil and cook about 2 minutes, stirring occasionally. Add the meat and cook until it has lost its pink color, stirring occasionally.

4.   Remove from heat and stir in a mixture of the gravy-sauce and basil.

5.   Spoon about one third of the meat sauce over the bottom of a 2-quart baking dish. Arrange half the eggplant slices in a layer over the sauce. Place slices of cheese over the eggplant. Repeat with meat sauce and eggplant; end with remaining meat sauce. Sprinkle a mixture of the bread crumbs and butter over the top.

6.   Set in a 375°F oven about 20 minutes, or until mixture is thoroughly heated and topping is browned. Accompany with *buttered noodles* and a crisp *green salad.*   ABOUT 8 SERVINGS

GROUND BEEF À LA STROGANOFF

2 tablespoons butter or margarine
½ cup finely chopped onion
1 clove garlic, minced
1 lb. ground beef
2 tablespoons flour
2 teaspoons salt
¼ teaspoon pepper
½ teaspoon tarragon
¼ teaspoon basil
1 can (6 oz.) tomato paste
1 can (10½ oz.) condensed beef consommé
1 tablespoon wine vinegar
1 can (4 oz.) sliced mushrooms, drained
1 cup dairy sour cream
¼ cup snipped parsley
8 oz. noodles, cooked according to pkg. directions and drained

1.   Heat butter in a skillet; add onion and garlic. Cook about 5 minutes, stirring occasionally. Add the ground beef, separate into pieces, and brown lightly.

2.   Sprinkle a mixture of flour, salt, pepper, tarragon, and basil over the meat. Stir in tomato paste, consommé, and vinegar. Simmer, uncovered, 10 minutes, stirring occasionally. Remove from heat; stir in mushrooms and sour cream. Heat thoroughly, stirring occasionally (do not boil).

3.   Toss parsley with noodles and top with sauce.
                                    ABOUT 6 SERVINGS

CORNED BEEF 'N' CABBAGE

8 large cabbage leaves
½ lb. corned beef
¼ lb. Swiss cheese
½ cup dairy sour cream
¼ cup snipped parsley
2 tablespoons butter or margarine
½ cup commercial barbecue sauce
½ cup water

1.   Cook cabbage leaves in boiling *salted water* about 5 minutes, or until tender.

2.   Meanwhile, grind corned beef and Swiss cheese, using the medium blade of a food chopper. Blend in sour cream and parsley.

3.   Drain cabbage leaves and spoon about 5 tablespoonfuls of corned beef mixture onto center of each leaf. Roll each leaf, tucking the ends in toward center. Secure with wooden picks.

4.   Heat butter in a skillet; add stuffed cabbage and cook about 2 minutes on each side, or until golden brown. Add a mixture of the barbecue sauce and water; cover and simmer 30 minutes.

5.   To serve, arrange stuffed cabbage leaves on a warm serving platter and spoon the sauce over them.   8 SERVINGS

Ground Pork

CHINESE SIZZLED MEATBALLS WITH VEGETABLES AND RICE

1 lb. lean ground pork
or beef round steak
1 teaspoon salt
½ teaspoon crushed
marjoram leaves
¼ teaspoon garlic
powder
1 egg, fork beaten
2 tablespoons bottled
sweet and sour sauce
1 tablespoon peanut oil

2 cans (12 to 14 oz.
each) fried rice with
meat, heated follow-
ing label directions
2 pkgs. (10 oz. each)
frozen cauliflower,
cooked
1 divider-pak can (43
oz.) mushroom chow
mein or beef chop
suey, heated follow-
ing label directions

1. Lightly and thoroughly mix meat with a blend of salt, marjoram, and garlic powder; mix in egg and sweet and sour sauce. Gently shape into 1-inch balls.
2. Brown meatballs evenly on all sides in hot oil in a skillet. Cover while cooking.
3. To serve, turn hot fried rice onto a serving platter; add the cauliflower, sprinkle with *monosodium glutamate*, drizzle with *sweet and sour sauce or soy sauce*, spoon on chow mein, and top with the meatballs.
4. Garnish with *parsley* and *orange fans* made by cutting navel oranges into ¼-inch slices, cutting each slice into thirds, and overlapping pieces to resemble open fans.   ABOUT 6 SERVINGS

DANISH MEATBALLS
(Frikadeller)

1½ lbs. lean ground
pork
1 medium-sized onion,
quartered or minced
2 tablespoons flour
1¼ cups milk

1½ teaspoons salt
⅛ teaspoon black
pepper
2 egg whites
½ cup butter

1. Force ground pork and onion through the medium blade of a meat grinder three times into a large mixing bowl. Or, have meat market grind the pork three times; mix in the minced onion.
2. Mix in flour. Add milk, about 4 tablespoons at a time, beating thoroughly after each addition. Mix in a blend of salt and pepper.

3. Beat egg whites to stiff, not dry, peaks and fold into meat mixture until blended.
4. Thoroughly heat butter, all at one time, in a large skillet. Spoon meat mixture by tablespoonfuls (keeping oval shape) into hot butter. Fry until browned on all sides.   2½ DOZEN MEATBALLS
NOTE: If using an electric blender, pour half of the milk into the container, add the quartered onion, and about ¼ of the meat. Blend, continuing to add milk and as much meat as container will hold. Empty into a large mixing bowl. Put milk and remainder of meat into container and blend until smooth. Empty into bowl. Mix in flour and seasonings; proceed with steps 3 and 4.

CHEESE BALL CASSEROLE À LA MEXICANA

1 lb. lean ground pork,
cooked until lightly
browned, drained
½ lb. ground smoked
ham
1 green pepper, finely
chopped
1 small onion, finely
chopped
3 cloves garlic,
minced
2 tablespoons snipped
parsley
1 can (16 oz.) tomatoes,
well drained
2 tablespoons tomato
juice

2 teaspoons sugar
½ teaspoon salt
¼ teaspoon pepper
½ cup dark seedless
raisins
¼ cup chopped green
olives
1 tablespoon capers
Shredded tortillas
(enough to make 2
cups)
½ lb. sharp Cheddar
cheese, thinly sliced
1 egg, beaten
Tortillas

1. Mix pork and ham thoroughly; blend in green pepper, onion, garlic, parsley, tomatoes, tomato juice, sugar, salt, pepper, raisins, olives, capers, and shredded tortillas. Heat about 20 minutes in a large saucepan, stirring occasionally.
2. Meanwhile, cover bottom and sides of a 1½-quart casserole with overlapping cheese slices.
3. When meat mixture is hot, quickly stir in egg and spoon into lined casserole. Around edge of dish overlap small pieces (quarters) of tortillas and remaining cheese slices.

4. Set in a 325°F oven 15 minutes, or until cheese is bubbly.
5. Serve with warm tortillas. 8 SERVINGS

STUFFED PEPPERS WITH NOGADA SAUCE
(Chiles Rellenos en Nogada)
A Mexican recipe well worth the preparation time.

6 medium-sized green peppers	5 peppercorns, crushed
3 tablespoons lard	¼ teaspoon ground nutmeg
2 cloves garlic, minced	⅛ teaspoon powdered saffron
¼ cup chopped onion	¼ cup finely chopped almonds
1 lb. lean ground pork	¼ cup dark seedless raisins
½ lb. ham with fat, ground	1 teaspoon chopped capers
2 cups chopped ripe tomatoes	2 tablespoons chopped candied lemon peel
2 tablespoons snipped parsley	¼ cup pitted chopped green olives
3 tablespoons cider vinegar	Lard for deep frying heated to 365°F
½ teaspoon vanilla extract	2 eggs, beaten
2 tablespoons sugar	Nogada Sauce, *below*
4 whole cloves, crushed	Pomegranate seeds

1. Cut out stems of peppers; remove seeds and membrane. Place peppers in a large saucepan; cover with boiling water, bring to boiling, and cook about 2 minutes. Drain and invert on absorbent paper.
2. Heat the 3 tablespoons lard in a heavy skillet; add garlic, onion, and ground meat. Cook until meat is browned, stirring occasionally. Blend in tomatoes, parsley, vinegar, extract, and a mixture of the sugar, cloves, peppercorns, nutmeg, and saffron. Then stir in almonds, raisins, capers, lemon peel, and olives.
3. Cook over low heat, stirring frequently, until mixture is almost dry (30 to 40 minutes). Meanwhile, heat lard for deep frying.
4. Spoon filling into peppers, packing lightly so mixture will remain in cavities during frying.
5. Roll peppers in *flour*, coating entire surface. Dip in beaten eggs.
6. Fry peppers in hot deep fat until coating is golden. (Or fry in 2 inches of hot fat in a deep skil-

let, turning to brown evenly.) Remove peppers with a slotted spoon and drain on absorbent paper.
7. Arrange on serving plate and top with the Nogada Sauce. Sprinkle with pomegranate seeds.
6 SERVINGS

NOGADA SAUCE

1 cup walnuts, ground	½ teaspoon salt
½ clove garlic, ground	2 tablespoons cider vinegar
5 peppercorns, crushed	
¼ cup fine dry bread crumbs	6 to 8 tablespoons water
2 tablespoons sugar	

Mix walnuts, garlic, peppercorns, crumbs, sugar, and salt with vinegar. Stir in enough water to make a very thick sauce. Let stand 30 minutes.

Ground Ham

HAM-VEAL LOAF WITH SAUCY TOPPING

1½ lbs. ground cooked ham	¼ teaspoon ground thyme
½ lb. ground veal	¼ cup finely chopped onion
½ lb. ground pork	
2 eggs, fork beaten	½ cup finely chopped green pepper
½ teaspoon salt	2 tablespoons finely chopped parsley
⅛ teaspoon black pepper	
½ teaspoon ground nutmeg	¾ cup soft bread crumbs
½ teaspoon dry mustard	¾ cup apple juice
	Topping, *below*

1. Combine ground meat with eggs, salt, pepper, nutmeg, dry mustard, and thyme in a large bowl. Add onion, green pepper, and parsley and toss.
2. Add the crumbs and apple juice; mix thoroughly but lightly. Turn into a 9x5x3-inch loaf pan and flatten top.
3. Bake at 350°F 1 hour. Remove from oven; drain and reserve juices. Unmold loaf in a shallow baking pan and spoon some of the juices over loaf. Spoon the Topping over loaf; return to oven 30 minutes.
4. Remove loaf to a warm platter. 1 MEAT LOAF
TOPPING: Blend *⅔ cup packed light brown sugar, 2 teaspoons cornstarch, 1 teaspoon dry mustard,* and *1 teaspoon ground allspice* in a small saucepan. Add *⅔ cup apricot nectar, 3 tablespoons lemon juice,* and *2 teaspoons cider vinegar.* Bring rapidly

to boiling and cook about 2 minutes, stirring constantly. Reduce heat and simmer 10 minutes.

ABOUT 1¼ CUPS TOPPING

PARTY HAM LOAF

¼ cup pineapple syrup	2 eggs, beaten
¾ cup packed brown sugar	1 teaspoon dry mustard
1 tablespoon cider vinegar	¾ teaspoon salt
24 whole cloves	⅛ teaspoon pepper
24 canned pineapple chunks	½ teaspoon ground nutmeg
4 slices bread, cut in cubes	⅓ cup chopped onion
½ cup milk	1½ lbs. ground cooked ham
	½ lb. ground pork
	½ lb. ground veal

1. Mix the pineapple syrup, brown sugar, and vinegar in a small saucepan; heat until sugar is dissolved, stirring constantly. Pour ¼ cup syrup into a 9x5x3-inch loaf pan.
2. Insert cloves in pineapple chunks; with cloves down, arrange in pan in the shape of a pineapple.
3. Mix bread cubes, milk, and eggs together in a large bowl; lightly mix in, in order, a mixture of the mustard, salt, and pepper, the onion, ground meat, and remaining syrup. Spoon lightly into pan.
4. Bake at 350°F about 1½ hours.
5. To unmold, loosen meat from sides of pan. Pour off excess juices, invert onto warm platter, and remove pan. Form leaves with *green pepper strips* to resemble pineapple crown.

ABOUT 8 SERVINGS

HAM PINWHEEL RING

1½ cups ground ham	Baking Powder Biscuit dough, *page 93*
⅓ cup sweetened condensed milk	1 to 2 tablespoons melted butter or margarine
¼ cup pickle relish	Sauce Par Excellence, *below*
2 teaspoons prepared mustard	
2 tablespoons minced parsley	

1. Lightly mix ham with condensed milk, relish, mustard, and parsley; set aside.
2. Prepare biscuit dough. Roll into a rectangle about ¼ inch thick on a lightly floured surface. Spread ham mixture evenly over dough. Starting with long side of dough, roll up and pinch long edge to seal. (Do not pinch ends of roll.)

3. Place roll on a baking sheet, sealed edge down. Bring ends of roll together to form a ring. Brush lightly with the melted butter. With scissors or sharp knife, make cuts at 1 inch intervals around outside of ring to within ¼ inch of center. Slightly pull out and twist each section so that cut sides rest almost flat on baking sheet.
4. Bake at 400°F 20 to 30 minutes, or until ring is golden brown.
5. Meanwhile, prepare sauce and serve with ham ring garnished with *parsley*. 6 TO 8 SERVINGS

SAUCE PAR EXCELLENCE

¾ lb. fresh mushrooms, sliced lengthwise	3 tablespoons milk
½ cup butter or margarine	1½ teaspoons Worcestershire sauce
1¾ cups plus 2 tablespoons (1½ 10½-oz. cans) condensed cream of chicken soup	1½ cups dairy sour cream

1. Cook mushrooms in hot butter in a large skillet until lightly browned, stirring occasionally. Stir a blend of soup, milk, and Worcestershire sauce into skillet. Simmer, stirring constantly until heated.
2. Remove from heat. Add sour cream in very small amounts, blending after each addition. Cook over low heat, stirring constantly, until thoroughly heated (do not boil). ABOUT 4 CUPS SAUCE

SWEET-SOUR HAM PATTIES

1 cup packed brown sugar	¾ cup chopped green pepper
⅓ cup cider vinegar	¼ cup chopped onion
1 tablespoon prepared mustard	½ cup fine dry bread crumbs
3 cups ground cooked ham (about 1½ lbs.)	⅓ cup ketchup
1 egg, slightly beaten	6 canned pineapple slices, drained

1. Combine the brown sugar, vinegar, and mustard in a bowl; set aside.
2. Toss lightly in a bowl the ground ham, egg, green pepper, onion, crumbs, and ketchup. Shape mixture into 12 patties about 3½-inches in diameter. Place 6 of the patties in a lightly greased baking dish. Top each patty with a pineapple slice. Cover pineapple with another ham patty.

3. Make a hole just through top patty. Spoon about 1 tablespoon of the sauce into each hole. Brush remaining sauce over the tops of patties.
4. Set in a 350°F oven 25 minutes, or until thoroughly heated, basting several times with the sauce in baking dish. 6 SERVINGS

HAM SURPRISES

4 canned pineapple slices, drained (reserve ⅓ cup syrup)	1 egg
	3 slices bread, cut in small pieces
2 tablespoons butter	3 cups ground ham

1. Brown pineapple slices in butter in a skillet.
2. Combine syrup and egg; add bread pieces; set aside 10 minutes. Mix in ham. Shape into 8 thin patties slightly larger than pineapple slices.
3. Coat pineapple slices with brown sugar. Place on 4 ham patties; top with remaining ham patties; press edges to seal completely.
4. Lightly brown on both sides. 4 SERVINGS

Ground Lamb

ARMENIAN MEATBALLS

1 lb. ground lamb	1 cup chopped parsley
1 egg, beaten	⅓ cup finely chopped onion
½ teaspoon salt	
⅛ teaspoon black pepper	2 tablespoons butter
¼ teaspoon garlic salt	1 can (8 oz.) tomato sauce
1 cup shredded Cheddar cheese	¼ cup shredded Parmesan cheese
1 cup small soft bread cubes	

1. Lightly mix ground lamb and egg in a bowl. Blend in a mixture of the salt, pepper, and garlic salt. Add Cheddar cheese, bread cubes, parsley, and onion; mix lightly to blend. Shape into 18 2-inch balls.
2. Heat butter in a skillet. Add meatballs and brown evenly on all sides, turning gently.
3. Remove meatballs to a 1-quart shallow baking dish. Pour tomato sauce over meatballs and top with the Parmesan cheese. Cover the baking dish.
4. Set in a 350°F oven 20 minutes. Remove cover and heat an additional 10 minutes. 6 SERVINGS

CURRIED LAMB-PRUNE BURGERS

Prunes and ketchup greatly enhance the flavor of these broiled bacon-wrapped patties.

1¼ lbs. ground lamb	1 cup soft bread crumbs
½ cup ketchup	
⅔ cup snipped dried prunes	¼ cup minced parsley
	2 tablespoons minced onion
¾ teaspoon salt	
Few grains pepper	8 slices bacon
1 teaspoon curry powder	

1. Lightly mix ground lamb, ketchup, and prunes in a bowl. Blend in a mixture of seasonings. Add bread crumbs, parsley, and onion; toss lightly to blend.
2. Shape into 8 patties, fasten a slice of bacon around each, and place on broiler rack. Broil with top of meat about 5 inches from heat source 6 minutes on each side, or until desired doneness.
3. Serve with *French fries, dill pickles,* and a *tossed salad* or *cole slaw* with *cherry tomatoes.*
8 SERVINGS

LAMBURGER BROIL WITH BANANAS

1½ lbs. ground lamb	½ teaspoon salt
1½ teaspoons salt	½ teaspoon dry mustard
⅛ teaspoon pepper	½ teaspoon celery salt
2 tablespoons chopped parsley	Few grains cayenne pepper
1 medium-sized onion, chopped	½ teaspoon Worcestershire sauce
6 brown-and-serve sausage links	3 large green-tipped bananas
¼ cup butter or margarine, melted	1 large pear, halved

1. Combine ground lamb with 1½ teaspoons salt, the pepper, parsley, and onions in a bowl; mix lightly with a fork. Form into 6 thick oval-shaped patties; press a sausage lengthwise into center of each. Place on broiler rack in broiler pan.
2. Combine butter and the ½ teaspoon salt, celery salt, dry mustard, cayenne pepper, and Worcestershire sauce; blend well. Brush over the meat.
3. Broil 4 or 5 inches from source of heat about 10 minutes on each side; brush patties frequently with the seasoned butter during broiling.
4. Peel bananas; cut in half lengthwise, then crosswise. Place on broiler rack with patties; brush with seasoned butter and broil 5 minutes.

5. Arrange lamburgers on a heated serving plate with bananas in center. Garnish plate with the pear halves and sprigs of *watercress* or *parsley*.

6 LAMBURGERS

BALKAN LAMB AND EGGPLANT CASSEROLE
(Moussaka)

3 cloves garlic, minced	Freshly ground black
2 large onions, chopped	pepper
	2 teaspoons paprika
1 large green pepper, chopped	2 large eggplant, pared and cut in
1 tablespoon olive oil	½-in. slices
1½ lbs. lean ground lamb	1 cup yogurt
	4 egg yolks
1½ teaspoons salt	½ cup flour

1. Cook garlic, onion, and green pepper 3 minutes in hot oil in a large skillet. Add ground lamb and season with salt, pepper, and paprika. Separate meat and cook until pink color is gone. Using a slotted spoon, remove mixture from skillet; set aside.
2. Coat eggplant with *flour*. Lightly brown slices in hot *butter or margarine* in the skillet.
3. In a 2½-quart casserole, alternate layers of eggplant and meat; cover.
4. Bake at 350°F 45 minutes.
5. Mix remaining ingredients and spoon over mixture in casserole. Cover and continue baking 15 minutes; uncover and brown top under broiler.

8 TO 10 SERVINGS

SOUTH AFRICAN CURRY
(Bobotie)
This distinctive curried lamb recipe is from Chocolate House, Princess Street, Edinburgh, Scotland.

1 thick slice bread, crumbled (about 1 cup)	1 to 2 tablespoons sugar
	⅓ cup seedless raisins
1 cup milk	8 almonds, finely chopped
2 medium-sized onions, sliced	
	1 egg, fork beaten
1 apple, pared and sliced	2 lbs. cooked lamb or mutton, finely chopped
3 tablespoons butter	
2 tablespoons curry powder	1 egg, fork beaten

1. Soak bread crumbs in milk. Drain off milk and reserve (about ½ cup); set crumbs aside.

2. Cook onions and apple in heated butter in a large skillet until just tender, stirring occasionally. Mix in curry powder, sugar, raisins, and almonds. Blend in 1 egg, bread crumbs, then lamb. Cook a few minutes over medium heat, stirring constantly. Season to taste with *salt* and *pepper*. Turn into a buttered 2½-quart baking dish.
3. Mix reserved milk and remaining egg; season to taste with *salt* and *white pepper*. Pour over meat mixture.
4. Set in a 350°F oven about 15 minutes, or until custard is set.

ABOUT 8 SERVINGS

TOP-NOTCH LAMB BAKE

¾ lb. ground lamb	½ teaspoon salt
2 tablespoons bacon drippings	2 large tomatoes, peeled and sliced
1 teaspoon salt	1 can (4-oz.) mushrooms, drained
⅛ teaspoon pepper	
⅛ teaspoon ground allspice	4 oz. Cheddar cheese, shredded
3 tablespoons butter	1 cup soft bread crumbs
1 small onion, thinly sliced	2 tablespoons melted butter
1 lb. eggplant, pared and diced	

1. Add ground lamb to bacon drippings in a large heavy skillet; separate into small pieces and cook until lightly browned. Sprinkle evenly with a mixture of 1 teaspoon salt, pepper, and allspice. Transfer meat to a buttered 1½-quart casserole.
2. Heat 3 tablespoons butter in skillet. Add onion and cook until golden. Arrange onion over meat in casserole.
3. Add eggplant to skillet and cook until lightly browned, turning frequently. Sprinkle with ½ teaspoon salt. Put half of the eggplant over onions and arrange tomato slices over eggplant. Cover with mushrooms and remaining eggplant. Sprinkle with the cheese and then the bread crumbs which have been tossed in melted butter.
4. Set in a 400°F oven 20 minutes, or until mixture is thoroughly heated.

4 TO 6 SERVINGS

Ground Veal

SKILLET VEAL LOAF FIRENZE

1 lb. ground veal	1 medium-sized carrot,
¼ lb. ham	finely chopped
½ teaspoon salt	1 stalk celery, finely
⅛ teaspoon pepper	chopped
⅛ teaspoon ground	2 tablespoons finely
cinnamon	chopped parsley
1 teaspoon grated	¼ cup olive oil
lemon peel	2 tablespoons butter
3 eggs, beaten	or margarine
2 tablespoons flour	1 cup vegetable broth
1 medium-sized onion,	(dissolve 1 vegetable
finely chopped	bouillon cube in 1
	cup boiling water)

1. Have meat dealer grind veal and ham together three times.
2. Add salt, pepper, cinnamon, and lemon peel to beaten eggs; blend well. Lightly mix in meat. Turn onto waxed paper or aluminum foil and gently shape into a large patty. Coat with flour; set aside.
3. Add the onion, carrot, celery, and parsley to hot oil and butter in a 10-inch skillet. Cook about 5 minutes, stirring occasionally. Add meat and brown on both sides.
4. When meat is browned, add about ½ of the vegetable broth to the skillet. Cover and simmer about 25 minutes, or until meat is cooked. If necessary, add a little more hot broth to keep meat from sticking. Place meat on a hot platter; keep hot.
5. Add remaining broth to skillet; force the mixture through a coarse sieve, or purée in an electric blender. Heat the sauce; pour some over meat loaf and serve the remaining sauce in a gravy boat.

6 SERVINGS

VEAL-OYSTER LOAF

½ pt. oysters, drained	1 egg, fork beaten
1 lb. ground veal	¾ teaspoon salt
1¼ cups crushed corn	¼ teaspoon paprika
flakes	¼ teaspoon marjoram
½ cup minced onion	⅛ teaspoon thyme
¾ cup undiluted	
evaporated milk	

1. Pick over oysters to remove any shell particles; finely chop. (If oysters are frozen, thaw before using.) Combine oysters with ground veal, corn flakes, onion, evaporated milk, and egg and a mixture of the remaining ingredients.
2. Pack lightly into a greased 9x5x3-inch loaf pan.
3. Bake at 350°F about 1½ hours.
4. To unmold, loosen loaf gently from sides of pan with a spatula. Invert onto a hot serving platter and remove pan. Garnish with *parsley sprigs*.

6 TO 8 SERVINGS

VEAL-SPINACH PINWHEELS

1 pkg. (12 oz.) frozen	1 egg, beaten
chopped spinach	1½ teaspoons salt
¼ cup shredded	⅛ teaspoon black
Parmesan cheese	pepper
1 lb. ground veal	¼ teaspoon marjoram
¼ cup chopped onion	⅛ teaspoon thyme
⅔ cup soft bread	2 tablespoons butter
crumbs	or margarine

1. Cook spinach according to directions on package; drain thoroughly. Lightly toss with cheese.
2. Toss lightly the ground veal, onion, bread crumbs, egg, salt, pepper, marjoram, and thyme.
3. Put veal mixture between two pieces of waxed paper; press into a 10x6-inch rectangle. Remove top piece of paper.
4. Spread spinach mixture evenly over meat. Roll up, starting with shorter side. Wrap meat roll and chill about 30 minutes.
5. Cut meat roll into 4 slices; arrange on broiler rack. Dot with 1 tablespoon butter.
6. Broil with top of meat about 4 inches from source of heat about 8 minutes; turn and dot slices with remaining butter; broil about 3 minutes.

4 SERVINGS

PARTY VEAL LOAF WITH SAUCE

1½ lbs. ground veal	1 teaspoon dry mustard
1 lb. ground ham	1 teaspoon water
1 cup instant nonfat	1 cup fine dry bread
dry milk	crumbs
¼ cup grated onion	½ teaspoon salt
1 egg, fork beaten	⅛ teaspoon pepper
2 cans (29 oz. each)	¼ teaspoon ground
cling peach halves,	cloves
drained (reserve 3	Sauce, *page 234*
cups syrup)	

1. In a large bowl, mix the veal, ham, and dry milk with a fork. Add onion, egg, 1 cup of the reserved peach syrup, a blend of dry mustard and water, and

a mixture of bread crumbs, salt, pepper, and cloves; mix lightly but thoroughly.

2. Shape mixture into a loaf and place on a rack in a large shallow baking pan. Insert *whole cloves* into meat loaf.

3. Bake at 350°F 1½ hours. Generously spoon Sauce over loaf every 20 minutes during baking.

4. About 15 minutes before baking time is up, put the peach halves into pan around the meat loaf and spoon Sauce over them. Continue baking.

5. Let meat loaf stand a few minutes before slicing. Transfer to a serving platter and surround with peaches. Fill cavities with Sauce and pour remainder into a sauceboat.   ABOUT 12 SERVINGS

SAUCE: In a saucepan, mix the remaining 2 cups reserved peach syrup, *1 cup packed brown sugar, ¼ cup cider vinegar*, and *12 whole cloves*. Bring to boiling; simmer 5 minutes.

CANNELLONI ALLA PIEMONTESE "MAISON"

This interpretation of cannelloni served at Hotel Limone, Limone Piemonte, Italy, differs from the usual cannelloni inasmuch as squares cut from pancakes are used instead of pasta.

6 thin 10-in. pancakes	1 egg
⅓ cup finely chopped onion	⅓ cup grated Parmesan cheese
3 tablespoons olive oil	¼ teaspoon salt
½ lb. ground veal, cooked (or other cooked meat)	Pinch pepper
	Pinch nutmeg
1 pkg. (10 oz.) frozen chopped spinach, cooked and drained	1½ cups Béchamel Sauce, *page 342*

1. Cut pancakes into 2½-inch squares; keep warm.

2. Cook onion in heated olive oil in a skillet about 3 minutes. Add ground meat and cook until lightly browned. Mix spinach with meat mixture; force mixture through medium blade of food chopper.

3. Mix egg, cheese, salt, pepper, and nutmeg with meat mixture until thoroughly blended. Place about 1 tablespoon meat mixture on each pancake square and roll each into a sausage shape.

4. Arrange the filled cannelloni in a shallow buttered baking dish; cover with Béchamel Sauce.

5. Heat in a 375°F oven until golden brown. Serve very hot.   4 TO 6 SERVINGS

STUFFED CABBAGE ROLLS
(Kaldomar)

1 large head cabbage (3 to 3½ lbs.)	2 teaspoons salt
1 lb. ground veal	1 teaspoon ground nutmeg
1 lb. ground beef	2 cans (10½ oz. each) condensed beef broth
1¼ cups milk	2 soup cans water
⅔ cup fine dry bread crumbs	¼ cup flour
4 teaspoons grated onion	½ cup water

1. Remove and discard wilted outer leaves from head of cabbage; rinse and cut out the core.

2. Put cabbage in kettle; add boiling water to cover and *1 teaspoon salt*. Cover and bring water to boiling; reduce heat and simmer until cabbage leaves are softened, about 5 minutes. Carefully separate the leaves and set aside 16 large and 16 small leaves to drain on absorbent paper.

3. Combine the ground meat and the milk, crumbs, onion, salt, and nutmeg; mix thoroughly.

4. Place a small cabbage leaf in center of a large leaf. Put about ⅓ cup of the meat mixture onto the center of each small leaf. Roll each leaf, tucking ends in toward center. Fasten securely with wooden picks and tie with cord.

5. Combine beef broth and water in a saucepot and bring to boiling. Add cabbage rolls one at a time so that water continues to boil. Reduce heat; cover and cook about 25 minutes, or until the cabbage rolls are tender.

6. Remove rolls with slotted spoon; reserve broth for sauce or gravy. Remove wooden picks and cord from rolls and keep rolls warm.

7. Combine the flour and water in a saucepan and blend thoroughly. Add 2 cups of the reserved broth slowly, stirring constantly. Cook and stir over medium heat until sauce comes to boiling; cook 3 minutes longer until thickened and smooth.

8. Pour sauce over cabbage rolls in a serving dish. If desired, use *Cream Gravy, below*, instead of the sauce.   8 SERVINGS

CREAM GRAVY: Heat *3 tablespoons butter or margarine* in a saucepan; blend in *3 tablespoons flour* and cook over medium heat until bubbly. Stir in 1 cup reserved beef broth and cook, stirring constantly until boiling. Stir in *1 cup milk* and a mixture of ½ *teaspoon salt, ¼ teaspoon ground cardamon*, and a *few grains sugar*. Bring to boiling; cook 3 minutes, stirring until thickened.

Chapter 7

POULTRY & STUFFINGS

Some of us still hold to our early conviction that no special occasion dinner could be properly observed without some type of poultry being served. Turkey or goose for Thanksgiving and Christmas are traditional and much improved from the birds that graced the pilgrims' table. Modern poultry has steadily increased in popularity and, with the growth of scientifically controlled methods, prices have decreased dramatically.

To many persons poultry is best known as roasted, fried, or broiled. But there are many additional ways, some regional and international, of preparing the favorite bird and many new touches for the time-tested ways.

Poultry includes all domesticated birds used for food: chicken (including capon), turkey, duckling, goose, Rock Cornish game hen (a delicious hybrid), squab, and guinea.

CLASSES

Chicken and turkeys are classified according to size, age, and sex. Age influences tenderness of the meat and therefore determines the cooking method. Size determines the cooking time.

Chicken—Broiler, either sex, 1½ to 2½ pounds ready-to-cook weight, 10 to 12 weeks old; *fryer*, either sex, 2 to 3 pounds ready-to-cook weight, 12 to 16 weeks old; *broiler-fryer*, a meatier, more tender all-purpose young chicken varying in weight from 1½ to 4 pounds ready-to-cook weight; *roaster*, either sex, usually over 3½ pounds, and about 3 months old; *capon*, unsexed male, usually over 10 months old, 4 pounds or over, exceptionally good flavor, especially tender, with large proportion of white meat; *stewing chicken*, female, more than 10 months old, 3 to 5 pounds ready-to-cook weight.

Turkey—Fryer-roaster, either sex, usually under 16 weeks old, 4 to 8 pounds ready-to-cook weight; *young hen or tom*, female or male, usually under 8 months old, 8 to 24 pounds ready-to-cook weight; *mature hen or tom*, over 10 months old, less tender,

and seldom found on the consumer market; *frozen boned turkey* (rolls, loaves, or slices in gravy), cooked according to directions on label.

Duckling—Either sex, 8 to 9 weeks old, 3½ to 5 pounds ready-to-cook weight.

Goose—Classifications less well established, but weights range from 4 to 8 pounds ready-to-cook weight for young birds, up to 14 pounds for mature birds.

STYLES

Dressed poultry refers to birds which have been bled and feather-dressed but have head, feet, and viscera intact. *Ready-to-cook poultry* is fully cleaned and ready for cooking. Today almost all chickens, turkeys, and ducklings are completely eviscerated, vacuum-sealed in sturdy plastic bags which eliminate air pockets (and thus freezer burn), then quick-frozen and held at 0°F from processing plant to the consumer. Ready-to-cook poultry is sold fresh or ice-chilled in a few markets, but as a rule it is not easily obtainable.

Since 1953 only ready-to-cook poultry is permitted to carry United States Department of Agriculture grades on individual birds; but the use of official inspection and grading services is entirely voluntary on the part of the packers.

In many markets, chicken and turkey halves, quarters, pieces, and giblets are sold separately, usually quick-frozen. These pieces—especially breasts, thighs, and drumsticks—greatly simplify cooking and serving poultry, and facilitate meal-planning. Quick-frozen *stuffed* turkeys must be cooked without thawing. *Do not freeze your own stuffed turkeys* as the long time required to freeze them encourages the growth of bacteria.

PURCHASING GUIDE

Where tags or stamps provide information as to quality established by inspection or grading or both, this is the consumer's most reliable guide in the selection of poultry. The grading and inspection program of the United States Department of Agriculture employs three recognizable marks: 1) *inspection mark*, indicating that the bird has been processed under sanitary conditions and is wholesome food; 2) *grade mark*, indicating the quality, class, and kind—there are three grades, A, B, and C; 3) *grade and inspection mark*. Poultry bearing the combined grade and inspection marks is guaranteed to be of top quality.

When grading and inspection labels are not present, the consumer may be guided by some of the standards used in official grading. Young birds have smooth, soft, thin skin, little fat, and flexible-tipped breastbones; as the bird ages, the skin coarsens, more fat is deposited along the backbone, and the breastbone becomes more rigid. Grade A quality requires that a bird be well-formed and full-fleshed, with no defects, tears, or bruises in the skin, clean and free from pinfeathers.

STORAGE

Poultry is a perishable food and must be safeguarded against spoilage or deterioration of flavor.
Fresh poultry—To store fresh or ice-chilled ready-to-cook chicken or turkey, remove from store wrappings. Remove neck and giblets. Wrap bird (whole or cut in pieces) loosely in waxed paper or transparent, moisture-vaporproof material, ends open to let in air. Place in a shallow pan and store in the coldest part of the refrigerator. Use within 48 hours. If poultry is to be frozen, wrap securely in freezer wrap and place immediately in freezer.
Quick-frozen poultry must be kept frozen until ready to use and once thawed must not be refrozen. In thawing frozen poultry before cooking, follow directions on the label, if available. Or use one of

the following methods: *Refrigerator thawing*—Keep in original wrapping and place on a tray in refrigerator from 1 to 3 days. A 4-pound chicken or turkey requires about 1 day while a 20- to 24-pound turkey may take as long as 3 to 3½ days. *Cold-water thawing*—Place bird in its original wrapper in a large pan or in the sink; cover completely with very cold water. Change water frequently so that it will remain cold. An 8- to 12-pound bird requires 3 to 6 hours; 12- to 20-pound bird 6 to 8 hours; 20- to 24-pound bird 10 to 12 hours. Once it is thawed, refrigerate poultry if not cooking immediately. *Room-temperature thawing*—This method is less satisfactory than other methods. If time permits, refrigerator thawing is the most satisfactory method.
Cooked poultry, gravy, and stuffing should not be left at room temperature for longer than it takes to finish the meal. Never store bird with stuffing; remove stuffing and store it covered in refrigerator; cover gravy and refrigerate. If only one side of a roast bird has been carved, wrap remainder of bird in waxed paper, aluminum foil, or moisture-vapor-proof material; store in refrigerator. If more than one half of the meat has been used, remove the remaining meat from the bones and wrap tightly before storing. Cooked pieces should be tightly wrapped and refrigerated. Do not keep cooked poultry, however carefully stored, for more than a few days. If keeping leftover turkey or other poultry for more than several days, immediately remove meat from bones, wrap meat in moisture-vapor-proof material, and store in freezer.

PREPARATION FOR COOKING

Ready-to-cook poultry, whole or in pieces, should be rinsed in cold water, drained immediately, and patted dry. It should never be allowed to soak in water, as soaking dissipates flavor. *Dressed poultry* should be drawn immediately, preferably at the market. Remove pinfeathers with a sharp-pointed knife or a strawberry huller. Singe the bird over a flame, turning quickly until all down and hair are burnt off. Then wash as for ready-to-cook poultry.

Before roasting, neck and body cavities of whole birds are rubbed with salt, then usually are stuffed (never stuff until ready to roast), then trussed, and a meat thermometer inserted. Poultry pieces are often coated with a mixture of flour, salt, pepper, and other seasonings before frying; before broiling they are seasoned with salt and pepper.
To coat poultry pieces evenly—Put a mixture of

flour and seasonings into a bowl or onto a piece of waxed paper. Coat one or a few pieces of poultry at a time. Or shake a few pieces at a time with flour in a plastic or clean paper bag.

COOKING POULTRY

Two general principles apply to the cooking of all kinds of poultry: 1) Cook at low to moderate heat for a suitable length of time. High temperatures shrink the muscle tissue and make the meat tough, dry, and hard. Poultry should always be cooked until well done; the meat should separate easily from the bone and should be tender to the fork. 2) Suit the method of cooking to the age or class of the bird. Young birds of all kinds may be broiled, fried, or roasted in an open pan. Older, less tender birds require cooking by moist heat in a covered casserole or Dutch oven, or in water or steam.

A recommended method of cooking turkey when a moist product is desired is wrapping the bird in heavy-duty aluminum foil and cooking it at a comparatively high oven temperature for a shorter time than is required for roasting, uncovered, at a lower temperature. Directions for roasting in foil are often included on the box in which foil is packed.

Another satisfactory method may be used if one prefers an especially moist bird. Encase the bird securely in a brown carry-out grocery bag and place, seam side of bag up, on the rack in a roasting pan. Use a moderate oven temperature (325°F) for a medium-sized bird and a slow temperature (275° to 300°F) for a bird 20 pounds and up.

Stuffing Poultry for Roasting

Ingredients for a stuffing should be mixed *just before needed* and the bird should be stuffed *just before roasting*. Never stuff a bird a day in advance and store in refrigerator or freezer. These are safety precautions to prevent food poisoning, since stuffing is the perfect medium for disease-producing bacteria. *Immediately* after the meal is served, remove the stuffing from the bird and store, covered, in the refrigerator. Use leftover stuffing within 2 or 3 days; heat thoroughly before serving.

Any extra stuffing which cannot be put into the bird may be put in a greased, covered baking dish or wrapped in aluminum foil and baked in the oven during the last hour of roasting.

Tests for Doneness of Roast Poultry

A meat thermometer used to test doneness should register 180°-185°F when inserted in center of thigh muscle or 165°F when inserted in center of stuffing. Poultry is also done when the thickest part of drumstick feels soft when pressed with fingers protected with clean cloth or paper napkin.

TIMETABLE FOR ROASTING*

Kind	Ready-to-Cook Weight (Pounds)	Oven Temperature Constant	Approx. Total Roasting Time (Hours)	Internal Temperature of Bird
Chicken	1½ to 2	400°F	1 to 1¼	
	2 to 2½	400°F	1¼ to 1½	
	2½ to 3	375°F	1½ to 2	
	3 to 4	375°F	2 to 2½	
Capon	5 to 6	325°F	2½	
Turkey**	6 to 8	325°F	3 to 3½	180°-185°F
	8 to 12	325°F	3½ to 4½	180°-185°F
	12 to 16	325°F	4½ to 5½	180°-185°F
	16 to 20	325°F	5½ to 6½	180°-185°F
	20 to 24	325°F	6½ to 7	180°-185°F
halves or quarters	5 to 8	325°F	2½ to 3½	180°-185°F
	8 to 10	325°F	3½ to 4	180°-185°F
	10 to 12	325°F	4 to 4½	180°-185°F
rolls, boneless***	3 to 5	325°F	2½ to 3	170°-175°F
	5 to 7	325°F	3 to 3½	170°-175°F
	7 to 9	325°F	3½ to 4	170°-175°F

Kind	Ready-to-Cook Weight (Pounds)	Oven Temperature Constant	Approx. Total Roasting Time (Hours)	Internal Temperature of Bird
Duckling	4 to 5	325°F	2½ to 3	
Goose	4 to 8	325°F	2¾ to 3½	
	8 to 12	325°F	3½ to 4¼	
	12 to 14	325°F	4¼ to 4¾	
Rock Cornish game hen	about 1	400°F	1	

*This timetable covers poultry thawed and stuffed at home. Decrease roasting time 15 to 20 minutes if poultry is not stuffed.

**When dinner is set for a definite hour, start roasting bird 20 to 30 minutes ahead of schedule to avoid delay should the turkey take longer to cook than was estimated from the timetable.

***Lengthen roasting time approximately 30 minutes if cooking rolls from the frozen state.

ROTISSERIE ROASTING

When using a rotisserie, check and follow manufacturer's directions for regulating the rotisserie temperature. Follow this guide for roasting time.
Chicken: Follow *Timetable for Roasting, page 237.*
Turkey: 4 to 6 pounds—2½ to 3 hours; 6 to 8 pounds—3 to 3½ hours; 8 to 10 pounds—3½ to 4 hours; 10 to 12 pounds—4 to 5 hours. *Boneless rolls:* 3 to 5 pounds—2 to 2½ hours; 5 to 7 pounds—3 to 3½ hours; 7 to 9 pounds—3½ to 4 hours.
Duckling: 4 to 5 pounds—1½ to 2 hours.
Rock Cornish game hen: 1 pound—1 to 1¼ hours.

CHICKEN

Roast Chicken

HONEY-GLAZED FILBERT ROAST CHICKEN
A new flavor twist in the stuffing and the glaze.

½ pkg. herb-seasoned stuffing mix (2 cups)	1 roaster chicken or capon, about 5 lbs.
1 cup toasted filberts, chopped	½ cup honey
½ cup chopped celery	2 tablespoons soy sauce
1 chicken liver, finely chopped	1 teaspoon grated orange peel
½ cup butter or margarine, melted	2 tablespoons orange juice
½ cup water	Green grapes
	Filbert Glacé, *page 606*

1. Combine stuffing mix with the filberts, celery, chicken liver, butter, and water; toss lightly. Stuff cavity of chicken with the mixture, then tie chicken legs and wings with cord to hold close to body.
2. Place chicken, breast up, on rack in a shallow roasting pan. Roast at 325°F 2½ to 3 hours, or until chicken tests done. (The thickest part of drumstick feels soft when pressed with fingers and meat thermometer registers 180° to 185°F.)

3. Meanwhile, combine honey, soy sauce, and orange peel and juice. Brush chicken frequently with the mixture during last hour of roasting.
4. Place chicken on a serving platter and garnish with grapes and Filbert Glacé.   6 SERVINGS
NOTE: To toast filberts, spread in a shallow pan and set in a 400°F oven 10 to 15 minutes, stirring occasionally to toast evenly.

PENNSYLVANIA DUTCH ROAST CHICKEN
This chicken, smothered with a coating which helps to hold in the natural juices, is steamed (not truly roasted) to succulent perfection.

1 roaster chicken, 3 to 4 lbs.	Bread Stuffing, *page 239*
Butter or margarine, softened	1 cup dairy sour cream

1. Rub inside of chicken with a mixture of *salt* and *pepper*, then rub generously with butter. Fill with stuffing; sew, or skewer and lace with cord.
2. Put chicken into a roasting pan; cover.
3. Roast at 400°F 1½ to 2 hours, or until chicken is tender; about every 15 minutes during roasting

spoon some of the sour cream over the chicken. Remove cover for the last 30 minutes of roasting if a darker brown is desired.

4.   For a thicker gravy, *1 tablespoon flour* may be stirred into the liquid in pan after removing the chicken. Set pan over heat and bring mixture to boiling, stirring constantly; boil 1 minute.

4 TO 6 SERVINGS

BREAD STUFFING: Soak *4 slices white bread* in *cold water* and squeeze out all excess moisture. Using a fork, fluff bread and drizzle with *2 tablespoons melted butter or margarine*. Blend into *1 slightly beaten egg* a mixture of *1 teaspoon salt*, *⅛ teaspoon black pepper*, and *¼ teaspoon poultry seasoning*, then *1 teaspoon chopped parsley* and *1 teaspoon grated onion*. Add egg mixture to bread mixture and toss lightly until thoroughly mixed. If desired, finely chopped *cooked giblets* may be added.

STUFFED CHICKEN, JAMAICAN STYLE

1 roaster chicken or capon, about 6 lbs.	Sweet Potato Stuffing, *below*

1.   Rub cavities of chicken with a mixture of *salt* and *pepper*. Lightly fill body and neck cavities with Sweet Potato Stuffing. Truss. Brush skin thoroughly with *melted butter or margarine*.

2.   Place chicken, breast up, on rack in a shallow roasting pan. Spread a piece of cheesecloth which has been dipped in melted butter or margarine over top and sides of chicken.

3.   Roast uncovered at 325°F 3 to 3½ hours, or until thickest part of drumstick is tender. Keep cloth moist during roasting by brushing occasionally with fat from pan.

ABOUT 6 SERVINGS

SWEET POTATO STUFFING: Combine *1¼ cups mashed sweet potatoes*, *7 slices bread*, toasted and cut into cubes, and *½ cup finely chopped celery* in a bowl. Put *6 pork sausage links* and *2 tablespoons water* into a cold skillet. Cover and cook slowly 8 to 10 minutes. Remove cover and pour off fat. With a fork break links into small pieces. Add *⅓ cup chopped onion* and cook over medium heat until onion is transparent and sausage is lightly browned. Remove from heat and stir in *1¼ teaspoons salt*, *¼ teaspoon pepper*, *½ teaspoon ground thyme*, *¼ teaspoon sage*, *¼ teaspoon crushed marjoram leaves*, and *2 tablespoons butter or margarine*. Add to sweet potato mixture and lightly mix together.

ABOUT 4½ CUPS STUFFING

NOTE: Any extra stuffing may be put into a greased covered baking dish or wrapped in aluminum foil and baked during the last hour of roasting.

Oven-Fried or Baked Chicken

OVEN-BARBECUED CHICKEN

3 broiler-fryers, 1½ to 2 lbs. each, quartered	¼ teaspoon freshly ground black pepper
6 tablespoons butter, melted	¾ to 1 cup Golden Barbecue Sauce, *below*
1½ teaspoons salt	

1.   Put chicken on rack in a roasting pan and brush generously with butter; sprinkle with salt and pepper.

2.   Roast at 350°F about 50 minutes, or until golden brown, brushing occasionally with butter.

3.   Brush browned chicken with Golden Barbecue Sauce and repeat every 5 minutes; continue to roast about 40 minutes, or until chicken is tender. Serve immediately.

6 SERVINGS

GOLDEN BARBECUE SAUCE: Pour *¾ cup light molasses* into a bowl; gradually add *½ cup prepared mustard*, *2 tablespoons plus 2 teaspoons Worcestershire sauce*, *¾ cup cider vinegar*, *1 teaspoon Tabasco*, *⅛ teaspoon marjoram*, and *⅛ teaspoon oregano*, blending well after each addition. Store, covered, in refrigerator. Mix thoroughly before using.

ABOUT 2 CUPS SAUCE

NOTE: This sauce may also be used in preparing barbecued frankfurters, spareribs, hamburgers, bologna, or canned luncheon meat.

PENNY-WISE CHICKEN CASSEROLE

1 small head cabbage, cut in 1½-in. wedges	2 tablespoons brown sugar
1 teaspoon flour	1 teaspoon flour
1 teaspoon caraway seed	1 broiler-fryer, 2 to 2-½ lbs., cut up
4 small tart red apples, cored and cut in ½-in. rings	½ cup cider vinegar
	1 tablespoon salt
	2 tablespoons butter or margarine, melted

1.   Arrange cabbage on bottom of a 2-quart shallow casserole; sprinkle with 1 teaspoon flour and the caraway seed.

2. Top with apple rings; sprinkle with a mixture of brown sugar and 1 teaspoon flour.

3. Arrange chicken pieces, skin side up, on top of cabbage-apple mixture. Pour a mixture of the vinegar and salt over chicken; pour melted butter evenly over chicken; cover casserole.

4. Bake at 350°F 45 minutes. Remove cover; bake 30 minutes or until chicken is browned and tender.

4 TO 6 SERVINGS

CHICKEN KUMQUAT

1 broiler-fryer, 2½ to 3 lbs., cut up	1 jar (8 oz.) kumquats and syrup
½ cup flour	3 tablespoons coarsely chopped crystallized ginger
1 teaspoon salt	
¼ teaspoon pepper	
½ teaspoon rosemary leaves, crushed	1 cup chicken broth
	Sliced almonds, toasted
½ cup butter or margarine	

1. Coat chicken pieces evenly with a mixture of flour, salt, pepper, and rosemary.

2. Heat butter in a skillet. Add chicken pieces and brown evenly over medium heat, about 15 minutes. When chicken is browned, arrange pieces in a shallow baking pan.

3. Put kumquats and syrup into an electric blender container; blend until smooth. Mix kumquat purée, ginger, and chicken broth with drippings in skillet. Heat to boiling. Pour sauce over chicken.

4. Bake at 350°F about 45 minutes, or until tender, basting several times. Garnish with almonds.

ABOUT 4 SERVINGS

CHICKEN AND SWEET POTATOES IN CREAM

4 chicken breasts	⅛ teaspoon ground cloves
1 cup cream	
2 tablespoons honey	2 tablespoons butter or margarine
½ teaspoon salt	
½ teaspoon ground nutmeg	1 can (18 oz.) sweet potatoes
¼ teaspoon ground allspice	

1. Arrange chicken, skin side up, in a shallow baking pan.

2. Mix together cream, honey, salt, nutmeg, allspice, and cloves. Pour over chicken. Dot with butter.

3. Bake at 350°F 30 minutes, basting with cream mixture. Remove from oven and arrange sweet potatoes around chicken; spoon sauce over potatoes, if desired. Return to oven and bake 30 minutes longer, or until chicken is tender. 4 SERVINGS

CHICKEN BRAZILIAN

Succulent coconut-stuffed chicken breasts, a zestful tomato sauce, browned bananas, pineapple, and sweet potatoes all add to the allure of this hearty South American meal.

4 large chicken breasts	6 tablespoons cooking oil
¼ cup butter or margarine, softened	Sauce, *below*
1 tablespoon chili powder	2 cooked sweet potatoes, quartered
¼ cup flaked coconut	4 slices pineapple
1 egg, fork beaten	2 firm bananas, peeled and cut in half lengthwise
½ cup fine dry bread crumbs	

1. Remove skin and bones from the chicken breasts, keeping breasts whole. Rinse and pat dry; set aside.

2. Cream the butter with the chili powder. Blend in the coconut. Divide the mixture into 4 portions.

3. Spoon one portion onto each breast, roll and skewer. Tuck in sides and skewer. Repeat for each chicken breast.

4. Dip breasts in the egg, then roll in bread crumbs to coat evenly.

5. Heat 3 tablespoons oil in a large heavy skillet. Add the chicken and brown evenly on all sides. Transfer to a shallow baking pan and bake at 400°F about 15 minutes, or until chicken is tender when pierced with a fork.

6. Prepare sauce; set aside and keep warm.

7. Meanwhile, heat remaining 3 tablespoons oil in the skillet. Lightly brown the pineapple, sweet potatoes, and bananas. Arrange with chicken on serving platter. Garnish with *leaf lettuce, toasted nuts,* and *coconut.* Serve with sauce. 4 SERVINGS

SAUCE: Heat *2 tablespoons cooking or salad oil;* add *¼ cup finely chopped onion* and cook 2 minutes, stirring occasionally. Blend in a mixture of *1 tablespoon flour* and *1 teaspoon curry powder.* Heat until bubbly, stirring constantly. Remove from heat; stir in *1 can (8 ounces) tomato sauce* and *¼ cup water.* Bring to boiling and cook 1 to 2 minutes longer, stirring constantly.

ORIENTAL OVEN-FRIED CHICKEN

2 tablespoons soy sauce
2 tablespoons honey
1 tablespoon lemon
   juice
1 clove garlic, minced
3 lbs. chicken pieces
   for frying

¾ cup flour
¾ cup all-vegetable
   shortening, melted in
   a skillet
2 cans (3 oz. each) chow
   mein noodles, finely
   crushed

1. In a large bowl or dish, mix the soy sauce, honey, lemon juice, and garlic. Put chicken into marinade and turn pieces to coat. Cover and refrigerate 2 to 3 hours, turning pieces once or twice.
2. Remove chicken and coat with flour (shake in a plastic bag, if desired). Dip pieces in melted shortening and then coat with crushed noodles. Arrange chicken pieces, skin side down, one layer deep in a large shallow baking dish; pour any remaining shortening over chicken.
3. Bake at 375°F 30 minutes. Turn chicken pieces over and bake about 15 minutes, or until tender.

6 SERVINGS

Broiled Chicken

FLAVOR-FULL BROILED CHICKEN

Spread *chicken pieces* generously with an *Herb Butter*, *Lemon Butter*, or *Honey Glaze*, *below*, spreading some of the butter or glaze between skin and meat. Arrange chicken, skin side down, in a shallow baking pan or broiler pan without rack. Broil about 9 inches from source of heat 25 to 30 minutes, brushing occasionally with butter or glaze. Turn and broil, continuing to brush, 20 minutes longer, or until tender.

HERB BUTTERS

Rosemary: Mix thoroughly with *½ cup butter or margarine*, softened, *1½ teaspoons crushed rosemary leaves* and *2 teaspoons snipped chives*.
Tarragon: Mix thoroughly with *½ cup butter or margarine*, softened, *1½ teaspoons crushed tarragon leaves*.
Herb-Garlic: Mix thoroughly with *½ cup butter or margarine*, softened, *1 clove garlic*, minced, *¾ teaspoon thyme*, and *¼ teaspoon curry powder*.
LEMON BUTTER: Blend *¼ cup melted butter or margarine*, *¼ cup cooking oil*, *3 tablespoons lemon juice*, *¼ teaspoon seasoned salt*, and *¼ teaspoon Tabasco*.

HONEY GLAZE: Blend *½ cup honey*, *⅓ cup soy sauce*, *6 tablespoons lemon juice*, *2 teaspoons dry mustard*, and *2 cloves garlic*, minced.

BROILED CHICKEN

2 broiler-fryer chickens,
   2 lbs. each
Melted butter or
   margarine

2 teaspoons salt
½ teaspoon mono-
   sodium glutamate
½ teaspoon pepper

1. Cook heart, gizzard, and liver for stock, if gravy is desired.
2. Split chickens into lengthwise halves. Cut away backbone and neck. Crack drumstick-joint and joints of wings. Skewer legs and wings to body.
3. Arrange chicken pieces, skin side down, in a broiler pan without rack. Brush generously with melted butter; sprinkle with a mixture of the salt, monosodium glutamate, and pepper.
4. Place pan under broiler with top of chicken 7 to 9 inches from source of heat. Broil 40 to 45 minutes, or until browned.
5. Turn pieces about every 10 minutes and brush each time with melted butter.
6. Place on serving platter and pour pan juice over pieces.

4 SERVINGS

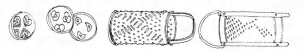

GOURMET FRIED CHICKEN

½ lb. Swiss cheese, cut
   in pieces
4 slices bacon, cut in
   pieces
¾ green pepper, seeded,
   rinsed, and cut in
   pieces

½ onion, peeled and cut
   in pieces
¼ cup mayonnaise
3 lbs. fried chicken
   pieces

1. Grind cheese, bacon, green pepper and onion together, using medium blade of a food chopper. Mix with mayonnaise.
2. Arrange fried chicken on a broiler rack; spread with cheese mixture.
3. Place under broiler about 6 inches from source of heat, until bubbly hot and brown, about 7 minutes.

4 TO 6 SERVINGS

Fried Chicken

HINTS FOR FRIED CHICKEN

Generally the pieces of chicken are dipped in liquid before coating with flour or other dry ingredients.

Materials for dipping: Beaten egg with water, milk, orange juice, lemon juice, or herbs; undiluted evaporated milk; buttermilk; a marinade.

Materials for coating: Seasoned flour with herbs such as tarragon, thyme, sage, oregano, or basil; instant potato flakes; crushed corn flakes or other dry cereals; finely crushed pretzels or herb stuffing mix; pancake or waffle mix or cornbread mix.

Methods of frying:

Pan frying—Heat in a heavy skillet over medium heat enough fat or cooking oil to cover bottom to a depth of ½ inch. Put meatiest pieces of chicken skin side down in skillet. Add less meaty pieces as first ones brown. Turn with tongs or two spoons to brown all sides. When evenly browned, reduce heat, add 1 to 2 tablespoons water, and cover skillet. Cook slowly 25 to 40 minutes, or until thickest pieces are tender when pierced with a fork. Uncover skillet last 10 minutes of cooking to crisp the crust.

Deep frying—Heat fat for deep frying (see *page 19*) to 350°F. Deep fry only as many pieces of chicken at one time as will lie uncrowded one layer deep in the hot fat. Deep fry chicken 10 to 13 minutes, or until tender and golden brown. (Chicken livers require only about 1 minute frying time.) Turn pieces with tongs several times. Drain over fat a few seconds; remove to absorbent paper to drain thoroughly. Be sure fat is heated to 350°F before frying each layer of chicken.

EMPRESS CHICKEN

½ cup butter or margarine	1 teaspoon salt
1 clove garlic, crushed	½ teaspoon black pepper
1 broiler-fryer, 2½ lbs., cut up	½ teaspoon paprika
½ cup herb-seasoned stuffing mix, rolled fine	1 tablespoon snipped parsley

1. Put butter and garlic into a large electric skillet and heat to 360°F.
2. Coat chicken pieces with a mixture of the stuff-ing mix, salt, pepper and paprika. Put chicken pieces into the skillet; brown evenly on all sides.
3. Reduce heat to 260°F and allow chicken to cook, uncovered, until tender, about 30 minutes, turning occasionally. Sprinkle with parsley and serve with *Cherry-Filled Peaches, page 386.*

4 SERVINGS

FRIED CHICKEN À LA SOUTHERN BELLE

1 broiler-fryer, 2½ to 3 lbs., cut up	1½ teaspoons salt
1½ cups cream	1 teaspoon monosodium glutamate
1½ teaspoons savory	¼ teaspoon freshly ground black pepper
1 teaspoon freshly ground black pepper	Shortening and butter (equal parts)
¾ cup all-purpose flour	
1½ teaspoons paprika	

1. Marinate chicken pieces 1 hour in a mixture of cream, savory, and 1 teaspoon pepper, turning once.
2. Remove chicken from cream. (Cream may be used for gravy.) Coat with a mixture of the flour, paprika, salt, monosodium glutamate, and the ¼ teaspoon pepper. Set aside 30 minutes.
3. Meanwhile, fill a large heavy skillet one-half full with the fat. Heat to 360°F.
4. Fry only a few chicken pieces at a time 10 to 13 minutes (about 5 minutes for wings), or until tender and browned; turn pieces several times during cooking. Drain over fat a few seconds; remove to absorbent paper-lined platter. Keep warm.
5. Serve with *fruit kabobs.* (Thread pineapple half-slices, Spicy Prunes, *page 387*, and maraschino cherries onto skewers). Heat, if desired.

4 SERVINGS

SWISS-CAPPED GLAZED CHICKEN

2 broiler-fryers, 2½ to 3 lbs. each, cut up	⅔ cup orange juice
½ cup all-purpose flour	2 tablespoons lemon juice
2 teaspoons salt	1 cup finely shredded Swiss cheese
¼ teaspoon pepper	½ cup toasted slivered blanched almonds
¼ to ½ cup butter or margarine	½ teaspoon paprika
1½ cups currant jelly	

1. Coat chicken pieces with a mixture of the flour, salt, and pepper.
2. Heat butter in a large skillet. Add chicken pieces, skin side down, and brown evenly.

3. Meanwhile, beat together the jelly and orange and lemon juices.

4. Pour jelly mixture over browned chicken pieces. Cover skillet and simmer about 45 minutes, or until chicken is tender. Spoon glaze over chicken occasionally during cooking.

5. Top evenly with cheese, almonds, and paprika. Place under broiler 4 inches from source of heat until cheese is melted, about 1 minute. Serve immediately.   ABOUT 8 SERVINGS

CHICKEN PILAF

Also know as pilau, pilaw, or pilav in various Middle-East countries, this rice dish is usually served as a meat accompaniment. However, sometimes meat, chicken, or vegetables are combined with the rice and the dish is served as an entrée.

2 broiler-fryers, 2 lbs. each, cut up	4¼ cups chicken stock*
2 teaspoons salt	6 slices bacon, diced
½ teaspoon pepper	2 medium-sized onions, chopped
1½ teaspoons monosodium glutamate	2 medium-sized green peppers, chopped
¼ cup butter (use half olive oil, if desired)	3 medium-sized ripe tomatoes, cut in eighths
1 large clove garlic, minced	1 teaspoon celery salt
1 teaspoon crushed marjoram	2½ cups uncooked rice
	1 can (30 oz.) sliced pineapple, drained

1. Season chicken breasts, thighs, and drumsticks with a mixture of salt, pepper, and monosodium glutamate.

2. Heat butter and garlic in a Dutch oven. Add chicken and brown on all sides. Sprinkle with marjoram and add ½ cup hot chicken stock. Cover and simmer 20 to 30 minutes, or until chicken is tender. Transfer chicken and drippings to a large bowl.

3. In same Dutch oven, fry bacon until crisp; remove to bowl with chicken. Measure fat and set aside ¼ cup. Add enough butter to remaining fat to make 3 tablespoonfuls and return to Dutch oven.

4. Add onion and green pepper to fat and cook 3 minutes, stirring occasionally. Stir in tomatoes and celery salt; cook only until tomatoes are heated but not soft. Season mixture with *¼ teaspoon salt* and *⅛ teaspoon pepper*; spoon over chicken.

5. Return the ¼ cup fat to Dutch oven; add rice. Cook slowly, stirring frequently, until rice is golden.

6. Heat remaining 3¾ cups chicken stock to boiling; add to rice with *2 teaspoons salt* and *½ teaspoon freshly ground black pepper*. Cover closely and cook over low heat until liquid is absorbed, about 25 minutes. Gently stir in the vegetables and bacon. Spoon chicken (with drippings in bowl) over vegetables and put 3 pineapple slices (cut in wedges) on top. Cover and cook over low heat until mixture is heated through.

7. To serve, pile rice and vegetables onto a large platter; place chicken on top. Surround with remaining pineapple slices, lightly browned in *2 tablespoons butter*.   ABOUT 8 SERVINGS

*To prepare stock, put chicken backs, necks, wings and gizzards into a saucepot. Cover with *6 cups water*. Add *¼ cup chopped onion, celery tops, 2 sprigs parsley, 2 teaspoons salt, 6 whole cloves,* and *3 peppercorns*. Cover and simmer until broth is richly flavored; cool, strain, and refrigerate.

GOOD FORTUNE CHICKEN WITH PINEAPPLE PIQUANT

1 egg, fork beaten	½ cup onion chunks
⅓ cup water	1 tablespoon cooking oil
1 tablespoon milk	1 can (about 15 oz.) pineapple chunks (reserve syrup)
¼ cup flour	
1 tablespoon cornstarch	½ cup cider vinegar
1 tablespoon cornmeal	½ cup packed brown sugar
⅛ teaspoon baking powder	
12 small chicken legs	2 tablespoons soy sauce
Fat for deep frying heated to 350°F	¼ cup water
	1 tablespoon cornstarch
½ cup green pepper chunks	

1. Beat the egg, water, and milk with a mixture of flour, cornstarch, cornmeal, and baking powder in a bowl until smooth. Dip each chicken leg into the batter and drain over bowl a few seconds.

2. Fry pieces in hot fat 15 minutes, or until chicken is crisp brown and tender. Remove with slotted spoon and drain over fat; place on absorbent paper.

3. Meanwhile, cook green pepper and onion in the hot cooking oil in a large skillet until crisp-tender, stirring occasionally. Push vegetables to one side of skillet.

4. Pour in reserved pineapple syrup; add vinegar, brown sugar, soy sauce, and a mixture of water and cornstarch. Stir until blended. Mix in pineapple.

Bring rapidly to boiling, stirring constantly; cook 3 minutes.

5. Serve chicken legs with sauce as an appetizer or main dish. If desired, add *1 tablespoon sesame seed* to sauce, or sprinkle over chicken when served. 4 TO 6 SERVINGS

MANCHA MANTELES

Mexicans have given this incomparable creation its strangely apt name which translates as Tablecloth Stainer!

3 tablespoons butter	¼ cup sugar
3 tablespoons olive oil	1½ teaspoons salt
1 lb. lean boneless pork, cut in 1-in. pieces	1 tablespoon chili powder
2 broiler-fryers, 2½ to 3 lbs. each, cut up, seasoned, and floured*	1 teaspoon ground cinnamon
	3 whole cloves
1 large onion, sliced	1 bay leaf
1 green pepper, sliced	2 cups cubed raw sweet potato
1 can (6 oz.) tomato paste	1 cup fresh pineapple pieces
¼ cup unblanched almonds, toasted	1 cup diced tart apple
1 tablespoon sesame seed, toasted	

1. Heat half the butter and half the olive oil in a large skillet. Add pork and brown well; remove to a large saucepot. Set aside.
2. Brown chicken evenly in skillet adding the remaining butter and olive oil as needed. Transfer chicken to the saucepot.
3. Add onion and green pepper to drippings in skillet and cook about 5 minutes, stirring occasionally. Remove from heat and spoon into an electric blender container. Add tomato paste, almonds, and sesame seed; blend until smooth.
4. Return mixture to skillet; stir in *4 cups hot water* and sugar, salt, chili powder, cinnamon, cloves, and bay leaf. Bring to boiling; simmer, uncovered, about 15 minutes.
5. Pour the sauce over chicken and pork in saucepot. Bring to boiling and simmer, covered, about 30 minutes. Add the sweet potato and cook 15 minutes longer. Stir in the pineapple and apple; heat thoroughly.
6. Serve in soup plates. 8 TO 10 SERVINGS
*If available, use a 4- to 5-pound chicken and adjust the cooking time accordingly.

CHICKEN AMANDE

1 broiler-fryer, about 3 lbs., cut up	1 teaspoon seasoned salt
3 tablespoons shortening	½ teaspoon black pepper
1 clove garlic, minced	½ teaspoon crushed tarragon
¼ cup chopped onion	½ cup toasted slivered blanched almonds
2 tablespoons flour	
2 tablespoons tomato paste	¾ cup dairy sour cream
1½ cups chicken broth (dissolve 2 chicken bouillon cubes in 1½ cups boiling water)	2 tablespoons shredded Parmesan cheese

1. Brown chicken on all sides in hot shortening in a large skillet; remove pieces as they brown.
2. Add garlic and onion to skillet and cook, stirring occasionally.
3. Stir in flour and tomato paste; pour in chicken broth. Cook slowly, stirring constantly, until mixture boils. Return chicken to skillet. Sprinkle with a mixture of seasoned salt, pepper, and tarragon; top with ¼ cup of the almonds. Cover and cook over low heat 45 to 60 minutes, or until tender. Remove chicken pieces to a hot serving dish.
4. Add sour cream gradually to the sauce, stirring constantly. Heat thoroughly (do not boil). Pour over chicken. Sprinkle with the Parmesan cheese and remaining almonds. ABOUT 6 SERVINGS

CHICKEN PAPRIKA

A favorite recipe from famous newspaper columnist Abigail Van Buren.

¼ cup butter or margarine	3 tablespoons flour
	1½ teaspoons salt
2 tablespoons cooking oil	¼ teaspoon freshly ground black pepper
2 broiler-fryers, 2½ to 3 lbs. each, cut up	1 tablespoon ketchup
½ cup sliced onion	1¾ cups chicken broth (dissolve 2 chicken bouillon cubes in 1¾ cups boiling water)
½ cup sliced carrot	
½ cup sliced celery	
2 tablespoons paprika	½ cup dairy sour cream

1. Heat half of the butter and half of the oil in a Dutch oven or large skillet. Add chicken a few pieces at a time and brown evenly; remove chicken as it browns. If needed, add more butter and oil.
2. Add any remaining butter and oil to skillet, stir

in vegetables, and cook 5 minutes, stirring occasionally.

3. Stir in paprika and cook 1 minute. Blend in flour and heat until bubbly. Stir in salt, pepper, ketchup, and broth. Bring to boiling, stirring constantly, and cook 1 to 2 minutes. Reduce heat and simmer, covered, 10 minutes.

4. Add chicken; simmer, covered, 35 to 40 minutes, or until chicken is tender.

5. Remove chicken and vegetables to a hot platter; keep hot.

6. Gradually add sour cream to sauce, stirring constantly; heat thoroughly (do not boil). Spoon some of the sauce over chicken; serve remaining sauce in a bowl. 6 SERVINGS

CHICKEN À LA KISMIS

3 lbs. chicken pieces for frying (legs, thighs, and breasts)
1 tablespoon flour
1 teaspoon seasoned salt
¾ teaspoon paprika
1½ tablespoons cooking oil
1½ tablespoons butter or margarine
1 clove garlic, minced
⅓ cup chicken broth
2 tablespoons cider vinegar
1 tablespoon brown sugar
¼ teaspoon rosemary
1 can (11 oz.) mandarin oranges, drained (reserve syrup)
1 jar (4 oz.) maraschino cherries, drained (reserve syrup)
1 tablespoon water
1 tablespoon cornstarch
½ cup dark seedless raisins

1. Coat the chicken pieces with a mixture of the flour, seasoned salt, and paprika. Heat cooking oil, butter, and garlic in a large, heavy skillet. Add chicken pieces and brown well on all sides.

2. Mix the chicken broth, vinegar, brown sugar, and rosemary with the reserved syrups. Pour into skillet; cover and cook slowly 25 minutes, or until chicken is tender.

3. Remove chicken pieces to a serving dish and keep warm; skim any excess fat from liquid in skillet. Blend water with cornstarch and stir into liquid in skillet. Add raisins, bring to boiling, and cook, stirring constantly, about 5 minutes, or until mixture is thickened and smooth.

4. Mix in oranges and cherries; heat thoroughly. Pour over chicken and serve with fluffy *cooked rice*.
ABOUT 6 SERVINGS

CHICKEN CACCIATORE

Cacciatore, meaning "hunter" in Italian, indicates that the food, usually chicken, is prepared in the "hunter's style," that is, simmering the fowl in a well-seasoned tomato and wine sauce.

¼ cup cooking oil
1 broiler-fryer, 2½ lbs., cut up
2 onions, sliced
2 cloves garlic, minced
3 tomatoes, quartered
2 green peppers, sliced
1 small bay leaf
1 teaspoon salt
¼ teaspoon pepper
½ teaspoon celery seed
1 teaspoon crushed oregano or basil
1 can (8 oz.) tomato sauce
¼ cup sauterne
8 oz. spaghetti, cooked according to pkg. directions

1. Heat oil in a large heavy skillet; add chicken and brown on all sides. Remove from skillet.

2. Add onion and garlic to oil remaining in skillet and cook until onion is tender but not brown; stir occasionally.

3. Return chicken to skillet and add the tomatoes, green pepper, and bay leaf.

4. Mix the salt, pepper, celery seed, and oregano and blend with tomato sauce; pour over all.

5. Cover and cook over low heat 45 minutes. Blend in wine and cook, uncovered, 20 minutes longer. Discard bay leaf.

6. Put the cooked spaghetti onto a hot serving platter and top with the chicken and sauce.
ABOUT 6 SERVINGS

CASA CHICKEN

Oriental and Southwestern influences meet.

1 broiler-fryer, 2 to 2½ lbs., cut up
¾ teaspoon onion salt
¾ teaspoon pepper
3 tablespoons shortening
½ cup ketchup
¼ cup soy sauce
2 tablespoons prepared mustard
½ teaspoon curry powder
2¼ cups water
2 bay leaves
2 tablespoons cornstarch
2 tablespoons water

1. Sprinkle chicken evenly with a mixture of the onion salt and pepper.

2. Heat the shortening in a large heavy skillet. Place chicken pieces, skin side down, in skillet and brown all sides.

3. Blend ketchup, soy sauce, mustard, curry powder, and water; add bay leaves. Pour mixture

over chicken. Cover and cook over low heat until chicken is tender, about 45 minutes. Remove chicken to a warm serving platter.

4. If sauce is thick, add about 1 cup water and bring to boiling. Stirring constantly, gradually add a blend of cornstarch and 2 tablespoons water. Bring to boiling; cook and stir until thickened.

5. Serve with fluffy *cooked rice.* Spoon sauce over chicken and rice. ABOUT 4 SERVINGS

CHICKEN ENCHANTÉE

2 lbs. frozen chicken
  pieces, thawed
½ cup all-purpose flour
1 teaspoon salt
⅛ teaspoon black pepper
¼ cup butter or
  margarine
1 cup sliced fresh
  mushrooms
1 cup (about ½ lb.)
  cubed cooked ham
  (½-in. cubes)

1 clove garlic, minced
1½ cups reconstituted
  frozen pineapple-
  orange juice
  concentrate
1 pkg. (10 oz.) frozen
  cut green beans,
  cooked and drained
½ cup dairy sour cream

1. Coat chicken with a mixture of flour, salt, and pepper.

2. Heat butter in a large heavy skillet. Place chicken in skillet and brown evenly. Remove chicken, set aside and keep warm.

3. Add mushrooms to skillet and cook until lightly browned. Stir in ham, garlic, and 1¼ cups of the pineapple-orange juice. Return chicken to skillet. Cover and simmer 25 to 30 minutes, or until chicken is tender when pierced with a fork; occasionally spoon sauce over chicken.

4. Remove chicken from skillet to a warm serving dish. Add beans to mixture remaining in skillet. Gently mix together to coat beans thoroughly. Spoon mixture over the chicken; set aside and keep warm.

5. Pour the remaining ¼ cup fruit juice into skillet. Heat thoroughly. Stirring vigorously, blend in sour cream. Cook over low heat 3 to 5 minutes, or until thoroughly heated (do not boil). Pour sauce over chicken. ABOUT 6 SERVINGS

ANTOINE'S CHICKEN CREOLE

Crisply fried chicken served in a wonderfully flavored creole sauce is a popular item at Antoine's in New Orleans, Louisiana. For elegance, each portion of chicken may be placed on a ripe avocado half and the sauce poured over all.

1 broiler-fryer, 2½ to
  3 lbs., cut up
¼ cup olive oil
1 can (16 oz.) tomatoes
2 tablespoons butter
1 teaspoon salt
⅛ teaspoon pepper
⅛ teaspoon cayenne
  pepper
1 sprig thyme
1 bay leaf

1 tablespoon minced
  parsley
3 cloves garlic, minced
1 tablespoon butter
1 tablespoon flour
6 chopped shallots (or
  ½ cup minced onion)
5 tablespoons chopped
  green pepper
½ cup white wine

1. Wipe chicken pieces with a damp cloth. Sauté in olive oil, turning to brown all sides.

2. Combine tomatoes and 2 tablespoons butter in a saucepan and simmer 10 minutes, stirring occasionally. Add salt and peppers. Cook 10 minutes. Add thyme, parsley, bay leaf, and garlic. Cook 15 minutes, or until sauce is thick.

3. Melt 1 tablespoon butter in a heavy saucepot or deep skillet; blend in flour and cook until browned. Add shallots and green pepper; brown slightly. Add chicken and wine; cover and simmer 45 minutes, or until chicken is tender. 4 TO 6 SERVINGS

ORIENTAL PINEAPPLE CHICKEN

12 chicken wings
½ teaspoon mono-
  sodium glutamate
¼ teaspoon ground
  ginger
1 clove garlic, minced
2 tablespoons cooking
  oil
Chicken broth (1½ cups)
1 can (8½ oz.) pineapple
  slices (reserve syrup)
½ cup soy sauce
2 tablespoons cider
  vinegar

2 tablespoons
  cornstarch
1 cup diagonally sliced
  celery
4 green onions,
  diagonally sliced
1 can (5 oz.) water
  chestnuts, drained
  and halved
1 can (16 oz.) bean
  sprouts, drained and
  rinsed
¼ cup toasted blanched
  almonds

1. Remove and discard tips from chicken wings; cut wings in half at joint. Toss with a mixture of monosodium glutamate and ginger.

2. Heat garlic and oil in a large heavy skillet. Brown chicken.

3. Add enough chicken broth to the pineapple syrup to make 1⅔ cups; gradually pour into skillet. Cover and simmer 15 minutes, or until wings are tender.

4. Push chicken to side of skillet. Stir in a mixture of soy sauce, vinegar, and cornstarch. Add celery and green onion. Bring to boiling and cook 3 minutes, stirring constantly. Mix in the water chestnuts, bean sprouts, almonds, and 2 of the pineapple slices, cut in large pieces: Move chicken through mixture. Heat thoroughly.

5. Turn into a heated serving dish. Garnish top with remaining pineapple slices.   4 SERVINGS

Fricasseed & Stewed Chicken

CHICKEN FRICASSEE

1 stewing chicken, 4 to 5 lbs., cut up	1 bay leaf
1 large onion, quartered	2 teaspoons salt
6 stalks celery with leaves, cut in pieces	3 peppercorns
½ bunch parsley	¼ cup flour
	1 cup cream
	2 teaspoons lemon juice

1. Put chicken, gizzard, heart, and neck into a kettle. Refrigerate liver. (If desired, brown chicken pieces in a skillet with hot fat; pieces may be coated with seasoned flour before frying.)

2. Add hot water to kettle to barely cover; add onion, celery, parsley, bay leaf, salt, and peppercorns. Bring water to boiling; remove foam.

3. Cover kettle tightly and simmer 2 to 3 hours, or until thickest pieces of chicken are tender when pierced with a fork, Add liver last 15 minutes of cooking.

4. Remove chicken and giblets from broth. Strain broth and cool slightly; skim off fat.

5. Heat 4 tablespoons of chicken fat in the kettle; blend in flour and heat until bubbly, stirring constantly.

6. Continue stirring and gradually add 2 cups of the chicken broth and the cream. Bring to boiling; cook and stir 1 to 2 minutes. Mix in the lemon juice and chicken pieces; heat thoroughly.

7. Serve chicken and gravy in a warm serving dish and garnish with *parsley*.   ABOUT 6 SERVINGS

NOTE: For additional flavor, add *1½ teaspoons monosodium glutamate* and *1 chicken bouillon cube* to cooking liquid.

CHICKEN AND DUMPLINGS: Follow recipe for Chicken Fricassee. For the last 12 minutes of cooking, add liver and *Cornmeal Dumplings, below*, to kettle. Cover tightly and continue cooking over medium heat 12 minutes without removing cover. Remove dumplings and chicken to a warm serving dish; keep warm. Prepare gravy and spoon over chicken and dumplings.   ABOUT 6 SERVINGS

CORNMEAL DUMPLINGS

1 cup all-purpose flour	3 tablespoons shortening
3 teaspoons baking powder	1 egg, well beaten
½ teaspoon salt	¾ cup milk
1 cup cornmeal	

1. Sift the flour, baking powder, and salt together into a bowl. Stir in cornmeal. Cut in shortening with pastry blender until pieces are the size of peas. Add a blend of egg and milk; with a fork, stir until just blended.

2. Drop batter by tablespoonfuls onto hot chicken mixture and proceed as directed.

COUNTRY CHICKEN FRICASSEE

1 broiler-fryer, about 3 lbs., cut up	2 crookneck squash, cut in halves lengthwise
1 teaspoon salt	2 pattypan squash, cut in half
1 teaspoon monosodium glutamate	Green beans (about 6 oz.), tips cut off
1 bay leaf	1 cup pitted ripe olives
2 cups sliced carrots	1 tablespoon cornstarch
2 onions, quartered	

1. Place chicken pieces with the salt, monosodium glutamate, and bay leaf in a Dutch oven or saucepot. Add enough water to just cover chicken. Bring to boiling, cover; simmer 25 minutes until chicken is almost tender.

2. Add carrots and onions to cooking liquid; cover and cook 10 minutes. Add squash and beans; cover and cook 10 minutes, or until chicken and vegetables are tender. Remove chicken and vegetables to a warm serving dish; add olives; keep hot.

3. Bring cooking liquid to boiling and stir in a blend of cornstarch and about 2 tablespoons water. Boil and stir 2 to 3 minutes. Pour gravy over chicken.   4 SERVINGS

LE COQ AU VIN
This version of the well-known chicken and wine dish is a specialty of La Cremaillere, Banksville, New York.

2 broiler-fryers, 2 lbs. each	8 small white onions
2 tablespoons flour	1 slice salt pork, diced
¼ cup butter	2 cups red wine
6 fresh mushrooms	1 cup brown gravy
	Bouquet garni, *page 21*

1. Separate legs and breasts of chickens. Season with *salt* and *pepper* to taste and roll in flour.
2. Heat the butter in a large saucepan, add the chicken, mushrooms, onions, and salt pork. Cover and cook slowly for 15 minutes.
3. Drain all the fat from saucepan, add the wine, gravy, and bouquet garni; cook 15 minutes longer. Season to taste and serve.   4 SERVINGS

Cooked-Chicken Dishes

OLD-FASHIONED CHICKEN PIE

1 stewing chicken, 4 to 5 lbs., cut up	4 carrots, scraped and sliced
1 small onion	3 stalks celery, cut in pieces
2 pieces (3 in. each) celery with leaves	2 small onions
3 sprigs parsley	¼ to ½ teaspoon salt
2 teaspoons salt	Biscuit dough (made from 1½ cups flour, or use a mix), rolled out
2 or 3 peppercorns	
1 small bay leaf	
4 medium-sized potatoes, pared and quartered	

1. Put chicken pieces into a 4-quart kettle. Add *1 quart hot water*, 1 onion, celery, parsley, 2 teaspoons salt, peppercorns, and bay leaf. Cover; bring to boiling; remove foam. Cover tightly and simmer 2 to 3 hours, or until thickest pieces are fork-tender.
2. Remove chicken from broth and cool slightly; remove meat from bones. Cut meat in 1-inch pieces. Set aside. Strain and cool broth; remove fat. Reserve broth.
3. Bring reserved chicken broth to boiling. Add the vegetables and salt. Cook, covered, about 20 minutes, or until tender. Remove vegetables with slotted spoon and place in a 2-quart deep casserole along with the chicken pieces.

4. To prepare gravy, combine *½ cup water* and *¼ cup flour* in a jar. Cover and shake until blended. Stirring constantly, add gradually to boiling broth; cook and stir 3 to 5 minutes.
5. Pour gravy into casserole. (There should be enough gravy to "float" chicken and vegetable pieces without mixture being too liquid.) Top with cutout biscuits placed so they just touch.
6. Bake at 425°F 15 to 20 minutes, or until biscuits are golden brown.   6 TO 8 SERVINGS

WITCHES' HAT CASSEROLE
A casserole with a Halloween motif.

2 tablespoons water	2 cups cream
2 tablespoons instant minced onion	3 cups coarsely diced cooked chicken, or 3 cans (6½ or 7 oz. each) tuna, drained and separated in pieces
½ cup butter or margarine	
½ cup sliced celery	
⅓ cup chopped green pepper	1 can (8 oz.) green beans, drained
⅛ teaspoon garlic powder	½ cup sliced pitted ripe olives
¾ cup flour	2 tablespoons chopped pimiento
1 teaspoon salt	
¼ teaspoon crushed rosemary	Parmesan Pastry Cutouts, *below*
2 cups chicken broth	

1. Add water to onion; let stand a few minutes.
2. Heat butter in a large saucepan. Add onion, celery, green pepper, and garlic powder. Cook until vegetables are tender, stirring occasionally. Blend in flour, salt, and rosemary. Heat until bubbly.
3. Gradually add the broth and cream, blending well. Stirring constantly, cook until mixture is thickened and smooth, about 8 minutes.
4. Mix in chicken, beans, olives, and pimiento. Turn into a 2-quart casserole. Sprinkle with *shredded Parmesan cheese.*
5. Heat in a 400°F oven about 10 minutes, or until mixture is bubbly. Arrange Parmesan Pastry Cutouts on top.   6 TO 8 SERVINGS

PARMESAN PASTRY CUTOUTS: Prepare *pastry for a 1-crust pie*, adding *¼ cup shredded Parmesan cheese* to the dry ingredients. Roll dough about ⅛ inch thick. For "witches' hat," cut 6 wedge-shaped pieces (for hats) and 6 crescent-shaped pieces (for brims). Place on baking sheet. Bake at 425°F 6 to 8 minutes, or until golden.

AVOCADO-CHICKEN CASSEROLE

1 small ripe avocado
1 tablespoon lemon juice
¼ cup butter or
    margarine
5 tablespoons flour
½ teaspoon salt
⅛ teaspoon white pepper
1½ cups cream
¾ cup milk

1 cup shredded sharp
    Cheddar cheese
1 cup wide noodles,
    cooked and drained
2 chicken breasts,
    cooked, skinned,
    boned, and sliced
    (white meat of roast
    turkey or capon may
    be used)

1. Peel avocado; cut into slices ¼ to ½ inch thick. Put slices into a bowl and drizzle with lemon juice; turn slices gently a few times.
2. Heat the butter in a saucepan. Blend in flour, salt, and pepper; heat until bubbly. Gradually add cream and milk, stirring constantly. Bring to boiling; cook and stir 1 to 2 minutes.
3. Remove from heat. Add the cheese all at one time and stir until cheese is melted; remove 1 cup of the sauce and set aside. Mix the cooked noodles into remaining sauce.
4. Arrange the chicken slices on the bottom of a greased 1-quart shallow baking dish. Spoon the sauced noodles over chicken slices, arrange avocado slices on top, and carefully spoon the reserved sauce over avocado. Sprinkle lightly with *paprika*.
5. Heat in a 350°F oven about 25 minutes, or until thoroughly heated and top is delicately browned.
4 SERVINGS

CHICKEN DIVAN

1½ lbs. broccoli, or 2
    pkgs. (10 oz. each)
    frozen broccoli spears
¼ cup butter
¼ cup flour
½ teaspoon salt
2 cups chicken broth
½ teaspoon marjoram

¼ cup crumbled blue
    cheese
½ cup heavy cream,
    whipped
3 chicken breasts,
    cooked, skinned,
    boned, and sliced
1 cup shredded
    Parmesan cheese

1. Cook broccoli until just tender; drain.
2. Heat butter in a saucepan. Blend in flour and salt. Heat until mixture bubbles; remove from heat.
3. Add the chicken broth gradually, stirring constantly. Bring to boiling and cook about 2 minutes, or until sauce thickens slightly. Remove from heat. Add the marjoram and blue cheese and stir until cheese is melted. Blend in the whipped cream.

4. Divide broccoli among 6 ramekins. Using one half of the sauce, spoon some of it over each portion of broccoli. Top each serving with chicken.
5. Blend ½ cup of the Parmesan cheese into the remaining sauce. Spoon sauce over chicken and sprinkle with the remaining cheese and *paprika*.
6. Set ramekins under broiler 4 inches from source of heat 3 minutes, or until tops are lightly browned. Serve hot.
6 SERVINGS

CURRY OF CHICKEN

⅓ cup butter or
    margarine
3 tablespoons chopped
    onion
3 tablespoons chopped
    celery
3 tablespoons chopped
    green apple
12 peppercorns
1 bay leaf
⅓ cup flour
2½ teaspoons curry
    powder

½ teaspoon mono-
    sodium glutamate
¼ teaspoon sugar
⅛ teaspoon ground
    nutmeg
2½ cups milk
2 teaspoons lemon juice
½ teaspoon Worcester-
    shire sauce
3 cups cubed cooked
    chicken
¼ cup cream
¼ teaspoon Worcester-
    shire sauce

1. Heat butter in a heavy 3-quart saucepan. Add onion, celery, apple, peppercorns, and bay leaf; cook until onion is golden.
2. Blend in a mixture of flour, curry powder, monosodium glutamate, sugar, and nutmeg; heat until bubbly.
3. Gradually add milk, stirring constantly. Bring to boiling, stirring until mixture thickens; cook 1 to 2 minutes.
4. Remove from heat; stir in lemon juice and the ½ teaspoon Worcestershire sauce. Strain through a fine sieve, pressing vegetables against sieve to extract all sauce.*
5. Return sauce to pan; blend in cream and the ¼ teaspoon Worcestershire sauce. Add chicken and cook over medium heat 2 to 3 minutes, or until thoroughly heated.
6. Serve with *fluffy cooked rice* and accompaniments such as *chutney, golden raisins, preserved kumquats*, and *cashew nuts*.　ABOUT 4 SERVINGS
*If desired, this sauce may be prepared ahead of time and stored, covered, in the refrigerator for several hours. If this is done, reheat sauce and proceed with step 5 just before serving.

CAPON AND LOBSTER CURRY

A specialty of The Imperial House in Chicago.

½ cup butter
1 large apple, cored and sliced
¾ cup sliced onion
½ cup coarsely chopped celery
2 bay leaves
½ cup all-purpose flour
1 to 2 tablespoons curry powder
1 qt. chicken broth
1 cup grated coconut
1 cup heavy cream
1 lb. cooked lobster meat, cubed
1½ lbs. cooked capon or chicken, cubed

1. Heat butter in a deep, heavy-bottomed pan; add apple, onion, celery, and bay leaves. Cover pan and cook over medium heat 15 minutes.
2. Remove from heat; sprinkle apple mixture with a blend of flour and curry powder; stir until blended. Cook and stir over low heat 5 minutes.
3. Gradually add broth, coconut, and cream, stirring constantly. Cook, uncovered, over low heat 15 minutes; stir frequently.
4. Force sauce through a fine sieve into a large saucepan. Stir in lobster and chicken; cook and stir gently over low heat just until meat is heated through. Season to taste with *salt* and *pepper*.
5. Serve immediately over *rice* with a spoonful of *chutney* over each serving.   8 SERVINGS

CHICKEN IN RICH CREAM SAUCE

½ cup butter or margarine
¼ lb. fresh mushrooms, sliced
1 tablespoon minced onion
⅓ cup flour
½ teaspoon monosodium glutamate
¼ teaspoon salt
⅛ teaspoon white pepper
2 cups chicken broth
¾ cup milk
3 oz. cream cheese, cut in pieces
Cooked white meat of chicken, cut in pieces (about 2 cups)
¼ cup short slivers green pepper
¼ cup canned sweet corn, golden or shoe peg white
1 teaspoon lemon juice
¾ cup seasoned whipped cream
Baking powder biscuits (prepared from a mix, refrigerated fresh dough, or favorite recipe)

1. Heat about 2 tablespoons butter in a large heavy saucepan. Add mushrooms and onion and cook 5 minutes, stirring occasionally. Remove mushrooms.
2. Heat remaining butter in the saucepan and stir in the flour, monosodium glutamate, salt, and pepper. Cook and stir until bubbly. Gradually add broth and milk, mixing until smooth. Bring to boiling, stirring constantly; cook 1 to 2 minutes.
3. Add cream cheese and stir until blended. Mix in the mushrooms, chicken, green pepper, and corn; heat thoroughly.
4. Just before serving, stir in the lemon juice. Fold in whipped cream.
5. Split hot biscuits, butter, and place on heat-resistant platter. Immediately spoon over the creamed chicken. Set under broiler 4 inches from heat until delicately browned.   ABOUT 6 SERVINGS

CHICKEN ALOHA

Pastry for a 1-crust pie
⅓ cup butter or margarine
½ cup flour
1½ teaspoons monosodium glutamate
¾ teaspoon salt
⅛ teaspoon white pepper
2 large fresh coconuts (reserve 1 cup coconut liquid, ½ cup shredded coconut, and shells)
2 cups chicken broth
2 egg yolks, slightly beaten
1 can (about 13 oz.) pineapple tidbits, drained (reserve ¼ cup syrup)
¼ cup cream
2 tablespoons butter or margarine
½ lb. fresh mushrooms, sliced lengthwise
1 cup smoked ham strips
½ cup chopped onion
2 cups cooked chicken pieces
1 can (16 oz.) artichoke hearts, drained and cut in halves lengthwise
½ cup salted macadamia nuts, almonds, or cashews

1. Prepare pastry, form into a ball, wrap in waxed paper, and refrigerate.
2. Heat the ⅓ cup butter in a heavy saucepan. Blend in a mixture of flour, monosodium glutamate, salt, and pepper. Heat until bubbly.
3. Gradually add the reserved coconut liquid and the chicken broth. Bring to boiling; stir and cook 1 to 2 minutes. Stir about 3 tablespoons of hot mixture into beaten egg yolks. Immediately blend into mixture in saucepan. Cook, stirring constantly, 3 to 5 minutes or until slightly thicker.
4. Remove from heat; blend in reserved pineapple syrup and cream. Set aside and keep warm.

5. Heat the 2 tablespoons butter in a skillet. Add mushrooms, ham, and onion; cook, stirring frequently, until mushrooms are delicately browned. Combine with chicken, pineapple, artichoke hearts, shredded coconut, sauce, and nuts. Mix gently and thoroughly.

6. Roll pastry into a rectangle ⅛ inch thick. With a sharp knife or pastry wheel, cut into strips 1 inch wide. Set aside.

7. Stand the coconut shells upright in ramekins or bowls. Fill with the chicken mixture. Cover with coconut tops. Seal covers to shells by wrapping a strip of pastry around each seam. Moisten ends of strips with cold water; press gently together and press strips against shells.

8. Set in a 350°F oven about 45 minutes, or until heated through.

9. Transfer to a serving platter. Just before serving, remove and discard pastry strips and top of coconuts. Sprinkle *toasted shredded coconut* over top of mixture. 4 SERVINGS

CHICKEN-CRAB MEAT CASSEROLE ROSEMARY

A rich combination of chicken, seafood, and avocado — luncheon fare for sophisticated tastes.

½ cup butter	2 cans (6½ oz. each)
2 tablespoons finely	crab meat, drained
chopped onion	and flaked (bony
7 tablespoons flour	tissue removed)
¾ teaspoon salt	1½ cups avocado
¾ teaspoon paprika	chunks
1 teaspoon rosemary,	Lemon juice
crushed	1 cup coarse fresh bread
2 cups chicken broth	crumbs, browned in 2
2 cups dairy sour cream	tablespoons butter
3 cups cooked chicken	
pieces	

1. Heat the butter and onion in a saucepan until onion is golden. Blend in a mixture of flour, salt, paprika, and rosemary. Heat until bubbly. Remove from heat.

2. Gradually add the chicken broth, stirring constantly. Bring to boiling, stirring constantly, and boil 1 to 2 minutes. Remove from heat and blend in the sour cream in small amounts, then the chicken and crab meat.

3. Drizzle avocado with lemon juice to prevent discoloration. Blend into the mixture. Turn into a 2-quart baking dish. Top evenly with the browned bread crumbs.

4. Heat in a 350°F oven about 30 minutes. Remove from oven and garnish one corner of the dish with a small bunch of *watercress*.

8 TO 10 SERVINGS

CHICKEN RISSOLES DE LUXE

Pie crust mix for a 2-	½ teaspoon crushed
crust pie	rosemary
¼ cup butter or	½ teaspoon Worcester-
margarine, chilled	shire sauce
3 tablespoons flour	1½ cups finely chopped
Few grains pepper	cooked chicken
2 tablespoons butter or	¼ cup finely chopped
margarine	cooked or canned
½ cup milk	mushrooms
½ cup chicken broth	¼ cup finely chopped
1 tablespoon snipped	salted almonds
parsley	Fat for deep frying
2 teaspoons grated onion	heated to 375°F
2 teaspoons drained	
capers	

1. Prepare pie crust mix according to directions on package. Roll pastry ¼ inch thick on a lightly floured surface. Dot with 2 tablespoons of the chilled butter. Fold two sides to center and press slightly to flatten. Fold ends to center and seal edges. Wrap in moisture-vaporproof material and chill thoroughly. Roll pastry ¼ inch thick. Dot with the remaining butter. Fold, wrap, and chill thoroughly.

2. Meanwhile, add flour and pepper to the 2 tablespoons butter in a saucepan. Heat until bubbly. Gradually add milk and chicken broth, stirring constantly. Bring to boiling; cook 1 to 2 minutes.

3. Remove from heat and mix in the parsley, onion, capers, rosemary, Worcestershire sauce, chicken, mushrooms, and almonds; set aside.

4. Roll out pastry about ⅛ inch thick and cut, using a cardboard pattern and a pastry wheel, into sixteen 4-inch rounds. Spoon about ¼ cup filling onto half of the rounds; spread into an even layer leaving about a ½-inch border of pastry. Moisten pastry edges, cover with remaining rounds, and press with a fork to seal completely.

5. Fry in hot fat about 3 minutes, or until golden brown. Remove from fat with a large slotted turner. Garnish each rissole with a *cherry tomato* on a pick and sprigs of *watercress*. 8 RISSOLES

Chicken Livers

SAUTÉED CHICKEN LIVERS

2 pounds chicken livers, rinsed and drained	1 teaspoon salt
1 cup cream	¼ teaspoon white pepper
½ cup all-purpose flour	½ cup butter or margarine

1. Marinate chicken livers in cream in refrigerator overnight.
2. Drain chicken livers (reserve cream); coat evenly with a mixture of the flour, salt, and pepper.
3. Heat butter in a large skillet, add livers, and cook, turning occasionally, until lightly browned.
4. The reserved cream may be thickened, seasoned, and served as gravy.   ABOUT 6 SERVINGS

CHICKEN LIVERS SUPERB

¼ cup flour	2 tablespoons Worcestershire sauce
1 cup finely chopped onion	2 tablespoons chili sauce
½ cup butter	1 teaspoon salt
2 lbs. chicken livers	¼ teaspoon black pepper
5 oz. fresh mushrooms, cleaned, sliced lengthwise through stems and caps, and lightly browned in butter	½ teaspoon rosemary
	½ teaspoon thyme
	2 cups dairy sour cream

1. Rinse and drain chicken livers. Pat free of excess moisture with absorbent paper. Coat lightly with flour. Set aside.
2. Lightly brown the onion in heated butter in a large skillet, stirring occasionally. Remove one half of onion-butter mixture and set aside for second frying of livers. Add half of the chicken livers and cook, occasionally moving and turning with a spoon, about 5 minutes, or until lightly browned. Turn into the blazer pan of a chafing dish. Fry remaining livers, using all of the onion-butter mixture; turn into the blazer pan. Set aside.
3. After browning mushrooms, blend a mixture of the Worcestershire sauce, chili sauce, salt, pepper, rosemary, and thyme with the mushrooms. Heat thoroughly.
4. Adding sour cream in small amounts at a time and stirring constantly, quickly blend with mushroom mixture. Heat thoroughly (do not boil). Mix gently with livers to coat.
5. Set blazer pan over simmering water. Before serving, garnish with wreaths of *sieved hard-cooked egg white, watercress,* and *sieved hard-cooked egg yolk.* Serve with buttered toasted *English muffins.*
ABOUT 8 SERVINGS

NOTE: If desired, blend in ¼ *cup dry sauterne or sherry* with the sour cream.

BELGIAN ENDIVE AND CHICKEN LIVERS
A favorite of Hermione Gingold, motion picture and TV personality.

6 small stalks Belgian endive	1 cup sliced fresh mushrooms
½ cup butter	½ cup dry sherry
1 lb. chicken livers	½ cup heavy cream
	1 teaspoon salt

1. Cut endive into quarters and parboil 15 minutes. Drain thoroughly.
2. Sauté endive in butter 15 minutes, remove from skillet with slotted spoon and keep endive warm.
3. Cut up chicken livers and sauté with mushrooms 10 minutes in butter remaining in the skillet. Add sherry, cream, and salt. Simmer, stirring frequently until hot (do not boil).
4. Return endive to sauce, simmer gently until the entire mixture is piping hot.   6 SERVINGS

CHICKEN LIVERS TAIPEI
A recipe from the Golden Dragon Room of The Grand Hotel in Taipei, Taiwan.

2 cups chicken livers (about 1 lb.), rinsed, dried, and halved or quartered	2 tablespoons minced onion
	1 tablespoon thinly sliced gingerroot
Fat for deep frying heated to 350°F	2 tablespoons ketchup
	2 tablespoons sugar
1 tablespoon lard	1 teaspoon salt

1. Fry the chicken livers in deep fat to a golden brown.
2. Heat the lard in a skillet and add the onion, gingerroot, and livers; heat and stir a few minutes.
3. Stir in the ketchup, sugar, and salt. Heat the mixture 2 to 3 minutes, stirring constantly. Add a dash of *sesame oil.* Serve hot.   ABOUT 4 SERVINGS

TURKEY

ROAST TURKEY

1 ready-to-cook turkey   Melted fat

1. Rinse bird with cold water. Drain and pat dry with absorbent paper or soft cloth.
2. Prepare cooked giblets and broth for gravy (see instructions).
3. Prepare favorite stuffing.
4. Rub body and neck cavities with *salt*. Fill lightly with stuffing. (Extra stuffing may be put into a greased covered baking dish or wrapped in aluminum foil and baked with turkey the last hour of roasting time.)
5. Fasten neck skin to back with skewer and bring wing tips onto back. Push drumsticks under band of skin at tail, or tie with cord. Set, breast up, on rack in shallow roasting pan. Brush with melted fat.
6. If meat thermometer is used, place it in center of inside thigh muscle or thickest part of breast meat. Be sure that tip does not touch bone. If desired, cover top and sides of turkey with cheesecloth moistened with melted fat. Keep cloth moist during roasting by brushing occasionally with fat from the bottom of pan.
7. Roast, uncovered, at 325°F until turkey tests done (the thickest part of the drumstick feels soft when pressed with fingers and meat thermometer registers 180°F to 185°F).
8. When turkey is two thirds done, cut band of skin or cord at drumsticks. Roast until done. For easier carving, let turkey stand 20 to 30 minutes, keeping it warm. Meanwhile, if desired, prepare gravy from drippings.
9. Remove cord and skewers from turkey and place on heated platter. Garnish platter and, if desired, put paper frills on drumsticks.

NOTE: If desired, turkey may be roasted in heavy-duty aluminum foil. Brush bird thoroughly with melted fat; wrap securely in foil; close with a drugstore or lock fold to prevent leakage of drippings. Place, breast up, in roasting pan (omit rack). Roast a 10- to 12-pound turkey at 450°F about 3 hours. About 20 minutes before end of roasting time, remove from oven. Quickly unfold foil to edge of pan. Insert meat thermometer. Return uncovered bird to oven and complete cooking. (Turkey will brown sufficiently in this time.)

ROAST HALF TURKEY: Follow recipe for Roast Turkey, using a half or quarter turkey, 3½ to 5 pounds. Rub cut side with *salt*. Skewer skin along cut edges to prevent shrinking. Tie leg to tail and wing flat against breast. Place, skin side up, on rack. Roast at 325°F about 2 hours. Meanwhile, prepare stuffing for half-turkey. Remove turkey from rack and spoon stuffing onto a piece of aluminum foil; return to rack. Cover stuffing with half-turkey. Roast 1 to 1½ hours longer. 3 TO 5 SERVINGS

COOKED GIBLETS AND BROTH: Put *turkey neck* and *giblets* (except liver) into a saucepan with *1 large onion*, sliced, *parsley, celery with leaves, 1 medium-sized bay leaf, 2 teaspoons salt,* and *1 quart water*. Cover and simmer until giblets are tender, about 2 hours; add the *liver* the last 15 minutes of cooking. Strain; reserve broth for gravy. Chop the giblets; set aside for gravy.

For paper frills: Select a sheet of white paper twice as wide as desired for length of frills; fold lengthwise. With fold toward you, make parallel cuts through fold ⅛ inch apart to within ½ inch of opposite side. Cut paper desired length; turn inside out. Wind around drumsticks. Fluff fringed ends with fingers. Fasten in place with cellulose tape.

BUTTER-ROASTED TURKEY
These instructions for roasting make use of an aluminum-foil tent.

1. Rinse a *ready-to-cook turkey*, drain, and pat dry. Rub the body and neck cavities with *salt*. Fill lightly with desired stuffing. (Extra stuffing may be put into a greased covered baking dish or wrapped in aluminum foil and baked with turkey the last hour of roasting time.) Fasten neck skin to back with skewer and bring wing tips onto back. Push drumsticks under band of skin at tail, or tie with cord.
2. Place turkey, breast down, on foil band* put crosswise onto a rack in a foil-lined roasting pan. Brush turkey with *softened butter*. Roast at 325°F according to the timetable, *page 237*.

3. When turkey has roasted for about two-thirds the required time, remove from oven. Use the foil band to flip turkey first on the side then breast up. Brush breast with softened butter. Insert meat thermometer into the thickest part of the thigh during this final one-third of roasting time.

4. Crease a large piece of foil lengthwise to make a tent, and arrange it loosely over bird. Return to oven and continue roasting. The tent keeps turkey moist and prevents overbrowning. The turkey is done when thermometer registers 180° to 185°F, or the thickest part of drumstick feels soft when pressed with fingers protected with clean cloth or paper napkin.

5. Transfer turkey to a heated serving platter, lifting it with the foil band; remove band. Let turkey stand covered with the foil tent for about 30 minutes for easier carving; remove tent. Garnish platter with *chutney filled oranges*, or as desired.

*To make the band, fold a long piece of heavy-duty aluminum foil lengthwise over and over to make a 3 inch wide band.

FRIED TURKEY

2 roaster-fryer turkeys, 4 to 5 lbs. each, cut in serving-sized pieces
Seasoned flour
Shortening
1 to 2 tablespoons water

1. Coat turkey pieces well with seasoned flour. Put, skin side down, in a large skillet of heated shortening (about ½ inch deep). Cook, turning to brown evenly on all sides.

2. Reduce heat, add water, and cover skillet tightly. Cook slowly 50 to 60 minutes, or until turkey is tender. Cook uncovered last 10 minutes to crisp skin. 12 SERVINGS

CHILI TURKEY PIE

Frozen boned turkey roast is an easy source of meat for this flavorful turkey pie.

2 tablespoons lemon juice
4 cups diced cooked turkey
¾ cup chopped onion
1 clove garlic, minced
¼ cup butter or margarine
2 cans (10½ oz. each) condensed cream of mushroom soup
½ cup milk
1 teaspoon chili powder
½ teaspoon seasoned salt
1 can (12 oz.) whole kernel corn with peppers
½ cup sliced celery
¼ cup whole Spanish peanuts
2 tablespoons snipped parsley
Herbed Pastry, *below*

1. Drizzle lemon juice over turkey and set aside while preparing sauce.

2. Cook the onion and garlic in hot butter in a large skillet about 3 minutes, stirring occasionally.

3. Blend the soup, milk, and a mixture of the chili powder and seasoned salt. Add to the skillet with the turkey, corn, celery, peanuts, and parsley; blend thoroughly.

4. Turn mixture into a greased 2-quart shallow baking dish. Top with Herbed Pastry; flute edge. Slit top in several places or make cutouts in pastry topping to allow steam to escape. Brush the pastry lightly with *milk*.

5. Bake at 450°F 15 minutes. Reduce oven temperature to 350°F and bake 25 minutes, or until crust is browned. Garnish one end of dish with a bouquet of *parsley*. Serve with an assortment of crisp *relishes*. ABOUT 8 SERVINGS

HERBED PASTRY: Blend *1½ cups all-purpose flour, 2 tablespoons finely snipped parsley, ¾ teaspoon salt, ½ teaspoon chili powder,* and *½ teaspoon chervil,* crushed, in a bowl. Cut in *½ cup lard*

TIMETABLE FOR ROASTING TURKEY IN ALUMINUM FOIL

Ready-to-Cook Weight (Pounds)	Oven Temperature Constant	Approx. Total Roasting Time (Hours)	Internal Temperature of Bird
8 to 12	450°F	2 to 2½	185°F
12 to 16	450°F	2½ to 3	185°F
16 to 20	450°F	3 to 3½	185°F
20 to 24	450°F	3½ to 4	185°F

NOTE: Open foil during last 30 to 40 minutes for browning.

or vegetable shortening with a pastry blender or two knives until pieces are the size of small peas. Sprinkle *4 to 5 tablespoons cold water* gradually over the mixture, mixing lightly with a fork after each addition. Use only enough water to hold pastry together. Roll out about ⅛ to ¼ inch thick and a little larger than baking dish. Complete as directed.

TURKEY KABOBS

1½ lbs. boned cooked turkey, cut in chunks	¼ cup honey
	¼ cup cooking oil
1 can (about 20 oz.) pineapple chunks, drained (reserve ¼ cup syrup)	1 teaspoon dry mustard
	2 tablespoons finely chopped green onion
½ cup soy sauce	Cherry tomatoes
½ cup ketchup	2 cans (5 oz. each) whole water chestnuts
⅓ cup white wine vinegar	

1. Marinate the turkey chunks overnight in a mixture of the reserved pineapple syrup, soy sauce, ketchup, vinegar, honey, oil, dry mustard, and onion; turn chunks occasionally. Drain and reserve marinade.
2. Thread turkey, pineapple, tomatoes (if large, cut in half), and water chestnuts onto ten 8-inch skewers. Brush generously with marinade.
3. Broil about 2 inches from source of heat 3 to 5 minutes or until lightly browned, turning and brushing frequently with the marinade.   10 KABOBS

CREAMED TURKEY AND AVOCADO

½ cup butter or margarine	⅛ teaspoon ground nutmeg
½ lb. fresh mushrooms, sliced lengthwise through caps and stems	1½ cups cream
	1½ cups chicken broth (dissolve 2 chicken bouillon cubes in 1½ cups boiling water)
¼ cup finely chopped onion	
½ cup flour	3 cups cooked turkey pieces
½ teaspoon seasoned salt	2 medium-sized avocados
⅛ teaspoon pepper	Lemon juice

1. Heat butter in a chafing dish blazer pan or skillet over direct heat. Add the mushrooms and onion. Cook, stirring frequently, until onion is soft and mushrooms are tender and lightly browned. With a slotted spoon remove mushrooms, allowing butter to drain back into pan; set the mushrooms aside.
2. Blend flour, seasoned salt, pepper, and nutmeg into butter in pan. Heat until bubbly. Stir in cream and chicken broth, bringing rapidly to boiling; cook and stir 1 to 2 minutes. Mix in mushrooms and turkey pieces; heat thoroughly.
3. Cut avocados into halves lengthwise and remove pits. Using a melon-ball cutter, cut avocados into balls. Drizzle with lemon juice to prevent discoloration. Combine with creamed turkey just before serving. Keep warm over pan of hot water. Serve in heated *patty shells*.   6 TO 8 SERVINGS

TURKEY IN BUNS

¾ cup ketchup	1 teaspoon salt
1 cup currant jelly	¼ teaspoon garlic salt
¼ cup finely chopped onion	3 cups diced cooked turkey
2 tablespoons Worcestershire sauce	

1. Combine ketchup, jelly, onion, Worcestershire sauce, salt, and garlic salt in a heavy saucepan. Simmer about 20 minutes.
2. Stir in turkey. Heat. Spoon onto *toasted buttered buns*.   8 TO 10 SERVINGS

TURKEY MOLE POBLANO

½ cup cooking oil	2 tablespoons seedless raisins
2 cloves garlic, minced	
2 tablespoons puréed fresh small red chiles (seeds and stems removed before forcing through a food mill)	½ cup fine bread crumbs
	1 tablespoon chili powder
	1 teaspoon salt
½ cup almonds	¼ teaspoon pepper
2 tablespoons peanuts	¼ teaspoon ground coriander
2 tablespoons sesame seed	
1 cup drained canned tomatoes	⅛ teaspoon ground cloves
1 cup chicken broth	Few grains ground ginger
½ oz. (½ sq.) unsweetened chocolate, melted	1 piece (3 in.) stick cinnamon
	Turkey slices

1. Heat oil and garlic together in a heavy skillet, then add chile pulp.

2. Meanwhile, put nuts and sesame seed into an electric blender container. Chop finely.
3. Add remaining ingredients except stick cinnamon and turkey to blender container and blend to a smooth paste. Stir into the oil in skillet and add the stick cinnamon; simmer, stirring frequently, until thickened, about 15 minutes.
4. Pour mole over cooked sliced turkey in a shallow baking dish. Cover; heat in a 350°F oven 20 minutes. SAUCE FOR 6 TO 8 SERVINGS

DUCKLING

ROAST DUCKLING À L'ORANGE

2 ready-to-cook
   ducklings, 4 lbs. each
1 to 2 teaspoons salt
Apricot-Rice Stuffing,
   page 260
1 cup orange juice
2 tablespoons butter or
   margarine
Orange Gravy, *below*

1. Rinse ducklings and pat dry with absorbent paper. Rub cavities of ducklings with salt.
2. Prepare Apricot-Rice Stuffing and set aside.
3. Heat orange juice and butter together over low heat until butter is melted. Remove from heat and, using a pastry brush, brush cavities with the mixture.
4. Lightly fill body and neck cavities with the stuffing; do not pack. To close body cavities, sew, or skewer and lace with cord; fasten neck skin to backs and wings to bodies with skewers. Place ducklings, breast up, on rack in roasting pan. Brush with juice mixture.
5. Roast, uncovered, at 325°F 2½ to 3 hours. To test doneness, move leg gently by grasping end bone; drumstick-thigh joint should move easily. Brush frequently with orange juice mixture; pour off and reserve drippings as they accumulate.
6. Place ducklings on a heated platter; remove skewers and cord. Garnish with *broiled orange slices* and *parsley*; serve with Orange Gravy.

6 TO 8 SERVINGS

ORANGE GRAVY: Leaving brown residue in roasting pan, pour drippings and fat into a bowl. Allow fat to rise to surface; skim off fat and reserve 3 tablespoons; put reserved fat into roasting pan. Blend in *3 tablespoons flour, ¼ teaspoon salt,* and *⅛ teaspoon black pepper.* Stirring constantly, heat until mixture bubbles. Remove from heat. Continue to stir while slowly adding *2 cups reserved drippings* plus orange juice. Return to heat and cook rapidly, stirring constantly, until gravy thickens. Cook 1 to 2 minutes longer. While stirring, scrape bottom and sides of pan to blend in brown residue.

Blend in *⅓ cup orange marmalade.* Remove from heat; pour into gravy boat and serve hot.

DUCKLING A LÀ GOURMET

1 ready-to-cook
   duckling, 4 to 5 lbs.,
   cut in quarters
1 egg, slightly beaten
½ cup packaged grated
   coconut
¼ cup flour
1½ teaspoons salt
⅛ teaspoon black
   pepper
Sauce Oriental, *page 346*

1. Prick skin of duckling with a fork. Place, skin side up, on rack in a shallow roasting pan.
2. Roast at 400°F 1 hour. Remove excess fat from pan as it collects.
3. Brush duckling with the beaten egg. Coat with a mixture of the coconut, flour, salt, and pepper.
4. Return to oven and continue to roast 15 minutes, basting once with the drippings.
5. Serve with Sauce Oriental. 4 SERVINGS

DUCK WITH OLIVES
(Canard aux Olives)

This recipe is from the Hotel Aiglon, Menton, France.

1 ready-to-cook
   duckling, 4 lbs.
⅓ cup olive oil
1 cup carrot slices
1 cup coarsely chopped
   onion
½ teaspoon salt
⅛ teaspoon pepper
¼ teaspoon rosemary
2 small stalks celery
2 to 3 sprigs parsley
1 bay leaf
⅓ cup cognac
2 tablespoons tomato
   paste
2 cups chicken broth
⅓ cup white wine
16 whole pitted green
   olives

1. Rinse duckling and cut into quarters. Cut away and discard excess fat.
2. Brown duck in olive oil in a large heavy skillet.

Honey-Glazed Filbert Roast Chicken

Add the carrots, onion, salt, pepper, and rosemary. Tie the celery, parsley, and bay leaf together and add to skillet. Brown the vegetables. Pour off excess fat. Add cognac and ignite.

3. When flaming stops, add a blend of the tomato paste, broth, and wine to skillet.

4. Cover and roast at 350°F about 1½ hours, or until duck is tender.

5. Place duck pieces on heated platter.

6. Strain the sauce into a saucepan; add the olives. Heat until very hot. Immediately pour over the duck. Serve immediately.   4 SERVINGS

GOOSE

ROAST GOOSE

1 ready-to-cook goose, 8 to 10 lbs.	¾ lb. prunes (soaked in warm water, drained, and pitted)
1 tablespoon salt	1 tablespoon sugar
¼ teaspoon black pepper	
1 lb. cooking apples, pared and quartered	

1. Rinse goose and remove any large layers of fat from the body cavity. Pat dry with absorbent paper. Rub body and neck cavities with a mixture of the salt and pepper.

2. Mix apples, prunes, and sugar together; lightly spoon mixture into cavities. To close body cavity, sew, or skewer and lace with a cord. Fasten neck skin to back with skewer. Loop cord around legs, tighten slightly, and tie around a skewer inserted on the back above tail. Rub skin of goose with a little *salt.*

3. Place goose, breast down, on a rack in a shallow roasting pan.

4. Roast, uncovered, at 325°F 2½ hours, removing fat from pan several times during this period. Turn goose, breast up, and roast 45 to 60 minutes longer, or until goose tests done. To test for doneness, move leg gently by grasping end of bone. When done, drumstick-thigh joint moves easily or twists out.

5. Transfer goose to a carving board or heated serving platter while preparing Gravy, *below.* Garnish as desired.   ABOUT 8 SERVINGS

GRAVY: Pour off all but ¼ cup of drippings from roasting pan. Add about *2 cups hot water;* bring to boiling, stirring to loosen browned residue. Stir in a smooth mixture of *½ cup cold water* and *¼ cup flour.* Bring to boiling and boil 1 to 2 minutes, stirring constantly. Season to taste. If desired, add *2 tablespoons currant jelly* and *cooked giblets.*

ROCK CORNISH GAME HENS

GAME HENS WITH SPICY STUFFING

3½ cups slightly dry bread cubes	½ cup chopped celery
½ cup chopped, drained sweet mixed pickles	¼ cup butter or margarine
½ cup diced dried figs	4 frozen Rock Cornish game hens (1 lb. each), thawed
1 egg, slightly beaten	
¼ teaspoon salt	2 tablespoons butter or margarine, melted
⅛ teaspoon poultry seasoning	

1. Toss together lightly in a bowl the bread cubes, pickles, figs, egg, salt, and poultry seasoning.

2. Sauté celery in ¼ cup butter 1 minute. Toss with bread mixture. Spoon into cavities of hens; truss and arrange securely on a spit.

3. Roast hens on rotisserie about 1 hour, or until well browned and tender, brushing occasionally with melted butter.   4 SERVINGS

LIME-GLAZED GAME HENS

½ cup butter or margarine, melted	2 teaspoons soy sauce
2 tablespoons brown sugar	4 frozen Rock Cornish game hens, 1 to 1¼ lbs. each, thawed
3 to 4 tablespoons lime juice	2 teaspoons salt

1. Blend butter, brown sugar, lime juice, and soy sauce; set aside.

2. Clean, rinse, and pat hens dry with absorbent

Game Hens with Spicy Stuffing

paper. Rub cavities with salt and brush with some of the butter mixture.

3. To close cavities fasten with skewers. Skewer neck skin to backs and wings to bodies. Place hens, breast up, in a shallow roasting pan. Brush hens with butter mixture.

4. Roast, uncovered, following package directions for time and temperature. While roasting, baste hens with any remaining butter mixture. Roast until hens test done (drumstick-thigh joints move easily). Arrange hens on a warm serving platter.

4 SERVINGS

ROAST ROCK CORNISH GAME HENS

Wild Rice Stuffing, *page 260*	4 teaspoons salt
8 Rock Cornish game hens, about 1 lb. each	½ cup unsalted butter, melted

1. Prepare stuffing and set aside.
2. Clean, rinse, and pat game hens dry with absorbent paper. Rub cavities of the hens with the salt. Lightly fill body cavities with the stuffing. To close body cavities, sew or skewer and lace with cord. Fasten neck skin to backs and wings to bodies with skewers.

3. Place game hens, breast up, on rack in roasting pan. Brush each hen with butter (about 1 tablespoon).

4. Roast, uncovered, at 350°F; frequently baste hens during roasting period with drippings from roasting pan. Roast 1 to 1½ hours, or until hens test done. To test for doneness, move leg gently by grasping end bone; drumstick-thigh joint moves easily when hens are done. Remove skewers, if used.

5. Transfer hens to a heated serving platter and garnish with sprigs of *watercress*, or as desired.

8 SERVINGS

ROAST SQUAB: Follow directions for Roast Rock Cornish Game Hens. Substitute *squab* weighing ¾ to 1 pound each (ready-to-cook weight).

STUFFINGS FOR POULTRY

APPLE STUFFING

2 medium-sized apples, pared and diced (about 2 cups, diced)	8 cups soft bread cubes
	¾ cup melted butter
	2 teaspoons salt
⅓ cup chopped celery with leaves	¼ teaspoon pepper
	1 teaspoon marjoram
⅓ cup chopped onion	¾ cup apple cider

1. Combine apple, celery, and onion with bread cubes in a large bowl. Toss with butter, salt, pepper, and marjoram.
2. Pour cider over bread mixture and toss until thoroughly mixed. Spoon the stuffing lightly into neck and body cavities of bird (do not pack).

STUFFING FOR THREE 4-POUND DUCKLINGS

APRICOT-PRUNE STUFFING

1 pkg. (8 oz.) stuffing mix	½ cup finely cut dried prunes
⅔ cup finely cut dried apricots	¼ cup finely chopped onion

1. Prepare stuffing mix according to directions on package for moist stuffing.
2. Add apricots, prunes, and onion; toss. Lightly spoon stuffing into body and neck cavities of bird (do not pack).

ABOUT 5½ CUPS STUFFING

CHESTNUT STUFFING

¼ cup butter	1 teaspoon salt
1 small onion, chopped	⅛ teaspoon pepper
½ cup chopped celery	2 lbs. chestnuts, cooked* and cut in pieces
1 cup soft bread crumbs	
1 tablespoon chopped parsley	½ cup cream

1. Heat butter in a skillet; add onion and celery; cook until onion is transparent and celery tender.
2. Remove skillet from heat. Add bread crumbs, parsley, salt, and pepper; mix well.
3. Put half of the chestnuts through a ricer or food mill; coarsely chop remaining ones.
4. Combine the chestnuts with bread mixture; drizzle cream over stuffing and toss lightly.
5. Lightly spoon stuffing into neck and body cavities of bird (do not pack). ABOUT 3⅓ CUPS STUFFING
*Roast chestnuts as directed on *page 20*. Put shelled chestnuts into boiling *salted water* to cover and boil 20 minutes, or until tender. Cool.

WATER CHESTNUT-CELERY STUFFING

1 pkg. (8 oz.) stuffing mix
1 cup diced celery
¼ cup finely chopped onion

1 can (8 oz.) water chestnuts, drained and sliced
2 tablespoons dried parsley flakes

1. Prepare stuffing mix according to directions on package for moist stuffing.
2. Add celery, onion, water chestnuts, and parsley flakes; toss lightly to mix. Lightly spoon stuffing into body and neck cavities of bird (do not pack). ABOUT 5⅓ CUPS STUFFING

TURKEY STUFFING

A recipe from Mrs. Lyndon B. Johnson, former First Lady of the United States.

4 slices toasted bread, crumbled
1 medium-sized pan cornbread, crumbled
Turkey stock

6 eggs
1 stalk celery, chopped
3 large onions, chopped
¼ cup butter

1. Mix toast and cornbread crumbs with enough turkey stock so that mixture will not be stiff.
2. Add the eggs, celery, onion, and butter. Season to taste with *salt*, *pepper*, and *sage*.
3. Bake at 325°F about 1 hour. 8 SERVINGS

OLD-FASHIONED CORNBREAD STUFFING

1 cup dark or golden seedless raisins
1½ cups thinly sliced celery
8 cups soft white-bread crumbs
6 cups cornbread crumbs
1 cup coarsely chopped salted toasted almonds
½ cup chopped parsley
1 teaspoon poultry seasoning

1 teaspoon ground nutmeg
1 teaspoon salt
½ teaspoon pepper
⅔ cup giblet broth
½ cup instant minced onion
¾ cup butter or margarine, melted
2 eggs, beaten

1. Combine raisins, celery, crumbs, almonds, and parsley. Sprinkle with a mixture of the poultry seasoning, nutmeg, salt, and pepper.
2. Add broth and onion to butter; add butter mixture and eggs to crumb mixture, mixing lightly.
3. Spoon mixture lightly into turkey; or shape into stuffing balls, place on greased baking sheet, and bake at 350°F 20 minutes, or until lightly browned.
STUFFING FOR A 15-POUND TURKEY OR 20 BALLS

HERBED STUFFING

Cooked Giblets and Broth, *page 253*
4 qts. ½-in. bread cubes
1 cup snipped parsley
2 to 2½ teaspoons salt
2 teaspoons thyme
2 teaspoons rosemary, crushed

2 teaspoons marjoram
1 teaspoon ground sage
1 cup butter or margarine
1 cup coarsely chopped onion
1 cup coarsely chopped celery with leaves

1. Prepare Cooked Giblets and Broth. Set aside 1 cup chopped cooked giblets and the broth.
2. In a large bowl, toss bread cubes with the reserved chopped giblets, parsley, and a mixture of salt, thyme, rosemary, marjoram, and sage.
3. Melt butter in a skillet; add chopped onion and celery. Cook over medium heat about 5 minutes, stirring occasionally. Toss with the bread mixture.
4. Add 1 to 2 cups broth (depending upon how moist a stuffing is desired), mixing lightly until ingredients are thoroughly blended. Lightly fill body and neck cavities of turkey (do not pack).
STUFFING FOR A 14- TO 15-POUND TURKEY

FILBERT STUFFING FOR TURKEY

4 qts. bread cubes
2 cups coarsely chopped filberts, toasted*
¾ cup snipped parsley
¼ cup chopped celery

1 turkey liver, cut in small pieces
½ cup milk
¾ cup chopped onion
1 cup butter or margarine

1. Put all ingredients except onion and butter into a large bowl; set aside.
2. Cook onion about 3 minutes in hot butter in a skillet. Add to ingredients in bowl; toss lightly to mix. Lightly spoon into body and neck cavities of turkey (do not pack).
STUFFING FOR A 14- TO 16-POUND TURKEY
*To toast filberts, spread nuts in a shallow baking pan and set in a 400°F oven 10 minutes, or until browned, stirring occasionally.

CRANBERRY STUFFING

1 lb. fresh cranberries	2 teaspoons salt
¾ cup sugar	1 teaspoon ground
1 cup butter or	cinnamon
margarine, melted	Grated peel of 3 lemons
6 qts. bread cubes	1 cup water or giblet
2 cups seedless raisins,	broth
plumped	

Coarsely chop cranberries and mix with the sugar.
Toss butter with bread cubes in a large bowl; add
cranberry mixture and remaining ingredients. Mix
lightly.   STUFFING FOR A 14- TO 16-POUND TURKEY

OYSTER-MUSHROOM STUFFING

½ cup butter or	2 qts. bread cubes
margarine	2 tablespoons chopped
1 lb. mushrooms,	parsley
coarsely chopped	2 teaspoons salt
1 cup chopped onion	1 teaspoon mono-
1 cup chopped celery	sodium glutamate
with leaves	¼ teaspoon pepper
1 qt. oysters, cut in	1 to 1½ teaspoons
halves (reserve	poultry seasoning
liquor)	2 or 3 eggs, beaten

1.   Heat butter in a large skillet. Add mushrooms,
onion, and celery; cook 5 to 8 minutes over medium
heat, stirring occasionally. Set aside.
2.   In a large bowl, mix the oysters, bread cubes,
parsley, and a mixture of the salt, monosodium glutamate, pepper, and poultry seasoning. Add vegetables, the reserved oyster liquor, and the beaten
eggs; toss lightly to mix.
STUFFING FOR A 14- TO 16-POUND TURKEY

APRICOT-RICE STUFFING

¼ cup orange juice	3½ cups cooked rice
¼ cup butter or	1 cup finely chopped
margarine, melted	dried apricots
½ teaspoon salt	¼ cup finely chopped
¼ teaspoon pepper	onion
⅛ teaspoon thyme	¼ cup finely chopped
⅛ teaspoon ground	celery
nutmeg	2 tablespoons finely
⅛ teaspoon ground	chopped parsley
cloves	

Combine all ingredients in a large bowl. Toss lightly until thoroughly mixed.   ABOUT 5 CUPS STUFFING

WALNUT STUFFING

2 pkgs. (7 to 8 oz.	1 can (6 oz.) broiled
each) herb-seasoned	sliced mushrooms,
stuffing mix	undrained
¾ cup butter or	1½ cups chopped
margarine, melted	toasted walnuts
2 cups chicken broth	

Toss stuffing mix with the melted butter in a bowl.
Lightly mix in remaining ingredients.
STUFFING FOR A 14- TO 16-POUND TURKEY

WILD RICE STUFFING

1 cup wild rice, cooked,	½ cup butter or
page 19	margarine
½ lb. fresh mushrooms,	½ teaspoon crushed
sliced	sage leaves (optional)
2 tablespoons chopped	Dash thyme (optional)
onion	

1.   While wild rice is cooking, lightly brown the
mushrooms with onion in ¼ cup heated butter in a
skillet. Toss gently with the wild rice and herbs.
2.   Add remaining ¼ cup butter, melted, and continue tossing until thoroughly mixed. Add *salt* and
pepper to taste.   ABOUT 4 CUPS STUFFING

WINE STUFFING FOR TURKEY

3 qts. bread cubes	2 cloves garlic, minced
2 cups chopped	3 eggs, slightly beaten
blanched almonds	1 tablespoon salt
4 cups diced celery	¼ teaspoon cracked
2 cups chopped celery	black pepper
leaves	½ teaspoon ground
¼ cup butter or	nutmeg
margarine	½ teaspoon ground
½ cup finely chopped	mace
green onion	½ cup dry red wine

1.   Combine the bread cubes, almonds, celery,
and celery leaves; toss lightly until well mixed.
2.   Heat the butter in a skillet. Add the green onion and garlic and cook, stirring occasionally, until
lightly browned. Add contents of skillet to bread
mixture.
3.   Combine the eggs, salt, pepper, nutmeg, and
mace. Pour egg mixture and wine over bread
cubes; toss lightly to mix thoroughly.
4.   Lightly spoon into body and neck cavities of
turkey (do not pack).   ABOUT 16 CUPS STUFFING

Chapter 8
FISH & SHELLFISH

Fish and shellfish have always been highly prized as delicious food by those who have had access to fresh supplies. Refrigerated shipping facilities now make supplies available to everyone.

Fish are especially valuable for their excellent sources of highly digestible protein and for their fine mineral and vitamin content. Fat fish, such as salmon and mackerel, are rich in both vitamins A and D.

Research has determined that the fish flesh of all species is approximately equal in nutritional properties. The homemaker can, therefore, determine her choice by flavor, texture, and color.

FISH

AVAILABILITY

Fresh fish are best prepared as soon as possible after being caught. When fresh, they have red gills, bright eyes, and bright-colored scales adhering tightly. The flesh is firm and elastic, and practically free from odor. Fresh fish should be packed in ice until purchased; at home, wrap in foil or moisture-vaporproof material and store in the refrigerator.

Frozen fish is available the year around in market forms such as steaks, fillets, and sticks. It should be solidly frozen and *never refrozen after thawing.*

Salted fish are prepared either by "dry-salting" or by pickling in a brine. Firm, coarse-fleshed fish such as cod, hake, and haddock are dry-salted by packing in dry salt after cleaning. Fat and oily fish are "salted" in brine, then are frequently smoked. Finnan Haddie is prepared in this way.

Smoked fish is a delicacy; salmon, whitefish, and haddock are popular varieties. It is usually eaten without further cooking.

Canned fish is easy to store and convenient to serve. Sardines, tuna, cod, salmon, mackerel, and kippered herring are some of the varieties.

MARKET FORMS

Whole or round fish are just as they come from the water; before cooking they must be scaled and the entrails removed; the head, tail, and fins may be removed if desired.

Caviar is the salted eggs of sturgeon, the best coming from Russia. Eggs of other fish are also used, but must be labeled to indicate the source.

Drawn fish have only the entrails removed; before cooking they must be scaled; the head, tail, and fins may be removed if desired.

Dressed fish (ready-to-cook) have been scaled and the entrails, head, tail, and fins removed.

Fish steaks are cross sections of larger dressed fish, ready-to-cook as purchased.

Fish fillets are the sides of a dressed fish cut lengthwise away from the backbone and practically boneless.

Fish sticks are uniform pieces of fish dipped in batter, then breaded and frozen. They resemble French fried potatoes in appearance and can be purchased uncooked or precooked. Precooked sticks are deep-fried before freezing and need only be heated.

STORAGE

To store fresh fish, wrap the whole fish or fillets or steaks in moisture-vaporproof material or in waxed paper. Use fish the same day as purchased, if possible. Place in freezer if fish is not to be used in one or two days.

PURCHASING GUIDE

Kind	How to Cook	Size (Pounds)	Season	Market Unit	Type
Fish					
Bass,					
black sea	bake, broil, fry	½ to 4	all year	whole, fillets	lean
striped	bake, broil, fry	2 to 5	all year	whole	lean
Bluefish	bake, broil, fry	3 to 6	winter, spring, summer	whole	lean
Butterfish	bake, broil, fry	¼ to 1	spring, summer, fall	whole (fresh, smoked)	fat
Carp	bake, broil, fry	2 to 8	all year	whole, fillets (fresh, smoked)	lean
Catfish	bake, fry	1 to 40	all year	whole, fillets, steak	lean
Cod	bake, broil, boil, fry	4 to 75	all year	whole, fillets, steak (fresh, salted, canned)	lean
Eel	broil, boil, fry	½ to 10	all year	(fresh, smoked, pickled)	fat
Flounder	bake, broil, fry	½ to 6	all year	whole, fillets	lean
Grouper	bake, broil, boil, fry	5 to 12	all year	whole, fillets, steak	lean
Haddock	bake, broil, boil, fry	2 to 8	all year	whole, fillets (fresh, smoked as finnan haddie, canned)	lean
Hake	broil, boil	3 to 8	all year	pound, fillets (fresh, salted, smoked)	lean
Halibut	bake, broil, boil, fry	5 to 80	all year	whole, fillets, steak (fresh, smoked)	lean
Herring	bake, broil, boil, fry	½ to 1	all year	whole (fresh, salted canned, smoked, pickled)	fat
Mackerel	bake, broil, boil, fry	¾ to 10	all year	whole, fillets, steak (fresh, pickled, salted, smoked, canned)	fat
Mullet	bake, broil, fry	1 to 5	all year	whole (fresh, salted)	lean
Perch	bake, broil, fry	½ to 5	all year	whole, fillets	lean
Pickerel	bake, broil, boil, fry	2 to 40	all year	whole, steak	lean
Pike	bake, broil, fry	1 to 40	all year	whole, fillets	lean
Pompano	bake, broil	1 to 2	winter	whole	fat
Red snapper	bake, broil, boil, fry	10 to 20	all year	pound	lean
Salmon	bake, broil, boil, fry	4 to 25	summer, fall	whole, fillets, steak (fresh, smoked, salted, canned)	fat
Shad	bake, broil, boil, fry	1½ to 6	fall, winter, spring	whole (fresh, salted)	fat
Sheepshead	bake, broil, boil, fry	4 to 15	fall, winter	whole	lean
Smelt	bake, boil, fry	¼	fall, winter, spring	pound	fat
Sturgeon	bake, broil, boil	50 to 500	spring, summer, fall	pound, fillets, steak (fresh, smoked)	fat
Swordfish	bake, boil, fry	up to 800	summer, fall	pound, steak	lean
Trout	bake, broil, boil, fry	1 to 20	spring, summer, fall	whole (fresh, smoked)	fat

Kind	How to Cook	Size (Pounds)	Season	Market Unit	Type
Tuna	bake, broil, boil	30 up	spring, summer, fall	pound, steak (fresh, canned)	fat
Weakfish	bake, broil, boil, fry	1 to 6	summer, fall	whole	lean
Whitefish	bake, boil, broil, fry	1 to 30	spring, summer, fall	whole, steak, fillets (fresh, salted, smoked)	fat
Whiting	bake, broil, boil, fry	½ to 2	summer, fall	whole (fresh, salted)	lean
Shellfish					
Clams	fry, steam		all year	dozen or quart (fresh, canned)	lean
Crabs, alive meat	boil (hard-shell) fry, boil (soft-shell)		all year	dozen pound (fresh, canned)	lean
Lobsters, alive meat	boil, broil, bake		all year	whole pound (fresh or canned)	lean
Oysters	bake, broil, fry		fall, winter, spring	dozen, quart (fresh, canned)	lean
Scallops	broil, fry		fall, winter, spring	pound, quart (fresh, canned)	lean
Shrimp	boil		spring, fall	pound (fresh, canned)	lean

NOTE: For whole or round fish allow 1 pound per serving. Dressed fish or fish steaks allow ½ pound per serving. Allow ⅓ pound per serving of fish fillets or frozen fish sticks.

Baked Fish

BAKED FISH WITH SHRIMP STUFFING

1 dressed whitefish, bass, or lake trout, 2 to 3 lbs.
1 cup chopped cooked shrimp
1 cup chopped fresh mushrooms
1 cup soft bread crumbs
½ cup chopped celery
¼ cup chopped onion
2 tablespoons chopped parsley
¾ teaspoon salt
Few grains pepper
½ teaspoon thyme
¼ cup melted butter or margarine
2 to 3 tablespoons apple cider
2 tablespoons melted butter or margarine

1. Rinse fish under cold water; drain well and pat dry with absorbent paper. Sprinkle fish cavity generously with *salt*.
2. Combine in a bowl the shrimp, mushrooms, bread crumbs, celery, onion, parsley, salt, pepper, and thyme. Gradually pour ¼ cup melted butter over bread mixture, tossing lightly.
3. Lightly pile stuffing into fish. Fasten with skewers and lace with cord. Place fish in a greased shallow baking pan and brush with a mixture of the cider and 2 tablespoons melted butter.
4. Bake at 375°F, brushing occasionally with cider mixture, 25 to 30 minutes, or until fish flakes easily when pierced with a fork. If desired, place fish under broiler 3 to 5 minutes.
5. Transfer to a heated platter and remove skewers and cord. Garnish platter with sprigs of *parsley*. Serve with *scalloped potatoes* and *buttered French-style green beans*.   4 TO 6 SERVINGS

RED SNAPPER WITH CAPER STUFFING

1 dressed red snapper, 4 to 5 lbs.
Caper Stuffing, *page 264*
1 tablespoon cider vinegar or lemon juice
1 tablespoon salt
1 egg white, slightly beaten
½ cup fine dry bread crumbs
1 teaspoon grated lemon peel
½ to ⅔ cup butter, melted
Creamy Caper Sauce, *page 264*

1. Rinse fish under running cold water; drain well and pat dry with absorbent paper.
2. Lightly spoon the stuffing into fish and close

opening by fastening securely with skewers. Put in a greased large shallow baking pan.

3. Brush surface of fish with a mixture of the vinegar and salt. Brush with egg white; sprinkle with a mixture of the bread crumbs and lemon peel. Drizzle generously with some of the melted butter.

4. Bake at 350°F 45 minutes, or until fish flakes easily when tested with a fork; drizzle with the melted butter twice during baking.

5. Transfer fish to heated serving platter and remove skewers. Garnish top of fish with five notched *lime slices*, placing a *ripe olive ring* and a small piece of *pimiento* in the center of each. Serve immediately with the hot sauce.   ABOUT 8 SERVINGS

CAPER STUFFING: Mix together *2 cups fine dry bread crumbs, ½ cup capers, ¼ cup finely chopped green onion*, and *¼ cup finely chopped parsley*. Pour a blend of *2 beaten eggs* and *⅔ cup cream* evenly over all, mixing well.

CREAMY CAPER SAUCE: Heat *2 tablespoons butter* in a saucepan. Stir in *2 tablespoons flour, ½ teaspoon salt*, and *¼ teaspoon black pepper*; heat until mixture bubbles, stirring constantly. Remove from heat and slowly add *1½ cups heavy cream* and *1 tablespoon tomato paste*, stirring until well blended. Continue to stir, bring to boiling, and boil 1 to 2 minutes. Mix in *4 teaspoons capers*.

FLOUNDER STUFFED WITH CRAB MEAT
This truly memorable baked fish dish is served at the Ben Gross Restaurant, Irwin, Pennsylvania.

1 lb. lump crab meat, bony membrane removed	¼ teaspoon Tabasco
	¾ teaspoon salt
	¾ teaspoon dry mustard
1 slice white bread, crusts trimmed and bread cut in ¼-in. cubes	⅛ teaspoon seasoned salt
	1 cup Medium White Sauce, *page 342*
3 tablespoons lemon juice	1 egg yolk
	Butter
1 tablespoon dry sherry	4 fresh flounder fillets (about 2 lbs.) with pockets cut in sides
¾ teaspoon Worcestershire sauce	

1. Combine the crab meat (do not break up lumps) with bread cubes, lemon juice, sherry, Worcestershire sauce, Tabasco, salt, dry mustard, and seasoned salt. Mix gently; add a mixture of the white sauce and egg yolk. Continue tossing lightly.

2. Butter flounder and fill pockets with the crab meat stuffing. Put into a shallow baking dish. Sprinkle generously with *paprika*.

3. Bake at 350°F 10 to 12 minutes and brown under broiler before serving.   4 SERVINGS

BAKED FISH STEAKS

2 lbs. fish steaks or fillets, such as cod, haddock, halibut, or salmon, 1 in. thick	1½ teaspoons curry powder or tarragon
	½ teaspoon salt
	⅛ teaspoon pepper
	4 bacon slices

1. Wash, coarsely chop, and mix together equal amounts of *parsley, celery leaves*, and *onion* (enough to line a shallow baking dish).

2. Sprinkle both sides of fish steaks with a mixture of the curry powder, salt, and pepper. Arrange on parsley mixture. Place a bacon slice on each steak.

3. Bake uncovered at 350°F 25 to 30 minutes, or until fish flakes easily.

4. Serve with a *lemon-butter sauce*.   4 SERVINGS

BAKED RESTIGOUCHE SALMON BREVAL
The chef de cuisine of the Royal York Hotel, Toronto, Canada, contributed this recipe. Restigouche salmon, noted for its fine texture and delicate flavor, comes from the wide, scenic Restigouche River in the province of New Brunswick, Canada. It normally commands a high price due to a short fishing season and a limited supply. If this salmon is not available, substitute any salmon steaks.

4 Restigouche salmon steaks, 8 oz. each	¾ cup fish stock or water
1 cup sliced fresh mushrooms	3 tablespoons butter
	2 tablespoons flour
4 green onions, finely chopped	1 egg yolk, beaten
	⅓ cup heavy cream, whipped
2 tomatoes, peeled and finely diced	1 tablespoon chopped parsley
1 tablespoon lemon juice	
1 cup dry white wine	

1. Place fish in a buttered shallow baking dish; sprinkle with *salt* and *pepper*.

2. Combine the mushrooms, green onions, tomatoes, and lemon juice and spoon over the steaks.

3. Bring wine and stock to boiling and pour over steaks. Cover with buttered brown paper.

4. Bake at 350°F about 20 minutes. Remove salmon to heat-resistant platter; trim off skin and remove center bones.

5. Pour liquid into a saucepan, set over low heat and reduce liquid by one third. Blend butter and flour, add to liquid and cook, stirring until smooth and thickened.

6. Stir a little sauce into beaten egg yolk and blend into hot mixture; cook about 1 minute. Fold in whipped cream and parsley. Remove from heat immediately and taste for seasoning, adding *salt* and *cayenne pepper* as needed. Pour sauce over fish.

7. Place under broiler 2 to 3 minutes to glaze to a golden color. 4 SERVINGS

STUFFED SOLE HOLLANDAISE

This gourmet recipe is a favorite of Pat O'Brien, long-time star of screen and stage.

1 teaspoon seasoned salt	2 teaspoons water
1 teaspoon dill weed	1 can (3 oz.) sliced
⅛ teaspoon freshly	mushrooms, drained
ground pepper	1 can (7½ oz.) Alaska
1 tablespoon fresh lemon	king crab meat
juice	1 can (6 oz.)
4 medium fillets of	hollandaise sauce,
sole, 1 to 1¼ lbs.	or Hollandaise Sauce,
2 teaspoons instant	*page 344*)
minced onion	2 tablespoons butter
	or margarine, melted

1. Spread a mixture of seasoned salt, dill, pepper, and lemon juice over fillets.

2. Mix the instant minced onion with water, then combine with the mushrooms, crab meat, and 2 tablespoons of the hollandaise sauce.

3. Divide mixture into 4 portions and place one portion on center of each fillet. Roll each fillet around the filling and secure with wooden picks.

4. Place rolls, opened side up, in a greased shallow baking dish. Brush with melted butter.

5. Bake at 375°F 45 minutes, or until fish flakes easily.

6. Heat remaining hollandaise sauce over very low heat. Transfer fish rolls to serving plate, remove picks, and spoon sauce over rolls. 4 SERVINGS

FISH FILLETS VIENNESE

2 lbs. fresh or thawed	6 slices bacon, diced,
frozen sole fillets	panbroiled, and
1 teaspoon salt	drained
4 teaspoons lemon juice	¾ cup diced cucumber
1½ cups dairy sour cream	1 tablespoon capers
1 tablespoon prepared	¼ cup shredded
English mustard	Parmesan cheese
1 tablespoon flour	

1. Sprinkle fish evenly with salt. Arrange one third of the fish fillets in a buttered 2-quart shallow casserole. Sprinkle evenly with the lemon juice.

2. Combine sour cream, mustard, and *few grains salt*, and blend in the flour.

3. Cover fish fillets with one third of sour cream mixture. Top with one third of bacon, one fourth cup of cucumber, and 1 teaspoon capers; repeat twice. Top with cheese.

4. Bake at 375°F about 25 minutes.

6 TO 8 SERVINGS

FILLET OF SOLE BONNE FEMME

La Cremaillere, a Banksville, New York, restaurant, serves this epicurean fish dish.

1 lb. fresh mushrooms,	2 glasses dry white wine
cleaned and sliced	2 tablespoons flour
1 onion, chopped	½ cup melted butter
2 sprigs parsley,	½ cup heavy cream
chopped	1 egg yolk
6 fillets of sole or	
flounder	

1. Place half the mushrooms in a buttered baking dish (for top-of-range and oven use). Sprinkle a mixture of half the onion and parsley over mushrooms. Season with *salt* and *pepper* to taste.

2. Arrange fillets over mushroom mixture; sprinkle with remaining vegetables; add wine and dot with *butter*.

3. Cover and cook over medium heat until the liquid comes to boiling. Set in a 350°F oven 10 minutes. Remove from oven and drain liquid into a saucepan. Cook until liquid is reduced to half.

4. Blend flour with melted butter in a small bowl. Add to the liquid in saucepan; cook and stir until sauce thickens. Combine cream with egg yolk, mix thoroughly and stir into sauce.

5. Make sure the fillets are thoroughly dry before spooning sauce over them. Place under broiler until well browned. ABOUT 6 SERVINGS

Broiled Fish

POMPANO FLORENTINE

Mornay Sauce, *page 343*
1 pkg. (10 oz.) frozen
  chopped spinach
4 pompano fillets, 6 oz.
  each
¼ cup butter or
  margarine, melted

2 tablespoons lemon
  juice
1 teaspoon salt
⅛ teaspoon black
  pepper

1. Prepare Mornay Sauce; set aside. Cook spinach according to package directions.
2. Meanwhile, place pompano fillets, skin side down, on a greased broiler rack. Brush with one half of a mixture of the butter and lemon juice. Broil 2 inches from source of heat about 8 minutes, or until fish flakes easily. During broiling, brush fillets with remaining butter mixture.
3. When spinach is tender, drain thoroughly. Combine with 1 cup of the Mornay Sauce; keep hot.
4. When fillets are done, sprinkle with a mixture of salt and pepper. Spoon about ¾ cup Mornay Sauce over fillets. Broil 2 to 3 minutes, or just until sauce is lightly browned.
5. Arrange spinach mixture in four servings on a heated serving platter. Carefully place fillets over the spinach. Pour remaining Mornay Sauce around fillets. Garnish platter with *parsley sprigs* and *lemon wedges*.   4 SERVINGS

BROILED SALMON

1 cup sauterne
½ cup cooking or salad
  oil
2 tablespoons wine
  vinegar

2 teaspoons soy sauce
2 tablespoons chopped
  green onion
6 salmon steaks, cut ½
  in. thick

1. Blend sauterne, oil, vinegar, soy sauce, and green onion and pour over salmon steaks in a large shallow dish. Marinate in refrigerator several hours or overnight, turning occasionally.
2. To broil, remove steaks from marinade to broiler rack. Broil 6 inches from source of heat about 5 minutes on each side, brushing generously several times with marinade.
3. Put steaks onto a hot platter and garnish with *lemon slices* and *grape clusters*.   6 SERVINGS

BROILED RED SNAPPER WITH WINE SAUCE

1. Select a *red snapper* weighing 3½ to 4 pounds without the head. Split alongside the backbone from inside, severing both sets of ribs, and lay the fish open. Trim out rib bones and remove fins but not tail. Marinate fish about 30 minutes in *Gourmet Wine Sauce, below*.
2. Place a sheet of heavy-duty aluminum foil on broiler rack and lay the fish on foil, skin side down. Place under broiler about 5 inches from source of heat and broil 6 to 10 minutes, or until well browned. Brush with marinade during broiling.
3. Remove broiler pan and place a second sheet of foil over the fish. Then, holding both foil sheets firmly, turn. Remove the first foil sheet and broil skin side 3 to 5 minutes. Test fish for doneness. If the flesh flakes easily the fish is done. For well-browned fish, dust with *paprika* or brush with *melted butter*.
4. Serve on a platter and garnish with *lemon wedges* and *parsley*. If there is any wine sauce left, serve separately with the fish.

   6 TO 8 SERVINGS

GOURMET WINE SAUCE

1 medium onion, minced
1 clove garlic, minced
2 teaspoons minced
  parsley
1 teaspoon salt
½ teaspoon pepper

1 teaspoon oregano
1 teaspoon Italian
  seasoning
1 cup olive oil
1 cup dry sherry or
  other white wine

Mix all ingredients and, if possible, let stand 1 hour or longer to blend flavors.

BROILED TROUT

Purchase one 8- to 10-ounce *trout* for each serving; if desired, remove head and fins. Rinse trout quickly under cold running water and dry thoroughly. Brush cavity of fish with tart *French dressing* and sprinkle generously with *instant minced onion* and *salt*. Brush trout generously with French dressing and arrange in a greased large shallow baking pan or on a broiler rack. Broil trout about 3 inches from source of heat 5 to 8 minutes on each side, or until fish flakes easily; brush with dressing during broiling. Remove trout to heated platter.

Fried Fish

FISH FILLETS MORNAY

2 lbs. fresh or frozen fish fillets, thawed	⅛ teaspoon pepper
½ cup yellow cornmeal	Butter or margarine
1½ teaspoons salt	Toasted blanched almonds
	Mornay Sauce, *page 343*

1. Cut the fillets into serving-sized pieces. Coat with a mixture of cornmeal, salt, and pepper.
2. Fry in hot butter in a skillet until crisp and browned on both sides.
3. Serve fish, topped with almonds, on heated platter; surround with the sauce. ABOUT 6 SERVINGS

FRIED KIPPERS IN CREAM

4 kippered herring	3 medium onions, cut in ¼-in. slices and separated in rings
3 to 4 tablespoons butter or margarine	1¼ cups cream, scalded

1. Cover herring with cold water and bring to boiling. Drain and dry well with absorbent paper.
2. Meanwhile, heat butter in a skillet. Add onion rings and cook until soft, turning occasionally. Remove onion with slotted spoon and keep warm.
3. Place herring in skillet. Brown over low heat about 5 minutes on each side.
4. Slowly pour one half of the scalded cream into skillet with herring and simmer 2 minutes. Add remaining cream and simmer 3 minutes longer. Serve at once; garnish with the onion rings.

4 SERVINGS

FISH IN COCONUT-MUSHROOM SAUCE

1⅓ cups water	2 teaspoons cornstarch
1⅓ cups flaked coconut	1 scallion, sliced
1 pkg. (2 oz.) dried Japanese mushrooms	¼ cup sugar
	¼ to ½ teaspoon salt
1 lb. sole or other fish fillets	3 to 4 teaspoons lemon juice
1 egg, slightly beaten	1½ teaspoons Japanese soy sauce (shoyu)
Butter or margarine	

1. Bring water with coconut to boiling in a saucepan. Strain, pressing coconut to extract liquid; reserve ½ cup of the coconut for garnish (see *Toasted Coconut, below*). Return liquid to saucepan.

2. Soak mushrooms according to package directions until softened. Drain and reserve liquid. Set 8 or 9 mushrooms aside for garnish; slice remaining mushrooms and reserve.
3. Dip fillets into *cornstarch*, then egg, and again into cornstarch, coating all sides. Heat enough butter to cover the bottom of a large skillet. Add fillets and cook about 2 minutes on each side, or until lightly browned and fish flakes easily. Arrange fillets on a heated platter and keep warm.
4. Blend 2 tablespoons of the mushroom liquid into the 2 teaspoons cornstarch until smooth. Add with the sliced mushrooms, scallion, sugar, salt, lemon juice, and soy sauce to the coconut liquid in saucepan. Bring rapidly to boiling, stirring constantly, and cook until slightly thickened.
5. Spoon sauce over fish; garnish with Toasted Coconut and whole mushrooms, heated in some of their liquid. ABOUT 4 SERVINGS

TOASTED COCONUT: Heat *1 tablespoon butter or margarine* in a skillet; add the ½ cup drained coconut and heat until lightly browned, stirring occasionally.

CODFISH CAKES

1 lb. salt codfish	2 eggs, beaten
4 to 6 medium-sized potatoes (about 2 lbs.)	½ teaspoon paprika
	⅛ teaspoon pepper
2 tablespoons butter or margarine	Fat for deep frying heated to 365°F

1. Cover codfish with cold water to freshen. Let stand in the cold water at least 4 hours; change water 3 or 4 times during that period. (Or follow directions on package.) Drain fish and remove any pieces of bone. Flake and set aside.
2. Wash, pare, and cut potatoes into pieces. Combine fish and potatoes in a saucepan. Cook covered, in boiling water to cover, about 20 minutes, or until potatoes are tender.
3. Thoroughly drain and mash potatoes and fish. Whip in the butter and a mixture of the eggs, paprika, and pepper until mixture is fluffy.
4. Deep fry by dropping spoonfuls of the mixture into the hot fat. Drop only as many at one time as will float uncrowded one layer deep. Turn cakes as they brown, cooking each 2 to 5 minutes or until golden brown. Drain on absorbent paper.
5. Serve with a *tomato sauce* or *cream sauce.*

6 SERVINGS

FRIED SMELTS

2 doz. smelts	Fine bread crumbs
1 egg, beaten	Fat for deep frying
1 tablespoon water	heated to 360°F

1. Clean the smelts, leaving on the heads and tails; rinse and pat dry.
2. Sprinkle with *salt* and *pepper*; shake in a bag with *flour*; dip in a mixture of the egg and water; roll in crumbs. Let stand about 15 minutes.
3. Fry smelts without crowding in heated fat 3 to 4 minutes. Drain on absorbent paper.
4. Garnish with *parsley*; serve with *tartar sauce*.

4 SERVINGS

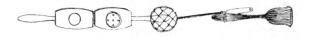

CORNMEAL-CRUSTED MOUNTAIN TROUT

Pour *peanut oil*, to a depth of ½ inch, into a skillet and heat oil to 350°F. Meanwhile, rinse and dry *trout* (do not scale); allow 1 trout per person. Coat trout with a mixture of *cornmeal* and *salt* and *pepper* to taste. Place in hot oil (do not crowd) and cook until golden on both sides, turning only once.

FRESH TROUT WITH SAUCE SUPREME

6 cleaned fresh trout, 8 to 10 oz. each	3 tablespoons tomato paste
6 tablespoons butter or margarine	¼ cup chopped pimiento-stuffed olives
Sauce Supreme:	
¼ cup finely chopped onion	¼ to ½ teaspoon salt
1 large clove garlic, cut in halves	1 cup heavy cream

1. Remove heads and fins from trout, if desired; rinse trout quickly under cold running water and pat dry with absorbent paper. Coat lightly with *seasoned flour*.
2. Heat butter in a large skillet over medium heat. Add trout to skillet and cook 5 to 8 minutes on each side, or until lightly browned and fish flakes easily. Transfer to a heated serving platter and keep hot.
3. To prepare the sauce, add the onion and garlic to butter in skillet. Cook until onion is golden. Remove and discard the garlic. Mix in tomato paste, olives, and salt. Gradually add the cream, stirring constantly. Heat thoroughly.
4. Serve sauce hot with the trout. Garnish platter with *watercress* or *parsley sprigs*.   6 SERVINGS

TROUT WITH LEMON-CAPER BUTTER: Prepare and cook trout as in recipe for Fresh Trout with Sauce Supreme. To prepare sauce, melt ½ *cup butter or margarine* over low heat; stir in *1 tablespoon lemon juice* and ¼ *cup drained capers*. Serve hot with the trout.

Poached Fish

POACHED SALMON AROMATIC

Salmon poached in a well-seasoned court bouillon was one of the reasons for Anthony Dardanelli's fine reputation as a gourmet chef in one of Philadelphia, Pennsylvania's hotel dining rooms.

2 qts. water	2 whole cloves
1 teaspoon salt	¼ stick cinnamon
1 cup cider vinegar	¼ teaspoon oregano
½ medium-sized onion	¼ teaspoon thyme
½ carrot, cut in pieces	¼ teaspoon rosemary
½ stalk celery, cut in pieces	¼ teaspoon basil
	⅛ teaspoon nutmeg
1 large clove garlic	6 salmon steaks
2 bay leaves	

1. Combine in a large kettle the water, salt, vinegar, vegetables, and spices and herbs (tied in a square of cheesecloth). Bring to boiling; cook 10 minutes.
2. Tie salmon in cheesecloth and place in boiling bouillon. Allow to simmer about 12 minutes.
3. Remove salmon from bouillon and serve with *lemon wedges* and *Hollandaise Sauce, page 344.*

6 SERVINGS

FISH POACHED IN COURT BOUILLON

1 qt. water	½ lemon, sliced
½ cup vinegar	1 teaspoon salt
1 carrot, sliced	Herb bouquet, *page 12*
2 small onions, sliced	4 peppercorns
3 or 4 shallots, minced	Fish

1. Heat the water in a large kettle with vinegar, carrot, onions, shallots, lemon, salt, and herb bouquet. Bring to boiling; reduce heat, cover, and simmer 20 minutes.

2. Add peppercorns and cook 10 minutes longer; strain and set aside.

3. Place fish in a large skillet. Cover with hot court bouillon and poach, covered, over low heat. Allow about 8 minutes per pound, or until fish flakes easily. Drain.

4. Serve hot with *melted butter*, or *Hollandaise Sauce, page 344*, or *Bercy Sauce, page 342*. If fish is to be served cold, let it remain in the court bouillon until completely cool to prevent drying.

ABOUT 1 QUART COURT BOUILLON

NOTE: Refrigerate court bouillon if not used immediately.

Canned- & Frozen-Fish Dishes

SAVORY SALMON KABOBS

1 can (16 oz.) salmon, drained and flaked	¼ cup finely chopped onion
1 egg, slightly beaten	¼ teaspoon Worcestershire sauce
1 cup shredded Cheddar cheese	⅛ teaspoon Tabasco
½ cup fine dry bread crumbs	¼ cup butter

1. Combine in a bowl all ingredients except the butter. Divide mixture into 6 portions and press firmly around wooden skewers into oblong shapes.

2. Melt butter over medium heat in a large heavy skillet. Add kabobs and brown evenly, turning frequently. Serve with *Tangy Cheese-Broccoli Sauce, below.*

6 SERVINGS

TANGY CHEESE-BROCCOLI SAUCE

2 tablespoons butter	1 tablespoon lemon juice
2 tablespoons flour	1 teaspoon Worcestershire sauce
½ teaspoon salt	
1 can (14½ oz.) evaporated milk	1 pkg. (10 oz.) frozen chopped broccoli, cooked and drained
1 cup shredded Cheddar cheese	

1. Melt butter in a heavy saucepan over medium heat. Blend in a mixture of the flour and salt; cook until bubbly. Remove from heat and add evaporated milk gradually, stirring constantly. Return to heat; cook and stir until sauce comes to boiling and is thickened and smooth. Cook 1 to 2 minutes.

2. Reduce heat to low and stir in the cheese, lemon juice, Worcestershire sauce, and cooked broccoli; heat only until cheese is melted.

3. Serve immediately over salmon kabobs.

ABOUT 3½ CUPS SAUCE

TUNA-CHILI CHOWDER

It is said that this is the chowder served on the famous tuna fishing boats.

3 cans (6½ or 7 oz. each) tuna packed in oil, drained and separated in large pieces (reserve ¼ cup oil)	3 soup cans water
	2 tablespoons tomato paste
	2 tablespoons cider vinegar
1 cup sliced celery	1 teaspoon salt
1 cup chopped green pepper	¼ teaspoon pepper
3 onions, chopped	1½ teaspoons chili powder
1½ teaspoons paprika	2 cans (about 16 oz. each) red kidney beans, drained
1 can (10¾ oz.) condensed tomato soup	

1. Heat the tuna oil in a large saucepan. Add the celery, green pepper, onion, and paprika; cook over medium heat, stirring occasionally, until celery is just tender.

2. Mix in remaining ingredients and the tuna. Cover and simmer to blend flavors.

ABOUT 8 SERVINGS

SKILLET TUNA SUPREME

Serve your family this quick-as-a-wink entrée with a flourish — it's mighty fine eating.

⅔ cup chopped onion	2 to 3 tablespoons brown sugar
1 green pepper, cut in slivers	1 teaspoon grated lemon peel
2 tablespoons cooking or salad oil	3 tablespoons lemon juice
1 can (10¾ oz.) condensed tomato soup	2 cans (6½ or 7 oz. each) tuna, drained
2 teaspoons soy sauce	

1. Cook onion and green pepper until almost tender in hot oil in a large skillet; stir occasionally.

2. Mix in the tomato soup, soy sauce, brown sugar, and lemon peel and juice. Bring to boiling; simmer 5 minutes.

3. Mix in the tuna, separating it into small pieces. Heat thoroughly.

4. Serve with fluffy hot *cooked rice*. Garnish with *toasted sesame seed* and *chow mein noodles*.

ABOUT 6 SERVINGS

BLUSHING TUNA PIE

3 cans (6½ or 7 oz. each) chunk-style tuna packed in oil, drained (reserve 3 tablespoons oil)
⅔ cup ketchup
½ teaspoon salt
2 tablespoons flour
¼ teaspoon pepper
1½ cups milk
1 cup shredded sharp Cheddar cheese
½ teaspoon Worcestershire sauce
1 unbaked 9-in. pastry shell

1. Mix tuna, ketchup, and salt in a bowl.
2. Put reserved tuna oil into a saucepan. Blend in flour and pepper. Heat until bubbly. Gradually add the milk, stirring constantly. Bring to boiling; cook 1 to 2 minutes.
3. Remove from heat. Add the cheese and stir until melted. Add the Worcestershire sauce and tuna; mix well. Turn into the unbaked pastry shell. Sprinkle with *paprika*.
4. Bake at 400°F 30 to 35 minutes, or until pastry is golden brown and mixture is bubbly.
5. Remove from oven and sprinkle lightly with *snipped parsley*.

4 SERVINGS

FISH STICK SPECIAL

1 pkg. (10 oz.) frozen fish sticks
¼ cup chopped toasted almonds
1 cup shredded Cheddar cheese
2 tablespoons chopped onion
¼ cup milk
½ cup chopped sweet mixed pickles
2 tablespoons buttered dry bread crumbs

1. Arrange fish sticks in a shallow baking dish.
2. Mix the remaining ingredients except bread crumbs and spoon over fish. Top with crumbs.
3. Heat in a 425°F oven 15 to 20 minutes.

ABOUT 4 SERVINGS

Stuffings for Fish

BREAD STUFFING FOR FISH

2 cups soft bread crumbs
1 teaspoon grated onion
½ cup chopped celery
1 tablespoon lemon juice
½ teaspoon salt
3 tablespoons butter or margarine, melted
2 tablespoons water

Toss all ingredients lightly but thoroughly.

STUFFING FOR A 3- TO 4-POUND FISH

MUSHROOM STUFFING: Follow recipe for Bread Stuffing for Fish. Omit lemon juice. Cook ½ to 1 *cup sliced fresh mushrooms* in the butter.

SAVORY STUFFING: Follow recipe for Bread Stuffing for Fish. Omit lemon juice. Add *2 tablespoons minced parsley, ¼ teaspoon savory seasoning*, and *¼ teaspoon celery seed*.

SPICY STUFFING: Follow recipe for Bread Stuffing for Fish. Omit celery. Add *2 tablespoons chopped green pepper* and *¼ teaspoon mace*.

VEGETABLE STUFFING: Follow recipe for Bread Stuffing for Fish. Omit lemon juice and water. Increase salt to 1 teaspoon salt and add *¾ cup shredded raw carrots*.

OYSTER OR CLAM STUFFING

½ cup chopped oysters or clams
2 cups fine cracker crumbs
2 tablespoons butter or margarine, melted
1 teaspoon salt
2 teaspoons chopped pickle
2 tablespoons lemon juice
½ cup water

Mix ingredients in order given, adding more water if stuffing seems dry.

STUFFING FOR A 3- TO 4-POUND FISH

SHELLFISH

MARKET FORMS

Live shellfish are those which should be alive when purchased, such as crabs, lobsters, clams, and oysters (except when purchasing cooked lobsters and crabs in the shell).

Shucked shellfish are those which have been removed from their shells.

Headless shellfish are shrimp and rock lobster tail (spiny lobster).

Cooked meat is the edible portion of the shellfish, cooked and ready to eat; shrimp, crab, and lobster meat are marketed this way.

Frozen shellfish available are shrimp, crab, lobster, lobster tails, scallops, and oysters.

Clams

There are two general types of clams, the soft clams and the hard or quahog clams. The latter group is divided into three classes: the little-necks, small in size; the cherrystones, medium-sized; and the large chowder clams. The little-neck and cherrystone clams may be used raw.

When purchased, the shells should be tightly closed or should close at a touch. They may be opened with a knife or be steamed open.

Shell clams kept in the refrigerator at 40°F will remain alive several days. *Fresh shucked clams*, sold by the pint or quart should be plump, with clear liquid, and free from shell particles. They are packed in metal or waxed containers and should be refrigerated or packed in ice; they will stay fresh for a week or 10 days if properly handled. *Frozen shucked clams* should not be thawed until ready to use and never refrozen. Clams are canned whole or minced, or as chowder. Clam juice, broth, and nectar are also canned.

PAELLA

1 cup olive or other cooking oil	2 cups uncooked long grain white rice
1 broiler-fryer chicken, 2 lbs., cup up	4 cups hot water
½ cup diced boiled ham or smoky sausage	1 cup fresh or frozen green peas
1 tablespoon minced onion	¼ cup coarsely chopped parsley
2 cloves garlic, minced	Few shreds saffron
2 ripe tomatoes, peeled and coarsely chopped	1 rock lobster tail, cooked and meat cut in pieces, or 1 pkg. frozen crab meat, thawed and drained
1½ teaspoons salt	
1½ lbs. fresh shrimp, shelled and deveined	
12 small clams in shells, scrubbed	1 can or jar (7 oz.) whole pimientos

1.   Heat oil in paellera or large skillet; cook chicken and ham about 10 minutes, turning chicken to brown on all sides. Add onion and garlic and cook 2 minutes. Add tomatoes, salt, shrimp, and clams; cover and cook 5 to 10 minutes, or until clam shells open. Remove clams and keep warm.
2.   Stir in rice, water, peas, parsley, and saffron. Cover and cook, stirring occasionally, 25 minutes, or until rice is just tender. Mix in the lobster, half of the pimiento, and the reserved clams in shells; heat until very hot. Serve garnished with remaining pimiento.   8 TO 10 SERVINGS

CLAM PIE

3 tablespoons butter or margarine	½ cup milk
½ cup chopped onion	1 can (16 oz.) whole cooked potatoes, drained and diced
2 tablespoons flour	
½ teaspoon salt	2 tablespoons snipped parsley
3 cans (7½ oz. each) minced clams, drained (reserve ½ cup liquid)	Pastry for a 1-crust 8-in. pie

1.   Heat butter in a large skillet; add the onion and cook until transparent.
2.   Blend in flour, salt, and a *few grains pepper.* Heat until bubbly. Add the reserved clam liquid and the milk gradually, stirring constantly. Bring to boiling; cook and stir 1 to 2 minutes.
3.   Remove from heat. Mix in potatoes, clams, and parsley. Turn into an 8-inch pie pan.
4.   Prepare pastry and roll out to fit over clam mixture. Cut a simple design near center of pastry to allow steam to escape during baking. Place pastry on clam mixture and flute edge.
5.   Bake at 450°F about 20 minutes, or until pastry is lightly browned.   4 TO 6 SERVINGS

Crabs & Crab Meat

Crabs are generally divided into two classes, the hard-shelled crab and the soft-shelled crab. The latter is not a different variety, but merely a crab caught after it has shed its shell and before it has developed a new one. Crabs when purchased alive should be vigorous and lively. The cooked crab meat may be purchased iced or frozen (it is very perishable) or in cans. Soft-shelled crabs are usually fried or broiled, while the hard-shelled crabs are boiled and the meat removed for use in various dishes. Cooked crab meat may be one of the following: *Blue Crab*—Lump meat comes from the large muscles which operate the swimming legs; it is white in color and is sometimes called "special" or "back fin" lump crab meat. Flake meat is the remaining portion of the body meat; it is also white. Claw meat is the brownish meat removed from the claws. *Rock Crab*—Meat is brownish in color; there is only one grade. *Dungeness Crab*—Claw and body meat is reddish in color. *King Crab*—Meat from the king crab of Alaska is mostly removed from the legs, frozen and packed. Entire leg sections, cooked and frozen, are also marketed.

To kill soft-shelled crab—Insert a small sharp knife into the body between the eyes or cut off the face. Lift up the pointed end of the soft shell and remove the spongy white fibers between the two halves of the body and between the sides of the top shell and the body. Turn crab on its back and remove the apron or ventral placque—the small loose shell running to a point about the middle of the undershell. Wash crab and cook at once.

CRAB MEAT À LA SARDI
From Sardi's in New York City.

1½ cups cooked crab meat (bony tissue removed)
¼ cup sherry, warmed
12 asparagus spears, cooked just tender

1 cup Sardi Sauce, *below*
2 tablespoons grated Parmesan cheese

1.　Sprinkle crab meat with sherry; set aside for 10 minutes.
2.　Turn crab-sherry mixture into a heated shallow baking dish; arrange asparagus spears on the top, cover with Sardi Sauce, and sprinkle with cheese.
3.　Place under broiler until cheese is lightly browned, and serve piping hot.　　　2 SERVINGS

SARDI SAUCE

½ cup sherry
¼ cup light cream
1¾ cups Sauce Velouté, *below*

½ cup Hollandaise Sauce, *page 344*
½ cup whipped cream

1.　Reduce sherry by cooking it rapidly 3 minutes; heat light cream.
2.　Add reduced sherry and heated cream to Sauce Velouté; let cool.
3.　Fold in Hollandaise Sauce and whipped cream.　　　ABOUT 3 CUPS SAUCE

SAUCE VELOUTÉ (Sardi's): Make a white roux by melting *½ cup butter* and blending with about *½ cup all-purpose flour.* Cook and stir until bubbly but do not allow it to color. Add about *5 cups white veal broth*, a little at a time, stirring constantly with a whisk. Bring to boiling and continue cooking

slowly for 30 minutes without stirring. Season the sauce very lightly since it is the basis for a number of white sauces. As soon as it is done remove all fat and strain into a bowl through a pointed sieve. While it cools stir from time to time to prevent a skin from forming. It will keep well for several days in the refrigerator. Store in freezer if kept for a longer period.

DEVILED CRAB

Mustard Sauce:
1 tablespoon dry mustard
2 tablespoons water
2 tablespoons olive oil
1 teaspoon ketchup
¼ teaspoon salt
¼ teaspoon Worcestershire sauce
Crab Meat Mixture:
6 tablespoons butter or margarine
4 teaspoons finely chopped green pepper
2 teaspoons finely chopped onion
6 tablespoons flour

1 teaspoon salt
½ teaspoon dry mustard
1½ cups milk
1 teaspoon Worcestershire sauce
2 egg yolks, slightly beaten
1 lb. lump crab meat, drained
2 teaspoons chopped pimiento
2 tablespoons dry sherry
1 cup fine dry bread crumbs
Paprika

1.　For mustard sauce, blend the sauce ingredients in a small bowl; set aside.
2.　For crab meat mixture, melt butter in a large heavy saucepan. Add the green pepper and onion; cook until onion is golden in color.
3.　Blend in a mixture of the flour, salt, and dry mustard. Heat until bubbly. Gradually add the milk, stirring until smooth. Stir in the Worcestershire sauce. Bring rapidly to boiling; cook 1 to 2 minutes longer.
4.　Stir a small amount of hot mixture into the egg yolks; return to saucepan and cook 3 to 5 minutes, stirring constantly.
5.　Stir in the crab meat and pimiento; heat thoroughly. Remove from heat and blend in the sherry and mustard sauce.
6.　Spoon into 6 shell-shaped ramekins, allowing about ½ cup mixture for each. Sprinkle top with the crumbs and paprika; drizzle with *melted butter or margarine.*
7.　Set in a 450°F oven 6 to 7 minutes, or until tops are lightly browned and mixture is thoroughly heated. Serve hot.　　　6 SERVINGS

CRAB MEAT AU GRATIN

A delicately rich dish—excellent with broccoli or asparagus accented with browned butter sauce.

½ cup butter
⅔ cup all-purpose flour
2 teaspoons salt
2⅔ cups milk
2 cans (6½ oz. each) crab meat, drained and separated in pieces
4 cups chopped celery
½ cup chopped green pepper
2 pimientos, drained and chopped

2 tablespoons grated onion
⅓ cup slivered blanched almonds, toasted
4 hard-cooked eggs, chopped
1 cup shredded sharp Cheddar cheese
1 tablespoon butter
2½ cups small bread cubes

1.   Heat ½ cup butter in a saucepan. Add a mixture of the flour and salt; blend well. Heat until bubbly, stirring constantly. Gradually add milk, stirring until blended. Bring to boiling; cook and stir 1 to 2 minutes.
2.   Mix crab meat, celery, green pepper, pimiento, onion, almonds, and eggs into sauce. Turn into a 2-quart shallow casserole. Sprinkle with cheese.
3.   Heat 1 tablespoon butter in a skillet. Add bread cubes and toss until coated. Spoon cubes over casserole.
4.   Heat in a 350°F oven 35 minutes. If desired, garnish with slices of *hard-cooked eggs*.

8 TO 10 SERVINGS

CRAB RAVIGOTE

A recipe from Brennan's Restaurant in New Orleans.

2 tablespoons butter
2 tablespoons flour
½ teaspoon salt
Few grains cayenne pepper
1 cup milk
⅓ cup chopped cooked green pepper

⅓ cup coarsely chopped pimiento
1 tablespoon capers
1 teaspoon tarragon vinegar
1 cup lump crab meat
⅓ cup Hollandaise Sauce, *page 344*

1.   Heat butter in a saucepan; blend in flour, salt, and cayenne pepper and heat until bubbly. Gradually add milk, stirring constantly. Cook and stir until boiling; cook 1 minute.
2.   Stir in remaining ingredients and heat thoroughly.
3.   Serve in 8-ounce individual casseroles or on *rusks*.

2 SERVINGS

HAMPTON CRAB MEAT IMPERIAL

As served at the famous Williamsburg Inn in Williamsburg, Virginia.

1 lb. cooked crab meat (3 cups)
½ cup diced green pepper
¼ cup butter
2 tablespoons pimiento strips
½ cup butter
½ cup all-purpose flour

4 cups milk, scalded
Dash cayenne pepper
½ teaspoon dry mustard
½ teaspoon salt
Dash Worcestershire sauce
¼ cup mayonnaise

1.   Remove bony membrane from crab meat; separate, reserving 6 pieces of red claw meat for garnish.
2.   Cook green pepper until tender in ¼ cup butter in a large skillet. Add crab meat and pimiento and stir over medium heat 5 minutes.
3.   Heat the ½ cup butter in a heavy saucepan; blend in flour and cook until bubbly. Pour in hot milk gradually, cooking and stirring with whisk or slotted spoon until sauce comes to boiling; cook 1 minute longer.
4.   Stir in a blend of remaining ingredients. Mix in crab meat and vegetables.
5.   Spoon crab mixture into 6 shell ramekins or cleaned crab shells. If desired, top each serving with additional mayonnaise or with fine *bread crumbs*; garnish with a piece of red claw meat. Place shells or ramekins on a baking sheet.
6.   Heat in a 375°F oven 15 to 20 minutes, or until sauce is lightly browned and bubbling; sprinkle lightly with *paprika*.

6 SERVINGS

BOOKY BAKED CRAB

This recipe is from Bookbinder's Sea Food House, Philadelphia, Pennsylvania.

½ cup butter
¾ cup all-purpose flour
1 cup milk
3 egg yolks, beaten
Few grains salt
Few grains pepper

Pinch dry mustard
1 teaspoon Worcestershire sauce
3 lbs. large lump crab meat

1.   Melt butter in a saucepan; stir in flour to make a paste. Remove from heat and stir in the milk.
2.   Cook and stir until very thick and smooth. Blend a little sauce into egg yolks and return to sauce; mix well. Mix in the salt, pepper, dry mustard, Worcestershire sauce, and the crab meat.

3. Form into 6 patties and place in a shallow baking dish.
4. Bake at 350°F 15 to 20 minutes.   6 SERVINGS

CRAB CRÊPES ROSEMARY

Here's cuisine of distinction, a luncheon or supper dish worthy of your most discriminating guests.

Crêpes, *below*	Few grains pepper
1 tablespoon butter or margarine	1½ cups chicken broth
4 to 6 oz. fresh mushrooms, sliced lengthwise	1½ cups dairy sour cream
2 tablespoons finely chopped onion	1 tablespoon snipped parsley
6 tablespoons butter or margarine	3 pkgs. (6 oz. each) thawed frozen or 2 cans (7½ oz. each) drained Alaska king crab meat, sliced
⅓ cup flour	
1 teaspoon crushed rosemary	1 cup shredded Swiss cheese
½ teaspoon seasoned salt	

1. Prepare Crêpes and keep warm.
2. Heat 1 tablespoon butter in a large saucepan. Add mushrooms and onion and cook until lightly browned. Remove mushrooms from saucepan with a slotted spoon and keep warm.
3. Heat remaining butter in saucepan and blend in flour, rosemary, seasoned salt, and pepper. Gradually add chicken broth, stirring constantly until smooth. Bring to boiling; stir and cook about 2 minutes.
4. Remove from heat. Blend in sour cream in small amounts, then mix in parsley, mushrooms, and crab.
5. Spoon about ¼ cup filling along center of each crêpe and roll up. Arrange, overlapping side down, in a single layer in shallow baking dishes. Top with cheese and sprinkle with *paprika*.
6. Set in a 350°F oven 10 to 15 minutes, or until cheese is melted and crêpes are thoroughly heated. Garnish with *parsley*.   6 TO 8 SERVINGS

CRÊPES: Sift *¾ cup all-purpose flour* and *½ teaspoon salt* into a bowl. Add a mixture of *4 well-beaten eggs* (about 1 cup), *2 cups milk*, and *3 tablespoons melted butter or margarine*; beat until smooth. Cover and refrigerate at least 2 hours. For each crêpe, pour about 3 tablespoons batter into a greased hot 6-inch skillet. Immediately tilt skillet back and forth to spread batter thinly and evenly. Bake until browned on first side. Turn and brown on second side. Grease skillet as necessary. Keep crêpes warm until ready to fill.   16 TO 18 CRÊPES

CRAB MEAT BROCHETTE

These crab meat balls from The Pump Room, Ambassador East Hotel, Chicago, Illinois, are equally delightful served as an appetizer or a main dish.

1 lb. fresh crab meat	1 cup white bread crumbs
1 teaspoon salt	
1 teaspoon dry mustard	Bacon strips, cut in halves or thirds
1 teaspoon chopped chives	Hollandaise Sauce, *page 344*
3 tablespoons sherry	Finely chopped chives

1. Combine crab meat, salt, dry mustard, chives, sherry, and bread crumbs; mix thoroughly. Form into balls the size of walnuts. Wrap a piece of bacon around each ball; secure with a wooden pick.
2. Broil about 15 minutes, turning occasionally to brown bacon evenly on all sides.
3. Serve with Hollandaise Sauce sprinkled with chives.   4 TO 6 SERVINGS

Lobsters & Lobster Meat

Lobster is the aristocrat of shellfish. It is one of those seasonal luxuries that modern air transport and the frozen food industry have made available any season. Those that come from along New England's cold coastal waters are the choicest of seafood because they have the largest claws which contain more meat than most.

Lobsters may be purchased *live in the shell*, *cooked in the shell*, as *lobster meat*, or *canned*. Live lobsters are dark bluish-green to brownish-olive in color; they must be kept alive up to the moment of cooking. The weight may vary from ¾ to 3 pounds. Lobsters cooked in the shell are red in color; they are not generally available in large quantities. Lobster meat is picked from cooked lobsters and chilled. It is sold by the pound, fresh or frozen.

How to kill and clean a lobster—Live lobsters may be killed by plunging into boiling water. Or they may be killed by the following method: Place lobster on a cutting board with back or smooth shell up. Hold a towel firmly over head and claws. Quickly insert the point of a sharp heavy knife into center of the small cross on the back of the head. This kills the lobster by severing the spinal cord. Before removing knife, bear down heavily, cutting through entire body and tail. Pull halves apart; remove and discard the stomach (a small sac which lies in the head) and the spongy lungs (which lie in upper body cavity between meat and shell). Remove and discard the dark intestinal vein running through center of body. Crack claws with a nutcracker.

How to boil lobster—Have a kettle large enough to hold all the lobsters to be cooked at the same time. The water must cover them. For each gallon of water, add 2 tablespoons salt, a few sprigs parsley, and 2 slices each of washed carrot, onion, and lemon. Bring water to boiling rapidly, then one at a time, grasp lobsters firmly by back near head and plunge them head first into the water. They are killed instantly and turn a vivid red.

When all lobsters have been added, cover kettle and again bring water to full boil; reduce the heat so that water simmers or "quivers" and continue cooking until lobsters are done. Allow 15 minutes for 1 pound; 16 minutes for 1¼ pound; 17 minutes for 1½ pound; and 20 minutes for 2 pound lobsters. Do not overcook as the meat becomes toughened.

When done, lift lobsters, using tongs, to rack to drain and cool. If serving them whole and cold, rub shell parts with salad oil to improve color. If saving shell parts for Thermidor, brush them with oil.

How to clean a cooked lobster—Slit the lobster down the center from head to tail, separating it into two halves by cutting through the shell. Remove and discard the "lady" (stomach), which is the inedible part near the head. Remove intestinal vein which runs from the "lady" to the tail. Remove and reserve the tomalley (greenish-colored liver), also the coral if any is present (in female only). These are considered to be great delicacies and are used along with the meat. Lobster is now ready to serve or use in other mixtures.

How to eat a lobster—Eat meat from tail and body cavity. Use an oyster fork to dip each morsel into melted butter. Pull apart bony structure on either half of lobster body; pick out and eat tidbits from it. Crack large claws and the "arms," using a nutcracker. Pull out the meat, dip into butter, and eat. If claw meat comes out in too large a piece, cut with knife and fork. The four pairs of small claws at sides of body contain delicious bits of lobster. A nut pick may be helpful in removing them.

How to remove cooked lobster from shell—After cooking and cooling the lobster twist off the large claws and the four pairs of small claws; break with hammer or nutcracker and remove the meat.

Twist off tail; slit it full length with kitchen shears or a heavy knife and break away tail meat in one section. Run sharp knife through meat to get out intestinal vein; discard vein.

Draw out body meat with thumb and first two fingers. Leave the "lady" and spongy "lungs" in the body; or discard these if using shell for lobster service later on. Save liver and coral, if any. Cut up the meat as directed in desired recipe.

Rock lobster tail is the name for crayfish or spiny lobster tail; the meaty tail is the only portion marketed. Usually sold frozen, the meat should be a clear whitish color. Shell color depends on the kind. *Canned rock lobster meat* is available.

LOBSTER TAILS, THERMIDOR

2 (1½ lbs. each) frozen rock lobster tails	2 cups (½ lb.) shredded Cheddar cheese
2 tablespoons butter	1 teaspoon Worcestershire sauce
2 tablespoons flour	¼ cup butter
½ teaspoon salt	¼ cup chopped green pepper
1 teaspoon paprika	½ lb. fresh mushrooms, sliced lengthwise
⅛ teaspoon Tabasco	
1 teaspoon prepared mustard	
1½ cups cream	

1. Drop frozen lobster tails into boiling *salted water*. Bring to boiling; simmer 25 to 30 minutes.

2. Meanwhile, heat the 2 tablespoons butter in a large saucepan. Stir in the flour, salt, and paprika and cook until mixture bubbles; blend in Tabasco and mustard. Add cream gradually, stirring until well blended. Bring rapidly to boiling and boil 1 to 2 minutes, stirring constantly. Remove from heat. Add cheese and Worcestershire sauce; stir until cheese is melted. Cover; set aside and keep warm.

3. Remove cooked lobster tails and place under running cold water for 1 minute, or until cool enough to handle. With scissors, cut along each edge of bony membrane on the underside of each shell; remove and discard the membrane.

4. Gently remove meat from shells, cut into ½-inch pieces, and add to sauce. Reserve shells.

5. Heat the ¼ cup butter in a skillet; add green pepper and mushrooms and cook about 5 minutes, or until mushrooms are lightly browned, stirring

occasionally. Blend green pepper-mushroom mixture into the cheese sauce.

6.   Fill lobster shells with mixture and top with a mixture of *2 tablespoons cracker crumbs, ¼ cup shredded Parmesan cheese*, and *2 tablespoons melted butter*.

7.   Set under broiler 4 inches from source of heat 2 to 3 minutes, or until sauce is bubbly and top is lightly browned. Garnish base of each tail with *watercress* and serve immediately.   6 SERVINGS

ROCK LOBSTER, CANTONESE STYLE

6 South African rock lobster tails (3 to 5 oz. each), thawed	4 carrots, cut in thin diagonal slices
2 cups shredded cabbage	¼ cup cooking or salad oil
1½ cups diagonally sliced celery	1 cup vegetable broth
1 cup thawed frozen or fresh peas	¼ cup soy sauce
6 green onions, cut into ½-in. pieces	1 teaspoon monosodium glutamate
	1 teaspoon sugar
	Lime butter or margarine*

1.   Using scissors, cut away the thin underside membrane of lobster tails. Remove meat and cut into ½- to ¾-inch pieces. Set aside.

2.   Cook vegetables 5 minutes in hot oil in a heavy skillet over medium heat, stirring frequently. Stir in vegetable broth, soy sauce, monosodium glutamate, and sugar. Simmer uncovered 10 minutes.

3.   Meanwhile, cook lobster pieces slowly in hot lime butter in a heavy skillet or saucepan 5 minutes, or until lobster is opaque and tender.

4.   Toss lobster with vegetables; serve with fluffy hot *rice*.   6 TO 8 SERVINGS

*Blend desired amount of *lime juice* with *melted butter or margarine*.

SHRIMP AND LOBSTER STEW
(El Pescador Caribe Hilton)

A recipe from the Hilton Hotel, San Juan, Puerto Rico.

1.   For each serving allow *6 fresh shrimp* and *3 medallions (rounds) raw lobster meat*. Melt *2 ounces lard or other fat* in a copper skillet and sauté shrimp and lobster meat with *1 shallot, 1 tablespoon diced peeled tomato, 1 teaspoon chopped onion, 1 teaspoon chopped green pepper*, and *½ tea-*

spoon chopped parsley. Stir the mixture and add *2 ounces dry sherry*.

2.   In another pan, sauté *3 diced fresh mushrooms* in *1 tablespoon butter* 3 minutes. Add *3 tablespoons cooked rice* and *½ cup cooked green peas*; sauté 5 minutes. Add the shrimp and lobster mixture, blending well. Correct the seasoning with *salt and pepper* and cook 5 minutes longer.

3.   Deglaze the copper skillet with *1 ounce brandy*; flame the spirit and add *3 tablespoons beef stock* and *juice of ½ lemon*. Pour the sauce over the seafood mixture and serve in a soup plate.

Mussels

A form of shellfish belonging to the mollusk family. Mussels are found in all the oceans of the world.

MUSSELS IN PINK SAUCE

This recipe is contributed by The Four Seasons restaurant in New York City.

5 doz. mussels	½ small onion, minced
2 cups water	½ cup water
Pink Sauce:	2 cups mayonnaise
2 tablespoons tomato purée	1½ tablespoons dairy sour cream
2 tablespoons lemon juice	1 teaspoon prepared horseradish
1 tablespoon sherry	Salt
½ tablespoon cognac	Paprika
1 clove garlic, minced	Red caviar

1.   Put mussels and 2 cups water into a saucepot, cover tightly, and bring to boiling. Steam until the shells open. Remove top shells.

2.   To prepare sauce, combine tomato purée, lemon juice, sherry, cognac, garlic, onion, and ½ cup water in a saucepan and cook until the mixture is reduced to one third of its original quantity. Strain the sauce; cool.

3.   Add mayonnaise, sour cream, and horseradish to the cooled sauce. Season to taste with salt and paprika. Chill 1 to 2 hours.

4.   Top each mussel with the Pink Sauce and garnish with caviar.   8 SERVINGS

MOULES À LA CREMAILLERE

Mussels cooked in wine as served at La Cremaillere, Banksville, New York.

2 qts. mussels	Freshly ground white
2 cups Chablis	pepper
1 cup finely chopped	1 cup Hollandaise
shallots	Sauce, *page 344*
½ cup finely chopped	Juice of ½ lemon
parsley	Salt
⅓ cup unsalted butter	

1. Scrub mussels under running water and trim off the beards.
2. Pour wine over mussels in a saucepot; add shallots, parsley, butter, and white pepper to taste. Cover tightly and cook over high heat about 2 minutes. Stir the mixture and cook, covered, 2 minutes longer, or until mussel shells open.
3. Remove the mussels from saucepot; remove and discard top shells, placing the filled bottom shells in a serving dish. Keep warm.
4. Cook the pan juice over high heat to reduce the amount by one half. Remove from heat. Stir in hot Hollandaise Sauce and lemon juice. Add salt and white pepper to taste.
5. Pour the sauce over the mussels and serve immediately.   4 SERVINGS

Oysters

Oysters in the shell are sold by the dozen. They must be alive with shells tightly closed; when dead, the shells open automatically and shellfish are no longer edible.

Shucked oysters are graded as to size and are sold by the pint, quart, or gallon. They should be plump with no sunken areas or evidence of shrinkage. The liquor should be clear, fresh, and sweet smelling. The dealer should have them well iced.

Shucked oysters may be purchased in cans or frozen. Fresh shucked oysters packed in cans and labeled "Perishable, Keep Refrigerated" must be refrigerated in the home. Frozen oysters should not be thawed until ready to use and never refrozen.

How to open oysters — Wash oyster shells thoroughly and rinse in cold water but do not soak. Insert a strong thin knife between shells near the thick end and run it around back of shell until muscle holding shells is cut. Discard flat shell, save liquor from oysters, and remove any small pieces of shell from oysters. Serve oysters on the deep half of the shell.

OYSTERS PIQUANTE IN THE HALF SHELL

Serve as an appetizer or the fish course of a dinner.

1 qt. (about 36) large	1 teaspoon lemon juice
oysters	3 to 4 drops Tabasco
1 cup mayonnaise	¼ teaspoon salt
2 tablespoons chili	Few grains pepper
sauce	⅛ teaspoon paprika
1 tablespoon butter or	1 cup buttered soft
margarine, melted	bread crumbs
1½ teaspoons prepared	
mustard	

1. Set out 12 small shell-shaped ramekins. (If oysters are purchased in shells, use deep half of each shell.)
2. Drain oysters; discard liquor; place 3 oysters in each ramekin or shell.
3. Blend the mayonnaise, chili sauce, butter, mustard, lemon juice, Tabasco, and a mixture of salt, pepper, and paprika. Spoon mayonnaise mixture over oysters. Top with the buttered crumbs.
4. Broil about 3 inches from source of heat 5 minutes, or until oysters begin to curl at edges and crumbs are golden brown.   12 SERVINGS

OYSTERS ROYALE

6 tablespoons butter	2 cups cream
½ clove garlic, minced	1½ pts. oysters, drained
½ cup diced celery	(reserve ⅓ cup
½ cup diced green	liquor)*
pepper	1 teaspoon prepared
6 or 7 tablespoons flour	mustard
½ teaspoon salt	2 oz. Gruyère cheese,
¼ teaspoon white	cut in pieces
pepper	¼ cup dry sherry
Few grains cayenne	
pepper	

1. Heat butter in a saucepan. Add garlic, celery, and green pepper; cook about 5 minutes, or until vegetables are crisp-tender. Remove vegetables with a slotted spoon and set aside.
2. Blend a mixture of flour, salt, and peppers into the butter in saucepan; heat until mixture bubbles. Remove from heat; add cream and reserved oyster liquor gradually, stirring constantly. Continue stirring, bring to boiling, and boil 1 to 2 minutes. Remove from heat.
3. Blend in the mustard and cheese, stirring until cheese is melted. Mix in the wine, vegetables, and

oysters. Bring just to boiling and remove from heat. (Edges of oysters should just begin to curl.) Turn into blazer pan of chafing dish and set over simmering water.

4.   Accompany with a basket of *toasted buttered 3½-inch bread rounds* sprinkled lightly with *ground nutmeg.*   10 TO 12 SERVINGS

*The amount of liquor in a pint of oysters varies. This recipe was tested using ⅓ cup but slightly less will not affect the recipe.

SCALLOPED OYSTERS

1 qt. oysters	Cream or milk
3 cups cracker crumbs (about 48 saltines, crushed)	1 teaspoon salt
	⅛ teaspoon pepper
	⅓ cup finely chopped onion
2 to 4 tablespoons butter or margarine, melted	½ cup butter or margarine

1.   Drain oysters, reserving liquor in a 2-cup measuring cup. Pick over oysters and remove any shell particles. Set aside.
2.   Lightly toss 1 cup of the cracker crumbs with melted butter; set aside.
3.   Add enough cream or milk to reserved oyster liquor to make 2 cups. Stir in the salt and pepper.
4.   Line a greased 2-quart shallow casserole with 1 cup of the unbuttered crumbs. Spoon half of the oysters over crumbs. Pour 1 cup of liquid over all. Sprinkle with half of the onion and dot with half of the butter. Repeat. Top with the buttered crumbs.
5.   Bake at 350°F 20 to 25 minutes, or until thoroughly heated.   6 TO 8 SERVINGS

OYSTER-POTATO FRIES

A crisp potato coating adds flavor and texture to oysters served as an appetizer or supper entrée.

¼ cup dairy sour cream	2 cups finely shredded potatoes, drained
¼ cup flour	
½ teaspoon salt	1 pt. oysters, well drained
½ teaspoon seasoned salt	
	Fat for deep frying heated to 365°F
1 egg, beaten	

1.   Stir the sour cream and a mixture of flour, salt, and seasoned salt into the beaten egg. Combine with the potatoes and blend thoroughly. Add 4 or 5 oysters at a time to potato mixture.

2.   Drop mixture by tablespoonfuls with an oyster in each spoonful into the hot fat. Do not crowd the oysters; they should be free to float one layer deep. Fry 2 to 3 minutes, or until golden brown.
3.   Remove with slotted spoon and drain over fat before removing to absorbent paper.   ABOUT 30

Scallops

Scallops are derived from a variety of shellfish of which the only part considered edible is the eye muscle which opens the shell. This muscle is cut out and the remainder discarded. There are two types, the tiny *bay scallop* and the larger *sea scallop.* Scallops should be cream colored rather than white and are sold by the pound. They are also available frozen and should have a sweetish odor.

SCALLOPS GOURMET IN PATTY SHELLS

2 lbs. frozen scallops, thawed and rinsed (under running cold water)	2 tablespoons flour
	¼ cup butter or margarine
	½ lb. fresh mushrooms, sliced lengthwise
1 cup boiling water	3 medium-sized tomatoes, cut in pieces
¼ cup lemon juice	
1 medium-sized onion, sliced	½ lb. sliced bacon, cut into ½-in. crosswise strips and fried until golden brown
2 large parsley sprigs	
1 bay leaf	
1 teaspoon salt	
2 tablespoons butter or margarine	6 puff paste patty shells, heated
1 large clove garlic, minced	

1.   Cut scallops in half, then cut into thin crosswise slices. Combine with the boiling water, lemon juice, onion, parsley, bay leaf, and salt in a large saucepan; simmer, uncovered, for 3 minutes. Drain, reserving 1 cup liquid, and set aside.
2.   Heat 2 tablespoons butter with the garlic in the saucepan; blend in the flour and cook until mixture bubbles. Remove from heat. Add the 1 cup reserved scallop liquid gradually, blending well. Bring rapidly to boiling and boil 1 to 2 minutes, stirring constantly. Set aside and keep warm.
3.   Heat the ¼ cup butter in a skillet; add mushrooms and cook about 5 minutes, or until lightly browned, stirring occasionally.
4.   Blend the mushrooms, tomatoes, and scallops

into the sauce and heat thoroughly. Stir in the bacon; spoon mixture into patty shells; replace pastry lids. Reserve remaining mixture for sauce.

5. Thread colored picks with a *carrot curl*, small *gherkin*, cut in half lengthwise, and a *bacon curl*; insert securely in rim of patty shell.

6. Serve immediately with the hot sauce in a gravy boat. **6 SERVINGS**

Shrimp

Fresh shrimp with heads removed are sold by the pound either fresh or frozen. Shrimp are graded according to the number per pound—jumbo (under 25); large (25 to 30); medium (30 to 42); and small (42 and over). *Cooked shrimp* with shells removed are also sold by the pound; the meat is pink. *Canned shrimp* are available in several sizes of cans and may be used in place of cooked shrimp.

COOKED SHRIMP

1 lb. fresh shrimp with shells	3 tablespoons lemon juice
2 cups water	1 tablespoon salt

1. Wash the shrimp in cold water. Drop shrimp into a boiling mixture of remaining ingredients. Cover tightly. Simmer 5 minutes, or only until shrimp are pink in color. (Avoid overcooking as it toughens shrimp.) Drain and cover with cold water to chill. Drain shrimp again.

2. Remove tiny legs from shrimp; peel off shells. Cut a slit along back (curved surface) of each shrimp just deep enough to expose the black vein. With knife point remove vein in one piece. Rinse quickly in running cold water. Drain on absorbent paper. Store in refrigerator until ready to use.

½ TO ¾ POUND COOKED SHRIMP

FRIED SHRIMP DE LUXE

2 lbs. Cooked Shrimp, *above*	1 env. (about 1⅜ oz.) dry onion soup mix
1 or 2 eggs, fork beaten	¼ cup chopped parsley
1½ cups corn flake crumbs	3 tablespoons shredded Parmesan cheese
	Butter or margarine

1. Dip shrimp into egg, then into a mixture of the corn flake crumbs, soup mix, parsley, and cheese. (Store leftover crumb mixture, tightly covered, in

refrigerator to use for coating meat, poultry, and shellfish, or as topping for casseroles.)

2. Fry the shrimp until lightly browned in hot butter in a heavy skillet.

3. Serve immediately. **ABOUT 8 SERVINGS**

SHRIMP ERNIE

Named for the owner, Ernest Coker, these shrimp are served at Ye Old College Inn, Houston, Texas, as an hors d'oeuvre or an entrée.

2 lbs. fresh shrimp, peeled and deveined	¼ cup ketchup
	1 teaspoon paprika
2 cups cooking or salad oil	1 small clove garlic, minced
1 tablespoon salt	

1. Marinate shrimp overnight in refrigerator in a mixture of remaining ingredients.

2. When ready to broil, put shrimp on sides in a large shallow pan, pour some marinade over them and broil slowly until lightly browned on both sides, allowing 7 to 8 minutes for each side and brushing occasionally with marinade.

3. Serve shrimp on frilled wooden picks from a heated platter. **6 TO 8 SERVINGS**

SHRIMP JAMBALAYA

3 tablespoons butter or margarine	¼ cup chopped parsley
	½ teaspoon salt
½ cup chopped onion	⅛ teaspoon pepper
½ cup chopped green onion	¼ teaspoon thyme
	⅛ teaspoon cayenne pepper
½ cup chopped green pepper	
	1 bay leaf
½ cup chopped celery	1 cup uncooked rice
¼ lb. diced cooked ham	3 cans (4½ oz. each) shrimp, rinsed under running cold water
2 cloves garlic, minced	
2 cups chicken broth	
3 large tomatoes, coarsely chopped	¼ cup coarsely chopped green pepper

1. Heat butter in a large heavy skillet over low heat. Stir in onion, green onion, green pepper, celery, ham, and garlic. Cook over medium heat about 5 minutes, or until onion is tender, stirring occasionally.

2. Stir in chicken broth, tomatoes, parsley, salt, pepper, thyme, cayenne pepper, and bay leaf; cover and bring to boiling.

3. Add rice gradually, stirring with a fork. Simmer, covered, 20 minutes, or until rice is tender.

4. Mix in shrimp and remaining green pepper. Simmer, uncovered, about 5 minutes longer.

6 to 8 SERVINGS

SHRIMP À LA CREOLE

After sampling food the world over, actor Robert Taylor once concluded that this easily prepared shrimp dish was one of his favorites.

½ cup chopped onion	½ cup chopped celery
1 large clove garlic, crushed	1½ to 2 teaspoons salt
2 tablespoons butter or margarine	¼ teaspoon thyme
	Cayenne pepper
1 tablespoon flour	2 bay leaves
6 large ripe tomatoes, peeled and chopped (about 5 cups)	2 lbs. fresh shrimp, peeled and deveined

1. Lightly brown onion and garlic in heated butter in a large heavy skillet, stirring occasionally. Blend flour into mixture. Stir in tomatoes, celery, salt, thyme, cayenne pepper to taste, and bay leaves. Simmer about 10 minutes, stirring occasionally.

2. Add shrimp, cover skillet and cook over low heat 10 minutes.

3. Serve immediately over *hot rice.* 6 SERVINGS

CURRIED PRAWNS

The El Prado in the Clift Hotel, San Francisco, serves this delightful curried shrimp.

1 lb. large Louisiana prawns, peeled and deveined	1 tablespoon flour
	1 teaspoon curry powder
2 tablespoons butter	¼ cup sauterne
1 tablespoon chopped scallions	2 cups cream

1. Sauté prawns in heated butter in skillet 2 to 3 minutes; add scallions and sauté 3 to 4 minutes longer. Sprinkle with a mixture of flour and curry powder. Cook and stir about 3 minutes.

2. Stir in the wine and cream and simmer mixture 10 minutes, stirring occasionally. Transfer prawns to a chafing dish using a slotted spoon.

3. Continue cooking the sauce over low heat to desired consistency. Correct the seasoning and pour over the prawns. Serve with *hot rice.*

2 SERVINGS

SHRIMP À LA KING

A luncheon dish that has remained a favorite at Antoine's in New Orleans for almost a century.

2 cups white wine	2 tablespoons flour
2 minced shallots, or ¼ cup minced onion	2 tablespoons butter
	Juice of ¼ lemon (about 2 teaspoons)
1 cup oyster liquid, fish stock, or chicken broth	½ cup light cream
	2 egg yolks, well beaten
1½ lbs. fresh shrimp, peeled and deveined	Toast points

1. Combine wine, shallots, and oyster liquid in a saucepan; bring to boiling and add shrimp. Simmer 15 minutes. Drain and reserve ¾ cup stock.

2. Meanwhile, stir flour into melted butter in a saucepan, making a roux. Blend in reserved stock; cook and stir until mixture thickens. Add shrimp and cook over low heat. Stir in lemon juice.

3. Add cream to beaten yolks. Mix well and add hot shrimp mixture, stirring constantly. Serve on toast points and garnish with *parsley.*

4 TO 6 SERVINGS

SCAMPI FLAMINGO

A recipe from the Danieli Royal Excelsior in Venice, Italy.

½ cup butter	3 tablespoons cognac
1 cup chopped celery	2 cups light cream
¼ cup chopped carrot	⅓ cup sherry
¼ cup chopped onion	¼ cup Sauce, *below*
¼ teaspoon thyme	½ cup butter
2 lbs. fresh shrimp with shells	½ teaspoon lemon juice

1. Heat ½ cup butter in a large skillet. Sauté vegetables with thyme until lightly browned. Add shrimp and brown carefully.

2. Add cognac and flame it. Add cream, sherry, and Sauce; cook 15 minutes.

3. Remove shrimp; shell and devein them; keep warm.

4. Add ½ cup butter and the lemon juice to sauce; cook about 5 minutes. Strain through a fine sieve and pour over the shrimp.

5. Serve sauce and shrimp separately with *rice.*

ABOUT 4 SERVINGS

SAUCE: Follow recipe for *Béchamel Sauce, page 342.* Use ½ *cup broth* and ½ *cup cream* for the liquid. Stir in ½ *teaspoon ground nutmeg* after sauce thickens.

Chapter 9

PASTAS & RICE DISHES

Say *pasta* and many Americans think only of macaroni and spaghetti dishes—specifically of macaroni with cheese or spaghetti with meatballs. Yet this versatile low-cost food has dozens of different forms and shapes with as many exciting ways to use them. Their bland flavor is a foil for all sorts of other ingredients.

In the United States the generic term *macaroni* is used to describe macaroni, spaghetti, noodles, and over 300 different pasta shapes available on the market.

Rice, like pasta, blends with and assumes the flavor of all sorts of other ingredients.

Grains of rice may be either *short, medium,* or *long.* Short and medium varieties have short plump grains which cook tender and moist with the particles tending to cling together. This cooking characteristic is especially good for croquettes, rice puddings, or rice ring molds.

Long grain rice is about five times as long as the grain is wide. When cooked, the grains are more light and fluffy than short grains and tend to separate. These characteristics adapt themselves to dishes such as salads and curries.

Types of Rice

Regular milled white rice (short, medium or long grain)—The rice is cleaned and graded in the milling process and requires no washing by the homemaker. The method of cooking is described on the package.   YIELD—1 cup will yield 3 cups cooked

Parboiled rice—The grains are parboiled before milling by a steam-pressure process which gelatinizes the starch in the grain and helps retain much of the natural vitamin and mineral content. To cook, 2½ cups water are used for each cup of rice. After cooking, parboiled rice grains tend to be fluffy, plump, and separate.

YIELD—1 cup will yield 4 cups cooked

Precooked rice—This variety requires a minimum cooking time and is ideal for hurry-up meals. Preparation instructions are on the package.

YIELD—1 cup will yield 2 to 3 cups cooked

Brown rice—The grains are unpolished and only the outer hull and a little of the bran are removed. This rice requires more liquid and longer cooking.

YIELD—1 cup will yield about 3 cups cooked

Wild rice—The long grains of wild rice are really seeds of a water grass. For cooking directions see *page 19.*   YIELD—1 cup will yield 3 cups cooked

MACARONI DISHES

GARLIC-BUTTERED FUSILLI

5 tablespoons butter
1 clove garlic

8 oz. fusilli, cooked
   and drained
Finely snipped parsley

1. Heat butter and garlic in a small skillet.

2. Pour garlic butter over cooked fusilli, add a generous amount of parsley, and toss until mixed. Serve immediately accompanied by a *tossed green salad* with *Italian dressing*, a basket of *crusty rolls or bread sticks*, and a bottle of *Italian red wine*, if desired.   ABOUT 6 SERVINGS

TORTELLINI

This recipe is from Ernie's, a popular San Francisco restaurant.

72 tortellini (snail-shaped pasta)
2 tablespoons butter
1½ cups half and half

1 cup grated Parmesan cheese
2 egg yolks, fork beaten

1. Cook tortellini in boiling *salted water* 10 minutes.
2. Drain, put into a saucepan, add butter and cream, and heat thoroughly over low heat (do not boil). Add cheese and stir until thick. Remove from heat.
3. Add a little *salt* and *pepper* and the beaten egg yolks; mix well. Serve hot.   6 SERVINGS

PEACHES-IN-PASTA CASSEROLE

Green pepper rings and peach halves form an interesting and attractive topping.

¼ cup butter or margarine
¼ cup flour
3 teaspoons dry mustard
½ teaspoon salt
1 cup milk
¾ lb. sharp Cheddar cheese, shredded
1 can (16 oz.) stewed tomatoes (2 cups) cut in pieces

7 oz. elbow macaroni, cooked and drained
6 to 8 green pepper rings, 1½ in. thick, cooked in boiling water 5 min. and drained
1 can (29 oz.) cling peach halves, drained
Grated Parmesan-Romano cheese

1. Heat butter in a large saucepan. Blend in flour, dry mustard, and salt. Heat until bubbly.

2. Gradually add milk, stirring until smooth. Bring to boiling; stir and cook 1 to 2 minutes. Add Cheddar cheese and heat, stirring until melted. Mix in the stewed tomatoes and drained macaroni.
3. Turn mixture into a greased 2½-quart shallow baking dish. Press pepper rings into mixture and top each with a peach half, rounded side up. Sprinkle generously with Parmesan-Romano cheese.
4. Set in a 350°F oven until sauce is bubbly, about 25 minutes.   6 TO 8 SERVINGS

TURKEY-TOMATO MAC

1 tablespoon cooking or salad oil
1¼ cups minced onion
1 miniature green cherry pepper, seeds removed and pepper minced
1 miniature red pepper, seeds removed and pepper minced
3 small cloves garlic, minced
1 tablespoon sugar

½ teaspoon basil, crushed
1 can (28 oz.) Italian-style tomatoes
1 can (6 oz.) tomato paste
8 oz. macaroni or spaghetti, broken
12 oz. extra sharp Cheddar cheese, shredded
Roast turkey or chicken, sliced or cut in bite-size pieces

1. Heat oil in a large skillet. Add onion, peppers, and garlic. Cook until tender, stirring occasionally. Stir in sugar, basil, tomatoes, and tomato paste; season to taste with *salt* and *freshly ground black pepper.* Cover and simmer 30 minutes.
2. Meanwhile, cook macaroni according to package directions; drain. Toss with *melted butter or margarine* and half of the cheese.

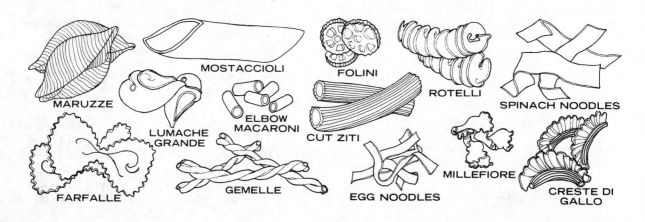

MARUZZE
MOSTACCIOLI
LUMACHE GRANDE
ELBOW MACARONI
FOLINI
ROTELLI
SPINACH NOODLES
FARFALLE
GEMELLE
CUT ZITI
EGG NOODLES
MILLEFIORE
CRESTE DI GALLO

3. Spoon a small amount of the sauce onto the bottom of a 2-quart shallow casserole. Add half the cooked macaroni and half the turkey, then spoon half the sauce over turkey. Repeat layering, ending with sauce. Sprinkle remaining cheese over top.
4. Set in a 325°F oven until thoroughly heated.

6 TO 8 SERVINGS

CHICKEN CANNELLONI

While many bachelors stick to barbecuing a steak and tossing a salad together, Rock Hudson became so fond of Chicken Cannelloni served at Frascati's restaurant in Los Angeles, California, that he asked for this recipe and now makes it whenever he has company.

Bolognese Sauce, *below*	5 celery stalks, chopped
4 cans chicken broth	2 small onions, chopped
¼ cup butter or margarine	¾ cup chopped raw spinach
16 tufoli macaroni shells (add a few extra to allow for breakage)	1 teaspoon salt
	¼ teaspoon pepper
3 shallots, chopped	3 bay leaves
3 cloves garlic, minced	¾ teaspoon oregano
½ cup unsalted butter	½ teaspoon thyme
3 whole chicken breasts, halved, boned and cut in chunks	4 egg yolks
	Grated Parmesan cheese

1. Prepare the Bolognese Sauce; refrigerate.
2. Bring chicken broth and ¼ cup butter to boiling in a large skillet; add tufoli and cook, covered, until tender, about 20 to 30 minutes. Carefully remove; cool.
3. Sauté shallots and garlic in sweet butter for 2 minutes. Add chicken, celery, onion, spinach, and dry seasonings. Simmer, covered, until chicken is tender, about 10 minutes. Discard bay leaves. Quickly stir in egg yolks; remove from heat.
4. Finely chop mixture and use to stuff tufoli. If not used immediately, refrigerate.
5. In each of 4 buttered individual shallow casseroles, arrange 4 of the stuffed tufoli, add one fourth of the Bolognese Sauce, and sprinkle generously with cheese.
6. Bake at 375°F until golden brown on top and thoroughly heated, about 25 minutes.
7. Serve with *crisp crackers.*

4 SERVINGS

BOLOGNESE SAUCE: In a saucepan over medium heat, melt *6 tablespoons butter* with *¼ cup finely diced cooked ham or prosciutto.* Stir in *1 small onion,* minced, *¼ cup grated raw carrot,* and *¼ pound ground chuck;* brown meat, stirring occasionally. Stir in *1 thin 2x1-inch piece lemon peel, ⅛ teaspoon nutmeg, 2 tablespoons tomato paste, 2 cans (10½ ounces each) condensed beef broth, 1 teaspoon salt,* and *¼ teaspoon pepper.* Simmer, covered, 1 hour, stirring occasionally. Remove lemon peel. Stir in *¼ cup heavy cream;* simmer 2 minutes.

SHRIMP FROMAGE

There's an intriguing combination of cheeses in this rich seafood dish . . . a blend to please your most discriminating guests.

2¼ cups cooked shrimp pieces*	4 oz. sharp Cheddar cheese, shredded
1 clove garlic, minced	2 oz. mozzarella cheese, shredded
½ cup chopped fresh mushrooms	2 tablespoons shredded Parmesan cheese
3 tablespoons chopped onion	½ cup creamed cottage cheese
½ cup butter or margarine	½ cup dairy sour cream
¼ cup flour	1 pkg. (10 oz.) elbow macaroni, cooked and drained.
½ teaspoon salt	
⅛ teaspoon pepper	½ cup soft bread crumbs or cracker crumbs, buttered
½ teaspoon monosodium glutamate	
2 cups milk	
4 oz. process Cheddar cheese, shredded	

1. Prepare shrimp, *page 284,* and set aside.
2. Cook garlic, mushrooms, and onion in ¼ cup butter in a skillet until onion is soft; set aside.
3. Heat ¼ cup butter in a saucepan. Blend in a mixture of flour, salt, pepper, and monosodium glutamate; heat until bubbly. Remove from heat. Add milk gradually, stirring constantly. Cook until sauce thickens; stir and cook 1 to 2 minutes.
4. Stir in the Cheddar, mozzarella, and Parmesan cheeses until melted. Remove from heat and blend in cottage cheese and sour cream.
5. Mix the cheese sauce, onion mixture, shrimp, and macaroni. Turn into a 2½-quart casserole. Top with buttered crumbs.
6. Bake at 350°F about 30 minutes, or until golden brown and bubbly.

8 TO 10 SERVINGS

To prepare shrimp—Rinse about *1½ pounds shrimp* in cold water. Drop into a rapidly boiling mixture of *1 quart water, celery leaves, 2 whole cloves, 1 small onion*, sliced, *3 to 4 parsley sprigs*, and *1 tablespoon salt*. Cover and return to boiling. Remove from heat and let stand 5 minutes. Drain shrimp and cool; remove legs, shells, and black veins. Drain. Cut into ½-inch pieces.

CHEESERONI CASSEROLE

7 oz. elbow macaroni, cooked and drained	1 small onion, thinly sliced and separated in rings
2 cups shredded sharp Cheddar cheese	1⅔ cups undiluted evaporated milk
1 teaspoon salt	2 tablespoons shredded Parmesan cheese
¼ teaspoon pepper	1 medium-sized ripe tomato, cut in eight wedges
⅛ teaspoon oregano, crushed	

1.   Using half of each at a time, layer the following ingredients in a buttered 2-quart casserole: macaroni, cheese, a mixture of salt, pepper, and oregano, onion rings, and evaporated milk. Sprinkle Parmesan cheese over top.
2.   Heat in a 350°F oven about 20 minutes. Arrange tomato wedges on top and heat 10 minutes.
6 TO 8 SERVINGS

MACARONI ALLA SAVONAROLA
A recipe from Al Doro Restaurant, Ferrara, Italy.

½ lb. ground veal	1 cup finely chopped cooked ham
¾ cup fine dry bread crumbs	3 tablespoons butter
1 egg, beaten	3 hard-cooked eggs, cut in ¼-in. cubes
2 tablespoons shredded Parmesan cheese	2 cups heavy cream
¼ teaspoon ground nutmeg	1 lb. maccaroncini (big spaghetti with a hole), cooked and drained
¼ teaspoon salt	
1 cup uncooked peas, fresh or frozen	½ cup shredded Parmesan cheese
2 tablespoons butter	
⅓ cup finely chopped onion	

1.   Mix half of the ground veal with bread crumbs, egg, 2 tablespoons cheese, nutmeg, and salt to make a smooth mixture. Form into small balls.
2.   In a large ovenproof skillet, cook peas in 2 tablespoons hot butter until lightly browned. Add the meatballs to the skillet. Set in a 375°F oven for 20 minutes.
3.   Lightly brown onion, ham, and remaining veal in 3 tablespoons butter in a saucepan.
4.   Add to the skillet the ham-veal mixture, hardcooked eggs, and cream; mix well. Bring to boiling; simmer about 15 minutes.
5.   Turn maccaroncini onto a platter, pour sauce over it and sprinkle remaining Parmesan cheese over all.
6 TO 8 SERVINGS

CASSEROLE ITALIANO

1 tablespoon butter or margarine	1 clove garlic, minced
1 lb. ground beef	2 pkgs. (3 oz. each) cream cheese, softened
2 cans (8 oz. each) tomato sauce	1 cup creamed cottage cheese
1 teaspoon salt	3 tablespoons dairy sour cream
⅛ teaspoon pepper	¼ cup finely chopped green onion
½ teaspoon dried parsley flakes	2 tablespoons finely chopped green pepper
½ teaspoon dried celery flakes	6 oz. (about 2 cups) small macaroni shells, cooked and drained
½ teaspoon basil	
⅛ teaspoon thyme	
Few grains cayenne pepper	1 tablespoon butter or margarine, melted
Few drops Worcestershire sauce	
1 small bay leaf	

1.   Heat 1 tablespoon butter in a large heavy skillet. Add the ground beef and cook until browned, separating meat into pieces with a spoon.
2.   Stir in a mixture of tomato sauce and seasonings. Cook uncovered over very low heat about 30 minutes, stirring occasionally. Remove from heat and discard bay leaf.
3.   Blend the cream cheese, cottage cheese, sour cream, green onion, and green pepper.
4.   Turn one half of cooked macaroni into a 2-quart casserole. Drizzle with one half of melted butter. Spread cheese mixture over macaroni and cover with the meat mixture. Top with remaining macaroni and drizzle with melted butter. Sprinkle with *paprika*.
5.   Cover and bake at 375°F 30 minutes. Remove cover; heat 15 minutes longer.   ABOUT 6 SERVINGS

SPAGHETTI DISHES

HAM 'N' CHICKEN SPECIALTY

6 green onions with tops, finely chopped	½ teaspoon pepper
¼ lb. fresh mushrooms, sliced lengthwise	½ teaspoon celery salt
¼ cup butter	1 cup dairy sour cream
1½ cups cooked ham pieces	1 cup creamed cottage cheese
1 cup cooked chicken pieces	1½ cups thin spaghetti pieces (1½ in.), cooked and drained
½ teaspoon salt	1 cup shredded sharp Cheddar cheese

1. Cook green onion and mushrooms until just tender in hot butter in a large skillet or saucepan. Mix in ham, chicken, and a mixture of salt, pepper, and celery salt; heat thoroughly.
2. Blend sour cream and cottage cheese. Add to spaghetti and toss lightly until thoroughly mixed. Add ham mixture and toss lightly.
3. Turn into buttered 1½-quart casserole or baking dish. Top evenly with shredded cheese.
4. Broil 3 inches from source of heat about 15 minutes, or until mixture is bubbly and cheese is delicately browned. Garnish with *parsley*.

ABOUT 6 SERVINGS

HAM DI PARMA

8 oz. spaghetti, cooked and drained	¾ cup dry white wine
¾ cup shredded Parmesan cheese	1 lb. cooked ham, cut in strips
6 oz. mushrooms, sliced lengthwise	⅓ cup sliced green olives
2 tablespoons grated onion	1 pimiento, cut in thin strips
⅓ cup butter or margarine	¼ teaspoon oregano, crushed
¼ cup flour	⅛ teaspoon black pepper
2 cups cream	

1. Toss spaghetti with ½ cup cheese; keep hot.
2. Cook mushrooms and onion 5 minutes in hot butter in a large skillet. With a slotted spoon, remove mushrooms; set aside.
3. Blend flour into butter in skillet. Remove from heat and gradually add cream, stirring constantly. Bring to boiling; cook 1 minute. Blend in wine, ham strips, olives, pimiento, oregano, and pepper.

4. Put hot spaghetti into a large shallow baking dish. Spoon hot creamed ham mixture over spaghetti. Sprinkle with remaining Parmesan cheese.
5. Broil 4 to 6 inches from source of heat until lightly browned and thoroughly heated.

ABOUT 8 SERVINGS

SPAGHETTI SUPREME

2 tablespoons chopped parsley	⅛ teaspoon salt
1 teaspoon basil	⅛ teaspoon freshly ground black pepper
3 cloves garlic, minced	¼ cup water
3 tablespoons olive oil	7 oz. spaghetti, cooked and drained
2 teaspoons French mustard	½ cup shredded Parmesan cheese
1 teaspoon anchovy paste	½ cup heavy cream

1. Add parsley, basil, and garlic to hot olive oil in a skillet and cook about 3 minutes.
2. Stir in mustard, anchovy paste, salt, pepper, and water; cook about 5 minutes.
3. Meanwhile, alternate layers of hot spaghetti and Parmesan cheese on a warm platter.
4. Stir cream into the sauce, heat thoroughly (do not boil), and pour over the spaghetti. Serve hot.

ABOUT 4 SERVINGS

SALMON 'N' SPAGHETTI

2 cans (6 oz. each) evaporated milk	1 teaspoon chopped chives
1 teaspoon salt	⅛ teaspoon cayenne pepper
4 cups (1 lb.) shredded sharp Cheddar cheese	½ cup butter or margarine
¾ cup sliced pimiento-stuffed olives	2 cloves garlic, minced
1 can (16 oz.) salmon, drained and separated into pieces	1 lb. spaghetti, cooked and drained

1. Mix evaporated milk and salt in a saucepan; set over low heat and bring just to boiling.
2. Blend the cheese, olives, salmon, chives, and cayenne pepper into milk in saucepan and heat thoroughly, stirring until cheese is melted.
3. Heat butter and garlic in a small skillet over low heat until butter is melted.

4. Pour garlic butter over hot cooked spaghetti and toss until mixed. Put buttered spaghetti on a serving platter and top with the hot salmon sauce. Serve at once. 6 SERVINGS

SPAGHETTI WITH TUNA-TOMATO SAUCE

1 cup finely chopped onion	½ teaspoon mono- sodium glutamate
1 clove garlic, minced	⅛ teaspoon pepper
¼ cup butter or margarine	½ teaspoon sugar
1 can (28 oz.) tomatoes	½ teaspoon basil
1 can (8 oz.) tomato sauce	½ teaspoon oregano
½ cup shredded Parmesan cheese	1 can (9¼ oz.) chunk- style tuna, drained and flaked
¼ cup minced parsley	7 or 8 oz. spaghetti, cooked and drained
1 teaspoon salt	2 tablespoons butter or margarine

1. Cook onion and garlic about 5 minutes in ¼ cup hot butter in a large saucepan or skillet. Stir in tomatoes, tomato sauce, cheese, parsley, and seasonings. Bring to boiling, stirring occasionally; simmer about 20 minutes. Add tuna and simmer about 15 minutes, stirring frequently.
2. Toss spaghetti with 2 tablespoons butter until melted. Serve hot sauce over spaghetti.

ABOUT 6 SERVINGS

TUNA-SPAGHETTI CASSEROLE

½ clove garlic, minced	4 large pimiento- stuffed olives, sliced
3 tablespoons chopped green pepper	2 cans (6½ or 7 oz. each) tuna, drained and separated in large pieces
2 tablespoons butter or margarine	
2 tablespoons flour	8 oz. spaghetti, cooked and drained
½ teaspoon salt	
1 teaspoon paprika	2 tablespoons butter or margarine, melted
1 teaspoon Worcester- shire sauce	
1 teaspoon prepared mustard	⅓ cup fine dry bread crumbs
1 can (10½ oz.) con- densed cream of celery soup	1 tablespoon shredded Parmesan cheese
1½ cups milk	2 hard-cooked eggs, sliced
1 tablespoon lemon juice	

1. Cook garlic and green pepper 5 minutes in hot butter in a saucepan. Blend in a mixture of flour, salt, and paprika. Heat until bubbly.
2. Remove from heat. Blend in Worcestershire sauce and mustard. Add soup and milk gradually, stirring constantly. Cook until sauce is smooth and slightly thickened.
3. Remove from heat. Stir in lemon juice, olives, tuna, and spaghetti. Turn mixture into a greased 2-quart casserole. Sprinkle outer edge with a mixture of melted butter, bread crumbs, and Parmesan cheese.
4. Heat in a 350°F oven about 25 minutes, or until mixture is thoroughly heated and crumbs are browned.
5. Garnish with slices of hard-cooked egg and sprinkle with *paprika*. ABOUT 8 SERVINGS

FIESTA ZUCCHINI-TOMATO CASSEROLE

2 env. (about 1½ oz. each) dry onion soup mix	2 to 3 zucchini (about ¾ lb.), washed and cut in about ½-in. slices
4 oz. spaghetti, broken	
1½ qts. boiling water	4 medium-sized tomatoes, peeled and cut in wedges
⅔ cup coarsely chopped onion	
1 cup green pepper strips	¼ cup snipped parsley
⅓ cup butter or margarine	1 teaspoon seasoned salt
	⅛ teaspoon black pepper
	⅔ cup shredded Swiss cheese

1. Add onion soup mix and spaghetti to boiling water. Partially cover and boil gently about 10 minutes, or until spaghetti is tender. Drain and set spaghetti mixture aside.
2. Cook onion and green pepper in hot butter in a large heavy skillet about 3 minutes, or until tender. Add zucchini, cover and cook 5 minutes. Stir in tomatoes, parsley, salt, and pepper. Cover and cook about 2 minutes, or just until heated.
3. Turn contents of skillet into a 2-quart casserole. Add spaghetti and toss gently to mix. Sprinkle cheese over top. If necessary to reheat mixture, set in a 350°F oven until thoroughly heated before placing under broiler.
4. Broil with top about 5 inches from source of heat until cheese is melted and lightly browned.

6 TO 8 SERVINGS

TURKEY PARMAZZINI

This dish may not be authentically Italian—but certainly worthy of the tradition.

2 tablespoons butter or margarine	4 cups julienne of cooked turkey
1¼ cups sliced fresh mushrooms	⅔ cup julienne of cooked ham
¼ cup butter or margarine	2 cups shredded Parmesan cheese
¼ cup flour	2 tablespoons butter or margarine
¼ teaspoon salt	8 oz. long spaghetti, cooked and drained
2 cups milk	
1¼ cups cream	1 tablespoon butter or margarine, melted
2 teaspoons paprika	
2 egg yolks, slightly beaten	

1. Heat 2 tablespoons butter in a skillet; add the mushrooms and cook over medium heat until mushrooms are lightly browned and tender.
2. Heat ¼ cup butter in a large heavy saucepan. Blend in flour and salt; heat until mixture bubbles. Gradually add milk, stirring constantly. Bring to boiling; stir and cook 1 to 2 minutes.
3. Blend in the cream and paprika; heat thoroughly over medium heat.
4. Vigorously stir about 3 tablespoons hot sauce into egg yolks; immediately blend into mixture in saucepan. Stir and cook about 2 minutes.
5. Blend in the turkey, ham, cooked mushrooms, and ½ cup Parmesan cheese; heat thoroughly.
6. Add 2 tablespoons butter to hot cooked spaghetti and toss until butter is melted. Add 1 cup Parmesan cheese to the spaghetti and toss to mix.
7. Turn spaghetti into a 2½-quart casserole and pull up around edge of casserole. Spoon sauce into center, sprinkle remaining Parmesan cheese over sauce, and drizzle the melted butter evenly over all. Sprinkle with *paprika*.
8. Heat in a 350°F oven about 15 minutes.

6 TO 8 SERVINGS

LASAGNE I

Tomato Sauce, *page 289*	1 lb. mozzarella or scamorze cheese, shredded
1 lb. lasagne noodles, cooked, drained and rinsed	
2 lbs. ricotta cheese	1 cup shredded Parmesan cheese

1. Prepare Tomato Sauce.
2. Spread about 1 cup Tomato Sauce in a but-tered 13x9x2-inch baking dish. Using a fourth of each, add a layer of noodles and then one of tomato sauce. Using a third of each, top evenly with 3 cheeses. Repeat layering and end with sauce.
3. Heat in a 375°F oven about 30 minutes, or until bubbly. Allow to stand 10 to 15 minutes to set layers before serving. Cut into squares.

12 TO 15 SERVINGS

LASAGNE II

It is said that on Christmas Eve the grandmother in an Italian household measures the width of the children's mouths to know how wide to make the lasagne noodles.

Tomato Meat Sauce, *page 289*	¾ lb. mozzarella cheese, sliced
8 qts. water	2 eggs, hard-cooked
¼ cup salt	¼ cup grated Parmesan cheese
1 tablespoon olive oil	
1 lb. lasagne noodles	½ teaspoon pepper
1 lb. ground beef	1 cup ricotta cheese
3 tablespoons olive oil	

1. Prepare sauce, allowing 4½ hours for cooking.
2. When sauce is partially done, heat the water, salt, and olive oil in a large saucepot. When boiling, gradually add the noodles and bring rapidly to boiling; cook about 15 minutes, or until noodles are tender. Test tenderness by pressing a piece against side of pot with fork. Drain through a colander.
3. Brown the beef in heated olive oil in a large skillet, breaking meat apart with a fork.
4. Pour about ½ cup Tomato Meat Sauce into an 8x8x2-inch baking dish. Top with one third of the noodles and half of the mozzarella cheese. Add half of the meat and 1 sliced egg. Sprinkle with half of the Parmesan cheese and pepper. Top with half of the ricotta cheese.
5. Beginning with the sauce, repeat the layering, ending with ricotta cheese. Top with ½ cup sauce. Arrange remaining noodles over the dish and top with more sauce.
6. Set in a 350°F oven about 30 minutes, or until mixture is bubbling. Remove from oven and let stand 5 to 10 minutes to set the layers.
7. To serve, cut in 2-inch squares and top with remaining sauce. ABOUT 6 SERVINGS

FRANKS LASAGNE

1 lb. frankfurters, cut in ¼-in. slices	12 oz. cottage cheese with chives
1 can (8 oz.) spaghetti sauce with mushrooms	1 tablespoon parsley flakes
1 can (6 oz.) tomato paste	1 teaspoon salt
1 tablespoon parsley flakes	½ teaspoon pepper
½ teaspoon salt	¼ cup grated Parmesan cheese
½ teaspoon garlic powder	12 oz. lasagne noodles, cooked, drained and rinsed
1 egg, well beaten	½ lb. mozzarella cheese, thinly sliced

1. Mix the frankfurters with the spaghetti sauce, tomato paste, 1 tablespoon parsley flakes, ½ teaspoon salt, and garlic powder.
2. Combine the egg with cottage cheese, 1 tablespoon parsley flakes, 1 teaspoon salt, pepper, and Parmesan cheese.
3. Arrange cooked noodles in a 13x9x2-inch baking dish; spread evenly with cottage cheese mixture; arrange mozzarella cheese slices on top. Spread frankfurter mixture over cheese.
4. Bake at 375°F 30 minutes, until mixture bubbles. Remove from oven and let stand 5 to 10 minutes to set layers. **ABOUT 12 SERVINGS**

TURKEY LASAGNE

¼ lb. bulk pork sausage, browned	¼ cup finely chopped parsley
1 can (28 oz.) tomatoes, drained	2 eggs, beaten
2 tablespoons chopped parsley	½ teaspoon seasoned salt
½ teaspoon salt	½ teaspoon mono-sodium glutamate
1 teaspoon crushed basil	¼ teaspoon pepper
1 teaspoon crushed rosemary	½ lb. lasagne noodles, cooked, drained and rinsed
1 bay leaf	½ cup shredded Parmesan cheese
1 clove garlic, minced	½ lb. Swiss cheese, thinly sliced
1 to 1½ cups cooked turkey pieces	
1½ cups creamed cottage cheese	

1. Simmer the sausage, tomatoes, 2 tablespoons parsley, salt, basil, rosemary, bay leaf, and garlic together in an uncovered skillet until thick, about 30 minutes. Remove bay leaf; mix in turkey and heat sauce thoroughly.
2. Meanwhile, mix cottage cheese, ¼ cup parsley, and a blend of beaten eggs and seasonings.
3. Spread one fourth of sauce in a 2-quart shallow casserole. Top with a third of noodles. Using a third of each, spread noodles with cottage cheese mixture, then sprinkle with Parmesan cheese, and arrange Swiss cheese slices on top. Repeat layering and end with sauce.
4. Bake at 350°F about 30 minutes, or until bubbly. Remove from oven and let stand 5 minutes. **8 SERVINGS**

LINGUINE WITH MARINARA SAUCE

Long, thin, flat Italian noodles are called linguine, that being the Italian word for tongue.

2 medium-sized cloves garlic, sliced	⅛ teaspoon pepper
½ cup olive oil	1 teaspoon oregano
1 can (28 oz.) tomatoes, sieved	¼ teaspoon chopped parsley
1¼ teaspoons salt	8 oz. linguine, cooked and drained

1. Brown garlic in hot olive oil in a large deep skillet. Add gradually, stirring constantly, a mixture of the tomatoes, salt, pepper, oregano, and parsley. Cook rapidly uncovered about 15 minutes, or until sauce is thickened; stir occasionally. If sauce becomes too thick, stir in ¼ to ½ cup water.
2. Serve sauce hot with the linguine. **ABOUT 6 SERVINGS**

QUICKIE TUNA-SPAGHETTI CASSEROLE

1 can (6½ or 7 oz.) tuna, drained	1 can (4 oz.) sliced mushrooms, drained
1 can (about 15 oz.) spaghetti in tomato sauce with cheese	2 tablespoons shredded Parmesan cheese
1 can (10¾ oz.) condensed minestrone soup	1 teaspoon seasoned salt
	¼ cup shredded Parmesan cheese
	2 slices bacon, diced

1. Mix tuna, spaghetti, soup, mushrooms, 2 tablespoons cheese, and seasoned salt. Turn into a greased 1-quart casserole. Top evenly with ¼ cup cheese and then bacon.
2. Heat in a 350°F oven 25 minutes, or until hot. **ABOUT 4 SERVINGS**

SPAGHETTI CASSEROLE

1 onion	1 lb. fresh mushrooms,
1 large green pepper	sliced lengthwise
1 cup pimiento-stuffed	½ lb. sharp Cheddar
olives	cheese, shredded
8 oz. spaghetti, cooked	Bread crumbs
and drained	3 tablespoons butter
1 can (16 oz.) tomatoes	½ cup heavy cream

1. Put onion, green pepper, and olives through meat grinder. Mix with spaghetti, tomatoes, and mushrooms. Season to taste with *salt* and *pepper*.
2. Turn into a greased 2½-quart casserole. Sprinkle with cheese and bread crumbs. Dot with butter. Pour cream over top.
3. Bake at 350°F 1½ hours. 6 TO 8 SERVINGS

Spaghetti Sauces

TOMATO SAUCE

1 cup chopped onion	3 cans (6 oz. each)
1 clove garlic, minced	tomato paste
3 tablespoons olive oil	2 cups water
½ lb. ground beef	2½ teaspoons salt
½ lb. ground pork	½ teaspoon pepper
1 can (28 oz.) Italian-	1 teaspoon oregano
style tomatoes,	
drained	

1. Add the onion and garlic to hot oil in a large deep skillet and cook until onion is soft.
2. Add the ground meat, separate it into small pieces, and cook until lightly browned. Stir in tomatoes, tomato paste, water, and a mixture of salt, pepper, and oregano. Cook uncovered over low heat about 1 hour, stirring occasionally.
ABOUT 7½ CUPS SAUCE

TOMATO MEAT SAUCE

¼ cup olive oil	1 tablespoon salt
½ cup chopped onion	1 bay leaf
½ lb. beef chuck	1 can (6 oz.) tomato
½ lb. pork shoulder	paste
7 cups canned tomatoes	
with liquid, sieved	

1. Heat the olive oil in a saucepot. Add onion and cook until lightly browned. Put the meat into saucepot and brown on all sides. Stir in tomatoes and

salt. Add bay leaf. Cover; simmer about 2½ hours.
2. Mix tomato paste into sauce. Simmer, uncovered, stirring occasionally, about 2 hours, or until thickened. If sauce becomes too thick, add ½ *cup water.*
3. Remove meat and bay leaf from sauce. Serve sauce over *cooked spaghetti.* ABOUT 4 CUPS SAUCE

TOMATO SAUCE WITH GROUND MEAT: Follow recipe for Tomato Meat Sauce. When cooking is almost completed, brown ½ *pound ground beef* in *3 tablespoons olive oil*, cutting beef into small pieces with fork or spoon. After removing meat from sauce, add ground meat and simmer 10 minutes.

TOMATO SAUCE WITH MUSHROOMS: Follow recipe for Tomato Meat Sauce. When cooking is almost completed, lightly brown ½ *lb. fresh mushrooms*, sliced, in *3 tablespoons melted butter*. After removing meat, add mushrooms and cook 10 minutes.

TOMATO SAUCE WITH CHICKEN LIVERS: Follow recipe for Tomato Meat Sauce. When cooking is almost completed, rinse and pat dry with absorbent paper ½ *pound chicken livers* and brown in *3 tablespoons olive oil*. After removing meat from sauce, add chicken livers and simmer 10 minutes.

TOMATO SAUCE WITH SAUSAGE: Follow recipe for Tomato Meat Sauce. When cooking is almost completed, brown about ½ *pound Italian sausage*, cut in 2-inch pieces, in *1 tablespoon olive oil*. After removing meat from sauce, add sausage and simmer 10 minutes.

CHICKEN SPAGHETTI SAUCE

¼ cup olive oil	2 cans (8 oz. each)
¾ cup chopped onion	tomato sauce
1 clove garlic, minced	¾ cup water
1 tablespoon chopped	¾ cup port wine
celery	½ teaspoon salt
2 teaspoons snipped	¼ teaspoon pepper
parsley	4 to 6 cups cubed,
	cooked chicken breast

1. Heat the olive oil in a large skillet. Stir in the onion, garlic, celery, and parsley; cook until onion is lightly browned.
2. Stir in the tomato sauce, water, wine, salt, and pepper; simmer, uncovered, about 1¼ hours, or until of desired consistency, stirring occasionally. Mix in desired amount of chicken; heat thoroughly.
3. Serve sauce over *cooked spaghetti* and sprinkle with *grated Parmesan cheese.* ABOUT 2 PINTS SAUCE

ITALIAN SPAGHETTI SAUCE

A sauce well worth the time spent in preparation.

½ cup olive oil
1½ cups finely chopped onion
4 cloves garlic, finely chopped
1 lb. ground beef
½ lb. ground veal
½ lb. sweet Italian sausage, cut in small pieces
1 (28 oz.) can Italian-style tomatoes
2 cans (6 oz. each) tomato paste
1 can (10¾ oz.) condensed tomato soup
1 cup water
1½ cups dry red wine
1½ teaspoons Worcestershire sauce
1 teaspoon salt

1 teaspoon sugar
½ teaspoon celery salt
½ teaspoon crushed red pepper
Dash chili powder
Dash ground cinnamon
Dash fennel seed
Dash oregano
3 bay leaves
4 whole allspice, crushed
1 green pepper, chopped (about ¾ cup)
½ lb. fresh mushrooms, sliced lengthwise
½ cup chopped pimiento-stuffed olives
1 jar (4 oz.) pimientos, drained and chopped

1.   Heat the olive oil in a large skillet. Add the onion and garlic and cook until onion is tender, about 5 minutes. Add the beef, veal, and sausage. Brown well, stirring occasionally.
2.   Combine in a large heavy saucepan or saucepot the remaining ingredients except mushrooms, olives, and pimientos. Stir in the meat and onion.
3.   Simmer, uncovered, at least 4 hours, stirring occasionally. If necessary, add a little hot water as sauce thickens during cooking. Remove bay leaves.
4.   About 30 minutes before sauce is done, stir in mushrooms, olives and pimientos.
5.   Serve sauce over *cooked spaghetti* and top with *grated Romano cheese.*   ABOUT 4½ PINTS SAUCE

TOMATO-COTTAGE CHEESE SAUCE

1 pkg. (1½ oz.) spaghetti sauce mix
1 can (6 oz.) tomato paste
1½ cups water
2 tablespoons butter
1 teaspoon salt
½ lb. ground beef

1 tablespoon instant minced onion
½ teaspoon seasoned salt
½ cup small-curd creamed cottage cheese

1.   Blend sauce mix, tomato paste, water, butter,

and salt in a saucepan. Bring to boiling and simmer about 25 minutes, stirring occasionally.
2.   Mix the beef, onion, and seasoned salt in a skillet; cook until meat is well browned.
3.   Blend meat and cottage cheese into sauce. Serve hot over *spaghetti or noodles.*
ABOUT 2½ CUPS SAUCE

SEAFOOD SPAGHETTI SAUCE

The San Francisco, Paris, France, serves Spaghetti aux Fruits de Mer, which is similar to this recipe.

1 lb. cooked shrimp, peeled and deveined
1 lb. cooked lobster meat, cut in pieces
1 env. Italian salad dressing mix, prepared according to directions
½ cup olive oil
2½ cups chopped onion

6 large ripe tomatoes, peeled and chopped
2 teaspoons tarragon, crushed
¼ teaspoon ground saffron
¾ teaspoon salt
¼ teaspoon pepper
2 tablespoons snipped parsley

1.   Marinate the shrimp and lobster meat in the prepared dressing for 1½ hours; drain thoroughly.
2.   Meanwhile, heat the olive oil in a large saucepan. Add the onion and cook until tender.
3.   Stir in the tomatoes, tarragon, saffron, salt, and pepper; simmer, covered, 30 minutes, stirring occasionally.
4.   Stir the drained marinated seafood into the tomato sauce and heat thoroughly. Stir in the parsley and serve over *cooked spaghetti.*
ABOUT 3½ PINTS SAUCE

EGGPLANT-PEPPER SPAGHETTI SAUCE

½ cup olive oil
2 cloves garlic, minced
1½ cups pared and diced eggplant
6 to 8 ripe tomatoes, peeled and cut in pieces
1 teaspoon basil
¼ teaspoon salt

⅛ teaspoon pepper
½ cup quartered ripe olives
4 anchovy fillets, cut in small pieces
1 tablespoon capers
2 medium-sized green peppers, cut in thin strips

1.   Heat the olive oil in a large skillet. Add the garlic and cook until slightly browned.
2.   Stir in the eggplant and tomatoes. Simmer, covered, about 30 minutes, stirring occasionally. Uncover and simmer about 15 minutes longer, stirring occasionally.

3. Blend in remaining ingredients; simmer 10 to 15 minutes, or until of desired consistency. Serve immediately over *cooked spaghetti*.

ABOUT 2½ PINTS SAUCE

WHITE CLAM SAUCE FOR LINGUINE

If clam sauce is one of your favorites, be sure to double this sauce recipe.

2 doz. cherrystone clams, washed*	3 cloves garlic, minced
	¼ cup olive oil
½ cup chopped onion	2 tablespoons flour
¼ cup snipped parsley	¼ to ½ teaspoon salt

1. Bring *2 cups water* to boiling in a large saucepot or Dutch oven. Add clams. Cover and steam until shells are partially opened.

2. Drain, reserving 1½ cups of the cooking liquid. Remove clams from shells; coarsely chop clams and set aside.

3. Add onion, parsley, and garlic to hot oil in a large skillet; cook about 3 minutes, stirring occasionally.

4. Mix in flour, salt, and a *few grains pepper*; cook until bubbly. Add reserved clam liquid gradually, while blending thoroughly. Bring rapidly to boiling, stirring constantly, and boil 1 to 2 minutes. Mix in the chopped clams and heat (do not boil).

5. Serve clam sauce on *8 ounces cooked linguine*.

4 SERVINGS

*Canned minced clams (three 7½-ounce cans) and the drained liquid (about 1½ cups) may be substituted for the whole clams and the reserved liquid.

NOODLE DISHES

GROUND BEEF-NOODLE SCALLOP

2 to 3 tablespoons shortening	¼ teaspoon pepper
	¼ cup soy sauce
2 cups chopped onion	1 teaspoon Worcestershire sauce
2 lbs. ground beef	
1 can (4 oz.) sliced mushrooms, drained	8 oz. fine noodles, cooked and drained
1 can (10½ oz.) condensed cream of chicken soup	8 oz. sharp Cheddar cheese, shredded
1¼ cups milk	1 can (5 oz.) chow mein noodles
2 teaspoons salt	¼ lb. salted mixed nuts

1. Heat shortening in a large skillet. Add the onion and cook about 5 minutes, turning occasionally with a spoon. Add the meat and separate into pieces. Cook until meat is browned and onion is tender.

2. Combine mushrooms and soup. Add the milk gradually, stirring until smooth. Blend in the salt, pepper, soy sauce, and Worcestershire sauce. Stir into meat mixture in skillet and cook until heated thoroughly.

3. Turn cooked noodles into a 3-quart shallow baking dish. Spread the meat-soup mixture over the noodles. Top with the shredded cheese.

4. Heat in a 350°F oven 15 minutes. Remove from oven and distribute chow mein noodles and nuts over surface. Return to oven and heat 10 minutes.

ABOUT 10 SERVINGS

CHILI DON PEDRO

Here's Italian pasta with Mexican overtones.

8 oz. noodles, cooked and drained	½ lb. creamed cottage cheese
1 tablespoon butter or margarine	½ cup dairy sour cream
	8 oz. cream cheese, cut in ¾-inch cubes
3 cans (about 16 oz. each) chili with beans	

1. Toss cooked noodles with butter; keep warm.

2. Mix remaining ingredients in a saucepan. Cover and simmer until the mixture is thoroughly heated, stirring occasionally. If necessary, blend in additional sour cream until of desired consistency.

3. To serve, combine noodles with the chili mixture and turn into a warm serving dish. Toss snipped *parsley* over top.

8 SERVINGS

GERMAN NOODLE RING

1 cup medium noodles, cooked and drained	3 tablespoons butter or margarine
3 tablespoons flour	1½ cups milk
½ teaspoon salt	6 oz. Swiss cheese, cut in pieces
½ teaspoon paprika	2 eggs, well beaten

1. Spoon noodles into a buttered 1½-quart ring mold.

2. Blend flour, salt, and paprika into hot butter in

a saucepan. Heat until bubbly. Remove from heat. Add milk gradually, stirring constantly. Bring to boiling; cook 1 to 2 minutes.
3. Remove from heat and add cheese all at one time; stir rapidly until cheese is melted. Reserve half of sauce to use later.
4. Add beaten eggs gradually to remaining sauce, blending well. Pour over noodles in mold.
5. Set mold in a pan in a 350°F oven. Pour hot water into pan to a depth of 1 inch. Bake about 40 minutes, or until mixture is set.
6. Unmold onto a large platter and pour remaining cheese sauce over mold. ABOUT 8 SERVINGS

HAM NAPOLI RING

Attractive party fare this . . . a custard-like noodle ring, filled with an excellent creamy sauce.

3 eggs
1½ cups milk
1 teaspoon salt
8 oz. noodles, cooked and drained
⅓ cup butter
½ cup sliced fresh mushrooms
¼ cup flour
½ teaspoon salt
2 cups milk
Cooked ham (enough to yield 1 cup pieces)
½ cup ripe olive pieces
¼ cup toasted, blanched almonds, coarsely chopped
2 tablespoons chopped parsley

1. Beat eggs slightly. Blend in 1½ cups milk and 1 teaspoon salt. Mix in cooked noodles. Turn mixture into a buttered 9-inch ring mold. Set in a pan containing boiling water to a depth of 1 inch.
2. Bake at 325°F 1½ hours, or until a knife inserted in center of mixture comes out clean.
3. Heat butter in a heavy saucepan. Add mushrooms and cook, stirring occasionally, until mushrooms are lightly browned and tender. With slotted spoon, remove mushrooms and set aside.
4. Blend flour and salt into butter in pan. Heat until bubbly. Gradually add remaining 2 cups milk, stirring to blend. Bring to boiling, stirring constantly; cook 1 to 2 minutes.
5. Stir in ham, olives, mushrooms, almonds, and parsley; heat thoroughly.
6. Unmold noodle ring onto hot platter and fill with creamed mixture. Garnish with *ripe olives, radish fans*, and *sprigs of parsley*. 6 SERVINGS

CHICKEN-HAM NAPOLI RING: Follow recipe for Ham Napoli Ring. Substitute *cooked chicken* for half of ham and *chicken broth* for half of milk.

DEVILED HAM-NOODLE RING

A decorative layer of deviled ham over a custard-like cheese and noodle ring makes this dish quite impressive.

6 oz. narrow noodles (about ⅛ in.), cooked and well drained
2 cans (4½ oz. each) deviled ham
3 tablespoons melted butter or margarine
1 carton (12 oz.) ricotta cheese
⅔ cup dairy sour cream
½ cup fine soft bread crumbs
¼ cup chopped onion
2 tablespoons chopped parsley
2 whole pimientos, drained and coarsely chopped
3 eggs, slightly beaten
1 teaspoon salt
⅛ teaspoon pepper
⅛ teaspoon ground nutmeg

1. Just before draining noodles, generously grease a 6½-cup ring mold. Press the deviled ham evenly into bottom of mold and set aside.
2. Toss hot noodles with butter, then with a mixture of remaining ingredients until mixed. Turn mixture into the mold over the deviled ham layer.
3. Set mold in a pan in a 350°F oven. Pour boiling water into pan to a depth of 1 inch. Bake 50 to 60 minutes, or until mixture is set.
4. Unmold onto a warm serving plate.
ABOUT 8 SERVINGS

SMOTHERED FRANKS WITH "CROUTONNED" NOODLES

Ingenious is the word to describe this tasty dish.

2 cups chopped onion
½ cup chopped green pepper
¼ cup butter or margarine
¼ cup flour
1 can (10½ oz.) condensed beef broth
1 lb. frankfurters, cut in ½-in. pieces
1 can (4 oz.) mushroom stems and pieces
8 oz. medium noodles, cooked, drained, and rinsed
¼ cup butter
½ teaspoon celery seed
2 cups Rye Croutons, *page 293*
1 cup dairy sour cream

1. Cook onion and green pepper in ¼ cup butter in a skillet until onion is transparent and green pepper is just tender. Blend in flour. Add bouillon gradually, blending thoroughly. Stir in frankfurters and mushrooms. Simmer, uncovered, 20 minutes, stirring occasionally.
2. Meanwhile, toss cooked noodles with remain-

ing butter and celery seed. Keep hot. Just before serving, toss in the croutons.

3. When frankfurter mixture has simmered 20 minutes, remove from heat and vigorously stir in sour cream, 1 tablespoon at a time. Stirring constantly, cook over low heat until just heated, about 3 minutes (do not boil). Serve hot over noodles. ABOUT 6 SERVINGS

RYE CROUTONS: Heat *6 tablespoons butter* in a large, heavy skillet over low heat. Add *6 slices toasted rye bread*, cut into ¼- to ½-inch cubes; turn and toss cubes until all sides are coated and croutons are browned. Remove from heat.

2 CUPS CROUTONS

TAGLIARINI

3 tablespoons olive oil	1 can (12 oz.) whole
1 lb. ground beef	kernel corn with
1½ teaspoons salt	liquid
⅛ teaspoon pepper	1 can (7 oz.) pitted
Few grains cayenne	ripe olives, drained
pepper	½ cup olive liquid
1 medium-sized onion,	4 oz. (about 1½ cups)
chopped	medium noodles,
1 clove garlic, minced	uncooked
1 medium-sized green	¼ lb. sharp Cheddar
pepper, chopped	cheese, shredded
1 can (28 oz.) Italian-	
style tomatoes	

1. Heat olive oil in a large skillet. Brown meat in skillet. Add salt and peppers, onion, garlic, and green pepper; cook, stirring frequently, until onion is soft.
2. Add remaining ingredients except cheese; stir to blend well. Cover closely and cook over low heat about 35 minutes, or until noodles are tender; stir occasionally.
3. Before serving, blend in cheese and heat only until cheese is melted. 8 TO 10 SERVINGS

SHUPP NOODLES
When preparing these Pennsylvania Dutch noodles for soup, cut the strips about one-eighth inch wide.

Noodles, *below*	½ teaspoon salt
½ cup butter	Few grains pepper
3 eggs	

1. Cook noodles in boiling salted water about 10 minutes. Drain.

2. Melt the butter in a skillet. Add the cooked noodles and fry until lightly browned.
3. Beat the eggs with salt and pepper, and stir into the noodles. Cook, without stirring, until eggs are set. Serve at once. 4 TO 6 SERVINGS

NOODLES

1 cup all-purpose flour	2 eggs, beaten
½ teaspoon salt	

1. Mix flour and salt in a bowl. Make a well in center and add eggs; blend thoroughly. Turn dough onto a floured surface; knead, cover, and let stand 30 minutes.
2. Roll about ⅛ inch thick. Turn dough over and continue rolling until paper thin. Allow dough to partially dry, about 1 hour.
3. Cut dough into lengthwise strips 2½-inches wide and stack on top of each other. Slice into short strips ¼ to ½ inch wide. Separate noodles and allow to dry thoroughly. Store tightly covered in refrigerator if not used immediately.

2 CUPS NOODLES

CRÊPES FARCIE
A recipe from Au Petit Jean Restaurant in Beverly Hills, California.

½ lb. spinach, cooked,	½ cup finely chopped
drained, and forced	fresh mushrooms
through food chopper	1 truffle, finely chopped
2 egg yolks, slightly	1½ cups finely chopped
beaten	cooked chicken
¼ teaspoon salt	breast
Few grains pepper	1 cup milk
1 cup all-purpose flour	1 tablespoon sherry
2 tablespoons butter	2 tablespoons grated
½ cup onion, finely	Parmesan cheese
chopped	Béchamel Sauce,
	page 342

1. Mix spinach with egg yolks, salt, and pepper. Add flour and mix until blended.
2. On a lightly floured surface, roll out dough ¹⁄₁₆ inch thick. Cut into 4-inch squares.
3. Add squares one at a time to boiling *salted water* and cook about 2 minutes, or until tender. Remove with a slotted spoon; cool separately.
4. Heat butter in a skillet. Add onion, mushrooms, truffle, and chicken; cook about 10 minutes, stirring occasionally. Gradually add milk, stirring constantly. Mix in sherry and cheese. Set aside.

5. Spoon filling along center of each pasta square and roll to form a tube. Arrange rolls in a shallow baking pan and pour Béchamel Sauce, thinned with a little *sherry* over all. Sprinkle with *grated Parmesan cheese*.

6. Set in a 350°F oven until thoroughly heated.

4 SERVINGS

SEAFOOD-SAUCED GREEN NOODLES

1½ lbs. medium-sized fresh shrimp	1 clove garlic, minced
3 tablespoons olive oil	2 tablespoons butter
2 tablespoons lemon juice	Clam Sauce, *below*
	8 oz. green noodles, cooked and drained

1. Shell and devein shrimp; rinse under running cold water and drain.

2. Mix olive oil, lemon juice, and garlic in a bowl. Add shrimp; cover and marinate about 2 hours, tossing occasionally. Remove shrimp; set marinade aside.

3. Add shrimp to hot butter in a skillet; cook, turning frequently, until pink and tender, about 10 minutes.

4. Remove shrimp with a slotted spoon. Cut about two thirds of shrimp into pieces; reserve remainder. Blend pieces into Clam Sauce; keep warm.

5. Add reserved marinade to skillet; heat. Toss cooked noodles with hot marinade; turn into a heated serving dish. Pour sauce over noodles, sprinkle with *grated Romano cheese*, and garnish with whole shrimp. ABOUT 6 SERVINGS

CLAM SAUCE

¼ cup finely chopped onion	3 tablespoons finely chopped parsley
3 tablespoons butter or margarine	¼ to ½ teaspoon thyme
2 tablespoons flour	1 jar (7½ oz.) whole clams, drained and cut in pieces
¼ teaspoon salt	
⅛ teaspoon white pepper	1 can (7½ oz.) minced clams, drained
1 can (12 oz.) clam juice	

1. Add onion to hot butter in a saucepan and cook until soft. Blend in a mixture of flour, salt, and pepper. Heat until bubbly.

2. Remove from heat and add the clam juice gradually, stirring constantly. Mix in parsley and thyme. Bring to boiling; stir and cook 1 to 2 minutes. Stir in the clam pieces and minced clams; heat thoroughly.

ABOUT 2¼ CUPS SAUCE

FETTUCCINE ALFREDO

Butter-tossed green noodles flavored with herb and garlic is an unforgettable experience when dining at Alfredo's in Rome, Italy.

1 lb. green noodles	1 teaspoon chopped fresh basil
2 tablespoons olive oil	1 clove garlic, minced

1. Cook noodles in boiling *salted water* until just tender; drain.

2. In a chafing dish, heat olive oil, basil, and garlic. Toss the noodles in hot oil with a fork until they are very hot.

3. Sprinkle generously with *grated Parmesan cheese*, adding a generous piece of *butter*, and toss again a moment before serving. ABOUT 8 SERVINGS

FETTUCCINE AL BURRO ALFREDO: Cook *egg noodles* in boiling *salted water* until barely tender, *al dente*; drain thoroughly. Bring quickly to the table in a heated serving bowl and rapidly toss and twirl with a generous amount of *fresh unsalted butter* and *finely grated Parmesan or Romano cheese* so that the butter and cheese melt so quickly that the fettuccine can be served piping hot.

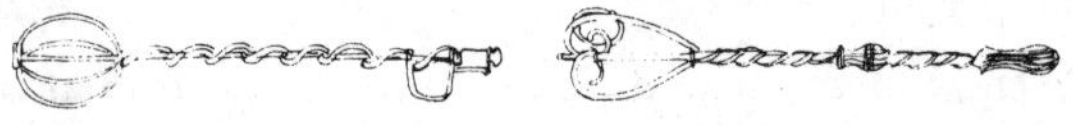

CREAMY GREEN NOODLES

3 tablespoons flour	8 oz. green noodles, cooked and drained
1 teaspoon salt	
Few grains pepper	¼ cup shredded Parmesan cheese
2 tablespoons butter or margarine	
2 cups cream	2 teaspoons grated lemon peel
¼ cup sliced pimiento-stuffed olives	

1. Blend a mixture of flour, salt, and pepper into hot butter in a saucepan. Heat until bubbly. Remove from heat. Add cream gradually, stirring constantly. Bring to boiling and cook 1 to 2 minutes.

2. Toss olives and sauce with noodles; turn into a warm serving dish. Sprinkle a mixture of Parmesan cheese and lemon peel evenly over top.

ABOUT 6 SERVINGS

RICE DISHES

FRIED RICE

¾ cup uncooked rice
2 tablespoons very
  finely chopped fresh
  mushrooms
2 tablespoons butter
¼ to ½ teaspoon grated
  onion

2½ cups chicken broth
  (dissolve 3 chicken
  bouillon cubes in 2½
  cups boiling water)
1 tablespoon finely
  chopped carrot
1 tablespoon finely
  chopped green pepper

1. Add rice, mushrooms, and onion to hot butter
in a large heavy skillet; cook until golden brown.
2. Stir broth into rice mixture. Cover and cook
over low heat 30 minutes, or until rice is tender.
3. Add carrot and green pepper and toss lightly.
ABOUT 8 SERVINGS

BEAUMONT RICE

From Beaumont Inn, Harrodsburg, Kentucky.

2 cups uncooked long
  grain rice
1 teaspoon bacon
  drippings
2 cups finely cut
  celery

1 cup finely cut onion
½ cup butter
¼ teaspoon salt
½ teaspoon pepper
6 cups hot liquid (beef
  or chicken broth)

1. Brown the rice in drippings in a large skillet
over low heat.
2. Sauté the celery and onion together in the butter until onion is soft.
3. Mix all ingredients thoroughly and turn into a
1½-quart casserole; cover and bake at 300°F until
rice is tender, about 1½ hours. (Or, mix all ingredients in the large skillet, cover tightly, and simmer
over low heat until rice is tender and all moisture
has been absorbed.)   8 TO 10 SERVINGS

HURRY-UP RICE MEDLEY

2 cups cooked rice
2 slices bacon, diced
½ cup diced celery
1 can (4½ oz.) deviled
  ham

1 egg, beaten
½ cup shredded
  Cheddar cheese

1. Fry bacon in a large skillet; remove and add
celery. Cook until tender. Stir in rice, deviled ham
and a mixture of the egg, *salt*, and *pepper* to taste.

Heat mixture thoroughly and continue stirring.
2. Spoon into a greased shallow casserole; sprinkle top with the cheese and bacon. Broil about 5
minutes, or until cheese melts.   4 SERVINGS

MEXICAN RICE

¼ cup finely chopped
  onion
1 small clove garlic,
  minced
1 cup uncooked rice

3 tablespoons cooking
  or salad oil
½ teaspoon chili
  powder
1 teaspoon salt
2½ cups water

1. Add onion, garlic, and rice to hot oil in a heavy
saucepan; fry about 3 minutes, or until golden, stirring occasionally.
2. Stir in a mixture of chili powder and salt. Add
water, stir, and cover tightly. Bring to boiling and
simmer until rice is tender, about 25 minutes.
ABOUT 8 SERVINGS

SPANISH RICE CASSEROLE

*Polly Bergen serves this as a main dish at family
dinners or at a big buffet. The amount of seasonings depends on whether you like food hot or mild.*

3 tablespoons olive oil
2 large onions, finely
  chopped
2 green peppers,
  finely chopped
1 clove garlic, minced
2 lbs. ground round
  steak or chuck
2 cans (28 oz. each)
  Italian-style
  tomatoes
1 can (6 oz.) tomato
  paste
1 tablespoon wine
  vinegar
1 tablespoon Worcester-
  shire sauce (optional)

1 dash Tabasco
  (optional)
2 teaspoons salt
Pepper to taste
1½ teaspoons chili
  powder
Few grains cayenne
  pepper
2 bay leaves
2 or 3 whole cloves
1 to 2 cups uncooked
  long grain rice,
  cooked
Grated Parmesan
  cheese

1. Heat olive oil in a large skillet or Dutch oven.
Add onion, green pepper, and garlic; cook over
medium heat until tender and lightly browned.
Remove vegetables with a slotted spoon; set aside.

2. Add ground meat to oil remaining in skillet. Cook over medium heat until lightly browned, stirring occasionally.

3. Add reserved cooked vegetables, tomatoes (including liquid), tomato paste, vinegar, Worcestershire sauce, Tabasco, salt, pepper, chili powder, cayenne pepper, bay leaves, and cloves; stir thoroughly to blend well.

4. Cover skillet and simmer "as long as you want to;" stir occasionally to prevent sticking.

5. Combine desired amounts of rice and sauce; mix until each rice kernel is coated with sauce. Turn into a large casserole. Sprinkle with Parmesan cheese.

6. Cover and set in a 300°F oven just until heated through, 30 to 45 minutes.   8 TO 10 SERVINGS

NOTE: Polly says the sauce improves with cooking—even as long as all day—and is good for spaghetti or, with addition of kidney beans, for chili. She makes up a large amount and freezes part of it.

YELLOW RICE PILAF

5 tablespoons finely chopped onion	1 qt. chicken broth
¼ cup butter	½ teaspoon salt
2 cups uncooked long grain rice	½ teaspoon turmeric

1. Add onion to hot butter in a large heavy saucepan; cook until onion is soft.

2. Add rice gradually to onion in saucepan, stirring constantly. Cook 2 to 3 minutes. Mix in chicken broth, salt, and turmeric. Bring to boiling. Remove from heat and turn into a lightly greased 1½-quart baking dish; cover.

3. Bake at 400°F 20 to 25 minutes, or until rice is tender.   6 TO 8 SERVINGS

RICE PILAF

A recipe from The Imperial House, Chicago, Illinois.

6 tablespoons olive oil	4 cups well-seasoned chicken broth
¼ cup finely chopped onion	1½ teaspoons salt
2 cups uncooked long grain rice	½ cup shredded Cheddar cheese

1. Heat oil in a large heavy skillet having a heat-resistant handle. Add onion and rice; cook over low heat 3 minutes, or until rice is golden.

2. Add chicken broth and salt; cover tightly.

3. Bake at 375°F 35 to 40 minutes. Remove from oven; fluff rice with a fork and stir in cheese.
8 SERVINGS

RICE PILAF DE LUXE

A dish served throughout the Middle East made with rice and raisins, this recipe includes pecans, which add a special flavor and texture.

1½ cups uncooked long grain rice	3 cans (about 14 oz. each) chicken broth
⅓ cup finely chopped onion	¾ cup golden raisins
⅓ cup butter	3 tablespoons butter
1½ teaspoons salt	¾ cup coarsely chopped pecans
	¾ teaspoon salt

1. Add rice and onion to ⅓ cup hot butter in a large heavy skillet; cook until lightly browned, moving and turning frequently with a spoon.

2. Stir in salt, broth, and raisins. Cover, bring to boiling, and cook over low heat about 25 minutes. Remove cover and cook 5 minutes, or until rice is tender and liquid is completely absorbed.

3. Meanwhile, heat remaining butter in a small skillet. Add pecans and ¾ teaspoon salt; heat 2 to 3 minutes, stirring occasionally.

4. Serve rice topped with buttered pecans.
8 SERVINGS

GREEN RICE

1½ cups packaged precooked rice	⅓ cup finely snipped parsley
½ cup shredded sharp Cheddar cheese	⅓ cup finely chopped green onion with tops
¼ cup butter or margarine	2 eggs, well beaten
⅓ cup finely chopped spinach	1½ cups milk, scalded

1. Cook rice according to package directions substituting chicken broth for water and omitting salt. (To prepare chicken broth, dissolve 1 chicken bouillon cube in the boiling water.)

2. Stir cheese and butter into hot cooked rice. Add spinach, parsley, and green onion; mix well. Add beaten eggs and milk; blend lightly but thoroughly. Turn into heat-resistant individual molds or custard cups or a 2-quart shallow baking dish.

3. Bake at 350°F about 30 minutes, or until set.

4. If rice is baked in molds, unmold and garnish

with sprigs of *watercress* inserted into top of each mold. If baked in a dish, garnish one corner of baking dish with strips of *green pepper* forming petals of a flower and *sieved hard-cooked egg yolk* for center of flower.   6 TO 8 SERVINGS

PARMESAN RICE

1⅓ cups packaged precooked rice	3 tablespoons shredded Parmesan cheese
3 tablespoons butter	2 tablespoons coarsely chopped pimiento

Cook rice according to package directions. Lightly toss with remaining ingredients.   ABOUT 4 SERVINGS

SAFFRON RICE

A richly seasoned dish from the Copper Kettle, Aspen, Colorado.

3 cups well-seasoned chicken broth	½ teaspoon coriander
1 cup dry white wine	½ teaspoon fennel
1 teaspoon chopped scallions	⅛ teaspoon mace
1 teaspoon chopped parsley	2 cups uncooked long grain rice
½ teaspoon powdered saffron	2 to 3 tablespoons butter

1.   In a large saucepan, combine chicken broth, wine, scallions, parsley, saffron, coriander, fennel, and mace. Bring rapidly to boiling over high heat.
2.   Add the rice all at once; do not stir. Cover tightly so that no steam escapes. Turn the heat as low as possible. Cook for 30 minutes.
3.   Stir in butter and serve.   ABOUT 8 SERVINGS

RICE PORRIDGE

On Christmas Eve the Danes begin their dinner with this rice porridge. The person who gets the hidden almond receives a present, usually a marzipan pig.

6 cups milk	1 blanched almond
1 cup uncooked long grain rice	5 tablespoons sugar
½ teaspoon salt	1 teaspoon ground cinnamon

1.   Bring milk to boiling in a heavy saucepan; add rice very gradually, stirring constantly, and continue to stir 1 to 2 minutes. Cover and cook over low heat, stirring occasionally, 45 to 60 minutes, or until almost all of milk is absorbed and rice is completely tender.
2.   Stir in the salt and almond. Transfer to a serving dish. Top with pats of *butter* and accompany with a mixture of the sugar and cinnamon.
ABOUT 8 SERVINGS

RICE AND CHICKEN AMANDINE

¼ cup chopped onion	2 tablespoons chopped pimiento
½ clove garlic, minced	
¼ cup butter	2 tablespoons chopped parsley
⅓ cup flour	
2 cups chicken broth	¼ teaspoon ground nutmeg
1 cup cream	
2½ cups cooked chicken pieces	¼ teaspoon thyme
	¼ teaspoon marjoram
3 cups cooked rice	1 teaspoon salt
½ cup toasted slivered blanched almonds	⅛ teaspoon pepper

1.   Add onion and garlic to hot butter in a large heavy skillet; cook until onion is soft. Blend in flour and heat until bubbly. Remove from heat.
2.   Add chicken broth gradually, stirring constantly. Bring to boiling; cook 1 to 2 minutes. Stir in cream; heat thoroughly (do not boil). Add remaining ingredients and mix well. Turn into a greased 2-quart casserole.
3.   Set in a 375°F oven for about 25 minutes, or until mixture is thoroughly heated.
ABOUT 6 SERVINGS

SWEET POTATO-RICE CASSEROLE
There's a wonderful blend of flavors in this mixture. Try it as a stuffing for poultry sometime . . . perfectly delicious!

1½ cups coarsely chopped celery	1 teaspoon ground coriander
1½ cups chopped onion	¾ teaspoon crushed rosemary
2 cups packaged precooked rice	¼ teaspoon ground ginger
½ cup butter	
2½ cups chicken broth	2 eggs, slightly beaten
2 tablespoons brown sugar	1 can (18 oz.) vacuum-packed sweet potatoes, cut in ½-in. pieces
1¾ teaspoons salt	
½ teaspoon black pepper	

1.   Stir celery, onion, and rice into hot butter in a

large heavy skillet; cook over low heat until rice is golden yellow, stirring occasionally.

2. Stir in 2 cups of the chicken broth and a mixture of brown sugar, salt, pepper, coriander, rosemary, and ginger. Cover skillet; bring mixture to boiling and cook over low heat 15 minutes, or until rice is tender; cool.

3. Mix eggs with remaining ½ cup chicken broth; blend into the rice mixture. Add sweet potatoes and toss lightly. Turn into a greased 2-quart shallow baking dish.

4. Heat in a 325°F oven 20 to 25 minutes.

ABOUT 8 SERVINGS

NOTE: Enough to stuff an 8-pound bird.

MOLDED GOURMET RICE

1 cup ripe olives, pitted and cut in large pieces	¼ cup finely chopped parsley
3 eggs, beaten	⅓ cup finely chopped onion
1 teaspoon salt	¼ cup butter or margarine, melted
⅛ teaspoon pepper	3 cups hot cooked rice
4 oz. sharp Cheddar cheese	

1. Blend all ingredients and turn into a well-greased 1-quart shallow baking dish. Set in a pan of hot water.

2. Bake at 350°F about 45 minutes, or until set.

3. Unmold rice onto serving plate and cut into squares. Garnish with sprigs of *watercress*.

6 SERVINGS

SAFFRON RICE RING

¼ cup butter or margarine	¼ cup finely chopped green onion
⅛ teaspoon saffron powder	4 cups hot cooked rice
	½ cup shredded Parmesan cheese

1. Heat butter and saffron in a skillet until butter is melted and bubbly, stirring occasionally to blend. Add the onion and cook 2 to 3 minutes, stirring occasionally.

2. Combine rice, cheese, and butter mixture; toss until thoroughly blended.

3. Turn rice mixture into a 1-quart ring mold and press with back of spoon. Unmold onto a warm serving plate. Fill center as desired.

ABOUT 6 SERVINGS

NASI GORENG

This Indonesian fried rice dish has become popular in Europe through the Dutch people and is now becoming popular in America as well.

¼ cup oil	3½ cups cooked rice
¾ cup chopped onion	¼ teaspoon salt
2 cloves garlic, finely chopped	Pancakes, *below*
1¼ teaspoons Tabasco	2 oz. cooked ham, cut in thin strips
¾ lb. cooked chicken, chopped	2 cucumber pickles, sliced
1 cup cooked small shrimp	

1. Heat oil in a large skillet. Add onion, garlic, and Tabasco and cook until onion is tender, but not brown.

2. Mix in chicken, shrimp, rice, and salt; heat thoroughly.

3. Turn mixture onto a heated large platter. Garnish the edge with rolled pancake strips and then top with ham strips and pickle slices.

4 TO 6 SERVINGS

PANCAKES

The addition of curry to the batter results in a greenish pancake.

¼ cup flour	¼ cup water
⅛ teaspoon salt	2 eggs, fork beaten
⅛ teaspoon curry powder	

1. Mix flour, salt, and curry powder in a bowl. Gradually add water, stirring well. Mix in eggs, stirring into a smooth batter.

2. Bake as for pancakes, then roll up pancakes and slice into ¼-inch wide strips.

WILD RICE WITH MUSHROOMS

½ lb. fresh mushrooms, sliced	1 cup wild rice, cooked, *page 19*, and drained
2 tablespoons finely chopped onion	⅓ cup melted butter or margarine
¼ cup butter or margarine	

1. Cook mushrooms and onion in ¼ cup butter in a skillet until mushrooms are lightly browned.

2. Combine mushrooms, wild rice, and melted butter; toss gently until mushrooms and butter are evenly distributed throughout rice. 8 SERVINGS

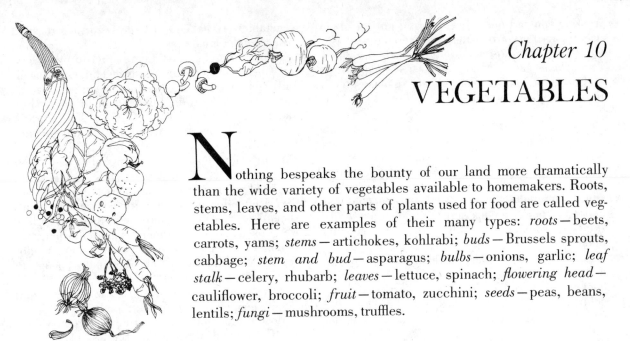

Chapter 10
VEGETABLES

Nothing bespeaks the bounty of our land more dramatically than the wide variety of vegetables available to homemakers. Roots, stems, leaves, and other parts of plants used for food are called vegetables. Here are examples of their many types: *roots*—beets, carrots, yams; *stems*—artichokes, kohlrabi; *buds*—Brussels sprouts, cabbage; *stem and bud*—asparagus; *bulbs*—onions, garlic; *leaf stalk*—celery, rhubarb; *leaves*—lettuce, spinach; *flowering head*—cauliflower, broccoli; *fruit*—tomato, zucchini; *seeds*—peas, beans, lentils; *fungi*—mushrooms, truffles.

SELECTION

Choose vegetables, whether fresh, frozen, or canned, according to the intended use. For example, appearance is of prime importance when selecting vegetables for a vegetable plate, while of lesser importance for soup.

Fresh vegetables should be firm and blemish-free. Buy from a reliable market where good methods of handling vegetables are practiced and where there is a quick turnover of the more perishable items.

Vegetables at the peak of their season are usually more flavorful and lower priced than when they are out of season.

When selecting vegetables at the market, refrain from pinching, squeezing, or unnecessary touching. Handle gently to prevent bruising.

Garden-fresh vegetables should be picked just before using if possible.

Frozen vegetables should be solidly frozen and never refrozen after thawing. The package should be in perfect condition.

Canned vegetables are subject to the regulations of the Federal Food, Drug, and Cosmetics Act, as are all canned foods shipped between states. Can labels must state the net weight or net fluid contents of the can and, in general, carry descriptions of the style of pack, size, maturity, seasoning, amount of food, and number of servings.

Dietetic-packed canned foods, including vegetables, are available for those on special diets such as low-sodium, diabetic, or weight reduction.

STORAGE

Fresh vegetables—Store less perishable vegetables, such as cabbage, potatoes, dry onions, winter squash, and rutabagas, in a cool, dry, well-ventilated place without beforehand washing. Keep onions separate from other vegetables. Store potatoes in a dark place and not directly on the floor.

Wash other vegetables, such as radishes, lettuce, and other leaf vegetables before storing; drain thoroughly and gently pat dry with a soft clean towel or absorbent paper. Rinse head lettuce under running water, drain, and shake off excess water thoroughly. For long storage do not remove core until lettuce is used. Place vegetables in refrigerator in vegetable drawers or plastic bags, or wrap tightly in waxed paper or moisture-vaporproof material to prevent vegetables from wilting unless refrigerator maintains a high humidity. Do not soak vegetables for any length of time when washing them. If they are wilted, put them in icy water for only a few minutes. Shake off all moisture left from washing, drain thoroughly, and gently pat dry.

Store peas and lima beans in the pod to keep fresh. Pods may be washed before storage; quickly rinse peas and lima beans after shelling.

Frozen vegetables—Store in home freezer or in

freezing compartment of refrigerator until ready to use. If package starts to thaw, use at once.

Canned vegetables—Store in a cool, dry place away from heat-producing objects. Rust on a can and dents in a can do not indicate spoilage unless there is evidence of leakage.

PREPARATION

Wash vegetables before cooking, even though they look clean. A vegetable brush is almost a necessity. Leave edible peel on vegetables or use a vegetable parer or sharp knife to keep parings as thin as possible. Many minerals and vitamins are located just under the peel, so cook scrubbed vegetables with skins on whenever possible. Peel after cooking them if desired.

Sometimes vegetables, particularly those of the bud and head groups (broccoli, cauliflower, artichokes, etc.), are immersed for a short time in icy cold salted water. This freshens the fiber and drives out any insects that have taken refuge in the crevices.

To clean leaf vegetables such as spinach, cut off and discard tough stems, roots, and bruised leaves. Rinse by lifting up and down several times in a large amount of water, changing water frequently. Do this until the water is clear and always lift the leaves out of the water rather than pouring off the rinsing water. This permits any sand to sink to the bottom.

To clean asparagus trim off the hard portion and the scales of stalks up to the heads. The French method for preparing it for cooking is to remove the outer flesh of the stalks or spears, especially around the tough lower portions. It is done with a sharp knife, shaving off the skin. Asparagus which has been "pared" in this manner requires less cooking time to tenderize it and almost the whole spear is edible except for the tough lower portion.

Cooking to Retain Food Values

Many vegetables can be and are eaten uncooked with all their values intact. But many more need to be cooked before they can be served. To prepare taste-tempting vegetables and to retain their abundant minerals and vitamins, use a cooking method which results in the least possible loss of these values.

Baking—Dry-bake in their skins such vegetables as whole potatoes, sweet potatoes, squash, onions, and tomatoes. Bake them in a hot oven until tender when pierced with a fork. Remove the skins when vegetables are baked in casseroles or in a roasting pan around a meat roast.

Au gratin and scalloping are other forms of baking especially good when fresh vegetables are used. In the latter method, layers of vegetable are alternated in a baking dish or ring mold with white sauce, cream or milk, and seasonings. For au gratin vegetables a covering of buttered crumbs or buttered crumbs with shredded cheese is added.

Boiling—This is the method probably used most by homemakers. To insure the best flavor, color, and food value in vegetables cook them only until they are tender. To shorten the cooking time, cut, slice, dice, or coarsely shred vegetables. The less water used in covering them the more nutrients are retained in the cooked vegetable. For young tender vegetables, ½ to 1 cup water is usually enough to cook enough vegetables for six servings. Mature root vegetables must be cooked a longer time and require enough water to cover them.

Most of the minerals occurring in vegetables are easily dissolved in water and the loss of vitamins during boiling takes place in several ways. They may be destroyed by overheating, by prolonged exposure to the air, and by dissolving in the cooking water. If this liquid is drained off the cooked vegetables and discarded, the principal food values gained by the intelligent buying of vegetables have been lost. Avoid this loss by using the least amount of water needed to keep the vegetable from scorching. By the time the vegetable is tender most of the cooking water will be evaporated. Liquid from vegetables may be used in soups, sauces, or gravies.

A desirable boiled vegetable is free from excess water, retains its original color, and is well seasoned. Pieces are uniform in size and attractive. *To cook leaf vegetables and greens,* such as spinach, chard, and dandelion, use only the water that clings to the leaves after the final washing. Put the greens into a saucepan, add the salt in layers throughout. Cover tightly and cook quickly until steam escapes from pan, then reduce heat and cook slowly so that leaves do not stick to the pan. *To cook asparagus,* after washing and trimming tie stalks in bundles and stand upright in a small, very deep pan or kettle (a deep coffee pot is convenient). Add boiling water to a depth of at least 2 inches, cover loosely, and cook until asparagus is just tender. Or, put asparagus into a skillet with boiling salted water to a depth of 1 inch. Cook, uncovered, 5 minutes; cover and cook until just tender.

To cook broccoli, after washing split the stalks which are over ½ inch thick through center lengthwise. Tie stalks in a bundle and stand upright in a deep pan. Add boiling water up to the flowerets. Cover pan loosely and cook until just tender.

To cook strong-flavored vegetables (cauliflower, mature cabbage, and Brussels sprouts), cover loosely and cook in a large amount of water. To restore color of red cabbage, add a small amount of vinegar at the end of the cooking period.

To heat canned vegetables, bring to boiling the liquid drained from the vegetable and boil until reduced to one half. Return vegetable to liquid and heat quickly. Do not boil.

To heat home-canned vegetables, boil 10 minutes (not required for tomatoes and sauerkraut).

To cook dried (dehydrated) vegetables, soak, then cook as directed for specific recipe. Dried beans should be soaked before cooking. *For quick method*, put beans and measured amount of water into a saucepan. Bring to boiling and boil rapidly 2 minutes. Cover tightly, remove from heat, and set aside 1 hour. Cook, using the soaking water. *For overnight method*, put beans and measured amount of water into a saucepan. Cover and let stand overnight. Cook, using the soaking water.

To cook frozen vegetables, follow directions on package. Do not thaw before cooking (thaw corn on the cob and partially thaw spinach). Break apart frozen block with a fork during cooking. Use as little boiling salted water as possible.

Broiling—Follow directions with specific recipes.

Frying and Deep-Frying—Follow directions with specific recipes.

Panning—Finely shred or slice vegetables. Cook slowly until just tender in a small amount of fat, in a covered, heavy pan. Occasionally move pieces with a spoon to prevent sticking and burning.

Steaming—Cooking in a pressure saucepan is a form of steaming. Follow directions given with saucepan as overcooking may occur in seconds.

NOTE: Some saucepans having tight-fitting covers may lend themselves to steaming vegetables in as little as 1 teaspoon water, no water, or in a small amount of butter, margarine, or shortening.

PURCHASING VEGETABLES

Artichokes, globe—Peak of crop comes in April and May. Select compact, heavy, plump globe; large, clinging, fleshy leaf scales; good green color. Age or injury produces areas of brown color on scales. Overmature artichokes have spreading scales, the centers may be fuzzy or purple, tips of scales hard and woody, and flavor will be strong. Look for worm injury at base of bud.

Asparagus—Peak of crop comes from April to June. Select tender, firm stalks with close compact tips. A rich green color should cover most of the stalk. Wilted stalks with spreading tips indicate that a long time has elapsed since cutting. Angular stalks are likely to be woody.

Beans, lima—Pods should be well-filled, bright, and dark green. Shelled beans should be plump, tender-skinned, greenish-white. Avoid dried, shriveled, spotted yellow, or flabby pods. Test shelled beans for tenderness.

Beans, snap (green or yellow)—Usually available throughout the year. Look for fresh, bright appearance with good color for the variety. Select young tender beans with firm crisp pods. Thick rough fibrous pods indicate overmaturity.

Beets—Usually available throughout the year. Look for deep red color, firm, round, smooth beets free from blemishes. Avoid shriveled beets. Beets which have been left in the field too long will have short necks covered with leaf scars.

Broccoli—Available throughout the year. Select firm, tender stalks with compact heads that have no evidence of flowering. Bud clusters should be dark green or sage green or green with a purple cast. Yellowing leaves may indicate woodiness. An open blossom does not indicate overmaturity.

Brussels sprouts—They are usually available ten months of the year, but the peak period is from October through December. Select firm, compact sprouts with fresh green color. Puffy sprouts indicate poor quality. Worm injury may cause considerable waste. Smudgy, dirty appearance may indicate the presence of plant lice.

Cabbage—Three major groups of cabbage varieties are available: *smooth-leaved green cabbage*, *crinkly-leaved green Savoy cabbage*, and *red cabbage*. Cabbage may be sold fresh or from storage. New cabbage is available the year-round. Select reasonably solid heads with all but 3 or 4 wrapper leaves removed and stem cut close to head. Early cabbage is less compact and firm than winter cabbage. Avoid worm injury, decay, yellowing of leaves, bursting heads. Cabbage only slightly affected can be trimmed and used. If bases of some of the outer leaves have separated from stem, cabbage may be strong-flavored and coarse. *Celery or*

Chinese cabbage has a long, loose head with pale-green to white leaves.

Carrots—Freshly harvested carrots are available all year long. Select firm, fresh, smooth, well-shaped carrots with good color. Avoid wilted, shriveled, cracked, excessively forked carrots. Masses of leaf stems indicate large cores in carrots.

Cauliflower—Available throughout the year with the peak supply appearing from September through January. Choose white to creamy-white, firm, crisp, compact curds with as few blemishes and bruises as possible. (The edible portion is called curd and the outer leafy covering the jacket leaves.) Avoid spreading of the curd.

Celeriac—A variety of celery with a root resembling a turnip. Select firm, crisp roots.

Celery—Available all year long. Select crisp stalks brittle enough to snap easily and with glossy surfaces. Avoid pithy, stringy stalks (detected by pressure). Open the head to detect rot, insect injury, and seed-stem formation. *Pascal celery*, an especially flavorful variety, has green stalks and leaves.

Chard—Leaves should be crisp, tender, and free from insect injury.

Chayote—Varies greatly in size and shape. Select firm chayote.

Chicory, Endive, Escarole—Usually available all year long. Look for crispness, freshness, tenderness. Tough coarse-leaved plants may be bitter. When selecting *Belgian endive* look for fresh, well-bleached heads 4 to 6 inches long.

Collards—Vegetable is similar to kale. Leaves should be large and curled at edges.

Corn—Sweet corn is available every month of the year, but it is most plentiful from May until mid-September. Select young corn that spurts milk when the kernels are pressed. Field corn may be as tender as sweet corn, but not as sweet. Sweet corn ears are usually smaller, husks are a darker green, and ribbon-like end hangs free. Dry, straw-colored husks are indicative of age or damage. Corn which is too immature lacks flavor. Worm injury confined to tips of ears can be cut out with little waste.

Cucumbers—Most plentiful during summer months, but available the year-round. Select firm, fresh, well-shaped cucumbers, deep green in color. Shriveled, withered cucumbers are rubbery and bitter. Overmaturity is indicated by puffiness, yellowing, rubbery flesh, and hard seeds. Overmature cucumbers are not suitable for slicing, but are usable for pickling.

Dandelions—Select plants with large, tender, fresh, green leaves. Use only plants which have not begun to blossom.

Eggplant—Usually available the year-round, but is most plentiful during the late summer. Select well-shaped, heavy, firm, shiny eggplant, free from blemish, and having a uniform, dark purple color. Wilted, shriveled, soft and flabby eggplant often has a bitter flavor.

Fennel—Select crisp bulbs and stalk.

Garlic—Should be dry and firm, not soft and spongy. Outer covering should be unbroken.

Kale—Leaves should have a dark bluish-green color and should be clean and fresh. Avoid wilted or yellow leaves.

Kohlrabi—Select small- or medium-sized bulbs with fresh tops. Avoid tough, woody tops.

Mushrooms—Select small- to medium-sized mushrooms with no mold or softness.

Okra—Choose fresh, tender pods that will snap easily. Dull, dry appearance shows woody, fibrous texture with hard seeds.

Onions, dry—They should be bright, clean, hard, and well-shaped with dry skins. Avoid developed seed stems or sprouts. Moisture at neck indicates decay.

Onions, green, Shallots, Leeks—Green onions should have fresh green tops well-blanched (whitened) 2 to 3 inches from the root. Onions should be young, crisp, and tender. Wilting and yellowing at top may indicate age or too long a period since pulling from ground. Shallots are similar to onions, but grow in clusters and they have no swelling at base. Leeks are larger than shallots and have a slight bulb formation and broad dark-green tops.

Parsley—See page 351.

Parsnips—Primarily a late winter vegetable, but available most of the year. (After long exposure to a cold temperature they become sweeter in flavor.) Select smooth, firm parsnips of medium size. Soft, flabby roots are pithy and fibrous. Large roots will have woody cores. Softness may indicate decay.

Peas—Select well-filled, fresh, bright-green pods. Flat, dark-green pods indicate immature peas. Swollen pods of poor color and flecked with grey specks indicate an advanced stage of maturity and the peas will be tough and the flavor poor. Avoid wet and mildewed pods.

Peppers, sweet green—They are available in varying amounts all year long. Fully matured peppers have a bright-red color. Select firm, thick-fleshed, well-shaped peppers of fresh appearance. Immature peppers are soft, pliable, thin-fleshed, and pale in color. Avoid limp peppers or those with surface blemishes.

Potatoes—Select only reasonably clean, sound, smooth, well-shaped potatoes with shallow eyes. Avoid leathery, wilted, discolored potatoes. Green color indicates sunburn and gives potatoes a bitter flavor. Hollow heart or black heart, often found in very large potatoes, can be discovered only by cutting. Frozen potatoes may be wet, have dark rings below the surface, and will turn black on cooking. If potatoes are purchased in a large quantity, sort them into similar sizes before storing. This insures uniform cooking when they are being prepared for eating.

Radishes—Select smooth, tender, crisp radishes with mild flavor. Leaves are not an indication of quality. Avoid pithy, spongy radishes.

Spinach—Select well-developed, stocky plants with fresh, crisp, clean leaves. Small straggly or over-grown stalky plants often have tough leaves. Avoid seed stems and yellow leaves.

Squash, summer—These include the varieties which are harvested while still immature and when the entire squash is tender and edible. Common varieties are: *Yellow crookneck, large yellow crookneck, green-white patty-pan, slender green zucchini,* and *Italian marrow.* Some of these squash are available at all times of the year. Look for tender, well-developed, firm, fresh-appearing, and well-formed squash. A tender squash has a glossy, not dull, skin and is neither hard nor tough.

Squash, winter—These are marketed only when fully mature. Some of the common varieties are: *Acorn, butternut, green and blue Hubbard, green and gold delicious,* and *banana.* Winter squash is most plentiful from early fall to late winter. Look for full maturity indicated by hard, tough rind. Squash should be heavy for its size, with a thick wall and much edible flesh.

Sweet potatoes, Yams—Available in varying amounts most of the year. They should be smooth, well-shaped, and unblemished. Misshapen, cracked sweet potatoes are undesirable only because of the waste. Decay may be a soft wet, or dry shriveled, sunken, discolored area. Small, dark, clay-colored spots uniting to form large dark blotches are only skin deep. Damp potatoes may have been badly frozen.

Tomatoes—Available all year round. They should be mature, firm, smooth, have good color, and be free from blemishes. Cracked tomatoes must be used at once. Many tomatoes are picked and shipped when color has begun to change from green to pink. Keep these in a warm place until fully ripe and do not store in the refrigerator until they are red in color.

Turnips, Rutabagas—The most popular turnip has white flesh, purplish near the top. Select smooth, firm, fairly round, small or medium-sized turnips with only a few leaf scars around the crown. The tops should be fresh, green, and young. If sold in bunches, the tops should be fresh and have a good green color. Rutabagas are yellow-fleshed, large-sized relatives of turnips. They are available generally in the fall and winter, but cold-storage rutabagas are also available in the spring. Late winter-storage rutabagas are often coated with a thin layer of paraffin in order to prevent loss of moisture and shriveling. The paraffin is removed with the paring before cooking. Look for firm, heavy weight rutabagas (for their size), generally smooth, and round or moderately elongated.

Watercress—This is a small, round-leaved plant that grows naturally (or may be cultivated) along the banks of fresh-water streams and ponds. Look for fresh, crisp, and rich green leaves. Avoid bunches with yellow, wilted, or decayed leaves.

HELPFUL HINTS ABOUT VEGETABLES

• To freshen fresh asparagus, stand the stalks upright in icy cold water.

• To remove the skins from carrots easily, cover them with boiling water and let stand for a few minutes until the skin loosens.

• To keep cauliflower white while cooking, use half milk and half water; cook, uncovered, until just tender.

• To make celery curls, cut stalks (about 3 inches long) lengthwise into thin strips to within 1 inch of end. Place in cold water until strips begin to curl.

• To make celery very crisp, let stand in icy cold water to which 1 teaspoon sugar per quart of water has been added.

• To garnish lettuce leaves sprinkle some paprika on waxed paper and dip edges of leaves into it.

• To keep onions from affecting eyes, peel them under running water.

• To prevent odor while cooking onions and cabbage, add 1 tablespoon lemon juice or a wedge of lemon to the cooking water.

- To extract juice from onion, cut a slice from the root end and scrape juice from center outward, using edge of a teaspoon.
- To finely cut onion, peel, cut off a slice, then cut exposed surface into ⅛-inch squares as deep as is needed. Then slice across thinly.
- To keep fresh parsley, mint, and watercress fresh and crisp, wash thoroughly, shake off excess water, and place uncrowded in a glass jar; cover and refrigerate.
- To freshen withered parsnips, carrots, potatoes, cabbage, lettuce, etc., let stand in icy cold salted water.
- To keep leftover pimientos from spoiling, put into a small jar, pour enough cooking or salad oil over top to cover, and place, tightly covered, in refrigerator.
- To keep potato skins soft and tender enough to eat, grease them before baking.
- To prevent sweet potatoes and apples from discoloring after paring, place them in salted water at once.
- To remove skin from a tomato quickly, place fork through stem end and plunge tomato into boiling water for a few seconds, then into cold water. Or hold tomato over direct heat for a few seconds; remove from heat and break the skin at blossom end; peel skin back.
- To restore sweetness to overmature vegetables, add a little sugar to cooking water.

VEGETABLES A TO Z

A Artichokes • Asparagus

ARTICHOKES VÉRONIQUE

A creamy sauce rich with lobster meat, Gruyère cheese, and grapes provides the flavor accent for cooked artichokes in this glamorous entrée.

6 large artichokes, cooked (see How to Cook Artichokes, *page 305*)	⅛ teaspoon dry mustard
	⅛ teaspoon ground nutmeg
	2½ cups milk
½ cup butter or margarine	1 cup heavy cream
	1 egg, slightly beaten
¼ cup finely chopped onion	4 oz. process Gruyère cheese, cut in pieces
⅓ cup flour	2 cups diced cooked South African rock lobster tail meat (reserve shells)
1½ teaspoons salt	
⅛ teaspoon pepper	
1 teaspoon mono-sodium glutamate	½ cup small grapes

1. While artichokes are cooking, heat butter in the top of a large double boiler. Add onion and cook over medium heat about 3 minutes. Stir in a mixture of the flour, salt, pepper, monosodium glutamate, dry mustard, and nutmeg. Heat until bubbly. Gradually add the milk and cream stirring constantly until smooth. Bring to boiling; boil 1 to 2 minutes, stirring to keep mixture cooking evenly.
2. Mix a small amount of the hot mixture with the egg and stir into the hot white sauce. Cook over boiling water 3 to 5 minutes, stirring occasionally.
3. Add the cheese and stir until cheese is melted. Stir in lobster meat and grapes; heat thoroughly.
4. Transfer artichokes to a heated platter. Fill with the sauce.
5. Garnish platter with lobster shells, *lemon wedges*, and clusters of *grapes*.   6 SERVINGS

HEARTS OF ARTICHOKE CASSEROLE

In the Netherlands Antilles, at Executive House's Aruba Caribbean Hotel-Casino this casserole is listed on the menu of the Papiamento Dining Room. Executive Chef Monsieur Robert Machax adapted the recipe for use in the American kitchen.

2 pkgs. (9 oz. each) frozen artichoke hearts	¼ cup grated Italian cheese
	2 tablespoons snipped parsley
½ loaf white bread, dried and finely grated	2 cloves garlic, minced

1. Cook artichoke hearts following package directions; drain.
2. Toss bread crumbs, cheese, parsley, garlic, *salt*, and *pepper* in a bowl.
3. Put artichoke hearts into an oiled casserole and cover with crumb mixture. Drizzle with *olive oil* to moisten well. Pour ½ *cup water* into bottom of casserole, being careful not to disturb oiled crumbs.
4. Bake at 350°F until lightly browned. 6 SERVINGS

HOW TO COOK ARTICHOKES

4 medium-sized artichokes	1 lemon slice
1 clove garlic, split	2 tablespoons olive oil
	1 teaspoon salt

1. Remove about 1 inch from tops of artichokes by cutting straight across with a sharp knife. Cut off stems about 1 inch from base; remove and discard lower outside leaves. With scissors, clip off tips of remaining leaves. If desired, soak the artichokes 20 to 30 minutes in cold *salted water*; rinse and drain.
2. Set the artichokes right side up in 1-inch boiling water in a saucepot. Add garlic, lemon slice, oil, and salt. Cook covered about 45 minutes, or until stem can be easily pierced with a fork.
3. Drain artichokes and cut off stems at base; spread each artichoke open and pull out center leaves. Using a spoon, remove and discard the "choke" or fuzzy part. (Center opening should hold about ⅓ cup filling.) Proceed as directed in recipe.

4 COOKED ARTICHOKES

ARTICHOKES IN MUSHROOM CREAM

Artichoke hearts in a creamy mushroom sauce served in crisp patty shells makes a distinctive dish.

2 pkgs. (9 oz. each) frozen artichoke hearts	⅛ teaspoon ground nutmeg
¼ cup butter	¾ cup chicken broth (dissolve 1 chicken bouillon cube in ¾ cup boiling water)
4 oz. fresh mushrooms, coarsely chopped	
2 tablespoons finely chopped onion	¾ cup cream
2½ tablespoons flour	2 egg yolks, slightly beaten
¼ teaspoon salt	
⅛ teaspoon white pepper	2 tablespoons snipped parsley
	½ teaspoon capers
	8 patty shells

1. Cook artichoke hearts according to package directions, substituting *seasoned salt* for salt. Drain and set aside.
2. Meanwhile, heat butter in a double-boiler top; add mushrooms and onion and cook, stirring occasionally, until mushrooms are lightly browned.
3. Blend in a mixture of the flour, salt, pepper, and nutmeg. Heat until bubbly. Remove from heat and add broth and cream gradually, stirring constantly; bring sauce to boiling and cook 1 to 2 minutes, stirring constantly.

4. Remove from heat and vigorously stir about 3 tablespoons of the mixture into egg yolks. Immediately return to double boiler. Cook over boiling water 3 to 5 minutes, stirring slowly so mixture cooks evenly.
5. Mix in artichoke hearts, parsley, and capers. Heat thoroughly.
6. Spoon mixture into warm patty shells. Replace patty shell tops or garnish with a tiny fancy shape cut from a crimson *cinnamon apple* or a *grenadine pear*.

8 SERVINGS

ASPARAGUS-ROSEMARY EN CRÈME

Usher in the spring elegance—put your guests in a party mood with this ham, chicken, and asparagus dish.

2 tablespoons finely chopped onion	5 oz. fresh mushrooms, sliced lengthwise and browned lightly in 1 tablespoon butter
½ cup butter	
7 tablespoons flour	
½ teaspoon salt	
½ teaspoon paprika	⅓ cup ripe olives, sliced lengthwise
½ to 1 teaspoon rosemary, crushed	
	8 thin slices baked ham
2 cups chicken broth	
2 cups dairy sour cream	8 slices cooked chicken (one half the size of ham slices)
	2 doz. asparagus spears, cooked and drained

1. Cook onion in hot butter in a saucepan until onion is golden. Blend in flour, salt, paprika, and rosemary; heat until bubbly.
2. Add chicken broth gradually, stirring to blend. Bring to boiling, stirring constantly, and cook 1 to 2 minutes. Remove from heat and quickly blend in sour cream in small amounts. Stir in mushrooms and olives; set aside.
3. Set out a large shallow baking dish. Place slices of ham in dish and spoon about a tablespoon of sauce over half of each slice; cover with chicken slices and spoon a tablespoon of sauce over each; fold the ham slices. Top each with 3 asparagus spears and spoon sauce evenly over all.
4. Set in a 350°F oven 20 minutes, or until thoroughly heated. Transfer each serving to a luncheon plate and garnish with *spiced crab apples*.

8 SERVINGS

ASPARAGUS-CAULIFLOWER PLATTER

Cook the desired amount of *frozen asparagus* and *cauliflower* according to package directions. Drain thoroughly and sprinkle with *seasoned salt*. Meanwhile, lightly brown *butter* in a skillet. Blend in *lemon juice* to taste and drizzle over vegetables on a warm serving platter. If desired, blend crushed *corn flakes* or *cracker crumbs* into butter before spooning over vegetables.

ASPARAGUS WITH RIPE OLIVE BUTTER

⅓ cup butter	¼ cup ripe olive rings
½ clove garlic, minced	2 pkgs. (10 oz. each)
2 teaspoons lemon juice	frozen asparagus spears, cooked and
Few grains black pepper	drained
	Seasoned salt

1. Heat butter and garlic about 5 minutes over low heat. Mix in lemon juice, pepper, and olive rings; heat thoroughly.
2. Arrange hot asparagus on a heated serving dish, sprinkle with seasoned salt, and top with olive butter. 6 SERVINGS

ASPARAGUS-GRAPEFRUIT AU GRATIN

¼ cup finely chopped onion	2 tablespoons finely chopped parsley
1 clove garlic, finely chopped	¼ teaspoon basil
¼ cup butter or margarine	¼ teaspoon rosemary
1 cup coarse bread crumbs (prepared from 3 slices lightly toasted bread)	1 can (16 oz.) grapefruit sections
	1¼ to 1½ lbs. fresh asparagus, or 2 pkgs. (10 oz. each) frozen asparagus spears, cooked and drained

1. Cook onion and garlic in hot butter in a small skillet until onion is soft, but not browned. Add bread crumbs, parsley, basil, and rosemary; continue heating, stirring until crumbs are well browned.
2. Put grapefruit with syrup into a small saucepan and heat just to serving temperature.

3. Arrange hot asparagus spears in heated serving dish; sprinkle with seasoned salt. Gently lift the grapefruit sections from syrup with a slotted spoon, drain thoroughly, and arrange around asparagus. Sprinkle crumbs over all. ABOUT 6 SERVINGS

ASPARAGUS SUPREME

2 tablespoons minced onion	1 cup undiluted evaporated milk
2 tablespoons butter or margarine	3 pkgs. (10 oz. each) frozen asparagus
1 tablespoon flour	pieces, cooked and
½ teaspoon salt	drained
½ teaspoon paprika	4 oz. process sharp
¼ teaspoon dry mustard	Cheddar cheese,
½ teaspoon Worcestershire sauce	shredded
	2 tablespoons fine dry bread crumbs

1. Cook onion in hot butter in a saucepan until onion is soft, but not browned. Blend in flour, salt, paprika, dry mustard, and Worcestershire sauce. Heat until bubbly.
2. Remove from heat. Add the evaporated milk gradually, stirring constantly. Bring to boiling; cook 1 to 2 minutes.
3. Turn asparagus into a 1-quart shallow baking dish. Pour sauce over asparagus and mix lightly with a fork. Sprinkle the cheese and bread crumbs over top.
4. Set under broiler with top of mixture 2 to 3 inches from source of heat and broil 3 to 5 minutes, or until crumbs are lightly browned and cheese is melted. ABOUT 8 SERVINGS

ASPARAGUS-MUSHROOM SUPREME

2 tablespoons butter or margarine	½ lb. fresh mushrooms, sliced and lightly
2 tablespoons flour	browned in butter
¾ teaspoon seasoned salt	½ cup very finely cut celery
¼ teaspoon freshly ground black pepper	2 pkgs. (10 oz. each) frozen asparagus
Few grains paprika	spears, or 1 lb.
1 cup cream	fresh asparagus,
½ cup shredded Swiss cheese	cooked and thoroughly drained

1. Heat butter in a saucepan and blend in flour,

seasoned salt, pepper, and paprika. Cook until bubbly. Add cream gradually, stirring until blended. Bring to boiling; cook and stir 1 to 2 minutes.

2. Remove from heat; add cheese and stir until cheese is melted. Mix in mushrooms and celery.

3. Line the bottom of a greased 1½-quart shallow casserole with half the asparagus. Pour sauce over asparagus and arrange the remaining asparagus on top. Sprinkle with *cracker crumbs*.

4. Set in a 350°F oven 25 minutes until thoroughly heated. 6 SERVINGS

B Beans • Beets • Broccoli • Brussels Sprouts

BROWN BEANS
(Bruna Bönor)

Brown beans are a favorite Swedish dish and an excellent smorgasbord item.

1 lb. dried brown or pinto beans, washed	1 tablespoon salt
1½ qts. water	1 cup dark corn syrup
	¼ cup cider vinegar

1. Put beans and water into a saucepan, bring to boiling and boil rapidly 2 minutes. Cover tightly, remove from heat and set aside 1 hour.

2. Add salt to beans and soaking water, bring to boiling and simmer covered about 2 hours, or until beans are tender.

3. Add the remaining ingredients to saucepan and blend thoroughly. Cook uncovered over medium heat until sauce is thickened; stir as necessary to prevent sticking.

4. Serve hot with *fried salt pork* or *Swedish Meatballs, page 222.* 6 SERVINGS

MEXICAN BEANS
(Frijoles)

This popular Mexican dish is usually made of seasoned red kidney beans, or cow peas, cooked, fried, and mashed. The mixture is then refried as needed.

1 lb. dried pinto beans	1 teaspoon salt
6 cups water	½ cup lard*

1. Wash beans; put into saucepan with water, bring to boiling and boil rapidly 2 minutes. Remove from heat and cover tightly 1 hour.

2. Add salt, bring to boiling and simmer 1 to 2

hours or until beans are tender. Drain and reserve liquid.

3. Heat the lard in a large heavy skillet and add some of the drained beans. Mash them well; add a small amount of the liquid and blend. Continue adding remainder of beans and liquid alternately, mashing and blending after each addition. Continue cooking over low heat 15 to 20 minutes, or until very thick, stirring frequently. 8 TO 10 SERVINGS
*¼ cup bacon drippings may be substituted.

MEXICAN REFRIED BEANS (Frijoles Refritos): Follow recipe for Frijoles. To refry, heat with additional lard in skillet, stirring until beans are thoroughly heated and fat is completely absorbed.

BUCKAROO BEANS

Beans are cooked leisurely, absorbing full flavor from the rich brown sauce formed during cooking.

1 lb. dried pinto or red beans	1 can (16 oz.) whole tomatoes
6 cups water	½ cup coarsely chopped green pepper
2 medium-sized onions, thinly sliced	2 tablespoons brown sugar
2 large cloves garlic, thinly sliced	2 teaspoons chili powder
1 small bay leaf	½ teaspoon dry mustard
1 teaspoon salt	¼ teaspoon crushed oregano or cumin
½ lb. salt pork, slab bacon, or smoked ham	

1. Wash beans, drain, and place in heavy kettle or saucepot with the water; bring rapidly to boiling. Boil 2 minutes and remove from heat. Set aside covered 1 hour. (If desired, pour the water over the washed beans in kettle, cover and let stand overnight. Do not drain.)

2. Stir in the onion, garlic, bay leaf, and salt. (If salt pork is used add salt later.)

3. Wash salt pork thoroughly. Slice through pork or bacon twice each way not quite to the rind. Cut ham into ½-inch cubes, if used. Add meat to beans and bring rapidly to boiling. (To prevent foam from forming, add *1 tablespoon butter or margarine.*) Cover tightly and cook slowly about 1½ hours.

4. Stir in tomatoes, green pepper, and a mixture of the remaining ingredients. Bring rapidly to boiling and reduce heat. Season to taste with *salt* and simmer, covered, 6 hours or longer; remove cover the last hour of cooking, if desired. If necessary, gently stir beans occasionally to avoid sticking on

bottom of kettle. There should be just enough liquid remaining on beans to resemble a medium-thick sauce.

5. Serve piping hot in soup plates.

ABOUT 6 SERVINGS

GOURMET BAKED BEANS

This modern version of an all-time favorite is reminiscent of the old-fashioned bean pot oozing with juicy goodness and filling the kitchen with an unforgettable aroma of beans as they baked for hours and hours.

1 tablespoon cider vinegar	½ teaspoon salt
Undiluted evaporated milk (about 1 cup)	1 tablespoon molasses
⅓ cup firmly packed brown sugar	¼ teaspoon Worcestershire sauce
¼ cup flour	2 drops Tabasco
1 teaspoon dry mustard	2 cans (about 16 oz. each) molasses-style baked beans

1. Pour vinegar into a 1-cup measuring cup for liquids; add enough evaporated milk to measure 1 cup liquid; blend thoroughly.
2. Mix in a bowl the brown sugar, flour, dry mustard, and salt. Add evaporated milk mixture gradually, blending thoroughly. Stir in remaining ingredients. Turn into a 1½-quart casserole.
3. Bake at 350°F 35 to 40 minutes; stir 2 or 3 times during baking. Garnish with *onion rings*.

6 TO 8 SERVINGS

BOURBON BAKED BEANS

3 cans (about 16 oz. each) baked beans	¼ cup strong coffee
¼ cup bourbon whiskey	5 pineapple slices, cut in half

1. About 3 hours before serving time, empty beans into a 2-quart casserole. Stir in bourbon and coffee. Cover and let stand at room temperature.
2. About 1¼ hours before serving time, remove cover. Bake at 350°F about 1 hour.
3. Remove casserole from oven and arrange pineapple around edge of beans. Return to oven and bake 15 minutes. 8 TO 10 SERVINGS

OLD-FASHIONED GREEN BEANS AND BACON

A Pennsylvania Dutch specialty.

¾ lb. fresh green beans, cut, cooked, and drained	2 medium-sized potatoes, pared and cut in ½-inch pieces
8 slices bacon, diced	1 small onion, sliced
	¼ cup water
	½ teaspoon salt

1. While beans are cooking, fry bacon until crisp.
2. Add potatoes, green beans, and remaining ingredients to bacon and fat. Cook covered about 15 minutes, or until potatoes are tender.

ABOUT 4 SERVINGS

FRENCH-STYLE GREEN BEANS WITH WATER CHESTNUTS

1 can (5 oz.) water chestnuts, drained, and sliced, then slivered	½ teaspoon salt
	Few grains pepper
	2 tablespoons lemon juice
3 tablespoons chopped onion	1 teaspoon soy sauce
¼ cup butter or margarine	1 lb. fresh green beans, Frenched, cooked, and drained

1. Brown water chestnuts and onion in hot butter in a large skillet. Stir in a mixture of salt, pepper, lemon juice, and soy sauce. Heat thoroughly.
2. Toss sauce with hot beans. ABOUT 6 SERVINGS

GREEN BEANS À LA POULET

1 pkg. (9 oz.) frozen cut green beans	½ teaspoon salt
½ cup plus 3 tablespoons chicken broth	⅛ teaspoon white pepper
	½ cup cream
½ cup finely chopped onion	2 egg yolks, fork beaten
2 tablespoons butter or margarine	3 tablespoons finely snipped parsley
1 tablespoon flour	4 teaspoons lemon juice

1. Cook beans in ½ cup chicken broth; drain.
2. Meanwhile, cook onion until soft in hot butter in a heavy saucepan. Blend in the flour, salt, and pepper. Heat until bubbly. Stir in the cream and the remaining 3 tablespoons chicken broth; bring to boiling. Cook and stir 1 to 2 minutes.

3. Remove from heat. Vigorously stir about 3 tablespoons hot mixture into egg yolks. Immediately blend into mixture in saucepan. Mix in parsley. Cook over low heat 3 to 5 minutes.

4. Remove from heat. Stir in lemon juice. Pour over hot beans and toss lightly.   ABOUT 4 SERVINGS

CREAMY GREEN BEAN CASSEROLE

1 can (5 oz.) water
   chestnuts, drained
   and sliced
1 can (16 oz.) bean
   sprouts, drained
1 can (4 oz.) mush-
   rooms, drained
1 can (10½ oz.) con-
   densed cream of
   mushroom soup

½ teaspoon salt
Few grains pepper
2 pkgs. (10 oz. each)
   frozen cut green
   beans, cooked and
   drained
1 can (3½ oz.) French-
   fried onion rings

1. Combine in a large bowl the water chestnuts, bean sprouts, mushrooms, and a mixture of soup, salt, and pepper.

2. Add beans and toss lightly. Turn into a 2-quart casserole. Top with onion rings.

3. Set in a 325°F oven about 25 minutes, or until thoroughly heated.   ABOUT 8 SERVINGS

GREEN BEANS WITH MAYONNAISE SAUCE

½ cup mayonnaise
2 tablespoons shredded
   Parmesan cheese
1 teaspoon celery seed
⅛ to ¼ teaspoon curry
   powder

2 pkgs. (9 oz. each)
   frozen cut green
   beans, cooked and
   drained

Blend mayonnaise, cheese, celery seed, and curry powder. Toss sauce with hot beans.

6 TO 8 SERVINGS

GREEN BEANS WITH GARLIC

2 cloves garlic,
   minced
1 cup chopped celery
¼ cup butter or
   margarine

2 pkgs. (9 oz. each)
   frozen French-style
   green beans

1. Cook garlic and celery until just tender in hot butter in a large heavy skillet.

2. Add beans; cover and cook (break frozen blocks apart with a fork as they thaw) about 5 minutes, or until beans are just tender.

3. Sprinkle hot beans with *seasoned salt*, turn into a heated serving bowl and top generously with buttered-browned sliced almonds.

ABOUT 8 SERVINGS

CRUNCHY WAX BEANS

2 cans (16 oz. each)
   wax beans
½ cup butter or
   margarine
2 teaspoons grated
   onion

1 teaspoon lime juice
1 cup corn flakes,
   coarsely crumbled
2 teaspoons snipped
   parsley

1. Heat beans with liquid in a saucepan; drain.

2. Meanwhile, heat butter and onion over low heat until butter is browned. Stir in lime juice and corn flakes; toss with hot beans and parsley.

ABOUT 8 SERVINGS

LIMA BEANS AU GRATIN

1 cup dry bread crumbs
2 tablespoons butter
   or margarine
1 tablespoon chopped
   parsley
½ teaspoon rosemary
½ teaspoon oregano
6 slices bacon, diced
   and panbroiled
¼ cup butter or
   margarine
½ clove garlic, minced
2 tablespoons flour
1½ teaspoons salt

1½ teaspoons dry
   mustard
2 cups milk
1½ tablespoons instant
   minced onion
6 oz. sharp Cheddar
   cheese, shredded
1 pimiento, chopped
   and well drained
5 cups cooked dried
   large lima beans
   (about 2 cups,
   uncooked)

1. Lightly brown the bread crumbs in 2 tablespoons hot butter in a skillet. Remove from heat and mix in parsley, rosemary, oregano, and bacon.

2. Heat the ¼ cup butter with garlic; blend in flour, salt, and dry mustard. Heat until bubbly.

3. Add milk gradually, stirring constantly. Add onion and bring to boiling, stirring constantly until sauce thickens; cook 1 to 2 minutes.

4. Remove from heat; add cheese and stir until melted. Mix in pimiento. Turn lima beans into a 2½-quart casserole. Add cheese sauce and mix with beans. Top with crumbs.

5. Bake at 350°F 30 to 35 minutes.   8 SERVINGS

BARBECUED LIMA BEANS

2 cups dried large
lima beans, sorted
and washed
5 cups boiling water
¼ lb. salt pork, diced
(about ½ cup)
½ cup chopped onion
¼ cup chopped green
pepper
1 clove garlic, minced
¼ cup fat

1 can (10¾ oz.) con-
densed tomato soup
⅓ cup cider vinegar
2 teaspoons Worcester-
shire sauce
1½ teaspoons dry
mustard
1 teaspoon salt
¾ teaspoon chili powder
⅛ teaspoon cayenne
pepper

1. Add lima beans to boiling water gradually so boiling will not stop. Simmer 2 minutes. Remove from heat; set aside 1 hour.
2. Add salt pork to lima beans in saucepan. Cover and bring rapidly to boiling. Simmer about 1 hour, stirring occasionally.
3. Cook onion, green pepper, and garlic in hot fat in a skillet. Add soup and remaining ingredients; mix well. Cook over low heat 10 minutes.
4. Drain lima beans and salt pork, reserving liquid. Blend liquid into soup mixture. Turn half of lima beans and salt pork into a greased 2-quart casserole. Cover with half of soup mixture. Repeat.
5. Bake at 350°F 20 to 30 minutes.

6 TO 8 SERVINGS

LANCASTER COUNTY LIMA BEANS

1 lb. fresh lima beans
(or frozen)
4 large potatoes,
pared and diced

2 cups milk
2 tablespoons butter
1½ teaspoons salt
⅛ teaspoon pepper

1. Partially cook lima beans in boiling water in covered saucepan. Add potatoes and continue cooking until vegetables are tender. Drain.
2. Add milk, butter, salt, and pepper to vegetables in saucepan; stir gently. Heat thoroughly.

ABOUT 10 SERVINGS

LIMA BEANS WITH WATER CHESTNUTS

1 pkg. (10 oz.) frozen
baby lima beans,
cooked and drained
½ cup sliced water
chestnuts
¼ cup butter

2 tablespoons wine
vinegar
2 teaspoons dill seed
½ teaspoon salt
¼ teaspoon black
pepper

1. Combine lima beans and water chestnuts.

2. Heat remaining ingredients thoroughly in a small saucepan. Pour over vegetables; toss lightly to coat.

ABOUT 4 SERVINGS

LIMA BEAN BAKE

2 pkgs. (10 oz. each)
frozen lima beans
2 tablespoons instant
minced onion
½ lb. frankfurters
½ cup ketchup
⅓ cup molasses
3 gingersnaps, crushed

2 tablespoons dark
brown sugar
1 tablespoon dry
mustard
½ teaspoon salt
½ teaspoon paprika
1½ teaspoons Worces-
tershire sauce

1. Cook lima beans with onion; drain.
2. Cut frankfurters into halves lengthwise; cut each in half crosswise. Set aside.
3. Mix hot beans with remaining ingredients.
4. Spoon half of bean mixture into a 1½-quart casserole. Arrange half of frankfurters spoke-fashion over beans. Repeat layering.
5. Heat in a 375°F oven about 15 minutes, or until thoroughly heated.

ABOUT 6 SERVINGS

LIMA BEANS DE LUXE

2 pkgs. (10 oz. each)
frozen lima beans,
broken apart
2 slices bacon, diced
and panbroiled

½ cup lightly packed
brown sugar
⅓ cup ketchup
½ teaspoon salt
½ cup cream

1. Mix lima beans, bacon, brown sugar, ketchup, and salt in a shallow 1½-quart baking dish. Add cream; cover.
2. Bake at 350°F 1 hour 15 minutes, or until beans are tender.

6 SERVINGS

BEETS IN ORANGE SAUCE

A recipe from Brae Loch Inn, Cazenovia, New York.

8 to 10 cooked beets,
sliced
1 small onion, grated
3 tablespoons sugar
1 tablespoon cider
vinegar

1 tablespoon butter,
melted
4 teaspoons grated
orange peel
½ cup orange juice
Salt to taste

Mix all ingredients in a saucepan. Cover tightly and simmer 15 minutes.

4 TO 6 SERVINGS

ZESTY BEETS

1 can or jar (16 oz.) small whole beets	½ teaspoon prepared mustard
2 tablespoons butter or margarine	½ teaspoon seasoned salt
2 tablespoons prepared horseradish	

Heat the beets with liquid; drain. Gently stir in the remaining ingredients. 4 SERVINGS

HARVARD BEETS

2 tablespoons sugar	3 tablespoons cider vinegar
1 tablespoon cornstarch	2 tablespoons butter or margarine
½ teaspoon salt	
1 can or jar (16 oz.) diced or sliced beets, drained (reserve liquid)	

1. Mix sugar, cornstarch, and salt in a saucepan. Stir in reserved beet liquid (add water if necessary to make ¾ cup) and vinegar. Bring to boiling, stirring constantly.
2. Add beets and butter. Bring to boiling, stirring gently. Simmer 8 to 10 minutes. 4 SERVINGS

BEETS À LA RUSSE

2 tablespoons butter	1 can or jar (16 oz.) small whole beets, drained and shredded
1 tablespoon flour	
2 tablespoons sugar	
2 tablespoons cider vinegar	½ cup dairy sour cream

Heat butter in a saucepan. Blend in flour and heat until bubbly. Stir in sugar, vinegar, and beets. Heat thoroughly. Blend in sour cream and heat thoroughly (do not boil). 6 SERVINGS

BROCCOLI WITH HORSERADISH CREAM

½ teaspoon prepared horseradish	⅛ teaspoon salt
	¾ cup dairy sour cream
½ teaspoon prepared mustard	2 lbs. broccoli, cooked and drained

Blend horseradish, mustard, salt, and sour cream in a small saucepan. Heat just until hot. Pour over hot broccoli. ABOUT 4 SERVINGS

BROCCOLI WITH BUTTERY LEMON CRUNCH

½ cup coarse dry bread crumbs	1 small clove garlic, minced
¼ cup butter	½ teaspoon salt
1 tablespoon grated lemon peel	Few grains pepper
3 tablespoons butter	1½ lbs. broccoli, cooked and drained

1. Lightly brown crumbs in ¼ cup butter in a large skillet. Remove from butter with slotted spoon and mix crumbs with lemon peel.
2. Put the 3 tablespoons butter, garlic, salt, and pepper into skillet; heat until butter is lightly browned. Add broccoli and turn gently until well coated with butter. Transfer broccoli to a heated vegetable dish and pour remaining garlic butter over it. Top with "lemoned" crumbs. ABOUT 6 SERVINGS

BROCCOLI, SICILIAN STYLE

1 onion, thinly sliced	4 anchovy fillets, chopped
1 clove garlic, thinly sliced	½ cup sliced ripe olives
2 tablespoons olive oil	
1½ tablespoons flour	2 cups shredded process Cheddar cheese
½ teaspoon salt	
⅛ teaspoon pepper	About 1¾ lbs. broccoli, cooked and drained
1 cup chicken broth	

1. Cook onion and garlic until onion is soft in hot olive oil in a saucepan. Blend in a mixture of flour, salt, and pepper. Heat until bubbly.
2. Add chicken broth, stirring constantly. Bring to boiling and cook 1 to 2 minutes, or until sauce thickens.
3. Blend in anchovies, olives, and cheese. Pour sauce over hot broccoli. ABOUT 6 SERVINGS

BROCCOLI RING

3 tablespoons flour	1 cup mayonnaise
½ teaspoon salt	6 eggs, beaten
Few grains black pepper	2 tablespoons grated onion
3 tablespoons butter or margarine	2 cups chopped cooked broccoli
1 cup milk	

1. Blend flour, salt, and pepper into hot butter in a saucepan. Heat until bubbly.

2.   Remove from heat. Add milk gradually, blending thoroughly. Bring to boiling; stir and cook 1 to 2 minutes.

3.   Blend mayonnaise into sauce. Add mixture slowly to beaten eggs, stirring well. Lightly mix in grated onion and cooked broccoli.

4.   Pour mixture into a greased 1½-quart ring mold. Set mold in a pan in a 300°F oven. Add boiling water to pan to a depth of 1 inch. Bake about 35 minutes, or until custard tests done.

5.   Unmold onto warm serving plate. Serve with *creamed chicken* garnished with strips of *pimiento* and *mushrooms* lightly browned in *butter*.

ABOUT 6 SERVINGS

BROCCOLI PARMESAN

1 tablespoon minced onion	⅛ teaspoon marjoram
2 tablespoons butter or margarine	1½ cups milk
2 tablespoons flour	1 chicken bouillon cube
½ teaspoon salt	½ cup shredded Parmesan cheese
Few grains pepper	1½ lbs. broccoli, cooked and drained
½ teaspoon dry mustard	Paprika

1.   Cook onion until soft in hot butter in a saucepan. Blend in a mixture of flour, salt, pepper, dry mustard, and marjoram. Heat until bubbly.

2.   Add milk gradually, stirring constantly. Add bouillon cube; bring to boiling and continue stirring. Cook 1 to 2 minutes. Remove from heat. Add about ⅓ cup of the Parmesan cheese and stir until melted.

3.   Arrange hot broccoli on a heat-resistant platter or in a shallow baking dish. Pour sauce over broccoli and sprinkle with remaining cheese, then with paprika.

4.   Broil about 3 inches from source of heat until cheese is melted and mixture is bubbly, about 4 minutes.

ABOUT 6 SERVINGS

BRUSSELS SPROUTS IN HERB BUTTER

⅓ cup butter	¼ teaspoon marjoram
1 tablespoon grated onion	¼ teaspoon savory
1 tablespoon lemon juice	¼ teaspoon thyme
¾ teaspoon salt	2 lbs. Brussels sprouts, cooked and drained

1.   Combine butter, onion, lemon juice, salt, marjoram, savory, and thyme in a saucepan. Set over low heat and stir until butter is melted.

2.   Pour the seasoned butter evenly over the hot Brussels sprouts.

ABOUT 8 SERVINGS

BRUSSELS SPROUTS WITH CHESTNUTS

½ lb. Brussels sprouts	Few grains ground nutmeg
1 beef bouillon cube	Butter or margarine
½ lb. chestnuts	¼ cup buttered bread crumbs
½ teaspoon salt	
Few grains pepper	

1.   Cook Brussels sprouts; drain, reserving ½ cup liquid. Dissolve bouillon cube in liquid; set aside.

2.   Rinse chestnuts, make a slit on two sides of each shell and put into a saucepan; cover with boiling water and boil about 20 minutes.

3.   Remove shells and skins; return nuts to saucepan and cover with boiling salted water. Cover and simmer 8 to 20 minutes or until chestnuts are tender; drain.

4.   Mix chestnuts with Brussels sprouts. Turn one half of mixture into a buttered 1-quart casserole. Sprinkle with half of a mixture of salt, pepper, and nutmeg. Dot generously with butter. Repeat procedure. Pour beef broth over all. Sprinkle with buttered crumbs.

5.   Heat in a 350°F oven 15 to 20 minutes, or until crumbs are lightly browned.

4 SERVINGS

TANGY BRUSSELS SPROUTS

1 lb. Brussels sprouts	¼ teaspoon salt
1 beef bouillon cube	Few grains white pepper
½ cup dairy sour cream	½ teaspoon paprika
¼ cup mayonnaise	¼ teaspoon dry mustard
1 teaspoon lemon juice	6 slices bacon, fried and crumbled
¼ teaspoon Worcestershire sauce	

1.   Cook Brussels sprouts until tender adding bouillon cube to cooking water; drain.

2.   Blend the remaining ingredients except bacon in a small saucepan. Set over low heat and heat thoroughly (do not boil).

3. Spoon sauce over hot Brussels sprouts. Sprinkle with crumbled bacon. 6 SERVINGS

BEST-EVER BRUSSELS SPROUTS

1 lb. Brussels sprouts, shredded	¼ cup heavy cream
½ cup butter or margarine	¾ teaspoon salt
	¾ teaspoon sugar
	Few grains pepper

1. Add shredded Brussels sprouts to hot butter in a saucepan. Cook, stirring constantly, about 5 minutes, or until just tender.
2. Add a mixture of remaining ingredients. Cook 2 to 3 minutes, or until thoroughly heated; stir constantly. 4 TO 6 SERVINGS

CREAMY BRUSSELS SPROUTS AMANDINE

2 pkgs. (10 oz. each) frozen Brussels sprouts	1½ cups chicken broth (dissolve 2 chicken bouillon cubes in 1½ cups boiling water)
4 stalks celery, cut in 1 in. pieces	⅔ cup undiluted evaporated milk
¼ cup flour	1½ cups toasted ½-in. bread cubes
¼ teaspoon seasoned salt	½ cup coarsely chopped salted almonds
¼ cup butter or margarine	
1 teaspoon dill weed	

1. Cook vegetables until tender; drain.
2. Blend flour and seasoned salt into hot butter in a saucepan. Heat until bubbly. Stir in the dill weed and a mixture of broth and evaporated milk. Bring to boiling; stir and cook 1 to 2 minutes.
3. Stir bread cubes into sauce and spoon over hot vegetables. Top with almonds. ABOUT 8 SERVINGS

BRUSSELS SPROUTS DE LUXE

1 lb. Brussels sprouts	4 whole cloves
½ cup chopped onion	¼ cup butter or margarine
1 bay leaf	

1. Cook Brussels sprouts adding onion, bay leaf, and cloves to cooking water; drain and remove bay leaf and cloves.
2. Add Brussels sprouts to hot butter in a skillet; stir until sprouts are delicately browned.

6 TO 8 SERVINGS

C Cabbage · Carrots · Cauliflower · Celery & Celery Root · Corn

NEW CABBAGE IN ORANGE SAUCE

2 tablespoons butter or margarine	¼ teaspoon salt
2 tablespoons sugar	¼ teaspoon pepper
1½ tablespoons lemon juice	3 cups (about ½ lb.) coarsely shredded new cabbage
1 teaspoon grated onion	1 orange, thinly sliced and quartered
½ teaspoon monosodium glutamate	½ cup orange juice

1. Melt butter in a skillet. Add sugar, lemon juice, onion, monosodium glutamate, salt, pepper, cabbage, and orange pieces. Stir to mix thoroughly. Pour in orange juice.
2. Simmer, stirring occasionally, until cabbage is just tender, about 3 minutes. Serve at once in individual sauce dishes. ABOUT 6 SERVINGS

CABBAGE STRUDEL

This popular Jewish pastry, usually served as a sweet, is treated differently here. Cabbage is used for the filling and the strudel is served with the main course, or as an hors d'oeuvre.

2½ cups all-purpose flour	6 cups finely shredded cabbage
½ teaspoon baking powder	½ cup chopped onion
½ teaspoon salt	1 teaspoon celery salt
1 egg	⅛ teaspoon seasoned pepper
6 tablespoons cooking or salad oil	½ teaspoon sugar
¾ cup ice water	½ teaspoon mustard seed
½ cup rendered chicken fat or butter	

1. Combine flour, baking powder, and salt in a bowl; make a well in center. Add egg, 4 tablespoons of the oil, and the water. Work in the flour until a dough is formed. If dough is too soft, add a little more flour. Turn dough onto a lightly floured surface and knead until smooth and elastic. Cover with a warm bowl while preparing filling.
2. Heat chicken fat in a skillet. Stir in remaining ingredients. Cook, stirring occasionally, 20 minutes, or until cabbage is tender. Remove from heat and cool 20 minutes.

3. Roll out dough as thin as possible on a lightly floured surface. Cover with cabbage mixture and roll up jelly-roll fashion. Place roll in a greased shallow baking pan. Brush with remaining 2 tablespoons oil.

4. Bake at 350°F about 45 minutes, or until crisp and brown. Slice while hot and serve as a meat accompaniment. Or, cut into very small slices for hors d'oeuvres.   6 SERVINGS

COMPANY CABBAGE

5 cups finely shredded cabbage	1 beef bouillon cube
1 cup finely shredded carrot	¼ cup boiling water
½ cup chopped green onion	1 teaspoon prepared mustard
½ teaspoon salt	⅓ cup chopped pecans
⅛ teaspoon pepper	¼ cup butter or margarine
	¼ teaspoon paprika

1. Combine cabbage, carrots, onion, salt, and pepper in a large heavy saucepan.

2. Dissolve bouillon cube in boiling water and add to vegetables in saucepan; toss with fork to blend thoroughly. Cover tightly and cook over low heat 5 minutes; stir once during cooking. Drain if necessary. Turn into a warm serving dish. Keep hot.

3. Stir mustard and pecans into hot butter in a small saucepan and heat thoroughly. Pour over vegetables. Sprinkle with paprika.   6 SERVINGS

RED CABBAGE, DANISH STYLE

1 large head red cabbage	½ teaspoon salt
⅓ cup butter	⅔ cup red currant syrup, or melted red currant jelly
6 tablespoons cider vinegar	
6 tablespoons water	2 large cooking apples, pared, cored, and sliced
1 teaspoon sugar	

1. Cut cabbage into quarters, cut out core, and remove tough outer leaves. Shred coarsely.

2. Add cabbage to hot butter in a large heavy skillet; cook about 5 minutes to soften, turning frequently with a spoon.

3. Stir in a mixture of vinegar, water, sugar, and salt, then the syrup and apples. Cover; simmer about 1½ hours, stirring occasionally.
          ABOUT 8 SERVINGS

FESTIVE CREAMY CARROTS

8 medium-sized carrots, pared	⅛ teaspoon ground nutmeg
2 tablespoons butter or margarine	⅛ teaspoon salt
1 teaspoon sugar	Few grains white pepper
1 egg yolk, beaten	2 teaspoons chopped parsley
¾ cup cream	

1. Cut the carrots into chip-like pieces. Cook covered about 2 minutes in boiling *salted water* to barely cover. Drain, reserving ¼ cup liquid.

2. Add reserved liquid to carrots with butter and sugar. Cover and simmer 15 minutes, or until carrots are tender.

3. Mix the egg yolk with remaining ingredients. Add to carrots and heat thoroughly. 4 TO 6 SERVINGS

BELGIAN CARROTS PHANTASIE

This recipe, created by Executive Chef Enrico Wintrich, is featured in the 71 Club atop Chicago's Executive House.

2 tablespoons butter	1 pound Belgian carrots, cooked and puréed
2 tablespoons sugar	
¼ teaspoon salt	
1 tablespoon honey	½ bunch green onions, finely chopped
4 oz. dried figs, snipped	

1. Put butter, sugar, salt, and honey into a saucepan. Set over heat about 2 minutes, or until butter is melted. Stir in the figs and simmer, covered, about 4 minutes.

2. Mix in carrots and heat thoroughly. Top with the green onions before serving.   6 SERVINGS

HERBED CARROTS WITH GRAPES

1½ lbs. carrots	½ teaspoon thyme
½ teaspoon salt	¼ teaspoon celery salt
1 teaspoon basil	1 cup seedless grapes
½ cup butter or margarine	1 tablespoon lemon juice
1 small clove garlic, minced	⅛ teaspoon salt
	Few grains pepper

1. Wash and pare carrots; cut into 3x¼-inch strips. Put into a saucepan; add the ½ teaspoon salt, basil, and enough boiling water to almost cover. Cook covered 12 to 15 minutes, or until carrots are crisp-tender.

2. Meanwhile, melt butter and add garlic, thyme, and celery salt. Set aside.

3. When carrots are cooked, remove from heat immediately. Add grapes and let stand covered 1 to 2 minutes; drain off liquid.

4. Stir lemon juice into garlic butter and pour over hot carrots. Season with salt and pepper; toss mixture gently.   6 TO 8 SERVINGS

GLOSSY CARROTS

24 small whole carrots, pared and cooked	2 teaspoons honey
¼ cup butter or margarine	½ teaspoon ground ginger
¼ cup thawed frozen orange juice concentrate	½ teaspoon salt

1. While carrots are cooking, melt butter in a skillet. Blend in the orange juice concentrate, honey, and a mixture of ginger and salt.

2. Add carrots to skillet and set over low heat, turning carrots until well glazed.

ABOUT 4 SERVINGS

BAKED CARROT RING

1½ lbs. carrots, pared	1 cup shredded Cheddar cheese
1 tablespoon grated onion	
½ teaspoon celery seed	3 tablespoons flour
¼ teaspoon crushed basil	½ teaspoon salt
1 teaspoon sugar	3 tablespoons butter or margarine
¾ teaspoon salt	1¼ cups milk
Few grains pepper	4 eggs, separated

1. Shred enough of the carrots to make 1 cup.

2. Cook remaining carrots in boiling *salted water* until just tender, but not soft. Drain and cool carrots until they can be handled. Shred enough to make 2 cups.

3. Combine the raw and cooked carrots in a large bowl. Blend in onion, celery seed, basil, sugar, ¾ teaspoon salt, pepper, and cheese; set aside.

4. Stir flour and ½ teaspoon salt into hot butter in a saucepan. Heat until bubbly. Remove from heat and add milk gradually, stirring constantly. Bring to boiling; stir and cook 1 to 2 minutes.

5. Beat egg yolks in a bowl and gradually add sauce, stirring constantly. Stir into carrot mixture.

6. Beat egg whites until stiff, not dry, peaks are formed. Gently fold into mixture. Turn into a generously greased 1½-quart ring mold. Set in a shallow pan of hot water.

7. Bake at 350°F until mixture is set, about 1 hour.

8. Remove from oven and let stand 10 minutes. Run a knife around edge of mold to loosen. Unmold onto a heated serving plate. Surround ring with seasoned *cooked broccoli spears* and fill center with *parsley or watercress*.   6 TO 8 SERVINGS

SPICED CARROTS

1 lb. small carrots, scraped	½ teaspoon salt
	Few grains white pepper
⅓ cup thawed frozen orange juice concentrate	1 piece (1 in.) stick cinnamon
⅓ cup hot water	2 whole cloves
1 thin slice lemon	2 whole allspice
1 teaspoon grated onion	Several blades whole mace
2 teaspoons brown sugar	2 tablespoons butter or margarine

1. Put carrots into a large heavy skillet or saucepan. Mix the orange juice concentrate, water, and remaining ingredients; pour over carrots.

2. Cover tightly and bring to boiling. Reduce heat and simmer until carrots are tender, about 20 minutes. Remove spices before serving.

ABOUT 6 SERVINGS

CARROTS LYONNAISE

2 tablespoons butter or margarine	1 teaspoon sugar
3 cups (about 1 lb.) thinly sliced carrots	¼ teaspoon thyme
	¼ teaspoon salt
¼ cup chopped onion	Few grains pepper

1. Heat butter in a saucepan. Add carrots and remaining ingredients.

2. Cover and cook over medium heat about 15 minutes, or until carrots are tender; stir occasionally.   ABOUT 4 SERVINGS

CAULIFLOWER SUPREME

½ lb. fresh mushrooms,
  sliced
½ cup butter
½ cup all-purpose flour
1 teaspoon salt
2 cups milk

2 pkgs. (10 oz. each)
  frozen cauliflower,
  cooked and drained
6 slices pasteurized
  process pimiento
  cheese
Paprika

1. Cook mushrooms in hot butter in a skillet until lightly browned. Remove mushrooms with slotted spoon and set aside.
2. Blend flour and salt into butter in skillet. Heat until bubbly. Add milk gradually, stirring constantly. Continue stirring and bring rapidly to boiling; cook 1 to 2 minutes. Stir in mushrooms.
3. Arrange half of cauliflower over bottom of lightly greased 1½-quart casserole. Cover with half of the sauce and 3 slices of cheese. Repeat layering. Sprinkle top with paprika.
4. Heat in a 350°F oven about 15 minutes, or until cheese is melted and mixture is bubbly.

6 TO 8 SERVINGS

CAULIFLOWER-SPINACH SENSATION

The combination of vegetables and the unusual way they are prepared makes this cold dish truly sensational.

⅓ cup chopped
  watercress
2 tablespoons chopped
  parsley
½ teaspoon tarragon,
  crushed
1 pkg. (10 oz.) frozen
  chopped spinach,
  cooked (do not drain)

½ cup mayonnaise
½ cup heavy cream,
  whipped
1 pkg. (10 oz.) frozen
  cauliflower, cooked,
  drained, and cooled

1. Stir watercress, parsley, and tarragon into undrained cooked spinach. Cook 1 minute.
2. Drain spinach mixture thoroughly and force through a food mill or sieve.
3. Blend mayonnaise and whipped cream. Mix with sieved spinach and cooled cauliflower. Chill.

ABOUT 4 SERVINGS

CELERY AND ALMONDS AU GRATIN

A recipe from Latham's on Cape Cod, Brewster, Massachusetts.

4 cups 1-in. celery
  pieces
½ cup coarsely chopped
  blanched almonds
3 tablespoons flour
¼ teaspoon salt
Few grains pepper

3 tablespoons butter
1½ cups chicken broth
½ cup cream
1 cup shredded sharp
  Cheddar cheese
Buttered coarse dry
  bread crumbs

1. Cook celery, covered, in a small amount of boiling water until crisp-tender; drain.
2. Mix celery and almonds in a 1½-quart casserole and set aside.
3. Blend a mixture of flour, salt, and pepper into hot butter and cook until bubbly. Gradually add chicken broth and cream, stirring constantly. Bring to boiling; stir and cook 1 to 2 minutes.
4. Pour over celery and almonds in casserole. Sprinkle with cheese and cover with bread crumbs.
5. Bake at 350°F 15 minutes, or until sauce is bubbly and crumbs are golden brown.

ABOUT 6 SERVINGS

BAKED CELERY NORWEGIAN

A recipe from the Copper Kettle, Aspen, Colorado.

1 large bunch Pascal
  celery
1 teaspoon salt
1 cup finely sliced
  scallions including
  green tops
1 cup chopped green
  pepper

2 tablespoons butter
3 oz. cream cheese,
  softened
3 oz. blue cheese
¾ cup heavy cream
3 tablespoons dry
  sherry
⅛ teaspoon pepper

1. Wash celery and trim leaves; slice into 1-inch diagonal pieces (about 4 cups). Add celery and salt to 1 inch of boiling water in a large saucepan. Cook, covered, just until celery is tender, about 15 minutes. Drain celery, reserving 1 cup liquid. Turn celery into a buttered 1-quart casserole.
2. Meanwhile, cook scallions and green pepper 5 minutes in hot butter in a heavy saucepan. Mix with celery in casserole.
3. Blend cheeses well in a bowl. Add the cream gradually while stirring. Mix in sherry, pepper, and reserved celery liquid. Pour sauce over vegetables in casserole.
4. Heat in a 400°F oven 15 minutes, or until bubbly.

6 SERVINGS

STEWED CELERY AND TOMATOES

3 lbs. celery
½ cup chopped onion
2 tablespoons grated
  carrot
2 tablespoons butter
  or margarine
3 tomatoes, peeled and
  cut in pieces
1¼ teaspoons salt

⅛ teaspoon pepper
¼ teaspoon sugar
¼ teaspoon crushed
  thyme
1 vegetable bouillon
  cube
2 tablespoons minced
  parsley

1. Cut celery on the diagonal into 1-inch pieces.
2. Cook onion and carrot in hot butter in a large saucepan until vegetables are softened, about 2 minutes. Add celery, tomatoes, a mixture of salt, pepper, sugar, and thyme, the bouillon cube, and parsley. Bring to boiling; simmer about 1 hour, or until sauce is reduced.
3. Serve in individual sauce dishes.

4 TO 6 SERVINGS

CELERY ROOT WITH MUSHROOMS AND CAPERS

2 cups cubed cooked
  celery root*
¼ cup fine dry bread
  crumbs
¼ cup butter

1 cup sliced fresh
  mushrooms
2 tablespoons butter
2 tablespoons capers

1. Coat celery root with bread crumbs.
2. Add celery root cubes to the ¼ cup hot butter in a skillet and turn frequently to brown all sides.
3. Cook mushrooms until tender in 2 tablespoons butter in a skillet.
4. Lightly mix mushrooms and capers with browned celery cubes.   ABOUT 6 SERVINGS
*To prepare and cook celery root—Wash, cut off ends, and pare one 1½-pound celery root. Cut into crosswise slices ½-inch thick. Put into a saucepan with 1 lemon, sliced. Pour in enough boiling water to cover celery root. Cover, bring to boiling and cook 5 to 10 minutes, or until tender. Drain.

Seasoned Butters for Corn on the Cob
Cook fresh ears of corn in boiling unsalted water just until tender, 3 to 5 minutes. Serve a platter of piping hot corn with small bowls of Herb or Curry Butter, below.
HERB BUTTER: Whip ½ cup butter or margarine with ½ teaspoon dill weed and ½ teaspoon crushed chervil until butter is light and fluffy. Chill until ready to use.
CURRY BUTTER: Whip ½ cup butter or margarine with 1 teaspoon curry powder until butter is light and fluffy. Chill until ready to use.

CORN "OYSTERS"
This version of Pennsylvania Dutch corn "oysters" is fritterlike.

1 cup sifted all-purpose
  flour
1 teaspoon baking
  powder
1 teaspoon sugar
1 teaspoon mono-
  sodium glutamate
½ teaspoon salt
¼ teaspoon paprika
2 teaspoons dill weed,
  crushed

2 cups fresh corn
  kernels cut from cob
  (about 4 ears)
6 tablespoons milk
2 egg yolks, beaten
2 egg whites, beaten
  to stiff, not dry,
  peaks
Fat for shallow frying
  heated to 365°F

1. Sift the flour, baking powder, sugar, monosodium glutamate, salt, and paprika together into a bowl. Stir in dill weed and a mixture of the corn, milk, and beaten egg yolks. Fold in stiffly beaten egg whites.
2. Drop by the teaspoonful into hot fat. Fry uncrowded until golden on both sides, turning once. Lift out of fat with slotted spoon and drain on absorbent paper-lined baking sheet. Serve hot.

ABOUT 2½ CUPS BATTER

CORN PUDDING

2¾ cups milk
6 or 7 fresh ears of
  corn
4 eggs, slightly beaten
1 tablespoon butter
1 teaspoon sugar
1 teaspoon salt
¼ teaspoon pepper

½ teaspoon mono-
  sodium glutamate
2 tablespoons finely
  cut pimiento
2 tablespoons finely
  chopped green pepper
2 tablespoons grated
  onion

1. Scald milk in the top of a double boiler over boiling water.
2. Meanwhile, cut corn kernels from cobs. Using a blender if desired, finely chop enough kernels to yield 2 cups. Put into a large saucepan with 1 cup of the scalded milk. Cover and simmer over low heat for 10 minutes, stirring occasionally.
3. Add a small amount of the scalded milk from

double boiler to eggs, stirring vigorously. Add to remaining scalded milk and blend. Mix in butter and a blend of the sugar, salt, monosodium glutamate, and pepper.

4. Stir pimiento, green pepper, and onion into the corn. Adding gradually, stir in the hot milk mixture and pour into a greased 1½-quart shallow baking dish.

5. Place filled baking dish in a pan set on oven rack. Pour in boiling water to a depth of 1-inch.

6. Bake at 325°F 55 to 60 minutes, or until a knife comes out clean when inserted halfway between center and edge of baking dish. 6 TO 8 SERVINGS

CORN-GOLD FRITTERS

1⅓ cups sifted all-purpose flour	1 teaspoon cooking or salad oil
1 teaspoon baking powder	2 eggs, well beaten
¾ teaspoon salt	1 can (12 oz.) whole kernel corn, drained
⅛ teaspoon pepper	Fat for deep frying heated to 365°F
⅔ cup milk	
1 teaspoon Worcestershire sauce	

1. Blend the flour, baking powder, salt, and pepper in a bowl.

2. Mix the milk, Worcestershire sauce, and oil with the eggs. Add all at one time to the dry ingredients and beat with a hand rotary beater just until smooth. Mix in the corn.

3. For each frying, drop batter by tablespoonfuls into the hot fat until surface is covered. Fry 2 to 3 minutes, or until golden brown, turning frequently. Drain fritters over fat for a few seconds before removing to absorbent paper. Allow 2 fritters per serving. ABOUT 6 SERVINGS

CORN WITH MUSHROOMS

¼ cup thinly sliced green onion	1 can (12 oz.) whole kernel corn, drained
⅔ cup coarsely chopped mushrooms	½ cup cream
2 tablespoons butter or margarine	½ teaspoon salt
	⅛ teaspoon pepper
	2 tablespoons snipped parsley

1. Cook onion and mushrooms in hot butter in skillet 5 minutes.

2. Add corn and stir mixture gently while heating thoroughly.

3. Add cream, salt, pepper, and parsley. Keep over very low heat until ready to serve.

4 TO 6 SERVINGS

SCALLOPED CORN

This recipe was contributed by Mrs. Hubert Humphrey, wife of the former Vice President.

1 egg	Butter
1 cup cream-style corn	⅓ cup half and half
1 cup canned whole kernel corn (including 3 tablespoons liquid)	24 to 30 soda crackers, crushed (reserve enough for topping)

1. Beat egg in a bowl with a fork until frothy. Blend in *salt* and *pepper* to taste and the corn. Add chunks of butter (about 2 tablespoons), half and half, and cracker crumbs; mix well.

2. Turn into a buttered 1-quart casserole. Top with reserved crumbs and dot generously with *butter*. Bake at 350°F 30 minutes. 6 SERVINGS

CORN SCALLOP FIESTA

Old-fashioned scalloped corn is given real red-carpet treatment in this colorful casserole.

1 can (17 oz.) cream-style corn	¼ cup chopped green pepper
2 eggs, beaten	1 tablespoon chopped celery
½ cup crushed soda crackers	1 teaspoon chopped onion
¼ cup butter or margarine, melted	6 drops Tabasco
¼ cup undiluted evaporated milk	½ teaspoon sugar
¼ cup finely shredded carrot	½ teaspoon salt
	½ cup shredded Cheddar cheese

1. Mix corn, eggs, crumbs, butter, evaporated milk, carrot, green pepper, celery, onion, and Tabasco in a bowl. Stir in a mixture of sugar and salt. Turn into a greased 8x8x2-inch baking dish. Top with cheese and sprinkle with *paprika*.

2. Bake at 350°F 30 minutes, or until custard is set and top is golden brown.

3. Remove from oven and mark off squares for serving with lines of *snipped parsley*. Put a *pimiento-stuffed olive slice* in center of each square.

ABOUT 6 SERVINGS

E Eggplant

EGGPLANT AMANDINE

1 medium-sized egg- plant, sliced, pared and cut in small cubes	1 small onion, finely chopped
¾ cup slivered blanched almonds	¼ cup finely snipped parsley
¼ cup butter or margarine	¾ cup cracker crumbs
	2 eggs, slightly beaten
	2 tablespoons milk
	1 cup thinly sliced Cheddar cheese

1. Cook eggplant in ½ *cup boiling salted water* until just tender. Drain thoroughly. Mash with a fork and beat until fluffy.
2. Lightly brown the almonds in 1 tablespoon butter in a skillet. Remove and keep warm.
3. Brown onion lightly in butter in skillet. Mix onion and parsley with eggplant.
4. Heat 3 tablespoons butter in the skillet. Add cracker crumbs and toss to coat crumbs. Blend crumbs and ½ cup almonds with eggplant mixture. Blend in a mixture of eggs and milk.
5. Turn into a greased 1-quart baking dish. Top with cheese and remaining almonds.
6. Bake at 350°F 30 minutes. Remove from oven. Sprinkle with *paprika* and garnish with *snipped parsley*. Return to oven and heat 10 minutes.

ABOUT 8 SERVINGS

EGGPLANT PARMIGIANA
A recipe contributed by movie star Mona Freeman.

2 medium-sized eggplants	2 medium onions, thinly sliced
1 egg, beaten	2 cloves garlic, minced
1 cup fine bread crumbs	½ lb. mozzarella cheese, thinly sliced
1 cup olive oil	½ cup grated Parmesan cheese
1 lb. ground beef	
1½ cups tomato sauce	¼ lb. ricotta cheese, cut in pieces
1½ teaspoons basil	
1½ teaspoons oregano	¼ cup grated Parmesan cheese
1 teaspoon salt	
⅛ teaspoon freshly ground black pepper	

1. Peel eggplants, cut into ½ inch thick slices, place in bowl of ice and water and let stand in refrigerator 30 minutes.

2. Drain eggplant on absorbent paper. Dip slices into beaten egg, then into bread crumbs.
3. Heat olive oil in a deep skillet, add eggplant slices, a few at a time, and cook on both sides until golden brown. Drain on absorbent paper.
4. Add ground beef to skillet, cook until pink color is gone and drain off excess fat.
5. Combine tomato sauce with basil, oregano, salt, pepper, onion, and garlic.
6. Place a layer of half of the eggplant on bottom of a buttered 2½-quart baking dish. Add half of the ground beef, half of each of the cheeses and half of the tomato sauce mixture.
7. Repeat layering with remaining ingredients; top with remaining ¼ cup Parmesan cheese.
8. Bake at 350°F 30 minutes, or until eggplant is tender.

ABOUT 6 SERVINGS

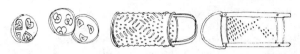

BRINGAL BERTIE GREEN
An eggplant-banana dish from The Astor Club, Berkeley Square, Mayfair, London, England.

1 large eggplant	1 clove garlic, minced
¼ cup olive oil	¼ teaspoon salt
¼ cup finely chopped onion	1 banana with brown- flecked peel
2 tablespoons butter	2 tablespoons grated Parmesan cheese
2 medium tomatoes, peeled and chopped	

1. Cut eggplant lengthwise into halves; score the cut surfaces with a knife. Add eggplant to hot olive oil in a large heavy skillet and cook about 15 minutes on each side, or until tender.
2. Carefully scoop out eggplant, reserving shells. Chop eggplant finely; set aside.
3. Cook onion in hot butter until tender. Mix in tomato, garlic, salt, and eggplant; cook about 10 minutes.
4. Spoon mixture into the eggplant shells.
5. Peel and slice banana lengthwise. Place a banana half on top of each filled shell and sprinkle with cheese.
6. Broil 4 inches from source of heat until cheese is melted, about 5 minutes.
7. Serve with *hollandaise sauce*.

4 SERVINGS

SKILLET EGGPLANT WITH PORK

1 eggplant, pared and cut in large pieces (about 2x1x1½ in.)	¼ teaspoon salt
¼ to ½ teaspoon salt	¼ teaspoon seasoned pepper
⅓ to ½ cup cooking oil	½ teaspoon monosodium glutamate
⅛ to ¼ teaspoon ground ginger	1 teaspoon cornstarch
1 clove garlic, crushed	1 teaspoon sugar
½ lb. pork tenderloin, cut in ¼-in. slices	½ cup cold water
	2 teaspoons soy sauce

1. Sprinkle eggplant with ¼ to ½ teaspoon salt; cook until partially tender, about 5 minutes, in a mixture of the hot oil and ginger in a large heavy skillet. Remove eggplant with a slotted spoon; set aside and keep warm until needed.

2. If necessary, add more oil to skillet and heat with the garlic. Add pork and fry slices a few minutes on each side.

3. Stir a mixture of the ¼ teaspoon salt, seasoned pepper, monosodium glutamate, cornstarch, and sugar into a blend of the water and soy sauce. Add to skillet, bring rapidly to boiling, and cook 2 minutes, stirring the mixture constantly.

4. Return eggplant to skillet. Cook mixture about 5 minutes, or until pork and eggplant are completely tender.

5. Just before serving, sprinkle with *minced parsley*. Transfer to a heated serving dish.

ABOUT 4 SERVINGS

PARMESAN-EGGPLANT SLIMS

In this recipe sliced eggplant is coated with a mixture of crumbs, Parmesan cheese, and Italian salad dressing mix. Crisply fried in olive oil these slices are irresistible.

32 round scalloped crackers, finely crushed (1⅓ cups)	½ cup olive oil
	1 clove garlic, cut in half
2 tablespoons shredded Parmesan cheese	1 medium-sized eggplant, cut crosswise in ¼-in. slices
2 teaspoons Italian salad dressing mix	1 egg, slightly beaten

1. Blend crumbs, cheese, and salad dressing mix.

2. In a large skillet, heat olive oil and garlic over low heat about 10 minutes; remove garlic.

3. Dip eggplant into crumb mixture, then into egg and again into crumbs. Pour off and reserve all but a few tablespoons of oil. Add enough slices to lie flat in skillet; fry about 3 minutes on each side, or until browned. Repeat with remaining slices, adding oil as needed.

4. To serve, overlap two rows of eggplant slices on a heated platter; garnish with *parsley*. If desired, mound *Crunchy Wax Beans, page 309*, on each side of eggplant. ABOUT 8 SERVINGS

STUFFED EGGPLANT GALATOIRE'S

This recipe is from Galatoire's in New Orleans, Louisiana.

1 large eggplant	Salt
3 scallions, chopped	Pepper
2 tablespoons chopped parsley	2 tablespoons bread crumbs
¼ cup butter	2 tablespoons grated Parmesan cheese
½ lb. cooked lump crab meat, diced, or ½ lb. cooked shrimp	

1. Cut eggplant in half and slash the cut surfaces. Bake at 350°F about 20 minutes, or until tender. Scoop out the pulp and reserve the shells.

2. Add scallions and parsley to butter heated in a large saucepan. Cook until the scallions are tender. Add the eggplant pulp, crab meat, and salt and pepper to taste. Heat thoroughly.

3. Spoon the stuffing into the shells and sprinkle with bread crumbs and Parmesan cheese.

4. Bake at 350°F until tops are brown. 2 SERVINGS

RATATOUILLE WITH SPANISH OLIVES

Ratatouille, a vegetable stew typical of the Provence countryside in France, is sometimes served as a cold hors d'oeuvre.

1 medium-sized eggplant, pared and cut in 3x½-in. slices	2 cloves garlic, minced
2 zucchini, cut in ¼-in slices	3 tomatoes, peeled and cut in strips
1 teaspoon salt	1 cup sliced pimiento-stuffed olives
½ cup olive oil	¼ cup chopped parsley
2 onions, thinly sliced	1 teaspoon salt
2 green peppers, thinly sliced	¼ teaspoon pepper

1. Toss eggplant and zucchini with 1 teaspoon salt and let stand 30 minutes. Drain and then dry on absorbent paper.

Kraut with Apples, Roast Loin of Pork, German Potato Salad, and Hazelnut Torte with Strawberry Whipped Cream

2. Heat ¼ cup of the oil in a large skillet and lightly brown eggplant strips and then zucchini slices. Remove with slotted spoon and set aside.

3. Heat remaining ¼ cup oil in the skillet; cook onion and green pepper until tender. Stir in garlic. Put tomato strips on top; cover and cook 5 minutes. Gently stir in eggplant, zucchini, olives, parsley, 1 teaspoon salt, and the pepper.

4. Simmer, covered, 20 minutes. Uncover and cook 5 minutes; baste with juices from bottom of pan. Serve hot or cold.   6 TO 8 SERVINGS

G Green Peppers

FRIED GREEN PEPPER STRIPS

2 large green peppers	1½ teaspoons salt
½ cup fine dry bread crumbs	⅛ teaspoon pepper
	1 egg, fork beaten
⅓ cup grated Parmesan cheese	2 tablespoons water
	Fat for frying

1. Clean green pepper and cut into ⅛ inch rings. Cut each ring into halves or thirds.

2. Coat with a mixture of bread crumbs, cheese, salt, and pepper. Dip into a mixture of egg and water. Coat again with crumb mixture. Chill 1 hour.

3. Heat a ½-inch layer of fat to 375°F in a skillet. Cover surface with chilled green pepper strips. Fry about 30 seconds, or until golden brown. Remove strips with fork or slotted spoon. Drain on absorbent paper.   4 SERVINGS

STUFFED PEPPERS

4 large green peppers	¼ teaspoon dry mustard
½ cup butter or margarine	¼ teaspoon garlic salt
	⅛ teaspoon pepper
2 cups diced ham	1½ cups tomato juice
1 cup cooked rice	¼ lb. Cheddar cheese, cut in 8 slices
2 tablespoons minced onion	

1. Cut green peppers into halves lengthwise; remove and discard white fiber and seeds. Drop pepper halves into boiling *salted water*; simmer 5 minutes. Remove and invert to drain.

2. Heat butter in a saucepan. Add ham and toss lightly with a fork. Mix in rice, onion, dry mustard, garlic salt, and pepper.

3. Pour tomato juice into a 2-quart shallow baking dish.

4. Spoon filling into pepper halves, heaping slightly. Place a slice of cheese on top of each filled pepper and set peppers in dish.

5. Bake at 350°F about 20 minutes. Increase temperature to 400°F and bake 10 minutes, or until cheese is lightly browned.

6. Spoon tomato juice over peppers before serving.   4 SERVINGS

M Mushrooms

GALLATIN'S MUSHROOMS À LA CRÈME GEORGE
A specialty of Gallatin's, Monterey, California.

½ lb. fresh mushrooms (stems chopped)	½ cup dairy sour cream
1 teaspoon butter	¼ teaspoon monosodium glutamate
1 teaspoon dry sherry or Madeira	

1. Sauté mushrooms in butter in a small pan 2 minutes. Add sherry and cook 1 minute.

2. Add sour cream, monosodium glutamate, and *salt* and *pepper* to taste; heat thoroughly (do not boil).

3. Serve on *toast points*.   2 SERVINGS

MUSHROOMS MAGNIFIQUE

12 large fresh mushrooms, cleaned	⅛ teaspoon thyme
2 tablespoons butter or margarine, softened	½ cup finely chopped pecans
	1½ tablespoons chopped parsley
½ clove garlic, minced	½ cup heavy cream
¼ teaspoon salt	

1. Remove stems from mushrooms; finely chop enough stems to make ¼ cup; salt caps lightly.

2. Mix butter with garlic, salt, thyme, pecans, parsley, and chopped mushroom stems until well blended.

3. Heap mixture into mushroom caps and place in a shallow baking dish. Pour cream over all.

4. Heat in a 350°F oven 20 minutes, or until mushrooms are tender, basting several times.

12 STUFFED MUSHROOMS

Bubble and Squeak with Cooked Corned Beef Brisket and English Mustard Sauce

FRESH MUSHROOM SOUS CLOCHE

These wine flavored mushrooms baked under glass bells are served at Antoine's, New Orleans.

1 cup water	1 tablespoon flour
½ cup white wine	Juice of ½ lemon
3 tablespoons butter	1 egg yolk
1 lb. fresh mushrooms, cleaned	¼ cup light cream
	Toast

1. Combine water, wine, and 1 tablespoon of the butter; add to the mushrooms in a saucepan. Bring to boiling; cover and let simmer 10 minutes. Drain, reserving broth.
2. Heat 2 tablespoons butter and blend in flour. Gradually add reserved broth, stirring constantly. Bring to boiling; stir and cook 1 to 2 minutes.
3. Thinly slice the mushrooms; mix into sauce with lemon juice. Cook 5 minutes.
4. Beat the egg yolk with cream. Gradually add mushroom mixture and mix well. Pour into heated glass bell, seal bottom of bell with round piece of toast cut to fit. Turn bell over into porcelain shirred-egg dish. Serve immediately. (The bell is removed at the table.) Or serve mushrooms on toast, omitting the bell. 4 SERVINGS

O   Onions

GLAZED ONIONS

2 tablespoons brown sugar	8 small onions (about 1 lb.), peeled, cooked and dried
¼ cup butter	

Blend brown sugar into hot butter in a skillet and stir until sugar is dissolved. Add cooked onions to skillet and turn several times to glaze evenly.
4 SERVINGS

CREAMED ONIONS WILLIAMSBURG

2 tablespoons flour	1 cup cream
¼ teaspoon salt	8 small onions, (about 1 lb.) cooked, drained, and dried
⅛ teaspoon ground nutmeg	
Few grains pepper	¼ cup chopped roasted peanuts
2 tablespoons butter or margarine	

1. Blend flour, salt, nutmeg, and pepper into hot butter in a saucepan. Heat until bubbly. Stir in the cream. Bring to boiling; cook and stir 1 to 2 minutes.
2. Add onions and peanuts to sauce; heat well.
ABOUT 4 SERVINGS

HERBED ONIONS

10 medium-sized onions, peeled	¼ teaspoon basil, crushed
1 cup vegetable broth	¼ teaspoon garlic powder
½ teaspoon salt	2 whole cloves
1 teaspoon sugar	1 large sprig parsley
¼ teaspoon oregano, crushed	½ small bay leaf
	1 tablespoon olive oil

1. Put onions into a skillet. Add a mixture of the broth and remaining ingredients. Cover tightly and bring to boiling. Reduce heat and simmer until onions are crisp-tender, about 25 minutes.
2. Season with *salt* and *pepper*. Serve hot.
6 TO 8 SERVINGS

ONION CASSEROLE

½ cup milk	2 egg yolks, fork beaten
¼ cup butter	½ cup dairy sour cream
¼ teaspoon salt	1 cup finely shredded sharp Cheddar cheese
⅛ teaspoon pepper	
1½ lbs. onions, peeled and thickly sliced	⅓ cup dry bread crumbs

1. Heat milk, butter, salt, and pepper in a saucepan. Add onion and cook covered until tender, about 15 minutes.
2. Turn onion mixture into a 1-quart casserole and pour a mixture of egg yolks, sour cream, and cheese over onions. Top with bread crumbs.
3. Heat in a 350°F oven 10 to 12 minutes.
ABOUT 6 SERVINGS

HOLIDAY ONIONS AND PEAS

¼ cup flour	1 pkg. (10 oz.) frozen green peas, cooked and drained
1 teaspoon seasoned salt	
¼ cup butter or margarine	2 tablespoons slivered pimiento
2 cups milk	1 cup corn flakes
24 small white onions (about 1½ lbs.), cooked and drained	2 tablespoons butter or margarine

1. Blend a mixture of flour and seasoned salt into

¼ cup hot butter in a saucepan. Heat until bubbly. Stir in the milk and bring to boiling; cook and stir 1 to 2 minutes.

2. Mix onions, peas, and pimiento into sauce. Turn mixture into a 1½-quart baking dish.

3. Coat corn flakes with 2 tablespoons hot butter in a skillet. Top creamed mixture with buttered corn flakes.

4. Heat in a 350°F oven until mixture is hot and bubbly, about 25 minutes.   ABOUT 8 SERVINGS

ONIONS SUPERB

Whole cloves	2 tablespoons flour
2 lbs. (about 20) small onions, peeled, cooked, and drained	1½ teaspoons seasoned salt
	Few grains pepper
2 tablespoons sugar	¾ cup cream
7 tablespoons butter or margarine	¾ cup chicken broth
	¾ cup bread crumbs

1. Insert a clove in each cooked onion.

2. Add sugar to 3 tablespoons hot butter in a skillet and stir until blended. Add a few onions at a time and cook until lightly browned, turning to glaze evenly. Remove onions with a slotted spoon to a shallow baking dish. Set aside.

3. Blend a mixture of flour, seasoned salt, and pepper into 2 tablespoons hot butter in a saucepan. Heat until bubbly. Stir in cream and chicken broth and bring to boiling; cook and stir 1 to 2 minutes. Pour sauce over onions in baking dish.

4. Lightly brown bread crumbs in 2 tablespoons hot butter. Sprinkle over creamed onions.

5. Heat in a 350°F oven 30 minutes.

4 TO 6 SERVINGS

BAKED ONIONS WITH MUSHROOM STUFFING

6 large onions (about 2 lbs.), cooked about 15 minutes and drained	1 cup packaged herb-seasoned stuffing mix
	¼ teaspoon salt
	¼ teaspoon ground thyme
1 cup chopped fresh mushrooms	Shredded Parmesan cheese
1 teaspoon lemon juice	
2 tablespoons butter or margarine	

1. Scoop out center of partially cooked onions, leaving shells about ¼ inch thick; set aside.

2. Add mushrooms and lemon juice to hot butter in a skillet; cook until mushrooms are tender and lightly browned.

3. Chop enough onion centers to yield 1 cup. Mix with mushrooms, stuffing mix, salt, and thyme. Spoon into onion shells; sprinkle with shredded Parmesan cheese.

4. Set onions in shallow baking dish; add boiling water to depth of ¼ inch. Bake at 350°F 35 minutes, or until onions are tender.   6 SERVINGS

LACY FRENCH-FRIED ONION RINGS

The popularity rating of these sweet, redolent onion rings will be great, so be sure to deep-fry plenty. They freeze well and can be oven-heated later for another occasion.

1 cup all-purpose flour	1 tablespoon cooking or salad oil
1 teaspoon baking powder	4 sweet Spanish onions
¼ teaspoon salt	Fat for deep frying heated to 375°F
1 egg, well beaten	
1 cup milk	

1. Blend the flour, baking powder, and salt; set aside.

2. Combine the egg, milk, and oil in a bowl and beat until thoroughly blended. Beat in the dry ingredients until batter is smooth. Cover and set aside while preparing onions.

3. Cut off root ends of onions; slip off the loose skins. Slice onions ¼ inch thick and separate into rings.

4. Using a long-handled two-tined fork, immerse a few onion rings at a time into the batter, lift out and drain over bowl a few seconds before dropping into heated fat. Turn only once as they brown. Do not crowd the rings.

5. When rings are golden brown on both sides, lift out and drain on absorbent paper-lined baking sheet. Serve hot with *salt* or *garlic salt*.

ABOUT 6 SERVINGS

LACY CORNMEAL FRIED ONION RINGS: Follow recipe for Lacy French-Fried Onion Rings. Reduce flour to ⅔ cup and blend in ½ *cup yellow cornmeal. To freeze french-fried onions*—leaving the crisp, tender rings on the absorbent paper-lined baking sheet on which they were drained, place in freezer and freeze quickly. Then carefully remove rings to moisture-vaporproof containers with layers of absorbent paper between layers of onions. The rings may overlap some, but do not have layers too deep. Cover container tightly, label, and freeze.

To reheat frozen french-fried onions—Removing the desired number of onion rings, arrange them (unthawed) in a single layer on a baking sheet. Heat in a 375°F oven several minutes, or only until the rings are crisp and as hot as when they came from the fat.

P Parsnips · Peas · Potatoes

BUTTERED PARSNIPS

Pare *parsnips*. Cook whole or cut into sticks or slices. Heat *salted water* (½ teaspoon salt to 1 cup water) to boiling. Add parsnips; cover and bring to boiling. Cook until tender, about 30 minutes for whole and 10 to 15 minutes for sticks or slice. Drain and season with *salt, pepper,* and *butter*; or glaze as for carrots (See *Glossy Carrots, page 315*).

PARSNIP FRITTERS

1 lb. parsnips (about 4), scrubbed and pared	1 teaspoon minced onion
2 eggs, well beaten	3 tablespoons flour
1 tablespoon butter or margarine	¼ teaspoon dill weed
½ cup milk	¾ teaspoon salt
	Few grains pepper
	Fat for deep frying heated to 365°F

1.   Cook the parsnips in boiling *salted water* until tender; drain thoroughly.
2.   Mash the parsnips, removing any fibrous portions. (There will be about 1¼ cups mashed.)
3.   Add eggs to parsnips; beat well. Beat in the butter, milk, onion, and a mixture of flour, dill weed, salt, and pepper until thoroughly blended.
4.   Drop batter by tablespoonfuls into hot fat and fry 2 to 3 minutes, turning several times until fritters are golden brown. Remove with slotted spoon, drain over fat and place on absorbent paper.
5.   Serve hot.   ABOUT 4 SERVINGS

PEAS AND ONIONS WITH LEMON BUTTER

2 pkgs. (10 oz. each) frozen green peas	1 tablespoon brown sugar
2 teaspoons sugar	½ teaspoon salt
1 jar (16 oz.) whole white onions, drained	¼ teaspoon pepper
¼ cup butter	1 tablespoon lemon juice

1.   Cook peas, adding sugar to water; drain.
2.   Chop enough onions to yield ½ cup; set remaining onions aside.
3.   Lightly brown chopped onions in hot butter in a saucepan. Blend in a mixture of brown sugar, salt, and pepper, then lemon juice and ¼ *cup water*; heat thoroughly.
4.   Toss hot peas and whole onions with lemon butter.   ABOUT 10 SERVINGS

PEAS WITH SWEET BASIL

½ cup sliced green onions with tops	½ teaspoon sugar
2 tablespoons butter or margarine	½ teaspoon salt
	⅛ teaspoon pepper
1 pkg. (10 oz.) frozen green peas, partially thawed	¼ teaspoon sweet basil
	1 tablespoon snipped parsley
	¼ cup water

1.   Cook green onion in hot butter in a skillet. Add peas and break apart with a fork.
2.   Stir in a mixture of sugar, salt, pepper, basil, and parsley, then water. Bring to boiling. Cook, tightly covered, about 10 minutes, or until peas are just tender.   4 SERVINGS

FRENCH PEAS
Fresh peas cooked in the French manner . . . with lettuce . . . is a gastronomical experience.

3 lbs. fresh green peas	1 teaspoon monosodium glutamate
1 small head lettuce	¼ teaspoon pepper
4 scallions or green onions	3 tablespoons butter, melted
3 tablespoons butter, cut in pieces	2 tablespoons finely chopped parsley
2 teaspoons sugar	2 tablespoons chopped chives
1½ teaspoons salt	

1.   Shell peas, reserving one third of tenderest

pods. Put reserved pods on a square of cheesecloth and tie corners securely together, forming a bag.

2. Cut out core of head lettuce. Tear solid portion of head into pieces. Put about half of lettuce pieces into a large saucepan; set remaining pieces aside.

3. Trim green tops of scallions to a length of 2 to 3 inches. Chop and add to saucepan with reserved peas, pea pods, 3 tablespoons butter, sugar, salt, monosodium glutamate, and pepper. Cover with remaining lettuce pieces. Cover and cook until peas are tender, 15 to 20 minutes. Remove from heat. Discard pea pods.

4. Add the remaining ingredients to saucepan. Toss lightly to mix thoroughly.   ABOUT 6 SERVINGS

PEAS DISTINCTIVE

1 pkg. (10 oz.) frozen green peas	⅛ teaspoon tarragon leaves, finely crushed
1 beef bouillon cube	
2 tablespoons butter or margarine, melted	⅛ teaspoon finely crushed chervil
¾ teaspoon sugar	Few grains pepper
½ teaspoon salt	

1. Cook peas, adding bouillon cube to water; drain.

2. Add a mixture of remaining ingredients to hot peas; toss lightly to coat thoroughly.

ABOUT 4 SERVINGS

CREAMY PEAS

3 slices bacon, diced and panbroiled (reserve drippings)	1 can (4 oz.) mushroom stems and pieces, drained (reserve liquid)
1 tablespoon flour	⅔ cup cream
½ teaspoon seasoned salt	1 teaspoon instant minced onion
½ teaspoon crushed sweet basil	1 can (17 oz.) green peas, drained

1. Put 2 tablespoons bacon drippings into a skillet. Blend in a mixture of flour, seasoned salt, and basil. Heat until bubbly.

2. Add mushroom liquid and cream gradually, stirring constantly, until sauce thickens. Stir in onion. Cook 1 to 2 minutes.

3. Mix mushrooms, peas, and *1 teaspoon diced pimiento* into sauce; heat thoroughly. Lightly mix in bacon.   ABOUT 6 SERVINGS

HERBED PEAS AND CELERY

½ cup thinly sliced celery	½ teaspoon sugar
1 tablespoon thinly sliced green onion	½ teaspoon salt
	Few grains pepper
¼ cup butter or margarine	¼ teaspoon ground nutmeg
1 pkg. (10 oz.) frozen green peas	¼ teaspoon chervil
	1 teaspoon lime juice

1. Partially cook celery and onion in hot butter in a saucepan. Add peas and a mixture of sugar, salt, pepper, nutmeg, and chervil.

2. Cover and cook until peas are tender, 5 to 7 minutes. Stir in lime juice.   ABOUT 4 SERVINGS

BAKED POTATOES

Wash and scrub *potatoes*; dry with absorbent paper. If desired, rub with *fat* for softer skins. Prick with a fork. Set potatoes on oven rack or baking sheet and bake at 400°F 45 to 60 minutes, or until potatoes are soft when pressed with fingers (protected from heat by paper napkin). Remove from oven. To make potatoes mealier, gently roll back and forth on a flat surface.

STUFFED POTATOES

6 medium-sized baking potatoes, baked	2 tablespoons milk
	2 tablespoons butter or margarine
½ cup coarsely chopped onion	
	2 teaspoons salt
½ cup coarsely chopped green pepper	¼ teaspoon white pepper
3 tablespoons butter or margarine	1 teaspoon paprika
1 medium-sized tomato, chopped	¼ teaspoon crushed rosemary leaves

1. While potatoes are baking, cook onion and green pepper in 3 tablespoons hot butter in a skillet. Add tomato and cook 1 minute.

2. Cut a thin lengthwise slice from each baked potato. With a spoon, scoop out each potato without breaking skin. Thoroughly mash or rice scooped-out potato. Whip in milk with remaining

ingredients until potatoes are fluffy. Blend in vegetable mixture.

3. Pile mixture lightly into potato shells. Arrange on baking sheet. Sprinkle with *paprika*.

4. Bake at 400°F 20 minutes, or until thoroughly heated and lightly browned.   6 SERVINGS

FRANCONIA POTATOES

(Oven-Browned)

Pare *potatoes* (cut very large potatoes into halves lengthwise). Cook in boiling *salted water* 10 to 15 minutes; drain. Arrange potatoes in shallow baking pan around a roast 40 to 50 minutes before end of roasting time. Turn potatoes often during baking, basting with drippings in roasting pan. When tender remove from pan and serve with roast.

PARISIAN POTATOES

Pare amount of *potatoes* desired and scoop out balls using a melon-ball cutter. Thoroughly dry potato balls with absorbent paper. Heat a generous amount of *butter* in a heavy skillet; add potatoes and cook over medium to high heat, shaking pan occasionally, until potatoes are browned. Season to taste with *salt* and *pepper*. Cover and cook over low heat about 20 minutes, or until tender. If desired, sprinkle with *parsley* before serving.

SCALLOPED POTATOES

6 medium-sized potatoes, pared and thinly sliced	1½ teaspoons salt
	⅛ teaspoon pepper
⅓ cup chopped onion	3 tablespoons butter or margarine
3 tablespoons flour	2½ cups milk, scalded

1. Put a third of the potato slices into a greased 2-quart casserole. Sprinkle with about a third of onion and a third of blended flour, salt, and pepper. Dot with 1 tablespoon of butter. Repeat layering twice, ending with butter. Pour the hot milk over potatoes. Cover casserole.

2. Bake at 350°F 30 minutes. Remove cover; bake 60 to 70 minutes, or until potatoes are tender. Remove from oven. Let stand about 5 minutes before serving.   ABOUT 6 SERVINGS

AU GRATIN POTATOES: Follow recipe for Scalloped Potatoes. After potatoes have baked for 30 minutes and cover has been removed, top with a layer of either buttered *bread crumbs*, shredded *Cheddar or Parmesan cheese*, or a blend of crumbs and cheese. Bake, uncovered, 60 to 70 minutes.

POTATOES ANNA

6 to 8 medium-sized potatoes, pared, and thinly sliced	½ cup butter or margarine

1. Dry potato slices thoroughly with absorbent paper. Arrange even layers of potatoes in a buttered 2-quart baking dish; overlap slices about ¼ inch. Sprinkle each layer with a mixture of *salt* and *pepper* and dot with some of the butter.

2. Bake at 425°F 40 to 60 minutes, or until potatoes are tender and golden brown.

3. To remove from dish for serving, run a spatula around edge to loosen. Invert onto warm serving plate.   6 TO 8 SERVINGS

POTATO-DEVILED HAM CASSEROLE

2 tablespoons butter or margarine	1 can (4½ oz.) deviled ham
1 slice toasted bread, cut in ¼-in. cubes	2 tablespoons butter or margarine
6 potatoes, pared, cooked, and cut in chunks	1 cup dairy sour cream
	1 tablespoon prepared horseradish
¼ cup cider vinegar	½ teaspoon sugar
1 teaspoon salt	⅛ teaspoon garlic powder
⅛ teaspoon pepper	Few drops Tabasco
1 small onion, sliced and separated into rings	

1. Melt the 2 tablespoons butter in a skillet. Add toast cubes and with a spoon move and turn until all sides are coated; remove from heat.

2. Put potatoes into an 11x7-inch shallow baking dish. Pour a mixture of vinegar, salt, and pepper over potatoes. Arrange onion rings over potatoes. Spoon the deviled ham over all. Dot with the remaining butter. Blend sour cream, horseradish, sugar, garlic powder, and Tabasco and spoon over all. Top with croutons.

3. Set in a 350°F oven 15 to 20 minutes, or until thoroughly heated.   6 SERVINGS

SUGAR-BROWNED POTATOES

This Danish specialty is almost as popular in Denmark as their famous pastries.

2 to 3 lbs. small potatoes	6 tablespoons sugar 3 tablespoons butter

1. Cook potatoes until almost tender. Drain and peel. Rinse with cold water; dry with absorbent paper.
2. Heat sugar in a heavy light-colored skillet. With back of a wooden spoon, gently keep sugar moving toward center of skillet until it is melted. Heat until syrup is a light golden brown.
3. Stir in butter and heat until butter and sugar are thoroughly blended.
4. Add potatoes and turn them gently to coat; remove from heat and before serving turn them until coated.   ABOUT 8 SERVINGS

HASHED BROWN POTATOES

1 lb. salt pork, diced 4 cups diced cooked potatoes	⅛ teaspoon salt ⅛ teaspoon black pepper

1. Fry salt pork until crisp in a skillet. Remove salt pork and add potatoes, salt, and pepper.
2. Fry 3 minutes, stirring constantly, then brown bottom. Fold as for an omelet.   6 SERVINGS

SUPERB HASH-BROWN POTATO PATTIES

1 tablespoon flour ½ teaspoon salt ½ teaspoon paprika 3 oz. cream cheese, softened 6 tablespoons shredded extra-sharp Cheddar cheese 1 tablespoon snipped parsley	3 tablespoons evaporated milk 1 teaspoon onion juice 1 egg, beaten until thick and piled softly 1 carton (12 oz.) frozen shredded hash brown potatoes, partially thawed and carefully separated

1. Blend a mixture of the flour, salt, and paprika with the cream cheese in a mixing bowl. Mix in the shredded cheese and parsley. Gradually add the evaporated milk and onion juice and stir until well blended. Gently blend in the well-beaten egg; then potatoes.
2. Heat *butter or margarine* in a heavy skillet over medium heat. Spoon about ¼ cup of mixture for each patty into hot skillet and cook until golden browned and crisp on one side. Turn patties and brown other side. Drain on absorbent paper. Serve on heated platter.   8 TO 10 PATTIES
NOTE: For large pancakes, use about ¾ cup of mixture.

O'BRIEN POTATOES

6 or 7 medium potatoes, cooked and peeled 3 to 4 tablespoons fat ¼ cup chopped onion ¼ cup minced green pepper	2 tablespoons minced pimiento ⅓ cup milk 1 teaspoon salt ¼ teaspoon pepper ¼ teaspoon paprika

1. Dice or coarsely chop the potatoes; set aside.
2. Heat the fat in a large skillet. Mix in the onion, green pepper, pimiento, and potatoes. Add the milk and sprinkle with a blend of seasonings; cook, stirring frequently, until potatoes are lightly browned.
3. Turn into a heated serving dish and garnish with *parsley sprigs*.   6 SERVINGS

SPANISH-STYLE POTATOES

Thinly slice equal portions of *raw potato* and *onion*; brown in hot *olive oil* with chopped *pimiento*. Blend a scant ¼ *teaspoon saffron* with *salt* to taste and sprinkle over vegetables. Add 1 *tablespoon water*, cover the skillet, and cook about 15 minutes, stirring occasionally. Loosen vegetables if sticking occurs. Blend in desired amount of *almonds* and heat thoroughly.

FRENCH-FRIED POTATOES

About 20 minutes before frying the potatoes, fill a deep saucepan two-thirds full with *vegetable shortening, all-purpose shortening, lard,* or *cooking oil* for deep frying and heat to 300°F. Meanwhile, wash and pare *6 medium-sized (about 2 pounds) potatoes.* Use a knife or fancy cutter to cut potatoes. Trim off sides and ends to form large blocks. Cut lengthwise into about ¾-inch slices; stack evenly. Cut lengthwise into sticks about ¾ inch wide. Pat dry with absorbent paper. Fry about 1 cup at a time in hot fat until potatoes are transparent but not browned. Remove from fat and drain on absorbent paper. Just before serving, heat fat to 360°F. Return potatoes to fat, frying 1 cup at a time. Fry until crisp and golden brown. Drain on absorbent paper. Sprinkle with *salt*. Serve immediately or keep warm in oven.

ABOUT 6 SERVINGS

POTATO PANCAKES

6 medium-sized potatoes	⅛ teaspoon pepper
Fat for frying	2 eggs, well beaten
2 tablespoons flour	1 tablespoon grated
1½ teaspoons salt	onion
¼ teaspoon baking	1 tablespoon minced
powder	parsley

1.   Pare and grate potatoes; set aside.
2.   Put fat (enough to make a layer ¼ inch deep) into a heavy skillet; set over low heat.
3.   Blend the flour, salt, baking powder, and pepper. Mix into beaten eggs along with onion and parsley.
4.   Drain liquid from grated potatoes; add potatoes to egg mixture and beat thoroughly with a spoon.
5.   When fat is hot, increase heat to medium. For each pancake, spoon about 2 tablespoons potato mixture into hot fat; leave about 1 inch between pancakes. Cook until golden brown and crisp on one side. Turn carefully and brown other side. Drain on absorbent paper. Repeat until all potato mixture is used.
6.   Serve with *applesauce* and *pancake syrup*.

ABOUT 20 MEDIUM-SIZED PANCAKES

POTATO KUGEL

Make individual little kugels in custard cups or muffin tins for those who like the crust.

6 potatoes, pared and grated	2 teaspoons baking powder
2 onions, grated	1½ teaspoons salt
2 eggs, fork beaten	¼ teaspoon white
¼ cup matzo meal or potato flour	pepper
	¼ cup rendered chicken fat or butter

1.   Drain potatoes; mix with onion. Beat in eggs. Stir in a mixture of matzo meal, baking powder, salt, and pepper. Blend in chicken fat or butter.
2.   Turn into a greased 9-inch pie pan or a shallow casserole. Dot with additional chicken fat or butter.
3.   Bake at 350°F about 1 hour, or until top is crisp and browned.

6 SERVINGS

Here are two versions of the ever-popular Swiss fried potatoes. Cooked potatoes are used in the first recipe and raw potatoes in the recipe following.

ONION-FLAVORED ROESTI

2 lbs. potatoes, cooked, peeled, and chilled	2 tablespoons butter
	3 tablespoons shortening
⅓ cup chopped onion	1 teaspoon salt

1.   Shred peeled potatoes on a coarse shredder and set them aside.
2.   Partially cook onion in hot butter and shortening in a heavy skillet. Add salt and potatoes; fry about 20 minutes, turning gently and occasionally until golden in color.
3.   Form potatoes into a cake. Add about *1 teaspoon butter* to skillet and fry until golden brown. Turn out onto a plate.

4 SERVINGS

POTATOES ROESTI

1 large potato, pared	¼ teaspoon salt
⅓ cup butter or margarine	

1.   Cut potato lengthwise into ⅛-inch slices. Cut each slice into lengthwise strips ⅛ inch thick. Pat potato strips dry with absorbent paper.
2.   Melt butter in a 6-inch skillet. Pour off and reserve all but 1 tablespoon.
3.   Arrange strips crisscross-fashion to a 1½-inch depth in hot skillet. Pour remaining melted butter over strips. Sprinkle with salt.
4.   Heat rapidly until butter sizzles. Reduce heat to medium and cook about 15 minutes, or until underside is browned.
5.   Drain off butter and reserve. Using wide spatula, turn carefully, keeping potato cake intact. Return about one half of butter to skillet; reserve remaining butter to use if frying additional potatoes. Cook 8 to 10 minutes longer over medium heat or until potatoes are browned on second side (butter should be sizzling).
6.   Drain off butter and remove potatoes from skillet.

1 SERVING

POTATO CROQUETTES

4 medium-sized
  potatoes, washed,
  pared, cut up, cooked,
  and drained
1 egg, well beaten
3 tablespoons butter
  or margarine, melted
2 tablespoons finely
  chopped parsley
1 tablespoon shredded
  Parmesan cheese

2 teaspoons chopped
  onion
1 teaspoon salt
½ teaspoon mono-
  sodium glutamate
⅛ teaspoon pepper
1 cup fine dry crumbs
1 egg, slightly beaten
1 tablespoon milk
Fat for deep frying
  heated to 365°F

1. Using a potato masher, food mill, or ricer, thoroughly mash potatoes in a bowl or rice them into a bowl. Whip in 1 egg, melted butter, parsley, Parmesan cheese, and onion and a mixture of salt, monosodium glutamate, and pepper. Continue whipping until mixture is fluffy. Chill at least 1 hour.
2. Allowing ¼ cup mixture for each croquette, shape mixture into balls, cylinders, or cones. Roll croquettes in bread crumbs and dip into a mixture of egg and milk. Roll again in bread crumbs.
3. Fry croquettes only one layer at a time and avoid crowding. Turn when underside is lightly browned and brown other side. Remove with slotted spoon and drain on absorbent paper.

ABOUT 6 SERVINGS

SKILLET POTATOES AU GRATIN

4 large potatoes,
  pared and sliced
½ cup finely chopped
  onion
1 teaspoon salt
¼ teaspoon black
  pepper
1 cup water
½ cup cream

¼ cup butter or
  margarine, melted
½ cup shredded sharp
  Cheddar cheese
½ cup bread crumbs
2 tablespoons butter
  or margarine
3 slices bacon, diced
  and pan broiled

1. Put sliced potatoes, onion, salt, pepper, and water into a heavy skillet; cover and bring to boiling. Cook about 10 minutes, or until potatoes are just tender.
2. Add cream, melted butter, and cheese to skillet and mix lightly. Cook uncovered over low heat about 10 minutes, or until thoroughly heated.
3. Meanwhile, lightly brown bread crumbs in 2 tablespoons butter in a small skillet.
4. Transfer potatoes to warm serving dish and top with crumbs and bacon. 6 SERVINGS

DUTCH STEWED POTATOES

1 onion, sliced
1 tablespoon butter or
  other shortening
2 cups diced raw
  potatoes
1 teaspoon salt

Few grains pepper
1 teaspoon minced
  parsley
¾ cup boiling water
1 tablespoon water
2 teaspoons flour

1. Cook onion 5 minutes in hot butter in a large skillet. Add potatoes and a mixture of salt, pepper, and parsley. Pour in boiling water and cook covered until tender, about 20 minutes.
2. Blend water and flour. Stir into mixture in skillet, bring to boiling and cook 1 to 2 minutes.

4 SERVINGS

PAPRIKA POTATOES

¼ cup chopped onion
2 tablespoons butter
  or margarine
2 tablespoons flour
1 teaspoon paprika
½ teaspoon salt
2 cups beef broth

1 cup dairy sour cream
2 tablespoons tomato
  paste
6 medium-sized
  potatoes, cooked and
  cut in cubes

1. Lightly brown the onion in hot butter in a large heavy skillet. Blend in flour, paprika, and salt. Heat until bubbly. Stir in the broth. Bring to boiling; cook and stir 1 to 2 minutes.
2. Remove from heat. Stirring vigorously, add a mixture of sour cream and tomato paste in very small amounts. Gently mix potatoes into sauce and cook over low heat stirring 3 to 5 minutes, or until thoroughly heated (do not boil). ABOUT 6 SERVINGS

POTATO LOAF

3 tablespoons flour
1½ teaspoons salt
⅛ teaspoon black
  pepper
3 tablespoons butter
  or margarine
1 cup milk
1 tablespoon minced
  parsley

2 tablespoons chopped
  pimiento
2 tablespoons grated
  onion
5 cups cubed cooked
  potatoes
1 cup shredded sharp
  Cheddar cheese

1. Blend a mixture of the flour, salt, and pepper into hot butter in a saucepan. Heat until bubbly. Stir in the milk. Bring to boiling; cook 1 to 2 minutes. Add parsley, pimiento, and onion; mix well.

2. Pour over cubed potatoes and toss lightly to mix thoroughly. Turn into a 9x5x3-inch loaf pan lined with waxed paper. Cover and chill overnight.

3. Unmold potato loaf onto a buttered heat-resistant platter. Remove waxed paper.

4. Heat in a 350°F oven 30 minutes. Remove from oven; sprinkle cheese evenly over top of loaf. Return to oven and heat 15 minutes, or until cheese is melted.   6 SERVINGS

DUCHESS POTATOES

4 cups hot seasoned mashed potatoes	Melted butter or margarine
2 egg yolks (or 1 whole egg), beaten	

1. Combine hot mashed potatoes and egg yolks; beat thoroughly.

2. Spoon into small mounds or force through a pastry bag and large star tube onto a greased baking sheet. Brush potatoes with melted butter.

3. Bake at 450°F about 10 minutes, or until browned. With spatula carefully remove potatoes to serving plate.   ABOUT 8 SERVINGS

NOTE: If potatoes are for planked meals, spoon or pipe potatoes onto seasoned plank in a border. Brush with melted butter. Set on broiler rack 4 to 6 inches from source of heat until browned.

POTATO-BACON PUFF

2 tablespoons butter or margarine	2 cups hot instant mashed potatoes
4 egg yolks, well beaten	½ cup shredded sharp Cheddar cheese
¼ cup grated onion	12 bacon slices, fried until crisp, drained and crumbled
½ teaspoon dry mustard	
⅛ teaspoon white pepper	½ cup snipped parsley
3 drops Tabasco	4 egg whites

1. Using an electric mixer, beat butter, egg yolks, onion, dry mustard, pepper, and Tabasco into potatoes. Blend in cheese, bacon, and parsley.

2. Beat egg whites until stiff, not dry, peaks are formed. Gently fold into potato mixture until thoroughly blended. Turn into a 1-quart soufflé dish or straight-sided casserole.

3. Bake at 325°F about 50 minutes.
ABOUT 6 SERVINGS

SPRINGTIME POTATOES

1 can (16 oz.) whole potatoes	1½ tablespoons chopped green onion
⅓ cup chopped cucumber	1 teaspoon salt
2 tablespoons chopped green pepper	Few grains black pepper
2 tablespoons sliced radishes	½ cup dairy sour cream

1. Heat potatoes thoroughly; drain.

2. Mix remaining ingredients in a saucepan. Heat over low heat, stirring frequently (do not boil).

3. Pour sour cream mixture over hot potatoes; toss lightly to coat evenly.   ABOUT 4 SERVINGS

R Rutabagas

WHIPPED RUTABAGAS

Scrub *rutabagas*; pare and cut into pieces. Cook, covered, in boiling *salted water* until tender, about 25 minutes. Drain; season and beat in the desired amount of *butter or margarine* and *hot milk or cream*, whipping until fluffy. If desired, beat in an equal amount or less of *seasoned whipped potatoes*.

RUTABAGA SOUFFLÉ

1 cup mashed cooked rutabaga	1 tablespoon brown sugar
½ cup hot instant mashed potatoes (prepared according to pkg. directions)	⅛ to ¼ teaspoon ground mace
	3 eggs, separated
1 cup milk	2 tablespoons fine dry bread crumbs
2 tablespoons cornstarch	1 tablespoon butter or margarine, melted
½ teaspoon salt	2 tablespoons shredded Parmesan cheese
⅛ teaspoon pepper	

1. Beat the mashed rutabaga and potatoes together; set aside.

2. Blend the milk with cornstarch in a saucepan. Bring to boiling over low heat; stir and cook about 3 minutes. Stir in the salt, pepper, brown sugar, and mace.

3. Add the hot mixture gradually to slightly beaten egg yolks, stirring constantly. Beat into mashed vegetables, blending thoroughly.

4. Beat egg whites until stiff, not dry, peaks are formed. Fold into rutabaga mixture. Turn into a 1½-quart casserole.

5. Toss bread crumbs with butter and cheese. Spoon over top of soufflé.

6. Bake at 325°F about 50 minutes, or until a silver knife comes out clean when inserted halfway between center and edge of casserole. Serve immediately. ABOUT 6 SERVINGS

S Sauerkraut · Spinach · Squash · Sweet Potatoes and Yams

KRAUT WITH APPLES
(Kraut mit Äpfeln)

Serve this adaptation of a German cooked sauerkraut speciality as an accompaniment to pork.

4 cups drained sauerkraut	1 tablespoon light brown sugar
2 apples, thinly sliced	2 tablespoons butter or margarine
½ cup apple cider	

Mix all ingredients. Cover and simmer 5 minutes, or until apples are tender. Garnish with *apple wedges* and *parsley*. ABOUT 8 SERVINGS

SAUERKRAUT WITH CARAWAY

An old Pennsylvania Dutch recipe.

½ cup chopped onion	1 potato, pared and grated (about ¾ cup)
2 tablespoons butter or margarine	1 teaspoon caraway seed
2 cans (16 oz. each) sauerkraut	Boiling water (about 2 cups)

1. Add onion to hot butter in a heavy saucepan and cook until onion is golden. Stir in sauerkraut and cook 8 minutes.

2. Mix in potato and caraway seed. Pour in boiling water to cover.

3. Cook, uncovered, over low heat about 30 minutes. Cover and continue cooking 30 minutes. If desired, *1 or 2 tablespoons brown sugar* may be blended into mixture during the last 5 minutes.

6 TO 8 SERVINGS

SPICED SPINACH

1 lb. fresh spinach	½ teaspoon salt
¼ cup melted butter or margarine	⅛ teaspoon seasoned pepper
½ to 1 teaspoon ground coriander	1 clove garlic, minced
	1 teaspoon lemon juice
½ teaspoon monosodium glutamate	1 hard-cooked egg, peeled and chopped

1. Rinse and drain spinach; put into a heavy saucepan; place over medium heat and cook in moisture remaining on leaves about 5 minutes, stirring occasionally with a fork. (Spinach should be wilted but not soft.) Drain.

2. Mix remaining ingredients except the egg.

3. Turn spinach into a serving dish. Pour butter mixture over spinach, and toss lightly. Sprinkle with chopped egg. Serve immediately. 4 SERVINGS

CREAMED SPINACH WITH ALMONDS

1 tablespoon flour	1 cup cream
¾ teaspoon salt	2 tablespoons toasted almond halves
⅛ teaspoon ground nutmeg	1 pkg. (10 oz.) frozen spinach, cooked and drained
1 tablespoon butter or margarine	

1. Blend flour, salt, and nutmeg into hot butter in a saucepan. Heat until bubbly. Gradually add cream, stirring constantly. Bring to boiling; stir and cook 1 to 2 minutes.

2. Add almonds and spinach to sauce; mix lightly to blend. Serve garnished with *tomato wedges*. ABOUT 4 SERVINGS

SPINACH CHEESE TART

Cheese Pastry for 1-Crust Pie, *page 454*	½ cup minced onion
3 cups coarsely chopped cooked spinach (about 2¼ lbs. raw)	¼ cup heavy cream
	¼ cup butter or margarine, melted
½ cup shredded Parmesan cheese	½ cup cracker crumbs
	2 tablespoons butter or margarine, melted

1. Prepare pastry shell; partially bake only about 8 minutes, or until slightly browned. Remove pastry shell from oven to a wire rack and reduce oven temperature to 375°F.

2. Meanwhile, combine spinach, cheese, onion, cream, and ¼ cup butter; mix thoroughly. Turn

spinach mixture into partially baked pastry shell. Sprinkle with a mixture of crumbs and remaining butter.

3.   Return tart to oven and bake about 15 minutes, or until pastry and crumbs are golden brown and spinach mixture is heated through.

ONE 9-INCH TART

CREAMED SPINACH WITH BACON

Adapted from popular dish served at Lawry's, The Prime Rib restaurant in Beverly Hills, California.

4 slices bacon, finely chopped	⅛ teaspoon freshly ground black pepper
1 medium-sized onion, finely chopped	1 cup milk
1 clove garlic, minced	1 pkg. (10 oz.) frozen chopped spinach, cooked and drained
2 tablespoons flour	
1 teaspoon seasoned salt	

1.   Fry bacon, onion, and garlic together until onion is tender, about 10 minutes.
2.   Stir in a mixture of flour, seasoned salt, and pepper. Remove from heat and stir in the milk. Bring to boiling; stir and cook 1 to 2 minutes. Mix in spinach and heat thoroughly.   4 TO 6 SERVINGS

HI-STYLE SPINACH

2 pkgs. (10 oz. each) frozen chopped spinach	1 teaspoon grated onion
¼ cup water	½ clove garlic, minced
3 slices white bread, (crusts removed), cut in ½-in. cubes	½ teaspoon seasoned salt
⅓ cup butter or margarine	3 tablespoons butter or margarine, melted
1½ teaspoons Worcestershire sauce	1 cup coarse fresh bread crumbs
	⅓ cup shredded Parmesan cheese

1.   Heat spinach with water only until thawed. Remove from heat (do not drain) and mix in the bread cubes, ⅓ cup butter, Worcestershire sauce, onion, garlic, and seasoned salt. Bring to boiling, reduce heat and simmer 10 minutes.
2.   Turn mixture into an 8-inch square pan.
3.   Toss 3 tablespoons butter into crumbs and cheese; sprinkle over top.
4.   Heat in a 400°F oven 10 to 12 minutes, or until crumbs are golden brown.   6 TO 8 SERVINGS

SPINACH TART
(La Tourte de Grand Mère)

This recipe for Grandmother's Tart is from the famous Lasserre Restaurant in Paris, France.

4 pkgs. (10 oz. each) frozen chopped spinach	2 tablespoons butter
1½ cups sifted flour	6 thin slices prosciutto, cut in squares
½ teaspoon salt	Mornay Sauce, *page 343*
½ cup lard	¾ cup shredded Parmesan cheese
2½ tablespoons water	

1.   Cook spinach according to package directions. Drain; press out excess moisture. Set aside.
2.   Sift flour and salt together. Cut in lard with pastry blender until pieces are the size of small peas. Gradually sprinkle water over mixture, mixing lightly with fork. Form into a ball. Roll out on floured surface and fit into a 10x1½-inch pie plate.
3.   Heat the butter in a skillet. Add prosciutto and heat 1 to 2 minutes.
4.   Evenly spread one half of the spinach in pastry shell. Top with prosciutto and butter. Spoon remaining spinach over prosciutto. Spread Mornay Sauce over spinach. Sprinkle with cheese.
5.   Bake at 350°F about 35 to 40 minutes, or until top is golden brown. Serve immediately.   8 SERVINGS

CORN-FILLED ACORN SQUASH

3 small acorn squash, washed, halved, and seedy centers removed	¼ teaspoon black pepper
½ cup chopped green pepper	1 teaspoon basil, crushed
1 clove garlic, minced	1 cup soft fine bread crumbs
3 tablespoons butter or margarine	3 tablespoons butter or margarine, melted
2 cups canned whole kernel corn, drained	3 tablespoons sesame seed, toasted
¼ teaspoon salt	3 tablespoons shredded Parmesan cheese
½ teaspoon monosodium glutamate	2 tablespoons snipped parsley

1.   Place squash halves, cut side down, in a shallow baking pan; pour in boiling water to a depth of ¼ inch. Bake at 400°F about 35 minutes, or until squash is almost tender.
2.   Meanwhile, cook green pepper and garlic in 3 tablespoons hot butter in a skillet about 5 minutes,

stirring occasionally. Remove from heat. Add corn and a mixture of salt, monosodium glutamate, pepper, and basil. Toss to mix; set aside.

3. Toss bread crumbs with remaining ingredients; set aside.

4. When squash is almost tender, remove from oven. Turn right side up. Butter each cavity generously and season with *salt* and *pepper*. Spoon the corn mixture into cavities. Sprinkle crumbs evenly over top.

5. Return to oven and continue baking until squash is tender and crumbs are browned, about 20 minutes.   6 SERVINGS

BAKED ACORN SQUASH: Follow step 1 of Corn-Filled Acorn Squash. Turn halves cavity side up and sprinkle with *salt*, *pepper*, and *brown sugar*; dot generously with *butter* or *margarine*. Return to oven and bake until tender.

ACORN SQUASH STUFFED WITH HAM AND APPLE

3 medium-sized acorn squash, washed, halved, and seedy centers removed	1 teaspoon dry mustard
	¼ teaspoon pepper
	2 tablespoons butter, melted
1 cup diced tart cooking apples	2 teaspoons chopped onion
2 cups diced ham	

1. Bake squash, following step 1 of *Corn-Filled Acorn Squash*, *page 332*. Invert squash halves and sprinkle lightly with *salt*.

2. Combine remaining ingredients and spoon into squash cavities.

3. Return to oven and bake 20 minutes, or until apples are tender.   6 SERVINGS

DILLED BUTTERNUT SQUASH

1 butternut squash (about 1½ lbs.), washed, halved, and seedy center removed	½ teaspoon dill weed
	¼ teaspoon salt
	Few grains black pepper
2 tablespoons butter or margarine	

1. Bake squash, following step 1 of *Corn-Filled Acorn Squash, page 332.*

2. Scoop out pulp, leaving one shell-half intact; discard extra shell.

3. Mash pulp and blend in remaining ingredients. Immediately spoon hot mixture into shell.

4. Wrap loosely in aluminum foil and heat in 400°F oven 5 to 10 minutes, or until very hot.
ABOUT 4 SERVINGS

BUTTER-PECAN SQUASH CASSEROLE

4 lbs. (about 4 cups cooked) acorn or butternut squash, halved and seed centers removed	1 tablespoon grated onion
	½ to 1 teaspoon crushed rosemary
	¼ to ½ teaspoon ground coriander
⅓ cup butter or margarine	1 teaspoon salt
2 tablespoons cream	

1. Bake squash, following step 1 of *Corn-Filled Acorn Squash*, page 332.

2. Scoop out pulp into a mixing bowl and beat with an electric mixer until smooth. Beat in the butter, cream, onion, rosemary, coriander, and salt. Turn into a buttered 1½-quart shallow baking dish. Sprinkle chopped *salted pecans* around edge and drizzle lightly with *melted butter*.

3. Heat in a 400°F oven about 20 minutes.
ABOUT 12 SERVINGS

SUMMER SQUASH WITH DILL

2 lbs. (about 4 small) summer squash (yellow straight-neck), washed	½ teaspoon salt
	1 cup dairy sour cream
	1 tablespoon lemon juice
½ cup boiling water	2 teaspoons sugar
2 teaspoons finely chopped fresh dill	½ teaspoon paprika

1. Trim ends from squash and cut squash into thin, crosswise slices. Put into a large saucepan with water, dill, and salt. Cover and simmer 15 minutes, or until just tender; drain.

2. Meanwhile, thoroughly heat remaining ingredients in the top of a double boiler over boiling water, stirring constantly.

3. Gently toss cooked squash with sauce.
ABOUT 6 SERVINGS

SUMMER SQUASH WITH BACON: Follow recipe for Summer Squash with Dill. Prepare squash; omit cooking. Panbroil *3 slices bacon*, diced, in a large skillet until pieces are crisp and brown; remove bacon and set aside. Return 3 tablespoons hot bacon fat to skillet; add squash, *¼ cup finely chopped* onion, *1 teaspoon salt*, and *a few grains black pepper*. Cover and cook over medium heat 12 minutes, or until squash is just tender. Mix in bacon.

STUFFED PATTYPAN SQUASH

6 white pattypan squash (about 4 lbs.)	¼ teaspoon salt
½ teaspoon salt	⅛ teaspoon pepper
1 teaspoon monosodium glutamate	½ cup fine dry bread crumbs
¼ cup butter or margarine	2 tablespoons butter or margarine, melted
1 tablespoon cream	1 tablespoon minced parsley
½ teaspoon grated onion	1 tablespoon shredded Parmesan cheese

1. Put squash into a heavy saucepot having a tight-fitting cover. Add about *½ cup boiling water*. Sprinkle with ½ teaspoon salt and monosodium glutamate. Cover and steam until just tender, about 35 minutes. Drain.
2. Cut a thin slice from top of each squash. Using a spoon, carefully scoop out squash into a bowl, leaving shells intact. Reserve shells.
3. Whip squash with ¼ cup butter, cream, onion, ¼ teaspoon salt, and pepper. Pile lightly into shells.
4. Toss bread crumbs, melted butter, parsley, and Parmesan cheese in a bowl; spoon onto filling in shells. Place squash in a baking pan.
5. Set in a 375°F oven until squash is thoroughly heated and topping is lightly browned.   6 SERVINGS

ELEGANT APRICOT-SWEET POTATOES

6 medium-sized (about 2 lbs.) sweet potatoes, cooked and peeled	1 cup lightly packed dark brown sugar
½ lb. dried apricots, cooked and drained (reserve ¼ cup liquid)	3 tablespoons butter or margarine, melted
	2 teaspoons orange juice
	1 teaspoon grated orange peel

1. Cut potatoes lengthwise into ½-inch slices. Arrange a layer of half the potatoes in a lightly greased 1-quart shallow baking dish. Cover with a layer of half the apricots. Sprinkle with half the brown sugar. Repeat layering.
2. Pour a mixture of butter, orange juice and peel, and reserved apricot liquid over all.

3. Heat in a 375°F oven 40 minutes, basting twice with liquid in bottom of dish. Remove dish from oven; arrange *¼ cup pecan halves* on top. Return to oven and heat 5 minutes.   6 TO 8 SERVINGS

SPICY WHIPPED SWEET POTATOES

6 medium-sized (about 2 lbs.) sweet potatoes, cooked, peeled, and mashed	½ teaspoon ground nutmeg
¼ cup butter or margarine	¼ teaspoon ground cinnamon
⅓ to ½ cup hot milk	¼ teaspoon ground ginger
¼ cup firmly packed light brown sugar	½ teaspoon salt
	⅛ teaspoon pepper

Whip potatoes with remaining ingredients until fluffy.   ABOUT 6 SERVINGS

SWEET POTATO PUDDING
Executive Chef Monsieur Robert Machax of the Executive House's Aruba Caribbean Hotel-Casino, Netherlands Antilles, adapted this recipe for American homemaker portions.

2 eggs	1 cup rich milk
2 cups pared and grated raw sweet potatoes	¼ cup melted butter
1 cup sugar	½ teaspoon grated lemon peel
½ teaspoon ground cinnamon	2 teaspoons lemon juice

1. Beat eggs in a bowl until light. Mix in the potatoes. Beat in sugar, cinnamon, and a *dash ground nutmeg*. Stir in remaining ingredients in order. Turn into a buttered 1½-quart baking dish.
2. Bake at 350°F about 30 minutes; stir pudding with a spoon, blending sides with center. Continue to bake 15 minutes.   6 TO 8 SERVINGS

YAM 'N' COCONUT CASSEROLE

12 medium-sized (about 4½ lbs.) yams, cooked and peeled	1 pkg. (7 oz.) flaked coconut
3 tablespoons brown sugar	2 cups diced tart apples
¾ cup cream	⅓ cup butter or margarine, melted

1. Cut yams into pieces; put into a large bowl.

2. With an electric mixer, beat in brown sugar, cream, and half of coconut. Beat until smooth. Stir in diced apples.

3. Turn mixture into a buttered 2½-quart baking dish. Toss remaining coconut with melted butter. Sprinkle evenly over top of yam mixture.

4. Bake at 325°F about 30 minutes, or until coconut is lightly browned. ABOUT 16 SERVINGS

CHERRY-GLAZED YAMS

Peel whole *cooked yams* and put into a shallow baking dish; spoon *cherry preserves* over them and heat in a 350°F oven 10 to 15 minutes.

RASPBERRY-CROWNED YAMS

8 medium-sized yams, cooked and peeled
½ cup butter or margarine, softened
½ cup lightly packed brown sugar
1 pkg. (10 oz.) frozen raspberries, thawed (do not drain)

1. Cut yams lengthwise into halves. Place in a shallow baking pan.

2. Cream butter with brown sugar.

3. Sprinkle cut surfaces of yams with *salt*, then spread with creamed mixture. Top each half with a spoonful of raspberries and syrup.

4. Heat in a 350°F oven about 20 minutes.
8 SERVINGS

YAMS AND BROCCOLI WITH PROVOLONE SAUCE

1 can (8 oz.) small onions
¼ teaspoon seasoned salt
1 pkg. (10 oz.) frozen broccoli spears
½ cup well-seasoned chicken broth
2 tablespoons butter or margarine, browned
⅓ cup maple-blended syrup, heated
4 medium-sized yams, cooked, peeled, and quartered
Provolone Sauce, *page 343*

1. Heat onions in their liquid with the seasoned salt; drain and keep warm.

2. Cook broccoli in the broth until just tender.

3. Drain broccoli and drizzle with browned butter. Pour the syrup over the hot yams. Arrange broccoli, yams, and onions in a heated 2-quart shallow baking dish.

4. Pour all but several tablespoonfuls of the hot Provolone Sauce over vegetables. Fold *2 or 3 tablespoons whipped cream* into remaining sauce and spoon over top. Set under broiler about 4 inches from source of heat until browned on top.
ABOUT 6 SERVINGS

T Tomatoes · Turnips

FRIED TOMATOES

4 firm ripe or green tomatoes
½ cup cornmeal
1 teaspoon salt
⅛ teaspoon pepper
¼ cup butter or margarine

1. Cut out stem ends of tomatoes and slice ½ inch thick.

2. Mix cornmeal, salt, and pepper in a shallow dish. Coat both sides of tomato slices with the mixture.

3. Heat butter in a skillet. Add as many tomato slices at one time as will lie flat in skillet. Lightly brown both sides, turning once; cook only until tender. Add butter as needed. ABOUT 4 SERVINGS

CREAMED TOMATOES: Follow recipe for Fried Tomatoes. Add ½ *teaspoon sugar* to cornmeal mixture. When tomatoes are lightly browned, stir to break up; cook 5 minutes. Just before serving, stir in *2 tablespoons cream.*

BAKED TOMATO HALVES WITH DANISH BLUE CHEESE

4 medium-sized firm ripe tomatoes, cut in halves
¼ teaspoon salt
⅛ teaspoon sugar
¼ teaspoon pepper
2 slices pumpernickel, crumbled
4 teaspoons melted butter
2 oz. Danish blue cheese, crumbled

1. Put the tomato halves, cut side up, in a buttered shallow baking dish. Sprinkle with a mixture of salt, sugar, and pepper.

2. Toss bread crumbs with melted butter. Mix in cheese. Spoon an equal amount onto each tomato half.

3. Bake at 350°F 15 minutes. Garnish with *watercress or parsley*.   8 TOMATO HALVES

BAKED STUFFED TOMATOES
A recipe from Mrs. Richard Nixon.

4 large or 6 medium-sized firm ripe tomatoes	¼ lb. fresh mushrooms, chopped
3 oz. (4 to 5 slices) bacon, cut in small pieces	1 tablespoon snipped chives
6 tablespoons olive oil	1 tablespoon snipped parsley
¾ cup chopped onion	1 egg, beaten
	½ teaspoon salt
	⅛ teaspoon pepper

1. Cut away stem ends of tomatoes. Scoop out ¾ of each tomato, leaving about a ¾-inch wall (if using a paring knife to cut away interior, be careful not to pierce skin).
2. Partially fry the bacon in a large skillet. Add 4 tablespoons of the olive oil; heat and mix in onion, mushrooms, chives, and parsley. Sauté for 10 minutes, stirring the mixture occasionally.
3. Remove skillet from heat. Quickly mix in the beaten egg, salt, and pepper. Immediately fill tomatoes and put in oiled baking dish. Top with *bread crumbs* and drizzle with remaining oil.
4. Bake at 400°F about 40 minutes.

4 TO 6 SERVINGS

CHEESE-RICE FILLED TOMATOES

6 large firm ripe tomatoes	½ lb. process Swiss cheese, shredded
½ cup chopped onion	½ cup drained sliced mushrooms (4-oz. can)
¼ cup chopped celery	
2 tablespoons butter or margarine	1 teaspoon salt
⅓ cup packaged precooked rice, cooked	⅛ teaspoon pepper
	¼ teaspoon marjoram

1. Cut ¼ inch slices from tops of tomatoes. Set aside. Scoop out and drain pulp; reserve. Invert tomatoes to drain.
2. Cook onion and celery in hot butter in a skillet until onion is tender. Add tomato pulp, rice, and remaining ingredients; mix well.
3. Put tomatoes into a greased baking dish. Spoon mixture into tomatoes. Replace tomato tops.
4. Bake at 350°F 15 minutes, or until thoroughly heated.   6 SERVINGS

STUFFED TOMATOES UNIQUE

4 medium-sized firm ripe tomatoes	3 tablespoons finely chopped parsley
4 slices bacon, diced and fried until crisp	1¼ cups coarsely crushed potato chips
1 can (8¾ oz.) crushed pineapple, well drained	½ teaspoon grated onion
	½ teaspoon salt
	⅛ teaspoon pepper

1. Cut a slice from stem end of each tomato; scoop out centers and cut pulp into small pieces.
2. Blend half of the bacon (reserve remaining for garnish), tomato pulp, and remaining ingredients. Put tomato shells into a greased shallow baking dish. Spoon filling into tomatoes.
3. Bake at 400°F 20 to 25 minutes. Garnish tops with reserved bacon.   4 SERVINGS

BAKED TOMATOES, GENOA STYLE
(Pomodori Genovese)

4 firm ripe tomatoes, cut in halves and seeded	1½ teaspoons marjoram, crushed
¼ cup olive oil	¼ cup finely snipped parsley
2 cloves garlic, minced	½ cup shredded Parmesan cheese
1½ teaspoons salt	
½ teaspoon pepper	

1. Put tomato halves, cut side up, in a shallow baking dish. Sprinkle lightly with *sugar*.
2. Mix the olive oil, garlic, salt, pepper, and marjoram. Spoon an equal amount onto each tomato half. Sprinkle with parsley and cheese.
3. Bake at 350°F about 20 minutes, or until lightly browned.   4 SERVINGS

SCALLOPED TOMATOES

1 cup chopped onion	1 teaspoon seasoned salt
1 can (29 oz.) tomatoes, drained and cut in pieces	1 cup dairy sour cream
	3 slices crisp toast, cut in ¼-to½-in. cubes
⅓ cup cheese cracker crumbs	
1 tablespoon parsley flakes	2 tablespoons butter
	Parsley flakes
1½ teaspoons sugar	

1. Mix the onion, tomatoes, crumbs, parsley

flakes, sugar, and salt in a greased 1¼-quart shallow baking dish. Spoon sour cream evenly over top.
2.   Add toast cubes to hot butter in a skillet and toss until all sides are coated.
3.   Spoon toast cubes over sour cream; sprinkle with parsley flakes.
4.   Heat thoroughly in a 325°F oven about 20 minutes. Serve in sauce dishes.   ABOUT 6 SERVINGS

TOMATO PUDDING

This is a version of a favorite recipe served at Hotel Dilworth, Boyne City, Michigan.

1 can (10 oz.) tomato purée	6 slices bread, cut in ½-in. cubes
¾ cup lightly packed brown sugar	½ cup melted butter or margarine
¼ teaspoon salt	

1.   Mix tomato purée, brown sugar, salt, and ¾ *cup boiling water* together in a saucepan; bring to boiling and boil 5 minutes.
2.   Arrange bread cubes in a 1½-quart baking dish; pour butter over them and toss lightly. Pour hot tomato sauce over bread cubes.
3.   Bake at 350°F 30 minutes. Garnish with overlapping slices of *tomatoes* sprinkled with *minced parsley*. Serve immediately.   6 TO 8 SERVINGS

TURNIP CUSTARD

2 lbs. turnips, pared, cooked, and mashed	⅔ cup undiluted evaporated milk
1 egg, well beaten	1 teaspoon salt
¼ cup finely crushed soda crackers	1 cup shredded sharp Cheddar cheese

1.   Blend mashed turnips with egg, crumbs, evaporated milk, salt, and a *few grains pepper*. Turn mixture into a buttered 1¼-quart baking dish.
2.   Set dish in a shallow pan in a 350°F oven. Pour boiling water into pan to a depth of 1 inch. Bake about 15 minutes.
3.   Remove from oven; sprinkle cheese over top. Bake 5 minutes, or until custard is "set."
ABOUT 6 SERVINGS

Z Zucchini

SEASONED ZUCCHINI

Wash desired amount of *zucchini*, trim off ends, and cut into thin slices. Heat a small amount of *butter*, *margarine*, *or olive oil* in a skillet. Add zucchini slices and cook quickly until tender. Season as desired.

ZUCCHINI PROVENÇALE

8 to 10 small (2½ lbs.) zucchini	2 cans (6 oz. each) tomato paste
⅔ cup coarsely chopped onion	1 clove garlic, minced
¼ lb. fresh mushrooms, sliced lengthwise	1 teaspoon salt
3 tablespoons olive oil	½ teaspoon monosodium glutamate
⅔ cup shredded Parmesan cheese	⅛ teaspoon pepper

1.   Wash, trim off ends, and cut zucchini crosswise into ⅛-inch slices.
2.   In a covered saucepan, cook zucchini, onion, and mushrooms in hot oil 10 to 15 minutes, or until zucchini is just tender; stir occasionally.
3.   Remove from heat and, with a fork, mix in about half of the cheese. Blend in a mixture of the tomato paste and remaining ingredients. Turn into a 2-quart casserole and sprinkle with remaining cheese.
4.   Heat in a 350°F oven 20 to 30 minutes, or until very hot.   8 SERVINGS

ZUCCHINI IN SALSA VERDE

¼ cup olive oil	2 anchovy fillets, finely chopped
2 tablespoons wine vinegar	Few grains pepper
2 tablespoons finely snipped parsley	4 zucchini, washed and thinly sliced
1 clove garlic, minced	Fat for deep frying heated to 365°F

1.   Combine oil, vinegar, parsley, garlic, anchovies, and pepper; set aside.
2.   Coat zucchini slices lightly with *flour*. Fry in hot fat, turning frequently, until lightly browned, 2 to 3 minutes. Remove with slotted spoon and drain on absorbent paper. Sprinkle lightly with *salt*.

3. Put zucchini into a bowl; pour sauce over it and toss lightly to coat well. Cover and set aside at least 1 hour before serving. 4 SERVINGS

ZUCCHINI IN SOUR CREAM
Zucchini takes on savory sophistication in this rich crouton-nut topped casserole dish.

2 tablespoons butter or margarine	1 cup dairy sour cream
6 medium-sized zucchini, thinly sliced (about 1½ lbs.)	2 tablespoons butter or margarine
1 large green pepper, cut in fine strips	1 cup small bread cubes
½ teaspoon salt	½ cup chopped blanched almonds
¼ teaspoon celery seed	Garlic salt
1 tablespoon grated onion	Paprika

1. Heat 2 tablespoons butter in a 1½-quart top-of-the-range casserole. Mix in zucchini, green pepper, salt, celery seed, and onion. Cover and simmer 5 minutes, or until vegetables are almost tender. Add sour cream gradually, blending well; heat thoroughly (do not boil).
2. Meanwhile, heat 2 tablespoons butter in a skillet over low heat. Add bread cubes and almonds; sprinkle with garlic salt. Stir frequently to brown all sides. Spoon bread cubes and nuts around edge of mixture in casserole. Sprinkle top with paprika. 6 TO 8 SERVINGS

STUFFED ZUCCHINI

4 zucchini (each about 4½ in. long), scrubbed and cut in halves lengthwise	2 tablespoons minced parsley
½ cup chopped onion	½ teaspoon lemon juice
1 tablespoon olive oil	½ teaspoon salt
3 tablespoons fine dry bread crumbs	Few grains pepper
2 cloves garlic, minced	1 egg yolk, beaten
	Fat for deep frying heated to 365°F

1. Hollow centers of zucchini by scooping out some of pulp; reserve. Drop shells into boiling *salted water;* cook until just tender, about 4 minutes. Drain. Chop reserved pulp; set aside.
2. Cook onion about 5 minutes in hot oil in a skillet. Remove from heat.

3. Add crumbs, garlic, parsley, lemon juice, salt, pepper, and egg yolk to onion along with chopped pulp; blend thoroughly.
4. Fill zucchini shells with mixture. Dip in a mixture of *1 egg yolk* beaten with *1 tablespoon olive oil.* Coat evenly with *fine dry bread crumbs.*
5. Fry zucchini in heated fat about 1 minute, or until lightly browned. Fry only as many stuffed shells at one time as will float uncrowded one layer deep in fat. Remove with slotted spoon and drain on absorbent paper. 8 SERVINGS

DEEP-FRIED ZUCCHINI

1¼ cups all-purpose flour	1 tablespoon butter or margarine, melted
1 teaspoon salt	6 medium-sized (about 2 lbs.) zucchini, cut in halves crosswise and in ⅜-in. sticks lengthwise
½ teaspoon monosodium glutamate	
¼ teaspoon pepper	
2 eggs, well beaten	
¾ cup milk	Fat for deep frying heated to 365°F
1 teaspoon Worcestershire sauce	

1. Blend the flour, salt, monosodium glutamate, and pepper in a bowl. Add a mixture of eggs, milk, Worcestershire sauce, and butter; beat just until smooth.
2. Dip zucchini sticks into batter, using a fork or slotted spoon to coat evenly. Allow any excess coating to drip off and then lower zucchini into hot fat.
3. Fry one layer at a time 2 to 3 minutes, or until golden brown, turning several times. Lift from fat with slotted spoon and drain a few seconds before removing to absorbent paper.
4. Sprinkle with *salt* and serve hot. 6 SERVINGS

ZUCCHINI ROMANO

8 small zucchini (about 1½ lbs.)	Few grains pepper
1 egg, fork beaten	2 tablespoons melted butter or margarine
⅓ cup shredded mozzarella cheese	½ lb. ground ham or veal
3 tablespoons Italian salad dressing	½ cup Salsa Italiana, *page 346*

1. Wash zucchini and trim ends. Slice off a narrow lengthwise strip. Using an apple corer remove seedy center to make a hollow about ¾ inch deep in

each zucchini. Cover with boiling water, simmer about 5 minutes and drain well.

2. Combine egg, cheese, salad dressing, pepper, and butter in a bowl. Lightly mix in meat. (If using veal, add ¼ teaspoon salt.) Fill zucchini with mixture using about 3 tablespoons in each hollow.

3. Arrange zucchini, stuffed side up, in a single layer in an oiled 1½-quart shallow baking dish; spread tops with Salsa Italiana. (Or omit Salsa Italiana and brush tops with olive or cooking oil.)

4. Bake at 375°F about 15 minutes, or until meat is cooked. Serve hot.   8 SERVINGS

MIXED-VEGETABLE DISHES

GARDEN VEGETABLE-RICE MEDLEY

1 cup diced celery	1 tablespoon lemon juice
⅓ cup coarsely chopped onion	1 teaspoon salt
1 clove garlic, minced	1 teaspoon mono-sodium glutamate
3 tablespoons butter or margarine	⅛ teaspoon seasoned pepper
2 cups diced pared cucumber	¼ teaspoon crushed thyme
1 tomato, peeled and cut up	¼ to ½ teaspoon ground ginger
1 medium-sized green pepper, cut in strips	1 tablespoon cornstarch
¼ cup snipped parsley	2 tablespoons water
1 can (10½ oz.) condensed beef broth diluted with ¾ cup boiling water	1⅓ cups packaged precooked rice

1. Cook the celery, onion, and garlic in hot butter in a large decorative skillet until celery is lightly browned. Add the cucumber, tomato, green pepper, parsley, ¾ cup of the hot broth, lemon juice, and a mixture of the salt, monosodium glutamate, seasoned pepper, thyme, and ginger. Stir lightly until the mixture is blended.

2. Combine cornstarch and water; stir into vegetable mixture and bring rapidly to boiling, stirring gently. Make a well in center of vegetables and add the rice. Pour the remaining hot broth over rice, moistening evenly. Cover skillet tightly and cook mixture over medium heat until rice is tender, about 5 minutes.

3. Garnish rice mound with *parsley* and serve the medley from skillet.   ABOUT 8 SERVINGS

BUBBLE AND SQUEAK
This dish of English origin is said to have taken its name from the sounds emitting from saucepot or skillet while the meat and vegetables are cooking or frying. Brussels sprouts, rather than the cabbage usually called for in traditional recipes, have been substituted in this version.

Cooked Corned Beef Brisket, *page 175*	2 lbs. fresh Brussels sprouts, or 4 pkgs. (10 oz. each) frozen Brussels sprouts
6 medium-sized potatoes, pared	
6 small whole white onions, peeled	English Mustard Sauce, *page 345*
1 lb. small whole carrots, pared	

1. Bring the corned beef cooking liquid to boiling; add potatoes and onions and return to boiling. Cook 20 minutes. Add carrots and Brussels sprouts and return to boiling. Cook, partially covered, until tender, 10 to 15 minutes.

2. Serve corned beef with the vegetables and English Mustard Sauce.   6 SERVINGS

SPANISH VEGETABLE MACÉDOINE
In France, vegetables macédoine usually refers to a medley of compatibly-flavored vegetables served hot with butter or a sauce or cold with mayonnaise. A Spanish touch has been added here.

2 medium-sized artichokes	Few grains pepper
2 medium-sized onions, chopped	½ teaspoon ground marjoram
2 large cloves garlic	¼ teaspoon celery salt
¼ cup olive oil	4 medium-sized tomatoes, coarsely chopped
1 cup chicken broth	
1 small zucchini, sliced	1 cup pimiento-stuffed olives
1 teaspoon salt	

1. Wash artichokes; trim 1 inch from tops and cut off stems about 1 inch from base; remove outside lower leaves. Trim and discard tips of remaining

leaves. Cut artichokes lengthwise into eighths and discard chokes.

2.   Cook onion and garlic in hot olive oil in a large skillet until onion is soft and lightly browned. Blend in the artichokes and broth. Cover and cook 15 minutes.

3.   Add zucchini and a mixture of salt, pepper, marjoram, and celery salt; cook covered 5 to 10 minutes, or until vegetables are almost tender. Blend in tomatoes and olives; cook 5 minutes. Remove garlic before serving.   4 TO 6 SERVINGS

VEGETABLE GOULASH

1½ cups fresh corn kernels (cut from about 3 ears)	1 can (8 oz.) tomato sauce
1 cup chopped onion	1 teaspoon mono-sodium glutamate
1 cup chopped celery	1 teaspoon brown sugar
½ cup chopped green pepper	½ to ¾ teaspoon chili powder
1 can (15 oz.) kidney beans, undrained	⅛ teaspoon black pepper

1.   Combine vegetables, tomato sauce, and remaining ingredients in a large saucepan; blend.
2.   Cover and bring to boiling; reduce heat and simmer 1 hour.
3.   Turn into a serving dish and serve hot.

ABOUT 6 SERVINGS

VEGETABLE TRIO IN CASSEROLE

½ lb. small white onions, peeled	½ teaspoon mono-sodium glutamate
1 lb. small new potatoes, pared and quartered	½ cup butter or margarine, melted
2 cups very thin carrot strips	1 teaspoon lemon juice
⅛ teaspoon salt	1 teaspoon sugar
⅛ teaspoon pepper	2 cloves garlic, minced
	½ cup chopped parsley

1.   Insert a whole clove into each onion. Combine vegetables in a 1½-quart shallow casserole.
2.   Sprinkle with the salt, pepper, and monosodium glutamate. Pour a mixture of the melted butter, lemon juice, sugar, and garlic over vegetables. Tightly cover casserole.
3.   Bake at 325°F about 1 hour. Mix in parsley; continue baking, uncovered, until vegetables are tender.   6 SERVINGS

GADO GADO

½ lb. fresh green beans	1 tablespoon cider vinegar
3 medium-sized carrots	2 teaspoons brown sugar
½ small head cauli-flower	1 teaspoon salt
1 cup peanuts, grated or finely chopped (use an electric blender, if desired)	Few grains red pepper

1.   Cut beans into 2-inch pieces and carrots into 2x½-inch strips. Separate cauliflower into florets. Cook vegetables separately in boiling salted water until tender. Drain; reserve about ¼ cup each of the carrot and bean liquid.
2.   Immediately blend the peanuts, vinegar, brown sugar, salt, red pepper, and enough vegetable liquid to make a thick sauce.
3.   Arrange vegetables on heated platter; spoon sauce over them. Garnish with sliced hard-cooked eggs. Sprinkle with paprika, if desired.

4 TO 6 SERVINGS

MIXED-VEGETABLE CASSEROLE

1 pkg. (10 oz.) frozen mixed vegetables	1 cup chicken broth
1 pkg. (10 oz.) frozen cauliflower	1 teaspoon prepared mustard
1 pkg. (10 oz.) frozen green peas	1 tablespoon prepared horseradish
¼ cup flour	4 drops Tabasco
¼ cup butter or margarine	1½ cups soft bread crumbs
½ cup milk	1 cup shredded sharp Cheddar cheese
½ cup cream	

1.   Cook each vegetable according to directions on package.
2.   Meanwhile, stir flour into hot butter in a saucepan and cook until bubbly. Stir in the milk, cream, and broth and bring to boiling; stir and cook 1 to 2 minutes. Blend in mustard, horseradish, and Tabasco.
3.   Drain cooked vegetables and mix lightly in a 1½-quart shallow casserole; pour sauce over them. Toss crumbs with cheese and sprinkle evenly over top.
4.   Heat in a 400°F oven 15 to 20 minutes, or until crumbs are golden brown and cheese is melted.

6 TO 8 SERVINGS

Chapter 11
SAUCES & GRAVIES

Sauces enhance the appearance and flavor of food and add to its nutritive value. They should offer pleasing contrasts in color, flavor, and consistency to the dishes they accompany. Usually they should be thin enough to flow, but thick enough not to saturate food.

Basic sauces for meat, poultry, fish, and vegetables are few in number, but their variations are almost limitless. Wherever spices, herbs, seasonings, and a few basic ingredients are available, the art of sauce making is open to amateur and professional alike.

White Sauce—Foremost among basic sauces is white sauce. This is the indispensable base for innumerable sauces and is frequently used in other food preparation as well—in cream soups, casserole dishes, croquettes, and soufflés. Four main groups are made from the basic sauce by varying the type of liquid used or by browning the flour.

White sauce, as the name implies, is made with milk or cream. Spices, seasonings, and condiments add their piquant flavor to many variations of white sauce. A second group is created by the substitution of meat or vegetable stock or water for milk, an example being *gravy*. To a third group belong the brown sauces which result when the flour used for thickening white sauce is browned before adding the liquid. Some gravies are also included in this group. A fourth group results from the substitution of tomato juice or purée for milk.

A white sauce provides the base for a group of French sauces often used to enhance meat, poultry, fish, or vegetable dishes. Included are:

Béchamel sauce—a white sauce with chicken stock and cream used for the liquid and often seasoned with onion.

Bercy sauce—a white sauce using fish stock for the liquid and cooking chopped shallots in the butter before adding the flour. There are variations of this sauce, some of which use wine for the liquid.

Mornay sauce—a white sauce to which cheese (Parmesan or Gruyère) and egg yolks have been added and using cream and chicken or veal stock for the liquid.

Velouté sauce—a white sauce using chicken or veal stock for the liquid and sometimes seasoned with ground nutmeg. Velouté sauce, when served with fish, may call for fish stock instead of chicken or veal.

One may find a variety of interpretations of these sauces in cookbooks and as they are prepared by famous chefs.

Hollandaise Sauce—Another well-known sauce used as a base for others. It is a rich sauce made with egg yolks, seasonings, lemon juice, and butter.

Béarnaise sauce—a Hollandaise based sauce with herbs such as tarragon, chervil, and parsley added to it. Some versions of Béarnaise sauce have wine as an ingredient.

BROWN ROUX

Used for thickening brown sauces, this paste may be made in advance and stored in refrigerator until needed.

Melt *1 cup butter or other fat* in a heavy skillet; blend in *1 cup all-purpose flour* to form a smooth paste. Stir and cook over low heat until mixture is light brown and roux is thoroughly cooked.

ABOUT 1 CUP

SAUCES

MEDIUM WHITE SAUCE
(Cream Sauce)

2 tablespoons butter or margarine	⅛ teaspoon pepper
2 tablespoons flour	1 cup milk (use light cream for richer sauce)
½ teaspoon salt	

1. Heat butter in a saucepan. Blend in flour, salt, and pepper; heat and stir until bubbly.
2. Gradually add the milk, stirring until smooth. Bring to boiling; cook and stir 1 to 2 minutes longer. ABOUT 1 CUP

THICK WHITE SAUCE: Follow recipe for Medium White Sauce. Use *3 to 4 tablespoons flour* and *3 to 4 tablespoons butter.* Use in preparation of soufflés and croquettes.

THIN WHITE SAUCE: Follow recipe for Medium White Sauce. Use *1 tablespoon flour* and *1 tablespoon butter.* Use as a base for cream soups.

BÉCHAMEL SAUCE
This sauce is named for its originator, Louis de Béchamel, Lord Steward of the Household in the Court of King Louis XIV.
Follow recipe for Medium White Sauce. Substitute *½ cup chicken broth* for *½ cup milk.* Stir in *1 tablespoon minced onion.* Serve hot on vegetables, fish, hard-cooked eggs, or poultry.

NORMANDY SAUCE
The flavor of almost any vegetable may be enhanced with this sauce. Use it freely with these—celery, carrots, cauliflower, asparagus, green peas, or salsify—all typical of Normandy, France.
Follow recipe for Medium White Sauce using 1½ times the recipe. Substitute *½ cup light cream* and *1 cup cider* for milk. Blend in *¼ teaspoon lemon juice* and *½ teaspoon ground nutmeg.*

BERCY SAUCE
A shallot sauce used as a topping for cooked fish before it is placed under broiler or in oven to brown.
Follow recipe for Medium White Sauce. Cook *1 tablespoon chopped shallots* in the butter before stirring in flour. Substitute *fish stock* for milk.

BROWN OR ESPAGNOLE SAUCE
This basic sauce is used as an ingredient in other sauces and may be stored about a week in the refrigerator or for a longer time in the freezer.

¼ cup chopped green onion	1 small bay leaf
½ cup chopped celery	Pinch ground thyme
½ cup chopped carrot	Few grains freshly ground black pepper
2 tablespoons cooking oil	2 tablespoons tomato sauce
2 qts. water	½ cup water
3 beef bouillon cubes	¼ cup flour
3 chicken bouillon cubes	

1. Using a large saucepot, cook onion, celery, and carrot in hot oil until dark brown; do not burn. Add 2 quarts water, bouillon cubes, bay leaf, thyme, and pepper; bring to boiling and then simmer until stock is reduced by half.
2. Strain. Stir in tomato sauce; bring to boiling.
3. Vigorously shake the water and flour in a screwtop jar. Gradually add to boiling mixture, stirring constantly. Cook 1 to 2 minutes, then simmer about 30 minutes, stirring occasionally. 1 QUART
NOTE: If desired, thicken sauce with *4 tablespoons Brown Roux, page 341,* instead of the flour-water mixture. Add the roux after the tomato sauce. To avoid lumping, blend some of the hot liquid mixture into roux, stirring until smooth. Then stir into remaining liquid and bring to boiling. Simmer as directed.

BORDELAISE SAUCE
A tasty sauce containing red wine usually served over broiled meat, often beef.

4 shallots, finely chopped	1 cup Brown Sauce, *above*
2 to 3 tablespoons butter	Few drops lemon juice
1 cup red wine	1 teaspoon finely minced parsley

1. Sauté shallots in butter in a small saucepan. Add the wine and cook over low heat until reduced to one half.
2. Strain. Add Brown Sauce and continue heating. Add lemon juice and parsley. ABOUT 1½ CUPS

MORNAY SAUCE
This French cheese sauce may be served over fish or vegetables, or as a topping for a casserole.

3 tablespoons flour	¾ cup light cream
3 tablespoons butter or margarine	2 egg yolks, fork beaten
¾ cup vegetable broth (dissolve 1 vegetable bouillon cube in ¾ cup boiling water)	½ cup shredded Parmesan cheese
	1 tablespoon butter or margarine

1. Blend the flour into 3 tablespoons hot butter in the top of a double boiler. Heat until bubbly. Stir in the broth and cream and bring to boiling; stir and cook 1 to 2 minutes longer.
2. Stir about ¼ cup of hot sauce into egg yolks. Immediately return to mixture in double boiler. Cook over boiling water about 5 minutes stirring occasionally.
3. Remove from heat and add cheese and remaining butter, stirring until cheese is melted.

ABOUT 1½ CUPS

NOTE: If desired, *1½ ounces Gruyère cheese*, cut in small pieces, may be substituted for Parmesan cheese.

NORMANDY CHEESE SAUCE

2 tablespoons flour	2 tablespoons butter or margarine
¼ teaspoon salt	
⅛ teaspoon pepper	1 can (14½ oz.) evaporated milk
1 teaspoon Worcestershire sauce	½ cup water
1 tablespoon prepared mustard	¼ lb. process American cheese

1. Blend flour, salt, pepper, Worcestershire sauce, and mustard with heated butter in a heavy saucepan; stir in evaporated milk and water. Cook and stir over low heat until thickened and smooth.
2. Add cheese and stir until melted.

ABOUT 2½ CUPS

PROVOLONE SAUCE

1½ tablespoons flour	1½ cups milk
¼ teaspoon celery seed	1½ cups (about 6 oz.) shredded provolone cheese
⅛ teaspoon pepper	
1½ tablespoons butter or margarine	

1. Stir a mixture of the flour, celery seed, and pepper into hot butter in a heavy saucepan. Cook until bubbly.
2. Add milk gradually, stirring constantly. Bring rapidly to boiling; stir and cook 2 minutes. Remove from heat and stir in the cheese until melted. Use immediately.

1½ CUPS SAUCE

HOT RAVIGOTE SAUCE
A French sauce made with veal or chicken stock flavored with herbs and white wine. It is served on hot or cold meat, fish, seafood, and vegetables.

½ cup white wine	1 teaspoon minced chervil
¼ cup vinegar	
5 tablespoons butter	1 teaspoon minced tarragon
¼ cup flour	
2 cups seasoned veal or chicken broth	1 teaspoon chopped chives
1 shallot, minced	

1. Cook wine and vinegar in a saucepan over low heat until reduced to one half.
2. Heat 3 tablespoons butter and blend in the flour. Stir in broth and cook until thickened, stirring constantly.
3. Add to wine and simmer 5 minutes. Add remaining butter and mix well. Stir in shallot and remaining ingredients. Season to taste with *salt* and *pepper*.

ABOUT 2½ CUPS

RAVIGOTE SAUCE

1 cup mayonnaise	1 teaspoon tarragon leaves, finely crushed
2 tablespoons finely chopped shallots	
2 teaspoons chopped parsley	⅛ teaspoon salt
2 teaspoons chopped chives	Few grains freshly ground black pepper
2 teaspoons finely crushed chervil	1 chilled hard-cooked egg, chopped

1. Thoroughly blend all ingredients, except chopped egg, in a small bowl. Mix in the chopped egg. Cover and refrigerate 1 to 2 hours to chill and allow flavors to blend.
2. Garnish, if desired, with a sprinkling of sieved hard-cooked egg yolk.

ABOUT 1 CUP SAUCE

TOMATO RAVIGOTE SAUCE: Follow recipe for Ravigote Sauce. Blend in *¼ cup ketchup* before mixing in the chopped egg.

JIFFY CURRY SAUCE

⅔ cup (½ can) condensed
  cream of celery
  soup, undiluted
1½ teaspoons instant
  minced onion
½ teaspoon curry
  powder
6 tablespoons milk
1 egg, slightly beaten
1½ teaspoons butter or
  margarine

1.   Combine the soup, onion, and curry powder in top of a double boiler; stir until well blended. Stir in the milk. Heat thoroughly over simmering water, stirring occasionally.
2.   Stir about ¼ cup of the hot sauce into the beaten egg; immediately return mixture to double boiler.
3.   Cook over simmering water 3 to 5 minutes, stirring occasionally to keep mixture cooking evenly. Blend in the butter.   ABOUT 1 CUP

HOLLANDAISE SAUCE

This rich sauce is used to enhance many foods . . . cooked green vegetables, chicken and turkey, egg dishes, and others.

2 egg yolks
2 tablespoons cream
¼ teaspoon salt
Few grains cayenne
  pepper
2 tablespoons lemon
  juice or tarragon
  vinegar
½ cup butter

1.   In the top of a double boiler, beat egg yolks, cream, salt, and cayenne pepper until thick with a whisk beater. Set over hot (not boiling) water. (Bottom of double-boiler top should not touch water.)
2.   Add the lemon juice gradually, while beating constantly. Cook, beating constantly with the whisk beater, until sauce is the consistency of thick cream. Remove double boiler from heat, leaving top in place.
3.   Beating constantly, add the butter, ½ teaspoon at a time. Beat with whisk beater until butter is melted and thoroughly blended in.   ABOUT 1 CUP
NOTE: If necessary, the sauce may be kept hot 15 to 30 minutes over hot water. Keep covered and stir sauce occasionally.
BÉARNAISE SAUCE: Follow recipe for Hollandaise Sauce. Add 1 peppercorn, crushed, with the salt. Blend in, after the butter, *3 tablespoons finely chopped fresh herbs* such as tarragon, chervil, shallots (or green onion or chives), and parsley.

CIDER SAUCE FOR HAM

This sauce accentuates the rich, full flavor of ham.

3 tablespoons brown
  sugar
1 tablespoon cornstarch
¼ teaspoon salt
¼ teaspoon ground
  cloves
⅛ teaspoon ground
  cinnamon
Few grains ground
  nutmeg
1 cup apple cider
1 teaspoon lemon juice

1.   Thoroughly mix the brown sugar, cornstarch, salt, cloves, cinnamon, and nutmeg in a saucepan. Stir in the cider. Bring rapidly to boiling over high heat; stirring constantly, continue cooking until mixture is thick and clear, about 3 minutes.
2.   Remove from heat and stir in lemon juice.
                                     ABOUT 2½ CUPS

AMBER RAISIN SAUCE

3 tablespoons brown
  sugar
½ teaspoon seasoned
  salt
½ teaspoon ground
  cinnamon
¼ teaspoon ground
  nutmeg
1 tablespoon cornstarch
1 cup apple juice
4 lemon slices
½ cup sauterne
2 tablespoons butter
½ cup dark seedless
  raisins

1.   Combine brown sugar, salt, cinnamon, nutmeg, and cornstarch in a saucepan. Stir in the apple juice. Add lemon slices. Stirring constantly, bring mixture to boiling and cook 1 minute.
2.   Reduce heat, stir in sauterne and simmer until slightly thickened, about 5 minutes.
3.   Stir in butter and raisins; heat a few minutes longer. Serve with roast ham.   ABOUT 1¾ CUPS

MINT SAUCE

An all-time favorite to complement the flavor of roast lamb or veal.

¼ cup vinegar
1 cup water
4 tablespoons dried
  mint
1½ tablespoons lemon
  juice
2 tablespoons sugar
Salt to taste

1.   Combine vinegar, ½ cup water, and 2 tablespoons mint in a saucepan. Simmer 5 minutes; strain.
2.   Add remaining water and mint, lemon juice, sugar, and salt; bring to boiling over low heat. Serve hot.   ABOUT 1 CUP

MUSTARD SAUCE

This satiny smooth sauce—served hot or cold—is equally delicious over vegetables, meat, or poultry.

1 cup undiluted evaporated milk	¼ cup sugar
2 tablespoons dry mustard	3 egg yolks, well beaten
	⅓ cup cider vinegar

1. Scald evaporated milk in the top of a double boiler over boiling water. Blend a small amount of hot evaporated milk with dry mustard until smooth; return to remaining evaporated milk along with the sugar and stir until sugar is dissolved. Add a small amount of the hot mixture to the beaten egg yolks, blending well, and return to double-boiler top.
2. Cook over boiling water about 3 minutes, stirring constantly.
3. Remove from heat. Mix in the vinegar. Serve hot; or cool, refrigerate, and serve cold.

ABOUT 1¼ CUPS SAUCE

ENGLISH MUSTARD SAUCE

A sauce that is especially compatible with hot corned beef.

1 tablespoon flour	1 tablespoon cider vinegar
1 teaspoon dry mustard	
⅛ teaspoon salt	1 tablespoon butter
⅛ teaspoon pepper	1 tablespoon prepared mustard
½ cup water	

1. Combine the flour, dry mustard, salt, and pepper in a heavy saucepan. Gradually add the water and vinegar; cook, stirring, until boiling; cook 1 to 2 minutes longer.
2. Remove from heat; stir in butter and mustard. Serve hot. ABOUT ½ CUP

DILLED MUSHROOM SAUCE

¼ cup chopped onion	Few grains pepper
¼ cup chopped fresh mushrooms	¼ teaspoon dill weed, crushed
2 tablespoons butter or margarine	1 cup milk
2 tablespoons flour	1 teaspoon grated lemon peel
¼ teaspoon salt	

1. Cook onion and mushrooms in hot butter in a heavy saucepan over medium heat about 5 minutes. Blend in a mixture of flour, salt, pepper, and dill weed. Cook, stirring constantly, until bubbly.

2. Remove from heat and gradually add milk, continuing to stir. Add lemon peel. Bring rapidly to boiling and boil 1 to 2 minutes, stirring constantly. Serve hot. ABOUT 1 CUP

MUSHROOM-CARAWAY SAUCE

A hint of lemon-lime flavor heightens the tasty zest of this unusual sauce … a perfect foil for creamy scrambled eggs.

1 can (10½ oz.) condensed cream of mushroom soup	¾ teaspoon caraway seed
	¼ teaspoon onion salt
1 bottle (7 oz.) lemon-lime carbonated beverage	⅛ teaspoon freshly ground black pepper
	1¾ teaspoons wine vinegar
¼ cup heavy cream	

1. Put mushroom soup into a heavy saucepan; stir until smooth.
2. Gradually add lemon-lime carbonated beverage and then cream, stirring constantly.
3. Blend in the remaining ingredients and heat until mixture begins to simmer. ABOUT 2 CUPS

QUICK TOMATO SAUCE

2 tablespoons butter or margarine	⅓ cup water
¼ cup coarsely chopped celery	2 tablespoons lemon juice
¼ cup coarsely chopped green pepper	1 tablespoon Worcestershire sauce
2 tablespoons finely chopped onion	2 tablespoons brown sugar
1 can (10¾ oz.) condensed tomato soup	1 teaspoon dry mustard
	½ teaspoon salt
	Few grains pepper

1. Heat the butter in a skillet. Add the vegetables and cook, stirring frequently, until celery and green pepper are tender.
2. Gradually add a mixture of soup, water, lemon juice, and Worcestershire sauce, stirring constantly. Mix in a blend of the remaining ingredients. Simmer, uncovered, about 5 minutes.

ABOUT 2 CUPS

FLAVORFUL TOMATO SAUCE

1 tablespoon grated
  onion
2 tablespoons butter
  or margarine
2 tablespoons flour
1 teaspoon dry mustard
1 teaspoon seasoned
  salt

2 cans (8 oz. each)
  tomato sauce
1/3 cup water
2 tablespoons brown
  sugar
1/2 teaspoon Worcester-
  shire sauce

1.   Cook the onion until soft in heated butter in a
saucepan. Blend in a mixture of the flour, dry mustard, and seasoned salt. Heat until mixture bubbles, stirring constantly.
2.   Add tomato sauce and remaining ingredients,
cooking and stirring until sauce thickens. Cook 1 to
2 minutes. Serve sauce hot.   ABOUT 1¾ CUPS

SALSA ITALIANA

A special sauce to complement many main dishes.

1 cup chopped onion
1/4 cup olive oil or
  cooking oil
1 clove garlic, minced
1/4 cup grated carrot
1 tablespoon finely
  snipped parsley
1/4 teaspoon basil,
  crushed

1/8 teaspoon thyme,
  crushed
2 cans (8 oz. each)
  tomato sauce
1/2 cup beef broth
  (dissolve 1/2 beef
  bouillon cube in 1/2
  cup boiling water)

1.   Add onion to hot oil in saucepan and cook until
tender. Stir in the garlic, carrot, and parsley; cook
about 3 minutes, stirring frequently.
2.   Blend in remaining ingredients. Simmer gently
until flavors are blended, about 10 minutes.
                                      ABOUT 3 CUPS

ORANGE BARBECUE SAUCE

1/4 cup packed brown
  sugar
1/2 teaspoon dry mustard
1/8 teaspoon ground
  cloves
1/2 teaspoon Worcester-
  shire sauce

1/3 cup chopped onion
1½ teaspoons grated
  orange peel
1/3 cup orange juice
3/4 cup ketchup
1½ cups water

Mix all ingredients in a heavy saucepan; bring to
boiling, stirring until sugar is dissolved. Reduce
heat; simmer, uncovered, about 30 minutes, stirring occasionally.   ABOUT 2¼ CUPS

SNAPPY BARBECUE SAUCE

A good accompaniment for steamed crab.

1/2 cup ketchup
1/4 cup water
2 tablespoons vinegar
2 tablespoons brown
  sugar

1/2 teaspoon dry mustard
1 teaspoon Worcester-
  shire sauce
1/8 teaspoon chili powder
1/4 teaspoon salt

Combine all ingredients in a small saucepan. Simmer over low heat 5 minutes.   ABOUT 3/4 CUP

SAUCE ORIENTAL

1½ tablespoons
  cornstarch
1 can (11 oz.) mandarin
  oranges, drained
  (reserve syrup)
1/2 cup maple syrup

2 tablespoons lemon
  juice
2 tablespoons dark
  seedless raisins
1 tablespoon butter or
  margarine

1.   Combine cornstarch, reserved orange syrup,
maple syrup, and lemon juice in a saucepan; stir
until smooth. Add raisins. Bring to boiling over
medium heat, stirring constantly; boil 3 minutes.
2.   Stir in butter and oranges; simmer 2 minutes.
3.   Serve hot with *roast duckling.*   ABOUT 1⅔ CUPS

TERIYAKI SAUCE

*A sauce complementary to shellfish, especially crab
meat.*

1/2 cup pineapple juice
1/4 cup brown sugar
2 tablespoons soy
  sauce
1 tablespoon salad oil

3/4 teaspoon ground
  ginger
1/4 teaspoon salt
1 clove garlic, minced

Combine all ingredients in small saucepan. Heat to
blend flavors.   ABOUT 2/3 CUP

TANGY PLUM SAUCE FOR POULTRY

1 can or jar (17 oz.)
  purple plums, drained
  (reserve 1/4 cup syrup)

1/2 cup frozen orange
  juice concentrate,
  thawed
1/2 teaspoon Worcester-
  shire sauce

1.   Pit plums, and force through a sieve or food
mill into a bowl. Blend in reserved syrup, orange
juice, and Worcestershire sauce.

2. During final hour of roasting, brush *turkey* (or other poultry) with the sauce at 15-minute intervals. If desired, blend remaining sauce into gravy. ABOUT 1½ CUPS

ROSEMARY PLUM SAUCE

This versatile sauce is a perfect complement for meat and poultry. Blended with only a small amount of the Rosemary Brew, it is also delightful over waffles, pancakes, and fritters.

1 jar or can (17 oz.)   Rosemary Brew, *below*
   purple plums, drained   3 to 4 tablespoons
   (reserve syrup)   butter or margarine
½ cup dark corn syrup

1. Pit plums and purée pulp in an electric blender.
2. Mix purée with corn syrup, Rosemary Brew, and butter in a saucepan.
3. Heat thoroughly, stirring occasionally.
ABOUT 2¾ CUPS

ROSEMARY BREW: In a small saucepan, bring 1 cup reserved plum syrup to boiling. Mix in *2 tablespoons rosemary leaves* and simmer. Remove from heat, cover, and let stand about 10 minutes. Strain through a fine sieve.

TARRAGON BUTTER

¼ cup butter, melted   ¼ teaspoon salt
2 tablespoons lemon   ½ teaspoon crushed
   juice   tarragon
1 teaspoon minced
   onion

Combine melted butter with remaining ingredients. Serve hot over fish or shellfish.
ABOUT 6 TABLESPOONS

WINE SAUCE FOR GAME OR TONGUE

1 tablespoon butter or   ½ cup water
   margarine   3 whole cloves
½ glass currant jelly   1 teaspoon salt
Juice of ½ lemon   ½ cup port wine
Dash cayenne pepper

Combine all ingredients except wine in a saucepan; simmer about 5 minutes. Strain and mix in wine and *3 tablespoons brown gravy*, if desired.
ABOUT 1 CUP

FLUFFY HORSERADISH SAUCE

¼ cup prepared   1 teaspoon sugar
   horseradish   ½ cup heavy cream,
1 tablespoon vinegar   whipped

Combine all ingredients and mix well. ABOUT 1 CUP

SOUR CREAM SAUCE

1 cup dairy sour cream   ½ teaspoon dry mustard
1 tablespoon sugar   1 to 2 tablespoons
Salt to taste   vinegar
Dash cayenne pepper

Combine all ingredients, mix thoroughly, and chill. Serve with *cold fish*, *poultry*, and *meats*. 1 CUP

MAYONNAISE-SOUR CREAM SAUCE: Follow recipe for Sour Cream Sauce. Add *1 to 2 teaspoons grated lemon peel*. Substitute *½ cup mayonnaise* for *½ cup dairy sour cream*.

CUCUMBER SAUCE: Follow recipe for Sour Cream Sauce. Add *1 cup chopped pared cucumber*. Omit the mustard and add *2 tablespoons prepared horseradish*.

TARTAR SAUCE

A favorite for hot or cold fish and shellfish.

1 to 2 teaspoons   1 to 2 tablespoons
   minced onion   chopped green olives,
1½ to 2 tablespoons   drained
   chopped sweet pickle,   ¾ cup mayonnaise
   drained

Combine all ingredients. Store in covered jar in refrigerator.
ABOUT 1 CUP

REMOULADE SAUCE

3 cups mayonnaise   1 tablespoon prepared
⅓ cup minced green   horseradish
   onion   1 tablespoon finely
3 tablespoons drained   chopped parsley
   capers   1 clove garlic, crushed
1 tablespoon Worcester-   Few drops Tabasco
   shire sauce

Combine all ingredients in a large bowl. Mix well and store in a covered container in the refrigerator. Serve with hot or cold cooked shrimp or other seafood.
ABOUT 3 CUPS

GRAVIES

BROWN GRAVY

Remove roasted meat or poultry from roasting pan. Leaving brown residue in the pan, pour the drippings into a bowl. Allow the fat to rise to surface; skim off fat and reserve. (Remaining drippings in bowl are meat juices which should be used as part of the liquid in the gravy.)

Method I:

3 tablespoons fat	2 cups liquid, warm or
3 tablespoons flour	cool (water; drippings;
½ teaspoon salt	meat, chicken, or
⅛ teaspoon pepper	vegetable broth; or
	milk)

1. Add the fat to roasting pan (with brown residue); stir in the flour and seasonings until smooth. Heat until bubbly. Brown slightly if desired.
2. Stir in the liquid and cook until sauce thickens; continue stirring and cooking 2 or 3 minutes longer, scraping bottom and sides of roasting pan to blend in the brown residue. ABOUT 2 CUPS GRAVY

Method II:

2 cups chicken or meat	¼ cup flour
broth (fat skimmed)	½ teaspoon salt
½ cup cold broth or	⅛ teaspoon pepper
water	

1. Bring the broth to boiling in a saucepan. Drippings from roasted meat or poultry may be substituted for part of the broth. If necessary, add milk or water to drippings to make 2 cups liquid.
2. Measure broth and flour into a screw-top glass jar or shaker. Cover jar and shake until flour and broth are blended. Stirring boiling broth constantly, add flour mixture, a small amount at a time and bring to boiling after each addition. Cook and stir, adding only enough flour mixture until gravy is desired consistency. Add seasonings to taste. When gravy is thickened, cook 2 or 3 minutes longer. ABOUT 2½ CUPS GRAVY

GIBLET GRAVY: Follow either method adding chopped *giblets* the last several minutes of cooking.

RED EYE GRAVY

Tennessee Ernie Ford says his Red Eye Gravy — which he also calls Poor Man's Au Jus — can only be made from country cured Tennessee ham, no other kind will work. He insists that the real country hams are a deep red color, which gives the gravy it's name. This ham can only be fried — not baked.

Fry thick slices of *Tennessee ham.* Remove meat from the skillet, skim off the excess fat that rises to the surface. Add 4 *tablespoons cold coffee.* That's it! Serve over *grits* and *hot biscuits.*

GINGERSNAP GRAVY

1. Drain *drippings* and *fat* from roasting pan. Allow fat to rise to surface and skim it off; reserve 3 tablespoons. Heat the fat and drippings (about ¾ cup) in a saucepan; blend in *6 finely crushed gingersnaps*; heat until mixture bubbles.
2. Remove from heat and gradually add *1 cup water*, blending well. Bring to boiling and boil 1 to 2 minutes, stirring constantly. Season with *salt* and *pepper* as desired. ABOUT 1½ CUPS GRAVY

GINGER GRAVY: Follow recipe for Gingersnap Gravy. Substitute a mixture of *3 tablespoons flour, ½ teaspoon monosodium glutamate, ¼ teaspoon salt, ⅛ teaspoon black pepper,* and *½ teaspoon ground ginger* for the gingersnaps.

TURKEY OR CHICKEN GRAVY

6 tablespoons flour	4 cups liquid (reserved
½ teaspoon salt	giblet broth and
¼ teaspoon pepper	turkey drippings, or
	chicken broth)

1. Remove roasted turkey from roasting pan. Leaving brown residue in pan, pour drippings into a bowl. Allow fat to rise to surface; skim off and reserve fat. Reserve remaining drippings for part of gravy liquid.
2. Measure 6 tablespoons reserved fat into roasting pan and blend in flour, salt, and pepper until smooth. Stirring constantly, heat until mixture bubbles. Brown slightly, if desired. Remove from heat and slowly blend in the liquid.
3. Return to heat and cook rapidly, stirring constantly, until gravy thickens. Cook 1 to 2 minutes longer. While stirring, scrape bottom and sides of pan to blend in brown residue. ABOUT 4 CUPS GRAVY

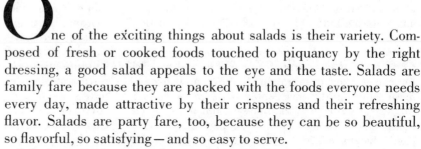

Chapter 12

SALADS & SALAD DRESSINGS

One of the exciting things about salads is their variety. Composed of fresh or cooked foods touched to piquancy by the right dressing, a good salad appeals to the eye and the taste. Salads are family fare because they are packed with the foods everyone needs every day, made attractive by their crispness and their refreshing flavor. Salads are party fare, too, because they can be so beautiful, so flavorful, so satisfying—and so easy to serve.

Salads come in many forms: they may be appetizers, garnitures, accompaniments, main dishes, desserts, or a whole meal; they may be made individually, or may be big enough to serve the whole party; and they may be crisp and cool, molded, frozen, or even hot. With all this variety, don't let yourself or your family get into a salad rut!

SALAD POINTERS

A salad is only as good as its makings so select the ingredients with care. Greens should be fresh, crisp, and dry, vegetables garden fresh, and fruits firm, fully ripe, and free from blemish. When using canned products, choose those of good quality and appearance.

Chill all salad ingredients, bowls, and plates thoroughly. With the exception of a few hot salads, coldness is essential to the appeal of all salads.

Trim and rinse greens under running cold water, handling them carefully to avoid bruising. Shake off the excess moisture and then gently pat dry before putting them into a plastic bag or the vegetable drawer and into your refrigerator. Wet greens not only make watery salads, they present a surface to which an oil dressing cannot cling.

Greens should always be broken or torn, never cut (except in the case of head lettuce which is to be served in wedges or quarters).

Tomatoes may be peeled or not, as your family prefers, for use in salads. Unpeeled tomato shells or tomato cups are sturdier and keep their shape better; peeled ones are easier to cut with a fork.

Tomato wedges or chunks should be added to tossed salads just before serving, as their juice tends to make the dressing watery.

Fruits that tend to discolor after peeling or paring (such as avocados, bananas, apples, fresh peaches and pears) should be brushed with pineapple or citrus fruit juice unless they are to be tossed immediately with an acid fruit or salad dressing.

Final assembling of ingredients for a salad of fresh fruits, vegetables, or greens should be done *just* before serving. Many main-dish salads, potato and macaroni salads, and cooked-vegetable salads improve in flavor when the mixture is prepared an hour or so ahead of serving time and allowed to stand in the refrigerator to chill and blend the individual flavors. But even these mixtures should be combined with their green garnishes at the last moment.

Avoid unnecessary handling of salad materials. Salads should always have that fresh-from-the-refrigerator look which is so appealing to the eye and tempting to the taste. Arrange fruits or vegetables on the salad plate if the salad requires it, but don't *rearrange* them.

SALAD CONTAINERS

Cabbage Bowls — Rinse firm green or red cabbage head. If necessary, level base by cutting a thin slice from core end. Form the bowl by cutting out center of cabbage head. Shred the cabbage removed from the head for cabbage salads. Spoon completed salad into the bowl and serve.

Grapefruit (or Orange) Baskets — Rinse grapefruit and cut into halves. With a grapefruit knife or sharp paring knife, loosen each section by cutting down along either side of dividing membranes. Cut completely around outer skin to loosen membrane from shell. Remove grapefruit sections and reserve for use in food preparation. Remove and discard membrane and fibrous center. *To make a handle for basket* — About ¼ inch down from top of each half-shell, carefully cut through peel and around shell, leaving a 1-inch piece attached at opposite sides of shell. Bring the strips up together at the center and secure with a small piece of thread or a short piece of wooden pick. Decorate handle with watercress or mint, or a small flower.

Green Pepper Shells — Rinse and cut a thin slice from stem end of chilled green peppers. Remove white fiber and seeds.

Melon Bowls — Rinse melons and cut into halves. If a scalloped edge is desired, using a narrow-pointed knife, carefully carve around each melon half. If a saw-toothed edge is desired, do not cut melons into halves. Using a narrow-pointed knife, mark points in a saw-toothed line at 1-inch intervals around center of melon. Cut on line between points and pull halves apart. With a knife or spoon, remove seedy center from melon halves. Using a spoon or melon-ball cutter, scoop out meat from melon halves, keeping surface smooth and leaving shells about ½ inch thick. Chill shells and pieces in refrigerator.

Pineapple Shells — Rinse pineapple. To prepare, cut whole pineapple into halves lengthwise through crown (spiny top). Cut out and discard core. With a grapefruit knife or sharp paring knife, carefully remove and reserve fruit from pineapple halves, leaving shells about ½ inch thick. Cut reserved pineapple into pieces and chill with the shells.

Tomato Shells — Rinse and chill firm tomatoes; peel, if desired. Cut a slice from top of each tomato. Using a spoon, remove pulp. Invert shells to drain. Sprinkle lightly with salt before filling.

SALAD GARNISHES & RELISHES

Use raw vegetables for colorful, easy-to-prepare garnishes. Select only those that are in prime condition — crisp, fresh, preferably young and tender. Clean them thoroughly; with a sharp knife, trim ends where necessary and cut the vegetables into varied shapes as suggested. Chill in ice and water.

Carrot Curls — Wash and pare or scrape carrots. Cut into halves lengthwise. Using a vegetable parer, shave into paper-thin strips. Curl each around finger and fasten with a wooden pick. Chill thoroughly in ice and water. Drain and remove picks before serving.

Carrot Sticks — Wash and pare or scrape carrots. Cut into narrow strips about 3 inches long. Chill in refrigerator. If desired, draw carrot sticks through pitted ripe or green olives; place as accents on relish tray or salad plates.

Cauliflowerets — Remove leaves, cut off all the woody base, and trim any blemishes from head of cauliflower. Separate into flowerets. Rinse, drain, and chill in refrigerator.

Double Celery Curls — Clean celery. Cut into 2½- to 3-inch lengths. Slit into narrow parallel strips, cutting from each end almost to center. Chill until curled in ice and water. Drain before serving.

Cucumber Balls — Cut large cucumbers into balls with a French vegetable cutter. Marinate in French dressing or sprinkle balls with paprika.

Cucumber Tulip — Cut the ends from an unpared, medium-sized cucumber. Cut 6 or 7 triangular sections down from cut edge, forming petals. Wooden picks may be used as markers so that all petals will be even. Scoop out center and remove remaining seeds, leaving a ¼-inch wall. Place a small rounded bit of carrot or rutabaga on a wooden pick and press into the center. Chill in ice and water. Drain before serving.

Fluted Cucumber Slices — Draw tines of fork lengthwise over entire surface. Cut into thin slices.

Frosted Grapes — Beat 1 egg white until frothy. Dip small clusters of rinsed, thoroughly drained grapes in the beaten egg white. Shake off excess egg white and dip grapes into granulated sugar. Set aside to dry. Chill, if desired.

Green or Red Pepper Strips — Rinse whole peppers and cut into halves lengthwise. Remove all fiber and seeds; slice lengthwise into strips. *For rings*, slice whole peppers crosswise.

Jellied Ginger Ale Cubes — Soften ½ tablespoon unflavored gelatin in 2 tablespoons cold water. Place over hot water to dissolve completely. Cool and add 1 cup ginger ale; mix thoroughly. Pour into a small square pan and chill until firm. Cut into small cubes.

Sweet Pickle Fans—Cut pickles into thin slices almost to the end. Spread and press uncut end carefully to hold fan in place.

Radish Fans—Wash firm red radishes. Cut off root ends. Cut thin lengthwise parallel slices almost to end. Chill in ice and water until slices spread apart. Drain.

Radish Roses—Wash firm red radishes. Trim off root ends, leaving a bit of the stem and several small leaves for color contrast. With a sharp pointed knife, mark petals. Pare each petal thinly away from tip toward stem end so that red outside covering stands out like the petals of a flower. Chill in ice and water until petals spread apart. Drain before serving.

Tomato Wedges—Rinse firm tomatoes and put into boiling water about ½ minute, or until skin loosens. Peel, cut out stem ends, and chill. Place chilled tomato on flat surface and cut lengthwise into six or eight wedges.

GREEN & VEGETABLE SALADS

SALAD GREEN VARIETIES & PREPARATION

The many varieties of greens star in the tossed salad and form the background of other salads. Select greens that are fresh and crisp and blemish-free. In general, rinse them before storing, drain thoroughly, and gently pat dry with a soft, clean cloth or absorbent paper. Put into the refrigerator in the vegetable drawer or a plastic bag, or wrap tightly in aluminum foil or other moisture-vaporproof material to prevent wilting. Avoid soaking greens when rinsing them. If necessary, crisp them by placing in ice and water for a short time. Before using, remove all moisture left from rinsing and crisping.

Lettuce—Discard bruised and wilted leaves; rinse, drain, and dry lettuce. (For lettuce cups, remove the core from head lettuce with a sharp pointed knife; let cold water run into the core cavity to loosen the leaves; drain thoroughly; gently pull leaves from head; cut off heavy coarse ends; pat dry.) The following are types of lettuce: *Head or Iceberg*—firm, compact head with medium-green outside leaves, pale-green heart. *Butterhead or Boston*—loose, lighter-weight head with light-green outside leaves, light-yellow heart; less crisp than Iceberg. *Romaine or Cos*—elongated green head with coarser leaves having stronger flavor than Iceberg. *Bibb or Limestone*—head similar in size and shape to Boston; deep-green leaves with delicate flavor. *Leaf*—leafy bunches of curly-edged leaves; many varieties are grown commercially and in the home garden. A bright attractive touch for lettuce is achieved by dipping the curly edges of leaves in a paste made of two parts paprika and one part water.

Cabbage—see *page 301*. Discard bruised and wilted outside leaves; rinse, quarter, and remove core; chop or shred as directed in the recipe.

Endive—Discard bruised and wilted leaves; rinse, drain, and dry. The following are varieties of endive: *Curly* (often called chicory)—bunchy head with narrow, ragged-edged curly leaves; dark-green outside, pale-yellow heart; pleasantly bitter flavor. *French* (Witloaf chicory)—thin, elongated stalk, usually bleached while growing. *Belgian*—well-bleached heads 4 to 6 inches long. *Escarole* (broad-leaf endive)—bunchy head of broad leaves that do not curl at tips; dark-green outer leaves, pale-yellow heart; less bitter than curly endive.

Parsley—Discard coarse stems and bruised leaves; rinse gently but thoroughly with cold water; shake off excess water and pat dry. Store in tightly covered jar or plastic bag in refrigerator.

Spinach—Discard tough stems, roots, and bruised or wilted leaves. Wash leaves thoroughly by lifting up and down several times in a large amount of water; lift leaves out completely and pour off water; repeat in several changes of water until all sand and grit are removed. Drain; pat dry.

Watercress—See *Parsley*. Watercress may be stored without rinsing, if preferred. Let the tied bunch stand in a jar or bowl containing enough water to reach about half way up stems. Cover and store in refrigerator. When ready to use, snip off the amount needed, rinse, drain, and shake off excess water.

Other greens—*Field salad*—spoon-shaped leaves; *finocchio*—anise-flavored stalk (serve like celery); *Swiss chard* and *beet, dandelion, mustard,* and *turnip greens*—use tops only.

ASPARAGUS VINAIGRETTE

In this version of the ever-appealing asparagus served in the French manner, flavor perfection is easily achieved using a salad dressing mix in preparing the "vinaigrette."

1 env. herb-flavored
   oil-and-vinegar salad
   dressing mix
Tarragon-flavored
   white wine vinegar
Water
Salad oil
2 tablespoons chopped
   parsley

1 tablespoon finely
   chopped chives
2 teaspoons capers
1 hard-cooked egg,
   finely chopped
Cooked asparagus
   spears, chilled

1.   Prepare salad dressing mix as directed on package, using vinegar, water, and salad oil.
2.   Using 1 cup of the dressing, mix well with parsley, chives, capers and egg. Chill thoroughly.
3.   To serve, arrange chilled asparagus in six bundles on a chilled serving plate lined with *Boston lettuce.* Garnish each bundle with a *pimiento strip.* Complete platter with *cucumber slices* and *radish roses.* Mix dressing well before spooning over asparagus.   6 SERVINGS

GARBANZO BEAN SALAD

2 cans (15 oz. each)
   garbanzos, drained
   (about 4 cups)
1 cup cut celery
2 green peppers, diced
   or slivered
2 or 3 tomatoes, peeled
   and cut in small
   pieces
½ cup finely chopped
   sweet onion
1 cup radish slices
¼ cup snipped parsley

1 cup quartered pitted
   ripe olives
1 env. Italian salad
   dressing mix
2 teaspoons Worcester-
   shire sauce
1 teaspoon mono-
   sodium glutamate
1 teaspoon ground
   coriander
¾ teaspoon lemon
   pepper marinade

1.   Combine the vegetables and olives in a bowl; toss lightly and refrigerate to chill.
2.   Meanwhile, prepare salad dressing following package directions, using wine vinegar and adding Worcestershire sauce and remaining ingredients with the mix. Shake thoroughly before using.
3.   About 1 hour before serving, toss salad ingredients lightly with dressing until well mixed, then chill.   10 TO 12 SERVINGS

SWEET-SOUR BEANS IN TOMATO SHELLS

⅓ cup cider vinegar
2½ tablespoons dark
   brown sugar
½ teaspoon salt
1 can (16 oz.)
   diagonally sliced
   green beans, drained

1 tablespoon finely
   chopped onion
6 tomato shells,
   chilled
1 tablespoon basil,
   crushed

1.   Pour a mixture of the vinegar, brown sugar, and salt over the beans and onion in a bowl; toss lightly. Set in refrigerator to marinate 1 hour, tossing occasionally.
2.   Sprinkle the inside of each tomato shell with crushed basil and *salt.* Spoon beans equally into tomato shells. Garnish with crisp *bacon curls.*
                                    6 SERVINGS

BACON-BEAN SALAD

Here's a salad bursting with good flavor and ideal to tote to a potluck supper or picnic.

⅔ cup cider vinegar
¾ cup sugar
1 teaspoon salt
1 can (16 oz.) cut
   green beans
1 can (16 oz.) cut wax
   beans
1 can (16 oz.) kidney
   beans, thoroughly
   rinsed and drained
1 can (16 oz.) lima
   beans

1 medium-sized onion,
   quartered and finely
   sliced
1 medium-sized green
   pepper, chopped
½ teaspoon freshly
   ground black pepper
⅓ cup salad oil
1 lb. bacon, cut in
   1-inch squares
   (optional)

1.   Blend vinegar, sugar, and salt in a small saucepan. Heat until the sugar is dissolved. Remove from heat and set aside.
2.   Drain all beans and toss with onion, green pepper, vinegar mixture, and the pepper. Pour oil over all and toss to coat evenly. Store in a large covered container in refrigerator.
3.   When ready to serve, fry bacon until crisp; drain on absorbent paper. Toss the bacon with bean mixture.   ABOUT 12 SERVINGS

Shrimp and Avocado Salad

COLIFLOR ACAPULCO
Mexico has contributed this flamboyant salad.

1 large head cauliflower	Lettuce
Marinade, *below*	1 jar (16 oz.) sliced pickled beets, drained and chilled
1 can (15 oz.) garbanzos, drained	1 large cucumber, thinly sliced and chilled
1 cup pimiento-stuffed olives	
Pimientos, drained and cut lengthwise in strips	Radish roses
	Guacamole II, *page 33*

1. Cook the cauliflower in boiling *salted water* about 10 minutes, or just until tender; drain. Place cauliflower, head down, in a deep bowl and pour the marinade over it. Chill several hours or overnight; occasionally spoon marinade over all.
2. Shortly before serving, thread garbanzos, pimiento-stuffed olives, and pimiento strips onto wooden picks for decorative kabobs. Set aside while arranging salad.
3. Drain the cauliflower. Line a chilled serving plate with crisp lettuce and place cauliflower, head up, in the center. Arrange the pickled beet and cucumber slices around the base, tucking in *parsley sprigs* and the radish roses.
4. Spoon and spread Guacamole II over the cauliflower. Decorate with *cashew nuts* and the kabobs. Serve cold. **6 TO 8 SERVINGS**

MARINADE: Combine *1½ cups salad oil, ½ cup lemon juice, 1½ teaspoons salt*, and *1 teaspoon chili powder*. Shake the marinade well before pouring it over the cauliflower.

PIQUANT PEPPER-CABBAGE SLAW

¼ to ⅓ cup sugar	2 tablespoons butter or margarine
2 tablespoons flour	1 teaspoon celery seed
1 teaspoon salt	1 head chilled cabbage, finely shredded
2 teaspoons dry mustard	
2 eggs, fork beaten	1 green pepper, chopped
1 cup milk, scalded	
¾ cup cider vinegar	1 red pepper, chopped

1. Mix sugar, flour, salt, and dry mustard together in top of a double boiler. Blend in the eggs and milk. Cook over boiling water about 5 minutes, stirring frequently.
2. Stir in the vinegar, a small amount at a time.

Cook and stir until mixture begins to thicken, then mix in the butter and celery seed. Remove from heat; cool and chill thoroughly.
3. To serve, toss the cabbage and peppers with enough dressing to coat evenly (store remaining dressing); mound onto fresh *spinach leaves*.
ABOUT 8 SERVINGS

CRUNCHY PEANUT COLE SLAW

3 cups finely chopped green cabbage	½ cup finely chopped cucumber
1 cup finely chopped red cabbage	¼ cup finely chopped green onion
1 cup finely chopped celery	¼ cup finely chopped green pepper
1 cup coarsely chopped cauliflower	1 tablespoon butter or margarine
1 cup dairy sour cream	½ cup coarsely chopped salted peanuts
1 cup mayonnaise	2 tablespoons shredded Parmesan cheese
1 tablespoon sugar	
1 teaspoon salt	
1 tablespoon tarragon vinegar	

1. Toss the green and red cabbage, celery, and cauliflower together and chill.
2. Combine the sour cream, mayonnaise, sugar, salt, vinegar, cucumber, green onion, and green pepper for the salad dressing and chill thoroughly.
3. Melt butter in a small skillet; add peanuts and heat several minutes until lightly browned. Remove from heat and immediately stir in the Parmesan cheese. Set aside.
4. Just before serving, toss chilled vegetables with the dressing and top with the peanut mixture.
8 SERVINGS

TOMATO-CREAM SLAW

1 cup dairy sour cream	2 tablespoons sugar
¼ cup mayonnaise	1 teaspoon celery seed
½ cup tomato sauce	1 small head cabbage, coarsely shredded
2 tablespoons cider vinegar	

1. Combine in a bowl the sour cream, mayonnaise, tomato sauce, vinegar, sugar, and celery seed. Refrigerate at least 1 hour for flavors to blend and dressing to chill.
2. Put shredded cabbage into a bowl and chill.
3. Just before serving, pour the dressing over the cabbage and toss lightly to mix. **ABOUT 6 SERVINGS**

Salade Niçoise

TURNIP-CARROT-CABBAGE SLAW

1 cup shredded white turnip	¼ cup chopped parsley
1 cup shredded carrot	¼ teaspoon salt
2 cups finely shredded cabbage	⅛ teaspoon pepper
¼ cup finely chopped onion	3 tablespoons mayonnaise

1.   Toss vegetables together gently with a mixture of salt, pepper, and mayonnaise until vegetables are evenly coated.
2.   Chill, covered, in refrigerator until ready to serve.   ABOUT 6 SERVINGS

PIQUANT CUCUMBER SLICES

2 tablespoons sugar	1 cucumber, rinsed (do not pare)
1 teaspoon salt	⅛ teaspoon white pepper	¼ cup coarsely chopped onion
1 teaspoon celery seed	2 tablespoons chopped parsley
¼ cup cider vinegar	
1 tablespoon lemon juice	

1.   Combine the sugar, salt, white pepper, celery seed, vinegar, and lemon juice in a bowl; blend thoroughly.
2.   Score cucumber by drawing tines of a fork lengthwise over entire surface. Cut into ⅛-inch slices.
3.   Add cucumber to vinegar mixture with onion and parsley; toss to coat evenly.
4.   Chill thoroughly, turning several times.
ABOUT 4 SERVINGS

WILTED LETTUCE

Visitors to Pennsylvania Dutch country are likely to be treated to this old-fashioned lettuce dish. Fresh tender leaf lettuce of early summer is often used.

1 large head lettuce	2 tablespoons heavy cream
6 slices bacon, diced	½ cup water	1 tablespoon sugar
¼ cup cider vinegar	¼ teaspoon salt

1.   Tear lettuce into pieces into a bowl; set aside.
2.   Fry bacon until crisp in a skillet; reserve ¼ cup drippings. Drain bacon on absorbent paper; set aside.
3.   Stir the remaining ingredients into drippings in skillet. Heat mixture just to boiling, stirring constantly.
4.   Immediately pour vinegar mixture over the lettuce and toss lightly to coat thoroughly. Top with the bacon.   ABOUT 8 SERVINGS

MUSHROOM-SOY SALAD

⅔ cup salad oil	1 can (5 oz.) water chestnuts, sliced
¼ cup pickle relish	¼ cup lemon juice	6 green onions, diagonally sliced
2 teaspoons sugar	⅛ teaspoon salt	4 radishes, thinly sliced
⅛ teaspoon curry powder	½ head iceberg lettuce, torn into chunks
1 cucumber, thinly sliced	1 tablespoon soy sauce
½ lb. fresh mushrooms, sliced	

1.   In a bottle or jar, put the salad oil, pickle relish, lemon juice, and a mixture of sugar, salt, and curry powder. Cover and shake well.
2.   In a bowl, combine cucumber, mushrooms, water chestnuts, and green onions; toss together. Shake dressing, pour desired amount over all, and toss. Cover and chill.
3.   Just before serving, add radishes and lettuce, drizzle with soy sauce, and toss again.
6 TO 8 SERVINGS

BLUE RIBBON POTATO-ONION SALAD

2 lbs. potatoes, cooked and peeled	3 hard-cooked eggs, chopped
2½ tablespoons cider vinegar	1 cup diced celery
1 tablespoon salad oil	Onion Sour Cream Dressing, *below*
1½ teaspoons salt	

1.   Cut potatoes into ½ inch cubes and put into a bowl. Toss with a mixture of vinegar, oil, and salt. Add eggs, celery, and dressing; toss until mixed. Cover and chill thoroughly.
2.   Turn salad into a chilled salad bowl.
10 TO 12 SERVINGS

ONION-SOUR CREAM DRESSING: Combine *1¾ cups dairy sour cream, ½ teaspoon sugar, few grains pepper, 2 tablespoons cider vinegar, 1½ teaspoons prepared mustard, ½ cup grated onion (or blender puréed), and ½ cup sliced ripe olives. Chill until ready to use.*   ABOUT 2½ CUPS DRESSING

GARDEN POTATO SALAD

2 cans (16 oz. each)
potato salad
²/₃ cup thinly sliced
radishes (about 8
radishes)
1 medium-sized cucum-
ber, rinsed, pared,
and diced
6 green onions, cut in
½-inch pieces

Turn potato salad into a bowl. Add the radishes, cucumber, and onion; lightly toss together. Chill thoroughly. Before serving, toss lightly.

ABOUT 8 SERVINGS

SPINACH-BEET SALAD

Wash, discard bruised leaves, drain, dry, and tear enough *spinach* into pieces to yield about 2 quarts. Turn into a salad bowl; cover and chill. Meanwhile, pour *French dressing* over *2 cups julienne beets*; chill. When ready to serve, add marinated beets and *Herb Croutons, below*, to spinach in bowl; gently turn and toss until greens are evenly coated with dressing. Garnish with *hard-cooked egg slices*. Serve immediately.

6 TO 8 SERVINGS

HERB CROUTONS: Trim crusts from *2 slices toasted white bread* and cut into ¼- to ½-inch cubes. Heat *2 tablespoons butter or margarine* in a small skillet over low heat. Add ¼ *teaspoon thyme*, crushed, ¼ *teaspoon marjoram*, crushed, and bread cubes. Turn and toss cubes until all sides are coated and croutons are browned.

ABOUT ²/₃ CUP

SHADES O' GREEN SALAD

3 oz. (about 3 cups)
fresh spinach,
chilled
½ head lettuce
4 stalks Pascal celery,
cut in slices
½ green pepper,
slivered
1 cucumber, sliced
2 tablespoons chopped
chives
French Dressing,
page 380
6 green olives, pitted
and sliced
1 small avocado, peeled
and sliced

1.   Line 6 chilled individual salad bowls with spinach leaves; tear remaining spinach and the lettuce into pieces.

2.   Toss lightly in a bowl the spinach, lettuce, celery, green pepper, cucumber, and chives. Pour about ½ cup dressing over salad and toss to coat greens evenly.

3.   Arrange individual portions of salad in bowls and garnish each with olive and avocado slices.

6 servings

NOTE: *Romaine* may be substituted for spinach; use *Tarragon French Dressing, page 381.*

ACCORDION TOMATO-CORN SALAD

8 medium-sized firm,
ripe tomatoes
4 ears corn, cooked,
cooled, and kernels
cut from cobs
1 medium-sized cucum-
ber, pared and diced
1 medium-sized green
pepper, chopped
½ cup Italian salad
dressing
2 tablespoons finely
chopped onion
1 teaspoon Worcester-
shire sauce
1 teaspoon salt
Seasoned salt

1.   Cut out around stem ends of tomatoes. Make 4 or 5 cuts in each tomato from bottom almost through to stem end. Pull pieces apart slightly to give accordion effect. Cover and chill tomatoes.

2.   Meanwhile, toss corn, cucumber, and green pepper together in a bowl.

3.   Blend salad dressing, onion, Worcestershire sauce, and salt. Pour over vegetables, cover, and marinate in refrigerator 1 hour.

4.   When ready to serve, sprinkle cut surfaces of tomatoes generously with seasoned salt. Spoon marinated vegetables between the slices and place each tomato on a bed of *salad greens*.   8 SERVINGS

SALADE PROVENÇALE

2 green peppers, cut
in strips
¼ cup oil (part salad
oil and part olive oil)
3 firm ripe tomatoes,
washed and cut in
pieces
½ Bermuda onion,
peeled and sliced
4 oz. fresh mushrooms,
cleaned and sliced
lengthwise
12 whole pitted ripe
olives

1.   Fry the green pepper strips in the oil until partially tender.

2.   Remove strips to a bowl. Add the tomatoes, onion, mushrooms, and olives; toss.

3.   Shake well in a covered jar, *4 parts oil* (half

salad oil and half olive oil, including the oil from frying), *1 part white wine vinegar, salt* and *pepper* to taste, and *1 cut clove garlic*. Remove garlic before pouring dressing over salad; toss gently until well coated. Marinate at room temperature about 1 hour, turning occasionally. Chill.

4. Sprinkle generously with *freshly ground black pepper*. ABOUT 6 SERVINGS

ROQUEFORT-VEGETABLE SALAD

Crisp salad greens
1 small onion, sliced
1 cup sliced raw
  cauliflower
1 can (16 oz.) cut
  green beans, chilled
  and drained

1 can (13 to 15 oz.)
  green asparagus
  spears, chilled and
  drained
Roquefort-Mayonnaise
  Dressing, *below*

1. Half-fill six individual salad bowls with the greens. Arrange vegetables on greens.
2. Accompany with a bowl of the dressing garnished with snipped *parsley*. 6 SERVINGS

ROQUEFORT-MAYONNAISE DRESSING: Blend *3 ounces cream cheese*, softened, in a bowl with *3 ounces Roquefort cheese*, crumbled. Stir in *½ cup light cream*, *½ cup mayonnaise*, *½ teaspoon Worcestershire sauce*, *¼ teaspoon garlic powder*, and *¼ teaspoon dry mustard*. Beat until fluffy and chill. ABOUT 1½ CUPS DRESSING

SARDINE-EGG SALAD-STUFFED TOMATOES

6 tomatoes
2 cans (3¾ oz. each)
  Norwegian sardines
6 hard-cooked eggs,
  diced
2 tablespoons capers
¼ cup dairy sour cream

3 tablespoons
  mayonnaise
1 tablespoon caper
  liquid
½ teaspoon dry mustard
¼ teaspoon salt

1. Rinse tomatoes (peel if desired) and chill thoroughly in refrigerator.
2. Drain 1 can of sardines, remove tails, and cut the sardines into pieces; reserve the other can of sardines for completing the salad. Lightly toss the sardines with the eggs and capers.
3. Combine the sour cream, mayonnaise, caper liquid, dry mustard, and salt. Add to egg-sardine mixture and toss lightly to mix well. Chill thoroughly.
4. When both the mixture and tomatoes are thoroughly chilled, cut a slice from the top of each tomato. Using a spoon, remove seeds. Invert shells to drain. Sprinkle insides with *seasoned salt* before stuffing. Fill center of tomatoes with the egg-sardine mixture.
5. Choose greenest *lettuce leaves* and use to line salad plates. Set tomatoes on lettuce. Place one sardine across each stuffed tomato and garnish with sprigs of *watercress*. 6 SERVINGS

FRUIT SALADS

FRUIT PREPARATION

Apples, pears—Rinse, cut into quarters, remove core, and, if desired, pare and cut into lengthwise slices. Toss with pineapple or citrus fruit juice to help prevent discoloration.

Avocados—Rinse, peel, cut into halves lenthwise, and remove pits. Brush surfaces with lemon juice to help prevent discoloration.

Bananas—Use bananas having brown-flecked peel. Remove peel and cut bananas into pieces or slices. Brush or gently toss with pineapple or citrus fruit juice to help prevent discoloration.

Blueberries, raspberries—Sort and rinse; drain thoroughly.

Cherries—Sort, rinse, and drain. Remove stems, cut into halves, and remove pits.

Grapes—Rinse and drain thoroughly. When using thick-skinned grapes in salad mixture, peel them, if desired; remove seeds if any. Cut large bunches into small clusters.

Melons—Rinse and cut into halves. With a knife or spoon, remove seedy center. *For melon rings*, rinse melon and cut into halves crosswise. With a knife or spoon, remove seedy center. Cut melon into ¾-inch slices, reserving ends. With a sharp paring knife, remove the rind from each ring. Using a melon-ball cutter, carefully cut balls from melon ends. Reserve balls for use in other food preparation. Chill melon rings and balls in refrigerator. *For melon balls*, use melon-ball cutter, carefully cutting out balls.

Nectarines—Rinse, halve, and remove pits.

Oranges, grapefruit — Rinse. With a sharp knife, cut away the peel and white membrane. Or fruit may be blanched as follows before removing peel and membrane: Cover fruit with boiling water in a saucepot; cover and bring quickly to boiling. Remove from heat and let stand, covered, about 3 minutes. Drain, then cover with cold water. When fruit is chilled, drain. (Refrigerate after draining, if desired.) Remove peel and membrane by cutting slits with a sharp pointed knife through peel from stem to blossom end. Then remove segments by cutting on either side of dividing membranes to the center of fruit. Discard seeds, if any.

Peaches — Rinse; plunge into boiling water to loosen skins. Immediately plunge into cold water; gently slip off skins. Cut into halves; remove pits. Brush cut surfaces with lemon juice.

Pineapples — Cut off and discard crown (spiny top) and rinse pineapple. Cut into slices or wedges. With a sharp knife, cut away and discard rind and "eyes" and the core from each piece. Cut slices or wedges into smaller pieces, if desired.

Strawberries — Sort, rinse, and drain. Remove hull or leave on if used for garnish.

HELPFUL HINTS ABOUT FRUITS

• To obtain maximum juice from lemons and limes, firmly roll the fruit on a hard surface before extracting juice.

• To extract juice from a lemon when only a small amount is needed, puncture fruit with a fork and gently squeeze out desired amount of juice.

• To keep juice in fruit which has been cut, cover exposed part with waxed paper and place fruit, cut side down, on a dish, or fit cut side with a transparent bowl cover.

• To remove pits from cherries, insert a new pen point into penholder, pointed end in, and remove pits with the rounded end of pen point.

WALDORF SALAD

An always-popular salad said to have been created by a chef at the Waldorf in New York.

2 medium-sized red apples, rinsed, cored, and diced (about 2 cups)	½ cup coarsely chopped walnuts
1 cup diced celery	¼ cup mayonnaise
	4 crisp cup-shaped lettuce leaves

1. Combine the apples, celery, and walnuts in a bowl; add mayonnaise and toss to mix thoroughly. Chill in refrigerator.

2. To serve, place lettuce leaves on individual salad plates, and spoon a portion of the salad mixture into each. 4 SERVINGS

NOTE: If desired, add about ⅓ *cup golden raisins* and/or ⅓ *cup seeded, halved Tokay grapes* to salad mixture. Increase mayonnaise to ½ cup. Or, omit celery and raisins and add about ⅓ *cut-up dates* and ⅓ *cup miniature marshmallows* to the salad. Use ½ cup mayonnaise and combine with about ½ *cup whipped cream*, if desired.

PIMIENTO-CHEESE AVOCADO SALAD

4 ripe avocados	1 tablespoon minced parsley
1 jar or can (7 oz.) whole pimientos, drained; pat dry with absorbent paper (keep pimientos in one piece)	Few grains cayenne pepper
	½ teaspoon seasoned salt
8 oz. cream cheese, softened	⅛ teaspoon freshly ground black pepper
½ cup minced ripe olives	Salad greens
	Creamy Pimiento Dressing, *below*

1. Cut avocados into halves; peel and remove pits. Enlarge the pit cavities with a spoon, reserving scooped-out avocado. Roughen the surfaces of cavities with a spoon or fork. Brush surfaces (except cavities) with *lemon juice*.

2. Line the cavities with pimientos and trim evenly around edges. Mince leftover pimiento.

3. Combine scooped-out avocado, minced pimiento, cream cheese, olives, parsley, cayenne pepper, seasoned salt, and black pepper; blend the mixture thoroughly.

4. Fill lined avocados with cheese mixture, spreading it smoothly on top. Wrap each half in moisture-vaporproof material; chill thoroughly.

5. When ready to serve, halve each filled avocado shell lengthwise and arrange quarters on crisp *salad greens*. Serve with Creamy Pimiento Dressing.

8 SERVINGS

CREAMY PIMIENTO DRESSING: Mix ½ cup *mayonnaise* with ½ cup *dairy sour cream*. Season with ¼ *teaspoon salt*, ⅛ *teaspoon pepper*, and 2 *tablespoons lemon juice*. Stir in 2 *tablespoons minced pimiento* and 2 *tablespoons minced parsley*. Garnish with additional pimiento and parsley. Serve as dressing for stuffed avocados and cucumbers.

ABOUT 1 CUP

NOTE: To use any leftover cheese mixture, try this salad (or appetizer) idea. Core a firm, nicely shaped *cucumber*, using a sharp knife or an apple corer, removing all the seeds. Score the cucumber hollow with a fork or sharp knife; stuff with paper toweling to absorb the moisture. Remove toweling and fill with cheese mixture; chill. Cut in slices to serve.

COCONUT-MALLOW SALAD IN CHEESE TARTS

1 can (29 oz.) pear halves	1 cup flaked coconut
1 can (30 oz.) pineapple chunks	2 cups dairy sour cream
14 marshmallows, quartered	Cheddar Cheese Tart Shells, *below*

1. Thoroughly drain pear halves and pineapple chunks. Cut pear halves into quarters.
2. Put drained fruit into a bowl with the marshmallows and coconut; add sour cream and toss lightly until mixed thoroughly. Cover; chill 12 to 24 hours.
3. When ready to serve, spoon salad into cheese tart shells on chilled salad plates. Garnish with *fresh mint* and serve as a luncheon entrée.

6 SERVINGS

CHEDDAR CHEESE TART SHELLS

2 cups all-purpose flour	2/3 cup shortening
1 teaspoon salt	5 to 6 tablespoons cold water
1 cup finely shredded Cheddar cheese	

1. Mix flour, salt, and cheese in a bowl. Cut in shortening with a pastry blender until pieces are the size of small peas.
2. Sprinkle water over mixture, a teaspoonful at a time; mix lightly with a fork after each addition. Add only enough water to hold pastry together; work quickly and do not overhandle to help insure tenderness.
3. Shape pastry into 6 equal balls. Flatten each on a lightly floured surface and roll into a round about 1/8-inch thick and no less than 7 inches in diameter.
4. Fit into six 4½ x 1½ inch tart pans; flute edges and prick pastry well.
5. Bake at 450°F about 10 minutes, or until lightly browned.

SIX 4½-INCH TART SHELLS

NOTE: This versatile salad may also be appropriately served as a bridge party dessert-salad. For a dinner salad, omit the cheese pastry shells and serve on chilled *salad greens*. Servings will vary from 8 to 10 depending on the type of service.

CHEF'S FRUIT SALAD

1 qt. shredded salad greens	1½ cups Swiss cheese strips
6 cups mixed fruit	1½ cups cooked ham or turkey strips
Creamy Lemon-Celery Seed Dressing, *page 383*, or Celery Seed Salad Dressing, *page 382*	Cinnamon-Buttered Raisins, *below*

Line a salad bowl with crisp *salad greens*. Add shredded greens. Arrange fruit in bowl. Spoon some of the desired dressing over all. Top with cheese and ham strips alternately with Cinnamon-Buttered Raisins. Serve with remaining dressing.

ABOUT 6 SERVINGS

CINNAMON-BUTTERED RAISINS: Mix *1 tablespoon butter or margarine*, melted, *1/4 cup dark raisins*, *1/2 cup golden raisins*, and *1/2 teaspoon ground cinnamon* in a skillet. Set over low heat and stir 5 minutes. Cool.

ABOUT 1 CUP RAISINS

CALIFORNIA FRUIT JUMBLE

Arrange on a platter or in an attractive bowl *4 fully ripe unpeeled avocados*, cut in serving-sized pieces with *crenshaw, casaba, Persian, cantaloupe, honeydew*, or *watermelon*, cut in serving-sized pieces. Brush cut surfaces of avocado with *lemon juice*. Top with *2 pints strawberries*. Serve with *Avocado Salad Dressing*.

AVOCADO SALAD DRESSING: Blend *1/4 cup orange juice*, *2 tablespoons cider vinegar*, and *1 envelope salad dressing mix* in an electric blender container. Add *2/3 cup salad oil* and blend. Peel *3 fully ripe avocados* and cut into pieces. Adding a few pieces at a time to the container, blend in avocado. Mix in about *1/2 cup dairy sour cream*. Remove to serving dish; cover and chill. ABOUT 3 CUPS DRESSING

MOLDED SALADS

GELATIN TECHNIQUES

Dissolve unflavored gelatin. Modern high quality unflavored gelatin softens almost instantly in cold water or other cold liquid so "soaking" is no longer necessary. Generally, ½ cup cold liquid is used to soften each envelope of gelatin. To completely dissolve gelatin, stir in a saucepan over low heat.

Whenever a recipe calls for more than 1 tablespoon of sugar, the gelatin may be combined with the sugar (omitting softening in cold water) and the mixture slowly heated in fruit juice, milk, cream, or whatever liquid is used in the recipe, heating only until gelatin and sugar are dissolved.

Chill gelatin mixtures either by setting the bowl in the refrigerator or by putting it in a pan containing ice and water. If placed in refrigerator, stir occasionally; if placed over ice and water (a quicker method), stir frequently. If the gelatin mixture is clear, chill until slightly thicker than the consistency of thick, unbeaten egg white before adding any solid ingredients. If the mixture contains ingredients which thicken it or make it opaque, chill until it begins to gel (becomes slightly thicker); mix in solid ingredients only after mixture begins to gel.

Prevent separation of layered molds by chilling gelatin mixtures until set but not firm (sticky to the touch and not smooth on surface); layers should be of almost the same consistency when turning one mixture onto another so that they will be fused when unmolded.

Unmold gelatin from a plain ring mold by carefully running a pointed knife around inside of mold to loosen. Loosen a fancy mold by running the knife almost to bottom of mold in several places. If gelatin mold does not loosen readily, dip it into warm (not hot) water for only about 10 seconds. Invert mold onto a chilled serving plate which has been rinsed with cold water (so mold may be centered).

Beat heavy (whipping) cream to a medium consistency (piles softly) when it is to be blended with a gelatin mixture.

Molded Fruit Salads

APRICOT SALAD SQUARES

2 cans (about 17 oz. each) apricot halves, drained (reserve syrup)	1 teaspoon whole cloves
	1¼ cups boiling water
1 piece (3 in.) stick cinnamon	2 pkgs. (3 oz. each) orange-flavored gelatin
1 teaspoon whole allspice	1 cup ginger ale
	Pitted ripe olives

1. Put the apricot syrup and spices into a saucepan; simmer 10 minutes.
2. Add apricots. Set aside to cool.
3. Pour boiling water over gelatin and stir until gelatin is dissolved.
4. Drain syrup from apricots (discard spices) and measure syrup; add water to yield 2 cups. Pour liquid and ginger ale into gelatin. Chill until mixture is slightly thickened.
5. Meanwhile, in a 2-quart shallow dish, arrange apricot halves, cavity sides up, in clusters. Put an olive into each cavity. Spoon thickened gelatin over apricots and olives. Chill in refrigerator until firm.
6. To serve, cut into squares. Garnish with crisp *salad greens.* 12 SERVINGS

AVOCADO MOUSSE

There's an appealing blend of flavors in this rich gelatin mold, a prestigious addition to a spring luncheon menu.

1 env. unflavored gelatin	2 tablespoons grated onion
1 cup water	1 teaspoon salt
3 cups mashed ripe avocado (about 4 medium-sized)	1 teaspoon grated lemon peel
½ cup mayonnaise	1 teaspoon prepared horseradish
2 tablespoons lemon juice	½ cup chilled heavy cream, whipped

1. Sprinkle gelatin over ½ cup of the water in a saucepan to soften. Stir over low heat until gelatin is dissolved. Remove from heat and stir in the remaining ½ cup water. Set the gelatin aside to cool.
2. Meanwhile, blend remaining ingredients except cream in a large bowl. Stir cooled gelatin into

the avocado mixture. Chill until mixture is slightly thickened.

3.   Fold in the whipped cream and turn into a 1½-quart ring mold. Chill until firm.

4.   When ready to serve, unmold onto a chilled serving plate. Fill center of ring with large sprigs of *watercress*.   ABOUT 12 SERVINGS

MOLDED AVOCADO-GRAPEFRUIT SALAD
A blend of tart and delicate fruit flavors.

1½ cups boiling water	¼ teaspoon salt
1 pkg. (3 oz.) lemon-flavored gelatin	1¼ cups diced avocado
½ cup grapefruit juice	1 cup grapefruit sections

1.   Pour boiling water over gelatin and stir until dissolved. Blend in the grapefruit juice and salt. Chill until mixture is slightly thickened.

2.   Mix avocado and grapefruit into thickened gelatin. Turn into a 1-quart mold and chill until firm.

3.   Unmold onto a chilled serving plate. Serve with *Creamy Lemon Mayonnaise, page 384.*
                                ABOUT 6 SERVINGS

CHERRY-COTTAGE CHEESE SALAD MOLD
A delicious combination of cherries, pineapple, cottage cheese, olives, and nuts with compatible seasonings in a decorative mold.

1 cup boiling water	1 can (13-oz.) crushed pineapple, drained (reserve ½ cup syrup)
1 pkg. (3 oz.) cherry-flavored gelatin	
1 can (17 oz.) pitted dark sweet cherries in heavy syrup, drained (reserve 1 cup syrup)	1½ cups creamed cottage cheese, sieved
	¼ cup chopped pecans
½ cup chopped pecans	1 teaspoon sugar
¼ cup finely chopped pitted green olives	½ teaspoon celery salt
	½ teaspoon celery seed
1 cup boiling water	1 teaspoon grated onion
1 pkg. (3 oz.) lemon-flavored gelatin	½ teaspoon grated lemon peel

1.   Pour 1 cup boiling water over cherry-flavored gelatin in a medium-sized bowl and stir until dissolved. Mix in the reserved cherry syrup (add water to make 1 cup if necessary). Chill until slightly thicker than thick, unbeaten egg white.

2.   Meanwhile, halve cherries. Fold cherries, the ½ cup chopped pecans, and olives into thickened

gelatin. Spoon into a 7-cup heart-shaped or other fancy mold. Chill until just set, but not firm.

3.   Meanwhile, pour 1 cup boiling water over lemon-flavored gelatin in a medium-sized bowl and stir until dissolved. Mix in the reserved pineapple syrup. Chill until slightly thicker than thick, unbeaten egg white.

4.   Blend pineapple, cottage cheese, and remaining ingredients and stir into thickened gelatin until thoroughly mixed. Spoon over cherry layer; chill until firm, at least 3 hours.

5.   Unmold onto chilled serving plate; garnish with *lettuce*. Pipe *dairy sour cream* around the outer top edge of mold.   8 TO 10 SERVINGS

COLA SALAD

2 cups boiling water	1 cup pecans, coarsely chopped
2 pkgs. (3 oz. each) raspberry-flavored gelatin	1 cup maraschino cherries, drained and cut in eighths
1⅔ cups carbonated cola beverage	

1.   Pour the boiling water over gelatin in a bowl and stir until gelatin is dissolved. Mix in the cola beverage.

2.   Chill until slightly thicker than thick, unbeaten egg white.

3.   Stir the pecans and cherries into gelatin. Turn into a 1½-quart mold and chill until firm.

4.   Unmold onto a chilled serving plate. Accompany with a bowl of *salad dressing or mayonnaise*.
                                6 TO 8 SERVINGS

FESTIVE SALAD

1 can (30 oz.) fruit cocktail, drained (reserve 1⅓ cups syrup)	3 oz. cream cheese, softened
1 pkg. (3 oz.) lime-flavored gelatin	1 cup chilled heavy cream, whipped

1.   Heat 1 cup of the reserved syrup to boiling. Pour over gelatin in a bowl and stir until gelatin is dissolved. Mix in remaining syrup.

2.   Chill until mixture is slightly thicker than thick, unbeaten egg white.

3.   Gradually add thickened gelatin to cream cheese, a small amount at a time, stirring until well blended after each addition.

4. Mix in fruit cocktail, then fold in whipped cream. Turn into a 1½-quart mold and chill until firm.

5. Unmold onto a chilled serving plate.

8 to 10 SERVINGS

CRANBERRY SALAD

Perky with horseradish, this relish-type salad is a perfect foil for roast turkey.

2 cups fresh cranberries	2 tablespoons prepared horseradish
1 large red apple, pared, quartered, and cored	¼ teaspoon salt
	4 teaspoons unflavored gelatin
1 lemon, peeled, quartered, and seeds removed	½ cup cold water
	¼ cup chilled heavy cream, whipped
1 cup orange marmalade	

1. Put cranberries, apple, and lemon through coarse blade of food chopper. Add marmalade, horseradish, and salt; blend thoroughly.

2. Sprinkle gelatin over cold water to soften. Stir over low heat until gelatin is dissolved. Blend in the fruit mixture. Chill until just set, but not firm.

3. Fold whipped cream into gelatin mixture and turn into a 1-quart fancy mold. Chill until firm.

4. Unmold onto a serving platter and garnish with sprigs of *watercress*.   6 TO 8 SERVINGS

GRAPEFRUIT-LIME MOLD

½ cup sugar	2 env. unflavored gelatin
1 cup fresh grapefruit sections (cut in pieces if very large)	1 can (8¾ oz.) crushed pineapple, drained (reserve syrup)
½ cup fresh lime juice	¼ cup quartered maraschino cherries, well drained
1 pt. lime sherbet, softened	

1. Sprinkle ¼ cup sugar over grapefruit.

2. Add lime juice to sherbet; as sherbet melts, stir occasionally to blend.

3. Combine remaining sugar and gelatin in a saucepan. Add enough water to pineapple syrup to make 2 cups liquid. Mix 1 cup of the liquid into the gelatin mixture. Stir over low heat until gelatin is dissolved. Remove from heat; add remaining liquid and the sherbet. If necessary, beat with hand rotary or electric beater until well mixed.

4. Chill until mixture is the consistency of thick, unbeaten egg white, stirring occasionally.

5. Fold in grapefruit (including syrup), pineapple, and cherries. Turn into a 5-cup star-shaped mold. Chill until firm.

6. Unmold onto serving plate.   6 TO 8 SERVINGS

GRAPEFRUIT RING

2 env. unflavored gelatin	6 tablespoons orange juice
1 cup sugar	2 tablespoons lemon or lime juice
1 cup cold water	
1½ cups unsweetened grapefruit juice	

1. Combine gelatin and sugar in a saucepan. Mix in water. Stir over low heat until gelatin and sugar are dissolved. Remove from heat and stir in fruit juices. Pour into a 1-quart ring mold. Chill until firm.

2. Unmold onto a chilled platter. Garnish with crisp *salad greens*.   ABOUT 8 SERVINGS

ORANGE-CROWNED CHEESE SALAD

1 cup boiling water	1½ cups creamed cottage cheese, sieved
1 pkg. (3 oz.) lemon-flavored gelatin	½ teaspoon salt
1 can (6 oz.) frozen orange juice concentrate, thawed	1 pt. ripe strawberries, rinsed
3 tablespoons cold water	1 medium-sized ripe avocado, sieved
16 large orange sections (about 2 large oranges)	

1. Pour boiling water over gelatin in a bowl and stir until gelatin is dissolved. Mix in the orange juice concentrate and cold water. Chill until slightly thicker than thick, unbeaten egg white.

2. Arrange orange sections in bottom of a 1½-quart fancy tubed mold.

3. Divide gelatin mixture into halves. Blend cottage cheese and salt into one half. Set other half aside. Turn cottage cheese mixture into mold. Chill until almost set, but not firm.

4. Meanwhile, hull ¾ cup of the strawberries and cut them into halves; reserve whole berries for garnish. Arrange berry halves on gelatin mixture in mold with rounded sides against mold.

5. Blend sieved avocado into other half of slightly thickened gelatin. Turn avocado mixture into mold over first layer. Chill until firm.

6. Unmold onto chilled serving plate and garnish with reserved whole strawberries. **6 TO 8 SERVINGS**

KUMQUAT-AVOCADO MOLD

¾ cup boiling water
1 pkg. (3 oz.) lemon-flavored gelatin
¼ teaspoon salt
1¼ cups chilled ginger ale

1 pt. fresh kumquats, rinsed and thinly sliced
2 ripe avocados, peeled and diced

1. Pour boiling water over gelatin in a bowl and stir until gelatin is dissolved. Mix in salt and ginger ale.

2. Chill until slightly thicker than thick, unbeaten egg white.

3. Mix in the kumquats and avocados. Turn into a 1-quart mold. Chill until firm.

4. Unmold onto a chilled serving plate. Garnish as desired. **6 SERVINGS**

PRESERVED KUMQUAT-AVOCADO MOLD: Follow recipe for Kumquat-Avocado Mold. Substitute ½ *cup thinly sliced preserved kumquats* for the fresh kumquats. Decrease water to ½ cup and add ¼ *cup preserved kumquat syrup;* bring to boiling. Proceed as directed.

MOLDED FRUIT COMPOTE SALAD

This beautiful salad is given distinction by an unusual and easily made dressing.

1 cup apricot nectar
1 pkg. (3 oz.) orange-flavored gelatin
¾ cup orange juice
¼ cup lemon juice

1 can (30 oz.) fruits for salad, drained and cut in pieces
Curry Mayonnaise Dressing, *below*

1. Heat apricot nectar to boiling. Pour over gelatin in a bowl and stir until gelatin is dissolved. Mix in orange and lemon juices.

2. Chill until gelatin is slightly thicker than thick, unbeaten egg white.

3. Stir in the fruit. Turn into 6 individual molds. Chill until firm.

4. Unmold onto a chilled serving plate. Garnish with crisp *lettuce* or *curly endive.* Serve with Curry-Mayonnaise Dressing. **6 SERVINGS**

CURRY-MAYONNAISE DRESSING

1 cup mayonnaise
2 tablespoons confectioners' sugar
1 teaspoon curry powder

1 teaspoon lemon juice
Few grains salt
¼ cup heavy cream, whipped

Blend the mayonnaise with the confectioners' sugar, curry powder, lemon juice, and salt. Fold in the whipped cream. Refrigerate until ready to use. **ABOUT 1½ CUPS DRESSING**

SPARKLING FRESH PEACH MOLD

2 env. unflavored gelatin
¼ cup sugar
¾ cup water
3 cups white grape juice

¼ cup lemon juice
4 medium-sized ripe peaches, peeled and sliced
1½ cups red raspberries or blueberries

1. Blend gelatin and sugar in a saucepan. Mix in water; stir over low heat until gelatin and sugar are dissolved.

2. Remove from heat and stir in the grape juice and lemon juice. Chill until mixture is the consistency of thick, unbeaten egg white.

3. Arrange half of the sliced peaches and raspberries in a 1½-quart ring mold. Spoon half of the chilled gelatin over fruit. Arrange the remaining fruit in the mold and spoon remaining gelatin over fruit. Chill until firm.

4. Unmold onto a chilled serving plate. **ABOUT 8 SERVINGS**

PEACHES AND CREAM CHEESE SALAD

1 can (29 oz.) cling peach slices
Cantaloupe or honeydew melon (about 3 cups purée)
3 env. unflavored gelatin
1½ cups cold water

1 tablespoon sugar
1 teaspoon seasoned salt
1 tablespoon grated onion
3 oz. cream cheese (for eight balls)
Roasted diced almonds

1. Using an electric blender mash peaches with syrup, adding about one third at a time to the blender container. As peaches are mashed, turn into a large bowl. Purée enough melon to make 3 cups. Turn purée into the bowl with peaches.

2. Sprinkle gelatin over water in a saucepan. Stir over low heat until gelatin is dissolved. Blend in fruit mixture along with sugar, seasoned salt, and

onion. Turn into a 13x9-inch pan. Chill until just set (see *Decorative Topping, below*), or until firm.

3. Meanwhile, shape cream cheese into balls and roll in almonds. Cover and chill.

4. Cut salad into squares. Place on *salad greens*. Top with cheese balls.

5. Accompany with *Orange Salad Dressing, page 382.*   8 TO 12 SERVINGS

DECORATIVE TOPPING: 1 *can (16 ounce) cling peach slices* will be needed for about 24 slices. When mixture in pan is partially set, carefully place drained peach slices at regular intervals, allowing two slices per serving. Chill until firm.

PARTY-PERFECT SALAD MOLDS

2 pkgs. (12 oz. each) frozen sliced peaches, thawed	½ cup lemon juice
	½ cup maraschino cherries, quartered
2 pkgs. (3 oz. each) orange-flavored gelatin	¼ cup chopped celery
	¼ cup chopped green pepper
2 cups ginger ale	

1. Drain and set peaches aside, reserving syrup. Add enough water to syrup to make 1½ cups; bring to boiling.

2. Add boiling liquid to gelatin in a bowl and stir until gelatin is dissolved. Mix in ginger ale and lemon juice.

3. Chill until slightly thicker than thick, unbeaten egg white.

4. Blend in peaches and remaining ingredients. Spoon into twelve ½-cup individual molds. Chill until firm.

5. Unmold onto chilled salad plates.   12 SERVINGS

MOLDED PINEAPPLE-VEGETABLE LOAF

1 can (30 oz.) sliced pineapple, drained (reserve syrup)	3 oz. cream cheese, softened
	1 tablespoon cream
1 can (18 oz.) unsweetened pineapple juice	¼ cup chopped pimiento-stuffed olives
1 pkg. (6 oz.) lemon-flavored gelatin	2 cups shredded cabbage
½ cup lemon juice	1 cup shredded carrots

1. Add enough pineapple juice to reserved syrup to make 2 cups; heat to boiling. Pour over the gela-

tin in a bowl and stir until gelatin is dissolved. Mix in 1½ cups pineapple juice and the lemon juice.

2. Chill until mixture is slightly thickened.

3. Blend cream cheese and cream thoroughly; stir in the olives. Shape mixture into 8 balls; fit one ball in center of each pineapple ring, pressing it into place. Arrange two slices on bottom of a 9x5x3-inch loaf pan, two slices on each side, and one on each end.

4. Stir cabbage and carrots into gelatin mixture; turn mixture into pan. Chill until firm.

5. Unmold onto a chilled serving platter.
                                          ABOUT 12 SERVINGS

COCONUT-CREAM SALAD

1 cup boiling water	1¼ cups (about 3½ oz.) flaked coconut
1 pkg. (3 oz.) lime-flavored gelatin	
¼ cup sugar	1 cup chilled heavy cream, whipped
1 can (8¾ oz.) crushed pineapple, drained (reserve syrup)	

1. Pour boiling water over gelatin and sugar in a bowl. Stir until gelatin is dissolved.

2. Add enough water to the pineapple syrup to measure ½ cup liquid. Mix into gelatin. Chill until mixture is slightly thickened.

3. Stir in the pineapple and coconut. Fold in the whipped cream. Turn into a 5-cup mold and chill until firm.

4. Unmold onto a chilled serving plate. Garnish with pieces of *maraschino cherries*.
                                          ABOUT 8 SERVINGS

RASPBERRY SALAD MOLD

1¼ cups boiling water	1 can (8¾ oz.) crushed pineapple
1 pkg. (3 oz.) raspberry-flavored gelatin	1 large banana, peeled and sliced
1 pkg. (10 oz.) frozen raspberries, partially thawed	½ cup chopped nuts

1. Pour boiling water over gelatin in a bowl. Stir until gelatin is dissolved.

2. Add partially thawed berries and stir until berries are completely thawed. Chill until mixture is slightly thickened.

3. Stir the undrained pineapple, banana, and nuts into the gelatin. Turn into a 1-quart mold and chill until firm.

4. Unmold onto chilled serving plate. Serve with *Sour Cream Dressing, below.* 6 TO 8 SERVINGS

SOUR CREAM DRESSING: Combine *1 cup dairy sour cream, 1½ cups miniature marshmallows,* and *1 tablespoon sugar* in a bowl. Add *3 tablespoons lemon juice* gradually, beating until mixture is well blended. Store, covered, in refrigerator overnight. ABOUT 1½ CUPS

RHUBARB-STRAWBERRY MOLD

1 lb. rhubarb	1 cup sliced sweetened
¾ cup sugar	fresh strawberries,
¼ cup water	or 1 pkg. (10 oz.)
1 pkg. (3 oz.) strawberry-	frozen strawberries,
flavored gelatin	thawed
1 cup cold water	

1. Wash rhubarb; cut off stem ends and leaves; peel stalks only if skin is tough. Cut into 1-inch pieces (about 3 cups, cut) and put into a saucepan with the sugar and ¼ cup water. Set over low heat and stir until sugar is dissolved. Cover and cook slowly about 15 minutes, or until rhubarb is tender.
2. Drain rhubarb, reserving the hot syrup. Set rhubarb aside to cool.
3. Add enough boiling water to syrup to make 1 cup liquid. Pour over gelatin in a bowl and stir until gelatin is dissolved. Blend in the cold water. Chill until gelatin is slightly thickened.
4. Blend in the cooked rhubarb and strawberries. Turn into a 1-quart mold. Chill until firm.
5. Unmold onto chilled serving plate and, if desired, garnish with *whole strawberries* sprinkled with *confectioners' sugar.* 6 TO 8 SERVINGS

WATERMELON RELISH MOLD

1 pkg. (3 oz.) lemon-	½ cup thawed frozen
flavored gelatin	whipped topping
⅛ teaspoon salt	¼ cup mayonnaise or
¾ cup boiling water	salad dressing
1 cup ginger ale	2 tablespoons chopped
½ cup chopped sweet	capers
pickled watermelon	
rind	

1. Mix gelatin and salt in a bowl. Add boiling water and stir until dissolved. Mix in ginger ale. Chill until gelatin is slightly thickened.
2. Blend the watermelon rind and a mixture of the remaining ingredients into the thickened gelatin.

Turn mixture into a 3-cup mold. Chill until firm.
3. Unmold onto a chilled serving plate and garnish with crisp *salad greens.* ABOUT 6 SERVINGS

Molded Vegetable Salads

ARTICHOKE MOUSSE
This exquisite artichoke mold, born of time and patience, reflects the artistry of the professional.

6 medium-sized arti-	2 teaspoons grated
chokes	onion
1 onion, peeled and	1 teaspoon Worcester-
sliced	shire sauce
1 lime, sliced	1 teaspoon salt
2 stalks celery with	Few grains freshly
leaves, cut in pieces	ground black pepper
3 tablespoons olive oil	2 env. unflavored
1½ teaspoons salt	gelatin
½ cup mayonnaise	1 cup cold water
3 tablespoons lime	½ cup white grape juice
juice	1 cup chilled heavy
	cream, whipped

1. Remove about 1 inch from tops of artichokes by cutting straight across with a sharp knife. Cut off stems about 1 inch from base; remove and discard lower outside leaves. Rinse and drain.
2. Set the artichokes right-side up in 1 inch boiling water in a large saucepot. Add sliced onion, lime, celery, oil, and 1½ teaspoons salt. Cook, covered, 1 to 1½ hours, or until artichokes are very tender and a leaf can easily be pulled out. Add more water if necessary during cooking.
3. Drain and cool artichokes. Scrape "meat" from leaves; remove thistle (or fuzzy choke) and discard. Remove heart and combine in an electric blender container with "meat," mayonnaise, lime juice, grated onion, Worcestershire sauce, salt, and pepper; blend until smooth. (Or use hand rotary or electric beater to blend.) Set aside.
4. Soften gelatin in cold water in a saucepan. Set over low heat and stir until gelatin is completely dissolved. Remove from heat and stir in the grape juice. Set aside until cold.
5. Place a 1½-quart ring mold in a bowl of ice and water. Coat bottom with a small amount of gelatin. Chill until just set, but not firm. Arrange slivers of *ripe olives, pimientos,* and *green onions* in a floral design on bottom of mold.

6. Gently spoon a small amount of gelatin over the design to hold in place. Chill until layer is set, but not firm.

7. Add remaining gelatin to artichoke mixture; blend well. Chill over ice and water, stirring frequently, until mixture mounds slightly when dropped from a spoon. Fold in the whipped cream. Pour over design in mold and chill until firm.

8. Unmold onto a chilled tray and garnish with *curly endive*. Serve with *Cooked Pineapple Salad Dressing, page 369.* ABOUT 8 SERVINGS

CREAMY CARROT-NUT MOLD

2 cups boiling water	1 can (13¼ oz.) crushed
2 pkgs. (3 oz. each)	pineapple, undrained
orange-flavored	2 cups grated carrots
gelatin	½ cup chopped walnuts
1 cup dairy sour cream	

1. Pour boiling water over gelatin in a bowl and stir until the gelatin is dissolved.

2. Gradually add gelatin mixture to sour cream, stirring until well blended. Chill until mixture is slightly thickened.

3. Stir in pineapple, carrots, and walnuts. Turn into a 2-quart mold and chill until firm.

4. Unmold onto a bed of *salad greens* on a chilled serving plate. Garnish as desired.

8 TO 10 SERVINGS

EXQUISITE CUCUMBER MOLD

4 to 5 medium-sized	2 tablespoons grated
cucumbers	onion
2 env. unflavored	10 to 15 drops green
gelatin	food coloring
½ cup cold water	1 teaspoon salt
1½ cups mayonnaise	¼ teaspoon white
2½ tablespoons prepared	pepper
horseradish	1 cup chilled heavy
	cream, whipped

1. Rinse cucumbers, pare, cut lengthwise into halves, and discard seeds. Cut cucumbers into pieces. Finely grind enough cucumbers in an electric blender to make 3 cups pulp. Set aside.

2. Sprinkle gelatin evenly over cold water in a small saucepan; stir over low heat until completely dissolved. Set aside.

3. Measure mayonnaise into a large bowl and mix in cucumber pulp, horseradish, onion, food color-

ing, and a blend of salt and white pepper. Add the dissolved gelatin gradually, stirring constantly until thoroughly blended.

4. Chill until mixture is slightly thickened. Fold in whipped cream and turn into a 2-quart fancy mold. Chill until firm, about 6 hours.

5. Unmold onto a chilled serving plate.

8 TO 10 SERVINGS

PERFECTION SALAD DE LUXE

1 cup boiling water	8 drops Tabasco
1 pkg. (3 oz.) lemon-	1 cup finely shredded
flavored gelatin	cabbage
¾ cup cold water	½ cup finely shredded
½ teaspoon salt	carrot
1 tablespoon lemon	¼ cup finely shredded
juice	green pepper
1 tablespoon white	¼ cup finely shredded
wine vinegar	celery
1 teaspoon grated	1 tablespoon chopped
onion	pimiento
¼ teaspoon Worcester-	¼ to ½ teaspoon celery
shire sauce	seed

1. Pour boiling water over gelatin in a bowl; stir until gelatin is dissolved. Mix in the cold water, salt, lemon juice, vinegar, onion, Worcestershire sauce, and Tabasco. Chill until slightly thickened.

2. Blend in remaining ingredients. Turn into six ½-cup molds. Chill until firm.

3. Unmold onto crisp *salad greens* on chilled salad plates. 6 SERVINGS

POTATO SALAD MOLD

1 env. unflavored	2 jars (16 oz. each)
gelatin	mayonnaise-style
¾ cup chicken broth,	potato salad
cooled (dissolve 2	½ cup sliced celery
chicken bouillon	¼ cup sliced green
cubes in ¾ cup	onions
boiling water)	1 teaspoon garlic salt
	1 cup dairy sour cream

1. Sprinkle gelatin over broth in a saucepan to soften. Stir over low heat until gelatin is dissolved. Chill until mixture is slightly thickened.

2. Blend in remaining ingredients. Turn into a 5½-cup ring mold. Chill until firm.

3. Unmold onto a chilled serving plate.

ABOUT 8 SERVINGS

MUSTARD-POTATO SALAD MOLD

Feature a sunny potato salad mold with a platter of cold meats and cheese and iced tea for a casual warm weather luncheon menu.

2 teaspoons unflavored gelatin	2½ cups diced cooked potatoes (about 1 lb.)
½ cup sugar	¼ cup Italian salad dressing
½ cup cold water	2 hard-cooked eggs, chopped
1 cup undiluted evaporated milk	½ cup chopped celery or radishes
½ cup mayonnaise	
3 to 4 tablespoons prepared mustard	1 cup sliced pimiento-stuffed olives
1 tablespoon cider vinegar	½ cup sliced green onions
⅛ teaspoon pepper	

1.   Mix gelatin and sugar thoroughly in a saucepan. Stir in water. Place over low heat and stir until gelatin is dissolved.
2.   Remove from heat. Blend in evaporated milk, mayonnaise, mustard, vinegar, and pepper. Chill until mixture is slightly thickened.
3.   Toss potatoes with salad dressing. Mix potatoes, eggs and remaining ingredients with slightly thickened gelatin mixture. Turn into a 5½-cup ring mold. Chill until firm, about 4 hours.
4.   Unmold onto a chilled platter. Garnish with *leaf lettuce* and fill center with *cherry tomatoes*.
6 TO 8 SERVINGS

TWO-TONE SOUFFLÉ SALAD

1¾ cups tomato juice	¼ cup lemon juice
2 pkgs. (3 oz. each) lemon-flavored gelatin	½ cup mayonnaise
	1 tablespoon prepared horseradish
½ teaspoon salt	2 teaspoons grated onion
2 tablespoons wine vinegar	
¼ teaspoon salt	½ cup chopped celery
1 cup boiling water	½ cup chopped pared cucumber
⅓ cup cold water	½ cup cooked peas

1.   Bring 1 cup of the tomato juice to boiling. Pour over 1 package gelatin and the ½ teaspoon salt; stir until dissolved. Stir in the remaining tomato juice and vinegar.
2.   Pour into a 1½-quart fancy ring mold and chill until just set, but not firm.
3.   Meanwhile, dissolve the remaining package of gelatin and ¼ teaspoon salt in the boiling water.

Add the cold water, lemon juice, mayonnaise, horseradish, and onion; beat until well blended.
4.   Turn into a refrigerator tray and set in freezer about 20 minutes, or until mixture is frozen about 1 inch in from edge of tray.
5.   Turn partially frozen mixture into a bowl and beat with a hand rotary or electric beater until fluffy. Stir in vegetables and spoon over tomato layer in mold. Chill until firm, about 4 hours.
6.   Unmold onto a chilled large platter. Surround with alternate slices of cold *roast turkey* and *ham*. Garnish with *parsley sprigs*.
6 TO 8 SERVINGS

Molded Meat, Chicken, Fish & Shellfish Salads

TONGUE-VEGETABLE SALAD MOLD

1 smoked tongue (2½ to 3 lbs.)	2 beef bouillon cubes
	½ cup lemon juice
½ cup cold water	2 teaspoons grated onion
1 env. unflavored gelatin	
1½ cups vegetable broth (dissolve 2 vegetable bouillon cubes in 1½ cups boiling water)	3 tablespoons sugar
	½ teaspoon Worcestershire sauce
	¼ cup prepared horseradish
2 hard-cooked eggs, chilled and cut crosswise into 10 uniform slices	⅓ cup chopped sweet pickle
	1 cup finely diced celery
2 env. unflavored gelatin	½ cup finely diced green pepper

1.   Cook tongue according to package directions; chill thoroughly; reserve 3 cups tongue stock. Cut about 9 thin, uniform center slices of tongue; prepare 1½ cups finely diced tongue.
2.   Prepare all remaining ingredients for both layers of the salad before starting mold.
3.   Lightly oil a 2-quart ring mold with salad oil (not olive oil); set aside to drain.
4.   For aspic layer, sprinkle 1 envelope gelatin evenly over ½ cup cold water to soften. Place over hot water to dissolve.
5.   Stir dissolved gelatin into hot vegetable broth and blend thoroughly. Pour 1 cup of the mixture into bottom of mold; place mold and remaining gelatin mixture in refrigerator to chill until slightly thickened.

6. Arrange egg slices over chilled gelatin mixture in mold; spoon remaining gelatin mixture over eggs; chill until just set, but not firm.

7. For tongue-vegetable layer, sprinkle 2 envelopes gelatin evenly over 1 cup cold tongue stock to soften.

8. Heat remaining 2 cups of tongue stock until very hot; add beef bouillon cubes and stir until blended; pour over softened gelatin and stir until gelatin is dissolved. Stir in the lemon juice, onion, sugar, Worcestershire sauce, and horseradish.

9. Chill over ice and water, stirring frequently, until mixture is slightly thickened. Blend in the tongue, pickle, celery, and green pepper.

10. To complete mold, arrange the slices of tongue, rounded end down, against the sides of the mold. Spoon vegetable-gelatin mixture into mold; be sure slices of tongue remain in place. (Both layers should be of the same consistency when combined.) Chill until firm.

11. Unmold onto a chilled serving plate.

ABOUT 10 SERVINGS

JELLIED BEEF MOLD

3 cups diced roast beef	1 cup cold water
½ cup diced celery	¼ cup chili sauce
½ cup diced green pepper	¼ cup red wine vinegar
1 pimiento, coarsely chopped	2 tablespoons sugar
2 env. unflavored gelatin	1 teaspoon salt
2 cups beef broth, cooled (dissolve 2 beef bouillon cubes in 2 cups boiling water)	¼ teaspoon pepper
	2 tablespoons lemon juice
	2 tablespoons grated onion
	1 tablespoon prepared horseradish
¼ cup mayonnaise	1 teaspoon Worcestershire sauce

1. Toss the beef, celery, green pepper, and pimiento together in a bowl; refrigerate.

2. Sprinkle gelatin over 1 cup broth in a saucepan to soften. Stir over low heat until gelatin is dissolved. Blend in mayonnaise.

3. Remove from heat and stir in remaining broth and cold water. Mix in a blend of remaining ingredients. Chill until mixture is slightly thickened.

4. Mix the gelatin with the beef and vegetables. Turn into a 2-quart mold and chill until firm.

5. Unmold onto a chilled serving plate; garnish with crisp *lettuce*. ABOUT 8 SERVINGS

JELLIED VEAL

2 lbs. veal shank	1 bay leaf
1 lb. veal shoulder	¾ teaspoon ground ginger
2 qts. boiling water	¼ teaspoon pepper
1 tablespoon salt	
10 peppercorns	

1. Put meat into a large heavy saucepot with boiling water, salt, peppercorns, and bay leaf. Bring to boiling. Skim off foam. Cover, reduce heat, and simmer about 2 hours, or until meat is tender. Remove meat from broth.

2. Strain broth and return it to saucepot. Bring to boiling and boil rapidly, uncovered, until 1 quart liquid remains.

3. Remove the meat from bones. Put through medium blade of a food chopper. Add meat to broth with the ginger and pepper.

4. Turn into two 9x5x3-inch loaf pans and cool. Chill until firm.

5. Unmold onto a chilled serving plate.

10 TO 12 SERVINGS

HAM MOUSSE

2 env. unflavored gelatin	4 cups finely chopped cooked ham
1 cup cold water	2 tablespoons chopped pimiento
1 tablespoon prepared mustard	2 tablespoons chopped sweet pickle
Few grains cayenne pepper	1 cup chilled heavy cream, whipped

1. Soften gelatin in cold water in a saucepan. Dissolve completely over low heat.

2. Remove from heat. Stir in the mustard and cayenne pepper; cool. Chill until mixture is slightly thickened.

3. Blend in the ham, pimiento, and pickle. Fold in whipped cream.

4. Turn into a 1½-quart mold. Chill until firm.

5. When ready to serve, unmold onto a chilled serving plate. Garnish top of mold with *pimiento strips*. Spoon *Spicy Gelatin Cubes, below,* around mold. ABOUT 8 SERVINGS

SPICY GELATIN CUBES: Measure *1⅔ cups spiced peach syrup.* Heat 1 cup of syrup until boiling; pour over *1 package (3 ounces) cherry-flavored gelatin* and stir until gelatin is dissolved. Stir in remaining syrup, *⅓ cup water,* and *¼ teaspoon almond extract.* Pour into an 8-inch square pan and chill until firm.

When ready to serve, cut gelatin into ½-inch cubes. Spoon cubes around Ham Mousse.

CHICKEN MOUSSE

2 env. unflavored gelatin	¼ teaspoon dry mustard
3 cups cold chicken broth	2½ cups (about 12 oz.) finely chopped cooked chicken or turkey
2 tablespoons sweet pickle liquid	½ cup finely chopped sweet pickles
1 tablespoon grated onion	½ cup chopped salted blanched almonds
1 teaspoon mono-sodium glutamate	2 cups chilled heavy cream, whipped
¼ teaspoon salt	

1. Soften gelatin in 1 cup of the broth in a saucepan. Stir over low heat until gelatin is dissolved.
2. Mix in remaining broth, pickle liquid, onion, monosodium glutamate, salt, and dry mustard. Chill until mixture is slightly thickened.
3. Fold a mixture of the chicken, pickles, and almonds, and then the whipped cream into the gelatin. Turn into a bell-shaped or other 2-quart fancy mold. Chill until firm.
4. Unmold onto a chilled serving plate. Garnish with *sweet pickle strips.*   8 TO 10 SERVINGS

DUBONNET CHICKEN SALAD MOLD

2 env. unflavored gelatin	1 cup mayonnaise
1 cup cranberry juice cocktail	1½ cups finely diced cooked chicken
1 cup red Dubonnet	½ cup finely chopped celery
1 cup red currant syrup	¼ cup toasted blanched almonds, finely chopped
1 env. unflavored gelatin	
¾ cup cold water	½ cup chilled heavy cream, whipped
1 tablespoon soy sauce	

1. Sprinkle 2 envelopes gelatin over the cranberry juice to soften in a saucepan; stir over low heat until gelatin is dissolved. Remove from heat and stir in the Dubonnet and syrup.
2. Pour into a 2-quart fancy tubed mold. Chill until almost set, but not firm.
3. Meanwhile, sprinkle the 1 envelope gelatin over cold water in a saucepan. Stir over low heat until gelatin is dissolved.

4. Remove from heat and stir in the soy sauce and mayonnaise until thoroughly blended. Chill until mixture is slightly thickened. Mix in the chicken, celery, and almonds. Fold in the whipped cream until blended.
5. Spoon mixture into mold over first layer. Chill until firm, 8 hours or overnight.
6. Unmold and garnish with *leaf lettuce*, scored *cucumber slices*, and pitted *ripe olives.*
ABOUT 10 SERVINGS

CRAB MEAT MOUSSE

1½ tablespoons unflavored gelatin	Few grains pepper
¼ cup cold water	2 cups crab meat, flaked
¼ cup lemon juice	1 cup heavy cream, whipped
1 teaspoon salt	
¼ teaspoon paprika	

1. Sprinkle gelatin over cold water and lemon juice in a bowl; dissolve over hot water. Mix in salt, paprika, and pepper. Remove from heat and place over ice water about 5 minutes, stirring frequently.
2. Stir in crab meat, then fold in whipped cream. Turn into a 1-quart mold and chill until firm.
3. Unmold onto chilled plate and serve with *Cucumber Mayonnaise, below.*   ABOUT 8 SERVINGS

CUCUMBER MAYONNAISE: Wash, pare, and finely chop *1 medium-sized cucumber;* blend *1 cup mayonnaise, 2 tablespoons lemon juice,* and *1 tablespoon minced parsley,* then mix in cucumber.
ABOUT 2 CUPS

CRAB MEAT SALAD

Cooked Pineapple Salad Dressing, *page 369*	½ cup finely chopped celery
2 cups boiling water	¼ cup finely chopped green pepper
2 pkgs. (3 oz. each) lemon-flavored gelatin	1 tablespoon grated onion
½ teaspoon salt	2 teaspoons chopped pimiento
1 cup cold water	¾ lb. fresh crab meat, separated in pieces (bony tissue removed)
3 tablespoons cider vinegar	
¼ cup large-curd creamed cottage cheese, sieved	½ cup chilled heavy cream, whipped
½ cup coarsely chopped salted almonds	Fresh pineapple, thinly sliced pieces

1. Prepare salad dressing; chill thoroughly.

2. Pour boiling water over gelatin and salt in a bowl; stir until gelatin is dissolved. Blend in the cold water and vinegar. Chill until mixture is slightly thickened.

3. Thoroughly mix cottage cheese, almonds, celery, green pepper, onion, and pimiento with ½ cup of the salad dressing. Gently blend in crab meat.

4. Stir the crab meat mixture into slightly thickened gelatin. Turn into a 2-quart fancy mold and chill until firm.

5. Fold the whipped cream into the remaining salad dressing. Chill until ready to serve.

6. Unmold salad onto chilled serving plate and surround mold with the chilled sliced pineapple. Serve with the salad dressing.   ABOUT 8 SERVINGS

COOKED PINEAPPLE SALAD DRESSING

½ cup butter or margarine	1 cup unsweetened pineapple juice
2 tablespoons flour	1 egg, slightly beaten
2 tablespoons sugar	2 tablespoons lemon juice
Few grains salt	

1. Melt the butter in a heavy saucepan. Blend in flour, sugar, and salt; heat until mixture bubbles.

2. Add pineapple juice gradually, stirring constantly. Bring to boiling; stir and cook 3 minutes.

3. Stir about 3 tablespoons of the hot mixture into the beaten egg. Immediately blend into the mixture in saucepan and cook 3 minutes, stirring constantly.

4. Remove from heat and stir in lemon juice. Cool; chill. Store in a covered jar.
   ABOUT 1½ CUPS DRESSING

SHRIMP SALAD DUO ÉLÉGANTE

2 lbs. cooked shrimp, peeled and deveined	1½ cups boiling water
½ cup chopped pickled watermelon rind (reserve ½ cup syrup)	1 can (29 oz.) pear halves, drained (reserve 1½ cups syrup)
⅔ cup lime juice	1½ cups sliced celery
4 teaspoons French dressing mix	¼ cup coarsely chopped pistachio nuts
2 pkgs. (3 oz. each) strawberry-flavored gelatin	French Mayonnaise, below

1. Put shrimp into a large shallow dish and pour a mixture of the reserved syrup, lime juice, and French dressing mix over the shrimp; cover and marinate 2 hours, turning occasionally. Drain, reserving marinade; set shrimp aside.

2. Dissolve gelatin in boiling water; stir in 1 cup of the marinade and the reserved pear syrup; chill until gelatin is slightly thickened.

3. Pour gelatin into a 2-quart ring mold to ¼-inch depth; set remaining gelatin aside. Cut three pear halves in half lengthwise, and arrange, rounded side down, in bottom of mold; chill until gelatin is just set, but not firm.

4. Meanwhile, cut remaining pears and 2 cups of the shrimp into small pieces; add to remaining gelatin with the watermelon rind and blend well.

5. Spoon mixture over layer in mold and chill until firm, about 3 hours.

6. Combine remaining shrimp (about 2 cups) with celery, nuts, and the French Mayonnaise; toss lightly to mix. Refrigerate.

7. Unmold salad onto a chilled large serving plate and garnish mold with *salad greens*. Spoon shrimp mixture into the center.   8 TO 10 SERVINGS

FRENCH MAYONNAISE: Mix together *½ cup mayonnaise, ¼ cup clear French dressing,* and *¼ teaspoon horseradish.*

MOLDED LOBSTER ELEGANCE

2½ env. unflavored gelatin	1 teaspoon prepared horseradish
1 cup cold water	3 cups cooked lobster meat
3 egg yolks	
1 cup strong chicken broth, cooled (dissolve 2 chicken bouillon cubes in 1 cup boiling water)	3 tablespoons lemon juice
	1½ cups chilled heavy cream, whipped
1¼ teaspoons salt	¼ cup finely chopped toasted almonds
¼ teaspoon pepper	¼ cup finely chopped celery
2 teaspoons grated onion	¼ cup finely chopped pimiento-stuffed olives
1 teaspoon prepared mustard	

1. Soften the gelatin in the cold water in a small bowl. Set aside.

2. Meanwhile, beat the egg yolks in the top of a double boiler. Add the broth gradually, stirring constantly. Mix in the salt and pepper. Stirring constantly, cook over simmering water until smooth and slightly thickened, 5 to 8 minutes.

3. Remove from simmering water, immediately

add the softened gelatin, and stir until gelatin is dissolved. Stir in the grated onion, mustard, and horseradish. Cool; chill until mixture is slightly thickened.

4. Cut the lobster meat into small pieces and put into a large bowl. Drizzle lemon juice evenly over lobster.

5. Fold whipped cream into the slightly thickened gelatin mixture. Mix almonds, celery, and olives with the lobster. Pour the whipped cream mixture over lobster and fold together. Turn mixture into a 1½-quart mold. Chill until firm, 4 to 5 hours or overnight.

6. Unmold onto a chilled serving plate. Garnish with *watercress*.   10 TO 12 SERVINGS

CUCUMBER-SALMON RING

1 pkg. (3 oz.) lime-flavored gelatin	¼ cup cold water
½ teaspoon seasoned salt	1 cup mayonnaise
	1 teaspoon seasoned salt
1 cup boiling water	2 tablespoons cider vinegar
1 cup cold water	
2 tablespoons lemon juice	1 can (16 oz.) salmon, drained and flaked
1 cup grated pared cucumber	½ cup chopped celery
1 env. unflavored gelatin	⅓ cup chopped sweet pickle

1. Dissolve lime-flavored gelatin with ½ teaspoon seasoned salt in boiling water. Stir in 1 cup cold water and the lemon juice. Chill until slightly thicker than thick, unbeaten egg white.

2. Stir in cucumber; turn into a 1½-quart ring mold. Chill until just set, but not firm.

3. Meanwhile, soften unflavored gelatin in ¼ cup cold water; set over low heat and stir until gelatin is dissolved. Blend with a mixture of the mayonnaise, 1 teaspoon seasoned salt, and vinegar. Mix in salmon, celery, and pickle.

4. Spoon salmon mixture into mold over first layer. Chill until firm.

5. Unmold onto a serving plate and garnish with *salad greens*.   ABOUT 8 SERVINGS

SUPER TUNA RING

8 oz. cream cheese	¼ teaspoon marjoram, crushed
1 can (10¾ oz.) condensed tomato soup	4 teaspoons Worcestershire sauce
2 env. unflavored gelatin	1½ cups chopped celery
1 cup cold water	¼ cup chopped green onion
1 cup mayonnaise	
¼ teaspoon salt	2 cans (6½ or 7 oz. each) tuna, drained and flaked
⅛ teaspoon pepper	

1. Melt the cream cheese in the top of a double boiler over boiling water, stirring occasionally. Blend in the tomato soup until smooth. Remove from heat.

2. Soften gelatin in water in a small saucepan. Set over low heat and stir until gelatin is dissolved. Blend into cheese-tomato mixture. Stir in mayonnaise, salt, pepper, marjoram, and Worcestershire sauce until blended. Cover and chill until mixture is slightly thickened.

3. Mix the celery, onion, and tuna into chilled gelatin until well blended. Turn into a 1½-quart ring mold. Chill until firm, at least 8 hours or overnight.

4. Unmold onto a chilled serving plate. Fill center and garnish edge with *watercress*.   12 SERVINGS

TUNA MOUSSE

1 env. unflavored gelatin	2 tablespoons lemon juice
½ cup cold water	1½ tablespoons butter or margarine
2 eggs, beaten	
¾ cup milk	2 cans (6½ or 7 oz. each) tuna, drained and flaked
1½ teaspoons flour	
1½ teaspoons curry powder	¼ cup chopped pimiento stuffed olives
1 teaspoon seasoned salt	⅔ cup chilled heavy cream, whipped
Few grains pepper	

1. Sprinkle gelatin over the cold water to soften.

2. Using a wire whisk, beat the eggs with milk, flour, curry powder, seasoned salt, and pepper in the top of a double boiler. Set over hot (not boiling) water; bottom of double boiler top should not touch water. Cook, stirring constantly, until mixture is slightly thickened.

3. Remove from water; immediately add gelatin and stir until dissolved. Blend in lemon juice and

butter. Cool; chill until mixture is slightly thickened.

4. Mix tuna and olives into gelatin. Fold in whipped cream until blended. Turn mixture into a 1-quart mold. Chill until firm.

5. Unmold onto a chilled serving plate. Garnish with crisp *salad greens*. ABOUT 6 SERVINGS

Aspics

ARTICHOKE-ALMOND TOMATO ASPIC

1 can (46 oz.) tomato juice	4 env. unflavored gelatin
3 tablespoons lemon juice	1½ cups cold water
1 small onion, chopped	1 cup sliced pimiento-stuffed olives
1 teaspoon salt	1 cup slivered blanched almonds, toasted
¼ teaspoon pepper	
½ teaspoon celery salt	1 can (4½ oz.) artichoke hearts, drained and cut in wedges
½ teaspoon paprika	
¼ teaspoon cayenne pepper	

1. Put tomato juice, lemon juice, onion, salt, pepper, celery salt, paprika and cayenne pepper into a saucepan; bring to boiling.

2. Soften gelatin in cold water in a large bowl.

3. Strain hot tomato mixture into gelatin and stir until gelatin is dissolved; cool thoroughly.

4. Distribute the sliced olives, slivered almonds, and artichoke wedges evenly over bottom of a 13x9-inch pan. Gently pour the cooled tomato mixture over them. Chill until firm.

5. Cut into individual servings and place on chilled *salad greens*. Garnish as desired.

ABOUT 16 SERVINGS

TOMATO ASPIC RING

2 env. unflavored gelatin	1 tablespoon prepared horseradish
½ cup cold water	1 tablespoon grated onion
2 cans (16 oz. each) stewed tomatoes	½ teaspoon Worcestershire sauce
2 tablespoons sugar	3 hard-cooked eggs, cut in quarters
½ teaspoon salt	
2 tablespoons cider vinegar	

1. Sprinkle gelatin over cold water to soften.

2. Turn tomatoes into a saucepan and break up large pieces with a spoon. Stir in sugar, salt, vinegar, horseradish, onion, and Worcestershire sauce and heat to boiling. Add the softened gelatin and stir until dissolved.

3. Chill until mixture is slightly thickened.

4. Arrange egg quarters around bottom of a 5½-cup ring mold. Spoon slightly thickened gelatin mixture into mold. Chill until firm.

5. Unmold and fill center with *Marinated Green Peas, below*. 6 TO 8 SERVINGS

MARINATED GREEN PEAS: Drain *2 cans (17 ounces each) green peas*. Mix in *¼ cup sliced green onions*. Toss with *1 cup French dressing*; chill.

SENATE SALAD BOWL WITH SHRIMP-TOMATO ASPIC

A variation of the Senate Salad served in the United States Senate dining room.

1½ cups tomato juice	1 pkg. (9 oz.) frozen artichoke hearts
1 pkg. (3 oz.) lemon-flavored gelatin	Curly endive, lettuce, spinach, watercress
1 teaspoon salt	1 can frozen grapefruit sections, thawed and drained
Few grains cayenne pepper	
1½ teaspoons grated onion	½ cup sliced ripe olives
1½ teaspoons prepared horseradish	½ cup crumbled blue cheese
¾ lb. cooked shrimp, peeled and deveined	

1. Heat 1 cup of the tomato juice until very hot. Pour over gelatin in a bowl and stir until gelatin is dissolved. Stir in remaining tomato juice with salt, cayenne pepper, onion, and horseradish.

2. Pour mixture into an 8x4x2-inch loaf pan. Chill until mixture is slightly thickened.

3. Arrange 12 of the shrimp in 2 even rows in the gelatin mixture, with shrimp extending partly above surface. (Chill remaining shrimp for use in salad bowl.) Chill until firm, about 1½ hours.

4. Meanwhile, cook artichoke hearts according to package directions; cool; chill thoroughly.

5. Tear greens into pieces to yield about 2 cups of each. Mix in a large salad bowl; chill.

6. Just before serving, toss drained grapefruit sections, reserved shrimp, artichoke hearts, and ripe olives with greens; top with blue cheese.

7. Cut aspic into 12 squares with shrimp in the

center of each. Arrange aspic squares on salad. Serve with *French dressing*.   6 SERVINGS

LAYERED AVOCADO-TOMATO SALAD

1 env. unflavored gelatin	1¾ cups cold tomato juice
1 tablespoon sugar	¼ cup ketchup
1½ teaspoons salt	1 tablespoon lemon juice
1½ cups cold water	
2 cups sieved avocado (about 2 avocados)	½ teaspoon salt
	⅛ teaspoon onion salt
¼ cup lemon juice	1 teaspoon Worcestershire sauce
1 env. unflavored gelatin	2 drops Tabasco

1.   Combine 1 envelope gelatin, sugar, and 1½ teaspoons salt in a saucepan. Mix in ½ cup water. Stir over low heat until gelatin is dissolved.
2.   Remove from heat. Mix in remaining cold water, avocado, and ¼ cup lemon juice. Turn into a 1½-quart ring mold; chill until just set, but not firm.
3.   Meanwhile, soften 1 envelope gelatin in ½ cup of the cold tomato juice. Stir over low heat until gelatin is dissolved.
4.   Remove from heat. Mix in remaining ingredients. Chill until mixture is slightly thickened.
5.   When avocado layer in mold is just set, turn tomato mixture into the mold. Chill until firm.
6.   Unmold onto a chilled serving plate. Garnish with *parsley* and fill center with *ripe olives*.
                              8 TO 10 SERVINGS

VEGETABLE ASPIC

1 pkg. (10 oz.) frozen mixed vegetables	2 tablespoons lemon juice
½ teaspoon monosodium glutamate	1 tablespoon prepared horseradish
4 teaspoons unflavored gelatin	1 teaspoon grated onion
¾ cup cold water	½ teaspoon celery seed
1½ cups vegetable broth (dissolve 2 vegetable bouillon cubes in 1½ cups boiling water)	½ teaspoon salt
	⅛ teaspoon pepper
	½ cup finely shredded cabbage
	2 tablespoons finely snipped parsley

1.   Cook mixed vegetables according to package directions, adding monosodium glutamate with the salt; drain and chill the vegetables.

2.   Soften gelatin in cold water in a saucepan. Stir over low heat until gelatin is dissolved. Blend in the broth, lemon juice, horseradish, onion, celery seed, salt, and pepper.
3.   Chill until gelatin is the consistency of thick, unbeaten egg white. Stir in the chilled cooked vegetables, cabbage, and parsley. Turn into a 1-quart mold. Chill until firm.
4.   Unmold onto chilled serving plate.
                              ABOUT 6 SERVINGS

FRANKS IN TOMATO ASPIC

1 can (16 oz.) tomatoes	1 env. unflavored gelatin
1 onion, chopped	
1 teaspoon salt	¼ cup cold water
⅛ teaspoon pepper	4 to 6 frankfurters, cut in pieces
Few grains ground cloves	

1.   Mix together in a saucepan the tomatoes, onion, salt, pepper, and cloves; simmer, uncovered, 10 minutes.
2.   Meanwhile, soften gelatin in cold water.
3.   Remove tomato mixture from heat; strain into a bowl. Immediately add the softened gelatin and stir until gelatin is dissolved.
4.   Chill until mixture is slightly thicker than thick, unbeaten egg white.
5.   Mix in the frankfurter pieces. Turn into a shallow pan and chill until firm.
6.   To serve, cut into squares and serve with a *horseradish dressing*.   4 TO 6 SERVINGS

Novelty Molded Salads

SOUFFLÉ MONT BLANC
This cheese-rich cold soufflé may be served as a luncheon entrée with tossed salad and crisp rolls.

1 env. unflavored gelatin	Few drops Tabasco
	½ teaspoon salt
½ cup milk	¼ teaspoon dry mustard
¼ cup water	2 cups finely shredded Parmesan cheese
1 teaspoon lemon juice	
1 teaspoon grated onion	2 cups chilled heavy cream, whipped

1.   Sprinkle gelatin evenly over milk and water in a saucepan. Stir over low heat until gelatin is dissolved.

2. Blend lemon juice, onion, Tabasco, and a mixture of salt and dry mustard into dissolved gelatin; stir in cheese. Fold with whipped cream. Turn mixture into a 1½-quart mold. Chill until firm.

3. Unmold onto a chilled serving plate.

ABOUT 8 SERVINGS

DANISH BLUE CHEESE MOUSSE
An elegant salad or appetizer party mold.

1 env. unflavored gelatin	2 egg whites, beaten to stiff, not dry, peaks
½ cup cold water	
½ cup toasted chopped almonds	1 cup chilled heavy cream, whipped to soft peaks
¼ lb. Samsoe cheese, grated	½ teaspoon salt
¼ lb. Danish blue cheese	⅛ teaspoon white pepper
	¼ teaspoon dry mustard

1. Soften gelatin in cold water in a saucepan; stir over low heat until gelatin is dissolved.

2. Using a fork, gently mix almonds and Samsoe cheese in a large bowl. Using fork, break off small pieces of the blue cheese. Gently and quickly, using fingertips, crumble pieces into the bowl with the Samsoe cheese and almonds. Toss lightly with fork just until mixed.

3. Fold beaten egg whites and whipped cream together and then fold into cheese. Mix in gelatin and a blend of salt, pepper, and dry mustard. Turn into a loaf pan. Chill until firm, about 4 hours.

4. Unmold. Garnish top with a row of *lettuce-heart leaves*; put a *maraschino cherry* in each.

12 SERVINGS

CONTINENTAL CHESTNUT MOLD

Canned whole chestnuts, drained (about 13 oz.)	¾ teaspoon celery salt
	⅛ teaspoon white pepper
1 cup strong chicken broth	2 tablespoons white wine vinegar
2 env. unflavored gelatin	1 cup heavy cream
1 cup cold water	Marinated Brussels Sprouts, *below*
2 teaspoons sugar	

1. Using an electric blender, purée about half of the chestnuts with ¼ cup of the chicken broth; set aside. Chop the remaining chestnuts; set aside.

2. Soften gelatin in the cold water in a saucepan.

Stir over low heat until gelatin is dissolved. Remove from heat. Blend in, in order, a mixture of sugar, celery salt, and pepper, then the remaining broth, the vinegar, cream, and puréed chestnuts. Chill until mixture is slightly thickened.

3. Mix the chopped chestnuts into gelatin. Turn into a 1-quart fancy mold. Chill until firm.

4. Unmold onto a chilled large serving plate and surround the mold with the Brussels sprouts.

8 SERVINGS

MARINATED BRUSSELS SPROUTS

4 pkgs. (10 oz. each) frozen Brussels sprouts, cooked	⅛ teaspoon pepper
	½ cup apple cider
1 tablespoon light brown sugar	¼ cup white wine vinegar
1½ teaspoons chervil, crushed	3 teaspoons grated lemon peel
1 teaspoon monosodium glutamate	2 tablespoons lemon juice
¼ teaspoon garlic salt	2 tablespoons cooking oil

1. Drain Brussels sprouts and turn into a bowl.

2. Meanwhile, mix the brown sugar, chervil, monosodium glutamate, garlic salt, and pepper. Stir in the remaining ingredients.

3. Pour marinade over hot Brussels sprouts. Chill.

DEVILED EGG SALAD

6 eggs	1 teaspoon salt
1 env. unflavored gelatin	3 drops Tabasco
¼ cup cold water	¼ cup chopped green pepper
¼ cup ketchup	¼ cup chopped celery
2 tablespoons cider vinegar	2 tablespoons finely chopped pimiento
3 oz. cream cheese	1 tablespoon finely chopped parsley
½ cup mayonnaise	
1 teaspoon grated onion	

1. Hard-cook, chop, and chill the eggs.

2. Soften gelatin in cold water in a saucepan; dissolve over low heat. Stir in the ketchup and vinegar.

3. Beat together cream cheese, mayonnaise, onion, salt, and Tabasco until fluffy. Gradually add gelatin mixture, blending well. Mix in the eggs and remaining ingredients. Turn into six ½-cup molds. Chill until firm.

4. Unmold onto *lettuce*.

6 SERVINGS

MAIN-DISH SALADS

ALL-SEASONS MACARONI SALAD

1 cup dairy sour cream
½ cup Italian salad dressing
½ teaspoon salt
¼ teaspoon seasoned salt
Few grains pepper
2 cups (8 oz.) elbow macaroni, cooked and drained
1½ cups diced cooked chicken

½ lb. bacon, panbroiled and crumbled
2 hard-cooked eggs, chopped
¼ cup chopped pimiento
1 large tomato, diced
2 tablespoons lemon juice
1 avocado, peeled and sliced
Curly endive

1. Mix together in a bowl the sour cream, salad dressing, salts, and pepper; add macaroni and chicken and mix well. Chill thoroughly.
2. Add bacon, eggs, pimiento, and tomato to macaroni; toss lightly. Turn into salad bowl.
3. Sprinkle lemon juice over avocado slices. Garnish salad with avocado and endive. Additional bacon, chicken, eggs, pimiento, and tomato may be used to garnish, if desired.   6 SERVINGS

PERFECT PATIO SALAD

1 lemon
1 tablespoon seasoned salt
1 bay leaf
1 medium-sized onion, quartered
3 qts. boiling water
2 cups (8 oz.) elbow macaroni
1 env. Italian salad dressing mix
½ cup mayonnaise
½ cup chopped onion
½ teaspoon monosodium glutamate

Seasoned salt
Freshly ground black pepper
2 pkgs. (10 oz. each) frozen broccoli spears, cooked, drained, cut in pieces, and chilled
2 cups shredded iceberg lettuce
1 cup cherry tomatoes
6 lemon wedges
½ lb. sliced bacon, diced and fried until crisp

1. Cut lemon into halves; extract juice and reserve for preparing the salad dressing mix.
2. Add the lemon halves, seasoned salt, bay leaf, and onion to the boiling water. Following package directions, add macaroni and cook until tender. Drain and rinse.

3. Meanwhile, prepare the salad dressing mix, substituting lemon juice for vinegar. Pour enough salad dressing over hot macaroni to coat, tossing to mix well; cover and chill thoroughly.
4. If desired, thin mayonnaise with some of the remaining salad dressing. Toss with chilled macaroni mixture, onion, monosodium glutamate, and seasoned salt and pepper to taste. Lightly mix in the chilled broccoli.
5. Line a large salad bowl with the lettuce, turn salad mixture into bowl, and garnish top with cherry tomatoes and lemon wedges. Top individual servings with bacon pieces.   ABOUT 6 SERVINGS

PARTY CHICKEN SALAD

Celery Seed-Cream Dressing, *below*
3 cups cooked chicken cubes (use white meat)
1½ cups chopped celery

1 cup halved seedless grapes
¼ cup finely cut coconut
⅓ cup chopped toasted blanched almonds

1. Prepare Celery Seed-Cream Dressing.
2. Lightly toss chicken and remaining ingredients. Using just enough to coat evenly, add the dressing and toss gently. Garnish with *parsley*.
          ABOUT 6 SERVINGS

CELERY SEED-CREAM DRESSING

¼ cup sugar
1 tablespoon flour
½ teaspoon dry mustard
½ teaspoon salt
⅛ teaspoon pepper
1¼ cups lemon-lime carbonated beverage (room temperature)
4 egg yolks, slightly beaten

2 tablespoons butter or margarine
2 teaspoons confectioners' sugar
½ teaspoon dry mustard
½ cup chilled heavy cream, whipped
2 teaspoons celery seed

1. Combine sugar, flour, ½ teaspoon dry mustard, salt, and pepper together in top of a double boiler. Add 1 cup of the carbonated beverage gradually, blending well.
2. Cook and stir until mixture comes to boiling; cook 1 to 2 minutes. Stir in remaining ¼ cup carbonated beverage.
3. Vigorously stir about 3 tablespoons of the hot

mixture into the beaten egg yolks; immediately blend into mixture in top of double boiler. Set over simmering water and cook 3 to 5 minutes, stirring occasionally.

4. Remove from heat and stir in the butter. Cool; chill thoroughly.

5. Before serving, with a final few strokes, blend a mixture of confectioners' sugar and ½ teaspoon dry mustard into whipped cream. Blend whipped cream and celery seed into salad dressing.

ABOUT 2¼ CUPS DRESSING

CURRIED RICE-TURKEY PARTY SALAD

Don't pass up this unique rice, turkey, vegetable combination with flavor overtones of the Far East . . . a real taste-tempter.

½ cup creamy onion salad dressing
6 cups cooked rice, chilled
½ cup diced unpared cucumber, coarsely shredded zucchini, or sliced cauliflower
¾ cup mayonnaise
1 teaspoon monosodium glutamate
½ teaspoon salt
¼ teaspoon pepper
½ teaspoon celery salt

2 teaspoons curry powder
Turkey, cooked, cut in pieces, and chilled (about 3 cups)
½ cup thin green pepper strips
½ cup diagonally sliced celery
½ cup thinly sliced sweet red onion
¼ cup shredded radishes
Romaine or lettuce

1. Pour onion salad dressing over rice and cucumber in a large bowl; toss lightly until mixed. Cover and chill at least 1 hour.

2. Blend mayonnaise, monosodium glutamate, salt, pepper, celery salt, and curry powder; toss with turkey. Cover and chill at least 1 hour.

3. Just before serving, add turkey to the rice mixture; toss lightly until mixed. Add vegetables and again toss lightly.

4. Line a large salad bowl or chop plate with the romaine or lettuce leaves, lightly pile salad into bowl or onto plate, and garnish with *parsley sprigs*.

5. Accompany the salad with small side dishes of *flaked coconut, salted peanuts, chutney, raisins, chopped hard-cooked egg, sliced avocado,* and *grated orange peel.*   12 TO 14 SERVINGS

SALDE SICILIANO

This salad, a combination of novel ingredients, was served as a "meal in itself" for luncheon, or as the appetizer-salad course before the entrée at dinner in the Salon Reál dining room of the Executive House's Condado Beach Hotel in San Juan, Puerto Rico. It is a creation of Executive Chef Robert Halberg.

1 whole clove garlic
4 anchovy fillets
Juice of 1 lemon
6 tablespoons Burgundy
¾ cup olive oil
Oregano leaves (¼ oz. or 2½ tablespoons)
Peppercorns, crushed (⅛ oz. or ¾ teaspoon)
2 cloves garlic, minced
1 pimiento, diced
3 tomatoes, diced
1 cup cooked green beans

1 cup diced hearts of artichoke
1 cup diced hearts of palm
1 head romaine lettuce, torn in pieces
1 head iceberg lettuce, torn in chunks
2 slices bread, toasted and cut in cubes
¼ lb. Gorgonzola cheese, crumbled

1. Rub a large wooden salad bowl with the whole clove of garlic. Add anchovy fillets. Rub bowl again with the garlic and anchovies; mash together forming a paste. Blend in, stirring vigorously, the lemon juice, Burgundy, olive oil, oregano, and pepper. (If necessary, correct seasonings to taste.)

2. Blend in minced garlic, diced pimiento, and tomatoes. Add green beans, hearts of artichoke and palm, romaine, and iceberg lettuce. Toss lightly.

3. Add croutons and cheese. Again, toss lightly. Serve on chilled salad plates immediately.

4 TO 8 SERVINGS

CRAB LOUIS

A well-known salad which back in 1904 the metropolitan tenor, Enrico Caruso, was reputed to have repeatedly ordered at the Seattle's Olympic Club until the supply was exhausted.

1 cup mayonnaise
¼ cup chili sauce
1 tablespoon lemon juice
1 teaspoon Worcestershire sauce
1 teaspoon prepared horseradish
¼ teaspoon salt

¼ cup finely chopped onion
¼ cup finely chopped green pepper
2 tablespoons chopped green olives
Shredded lettuce
Crab meat (about 3 cups)

1. Blend all ingredients, except lettuce and crab meat.

2. Prepare desired amount of lettuce and put on chilled salad plates. Arrange crab meat on lettuce and spoon a generous amount of dressing over each serving. Garnish with *ripe olives*, wedges of *hard-cooked egg*, *tomato*, and *lemon*.   ABOUT 8 SERVINGS

GALA LOBSTER SALAD

1 cup mayonnaise	¼ small cucumber,
½ cup chili sauce	scored, sliced, and
¼ cup orange juice	cut in wedges
2 tablespoons lemon	1 ripe banana, peeled
juice	and diced
1 tablespoon chopped	1 small apple, pared and
parsley	diced
1 tablespoon chopped	3 tablespoons capers
hard-cooked egg	2½ cups chilled lobster
2 tomatoes, peeled and	meat, separated in
diced	pieces

1. Blend mayonnaise, chili sauce, orange and lemon juices, parsley, and egg; chill.
2. Combine remaining ingredients. Lightly toss with enough chilled dressing to coat evenly.
3. Mound individual servings on chilled plates lined with *salad greens*.   8 SERVINGS

HERRING SALAD
(Sillsalat)

A smorgasbord always includes herring if the true Scandinavian spirit of the occasion is observed.

1 lb. salt herring	1½ tablespoons white
fillets	vinegar
½ lb. veal, cut in ½-	½ teaspoon sugar
inch cubes	½ teaspoon salt
1 lb. medium-sized beets,	Few grains pepper
cooked and peeled	1 cup chilled heavy
2 small potatoes, cooked,	cream, whipped
peeled, diced and	3 hard-cooked eggs (2
chilled	eggs, yolks and whites
2 medium-sized onions,	finely chopped sep-
finely chopped	arately; 1 egg, cut in
1 large apple, washed	slices crosswise)
and diced	

1. Put herring into a large bowl, add 2 quarts cold water, and soak 3 hours.
2. Put veal into a saucepan with 3 cups water. Simmer about 1 hour, or until meat is tender. Drain and chill.

3. Cut beets into ¼ inch thick slices; cut slices into strips, ¼ inch wide. Chill.
4. Drain the herring, dry on absorbent paper, and cut into ½- to ¾-inch pieces. Combine herring, veal, potatoes, onion, and apple in a large bowl. Add a mixture of the vinegar, sugar, salt, and pepper; toss lightly to coat evenly.
5. Turn the whipped cream over the herring mixture and toss lightly until thoroughly mixed. Add the beets and toss, being careful not to break the strips. Turn into a serving bowl and chill thoroughly. (If desired, the salad may be packed lightly into a 2-quart mold.)
6. When ready to serve, spoon the chopped egg white around the edge of the salad, the chopped egg yolk over center. Arrange the hard-cooked egg slices in a circle between the chopped egg white and yolk. Complete the garnish with sprigs of *parsley*. Place a cruet of *white vinegar*, colored with beet juice, and a cruet of *cream* on the table so that each person may sour the salad to his own taste.
   10 TO 12 SERVINGS

SEAFOOD SALAD SUPREME
Seafood is dressed up with extra gourmet touches in this salad . . . truly superb cuisine.

1 can (6½ oz.) crab meat,	¼ cup sliced green
drained and separated	onions
1 can (7 oz.) shrimp,	1 medium-sized ripe
drained and cut in	avocado, chilled
pieces	3 tablespoons lemon
1 can (6 oz.) lobster,	juice
drained and cut in	3 hard-cooked eggs,
pieces	finely diced
1 can (6½ or 7 oz.) tuna,	2 medium-sized ripe
drained and separated	tomatoes, chilled and
in small pieces	diced
2 quarts (1 head)	1 cup mayonnaise
shredded lettuce	¼ cup cream
1 cup diced celery	1 teaspoon salt
½ cup chopped walnuts	¼ teaspoon pepper
⅓ cup sliced radishes	

1. Combine seafood in a bowl, cover and refrigerate.
2. Put into a large salad bowl the lettuce, celery, walnuts, radishes, and green onions. Chill 1 hour.
3. When ready to serve, dice the avocado. Drizzle with lemon juice and toss lightly. Add avocado to salad bowl along with seafood, eggs, and tomatoes.
4. Combine the mayonnaise, cream, salt, and

pepper. Pour over salad ingredients and toss lightly.

5.   Serve in crisp *lettuce cups*.   8 TO 10 SERVINGS

SHRIMP AND AVOCADO SALAD

1 cup wine vinegar	1 teaspoon thyme, crushed
⅓ cup water	
½ cup lemon juice	1 teaspoon oregano, crushed
1 cup salad oil	
¼ cup chopped parsley	2 lbs. large cooked shrimp, peeled, and deveined
2 cloves garlic, minced	
1 tablespoon salt	
¼ teaspoon freshly ground black pepper	3 small onions, sliced
	⅓ cup chopped green pepper
1 tablespoon sugar	
1 teaspoon dry mustard	2 ripe avocados, peeled and sliced

1.   For marinade, combine vinegar, water, lemon juice, oil, parsley, and garlic in a bowl or a screw-top jar. Add a mixture of salt, pepper, sugar, dry mustard, thyme, and oregano; blend thoroughly.

2.   Put shrimp, onions, and green pepper into a large shallow dish. Pour marinade over all, cover, and refrigerate 8 hours or overnight.

3.   About 1 hour before serving, put avocado slices into a bowl. Pour enough marinade from shrimp over the avocado to cover completely.

4.   To serve, remove avocado slices and shrimp from marinade and arrange on crisp *lettuce* in a large serving bowl.   ABOUT 8 SERVINGS

RUSSIAN SALAD

A recipe from the Albergo Ristorante "Allegri," Cervia, Italy.

2 cups diced cooked potatoes	¼ teaspoon freshly ground black pepper
2 cups cooked green beans, cut in 1-in. pieces	1½ teaspoons grated lemon peel
	1 can (6½ or 7 oz.) tuna, drained and flaked
2 cups cooked green peas	
2 cups diced cooked carrots	1 can (2 oz.) anchovies, drained and coarsely chopped
2 cups diced cooked celery	
¼ cup olive oil	1 tablespoon chopped gherkins
1 teaspoon salt	Mayonnaise

1.   Combine the vegetables in a large bowl. Pour a

blend of olive oil, salt, pepper, and lemon peel over vegetables; toss lightly. Add tuna, anchovies, pickle, and desired amount of mayonnaise.

2.   Mound salad on serving plate and cover with a thin layer of mayonnaise. Garnish as desired with *capers, gherkin slices,* and *hard-cooked egg slices or pieces.*   ABOUT 12 SERVINGS

SALADE NIÇOISE

A salad served in restaurants in Nice, France, probably inspired the many variations which bear this name appearing on European menus.

Salad Dressing, *below*	1 mild onion, quartered and thinly sliced
3 medium-sized cooked potatoes, sliced	
	2 ripe tomatoes, cut in wedges
1 pkg. (9 oz.) frozen green beans, cooked	
	2 hard-cooked eggs, quartered
1 clove garlic, cut in half	
	1 can (2 oz.) rolled anchovy fillets, drained
1 small head Boston lettuce	
	¾ cup pitted ripe olives
2 cans (6½ or 7 oz. each) tuna, drained	1 tablespoon capers

1.   Pour enough salad dressing over warm potato slices and cooked beans (in separate bowls) to coat vegetables.

2.   Before serving, rub the inside of a large shallow salad bowl with the cut surface of the garlic. Line the bowl or a large serving platter with the lettuce.

3.   Unmold the tuna in center of bowl and separate into chunks.

4.   Arrange separate mounds of the potatoes, green beans, onion, tomatoes, and hard-cooked eggs in colorful groupings around the tuna. Garnish with anchovies, olives, and capers.

5.   Pour dressing over all before serving.
     6 TO 8 SERVINGS

SALAD DRESSING: Combine in a jar or bottle *½ cup olive oil or salad oil, 2 tablespoons red wine vinegar,* a mixture of *1 teaspoon salt, ½ teaspoon pepper,* and *1 teaspoon dry mustard, 1 tablespoon finely chopped chives,* and *1 tablespoon finely chopped parsley.* Shake vigorously to blend well before pouring over salad.   ABOUT ⅔ CUP

TUNA SALAD GRANADA

½ cup strong beef broth (dissolve 1 beef bouillon cube in ½ cup boiling water)
½ cup cider vinegar
3 tablespoons olive oil
1 teaspoon salt
¼ teaspoon pepper
½ teaspoon dry mustard
2 tablespoons chopped onion
1 clove garlic, minced
2 cans (6½ or 7 oz. each) tuna, drained and flaked
1 cup diced cooked potato
Crisp lettuce
½ cup thinly sliced green pepper
¼ cup thinly sliced sweet red pepper
½ cup pimiento-stuffed olive slices
2 medium-sized tomatoes, quartered
4 hard-cooked eggs, cut lengthwise into halves

1. Mix broth, vinegar, oil, salt, pepper, dry mustard, onion, and garlic in a saucepan; heat to boiling. Cool.
2. Combine tuna, potato, and vinegar mixture; mix lightly. Cover and refrigerate about 2 hours, tossing occasionally.
3. When ready to serve, drain tuna mixture. Arrange lettuce on a chilled serving plate. Mound tuna and potato in center; top with the pepper strips and the olive slices. Arrange tomatoes and hard-cooked egg halves alternately around the plate. Drizzle remaining marinade over vegetables, if desired. 8 SERVINGS

TUNA-VEGETABLE PLATTER

A handsome and easy-to-arrange salad platter worthy of highlighting a summer buffet table.

1 cup dairy sour cream
¼ teaspoon seasoned salt
Few grains pepper
1¼ teaspoons prepared horseradish
1 teaspoon white wine vinegar
½ cup sliced ripe olives
¼ cup thin ¼-in. green pepper strips
2 teaspoons capers
2 cans (6½ or 7 oz. each) tuna, drained and flaked
1 pkg. (10 oz.) frozen asparagus spears
3 cups 3-inch carrot sticks
1 medium cauliflower, broken into flowerets

1. Blend sour cream with seasoned salt, pepper, horseradish, vinegar, olives, green pepper strips, and capers; toss with tuna. Chill thoroughly.
2. Cook each vegetable until just tender; drain.
3. Pour *French dressing* over vegetables and refrigerate at least 1 hour.
4. When ready to serve, spoon tuna mixture onto center of a large round platter and radiate the drained vegetables alternately out from the tuna. Garnish with *green pepper strips*. 6 SERVINGS

FROZEN SALADS

FROZEN FRUIT SALAD

8 oz. cream cheese, softened
1 can (20 oz.) crushed pineapple, drained (reserve 3 tablespoons syrup)
¼ cup mayonnaise
½ cup coarsely chopped salted almonds
½ cup maraschino cherries, drained and quartered
½ cup pitted dates, cut in slivers
24 large marshmallows, cut in eighths
1 cup chilled heavy cream, whipped

1. Blend cream cheese, pineapple syrup, and mayonnaise in a bowl. Mix in crushed pineapple, almonds, maraschino cherries, dates, and marshmallows. Fold in whipped cream. Turn into a 1½-quart mold. Freeze until firm.
2. Serve on chilled salad greens with *Pineapple Salad Dressing, page 384.* 8 TO 10 SERVINGS

FROZEN CHEDDAR CHEESE SALAD SENSATION

1 can (29 oz.) greengage plums, drained and pits removed
¼ cup lemon juice
2 tablespoons sugar
¼ teaspoon salt
1 cup shredded Cheddar cheese
1 cup chilled heavy cream, whipped
1 or 2 drops green food coloring

1. Cut plums into small pieces. Mix in the lemon juice, sugar, salt, and cheese. Fold in the whipped cream, then blend in the desired amount of green food coloring.
2. Turn mixture into a refrigerator tray. Freeze until firm, 3 to 4 hours.
3. Before serving, thaw slightly; cut into squares or wedges. Serve on crisp *salad greens* on chilled individual salad plates. ABOUT 8 SERVINGS

BUTTERED PINEAPPLE FROZEN SALAD

½ cup butter or margarine
2 tablespoons flour
2 tablespoons sugar
Few grains salt
1 can (about 13 oz.) pineapple tidbits, drained (reserve syrup)
1 can (15 to 16 oz.) crushed pineapple, drained (reserve syrup)
1 teaspoon lemon juice
¾ cup orange sections (about 2 medium-sized oranges), cut in ½-inch pieces
½ cup maraschino cherries, quartered and drained
2 cups miniature marshmallows
¼ cup chopped salted pecans
1 cup chilled heavy cream, whipped

1. Heat butter in a heavy saucepan. Blend in a mixture of flour, sugar, and salt. Heat until bubbly.
2. Gradually add 1¼ cups reserved pineapple syrup, stirring constantly. Bring to boiling; stir and boil 2 minutes.
3. Remove from heat and stir in lemon juice. Cool; chill thoroughly.
4. Lightly toss pineapple with oranges, cherries, marshmallows, and pecans in a large bowl. Add the chilled dressing and mix to coat. Fold in the whipped cream.
5. Turn into a 13x9-inch pan. Cover pan with aluminum foil; freeze until firm.
6. Allow salad to soften slightly. Cut into squares and place on chilled salad plates. Garnish with sprigs of *watercress*.   ABOUT 16 SERVINGS

FROSTY FRUIT SALAD

1 cup drained pineapple tidbits (reserve ¼ cup syrup)
1 cup orange pieces (1 to 2 medium-sized oranges)
1 cup chopped pitted softened prunes*
½ cup sliced maraschino cherries, well drained on absorbent paper
1 large banana
2 teaspoons unflavored gelatin
⅓ cup cold water
1 cup dairy sour cream
1 cup chilled heavy cream, whipped
¾ cup sugar
¾ teaspoon salt
2 cups small-curd creamed cottage cheese, sieved
½ cup chopped salted almonds

1. Prepare fruits except banana; set aside.
2. Soften gelatin in cold water in a small saucepan; set over low heat and stir until gelatin is dissolved.
3. Blend the sour cream, whipped cream, reserved pineapple syrup, sugar, and salt into cottage cheese; stir in the gelatin.
4. Peel and slice the banana. Add with the prepared fruits and the almonds to the cottage cheese mixture and mix until well blended. Turn into refrigerator trays and freeze until firm, about 4 hours.
5. Allow salad to soften slightly at room temperature before serving. To serve, cut into wedges.
                                    ABOUT 12 SERVINGS
*Put prunes into a colander and set over boiling water 30 minutes, or until softened and moist.

HOT SALADS

HOT POTATO SALAD
A Pennsylvania Dutch version of hot potato salad.

6 medium-sized potatoes, cooked, peeled, and sliced
2 hard-cooked eggs, chopped
4 slices bacon, diced
¼ cup finely chopped onion
1 egg, beaten
¼ cup cider vinegar
1¾ teaspoons salt

1. Combine potato slices and chopped eggs in a bowl. Fry bacon and onion together until delicately browned. Strain, reserving bacon drippings.
2. Add onion and bacon to the potato mixture; toss lightly. Add bacon drippings slowly to beaten egg, beating well. Blend in the vinegar and salt.

3. Pour dressing over potato mixture, mixing lightly to blend well. Serve hot.   6 SERVINGS

PEPPER CABBAGE
Crisp fried bacon is a good addition to this salad of Pennsylvania Dutch origin.

2 cups shredded cabbage
1 green or red pepper, finely chopped
1 teaspoon salt
Hot Salad Dressing, *page 380*

1. Combine the cabbage and pepper in a bowl; sprinkle with salt. Set aside about 1 hour. Drain off the liquid.

2. Pour the desired amount of Hot Salad Dressing over the drained vegetables, tossing until well mixed. Serve at once. 4 SERVINGS

HOT SALAD DRESSING

1 tablespoon butter or bacon fat	2 tablespoons sugar
1 teaspoon flour	½ teaspoon salt
¼ cup vinegar	⅛ teaspoon pepper
¼ cup water	½ teaspoon dry mustard
	1 egg, slightly beaten

1. Heat fat in a small heavy saucepan over low heat and blend in the flour. Heat until bubbly. Stir in the vinegar and water. Bring to boiling and cook 1 to 2 minutes, stirring constantly. Mix in a blend of sugar, salt, pepper, and dry mustard. Cook 4 minutes.
2. Gradually add hot mixture to beaten egg, mixing well. Immediately return to saucepan and cook 1 minute, stirring constantly. ¾ CUP DRESSING

GERMAN POTATO SALAD
(Kartoffelsalat)

The amount of potatoes used for this tangy hot potato salad will determine the number of servings.

12 slices bacon, diced and fried until crisp (reserve 6 tablespoons drippings)	1½ tablespoons sugar
	1½ teaspoons salt
	¾ teaspoon mono-sodium glutamate
3 medium-sized onions, chopped (2 cups)	¼ teaspoon pepper
1 cup less 2 tablespoons cider vinegar	2 to 3 lbs. potatoes, cooked, peeled, and cut in ¼-inch slices

1. Heat bacon drippings in a skillet. Add onion and cook until tender, stirring occasionally. Stir in vinegar, sugar, salt, monosodium glutamate, and pepper; heat to boiling. Mix in bacon.
2. Pour over potato slices in a serving dish and toss lightly to coat evenly. Garnish with snipped *parsley* and *paprika*. Serve hot. ABOUT 6 SERVINGS

SALAD DRESSINGS

A salad is complemented by the dressing, so suit it to the salad. Dressings should coat the greens, not drown them; they should accompany the salad, not hide it. Endless variations are possible using the basic French, mayonnaise, and cooked dressings. Others are the sweet or sour cream, cream or cottage cheese and yogurt dressings, and the bacon-vinegar type for wilted greens.

Mayonnaise has caused many a tear when it has broken or separated, probably because the oil was added too rapidly at the beginning or ingredients (egg yolk and oil) were not of the same temperature when combined. If separation occurs, it is possible to begin again and obtain a perfect *emulsion* of salad oil and egg yolk as follows: Combine 1 egg yolk, 1 tablespoon cold water, and a small amount of vinegar in a small mixer bowl or an electric blender container. Mix well and add the separated mayonnaise, a small amount at a time, beating constantly until an emulsion has re-formed.

FRENCH DRESSING

¼ cup lemon juice or cider vinegar	¼ teaspoon dry mustard
1 tablespoon sugar	¼ teaspoon pepper
¾ teaspoon salt	¾ cup salad oil or olive oil
¼ teaspoon paprika	

Combine all ingredients in a screw-top jar; shake well. Chill. Shake before using. ABOUT 1 CUP

CREAMY FRENCH DRESSING: Follow recipe for French Dressing. Blend ¼ *cup dairy sour cream* with the dressing.

CURRIED FRENCH DRESSING: Follow recipe for French Dressing. Mix ¼ *teaspoon curry powder* with seasonings.

LORENZO FRENCH DRESSING: Follow recipe for French Dressing. Add ¼ *cup finely chopped watercress* and *2 tablespoons chili sauce* to the dressing; shake well.

HONEY FRENCH DRESSING: Follow recipe for French Dressing, using lemon juice. Add ½ *cup honey* and ¼ *teaspoon grated lemon peel* to dressing and shake well. For added flavor, add ½ *teaspoon celery seed* and shake well.

HONEY-LIME FRENCH DRESSING: Follow recipe for French Dressing. Substitute ¼ *cup lime juice* for the lemon juice. Add *½ cup honey* and *¼ teaspoon grated lime peel* to dressing; shake well.

TANGY FRENCH DRESSING: Follow recipe for French Dressing. Add *3 to 4 tablespoons prepared horseradish* to the dressing and shake well.

TOMATO SOUP FRENCH DRESSING: Follow recipe for French Dressing. ADD *⅔ cup condensed tomato soup, 1 tablespoon chopped onion,* and *½ teaspoon marjoram* to the dressing; shake well.

TARRAGON FRENCH DRESSING

¾ cup olive oil or salad oil	1 teaspoon sugar
¼ cup tarragon vinegar	½ teaspoon salt
¼ teaspoon Worcestershire sauce	⅛ teaspoon pepper
1 clove garlic, cut in halves	¼ teaspoon paprika
	¼ teaspoon dry mustard
	⅛ teaspoon ground thyme

Combine all ingredients in a screw-top jar or bottle; shake well to blend. Chill. Before serving, discard garlic and shake dressing to blend thoroughly.

ABOUT 1 CUP

FRENCH DRESSING À LA CHIFFONADE

1 clove garlic, cut in halves	½ teaspoon paprika
1 hard-cooked egg (yolk sieved, white finely chopped)	¼ teaspoon dry mustard
	½ cup salad oil
1 teaspoon salt	¼ cup wine vinegar
¼ teaspoon pepper	2 tablespoons chopped parsley

1. Rub a bowl with the cut surfaces of garlic. Blend sieved egg yolk with salt, pepper, paprika, and dry mustard in the bowl. Adding gradually, vigorously stir in oil and vinegar. Blend in egg white and parsley.
2. Store covered in refrigerator; stir or shake well before using.

ABOUT ¾ CUP

QUICK FRENCH DRESSING

Here's a timesaving basic mixture to keep in the refrigerator.

1 cup vinegar	¼ teaspoon white pepper
1 clove garlic, crushed	1 teaspoon dry mustard
1½ teaspoons salt	

1. Bring the vinegar and garlic to boiling in a

small saucepan; strain mixture into a screw-top jar.
2. Add salt, pepper, and dry mustard (add sugar if desired). Cover tightly and shake well.
3. Add desired amount of *salad oil* or *olive oil* to a portion of the vinegar mixture just before salad dressing is needed.

GOURMET SALAD DRESSING

⅓ cup olive oil	½ teaspoon dry mustard
2 tablespoons red wine vinegar	⅛ teaspoon basil, crushed
3 tablespoons dry red wine	⅛ teaspoon tarragon, crushed
1½ teaspoons sugar	½ teaspoon Worcestershire sauce
1 teaspoon salt	
½ teaspoon freshly ground black pepper	

1. Combine oil, vinegar, wine, a mixture of sugar, salt, pepper, dry mustard, basil, and tarragon, and the Worcestershire sauce in a screw-top jar. Shake well to blend; chill thoroughly.
2. Just before serving, shake dressing vigorously and pour over *salad greens* and *artichoke hearts*; toss lightly.

ABOUT ⅔ CUP

GRENADINE SALAD DRESSING

¾ cup grenadine	1 teaspoon salt
¼ cup lemon juice	Few grains white pepper
1½ teaspoons celery seed	½ teaspoon grated onion
1 teaspoon dry mustard	¾ cup salad oil

1. Combine all ingredients except oil and beat with a hand rotary beater until thoroughly mixed.
2. Add the salad oil very gradually, beating constantly; continue beating until dressing thickens slightly. Chill; stir or shake before using.

ABOUT 1½ CUPS

SWEET 'N' TART SALAD DRESSING

½ cup sugar	1 cup salad oil
1 teaspoon salt	⅓ cup cider vinegar
1½ teaspoons celery seed	1 teaspoon grated onion
1 teaspoon paprika	1 clove garlic, cut in halves
1 teaspoon dry mustard	

1. Combine sugar, salt, celery seed, paprika, and

dry mustard in a bowl. Add oil and vinegar alternately, beating with a rotary beater until thoroughly blended and thickened.

2. Add grated onion and garlic, cover and let stand about 30 minutes. Remove garlic before serving. ABOUT 2 CUPS

CELERY SEED SALAD DRESSING
A delicious complement to fruit salads.

¼ cup sugar	1 teaspoon dry mustard
⅓ cup light corn syrup	1 teaspoon salt
¼ cup vinegar	Few grains white pepper
1½ to 2 teaspoons celery seed	1 teaspoon grated onion
	1 cup salad oil

1. Combine all ingredients except the oil in a small bowl. Beat with a hand rotary beater until mixture is thoroughly blended.
2. Add the oil very gradually beating constantly. Continue beating until mixture thickens.
3. Chill thoroughly in covered container in refrigerator. Shake well before serving. ABOUT 2 CUPS

POPPY SEED DRESSING
This delicious dressing comes from Ye Old College Inn, Houston, Texas.

⅔ cup honey	5 tablespoons poppy seed
1 teaspoon salt	
⅔ cup vinegar	2½ cups salad oil
6 tablespoons prepared mustard	1 medium-sized onion, finely grated (optional)

1. Combine ingredients in order listed in an electric blender container or electric mixer bowl. Blend or beat until oil is incorporated.
2. Store in covered container in refrigerator.
4½ CUPS

ORANGE SALAD DRESSING

¼ cup sugar	2 tablespoons tarragon vinegar
1 teaspoon salt	
½ teaspoon dry mustard	½ teaspoon grated onion
¼ cup orange juice	¾ cup salad oil
¼ cup light corn syrup	

1. Combine sugar, salt, and dry mustard in a small bowl. Add remaining ingredients except oil and beat with a hand rotary beater until blended.

2. Very gradually add the oil while beating constantly. Continue beating until mixture is of desired consistency. Chill. Stir before serving.
ABOUT 1½ CUPS

VEGETABLE MEDLEY SALAD DRESSING DE LUXE

1 cup salad oil	1 medium-sized ripe tomato, peeled and cut in pieces
3 tablespoons cider vinegar	
2 tablespoons prepared horseradish	1 small onion, peeled and cut in pieces
1 tablespoon sugar	½ small cucumber, pared and cut in pieces
1 teaspoon dry mustard	
1 teaspoon paprika	
¾ teaspoon salt	⅓ small ripe avocado, peeled and cut in pieces
⅛ teaspoon pepper	
½ teaspoon seasoned salt	
Few grains cayenne pepper	1 large clove garlic, crushed

Put all ingredients into an electric blender container and blend thoroughly. Chill before serving over a tossed vegetable or fruit salad. ABOUT 3½ CUPS

MAYONNAISE

2 egg yolks	Few grains cayenne pepper
1 tablespoon cider vinegar	
½ teaspoon salt	½ teaspoon dry mustard
¼ teaspoon sugar	1 cup salad oil
⅛ teaspoon white pepper	1 tablespoon lemon juice

1. Put the egg yolks, vinegar, salt, sugar, peppers, and dry mustard into a small bowl. Beat with a hand rotary beater until well blended. Add oil, 1 teaspoon at a time at first, beating vigorously after each addition. Gradually increase amounts added until one half of the oil has been used.
2. Alternately beat in small amounts of remaining oil and a few drops lemon juice. (If mayonnaise separates because oil has been added too rapidly, beat it slowly and thoroughly into 1 egg yolk, 1 tablespoon cold water, small quantity of vinegar, or a small portion of smooth mayonnaise.) Store in covered container in refrigerator. ABOUT 1½ CUPS

ELEGANT MAYONNAISE: Follow recipe for Mayonnaise. Into *1 cup chilled mayonnaise,* blend *1 teaspoon lemon juice, 1 teaspoon curry powder,* and *a few grains salt.* Beat *⅓ cup chilled heavy cream* to soft peaks. With final few strokes, beat in *2 table-spoons confectioners' sugar*. Fold into mayonnaise.

THOUSAND ISLAND DRESSING: Follow recipe for Mayonnaise. Into *½ cup mayonnaise*, mix *1 or 2 hard-cooked eggs*, sieved or finely chopped, *2 table-spoons chili sauce, 2 tablespoons finely chopped scallions* (with tops), *2 tablespoons chopped sweet pickle, 1 tablespoon chopped green olives*, and *½ teaspoon paprika*.

RUSSIAN DRESSING: Follow recipe for Mayonnaise. Into *½ cup mayonnaise*, blend *3 tablespoons chili sauce, 1 tablespoon minced onion*, and *½ tea-spoon prepared horseradish*.

SOUR CREAM MAYONNAISE: Follow recipe for Mayonnaise. Into *½ cup mayonnaise*, blend *½ cup dairy sour cream, 2 teaspoons cider vinegar, 1 tea-spoon sugar*, and *½ teaspoon dry mustard*.

AVOCADO FLUFF SALAD DRESSING

Sea Grape Lodge on Demere Key in the Gulf of Mex-ico is famous for fresh grapefruit salad served with this creamy green topper.

1 medium-sized soft-ripe avocado	1 tablespoon mayonnaise
1 tablespoon lime juice	¼ teaspoon salt
1 tablespoon sugar	¼ cup heavy cream, whipped

1.   Peel and pit avocado; cut into pieces. Put avocado pieces into an electric blender container with lime juice, sugar, mayonnaise, and salt; blend until smooth.
2.   Fold whipped cream into avocado mixture until blended; chill thoroughly.   ABOUT 1 CUP

GREEN GODDESS SALAD DRESSING

1 cup mayonnaise	3 tablespoons mashed anchovy fillets
½ cup dairy sour cream	1 tablespoon chopped chives
3 tablespoons tarragon vinegar	2 teaspoons chopped capers
1 tablespoon lemon juice	1 clove garlic, crushed
⅓ cup finely snipped parsley	⅛ teaspoon salt
3 tablespoons finely chopped onion	⅛ teaspoon pepper

1.   Blend all ingredients thoroughly. Cover tightly and chill in refrigerator 3 to 4 hours.

2.   To serve, add the dressing to crisp *salad greens* and gently turn and toss until greens are evenly coated. Serve immediately.   ABOUT 2½ CUPS

ROQUEFORT CHEESE DRESSING

This quick-as-a-wink dressing for garden-fresh salad is a favorite at Idle Spurs (Steak House) in Barstow, California.

½ cup Roquefort cheese, crumbled or mashed	¼ teaspoon pepper
	1 tablespoon paprika
⅔ cup half and half	⅔ cup salad oil
1 teaspoon dry mustard	2 tablespoons lemon juice
½ teaspoon salt	

1.   Blend cheese, cream, dry mustard, salt, pepper, and paprika together in an electric blender or beat in a bowl with a hand rotary beater.
2.   Add oil, a tablespoon at a time, beating until thickened and smooth. Beat in lemon juice.
3.   Store, covered, in refrigerator.   ABOUT 2½ CUPS

CREAMY LEMON-CELERY SEED DRESSING

1½ cups mayonnaise	1 tablespoon lemon juice
¼ cup unsweetened pineapple juice	½ teaspoon celery seed
1 teaspoon grated lemon peel	

Blend thoroughly mayonnaise, pineapple juice, lemon peel and juice, celery seed, and a *few drops Tabasco*. Cover and refrigerate at least 1 hour to blend flavors.   ABOUT 1½ CUPS

CRUNCHY SESAME SEED DRESSING

¼ cup finely chopped green pepper	1 tablespoon sugar
¼ cup finely diced pared cucumber	1 teaspoon salt
	Few grains pepper
2 tablespoons minced onion	1 clove garlic, minced
1 cup dairy sour cream	1 tablespoon butter or margarine
½ cup mayonnaise	½ cup sesame seed
1 tablespoon tarragon vinegar	¼ cup (1 oz.) grated Parmesan cheese

1.   Mix the green pepper, cucumber, and onion together; drain if necessary. Blend sour cream,

mayonnaise, vinegar, sugar, salt, pepper, and garlic; add to vegetables and mix well. Chill thoroughly.

2. Meanwhile, heat butter in a skillet. Add sesame seed and stir constantly until lightly browned. Remove from heat; add the grated Parmesan cheese and toss until well blended. Cool.

3. Serve the chilled dressing on chilled mixed *salad greens.* Sprinkle the sesame seed topping generously over the dressing.   2 CUPS

CREAMY LEMON MAYONNAISE

1 cup mayonnaise	⅓ cup chilled heavy
3 tablespoons lemon	cream
juice	3 tablespoons confec-
1 teaspoon grated lemon	tioners' sugar
peel	

1. Combine mayonnaise and lemon juice and peel in a bowl; mix well.

2. Beat heavy cream until peaks are formed; beat in the confectioners' sugar with final few strokes. Fold into the lemon mayonnaise.   ABOUT 1½ CUPS

PINEAPPLE SALAD DRESSING

A luncheon fruit salad plate will be enhanced with this fluffy, creamy, rich, delicately flavored dressing.

½ cup sugar	2 egg whites
1 tablespoon cornstarch	2 tablespoons sugar
⅛ teaspoon salt	2 tablespoons butter
1½ cups unsweetened	¾ cup chilled heavy
pineapple juice	cream, whipped to soft
2 egg yolks, slightly	peaks
beaten	

1. Blend the ½ cup of sugar, cornstarch, and salt in the top of a double boiler; stir in ½ cup of the pineapple juice. Over direct heat, bring mixture rapidly to boiling, stirring constantly; cook 2 to 3 minutes. Set over simmering water.

2. Vigorously stir about 3 tablespoons of the hot mixture into the egg yolks in a bowl and immediately blend into mixture in double boiler. Cook over simmering water 3 to 5 minutes. Stir slowly to keep mixture cooking evenly. Remove double boiler from heat.

3. Beat egg whites until frothy. Add the 2 tablespoons sugar gradually, beating well after each addition. Beat until glossy peaks are formed. Gen-

tly blend into the mixture in top of double boiler.

4. Heat the remaining 1 cup pineapple juice to lukewarm. Stirring constantly, gradually add to cooked pineapple-egg white mixture. Cook over simmering water until thick and smooth, stirring constantly, about 10 minutes. Add the butter and stir until melted.

5. Remove from heat and set aside to cool. Set in refrigerator to chill.

6. When pineapple mixture is chilled, gently fold into whipped cream.   ABOUT 4 CUPS DRESSING

COOKED SALAD DRESSING

¼ cup sugar	1 cup water
1 tablespoon flour	¼ cup cider vinegar
½ teaspoon dry mustard	4 egg yolks, fork beaten
½ teaspoon salt	2 tablespoons butter or
⅛ teaspoon pepper	margarine

1. Blend sugar, flour, dry mustard, salt, and pepper in the top of a double boiler. Add water gradually, stirring constantly. Bring to boiling; cook and stir mixture 2 minutes. Stir in vinegar.

2. Remove from heat. Stir about 3 tablespoons of the hot mixture into the beaten egg yolks. Immediately blend into mixture in double-boiler top. Set over boiling water and cook 5 minutes, stirring occasionally.

3. Remove from heat and blend in the butter. Cool, chill. Store in a tightly covered jar in refrigerator.   ABOUT 1½ CUPS

COOKED ORANGE SALAD DRESSING

A dressing for fruit salads from Ye Old College Inn, Houston, Texas.

2 eggs, beaten	1 teaspoon flour
Grated peel and juice of	Few grains salt
2 oranges	2 tablespoons butter
Grated peel and juice of	1 cup heavy cream,
1 lemon	whipped
¾ cup sugar	

1. Mix eggs, orange and lemon peels and juices in top of a double boiler. Gradually add a mixture of sugar, flour, and salt, blending well. Add butter.

2. Cook over boiling water, stirring constantly, until thick, about 10 minutes. Cool.

3. Just before serving, blend cooled mixture with whipped cream.   3¾ CUPS

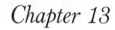

Chapter 13

RELISHES & GARNISHES

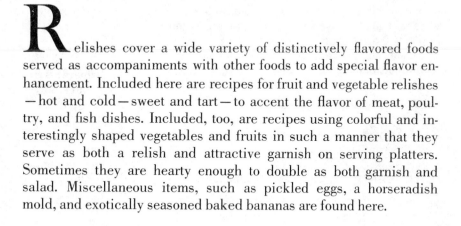

Relishes cover a wide variety of distinctively flavored foods served as accompaniments with other foods to add special flavor enhancement. Included here are recipes for fruit and vegetable relishes —hot and cold—sweet and tart—to accent the flavor of meat, poultry, and fish dishes. Included, too, are recipes using colorful and interestingly shaped vegetables and fruits in such a manner that they serve as both a relish and attractive garnish on serving platters. Sometimes they are hearty enough to double as both garnish and salad. Miscellaneous items, such as pickled eggs, a horseradish mold, and exotically seasoned baked bananas are found here.

HOT CINNAMON APPLES

3 cups sugar	½ teaspoon red food
1½ cups water	coloring
⅔ cup red cinnamon	6 small tart apples,
candies	cored and pared

1. Combine the sugar, water, cinnamon candies, and food coloring in a large deep saucepan; bring to boiling, stirring until candies are dissolved.
2. Add apples to syrup and simmer, uncovered, until apples are tender, about 10 minutes; turn frequently. Remove from heat and allow to stand about 20 minutes or until apples are evenly colored, turning frequently.
3. Serve hot as a meat accompaniment.

6 SERVINGS

GLAZED CURRIED APPLES

¼ cup butter or	3 tablespoons lemon
margarine	juice
1 tablespoon curry	4 medium-sized apples,
powder	halved, pared, and
1 cup water	cored
⅓ cup firmly packed	1 tablespoon cornstarch
dark brown sugar	1 tablespoon cold water

1. Melt butter in a skillet. Blend in curry powder

and heat until bubbly. Stir in 1 cup water, brown sugar, and lemon juice; bring to boiling. Add apple halves, cover, and simmer gently until tender, about 10 minutes, turning occasionally.
2. Remove apples with a slotted spoon and place, cut-side down, on a wire rack; stud generously with *whole cloves*.
3. Meanwhile, combine the cornstarch and cold water; stir into sauce in skillet. Bring rapidly to boiling, stirring constantly; boil 1 to 2 minutes. Return apples to skillet to reheat and coat with sauce.   8 CURRIED APPLE HALVES

SPICED BAKED BANANAS

3 firm bananas	Few grains ground
1½ tablespoons lime	cloves
juice	½ teaspoon grated
3 tablespoons sugar	orange peel
¼ teaspoon ground	¼ cup orange juice
cinnamon	1 tablespoon butter or
¼ teaspoon ground	margarine
nutmeg	

1. Cut bananas crosswise into halves, then lengthwise into halves. Dip pieces in the lime juice. Arrange in a 10x6x2-inch baking dish.

2. Blend remaining ingredients except butter. Pour over bananas. Dot with butter.

3. Bake at 350°F 20 minutes.   6 SERVINGS

MARASCHINO CHERRY CHUTNEY

¾ cup quartered
  maraschino cherries
  (about 30 cherries)
1 pkg. (10 oz.) frozen
  peach slices, thawed,
  drained, and cut in
  pieces

½ cup chopped walnuts
1 tablespoon finely
  chopped preserved
  ginger
2 tablespoons honey

Mix all ingredients in a small saucepan. Cover and cook over low heat 8 minutes, stirring occasionally. Cool. Serve as a curry accompaniment.

ABOUT 3 CUPS CHUTNEY

CRANBERRY RELISH BURGUNDY

1 can (16 oz.) whole
  cranberry sauce
1 can (8½ oz.) crushed
  pineapple, drained
⅓ to ½ cup Burgundy

½ teaspoon ground
  cinnamon
¼ teaspoon ground
  nutmeg
¼ teaspoon dry mustard
⅛ teaspoon salt

Mix all ingredients in a bowl and chill thoroughly (at least 8 hours) before serving.

ABOUT 1 PINT RELISH

GLAZED ORANGES

½ cup sugar
3 tablespoons water
1 tablespoon light corn
  syrup

7 whole cloves
2 oranges, cut in ½-in.
  slices

Combine sugar, water, corn syrup, and cloves in a skillet; heat to simmering, stirring constantly. Add orange slices; simmer 3 minutes on one side, turn slices, and simmer 2 minutes longer. Serve warm.

PIQUANT ORANGE CARTWHEELS
A delicious, delicately flavored orange relish.

3 medium-sized oranges
1 tablespoon sugar
1 tablespoon wine
  vinegar

2 teaspoons instant
  minced onion

Pare oranges and slice crosswise. Add a mixture of sugar, vinegar, and onion; toss lightly. Store covered in refrigerator.

PRESERVED ORANGES MAJESTIC

Water (about 5 to 6
  cups)
6 small navel oranges
  (1½ lbs.), washed
1½ cups water
½ cup white vinegar

½ cup light corn syrup
2 cups sugar
10 whole cloves
2 pieces (3 in. each)
  stick cinnamon

1. Bring water to boiling in a saucepan. Add oranges and simmer, uncovered, about 15 minutes or until tender. Drain oranges and cut into quarters.

2. Meanwhile, mix in a 3-quart saucepan the 1½ cups water, vinegar, corn syrup, and sugar. Stir over low heat until sugar is dissolved. Add the cloves and cinnamon and bring mixture to boiling. Boil vigorously, uncovered, without stirring, 15 to 18 minutes, or until syrup thickens slightly and turns to a light golden color.

3. Remove from heat and add the orange quarters; coat evenly with glaze. Turn into a bowl. Cool, turning pieces occasionally. Chill thoroughly.

4. Serve glazed oranges as a relish. (Relish may be stored in covered containers in refrigerator for weeks.)   ABOUT 12 SERVINGS

CHERRY-FILLED PEACHES

1 can (16 oz.) water-
  packed pitted tart
  red cherries, drained
  (reserve liquid)
1 can (29 oz.) peach
  halves, drained
  (reserve syrup)

2 tablespoons red wine
  vinegar
⅓ cup honey
1 teaspoon ground
  cinnamon
4 whole cloves

1. Mix in a saucepan the cherry liquid, peach syrup, the vinegar, honey, cinnamon, and cloves. Bring to boiling, then remove from heat. Pour over cherries and allow to stand several hours or overnight.

2. Heat marinade and cherries in a saucepan to boiling; add peaches and heat thoroughly.

3. Remove peach halves with a slotted spoon and arrange, cut side up, around *chicken pieces* on a platter. Spoon cherries into cavity of each peach half and sprinkle with *sugar*. Serve hot.

6 TO 8 SERVINGS

SPICY PEACHES

1 can (29 oz.) peach
  halves, drained
  (reserve ¾ cup syrup)
¼ cup thawed frozen
  orange juice
  concentrate
2 tablespoons brown
  sugar

3 tablespoons lemon
  juice
1 tablespoon soy sauce
1 teaspoon instant
  minced onion
Few grains salt
8 whole cloves
6 whole allspice

1. Combine the reserved pineapple syrup with the remaining ingredients, except peach halves, in a saucepan. Bring to boiling, stirring until sugar is dissolved. Cover and simmer about 10 minutes.
2. Pour hot syrup over peach halves in a bowl, cover and let stand 1 hour, turning occasionally.
3. Drain peach halves thoroughly.   6 SERVINGS

LIME-SPICED PEARS

Prepare these delicious spicy sweet-tart pears well in advance — even the day before — to allow the syrup flavor to permeate the fruit.

1 can (29 oz.) Bartlett
  pear halves, drained
  (reserve 1 cup syrup)
1 cup light corn syrup

2 pieces (3 in. each)
  stick cinnamon
2 teaspoons whole
  cloves
½ cup lime juice

1. Combine the reserved pear syrup with corn syrup and the spices in a saucepan; bring to boiling, stirring occasionally to mix well. Boil about 10 minutes. Stir in the lime juice and add the pear halves; bring the syrup to simmering.
2. Remove from heat; set aside to allow pears to absorb flavor.   ABOUT 7 SPICED PEAR HALVES

SPICY PRUNES

These prunes give just the right flavor accent to your favorite fried chicken.

1½ cups apricot nectar
1 piece (3 in.) stick
  cinnamon

4 whole cloves
1 lb. prunes (about 2½
  cups)

1. Combine apricot nectar, cinnamon, and cloves in a saucepan; heat to boiling.
2. Pour hot mixture with spices over prunes in a 1-quart jar. Cool.
3. Cover and refrigerate 2 or 3 days before serving.   1 QUART PRUNES

CELERY ROOT RELISH

1½-lb. celery root
1 lemon, sliced
French dressing
1 cup mayonnaise

1 teaspoon prepared
  mustard
1 teaspoon paprika
7 teaspoons sherry

1. Wash, cut off ends, and pare celery root. Cut into crosswise slices ½ inch thick. Put into a saucepan with lemon slices. Pour in enough boiling water to cover. Cover; bring to boiling; cook 5 to 7 minutes, or until just tender. Drain; cool.
2. Cut slices into sticks about ⅜ inch thick and 2½ inches long. Put sticks into a shallow dish. Add enough French dressing to coat evenly. Chill about 2 hours, turning occasionally.
3. Blend remaining ingredients together; chill.
4. Just before serving, drain celery root sticks and toss lightly with mayonnaise mixture.
  ABOUT 6 SERVINGS

CORA'S GREEN BEAN RELISH

2 pkgs. (9 oz. each)
  frozen cut green
  beans, cooked and
  drained
1 clove garlic
½ teaspoon salt
⅓ cup cider vinegar
1 teaspoon sugar
½ teaspoon oregano

½ teaspoon basil
¼ teaspoon crushed
  rosemary
⅔ cup salad oil
1 small red onion,
  thinly sliced and
  separated in rings
½ cup chopped dill
  pickle

1. While beans are cooking, crush garlic and salt together. Mix in vinegar, sugar, oregano, basil, and rosemary. Blend in salad oil.
2. Put beans, onion, and pickle into a bowl. Toss gently with the dressing. Cover; chill 2 to 3 hours.
  ABOUT 12 SERVINGS

CABBAGE-BEET-HORSERADISH RELISH

2 cups finely chopped
  or shredded cabbage
2 cups finely chopped
  or shredded cooked
  beets (about 4
  medium-sized)

2 tablespoons grated
  fresh horseradish
½ teaspoon salt
⅓ cup sugar
½ teaspoon mustard
  seed
1⅓ cups cider vinegar

1. Combine all ingredients in a bowl; mix well.
2. Store in tightly covered container in refrigerator. (Relish may be stored several weeks if kept well chilled.)   ABOUT 1 QUART RELISH

QUICK CORN RELISH

1 can (12 oz.) whole
    kernel corn, drained
½ cup chili sauce
3 tablespoons minced
    onion
2 tablespoons light
    brown sugar

1 tablespoon salad oil
1 tablespoon garlic-
    flavored wine vinegar
½ teaspoon mono-
    sodium glutamate

Combine all the ingredients in a saucepan. Bring to boiling. Reduce heat and simmer, covered, 5 minutes. Serve hot as a meat accompaniment.

ABOUT 1½ CUPS RELISH

SAUERKRAUT RELISH

Sweet and tart, this delicious "quickie" has no equal for true kraut lovers.

1 can (16 oz.) sauerkraut,
    thoroughly drained
1 cup coarsely chopped
    Spanish onion (1
    large onion)

½ cup coarsely chopped
    green pepper
1 jar (2 oz.) pimientos,
    drained and chopped
1 cup sugar
1 cup cider vinegar

1. Combine all ingredients in a bowl and toss lightly until well blended.
2. Store mixture in a tightly covered container in refrigerator at least 24 hours. ABOUT 1 QUART RELISH

GARDEN-RAISIN RELISH

Sun-drenched raisins and fresh vegetables are combined in this saucy hamburger relish.

¼ cup garlic-flavored
    wine vinegar
¼ cup lightly packed
    brown sugar
1 tablespoon cornstarch
1 teaspoon seasoned
    salt
½ cup dark seedless
    raisins

2 tablespoons snipped
    fresh mint, or ½
    tablespoon dried mint
1 cup diced firm ripe
    tomato
½ cup chopped firm
    cucumber
¼ cup chopped green
    onion
¼ cup chopped dill
    pickle

1. Blend vinegar into a mixture of the brown sugar, cornstarch, and salt in a heavy saucepan. Stir in the raisins. Cook and stir over medium heat until mixture comes to boiling; cook about 3 minutes longer. Cool completely.
2. When ready to serve, mix in mint and remaining chilled ingredients. Relish should stay fresh 2 to 3 days if covered and stored in the refrigerator.

ABOUT 2 CUPS RELISH

HOT CUCUMBER RELISH

4 slices bacon, diced
1 large cucumber,
    thinly sliced

¼ cup cider vinegar
¼ cup sugar
1 teaspoon cornstarch

1. Fry bacon until crisp in a skillet. Add cucumber, vinegar, and sugar. Mix well and cook, covered, over low heat until cucumber is just tender.
2. Blend cornstarch with a small amount of cold water and stir into liquid in skillet. Cook and stir until thickened and smooth.
3. Season with *salt* and *pepper*. Serve hot.

ABOUT 1 CUP RELISH

NIPPY HORSERADISH MOLD

1 env. unflavored gelatin
2 tablespoons sugar
1 teaspoon salt
½ cup cold water

¾ cup prepared
    horseradish
¾ cup heavy cream,
    whipped

1. Blend gelatin, sugar, and salt in a saucepan. Mix in water. Stir over low heat until gelatin is dissolved.
2. Remove from heat. Stir in horseradish. Chill until slightly thickened.
3. Fold whipped cream into horseradish mixture.
4. Turn into a 3-cup fancy mold. Chill until firm. Unmold onto chilled serving plate. 3-CUP MOLD

PICKLED EGGS

1 medium-sized onion,
    sliced
1¾ cups white vinegar
¾ cup water
3 tablespoons brown
    sugar
½ teaspoon salt

5 peppercorns
1 whole clove
¼ teaspoon dill seed
Piece of ginger root
¼ teaspoon garlic salt
18 hard-cooked eggs,
    peeled

1. Combine onion and remaining ingredients except eggs in a saucepan; bring to boiling and simmer about 5 minutes.
2. Put the eggs into two 1-quart jars; pour half the vinegar mixture over eggs in each jar. Cover jars, cool, and refrigerate at least overnight to develop flavor. (Eggs may be kept in refrigerator up to 2 weeks.)

2 QUARTS EGGS

Chapter 14

CAKES & TORTES— FROSTINGS & FILLINGS

For many years the art of cakemaking remained unchanged. There were two basic types of cakes—the so-called "butter" cakes, and the cakes without butter or the sponge-type cakes. In recent years, however, quite different methods of mixing cakes have been developed, resulting in cakes of still other types. Standard methods of mixing and the more recent simplified methods are described here.

Butter-type (shortening) *Cakes*—These contain fat (butter, margarine, vegetable or all-purpose shortening, or lard) and a chemical leavening agent. They are prepared using the conventional "creaming" method which is probably the one most familiar to homemakers. Mixing is done manually or with an electric mixer. The shortening is creamed with the sugar and flavoring (or the flavoring is added with the liquid). Beaten eggs are then beaten into the creamed mixture and the dry and liquid ingredients added alternately, beginning and ending with dry ingredients. When using the electric mixer the unbeaten eggs may be added, one at a time, to the creamed mixture, beating thoroughly after each addition. Then, with the mixer at low speed, the dry ingredients and liquids are added alternately, beating only until the batter is smooth after each addition. At this point overbeating must be avoided as this reduces volume. Nuts, raisins, etc., are usually added last. Exceptions are recipes in which egg whites are beaten separately and gently folded into the batter.

One-Bowl Cakes (Quick Method)—For best results use vegetable or all-purpose shortening for these cakes. The method is to add the soft shortening to the sifted dry ingredients. Then add two thirds of the liquid to which the flavoring has been added. (When using all-purpose flour, add all the liquid at one time.) Beat mixture at medium speed of electric mixer for 2 minutes, scraping down the bowl, or beat by hand 2 minutes, 150 strokes per minute. Add remaining liquid and unbeaten eggs and beat 2 minutes longer, scraping down the bowl.

Cakes without Butter—This group includes angel food and sponge cakes. Well-beaten eggs are used as the leavening agent and the air beaten into them, along with the steam formed in the batter, causes the cake to rise. These cakes contain no fat or baking powder, except in an occasional recipe when a small amount of each is used. The old method of baking these cakes was to place them in a cold oven and bake them for an hour or longer at 300°F. Opinions vary today on the use of a preheated 325° or 350°F oven for a shorter period, or 375° or 400°F oven for an even shorter time.

Chiffon Cakes—These cakes contain cooking oil and baking powder. They have the lightness of a sponge cake and the richness of a "butter" cake.

Cake-Mix Cakes—The formulas and the mixing methods of these packaged mixes are almost foolproof (if directions on package are followed).

Tortes—These, as a class, are cake-like desserts, made light with eggs and often enriched with nuts. Bread crumbs, cracker or cookie crumbs, or grated nuts may take (wholly or in part) the place of flour. Tortes are coarser and more compact than cakes.

INGREDIENTS

Baking Powder — Use double-action baking powder unless otherwise specified in recipe.

Eggs — To obtain greatest volume, allow whole eggs or whites or yolks to stand at room temperature for one or two hours before beating them. If yolks and whites must be separated before beating, do this as soon as eggs are removed from refrigerator. In separating eggs it is important that none of the yolk gets into the whites. If this occurs whites may not whip to greatest volume and stiff peaks will not form.

Flour — Formerly most cakes were made using cake flour in order to produce a light, very tender cake texture. Modern milling processes have now produced an all-purpose flour which often may be used with satisfactory results. This is especially true when making cakes containing shortening. To substitute all-purpose flour for cake flour, reduce the amount by 2 tablespoons per cup. Avoid overbeating of the batter when all-purpose flour is used.

Liquid — The liquid most commonly used in cake is milk (sweet, sour, or buttermilk). In addition, cream, dairy sour cream, water, fruit juices, and coffee are used. These may not be substituted for sweet milk without making other changes in the recipe, especially in the kind and amount of leavening agent used. Never make substitutions in prepared cake mixes unless they are included in package directions. Sour milk and buttermilk may often be used interchangeably without making other changes in the recipe. To sour milk, see *page 20*.

TECHNIQUES FOR MAKING CAKES

(Read also *Use Correct Techniques, page 10*.)

To measure dry ingredients, liquids, and shortening, see *page 10*.

To prepare pans — Use pans of proper size. The cake batter should fill the pan one half to two thirds full. Batter should rise just to the top of the pan.

Before mixing the batter, grease bottoms of cake pans for cakes containing shortening. Line bottoms of pans with waxed paper and grease paper lightly. Do not grease or line bottoms of pans when preparing cakes without shortening (sponge type).

To beat eggs, see *page 10*.

To cream shortening, see *page 14*.

To bake cake — Start heating oven before mixing batter. When placing pans on oven racks, do not place one pan directly over another. For a single cake, place pan so that the center of the product is as near to the center of the oven as possible. Refrain from opening oven door during baking.

To test cakes — Test when minimum baking time is up. Touch surface lightly at center. If cake springs back and leaves no indention it is done. It also shrinks slightly from sides of pan. When cake tester or wooden pick inserted into center of cake comes out clean, the cake is done.

To cool and remove cakes and tortes from pan — Cool butter-type cake in pan on a wire rack about 10 minutes and a torte about 15 minutes. Then run spatula gently around sides of pan. Cover cake or torte with wire rack and invert. Lift off pan and immediately turn cake right side up on wire rack. Peel off waxed paper, if used. Cool cake completely before frosting unless otherwise directed in recipe.

Invert sponge-type cake (baked in tubed pan) on end of tube immediately after removing from oven. If cake is higher than the pan, invert it on the neck of a bottle, or invert it between two wire racks so that top of cake does not touch any surface. Let cake hang until completely cooled. Then cut around cake with a pointed knife. Loosen with a spatula and gently remove the cake.

To fill and frost layer cake, see *Frostings & Fillings, page 430*.

STORING CAKES

Cakes (except fruitcakes) are usually at their best when served the day they are baked. However, if stored properly, most cakes will remain fresh and delicious for several days.

Plain or frosted cakes — Store in a cake keeper in a cool, dry place. If it is a butter-type cake and has been baked in an oblong or square pan, the cake may be frosted and left in the pan. Cover the pan with foil and store in the refrigerator. Cake will remain fresh for a week. For longer periods, freeze.

Cream-filled or whipped-cream frosted and filled cakes — Assemble the cake shortly before serving. Always keep frosted cake in refrigerator until ready to serve. Leftover cake must be refrigerated.

Fruitcake — When cake is completely cooled, wrap it tightly in aluminum foil or moisture-vaporproof material and store in a cool place several weeks. If desired, once or twice a week, using a pastry brush, paint the cake with rum, brandy, or fruit juices. Rewrap and store. Properly wrapped fruitcakes may be stored in freezer for many months.

AN IMPERFECT CAKE

May have this fault...	For these reasons...	
	A BUTTER-TYPE CAKE	**A SPONGE-TYPE CAKE**
Coarse grain	Use of all-purpose instead of cake flour	Use of all-purpose instead of cake flour
	Excess of leavening	Omission of cream of tartar
	Not enough creaming	(in angel food)
	Undermixing	Undermixing
	Oven temperature too low	
Heaviness or compactness	Excess of liquid, shortening, or eggs	Underbeating of egg yolks or overbeating of egg whites
	Not enough leavening for flour	Overmixing
	Overmixing	
	Oven temperature too high	
Heavy, soggy layer at bottom of cake	Excess of liquid	Excess of eggs or egg yolks
	Shortening too soft	Underbeating of egg yolks
	Underbeating of eggs	Undermixing
	Undermixing	Failing to bake batter
	Baking time too short	promptly
Cracked or humped top	Excess of flour	Excess of flour or sugar
	Not enough liquid	Oven temperature too high
	Overmixing	
	Uneven spreading of batter	
	Oven temperature too high	
Sticky top crust	Excess of sugar	Excess of sugar
	Baking time too short	
Falling	Excess of sugar, liquid, leavening, or shortening	Excess of sugar
		Overbeating of egg whites
		Undermixing
Crumbling or falling apart	Excess of leavening, sugar, or shortening	
	Undermixing	
	Incorrect preparation of pan; or cooling	
Pale top crust	Oven temperature too low	Oven temperature too low
	Not enough sugar or shortening	Not enough sugar
	Excess of flour	Excess of flour
	Pan too large	
	Overmixing	
Falling out of pan before cooling is complete		Baking time too long
		Excess of sugar
		Greasing of pan
One side higher	Uneven spreading of batter	Pan warped
	Pan warped	Range or oven rack not level
	Range or oven rack not level	
	Pan too close to wall of oven	
	Uneven oven heat	
Dry crumb	Excess of flour	Excess of flour
	Not enough shortening or liquid	Overbeating of egg whites
	Overbeating of egg whites	Baking time too long
	Baking time too long	

HELPFUL HINTS ABOUT CAKES

• Use fluted paper baking cups when preparing cupcakes. They save greasing of pans and eliminate sticking. They also make pan washing easy.
• Line cake pans with baking parchment or waxed paper for easy removal of cakes after baking. Grease pans (bottoms only) before lining with paper and grease the paper. Cut several pieces at one time to fit pans and keep on hand for future use. (Cut the circles for layer cake pans about ¼ inch smaller than size of pan.) After baked cakes are removed from pans, peel off paper immediately.
• For baking fruitcake, line the pan with heavy brown paper extending 1 inch above top of pan. When cake is baked, place on wire rack. When completely cooled, lift cake from pan and peel off paper.
• When baking an upside-down cake, line cake pan with aluminum foil, folding foil over the edges of pan. After cake is baked, let cool on rack about 5 minutes. Then place serving plate on top of cake, turn cake upside down and remove the pan. Carefully lift off the foil. Cake comes out of pan easily and pan is easy to clean.

• When making cakes (or cookies) which use shortening and call for flavoring extracts and/or ground spices, add them to the shortening before creaming with the sugar. The fat "carries" the extract and spice flavors through the batter.
• To make a lace-like decoration on a sponge or angel food cake or other unfrosted cake, place a sheer, lace paper doily on top of cake; sift confectioners' sugar over top; then carefully lift off doily.
• To make your own cinnamon sugar to be used for sprinkling over warm, not-to-be-frosted cakes and cupcakes, combine ½ *cup fine granulated sugar* with *1 tablespoon ground cinnamon*. Keep the mixture on hand stored in a covered jar.
• If cooked white frosting has "sugared" somewhat, beat in a small amount of *lemon juice* until frosting is smooth.
• To make marshmallow flowers for cake decorating, use large white or colored *marshmallows*. With kitchen shears dipped in water, cut off strips about ⅛ inch thick. Place strips between 2 pieces of waxed paper and roll with rolling pin to make thin "petals." Arrange petals on frosted cake to simulate open flowers.

CONVENTIONAL CAKES

White Cakes

DELICATE WHITE CAKE

2¾ cups sifted cake flour	1½ teaspoons vanilla extract
3 teaspoons baking powder	1½ cups sugar
¾ teaspoon salt	1 cup milk
1 cup vegetable shortening	8 egg whites
	½ cup sugar
	Rich Coconut Fruit Filling, *below*

1. Sift flour, baking powder, and salt together.
2. Cream shortening with the extract and the 1½ cups sugar, beating until mixture is fluffy.
3. Beating only until smooth after each addition, alternately add flour mixture and milk.
4. In a large bowl, beat egg whites until frothy; beating constantly, add remaining sugar gradually and continue beating until stiff shiny peaks are formed. Fold into cake batter.

5. Turn batter into three 9-inch layer cake pans which have been lined on bottoms with waxed paper.
6. Bake at 350°F 20 to 25 minutes, or until cake tests done.
7. Cool in pans 10 minutes before removing to wire racks to cool thoroughly. Spread the filling between and on top of cake layers. Store overnight or about 8 hours in a cool place before serving.
ONE 9-INCH 3-LAYER CAKE

RICH COCONUT FRUIT FILLING

8 egg yolks, slightly beaten	1 cup coarsely chopped pecans
1 cup sugar	¾ cup quartered candied cherries
½ cup butter (at room temperature)	¾ cup coarsely chopped seeded raisins
⅓ cup bourbon	
1⅓ cups flaked coconut	

1. In a medium-sized saucepan combine the egg yolks, sugar, and butter. Cook over medium heat,

stirring constantly until sugar is dissolved and mixture is slightly thickened, 5 to 7 minutes.

2. Remove from heat and turn into a bowl. Cool slightly. Blend in the bourbon thoroughly.

3. Stir in the remaining ingredients. Cool thoroughly at room temperature before spreading on cooled cake layers. *3½ CUPS FILLING*

NOTE: *2 tablespoons brandy flavoring and 2 tablespoons water* may be substituted for the bourbon.

SUNNY POPPY-SEED CAKE

An aura of Old World charm surrounds this dessert creation—cake "nutty" with poppy seeds, sliced and layered with velvety-rich custard filling.

½ cup poppy seed (about 2½ oz.)	1 teaspoon vanilla extract
¾ cup milk	1½ cups sugar
2¼ cups sifted cake flour	4 egg whites (⅔ cup), beaten to stiff, not dry, peaks
2 teaspoons baking powder	Vanilla Custard Filling, *page 443*
½ teaspoon salt	
¾ cup butter or margarine	1 cup coarsely chopped walnuts

1. Soak poppy seed in milk for 2 hours.

2. Sift the flour, baking powder, and salt together; set aside.

3. Cream butter with extract. Gradually add sugar, creaming until fluffy.

4. Beating only until smooth after each addition, alternately add dry ingredients in fourths and poppy seed-milk mixture in thirds.

5. Gently fold egg whites into batter until blended. Turn batter into a greased (bottom only) 13x9x2-inch baking pan.

6. Bake at 350°F 25 to 30 minutes, or until cake tests done.

7. Cool and remove from pan as directed for butter-type cakes. Using a long thin sharp knife, cut cake in half lengthwise and then in half crosswise, making four 9x6½-inch cake layers.

8. Spread about 6 tablespoons Vanilla Custard Filling on one layer and sprinkle with about ¼ cup of walnuts. Repeat layering, ending with filling and nuts. Refrigerate until ready to serve.

ONE 4-LAYER CAKE

NOTE: If desired, make two 9-inch round cake layers. Fill and frost with *White Mountain Frosting, page 431,* and sprinkle with *poppy seed.*

LANE CAKE

This Southern belle of cakes is named for an Alabama lady who authored a cookbook at the turn of the century. Mrs. Lane may have often used citrus-cheese filling, but most popular are the raisin-nut-coconut mixtures varying with the use of wines, fruit juices, and spices.

3 cups sifted cake flour	1 cup milk
3 teaspoons baking powder	6 egg whites (about ¾ cup)
½ teaspoon salt	¾ cup sugar
1 cup butter	Filling for Lane Cake, *below*
1 tablespoon vanilla extract	White Frosting, *page 437*
1 cup sugar	

1. Sift the flour, baking powder, and salt together; set aside.

2. Cream butter with extract. Add 1 cup sugar gradually, creaming well.

3. Beating only until smooth after each addition, alternately add dry ingredients in fourths and milk in thirds to creamed mixture.

4. Beat egg whites until frothy. Add ¾ cup sugar gradually, continuing to beat until stiff peaks are formed. Gently fold meringue into batter just until blended. Turn into 2 prepared 9-inch layer cake pans and spread evenly to edges.

5. Bake at 350°F about 30 minutes, or until cake tests done.

6. Cool and remove from pans as directed for butter-type cakes. Fill and frost cake.

ONE 9-INCH 2-LAYER CAKE

NOTE: If desired, make cake in three 8-inch layers.

FILLING FOR LANE CAKE

1½ cups pecans	⅓ cup butter
1 cup raisins	1½ cups freshly grated coconut
6 egg yolks (½ cup)	
1¼ cups sugar	Brandy (about ¼ cup)

1. Grind pecans and raisins together; set aside.

2. Beat egg yolks and sugar until very thick.

3. Melt butter in top of a double boiler. Stir in egg yolk mixture. Cook over simmering water about 15 minutes, stirring constantly. Remove from heat and blend in pecan-raisin mixture and coconut.

4. Stir in enough brandy until filling is of spreading consistency. *3¼ CUPS FILLING*

SWEETHEART CAKE: Follow recipe for Lane Cake. If desired, for liquid use *½ cup water* and *½ cup* *milk*. Use 2 prepared 9-inch heart-shaped layer cake pans. Fill cooled layers with *Pineapple Cream Filling, page 443*. Frost with *Seven-Minute Frosting, page 430*; if desired, remove 3 tablespoons frosting, tint as desired with *food coloring*, put into a small pastry bag with No. 3 stem decorating tube, and write desired message.

LINCOLN'S FAVORITE CAKE

Mary Todd, before her marriage to Abraham Lincoln, is said to have made this cake for him, and the verdict was — "the best in Kentucky."

3 cups sifted all-purpose flour	1 cup sugar
3 teaspoons baking powder	1 cup milk
¼ teaspoon salt	1¼ cups (about 7 oz.) toasted blanched almonds, finely chopped
1 cup butter	
1½ teaspoons vanilla extract	
¼ teaspoon almond extract	6 egg whites
	1 cup sugar
	Fluffy White Frosting, *page 431*

1. Grease bottom only of a 10-inch tubed pan. Line with waxed paper cut to fit bottom; grease waxed paper. Set aside.
2. Sift the flour, baking powder, and salt together.
3. Cream butter with extracts. Add 1 cup sugar gradually, creaming until fluffy.
4. Beating only until smooth after each addition, alternately add dry ingredients in fourths and milk in thirds to the creamed mixture. Stir in the almonds.
5. Beat egg whites until frothy; add 1 cup sugar gradually, beating well. Continue beating until stiff peaks are formed. Gently fold meringue into batter just until blended. Turn batter into prepared pan and spread evenly.
6. Bake at 350°F about 1 hour, or until cake tests done.
7. Remove from oven and cool 15 minutes in pan on wire rack. Remove from pan; cool completely.
8. Frost with Fluffy White Frosting. Decorate with finely cut *candied cherries*.

ONE 10-INCH TUBED CAKE

LADY BALTIMORE CAKE

3 cups sifted cake flour	1 cup milk
3 teaspoons baking powder	6 egg whites (about ¾ cup)
½ teaspoon salt	¾ cup sugar
1 cup butter	Glaze, *below*
1½ teaspoons vanilla extract	Lady Baltimore Frosting, *below*
¾ cup sugar	

1. Sift flour, baking powder, and salt together.
2. Cream butter with extract. Add ¾ cup sugar gradually, creaming well.
3. Beating only until smooth after each addition, alternately add dry ingredients in fourths and milk in thirds to creamed mixture.
4. Beat egg whites until frothy. Add remaining ¾ cup sugar gradually, continuing to beat until stiff peaks are formed. Gently fold meringue into batter just until blended. Turn into 2 prepared 9-inch layer cake pans and spread to edges.
5. Bake at 350°F about 30 minutes, or until cake tests done.
6. Cool and remove from pans as directed for butter-type cakes. Immediately spread with hot glaze. Cool. Fill and frost with Lady Baltimore Frosting.   ONE 9-INCH 2-LAYER CAKE

GLAZE: Combine *1 cup sugar* and *½ cup water* in a saucepan. Stir over low heat until sugar is dissolved. Increase heat and bring mixture to boiling. Cover and boil gently 5 minutes. Uncover pan and set a candy thermometer in place. Continue cooking, stirring occasionally, until thermometer registers 230° to 234°F. Using a pastry brush dipped in water, wash down sides of pan as necessary; change water each time. Remove from heat and remove thermometer. Stir in *1 teaspoon vanilla extract* and *½ teaspoon almond extract*. Use hot.

LADY BALTIMORE FROSTING

2 cups sugar	½ teaspoon orange extract
6 tablespoons cold water	
2 tablespoons light corn syrup	½ teaspoon lemon extract
⅓ cup (2 large) egg whites	1 cup seedless raisins, coarsely chopped
	1 cup chopped walnuts

1. In top of a double boiler, combine sugar, water, corn syrup, and egg whites; stir until sugar is moistened. Wash down any crystals with wet brush.

2. Place over boiling water and at once start beating with a hand rotary or electric beater. Continue beating, moving beater around, until mixture holds up in peaks.

3. Remove from hot water and place over cold water. With final few strokes, beat in extracts. Set one third of frosting aside.

4. For filling, stir the raisins and walnuts into remaining frosting.

5. Spread filling between layers; frost with reserved frosting.

MARBLE CAKE

2 cups sifted cake flour	3 egg whites
2 teaspoons baking powder	1½ oz. (1½ sq.) unsweetened chocolate, melted and cooled
½ teaspoon salt	
½ cup butter or margarine	
2 teaspoons vanilla extract	2 tablespoons hot water
	1 tablespoon sugar
1 cup sugar	½ teaspoon baking soda
¾ cup milk	Beige Seven-Minute Frosting, *below*

1. Sift flour, baking powder, and salt together.

2. Cream the butter with extract; gradually add sugar, creaming until fluffy.

3. Beating only until smooth after each addition, alternately add dry ingredients in fourths and milk in thirds to the creamed mixture.

4. Beat egg whites until stiff, not dry, peaks are formed. Fold beaten egg whites gently into batter until thoroughly blended. Turn one half of the batter into a prepared 8x8x2-inch baking pan.

5. Lightly, but quickly, stir a mixture of the remaining ingredients into batter in bowl. Spoon chocolate batter into pan. Gently lift white batter through chocolate until marbled effect is produced. Spread batter evenly to edges of pan.

6. Bake at 350°F 40 to 45 minutes, or until cake tests done.

7. Set pan on wire rack and cool completely before frosting. Frost cake with Beige Seven-Minute Frosting. Decorate with toasted *pecan halves*.

ONE 8-INCH SQUARE CAKE

BEIGE SEVEN-MINUTE FROSTING: Combine *¾ cup sugar, ¾ cup firmly packed brown sugar, 2 egg whites, 1 tablespoon light corn syrup,* and *⅛ teaspoon salt* in the top of a double boiler. Beat until blended. Place over boiling water; beat constantly until mixture will hold peaks. Remove from water; add *1 teaspoon vanilla extract*. Beat until cool and thick enough to spread.

Yellow Cakes

GOLD CAKE

2½ cups sifted cake flour	1½ teaspoons vanilla extract
4 teaspoons baking powder	1¼ cups sugar
½ teaspoon salt	6 egg yolks (½ cup), well beaten
⅔ cup butter or other shortening	⅔ cup milk

1. Sift flour, baking powder, and salt together.

2. Cream the butter with extract; gradually add the sugar, creaming well. Add the beaten egg yolks in thirds, beating thoroughly after each addition.

3. Beating until just blended after each addition, alternately add dry ingredients in thirds and liquid in halves to creamed mixture. Turn batter into a prepared 9-inch tubed pan.

4. Bake at 350°F about 55 minutes or until cake tests done.

5. Cool and remove from pans as directed for butter-type cakes. Sift *confectioners' sugar* over top.

ONE 9-INCH TUBED CAKE

ALMOND CAKE

2¼ cups sifted all-purpose flour	1 cup sugar
2 teaspoons baking powder	3 eggs
½ teaspoon salt	1 can (12 oz.) almond cake and pastry filling (about 1¼ cups)
1 cup butter	¼ cup milk
½ teaspoon vanilla extract	Almond Icing, *page 396*

1. Sift flour, baking powder, and salt together; set aside.

2. Cream the butter with extract. Add sugar gradually, beating vigorously. Add the eggs, one at a time, beating until light and fluffy after each addition. Mix in the almond filling.

3. Beating only until blended after each addition, alternately add dry ingredients in thirds and milk in halves to creamed mixture. Turn batter into a prepared 9-inch tubed pan.

4.   Bake at 350°F 50 to 60 minutes, or until cake tests done.

5.   Cool on wire rack as directed for butter-type cakes. Spoon Almond Icing over cake.

ONE 9-INCH TUBED CAKE

ALMOND ICING: Beat *¾ cup confectioners' sugar, 1 teaspoon soft butter, 1 teaspoon light corn syrup, ⅛ teaspoon almond extract, and 1 tablespoon plus 1 teaspoon heavy cream* until smooth and of spreading consistency.   ABOUT ⅓ CUP ICING

BANANA CAKE ROYALE

2 cups sifted all-purpose flour	⅔ cup vegetable shortening
3 teaspoons baking powder	2 teaspoons vanilla extract
½ teaspoon baking soda	⅔ cup sugar
1 teaspoon salt	3 egg yolks, well beaten
1 cup graham cracker crumbs (granular rather than fine)	3 egg whites
	½ cup sugar
1 teaspoon lemon juice	Filling and Topping:
⅓ cup milk	3 medium-sized ripe bananas
1⅓ cups sieved ripe banana (3 to 4 bananas)	Pineapple juice
	Sweetened Whipped Cream, *page 441*
	½ cup walnuts, chopped

1.   Blend the flour, baking powder, baking soda, salt, and graham cracker crumbs; set aside.

2.   Add lemon juice to milk and stir in the sieved banana; set aside.

3.   Blend shortening and extract. Add the ⅔ cup sugar gradually, creaming until fluffy. Add the beaten egg yolks in halves, beating thoroughly after each addition.

4.   Beating only until smooth after each addition, alternately add dry ingredients in fourths and banana-milk mixture in thirds to creamed mixture.

5.   Beat egg whites until frothy. Add the ½ cup sugar gradually, continuing to beat until stiff peaks are formed. Gently fold meringue into batter just until blended. Turn batter into 3 prepared 8-inch layer cake pans.

6.   Bake at 350°F 30 to 35 minutes, or until cake tests done.

7.   Cool and remove from pans as directed for butter-type cakes. Cool completely.

8.   For filling and topping, peel bananas and cut into slices; dip slices into pineapple juice. Place one cooled cake layer on serving plate and spread about one third of the Sweetened Whipped Cream over it. Arrange one third of the banana slices over the cream. Cover with the second layer and repeat procedure. Cover with third layer, spread remaining whipped cream over, and arrange remaining banana slices and chopped walnuts attractively on top. Serve immediately.   ONE 8-INCH 3-LAYER CAKE

TURBAN CAKE
(Napfkuchen)

This cake of German origin is baked in a fluted mold. A semisweet chocolate glaze will add to its enhancement.

2¼ cups sifted all-purpose flour	½ cup sugar
2¼ teaspoons baking powder	4 egg yolks (⅓ cup), well beaten
½ cup butter	¾ cup milk
1 tablespoon grated lemon peel	4 egg whites (½ cup)
1 teaspoon vanilla extract	½ cup sugar
	Chocolate Glaze, *below*

1.   Sift the flour and baking powder together; set aside.

2.   Cream butter with lemon peel and extract. Add ½ cup sugar gradually, creaming until fluffy after each addition. Add the beaten egg yolks in thirds, beating well after each addition.

3.   Beating only until smooth after each addition, alternately add dry ingredients in thirds and milk in halves to creamed mixture.

4.   Beat the egg whites until frothy. Add ½ cup sugar gradually, beating well after each addition. Beat until stiff peaks are formed. Gently fold into batter. Turn into a greased 2-quart (8 inch) fluted tubed or turk's-head mold.

5.   Bake at 350°F about 55 minutes, or until cake tests done.

6.   Invert pan and let cake hang in pan 1 hour. Loosen from pan by running a small spatula carefully around tube and around edge of cake. Invert and remove pan. Spread warm Chocolate Glaze over the cake. Allow 2 to 3 hours for glaze to set.   ONE 8-INCH CAKE

CHOCOLATE GLAZE: Melt *4 ounces semisweet chocolate pieces* over hot (not steaming) water. Remove from heat and stir until chocolate is melted. Blend in *¼ cup butter.*

BANANA CAKE

Contributed by Mrs. Edmund G. Brown, former First Lady of California.

2 cups all-purpose flour	3 medium-sized fully
2 teaspoons baking	ripe bananas, sieved
powder	(about 1¼ cups)
1 teaspoon baking soda	¾ cup buttermilk
½ cup butter	1 cup chopped walnuts
1 teaspoon vanilla	2 egg whites, beaten to
extract	stiff, not dry, peaks
1½ cups sugar	
2 egg yolks	

1. Sift the flour, baking powder, and baking soda together; set aside.
2. Cream butter with extract. Gradually add sugar, creaming thoroughly. Add egg yolks, one at a time, beating well after each addition.
3. Beating only until smooth after each addition, alternately add dry ingredients in fourths and a mixture of the sieved bananas and buttermilk in thirds to creamed mixture. Stir in the walnuts.
4. Fold the beaten egg whites gently into batter until thoroughly blended. Turn batter into 2 prepared 9-inch layer cake pans; spread evenly to edges.
5. Bake at 350°F 25 to 30 minutes, or until cake tests done.
6. Cool and remove from pans as directed for butter-type cakes. Fill and frost with a *butter cream frosting.*   ONE 9-INCH 2-LAYER CAKE

PRALINE CARROT CAKE

Caramel Syrup, *below*	1½ teaspoons vanilla
Cooked Carrots, *below*	extract
2½ cups sifted all-	2 eggs, well beaten
purpose flour	2 cups pecans, coarsely
2 teaspoons baking	chopped
powder	Caramel Frosting,
1 teaspoon salt	*page 438*
½ cup butter or	
margarine	

1. Prepare Caramel Syrup and Cooked Carrots; set aside.
2. Sift the flour, baking powder, and salt together.
3. Cream butter with extract; add the Caramel Syrup gradually, blending well. Add the eggs in thirds, beating thoroughly after each addition. Beat in the carrots.

4. Beating only until smooth after each addition, alternately add the dry ingredients in fourths and reserved 1 cup carrot syrup in thirds to creamed mixture. Mix in the pecans. Turn batter into a prepared 13x9x2-inch baking pan and spread evenly.
5. Bake at 350°F 45 to 50 minutes, or until cake tests done.
6. Set on a wire rack and cool completely in pan. Frost with Caramel Frosting.   ONE 13x9-INCH CAKE
CARAMEL SYRUP: Melt *1 cup sugar* in a heavy light-colored skillet (a black skillet makes it difficult to see the color of the syrup). With back of a wooden spoon, gently keep sugar moving toward center of skillet until sugar is completely melted and of a golden-brown color. Remove from heat. Being careful that steam does not burn hand, stir and gradually add *1 cup milk* a small amount at a time. Return to low heat and add *1 cup sugar* gradually, stirring constantly until completely dissolved. Remove from heat, blend in *1 tablespoon butter or margarine*, and cool to lukewarm.
COOKED CARROTS: Put *2 cups sliced carrots, 1 cup sugar*, and *1 cup boiling water* into a saucepan; stir until sugar is dissolved. Cover and simmer about 10 minutes, or until carrots are tender and syrup is clear. Drain carrots, reserving 1 cup syrup. Force carrots through a sieve or food mill. (If an electric mixer is to be used for mixing cake batter, do not sieve carrots.) Set aside to cool.

COCONUT CAKE SUPREME

3¼ cups sifted cake	2 egg yolks
flour	¾ cup water
4½ teaspoons baking	½ cup orange juice
powder	½ cup flaked coconut
½ teaspoon salt	4 egg whites (about ½
¾ cup butter	cup)
1½ teaspoons grated	½ cup sugar
orange peel	Coconut-Marshmallow
1½ cups sugar	Frosting, *page 432*

1. Sift flour, baking powder and salt together; set aside.
2. Cream butter and orange peel. Add the 1½ cups sugar gradually, creaming until fluffy. Add egg yolks and beat thoroughly.
3. Beating only until smooth after each addition, alternately add dry ingredients in fourths and a mixture of water and orange juice in thirds to creamed mixture. Blend in the coconut.

4. Beat egg whites until frothy. Add the ½ cup sugar gradually, beating well. Continue beating until stiff peaks are formed. Gently fold into batter until blended. Turn batter into 3 prepared 9-inch layer cake pans and spread evenly to edges.

5. Bake at 350°F about 30 minutes, or until cake tests done.

6. Cool and remove from pans as directed for butter-type cake. Fill and frost with Coconut-Marshmallow Frosting.   ONE 9-INCH 3-LAYER CAKE

FILBERT FORM CAKE
Another cake baked in a fancy mold.

¼ cup graham cracker crumbs
⅓ cup toasted whole filberts
1 cup butter or margarine
2 teaspoons grated lemon peel
1 teaspoon vanilla extract
2 cups sugar
6 egg yolks (about ½ cup)

1½ cups sifted all-purpose flour
2 teaspoons baking powder
½ teaspoon salt
6 tablespoons milk
6 egg whites (about 1 cup)
1 cup toasted chopped filberts
⅓ cup semisweet chocolate pieces

1. Generously grease a 3-quart fancy tubed or turk's-head mold; coat with graham cracker crumbs and arrange the whole filberts on bottom of mold. Set aside.

2. Cream butter with lemon peel and extract. Add 1½ cups of the sugar gradually, creaming thoroughly. Add egg yolks gradually, beating thoroughly. Beat until light and fluffy.

3. Sift flour, baking powder, and salt together. Add alternately with milk to creamed mixture, blending well.

4. Beat egg whites until frothy. Add remaining ½ cup sugar gradually, beating until stiff peaks are formed. Fold into batter until well blended.

5. Spoon one third of batter into prepared mold; sprinkle with half of a mixture of chopped filberts and chocolate pieces. Repeat layering, ending with the batter.

6. Bake at 350°F 50 to 55 minutes, or until cake tests done. Cake will be well browned on top.

7. Remove to wire rack; cool in pan 15 minutes. Gently loosen cake around tube and sides of pan; invert on cake plate.

8. When cake is cool, sift *confectioners' sugar* over top.   ONE TUBED CAKE

FORM CAKE (Gugelhupf): Follow recipe for Filbert Form Cake. Omit crumbs, filberts, and chocolate pieces. Turn batter into the greased mold and bake as directed.

HONEY CAKE

2 cups sifted cake flour
1 teaspoon baking soda
¼ teaspoon salt
½ teaspoon ground cinnamon
½ teaspoon ground ginger

½ cup vegetable shortening
1 cup honey
1 egg
½ cup sour milk, *page 20*, or buttermilk
Fluffy Honey Frosting, *page 440*

1. Sift the flour, baking soda, salt, cinnamon, and ginger together and blend thoroughly; set aside.

2. Beat shortening and honey until light and thick. Add egg and beat thoroughly.

3. Beating only until blended after each addition, alternately add the dry ingredients in fourths and sour milk in thirds to creamed mixture. Turn batter into 2 prepared 8-inch layer cake pans and spread evenly to edges.

4. Bake at 375°F about 25 minutes, or until cake tests done.

5. Cool and remove from pans as directed for butter-type cakes. Fill cake layers and frost with Fluffy Honey Frosting.   ONE 8-INCH 2-LAYER CAKE

GRAHAM CRACKER CAKE

½ cup sifted cake flour
2 teaspoons baking powder
¼ teaspoon salt
24 graham crackers, finely crushed (2 cups)
¾ cup chopped pecans
1 cup butter or margarine

1½ teaspoons vanilla extract
1 cup sugar
3 egg yolks, well beaten
1 cup milk
3 egg whites
⅓ cup sugar
Creamy Vanilla Filling, *page 442*

1. Blend the flour, baking powder, salt, graham cracker crumbs, and pecans; set aside.

2. Cream the butter with extract. Add the 1 cup sugar gradually, creaming until fluffy. Add egg yolks in thirds, beating thoroughly after each addition.

3. Beating only until smooth after each addition, alternately add dry ingredients in fourths and milk in thirds to the creamed mixture.

4. Beat egg whites until frothy; add ⅓ cup sugar gradually, continuing to beat until stiff peaks are formed. Gently fold meringue into batter until just blended. Turn batter into 2 lightly greased (bottoms only) 9-inch layer cake pans.

5. Bake at 350°F 30 to 35 minutes, or until cake tests done.

6. Cool and remove from pans as directed for butter-type cakes. Cool completely.

7. Spread the chilled Creamy Vanilla Filling over one layer of cooled cake. Cover with second layer. Place a lace paper doily over the cake; sift evenly with *confectioners' sugar* and carefully lift off doily. ONE 9-INCH 2-LAYER CAKE

MAPLE SYRUP CAKE

One bite and it's easily understood why Vermonters are especially partial to this kind of cake.

2⅔ cups sifted cake flour	⅔ cup lightly packed light brown sugar
3 teaspoons baking powder	7 egg yolks, well beaten
¾ teaspoon salt	⅔ cup milk
¾ cup butter or margarine	⅔ cup maple syrup
	Maple Sugar Frosting, page 436
	½ cup chopped walnuts

1. Sift the flour, baking powder, and salt together; set aside.

2. Cream butter; gradually add brown sugar, creaming until fluffy. Add egg yolks in thirds, beating thoroughly after each addition.

3. Beating until smooth after each addition, alternately add the dry ingredients in fourths and a mixture of milk and maple syrup in thirds to the creamed mixture. Turn batter into 3 prepared 8-inch layer cake pans and spread evenly to edges.

4. Bake at 350°F 45 to 50 minutes, or until cake tests done.

5. Cool and remove from pans as directed for butter-type cakes. Fill and frost cake with Maple Sugar Frosting. Sprinkle walnuts around outside edge of top. ONE 8-INCH 3-LAYER CAKE

MAPLE-BUTTERNUT CAKE: Follow recipe for Maple Syrup Cake. Blend in *½ cup coarsely chopped butternuts* just before turning batter into pans. Substitute butternuts for walnuts as topping.

BURNT-SUGAR CAKE

3 cups sifted cake flour	1½ cups sugar
3 teaspoons baking powder	3 eggs, well beaten
1 teaspoon salt	⅓ cup cooled Burnt-Sugar Syrup, below
¾ cup butter or margarine	¾ cup milk
1 teaspoon vanilla extract	Burnt-Sugar Butter Frosting, page 436

1. Sift the flour, baking powder, and salt together.

2. Cream butter with extract. Add sugar gradually, creaming well after each addition. Add eggs in thirds, beating thoroughly after each addition.

3. Thoroughly blend the Burnt-Sugar Syrup and milk. Beating only until blended after each addition, alternately add dry ingredients in fourths and milk mixture in thirds to creamed mixture. Turn into 2 prepared 9-inch layer cake pans.

4. Bake at 350°F 30 to 35 minutes, or until cake tests done.

5. Cool and remove from pans as directed for butter-type cakes. Fill and frost with Burnt-Sugar Butter Frosting. Sprinkle top with chopped toasted *pecans*, if desired. ONE 9-INCH 2-LAYER CAKE

BURNT-SUGAR SYRUP: Heat *1 cup sugar* in a heavy, light colored skillet over low heat; using back of wooden spoon, gently keep sugar moving toward center of skillet until melted. Heat until syrup is a rich brown and foam appears. Remove from heat and very gradually add *¾ cup boiling water*, stirring constantly. Return to heat and stir until bubbles are the size of dimes, about 5 minutes. Cool completely. ABOUT ¾ CUP SYRUP

ORANGE BLOSSOM CAKE

2½ cups sifted cake flour	2 teaspoons grated orange peel
2½ teaspoons baking powder	½ teaspoon grated lemon peel
½ teaspoon salt	1½ cups sugar
⅔ cup butter or margarine	3 eggs plus 2 yolks, well beaten
	1 cup orange juice

1. Sift the flour, baking powder, and salt together.

2. Cream the butter with orange and lemon peels. Add the sugar gradually, beating well. Add beaten eggs in thirds, beating well after each addition.

3. Beating until smooth after each addition, alter-

nately add dry ingredients in fourths and orange juice in thirds to creamed mixture. Turn batter into 2 prepared 9-inch layer cake pans and spread evenly to edges.

4. Bake at 350°F 25 to 30 minutes, or until cake tests done.

5. Cool and remove from pans as directed for butter-type cakes. Fill and frost layers with an *orange butter cream frosting*.

ONE 9-INCH 2-LAYER CAKE

GOLDEN ORANGE CRUNCH CAKE

1½ cups very finely chopped walnuts, unblanched almonds, or filberts	2 teaspoons baking powder
⅓ cup butter, melted	½ teaspoon salt
¼ cup fine dry bread crumbs	¾ cup butter
½ cup lightly packed light brown sugar	2 tablespoons grated orange peel
¼ teaspoon ground cinnamon	1 teaspoon vanilla extract
2¾ cups sifted cake flour	1½ cups sugar
	4 eggs
	½ cup undiluted evaporated milk
	¼ cup orange juice

1. Thoroughly mix the walnuts, melted butter, bread crumbs, brown sugar, and cinnamon. Turn mixture into a 9-inch tubed pan and press firmly into an even layer on bottom and sides of pan.

2. Sift flour, baking powder, and salt together.

3. Cream the ¾ cup butter with orange peel and extract. Add the 1½ cups sugar gradually, creaming until fluffy. Add the eggs, one at a time, beating thoroughly after each addition.

4. Beating just until smooth after each addition, alternately add the dry ingredients in fourths and a mixture of the evaporated milk and orange juice in thirds to creamed mixture. Turn batter into the prepared pan and spread evenly to edges.

5. Bake at 375°F 55 to 60 minutes, or until cake tests done.

6. Remove cake from oven to a wire rack and cool in pan 30 minutes. Invert onto rack and remove pan. Cool thoroughly before cutting.

ONE 9-INCH TUBED CAKE

SALTED PEANUT CAKE

1½ cups sifted all-purpose flour	1 cup sugar
½ teaspoon baking soda	1 egg
⅓ cup butter or margarine	¾ cup buttermilk
1 teaspoon vanilla extract	1 cup (about 5 oz.) salted peanuts, finely chopped

1. Sift flour and baking soda together; set aside.

2. Cream butter with extract. Gradually add sugar, creaming until fluffy. Add egg; beat thoroughly.

3. Beating only until smooth after each addition, alternately add dry ingredients in thirds and buttermilk in halves. Mix in peanuts. Turn batter into a greased 8x8x2-inch baking pan; spread evenly to edges.

4. Bake at 350°F about 50 minutes, or until cake tests done.

5. Cool completely in pan on wire rack. Sift *confectioners' sugar* evenly over top.

ONE 8-INCH SQUARE CAKE

RASPBERRY RING CAKE

½ cup butter	½ teaspoon salt
1 teaspoon vanilla extract	¾ cup milk
1 cup sugar	6 tablespoons red raspberry jam
1 egg	⅛ teaspoon red food coloring
2 cups sifted cake flour	Raspberry Ripple Icing, *below*
2 teaspoons baking powder	

1. Cream the butter with extract. Add sugar gradually, creaming until fluffy. Add beaten egg, beating well.

2. Sift the flour, baking powder, and salt together.

3. Beating only until smooth after each addition, alternately add dry ingredients in fourths and milk in thirds to creamed mixture.

4. Remove one third of the batter to another bowl and blend in the jam and food coloring. Pour one half of the plain batter into a greased (bottom only) 2-quart ring mold; pour raspberry batter over first layer. Top with remaining batter.

5. Bake at 325°F 50 to 55 minutes, or until cake tests done.

6. Cool and remove from mold as directed for butter-type cakes. Decorate with Raspberry Ripple Icing.

ONE RING-SHAPED CAKE

RASPBERRY RIPPLE ICING: Combine *1 cup*

confectioners' sugar, 2 tablespoons cream, and *¼ teaspoon vanilla extract*; beat until smooth. With a spoon, drizzle frosting over top of cake allowing it to run down sides. Stir *⅓ cup red raspberry jam, 2 teaspoons water*, and *½ teaspoon red food coloring* together in a saucepan; heat until mixture thins. Spoon over cake.

MARBLEIZED TUBED CAKE

½ cup sugar	1½ teaspoons vanilla
¾ teaspoon ground	extract
cinnamon	1 cup sugar
2 tablespoons cocoa	4 egg yolks, well beaten
3 cups sifted all-	1 cup milk
purpose flour	4 egg whites
3 teaspoons baking	½ cup sugar
powder	2 tablespoons butter or
½ teaspoon salt	margarine
1 cup butter or	
margarine	

1. Blend ½ cup sugar, cinnamon, and cocoa; set aside.
2. Sift the flour, baking powder, and salt together; set aside.
3. Cream the 1 cup butter with extract. Add the 1 cup sugar gradually, creaming until fluffy. Add beaten egg yolks in thirds, beating thoroughly after each addition.
4. Beating only until smooth after each addition, alternately add dry ingredients in fourths and milk in thirds to creamed mixture.
5. Beat egg whites until frothy; add the remaining ½ cup sugar gradually, beating well. Continue beating until stiff peaks are formed. Fold batter gently into beaten egg whites until just blended.
6. Gently turn one third of the batter into a greased and floured (bottom only) 10-inch tubed pan, spreading evenly. Sprinkle batter in pan with one third of the sugar mixture. Alternately layer remaining batter and sugar mixture, ending with sugar mixture on top. Cut through batter from center to outer edge at 1 to 2 inch intervals with a spatula to swirl sugar mixture through batter. Dot with remaining butter.
7. Bake at 375°F about 1 hour, or until cake tests done.
8. Remove from oven to wire rack and cool completely in pan. Sprinkle top lightly with *confectioners' sugar*.   ONE 10-INCH TUBED CAKE

YUM YUM CAKE

2 tablespoons butter or	½ cup butter or
margarine	margarine
¼ cup lightly packed	1 teaspoon vanilla
dark brown sugar	extract
½ cup coarsely chopped	1 cup sugar
pecans	1 egg
2 cups sifted all-	¾ cup buttermilk
purpose flour	12 marshmallows, cut in
1½ teaspoons baking	small pieces
powder	½ cup (3 oz.) semisweet
¼ teaspoon baking soda	chocolate pieces,
¼ teaspoon salt	coarsely chopped

1. Cream the 2 tablespoons butter with brown sugar until well blended. Mix in pecans; set aside.
2. Sift the flour, baking powder, baking soda, and salt together; set aside.
3. Cream the ½ cup butter and extract. Add the sugar gradually, creaming until fluffy. Add egg and beat well.
4. Beating only until smooth after each addition, alternately add the dry ingredients in fourths and buttermilk in thirds. Stir in marshmallows and chocolate pieces. Turn into a greased (bottom only) 9x9x2-inch baking pan. Cover evenly with topping.
5. Bake at 350°F about 45 minutes, or until cake tests done.
6. Remove from oven to wire rack and cool completely in pan. Cut into squares.

ONE 9-INCH SQUARE CAKE

Spice Cakes

SPICE CAKE WITH PRALINE FROSTING

3 cups sifted cake flour	¾ cup butter
1½ teaspoons baking	1 cup lightly packed
powder	light brown sugar
¾ teaspoon baking soda	1 cup sugar
¾ teaspoon salt	3 eggs, well beaten
1½ teaspoons ground	1½ cups buttermilk
cinnamon	Praline Frosting:
¾ teaspoon ground	2 egg whites
nutmeg	¼ teaspoon salt
½ teaspoon ground	1¾ cups lightly
allspice	packed brown sugar
½ teaspoon ground	½ cup chopped pecans
cloves	

1. Sift the flour, baking powder, baking soda, salt,

and spices together and blend thoroughly; set aside.

2. Cream butter; gradually add the sugars, creaming until fluffy. Add the beaten eggs in thirds, beating thoroughly after each addition.

3. Beating only until blended after each addition, alternately add dry ingredients in fourths and buttermilk in thirds to creamed mixture. Turn batter into a greased (bottom only) 13x9x2-inch baking pan and spread evenly.

4. Bake at 350°F 55 to 60 minutes, or until cake tests done.

5. Set on wire rack while preparing frosting.

6. Beat the egg whites with salt until rounded peaks are formed. Gradually add the brown sugar, beating thoroughly. (If mixture becomes too thick to beat, blend in remaining sugar with a spoon.) Add the pecans and mix well.

7. Spread frosting over the partially cooled cake in pan. Return to oven and bake about 18 minutes, or until frosting is delicately browned.

8. Set on wire rack for 10 to 15 minutes to cool before cutting into squares. Serve warm.

ONE 13x9-INCH CAKE

APPLE BUTTER SPICE CAKE

Topping:	1 teaspoon baking soda
½ cup lightly packed	½ teaspoon salt
light brown sugar	½ cup butter or
¾ cup chopped pecans	margarine
1 teaspoon ground	1 teaspoon vanilla
cinnamon	extract
½ teaspoon ground	1 cup sugar
nutmeg	2 eggs
Batter:	¾ cup apple butter
2 cups sifted all-	½ cup whole bran cereal
purpose flour	1 cup dairy sour cream
1 teaspoon baking	
powder	

1. Combine the ingredients for topping and set aside.

2. Sift the flour, baking powder, baking soda, and salt together; set aside.

3. Cream butter with extract; gradually add the sugar, beating until fluffy. Add the eggs, one at a time, beating thoroughly after each addition. Blend in the apple butter and cereal.

4. Beating only until smooth after each addition, alternately add dry ingredients in fourths and sour cream in thirds to creamed mixture. Turn half the batter into a greased (bottom only) 13x9x2-inch baking pan. Spread evenly to edges. Sprinkle half of the topping mixture over batter in pan. Spoon remaining batter into pan and spread evenly. Sprinkle with remaining topping.

5. Bake at 350°F about 30 minutes, or until cake tests done.

6. Cool cake completely in pan. Cut into squares and serve warm or cold. Top with *whipped cream*, if desired.

ONE 13x9-INCH CAKE

JAM CAKE

The flavor-blend of spices and blackberry jam in this buttermilk cake adds to its distinctiveness.

4 cups sifted all-	½ cup butter
purpose flour	½ cup vegetable
2 teaspoons baking soda	shortening
2 teaspoons ground	2 cups sugar
allspice	5 eggs
2 teaspoons ground	1 cup blackberry jam
cinnamon	1½ cups buttermilk
2 teaspoons ground	Orange Filling, *below*
nutmeg	Orange Butter Frosting,
1 teaspoon ground cloves	*page 436*

1. Sift the flour, baking soda, and spices together and blend thoroughly; set aside.

2. Cream butter and shortening. Add sugar gradually, creaming thoroughly. Add eggs, one at a time, beating until light and fluffy after each addition. Mix in the jam.

3. Beating only until blended after each addition, alternately add dry ingredients in fourths and buttermilk in thirds to creamed mixture. Turn batter into 4 prepared 9-inch layer cake pans.

4. Bake at 350°F about 30 minutes, or until cake tests done.

5. Cool and remove from pans as directed for butter-type cakes. Fill with Orange Filling. Frost sides and top with Orange Butter Frosting.

ONE 9-INCH 4-LAYER CAKE

ORANGE FILLING: Quarter *3 medium-sized oranges*, discard seeds, and force through fine blade of food chopper. Put into a small saucepan with *2 cups sugar* and *3 egg yolks*. Cook over medium heat, stirring constantly, until mixture is thickened, about 10 minutes. Remove from heat and stir in *2 tablespoons butter*. Beat vigorously until of spreading consistency. Cool before filling cake.

ABOUT 3 CUPS FILLING

BITTERSWEET CHOCOLATE SPICE CAKE

2¼ cups sifted all-
    purpose flour
2 teaspoons baking
    powder
½ teaspoon salt
1 teaspoon ground
    cinnamon
½ teaspoon ground
    allspice
½ teaspoon ground
    nutmeg
¼ teaspoon ground
    coriander

¾ cup butter or
    margarine
2 teaspoons vanilla
    extract
½ teaspoon almond
    extract
2 cups sugar
4 eggs, well beaten
1 cup milk
5 oz. (5 sq.)
    unsweetened
    chocolate, grated
Caramel Fudge Frosting,
    page 434

1. Sift the flour, baking powder, salt, and spices together and blend thoroughly; set aside.
2. Cream the butter with extracts. Gradually add the sugar, creaming thoroughly. Add the eggs in fourths, beating thoroughly after each addition.
3. Beating only until blended after each addition, alternately add dry ingredients in fourths and milk in thirds to creamed mixture. Fold in chocolate until blended. Turn batter into 2 prepared 9-inch layer cake pans and spread evenly to edges.
4. Bake at 375°F 30 minutes, or until cake tests done.
5. Cool and remove from pans as directed for butter-type cakes. Fill and frost.

ONE 9-INCH 2-LAYER CAKE

SOFT GINGERBREAD

Gingerbread was recorded in early colonial accounts and is still greatly appreciated in America.

3 cups sifted all-
    purpose flour
1 teaspoon baking soda
¼ teaspoon salt
2 teaspoons ground
    cinnamon
2 teaspoons ground
    ginger
1 teaspoon ground cloves

¼ teaspoon ground
    nutmeg
½ cup butter
1 cup sugar
2 eggs, well beaten
1 cup light molasses
¼ cup boiling water
1 cup sour milk,
    page 20

1. Sift the flour, baking soda, salt, and spices together and blend thoroughly; set aside.
2. Cream butter; gradually add sugar, creaming until fluffy. Add eggs in thirds, beating well after each addition. Add a mixture of molasses and boiling water gradually, mixing well.

3. Beating only until smooth after each addition, alternately add dry ingredients in fourths and sour milk in thirds to creamed mixture. Turn batter into a well greased (bottom only) 13x9x2-inch baking pan.
4. Bake at 350°F about 35 minutes, or until gingerbread tests done.
5. Cool in pan on wire rack. ONE 13x9-INCH CAKE

DATE DELIGHT CAKE

2 cups sifted all-
    purpose flour
1 teaspoon baking soda
1 teaspoon salt
1 teaspoon ground
    allspice
1 teaspoon ground
    cinnamon
1 teaspoon ground
    nutmeg
1 cup cooking oil

3 eggs
1 teaspoon vanilla
    extract
1½ cups sugar
1 cup buttermilk
1 cup chopped walnuts
1 cup chopped pitted
    dates
Caramel Frosting,
    page 438

1. Sift the flour, baking soda, salt, and spices together and blend thoroughly; set aside.
2. Combine the oil, eggs, extract, and sugar in a large bowl. Beat until smooth and creamy.
3. Beating only until smooth after each addition, alternately add dry ingredients in fourths and buttermilk in thirds to the creamed mixture.
4. Stir in the walnuts and dates until thoroughly blended. Turn batter into a greased (bottom only) 13x9x2-inch baking pan; spread evenly to edges.
5. Bake at 300°F 55 to 60 minutes, or until cake tests done.
6. Cool cake completely in pan. Frost.

ONE 13x9-INCH CAKE

OLD-FASHIONED MOLASSES CAKE

4⅓ cups sifted all-
    purpose flour
3 teaspoons baking
    powder
¾ teaspoon baking soda
1 teaspoon salt
3 teaspoons ground
    cinnamon

1½ teaspoons ground
    ginger
¾ teaspoon ground
    cloves
¾ cup butter
¾ cup sugar
1½ cups light molasses
3 eggs, well beaten
1½ cups hot water

1. Sift the flour, baking powder, baking soda, salt, and spices together and blend thoroughly.

2. Cream butter; gradually add sugar, creaming until fluffy. Add molasses gradually, mixing well. Blend in ½ cup of the dry ingredients. Add eggs in thirds, beating well after each addition.

3. Beating only until smooth after each addition, alternately add the remaining dry ingredients in fourths and hot water in thirds. Turn batter into a greased (bottom only) 13x9x2-inch baking pan and spread evenly to edges.

4. Bake at 350°F 50 minutes, or until cake tests done.

5. Cool cake completely in pan. Cut into squares and, if desired, serve with warm *applesauce.*

ONE 13x9-INCH CAKE

PUMPKIN CAKE

2¼ cups sifted cake flour	½ cup butter or margarine
3 teaspoons baking powder	½ cup sugar
½ teaspoon baking soda	1 cup lightly packed dark brown sugar
½ teaspoon salt	2 eggs
1½ teaspoons ground cinnamon	¾ cup buttermilk
½ teaspoon ground allspice	¾ cup canned pumpkin
½ teaspoon ground ginger	½ cup finely snipped or chopped golden raisins

1. Sift the flour, baking powder, baking soda, salt, and spices together and blend thoroughly; set aside.

2. Cream butter; gradually add sugars, creaming until fluffy. Add eggs, one at a time, beating thoroughly after each addition.

3. Beating only until smooth after each addition, alternately add dry ingredients in fourths and a mixture of the buttermilk, pumpkin, and raisins in thirds to creamed mixture. Turn batter into 2 prepared 9-inch layer cake pans and spread evenly.

4. Bake at 350°F about 30 minutes, or until cake tests done.

5. Cool and remove from pans as directed for butter-type cakes. TWO 9-INCH CAKE LAYERS

PUMPKIN MINIATURES: Follow recipe for Pumpkin Cake. Spoon batter into 1¾-inch muffin-pan wells lined with paper baking cups, half filling each. Bake at 375°F about 13 minutes, or until cupcakes test done. Remove from pans and cool on racks. Frost with *butter cream frosting.*

6½ DOZEN CUPCAKES

Chocolate Cakes

OLD-FASHIONED CHOCOLATE CAKE

Said to have been a favorite of President William McKinley.

2 egg yolks, fork beaten	1½ teaspoons vanilla extract
6 oz. (6 sq.) unsweetened chocolate, melted	2 cups lightly packed brown sugar
½ cup hot water	1 cup sour milk, *page 20*
2 cups sifted cake flour	White Velvet Frosting, *page 437*
1 teaspoon baking soda	
½ teaspoon salt	
½ cup butter	

1. Stir egg yolks into melted chocolate. Gradually add the hot water, stirring constantly until smooth. Set aside to cool.

2. Sift flour, baking soda, and salt together; set aside.

3. Cream butter with extract; gradually add brown sugar, creaming thoroughly. Blend in chocolate mixture.

4. Beating only until blended after each addition, alternately add the dry ingredients in fourths and the sour milk in thirds to the creamed mixture. Turn into 2 prepared 8-inch layer cake pans and spread evenly to edges.

5. Bake at 350°F 30 minutes, or until cake tests done.

6. Cool and remove from pans as directed for butter-type cakes. Fill and frost.

ONE 8-INCH 2-LAYER CAKE

JERRY LEWIS' CHOCOLATE CAKE

Actor, producer, director Jerry Lewis is always on the go, but when wife Patti bakes his favorite cake, Jerry makes sure he has time to enjoy its chocolaty goodness.

2 cups sifted cake flour	2 oz. (2 sq.) unsweetened chocolate, melted and cooled
½ teaspoon salt	1 cup sour milk, *page 20*
½ cup butter or margarine	1 teaspoon baking soda
1 teaspoon vanilla extract	1 tablespoon vinegar
1½ cups sugar	
2 eggs	

1. Sift flour and salt together; set aside.

2. Cream butter with extract. Gradually add sugar, creaming until light and fluffy. Add eggs, one at

a time, beating thoroughly after each addition. Blend in chocolate.

3. Beating only until smooth after each addition, alternately add dry ingredients in thirds and sour milk in halves to creamed mixture. Stir baking soda and vinegar together; immediately blend into batter. Turn into 2 prepared 9-inch layer cake pans and spread evenly to edges.

4. Bake at 375°F 25 minutes, or until cake tests done.

5. Cool and remove from pans as directed for butter-type cakes. Frost as desired.

TWO 9-INCH CAKE LAYERS

CHOCOLATE BROWN SUGAR CAKE

2¼ cups sifted cake flour	3 eggs
1 teaspoon baking soda	3 oz. (3 sq.)
½ teaspoon salt	unsweetened
½ cup butter	chocolate, melted
1 teaspoon vanilla	and cooled
extract	1 cup buttermilk
1½ cups lightly packed	Buttermilk Fudge
dark brown sugar	Frosting, *page 434*

1. Sift flour, baking soda, and salt; set aside.

2. Cream the butter with extract. Gradually add sugar, creaming thoroughly. Add eggs, one at a time, beating until light and fluffy after each addition. Mix in the chocolate.

3. Beating only until blended after each addition, alternately add dry ingredients in thirds and buttermilk in halves to creamed mixture. Turn batter into 2 prepared 9-inch layer cake pans.

4. Bake at 350°F 30 minutes, or until cake tests done.

5. Cool and remove from pans as directed for butter-type cakes. Fill and frost.

ONE 9-INCH 2-LAYER CAKE

CHOCOLATE POTATO CAKE

Instant mashed potatoes	2 teaspoons grated
½ cup milk	lemon peel
2 cups sifted cake flour	2 cups sugar
2 teaspoons baking	4 eggs, well beaten
powder	1 oz. (1 sq.)
½ teaspoon salt	unsweetened
1 cup butter or	chocolate, melted
margarine	and cooled

1. Prepare 1 cup lightly packed riced or sieved potato from instant mashed potatoes according to package directions, using only the water (omit milk, butter, and seasonings). Blend potato with the ½ cup milk; set aside.

2. Sift flour, baking powder, and salt together; set aside.

3. Cream butter with lemon peel. Add sugar gradually, creaming until fluffy after each addition. Add beaten eggs in thirds; beat well after each addition.

4. Beating only until blended after each addition, alternately add dry ingredients in fourths and potato mixture in thirds to creamed mixture. Stir in the cooled chocolate. Turn batter into 2 prepared 9-inch layer cake pans.

5. Bake at 350°F about 40 minutes, or until cake tests done.

6. Cool and remove from pans as directed for butter-type cakes. Fill and frost with *Potato Fudge Frosting, page 435.* ONE 9-INCH 2-LAYER CAKE

MRS. EISENHOWER'S DEVIL'S FOOD CAKE

A recipe from the wife of former President Dwight David Eisenhower.

⅔ cup cocoa	1 teaspoon vanilla
½ cup boiling water	extract
2½ cups sifted cake	2 cups sugar
flour	3 egg yolks
1¼ teaspoons baking	1 cup sour milk,
powder	*page 20*
1 teaspoon baking soda	3 egg whites, beaten to
¼ teaspoon salt	stiff, not dry, peaks
½ cup butter	Seven-Minute Frosting,
	page 430

1. Mix cocoa and water together; set aside to cool.

2. Sift flour, baking powder, baking soda, and salt together; set aside.

3. Cream butter with extract; gradually add sugar, creaming thoroughly. Add egg yolks, one at a time, beating thoroughly after each addition. Add cocoa mixture and beat until well blended.

4. Beating only until blended after each addition, alternately add dry ingredients in thirds and sour milk in halves to creamed mixture. Fold in beaten egg whites. Turn batter into 2 prepared 9-inch layer cake pans and spread evenly to edges.

5. Bake at 375°F 25 to 30 minutes, or until cake tests done.

6. Cool and remove from pans as directed for butter-type cakes. Fill and frost with Seven-Minute Frosting. ONE 9-INCH 2-LAYER CAKE

WELLESLEY FUDGE CAKE

A favorite with the students of Wellesley, a school in the Massachusetts town of the same name.

4 oz. (4 sq.) unsweet-ened chocolate	½ cup butter or margarine
½ cup hot water	2 teaspoons vanilla extract
½ cup sugar	1¼ cups sugar
2 cups sifted cake flour	4 eggs, well beaten
1½ teaspoons baking powder	⅔ cup milk
½ teaspoon baking soda	Fudge Frosting II, *page 435*
½ teaspoon salt	

1. Combine chocolate and water in a heavy saucepan. Place over very low heat, stirring constantly, until chocolate is melted. Add the ½ cup sugar and stir until dissolved. Set aside to cool.
2. Sift flour, baking powder, baking soda, and salt together; set aside.
3. Cream butter with extract; gradually add the 1¼ cups sugar, creaming until fluffy. Add eggs in thirds, beating thoroughly after each addition. Blend in chocolate mixture.
4. Beating only until smooth after each addition, alternately add dry ingredients in fourths and milk in thirds to creamed mixture. Turn batter into 2 prepared 8x8x2-inch baking pans and spread evenly to edges.
5. Bake at 350°F 25 to 30 minutes, or until cake tests done.
6. Cool and remove from pans as directed for butter-type cakes. Fill and frost with Fudge Frosting II. ONE 8-INCH SQUARE 2-LAYER CAKE

THE VASSAR DEVIL

A popular dessert at Vassar for more than forty years, it is now featured at The Treasure Chest Restaurant in Poughkeepsie, New York.

2 oz. (2 sq.) unsweet-ened chocolate	1 teaspoon vanilla extract
¼ cup boiling water	½ cup sugar
1 cup sifted all-purpose flour	1 egg
1 teaspoon baking powder	½ teaspoon baking soda
¼ teaspoon salt	½ cup sour milk, *page 20*
⅓ cup butter or margarine	Vassar Devil Icing, *below*

1. Put chocolate and water into a heavy sauce-pan. Set over very low heat and stir until chocolate is melted. Set aside.
2. Sift flour, baking powder, and salt together; set aside.
3. Cream butter with extract. Gradually add sugar, creaming thoroughly. Add egg and beat well.
4. Dissolve baking soda in sour milk and stir into creamed mixture. Beat in chocolate. Add dry ingredients and beat until smooth. Turn batter into a greased (bottom only) 8x8x2-inch baking pan and spread evenly to edges.
5. Bake at 325°F 25 minutes, or until cake tests done.
6. Cool and remove from pan as directed for butter-type cakes. Spread Vassar Devil Icing over top of cooled cake.
7. To serve, cut cake into squares and split each. Sandwich a small slice of *vanilla ice cream* between each split cake square. Spoon *chocolate sauce* over each serving and top with *whipped cream*. 16 SERVINGS

VASSAR DEVIL ICING: Put *1 cup sugar, 2 ounces (2 squares) unsweetened chocolate*, grated, *½ cup milk*, and *2 tablespoons butter or margarine* into a heavy saucepan. Stir over low heat until sugar is dissolved. Bring rapidly to boiling. Wash down sides of pan and set candy thermometer in place. Cook to 232°F, stirring occasionally. Remove from heat and set aside to cool to 110°F. Do not stir. Add *1 teaspoon vanilla extract* and beat just until icing is of spreading consistency. Immediately spread over cake. ABOUT ¾ CUP ICING

CHOCOLATE APPLESAUCE CAKE

3 cups sifted cake flour	½ cup vegetable shortening
¾ cup cocoa, sifted	½ cup butter or margarine
2½ teaspoons baking powder	1½ cups sugar
½ teaspoon baking soda	2 eggs, well beaten
¾ teaspoon salt	1 cup thick sweetened applesauce
1½ teaspoons ground cinnamon	¾ cup sour milk, *page 20*, or buttermilk
¾ teaspoon ground nutmeg	¾ cup nuts, chopped
½ teaspoon ground cloves	

1. Sift flour, cocoa, baking powder, baking soda, salt, and spices together and blend; set aside.
2. Cream shortening and butter; gradually add

sugar, creaming until fluffy. Add eggs in thirds, beating thoroughly after each addition.

3.　Beating only until smooth after each addition, alternately add dry ingredients in fourths and a mixture of the applesauce and sour milk in thirds to the creamed mixture. Stir in the chopped nuts. Turn batter into an ungreased 10-inch tubed pan having a removable bottom.

4.　Bake at 350°F about 1 hour, or until cake tests done.

5.　Cool 15 minutes before removing from pan.

ONE 10-INCH TUBED CAKE

TEXAS CHOCOLATE CAKE
This chocolate cake is said to be a favorite of former President Lyndon B. Johnson.

4 oz. sweet chocolate	2 cups sugar
½ cup boiling water	4 egg yolks
2½ cups sifted cake flour	1 cup buttermilk
1 teaspoon baking soda	4 egg whites, beaten to stiff, not dry, peaks
½ teaspoon salt	Texas Coconut-Pecan Frosting, *below*
1 cup butter	
1 teaspoon vanilla extract	

1.　Combine chocolate and boiling water in a heavy saucepan. Place over very low heat, stirring constantly, until chocolate is melted. Set aside to cool.

2.　Sift flour, baking soda, and salt together.

3.　Cream butter with extract; gradually add sugar, creaming until fluffy. Add egg yolks, one at a time, and beat well after each addition. Mix in chocolate.

4.　Beating until blended after each addition, alternately add dry ingredients in fourths and buttermilk in thirds to creamed mixture.

5.　Fold beaten egg whites into batter. Turn into 3 prepared 9-inch layer cake pans and spread evenly to edges.

6.　Bake at 350°F 30 to 40 minutes, or until cake tests done.

7.　Cool and remove from pans as directed for butter-type cakes before spreading Texas Coconut-Pecan Frosting between layers and on top.

ONE 9-INCH 3-LAYER CAKE

TEXAS COCONUT-PECAN FROSTING: Combine *1 cup undiluted evaporated milk, 1 cup sugar, 3 egg yolks, ½ cup butter or margarine, and 1 teaspoon vanilla extract. Cook and stir over medium heat* until thickened, about 12 minutes. Remove from heat. Add *1⅓ cups flaked coconut and 1 cup chopped pecans.* Beat until cool and thick enough to spread.

Special-Flavor Cakes

UPSIDE-DOWN LEMON CAKE
More pudding than cake and redolent with the fresh flavor of lemon, the whole family should give this dessert a high rating.

12 lemon slices (about 1½ lemons)	Cake batter:
Sauce:	1½ cups sifted cake flour
½ cup sugar	2 teaspoons baking powder
4 teaspoons cornstarch	½ teaspoon salt
⅛ teaspoon salt	¼ cup butter
¾ cup water	1 teaspoon grated lemon peel
2 teaspoons grated lemon peel	¾ cup sugar
2 tablespoons lemon juice	1 egg
1½ tablespoons butter	½ cup milk
1 drop yellow food coloring	

1.　Rinse, slice very thin, and remove seeds from enough lemons to yield 12 slices.

2.　At four equal intervals around each slice, make cuts through peel almost to center. Arrange lemon slices on bottom of a greased (bottom only) 9x9x2-inch baking pan. (For a distinctive topping, slice about 3 lemons as indicated above, and overlap slices in rows to cover bottom of pan.)

3.　For sauce, mix sugar, cornstarch, and salt together in a saucepan. Add water gradually, blending thoroughly.

4.　Stirring constantly, bring mixture to boiling. Continue to stir and cook about 3 minutes.

5.　Remove from heat and blend in lemon peel and juice, butter, and yellow food coloring.

6.　Spoon about one half of the sauce into the pan to cover the lemon slices; reserve remaining sauce.

7.　For cake batter, sift the flour, baking powder, and salt together; set aside.

8.　Cream butter with lemon peel. Add sugar gradually, creaming until fluffy. Add egg, beating thoroughly.

9.　Beating only until smooth after each addition,

alternately add dry ingredients in thirds and milk in halves to creamed mixture. Turn batter into pan over lemon slices and spread evenly to edges.

10. Bake at 350°F about 40 minutes, or until cake tests done.

11. Remove from oven; let stand 2 to 3 minutes in pan on wire rack. Using a spatula, loosen cake from sides of pan and invert onto a serving plate. Allow pan to remain over cake 1 to 2 minutes. Remove pan. Spoon remaining lemon sauce evenly over top of cake. Serve warm.   1 UPSIDE-DOWN CAKE

PINEAPPLE UPSIDE-DOWN CAKE

Topping:
1/4 cup butter or margarine
2/3 cup lightly packed brown sugar
5 canned pineapple slices (reserve 1/2 cup syrup)
5 maraschino cherries
Cake batter:
1 1/2 cups sifted cake flour

2 teaspoons baking powder
1/2 teaspoon salt
1/2 cup butter or margarine
1 teaspoon vanilla extract
1/2 cup sugar
1 egg

1. For topping, heat the butter in an 8x8x2-inch baking pan (or in a 10-inch skillet with a heat-resistant handle); blend in the brown sugar and spread evenly. Arrange pineapple slices on top of the brown sugar mixture with a cherry in the center of each. Set aside.

2. For cake batter, sift the flour, baking powder, and salt together; set aside.

3. Cream the butter with extract. Add the sugar gradually, creaming until fluffy. Add egg and beat thoroughly.

4. Beating only until smooth after each addition, alternately add the dry ingredients in thirds and reserved pineapple syrup in halves to the creamed mixture. Turn batter over pineapple slices and spread evenly to edges of pan.

5. Bake at 350°F about 45 minutes (about 35 minutes for skillet), or until cake tests done.

6. Remove from oven; let stand 1 to 2 minutes in pan on wire rack. Using a spatula, loosen cake from sides of pan and invert onto a serving plate. Allow pan to remain over cake 1 to 2 minutes so syrup will drain onto cake. Remove from pan. Serve warm or cool.   ONE UPSIDE-DOWN CAKE

CRANBERRY UPSIDE-DOWN CAKE: Follow recipe for Pineapple Upside-Down Cake. In topping, substitute *2/3 cup granulated sugar* for brown sugar. Blend *1 tablespoon grated orange peel* and *1/2 teaspoon vanilla extract* with sugar and butter in pan. Spread mixture evenly in pan. Omit pineapple and cherries; spoon a mixture of *2 cups cranberries,* washed and coarsely chopped, and *1/3 cup sugar* over mixture in pan. Proceed as directed for cake, substituting *1/2 cup milk* for pineapple syrup.

APRICOT UPSIDE-DOWN CAKE: Follow recipe for Pineapple Upside-Down Cake. Substitute the following topping: Simmer *1/2 pound dried apricots* in *2 cups water* until fruit is plump and tender. Cool and drain well. Thoroughly blend *3 tablespoons melted butter or margarine, 1/2 cup lightly packed brown sugar,* and *1/3 cup drained crushed pineapple.* Arrange apricots in lightly greased (bottom only) pan. Spoon pineapple mixture over apricots. Proceed as directed for cake, substituting *1/2 cup milk* for pineapple syrup.

PEACHY NUT UPSIDE-DOWN CAKE: Follow recipe for Apricot Upside-Down Cake. Substitute *1/2 pound dried peaches* for apricots. Put a *pecan half* in cavity of each peach and arrange nut side down in prepared pan.

ELEGANT LOAF CAKE

2 cups sifted cake flour
2 1/2 teaspoons baking powder
3/4 teaspoon salt
2/3 cup butter or margarine
1 teaspoon almond extract
1/2 teaspoon vanilla extract
1/2 cup sugar
2 egg yolks, well beaten
2/3 cup milk
1 cup walnuts, very finely chopped

3/4 cup (about 6 oz.) candied cherries, very finely chopped
1/4 cup (about 2 oz.) candied citron, very finely chopped
4 egg whites
1/4 cup sugar
Glossy Vanilla Icing, page 440
1/2 cup walnuts or toasted filberts, chopped

1. Sift the flour, baking powder, and salt together.

2. Cream butter with extracts. Gradually add the 1/2 cup sugar, creaming until fluffy. Add egg yolks in halves, beating thoroughly after each addition.

3. Beating only until smooth after each addition, alternately add dry ingredients in fourths and milk

in thirds to creamed mixture. Stir in the finely chopped walnuts, cherries, and citron.

4. Beat egg whites until frothy; gradually add the ¼ cup sugar, beating well. Continue beating until stiff peaks are formed. Gently fold meringue into batter until just blended. Turn batter into a prepared 9x5x3-inch loaf pan.

5. Bake at 350°F 70 minutes, or until done.

6. Cool and remove from pan as directed for butter-type cakes. Spread Glossy Vanilla Icing on top of cake allowing some frosting to drip slightly down sides of cake. Decorate with the coarsely chopped walnuts.   ONE 9x5-INCH LOAF CAKE

MARASCHINO DATE-NUT CAKE

2 cups sifted all-purpose flour	¼ cup all-purpose flour
2 teaspoons baking powder	¾ cup butter or margarine
¼ teaspoon salt	½ teaspoon vanilla extract
1 teaspoon ground allspice	2 cups sugar
1 teaspoon ground cinnamon	4 eggs
1½ cups drained maraschino cherries, sliced	2 oz. (2 sq.) unsweetened chocolate, grated
1 cup (about 7 oz.) dates, cut in pieces	1 cup cold unseasoned mashed potatoes
2 cups coarsely chopped pecans	½ cup milk

1. Sift the flour, baking powder, salt, allspice, and cinnamon together and blend well; set aside.

2. Mix cherries, dates, pecans, and the ¼ cup flour; set aside.

3. Cream butter with extract. Add sugar gradually, creaming until fluffy. Add eggs, one at a time, beating thoroughly after each addition. Mix in the grated chocolate and cooled mashed potatoes.

4. Beating only until blended after each addition, alternately add dry ingredients in thirds and milk in halves to creamed mixture. Blend in fruit-nut mixture. Turn batter into a greased (bottom only) 13x9x2-inch baking pan and spread evenly to edges.

5. Bake at 300°F about 1½ hours, or until cake tests done.

6. Remove from oven to wire rack and cool cake completely in pan.   ONE 13x9-INCH CAKE

PRUNELLA CAKE

¼ lb. (about ⅔ cup) dried prunes	½ teaspoon ground cinnamon
1⅓ cups sifted all-purpose flour	½ teaspoon ground nutmeg
½ teaspoon baking powder	1 cup sugar
½ teaspoon baking soda	½ cup vegetable shortening
½ teaspoon salt	2 eggs, well beaten
	⅔ cup buttermilk

1. Rinse the prunes and cover with *1 cup hot water* in a saucepan. Cover and let prunes soak 1 hour. Simmer prunes in soaking water 45 to 60 minutes, or until fruit is plump and tender. Drain and cool slightly; reserve liquid for topping. Remove pits and cut prunes finely with scissors.

2. Sift the flour, baking powder, baking soda, salt, cinnamon, and nutmeg together; combine with the prunes and set aside.

3. Gradually add sugar to shortening, creaming until fluffy. Add the eggs in thirds, beating well after each addition.

4. Beating until smooth after each addition, alternately add dry ingredients in fourths and buttermilk in thirds to creamed mixture. Turn batter into a prepared 9x9x2-inch baking pan.

5. Bake at 350°F 40 to 45 minutes, or until cake tests done.

6. Cool. Serve with *Prune Topping, below.*
ONE 9-INCH SQUARE CAKE

PRUNE TOPPING

1 cup sugar	1 cup pecans, coarsely chopped
1 tablespoon flour	
1 tablespoon cornstarch	1 cup (about 7 oz.) uncooked prunes, cut in small pieces
¾ cup reserved prune liquid or bottled prune juice	
	2 tablespoons butter or margarine
1 egg, slightly beaten	

1. Mix sugar, flour, and cornstarch in the top of a double boiler. Add prune liquid gradually, stirring constantly. Bring to boiling over direct heat and cook 3 minutes, stirring constantly.

2. Place over simmering water; cover and cook 12 minutes, stirring occasionally. Vigorously stir about 2 tablespoons hot mixture into egg. Immediately blend into mixture in double boiler. Cook over simmering water 3 to 5 minutes, stirring constantly.

3. Remove from heat and blend in the pecans, prunes, and butter. Serve warm.

CRUNCH-TOP RAISIN CAKE

⅓ cup lightly packed brown sugar
1 tablespoon flour
¼ teaspoon ground nutmeg
2 tablespoons butter or margarine
¼ cup blanched almonds, slivered
1½ cups sifted cake flour
2 teaspoons baking powder
½ teaspoon ground nutmeg

⅛ teaspoon salt
⅓ cup butter or margarine
2 teaspoons grated lemon peel
¾ cup sugar
1 egg
¼ cup water
3 tablespoons lemon juice
¾ cup dark seedless raisins, coarsely chopped

1. Blend the brown sugar, flour, and ¼ teaspoon nutmeg in a bowl. Using a pastry blender or two knives, cut in the 2 tablespoons butter until mixture is crumbly. Stir in the almonds; set aside.
2. Sift the cake flour, baking powder, ½ teaspoon nutmeg, and salt together; set aside.
3. Cream the ⅓ cup butter with lemon peel. Gradually add sugar, creaming until fluffy. Add egg and beat thoroughly.
4. Beating only until smooth after each addition, alternately add dry ingredients in thirds and a mixture of the water and lemon juice in halves to creamed mixture. Stir in the chopped raisins. Turn batter into a greased (bottom only) 8x8x2-inch baking pan and spread evenly to edges. Spoon almond mixture evenly over batter and press lightly.
5. Bake at 350°F 45 minutes, or until cake tests done.
6. Cool in pan on wire rack. Cut into squares and serve warm or cool. ONE 8-INCH SQUARE CAKE

Pound Cakes & Fruitcakes

POUND CAKE RING

2 cups sifted cake flour
1½ teaspoons baking powder
½ teaspoon salt
1 cup butter

1½ teaspoons vanilla extract
1¼ cups sugar
4 eggs, well beaten
½ cup milk
Citrus Glaze, *below*

1. Sift the flour, baking powder, and salt together; set aside.

2. Cream butter with extract. Gradually add sugar, creaming until fluffy. Add eggs in thirds, beating thoroughly after each addition.
3. Beating only until smooth after each addition, alternately add dry ingredients in thirds and milk in halves to creamed mixture. Turn batter into a greased (bottom only) 3-quart ring mold.
4. Bake at 325°F about 40 minutes, or until cake tests done.
5. Cool 10 minutes in pan on wire rack; remove and cool completely. Spoon hot Citrus Glaze over cake on serving plate. 1 RING-SHAPED CAKE
CITRUS GLAZE: Combine ½ *cup light corn syrup,* ½ *cup sugar,* ½ *cup orange juice,* and ¼ *cup lemon juice* in a saucepan. Stir over low heat until sugar is dissolved. Increase heat and boil 5 minutes.

CHOCOLATE POUND CAKE

3 cups sifted all-purpose flour
2 teaspoons baking powder
¼ teaspoon salt
½ cup cocoa, sifted
1 cup butter or margarine

½ cup lard
1 tablespoon vanilla extract
½ teaspoon almond extract
3 cups sugar
5 eggs
1¼ cups milk

1. Sift the flour, baking powder, salt, and cocoa together and blend thoroughly; set aside.
2. Cream butter and lard with extracts. Gradually add sugar, creaming thoroughly. Add eggs, one at a time, beating thoroughly after each addition.
3. Beating only until blended after each addition, alternately add dry ingredients in fourths and milk in thirds to creamed mixture. Turn batter into a greased (bottom only) 10-inch tubed pan.
4. Bake at 325°F 1½ hours, or until cake tests done.
5. Cool 15 minutes in pan on wire rack; remove and cool completely. ONE 10-INCH TUBED CAKE
CHOCOLATE POUND CAKE LOAF: Follow recipe for Chocolate Pound Cake. Divide ingredients in half, except use 3 eggs. Turn batter into a greased (bottom only) 9x5x3-inch loaf pan. Bake at 325°F about 65 minutes.

OLD WILLIAMSBURG-STYLE FRUITCAKE

1 cup butter or margarine	8 oz. (1⅓ cups) diced candied pineapple
2⅓ cups sugar	8 oz. (1 cup) diced candied citron
4 egg yolks	
4 cups sifted all-purpose flour	2 cups flaked coconut, finely chopped
½ cup sherry	4 egg whites, beaten to stiff, not dry, peaks
1 lb. walnuts, chopped	
1 pkg. (15 oz.) golden raisins	Almond Paste, *below*
8 oz. (1 cup) finely chopped candied red cherries	Icing, *below*

1. Cream butter. Gradually add sugar, beating thoroughly after each addition. Add egg yolks, one at a time, beating until light and fluffy after each addition. Blend in 1 cup flour, then the sherry.
2. Mix the remaining flour, walnuts, the fruits, and coconut. Stir into mixture in bowl. Fold in beaten egg whites. Turn batter into a greased 10-inch tubed pan lined with greased brown paper or baking parchment. Spread evenly in pan.
3. Bake at 300°F 2¾ hours, or until cake tests done.
4. Cool completely on wire rack before removing the cake from the pan.
5. Brush cake with *sherry*. Wrap tightly in aluminum foil. Store in a cool place.
6. The day before the cake is to be served, brush top and sides of cake with a slightly beaten *egg white*. Place the round of Almond Paste on top of the cake and arrange pieces on sides; press edges to seal. Let dry at room temperature about 8 hours.
7. Reserving about 1 cup, spread Icing over sides and top of cake. Using a pastry bag and tube, decorate with reserved icing. Garnish with *flaked coconut* and *candied red and green cherries*. Let dry at room temperature about 4 hours.

ONE 10-POUND DECORATED FRUITCAKE

ALMOND PASTE: Blend *1 pound (about 4 cups) ground blanched almonds, 1 pound confectioners' sugar, 3 egg whites, 1 tablespoon lemon juice, ½ teaspoon orange extract,* and *⅛ teaspoon almond extract.* Press into a ball. Roll out about one third of the ball into an 8-inch round on waxed paper dusted with *confectioners' sugar.* Roll remainder of ball into a 28x4-inch strip; cut into 4 pieces.

ICING: Add *3 cups confectioners' sugar* to *2 egg whites* and beat with electric mixer at high speed about 5 minutes. Blend in *2 tablespoons lemon juice.* Add *3 cups confectioners' sugar* gradually, beating the mixture well.

PECAN FRUITCAKE

1 lb. (about 2½ cups) candied red cherries, cut in pieces	4 cups sifted all-purpose flour
	2 teaspoons baking powder
1 lb. (about 3 cups) golden raisins	2 cups butter or margarine
1 lb. (about 4 cups) pecans, coarsely chopped	4 teaspoons lemon juice
	2¼ cups sugar
	6 large eggs

1. Combine cherries, raisins, pecans, and 1 cup of the flour. Blend the remaining flour and baking powder; set aside.
2. Cream butter with lemon juice. Add sugar gradually, creaming until fluffy after each addition. Add eggs, one at a time, beating thoroughly after each addition.
3. Beating only until smooth after each addition, add dry ingredients in fourths to creamed mixture. Blend in the fruit mixture. Turn batter into a well greased 10-inch tubed pan and spread evenly.
4. Place a shallow pan containing water on bottom rack of oven during baking time.
5. Bake at 275°F about 4½ hours, or until cake tests done.
6. Remove from oven to wire rack. Remove from pan before entirely cooled. Cool completely.

ABOUT 7 POUNDS FRUITCAKE

UNBAKED FRUITCAKE

8 oz. (1½ cups) raisins	¾ cup butter or margarine
1 cup chopped figs	1 tablespoon grated orange peel
1 cup chopped dried pears	
1 cup chopped walnuts	¾ cup confectioners' sugar
6 oz. (1 cup) chopped candied pineapple	3 doz. vanilla wafers, finely crushed (about 7 cups crumbs)
6 oz. (1 cup) chopped candied cherries	
4 oz. (½ cup) chopped candied citron	¼ teaspoon salt
	1 cup honey
8 oz. (1 cup) chopped candied orange peel	

1. Pour 2 cups boiling water over dried fruits;

bring to boiling and drain. Mix with walnuts and candied fruits.

2.   Cream butter with orange peel; gradually add confectioners' sugar, creaming well. Blend in

crumbs, salt, and honey. Mix with fruit-nut mixture. Press into a well-greased 2-quart fluted mold.

3.   Refrigerate 2 to 3 days before unmolding to serve.   ABOUT 5 POUNDS FRUITCAKE

ONE-BOWL & QUICK CAKES

MERRIE COMPANIE CAKE
(One-Bowl Method)

2¾ cups sifted cake flour	¾ teaspoon orange extract
1¾ cups sugar	¾ teaspoon lemon extract
2 teaspoons baking powder	3 eggs
1¼ teaspoons salt	1 egg yolk
1 cup vegetable shortening	Fruit 'n' Nut White Mountain Frosting, *page 431*
¾ cup milk	

1.   Sift the flour, sugar, baking powder, and salt into a large bowl. Add shortening, about ½ cup milk, and extracts. Beat 2 minutes with electric mixer at medium speed. Scrape down bowl.

2.   Add remaining milk, eggs, and egg yolk and beat 2 minutes. Turn batter into a prepared 9-inch tubed pan.

3.   Bake at 375°F about 45 minutes, or until cake tests done.

4.   Cool and remove from pan as directed for butter-type cakes. Frost with Fruit 'n' Nut White Mountain Frosting.   ONE 9-INCH TUBED CAKE

CHOCOLATE TUBED CAKE
(One-Bowl Method)

4 cups sifted all-purpose flour	4 sq. (4 oz.) unsweetened chocolate, melted and cooled
3 cups sugar	2 cups milk
3 teaspoons baking powder	6 eggs (about 1⅓ cups), well beaten
2 teaspoons salt	2 teaspoons vanilla extract
1⅓ cups vegetable shortening	1 cup finely chopped walnuts

1.   Sift the flour, sugar, baking powder, and salt together; add shortening, cooled chocolate, and 1½ cups milk. Stir only enough to moisten.

2.   Beat 2 minutes with electric mixer at medium speed or 300 strokes by hand; scrape sides of the bowl frequently.

3.   Blend in beaten eggs, remaining milk, and extract. Beat 2 minutes; stir in the walnuts.

4.   Turn batter into a greased (bottom only), waxed-paper lined, and greased again 10-inch tubed pan; spread evenly. Tap bottom of pan sharply to release air bubbles.

5.   Bake at 325°F 1 hour and 45 minutes, or until cake tests done.

6.   Cool 20 minutes in pan on wire rack. Remove from pan, peel off waxed paper, and cool cake completely on rack.

7.   Sprinkle cake with *vanilla confectioners' sugar.*   ONE 10-INCH TUBED CAKE

QUICK COCOA CAKE
(One-Bowl Method)

1⅓ cups sifted cake flour	2 eggs
1 cup sugar	¼ cup milk
½ cup cocoa	1½ teaspoons vanilla extract
1 teaspoon baking powder	½ cup milk
½ teaspoon baking soda	2 teaspoons cider vinegar
¼ teaspoon salt	½ recipe Rich Chocolate Frosting, *page 438*
6 tablespoons vegetable shortening or all-purpose shortening	

1.   Sift flour, sugar, cocoa, baking powder, baking soda, and salt together into a large bowl; blend to distribute cocoa. Add shortening.

2.   Add a mixture of the eggs, ¼ cup milk, and extract to dry ingredients. Beat with electric mixer at medium speed for 2 minutes (or beat vigorously about 300 strokes). Scrape sides and bottom of bowl occasionally.

3.   Add a mixture of ½ cup milk and the vinegar to batter. Beat at medium speed for 1 minute (or beat

vigorously about 150 strokes). Turn batter into a greased 2-quart ring mold or an 8x8x2-inch baking pan.

4. Bake at 350°F about 30 minutes for cake ring and 35 minutes for square cake, or until cake tests done.

5. Remove from oven to wire rack and cool cake ring about 5 minutes before removing cake. If using a square pan, cool the cake completely in pan. Frost with Rich Chocolate Frosting.

ONE CAKE MOLD OR 8-INCH SQUARE CAKE

CARAWAY CAKE

1½ cups sifted all-purpose flour	¼ cup lard
1 cup sugar	1 egg, beaten
2 teaspoons baking powder	¾ cup milk
¼ teaspoon salt	½ teaspoon vanilla extract
2 tablespoons caraway seed	2 tablespoons sugar

1. Sift the flour, 1 cup sugar, baking powder, and salt together into a bowl and mix in the caraway seed. Cut in lard with pastry blender or two knives until particles resemble rice kernels.

2. Add a mixture of egg, milk, and extract; mix until all ingredients are moistened. Turn batter into a prepared 11x7x1½-inch baking pan. Sprinkle the 2 tablespoons sugar over top.

3. Bake at 375°F 30 minutes, or until cake tests done.

4. Cool in pan on wire rack. Cut into squares.

ONE 11x7-INCH CAKE

WHIPPED CREAM CAKE

1½ cups sifted cake flour	1½ teaspoons vanilla extract
1 cup sugar	¼ teaspoon lemon extract
2 teaspoons baking powder	1 cup chilled heavy cream, whipped to soft peaks
¼ teaspoon salt	
2 eggs	

1. Sift the flour, sugar, baking powder, and salt together; set aside.

2. Beat eggs and extracts in a large bowl until thick and piled softly. Gently fold in whipped cream. Sift about one fourth of the flour mixture at a time over the cream mixture, gently folding until just blended after each addition. Turn batter into 2

greased (bottoms only) 8-inch layer cake pans which have been lined on bottoms with waxed paper and greased again. Spread batter evenly to edges.

3. Bake at 350°F 30 minutes, or until cake tests done.

4. Cool and remove from pans as directed for butter-type cakes. Fill and frost as desired.

TWO 8-INCH CAKE LAYERS

RUM RING CAKE

We can attest to the excellence of this simple, rum-syrup drenched cake. The recipe is from a home-maker in Switzerland who is always proud to present her glamorous cake to guests.

1¼ cups sifted cake flour	1½ teaspoons grated lemon peel
¾ cup sugar	2 cups water
3 teaspoons baking powder	1 cup sugar
Few grains salt	2 to 3 tablespoons lemon juice, strained
¼ cup butter, softened	¼ cup dark rum
4 eggs (about 1 cup), fork beaten	1 can (16 oz.) whole peeled apricots, drained and chilled

1. Blend the cake flour, sugar, baking powder, and salt in a mixing bowl. Make a well in the center of the dry ingredients and add the softened butter, eggs, and lemon peel. Beat until batter is smooth, about 5 minutes. Turn batter into a generously greased (bottom only) 6½-cup ring mold, spreading evenly.

2. Bake at 350°F about 20 minutes, or until cake tests done.

3. Cool on wire rack 10 minutes. Run a knife around tube and edge of cake to loosen. Invert onto the rack and remove ring mold. Cool completely.

4. Transfer to serving plate deep enough to hold the syrup.

5. Combine water and sugar in a saucepan. Stir over low heat until sugar is dissolved. Increase heat and bring to boiling; remove syrup from heat and cool slightly. Stir in the lemon juice and rum.

6. About 30 minutes before serving, gradually pour about ¼ of the syrup at one time over cake, allowing it to be absorbed before pouring more syrup. (Cake should be well saturated.) Fill center of ring with apricots. Garnish top and sides of cake with sweetened *whipped cream rosettes* in a decorative pattern.

ONE 9-INCH CAKE RING

ANGEL FOOD & SPONGE CAKES

ANGEL FOOD CAKE

1 cup sifted cake flour	½ teaspoon salt
¾ cup sugar	1 teaspoon vanilla
1½ cups (about 12) egg whites	extract
	½ teaspoon almond
1 teaspoon cream of tartar	extract
	¾ cup sugar

1. Sift flour and ¾ cup sugar together four times; set aside.
2. Beat egg whites with cream of tartar, salt, and extracts until stiff, not dry, peaks are formed. Lightly fold in remaining sugar, 2 tablespoons at a time.
3. Gently folding until blended after each addition, sift about 4 tablespoons of the flour mixture at a time over meringue. Carefully slide batter into an ungreased 10-inch tubed pan, turning pan as batter is poured. Cut through batter with knife or spatula to break large air bubbles.
4. Bake at 350°F about 45 minutes, or until cake tests done.
5. Immediately invert pan and cool cake completely. Remove from pan as directed for sponge-type cakes. ONE 10-INCH TUBED CAKE

CHERRY-NUT ANGEL FOOD CAKE: Follow recipe for Angel Food Cake. Fold in *½ cup finely chopped nuts* and *¼ cup finely chopped, well-drained maraschino cherries* with last addition of flour mixture.

TOASTY-COCONUT ANGEL FOOD CAKE: Follow recipe for Angel Food Cake. Fold in *1 cup toasted flaked coconut* with last addition of flour mixture.

RAINBOW ANGEL FOOD CAKE: Follow recipe for Angel Food Cake. Divide batter equally among 3 bowls. Fold *2 drops red food coloring* into one portion, *2 drops yellow food coloring* and *¼ teaspoon lemon extract* into another, and *2 drops green food coloring* and *¼ teaspoon peppermint extract* into the third portion. Form 3 layers in pan.

MOCHA ANGEL DESSERT: Follow recipe for Angel Food Cake. Substitute four 9-inch layer cake pans for tubed pan. Lightly grease bottoms and line with waxed paper. Divide batter equally among the pans. Bake at 325°F 25 to 30 minutes, or until cake tests done. Meanwhile, prepare *Mocha-Mallow Whipped Cream, page 442.* Invert cake pans on wire racks; allow to cool completely. Remove layers from pans, peel off paper, and turn layers right side up. Place 1 cake layer on serving plate; spread about one fourth of Mocha-Mallow Whipped Cream over top. Cover with second layer; repeat procedure with remaining filling and layers. Chill. If desired, top with *chocolate curls.* ONE 9-INCH 4-LAYER CAKE

COCOA ANGEL FOOD CAKE

1 cup sifted cake flour	1 teaspoon cream of tartar
1 cup sugar	
½ cup cocoa, sifted	¼ teaspoon salt
1½ cups (about 12) egg whites	1 teaspoon vanilla extract
2 tablespoons cold water	1 cup sugar

1. Sift the flour, 1 cup sugar, and cocoa together four times to distribute cocoa evenly; set aside.
2. Beat egg whites with water, cream of tartar, salt, and extract until stiff, not dry, peaks are formed. Lightly fold in the remaining sugar, 2 tablespoons at a time.
3. Gently folding until blended after each addition, sift about 4 tablespoons of dry ingredients at a time over meringue. Carefully slide batter into an ungreased 10-inch tubed pan. Cut through batter to remove any large air bubbles.
4. Bake at 350°F about 45 minutes, or until cake tests done.
5. Immediately invert pan and cool cake completely. Remove from pan as directed for sponge-type cakes. Sift *confectioners' sugar* over cake top. ONE 10-INCH TUBED CAKE

ANGEL FOOD SPICE CAKE

1 cup sifted cake flour	¼ teaspoon ground cloves
¾ cup sugar	
¼ cup cocoa, sifted	1½ cups (about 12) egg whites
1 teaspoon ground cinnamon	
	1½ teaspoons cream of tartar
½ teaspoon ground allspice	
	½ teaspoon salt
½ teaspoon ground nutmeg	1 teaspoon vanilla extract
	1 cup sugar

1. Sift flour, ¾ cup sugar, cocoa, and spices together and blend thoroughly; set aside.

2. Beat egg whites with cream of tartar, salt, and extract until stiff, not dry, peaks are formed. Lightly fold in remaining sugar, 2 tablespoons at a time.

3. Gently folding until blended after each addition, sift about 4 tablespoons flour mixture at a time over beaten egg whites. Carefully slide batter into an ungreased 10-inch tubed pan. Cut through batter with knife or spatula to break large air bubbles.

4. Bake at 350°F 45 to 50 minutes, or until cake tests done.

5. Immediately invert pan and cool completely. Remove cake from pan as directed for sponge-type cakes. ONE 10-INCH TUBED CAKE

SPONGE CAKE

¾ cup (about 9) egg yolks	1½ cups sifted all-purpose flour
¾ cup sugar	1¼ cups (about 9) egg whites
1½ tablespoons grated lemon peel	¾ teaspoon cream of tartar
1½ teaspoons vanilla extract	½ teaspoon salt
	¾ cup sugar

1. Beat egg yolks, ¾ cup sugar, lemon peel, and extract together until very thick.

2. Sift about one third of the flour at a time over egg yolk mixture, gently folding until just blended after each addition. Set aside.

3. Beat the egg whites with cream of tartar and salt until frothy. Gradually add the remaining ¾ cup sugar, continuing to beat until stiff peaks are formed. Gently fold egg yolk mixture into meringue. Turn batter into an ungreased 10-inch tubed pan.

4. Bake at 325°F about 50 minutes, or until cake tests done.

5. Immediately invert pan and cool cake completely. ONE 10-INCH TUBED CAKE

EGG YOLK SPONGE CAKE

3¾ cups sifted cake flour	1 teaspoon vanilla extract
3 teaspoons baking powder	½ teaspoon lemon extract
1 teaspoon salt	½ teaspoon orange extract
1 cup (about 12) egg yolks	2 cups sugar

1. Sift flour, baking powder, and salt; set aside.

2. Beat egg yolks and extracts together until very thick and lemon colored.

3. Alternately add sugar in fourths and *1 cup hot water* in thirds to egg yolk mixture, beating until very thick after each addition.

4. Sift about one fourth of dry ingredients at a time over egg yolk mixture, gently folding until just blended after each addition. Turn into an ungreased 10-inch tubed pan.

5. Bake at 350°F 55 to 60 minutes, or until cake tests done.

6. Immediately invert pan and cool cake completely. ONE 10-INCH TUBED CAKE

HOT MILK SPONGE CAKE
The versatility of this easily achieved, light sponge cake extends to such familiar desserts as Boston Cream Pie and Washington Pie.

1 cup sifted cake flour	3 eggs, well beaten
1 teaspoon baking powder	2 or 3 teaspoons lemon juice
¼ teaspoon salt	6 tablespoons hot milk (do not boil)
1 cup sugar	

1. Sift the flour, baking powder, and salt together.

2. Add sugar gradually to the beaten eggs, beating until very thick and piled softly. Mix in lemon juice.

3. Sprinkle dry ingredients over egg mixture about one fourth at a time; gently fold in until just blended after each addition.

4. Add hot milk all at one time and quickly mix just until smooth. Turn batter into a greased (bottom only) 9x9x2-inch baking pan or two 9-inch layer cake pans.

5. Bake at 375°F 15 to 25 minutes, or until cake tests done.

6. Cool 8 to 10 minutes in pan on wire rack. Remove cake from pan and cool completely on rack. ONE 9-INCH SQUARE OR TWO 9-INCH CAKE LAYERS

LEMON HOT MILK SPONGE CAKE: Follow recipe for Hot Milk Sponge Cake. Increase lemon juice to 2 tablespoons and add *1½ teaspoons grated lemon peel.*

ORANGE HOT MILK SPONGE CAKE: Follow recipe for Hot Milk Sponge Cake. Substitute *2 tablespoons orange juice* and *1 teaspoon grated orange peel* for the lemon juice.

PINEAPPLE HOT MILK SPONGE CAKE: Follow recipe for Hot Milk Sponge Cake. Decrease lemon juice to 1 teaspoon and add *2 tablespoons pineapple juice.*

SPONGE CAKE À LA GLAMOUR: Follow recipe for Lemon or Orange Hot Milk Sponge Cake; use layer cake pans. While cake is cooling, prepare *½ recipe Lemon Filling I, page 444,* for lemon cake or *½ recipe Orange Filling I, page 444,* for orange cake. Gently spread top of each layer with the filling. Set layers side by side in refrigerator for at least 3 hours. An hour before serving, prepare *1¼ times recipe for Sweetened Whipped Cream, page 441.* Spread top of bottom layer with whipped cream. Cover with top layer and spread entire cake with remaining whipped cream. Set in refrigerator until ready to serve.

BOSTON CREAM PIE: Follow recipe for Hot Milk Sponge Cake; use layer cake pans. Prepare *Creamy Vanilla Filling, page 442.* Place one cake layer on serving plate and spread with chilled filling. Cover with second layer. Sift *¼ cup confectioners' sugar* over top of cake. For a lacy design, sift confectioners' sugar over a lace paper doily on top of cake; carefully remove doily.

CHOCOLATE CREAM PIE: Follow recipe for Boston Cream Pie. Spread *Fudge Glaze, page 440,* over top of cake instead of sifting on confectioners' sugar.

WASHINGTON PIE: Follow recipe for Hot Milk Sponge Cake; use layer cake pans. When ready to serve, spread *raspberry jam or jelly* over bottom layer; cover with second layer. Sift *¼ cup confectioners' sugar* over top of cake.

SUNSHINE CAKE

1½ cups sifted cake flour	1 teaspoon grated lemon peel
1 teaspoon baking powder	1½ cups sugar
½ teaspoon salt	⅓ cup cold water
½ cup (about 6) egg yolks	1 scant cup (about 6) egg whites
1 teaspoon lemon extract	1 teaspoon cream of tartar

1. Sift the flour, baking powder, and salt together; set aside.
2. Beat the egg yolks, extract, and lemon peel together. Gradually add the sugar, continuing to beat until mixture is very thick.
3. Beating just until blended after each addition, alternately add dry ingredients in thirds and water in halves to egg yolk mixture; set aside.

4. Beat egg whites with cream of tartar until stiff, not dry, peaks are formed. Fold egg yolk mixture into beaten egg whites until blended. Turn batter into ungreased 10-inch tubed pan.
5. Bake at 325°F about 1 hour, or until cake tests done.
6. Immediately invert pan and cool cake completely. ONE 10-INCH TUBED CAKE

LEMON SUNSHINE CAKE SQUARES: Follow recipe for Sunshine Cake. Decrease cream of tartar to ½ teaspoon. If desired, blend *1 teaspoon rum extract* with the lemon. Turn batter into a 13x9x2-inch baking pan lined (bottom only) with waxed paper. Bake 35 to 40 minutes. Remove from oven to wire rack and cool 10 minutes in pan. Remove from pan immediately and peel off waxed paper; cool completely. Sprinkle lightly with *confectioners' sugar,* if desired. Cut into squares.

LEMON SUNSHINE LAYER CAKE: Follow recipe for batter of Lemon Sunshine Cake Squares. Divide batter equally into three 9-inch layer cake pans lined (bottom only) with waxed paper. Bake 15 to 18 minutes. Remove from oven to racks and cool 10 minutes. Remove from pans and peel off waxed paper; cool completely. For filling and frosting, blend fresh or frozen (thawed and well drained) *raspberries* with *Sweetened Whipped Cream, page 441.* Spread generously between cake layers. Frost top and sides of cake with additional Sweetened Whipped Cream and decorate with *raspberries.*

ONE 9-INCH 3-LAYER CAKE

MERINGUE SPONGE CAKE

½ cup water	1 tablespoon grated lemon peel
1¼ cups sugar	
¾ cup (about 6) egg whites	1 tablespoon lemon juice
¼ teaspoon salt	1 teaspoon vanilla extract
1 teaspoon cream of tartar	
½ cup (about 6) egg yolks	1 cup plus 2 tablespoons sifted cake flour

1. Mix water and sugar in a saucepan. Bring to boiling, stirring until sugar is dissolved. Boil until mixture reaches 238°F (soft-ball stage). Remove from heat.
2. Beat egg whites and salt until stiff, not dry, peaks are formed. Pour syrup slowly into egg whites, beating constantly. Add the cream of tartar and beat until mixture is cool.

Delicate White Cake with Rich Coconut Fruit Filling

3. Beat the egg yolks, lemon peel and juice, and extract until very thick. Fold into egg white mixture. Sift one fourth of flour at a time over egg mixture, folding until blended after each addition. Turn batter into an ungreased 9- or 10-inch tubed pan.

4. Bake at 325°F 50 minutes, or until cake tests done.

5. Immediately invert pan and cool cake completely. ONE 9- OR 10-INCH TUBED CAKE

BUTTER SPONGE CAKE
(Gâteau Génoise)

This moist, rich sponge cake of French origin is usually the basis for petits fours and other French pastries.

5 eggs (1 cup plus 1 tablespoon)	⅛ teaspoon almond extract
1 cup less 1 tablespoon sugar	1¼ cups sifted cake flour
¼ teaspoon vanilla extract	3 tablespoons butter, melted and cooled

1. Butter bottom of a 15x10x1-inch jelly roll pan; line with waxed paper and butter paper. Set aside.

2. Combine eggs and sugar in the top of a 3-quart double boiler. Set top over simmering water and beat constantly until mixture is thick and piles softly (about 10 minutes with electric mixer). Remove from heat; set top in cold water and continue beating until mixture is cooled, about 15 minutes. Blend in the extracts.

3. Sift one fourth of the flour at a time over egg mixture, gently folding just until blended after each addition.

4. Gradually add the melted butter, folding only until blended. Immediately turn batter into prepared pan and spread evenly.

5. Bake at 325°F about 25 minutes, or until cake tests done.

6. Loosen edges with a sharp knife and remove cake from pan. Carefully peel off paper and cool cake, top side up, on wire rack.

ONE 15x10-INCH CAKE

SMALL FANCY CAKES (Petits Fours): Follow recipe for Butter Sponge Cake. When cool, trim cake edges and cut cake into tiny diamonds, rounds, crescents, or ovals. Use shapes whole, or split and fill with sieved *raspberry or apricot jam.* Prepare *Petits Fours Icing, page 432.* Arrange like shapes on cake racks over trays and in turn pour the icing over them, covering completely. Immediately affix icing flowers, or later pipe on decorations with decorating icing. For the first set of cakes use white icing. Return "spillover" to original pan. Add *yellow food coloring* for a pale yellow color and pour over second set of cakes. Return "spillover" and add either *green* (for chartreuse shade) or a drop of *red food coloring* for a rosy shade. If there is a fourth set, add *melted chocolate* and thin icing with a little hot water. As soon as icing is set a little, carefully slide a metal spatula under each cake and transfer it to a glassine petits fours case; push the case up around the sides of the little cake.

FRENCH PASTRY CAKES: Follow recipe for Butter Sponge Cake. Prepare a recipe of *Creamy Butter Frosting, page 433,* and one of *Chocolate Butter Frosting, page 433.* When cake is cool, trim edges and cut cake into 3x1¾-inch rectangles, squares, and rounds. Split each and fill with sieved *strawberry, apricot, or raspberry jam.* Frost the sides with Creamy Butter Frosting or Chocolate Butter Frosting, then roll in flaked *toasted almonds, ground pistachios* or *pecans* or *walnuts,* or *toasted coconut,* or enclose square cakes with *Chocolate Slabs, page 430.* Frost the tops and decorate as desired with frosting swirls, *chocolate shot, candied cherries,* flaked *nuts, Chocolate Rolls, page 430,* piped *chocolate decorations* (see *Decorating Chocolate, page 430*).

PASSOVER SPONGE CAKE

1 cup matzo cake meal	1½ teaspoons grated lemon peel
¼ cup potato starch	
¾ cup (9) egg yolks	1½ cups sugar
¼ cup orange juice	1⅓ cups (9) egg whites
	½ teaspoon salt

1. Mix cake meal and potato starch; set aside.

2. Beat the egg yolks, orange juice, lemon peel, and sugar together until very thick, about 8 minutes. Fold in dry ingredients.

3. Beat egg whites with salt until stiff, not dry, peaks are formed. Fold egg yolk mixture into egg whites. Turn batter into an ungreased 10-inch tubed pan.

4. Bake at 325°F about 55 minutes, or until cake tests done.

5. Immediately invert pan and cool cake completely. ONE 10-INCH TUBED CAKE

Black Forest Torte

DAFFODIL CAKE

1¼ cups sifted cake flour	4 egg yolks
½ cup sugar	2 tablespoons orange juice
1¼ cups (about 10) egg whites	1½ teaspoons grated orange peel
¾ teaspoon salt	¼ teaspoon almond extract
1½ teaspoons cream of tartar	½ teaspoon vanilla extract
1 cup sugar	

1. Sift flour and the ½ cup sugar together.
2. Beat the egg whites with salt and cream of tartar until stiff, not dry, peaks are formed. Lightly fold in 1 cup sugar, 2 tablespoons at a time.
3. Sprinkle dry ingredients over egg whites, about one fourth at a time; gently fold in until just blended after each addition.
4. Beat egg yolks, orange juice and peel, and almond extract together until very thick. Fold one third of the egg white mixture into egg yolks.
5. Fold vanilla extract into remaining egg white mixture.
6. Turn alternate layers of yellow and white batter into an ungreased 10-inch tubed pan, ending with white batter on top. Lift white batter through yellow batter to produce a marbled effect.
7. Bake at 375°F 35 minutes, or until cake tests done.
8. Immediately invert pan and cool cake completely.　ONE 10-INCH TUBED CAKE

SPONGE CAKE RING DESSERT

½ cup sifted cake flour	¼ teaspoon cream of tartar
⅛ teaspoon salt	
3 egg yolks	3 tablespoons sugar
¼ cup sugar	Coffee-Butterscotch Glaze, *page 441*
2 tablespoons water	
1 teaspoon vanilla extract	Mocha Fudge Sauce, *page 552*
3 egg whites	

1. Sift flour and salt together; set aside.
2. Beat egg yolks, ¼ cup sugar, water, and extract together until very thick. Fold flour mixture into egg yolks until just blended. Set aside.
3. Beat egg whites with cream of tartar until frothy. Add the 3 tablespoons sugar gradually, continuing to beat until stiff peaks are formed.
4. Fold egg yolk mixture into meringue until

blended. Turn batter into an ungreased 1½-quart ring mold.
5. Bake at 325°F about 30 minutes, or until cake tests done.
6. Immediately invert mold and cool cake completely.
7. When ready to serve, place the cooled cake ring on a serving plate. Brush Coffee-Butterscotch Glaze over top of cake. Fill center of cake ring with scoops of *coffee or vanilla ice cream.* Drizzle Mocha Fudge Sauce over the ice cream. Pour remaining sauce into a pitcher and serve with the dessert.

6 TO 8 SERVINGS

JELLY ROLL

⅓ cup (about 4) egg yolks	½ cup (about 4) egg whites
½ cup sugar	½ teaspoon cream of tartar
¼ cup water	
1½ teaspoons vanilla extract	¼ teaspoon salt
	½ cup sugar
1 cup sifted cake flour	Jelly or jam

1. Grease bottom of a 15x10x1-inch jelly roll pan; line with waxed paper cut to fit bottom of pan; grease paper. Set aside.
2. Beat egg yolks, ½ cup sugar, water, and extract together until very thick. Fold in flour until just blended.
3. Beat egg whites with cream of tartar and salt until frothy. Add ½ cup sugar gradually, continuing to beat until stiff peaks are formed.
4. Fold egg yolk mixture into meringue until blended. Turn batter into the prepared pan and spread evenly.
5. Bake at 350°F 20 to 25 minutes, or until cake tests done.
6. Loosen edges of cake and immediately turn onto a towel with *confectioners' sugar* sifted over it. Peel off the paper and trim any crisp edges of cake.
7. To roll, begin at one end of cake. Using towel as a guide, tightly grasp nearest edge of towel and quickly pull it over beyond opposite edge. Cake will roll itself as you pull. Wrap roll in towel and set on wire rack to cool about 30 minutes.
8. When ready to fill, carefully unroll cooled cake, spread with jelly, and reroll.　ONE JELLY ROLL

CUSTARD-FILLED CAKE ROLL: Follow recipe for Jelly Roll. Omit jelly or jam. Prepare *Vanilla Custard Filling, page 443.* Stir chopped *black walnuts* or chopped *salted pecans, pistachio nuts, almonds,* or *other nuts* into filling. (If using salted nuts, omit salt in filling.) Fill cake roll and sift *confectioners' sugar* or *cocoa* over top. If desired, halved, hulled, thoroughly rinsed and drained *fresh strawberries* may be substituted for nuts in the filling. Garnish with whole strawberries with stems.

CHOCOLATE CAKE ROLL: Follow recipe for Jelly Roll. Decrease cake flour to ¾ cup and sift with 5 *tablespoons cocoa*. Bake at 325°F about 30 minutes, *or until cake tests done*. Fill with *Cocoa Whipped Cream I, page 441*, and reroll. Sift *confectioners' sugar* or *cocoa* over top.

CHIFFON CAKES

ORANGE CHIFFON CAKE

1 cup plus 2 tablespoons sifted cake flour	1 tablespoon grated orange peel
½ cup sugar	⅓ cup orange juice
1½ teaspoons baking powder	½ cup (4 to 5) egg whites
½ teaspoon salt	¼ teaspoon cream of tartar
¼ cup cooking oil	¼ cup sugar
2 egg yolks	

1. Sift the flour, ½ cup sugar, baking powder, and salt together into a bowl. Make a well in center and add the oil, egg yolks, and orange peel and juice in order listed. Beat until smooth; set aside.
2. Beat the egg whites with cream of tartar until frothy. Gradually add the ¼ cup sugar, continuing to beat until stiff peaks are formed.
3. Slowly pour egg yolk mixture over entire surface of beaten egg white. Gently fold together until just blended. Turn batter into an ungreased 9x9x2-inch baking pan.
4. Bake at 350°F 30 to 35 minutes, or until cake tests done.
5. Immediately invert pan and cool cake completely before removing from pan.

ONE 9-INCH SQUARE CAKE

COCOA CHIFFON CAKE

½ cup cocoa	7 egg yolks
¾ cup boiling water	2 teaspoons vanilla extract
1¾ cups sifted cake flour	1 cup (7 to 8) egg whites
1 cup sugar	½ teaspoon cream of tartar
3 teaspoons baking powder	¾ cup sugar
¾ teaspoon salt	
½ cup cooking oil	

1. Mix cocoa and boiling water together until smooth; set aside to cool.

2. Sift the flour, sugar, baking powder, and salt together into a bowl. Make a well in the center of the dry ingredients; add oil, egg yolks, cooled cocoa mixture, and extract. Beat until smooth. Set aside.
3. Beat egg whites with cream of tartar until frothy. Gradually add ¾ cup sugar, continuing to beat until stiff peaks are formed.
4. Slowly pour egg yolk mixture over entire surface of meringue. Carefully fold together until just blended. Turn batter into an ungreased 10-inch tubed pan, turning pan as you pour in batter.
5. Bake at 325°F 55 minutes; increase temperature to 350°F and bake for 10 to 15 minutes, or until cake tests done.
6. Immediately invert pan and cool cake completely.

ONE 10-INCH TUBED CAKE

LEMON CHIFFON CAKE

2¼ cups sifted cake flour	¾ cup cold water
1 cup sugar	1 teaspoon grated lemon peel
3 teaspoons baking powder	1 tablespoon lemon juice
1 teaspoon salt	¾ cup (6) egg whites
½ cup cooking oil	½ teaspoon cream of tartar
6 egg yolks	½ cup sugar

1. Sift the flour, 1 cup sugar, baking powder, and salt together into a bowl. Make a well in the center and add the oil, egg yolks, water, and lemon peel and juice. Beat until smooth; set aside.
2. Beat the egg whites with cream of tartar until frothy. Add the ½ cup sugar gradually, continuing to beat until stiff peaks are formed.
3. Slowly pour egg yolk mixture over entire surface of meringue. Carefully fold together until just blended. Gently pour batter into an ungreased 10-inch tubed pan, turning pan as you pour.

4. Bake at 325°F 55 minutes; increase temperature to 350°F and bake 10 to 15 minutes, or until cake tests done.

5. Immediately invert pan; cool cake completely. Frost cake with tinted *butter frosting*.

ONE 10-INCH TUBED CAKE

VALENTINE CAKE: Follow recipe for Lemon Chiffon Cake. Bake in three 9-inch heart shaped pans. Fill cooled layers with *Butter Cream Frosting I, page 432*; decorate sides and top with *Sweetened Whipped Cream, page 441*. Arrange pink icing roses on the top, if desired.

CUPCAKES & CAKELETS

CHOCOLATE CUPCAKES

½ cup milk
2 to 2½ oz. (2 to 2½ sq.) unsweetened chocolate
1 egg, slightly beaten
¼ cup sugar
1½ cups sifted cake flour
1¼ teaspoons baking powder

¼ teaspoon baking soda
⅛ teaspoon salt
½ cup butter or margarine
1 teaspoon vanilla extract
1 cup sugar
2 eggs, well beaten
½ cup dairy sour cream

1. Combine milk and chocolate in top of double boiler. Set over simmering water until milk is scalded and chocolate is melted. Stir until well blended.
2. Vigorously stir about 3 tablespoons of the hot milk mixture into the slightly beaten egg; immediately blend into mixture in double boiler. Cook 3 to 5 minutes, stirring constantly. Stir in the ¼ cup sugar.
3. Cook over simmering water about 5 minutes, stirring constantly. Remove from water and set aside to cool.
4. Sift flour, baking powder, baking soda, and salt together; set aside.
5. Cream butter with extract. Add the 1 cup sugar gradually, creaming until fluffy after each addition.
6. Add beaten eggs in thirds, beating thoroughly after each addition. Blend in the cooled chocolate mixture.
7. Beating only until smooth after each addition, alternately add dry ingredients in thirds and sour cream in halves to creamed mixture. Line 2½-inch muffin-pan wells with paper baking cups or grease (bottoms only). Fill each well about one half full with batter.
8. Bake at 350°F 20 to 25 minutes, or until cakes test done.
9. Remove from pans. Cool.

ABOUT 2 DOZEN CUPCAKES

COCOA CUPCAKES

1¼ cups sifted all-purpose flour
½ cup cocoa, sifted
½ teaspoon baking powder
½ teaspoon baking soda
Milk (about ½ cup)
1½ teaspoons cider vinegar

½ cup butter
1½ teaspoons vanilla extract
1 cup sugar
1 egg
½ cup hot water
Chocolate-Cola Frosting, *page 439*

1. Sift the flour, cocoa, baking powder, and baking soda together and blend thoroughly; set aside.
2. Add enough milk to vinegar to measure ½ cup liquid; set aside.
3. Cream the butter with extract. Gradually add sugar, creaming until fluffy. Add egg and beat thoroughly.
4. Beating only until smooth after each addition, alternately add dry ingredients in fourths and milk and hot water in thirds to creamed mixture. Spoon mixture into 2½-inch muffin-pan wells lined with paper baking cups or greased (bottoms only), filling each one half to two thirds full.
5. Bake at 375°F about 20 minutes, or until cakes test done.
6. Remove from pans and cool. Frost with Chocolate-Cola Frosting. ABOUT 16 CUPCAKES

BANANA CUPCAKES

2 cups sifted cake flour
1 teaspoon baking soda
1 teaspoon salt
½ cup butter or margarine
1 teaspoon vanilla extract

1 cup sugar
2 eggs
1 cup mashed ripe bananas (about 2 medium-sized bananas)
¼ cup dairy sour cream

1. Sift the flour, baking soda, and salt together.

2. Cream the butter with extract. Add the sugar gradually, beating thoroughly. Add the eggs, one at a time, beating until light and fluffy after each addition. Blend in banana.

3. Beating only until blended after each addition, alternately add dry ingredients in thirds and sour cream in halves to creamed mixture. Spoon batter into 2½-inch muffin-pan wells lined with paper baking cups or greased (bottoms only), filling each about two thirds full.

4. Bake at 350°F 25 to 28 minutes, or until cakes test done.

5. Remove from pans and cool. Cut a cone-shaped piece from top of each cupcake. Fill with *whipped dessert topping* or *sweetened whipped cream* and set tops in place.   18 CUPCAKES

AMBROSIA CAKES

If ambrosia is truly the food of the gods, then these delectable orange-saturated cakes are aptly named. To make them as magnificent to behold as they are wonderful to eat, serve them flambé—alight with the flames of burning brandy. For the full dramatic effect of this truly festive dessert at your party, turn out all the lights in the room before you ignite the brandy—and listen to the exclamations of delight!

1 cup sifted cake flour	1 egg
½ teaspoon baking soda	½ cup dairy sour cream
¼ teaspoon baking powder	⅔ cup pitted date pieces
¼ teaspoon salt	½ cup (about 2 oz.) pecans
¼ cup butter	Topping:
1½ teaspoons grated orange peel	⅔ cup sugar
½ teaspoon vanilla extract	½ cup orange juice
½ cup sugar	2½ tablespoons Cointreau

1. Sift the flour, baking soda, baking powder, and salt together; set aside.

2. Cream butter with orange peel and extract. Gradually add sugar, creaming until fluffy. Add egg and beat thoroughly.

3. Beating until smooth after each addition, alternately add dry ingredients in halves with sour cream to creamed mixture. Stir in dates and pecans. Spoon batter into greased (bottoms only) 2½-inch muffin-pan wells, filling each one half full.

4. Bake at 350°F 30 to 40 minutes, or until cakes test done.

5. Meanwhile, for topping, stir sugar, orange juice, and Cointreau together until sugar is dissolved; set aside.

6. Remove cakes from oven and immediately drizzle about 1 tablespoon of the orange juice mixture evenly over the top of each cake. When orange juice mixture has been absorbed, remove cakes from pans and cool on wire racks. If desired, serve with *sweetened whipped cream.*   16 CUPCAKES

FLAMING AMBROSIA CAKES: Follow recipe for Ambrosia Cakes. Omit Cointreau in topping and increase orange juice to ⅔ cup. To flame, heat ½ *cup brandy* in a small saucepan. Ignite brandy and pour flaming brandy over top of each cake.

CARAMEL PUDDING "COOKIES"

3 tablespoons butter or margarine	¼ cup sugar
⅓ cup sifted all-purpose flour	2 tablespoons milk
¼ teaspoon baking soda	1 teaspoon vanilla extract
¼ teaspoon salt	1 cup pecans, finely chopped
2 eggs	Chocolate Frosting, *below*
¼ cup firmly packed brown sugar	

1. Melt butter and set aside to cool.

2. Sift flour, baking soda, and salt together; set aside.

3. Beat the eggs and sugars until thick and piled softly.

4. Blend in cooled butter, milk, and extract. Add dry ingredients and blend in quickly. Stir in the pecans.

5. Line 1¾-inch muffin-pan wells with paper baking cups or lightly grease only bottoms of wells. Half fill with batter.

6. Bake at 375°F 10 to 12 minutes, or until tops of "cookies" spring back when lightly touched.

7. Immediately remove from muffin-pan wells and set on wire rack; cool completely. Spread cooled "cookies" with Chocolate Frosting and sprinkle with *pistachio nuts.*   3 DOZEN "COOKIES"

CHOCOLATE-PECAN MINIATURES: Follow recipe for Caramel Pudding "Cookies." Decrease butter to 2 tablespoons and melt with *1 ounce (1 square) unsweetened chocolate.*

CHOCOLATE FROSTING: Melt *2½ ounces (2½ squares) unsweetened chocolate;* set aside to cool. Cream *¼ cup butter* with *½ teaspoon vanilla ex-*

tract; beat in ½ *cup confectioners' sugar.* Add cooled chocolate and ½ *cup confectioners' sugar;* beat until fluffy. ABOUT ¾ CUP FROSTING

PEANUT BUTTER CUPCAKES

2 cups sifted cake flour	½ cup peanut butter
2½ teaspoons baking powder	2 eggs
½ teaspoon salt	½ cup lightly packed brown sugar
⅓ cup shortening	¾ cup milk
1 teaspoon vanilla extract	Creamy Peanut Butter Frosting, *page 437*
1 cup lightly packed brown sugar	

1. Blend flour, baking powder, and salt; set aside.
2. Cream shortening and extract; gradually add the 1 cup brown sugar, creaming well. Beat in the peanut butter until thoroughly blended.
3. Beat eggs with remaining ½ cup brown sugar until thick. Add to creamed mixture and beat well.
4. Beating only until smooth after each addition, alternately add dry ingredients in fourths and milk in thirds to creamed mixture. Line 2½-inch muffin-pan wells with paper baking cups or grease (bottoms only). Fill each well about one half full with batter.
5. Bake at 350°F 25 to 30 minutes, or until cakes test done.
6. Remove from pans and cool. Frost.
ABOUT 2 DOZEN CUPCAKES

RIBBON CAKES

1 cup butter or margarine, softened	1½ cups dairy sour cream
1 teaspoon vanilla extract	½ cup finely chopped pecans
1 cup sugar	6 tablespoons red raspberry jam
4 eggs	¼ cup apricot jam
2 cups all-purpose flour	
1 teaspoon salt	

1. Invert a 15x10x1-inch jelly roll pan; grease and flour the bottom.
2. Cream the butter with extract. Gradually add the sugar, creaming until fluffy. Add eggs, one at a time, beating well after each addition. Mix in the flour and salt.
3. Spread one third of the batter on the prepared pan. Spread evenly to ½ inch from edge of pan.

4. Bake at 350°F about 10 minutes. Remove from oven and carefully cut layer in half crosswise, forming two layers; remove to wire rack.
5. Repeat twice with the remaining batter, making a total of 6 thin layers. (Wash, grease, and flour pan before each baking.)
6. Mix the sour cream and pecans. Place one cake layer, top side up, on a cutting board. Spread evenly with about ¼ cup of the sour cream mixture. Then spread with about 2 tablespoons raspberry jam.
7. Add a second cake layer and spread with ¼ cup sour cream mixture and 2 tablespoons apricot jam. Repeat with remaining layers, leaving the top plain. Place a board on top to compress the layers; chill overnight or 24 hours.
8. Trim off crust edges and spread top with a *creamy butter frosting.* Lightly sprinkle with *colored decorators' sugar.* Cut crosswise into 12 strips, about ¾ inch wide; cut each strip into fourths. 48 RIBBON CAKES

CHOCOLATE-COATED PARTY CAKES

These delicate cream filled cakes are similar to a German specialty called Mohrenköpfe.

4 egg yolks	1 cup sifted cake flour
⅓ cup sugar	1 cup sweetened whipped cream
1 teaspoon grated lemon peel	Chocolate Glaze I, *page 440*
4 egg whites	
⅓ cup sugar	

1. Beat egg yolks, ⅓ cup sugar, and lemon peel until very thick and lemon colored. Set aside.
2. Beat egg whites until frothy; add ⅓ cup sugar gradually, continuing to beat until stiff peaks are formed.
3. Fold egg yolk mixture into beaten whites until blended. Sprinkle about one fourth of the flour at a time over the egg mixture; fold together gently until just blended after each addition.
4. Turn batter into 12 greased (bottoms only) 2½x1¼-inch muffin-pan wells, filling each about two thirds full.
5. Bake at 325°F 18 minutes, or until delicately browned.
6. Cool slightly; run a spatula gently around sides of cakes; lift out and set on wire racks to cool.
7. Cut a thin slice from bottom of each cake and carefully hollow out the cake. Fill with sweetened

whipped cream and replace cake slice. Spoon Chocolate Glaze I over tops of cakes and allow glaze to set slightly before serving.

1 DOZEN SMALL CAKES

LADYFINGERS

3 egg whites (⅓ cup)	¼ teaspoon orange
Few grains salt	extract
⅓ cup sugar	¼ teaspoon vanilla
2 egg yolks	extract
	⅓ cup all-purpose flour

1. Using an 18x12-inch baking pan, cut both brown and waxed paper to fit the bottom of pan.
2. Cut a ladyfinger pattern from paper or cardboard about 4½ inches long and ¾ inch wide. Trace the pattern on the brown paper in sets of six, forming 4 rows across. (There will be 24 patterns traced on paper with space between each pattern and between each row.)
3. Place brown paper in the pan and cover with the waxed paper. (This pattern will show through the waxed paper.)
4. Put egg whites and salt into a mixing bowl and beat until frothy; beat in the sugar gradually until stiff peaks are formed.
5. Beat egg yolks with extracts until very thick. Add to the meringue, folding gently until well blended. Sift the flour over all, a little at a time, folding gently after each addition.

6. Drop coupling into decorating bag; plug end with a cork and fill bag with batter. Pipe out dumbbell-shaped ladyfingers over the patterns.
7. Bake at 350°F 12 to 15 minutes, or until ladyfingers spring back when lightly touched.
8. Remove from oven and invert over a clean towel sprinkled with some *confectioners' sugar*. Discard the brown paper and immediately pull the waxed paper from ladyfinger halves. Put them together in pairs as soon as they are removed from paper. (After cooling, the halves will not adhere to each other.) Cool on wire racks and cover with a towel. Store in a covered container.

12 PAIRS LADYFINGERS

MINIATURE FRUITCAKES

Brush 2½-inch paper baking cups with cooking or salad oil and place in muffin-pan wells. Fill each two thirds full with your favorite *fruitcake batter*. Decorate tops with whole *candied cherries* or *almond halves*. Bake at 300°F about 45 minutes, placing shallow pan containing water on bottom rack of oven while baking. Glaze before serving.

TORTES

BLITZ TORTE

1 tablespoon sugar	½ cup sugar
½ teaspoon ground	4 egg yolks, well beaten
cinnamon	3 tablespoons milk
1 cup sifted cake flour	4 egg whites (about ½
1 teaspoon baking	cup)
powder	¾ cup sugar
⅛ teaspoon salt	⅔ cup slivered blanched
½ cup butter	almonds
1 teaspoon vanilla	Creamy Vanilla Filling,
extract	*page 442*

1. Mix the 1 tablespoon sugar with cinnamon; set aside.
2. Sift the flour, baking powder, and salt together.
3. Cream butter and extract. Add ½ cup sugar

gradually, creaming until fluffy. Add egg yolks in thirds, beating well after each addition.
4. Mixing only until well blended after each addition, alternately add dry ingredients and milk. Turn batter into 2 greased (bottom only) 8-inch layer cake pans; spread evenly to edges.
5. Beat the egg whites until frothy; gradually add the ¾ cup sugar, beating until stiff peaks form.
6. Spread one half of meringue over batter in each pan; sprinkle each layer with half of the slivered almonds and half of the sugar-cinnamon.
7. Bake at 325°F 1 hour, or until meringue is delicately browned.
8. Cool torte layers in pans on wire racks. Remove one torte layer from pan and place on serving plate, meringue side up. Spread with Creamy Va-

nilla Filling. Remove second layer from pan and place, meringue side up, on top of filling.

ONE 8-INCH TORTE

SPICY APPLESAUCE TORTE

1 cup sifted cake flour	1 cup fine gingersnap
4 teaspoons baking	crumbs (about 16
powder	gingersnaps)
½ teaspoon salt	⅓ cup butter or
1 teaspoon ground	margarine
cinnamon	¾ cup sugar
½ teaspoon ground	2 eggs, well beaten
nutmeg	1 cup thick unsweet-
¼ teaspoon ground	ened applesauce
cloves	½ cup walnuts, finely
	chopped

1. Sift the flour, baking powder, salt, and spices together and blend thoroughly. Mix in the crumbs; set aside.
2. Cream butter. Add sugar gradually, creaming until fluffy. Add beaten eggs in halves, beating thoroughly after each addition.
3. Beating only until smooth after each addition, alternately add dry ingredients in fourths and applesauce in thirds to creamed mixture. Blend in the walnuts. Turn batter into 2 prepared 8-inch layer cake pans and spread evenly to edges.
4. Bake at 350°F 35 to 40 minutes, or until torte layers test done.
5. Cool and remove from pans as directed for tortes. If desired, spread *Creamy Vanilla Filling, page 442*, between layers. ONE 8-INCH TORTE

LINZER TORTE

1 cup all-purpose flour	⅛ teaspoon ground
¾ cup finely chopped	cloves
blanched almonds	1 tablespoon grated
(reserve 2 tablespoons	lemon peel
for topping)	1 cup butter or
1 cup confectioners'	margarine, softened
sugar	1 egg
½ teaspoon ground	½ cup red raspberry jam
cinnamon	1 egg, slightly beaten

1. Mix the flour, almonds, confectioners' sugar, spices, lemon peel, butter, and egg together in a bowl until dough forms a ball. Cover and refrigerate dough several hours or until dough is very firm.
2. Remove bowl of dough from refrigerator and

set over ice and water. Press ⅔ of the dough onto bottom of an ungreased 8-inch springform pan or an 8-inch layer cake pan. Spread evenly with jam.
3. With remaining dough, make ten 8-inch rolls the thickness of a pencil and one roll ½ inch thick and 27 inches long. (Flour hands and rolling surface generously with flour since dough softens quickly when handled.) Place small rolls crisscross on top of jam to form a lattice design. Place the one long roll around top edge of torte; brush lattice with beaten egg. Sprinkle with remaining chopped almonds.
4. Bake at 375°F 40 minutes, or until torte is a golden brown.
5. Set torte on wire rack. If baking in a springform pan, let torte cool in pan 10 minutes. Remove the rim from the pan and continue cooling torte to room temperature. Cut torte away from pan bottom and slide off with spatula onto a serving plate. If baking in a layer cake pan, let torte cool 10 minutes; run knife around edge of pan to loosen. Cool completely.
6. Turn out onto cloth-covered wire rack; with another rack, turn cake right-side up. If desired, garnish with a border of *whipped cream*.

ONE 8-INCH TORTE

CARROT TORTE

6 egg yolks (about ½	½ cup plus 2 tablespoons
cup)	all-purpose flour
1¼ cups sugar	6 egg whites (about ¾
2 cups (about 12 oz.)	cup)
unblanched almonds,	Lemon Glaze, *page 425*
grated	Small marzipan carrots,
2 cups grated raw	split in half
carrots	lengthwise
1½ teaspoons grated	
lemon peel	

1. Beat egg yolks and sugar together until very thick. Stir in 1½ cups of the grated almonds, carrots, and lemon peel.
2. Sprinkle flour over carrot mixture and fold in until just blended.
3. Using a clean bowl and beater, beat egg whites until stiff, not dry, peaks are formed. Lightly fold half the beaten egg whites into carrot mixture; fold in remaining egg white. Turn into well-greased and floured (bottom only) 9-inch springform pan.
4. Bake at 300°F about 70 minutes, or until torte tests done.

5. Cool and remove from pan as directed for tortes. Spread torte with Lemon Glaze, covering sides lightly. Immediately press remaining grated almonds onto sides of torte. To garnish, arrange marzipan carrot halves, cut side down, spoke-fashion around top of torte. ONE 9-INCH TORTE

LEMON GLAZE: Put *1½ cups confectioners' sugar* into a bowl. Stir in *2 tablespoons lemon juice* and *2½ teaspoons water* until smooth.

VENETIAN CRÈME TORTE

2 cups sifted cake flour
½ cup cocoa, sifted
½ teaspoon baking soda
⅛ teaspoon salt
½ cup butter
2 teaspoons vanilla
  extract
1⅔ cups sugar
3 eggs
1 cup buttermilk
Venetian Crème Icing,
  below

1. Sift the flour, cocoa, baking soda, and salt together and blend thoroughly; set aside.
2. Cream butter and extract. Add sugar gradually, beating constantly until thoroughly creamed. Add the eggs, one at a time, beating until light and fluffy after each addition.
3. Beating only until blended after each addition, alternately add dry ingredients in thirds and buttermilk in halves to creamed mixture. Divide batter equally among 6 prepared 9-inch layer cake pans and spread evenly to edges.
4. Bake at 350°F about 10 minutes, or until torte layers test done.
5. Cool and remove from pans as directed for butter-type cakes. Spread Venetian Crème Icing between layers and on top of torte. Refrigerate until ready to serve. ONE 9-INCH TORTE

VENETIAN CRÈME ICING

½ cup sugar
½ cup all-purpose flour
½ teaspoon salt
1¾ cups milk
1 cup light or heavy
  cream
1 cup butter
1 teaspoon vanilla
  extract
1½ cups confectioners'
  sugar

1. Thoroughly mix sugar, flour, and salt together in a heavy saucepan. Gradually add milk, stirring until smooth. Blend in the cream. Stirring constantly, cook over medium heat until very thick; boil 1 minute. Remove from heat.
2. Cover saucepan and place in ice and water; chill until mixture is set.
3. Cream butter with extract. Add half of confectioners' sugar and beat until fluffy.
4. Beat chilled mixture until smooth. Beating thoroughly after each addition, alternately add chilled mixture and remaining confectioners' sugar to butter mixture. ABOUT 4 CUPS ICING

CHOCOLATE TORTE
(Schokoladentorte)

1½ cups blanched
  almonds, grated
  (about 2½ cups)
1¼ cups cocoa, sifted
1 teaspoon ground
  cinnamon
1 cup unsalted butter
1½ teaspoons vanilla
  extract
⅔ cup sugar
8 egg yolks (⅔ cup),
  well beaten
8 egg whites (about 1¼
  cups)
⅔ cup sugar
Chocolate-Mocha Butter
  Cream Frosting, *page
  433*

1. Blend the almonds, cocoa, and cinnamon. Divide into 4 portions by marking with a spatula; set aside.
2. Cream butter with extract. Gradually add ⅔ cup sugar, creaming until fluffy. Add the beaten egg yolks in thirds, beating thoroughly after each addition. Beat an additional 2 minutes after last addition. Set aside.
3. Using a clean bowl and beater, beat egg whites until frothy. Gradually add ⅔ cup sugar, continuing to beat until stiff peaks are formed. Gently fold egg yolk mixture and one portion of the cocoa mixture into meringue until only partially blended. Repeat with second and third portions. Spoon remaining portion over batter and gently fold until just blended. Gently turn batter into 3 prepared 9-inch layer cake pans and spread evenly to edges.
4. Bake at 350°F 30 to 35 minutes, or until torte layers test done.
5. Cool and remove from pans as directed for tortes. When completely cooled, fill and frost layers with Chocolate-Mocha Butter Cream Frosting. Refrigerate until ready to serve. ONE 9-INCH TORTE

PICTURE-PRETTY CHOCOLATE TORTE: Follow recipe for Chocolate Torte for baking and frosting torte layers. Cover sides of torte with *chocolate décors*. Arrange *Chocolate Rolls, page 430,* on top of torte so they radiate from the center and extend slightly over the edge, leaving center of torte clear.

Break several of the rolls into pieces and scatter over center of torte. Sift *Vanilla Confectioners' Sugar, page 558,* over chocolate.

BLACK FOREST TORTE

1½ cups toasted filberts, grated*	6 tablespoons kirsch
¼ cup flour	6 egg whites
½ cup butter or margarine	Cherry Filling, *below*
1 cup sugar	3 cups chilled heavy cream
6 egg yolks	⅓ cup confectioners' sugar
4 oz. (4 sq.) semisweet chocolate, melted and cooled	Chocolate curls

1. Grease and lightly flour an 8-inch springform pan; set aside.
2. Blend grated filberts and flour; set aside.
3. Cream butter until softened. Beat in sugar gradually until mixture is light and fluffy. Add egg yolks, one at a time, beating thoroughly after each addition.
4. Blend in the chocolate and 2 tablespoons of the kirsch. Stir in nut-flour mixture until blended.
5. Beat egg whites until stiff, not dry, peaks are formed. Fold into batter and turn into the pan.
6. Bake at 375°F about 1 hour, or until torte tests done. (Torte should be about 1½ inches high and top may have a slight crack.)
7. Cool 10 minutes in pan on a wire rack; remove from pan and cool.
8. Using a long sharp knife, carefully cut torte into 3 layers. Place top layer inverted on a cake plate; spread with Cherry Filling.
9. Whip cream (1½ cups at a time) until soft peaks are formed, gradually adding half of the confectioners' sugar and 2 tablespoons of the kirsch to each portion.
10. Generously spread some of the whipped cream over the Cherry Filling. Cover with second layer and remaining Cherry Filling. Spread generously with more whipped cream and top with third torte layer. Frost entire torte with remaining whipped cream.
11. Decorate torte with reserved cherries and chocolate curls. ONE 8-INCH TORTE
*To grate nuts, use a rotary-type grater with hand-operated crank.
CHERRY FILLING: Drain *1 jar (16 ounces) red mara-*

schino cherries, reserving ½ cup syrup. Set aside 13 cherries for decoration; slice remaining cherries. Set aside. Combine reserved syrup and *4 tablespoons kirsch.* In a saucepan, gradually blend syrup mixture into *1½ tablespoons cornstarch.* Mix in *1 tablespoon lemon juice.* Stir over medium heat until mixture boils ½ minute. Mix in sliced cherries and cool. 1⅓ CUPS FILLING

SACHER TORTE

There are many recipes claiming to be the "original" Sacher Torte of Viennese fame. This one is a favorite.

1 cup butter	⅔ cup fine dry bread crumbs
1 cup confectioners' sugar	8 egg whites (1 cup)
8 egg yolks (⅔ cup), well beaten	⅛ teaspoon salt
8 oz. (8 sq.) semisweet chocolate, melted and cooled	1 cup confectioners' sugar
	Frosting, *below*

1. Cream butter; gradually add 1 cup confectioners' sugar, beating until fluffy. Gradually add egg yolks, beating well after each addition. Blend in the chocolate and crumbs; set aside.
2. Using a clean bowl and beater, beat egg whites and salt together until frothy; add remaining confectioners' sugar gradually, beating well after each addition. Beat until stiff peaks are formed. Fold egg yolk mixture into meringue until just blended. Turn batter into a greased (bottom only) 9-inch springform pan. Cut through batter with a knife or spatula to break large air bubbles.
3. Bake at 350°F about 1 hour, or until torte tests done.
4. Immediately invert pan and cool cake completely in pan before removing. Frost sides and top with frosting. ONE 9-INCH TORTE
FROSTING: Partially melt *3 ounces (3 squares) semisweet chocolate* in top of double boiler over hot (not simmering) water. Remove chocolate from water and stir until completely melted. Add *½ cup unsalted butter* and stir until butter is melted. Use while slightly warm.

HAZELNUT TORTE WITH STRAWBERRY WHIPPED CREAM
(Haselnusstorte mit Erdbeer Schlagsahne)

Graham cracker crumbs (about 3 tablespoons)
2 cups sugar
½ teaspoon ground allspice
1 teaspoon grated lemon peel
4 cups (about 1 lb.) filberts or hazelnuts, grated in rotary-type grater

6 egg yolks (½ cup)
6 egg whites (¾ cup)
¼ teaspoon salt
1 tablespoon light corn syrup
1 teaspoon water
1 egg white, slightly beaten
Strawberry Whipped Cream, *page 441*

1.   Thoroughly grease a 6½-cup ring mold and coat evenly with graham cracker crumbs; set aside.
2.   Blend sugar, allspice, and lemon peel in a large bowl; mix in filberts until completely blended.
3.   Beat egg yolks until thick and lemon colored. Using a fork, blend into nut mixture.
4.   Using a clean bowl and beater, beat the egg whites with the salt until stiff, not dry, peaks are formed. Blend into nut mixture. Turn into prepared mold; spread evenly using the back of a spoon.
5.   Bake at 350°F 45 to 55 minutes.
6.   Remove torte from oven (leave oven on); cool 10 to 15 minutes on a wire rack. Loosen torte from mold and turn out onto an ungreased baking sheet.
7.   Blend corn syrup and water; brush over top of torte. Brush entire torte with egg white. Return torte to oven for 5 minutes.
8.   Transfer to cake plate. Serve warm or at room temperature with Strawberry Whipped Cream.

ONE 9-INCH TORTE

STRAWBERRY-CREAM FILLED GRAHAM CRACKER TORTE

8 egg yolks (about ¾ cup)
1½ cups sugar
1½ cups graham cracker crumbs (about 20 graham crackers)
1 teaspoon baking powder
1 cup very finely chopped pecans

8 egg whites (about 1 cup), beaten to stiff, not dry, peaks
2 cups strawberries, rinsed, hulled, and cut in halves
¼ cup sugar
1 cup chilled heavy cream, whipped to soft peaks

1.   Combine egg yolks and 1½ cups sugar; beat until very thick.

2.   Mix graham cracker crumbs and baking powder together. Folding until blended after each addition, add the crumb mixture and pecans in fourths to egg yolk mixture.
3.   Fold beaten egg whites into egg yolk-crumb mixture. Turn into an ungreased 9-inch springform pan and spread evenly to edges.
4.   Bake at 350°F 25 minutes; reduce oven temperature to 325°F and bake 25 to 30 minutes, or until torte tests done.
5.   Cool torte in pan on wire rack.
6.   Meanwhile, lightly toss strawberries and ¼ cup sugar together; refrigerate about 30 minutes; drain.
7.   Remove torte from pan. Using a long thin sharp knife, cut a 1-inch crosswise layer from top of torte, then from this cut a ½ inch thick ring from edge of layer and replace this ring on torte. Fill cavity with drained sweetened berries and spread with whipped cream. Put trimmed layer on top. Spread *Semisweet Chocolate Frosting, below*, over sides and top of torte. Refrigerate until ready to serve.

ONE 9-INCH TORTE

SEMISWEET CHOCOLATE FROSTING: Partially melt *6 ounces semisweet chocolate pieces* and *¼ cup butter or margarine* together in the top of a double boiler over hot water. Remove from heat and stir until completely melted. Beating until smooth after each addition, alternately add *2 cups confectioners' sugar* in fourths and *3 tablespoons hot water* in thirds to the chocolate mixture. Beat until frosting is of spreading consistency.

ABOUT 1½ CUPS FROSTING

MACAROON TORTE SURPRISE

2 cups sugar
2 teaspoons baking powder
6 egg whites
4 teaspoons almond extract
1½ cups finely chopped walnuts
30 square saltine crackers, crushed (about 1⅓ cups crumbs)
Filling:
1 teaspoon unflavored gelatin

¼ cup cold water
¼ cup boiling water
1 cup chilled heavy cream, whipped to soft peaks
½ cup finely chopped maraschino cherries, well drained
½ cup chopped pecans
1 teaspoon almond extract
Sweetened Whipped Cream, *page 441*

1.   Combine sugar and baking powder; set aside.

2. Beat egg whites until frothy. Gradually add sugar mixture, continuing to beat until stiff peaks are formed. Fold in the extract, walnuts, and cracker crumbs.

3. Turn 1 cup batter into 1 of 3 greased (bottoms only) 8-inch layer cake pans. Divide remaining batter between other 2 pans and spread evenly to edges.

4. Bake at 325°F about 35 minutes, or until layers are lightly browned; remove pan containing 1 cup batter from oven after 25 minutes.

5. Remove from oven to wire racks. Cool and remove from pans as directed for tortes. Crumble thin torte layer into fine pieces and set aside.

6. For filling, soften gelatin in cold water. Add to boiling water stirring until gelatin is completely dissolved. Chill until slightly thicker than consistency of thick unbeaten egg whites.

7. Fold whipped cream into gelatin mixture until just blended. Fold in the cherries, pecans, reserved torte crumbs, and extract.

8. Spread one half of the filling between the torte layers and remaining half over top. Chill 24 hours.

9. When ready to serve, frost sides and top of torte with Sweetened Whipped Cream and decorate with *maraschino cherries*.   ONE 8-INCH TORTE

DOBOS TORTE

Delicate layers, velvety rich chocolate filling, and a crunchy caramel-like topping were the inspiration of a gifted Hungarian pastry chef named Dobos.

Hungarian Chocolate
  Frosting, *below*
6 egg yolks
¼ cup sugar
6 egg whites (about ¾
  cup)

¼ cup sugar
1 cup sifted all-purpose
  flour
Caramel topping:
¾ cup confectioners'
  sugar

1. Prepare Hungarian Chocolate Frosting.

2. Beat egg yolks and ¼ cup sugar together until very thick; set aside.

3. Beat egg whites until frothy. Gradually add ¼ cup sugar, beating until stiff peaks are formed.

4. Gently fold egg yolk mixture into beaten egg whites. Sprinkle one fourth of the flour at a time over surface and gently fold until *just* blended after each addition. *Do not overmix!* Spoon an equal amount of batter into each of 6 greased (bottom only) waxed-paper lined and greased again 8-inch layer cake pans and spread evenly to edges.

5. Stagger pans in oven and bake at 350°F about 15 minutes, or until lightly browned.

6. Remove torte layers to wire racks. Carefully and quickly invert layers onto the racks. Beginning at center, tear paper and gently pull it off. Place layers right side up on racks and cool completely.

7. To assemble torte, beat the chilled frosting until fluffy. Spread ⅛ inch thick on 4 of the torte layers; stack layers. Add fifth layer but do not frost top. Spread frosting thinly on sides of torte. Put the 5 layers and remaining frosting in refrigerator.

8. Meanwhile, place the sixth layer on a baking sheet. Mark into 16 to 18 wedge-shaped pieces with back of knife blade; do not cut wedges apart. Grease a small area of the baking sheet around the torte layer (so topping will not stick to baking sheet if it runs off).

9. For caramel topping, stirring constantly, melt confectioners' sugar in a small heavy skillet over low heat until sugar is smooth and golden brown. Remove from heat and quickly pour onto top layer of torte. Spread topping evenly over layer with spatula, working rapidly before sugar hardens. Make indentations over those marked in torte layer, using back of knife blade. Then cut wedges apart.

10. Remove the stacked layers and frosting from refrigerator. Beat frosting until fluffy. Spread frosting ⅛ inch thick on top of fifth layer and arrange wedges on top of it. Frost sides of sixth layer. Using a pastry bag and a decorating tube, pipe a border of frosting around top edge of torte. Refrigerate until frosting is firm.   ONE 8-INCH TORTE

HUNGARIAN CHOCOLATE FROSTING

8 hazelnuts (filberts)
1 cup firm unsalted
  butter
1 teaspoon vanilla
  extract
1 cup sugar

¼ cup water
6 egg yolks
4 oz. (4 sq.) unsweet-
  ened chocolate,
  melted and cooled

1. Heat nuts in a 400°F oven 3 to 5 minutes, or until skins are loosened and nuts are lightly toasted. Remove from oven, cool slightly, and remove skins. Chop nuts finely and set aside.

2. Cream butter with extract until butter is light and fluffy. Set aside.

3. Mix sugar and water together in a small saucepan, cover, and bring syrup to boiling over low heat. Uncover pan, insert candy thermometer, and cook to 230°F (thread stage).

4. Meanwhile, beat egg yolks until very thick. Beating constantly, pour the hot syrup very gradually in a thin stream into egg yolks (do not scrape pan). Beat egg yolk mixture until very thick and of same consistency as the creamed butter. Cool.

5. Beat egg yolk mixture, about 2 tablespoonfuls at a time, into butter until just blended. Adding gradually, beat in chocolate and hazelnuts. Refrigerate until ready to use. Then frost torte as directed.

3 CUPS FROSTING

FROSTINGS & FILLINGS

A cake without frosting may be laden with virtues and be a fine creation. Yet somehow, cake seems to come into its glory only when it is decked in a sculptured or swirled coat of sweetness. Frostings may be plain or fancy, chocolate brown or pale as dawn, delicately laced with essence of fruits or flecked with fragments of nuts or candy. They may be prepared in many ways, but they are always designed for delight.

Sugar, in some form, is the main ingredient in cooked and uncooked frostings. As used in these recipes, *sugar* refers to granulated cane or beet sugar. Other forms of sugar and sweeteners used in frostings are confectioners' (powdered) sugar, brown sugar and granulated brown sugar, maple sugar and maple syrup, corn syrup, molasses, and honey. (See *page 13* for definitions.)

COOKED FROSTINGS

Seven-minute, white mountain, and fudge frostings are the basic cooked frostings. Special flavorings and other ingredients are added to create any number of frostings. These frostings are easy to make successfully if certain techniques and rules are followed.

The saucepan used for cooking a syrup or frosting should be large enough to allow contents to boil freely without running over. If a cover is needed, it should be tight fitting.

The double boiler should be large enough for the amount of frosting to be beaten.

All the sugar crystals must be dissolved before cooking starts to prevent unwanted graininess in the frosting. The steam formed during the first 5 minutes of cooking, when the saucepan is covered and the mixture boiling, helps to dissolve any crystals that may have formed on the sides of pan. Any crystals that form during cooking may be washed down from sides of pan with a pastry brush dipped in water.

Use a candy thermometer for accurate temperature readings. (To test thermometer before using, see *page 599*.) The cold water test (see *When You Cook Syrups, page 430*) may be used for syrup if a thermometer is not available.

When the humidity is high, cook frostings 2 to 4 degrees higher so frosting will hold its shape.

Separate egg whites very carefully from egg yolks. Any trace of yolk in the whites will cut down the volume of beaten egg whites and the quality of the frosting. To insure greater volume, allow egg whites to stand at room temperature before beating.

Use clean spoons for each process—stirring, testing, and beating. Otherwise, undissolved sugar crystals may be in the finished frosting and cause it to become grainy.

Seven-Minute Frosting—All the ingredients (except flavoring extracts) are combined in the top of a double boiler. As soon as the double-boiler top is set over boiling water the mixture should immediately be beaten with a hand rotary or electric beater. Beating should continue until frosting holds stiff peaks. Move the beater throughout the mixture while beating for thorough blending. Extract is blended in last.

White Mountain Frosting—A hot sugar syrup is cooked to a given temperature and then poured in a steady fine stream into stiffly beaten egg whites while beating constantly. If using a hand rotary beater, turn it over on its side and beat mixture with one hand while pouring syrup with the other. If the frosting is too slow to thicken, let it stand for several minutes; if too firm, blend in hot water, a few drops at a time, until it is of spreading consistency.

Fudge Frosting—The frosting is cooked to a given temperature and beaten, when mixture has cooled sufficiently (bottom of pan should feel just comfortably warm), until it becomes creamy and begins to lose its gloss. If it hardens too quickly, beat in about one tablespoon of hot milk or water. It is important to use *clean* spoons each time the frosting is stirred, tested, or beaten; this helps to avoid graininess.

WHEN YOU COOK SYRUPS

A candy thermometer is an accurate guide to correct stage of cooking. Hang thermometer on pan so bulb does not touch side or bottom of pan.

Syrup Stages and Temperatures

Thread (230° to 234°F)—Spins 2-inch thread when allowed to drop from spoon or fork.

Soft Ball (234° to 240°F)—Forms a soft ball in very cold water; flattens when taken from water.

Firm Ball (244° to 248°F)—Forms a firm ball in very cold water; does not flatten in fingers.

Hard Ball (250° to 266°F)—Forms a ball which is pliable but holds its shape in very cold water.

Soft Crack (270° to 290°F)—Forms threads which are hard but not brittle in very cold water.

Hard Crack (300° to 310°F)—Forms threads which are hard and brittle in very cold water.

UNCOOKED FROSTINGS

Often the uncooked confectioners' sugar frosting is called butter frosting. From a few basic frostings, many variations result with the addition of flavorings, nuts, and fruits.

TO FILL AND FROST

Cool cake completely before frosting. Brush loose crumbs off cake. Cover cardboard, cut ½ inch larger than cake, with foil. Arrange cake or bottom cake layer on covered cardboard. For ease and convenience, put cake on a stand so it can be turned while frosting. Use a flexible spatula.

Tube, loaf, oblong, or square cake—Place cake on cake plate. Frost sides first, working rapidly. See that frosting touches plate, covering cardboard all around bottom, leaving no gaps. Pile remaining frosting on top of cake and spread lightly.

Layer cake—Place cake layer, bottom side up, on cake plate. Spread filling or frosting over top of layer. Cover with the second layer, bottom side down, fitting it so that cake is even. (Repeat procedure if more layers are used, with top layer bottom side down.) If necessary, hold layers in position with wooden picks or metal skewers; remove when filling is set. Frost sides of cake first, working rapidly. See that frosting touches plate all around the bottom, leaving no gaps. Pile remaining frosting on top of cake and spread lightly.

TO DECORATE

See *The Art of Cake Decorating,* page 445.

Decorating with Chocolate

CHOCOLATE ROLLS: Mark 3-inch squares on waxed paper on a baking sheet. Melt semisweet chocolate over hot (not simmering) water. Spread 1 teaspoon melted chocolate within borders of each 3-inch square. Cool at room temperature, then set in refrigerator to harden. To roll, loosen chocolate from paper. As chocolate softens and becomes pliable, roll it by slowly folding the waxed paper over itself, loosening the chocolate as you roll it. Chill immediately.

CHOCOLATE SLABS: Melt semisweet chocolate over hot (not simmering) water, then pour onto waxed paper on a baking sheet; spread to ¹⁄₁₆- to ⅛-inch thickness. When chocolate has cooled and set, cut into slabs to fit sides of pastries or to decorate tops.

DECORATING CHOCOLATE: Melt semisweet chocolate over hot (not simmering) water, then cool it enough so it can be piped through decorating tubes (if chocolate is too thin, stir in a bit of confectioners' sugar).

Cooked Frostings

SEVEN-MINUTE FROSTING

1½ cups sugar	⅛ teaspoon salt
⅓ cup water	1 teaspoon vanilla
2 egg whites	extract
1 tablespoon light corn	
syrup	

1. Combine all ingredients except extract in the top of a double boiler; beat with hand rotary or electric beater until blended.
2. Place over boiling water; beat constantly until mixture will hold peaks.
3. Remove from water; add extract. Beat until cool and thick enough to spread.

ENOUGH TO FILL AND FROST ONE 9-INCH 2-LAYER CAKE
NOTE: Mixture may be tinted by gently stirring in one or more drops of *food coloring.*

CHOCOLATE SEVEN-MINUTE FROSTING: Melt *3 ounces (3 squares) unsweetened chocolate* and set aside to cool. Follow recipe for Seven-Minute Frosting; blend in chocolate when mixture holds peaks.

MARSHMALLOW FROSTING: Follow recipe for

Seven-Minute Frosting. Add *16 marshmallows*, quartered, to hot frosting and beat until fluffy.

MOCHA SEVEN-MINUTE FROSTING: Follow recipe for Seven-Minute Frosting. Increase corn syrup to 2 tablespoons, omit extract, and add *2 tablespoons instant coffee* to sugar mixture. When frosting forms peaks, beat in *1 tablespoon maple extract*.

ORANGE SEVEN-MINUTE FROSTING: Follow recipe for Seven-Minute Frosting. Use only 2 tablespoons water and add *3 tablespoons orange juice*. Omit extract.

PEPPERMINT SEVEN-MINUTE FROSTING: Follow recipe for Seven-Minute Frosting. Omit vanilla extract; add *¼ teaspoon peppermint extract* and several drops *red food coloring*.

PISTACHIO SEVEN-MINUTE FROSTING: Follow recipe for Seven-Minute Frosting. Substitute *½ to 1 teaspoon pistachio extract* for vanilla extract. Blend in *1 or 2 drops green food coloring*, if desired.

FLUFFY WHITE FROSTING

1 cup sugar	⅓ cup water
½ teaspoon cream of tartar	1 egg white
Few grains salt	1 teaspoon vanilla extract

1. Combine all ingredients except extract in top of a double boiler. Set over boiling water and beat with hand rotary or electric beater about 8 minutes, or until soft peaks are formed when beater is lifted upright.
2. Remove from water and add extract; beat 1 minute. ENOUGH TO FROST ONE 13x9-INCH CAKE

SNOWY ICING

1 cup sugar	1 egg white
¼ cup water	1 teaspoon vanilla extract
Few grains salt	

1. Mix the sugar, water, and salt in a small saucepan; stir over low heat until sugar is dissolved.
2. Cook without stirring until mixture spins a 2-inch thread (about 230°F) when a small amount is dropped from a spoon.
3. Beat egg white until stiff, not dry, peaks are formed. Continue beating egg white while pouring hot syrup over it in a steady thin stream. After all the syrup is added, continue beating until icing is very thick and forms rounded peaks (holds shape).

4. Blend in extract. ABOUT 2½ CUPS ICING OR ENOUGH TO FROST ONE 8-INCH SQUARE CAKE

WHITE MOUNTAIN FROSTING

2 cups sugar	½ cup egg whites (about 4)
¾ cup water	2 teaspoons vanilla extract
2 tablespoons light corn syrup	
⅛ teaspoon salt	

1. Blend sugar, water, corn syrup, and salt in a heavy saucepan. Stir over low heat until sugar is dissolved. Increase heat; cover and boil gently 5 minutes.
2. Set candy thermometer in place. Cook without stirring to 244°F (firm-ball stage). Wash sugar crystals from sides of pan with a pastry brush dipped in water; change water each time.
3. Beat egg whites until stiff, not dry, peaks are formed. Continue beating egg whites while pouring the hot syrup over them in a steady stream. (Do not scrape bottom and sides of pan.) Continue beating about 2 minutes, or until rounded peaks are formed.
4. Fold in extract until just blended. Immediately fill and frost cake.

ENOUGH TO FILL AND FROST ONE 9-INCH 2-LAYER CAKE

FRUIT 'N' NUT WHITE MOUNTAIN FROSTING

½ cup sugar	½ teaspoon almond extract
2 tablespoons water	½ cup (4-oz. jar) diced candied fruits
¼ cup light corn syrup	½ cup chopped walnuts
2 egg whites	

1. Mix sugar, water, and corn syrup in a small saucepan. Cover and bring to a rolling boil. Remove cover and set candy thermometer in place. Cook until thermometer registers 242°F, or syrup spins a 6- to 8-inch thread.
2. Meanwhile, beat egg whites until stiff, not dry, peaks are formed. Continue beating and pour hot syrup slowly in a thin stream over the egg whites. Beat until of spreading consistency.
3. Blend in extract. With final few strokes fold in the fruits and walnuts.

ENOUGH TO FROST ONE 9-INCH TUBED CAKE OR TWO 8- OR 9-INCH CAKE LAYERS

MARSHMALLOW CREAM FROSTING

1 cup sugar
1 cup marshmallow
   cream
2 egg whites
¼ cup water

¼ teaspoon cream of
   tartar
⅛ teaspoon salt
1 teaspoon vanilla
   extract

1. Combine all ingredients except extract in top of a double boiler. Place over boiling water and beat with a hand rotary or electric beater about 5 minutes, or until frosting holds soft peaks.
2. Remove from water and add extract. Beat until frosting is cool before spreading on cake.

ENOUGH TO FILL AND FROST ONE 9-INCH 2-LAYER CAKE

COCONUT-MARSHMALLOW FROSTING

1½ cups sugar
¾ cup boiling water
½ teaspoon vinegar
3 egg whites

10 large fresh
   marshmallows, cut
   in small pieces
1 cup flaked coconut,
   lightly toasted

1. Combine sugar, water, and vinegar in a saucepan. Stir over low heat until sugar is dissolved. Bring to boiling; cover and boil 5 minutes.
2. Remove cover; set candy thermometer in place and cook, without stirring, to 244°F (firm-ball stage). Wash away any crystals from sides of pan with a pastry brush dipped in hot water.
3. Meanwhile, beat egg whites until stiff, not dry, peaks are formed. Continue beating while pouring hot syrup in a fine stream. Add cut marshmallows and continue beating until frosting is thick.
4. Quickly spread between layers and over top and sides. Sprinkle coconut over all.

ENOUGH TO FILL AND FROST ONE 9-INCH 2-LAYER CAKE

DIVINITY FROSTING

2½ cups sugar
½ cup water
½ cup light corn syrup
¼ teaspoon salt
2 egg whites

¼ cup marshmallow
   cream
1½ teaspoons lemon
   extract

1. Put the sugar, water, corn syrup, and salt into a deep 2-quart saucepan. Bring to boiling; cover pan and boil for 3 minutes.
2. Uncover pan, set candy thermometer in place, and cook gently to 248°F (firm-ball stage).

3. Meanwhile, beat egg whites in a large bowl until stiff, not dry, peaks are formed.
4. Remove syrup from heat and stir in the marshmallow cream.
5. Continue beating the egg whites, pouring the hot syrup in a thin stream over them. Beat at medium speed until frosting is cool and loses its shine. This may be speeded up by setting the bowl of frosting over another bowl of cold water. While beating, add extract. *Use the frosting right away, as it starts to set up quickly.*

ENOUGH TO FILL AND FROST ONE 9-INCH 3-LAYER CAKE
NOTE: If frosting becomes too stiff, beat in a little hot water until frosting is of spreading consistency. If frosting is too soft from undercooking, put it into double boiler top over boiling water until of proper consistency.

PETITS FOURS ICING

2 cups sugar
⅛ teaspoon cream of
   tartar

1 cup hot water
1¼ to 1½ cups
   confectioners' sugar

1. Combine the sugar, cream of tartar, and hot water in a saucepan. Bring to boiling; set candy thermometer in place and cook to 226°F (thin syrup). Cool to lukewarm, 100°F.
2. Mix in confectioners' sugar. Heat over boiling water in top of double boiler until of pouring consistency. Stir in 1 teaspoon desired *extract* and, if desired, *food coloring.*
3. Pour over small cakes that have been placed on rack over a tray. Pick up icing that drops, reheat, and use again and again. If it becomes too stiff, add a little hot water.

ENOUGH TO FROST ABOUT 2 DOZEN SMALL CAKES

BUTTER CREAM FROSTING I

6 egg yolks
¾ cup sugar
½ teaspoon cornstarch
¾ cup cream

2 teaspoons vanilla
   extract
1½ cups firm unsalted
   butter

1. In top of a double boiler, beat the egg yolks until very thick. Gradually add a mixture of sugar and cornstarch, beating constantly. Gradually add the cream, stirring until well blended. Set over boiling water and cook, stirring constantly, until thickened, about 15 minutes.

2. Remove from heat and stir in the extract. Cover; cool slightly. Set in refrigerator to chill.

3. Put butter into a large mixer bowl. Beginning with medium speed of electric mixer, and as soon as possible increasing to high, beat butter until fluffy. Gradually add the chilled mixture to the creamed butter, beating until just blended after each addition. If necessary, set frosting over ice and water until firm enough to spread. If frosting should curdle, beat again until just smooth.

4. This frosting will keep several days, tightly covered, in the refrigerator. Beat just until smooth before using. ENOUGH TO FROST SIDES AND TOPS OF THREE 9-INCH TORTE LAYERS

HAZELNUT BUTTER CREAM FROSTING: Grate *½ cup (about 2½ ounces) hazelnuts (filberts)*. Follow recipe for Butter Cream Frosting. Blend the grated nuts into the frosting after blending in the chilled mixture.

MOCHA BUTTER CREAM FROSTING: Dissolve *1¾ teaspoons instant coffee in 1 teaspoon boiling water*. Set aside to cool. Follow recipe for Butter Cream Frosting. Omit extract. Blend cooled coffee into the butter.

CHOCOLATE-MOCHA BUTTER CREAM FROSTING: Melt *1½ ounces (1½ squares) unsweetened chocolate* and set aside to cool. Follow recipe for Mocha Butter Cream Frosting. Gradually blend chocolate into whipped butter after adding coffee.

MERINGUE BUTTER FROSTING

1 cup plus 2 tablespoons sugar	½ teaspoon vanilla extract
⅓ cup water	½ teaspoon rum
2 egg whites	2 egg yolks
1½ cups firm unsalted butter	½ cup walnuts, grated

1. Combine sugar and water in a small saucepan. Bring to boiling, stirring until sugar is dissolved. Cover tightly and boil gently for 5 minutes.

2. Uncover and set candy thermometer in place. Continue cooking, without stirring, until thermometer registers 230°F (thread stage). Using pastry brush dipped in water, wash down crystals from sides of pan from time to time during cooking. Remove from heat.

3. Beat egg whites until stiff, not dry, peaks are formed. Continue beating egg whites while pouring hot syrup over them in a steady thin stream. (Do not scrape pan.) Continue beating a few minutes until mixture is very thick (piles softly). Cool completely.

4. Cream butter with extract and rum until light and fluffy. Add egg yolks, one at a time, beating after each addition. Add about 2 tablespoons egg white mixture at a time to creamed butter, beating until just blended after each addition. (Egg white mixture and creamed butter should be of same consistency before mixing together.) Mix in grated walnuts.

5. If necessary, chill frosting until firm enough to spread.
ENOUGH TO FILL AND FROST ONE 9-INCH 2-LAYER CAKE

CHOCOLATE BUTTER FROSTING
(Crème au Beurre Chocolat)

6 oz. semisweet chocolate	1½ teaspoons vanilla extract
¼ cup strong coffee	¾ cup light corn syrup
1½ cups firm unsalted butter	4 egg yolks

1. Put chocolate and coffee into the top of a double boiler. Set over hot (not simmering) water until chocolate is melted; blend well. Set aside to cool.

2. Cream butter and extract until light and fluffy; set aside.

3. Pour the corn syrup into a saucepan. Set candy thermometer in place. Boil corn syrup gently to 230° to 234°F (thread stage).

4. Meanwhile, beat the egg yolks until very thick. Continue beating constantly while pouring syrup very slowly into egg yolks. Beat until mixture is very thick and of same consistency as the whipped butter. Cool completely.

5. Beat egg yolk mixture, about 2 tablespoons at a time, into butter until just blended. Gradually blend in the chocolate. (If tightly covered, this frosting may be stored for several days in refrigerator.) ENOUGH TO FILL AND FROST ONE 8-INCH 2-LAYER CAKE

CREAMY BUTTER FROSTING (Crème au Beurre Vanille): Follow recipe for Chocolate Butter Frosting. Omit chocolate and coffee.

LIQUEUR BUTTER FROSTING (Crème au Beurre au Liqueur): Follow recipe for Chocolate Butter Frosting or prepare Creamy Butter Frosting. Substitute *1 tablespoon liqueur* such as kirsch, curaçao, or Cointreau for the vanilla extract.

BROWNIE CARAMEL FROSTING

1¼ cups sugar
⅔ cup cream
¾ cup lightly packed
  brown sugar

1 teaspoon vanilla
  extract

1. Combine the sugar and cream in a medium-sized saucepan. Stir over low heat until sugar is dissolved. Increase heat and bring mixture to boiling. Set candy thermometer in place. Cook to 234°F (soft-ball stage). Using a pastry brush dipped in water, wash down crystals from sides of pan during cooking.
2. Meanwhile, heat the brown sugar in a heavy skillet; with back of wooden spoon, gently keep sugar moving toward center of skillet until sugar is melted. Stir melted brown sugar rapidly into the syrup. Boil again to soft ball stage (do not overcook).
3. Remove from heat. Set aside to cool to 110°F, or until just cool enough to hold pan on palm of hand.
4. Blend in extract and beat until creamy and of spreading consistency. Place frosting over hot water if it becomes too stiff while spreading on cake.
ENOUGH TO FROST SIDES AND TOPS OF TWO 8-INCH CAKE LAYERS OR 2 DOZEN CUPCAKES

CARAMEL ICING

¾ cup buttermilk
1½ cups lightly packed
  dark brown sugar

⅛ teaspoon baking soda
1 tablespoon butter

1. Combine buttermilk and brown sugar in a saucepan. Set candy thermometer in place. Cook to 234°F (soft-ball stage); stir often to prevent scorching.
2. Remove from heat and stir in baking soda and butter. Cool to 110°F. Beat until of spreading consistency. ENOUGH TO FROST TOP AND SIDES OF ONE 8-INCH SQUARE CAKE

BUTTERMILK FUDGE FROSTING

¾ cup butter or
  margarine
1 cup buttermilk
2 cups sugar
1 teaspoon baking soda

2 tablespoons butter or
  margarine
1 teaspoon vanilla
  extract

1. Put the butter, buttermilk, sugar, and baking soda into a heavy 3-quart saucepan. Stir over low heat until sugar is completely dissolved.

2. Increase heat and bring mixture to boiling. Set candy thermometer in place. Cook, stirring constantly, until thermometer registers 232°F.
3. Remove from heat and put the 2 tablespoons butter on top of frosting. Set frosting aside to cool to 110°F. Do not disturb during cooling.
4. When cool, stir in extract and beat until creamy and of spreading consistency. If frosting becomes too thick to spread smoothly, add a few drops of hot water. ENOUGH TO FILL AND FROST ONE 9-INCH 2-LAYER CAKE

VANILLA FUDGE FROSTING
A wonderful frosting for lemon cake.

2¼ cups sugar
¾ cup milk
¼ teaspoon cream of
  tartar
¼ teaspoon salt

1½ tablespoons butter
¾ teaspoon vanilla
  extract
1 to 2 tablespoons
  cream

1. Combine the sugar, milk, cream of tartar, and salt in a 2-quart saucepan. Stir over low heat until sugar is dissolved.
2. Increase heat and bring mixture to boiling. Set candy thermometer in place. Cook, stirring occasionally, to 234°F (soft-ball stage). Using a pastry brush dipped in water, wash down crystals from sides of saucepan from time to time during cooking.
3. Remove from heat. Set aside to cool to 110°F, or until just cool enough to hold pan on palm of hand. Do not stir.
4. When cooled, blend in butter and extract. Mix in enough cream for spreading consistency.
ENOUGH TO FILL AND FROST ONE 8-INCH 2-LAYER CAKE

CARAMEL FUDGE FROSTING
Ice your favorite cake—white, yellow, or chocolate—with this luscious fudgy frosting and cut cake into squares.

3 cups lightly packed
  light brown sugar
1 cup milk
½ cup butter or
  margarine
Few grains salt

½ oz. (½ sq.)
  unsweetened
  chocolate, cut in
  pieces
1 teaspoon vanilla
  extract

1. Combine all ingredients except extract in a heavy 3-quart saucepan. Stir over low heat until sugar is completely dissolved.

2. Increase heat and bring mixture to boiling. Wash down crystals from sides of pan with a pastry brush dipped in water. Set candy thermometer in place. Cook, stirring occasionally, until thermometer registers 234°F, washing down crystals from sides of pan and changing water each time.
3. Remove from heat and set aside to cool to 110°F, or until just cool enough to hold pan on palm of hand. Do not disturb frosting during cooling.
4. When cool, stir in the extract and beat until creamy and of spreading consistency.
Enough to fill and frost one 8-inch 2-layer cake

FUDGE FROSTING I

2 oz. (2 sq.) unsweetened chocolate, grated or cut in pieces	1 cup cream
	1/8 teaspoon salt
	1 teaspoon vanilla extract
2 cups sugar	

1. Put chocolate, sugar, cream, and salt into a heavy saucepan. Stir over low heat until sugar is dissolved and chocolate is melted.
2. Increase heat and bring mixture to boiling. Set candy thermometer in place. Continue cooking, stirring occasionally to prevent scorching, until mixture reaches 234°F (soft-ball stage). Using a pastry brush dipped in water, wash down crystals from sides of pan from time to time during cooking.
3. Remove from heat. Set aside to cool to 110°F, or until just cool enough to hold pan on palm of hand. Do not stir.
4. When cooled, blend in the extract. Beat vigorously just until mixture loses its gloss and is of spreading consistency. If frosting becomes too thick, beat in a small amount of *cream*.
Enough to fill and frost one 9-inch 2-layer cake

FUDGE FROSTING II

4 oz. (4 sq.) unsweetened chocolate, cut in pieces	1/2 cup butter or margarine
3 cups sugar	2 tablespoons light corn syrup
1 cup milk	1 tablespoon vanilla extract

1. Combine all ingredients except extract in a heavy 3-quart saucepan. Heat slowly until mixture boils rapidly, stirring constantly.

2. Set candy thermometer in place. Cook to 234°F (soft-ball stage; remove from heat while testing). Using a pastry brush dipped in water, wash down the crystals from sides of saucepan from time to time during cooking.
3. Remove from heat and cool to 110°F without stirring or jarring.
4. Mix in extract. Beat until of spreading consistency.
Enough to fill and frost one 9-inch 2-layer cake

POTATO FUDGE FROSTING

Instant mashed potatoes	1/8 teaspoon salt
1/4 cup milk	2 teaspoons vanilla extract
1/2 cup butter or margarine	4 1/2 cups confectioners' sugar
3 oz. (3 sq.) unsweetened chocolate	1/4 cup milk

1. Prepare 1/2 cup lightly packed riced or sieved potato from instant mashed potatoes according to package directions, using only the water (omit milk, butter, and seasonings). Blend potato with the 1/4 cup milk; set aside.
2. Heat butter in a saucepan over low heat until lightly browned. Add chocolate and stir just until melted; remove from heat.
3. Add potatoes, salt, and extract and beat until well blended. Alternately add confectioners' sugar and 1/4 cup milk, beating well after each addition.
Enough to frost and fill one 9-inch 2-layer cake

HONEY-CHOCOLATE FROSTING

The hint of honey in this frosting gives it an intriguingly "different" flavor.

1/2 cup butter or margarine	1/8 teaspoon salt
2 oz. (2 sq.) unsweetened chocolate, cut in pieces	1/3 cup honey
	1/4 cup cream or rich milk
1/2 cup sugar	2 egg yolks, slightly beaten

1. Combine all ingredients except egg yolks in the top of a double boiler and place over boiling water. When chocolate is melted, blend well with hand rotary or electric beater.
2. Vigorously stir about 3 tablespoons of the hot mixture into the egg yolks. Immediately blend into the mixture in top of double boiler.
3. Cook over boiling water, stirring constantly.

When slightly thickened (about 2 minutes), remove from heat; set double boiler top in ice and water; beat frosting until of spreading consistency.

ENOUGH TO FILL AND FROST ONE 8-INCH 2-LAYER CAKE

MAPLE SUGAR FROSTING

1 cup sugar
1 cup lightly packed
  maple sugar (see note)

1 cup dairy sour cream

1. Combine all ingredients in a medium-sized heavy saucepan. Set over low heat and stir until sugar is dissolved.
2. Increase heat and bring to boiling. Set candy thermometer in place and cook without stirring to 238°F (soft-ball stage); during cooking, wash sugar crystals from sides of pan occasionally with pastry brush dipped in water.
3. Remove saucepan to a wire rack and cool to 110°F without stirring or moving the pan.
4. Beat vigorously with wooden spoon or electric mixer until mixture begins to lose its gloss and is of spreading consistency.
5. Spread on cake immediately. If frosting becomes too thick to spread, beat in a few drops of *cream* or *milk*.

ENOUGH TO FILL AND FROST ONE 8-INCH 3-LAYER CAKE

NOTE: If maple sugar is available only in solid form, grate, using a fine grater, before using.

BROWN SUGAR FROSTING: Follow recipe for Maple Sugar Frosting. Substitute *1 cup lightly packed light brown sugar* for the maple sugar. Add *1 teaspoon vanilla extract* just before beating.

Uncooked Frostings

BASIC BUTTER FROSTING

6 tablespoons butter
1½ teaspoons vanilla
  extract

3 cups confectioners'
  sugar
1½ tablespoons milk or
  cream

1. Cream butter with extract. Add confectioners' sugar gradually, beating thoroughly after each addition.
2. Stir in milk and beat until frosting is of spreading consistency.

ENOUGH TO FILL AND FROST ONE 8- OR 9-INCH 2-LAYER CAKE

LEMON BUTTER FROSTING: Follow recipe for Basic Butter Frosting. Substitute *lemon juice* for milk and add *1½ teaspoons grated lemon peel*. If desired, add a few drops *yellow food coloring*.

MOCHA BUTTER FROSTING: Follow recipe for Basic Butter Frosting. Sift *1½ teaspoons instant coffee* with the confectioners' sugar. Melt and cool *3 ounces (3 squares) unsweetened chocolate* and blend in after adding sugar.

CHOCOLATE BUTTER FROSTING: Follow recipe for Basic Butter Frosting. Melt and cool *3 ounces (3 squares) unsweetened chocolate* and blend in after adding sugar.

BURNT-SUGAR BUTTER FROSTING: Follow recipe for Basic Butter Frosting. After adding sugar, blend in *½ cup Burnt-Sugar Syrup, page 399*, and a few grains *salt*; increase milk to 2 tablespoons.

RAISIN-RUM BUTTER FROSTING: Follow recipe for Basic Butter Frosting. Decrease vanilla extract to *½ teaspoon* and add *1 teaspoon rum*. Increase milk to about 3 tablespoons and add *1 drop red food coloring* and *¼ cup finely chopped golden raisins*.

ORANGE BUTTER FROSTING: Follow recipe for Basic Butter Frosting. Substitute *1½ teaspoons grated orange peel* for the vanilla extract and *1½ to 2½ tablespoons orange juice* for the milk. If a deeper orange color is desired, mix *4 drops red food coloring* and *3 drops yellow food coloring* with orange juice.

BLACK WALNUT BUTTER FROSTING: Follow recipe for Basic Butter Frosting. Cream *2 teaspoons grated orange peel* with butter and extract. Stir in *¼ cup finely chopped black walnuts*.

CREAM CHEESE BUTTER FROSTING: Follow recipe for Basic Butter Frosting, doubling recipe and creaming *3 ounces softened cream cheese* with the butter.

BUTTER CREAM FROSTING II

½ cup butter
½ teaspoon almond
  extract

5 cups confectioners'
  sugar
4 to 5 tablespoons milk
  or cream

Cream butter with extract. Alternately add confectioners' sugar and milk, beating thoroughly after each addition. Beat until of spreading consistency. If desired, tint with *green food coloring*.

ENOUGH TO FILL AND FROST ONE 9-INCH 3-LAYER CAKE

TINTED BUTTER FROSTING

2 tablespoons butter or
  margarine
½ teaspoon vanilla
  extract

1½ cups confectioners'
  sugar
1 tablespoon warm
  cream
Food coloring

1. Cream butter with extract. Alternately add confectioners' sugar and cream, blending thoroughly after each addition.
2. Tint as desired with a drop or two of food coloring. Use for decorating petits fours and other small cakes.   About ¾ cup frosting

WHITE FROSTING

⅔ cup butter
1½ teaspoons vanilla
  extract
¼ teaspoon almond
  extract

7 cups confectioners'
  sugar
1 egg white, unbeaten
4 to 6 tablespoons
  cream, heated

1. Cream butter with extracts. Gradually add confectioners' sugar, beating until creamy. Add egg white and beat until fluffy.
2. Add the hot cream gradually, a tablespoonful at a time, beating until frosting is of spreading consistency.   Enough to generously fill and frost one 9-inch 3-layer cake

WHITE VELVET FROSTING

¼ cup butter or
  margarine
1½ teaspoons vanilla
  extract
⅛ teaspoon salt

1 egg yolk
3 cups confectioners'
  sugar
3 tablespoons milk or
  cream

1. Cream butter with extract, salt, and egg yolk until light and fluffy.
2. Alternately add confectioners' sugar and milk, beating after each addition. Beat until frosting is of spreading consistency.   Enough to fill and frost one 8- or 9-inch 2-layer cake

LEMON VELVET FROSTING: Follow recipe for White Velvet Frosting. Substitute *1 teaspoon lemon extract* for vanilla extract.

BROWN VELVET FROSTING: Melt and cool *2 ounces (2 squares) unsweetened chocolate.* Follow recipe for White Velvet Frosting. Stir chocolate into frosting after addition of egg yolk.

QUICK BANANA FROSTING

⅓ cup sieved ripe
  banana
¼ teaspoon lemon juice
Few grains salt

¼ cup butter or
  margarine
2½ cups confectioners'
  sugar

1. Mix sieved banana with lemon juice and salt; set aside.
2. Cream butter until softened. Alternately add confectioners' sugar and banana, beating thoroughly after each addition. Beat until smooth and of spreading consistency.   Enough to fill and frost one 8-inch 2-layer cake

CINNAMON CANDY FROSTING

1 tablespoon butter or
  margarine
2 cups confectioners'
  sugar

Milk (about 3
  tablespoons)
2 tablespoons finely
  crushed red cinnamon
  candies

Cream butter; alternately add confectioners' sugar and milk, beating until of spreading consistency. Stir in crushed candy.   Enough to fill and frost one 8-inch square cake

HONEY-DO FROSTING

1 tablespoon butter or
  margarine
¼ cup honey
2 cups confectioners'
  sugar

½ cup lightly packed
  brown sugar
2 tablespoons
  sweetened condensed
  milk

Beat the butter and honey together. Blend in remaining ingredients in order. Beat until frosting is of spreading consistency.   Enough to frost one 8- or 9-inch square cake

CREAMY PEANUT BUTTER FROSTING

6 tablespoons butter
1½ tablespoons peanut
  butter
¾ teaspoon vanilla
  extract

2½ cups confectioners'
  sugar
1 egg yolk
1½ tablespoons milk

1. Cream butter with peanut butter and extract.
2. Gradually add the confectioners' sugar, beating well after each addition. Beat in the egg yolk.
3. Beat in enough of the milk until frosting is of spreading consistency.   Enough to frost one 8- or 9-inch square cake

CARAMEL MOCHA FROSTING

½ cup butter or
  margarine
1 tablespoon vanilla
  extract
2 teaspoons cocoa

3½ cups confectioners'
  sugar
1 egg yolk
3 tablespoons strong
  coffee

1. Cream butter with extract. Blend in cocoa. Gradually add confectioners' sugar, beating until smooth. Beat in the egg yolk.
2. Blend in the coffee a small amount at a time and beat until frosting is of spreading consistency.

ENOUGH TO FILL AND FROST ONE 9-INCH 2-LAYER CAKE

PEPPERMINT BUTTER FROSTING

½ cup butter
½ teaspoon peppermint
  extract
⅛ teaspoon salt

3½ cups confectioners'
  sugar
1 egg
1 to 2 tablespoons milk
  or cream

1. Cream butter, extract, and salt. Gradually add the confectioners' sugar, beating until smooth after each addition.
2. Add egg and beat thoroughly. If necessary, blend in milk. Beat until frosting is of spreading consistency.
3. Tint as desired with *red food coloring*.

ENOUGH TO FROST TWO 8- OR 9-INCH CAKE
LAYERS OR ONE 13x9-INCH CAKE

RAISIN BUTTER FROSTING

¼ cup water
¼ cup dark seedless
  raisins
½ cup butter
½ teaspoon grated
  lemon peel

1 to 2 teaspoons lemon
  juice
3½ cups confectioners'
  sugar
¼ cup cream

1. Bring water to boiling. Add raisins and again bring to boiling. Remove from heat, cover, and set aside to cool. Drain raisins, reserving liquid. Coarsely cut raisins.
2. Cream butter with lemon peel and juice. Add confectioners' sugar gradually, beating well after each addition.
3. Add cream slowly, beating in. Mix in the raisins. Blend in enough reserved raisin liquid for a spreading consistency. ENOUGH TO FROST ONE
10-INCH TUBED CAKE

SPICE BUTTER FROSTING

¼ cup butter
1 teaspoon vanilla
  extract
1 teaspoon cocoa
¼ teaspoon salt
¼ teaspoon ground
  cinnamon

⅛ teaspoon ground
  cloves
⅛ teaspoon ground
  nutmeg
4 cups confectioners'
  sugar
⅓ to ½ cup cream

Cream butter with extract. Blend in a mixture of cocoa, salt, and spices. Alternately add confectioners' sugar and cream, beating until frosting is of spreading consistency. ENOUGH TO FROST ONE
10-INCH TUBED CAKE

BROWNED BUTTER FROSTING

¼ cup butter
2½ cups confectioners'
  sugar

3 tablespoons cream
1 teaspoon vanilla
  extract

Heat the butter in a saucepan until lightly browned. Remove from heat. Blend in the sugar, cream, and extract; beat until smooth. If necessary, blend in more cream for desired spreading consistency.

ABOUT 1½ CUPS FROSTING

CARAMEL FROSTING

½ cup butter
1 cup lightly packed
  brown sugar

¼ cup cream
1½ cups confectioners'
  sugar

1. Melt butter in a heavy skillet over low heat. Blend in the brown sugar and cream. Stirring constantly, bring to boiling and cook 1 minute, or until sugar is completely dissolved.
2. Remove from heat and cool to 110°F.
3. When syrup has cooled, gradually add the confectioners' sugar, beating until blended after each addition. If necessary, continue beating until thick enough to spread. ENOUGH TO FROST
ONE 13x9-INCH CAKE

RICH CHOCOLATE FROSTING

½ cup butter or
  margarine
4 oz. (4 sq.) unsweet-
  ened chocolate
2⅔ cups confectioners'
  sugar

1 egg
6 tablespoons water
2 teaspoons vanilla
  extract
⅛ teaspoon salt

1. Melt butter and chocolate together. Pour into a

bowl. Beat in, in order, the confectioners' sugar, egg, water, extract, and salt.

2. Set bowl in a larger bowl of ice and water. Beat with electric mixer about 5 minutes, or until frosting is of spreading consistency.

ABOUT 3 CUPS FROSTING OR ENOUGH TO GENEROUSLY FROST ONE 8-INCH SQUARE CAKE

POURED CHOCOLATE FROSTING

5 tablespoons milk	6 tablespoons cocoa
¼ cup butter or margarine	⅛ teaspoon salt
2 cups confectioners' sugar	⅛ teaspoon vanilla extract

1. Put milk and butter into a heavy saucepan. Set over low heat until butter is melted and milk is scalded.

2. Remove from heat and beat in a mixture of the confectioners' sugar, cocoa, and salt. Blend in extract. Cool.

3. Pour frosting (frosting will be thin) in center of cake, spreading and working with spatula over top and sides of cake until frosting sets in desired swirls.

ENOUGH TO FROST TOP AND SIDES OF TWO 8-INCH CAKE LAYERS

CHOCOLATE-COLA FROSTING

1 pkg. chocolate fudge frosting mix	Cola beverage

Prepare frosting mix as directed on package, substituting cola beverage for the liquid. Beat until of spreading consistency.

ENOUGH TO FILL AND FROST ONE 8- OR 9-INCH 2-LAYER CAKE

CHOCO-MARSHMALLOW FROSTING

6 tablespoons butter or margarine	½ cup golden raisins, rinsed and coarsely chopped
6 tablespoons cocoa	
½ cup milk	½ cup walnuts, coarsely chopped
3 cups confectioners' sugar	⅔ cup (about 1 oz.) miniature marshmallows
1 teaspoon vanilla extract	

1. Melt butter in a heavy saucepan over low heat. Blend in the cocoa, then the milk. Stirring constantly, cook until mixture thickens, about 3 minutes.

2. Remove from heat. Add confectioners' sugar

gradually, stirring until smooth after each addition. Stir in the remaining ingredients.

ENOUGH TO FROST ONE 13x9-INCH CAKE

CREAM CHEESE FROSTING

3 oz. cream cheese, softened	1 teaspoon vanilla extract
1½ cups confectioners' sugar	

Cream all ingredients together until fluffy.

ENOUGH TO FROST ONE 8x4-INCH LOAF CAKE

COFFEE-CREAM CHEESE FROSTING

1 tablespoon instant coffee	6 oz. cream cheese, softened
1 teaspoon vanilla extract	5 cups confectioners' sugar
½ teaspoon water	

1. Blend the coffee, extract, and water with the cream cheese and mix until smooth.

2. Add the confectioners' sugar gradually, beating until frosting is of spreading consistency.

ENOUGH TO FILL AND FROST ONE 9-INCH 2-LAYER CAKE

LEMON CREAM CHEESE FROSTING

6 oz. cream cheese, softened	½ teaspoon grated lemon peel
1½ teaspoons lemon juice	4 cups confectioners' sugar
	Milk or light cream

1. Blend cream cheese with lemon juice and peel. Gradually add the confectioners' sugar, beating until smooth.

2. If necessary, beat in milk, 1 teaspoon at a time, until frosting is of desired consistency.

ENOUGH TO FILL AND FROST ONE 9-INCH 2-LAYER CAKE

ORANGE CREAM CHEESE FROSTING: Follow recipe for Lemon Cream Cheese Frosting. Omit lemon juice and peel. Blend *2 tablespoons plus 2 teaspoons thawed frozen orange juice concentrate* with cream cheese. Chill frosting in refrigerator until of spreading consistency, about 30 minutes. Store frosted cake in refrigerator.

CHOCOLATE CREAM CHEESE FROSTING: Follow recipe for Lemon Cream Cheese Frosting. Omit lemon juice and peel. Blend *1 teaspoon vanilla extract* with cream cheese. After beating in sugar, blend in *2 ounces (2 squares) unsweetened chocolate*, melted.

GLOSSY VANILLA ICING

½ cup sugar	3⅓ cups confectioners'
½ cup cream	sugar
1 tablespoon light corn	2½ teaspoons vanilla
syrup	extract
1 tablespoon butter or	
margarine	

1. Combine sugar, cream, corn syrup, and butter in a heavy saucepan. Set over low heat and stir until butter is melted.
2. Remove from heat and gradually add confectioners' sugar, blending until smooth. Mix in extract. If frosting is too stiff, blend in *cream.*
3. With spatula, spread frosting on top of cake, allowing it to drip slightly down sides of cake.

ENOUGH TO FROST TOP OF LOAF CAKE OR
TOPS OF TWO 8- OR 9-INCH CAKE LAYERS

GLOSSY CHOCOLATE ICING: Follow recipe for Glossy Vanilla Icing. Melt *1 ounce (1 square) unsweetened chocolate* in butter mixture.

FLUFFY HONEY FROSTING

1 cup honey	2 egg whites
Few grains salt	

1. Bring honey to boiling in a small saucepan over low heat.
2. Add salt to egg whites and beat until stiff, not dry, peaks are formed. Beating constantly, pour the hot honey very slowly in a thin stream over the egg whites. Continue beating 2 to 3 minutes, or until frosting forms rounded peaks.

ENOUGH TO FILL AND FROST ONE
8- OR 9-INCH 2-LAYER CAKE

FLUFFY FILBERT FROSTING

2 tablespoons butter	1 lb. confectioners'
1 cup chopped filberts	sugar
½ cup butter	1 egg, fork beaten
1 teaspoon vanilla	1 to 2 tablespoons
extract	cream

1. Melt the 2 tablespoons butter in a heavy skillet over low heat. Stir in filberts and continue heating, stirring constantly, until nuts are browned. Cool.

2. Cream the ½ cup butter with extract. Add half the confectioners' sugar gradually, creaming thoroughly. Beat in the egg and then the remaining sugar. Beat in enough of the cream to make a fluffy frosting. Mix in the nuts. ENOUGH TO FILL AND FROST ONE 8-INCH 3-LAYER TORTE

Glazes & Toppings

CHOCOLATE GLAZE I

3 oz. (½ cup) semisweet	3 tablespoons butter
chocolate pieces	

Partially melt chocolate pieces in the top of a double boiler over hot (not simmering) water. Remove from heat and stir until chocolate is melted. Blend in butter. ENOUGH TO GLAZE ONE 8-INCH TUBED CAKE

CHOCOLATE GLAZE II

4 oz. semisweet	¼ cup cream
chocolate, melted	3 tablespoons boiling
3 cups confectioners'	water
sugar	4 teaspoons butter
4 teaspoons dark corn	2 teaspoons vanilla
syrup	extract

1. Mix all ingredients except extract in a heavy saucepan. Place over low heat and stir constantly until smooth; remove from heat.
2. Stir in extract; cool slightly.

ENOUGH TO GLAZE 3 DOZEN COOKIES

FUDGE GLAZE

2 oz. (2 sq.) unsweet-	1¼ cups confectioners'
ened chocolate	sugar
3 tablespoons butter	⅛ teaspoon salt
¼ cup cream	

1. Melt the chocolate and butter together; set aside.
2. Beat cream and mix with confectioners' sugar and salt. Add the melted chocolate and butter; stir vigorously until glaze is smooth. Spread over top of cake. ENOUGH TO GLAZE ONE 9-INCH CAKE LAYER

COFFEE-BUTTERSCOTCH GLAZE

⅓ cup lightly packed
 light brown sugar

⅓ cup strong coffee
2 tablespoons butter

1. Mix the brown sugar and coffee in a small saucepan. Set over medium heat and bring to boiling, stirring constantly. Continue to stir and boil 8 to 10 minutes, or until slightly thickened.
2. Remove from heat and blend in the butter. Cool slightly before brushing on cake.

ENOUGH TO GLAZE 1 RING-SHAPED CAKE

SWEETENED WHIPPED CREAM

1 cup chilled heavy
 cream
3 tablespoons
 confectioners' sugar

1 teaspoon vanilla
 extract

1. Beat the cream until it stands in soft peaks. With final few strokes, beat in the confectioners' sugar and extract until blended.
2. Set in refrigerator if not used immediately. If whipped cream is not stiff enough when ready to use, beat again. ABOUT 2 CUPS WHIPPED CREAM

ALMOND WHIPPED CREAM: Follow recipe for Sweetened Whipped Cream. Substitute *¼ teaspoon almond extract* for vanilla extract. Fold in *½ cup toasted slivered blanched almonds.*

COCOA WHIPPED CREAM I: Follow recipe for Sweetened Whipped Cream. Omit sugar, and add *¼ cup instant cocoa.*

DUTCH COCOA WHIPPED CREAM: Follow recipe for Sweetened Whipped Cream. Mix *3 tablespoons Dutch process cocoa* with the sugar.

COINTREAU WHIPPED CREAM: Follow recipe for Sweetened Whipped Cream. Decrease sugar to 4 teaspoons and substitute *2 tablespoons Cointreau* for the extract.

CRÈME DE CACAO WHIPPED CREAM: Follow recipe for Sweetened Whipped Cream. Omit sugar and extract and add *3 tablespoons creme de cacao.*

CRÈME DE MENTHE WHIPPED CREAM: Follow recipe for Sweetened Whipped Cream. Decrease sugar to 2 tablespoons and substitute *2 tablespoons crème de menthe* for the extract.

MOCHA WHIPPED CREAM: Follow recipe for Sweetened Whipped Cream. Mix *1 teaspoon instant coffee* with the sugar.

MOLASSES WHIPPED CREAM: Follow recipe for Sweetened Whipped Cream. Omit sugar and add *2 tablespoons molasses* and a few grains *salt.*

ORANGE WHIPPED CREAM: Follow recipe for Sweetened Whipped Cream. Omit extract; beat in *1 teaspoon grated orange peel* and *¼ cup orange juice* with the sugar. Blend in *8 drops yellow food coloring* and *1 drop red food coloring.*

RUM WHIPPED CREAM: Follow recipe for Sweetened Whipped Cream. Substitute *1 to 1½ tablespoons rum* for extract.

STRAWBERRY WHIPPED CREAM: Follow recipe for Sweetened Whipped Cream, preparing 1½ times recipe. Slice *2 pints rinsed, hulled, fresh strawberries* (reserve a few whole berries for garnish, if desired). Fold berries into the cream.

COCOA WHIPPED CREAM II

5 tablespoons sugar
3 tablespoons cocoa
¼ teaspoon salt

1 cup heavy cream
2 teaspoons vanilla
 extract

1. Mix ingredients in order in a bowl. Chill, covered, 2 hours or longer.
2. Whip chilled mixture until cream stands in peaks. ENOUGH TO FILL ONE 15x10-INCH CAKE ROLL OR FILL AND FROST ONE 8-INCH 2-LAYER CAKE

COFFEE WHIPPED CREAM

1 cup chilled heavy
 cream
⅓ cup light corn syrup

1 tablespoon instant
 coffee
1 teaspoon vanilla
 extract

1. Combine the cream, corn syrup, and coffee in a large bowl. Cover; refrigerate about 1 hour.
2. Beat chilled mixture with electric mixer at medium speed until it thickens slightly. Add extract and continue beating until soft peaks form.

ABOUT 2 CUPS WHIPPED CREAM

MOCHA GINGER CREAM

1 cup sugar
½ cup strong coffee
3 egg yolks
1 cup heavy cream,
 whipped

½ cup (about 3 oz.)
 chopped candied
 ginger

1. Combine sugar and coffee in a 1-quart saucepan. Set over low heat and stir until sugar is dissolved. Increase heat and bring mixture to boiling. Cover saucepan and boil gently for 5 minutes to dissolve any crystals that may have formed.

2. Uncover and set candy thermometer in place. Cook, stirring occasionally, to 234°F (soft-ball stage; remove from heat while testing). During cooking, wash down crystals from sides of pan with pastry brush dipped in water.

3. Using electric mixer, beat the egg yolks at high speed until very thick. Gradually pour syrup over beaten egg yolks, beating constantly. Continue beating until very stiff. Chill in refrigerator.

4. Gently fold the whipped cream into the chilled mixture along with the chopped ginger.

5. Serve as a topping for gingerbread or other cake.   ABOUT 1 QUART TOPPING

MOCHA MAPLE CREAM: Follow recipe for Mocha Ginger Cream. Add *3 tablespoons maple syrup* to ingredients in saucepan. Fold *½ teaspoon maple extract* in with whipped cream. Omit candied ginger.

MOCHA-MALLOW WHIPPED CREAM

16 (4 oz.) marshmallows   2 cups heavy cream
⅓ cup strong coffee
   (dissolve 4 teaspoons
   instant coffee in ⅓
   cup boiling water)

1. Heat the marshmallows and coffee together in top of a double boiler over boiling water until marshmallows are melted; stir occasionally.

2. Remove from heat. Cool; chill in refrigerator until mixture thickens.

3. Whip cream to soft peaks. Fold into chilled mixture.   ENOUGH TO FILL AND FROST ONE
8- OR 9-INCH 2-LAYER CAKE

BROILER FUDGE TOPPING

2 tablespoons butter or   2 tablespoons cocoa
  margarine, softened   2 tablespoons cream
½ cup lightly packed   ½ cup nuts, coarsely
  brown sugar   chopped

1. Cream butter, brown sugar, and cocoa until fluffy. Beat in the cream. Stir in nuts.

2. Spread lightly over cake after it has cooled in pan 10 to 15 minutes.

3. Place under broiler with top about 4 inches from source of heat. Broil about 1 minute, or until frosting bubbles; watch closely to avoid scorching.
ENOUGH TO FROST TOP OF
ONE 8-INCH SQUARE CAKE

SPICED HONEY TOPPING

½ cup honey   ⅛ teaspoon ground
1 teaspoon thick sweet-   cloves
  ened applesauce   ⅛ teaspoon salt
⅛ teaspoon ground ginger   1 egg white, unbeaten

Combine all ingredients in a bowl. Using hand rotary beater or electric mixer, beat until topping is of spreading consistency, about 5 minutes.

ENOUGH TO FROST TOP AND SIDES
OF TWO 8-INCH CAKE LAYERS

Fillings

CREAM FILLING I

3 tablespoons flour   1½ cups milk, scalded
6 tablespoons sugar   4 egg yolks, fork beaten
¼ teaspoon salt   1 teaspoon vanilla
½ cup cold milk   extract

1. Combine the flour, sugar, and salt in the top of a double boiler; mix well. Add the cold milk, stirring to blend thoroughly.

2. Gradually add the scalded milk, stirring to blend. Set over low heat and bring mixture to boiling, stirring constantly; cook about 2 minutes.

3. Vigorously stir about 3 tablespoons hot mixture into the egg yolks. Immediately return to mixture in double-boiler top.

4. Set over boiling water about 5 minutes, stirring to keep mixture cooking evenly. Remove from heat and pour into a bowl. Stir in the extract. Cover and cool slightly. Chill before spreading between layers.
2 CUPS FILLING

CREAMY VANILLA FILLING

⅓ cup sugar   1 tablespoon butter or
2½ tablespoons flour   margarine
¼ teaspoon salt   2 teaspoons vanilla
1½ cups cream   extract
3 egg yolks, slightly   ¼ teaspoon almond
  beaten   extract

1. Mix sugar, flour, and salt in a heavy saucepan. Stir constantly while gradually adding the cream. Bring to boiling; stir and cook 3 minutes.

2. Vigorously stir about 3 tablespoons of the hot mixture into the egg yolks; immediately blend into cream mixture. Stir and cook about 1 minute.

3. Remove from heat and blend in the remaining

ingredients. Press a circle of waxed paper onto top (this prevents a crust from forming). Cool slightly, then chill. ABOUT 1½ CUPS FILLING

CREAMY CHERRY FILLING: Follow recipe for Creamy Vanilla Filling. Omit almond extract. Mix in *1 to 2 tablespoons maraschino cherry syrup.* Mix *½ cup chopped maraschino cherries* into chilled filling.

CREAMY CHOCOLATE FILLING: Follow recipe for Creamy Vanilla Filling. Increase sugar to ½ cup. Add *1½ ounces (1½ squares) unsweetened chocolate* to cream mixture.

PINEAPPLE CREAM FILLING: Follow recipe for Creamy Vanilla Filling. Drain contents of *1 can (8½ ounces) crushed pineapple.* Mix crushed pineapple into chilled filling.

VANILLA CREAM FILLING

½ cup sugar
2½ tablespoons flour
¼ teaspoon salt
½ cup cream
½ cup cream, scalded
3 egg yolks, slightly beaten
1 tablespoon butter or margarine
2 teaspoons vanilla extract
½ cup dairy sour cream

1. Mix sugar, flour, and salt in the top of a double boiler. Blend in the cold cream. Gradually add the scalded cream, stirring constantly. Bring to boiling over direct heat and cook 3 minutes, stirring constantly.
2. Remove from heat. Stir about 3 tablespoons of the hot mixture into beaten egg yolks; immediately blend into mixture in double boiler. Set over boiling water and cook about 5 minutes, stirring constantly.
3. Remove from heat. Blend in butter, extract, and sour cream. Cover and cool slightly; chill.
ABOUT 1½ CUPS FILLING

VANILLA CUSTARD FILLING

½ cup sugar
2 tablespoons cornstarch
¼ teaspoon salt
½ cup cold milk
1 cup milk, scalded
4 egg yolks, beaten
2 teaspoons vanilla extract

1. Mix sugar, cornstarch, and salt together in the top of a double boiler. Blend in the cold milk, stirring until mixture is smooth. Add scalded milk gradually, stirring constantly. Bring mixture rapid-

ly to boiling over direct heat and cook 3 minutes, stirring constantly.
2. Remove from heat. Stir about 3 tablespoons of the hot mixture into egg yolks; immediately blend into mixture in double boiler. Set over boiling water and cook about 5 minutes, stirring constantly.
3. Remove from heat; blend in the extract. Cool slightly; refrigerate until ready to use.
ABOUT 1½ CUPS FILLING

CHOCOLATE FILLING

1 cup sugar
¼ cup cornstarch
½ teaspoon salt
¼ cup cold water
¾ cup boiling water
2 oz. (2 sq.) unsweetened chocolate, melted
¼ cup butter or margarine
2 teaspoons vanilla extract

1. Thoroughly blend the sugar, cornstarch, and salt in the top of a double boiler. Add the cold water and blend well. Gradually add the boiling water.
2. Stirring gently and constantly, bring mixture to boiling over direct heat, and cook 3 minutes. Place over simmering water; cover and cook 12 minutes, stirring 3 or 4 times.
3. Remove from heat; stir in melted chocolate, butter, and extract. Cool slightly.
ABOUT 1 CUP FILLING

CHOCOLATE-ALMOND FILLING
An especially delicious filling for devil's food cake. If this filling recipe is doubled, it will fill and frost an 8-inch 2-layer cake.

¼ cup sugar
3 tablespoons flour
⅛ teaspoon salt
¾ cup milk
1 oz. (1 sq.) unsweetened chocolate, grated
1 tablespoon butter or margarine
1½ teaspoons vanilla extract
Few drops almond extract
½ cup chilled heavy cream, whipped to soft peaks
½ cup toasted blanched almonds, finely chopped

1. Mix together sugar, flour, and salt in a heavy saucepan. Gradually add the milk and grated chocolate, stirring constantly. Cook and stir until the mixture is thick and smooth.
2. Remove from heat. Stir in butter and extracts. Set in refrigerator to chill thoroughly.
3. Spread the whipped cream and nuts over the

chocolate mixture and gently fold together. Chill.

ABOUT 2 CUPS FILLING

SEMISWEET CHOCOLATE FILLING

1 pkg. (6 oz.) semisweet chocolate pieces	2 tablespoons cornstarch
1½ cups milk	2 tablespoons cold water
2 teaspoons instant coffee	2 eggs, beaten
⅛ teaspoon salt	1 teaspoon vanilla extract

1. Put chocolate pieces, milk, instant coffee, and salt into double-boiler top; heat over boiling water, stirring constantly until chocolate is melted.
2. Mix a blend of cornstarch and cold water and stir into eggs; stir about ½ cup of the melted chocolate mixture into eggs and blend thoroughly. Stir into mixture in double boiler and cook over boiling water, stirring constantly until very thick and smooth.
3. Remove from heat and stir in extract; cool thoroughly. (If a slightly sweeter filling is desired, blend in 1 to 2 tablespoons sugar.)

ABOUT 2¼ CUPS FILLING

SWEET CHOCOLATE FILLING

6 oz. sweet chocolate	3 egg yolks, well beaten
2 tablespoons confectioners' sugar	3 egg whites
2 tablespoons water	¼ teaspoon vanilla extract

1. Melt chocolate in the top of a double boiler over hot (not simmering) water. Stir in confectioners' sugar, water, and egg yolks. Cook, stirring constantly, until thickened. Remove from water and cool.
2. Beat egg whites until stiff, not dry, peaks are formed. Fold egg whites and extract into chocolate mixture. 1½ CUPS FILLING

LEMON FILLING I

3 egg whites	1 teaspoon grated lemon peel
1 cup sugar	
3 tablespoons lemon juice	3 egg yolks, slightly beaten

1. Combine all ingredients except egg yolks in double-boiler top and beat slightly with hand rotary or electric beater.

2. Place over simmering water. Cook about 5 minutes, or until thickened, stirring constantly.
3. Vigorously stir about 3 tablespoons of hot mixture into the egg yolks. Immediately blend into mixture in double boiler. Cook over simmering water 10 minutes; stir slowly to keep mixture cooking evenly. Remove from heat and cool thoroughly.

ABOUT 1 CUP FILLING

ORANGE FILLING I

½ cup sugar	1 tablespoon lemon juice
2½ tablespoons cornstarch	1 tablespoon grated orange peel
⅛ teaspoon salt	2 teaspoons butter or margarine
½ cup water	
½ cup orange juice	
1 egg yolk, slightly beaten	

1. Mix sugar, cornstarch, and salt together in the top of a double boiler. Blend in water and orange juice. Stirring gently and constantly, bring to boiling over direct heat and cook for 3 minutes. Cover and cook over simmering water 12 minutes, stirring 3 or 4 times.
2. Vigorously stir about 2 tablespoons hot mixture into egg yolk. Immediately blend into mixture in double boiler. Cook over simmering water 3 to 5 minutes, stirring slowly and constantly to keep mixture cooking evenly.
3. Remove from heat and blend in lemon juice, orange peel, and butter. Cool filling before spreading on the cake. ABOUT 1 CUP FILLING

ORANGE FILLING II

¾ cup orange juice	2 egg whites
½ cup sugar	¼ cup sugar
1 tablespoon grated orange peel	

1. Combine orange juice, sugar, and orange peel; set aside.
2. Beat egg whites until frothy; gradually add ¼ cup sugar, beating well. Continue beating until stiff peaks are formed.
3. Gently fold orange mixture into meringue.

ENOUGH TO FILL ONE 9-INCH LAYER CAKE

LEMON FILLING II: Follow recipe for Orange Filling II. Substitute *lemon juice* and *lemon peel* for orange juice and peel.

Chapter 15

The Art of
CAKE DECORATING

Whether a cake is made from "scratch" or from a packaged mix or bought unfrosted at a shop, you can make it a work of art through the medium of frostings, whipped cream, or meringue. Cake decorating may be simple or very elaborate depending upon the skill of the decorator or the occasion. In any case, the cake must be nicely frosted and the design give pleasure to the beholder.

Time, patience, and practice are needed to perfect the making of flowers and intricate borders as well as the application of them on the cake. It is much like the preparation of a beautiful meal. It is not enough just to prepare fine tasting food; it must be presented attractively in a proper setting.

ICINGS FOR DECORATING

Almost any icing can be used for piping borders and designs, even the making of flowers, by adding confectioners' sugar until the icing is the right consistency for piping. First, remove the amount of icing needed for decorating, then apply the remainder to surfaces of cake.

However, for flowers and other shapes that are made up in advance, it is advisable to use Royal Icing. These decorations will be hard but will hold their shape regardless of the weather.

ROYAL ICING

1 large egg white	1 teaspoon lemon juice,
Sifted confectioners'	or ⅛ teaspoon cream
sugar	of tartar

1. Beat egg white slightly, then add 1 tablespoon confectioners' sugar and beat at high speed of electric mixer about 2 minutes.
2. Gradually add more confectioners' sugar, beating until mixture will hold its shape. Amount of sugar will depend upon size of egg white—generally about 1¼ cups.
3. Beat in lemon juice or cream of tartar. Keep icing covered while decorating cake, and if it gets lumpy, beat it again.

BUTTER CREAM DECORATING FROSTING

½ cup all-purpose shortening	1 teaspoon lemon extract
¼ cup butter or margarine	3 cups sifted confectioners' sugar

In an electric mixer bowl beat the shortening, margarine, and extract together. Gradually beat in the confectioners' sugar until frosting will hold the shape of a tube design.

COLORS FOR DECORATING

It is very important to have color harmony in your decorating work. There are only three basic colors, red, blue, and yellow, from which all others are derived. Certified food colors may be purchased in liquid and paste form. The pastes and new concentrated liquids do not thin icings as some others do. Paste colors which have dried out in jars usually can be reconditioned by blending them with a few drops of glycerin (obtainable at a drugstore).

It is recommended that one have a set of four colors: lemon yellow, clear red, electric blue, and green. Blue and yellow make green, but because this is the most used color in cake decorating, it is handy to have it readily available. The shade of green may be varied by the addition of either yellow or blue to obtain what is often referred to as a mint-green or a leaf-green. Also, greens may be toned down with a little melted chocolate or brown color to simulate a true leaf color.

Many companies who make and sell food colors have charts available with instructions for proper blending of them.

Instead of coloring the icings, flowers may be made untinted, then sprayed with an atomizer in which water has been mixed with the color.

CAKE DECORATING EQUIPMENT

A large investment in equipment for cake decorating is not always necessary since much can be done using paper cones which may be handmade. However, a few items such as those listed below will help you give a professional finish to your cakes. They are usually obtainable at department stores or at school or bakery supply houses. Some grocery and variety stores offer tubes of colored frostings onto which different tubes can be attached.

Decorating bags
Decorating tubes or tips for forming flowers
Decorating comb for quick lines on cakes
Nails for use when making flowers separately
Coupling or adapter for changing tubes
Revolving decorating stand

CAKE DECORATING BAGS are available in an assortment of materials: canvas, plastic, plastic-coated fabrics, and other synthetic materials. Then there is the small parchment bag (or cornet cone) to be made as one needs it. Nothing surpasses it for simple decorating jobs as it is easy to fill and use, easy to retrieve any unused icing, and easy of disposal.

Bags range in size from 7 to 18 inches; the larger size being used for meringues, mashed potatoes, French doughnuts, etc. Instead of bags, a metal decorating gun or syringe may be used.

Plastic bags should not be subjected to high temperatures when washing them, not over 135°F, whereas canvas bags may be put into a washing machine. The disadvantage of the canvas bag is that icing or cheese or even chou paste will seep through it. However, it has the longest life.

Fill bags not more than two-thirds full. Close them properly by folding down or by twisting so that the icing will not squeeze out the top.

Paper cones are made from parchment or heavy grease-proof paper. Make paper cones following directions below, or purchase them already made.

Use the paper cone with or without the decorating tips. For fine writing, simply snip off the point and fill bag one half full of icing. Pressure on the bag will determine the width of the line.

When using tips with the bag, cut an opening with scissors just large enough to permit design of tip to be free.

HOW TO MAKE A PAPER CONE

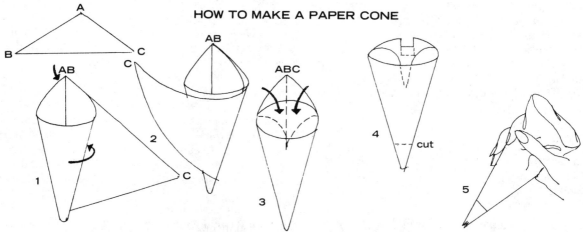

Cut a 24x17x17-inch triangle from baking parchment.   1) Bring points A and B together.   2) Bring C around so that A, B, and C meet.   3) Fold point ABC into cone.   4) Cut a tab in rim; fold tab outward. Trim ½ to ¾ inch from tip.   5) Insert tube into tip; fill bag half-full; hold bag as shown and press.

DECORATING TUBES OR TIPS are available in brass-nickel, aluminum, or plastic. There are dozens of different designs on the tubes, but for the cake decorating beginner the following designs should be sufficient.

Leaf tube for leaves, flowers, and borders

Stem tube for writing, borders, and some flowers

Star (small or medium large) tube for flowers and borders

Ribbon tube for borders and designs

Drop flower tube for many flowers, including roses

To facilitate flower making, double-shank tubes are available. Using these, all one has to do to make beautiful flowers is to twist the wrist.

Care of decorating tubes—Good tubes have fine points which make the designs in the icing. Keep them in good condition and avoid poking nails or an ice pick through the tubes to clean them. Use a wooden pick to remove any icing, then an artist's brush, hot water, and detergent to clean the tubes. Rinse in clear hot water and place upright on absorbent paper on a tray. Set in a warm place to dry thoroughly. Store in a cardboard or plastic box to prevent damage. To speed up cleaning of tubes, drop them into a cupful of cold water on the work table as you finish using them.

LEAF TUBE

Leaf tube—This is one of the most useful tubes for fast decorating and also the simplest to operate. It is available in a wide range of sizes, from very tiny for sugar-cube decorating to very wide for large wedding cakes. It is best to start with an average size one (No. 67) as it can be used for floral arrangements or for piping borders.

For practice work use the back of a cake pan, a smooth tile, or a piece of glass. The glass is particularly useful because a pattern or design can be drawn on paper and placed under the glass for a guide.

Hold the partially filled bag of icing between the first and second fingers and press down on the folded ends with the thumb. Do not squeeze across the middle as this causes the icing to ooze out the top.

When a large bag is being used, the left hand may be used to guide and balance it.

Holding the flat side of the tube parallel to the pan, contact the pan and start pressing out the icing. Lift the tube slightly and, with even pressure, continue pushing for a short distance, then stop pushing and twist the tube away. The consistency of the icing is important if the leaves are to hold their shapes and if they are to be pointed. Practice holding the tube in different positions.

Wavy leaf border—Make this either by placing the flat side of the leaf tube parallel to cake edge or by turning the tube on end. Make contact and start pushing out the icing while at the same time weaving the bag back and forth in uniform movements around the rim of cake top or base.

Daffodils and jonquils—Using the leaf tube, make 6 petals for each flower and a tall "trumpet." The daffodil may be made in a variety of colors while the jonquil is usually yellow with a yellow center cup or trumpet.

On a cardboard, trace around the base of a juice glass to make a circle about 1¼ inches in diameter. At center, draw a triangle with ¼-inch sides. With bag of icing and leaf tube held flat, pipe 3 short petals outward from sides of triangle. Pipe 3 more petals between the first ones, starting at center of triangle. Then holding the bag upright pipe 3 upstanding petals at center for the trumpet.

After you become familiar with making the flower, it will not be necessary to draw the circle or the triangle; also, you can use waxed paper and a rose nail for speedy work. These flowers can be piped directly onto frosted cake or cupcakes.

Jane and Bill

STEM TUBE

Stem tube—This is often called the writing tube and comes in sizes from pinpoint to ¾ inch. Start practice work with a No. 3 or 4 tube, then as you acquire skill in writing and line work start using smaller openings.

When applying a name or writing to the cake, have it properly balanced in the available area. For example, count the number of letters in a name and find the center one; place this one at the center of the area or mark the spot with a wooden pick. Writing is somewhat difficult for some people so if in need of practice, one can write the name on a special little cake easel (washable and reusable) before applying the name to the cake.

The stem tube may be used for border work, some flowers, and flower stems.

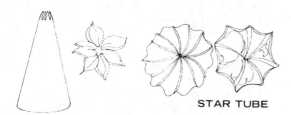

STAR TUBE

Star tube — This is also referred to as a rose tube since it is used to make small flowers (rosettes). For larger roses there are special straight and curved rose tubes in many sizes.

The star tube can be used for borders, either holding the tube straight, or on a slant for a variety of shell-like edgings. Fine-tipped tubes may be used for printing or outline work. Uniform pressure is important so that the stars or circle rosettes are all the same size.

Ribbon tube — This is available in different sizes, some plain on both sides of the slot, others having one serrated side. The tube is used for borders, ribbons, and for basket weaving.

DROP FLOWER TUBE

Drop flower tube — The drop flower tubes have different numbers of cuts to correspond to the petals on flowers. They are available in assorted sizes. All have the shank on the inside. It is this feature which gives you a flower with a hole in the center for placing the stamen of the flower.

Place waxed or parchment paper on a flat surface. Hold the bag perpendicular to the paper and rest the exposed shank on paper. Turn your hand as far left as possible, then start pressing out the

icing as you swing the bag to the right. Stop pressure and lift off tube. Your flower is completed after you pipe stamens in the center with a stem tube, or you may use artificial stamens.

For a variegated effect, place two or three colors of icing in same bag. Consult a flower catalog or your garden for ideas on centers to use.

USE OF THE ROSE NAIL — This may be used for the making of a large number of flowers: daffodils, carnations, pansies, sweet peas, gardenias, poinsettias, and, of course, roses. The ideal is to have a nail for each flower to be made, but this can be costly. Therefore, cut waxed paper or parchment squares to fit over nail, having one for each flower.

Place a dab of icing on nail, cover with a paper square, then put another dab of icing in center on which you will make your flower. Hold nail in left hand, about one third of the way down. As you squeeze the icing with the right hand, pivot the nail with the left. When flower is completed, slip paper to a flat surface and continue making other flowers.

How to make a rose (see illustration on *page 449*) — Use a No. 103 or 104 straight tube. Affix waxed paper to rose nail, then pipe a small amount of frosting or icing at the center. Hold the tube, wide end down, and touch it to the frosting. Gently force out the frosting to form a bud by working around the center, slanting top of tube slightly to the left for a closed-at-the-top center cone. While piping, pivot the nail head.

Pipe 3 short petals around the cone, starting close to base and overlapping petals slightly. Make outer petals longer and slant bag to the right to get a flared effect. Be sure all petals touch at the base.

Remove paper and rose to flat surface. If a butter cream frosting or cream cheese has been used, refrigerate roses until ready to apply.

COUPLING — This consists of 2 pieces of strong synthetic material. The shank part goes inside the decorating bag, then a tube is slipped over the end and this is secured in place with a coupling nut. The advantage of it is that a variety of designs can be made with the same bag of icing.

Many of the fabric bags have openings small enough to accommodate the small tubes only, and when a coupling is wanted, it is necessary to enlarge the opening. When doing this cutting, work carefully and make a few tests with the shank so that the opening will not be too large. The hole for the coupling will be the right size for large rose and leaf tubes as well as the large stems and stars.

PREPARING THE CAKE

Decorating is the final touch so make sure you have a neatly frosted cake on which to work.

Select a flat plate or tray a little larger than your cake. Place cake in center; slip strips of waxed paper under cake to protect the plate. Set on a revolving cake stand, if you have one, and apply frosting. Use a broad-bladed, flexible metal spatula with straight edge and a 10- or 12-inch blade.

If desired, dip the teeth of a decorating comb in hot water and quickly draw it around the sides of the cake, taking care not to dig into frosting. Should this happen, smooth out frosting again and repeat.

For an added flair, arrange greaseproof ruffling (obtainable in many colors) around base of cake. Then pipe a border where the cake joins the ruffle. Pull out paper strips.

HOW TO MAKE A ROSE

EASTER LAMB CAKE

Thoroughly mix *2 tablespoons shortening* and *1 tablespoon flour*; generously coat inner sides of a lamb mold. Prepare *1 package pound cake mix* according to package directions. Turn batter into face side of mold, filling it level. Spoon a small amount of batter into back side of mold, being careful to fill ears. Cover face side with back side. Set on a baking sheet. Bake at 375°F 50 to 55 minutes. Remove from oven and carefully remove top of mold. Let stand in mold 10 minutes. Turn out onto wire rack. Cool completely. Frost generously with *fluffy white frosting* and sprinkle with *flaked coconut.* Use *raisins* for eyes and nose and a *candied cherry* for mouth. Transfer to a plate.

BOUQUET CAKE

Prepare *1 package pound cake mix* according to package directions. Turn batter into a 1½-quart round casserole. Bake at 325°F 1 hour. Cool. Invert on a serving plate. Frost generously with *fluffy white frosting* (from a mix, if desired). Press *Gumdrop Roses, below,* into frosting in concentric rings around cake; use a different color for each ring. Press a few *gumdrop leaves* (flatten green gumdrops) into frosting among the roses.

GUMDROP ROSES: For each rose, flatten *4 small gumdrops* of the same color with a rolling pin on a lightly sugared surface. Roll one petal tightly to form center. Overlap remaining petals around center and pinch together firmly at the base.

DECORATOR'S GUIDE

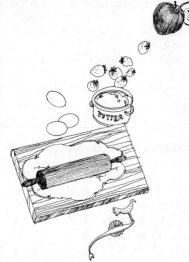

Chapter 16

PIES

Pies offer an endless variety of textures and flavors in both the pie crust (or shell) and the filling. It is essential that the pastry for the pie crust be tender, digestible, and pleasing to the eye.

When making pastry it is advisable to work quickly and handle the pastry dough as little as possible. For the homemaker, all-purpose flour and cake flour are available for making pastry. The latter makes a very tender, but crumbly, pie crust. All-purpose flour makes a more flaky crust and also a tender one, providing sufficient fat is used and the dough is not overhandled.

While most pie shells are made using flour as the main ingredient, many "crumb" crusts are made using crushed wafer-type cookies, crackers, or ready-to-eat dry cereals. Meringue pie shells are also made using egg whites as their main ingredient. Baked meringue shells are usually filled with custard or fruit fillings or with ice cream.

Basic (plain) pastry may be prepared using several methods:

Method I — Cold shortening (lard, vegetable or all-purpose shortening, butter or margarine, or a combination of several shortenings) is cut into a mixture of flour and salt, using a pastry blender or two knives. Then only enough water is added to hold the mixture together to form a ball.

Method II — Cooking or salad oil (not olive oil) is thoroughly beaten with icy-cold water, then combined with flour and salt, mixing only until flour is moistened enough to hold mixture together and shape into a ball.

Method III — Boiling water is added to cold shortening (not oil), mixing with a fork until mixture is creamy and thickened. Flour with salt is added, stirring only until mixture can be shaped into a ball.

Today's homemaker has available on her grocers' shelves a number of packaged pie crust mixes. These are not only timesavers, but their uniformity aids the homemaker in making excellent pastry products.

TECHNIQUES FOR MAKING PIES

(Read also *Use Correct Techniques, page 10*.)

Assemble utensils — A pastry blender cuts shortening into flour evenly and quickly. A pastry canvas and a stockinet-covered rolling pin help prevent pastry from sticking to surface when rolling it out. A floured canvas also requires less flour for rolling out the dough than when rolling on a floured board.

Select pie pans of proper size — Measure inside from rim to rim.

To measure dry ingredients, liquids, and fats, see *page 10*.

Use only enough water to hold dough together to form a smooth ball. Too much moisture tends to cause shrinkage in the pie shell and also results in a less tender pastry. Avoid overmixing.

Chill pastry dough in refrigerator. This is especially advisable if the room is warm. Chilling will aid in insuring a more tender pastry.

To roll pastry for 1-crust pie, shape the dough into a slightly flattened ball. Put onto floured surface and gently roll with rolling pin from center to edge, keeping dough the same thickness throughout. Test the thickness of dough by pressing with finger; it should make only a slight dent. Roll into a circle about 1½ inches larger in diameter than the diameter of pie pan (measuring from outer rim of pan). Fold dough in half; transfer to pie pan; unfold and fit loosely into pan, pressing gently against bottom and sides to remove any air bubbles. Do not stretch the dough. Handle carefully to avoid tearing dough. If cracks or tears do occur, mend them by pressing the pastry together or by patching with another piece of dough. Cracks in the bottom permit the filling to soak through and cause the pie to stick to the pan. Allowing 1 inch pastry beyond rim of pan, trim evenly with kitchen shears. Fold the overhung pastry back and under, then press to itself to form a stand-up edge.

Flute the edge by pressing index finger on edge of pastry and pinch pastry with thumb and index finger of other hand. Lift fingers and repeat procedure to flute around entire edge. For other edgings, see *page 457*.

Prick pastry shell thoroughly with a fork before baking to prevent buckling and large blisters from forming while pie shell is baking. If blisters do occur during first few minutes of baking, prick them. Omit pricking if the pie filling is to be baked with the pie shell.

To roll pastry for a 2-crust pie, divide the dough almost in half, leaving the slightly larger portion for the top crust. Refrigerate the larger portion until ready to roll out. Roll the bottom crust, following directions for 1-crust pie, except do not allow the extra pastry for tucking under itself; instead, trim the crust even with edge of pan.

To complete 2-crust pie, add the filling and moisten the edge of bottom crust with water. Roll the remaining dough into a circle about 1 inch larger in diameter than diameter of pan. Fold in half and place carefully over filling; gently press edges of top and bottom crust together. Tuck the extra pastry under edge of bottom crust. Seal by fluting edges together or press edges with a fork. Cut enough slits in top crust to allow steam to escape while pie is baking.

TECHNIQUES FOR MAKING
SOFT MERINGUES AND PIE FILLINGS

To beat whole eggs, egg whites, and egg yolks, see *page 10*.

To prepare meringue, begin adding sugar gradually to egg whites as soon as they have been beaten until frothy. Adding sugar at an early stage lessens the tendency toward formation of syrup beads and leaking of meringue after baking. Beating in the sugar instead of folding it in gives a more stable meringue. Beat meringue until stiff peaks are formed. Generally 2 tablespoons sugar per egg

white is the proportion used for soft meringues. Too much sugar tends to produce beading and results in a meringue with a sticky crust; too little sugar results in a less tender meringue that is less fluffy in appearance and flat in taste.

Seal meringue to edge of crust to help prevent meringue from shrinking.

To bake meringue topping on pies a high temperature (425° to 450°F) for 5 to 6 minutes may be used if pie is to be served soon after baking. A moderate temperature (350°F) for about 15 minutes, or until meringue is delicately browned, is recommended if pie is to stand for several hours. The meringue must be cooked through to avoid a tendency to "weep" next to filling, in which case the topping may slide off when pie is cut.

Cook cream filling by vigorously stirring about 3 tablespoons of hot filling mixture into beaten egg yolks and immediately blending into mixture in top of double boiler or heavy saucepan. This method blends the egg yolks evenly into the hot mixture without lowering the temperature. For maximum thickening power of the egg the temperature of the mixture must not be lowered. Help prevent the filling from becoming thin and runny after standing a short time (when it was once of serving consistency) by cooking the mixture 3 to 5 minutes over simmering water or about 3 minutes over direct heat after the egg yolks have been blended in.

High-acid fruit or fruit juice fillings (such as lemon, lime, or strawberry) usually require more cornstarch or flour than other fillings because of the thinning effect of the acid of the fruit or fruit juice upon starch when subjected to heat. For example, lemon fillings should call for the lemon juice to be blended in after the mixture has been cooked and removed from heat; this ensures a filling which should not thin.

Cool cream filling by covering cooked filling and cooling slightly, stirring occasionally to prevent film from forming; cool to lukewarm in refrigerator. (Cooling filling before turning into pie shell helps prevent soaking of crust.) Turn filling into baked and cooled pie shell and chill in refrigerator until ready to serve.

Thoroughly mix fruit and sugar-flour mixture for fruit filled pie to prevent hard sugar lumps in baked pie and produce even thickening.

Baking fruit pies at two temperatures helps to prevent soaking of crust; higher temperature sets crust, lower temperature finishes baking pie.

To prevent soaking of crust of a custard pie, (1) scald milk before adding to other ingredients as this shortens the time for the custard to set during baking; (2) bake pie shell and custard separately, then slip custard into shell (see *Slipped Custard Pie, page 470*).

Keep cooled custard-type, cream, whipped cream topped and filled pies in refrigerator until ready to serve; return any leftover pie to refrigerator. *Do not allow to stand at room temperature* because these pies spoil easily and have been known to cause food poisoning if not adequately refrigerated.

MERINGUE I

3 egg whites 6 tablespoons sugar
⅛ teaspoon salt

1. Beat egg whites with salt until frothy; gradually add sugar, beating constantly until stiff peaks are formed.
2. Pile meringue lightly over pie filling. Swirl with back of spoon; seal meringue to edge of crust.
3. Bake at 350°F about 15 minutes, or until meringue is delicately browned. Or, if serving pie soon after baking, bake at 450°F about 5 minutes.

TOPPING FOR ONE 9-INCH PIE

MERINGUE II: Follow recipe for Meringue I. Decrease egg whites to 2 and sugar to ¼ cup.

TOPPING FOR ONE 8-INCH PIE

FESTIVE MERINGUE: Follow recipe for Meringue I or II. Before baking, sprinkle *slivered almonds*, finely chopped *crystallized ginger*, or finely chopped *candied cherries* over meringue.

HELPFUL HINTS ABOUT PIES

• To prevent juice from cooking out of pies into the oven, place a strip of dampened cloth or pastry tape around the edge of the pie or place a tiny funnel or 4-inch stick of uncooked macaroni in the center of the pie.

• To avoid shrinkage of a pastry crust, roll out the pastry, place in a pie pan without stretching, and set aside about 5 minutes before fluting the edge. Or place a second pie pan on the pastry before baking. Remove the second pan after about 10 minutes of baking to allow the pastry shell to brown on the inside.

• To make a crunchy topping for a 2-crust pie, combine 1 tablespoon butter or other shortening, 1 tablespoon sugar, ⅛ teaspoon grated lemon peel, few grains salt, and 3 tablespoons flour; mix until consistency of coarse crumbs. Brush top of unbaked pie with milk, then sprinkle with the crumb mixture. Bake pie as directed in recipe.

PASTRY CRUSTS

PASTRY I FOR 1-CRUST PIE

1 cup sifted all-purpose flour
½ teaspoon salt
⅓ cup lard, vegetable shortening, or all-purpose shortening
2 to 3 tablespoons cold water

1. Sift flour and salt together into a bowl. Cut in shortening with pastry blender or two knives until pieces are the size of small peas.
2. Sprinkle the water over mixture, a teaspoonful at a time, mixing lightly with a fork after each addition. Add only enough water to hold pastry together. Work quickly; do not overhandle. Shape into a ball and flatten on a lightly floured surface.
3. Roll from center to edge into a round about ⅛ inch thick and about 1 inch larger than overall size of pan.
4. Loosen pastry from surface with spatula and fold in quarters. Gently lay pastry in pan and unfold it, fitting it to pan so it is not stretched.
5. Trim edge with scissors or sharp knife so pastry extends about ½ inch beyond edge of pie pan. Fold extra pastry under at edge, and flute.
6. Thoroughly prick bottom and sides of shell with a fork. (Omit pricking if filling is to be baked in shell.)
7. Bake at 450°F 10 to 15 minutes, or until crust is light golden brown.
8. Cool on rack. ONE 8- OR 9-INCH PIE SHELL

PASTRY FOR 2-CRUST PIE: Double the recipe for Pastry I. Divide pastry into halves and shape into a ball. Roll each ball as in Pastry I. For top crust, roll out one ball of pastry and cut 1 inch larger than pie pan. Slit pastry with knife in several places to allow steam to escape during baking. Gently fold in half and set aside while rolling bottom crust. Roll second ball of pastry and gently fit pastry into pie pan; avoid stretching. Trim pastry with scissors or sharp knife around edge of pan. Do not prick. Fill as directed in specific recipe. Moisten edge with water for a tight seal. Carefully arrange top crust over filling. Gently press edges to seal. Fold extra top pastry under bottom pastry. Flute or complete with desired *Pastry Edging, page 457.*

PASTRY FOR 1-CRUST 10-INCH PIE: Follow recipe for Pastry I. Increase flour to 1⅓ cups, salt to ¾ teaspoon, shortening to ½ cup, and water to about 3 tablespoons.

PASTRY FOR LATTICE-TOP PIE: Prepare pastry as in recipe for Pastry for 2-Crust Pie. Divide pastry into halves and shape into two balls. Follow directions in Pastry I for rolling pastry. Roll one pastry ball for bottom crust; fit gently into pie pan. Roll the second pastry ball into a rectangle about ⅛ inch thick and at least 10 inches long. Cut pastry with a sharp knife or pastry wheel into strips that are about ½ inch wide. Fill pastry shell as directed in specific recipe. *To Make a Lattice Top:* Cross two strips over the pie at the center. Working out from center to edge of pie, add the remaining strips one at a time, weaving the strips under and over each other in crisscross fashion; leave about 1 inch between the strips. Or, if desired, arrange half the strips over top, twisting each strip several times. Repeat using remaining pastry strips and placing them diagonally to first strips. Trim the strips even with the edge of the pastry. Moisten the edge of pastry shell with water for a tight seal. Fold edge of bottom crust over ends of strips. Flute or complete with desired *Pastry Edging, page 457.* Bake as directed in specific recipe.

PASTRY FOR LITTLE PIES AND TARTS: Prepare recipe for Pastry I. Roll pastry ⅛ inch thick and cut about ½ inch larger than overall size of pans. Carefully fit rounds into pans without stretching. Fold excess pastry under at edge. Flute or complete with desired *Pastry Edging, page 457.* Prick bottom and sides of shell with fork. (Omit pricking if filling is to be baked in shell.) Bake at 450°F 8 to 10 minutes, or until light golden brown. Cool on wire rack. THREE 6-INCH PIES, SIX 3½ INCH TARTS, OR NINE 1½-INCH TARTS

PASTRY FOR ROSE-PETAL TARTS: Double recipe for Pastry I. Roll pastry ⅛ inch thick. Cut pastry into rounds, using 2½-inch round cutter. Place one pastry round in bottom of each 2¾-inch muffin-pan well. Fit 5 pastry rounds around inside of each well, overlapping edges. Press overlapping edges together. Prick bottom and sides well with fork. Bake at 450°F 8 to 10 minutes, or until light golden brown. Cool on wire rack. Carefully remove from pans. SIX 2¾-INCH TARTS

SPICE PASTRY FOR 1-CRUST PIE: Follow recipe for Pastry I. Sift *2 tablespoons sugar, ¼ teaspoon cinnamon, ⅛ teaspoon ginger, and ⅛ teaspoon cloves* with flour and salt. Substitute *orange juice* for cold water.

CHEESE PASTRY FOR 1-CRUST PIE: Follow recipe for Pastry I. Cut in *½ cup (2 ounces) finely shredded Cheddar cheese* with the lard or shortening.

CHEESE PASTRY FOR 2-CRUST PIE: Follow recipe for Pastry for 2-Crust Pie. Cut in *1 cup (4 ounces) finely shredded Cheddar cheese* with the lard or shortening.

ROLLED OAT PASTRY FOR 1-CRUST PIE: Follow recipe for Pastry I. Mix *½ cup uncooked rolled oats* with the flour. Increase shortening to ½ cup. Bake at 400°F 15 minutes or until crust is lightly browned.

PASTRY TOPPING: Follow recipe for Pastry I. Roll out pastry 1 inch larger than overall size of baking dish or casserole and cut slits near center to allow steam to escape. Bake as directed in specific recipe.

PASTRY II FOR 1-CRUST PIE

1 cup sifted all-purpose flour	5 tablespoons butter
1½ teaspoon sugar	2 to 3 tablespoons icy cold water
⅛ teaspoon salt	

1. Sift flour, sugar, and salt together into a bowl. Cut in butter with a pastry blender or two knives until pieces are the size of small peas.

2. Proceed as in *Pastry I for 1-Crust Pie, page 453.*
ONE 8- OR 9-INCH PIE SHELL

PROBLEMS WITH PASTRY

The Problem	The Causes	The Prevention
Tough crust	Not enough fat	Use ⅓ cup fat to 1 cup flour for plain pastry.
	Too much liquid	Add liquid slowly; mix just enough to moisten flour.
	Too much flour for rolling	Roll between sheets of waxed paper or on lightly floured surface.
Pastry does not brown	Oven temperature too low	Be sure oven is heating properly; follow directions for correcting baking temperatures for individual pies.
Crust too solid	Not enough fat, or over-mixing, or temperature too low	Same as for tough crust; also, mix fat until fine particles and some large particles; adjust oven temperature.
Soggy undercrust	Oven temperature too low	Same as browning problem.
	Pie placed too high in oven	Make sure top of pie is in center of oven.
	Too much filling or filling too moist	Use tested recipes. Mix fresh (juicy) fruits with flour; thicken liquid from canned fruits with flour or cornstarch.
	Soaking started before baking	Chill unbaked pie shell 15 minutes before making filling; add filling just before baking. Or bake undercrust 10 minutes before adding filling.
Crust burns easily	Too much fat and/or pastry rolled too thin	Same as tough crust; roll to ⅛ inch.
Crust doughy, too thick and soft	Not enough fat and/or too much liquid; ingredients, especially fat and liquid, not cold enough	Use standard recipes and measure accurately. Use iced water (except for hot water pastry).
	Oven temperature too low	Adjust oven temperature.
	Pastry rolled too thick	Roll as recipe directs.
Baked pastry shell shrinks	Pastry stretched in pan before rolling	Fit rolled pastry into pan loosely.
	Oven temperature too low	Bake at 450°F 10 to 12 minutes.
	Overmixing	Same as for tough crust.
Baked pastry shell blisters	Pastry stretched in pan	Same as for shrinking.
	Pastry not pricked enough	Prick in many places.
	Oven temperature too low	Same as for shrinking.

PASTRY III FOR 1-CRUST PIE

1 cup sifted all-purpose flour	¼ cup cooking or salad oil (not olive oil)
½ teaspoon salt	2½ tablespoons icy cold water

1.   Sift flour and salt together into a bowl. Beat oil and water together with a fork until thickened and creamy.

2.   Immediately pour the oil-water mixture over entire surface of flour. Toss and mix with fork until all flour is moistened.

3.   Form dough into ball. Place dough between squares of waxed paper. Roll lightly from center to edge into a 12-inch round. Peel off top sheet of paper.

4.   Place pastry in a pie pan; peel off remaining waxed paper. Fit into pan; fold edge under, and flute.

5.   If pastry is to be baked before filling, prick bottom and sides with a fork.

6.   Bake at 475°F 10 to 12 minutes, or until golden brown.   ONE 8- OR 9-INCH PIE SHELL

PASTRY FOR HIGH-COLLARED 1-CRUST PIE

1⅓ cups sifted all-purpose flour	½ cup all-vegetable shortening (not oil)
½ teaspoon salt	2½ tablespoons cold water

1.   Sift the flour and salt together into a bowl. Cut in shortening with pastry blender or two knives until particles resemble coarse crumbs.

2.   Proceed as directed in *Pastry I for 1-Crust Pie, page 453*, through step 6, except roll pastry 1½ inches larger than pan. Flute edge forming a high collar.   ONE 9-INCH PIE SHELL

CAKE FLOUR PASTRY

2 cups sifted cake flour	3 to 6 teaspoons icy cold water
¼ teaspoon salt	
½ cup firm butter or margarine	

1.   Mix the flour and salt in a bowl. Cut in the butter with a pastry blender. Stirring with a fork, add enough water until pastry can be pressed into a ball.

2.   Roll out on a floured surface and fit into a 10-inch pie pan, being careful not to stretch pastry. Flute edge as desired.   ONE 10-INCH PIE SHELL

FILBERT PASTRY

1⅓ cups sifted all-purpose flour	½ cup all-vegetable shortening (not oil)
½ cup toasted filberts, finely chopped	¼ cup water
¾ teaspoon salt	Sugar

1.   Mix flour, filberts, and salt together in a bowl. Cut in shortening with pastry blender or two knives until mixture is crumbly.

2.   Proceed as directed in *Pastry I for 1-Crust Pie, page 453*, through step 6, except roll pastry 1½ inches larger than pan.

3.   Line inside of pie shell with a sheet of aluminum foil or waxed paper. Half fill with *dried beans or rice.*

4.   Bake at 425°F 10 minutes. Remove beans and paper. Sprinkle shell lightly with sugar. Bake 5 minutes, or until pie shell is lightly browned. Cool.   ONE 9-INCH PIE SHELL

PEANUT BUTTER PASTRY

1½ cups sifted all-purpose flour	3 tablespoons peanut butter
½ teaspoon salt	2 to 3 tablespoons cold water
½ cup vegetable shortening or all-purpose shortening	

1.   Sift flour and salt together into a bowl. Add a blend of shortening and peanut butter. Proceed as in *Pastry I for 1-Crust Pie, page 453*, using a 9- or 10-inch pie pan.

2.   Bake at 450°F 10 minutes.

          ONE 9- OR 10-INCH PIE SHELL

SOUR CREAM PASTRY

1 cup sifted all-purpose flour	4½ tablespoons dairy sour cream
½ teaspoon salt	1 tablespoon butter or margarine, cut in small pieces
¼ cup butter or margarine, chilled and cut in pieces	

1.   Sift flour and salt together into a bowl. Using

pastry blender or two knives, cut ¼ cup butter into flour until pieces are the size of peas.

2.   Blend in sour cream, a little at a time, until pastry holds together; mix lightly with a fork after each addition. Add only enough sour cream to hold pastry together; do not overhandle.

3.   Shape pastry into a ball and flatten on a lightly floured surface. Roll into a rectangle about ½ inch thick.

4.   Dot two thirds of the pastry with the 1 tablespoon butter. Cover the center third of dough with the unbuttered third; fold remaining third over to form three thicknesses.

5.   Roll into a rectangle ¼ inch thick and repeat folding to form three thicknesses. Chill thoroughly, about 30 minutes.

6.   Proceed as in *Pastry I for 1-Crust Pie, page 453.*   ONE 8- OR 9-INCH PIE SHELL

BUTTER PASTRY FOR TARTS

1½ cups sifted all-purpose flour	1 egg yolk
⅛ teaspoon salt	2 to 3 tablespoons cold water
½ cup butter	

1.   Combine flour and salt in a bowl. Using a pastry blender or two knives, cut in butter as for pastry; mix in the egg yolk.

2.   Add water gradually, mixing with a fork until pastry holds together. Shape dough into a ball; wrap and refrigerate until thoroughly chilled.

3.   Using one half of dough at a time, roll about ⅛ inch thick on a lightly floured surface. Using a scalloped cookie cutter, cut out 3-inch rounds of dough.

4.   Gently fit pastry rounds into 1¾-inch muffin pan wells; prick pastry with a fork.

5.   Bake at 375°F about 15 minutes or until lightly browned.

ABOUT 2 DOZEN TART SHELLS

PASTRY SPECIALTIES

Put ½ *regular package pie crust mix* or crumble *1 stick pie crust mix* into a bowl. Stir in additional ingredients as listed or as desired. Follow package directions for quantity and method of adding liquid, rolling dough, and baking pie shell.

Almond Pastry: *⅓ to ½ cup finely chopped unblanched almonds.*

Coconut Pastry: *½ cup flaked or chopped shredded coconut.*

Cheese Pastry: *½ cup shredded Swiss or Parmesan cheese.*

Orange Pastry: *¾ teaspoon grated orange peel*, and substitute *orange juice* for liquid suggested.

Lemon Pastry: Follow directions for Orange Pastry. Substitute *lemon peel and juice* for orange. Just before baking, brush with *melted butter or margarine* and sprinkle generously with *sugar*.

Puff Pastry: Prepare pie crust mix and roll out according to package directions. Dot with pieces of *butter or margarine* (3 tablespoons). Fold so the two sides meet in center. Seal by pressing edges with fingers. Fold ends to center and seal. Wrap in moisture-vaporproof material and chill. Follow package directions for rolling out, fluting, and baking pastry. Press fluted points firmly over edge of pan to secure pastry. For a 2-crust pie, double recipe and proceed according to package directions.

Toppers: Prepare any of the above pastries and cut out fancy shapes in sizes appropriate to top pies and tarts. Bake on an ungreased baking sheet.

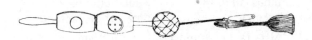

Pastry Edgings

For an attractive edge on a 1-crust pie, trim excess pastry to ½ inch beyond edge of pan. Fold pastry under, allowing it to rest on pie pan and extend just to edge of pan; complete pastry edging as desired.

For a 2-crust pie, trim edge of bottom pastry even with pie pan; fill pie; arrange top pastry over filling. Put top crust in place. Gently press edges of bottom and top crusts together for a tight seal. Fold extra pastry of top crust under edge of bottom crust; then flute as desired.

Fluted edge—Press index finger on edge of pastry, then pinch pastry with thumb and index finger of other hand. Lift fingers and repeat procedure to flute entire edge.

Diagonal flute—Place index fingers diagonally and slightly apart on edge of pastry. Push one finger toward the other, bringing pastry up to form a flute. Lift fingers and repeat to flute entire edge.

Twisted flute (also called rope or shell edge)—Hold edge of pastry firmly between thumbs and knuckle of index finger. Press and twist the fingers toward center of pan. Lift fingers and repeat procedure to flute entire edge.

Fork flute — Press edge of pastry with four-tined fork at ½-inch intervals. To prevent sticking, occasionally dip fork in flour.

Coin edge — Trim pastry with scissors or sharp knife around edge of pan. Using a ¾-inch cookie cutter or a large thimble, cut rounds from remaining pastry. Brush rim of pastry shell with water and overlap rounds, pressing lightly.

Leaf edge — Trim pastry with scissors or sharp knife around edge of pan. Using a waxed-paper pattern as a guide, cut out leaves from remaining pastry. Brush rim of pastry shell with water and overlap leaves, pressing lightly.

Designers edge — Using the tip of an inverted teaspoon, mark edge of pastry as desired.

Twisted edge — Prepare extra pastry. Roll pastry into a rectangle ⅛ inch thick. Cut strips about ¼ inch wide. With strips on flat surface, carefully twist two strips together loosely. Repeat twisting with other strips. Brush rim of pastry shell with water and place the twisted strips on rim. Join by overlapping and pressing ends of strips together.

Braided edge — Prepare extra pastry. Roll pastry into a rectangle ⅛ inch thick. Cut 9 strips about 14 inches long and ¼ inch wide. With strips on flat surface, carefully braid three strips. Repeat braiding using remaining strips. Brush rim of pastry shell with water and place the braids on rim. Press gently to seal to rim. Join by overlapping and pressing ends of braids together.

PIE SHELLS

GRAHAM CRACKER CRUMB CRUST

1⅓ cups graham cracker crumbs (16 to 18 crackers)	¼ cup sugar
	¼ cup butter or margarine, softened

1. Mix cracker crumbs with sugar. Using a fork or pastry blender, blend butter evenly with crumb mixture.
2. With back of spoon, press crumb mixture firmly into an even layer on bottom and sides of an 8- or 9-inch pie pan. Level edges of the pie shell.
3. Bake at 375°F 8 minutes. Cool thoroughly before filling. ONE 8- OR 9-INCH PIE SHELL

10-INCH GRAHAM CRACKER CRUST: Follow recipe for Graham Cracker Crumb Crust. Increase crumbs to 1⅔ cups, sugar to 5 tablespoons, and butter to 5 tablespoons. Press into a 10-inch pie pan.

NUT-CRUMB CRUST: Follow recipe for Graham Cracker Crumb Crust. Decrease graham cracker crumbs to 1 cup and mix in *½ cup finely chopped nuts.*

COOKIE CRUMB CRUST: Follow recipe for Graham Cracker Crumb Crust. Substitute *1⅓ cups cookie crumbs* (about twenty-four 2⅛-inch cookies, such as vanilla or chocolate wafers) for graham cracker crumbs. Omit sugar. Bake vanilla crumb crust at 375°F 8 minutes; bake chocolate crumb crust at 325°F 10 minutes. *For a 10-inch cookie crumb crust:* Increase cookie crumbs to 1¾ cups and butter to 5 tablespoons.

GRAHAM CRACKER TART SHELLS: Follow recipe for Graham Cracker Crumb Crust. Line eight 2½-inch muffin-pan wells with paper baking cups. Using back of spoon, press crumb mixture firmly into an even layer on bottom and sides of the paper cups. Bake at 375°F 6 minutes. Cool thoroughly on wire rack; remove paper baking cups.

PEANUT BUTTER-CEREAL CRUST

Ice cream frozen in this crust makes a delicious pie.

⅓ cup peanut butter	2 cups oven-toasted rice cereal
⅓ cup corn syrup	

Blend peanut butter and corn syrup in a bowl. Add the cereal and mix until well coated. Turn mixture into a buttered 9-inch pie pan and press firmly and evenly on bottom and sides. Chill until firm.

ONE 9-INCH PIE SHELL

CEREAL CRUMB CRUST

4 cups ready-to-eat high protein cereal, finely crushed	¼ cup butter or margarine, softened
	2 tablespoons sugar

1. Blend all ingredients until well mixed. Reserve 2 tablespoons mixture for topping. Turn crumb mixture into a 9-inch pie pan and press firmly and evenly on bottom and sides. Chill.
2. Fill as desired and sprinkle with reserved crumbs. ONE 9-INCH PIE SHELL

COCONUT-CEREAL CRUMB CRUST: Follow recipe for Cereal Crumb Crust. Stir *½ cup flaked coconut* into crumb mixture.

CHOCOLATE-CEREAL FLAKE CRUST

1 cup (6 oz.) semisweet chocolate pieces	2 cups presweetened corn flakes
2 tablespoons butter or margarine	

1.   Melt chocolate and butter together over hot, not boiling, water.
2.   Remove from heat and mix in the cereal, stirring until flakes are well coated.
3.   Turn mixture into a buttered 8-inch pie pan and press firmly and evenly on bottom and sides. Set in a cool place until firm.
4.   Fill with desired cream filling.

ONE 8-INCH PIE SHELL

CHOCOLATE-RICE CEREAL CRUST: Follow recipe for Chocolate Cereal Flake Crust. Substitute *2 cups oven-toasted rice cereal*, slightly crushed, for the flakes. Use a 9-inch pie pan.

CHOCOLATE-COCONUT CRUST

2 oz. (2 sq.) unsweetened chocolate	⅔ cup confectioners' sugar
2 tablespoons butter or margarine	¾ cup flaked coconut, toasted
2 tablespoons hot milk	¾ cup corn flakes

1.   Heat chocolate and butter in a small heavy saucepan over low heat, stirring until well blended.
2.   Stir the hot milk into the confectioners' sugar; blend into the chocolate. Mix in the coconut and corn flakes evenly.
3.   Spread on the bottom and sides of a buttered 8-inch pie pan. Chill until firm.   ONE 8-INCH PIE SHELL

FILBERT CRUST

1¼ cups unblanched filberts, finely ground	¼ cup sugar
	¼ cup butter or margarine

1.   Mix the filberts and sugar in a bowl. Cut in the butter with a pastry blender or two knives. Turn mixture into a 9- or 10-inch pie pan; press firmly against the bottom and sides of pan.

2.   Bake at 375°F 5 minutes, until lightly browned. Cool and chill.   ONE 9- OR 10-INCH PIE SHELL

BRAZIL NUT CRUST: Follow recipe for Filbert Crust. Substitute *1¼ cups unblanched Brazil nuts* for the filberts.

SALTED PEANUT CRUST: Follow recipe for Filbert Crust. Substitute *1¼ cups salted peanuts*, coarsely ground, for the filberts.

MERINGUE SHELL

4 egg whites	1⅓ cups sugar
½ teaspoon cream of tartar	½ teaspoon cider vinegar

1.   Beat egg whites with cream of tartar until frothy; gradually add about one half of the sugar, beating constantly. Blend in the vinegar and gradually add remaining sugar, continuing to beat until stiff peaks are formed.
2.   Spread a 1-inch layer of meringue on bottom of a lightly greased 9-inch pie pan.
3.   Pile remaining meringue around edge of pan and swirl with a spatula to form the sides of the shell.
4.   Bake at 250°F about 2¼ hours, or until meringue is dry.
5.   Cool meringue in pan on a rack; store, if desired, in an airtight container.

ONE 9-INCH MERINGUE SHELL

ALMOND MERINGUE SHELL: Follow recipe for Meringue Shell. Blanch, toast, and grate *½ cup almonds*; fold into stiffly beaten egg white mixture.

10-INCH MERINGUE SHELL: Follow recipe for Meringue Shell. Increase egg whites to 6, cream of tartar to ¾ teaspoon, sugar to 2 cups, and vinegar to ¾ teaspoon.

COCONUT MERINGUE SHELL
A delicate shell for a party pie.

⅓ cup (2 to 3) egg whites	1 teaspoon lemon juice
⅛ teaspoon salt	⅛ teaspoon almond extract
¼ teaspoon cream of tartar	1 cup sugar
	⅓ cup flaked coconut

1.   Beat egg whites until frothy. Beat in the salt, cream of tartar, lemon juice, and extract; gradually add sugar, beating constantly until stiff peaks are formed.

2.   Reserve about ⅔ cup meringue; set aside.
3.   Fold coconut into remaining meringue. Spread over bottom and up sides of a lightly greased 9-inch pie pan.
4.   Using a pastry bag and star decorating tube, pipe the reserved meringue around top edge of shell, forming rosettes.
5.   Bake at 325°F 40 to 45 minutes, or until crisp and very lightly browned.

ONE 9-INCH MERINGUE SHELL

FRUIT PIES

APPLE PIE

Pastry for 2-crust pie	1 teaspoon ground cinnamon
6 to 8 tart cooking apples	¼ teaspoon ground nutmeg
1 tablespoon lemon juice	⅛ teaspoon salt
1 cup sugar	2 tablespoons butter or margarine
3 to 3½ tablespoons flour	

1.   Prepare a 9-inch pie shell; roll out remaining pastry for top crust. Set aside.
2.   Wash, quarter, core, pare, and thinly slice the apples. Turn into a bowl and drizzle with lemon juice. Toss lightly with mixture of sugar, flour, cinnamon, nutmeg, and salt.
3.   Turn mixture into unbaked pie shell. Dot apples with butter. Complete as for a 2-crust pie.
4.   Bake at 450°F 10 minutes; reduce oven temperature to 350°F and bake about 40 minutes, or until crust is lightly browned. Serve warm or cold.

ONE 9-INCH PIE

FULL-O'-FLAVOR APPLE PIE

Pastry for 2-crust pie	¼ teaspoon ground nutmeg
2 cans (20 oz. each) sliced apples packed in syrup	⅛ teaspoon salt
2 tablespoons lemon juice	2 tablespoons butter or margarine
½ cup firmly packed brown sugar	½ cup confectioners' sugar
2 tablespoons flour	1 tablespoon light cream
1 teaspoon ground cinnamon	¼ teaspoon vanilla extract

1.   Prepare a 9-inch pie shell; roll out remaining pastry for top crust. Set aside.
2.   Turn apples into a large bowl; lightly mix in the lemon juice. Add a mixture of brown sugar, flour, cinnamon, nutmeg, and salt; toss lightly.

3.   Spoon the apple mixture into unbaked pie shell, heaping slightly at the center. Dot with butter. Complete as directed for 2-crust pie.
4.   Bake at 450°F 10 minutes; reduce oven temperature to 350°F and bake 30 to 40 minutes, or until crust is lightly browned.
5.   While pie is baking, prepare glaze by thoroughly mixing the remaining ingredients.
6.   When pie is baked, remove from oven and set on wire rack. Using a pastry brush, evenly brush the glaze over top of pie. Serve warm or cool.

ONE 9-INCH PIE

VICTORIA PIE

A recipe from Rickey Restaurant Studio Inn, Palo Alto, California.

5 large tart apples, cut in eighths, pared, and cored	1 unbaked 10-in. pie shell
½ cup water	½ cup sugar
½ cup dark seedless raisins	4 oz. (½ cup) almond paste
⅓ to ½ cup sugar	6 egg yolks, beaten
½ teaspoon ground cinnamon	⅓ cup heavy cream
	Few grains salt

1.   Combine apples and water in a saucepan; cover and cook until apples are just tender.
2.   Add raisins and a mixture of ⅓ to ½ cup sugar and cinnamon; stir until sugar is dissolved. Cool slightly.
3.   Turn apple-raisin mixture into pie shell.
4.   Bake at 400°F 20 minutes.
5.   Meanwhile, add the ½ cup sugar to almond paste gradually, beating thoroughly; add beaten egg yolks in thirds, beating well after each addition. Blend in the cream and salt.
6.   Remove pie from oven; reduce oven temperature to 350°F. Spread almond mixture evenly over top. Return pie to oven and bake 10 to 15 minutes, or until top is lightly browned.

7.   Remove to wire rack. Cool pie completely.

ONE 10-INCH PIE

APPLEJACK APPLE PIE

Cheese Pastry for 2-
Crust Pie, *page 454*
5 cups sliced pared
apples
1 cup sugar
3 tablespoons
cornstarch
¼ teaspoon salt

½ teaspoon ground
nutmeg
¼ teaspoon ground
cinnamon
⅓ cup applejack
4 teaspoons currant
jelly
2 tablespoons butter or
margarine

1.   Prepare a 9-inch pie shell; roll out remaining pastry for top crust. Set aside.
2.   Gently toss apples with a mixture of sugar, cornstarch, salt, nutmeg, and cinnamon. Pour a mixture of the applejack and jelly over apples and toss lightly.
3.   Turn into the unbaked pie shell, heaping slightly at center; dot with butter. Complete as directed.
4.   Bake at 450°F 10 minutes; reduce oven temperature to 350°F and bake 30 to 40 minutes, or until pastry is lightly browned. Serve slightly warm.

ONE 9-INCH PIE

DUTCH APPLE PIE

3 to 4 (about 1 lb.)
tart cooking apples
1 unbaked 9-in. pie
shell
1 egg, slightly beaten
1 cup heavy cream
1½ teaspoons vanilla
extract
1 cup sugar
3 tablespoons flour
⅛ teaspoon salt

½ teaspoon ground
cinnamon
¼ teaspoon ground
nutmeg
4 teaspoons butter or
margarine
½ cup walnuts, coarsely
chopped
¾ cup shredded sharp
Cheddar cheese

1.   Wash, quarter, core, pare, and thinly slice apples. Turn slices into unbaked pie shell.
2.   Blend the egg, cream, and extract. Gradually add a mixture of sugar, flour, salt, cinnamon, and nutmeg, mixing well. Pour over apples in pie shell. Dot with butter. Sprinkle walnuts over top.
3.   Bake at 450°F 10 minutes; reduce oven temperature to 350°F and bake 35 to 40 minutes, or until apples are tender and top is lightly browned.
4.   Remove from oven and sprinkle cheese over top. Serve warm.

ONE 9-INCH PIE

MRS. EISENHOWER'S
DEEP-DISH APPLE PIE
A favorite recipe from the former First Lady.

Pastry for 1-crust pie
6 tart apples
½ cup sugar
½ cup firmly packed
brown sugar
½ teaspoon ground
nutmeg

Grated peel of 1 lemon
(about 1½ teaspoons)
Grated peel of 1 orange
(about 2 teaspoons)
3 tablespoons butter or
margarine

1.   Prepare pastry and roll out slightly larger than overall size of baking dish to be used. Prick in a design. Set aside.
2.   Pare and core apples; cut into eighths. Put into a greased deep 1½-quart baking dish.
3.   Combine sugars, nutmeg, and lemon and orange peels; sprinkle mixture over the apples. Dot with butter. Cover with the pastry.
4.   Bake at 425°F 40 to 45 minutes.

ABOUT 6 SERVINGS

FRESH APRICOT PIE

Pastry for Lattice-Top
Pie, *page 454*
1 cup sugar
⅓ cup all-purpose flour
⅛ teaspoon ground
nutmeg

4 cups fresh apricots,
halved and pitted
2 tablespoons butter or
margarine
2 tablespoons orange
juice

1.   Prepare a 9-inch pie shell and lattice strips for top crust; set aside.
2.   Combine sugar, flour, and nutmeg; spoon some into pie shell. Arrange apricots, cut side up, over bottom of shell. Sprinkle with remaining sugar mixture. Dot with butter and drizzle with orange juice. Complete as directed for lattice-top pie.
3.   Bake at 450°F 10 minutes; reduce oven temperature to 350°F and bake 30 to 35 minutes.

ONE 9-INCH PIE

FRESH RED RASPBERRY PIE

Pastry for 2-crust pie
5 cups red raspberries
1 tablespoon orange
juice

1 cup sugar
⅓ cup flour
¼ teaspoon salt

1.   Prepare an 8-inch pie shell; roll out remaining pastry for top crust. Set aside.
2.   Gently toss raspberries with orange juice and a mixture of the remaining ingredients.

3. Turn into unbaked pie shell, heaping slightly at center. Complete as directed for 2-crust pie.
4. Bake at 450°F for 10 minutes; reduce oven temperature to 350°F and bake 25 to 30 minutes, or until pastry is lightly browned. ONE 8-INCH PIE

FRESH BLUEBERRY PIE

Pastry for 2-crust pie
4 cups fresh blueberries
4 teaspoons lemon juice
¾ cup sugar
¼ cup flour
½ teaspoon ground cinnamon
¼ teaspoon ground nutmeg
⅛ teaspoon salt
1 teaspoon grated lemon peel
2 tablespoons butter or margarine

1. Prepare an 8-inch pie shell; roll out remaining pastry for top crust; set aside.
2. Rinse and drain blueberries. Toss gently with lemon juice, then with a mixture of the sugar, flour, cinnamon, nutmeg, salt, and lemon peel.
3. Turn into unbaked pie shell, heaping berries slightly at center; dot with butter. Complete as directed for 2-crust pie.
4. Bake at 450°F 10 minutes; reduce oven temperature to 350°F and bake 30 to 35 minutes, or until crust is lightly browned. Serve warm or cool.
ONE 8-INCH PIE

BRANDIED BLACKBERRY PIE

Pastry for Lattice-Top Pie, *page 454*
4 cups fresh ripe blackberries, rinsed and drained
1 cup sugar
3 tablespoons cornstarch
⅛ teaspoon salt
1 tablespoon grated orange peel
2 tablespoons butter or margarine
2 tablespoons blackberry-flavored brandy

1. Prepare an 8-inch pie shell and lattice strips for top crust; set aside.
2. Gently toss blackberries with a mixture of the sugar, cornstarch, salt, and orange peel.
3. Turn into unbaked pie shell, heaping berries slightly at center; dot with butter. Complete as directed for lattice-top pie.
4. Bake at 450°F 10 minutes; reduce oven temperature to 350°F and bake 25 to 30 minutes, or until pastry is lightly browned.
5. Drizzle brandy onto berries through lattice openings. Serve warm or cool. ONE 8-INCH PIE

SAUCY STRAWBERRY LATTICE PIE

Pastry for Lattice-Top Pie, *page 454*
1 qt. firm ripe strawberries, rinsed and hulled
1 cup sugar
3 tablespoons flour
½ teaspoon ground cinnamon
1 tablespoon lemon juice
3 tablespoons butter or margarine

1. Prepare a 9-inch pie shell; place in refrigerator to chill thoroughly.
2. Combine strawberries and a mixture of sugar, flour, and cinnamon in a large bowl. Let stand 5 minutes.
3. Meanwhile, roll out remaining pastry and cut lattice strips.
4. Mix lemon juice into strawberry mixture. Turn into chilled pie shell. Dot with butter. Top with pastry strips to form a lattice design; flute edge.
5. Bake at 450°F 10 minutes; reduce oven temperature to 375°F and bake 25 minutes, or until pastry is light brown.
6. Cool before serving. ONE 9-INCH PIE

GLAZED STRAWBERRY PIE

1 qt. strawberries, rinsed and hulled
6 tablespoons sugar
1½ tablespoons cornstarch
6 tablespoons water
1 teaspoon lemon juice
3 or 4 drops red food coloring
3 oz. cream cheese
1 tablespoon orange juice
1 baked 9-in. pie shell

1. Reserve 2 cups whole strawberries. Crush remaining strawberries with a fork; set aside.
2. Mix sugar and cornstarch thoroughly in a saucepan. Blend in the water. Stirring constantly, bring to boiling and boil for 3 minutes, or until clear.
3. Remove from heat; stir in crushed strawberries, lemon juice, and food coloring. Cool mixture slightly by setting pan in a bowl of ice and water. Cover and set aside.
4. Beat the cream cheese until softened, then beat in the orange juice until blended. Spread over bottom of baked pie shell. Turn whole strawberries into shell. Pour cooled strawberry mixture over berries. Chill in refrigerator.
5. If desired, serve with a *cream topping*.
ONE 9-INCH PIE

STRAWBERRY CRUMB PIE

6 cups halved fresh strawberries	Pastry for High-Collared 1-Crust Pie, *page 456*
¾ cup sugar	¼ cup packed light brown sugar
¼ cup quick-cooking tapioca	½ teaspoon ground cinnamon

1.   Toss strawberries with sugar and tapioca; set aside.

2.   Prepare pastry, reserving about ½ cup crumbs for topping, and make the pie shell. Turn strawberry mixture into shell. Cut an 8-inch round of aluminum foil and lay over filling.

3.   Bake at 400°F 35 minutes.

4.   Meanwhile, blend reserved flour mixture with brown sugar and cinnamon. Remove foil and sprinkle flour mixture evenly over pie. Continue baking 25 minutes, or until crust and topping are browned.

5.   Cool on wire rack. Serve with *whipped cream.*

ONE 9-INCH PIE

STRAWBERRY MAPLE CHEESE PIE

Pastry for High-Collared 1-Crust Pie, *page 456*	3 tablespoons maple syrup
4 oz. cream cheese, softened	½ cup dairy sour cream
	4 cups halved fresh strawberries

1.   Prepare pie shell, bake, and cool.

2.   Blend cream cheese with maple syrup; stir in sour cream. Pour into cooled pie shell, cover filling with waxed paper, and chill about 3 hours.

3.   Drizzle strawberries generously with maple syrup; chill.

4.   Top cheese filling with strawberries.

ONE 9-INCH PIE

LATTICE-TOP CHERRY PIE

¾ to 1 cup sugar	¼ teaspoon almond extract
2½ tablespoons cornstarch	4 or 5 drops red food coloring
⅛ teaspoon salt	Pastry for Lattice-Top Pie, *page 454*
2 cans (16 oz. each) pitted tart red cherries, drained (reserve ¾ cup liquid)	1 tablespoon butter or margarine
1 teaspoon lemon juice	

1.   Combine sugar, cornstarch, and salt in a heavy saucepan; stir in the reserved cherry liquid. Bring to boiling and boil 2 to 3 minutes, stirring constantly.

2.   Remove from heat; stir in lemon juice, extract, and food coloring, then the cherries. Set aside.

3.   Meanwhile, prepare an 8-inch pie shell and lattice strips for top crust; set aside.

4.   When filling is cool, spoon into unbaked pie shell. Dot with butter. Complete as directed for lattice-top pie.

5.   Bake at 450°F 10 minutes; reduce oven temperature to 350°F and bake about 35 minutes, or until pastry is lightly browned.

6.   Remove pie to wire rack to cool. ONE 8-INCH PIE

CRANBERRY-ORANGE PIE

Pastry for 1-crust pie	4 cups (1 lb.) cranberries, rinsed and drained
¼ teaspoon ground cinnamon	2 tablespoons cold water
⅛ teaspoon ground ginger	1 tablespoon cornstarch
⅛ teaspoon ground nutmeg	2 tablespoons butter or margarine
2¼ cups sugar	1 teaspoon grated lemon peel
¼ teaspoon salt	1 teaspoon grated orange peel
¼ cup orange juice	
2 tablespoons water	

1.   Prepare pastry, blending the ground spices into flour mixture; make a 9-inch pie shell and set aside.

2.   Combine the sugar, salt, and orange juice with 2 tablespoons water in a saucepan. Stir over medium heat until sugar is dissolved; increase heat and bring to boiling.

3.   Add cranberries; cook slowly 3 to 4 minutes, or until skins begin to pop.

4.   Blend cold water with cornstarch; add gradually to hot cranberries, stirring constantly. Bring to boiling; stir and cook 3 minutes.

5.   Remove from heat; stir in the butter and lemon and orange peels; cool.

6.   Brush unbaked pie shell with *melted butter.* Turn filling into shell.

7.   Bake at 450°F 10 minutes; reduce oven temperature to 350°F and bake about 20 minutes, or until pastry is lightly browned.

8.   Garnish with *orange sections.* Cool.

ONE 9-INCH PIE

FRESH FIG PIE

½ to ¾ lb. fresh figs
¾ cup sugar
1 tablespoon grated orange peel
3 tablespoons lemon juice
1 unbaked 9-in. pie shell
2 tablespoons butter or margarine

1. Peel and slice figs (enough for 3 cups). Stir sugar, orange peel, and lemon juice into figs. Turn fruit into unbaked pie shell. Dot with butter.
2. Bake at 450°F 10 minutes; reduce oven temperature to 350°F and bake about 25 minutes.

ONE 9-INCH PIE

GRAPE ARBOR PIE

Pastry for Lattice-Top Pie, *page 454*
3 cups Concord grapes
1 cup sugar
3 tablespoons cornstarch
¼ teaspoon salt
2 teaspoons grated orange peel
1 tablespoon orange juice
1 tablespoon lemon juice
1 tablespoon butter or margarine

1. Prepare an 8-inch pie shell and lattice strips for top crust; set aside.
2. Rinse and drain the grapes; slip off skins and chop; set aside in a bowl.
3. Bring skinned grapes to boiling in a saucepan; lower heat and simmer 5 minutes, or until seeds are loosened.
4. Drain pulp, reserving juice. Force pulp through fine sieve or food mill into bowl with chopped grape skins; set aside. Discard the seeds.
5. Thoroughly mix sugar, cornstarch, and salt in a saucepan. Stir in the reserved grape juice until well blended. Bring mixture to boiling; stir and cook 3 minutes.
6. Remove from heat; stir in the pulp mixture, orange peel, and the juices. Turn filling into unbaked pie shell. Dot with butter. Complete as directed for lattice-top pie.
7. Bake at 450°F 10 minutes; reduce oven temperature to 350°F and bake 20 to 25 minutes, or until pastry is lightly browned.
8. Cool on wire rack.

ONE 8-INCH PIE

MANGO PIE

½ cup all-purpose flour
⅓ cup firmly packed dark brown sugar
Few grains salt
⅓ cup butter or margarine
1 unbaked 8-in. pie shell
4 cups sliced pared mangos (about two 1-lb. mangos)
4 teaspoons lime juice
½ cup sugar
¼ teaspoon salt
3 tablespoons quick-cooking tapioca
1 teaspoon grated lime peel

1. Combine flour, brown sugar, and salt in a bowl; cut in butter with a pastry blender until pieces are the size of small peas. Chill.
2. Bake pie shell at 450°F 5 minutes and set aside.
3. Sprinkle mango slices with lime juice. Gently toss with a mixture of the remaining ingredients.
4. Turn into partially baked pie shell, heaping slightly at center. Sprinkle crumb mixture evenly over the top of fruit mixture.
5. Bake at 450°F 10 minutes; reduce oven temperature to 350°F and bake 15 to 20 minutes, or until crumb topping is golden brown and fruit is tender.
6. Serve warm with *vanilla ice cream.*

ONE 8-INCH PIE

FRESH PEACH-PLUM PIE

Pastry for 2-crust pie
2 cups sliced peeled ripe peaches
2 cups sliced ripe purple plums
2 to 4 teaspoons lemon juice
¼ teaspoon almond extract
1½ cups sugar
3 tablespoons quick-cooking tapioca
1 teaspoon grated lemon peel
¼ teaspoon salt
2 tablespoons butter or margarine

1. Prepare a 9-inch pie shell; roll out remaining pastry for top crust. Set aside.
2. Gently toss peaches and plums with the lemon juice and extract, then with a mixture of the sugar, tapioca, lemon peel, and salt.
3. Turn into unbaked pie shell, heaping slightly at center; dot with butter. Complete as directed for 2-crust pie.
4. Bake at 450°F 10 minutes; reduce oven temperature to 350°F and bake about 35 minutes, or until crust is lightly browned.
5. Serve warm.

ONE 9-INCH PIE

FRESH PEACH PIE: Follow recipe for Fresh Peach-Plum Pie. Increase peaches to 4 cups and omit plums. Omit almond extract. Use 1¼ cups sugar.

FRESH PLUM PIE: Follow recipe for Fresh Peach-Plum Pie. Increase plums to 5 cups and omit the peaches. Omit almond extract. Decrease sugar to 1 cup; add ¼ *cup firmly packed dark brown sugar.* Decrease lemon peel to ½ teaspoon.

GLAZED PEACH PIE

2½ cups fresh peach slices	2 tablespoons butter or margarine
1 tablespoon lemon juice	⅛ teaspoon salt
¼ cup sugar	⅛ teaspoon almond extract
½ cup sugar	
3 tablespoons cornstarch	1 baked 8-in. pie shell

1. Turn peach slices into a bowl. Drizzle lemon juice over them and mix lightly. Add ¼ cup sugar and toss gently. Set aside 1 hour.
2. Drain peaches, reserving syrup in a 1-cup measuring cup for liquids. Add enough water to syrup to measure 1 cup liquid.
3. Combine the ½ cup sugar and cornstarch in a saucepan. Stir in the reserved peach liquid until thoroughly blended. Stirring constantly, bring mixture to boiling; boil 3 minutes, or until thick and clear. Remove from heat.
4. Blend in the butter, salt, and extract. Add the peach slices and mix gently. Turn into baked pie shell; cool. If desired, serve with *whipped cream.*
ONE 8-INCH PIE

FRESH PEAR PIE

Pastry for 2-crust pie	4 large ripe pears, washed, quartered, cored, pared, and sliced (about 4 cups)
¾ cup sugar	
3 tablespoons cornstarch	
½ teaspoon ground nutmeg	
Few grains salt	2 tablespoons butter or margarine
2 tablespoons lemon juice	

1. Prepare an 8-inch pie shell; roll out remaining pastry for top crust. Set aside.
2. Mix the sugar, cornstarch, nutmeg, and salt.
3. Sprinkle lemon juice over sliced pears and mix lightly; toss gently with the sugar mixture. Turn filling into pastry shell. Dot top with butter. Complete as directed for a 2-crust pie.

4. Bake at 450°F 10 minutes; reduce oven temperature to 350°F and bake 30 to 35 minutes, or until crust is light golden brown.
5. Cool pie on wire rack.
ONE 8-INCH PIE

PEAR MERINGUE PIE

1 can (29 oz.) pear halves, drained	1 cup dairy sour cream
1 unbaked 8-in. pie shell	1 teaspoon vanilla extract
2 egg yolks, well beaten	¼ teaspoon grated lemon peel
½ cup sugar	1 teaspoon lemon juice
2 tablespoons flour	Meringue II, *page 453*
½ teaspoon salt	

1. Slice pears to make about 4 cups slices; arrange in unbaked pie shell.
2. Beat into egg yolks a mixture of sugar, flour, and salt. Add a blend of sour cream, extract, and lemon peel and juice; mix thoroughly. Spread evenly over pears.
3. Bake at 350°F 50 to 55 minutes.
4. Cool to lukewarm on wire rack.
5. Prepare Meringue II and complete pie as directed in meringue recipe.
ONE 8-INCH PIE

HOLIDAY PEAR AND CRANBERRY PIE
This delectable, attractive pie becomes a distinctive Christmas dessert with a partridge-in-a-pear-tree pastry topping.

Pastry for 2-crust pie	1 cup sugar
3 fresh winter pears, cored (do not pare) and sliced	2 teaspoons grated orange peel
	⅛ teaspoon salt
1½ cups fresh cranberries, rinsed and sorted	2 tablespoons quick-cooking tapioca

1. Using one half the pastry, line a 9-inch pie pan and flute the pastry edge. Roll out remaining pastry. Using a paper cutout of a pear tree with pears and a partridge, cut the tree from the pastry.
2. Combine pears and cranberries with remaining ingredients; mix well and spoon into pie shell. Carefully place the pear tree cutout over the pie filling.
3. Bake at 400°F about 40 minutes, or until fruit is tender and pie crust is light golden brown.
ONE 9-INCH PIE

ALMOND-CRUNCH PINEAPPLE PIE

Pastry for 2-crust pie
2 tablespoons sugar
3 tablespoons cornstarch
¼ teaspoon salt
1 can (20 oz.) crushed
　pineapple
2 tablespoons butter or
　margarine

1 tablespoon lime juice
1 tablespoon sugar
1½ teaspoons butter or
　margarine
¼ cup light corn syrup
1 teaspoon water
¾ cup sliced
　unblanched almonds

1. Prepare an 8-inch pie shell; roll out remaining pastry for top crust. Set aside.
2. Mix 2 tablespoons sugar, cornstarch, and salt in a saucepan; stir in undrained pineapple. Bring mixture to boiling over medium heat, stirring constantly. Boil until clear and thickened, 1 to 2 minutes. Stir in 2 tablespoons butter and lime juice.
3. Turn filling into the pie shell; cover with top crust. Seal and flute edges.
4. Bake at 425°F 20 minutes, or until pastry begins to brown.
5. Meanwhile, combine the 1 tablespoon sugar, 1½ teaspoons butter, corn syrup, and water in a small saucepan. Cook over low heat, stirring until sugar is dissolved and mixture boils.
6. Remove pie from oven. Sprinkle almonds over top crust. Spoon hot glaze evenly over nuts. Return pie to oven; bake about 8 minutes, or until topping is bubbly and lightly browned. Cool completely before cutting.　　　ONE 8-INCH PIE

ROSY RHUBARB PIE

Pastry for 2-crust pie
1 tablespoon quick-
　cooking tapioca
1¾ lbs. fresh rhubarb
¼ cup grenadine
¾ cup sugar
½ cup flour

¼ teaspoon salt
1 teaspoon grated
　orange peel
2 tablespoons butter or
　margarine
Egg white, beaten
2 teaspoons sugar

1. Prepare a 9-inch pie shell; roll out remaining pastry for top crust. Sprinkle tapioca over bottom of pie shell. Set aside.
2. Wash rhubarb, trim off leaves and ends of stems, and cut into 1-inch pieces to make 6 cups. (Peel only if skin is tough.)
3. Toss rhubarb with grenadine, then with a mixture of sugar, flour, salt, and orange peel. Turn into pie shell, heaping slightly in center; dot with butter. Complete as directed for a 2-crust pie.
4. Brush top lightly with egg white, then sprinkle with the 2 teaspoons sugar.
5. Bake at 450°F 15 minutes; reduce oven temperature to 375°F and bake 20 to 25 minutes, or until golden brown.　　　ONE 9-INCH PIE

CREAM PIES

CREAM PIE

¾ cup sugar
3 tablespoons cornstarch
2 tablespoons flour
½ teaspoon salt
3 cups milk
3 egg yolks, slightly
　beaten

1 tablespoon butter or
　margarine
1½ teaspoons vanilla
　extract
1 baked 9-in. pie shell
　or crumb crust

1. Mix sugar, cornstarch, flour, and salt in a 1½-quart saucepan. Stir in one half of the milk, then a blend of remaining milk and egg yolks. Bring to boiling over medium heat, stirring vigorously. Reduce heat; stir and cook about 5 minutes.
2. Remove from heat; blend in butter and extract. Cool slightly.
3. Turn filling into the pie shell. Chill.

ONE 9-INCH PIE

ALMOND MACAROON PIE

9 (1¾ in.) almond
　macaroon cookies
1 cup sugar
3 tablespoons flour
⅛ teaspoon salt
¼ cup cold milk
1 cup cream, scalded
3 egg yolks, slightly
　beaten

2 tablespoons butter or
　margarine
1 teaspoon almond
　extract
1 baked 9-in. pie shell
¼ cup blanched
　almonds, finely
　chopped

1. Heat cookies on a baking sheet in a 325°F oven for about 15 minutes; cool. Crush to make about ¾ cup fine crumbs.
2. Combine sugar, flour, and salt in top of double boiler; mix well and stir in the cold milk. Gradually add the scalded cream, stirring constantly. Bring to boiling and cook 3 minutes.

3. Stir about ½ cup of hot mixture into beaten egg yolks; immediately blend into mixture in double boiler. Place over boiling water and cook about 5 minutes, or until thickened, stirring occasionally.

4. Remove from water. Blend in butter, extract, and macaroon crumbs; cool to lukewarm.

5. Turn filling into pie shell. To complete pie, top with *sweetened whipped cream* and sprinkle with chopped almonds. ONE 9-INCH PIE

BANANA BUTTERSCOTCH PIE

¾ cup firmly packed brown sugar	2 tablespoons butter or margarine
5 tablespoons flour	1 teaspoon vanilla extract
½ teaspoon salt	3 ripe bananas
2 cups milk	1 baked 9-in. pie shell
2 egg yolks, slightly beaten	

1. Mix the brown sugar, flour, and salt together in the top of a double boiler. Add milk gradually, stirring until mixture is thoroughly blended.

2. Place over boiling water and cook, stirring constantly until thickened.

3. Vigorously stir about 3 tablespoons of the hot mixture into egg yolks, then blend into mixture in double-boiler top. Cook over boiling water about 5 minutes, stirring constantly. Remove from water. Blend in butter and extract; set aside.

4. Turn half of the lukewarm filling into the pastry shell. Cut bananas into crosswise slices and arrange over filling. Turn remaining filling over bananas. Top with *whipped cream.* ONE 9-INCH PIE

RICH DARK BUTTERSCOTCH PIE

5 tablespoons butter or margarine	¼ teaspoon salt
⅓ cup flour	1 teaspoon vanilla extract
¾ cup firmly packed light brown sugar	1 tablespoon firm butter or margarine
¼ cup sugar	Meringue I, *page 453*
2 cups milk, scalded	1 baked 9-in. pie shell, or 8 baked tart shells
3 egg yolks, beaten	

1. Melt 5 tablespoons butter in a heavy saucepan. Over medium heat, stir in flour, forming a smooth paste. Stir in sugars. Heat, stirring constantly, until sugars are melted and mixture is smooth.

2. Stirring constantly, gradually add ½ cup of the hot milk; continue stirring until mixture boils. Add the remaining milk, ½ cup at a time, stirring constantly; bring to boiling after each addition.

3. Vigorously stir about 3 tablespoons of the hot mixture into the egg yolks. Immediately return to mixture in saucepan. Cook about 3 minutes, stirring constantly.

4. Remove from heat and stir in the salt, extract, and remaining butter. Set aside to cool.

5. Turn filling into the pastry shell. Top with meringue and bake as directed in meringue recipe.

6. Cool completely before serving. ONE 9-INCH PIE

BLACK BOTTOM PIE

½ cup sugar	2 teaspoons vanilla extract
4 teaspoons cornstarch	1 baked 10-in. pie shell
½ cup cold milk	4 egg whites
1½ cups milk, scalded	¼ teaspoon salt
4 egg yolks, slightly beaten	¼ teaspoon cream of tartar
1 env. unflavored gelatin	½ cup sugar
¼ cup cold water	1 cup heavy cream, whipped
1 tablespoon rum extract	½ oz. (½ sq.) unsweetened chocolate
1½ oz. (1½ sq.) unsweetened chocolate, melted and cooled	

1. Blend ½ cup sugar and cornstarch in a saucepan. Stir in the cold milk, then the scalded milk, adding gradually. Bring rapidly to boiling, stirring constantly. Cook 3 minutes.

2. Turn mixture into a double-boiler top and set over boiling water. Vigorously stir about 3 tablespoons of hot mixture into egg yolks. Immediately blend into mixture in double boiler. Cook over simmering water, stirring constantly, 3 to 5 minutes, or until mixture coats a metal spoon. Remove double-boiler top from hot water immediately.

3. Soften gelatin in the cold water. Remove 1 cup of the cooked filling and set aside. Immediately stir softened gelatin into mixture in double boiler until completely dissolved. Cool until mixture sets slightly. Blend in rum extract.

4. Blend the melted chocolate and vanilla extract into the 1 cup reserved filling. Cool completely; turn into the baked pie shell, spreading evenly over bottom. Chill until set.

5. Beat egg whites with salt until frothy. Add cream of tartar and beat slightly. Gradually add

remaining ½ cup sugar, beating well after each addition; continue beating until stiff peaks are formed. Spread over gelatin mixture and gently fold together. Turn onto chocolate filling in pie shell. Chill until firm.

6.   Spread whipped cream over pie, swirling for a decorative effect. Top with chocolate curls shaved from the ½ ounce unsweetened chocolate. Chill until ready to serve.   ONE 10-INCH PIE

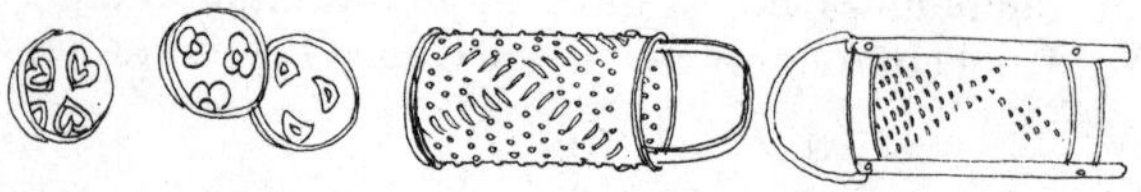

TOASTED COCONUT PIE

¾ cup sugar	1 teaspoon vanilla
¼ cup flour	extract
¼ teaspoon salt	1 cup toasted flaked
2 cups milk, scalded	coconut*
3 egg yolks, fork beaten	1 baked 9-in. pie shell
2 tablespoons butter or margarine	Meringue I, *page 453*

1.   Combine the sugar, flour, and salt in a heavy saucepan. Add scalded milk gradually, stirring constantly until mixture is thoroughly blended. Cook, stirring vigorously over medium heat until mixture thickens and comes to boiling; boil 1 to 2 minutes, stirring constantly.
2.   Stir about ½ cup of the hot mixture into egg yolks; blend thoroughly and return to saucepan. Reduce heat; stir and cook about 5 minutes.
3.   Remove from heat; stir in butter until thoroughly blended. Mix in the extract and toasted coconut; set aside to cool.
4.   Turn filling into baked pastry shell; top with meringue and bake as directed in meringue recipe. Or, instead of meringue, spread with *whipped cream* before serving.   • ONE 9-INCH PIE
*To toast coconut, spread in a shallow baking pan; heat in a 350°F oven about 10 minutes, or until coconut is golden brown, stirring occasionally.

TOASTED COCONUT-BANANA PIE: Follow recipe for Toasted Coconut Pie. Decrease coconut to ¾ cup. Spread about one-third of cooled filling in bottom of pastry shell; slice *1 medium-sized banana* over filling and cover with another third of filling. Slice a second banana over filling and cover with remaining filling. Top with meringue and bake as directed until lightly browned.

MOCHA CREAM PIE WITH CRUNCHY PEANUT BUTTER TOPPING

½ cup crunchy peanut butter	1 tablespoon instant coffee
¾ cup confectioners' sugar	1 can (14½ oz.) evaporated milk
1 baked 9-in. pie shell	2 eggs, fork beaten
½ cup sugar	2 tablespoons butter or margarine
2 teaspoons flour	½ teaspoon vanilla
⅛ teaspoon salt	extract

1.   Using a pastry blender or fork, mix peanut butter with confectioners' sugar until crumbly. Spread two thirds of mixture over bottom of pie shell; reserve remaining mixture for topping.
2.   Combine sugar, flour, salt, and instant coffee in a heavy saucepan. Mix in evaporated milk. Bring mixture rapidly to boiling, stirring constantly. Cook and stir 2 minutes.
3.   Gradually add about one third of hot mixture to beaten eggs, stirring constantly; blend into hot mixture. Cook and stir 5 minutes over low heat.
4.   Remove from heat and stir in butter and extract. Pour filling over crumb mixture in pie shell. Sprinkle remaining crumb mixture on filling to form a border. Chill pie before serving.
5.   If desired, serve with a *whipped dessert topping* or *sweetened whipped cream*.   ONE 9-INCH PIE

DOUBLE LEMON MERINGUE PIE
This lemon filling is equally delicious without the coriander or baked in plain pastry. Try it, too, as filling for tarts topped with meringue.

Pastry for 1-crust pie	2 tablespoons butter or margarine
1 teaspoon grated lemon peel	1 teaspoon ground coriander
1½ cups sugar	1 teaspoon grated lemon
7 tablespoons cornstarch	peel
¼ teaspoon salt	½ cup lemon juice
½ cup cold water	Lemon Meringue,
1 cup boiling water	*page 469*
3 egg yolks, slightly beaten	

1.   Prepare pastry, mixing 1 teaspoon lemon peel with the dry ingredients. Line a 9-inch pie pan with pastry. Bake pie shell; cool.
2.   Thoroughly mix sugar, cornstarch, and salt in a heavy saucepan. Stir in the cold water. Add the

boiling water gradually, stirring constantly. Bring mixture to boiling; lower heat. Cook and stir about 10 minutes.

3.   Stir about ½ cup of the hot mixture into beaten egg yolks. Immediately blend into mixture in saucepan. Stir and cook over low heat 3 minutes.

4.   Blend in butter, coriander, and the lemon peel and juice. Cool.

5.   Turn filling into pie shell. Top with meringue and bake as directed.

6.   Cool on wire rack.   ONE 9-INCH PIE

LEMON MERINGUE: Beat *3 egg whites* and *1 teaspoon lemon juice* until frothy. Gradually add *6 tablespoons sugar*, beating constantly until stiff peaks are formed. Pile lightly over pie filling, sealing meringue to pastry edge. Bake at 350°F 15 minutes, or until meringue is delicately browned.

LEMON-LIME MERINGUE PIE

2 bottles (7 oz. each) lemon-lime carbonated beverage	⅓ cup sugar
	⅓ cup lemon juice
	¼ cup lime juice
¾ cup sugar	1 teaspoon grated lemon peel
¼ cup cornstarch	
¼ cup flour	2 tablespoons butter or margarine
½ teaspoon salt	
3 egg yolks	1 baked 9-in. pie shell
	Meringue I, *page 453*

1.   Heat lemon-lime carbonated beverage to boiling.

2.   Combine the ¾ cup sugar, cornstarch, flour, and salt in a saucepan; add the hot beverage slowly, stirring until blended. Bring to boiling over medium heat, stirring constantly. Reduce heat; stir and cook 10 minutes.

3.   Beat egg yolks and ⅓ cup sugar together. Stir about ½ cup of hot mixture into the egg yolks. Then blend into mixture in saucepan.

4.   Add lemon and lime juices and cook over low heat until thickened, stirring constantly.

5.   Remove from heat; stir in lemon peel and butter. Turn filling into pie shell; cool slightly.

6.   Top with meringue and bake as directed in meringue recipe.   ONE 9-INCH PIE

LEMON-RAISIN PIE

2 cups seedless raisins	2 eggs, beaten
2 cups water	2 tablespoons butter or margarine
½ cup sugar	
3 tablespoons flour	1 teaspoon grated lemon peel
¼ teaspoon salt	
½ teaspoon ground cinnamon	3 tablespoons lemon juice
¼ teaspoon ground cloves	1 baked 9-in. pie shell
	¼ cup chopped walnuts

1.   Combine raisins and water in a heavy saucepan and bring to boiling; lower heat and cook 10 minutes.

2.   Thoroughly blend sugar, flour, salt, cinnamon, and cloves. Mix into hot raisins. Bring rapidly to boiling; cook and stir until thickened.

3.   Stir a small amount of hot mixture into beaten eggs. Immediately blend with remaining hot mixture in saucepan. Cook and stir 3 minutes over medium heat.

4.   Remove from heat. Stir in butter and lemon peel and juice. Turn filling into baked pie shell. Sprinkle walnuts in a circle on top. Cool.

5.   Garnish with a border of *whipped cream.*
                    ONE 9-INCH PIE

FLORIDA LIME PIE

A recipe from the Matson Navigation Company.

Crumb pie shell:	1 can (14 oz.) sweetened condensed milk
1½ cups corn flake crumbs	
½ cup sugar	3 egg yolks, slightly beaten
½ teaspoon ground cinnamon	Green food coloring
	3 egg whites
½ cup butter, melted	2 tablespoons sugar
Filling:	1 cup heavy cream, whipped
¼ cup lime juice	

1.   To prepare pie shell, combine the crumbs, sugar, and cinnamon in a bowl; stir in the butter and mix thoroughly.

2.   Line a 9-inch pie pan with the mixture, pressing it firmly against bottom and sides. Chill about 20 minutes.

3.   Combine the lime juice, condensed milk, and egg yolks; tint to desired color with food coloring.

4.   Beat egg whites until frothy; add 2 tablespoons sugar and continue beating until stiff peaks are formed. Fold into yolk mixture until thoroughly blended. Turn into chilled shell.

5. Set in a 350°F oven about 20 minutes, or until lightly browned.
6. Cool pie and top with whipped cream; decorate as desired.   ONE 9-INCH PIE

KEY LIME PIE

This popular pie originating in the Florida Keys takes on its piquant flavor from those small, yellow-green Key limes.

1 can (14 oz.) sweetened condensed milk	1 or 2 drops green food coloring
3 egg yolks	1 baked 9-in. pie shell
2/3 cup lime juice	3 egg whites
	1/3 cup sugar

1. Mix the condensed milk, egg yolks, lime juice, and food coloring until blended. Chill.
2. Turn mixture into baked pie shell.
3. Beat egg whites until frothy; add sugar gradually, beating well after each addition. Beat until stiff peaks are formed; spread the meringue over pie filling to edge of pastry.
4. Set in a 450°F oven about 5 minutes, or until meringue is delicately browned.   ONE 9-INCH PIE

TALBOTT INN ORANGE PIE

From Talbott Tavern, Bardstown, Kentucky.

3/4 cup sugar	2 tablespoons lemon juice
1/2 cup flour	
1/4 teaspoon salt	1 tablespoon orange extract
1 3/4 cups reconstituted frozen orange juice	1 baked 8-in. pie shell
2 egg yolks, slightly beaten	2 egg whites
	1/2 cup sugar
	2 tablespoons water

1. Mix sugar, flour, and salt in the top of a double boiler. Stir in orange juice and cook over direct heat until thickened, stirring constantly.
2. Add a small amount of hot mixture to egg yolks; blend well and return to double boiler. Cook over boiling water about 5 minutes, or until mixture is thick. Remove from heat; add lemon juice and orange extract. Chill and turn into baked pie shell.
3. Beat egg whites, sugar, and water in top of double boiler until blended. Place over boiling water and beat 1 minute. Remove from heat and beat until meringue stands in peaks.
4. Pile over the pie and garnish with *orange sections* and *flaked coconut*.   ONE 8-INCH PIE

CUSTARD PIES

CUSTARD PIE

4 eggs	3/4 cup cream, scalded
1/2 cup sugar	1 teaspoon vanilla extract
1/2 teaspoon nutmeg	
1/4 teaspoon salt	1 unbaked 8-in. pie shell
1 1/2 cups milk, scalded	

1. Beat the eggs slightly; add sugar, nutmeg, and salt and beat just until blended. Gradually add the scalded milk and cream, stirring constantly. Mix in the extract. Strain mixture into pie shell.
2. Bake at 450°F 10 minutes; reduce oven temperature to 350°F and bake 15 to 20 minutes, or until a knife inserted in custard halfway between center and edge comes out clean.
3. Cool on wire rack. Place in refrigerator until ready to serve.   ONE 8-INCH PIE

SLIPPED CUSTARD PIE: Follow recipe for Custard Pie for amounts of ingredients. Prepare, bake, and set pie shell aside to cool. Lightly butter a second 8-inch pie pan. Prepare custard and strain into the pan. Set in pan of hot water. Bake at 325°F 25 to 30 minutes, or until custard tests done. Remove from water and cool. Run tip of knife around edge of pan; hold pan level and shake gently to loosen custard. Hold pan at a slight angle and slip the custard carefully into pie shell. Work quickly to avoid breaking custard. Set aside a few minutes.

SHAKER SUGAR PIE

From The Golden Lamb Restaurant, Lebanon, Ohio.

1 unbaked 9-in. pie shell	1 teaspoon vanilla extract
3/4 cup firmly packed light brown sugar	Few grains ground nutmeg
1/4 cup flour	1/2 cup butter or margarine, softened
2 cups cream	

1. Prick pie shell and bake at 450°F 5 minutes. Set aside. Reduce oven temperature to 350°F.

2. Mix the brown sugar with flour until blended. Spoon over bottom of partially baked pie shell.

3. Combine the cream, extract, and nutmeg; pour over sugar in pie shell. Dot with the butter.

4. Bake at 350°F about 55 minutes, or until crust is lightly browned and filling is set. ONE 9-INCH PIE

SOUR CREAM-APPLE PIE

1 can (20 oz.) sliced apples (packed in syrup)
½ cup firmly packed brown sugar
1 egg, slightly beaten
2 cups dairy sour cream
3 tablespoons brown sugar
2 tablespoons flour

½ teaspoon ground cinnamon
⅛ teaspoon ground nutmeg
⅛ teaspoon ground mace
⅛ teaspoon salt
1 baked 9-in. Graham Cracker Crumb Crust, *page 458*

1. Toss apples gently with ½ cup brown sugar in a saucepan. Cook over medium heat until mixture bubbles; reduce heat and cook 5 minutes, stirring occasionally; remove from heat.

2. Blend beaten egg with sour cream and a mixture of remaining ingredients, except pie shell, until smooth.

3. Turn about one half of the sour cream mixture into pie shell; spread evenly.

4. Spoon apple mixture in an even layer over sour cream mixture; top with remaining sour cream mixture, spreading evenly.

5. Bake at 400°F 10 to 12 minutes, or until sour cream topping is set.

6. Cool on wire rack; chill thoroughly.
ONE 9-INCH PIE

APPLE-CUSTARD PIE

1½ cups thinly sliced pared apples
¼ cup sugar
¼ teaspoon ground cinnamon
¼ teaspoon ground nutmeg
1 unbaked 9-in. pie shell
¾ cup milk

½ cup cream
2 eggs, slightly beaten
½ cup sugar
⅛ teaspoon salt
1 teaspoon vanilla extract
1 cup small-curd creamed cottage cheese

1. Toss apples with ¼ cup sugar, cinnamon, and nutmeg. Turn into unbaked pie shell.

2. Bake at 425°F 15 minutes.

3. Meanwhile, scald milk and cream together.

4. Combine eggs with the remaining ingredients and beat only until blended. Add scalded milk and cream gradually, stirring constantly.

5. Remove pie from oven; reduce oven temperature to 325°F. Pour cheese mixture over apples in pie shell.

6. Return to oven and bake 45 minutes, or until mixture is "set" and lightly browned.

7. Serve slightly warm. ONE 9-INCH PIE

APRICOT CHEESE PIE

1 cup dried apricots
1 unbaked 9-in. pie shell
3 eggs
½ teaspoon grated lemon peel

1 teaspoon lemon juice
¾ cup sugar
1 tablespoon flour
½ teaspoon salt
1½ cups creamed cottage cheese, sieved

1. Rinse and drain apricots; cut into small pieces and distribute over bottom of pie shell.

2. Combine eggs and lemon peel and juice; beat slightly. Gradually add a mixture of sugar, flour, and salt, beating constantly. Add the cottage cheese and mix until blended. Pour over apricots.

3. Bake at 375°F about 35 minutes, or until a knife inserted near center comes out clean.

4. Set pie on wire rack to cool before serving.
ONE 9-INCH PIE

FRAU MOYER'S CHEESE CUSTARD PIE
This delicious pie is of Pennsylvania Dutch origin.

1 cup large-curd creamed cottage cheese
1 cup cream
½ cup confectioners' sugar
¼ teaspoon salt

¼ teaspoon ground nutmeg
5 egg yolks, slightly beaten
¼ cup butter, melted
5 egg whites
1 unbaked 9-in. pie shell

1. Force cottage cheese through a fine sieve into a bowl. Stir in the cream, confectioners' sugar, salt, nutmeg, beaten egg yolks, and melted butter.

2. Beat egg whites until stiff, not dry, peaks are formed. Fold into cheese mixture until blended. Turn into the pie shell.

3. Bake at 450°F 10 minutes. Reduce oven temperature to 350°F; bake about 20 minutes, or until custard tests done. Serve warm.   ONE 9-INCH PIE

STRAWBERRY-GLAZED CHEESE PIE

8 oz. cream cheese
½ cup sweetened
    condensed milk
¼ teaspoon vanilla
    extract
1 teaspoon grated lemon
    peel
2 tablespoons lemon
    juice

½ cup heavy cream,
    whipped
1 baked 10-inch Graham
    Cracker Crumb Crust,
    page 458
1 pkg. (16 oz.) frozen
    strawberries, thawed
    and drained (reserve
    syrup)
2 teaspoons cornstarch

1. Soften cream cheese in a bowl; beat in condensed milk, extract, and lemon peel and juice until thoroughly blended. Fold in the whipped cream. Turn mixture into baked pie shell; chill.
2. Stir ¾ cup of the reserved strawberry syrup into cornstarch in a saucepan. Cook and stir over medium heat until mixture comes to boiling; cook 3 minutes longer, or until mixture is clear. Cool about 10 minutes.
3. Gently mix in strawberries; spoon glaze over pie; chill thoroughly.   ONE 10-INCH PIE

PECAN-TOPPED PUMPKIN PIE

1 unbaked 9-in. pie
    shell
1 can (16 oz.) pumpkin,
    about 2 cups
⅔ cup firmly packed
    light brown sugar
1 teaspoon ground
    cinnamon
½ teaspoon ground
    ginger
½ teaspoon ground
    nutmeg

⅛ teaspoon ground
    cloves
½ teaspoon salt
2 eggs, slightly beaten
2 cups cream, scalded
3 tablespoons butter or
    margarine
1 cup pecan halves
¼ cup firmly packed
    light brown sugar

1. Prepare pie shell; set aside.
2. For filling, combine pumpkin, ⅔ cup brown sugar, and a mixture of spices and salt in a bowl. Add the eggs and mix well. Gradually add the scalded cream, stirring until mixture is smooth. Pour filling into unbaked pie shell.
3. Bake at 400°F about 50 minutes, or until a knife

inserted near center comes out clean. Cool on rack.
4. For topping, melt the butter in a small skillet. Add pecans; turn them with a spoon until coated with butter. Turn nuts into a bowl containing ¼ cup brown sugar; toss to coat thoroughly.
5. When pie is cool, arrange coated pecans, rounded side up, over the top in an attractive design. Place under broiler about 3 inches from source of heat. Broil 1 to 2 minutes.   ONE 9-INCH PIE

SOUR CREAM-RAISIN PIE

½ cup sugar
2 tablespoons flour
½ teaspoon ground
    cinnamon
¼ teaspoon ground
    nutmeg
¼ teaspoon salt

1 egg, well beaten
1½ cups dairy sour
    cream
1½ cups dark seedless
    raisins
1 unbaked 9-in. pie
    shell

1. Combine sugar, flour, spices, and salt.
2. Combine the egg with sour cream; gradually add dry ingredients, blending thoroughly. Stir in raisins. Turn filling into unbaked pie shell.
3. Bake at 450°F 10 minutes; reduce oven temperature to 350°F and bake 20 to 25 minutes, or until a knife inserted near center comes out clean.
4. Serve slightly warm.   ONE 9-INCH PIE
SOUR CREAM-DATE PIE: Follow recipe for Sour Cream-Raisin Pie. Omit spices and raisins. Stir *1 teaspoon grated lemon peel* into sugar mixture. Mix *2 cups date pieces* and *⅓ cup coarsely chopped pecans* into sour cream mixture.

SWEET POTATO PIE

1½ cups sieved cooked
    sweet potatoes or yams
2 tablespoons butter or
    margarine, melted
1 teaspoon grated orange
    peel
½ cup firmly packed
    light brown sugar
1 teaspoon ground
    cinnamon

½ teaspoon ground
    ginger
½ teaspoon ground
    nutmeg
¼ teaspoon ground
    cloves
½ teaspoon salt
2 eggs, beaten
1½ cups milk, scalded
1 unbaked 9-in. pie
    shell

1. Combine sweet potatoes with melted butter, orange peel, and a mixture of the brown sugar, spices, and salt; mix until thoroughly blended.

2. Add eggs and beat well. Blend in scalded milk. Turn filling into unbaked pie shell.

3. Bake at 450°F 10 minutes; reduce oven temperature to 350°F and bake 30 to 35 minutes, or until a knife inserted near center comes out clean.

4. Set on wire rack to cool. Serve with *sweetened whipped cream* sprinkled with ¼ cup chopped unblanched almonds.   ONE 9-INCH PIE

SPECIAL PIES

CHESS PIE

Cake Flour Pastry, *page 456*	2 cups sugar
1 cup butter or margarine	7 egg yolks (about ⅔ cup), beaten
1½ teaspoons vanilla extract	½ cup cream
	2 tablespoons cornmeal

1. Prepare a 10-inch pie shell; set aside.
2. Cream the butter with the extract until softened. Gradually add the sugar, beating well after each addition.
3. Add egg yolks and beat until blended. Stir in the cream and cornmeal. Turn into the top of a double boiler and cook over boiling water 15 to 20 minutes, stirring constantly. Turn into pie shell.
4. Bake at 350°F about 35 minutes.
5. Cool on wire rack.   ONE 10-INCH PIE

KENTUCKY CHESS PIE

Here is a popular recipe from the Beaumont Inn in Harrodsburg, Kentucky.

1 cup sugar	½ cup butter, melted
1 tablespoon flour	1 unbaked 8- or 9-in. pie shell
¼ teaspoon salt	Meringue:
2 egg yolks	2 egg whites
1 whole egg	2 tablespoons sugar
3 tablespoons water	
1 teaspoon white vinegar	

1. Mix the sugar, flour, and salt thoroughly.
2. Beat egg yolks with egg; beating constantly, slowly add the water, vinegar, and melted butter. Add dry ingredients and mix well. Turn into unbaked pie shell.
3. Bake at 350°F about 35 minutes, or until filling is "set."
4. Meanwhile, prepare meringue. Beat egg whites until foamy; add the sugar gradually, beating constantly until stiff peaks are formed.
5. Remove pie from oven; top with meringue and return to oven. Bake 12 to 15 minutes, or until meringue is lightly browned.   ONE 8- OR 9-INCH PIE

RICH CHOCOLATE-NUT PIE

½ cup butter or margarine	⅓ cup cocoa
1 teaspoon vanilla extract	½ teaspoon salt
1 cup sugar	¾ cup dark corn syrup
3 eggs	¾ cup milk
¼ cup flour	¾ cup pecan halves
	1 unbaked 9-in. pie shell

1. Cream the butter with the extract. Gradually add the sugar, creaming well after each addition. Add the eggs, one at a time, beating until fluffy after each addition.
2. Combine the flour, cocoa, and salt. Add to the creamed mixture, mixing well. Beat in the corn syrup and milk until thoroughly blended. Stir in the pecans. Pour the filling into unbaked pie shell.
3. Bake at 450°F 10 minutes; reduce oven temperature to 325°F and bake 40 to 45 minutes, or until the filling is set.
4. Serve slightly warm or cold with *unsweetened whipped cream.*   ONE 9-INCH PIE

HEAVENLY LEMON PIE

4 egg yolks	4 egg whites
⅔ cup sugar	¼ teaspoon salt
1 tablespoon grated lemon peel	½ cup sugar
⅓ cup lemon juice	1 baked 10-in. pie shell

1. In the top of a double boiler, beat the egg yolks with the ⅔ cup sugar until thoroughly blended; beat in the lemon peel and juice.
2. Cook and stir over simmering water 12 to 15 minutes, or until mixture is very thick. Turn into a bowl; cool.
3. Beat egg whites with salt until frothy; gradually

add the ½ cup sugar, beating constantly until stiff peaks are formed.

4. Carefully spread egg-white mixture over the cooled lemon mixture and gently fold together. Turn filling into baked pie shell.

5. Bake at 450°F 5 minutes, or until filling is puffy and lightly browned. Serve while warm.

ONE 10-INCH PIE

MINCE PIE

Pastry for a 2-crust pie
3½ cups moist mincemeat
1¼ cups chopped apple
1 teaspoon grated lemon peel
1 tablespoon lemon juice

1. Prepare a 9-inch pie shell; roll out remaining pastry for top crust. Set aside.

2. Blend mincemeat and remaining ingredients in a saucepan; heat thoroughly. Cool slightly.

3. Turn filling into unbaked pie shell. Complete as directed for 2-crust pie.

4. Bake at 425°F 35 minutes. Cool on wire rack.

ONE 9-INCH PIE

SHOOFLY PIE

Pennsylvania Dutch in origin, this old-fashioned pie has found favor in other sections of our country.

1 cup all-purpose flour
⅔ cup firmly packed dark brown sugar
¼ teaspoon salt
5 tablespoons butter or margarine
⅔ cup very hot water
5 tablespoons molasses
1 tablespoon dark brown sugar
½ teaspoon baking soda
1 unbaked 8-in. pie shell

1. Combine flour, ⅔ cup brown sugar, and salt in a bowl. Cut in butter until particles resemble rice kernels; set aside.

2. Blend hot water with the molasses, 1 tablespoon brown sugar, and baking soda.

3. Reserving 3 tablespoons crumb mixture for topping, stir molasses mixture into remaining crumb mixture. Pour into unbaked pie shell. Sprinkle reserved crumbs over filling.

4. Bake at 350°F 35 to 40 minutes, or until top springs back when touched lightly. ONE 8-INCH PIE

BUTTERNUT PIE

A favorite at Vermont House, Newbury, Vermont.

3 eggs
1 cup sugar
1 teaspoon salt
1 teaspoon vanilla extract
1 cup maple syrup
1 cup coarsely chopped butternuts*
1 unbaked 9-in. pie shell

1. Beat the eggs, sugar, salt, and extract together until thick and piled softly. Beat in the maple syrup, then stir in butternuts. Pour the filling into unbaked pie shell.

2. Bake at 350°F about 40 minutes, or until a knife inserted near center comes out clean.

ONE 9-INCH PIE

*If butternuts are not available, substitute walnuts.

PECAN PIE

3 tablespoons butter or margarine
2 teaspoons vanilla extract
¾ cup sugar
3 eggs
½ cup chopped pecans
1 cup dark corn syrup
⅛ teaspoon salt
1 unbaked 9-in. pie shell
½ cup pecan halves

1. Cream butter with extract. Gradually add sugar, creaming well. Add eggs, one at a time, beating thoroughly after each addition.

2. Beat in chopped pecans, corn syrup, and salt. Turn into the unbaked pie shell.

3. Bake at 450°F 10 minutes; reduce oven temperature to 350°F. Arrange pecan halves over top of filling. Bake 30 to 35 minutes longer, or until set. Cool on wire rack. ONE 9-INCH PIE

APPLE-PECAN PIE

Awarded a blue ribbon by apple-growers at their annual Apple Smorgasbord in Grand Rapids, Michigan.

2 tablespoons butter or margarine
1 teaspoon vanilla extract
1 cup firmly packed light brown sugar
3 eggs
1 cup coarsely chopped pecans
¾ cup dark corn syrup
½ cup thick applesauce
Few grains cinnamon
1 unbaked 9-in. pie shell

1. Cream butter with extract until softened; gradually add brown sugar, beating thoroughly. Add

eggs, one at a time, beating thoroughly after each addition.

2. Blend in the pecans, corn syrup, applesauce, and cinnamon. Turn filling into unbaked pie shell.

3. Bake at 450°F 10 minutes; reduce oven temperature to 350°F and bake 35 to 40 minutes.

4. Cool on wire rack. ONE 9-INCH PIE

GOLDEN RAISIN-PECAN PIE

1¾ cups sugar	2 tablespoons cider
3 tablespoons flour	vinegar
¼ teaspoon salt	1 teaspoon vanilla
½ teaspoon ground	extract
nutmeg	⅔ cup chopped pecans
3 egg yolks, well beaten	½ cup golden raisins
3 tablespoons butter or	3 egg whites
margarine, melted	1 unbaked 9-in. pie
½ cup undiluted	shell
evaporated milk	

1. Combine the sugar, flour, salt, and nutmeg; add to beaten egg yolks and blend thoroughly. Beat in the butter, evaporated milk, vinegar, and extract. Stir in the pecans and raisins.

2. Beat the egg whites until rounded peaks are formed, then fold into egg yolk mixture, blending thoroughly. Turn filling into pie shell.

3. Bake at 350°F 50 minutes, or until pastry is lightly browned.

4. Serve warm or cold. ONE 9-INCH PIE

BRIDGE PIE

¾ cup butter or	1 cup coarsely chopped
margarine	dates
¾ cup sugar	2 egg whites
2 egg yolks	1 unbaked 9-inch
¼ cup milk	Graham Cracker Crumb
¾ cup chopped pecans	Crust, *page 458*

1. Cream butter; gradually add sugar, beating thoroughly until light and fluffy. Add egg yolks and beat until smooth. Blend in the milk. Stir in pecans and dates.

2. Beat egg whites until stiff, not dry, peaks are formed; spread over date mixture and gently fold together. Turn filling into crust; spread evenly.

3. Bake at 350°F 35 to 40 minutes, or until "set."

4. Serve with *whipped cream*. ONE 9-INCH PIE

CHIFFON PIES

APRICOT-NUT CHIFFON PIE

Apricot-Nut Pastry,	1¼ cups apricot nectar
below	1 tablespoon lemon
1 env. unflavored	juice
gelatin	1 can (16 or 17 oz.)
½ cup sugar	apricot halves,
⅛ teaspoon salt	drained and sieved
¼ cup cold water	½ cup heavy cream,
¼ cup orange juice	whipped
	⅔ cup chopped nuts

1. Prepare and bake Apricot-Nut Pastry; set aside.

2. Thoroughly mix gelatin, sugar, and salt in a saucepan. Blend in cold water and orange juice. Stir over low heat until gelatin is dissolved. Remove from heat. Blend in apricot nectar and lemon juice.

3. Chill mixture until slightly thicker than consistency of thick, unbeaten egg white. Beat with hand rotary or electric beater until light and fluffy. Blend

in the sieved apricots. Fold in the whipped cream and nuts; turn filling into pastry shell. Chill until firm.

4. Serve topped with *whipped cream*, if desired.
ONE 9-INCH PIE

APRICOT-NUT PASTRY

7 tablespoons butter or	1¼ cups sifted all-
shortening	purpose flour
3 tablespoons apricot	½ teaspoon salt
nectar, heated	¼ cup chopped nuts
1 teaspoon milk	

1. Combine butter, hot apricot nectar, and the milk in a bowl; whip with a fork until mixture is smooth.

2. Sift flour and salt together into the butter mixture; stir quickly to a smooth dough.

3. Shape dough into a flat round and roll out between two 12-inch squares of waxed paper into a round about ⅛ inch thick.

4. Peel off top piece of paper and sprinkle dough

with 2 tablespoons of the nuts, leaving a 1-inch border plain. Cover with the paper and gently roll nuts into dough.

5. Turn pastry over and repeat step 4.

6. Peel off top paper and fit pastry into a 9-inch pie pan; remove other piece of paper.

7. Flute pastry edge and generously prick shell with a fork.

8. Bake at 450°F 8 to 9 minutes, or until pastry is lightly browned; cool. ONE 9-INCH PIE SHELL

BANANA CHIFFON PIE

1 cup undiluted evaporated milk	½ cup sugar
1 env. unflavored gelatin	¼ teaspoon salt
⅓ cup cold water	1 cup mashed fully ripe banana
⅓ cup thawed frozen orange juice concentrate	2 tablespoons lemon juice
	1 baked 9-in. pie shell

1. Pour evaporated milk into refrigerator tray and set in freezer until ice crystals form around edge.

2. Soften gelatin in cold water in a small saucepan. Stir over low heat until gelatin is dissolved.

3. Mix together the orange juice concentrate, sugar, and salt. Add the dissolved gelatin and stir until sugar is dissolved. Blend in the mashed banana. Chill until mixture is partially set.

4. Beat chilled evaporated milk until thick. Add lemon juice and continue beating until mixture is very stiff. Fold slightly thickened gelatin mixture into whipped evaporated milk. Pile mixture lightly into pie shell. Chill until firm.

5. Garnish with *banana slices* and, if desired, *orange slices*. ONE 9-INCH PIE

CHERRY CHIFFON PIE

2 cups stemmed, halved, and pitted dark sweet cherries (about 1 lb.)	2 drops red food coloring
½ cup sugar	¼ cup sugar
1 env. unflavored gelatin	½ cup heavy cream, whipped
¼ cup cold water	2 egg whites
2 tablespoons lemon juice	⅛ teaspoon salt
	¼ cup sugar
	1 baked 9-in. pie shell

1. Cut cherries into small pieces; mix with ½ cup

sugar. Cover and let stand 1 hour to let syrup form.

2. Soften gelatin in cold water; set aside.

3. Drain cherries, reserving syrup; add enough water to cherry syrup to measure 1 cup; heat until very hot.

4. Remove from heat and immediately stir in softened gelatin until dissolved. Blend in lemon juice and food coloring; cool.

5. Chill until mixture is slightly thickened.

6. Beat the ¼ cup sugar into whipped cream with final few strokes.

7. Beat egg whites with salt until frothy; gradually add remaining ¼ cup sugar, beating constantly until stiff peaks are formed.

8. Mix cherries into slightly thickened gelatin. Spread whipped cream and beaten egg whites over gelatin; fold together.

9. Turn filling into pie shell. Chill until firm.
ONE 9-INCH PIE

MOCHA-NOG PIE

2 env. unflavored gelatin	3 egg whites
½ cup cold water	1 cup chilled heavy cream, whipped
⅔ cup sugar	1½ teaspoons vanilla extract
½ teaspoon ground nutmeg	1 baked 10-in. pie shell
2 cups strong coffee	½ oz. (½ sq.) unsweetened chocolate
3 egg yolks, slightly beaten	

1. Soften gelatin in cold water; set aside.

2. Mix sugar, nutmeg, and coffee in top of double boiler. Bring to boiling. Remove from heat; add the gelatin and stir until gelatin is dissolved.

3. Stir about ½ cup hot coffee mixture into egg yolks, then blend into mixture in double boiler top. Cook over simmering water, stirring constantly, until mixture is slightly thickened. Remove from water; cool.

4. Chill until mixture is partially set.

5. Beat egg whites until stiff, not dry, peaks are formed. Spread beaten egg whites and a blend of whipped cream and extract over gelatin mixture and fold together. Turn filling into pie shell. Chill until firm.

6. Top with chocolate curls made by pulling the chocolate across a shredder. ONE 10-INCH PIE

REGAL MOCHA-NOG PIE: Follow recipe for Mocha-Nog Pie. Omit nutmeg and extract. When gelatin mixture is slightly thicker, blend in ½ *cup brandy* or ¼ *cup crème de cacao.* If brandy is used, beat egg whites until frothy; add *3 tablespoons sugar* gradually, continuing to beat until rounded peaks are formed.

CHOCOLATE PIE ELEGANTE

1 env. unflavored gelatin	2 egg yolks, slightly beaten
½ cup cold water	1 teaspoon vanilla extract
2 oz. (2 sq.) unsweetened chocolate	2 egg whites
1 cup milk, scalded	1 cup chilled heavy cream, whipped
½ cup sugar	1 baked 9-in. pie shell
¼ teaspoon salt	

1. Soften gelatin in cold water; set aside.
2. Combine chocolate and milk in the top of a double boiler over boiling water. Heat until chocolate is melted; stir until well blended and smooth.
3. Add sugar and salt to egg yolks; stir in several tablespoons of the milk-chocolate mixture, then blend into mixture in double boiler. Cook over boiling water 5 minutes, stirring frequently.
4. Remove from heat; add the softened gelatin and stir until dissolved. Blend in extract. Chill until mixture begins to thicken.
5. Beat egg whites until stiff, not dry, peaks are formed. Gently fold into whipped cream. Fold into gelatin mixture until thoroughly blended.
6. Turn filling into the pie shell. Sprinkle coarsely shredded *unsweetened chocolate* irregularly around outer edge of pie. Chill until firm. ONE 9-INCH PIE

FILBERT BLACK-TOP PIE

½ cup chopped filberts	2 egg yolks
1 cup graham cracker crumbs	¼ cup sugar
3 tablespoons sugar	1 teaspoon rum flavoring
⅓ cup butter or margarine, melted	1½ cups milk
1 env. unflavored gelatin	2 egg whites
	2 tablespoons sugar
¼ cup cold water	Chocolate Icing, *below*

1. Mix filberts, crumbs, 3 tablespoons sugar, and butter; press firmly into a 9-inch pie pan.
2. Bake at 350°F for 12 minutes; cool.
3. Soften gelatin in cold water; dissolve over boiling water.

4. Beat egg yolks with ¼ cup sugar and rum flavoring until thick.
5. Gradually add milk, beating well. Continue beating while adding dissolved gelatin. Chill until mixture is partially set.
6. Beat egg whites until frothy; add 2 tablespoons sugar and beat until stiff peaks are formed.
7. Beat gelatin mixture until fluffy; fold into beaten egg whites. Turn filling into pie shell. Chill until firm.
8. Spread Chocolate Icing over top of pie. Sprinkle with ½ *cup chopped toasted filberts.* Chill until icing is set. ONE 9-INCH PIE

CHOCOLATE ICING: Melt ½ *cup semisweet chocolate pieces* in the top of a double boiler over hot water. Add ¼ *cup confectioners' sugar, 1 tablespoon butter or margarine,* and *2 to 4 tablespoons cream.* Stir until smooth. ABOUT ⅔ CUP ICING

GRAPE CHIFFON PIE

1 env. unflavored gelatin	½ cup grapefruit juice
	2 tablespoons sugar
½ cup cold water	Few grains salt
1 can (6 oz.) frozen grape juice concentrate, thawed	1½ cups chilled heavy cream
	1 baked 8-in. pie shell

1. Soften gelatin in cold water; stir over low heat until gelatin is dissolved.
2. Remove from heat and blend in the concentrate. Stir in grapefruit juice, sugar, and salt until sugar is dissolved. Chill until slightly thickened.
3. Beat 1 cup cream until it piles softly. Spread whipped cream over gelatin and fold together. Turn filling into pie shell; chill until firm.
4. To serve, beat remaining cream to soft peaks. Pile lightly on top of pie and swirl gently with back of a spoon. ONE 8-INCH PIE

GRAPEFRUIT CHIFFON PIE

Ms. Newton Keith of the Royal Savage Inn, Plattsburgh, New York, contributed this recipe.

1 cup fresh grapefruit juice	1 teaspoon cream of tartar
1 env. unflavored gelatin	1 cup sugar
	½ cup boiling water
2 egg whites	1 baked 9-in. pie shell

1. Measure ½ cup grapefruit juice into a small

saucepan; sprinkle on gelatin. Stir over direct heat until dissolved. Remove from heat and stir in remaining grapefruit juice. Set in refrigerator until slightly thickened.

2. Meanwhile, combine egg whites, cream of tarter, and sugar in a mixing bowl. Pour boiling water over all and beat constantly with an electric beater 10 minutes.

3. Add slightly thickened gelatin to the beaten egg white mixture; beat until thoroughly blended, about 3 minutes. Turn into the baked pie shell. Refrigerate until ready to serve.   ONE 9-INCH PIE

NOTE: 1 cup of the following may be substituted for the grapefruit juice; strawberry, raspberry, cherry, apple, pineapple, loganberry, cranberry, grape, apricot or a blend of juices.

LIME CHIFFON PIE

1 env. unflavored gelatin	½ cup lime juice
¼ cup cold water	¼ teaspoon salt
4 egg yolks, slightly beaten	2 to 3 drops green food coloring
⅔ cup sugar	4 egg whites
2 teaspoons grated lime peel	½ cup sugar
	1 baked 9-in. pie shell

1. Soften gelatin in cold water; set aside.
2. Mix the egg yolks, sugar, lime peel and juice, and salt together in top of a double boiler. Cook over simmering water, stirring constantly, until mixture is slightly thickened.
3. Remove from water and blend in gelatin, stirring until gelatin is dissolved. Mix in the food coloring. Cool. Chill until mixture is partially set.
4. Beat egg whites until frothy; gradually add ½ cup sugar, beating constantly until stiff peaks are formed. Spread over gelatin mixture and fold together. Turn into pie shell. Chill until firm.
ONE 9-INCH PIE

LEMON CHIFFON PIE: Follow recipe for Lime Chiffon Pie. Substitute *lemon peel and juice* for lime peel and juice. Substitute *yellow food coloring* for green.

DAKKERI CHIFFON PIE: Follow recipe for Lime Chiffon Pie. Use an 8-inch pie pan. Decrease egg yolks and egg whites to 3. Blend ⅓ *cup light rum* into cooled gelatin mixture. Garnish with thin slices of *lime.*

ORANGE CHIFFON PIE: Follow recipe for Lime Chiffon Pie. Substitute *2 tablespoons lemon juice* for 2 tablespoons of the water. Substitute *orange peel and juice* for lime peel and juice. Omit food coloring.

LEMON CLOUD PIE

½ cup sugar	½ teaspoon vanilla extract
1 env. unflavored gelatin	1 teaspoon grated lemon peel
¼ teaspoon salt	5 egg whites
5 egg yolks	½ cup sugar
½ cup water	1 baked 9-in. pie shell
½ cup lemon juice	

1. Mix together in the top of a double boiler ½ cup sugar, the gelatin, and salt. Set aside.
2. Beat the egg yolks slightly. Mix in the water, lemon juice, and extract. Add gradually to gelatin mixture, stirring constantly until well mixed. Cook, stirring constantly over boiling water until gelatin is dissolved and mixture is slightly thickened.
3. Remove from water and stir in the lemon peel. Cool slightly. Chill until partially set.
4. Beat the egg whites until frothy; add ½ cup sugar gradually, beating constantly until stiff peaks are formed.
5. Turn slightly thickened gelatin mixture onto beaten egg whites and gently fold together. Turn into pie shell. Chill until firm.   ONE 9-INCH PIE

CANTA-LIME PIE

2 teaspoons unflavored gelatin	2 tablespoons butter or margarine
¼ cup cold water	½ cup dairy sour cream
¾ cup sugar	7 drops green food coloring
¼ cup flour	1 ripe cantaloupe, rinsed, cut in half and seeds removed
⅛ teaspoon salt	
1¼ cups water	2 egg whites
2 egg yolks, slightly beaten	2 tablespoons sugar
1½ teaspoons grated lime peel	1 baked 8-in. pie shell
3 tablespoons lime juice	

1. Soften gelatin in cold water; set aside.
2. Blend the ¾ cup sugar, flour, and salt together in a heavy saucepan. Gradually add 1¼ cups water, stirring until smooth. Bring to boiling, stirring constantly; cook and stir 3 minutes.

3. Stir about ¼ cup hot mixture into the egg yolks; immediately blend into hot mixture in saucepan. Cook, stirring constantly, 3 to 5 minutes. Remove from heat and mix in gelatin until dissolved.

4. Stir in lime peel and juice and butter; cool. Blend in the sour cream and food coloring. Chill until mixture is partially set.

5. Using a melon-ball cutter, carefully cut 6 balls from melon; reserve for garnish. Pare the remaining melon and coarsely chop enough to yield ¾ cup. Drain; refrigerate balls and chopped melon.

6. Beat egg whites until frothy; gradually add 2 tablespoons sugar, beating until stiff peaks are formed.

7. Spread over gelatin mixture; fold in melon pieces. Turn into pie shell. Chill until firm.

8. Garnish with reserved melon balls, *mint leaves*, and *whipped cream*. ONE 8-INCH PIE

GRASSHOPPER CHIFFON PIE

1 env. unflavored gelatin	1 cup chilled heavy cream
½ cup cold water	1 tablespoon confectioners' sugar
10 tablespoons white crème de cacao	2 egg whites
3 tablespoons green crème de menthe	¼ teaspoon salt
	¼ cup sugar
	1 baked 9-in. pie shell

1. Sprinkle gelatin evenly over the cold water in a saucepan. Set over low heat, stirring constantly, until gelatin is dissolved. Remove from heat.

2. Pour the crème de cacao and crème de menthe into a chilled large bowl. Stir the dissolved gelatin into the liqueurs. Chill until mixture is the consistency of thick, unbeaten egg white.

3. Meanwhile, whip the cream until soft peaks are formed. With final few strokes beat in confectioners' sugar until blended. Set in refrigerator while beating egg whites.

4. Using a clean beater, beat egg whites and salt until frothy. Add sugar gradually, continuing to beat until rounded peaks are formed when beater is slowly lifted upright.

5. Spread whipped cream and beaten egg white over the slightly gelled mixture and fold together until thoroughly blended (if necessary, rebeat whipped cream or egg white just to proper consistency before turning onto gelatin). Turn filling into baked pie shell and chill until firm.

6. Garnish pie with sprigs of fresh *mint* lightly sifted with *confectioners' sugar*. ONE 9-INCH PIE

ORANGE-BLOSSOM CHIFFON PIE

1 env. unflavored gelatin	1 cup chilled heavy cream
⅓ cup cold water	2 tablespoons confectioners' sugar
2 egg yolks	1 teaspoon vanilla extract
1 cup water	2 egg whites
¼ teaspoon salt	¼ cup sugar
1 can (6 oz.) frozen orange juice concentrate, partially thawed	1 baked 9-in. pie shell

1. Sprinkle gelatin over ⅓ cup water in top of a double boiler to soften. Beat egg yolks, 1 cup water, and salt together. Blend into gelatin. Cook over boiling water, stirring constantly, until gelatin is dissolved and mixture is slightly thickened, about 5 minutes.

2. Immediately remove from heat, add orange juice concentrate, and stir until blended. Chill, stirring occasionally, until mixture mounds when dropped from a spoon (or chill over ice and water, stirring frequently).

3. Meanwhile, whip cream until soft peaks are formed. With final few strokes, beat in confectioners' sugar and extract; set in the refrigerator.

4. Using a clean beater, beat egg whites until frothy. Gradually add sugar, continuing to beat until rounded peaks are formed. Fold in the gelatin mixture and then the whipped cream.

5. Turn into a baked pie shell. Using the back of a spoon swirl top. Chill thoroughly. Decorate with *orange sections* and *pastry cutouts*. ONE 9-INCH PIE

AVOCADO-ORANGE CHIFFON PIE

1 env. unflavored gelatin	1¼ cups orange juice
2 tablespoons cold water	⅓ cup sugar
2 tablespoons lemon juice	¼ teaspoon salt
¼ teaspoon grated orange peel	1 large ripe avocado
	1 cup heavy cream, whipped
	1 baked 9-in. pie shell

1. Soften gelatin in a mixture of the cold water and lemon juice; dissolve over hot water.

2. Mix together orange peel and juice, sugar, and

salt until sugar is dissolved; blend in dissolved gelatin. Chill until slightly thickened.

3. Meanwhile, cut into halves, pit, and peel avocado; force enough avocado through sieve or food mill to yield 1 cup. Blend sieved avocado into thickened gelatin mixture and then fold into whipped cream.

4. Turn filling into pie shell. Chill until firm.

ONE 9-INCH PIE

PEACHY PARFAIT PIE

6 almond macaroon cookies (1¾ in. each)	2 tablespoons sugar
1¼ cups boiling water	Few drops almond extract
1 pkg. (3 oz.) lemon-flavored gelatin	⅔ cup (about 3 oz.) salted almonds, coarsely chopped
1 pt. vanilla ice cream	1 baked 9-in. pie shell, or Graham Cracker Crumb Crust, *page 458*
2 medium-sized (about ½ lb.) firm ripe peaches	

1. Place cookies on a baking sheet and heat in a 325°F oven 15 minutes, or until cookies are dry. Cool on a wire rack; then crush enough to make ½ cup crumbs.

2. Pour boiling water over gelatin in a large bowl; stir until gelatin is dissolved. Add ice cream by heaping spoonfuls, blending well after each addition. Chill about 15 minutes, or until mixture mounds when dropped from a spoon.

3. Meanwhile, dip peaches into boiling water, then into cold water; slip off skins. Halve the peaches and remove pits. Chop enough of the peaches to yield about 1 cup. Sprinkle with sugar, add extract, and mix lightly.

4. Blend cookie crumbs, almonds, and peaches into thickened gelatin mixture. Turn filling into pie shell. Chill until set, 45 to 60 minutes.

ONE 9-INCH PIE

PIE OF GOLD: Follow recipe for Peachy Parfait Pie. Omit cookies, almonds, peaches, sugar, and extract. Substitute *orange-flavored gelatin* for the lemon-flavored gelatin and *1 pint orange sherbet* for the ice cream. Mix *2 cups orange sections*, cut in pieces, and *½ cup flaked coconut* into thickened gelatin. Proceed as directed.

DOUBLE STRAWBERRY PARFAIT PIE: Follow recipe for Peachy Parfait Pie. Omit cookies, almonds, peaches, sugar, and extract. Substitute *1 pint strawberry ice cream* for the vanilla ice cream. Mix *2 cups fresh ripe strawberries*, cut in pieces, into thickened gelatin. Proceed as directed.

PINEAPPLE VOLCANO CHIFFON PIE

2 env. unflavored gelatin	1 tablespoon lemon juice
½ cup sugar	3 egg whites
¼ teaspoon salt	1 baked 9-in. Graham Cracker Crumb Crust, *page 458*
3 egg yolks, fork beaten	
½ cup water	Frozen dessert topping, thawed, or whipped dessert topping
1 can (20 oz.) crushed pineapple	
¼ teaspoon grated lemon peel	1 can (8 oz.) crushed pineapple, drained

1. Mix gelatin, ¼ cup of the sugar, and salt in the top of a double boiler.

2. Beat egg yolks and water together. Stir into gelatin mixture with the undrained pineapple.

3. Set over boiling water. Thoroughly heat mixture and continue cooking 5 minutes to cook egg yolks and dissolve gelatin, stirring constantly.

4. Remove from water; mix in lemon peel and juice. Chill until mixture mounds slightly when dropped from a spoon.

5. Beat egg whites until frothy; gradually add the remaining ¼ cup sugar, beating constantly until stiff peaks are formed. Fold in gelatin mixture until blended. Turn into crust; chill.

6. Garnish pie with generous mounds of the dessert topping. Spoon on remaining crushed pineapple to resemble "volcanos." ONE 9-INCH PIE

PRUNE CHIFFON PIE

Coffee-Coconut Pie Shell, *page 481*	1 env. unflavored gelatin
1 cup chopped plumped prunes*	½ cup packed light brown sugar
⅓ cup bottled prune juice	¼ cup sugar
2 tablespoons grated orange peel	½ teaspoon salt
	1 cup dairy sour cream
3 eggs	1 cup chilled heavy cream

1. Prepare pie shell; bake and set aside.

2. Combine chopped prunes, prune juice, and orange peel in a heavy saucepan; mix well.

3. Beat eggs; add a mixture of the gelatin, sugars, and salt and blend thoroughly. Stir in the sour cream, then combine with the prune mixture. Cook, stirring constantly, over medium heat until thickened, about 10 minutes. Cool to lukewarm.

4. Beat ½ cup cream until it piles softly. Fold into

prune mixture. Turn filling into pie shell. Chill until firm.

5. Just before serving, beat remaining ½ cup cream. Decorate pie with the whipped cream, plumped *prune halves*, and *maraschino cherries*.
ONE 9-INCH PIE

*To plump dried prunes, steam them in a colander over a pan of boiling water for 30 minutes or until prunes are well plumped.

COFFEE-COCONUT PIE SHELL: Combine *1 can (3½ ounces) flaked coconut* and *1 cup double-strength coffee;* let stand 30 to 40 minutes. Drain coconut; spread on absorbent paper and pat dry. Spread *2 tablespoons softened butter or margarine* over a 9-inch pie pan; sprinkle coconut evenly over buttered surface and press against bottom and sides. Bake at 350°F 10 to 12 minutes, or until coconut is crisp.

RASPBERRY WINE PIE

1 env. unflavored gelatin	1 cup heavy cream, whipped
¼ cup sugar	1 pkg. (10 oz.) frozen red raspberries, thawed (do not drain)
⅛ teaspoon salt	
¼ cup cold water	
½ cup port wine	1 baked 8-in. pie shell

1. Combine gelatin, sugar, and salt in a saucepan. Mix well and stir in the cold water and wine. Stir over low heat until gelatin is dissolved. Chill mixture until slightly thickened.
2. Spread whipped cream over gelatin mixture; add raspberries and fold together. Turn filling into pie shell. Chill until firm.
ONE 8-INCH PIE

ROCK INN CUBAN RUM PIE

A specialty of Rock Inn, Adrian, Michigan.

3 egg yolks	1 cup chilled heavy cream
6 tablespoons sugar	
2 oz. dark rum	1 baked 8-in. Graham Cracker Crumb Crust, *page 458*
2 teaspoons unflavored gelatin	
¼ cup cold water	

1. Beat egg yolks and sugar together until thoroughly blended. Mix in the rum.
2. Soften gelatin in cold water; dissolve over hot water. Cool.
3. Whip cream just until fluffy. Continuing to beat

slowly, pour gelatin in a thin stream into cream. Beat until mixture stands in peaks. Fold in egg yolk mixture. Turn filling into crust shell. Chill.

4. Just before serving, garnish pie with *whipped cream, shaved chocolate,* or *candied fruit.*
ONE 8-INCH PIE

ENGLISH TOFFEE PIE

2 teaspoons unflavored gelatin	1 teaspoon vanilla extract
¼ cup cold water	2 egg whites
1 cup chilled heavy cream	⅛ teaspoon salt
¼ cup confectioners' sugar	½ lb. English toffee, coarsely crushed (about 1⅔ cups)
	1 baked 8-in. pie shell

1. Soften gelatin in cold water; stir over low heat until gelatin is dissolved. Set aside.
2. Beat cream until frothy; gradually add gelatin, beating continually until cream piles softly. Beat in confectioners' sugar and extract and continue to beat until cream stands in peaks.
3. Beat egg whites and salt until stiff, not dry, peaks are formed. Spread over whipped cream, add crushed toffee, and fold together. Turn filling into pie shell. Chill until firm.
ONE 8-INCH PIE

EYE-FULL TOWER PIE

Meringue Shell, *page 459*	Orange Whipped Cream, *page 441*
½ filling recipe for Lemon Chiffon Pie, *page 478*	½ cup sliced almonds, toasted
½ filling recipe for Lime Chiffon Pie, *page 478*	

1. Prepare Meringue Shell; bake as directed and cool.
2. Turn lemon filling into Meringue Shell; spread evenly. Spread lime filling over lemon layer; chill until firm.
3. When ready to serve, prepare Orange Whipped Cream; pile lightly on pie and swirl gently, using back of spoon. Sprinkle with almonds.
ONE 9-INCH PIE

ICE-CREAM PIES

VOODOO PIE

The name of this pie acknowledges the West Indian source of its chocolate-and-lime flavor.

2 eggs	1 pint chocolate ice
½ cup sugar	cream, softened
1 cup heavy cream	1 baked 10-in Chocolate
⅓ to ½ cup lime juice	Cookie Crumb
1 tablespoon grated lime	Crust, *page 526*
peel	Grated unsweetened
1 or 2 drops green food	chocolate
coloring	

1.   Beat eggs and sugar until thick and piled softly.
2.   Stir in cream and lime juice and peel until well blended; tint pale green with food coloring. Turn into refrigerator tray; freeze until mushlike in consistency.
3.   Beat until smooth and return to refrigerator tray. Freeze until almost firm.
4.   Spread ice cream over bottom of pie shell; spoon lime mixture over ice cream. Garnish top of pie with grated chocolate. Freeze until firm.

ONE 10-INCH PIE

PEPPERMINT CLOUD PIE

3 egg whites	Pastel Pink Pie Shell,
¼ teaspoon cream of	*below*
tartar	1 pint pink peppermint
6 tablespoons sugar	ice cream, slightly
	softened

1.   Beat egg whites and cream of tartar until frothy; add the sugar gradually, beating constantly until stiff peaks are formed. Spread evenly over bottom and up sides of baked pie shell, sealing meringue to top edge of pastry.
2.   Bake at 325°F 15 minutes. Cool on wire rack.
3.   Spoon ice cream over cooled meringue. Spread to form an even layer; swirl top. Garnish with *peppermint candies.* Set in freezer until serving time.

ONE 9-INCH PIE

PASTEL PINK PIE SHELL: Blend *1 cup all-purpose flour* and *½ teaspoon salt* in a bowl. Cut in *⅓ cup plus 1 tablespoon shortening* with a pastry blender until pieces are the size of small peas. Sprinkle a blend of *2 tablespoons water* and *4 drops red food coloring*, a tablespoon at a time, over mixture, tossing with a fork until mixture is evenly moistened.

Gather pastry into a ball. Roll out, on a lightly floured surface, 1 inch larger than an inverted 9-inch pie pan. Line the pie pan with pastry. Roll pastry edge under, even with outer rim of pan; flute edge. Prick bottom and sides with fork. Bake at 475°F 8 to 10 minutes. Cool on wire rack.

ONE BAKED 9-INCH PIE SHELL

STRAWBERRY ICE-CREAM PIE

2 pints vanilla ice cream,	2 drops red food
slightly softened	coloring
1 baked 9- or 10-in. pie	2 egg whites
shell	¼ teaspoon salt
16 large marshmallows	¼ cup sugar
2 tablespoons crushed	1 cup ripe strawberries,
ripe strawberries	rinsed, hulled, and
½ teaspoon vanilla	sliced
extract	

1.   Spoon ice cream into cooled pastry shell and spread evenly. Set in freezer until very firm.
2.   Combine the marshmallows and crushed strawberries in a heavy saucepan. Set over low heat, folding until marshmallows are half melted. Remove from heat and continue folding until mixture is smooth and foamy. Blend in the extract and food coloring; set aside to cool.
3.   Beat egg whites and salt until frothy; gradually add the sugar, beating constantly until stiff peaks form.
4.   Combine meringue with marshmallow mixture, folding until evenly blended. Remove filled pastry shell from freezer; cover with sliced strawberries. Top with meringue, sealing to edges.
5.   Place pie on a wooden board and set under broiler with top of meringue about 4 inches from source of heat until meringue is lightly browned. Serve immediately. Or, return to freezer until ready to serve.

6 TO 8 SERVINGS

ICE-CREAM PIE SPECTACULAR

1 egg white	1 pint coffee ice cream
¼ teaspoon salt	1 pint vanilla ice cream
¼ cup sugar	Raisin-Caramel Sauce,
1½ cups chopped walnuts	*page 483*

1.   Beat egg white with salt until frothy; add sugar

gradually, beating constantly until stiff peaks form.

2. Fold in the chopped walnuts. Turn into generously buttered 9-inch pie pan. With spoon, spread evenly over bottom and sides of pan, building up sides. Prick bottom and sides with a fork.

3. Bake at 400°F 10 to 12 minutes, or until lightly browned. Cool and chill.

4. Soften ice creams slightly. Spoon coffee ice cream into the chilled pie shell and top evenly with vanilla ice cream. Set in freezer until ready to serve.

5. Let pie stand at room temperature 10 minutes. Garnish with several spoonfuls of Raisin-Caramel Sauce and accompany with the remaining sauce.

ONE 9-INCH PIE

RAISIN-CARAMEL SAUCE

3 tablespoons butter	½ cup golden raisins,
1 cup packed light	plumped
brown sugar	1 teaspoon vanilla
½ cup cream	extract

Heat butter in a small saucepan. Add brown sugar and stir over low heat until smooth. Remove from heat. Add cream very slowly, stirring until blended after each addition. Heat about 1 minute. Stir in the raisins and extract. Serve warm or chilled.

LITTLE PIES & TARTS

REGAL ALMOND TARTLETS

Pastry for 2-crust pie	½ teaspoon almond
½ cup sugar	extract
2 tablespoons flour	2 eggs
1¼ cups (about 7 oz.)	2½ tablespoons butter
ground almonds	or margarine,
2 tablespoons orange	softened
juice	Raspberry jelly

1. Prepare tartlet shells from the pastry using muffin pans having 1¾x1-inch wells (about 24 wells). Using scallop-edged cookie cutter, cut pastry rounds about 1 inch larger than the overall size of the wells. Gently fit a round into each well, reserving the remaining pastry. Prick the entire surface of the pastry with a fork.

2. Bake the shells at 450°F 10 minutes. Remove to wire racks and cool slightly in the muffin pans.

3. To prepare filling, sift together and set aside the sugar and flour. Mix the almonds, orange juice, and extract; set aside.

4. Beat the eggs until piled softly, then beat in the sugar-flour mixture and the softened butter. Blend in the almond mixture thoroughly.

5. Spread about ½ teaspoon jelly over bottom of each tart shell, then fill each about three-fourths full with the filling mixture. Using a sharp knife, cut small strips from the reserved pastry. Place 2 strips crossed on each tart.

6. Bake at 350°F about 15 minutes, or until tarts are delicately browned and filling is set.

7. Cool slightly before removing from pans. Cool completely on wire racks. ABOUT 2 DOZEN TARTLETS

CREAMY COCONUT PETAL TARTS

1 pkg. (3 oz.) lemon-	½ cup coarsely chopped
flavored gelatin	walnuts
¼ cup sugar	1¼ cups (about 3½ oz.)
1 cup boiling water	flaked coconut
1 can (8½ oz.) crushed	1 cup heavy cream,
pineapple, drained	whipped
(reserve syrup)	12 baked Rose Petal
¼ cup sliced maraschino	Tart Shells, *page 454*
cherries, well drained	

1. Combine the gelatin and sugar in a bowl; add the boiling water. Stir until gelatin is dissolved.

2. Measure the reserved pineapple syrup; if necessary add enough water to measure ½ cup liquid; stir into the gelatin.

3. Chill until mixture is slightly thickened, and then mix in the pineapple, cherries, walnuts, and coconut. Fold in whipped cream. Spoon filling into tart shells.

4. Chill until firm. Decorate with *maraschino cherries* (with stems). 12 TARTS

BLUEBERRY TARTS

¾ cup dairy sour cream	1¼ cups cold milk
1 tablespoon	6 baked Nutmeg-Sour
confectioners' sugar	Cream Tart Shells,
1 pkg. instant lemon	*page 484*
pudding mix	Fresh blueberries

1. Blend the sour cream and confectioners' sugar.

2. Prepare the pudding mix according to direc-

tions on package, using the 1¼ cups milk. Fold in sour cream mixture.

3. Remove tart shells from pans: spoon about ⅓ cup of the pudding into each shell and top with blueberries. 6 TARTS

NUTMEG-SOUR CREAM TART SHELLS

Pie crust mix for a 1-crust pie	1 teaspoon ground nutmeg
1½ teaspoons sugar	3 tablespoons dairy sour cream

1. Blend the pie crust mix, sugar, and nutmeg in a bowl. Prepare pastry following directions on package, substituting the sour cream for the liquid. Shape pastry into a ball and flatten on a lightly floured surface.
2. Roll pastry to about ¹⁄₁₆-inch thickness and cut six rounds about ½ inch larger than overall size of a 3½-inch tart pan. Carefully fit rounds into six tart pans without stretching. Fold excess pastry under at edge and flute or press with a fork. Prick bottoms and sides of shells with fork.
3. Bake at 425°F about 8 minutes, or until lightly browned. Cool. Carefully remove from pans.

SIX 3½-INCH TART SHELLS

CURRANT TARTS

Pastry for Little Pies and Tarts, *page 454* (use ten 2¾ inch muffin-pan wells)	1¼ teaspoons vanilla extract
2 cups packed brown sugar	½ cup butter or margarine, melted
2 eggs, slightly beaten	1 cup (about 5 oz.) currants
Few grains salt	⅓ cup chopped pecans

1. Prepare unbaked tart shells, set aside.
2. Add the brown sugar gradually to the beaten eggs in a bowl, beating constantly until thoroughly blended. Beat in the salt, extract, and melted butter, then mix in the currants and pecans.
3. Spoon the filling into tart shells, allowing ¼ cup for each shell.
4. Bake at 350°F 30 to 35 minutes, or until tarts are lightly browned and filling is set.
5. Cool in pan on wire rack. 10 TARTS

NOTE: If desired, substitute for the plain currants *1 cup currants* which have been marinated for several days (or longer) in about *½ cup light rum*, then thoroughly drained before adding to the tart filling.

INDIVIDUAL DEEP-DISH APPLE PIES

¾ cup packed brown sugar	1 tablespoon grated lemon peel
¼ teaspoon ground nutmeg	7 cups sliced pared apples
2 tablespoons grated orange peel	3 tablespoons butter or margarine
	Pastry rounds*

1. Combine the brown sugar, nutmeg, and orange and lemon peels and toss gently with apple slices.
2. Fill 6 deep ramekins with apple slices. Dot each with 1½ teaspoons butter. Top with pastry rounds.
3. Bake at 425°F about 30 minutes, or until apples are tender. 6 SERVINGS

*Prepare pastry; roll out and cut into rounds slightly smaller than ramekins to be used.

DEEP-FRIED APPLE PIES

Pastry for 2-crust pie	½ teaspoon ground cinnamon
3 cups sliced pared tart apples	⅛ teaspoon ground nutmeg
½ cup water	Butter or margarine
1 teaspoon lemon juice	Fat for deep-frying heated to 375°F
¼ cup sugar	

1. Shape pastry into two balls. Using one ball at a time, flatten on a lightly floured surface and roll out ⅛ inch thick. Cut out rounds using a 3½ inch cutter; set aside.
2. Put apples into a saucepan; add water and lemon juice. Cover tightly and cook over low heat just until tender. Remove from heat; drain. Lightly mix in a blend of sugar, cinnamon, and nutmeg.
3. Place about 2 tablespoons apple mixture onto each pastry round; dot with butter. Moisten one half of the edge of each round with water to help form a tight seal. Fold the other half of round over filling. Press edges together with a fork. Be sure to seal to avoid leakage of filling while frying.
4. Lower pies into heated fat; add only as many as will float uncrowded in fat. Deep-fry about 3 minutes, or until golden brown. Turn pies as they rise to surface and several times during cooking.
5. Remove with a slotted spoon and drain over fat before removing to absorbent paper. Serve warm sprinkled with *confectioners' sugar*.

ABOUT 15 PIES

Chapter 17

DESSERTS & DESSERT SAUCES

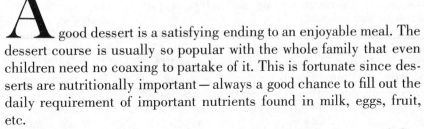

A good dessert is a satisfying ending to an enjoyable meal. The dessert course is usually so popular with the whole family that even children need no coaxing to partake of it. This is fortunate since desserts are nutritionally important — always a good chance to fill out the daily requirement of important nutrients found in milk, eggs, fruit, etc.

Following are desserts for every occasion; for luncheon and dinner menus, for the sole refreshment at a party, an afternoon tea or bridge game, a morning coffee, and numerous other occasions. Included are simple and elaborate desserts, light desserts to end hearty meals, and hearty desserts to conclude light meals.

Innumerable quick-and-easy packaged preparations are available to homemakers today. They include instant type gelatin desserts and puddings of many flavors, some requiring no cooking to thicken and others requiring a short cooking period after the addition of milk or other liquid. Canned, refrigerated, and frozen ready-to-serve puddings are available in a variety of flavors.

The desserts in this chapter are classified as follows:

Cake-Desserts, including cheese cakes which are not truly cakes, shortcakes, and desserts with a sponge or angel food cake base.

Pastries (other than pies) using puff paste or choux paste (cream puffs) and some doughs which traditionally would not be true pastry. Strudel and fruit dumplings are also included here.

Dessert Pancakes, Crêpes, and Blintzes, some of which are favorites from other countries.

Meringue Desserts, including Schaumtorte and individual meringues and meringue shells.

Custards, which are mixtures of sweetened and flavored eggs and milk. They may be cooked with constant stirring on top of the range, or cooked without stirring in the oven. Thickening is due to the coagulation of the egg proteins on heating.

Stirred (soft) custard—The custard mixture is cooked over simmering water with constant stirring until it is just thick enough to coat a metal spoon. The custard may not yet appear sufficiently thickened, but it becomes somewhat thicker on cooling. Curdling may occur in a fraction of a second when the mixture is nearing the proper consistency if the cooking is too rapid (that is, if the water under the custard is boiling rather than just simmering) or is continued too long.

Baked custard—The mixture thickens in the form of a "gel" in which the coagulated egg protein encloses and holds the liquid. As in all forms of egg cookery, custards should be baked at a low temperature, because too high a temperature (or too long baking) will cause the protein to toughen and squeeze out liquid, producing "weeping." A useful method of shortening baking time is to scald the milk before stirring it into the slightly beaten eggs. To insure uniform temperature throughout the mixture, custards are usually baked in a pan containing hot water. A baked custard is done when a metal knife inserted halfway between center and edge of custard comes out clean.

So-called "baked" custards are sometimes cooked on top of the range in a deep heavy skillet having a tight-fitting cover. The filled custard cups (each cup tightly covered with aluminum foil) are placed on a rack in the skillet, hot water is added to a depth of about 1 inch, and the covered skillet is placed over low heat so that a simmering temperature is maintained until the custards are "set."

Puddings—Top-of-the-range, baked, and steamed puddings are usually thickened with flour or cornstarch, or with starchy cereals such as tapioca, farina, rice, and cornmeal.

Starches and the above-mentioned starchy cereals thicken liquids because the starch granules, as they are heated in the liquid, gradually swell and absorb moisture. The extent of thickening, of course, depends primarily upon the proportion of starch to liquid. Thickening continues as the mixture cools. To make such mixtures smooth, the starch granules should be separated before hot liquid is added: blend until smooth with a little cold liquid after mixing the sugar in the recipe with the starch; help keep granules separated as they thicken by constantly stirring while cooking—this also insures uniform heating. Starch mixtures must be brought to boiling and cooked long enough to destroy the raw starch flavor.

Dessert Soufflés—These may be hot baked products or light chilled gelatin desserts prepared in soufflé dishes. The baked soufflés are made light and fluffy by the addition of beaten egg whites. For maximum volume and easy folding into mixture, beat egg whites until they form rounded peaks and do not slide when bowl is partially inverted.

A baked soufflé may be left in the oven for a short time with the heat turned off if it cannot be served immediately. As a soufflé cools it tends to shrink and fall because the volume of air decreases. An underbaked soufflé will fall rapidly; a soufflé baked until done and cooled slowly will fall slowly upon removal from oven.

Gelatin Desserts—These may range from plain fruit-flavored gelatin through elaborate refrigerator desserts made with gelatin.

Refrigerator Desserts are mixtures that may or may not have gelatin; they must be chilled in the refrigerator until firm enough to serve. An example is a rich dessert in a ladyfinger-lined springform pan, chilled several hours or overnight.

Frozen Desserts and Ice Creams—This takes in a number of different types of mixtures that can be frozen—in the refrigerator or an ice-cream freezer. Some frozen desserts should be agitated during freezing to break up large ice crystals while they are forming. The smaller the ice crystals in the frozen dessert, the smoother and creamier-seeming will be the texture of the dessert. Therefore, when the dessert is frozen to a mushy consistency it should be removed from the refrigerator and beaten or stirred until smooth. The whipped cream used in mousses prevents formation of large ice crystals by incorporating air into the mixture. Any substance, such as gelatin, eggs, flour, cornstarch, and rennet, which increases the viscosity (resistance to pouring) of the mixture tends to separate the crystals and prevent them from growing.

The following must be stirred (agitated) during the freezing process: *American ice cream*—mixture of cream, sugar, and flavoring. Cream that can be whipped is highly desirable since the incorporation of air during whipping gives a smooth texture to the ice cream. Whipping also distributes the fat evenly, creating added smoothness as the mixture becomes frozen. Because heavy cream is expensive, recipes have been developed which call for substitution of thin cream, evaporated milk, or milk thickened with gelatin, flour, eggs, or marshmallows for part or all of the heavy cream. *French ice cream*—a rich mixture of eggs, cream, sugar, and flavorings; virtually a frozen custard. *Philadelphia ice cream*—uncooked mixture of cream, sugar, and flavorings; never with gelatin or other binder added. *Frozen custard*—mixture with a custard base; also a frozen product, in the wholesale and retail trade, too low in butterfat content to be legally called ice cream. *Water ice*—fruit juice which is distilled and sweetened with sugar, syrup, or honey; has rather coarse texture, melts easily. *Granite*—water ice frozen with little stirring; rough and icy in texture. *Frappé*—water ice frozen to a mushy consistency. *Sherbet*—water ice (the base of which may be fruit juice or fruit pulp) with beaten egg white or gelatin added—this decreases the size of the crystals and gives a smoother product; milk sherbet uses milk as part of liquid in water ice. *Sorbet*—French frozen dessert similar to sherbet. *Coupe*—frozen cup usually composed of fruit and ice cream and attractively garnished with whipped cream, candied fruits and peels, chopped nuts, mint leaves, or fresh fruit; originally served in a special glass similar to the "champagne coupe."

The following frozen desserts need little or no stirring during the freezing process. They are ice creams made of heavy cream with or without eggs.

Parfait—made by pouring a hot thick syrup over beaten egg whites or beaten egg yolks, adding flavoring, and folding in whipped cream. *Biscuit*—parfait or similar mixture, partially frozen, then packed in small individual paper cases, and frozen until firm. *Bombe*—two or more frozen mixtures packed in a melon-shaped or round mold and refrozen. *Mousse*—sweetened and flavored whipped cream; may contain gelatin.

Fruit Desserts—Fresh fruits in season, with a dash of liqueur, sugar, and cream, or a topping, if desired, and unelaborated stewed, frozen, or canned fruits are probably the lightest and easiest to prepare of all desserts.

CAKE-DESSERTS

LUSCIOUS LEMON CHEESE CAKE

2⅔ cups zwieback crumbs (about 24 slices)	1¾ cups sugar
	3 tablespoons flour
½ cup confectioners' sugar	1½ teaspoons grated lemon peel
1½ teaspoons grated lemon peel	½ teaspoon vanilla extract
½ cup butter or margarine, softened	4 eggs, slightly beaten
	2 egg yolks
2½ lbs. cream cheese, softened	¼ cup heavy cream

1. Butter bottom and sides of a 9-inch springform pan.
2. Mix the crumbs, confectioners' sugar, and lemon peel in a bowl. Using a fork, mix in the butter. Reserve ¾ cup of the mixture for topping. Turn remainder into prepared pan; press crumbs firmly into an even layer on bottom and sides of pan. Set aside.
3. Combine the cream cheese, sugar, flour, lemon peel, and extract in a bowl. Beat until smooth and fluffy. Add the eggs and egg yolks in thirds, beating thoroughly after each addition. Blend in the cream.
4. Turn mixture into prepared crust, spreading evenly. Sprinkle reserved crumb mixture over top.
5. Bake at 250°F 2 hours. Turn off heat. Let cake stand in oven about 1 hour.
6. Remove to a wire rack to cool completely. Refrigerate several hours or overnight.
7. To serve, remove springform rim. Cut cake into wedges. ONE 9-INCH CHEESE CAKE

STRAWBERRY-GLAZED CHEESE CAKE: Follow recipe for Luscious Lemon Cheese Cake. Reduce zwieback crumbs to 2 cups and use to line springform pan. Prepare strawberry glaze for cooled cheese cake. Using *1 quart fresh ripe strawberries*, crush enough to make ½ cup crushed. Combine ½ cup sugar and *1 tablespoon cornstarch* in a saucepan. Stir in ¼ *cup water*. Bring rapidly to boiling, stirring constantly. Cook 2 minutes. Remove from heat and stir in *2 teaspoons butter* and *8 drops red food coloring*. Strain and set aside to cool slightly. Meanwhile, arrange remaining whole strawberries on top of cheese cake. (Halve the very large berries and arrange cut-side down on cake.) Spoon the glaze evenly over the berries.

CHEESE CAKE TOMASELLI

A delightful dessert served at Cafe Tomaselli, Salzburg, Austria.

5 egg yolks	¼ cup heavy cream
1 cup sugar	¼ cup flour
½ teaspoon salt	1 lb. farmer cheese*
½ teaspoon grated lemon peel	5 egg whites, beaten to stiff, not dry, peaks

1. Butter an 8-inch springform pan and coat it lightly with *fine dry bread crumbs*.
2. Beat egg yolks with sugar, salt, and lemon peel until thoroughly blended. Mix in a blend of cream and flour.
3. Force cheese through food mill or sieve; combine with the egg yolk mixture. Beat thoroughly until smooth. Fold in the beaten egg whites just until blended. Carefully turn into prepared springform pan.
4. Bake at 300°F 1 to 1¼ hours, or until cake is lightly browned and pulls away from sides of pan.
5. Cool cake on a rack about 15 minutes. Then remove the rim of springform pan and cool completely.
6. Sprinkle surface with a mixture of *cinnamon* and *sugar*. ABOUT 8 SERVINGS

*Essentially the same as cottage cheese produced in the United States.

CHOCOLATE-MINT CHEESE CAKE

1 env. unflavored
gelatin
½ cup cold water
½ cup boiling water
3 sq. (3 oz.) semisweet
chocolate
8 oz. cream cheese
1 cup sugar
1½ teaspoons vanilla
extract

¾ teaspoon peppermint
extract
1 can (14½ oz.)
evaporated milk
1⅓ cups chocolate wafer
crumbs (about 28
wafers)
¼ cup butter, melted
3 tablespoons lemon
juice

1. Soften gelatin in cold water in a bowl; add boiling water and stir until gelatin is completely dissolved. Set aside to cool.
2. Melt chocolate over hot water.
3. Meanwhile, cream the cream cheese, sugar, and extracts together. Blend in the melted chocolate. Add the gelatin gradually, blending thoroughly. Chill until mixture begins to gel.
4. Meanwhile, chill evaporated milk in a refrigerator tray in freezer until ice crystals begin to form around edge.
5. Mix wafer crumbs and melted butter.
6. Line the sides of a 9-inch springform pan with a double layer of waxed paper. Turn two-thirds of crumb mixture into the pan (remainder is for topping) and press into an even layer on bottom.
7. When chocolate mixture begins to gel, beat icy evaporated milk and lemon juice together until very stiff. Fold into chocolate mixture until thoroughly blended. Turn into the pan.
8. Sprinkle remaining crumbs in border around edge. Chill until set, 2 to 3 hours.   10 to 12 SERVINGS

WHIPPING CREAM CHEESE CAKE
This recipe, created by Executive Chef Enrico Wintrich, is featured in the "71 Club" atop Chicago's Executive House.

1 env. unflavored
gelatin
¼ cup cold water
1 lb. cream cheese
1 cup confectioners'
sugar, sifted
1 teaspoon vanilla
extract

1 tablespoon brandy
1½ cups heavy cream,
whipped to soft peaks
6 thin slices pound or
sponge cake
Chocolate curls

1. Sprinkle gelatin over water in a saucepan and stir over low heat until dissolved; set aside.

2. Blend cream cheese, confectioners' sugar, extract and brandy in a large bowl; beat until smooth. Beat in dissolved gelatin.
3. Gently fold whipped cream into cheese mixture until blended.
4. Arrange the thin slices of cake over bottom of an 8x8x2-inch pan. Spoon cheese-whipped cream mixture over cake and spread evenly to edges. Top with chocolate curls or chopped nuts.
5. Chill at least 2 hours. Cut into six servings, allowing 1 slice cake per serving.   6 SERVINGS

STRAWBERRY SHORTCAKE

1¾ cups all-purpose
flour
2 tablespoons sugar
1 tablespoon baking
powder

½ teaspoon salt
½ cup lard, chilled
¾ cup milk
Sweetened sliced ripe
strawberries

1. Blend the flour, sugar, baking powder, and salt in a bowl. Cut in the lard with a pastry blender or two knives until particles are about the size of coarse cornmeal. Make a well in the center and add milk all at one time. Stir with a fork 20 to 30 strokes.
2. Turn dough out onto a lightly floured surface and shape it into a ball. Knead lightly with the fingertips about 15 times.
3. Divide dough into halves. Roll each half about ¼ inch thick to fit an 8-inch layer cake pan. Place one round of dough in pan and brush with *melted butter or margarine.* Cover with the other round. Brush top with *milk.*
4. Bake at 425°F 15 to 18 minutes, or until top is delicately browned.
5. Split shortcake while hot and spread with *butter or margarine.* Arrange half of the strawberry slices over bottom layer. Spoon *whipped dessert topping, dairy sour cream,* or *sweetened whipped cream* over berries. Cover with top layer and arrange remaining berries over it. Spoon additional topping over all.   ABOUT 6 SERVINGS
NOTE: *Orange or lemon marmalade* or *strawberry jam* may be thinly spread over layers before adding strawberries and topping.

PEACH SHORTCAKE: Follow recipe for Strawberry Shortcake. Substitute sweetened *fresh peach slices* for strawberries.

SUNSHINE SHORTCAKE: Follow recipe for Strawberry Shortcake. Substitute *orange sections,* sliced *banana,* and *confectioners' sugar* for strawberries.

SHORTCAKE FOR PASSOVER

4 egg yolks
¾ teaspoon grated lemon
   peel
¾ cup sugar
½ cup sifted matzo meal
4 egg whites

Few grains salt
1 qt. strawberries,
   sweetened
Sweetened Whipped
   Cream, *page 441*

1. Mix the egg yolks, lemon peel, and ½ cup of the sugar; beat at high speed of electric mixer until very thick and light-colored.
2. Sprinkle the matzo meal over the egg yolk mixture and fold together gently just until blended.
3. Beat egg whites and salt until frothy; add the remaining ¼ cup sugar gradually, beating constantly until stiff, glossy peaks are formed. Spread egg yolk mixture over egg whites and gently fold together.
4. Turn batter into 2 greased (bottoms only) waxed-paper-lined, and greased again 8x8x2-inch baking pans.
5. Bake at 350°F 20 minutes, or until lightly browned.
6. Cool in pans on wire racks for 10 minutes. Cut around edges of cakes, invert and carefully remove waxed paper. Turn right side up and cool completely.
7. To serve, place one cake layer on a large serving plate and top with half of the strawberries; repeat with second cake layer and remaining strawberries. Top with whipped cream. ABOUT 9 SERVINGS

CHERRY-BANANA SPONGE CAKE DESSERT

1 can (17 oz.) pitted
   dark sweet cherries,
   drained (reserve
   liquid)
2 tablespoons cornstarch
3 tablespoons apricot
   preserves
⅛ teaspoon salt
¼ teaspoon grated lemon
   peel
1 cup chilled heavy
   cream
¼ cup confectioners'
   sugar

½ teaspoon vanilla
   extract
½ teaspoon almond
   extract
4 medium-sized all-
   yellow bananas
2 tablespoons orange
   juice
2 sponge cake layers,
   9-in. each (see Hot
   Milk Sponge Cake,
   page 415)

1. Add enough water to cherry syrup to yield 1 cup. Stir a small amount of the syrup into corn-starch in a saucepan; blend until smooth. Mix in apricot preserves. Add remaining cherry syrup and salt; bring to boiling and boil 3 minutes, stirring constantly. Stir in lemon peel and cherries (reserve about 12 for garnish); cool and chill.
2. Just before assembling cake, whip cream until soft peaks are formed; with final few strokes, blend in the confectioners' sugar and extracts. Set in refrigerator.
3. Cut 3 of the bananas in half crosswise; slice each half lengthwise into 3 or 4 petals; drizzle with orange juice.
4. Slice remaining banana into ¼-inch slices and mix into cherry filling.
5. Place one cake layer on serving plate and spoon on the filling; top with second cake layer. Arrange banana petals around top edge of cake and pile whipped cream in the center. Garnish with a ring of reserved cherries. ONE 9-INCH LAYER CAKE

RASPBERRY RIBBON CAKE

1 pkg. lemon-flavored,
   butter-type layer cake
   mix
1 pkg. (3 oz.) raspberry-
   flavored gelatin
¾ cup boiling water
½ cup orange juice

1 can (8½ oz.) crushed
   pineapple, drained
   (reserve ¼ cup syrup)
½ cup chopped toasted
   almonds
1 cup heavy cream
¼ cup confectioners'
   sugar

1. Prepare and bake cake layers according to package directions; set aside to cool.
2. To prepare gelatin topping, dissolve gelatin in boiling water in a bowl. Stir in orange juice and reserved pineapple syrup. Chill until mixture is thickened but not "set." Blend in drained pineapple and almonds. Set aside.
3. Meanwhile, place 2-inch strips of waxed paper across bottoms of 2 layer cake pans, extending strips over edges. Replace the cooled cake layers by placing one layer in the cake pan upside down and the other layer in second pan right side up. (This will give a better looking cake when gelatin-topped layers are put together.)
4. Spoon gelatin mixture evenly over the cake layers. Refrigerate until gelatin is firm. Remove from refrigerator and, grasping extended ends of waxed paper, lift cake layers out of pans.
5. Whip cream until soft peaks are formed, beating in confectioners' sugar with final few strokes.
6. Place one layer of cake, gelatin side up, on

serving plate. Spread ½ cup of the whipped cream over gelatin topping. Place second layer, gelatin side up, over bottom layer. Using remaining whipped cream, frost sides of cakes. Refrigerate until serving time.   ABOUT 10 SERVINGS

MARBLE CHOCOLATE FREEZE

The irregularity of the cake slices creates a marbled effect in this dessert.

2 tablespoons cocoa	2 cups confectioners'
1 pkg. angel food cake	sugar
mix	6 egg yolks, well beaten
1 cup unsalted butter	3 oz. (3 sq.) unsweet-
4 teaspoons vanilla	ened chocolate, melted
extract	and cooled
	6 egg whites

1. Blend cocoa with flour portion of cake mix. Prepare, bake, and cool cake according to directions on package for a 10-inch tubed cake.
2. Cream butter with extract until butter is softened. Add confectioners' sugar gradually, beating constantly until light and fluffy. Add egg yolks in thirds, beating well after each addition. Blend in the cooled chocolate.
3. Beat egg whites until stiff, not dry, peaks are formed. Fold into chocolate mixture.
4. Slice the cooled cake into ½-inch wedges (measured at outer edge). Layer bottom of a 9x9x2-inch baking pan with a third of cake wedges.
5. Spread half of filling over cake. Repeat layers,

ending with cake. Press lightly until top layer is even with edge of pan. Cover and freeze at least 8 hours.
6. Let stand at room temperature about 10 minutes before serving.   ABOUT 12 SERVINGS

CHERRY ICE-CREAM CAKE

1 pkg. devil's food cake	2 tablespoons
mix	confectioners' sugar
1 qt. vanilla ice cream,	1 teaspoon vanilla
softened	extract
½ cup (30) chopped green	1½ cups heavy cream,
maraschino cherries	whipped

1. Prepare cake mix according to package directions. Turn into 2 prepared 9-inch layer cake pans and bake according to package directions. Cool thoroughly.
2. Combine the ice cream and cherries; mix well.
3. Place one cake layer on an aluminum foil-covered cardboard and spread ice cream in an even layer over cake. Top with other cake layer. Place in freezer until ice cream is firm.
4. Blend confectioners' sugar and extract into whipped cream with final few strokes.
5. Frost sides and top of cake with whipped cream and pipe an edge on top of cake with a pastry bag and tube. Freeze until firm.
6. Allow cake to soften slightly before serving. Serve garnished with *green cherries*.

ONE 9-INCH 2-LAYER CAKE

PASTRIES

PUFF PASTE
(Pâte Feuilletées)

1 cup butter	½ teaspoon salt
2 cups sifted all-	7 tablespoons water
purpose flour	

1. Put butter into a large bowl of cold water and ice cubes or chipped ice. Work butter with hands. Break it into small portions and squeeze each in water about 20 times, or until butter is pliable and waxy. Remove and wipe off excess water. Reserve ¼ cup of this butter. Pat remainder ½ inch thick, divide into 5 equal portions, wrap each in waxed paper. Chill in refrigerator until firm.

2. Sift flour and salt together into a bowl. With pastry blender or two knives, cut in the ¼ cup butter until pieces are the size of small peas. Add water gradually, stir in with a fork. When blended, gather into a ball and knead on lightly floured surface until elastic and smooth. Cover with bowl and let ripen about 30 minutes.
3. Roll on a floured surface to form a rectangle ¼ inch thick. Keep corners square, gently pulling dough into shape where necessary. Remove one portion of chilled butter and cut into small pieces. Quickly pat pieces down center third of dough. Cover butter with right-hand third of dough. Fold left-hand third under butter section. With rolling

pin gently press down and seal the open edges. Wrap pastry in waxed paper. Chill in refrigerator about 1 hour.

4. Remove from refrigerator and place on the board with butter section near top, narrow width toward you. Turn folded dough one-quarter way around, to have open edge away from you. Roll to original size. Repeat four times the procedure for folding, sealing and chilling, using second, third, fourth, and fifth portions of butter. Each time place dough on floured surface, turn, and roll as directed.

6. With last rolling, fold four sides toward center. Gently press down with rolling pin. Fold in half. Wrap dough in waxed paper. Cover with a damp towel. Chill in refrigerator about 2 hours before using.

7. To store for several days, wrap dough in waxed paper and place in refrigerator.

PUFF PASTE FOR 12 NAPOLEONS
OR 6 VOL-AU-VENT SHELLS

PATTY SHELLS (Vol-au-Vent Shells)
(Croûtes de Vol-au-Vent)

For Individual Vol-au-Vent: Follow recipe for Puff Paste. Roll pastry ⅓ inch thick. With a sharp knife or 3-inch cookie cutter, cut out rounds. With 2-inch cookie cutter cut centers from one half the 3-inch rounds. Remove centers, leaving ½-inch rims. Moisten ½-inch edges of solid 3-inch rounds with cold water. Fit rims on top. Thoroughly prick through rims and bases with a fork. Gently and evenly press rims down. Transfer to baking sheet which has been rinsed with cold water and well drained. Roll the 2-inch centers to ¼-inch thickness. These are used as covers and may be cut into shapes such as stars or scalloped rounds. Transfer to baking sheet. Prick well. Chill shells and covers in refrigerator for 30 minutes. Bake at 450°F 8 minutes; reduce oven temperature to 350°F and bake about 20 minutes longer. If browning is too rapid, cover with a sheet of unglazed paper. Remove to rack to cool. Reheat before filling with hot creamed mixture.

For Large Vol-au-Vent: Divide pastry into halves. Roll each into a round or oval of the same size to ⅓-inch thick. From one, cut out center, leaving a rim about ¾-inch wide. Moisten ¾-inch edge of solid round with cold water. Transfer it to one end of ungreased baking sheet covered with three thicknesses of unglazed paper. Place rim over round. Prick well. Gently and evenly press rim down. Roll remaining center to ¼-inch thickness. Transfer it to

other end of baking sheet. Prick well. Chill in refrigerator 30 minutes. Bake as individual Vol-au-Vent Shells. Reheat before filling with hot creamed mixture. Use baked center as a cover.

NAPOLEONS (Petites Mille-Feuilles): Follow recipe for Puff Paste. Divide pastry into thirds. Immediately return two portions to refrigerator. Roll remaining portion into a rectangle ⅛ inch thick. Cut into even 3x5-inch strips. Trim ends so all strips are equal. Transfer to baking sheet rinsed with cold water and drained thoroughly. Prick well. Repeat process with each remaining portion of pastry. Chill in refrigerator 30 minutes. Bake at 425°F 10 minutes; reduce oven temperature to 325°F and bake 20 minutes, or until golden brown. Remove to racks. When cold, split each slice lengthwise. Let stand about 30 minutes to dry. Fill one split slice with *Almond Pastry Cream, below.* Gently press together. Spread more filling over top and cover with one half of another slice, cut-side down. Spread top with more filling and cover with remaining half of slice. This completes one Napoleon, excepting the glaze.

Napoleon Glaze: Mix in a heavy saucepan *¾ cup confectioners' sugar, 1 tablespoon hot water, 1 teaspoon light corn syrup,* and *2 teaspoons butter.* Place over low heat, stirring constantly until butter melts. Add *½ teaspoon vanilla extract.* Spread on tops of Napoleons. For design, pipe *Decorating Chocolate, page 430,* through No. 4 decorating tube in parallel lines across width of cake; draw wooden pick lengthwise across chocolate lines before chocolate sets.

ALMOND PASTRY CREAM
(Crème Pâtisserie d' Amandes)

⅓ lb. (about 1 cup) blanched almonds, finely ground	3 tablespoons butter
	2 egg yolks
	1 tablespoon rum or kirsch
½ cup confectioners' sugar	

1. Mix the almonds and confectioners' sugar.
2. Cream butter until softened. Beat in egg yolks, one at a time, then the rum. Continue beating until blended. Mix in the almond-sugar. 1 CUP PASTE

CREAM PUFF OR CHOUX PASTE
(Pâte à Choux)

Since this pastry puffs up in baking, it is used in many interesting ways by French pastry cooks. A popular use is for cream puffs and éclairs which are delightful in taste and appearance. These crisp, hollow shells also may be filled with a salad mixture or any hot, creamed food. To insure crispness, fill just before serving.

1 cup hot water	½ teaspoon salt
½ cup butter	1 cup all-purpose flour
1 tablespoon sugar	4 eggs

1. Put hot water, butter, sugar, and salt into a saucepan and bring to a rolling boil.
2. Add the flour all at one time. Beat vigorously with a wooden spoon until mixture leaves sides of pan and forms a smooth ball. Remove from heat.
3. Add eggs, one at a time, beating until smooth after each addition. Continue beating until mixture is thick and smooth.
4. Dough may be shaped and baked at once, or wrapped in waxed paper and stored in refrigerator overnight.
5. Complete as directed in any one of the following variations.

1 DOZEN LARGE OR 4 DOZEN MINIATURE PUFFS OR ÉCLAIRS

CREAM PUFFS (Choux à la Crème): Prepare recipe for Cream Puff or Choux Paste. Force dough through a pastry bag or drop by tablespoonfuls 2 inches apart onto a lightly greased baking sheet. Bake large puffs at 450°F 15 minutes; reduce oven temperature to 350°F and bake 20 to 25 minutes longer, or until golden in color. Bake small puffs at 450°F 10 minutes; reduce oven temperature to 350°F and bake 5 minutes longer, or until golden in color. Remove to rack and cool. Cut off tops of cream puffs, pull out any soft, moist dough, and fill shells with *French Pastry Cream*, or *Cocoa or Strawberry Filling, below.* Replace tops and sprinkle with *sifted confectioners' sugar.*

ÉCLAIRS (Éclairs de Crème au Chocolat): Follow recipe for Cream Puffs, forming dough into oblongs 1x4½ inches. When cool, cut a slit in the side of each éclair and pull out any soft, moist dough; force filling into éclair. Fill with *French Pastry Cream.* Frost with *Chocolate Glaze, below.*

Chocolate Glaze (Cooked): Melt *1 ounce (1 square) unsweetened chocolate.* Mix in heavy saucepan ¾ cup confectioners' sugar, 1 teaspoon dark corn syrup, 1 tablespoon cream, melted chocolate, 2 teaspoons boiling water, and 1 teaspoon butter. Place over low heat and stir constantly until butter melts. Remove from heat and add ½ teaspoon vanilla extract. Cool slightly. Spread evenly over tops of éclairs.

Chocolate Glaze (Uncooked): Blend *1½ cups confectioners' sugar* into *1 egg white.* Add ¾ teaspoon vanilla extract and 1½ ounces (1½ squares) unsweetened chocolate, melted. Mix thoroughly and spread over tops of éclairs.

CREAM PUFF CHRISTMAS TREE: Prepare recipe for Cream Puff or Choux Paste. Force dough through a pastry bag and tube, or drop by spoonfuls 2 inches apart onto lightly greased baking sheets. Bake at 425°F 20 minutes, or until golden brown. Turn off oven. Prick puffs with a fork and return to oven for 20 minutes. Remove puffs to wire racks and cool completely. Cut off tops of puffs. Spoon about 3 tablespoons *Eggnog Pineapple Filling, page 493,* into each shell. Replace tops. On a serving plate, arrange puffs to form a tree.

18 TO 24 CREAM PUFFS

FRENCH PASTRY CREAM
(Crème Pâtisserie)

3 tablespoons flour	4 egg yolks, slightly
6 tablespoons sugar	beaten
¼ teaspoon salt	1 teaspoon vanilla
½ cup cold milk	extract
1½ cups milk, scalded	

1. Thoroughly blend flour, sugar, and salt in the top of a double boiler. Add the cold milk, stirring well. Gradually stir in scalded milk. Bring to boiling over direct heat, stirring constantly; cook 2 minutes.
2. Set over boiling water. Vigorously stir about 3 tablespoons of hot mixture into egg yolks. Immediately blend into mixture in double boiler. Cook over simmering water 3 to 5 minutes; stir slowly to keep mixture cooking evenly.
3. Remove from heat and strain into a bowl. Stir in extract. Cover and cool. Chill.

ABOUT 2 CUPS PASTRY CREAM

COCOA FILLING: Prepare *3 envelopes dessert topping mix* according to package directions. Fold in *2 tablespoons Dutch process cocoa per package.*

ABOUT 6 CUPS FILLING

STRAWBERRY FILLING: Prepare *2 envelopes dessert topping mix* according to package directions. Fold in *2 packages (16 ounces each) frozen strawberries,* thawed and drained.

ABOUT 5 CUPS FILLING

EGGNOG PINEAPPLE FILLING

1½ tablespoons cornstarch	1 can (8½ oz.) crushed pineapple, well drained
2 tablespoons cold water	
3 cups dairy eggnog	1 cup quartered maraschino cherries
½ teaspoon vanilla extract	
	¼ cup flaked coconut

1. Mix a blend of the cornstarch and water and eggnog in a heavy saucepan. Stirring constantly, bring rapidly to boiling. Cook and stir 2 to 3 minutes. Remove from heat.

2. Immediately turn into a chilled bowl; do not scrape pan. Mix in remaining ingredients. Cool over ice and water, stirring occasionally. Use to fill cream puffs. ABOUT 3½ CUPS FILLING

LEMON PASTRY DESSERT

Lemon Filling, *below*	2 eggs, well beaten
Topping, *below*	2 tablespoons heavy cream
3 cups sifted all-purpose flour	
⅛ teaspoon salt	1 egg white
1 cup firm butter or margarine	½ cup flaked coconut, toasted

1. Prepare and chill the Lemon Filling and the mixture for Topping.

2. Blend flour and salt in a bowl. Cut in butter until particles are the size of rice kernels. Add a mixture of beaten eggs and 1 tablespoon of the cream; stir with a fork until dough holds together. Form into a ball and divide into halves.

3. On a lightly floured surface, roll half of the dough at a time into a 16x12-inch rectangle. Cut into halves, prick entire surface thoroughly with a fork and place on baking sheets. Brush pastry with a mixture of egg white and remaining 1 tablespoon cream.

4. Bake at 350°F 15 minutes, or until lightly browned. Leave pastry on baking sheets and set on wire racks to cool.

5. On a serving tray, stack and fill three of the pastries, topping each layer of filling with finely chopped drained *maraschino cherries*, if desired. Cover with the fourth pastry and spread the Topping evenly over surface. Sprinkle with the coconut. Chill thoroughly.

6. To serve, cut into rectangles. 12 TO 16 SERVINGS

LEMON FILLING: Prepare *1 package (3½ ounces) lemon pudding and pie filling mix* according to package directions for pudding; cool thoroughly. Fold *1 cup whipped chilled heavy cream* into cooled pudding. Chill the filling at least 1 hour.

NOTE: If desired, *¼ cup butter mints*, crushed, may be blended into the whipped cream.

TOPPING: Mix *1 cup heavy cream, ¼ cup lightly packed brown sugar,* and *1½ teaspoons grated lemon peel* in a deep bowl having straight sides; chill thoroughly. Whip the chilled mixture until stiff.

STRUDEL

4 cups sifted all-purpose flour	Lukewarm water (80° to 85°F)
1 egg, fork beaten	Melted butter
1 tablespoon melted butter	Flour
	Fine dry bread crumbs
1 tablespoon cider vinegar	Strudel Fillings, *page 494*

1. Put flour into a large bowl and make a well in center; add egg and butter. Put vinegar into a measuring cup and fill with lukewarm water to the 1-cup line. Gradually add to ingredients in bowl, mixing until all flour is moistened.

2. Turn dough onto a lightly floured pastry board and knead. Hold dough high above board and hit it hard against the board 100 to 125 times, or until dough is smooth and elastic and small bubbles appear on the surface. Knead dough occasionally during the hitting process. Shape dough into a smooth round ball and put onto a lightly floured board. Lightly brush top of dough with melted butter. Cover dough with an inverted bowl and allow to rest 30 minutes.

3. Cover a table (about 48x30 inches) with a clean cloth and sprinkle the cloth evenly with *½ cup flour*.

4. Place dough on center of cloth and sprinkle very lightly with flour. Roll dough into a rectangle ¼ to ⅛ inch thick.

5. Clench the fists, tucking the thumbs under the fingers. With the palm-side of fists down, reach under the dough to its center (dough will rest on back of hands). Being careful not to tear dough, stretch the center of the dough gently and steadily toward you as you slowly walk around the table. (Dough should not have any torn spots, if possible, but such perfection will come with practice.)

6. As the center becomes as thin as paper, con-

centrate the stretching motion closer to the edge of the dough. Continue until dough is as thin as tissue paper and hangs over edges of table. With kitchen shears, trim edges leaving about 2 inches of dough overhanging on all sides.

7. Allow stretched dough to dry about 5 minutes, or until it is no longer sticky. Avoid drying dough too long since it will become brittle.

8. Sprinkle melted butter and bread crumbs over dough. Cover dough with one of the *Strudel Fillings, below*.

9. Fold the overhanging dough on all sides over the filling, making strudel even with edge of table. Beginning at one narrow end of table, grasp the cloth with both hands; slowly lift cloth and fold over a strip of dough about 3 inches wide. Pull cloth toward you; again lift cloth and slowly and loosely roll dough, making roll about 3 inches wide. Brush off excess flour from the roll; cut roll into halves and place on a buttered 15x10x1-inch jelly roll pan. Brush top and sides with fork-beaten *egg*.

10. Bake at 350°F about 40 minutes, or until strudel is golden brown. Remove to wire rack. Sift *confectioners' sugar* over top of strudel. Cut into 2½-inch slices and serve warm or cooled.

1 DOZEN SLICES

Strudel Fillings

CHERRY FILLING: Drain *2 cans (20 ounces each) pitted tart red cherries*. Put cherries between layers of absorbent paper and pat gently to remove any excess liquid. Mix *¾ cup chopped toasted blanched almonds, 1 cup sugar,* and *½ teaspoon ground cinnamon*. Sprinkle prepared strudel dough with cherries and almond mixture.

POPPY SEED FILLING: Mix *½ pound freshly ground poppy seed, 1 cup sugar, ½ cup raisins,* and *2 teaspoons grated lemon peel* and spoon over prepared strudel dough.

APPLE AND CURRANT FILLING: Core and pare *1½ pounds tart apples*. Cut apples into ⅛-inch slices. Spoon apple slices and *½ cup currants or raisins* over prepared strudel dough. Sprinkle with a mixture of *¾ cup sugar, 1 teaspoon ground cinnamon, ⅛ teaspoon nutmeg,* and *1 teaspoon grated lemon or orange peel*.

COTTAGE CHEESE FILLING: Beat *2 egg yolks, ¼ cup sugar,* and *¼ teaspoon salt* until thick. Add *1 pound dry cottage cheese* gradually to egg mixture, beating well. Stir in *¼ cup raisins, ½ teaspoon vanilla extract,* and *½ teaspoon grated lemon peel*. Spoon filling in small mounds on prepared strudel

dough; spread evenly, then roll as directed.

DRIED FRUIT FILLING: Mix *1 cup finely chopped dried apricots, 1 cup finely chopped prunes, 1 teaspoon grated orange peel, 2 tablespoons orange juice, ½ cup sugar,* and *2 tablespoons honey,* warmed. Spread over prepared strudel dough. Sprinkle *½ teaspoon ground nutmeg* before rolling.

CHOPPED NUT FILLING: Mix *½ pound blanched almonds,* finely ground, *4 egg yolks, ½ cup sugar,* and *1 teaspoon grated lemon peel* to form a paste. Spread in rows on prepared strudel dough. Drizzle with *¼ cup melted butter* before rolling.

RAISIN AND CHERRY FILLING: Mix *4 cups ground raisins, 1 jar (8 ounce) maraschino cherries, 4 cups chopped filberts, 2 cups sugar, 2 cups ground bread or cake crumbs,* and *¼ cup lemon juice*. Place on prepared strudel dough in rows fairly close together. Cut *Turkish paste* into small cubes and wedge into rows every few inches. (Or use *orange marmalade* and drop half teaspoonfuls into rows.) Roll as for other strudels. When cut, the colors of the paste or marmalade show through filling.

JELLY FILLING: Sprinkle prepared strudel dough generously with *cinnamon* and *sugar*. Mix *¾ cup chopped nuts, 1 cup golden raisins, 1 pint cherry, plum, or watermelon preserves, 1 cup fine bread crumbs,* and *1 teaspoon grated lemon peel*. Place a row of filling on dough every few inches; roll.

SPICY PEAR DUMPLINGS

Tender pastry enhances the flavor of succulent Anjou pears in this hearty family dessert.

2¾ cups all-purpose flour	½ teaspoon ground mace, ground coriander, or anise seed, crushed
1 tablespoon sugar	
½ teaspoon salt	
¾ cup lard	2 tablespoons butter or margarine
½ to ⅔ cup cold water	
6 fresh Anjou pears, pared and cored (reserve peelings)	1 cup water
	1 teaspoon cornstarch
	⅛ teaspoon salt
1½ cups lightly packed brown sugar	1 tablespoon lemon juice
	1 tablespoon butter or margarine

1. Combine flour, sugar, and salt in a bowl. Cut in lard with a pastry blender or two knives until pieces are the size of small peas. Sprinkle enough water over mixture, about 1 tablespoon at a time,

mixing lightly with a fork after each addition until dough can be easily gathered into a ball.

2. Divide dough into halves and shape each into a ball. Roll each into a round about 14 inches in diameter. Using a pastry wheel, divide each round into 3 equal wedge-shaped pieces. Place one pear in the center of each portion and spoon about 1 tablespoon of a mixture of brown sugar and spice into each pear cavity. Dot pears with the 2 tablespoons butter. Fold pastry up over pears, moistening edges to seal. Place the dumplings in buttered individual ramekins; set aside.

3. Combine pear peelings and water in a saucepan; bring to boiling and simmer, covered, about 5 minutes. Strain, discarding peelings, and add enough water to make 1 cup liquid.

4. Blend remaining brown sugar mixture, cornstarch, and salt. Stir in pear liquid, lemon juice, and butter. Bring to boiling and boil about 3 minutes. Pour syrup equally over pears in ramekins; cover each closely with aluminum foil.

5. Bake at 425°F 10 minutes; reduce oven temperature to 375°F and continue baking about 30 minutes, or until pastry is golden brown and pears are tender. Uncover last 20 minutes of baking.

6. Serve pears warm, spooning some of the sauce in the bottom of the ramekins over them. Accompany with a pitcher of *cream.* 6 SERVINGS

DESSERT PANCAKES, CRÊPES & BLINTZES

DESSERT PANCAKES

3 eggs	Few grains salt
½ cup cold water	1 cup milk
1 cup all-purpose flour	½ cup cream
1 tablespoon sugar	Butter or margarine

1. Beat the eggs with cold water until thoroughly blended. Add a mixture of the flour, sugar, and salt. Beat until batter is smooth. Stir in the milk and cream and set aside 30 minutes.

2. Heat enough butter in a skillet or a griddle to grease surface well. Pour in the batter from end of a spoon to make pancakes about 6 inches in diameter. Cook until golden brown on both sides.

3. Serve pancakes, as for crêpes, filled with crushed *fresh berries* and topped with *whipped cream.* ABOUT 24 PANCAKES

PANCAKES À LA BAHAMAS

A charming restaurant in Nassau features this rich orange-flavored dessert.

Orange Butter, *below*	7 tablespoons flour
3 egg yolks	3 egg whites
1 cup milk	Butter
Few grains salt	

1. Prepare Orange Butter and chill thoroughly.

2. Beat egg yolks. Add milk and salt; beat until blended. Mix in flour until well blended.

3. Beat egg whites until stiff, not dry, peaks are formed. Fold egg whites into egg yolk mixture.

4. Heat butter (allowing about 2 tablespoons of butter for preparing each pancake) in an 8-inch skillet over low heat. When butter begins to foam, pour it into a small cup and use for all the pancakes.

5. Using about ½ cup for each pancake, pour batter into heated skillet; tilt to evenly coat bottom of skillet. Cook until the batter is set. (Stir batter each time before baking another pancake.)

6. As pancake bakes spoon a portion of the melted butter around the edges and underneath until pancake seems to "float." Cook pancake slowly in the butter until the underside is golden, about 4 minutes. Turn and cook until the other side is golden. Add more butter, if necessary, to keep the pancake free from the skillet at all times.

7. Transfer pancake to a hot platter and top with a spoonful of the Orange Butter; roll. Set platter in warm oven while preparing remaining pancakes. Top with any remaining Orange Butter and pour *Cointreau* over the warm pancakes. Serve immediately. ABOUT 6 PANCAKES

ORANGE BUTTER: Cream together 6 *tablespoons butter or margarine, ½ teaspoon grated orange peel,* and 3 *tablespoons orange juice* until butter is softened. Beat rapidly so that juice will be readily blended with the butter. Add 6 *tablespoons confectioners' sugar* while continuing to beat. Chill thoroughly. Orange Butter can be stored for days in the refrigerator.

NOTE: These pancakes can also be served from the blazer pan of a chafing dish.

GERMAN APPLE PANCAKES

¼ cup butter or margarine	4 eggs
3 small, firm cooking apples, cored, pared, and thinly sliced (about 2½ cups)	⅓ cup milk
	¼ cup flour
	1 tablespoon sugar
	¼ teaspoon salt
2 tablespoons sugar	6 tablespoons butter or margarine
1 teaspoon ground cinnamon	Confectioners' sugar

1. Heat the ¼ cup butter in a 10-inch skillet; add the apple slices, cover, and cook over medium heat until apples are almost tender, turning slices several times during cooking. When almost tender, sprinkle a mixture of the 2 tablespoons sugar and the cinnamon evenly over apples. Continue cooking, uncovered, until apples are just tender. Turn into a bowl and keep warm.
2. Beat the eggs thoroughly and blend in the milk. Add a mixture of the flour, 1 tablespoon sugar, and salt and beat with a hand rotary beater until smooth.
3. Heat 3 tablespoons of the butter in the skillet until moderately hot. Pour in enough batter to cover bottom of skillet. Spoon about one half of the apple mixture evenly over batter. Pour in just enough batter to cover apples.
4. Bake pancake over medium heat until golden brown on bottom. Loosen edges with spatula; carefully turn and brown other side.
5. When pancake is baked, remove skillet from heat and brush pancake generously with *melted butter*. Roll up and transfer to a warm serving platter. Sift confectioners' sugar over the top. Keep pancake hot. Repeat procedure with remaining batter and apples. 2 APPLE PANCAKES

SWEDISH PANCAKES

1½ cups sifted all-purpose flour	3 eggs
3 tablespoons sugar	2 cups milk
½ teaspoon salt	2 tablespoons butter or margarine, melted

1. Sift flour, sugar, and salt.
2. Beat the eggs until thick. Blend in the milk and melted butter. Combine egg mixture with the dry ingredients and beat with hand rotary beater until smooth.
3. For each pancake, spoon 1 tablespoon batter

into each round of a greased heated plätt pan (Swedish pancake pan available in the housewares section of most department stores). Or if using a griddle or skillet, form pancakes about 3 inches in diameter.
4. Bake over medium heat until lightly browned on bottom. Loosen edges with a spatula, turn, and lightly brown other side.
5. As pancakes are baked, transfer them to a heated plate. Arrange pancakes in a circle, slightly overlapping each other. In center, serve preserved *lingonberries*. 5 DOZEN 3-INCH PANCAKES

EMPEROR'S DESSERT
(Kaiserschmarren)

Dessert Crêpes, *page 497;* omit lemon peel	½ cup golden raisins, plumped
¾ cup butter	½ cup flaked almonds, toasted
¾ cup sugar	
½ teaspoon ground cinnamon	

1. Prepare crêpes only. Using two forks, gently tear the crêpes into about 1-inch irregular pieces and set aside to keep warm.
2. Melt butter in a large skillet and stir in the sugar. Mix in the cinnamon, raisins, and almonds, stirring occasionally until heated.
3. Add crêpe pieces and toss lightly to coat.
  8 TO 10 SERVINGS

ANTOINE'S FRENCH PANCAKES À LA GELÉE

From this pancake is also made the famous Crêpes Suzette as served at Antoine's, New Orleans, Louisiana. The batter is smooth and velvety and pours like cream.

½ cup all-purpose flour	5 tablespoons milk (about)
1 egg	
1 egg yolk	3 tablespoons currant or red raspberry jelly
⅛ teaspoon salt	Confectioners' sugar

1. Combine flour, egg, egg yolk, salt, and milk. Beat with hand rotary or electric beater until smooth. If necessary, add more milk to make batter the consistency of light cream. Cover; refrigerate about ½ hour.
2. Heat a heavy iron skillet; grease bottom with waxed paper which has been dipped in *melted but-*

ter. Pour in enough batter to barely cover bottom of skillet, tipping while adding batter. Brown each pancake on both sides.

3. Remove from skillet, spread with jelly and roll up jelly-roll fashion. Sprinkle with a little confectioners' sugar. Place under a broiler to glaze. Serve immediately. 12 TO 15 PANCAKES

DESSERT CRÊPES

2 tablespoons butter
1 cup all-purpose flour
¼ cup sugar
¼ teaspoon salt
3 eggs, beaten
1 cup milk

1 teaspoon grated lemon
  peel
Peach or Strawberry
  Butter Élégant,
  below

1. Melt the butter in a 6-inch heavy skillet and set aside.
2. Combine the flour, sugar, and salt in a bowl. Add a mixture of eggs, milk, melted butter, and lemon peel; beat with a hand rotary or electric beater until smooth.
3. Heat skillet to moderately hot. Pour in just enough batter to cover bottom. Immediately tilt skillet back and forth to spread batter thinly and evenly.
4. Cook each crêpe over medium heat until light brown on bottom and firm to touch on top. Loosen edges with spatula. Turn and brown second side. It should not be necessary to grease skillet for each crêpe.
5. As each crêpe is cooked, transfer to a hot platter, spread generously with the desired butter and roll up. Spread some of the butter over each rolled crêpe. Serve immediately. 16 TO 18 CRÊPES

PEACH BUTTER ÉLÉGANT

1 cup firm unsalted
  butter
½ cup confectioners'
  sugar

1 pkg. (10 oz.) frozen
  sliced peaches,
  thawed and cut in
  pieces

1. Using an electric beater, whip the butter, gradually beating in the confectioners' sugar.
2. Add the peaches, 1 tablespoon at a time, beating thoroughly. ABOUT 2⅔ CUPS BUTTER
STRAWBERRY BUTTER ÉLÉGANT: Follow recipe for Peach Butter Élégant. Substitute *1 package (10 ounces) frozen sliced strawberries* for the peaches; decrease sugar to ¼ cup.

CRÊPES SUZETTE
Served in the Gourmet Room of The Netherland Hilton in Cincinnati, Ohio.

Crêpes:
1 cup all-purpose flour
1 teaspoon sugar
1 pinch salt
1 egg, well beaten
1 cup milk
2 tablespoons butter

Sauce:
½ cup sugar
Peelings (white portion
  removed) and juices of
  1 orange and ½ lemon
¼ cup butter
1 oz. Grand Marnier
1 oz. cognac
1 oz. Cointreau

1. To prepare crêpes, mix all ingredients except butter in a bowl; beat until smooth (batter should be consistency of thin cream).
2. Put a small amount of butter in an 8-inch skillet; heat until the butter bubbles. Pour in enough batter to form a 6-inch circle, quickly rotating the pan to spread the batter thinly and evenly. Cook over medium heat about ½ minute; turn crêpe and cook other side.
3. With the aid of a fork and a spoon, carefully fold the crêpe. Transfer to a heated pan and keep warm. Repeat process until all the batter is used.
4. To prepare sauce, heat ¼ cup of the sugar in a skillet over low heat, stirring until sugar is caramelized. Add the citrus peelings and the butter; stir until butter is melted.
5. Add the citrus juices; cook and stir several minutes. Remove the peelings from sauce.
6. To serve, transfer folded crêpes to the sauce. Sprinkle the remaining sugar over crêpes. Add the liqueurs to sauce and ignite.
7. Serve 3 crêpes per person on hot dessert plates. 4 SERVINGS

CRÊPES AU CHOCOLAT
Here is our version of a mouth-watering dessert specialty served in a quiet, intimate Zurich, Switzerland, "Keller" renowned for its fine food.

¼ cup butter
2 oz. (2 sq.) unsweetened chocolate
¾ cup sugar
¼ cup cocoa
½ cup undiluted
  evaporated milk

2 teaspoons vanilla
  extract
Few grains salt
Dessert Crêpes,
  above

1. Melt butter and chocolate together in the top of a double boiler over simmering water, or in a small

heavy saucepan over low heat. Stir in the sugar and cocoa, then the evaporated milk, extract, and salt.

2. Continue cooking and stirring until sauce is thickened. Keep warm while preparing crêpes.

3. Prepare crêpes only, substituting *1 teaspoon vanilla extract* for lemon peel. As crêpes are cooked, transfer to baking sheets, two or three on each sheet. Spoon a generous amount of the hot chocolate sauce on one quarter of each crêpe, then fold one half of crêpe over other half; fold into quarters. Press surface lightly with a spatula to distribute chocolate sauce to edges of crêpe.

4. Sift *confectioners' sugar* lightly over each crêpe, then quickly place under broiler about 3 inches from source of heat. Heat about 30 seconds, or until sugar melts slightly.

5. Serve piping hot on heated serving platter or individual dessert plates.   ABOUT 10 CRÊPES

CRÊPES SUPERBE WITH WINE SAUCE

⅔ cup all-purpose flour
3 tablespoons sugar
¼ teaspoon salt
⅛ teaspoon baking soda
2 eggs
¾ cup milk
¼ cup butter or margarine, melted and cooled

1½ teaspoons grated orange peel
3 tablespoons orange juice
1 tablespoon rum
Wine Sauce, *below*

1. Combine the flour, sugar, salt, and baking soda in a mixing bowl; mix well.

2. Using an electric or hand rotary beater, beat the eggs; add milk, melted butter, orange peel and juice, and rum.

3. Combine egg mixture with dry ingredients and continue beating until smooth. (Batter should be consistency of heavy cream. Add more orange juice, if necessary.)

4. Heat and lightly butter the bottom of a 6- or 8-inch skillet. Pour in about 2 tablespoons of the batter and tilt skillet to spread batter evenly. Cook over medium heat until small bubbles form in the batter. Turn over and brown crêpe very lightly on second side. Repeat process using all the batter.

5. Keep crêpes warm by placing them in a pan over simmering water.

6. To serve, roll crêpes jelly-roll fashion on serving plates; allow 2 or 3 per serving. Ladle hot Wine Sauce over them.   6 TO 8 SERVINGS

WINE SAUCE: Heat *1½ tablespoons butter or margarine* in a chafing dish blazer over direct heat. Stir in *1½ teaspoons sugar*, *¾ cup apricot jam*, *1 cup port wine*, *3 tablespoons brandy*, and *3 tablespoons Cointreau* (or rum). Heat until mixture comes to boiling. Reduce heat and ignite the sauce. Serve immediately over crêpes.

CHEESE BLINTZES

1½ cups creamed cottage cheese, drained
¼ cup dairy sour cream
1½ tablespoons sugar
½ teaspoon salt
2 tablespoons butter or margarine

1½ cups all-purpose flour
3 tablespoons sugar
½ teaspoon salt
1¼ cups milk
2 eggs, well beaten

1. Combine cottage cheese, sour cream, 1½ tablespoons sugar, and salt in a bowl; mix well; refrigerate.

2. To prepare pancakes, heat 2 tablespoons butter until melted; set aside to cool.

3. Combine flour, 3 tablespoons sugar, and ½ teaspoon salt in a bowl; mix well.

4. Beat melted butter and milk into beaten eggs. Combine with dry ingredients and beat until smooth.

5. Heat a 6-inch skillet (it is hot enough when drops of water dance in small beads). Grease lightly with *butter or margarine*.

6. Pour into skillet only enough batter to coat skillet thinly; immediately tilt back and forth to spread batter evenly. Cook over medium heat about 2 minutes, or until lightly browned on bottom and firm to touch on top. With spatula, remove pancake to a plate, brown side up.

7. Repeat with remaining batter. (It should not be necessary to grease skillet for each pancake.) Stack pancakes as they are baked.

8. For blintzes, spoon about 1½ tablespoons filling into center of brown side of one pancake. Fold two opposite sides to center. Roll up. Press edges to seal. Repeat for each pancake.

9. Heat *1 tablespoon butter or margarine* in a large skillet. Arrange several blintzes in skillet, sealed sides down. Brown on all sides over medium heat, turning carefully with tongs.

10. Remove blintzes to a serving platter. Serve hot with *sour cream* and *blueberries, currant jelly,* or *blueberry or blackberry jam.*   ABOUT 12 BLINTZES

SOUFFLÉ OMELETTE CHEZ SOI
From the Jockey Restaurant, Madrid, Spain.

3 egg whites
1 to 2 tablespoons sugar
3 egg yolks, slightly
  beaten

3 tablespoons butter
1 tablespoon brandy
Confectioners' sugar

1. Beat egg whites until frothy; gradually sprinkle sugar over egg whites, beating constantly until stiff peaks are formed. Add the egg yolks, beating only until blended. (Do not overbeat.)
2. Heat butter in a large heavy skillet having a cover. Turn egg mixture into skillet; cover.
3. Cook over low to moderate heat until bottom of omelette becomes light brown. Fold omelette in half; slide onto preheated serving plate.
4. Drizzle with brandy and sprinkle with confectioners' sugar. 1 OR 2 SERVINGS

MERINGUE DESSERTS

MERINGUES

6 egg whites
¼ teaspoon salt
¾ teaspoon cream of
  tartar

1½ cups sugar
Custard Filling, *below*
Cherry-Cinnamon
  Sauce, *page 517*

1. Beat egg whites with salt and cream of tartar until frothy. Gradually add sugar, continuing to beat until stiff peaks are formed and sugar is dissolved.
2. Shape meringue shells with a spoon or force through a pastry bag and tube onto a baking sheet lined with unglazed paper.
3. Bake at 250°F 1 hour.
4. Transfer meringues from paper to wire racks to cool.
5. When ready to serve, spoon Custard Filling into meringue shells and top with Cherry-Cinnamon Sauce. 12 MERINGUE SHELLS

CUSTARD FILLING

½ cup sugar
2 teaspoons flour
¼ teaspoon salt
2 cups milk

6 egg yolks, beaten
1 teaspoon vanilla
  extract

1. Blend sugar, flour, and salt in a heavy saucepan. Stir in the milk. Bring to boiling; stir and cook 1 to 2 minutes.
2. Add a small amount of the hot mixture to egg yolks, stirring constantly. Blend into mixture in saucepan. Cook 1 minute.
3. Remove from heat and cool immediately by pouring custard into a chilled bowl and setting it in refrigerator or pan of cold water. Blend extract into cooled custard. Chill until serving time.
ABOUT 2½ CUPS FILLING

INDIVIDUAL MERINGUES AU CHOCOLAT

2 egg whites
½ teaspoon cream of
  tartar

1 teaspoon vanilla
  extract
½ cup sugar

1. Beat egg whites until frothy; add cream of tartar and extract and beat slightly. Add sugar gradually, beating constantly until stiff peaks are formed.
2. Drop meringue mixture from a spoon into mounds on a baking sheet lined with unglazed paper. Using back of spoon, start from center of each mound to form meringue shells or nests.
3. Bake at 250°F about 1 hour, or until dry to the touch.
4. Cool meringues. Fill meringue shells with *Chocolate-Mocha Cream Pudding, page 504*. Garnish with *unsweetened whipped cream* and coarsely chopped *salted nuts*. 6 MERINGUE SHELLS
NOTE: If desired, fill meringue shells with fresh *blueberries* and top each with a dollop of *dairy sour cream* and a sprinkling of *brown sugar*.

CHOCOLATE MERINGUE SHELLS

4 egg whites
¼ teaspoon cream of
  tartar

¼ teaspoon salt
1 cup sugar
¼ cup sifted cocoa

1. Lightly grease seven 4¼-inch tart pans. Flatten paper baking cups. Place one in each pan, pressing it to fit the pan. Set aside.
2. Beat the egg whites, cream of tartar, and salt until frothy; add gradually ½ cup of the sugar, beating constantly. Continue beating 5 minutes after the last addition.
3. Add remaining sugar gradually, beating constantly until very stiff peaks are formed. Quick-

ly sprinkle cocoa over meringue and beat just until blended. (As the meringue tends to lose volume when the cocoa is added, it is important to incorporate the cocoa as quickly as possible.)

4. Spread meringue ¼ inch thick over the liner on bottoms of pans. Spread remaining meringue on sides of pans and ½ inch above rim; keep meringue within pan rim for ease of removal.

5. Bake at 250°F about 2 hours, or until shells are dry. To assure even drying of meringues, turn pans occasionally.

6. Remove from oven; cool completely on rack. (If the meringue shells are to be stored, keep them in an airtight container so that the meringue will not absorb moisture and become soft.) The shells should be crisp and dry and fine textured.

7. Remove cooled meringues from pans. Carefully peel off papers. Spoon desired cream filling or ice cream into shells just before serving.

7 MERINGUE SHELLS

MERINGUE TORTE
(Schaumtorte)

6 egg whites (about ¾ cup)	½ teaspoon almond extract
2 teaspoons vinegar	¼ teaspoon salt
1 teaspoon vanilla extract	2 cups sugar

1. Grease bottoms only of two 9-inch layer cake pans with removable bottoms. (If using solid bottom pans, line with unglazed paper cut to fit bottoms.) Set aside.

2. Beat egg whites until frothy; beat in vinegar, extracts, and salt. Gradually add sugar, continuing to beat until stiff peaks are formed. Turn meringue into prepared pans and spread evenly to edges.

3. Bake at 300°F 40 minutes. Turn off oven, open oven door about 1 or 2 inches and allow torte layers to dry in oven 30 minutes.

4. Cool torte layers completely on wire racks before removing from pans. (It is likely that top surfaces may become slightly cracked when torte is being removed from pans.)

5. Fill layers with *Sweetened Whipped Cream, page 441.*

ONE 9-INCH TORTE

MERINGUE WITH BRANDY SAUCE

A recipe from Mrs. Newton Keith, Royal Savage Inn, Plattsburg, New York.

6 egg whites (¾ cup)	⅓ cup butter, melted
2 cups sugar	1 cup heavy cream, whipped
2 teaspoons lemon juice	
⅔ cup sugar	2 teaspoons brandy flavoring
1 egg, slightly beaten	

1. Beat egg whites until foamy; add the 2 cups sugar gradually, beating constantly until stiff peaks are formed. Beat in lemon juice.

2. Using a pastry tube, shape meringue mixture in a round on brown paper on a baking sheet. Build up sides of round.

3. Bake meringue shell at 275°F about 1 hour. Cool.

4. Meanwhile, to prepare sauce, add ⅔ cup sugar slowly to egg, beating constantly until thoroughly blended. Beat in the melted butter and fold mixture into whipped cream and brandy flavoring.

5. Fill meringue shell with your favorite *ice cream* and serve with the sauce. ABOUT 8 SERVINGS

GÂTEAU SUCCES PYRAMIDE

A recipe from Restaurant Pyramide, Vienne, France.

Praline Powder (use hazelnuts), *page 501*	¾ cup sweet butter
4 egg whites	1 oz. (1 sq.) semisweet chocolate, melted
10 tablespoons sugar	1 tablespoon coffee beverage
½ cup powdered blanched almonds	½ teaspoon dark rum
2 tablespoons flour	1¼ cups heavy cream, whipped
½ cup sugar	Finely chopped hazelnuts (filberts)
3 tablespoons water	1 teaspoon confectioners' sugar
1/16 teaspoon cream of tartar	
2 eggs, beaten	

1. Prepare Praline Powder. Measure ¼ cup.

2. Beat egg whites until frothy; add sugar, a little at a time, beating constantly until stiff peaks are formed.

3. Fold in powdered almonds and flour. Spread the mixture evenly in bottoms of four 8-inch layer cake pans lined with waxed paper.

4. Bake at 350°F for 10 minutes, or until meringue is "crusty" to the touch. Remove from oven; set aside to cool.

5. Meanwhile, combine ½ cup sugar, water, and cream of tartar in a saucepan. Bring to boiling and set candy thermometer in place. Cook until thermometer registers 230°F, or until syrup spins a thread.

6. Beating constantly with electric or hand rotary beater, gradually add syrup to beaten eggs. Beat in the butter, adding a small amount at a time. Continue beating until thoroughly blended.

7. Divide mixture in half and turn into 2 bowls. To one half, add melted chocolate, coffee beverage, and rum. Fold the reserved Praline Powder into the other half.

8. Put one of the baked meringue rounds on a round platter; spread with the chocolate cream. Cover with a second round and spread it with some of the whipped cream. Place a third round over whipped cream and spread with the hazelnut praline cream. Top with remaining meringue round. Spread the sides of the cake with remaining whipped cream and sprinkle with finely chopped hazelnuts. Sprinkle top with confectioners' sugar.

1 GÂTEAU

PRALINE POWDER

¾ cup sugar	½ cup toasted hazelnuts
¼ cup water	(filberts) or shredded
¼ teaspoon cream of	blanched almonds
tartar	

1. Combine all ingredients in a heavy saucepan; mix well. Bring mixture to boiling and set candy thermometer in place. Cook, without stirring, until thermometer registers 300°F, or until syrup turns golden.

2. Remove from heat and immediately pour syrup into a lightly buttered shallow pan. When thoroughly cooled, break into chunks and crush until pulverized, using a mortar and pestle.

3. Store the powder in a tightly covered jar in refrigerator. ABOUT 1¼ CUPS PRALINE POWDER

CUSTARDS & PUDDINGS

FLOATING ISLAND

Soft Custard, *below*	⅛ teaspoon salt
Poached Meringues:	¼ teaspoon vanilla
2 cups milk or water	extract
2 egg whites	¼ cup sugar

1. Prepare Soft Custard, substituting *2 egg yolks* for 1 of the eggs. Pour custard into a serving bowl or individual dessert dishes; chill.

2. Scald milk or heat water to boiling in a large heavy skillet or saucepan.

3. Beat egg whites, salt, and extract until frothy; add sugar gradually, beating constantly until stiff peaks are formed.

4. Drop egg white mixture by tablespoonfuls, forming 8 mounds, onto scalding milk or boiling water. Cook, uncovered, over low heat about 5 minutes, or until "set."

5. Remove meringues with a slotted spoon to waxed or absorbent paper.

6. To serve, put poached meringues, "floating islands," onto chilled custard. If desired, top each meringue with a *strawberry* and accompany with additional strawberries. 4 SERVINGS

NOTE: If desired, poach the meringues in the scalded milk and use the milk for preparing custard.

SOFT CUSTARD

¼ cup sugar	2 cups milk, scalded
⅛ teaspoon salt	2 teaspoons vanilla
3 eggs, slightly beaten	extract

1. Add sugar and salt to beaten eggs and beat just until blended. Stirring constantly, gradually add scalded milk.

2. Strain mixture into a double-boiler top and cook, stirring constantly, over simmering water until custard coats a metal spoon.

3. Remove from heat and cool to lukewarm over cold water. Stir in extract. Chill. 4 SERVINGS

TIPSY SQUIRE

Hot Milk Sponge Cake,	1 cup plus 2 tablespoons
page 415 (use one	sherry
layer of cake)	1 tablespoon
Soft Custard	confectioners' sugar
½ cup almonds	1 cup heavy cream,
	whipped

1. Have sponge cake layer ready.

2. Prepare Soft Custard.

3. Put the cake layer into a serving dish or casse-

role. Poke almonds upright into cake. Pour 1 cup sherry over all. Pour custard over cake.

4. Fold remaining 2 tablespoons sherry and confectioner's sugar into whipped cream. Spread over custard; chill thoroughly.   8 SERVINGS

TRIFLE

Day-old pound cake (enough to line bottom of casserole)	5 egg yolks, slightly beaten
½ cup brandy or rum	½ cup sugar
1 env. unflavored gelatin	1½ cups milk, scalded
¼ cup cold water	3 egg whites
	¼ cup heavy cream, whipped

1. Cut the pound cake into 1-inch pieces. Arrange over bottom of a 2-quart shallow casserole. Pour brandy over cake pieces.
2. Soften gelatin in the cold water. Combine egg yolks with ¼ cup of the sugar in top of a double boiler. Add the scalded milk gradually, blending well. Cook over simmering water, stirring constantly until mixture coats a metal spoon. Immediately remove from heat and stir in gelatin until dissolved. Cool and chill until mixture becomes slightly thicker.
3. Beat the egg whites until frothy; gradually add the remaining ¼ cup sugar, beating constantly until stiff peaks are formed.
4. Spread egg whites and whipped cream over gelatin mixture and gently fold together. Turn into the casserole. Chill until firm.
5. When ready to serve, garnish with *candied cherries, slivered almonds,* and pieces of *angelica.* If desired, garnish with a border of *sweetened whipped cream* forced through a pastry bag and star decorating tube.   ABOUT 12 SERVINGS

COLD ZABAGLIONE
Served at Quo Vadis restaurant in New York City.

4 egg yolks	¾ cup sherry
¾ cup sugar	

1. Combine all ingredients in the top of a double boiler; mix thoroughly.
2. Cook the mixture over simmering water about 10 minutes, beating constantly with electric or hand rotary beater until the mixture is so thick that it will float a spoon.

3. Set the double-boiler top in a bowl of cracked ice and continue to beat the zabaglione until it is cold. Turn into sherbet glasses and chill until serving time.   3 LARGE SERVINGS

HAWAIIAN COCONUT PUDDING
(Haupia)

4 cups milk	5 tablespoons cornstarch
1½ cups flaked coconut	6 tablespoons sugar

1. Combine ½ cup of the milk and half the coconut in an electric blender container; blend well. Add an additional 1½ cups milk; blend 5 minutes. Strain out coconut pieces through a double thickness of cheesecloth; reserve coconut. Repeat blending and straining, using remaining coconut and milk.
2. Mix cornstarch with sugar in a saucepan. Gradually add the coconut milk, stirring until smooth. Bring rapidly to boiling and cook 2 to 3 minutes, stirring constantly.
3. Pour into a buttered 8-inch square pan; cool. Refrigerate until firm. Before serving, sprinkle with about ¼ cup of the reserved coconut and cut into squares.   8 SERVINGS

CRÈME BRÛLÉE

4 egg yolks, slightly beaten	2 teaspoons vanilla extract
¼ cup sugar	½ cup firmly packed brown sugar
2 cups heavy cream, scalded	

1. Combine egg yolks with sugar; blend thoroughly. Gradually add hot cream, stirring until sugar is dissolved. Strain into a 1-quart baking dish.
2. Blend in extract. Place baking dish in a shallow pan with hot water and bake at 325°F 50 minutes, or until a knife inserted in custard comes out clean.
3. Remove from oven and set baking dish on wire rack to cool; chill thoroughly.
4. Before serving, sift brown sugar evenly over top. Place under broiler with top at least 5 inches from source of heat; broil until sugar is melted. Watch carefully so sugar will not burn.
5. Cool and refrigerate until ready to serve.
6. Serve plain or with *greengage plums* as an accompaniment.   ABOUT 6 SERVINGS

POTS DE CRÈME CHOCOLAT

2 cups heavy cream	6 egg yolks, beaten
1 tablespoon sugar	1½ teaspoons vanilla
4 oz. sweet chocolate, melted	extract

1. Heat the cream and sugar together in the top of a double boiler over simmering water until cream is scalded. Add the melted chocolate and stir until blended. Pour mixture into beaten egg yolks, beating constantly until blended. Stir in extract.
2. Strain through a fine sieve into 8 small earthenware pots or custard cups. Set pots in a pan of hot water.
3. Bake at 325°F 20 minutes. (Mixture will become thicker upon cooling.)
4. Set cups on wire rack to cool; chill thoroughly.

8 SERVINGS

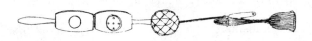

CHOCOLATE CUSTARD

1 cup (6-oz. pkg.) semisweet chocolate pieces	3 eggs
	1 teaspoon vanilla extract
3 tablespoons cream	⅓ cup sugar
3 cups milk	¼ teaspoon salt

1. Melt ⅔ cup of the chocolate pieces with the cream in the top of a double boiler over hot (not boiling) water. Stir until smooth; spoon about 1 tablespoon into each of 8 custard cups or 10 soufflé dishes. Spread evenly. Put cups into a shallow pan; set aside.
2. Scald milk. Melt remaining ⅓ cup chocolate and, adding gradually, stir in scalded milk until blended.
3. Beat eggs, extract, sugar, and salt together. Gradually add milk mixture, stirring constantly. Pour into chocolate-lined cups.
4. Set pan with filled cups on oven rack and pour boiling water into pan to a depth of 1 inch.
5. Bake at 325°F about 25 minutes, or until a metal knife inserted halfway between center and edge of custard comes out clean.
6. Set cups on wire rack to cool slightly. Refrigerate and serve when thoroughly cooled. Unmold if desired. Garnish with *whipped cream rosettes*.

8 TO 10 SERVINGS

BIRD'S NEST PUDDING

The origin of this odd title seems lost in antiquity, but several versions of this pudding flourish in New England. All of them have one thing in common — apples.

2 cups sugar	¼ cup sugar
1 cup water	⅛ teaspoon salt
¼ teaspoon red food coloring	2 teaspoons vanilla extract
6 medium-sized apples, washed, cored, and pared (keep whole)	3 eggs, fork beaten
	2 cups cream, scalded

1. Add the 2 cups sugar to the water in a large saucepan; bring to boiling, stirring until sugar is dissolved. Mix in the food coloring.
2. Add as many apples as will fit uncrowded in the saucepan; cover and cook slowly until apples are just tender, about 7 minutes, turning carefully several times to obtain an even color. With a slotted spoon, remove apples and place in a 1½-quart baking dish. Repeat with any remaining apples.
3. Meanwhile, blend the ¼ cup sugar, salt, and extract into the fork beaten eggs. Gradually add the hot cream, stirring until sugar is dissolved. Strain mixture through a fine sieve over and around apples in baking dish.
4. Place baking dish in a pan on oven rack; pour boiling water in pan to a depth of at least 1 inch.
5. Bake at 325°F 50 to 60 minutes, or until a metal knife inserted in custard about halfway between center and edge of baking dish comes out clean. Serve slightly warm.

6 SERVINGS

BRAZILIAN PUDIM MOKA WITH CHOCOLATE SAUCE

3 cups milk	½ cup sugar
1 cup cream	½ teaspoon salt
5 tablespoons instant coffee	1 teaspoon vanilla extract
2 teaspoons grated orange peel	Chocolate Sauce, *page 551*
4 eggs	1 cup coarsely chopped Brazil nuts
1 egg yolk	

1. Combine milk and cream in the top of a double boiler and heat over simmering water until scalded.
2. Add the instant coffee and orange peel and stir until the coffee is dissolved. Remove from simmer-

ing water and set aside to cool about 10 minutes.

3. Beat eggs and egg yolk slightly. Blend in sugar and salt.

4. Add coffee mixture gradually, stirring constantly; mix in extract. Strain through a fine sieve into eight 6-ounce custard cups. Sprinkle with *ground nutmeg.* Set cups in a pan of hot water.

5. Bake at 325°F 25 to 30 minutes, or until a knife inserted in center of custard comes out clean.

6. Cool and chill. To serve, invert each custard onto an individual serving plate. Pour Chocolate Sauce over top and sprinkle with Brazil nuts.

8 SERVINGS

LEMON SPONGE

1 cup sugar	2 tablespoons lemon
3 tablespoons flour	juice
Few grains salt	1 tablespoon butter,
2 egg yolks, slightly	melted
beaten	1 cup milk
2 teaspoons grated	2 egg whites
lemon peel	

1. Combine the sugar, flour, and salt in a bowl; add a mixture of the beaten egg yolks, lemon peel and juice, and melted butter; mix well. Stir in the milk.

2. Beat egg whites until stiff, not dry, peaks are formed. Fold into first mixture. Pour into 6 custard cups.

3. Bake in a pan with hot water in a 350°F oven about 35 minutes, or until golden brown on top. Serve slightly warm. 6 SERVINGS

NOTE: If desired, this sponge may be turned into an unbaked 8-inch pie shell and baked at 350°F 35 to 40 minutes, or until filling is set.

BANANA CREAM PARFAIT

1 pkg. vanilla pudding	¼ teaspoon banana
and pie filling mix	extract
2 cups milk	3 tablespoons grated un-
1 tablespoon butter	sweetened chocolate

1. Prepare pudding mix according to directions on package using the 2 cups milk. Remove from heat; stir in the butter and extract; cool slightly.

2. Alternate layers of pudding and grated chocolate in parfait glasses; chill in refrigerator; top with *chocolate curls.* ABOUT 3 SERVINGS

NOTE: For more banana flavor, alternate *banana*

slices with the chocolate between pudding layers.

COCONUT-BANANA CREAM PARFAIT: Follow recipe for Banana Cream Parfait. Mix ½ cup *flaked coconut* into the pudding.

BLUEBERRY-ORANGE PARFAITS

2 tablespoons cornstarch	½ teaspoon vanilla
1 cup sugar	extract
¼ to ½ teaspoon salt	2 tablespoons sugar
2 cups orange juice	2 cups fresh blueberries,
2 eggs, beaten	sorted and rinsed
¼ teaspoon grated	
lemon peel	

1. Mix cornstarch, sugar, and salt in a double-boiler top. Add a small amount of the orange juice and blend until smooth. Stir in remaining orange juice. Bring to boiling over direct heat and cook, stirring constantly, 3 to 5 minutes. Remove from heat.

2. Immediately blend about 3 tablespoons of the hot mixture into the beaten eggs; stir egg mixture into the orange juice mixture.

3. Set over simmering water and cook 3 to 5 minutes, or until thickened, stirring constantly. Remove from water and cool. Stir in lemon peel and extract. Chill.

4. Meanwhile, sprinkle the 2 tablespoons sugar over blueberries and let stand at least 30 minutes.

5. Spoon alternate layers of orange mixture and blueberries into parfait glasses, beginning with a layer of orange mixture and ending with blueberries. Top with *sweetened whipped cream.*

ABOUT 6 SERVINGS

CHOCOLATE-MOCHA CREAM PUDDING

2 oz. (2 sq.) unsweet-	1 cup milk
ened chocolate	3 egg yolks, slightly
1 cup double-strength	beaten
coffee	2 tablespoons butter or
⅔ cup sugar	margarine
¼ cup flour	2 teaspoons vanilla
¼ teaspoon salt	extract

1. Heat chocolate and coffee together over low heat until chocolate is melted; stir to blend.

2. Meanwhile, combine the sugar, flour, and salt in top of a double boiler. Blend in milk.

3. Add the hot coffee-chocolate mixture gradual-

ly, stirring until blended. Continue to stir and bring rapidly to boiling; boil 2 minutes.

4.   Stir a small amount of hot mixture into the egg yolks. Immediately blend into mixture in double boiler. Cook over simmering water 5 minutes; stir to keep it cooking evenly.

5.   Remove from simmering water and blend in the butter and extract. Chill thoroughly before spooning into *meringue shells* as a filling or serving as pudding.   4 TO 6 SERVINGS

RICH CHOCOLATE PUDDING

2 oz. (2 sq.) unsweet- ened chocolate	¼ teaspoon salt
2 cups milk	2 teaspoons vanilla extract
½ cup sugar	2 teaspoons butter or margarine
2 tablespoons corn- starch	

1.   Combine chocolate and milk into the top of a double boiler. Cook over simmering water until chocolate is melted, stirring occasionally.

2.   Combine sugar, cornstarch, and salt; gradually add to chocolate mixture, stirring constantly.

3.   Cook and stir over boiling water until thickened. Remove from heat; stir in extract and butter. Pour into serving dishes and chill.

4.   Serve with a *whipped cream* or *whipped dessert topping*.   ABOUT 4 SERVINGS

COFFEE TAPIOCA PARFAIT

2 egg whites	2 tablespoons instant coffee
¼ cup sugar	
2 egg yolks, slightly beaten	¼ teaspoon salt
3 cups milk	1 teaspoon vanilla extract
⅓ cup sugar	Salted pecans or almonds, chopped
⅓ cup quick-cooking tapioca	Whipped cream

1.   Beat egg whites until frothy; gradually add ¼ cup sugar, beating until stiff peaks are formed.

2.   Combine egg yolks with milk in a saucepan. Add ⅓ cup sugar, tapioca, instant coffee, and salt; mix well. Let stand 5 minutes.

3.   Cook and stir over medium heat until mixture comes to a full boil; do not overcook.

4.   Remove from heat and immediately stir a small amount of the hot mixture into egg white mixture.

Then quickly blend in the remaining hot mixture, extract, and nuts. Cool, stirring once after 15 minutes. Chill.

5.   To complete parfait, spoon one third of the tapioca into bottom of chilled parfait glasses; spoon on a layer of whipped cream, sprinkle with *instant coffee*, then *shaved unsweetened chocolate*, *ground cinnamon*, and *grated orange peel*. Repeat layering two more times, ending with a swirl of whipped cream sprinkled with instant coffee, chocolate, cinnamon, and orange peel.   ABOUT 8 SERVINGS

CELESTIAL LEMON CRÈME

This easy-on-the-cook dessert is decorated with strawberries and ladyfingers.

1 pkg. lemon pudding and pie filling mix	¼ cup confectioners' sugar
⅓ cup sugar	2 cups fresh straw- berries, sliced, or thawed frozen fruit (strawberry halves, raspberries, or sliced peaches)
1½ cups (12 oz. can) pineapple juice	
Few grains salt	
2 egg yolks	
1 cup water	
1 cup chilled heavy cream	4 ladyfingers, split in halves

1.   Combine pudding, ⅓ cup sugar, ¼ cup of the pineapple juice, and salt in a saucepan. Add egg yolks and blend well. Stir in remaining juice and water. Cook and stir until mixture boils and thickens. Remove from heat. Cool thoroughly, stirring frequently.

2.   Beat the cream until of medium consistency (piles softly); beat in confectioners' sugar with final few strokes. Fold into pudding. Chill at least 1 hour.

3.   Spoon one half of the pudding into a serving dish and layer with sliced strawberries (or well-drained fruit). If strawberries are used in a crystal bowl, arrange some slices or halves with the cut side against the glass. Place ladyfinger halves upright around edge of dish, allowing about 1 inch to extend above edge. Cover fruit with remaining pudding. Garnish with *whole strawberries or other fruit*, if desired.   6 TO 8 SERVINGS

GLAMOUR PUDDING 'N' PEACHES

Plump, juicy peaches filled with fruit and nuts rest on beds of creamy pudding in this dessert.

1 pkg. vanilla pudding and pie filling mix	1 can (29 oz.) cling peach halves, drained
1½ cups milk	½ cup chopped candied orange peel
½ cup white grape juice	
Chilled heavy cream, whipped to soft peaks and sweetened	2 tablespoons diced roasted almonds

1. Prepare pudding according to package directions using the 1½ cups milk.
2. Turn pudding into a bowl and cool slightly, stirring occasionally. Stirring constantly, gradually add grape juice to pudding. Fold in the desired amount of sweetened whipped cream.
3. Divide mixture equally among dessert dishes. Place a peach half, cut side up, in each.
4. Mix the remaining ingredients and spoon some onto each peach. Chill.   6 TO 8 SERVINGS

SPICY RICE PUDDING

2 cups milk	3 egg yolks, slightly beaten
⅔ cup sugar	
1 tablespoon flour	1 cup cooked rice
¼ teaspoon salt	½ cup golden raisins
¼ to ½ teaspoon ground mace	2 tablespoons butter
	½ teaspoon vanilla extract

1. Scald 1½ cups of the milk in the top of a double boiler over simmering water.
2. Combine in a bowl the sugar, flour, salt, and mace. Add the remaining milk and mix well.
3. Add the scalded milk gradually, stirring constantly. Pour mixture into double-boiler top. Cook and stir until boiling; cook 2 minutes longer.
4. Set over simmering water. Cover and cook 5 to 7 minutes, stirring occasionally.
5. Stir about 3 tablespoons of the hot mixture into the egg yolks; immediately blend into mixture in double boiler. Cook over simmering water 3 to 5 minutes, stirring occasionally.
6. Remove from heat. Fluff rice with a fork and stir into hot mixture. Stir in the raisins, butter, and extract. Cover and set pudding aside to cool slightly, stirring occasionally. Serve in sherbet glasses.   6 SERVINGS

CHOCOLATE RICE PUDDING: Follow recipe for Spicy Rice Pudding. Add *2 ounces (2 squares) unsweetened chocolate* to milk. Set over simmering water and heat until milk is scalded and chocolate is melted. Substitute for the mace, *⅛ teaspoon ground cinnamon* and *⅛ teaspoon ground cloves.* Omit raisins.

EMERALD-TOPPED LEMON RICE PUDDING

1 can (16½ to 18 oz.) ready-to-serve lemon pudding	¾ cup boiling water
	1 pkg. (3 oz.) lime-flavored gelatin
1 can (15¾ oz.) ready-to-serve rice pudding	¾ cup unsweetened pineapple juice

1. Empty the canned puddings into a bowl and mix thoroughly. Refrigerate several hours, allowing flavors to blend.
2. Pour boiling water over the gelatin and stir until dissolved; blend in the pineapple juice and pour into a shallow pan. Chill until very firm.
3. Turn gelatin onto a flat surface such as a baking sheet. Using the straight edge of a rubber spatula, chop through all of the gelatin, criss-crossing as you cut, until all is a shimmering mass.
4. Spoon about ¾ of the shimmering gelatin into a crystal bowl. Cover with the chilled pudding and pile remaining shimmering gelatin on top.

8 SERVINGS

APPLE CREAM

6 cups sliced apples (about 2 lbs.)	⅔ cup sugar
	1 egg
½ cup sugar	½ cup flour
1 teaspoon ground cinnamon	½ teaspoon baking powder
1 teaspoon ground nutmeg	½ teaspoon salt
¼ cup butter	1 cup heavy cream

1. Toss the apple slices with a mixture of the ½ cup sugar, cinnamon, and nutmeg. Spread evenly in bottom of a buttered 9x9x2-inch baking dish.
2. Cream butter and ⅔ cup sugar together thoroughly. Add egg and continue beating until mixture is light and fluffy.

3. Blend flour, baking powder, and salt; beat into creamed mixture until just blended. Spread evenly over apples in baking dish.

4. Bake at 350°F 30 minutes. Remove from oven and pour cream evenly over surface. Return to oven and bake 10 minutes, or until topping is golden brown.

5. Serve warm with cream, if desired.

ABOUT 8 SERVINGS

CRANBERRY PUDDING WITH BUTTER SAUCE

1½ cups sifted all-purpose flour	1½ cups (about 6 oz.) fresh cranberries, rinsed and coarsely chopped
¾ cup sugar	
3 teaspoons baking powder	
3 tablespoons butter, melted and cooled	⅔ cup milk
	Butter Sauce, *below*

1. Sift the flour, sugar, and baking powder into a bowl. Make a well in center and add the melted butter, cranberries, and milk. Stir just until dry ingredients are moistened.

2. Turn mixture into a greased 1-quart casserole.

3. Bake at 350°F 55 minutes. Serve warm with Butter Sauce. ABOUT 6 SERVINGS

BUTTER SAUCE: Melt ½ *cup butter* in the top of a double boiler. Gradually add *2 cups sugar* and ¾ *cup light cream*, stirring constantly. Place over simmering water and cook, stirring frequently, until sugar is completely dissolved, about 15 minutes. Serve with warm pudding. ABOUT 2 CUPS SAUCE

CHERRY COTTAGE PUDDING

Warm from the oven and topped with whipped sour cream and maraschino cherries, here is a treat for your family any time of the year.

1 can (16 oz.) water-pack tart red cherries, drained and halved	¼ teaspoon salt
	¼ cup butter
	½ teaspoon almond extract
2 cups sifted all-purpose flour	¾ cup sugar
	1 egg
2 teaspoons baking powder	1 cup dairy sour cream
	¼ cup milk
1 teaspoon baking soda	

1. Drain cherries on absorbent paper.

2. Mix flour, baking powder, baking soda, and salt.

3. Cream the butter with extract in a bowl. Add sugar and beat until thoroughly blended. Add egg and continue beating until light and fluffy.

4. Beating only until blended after each addition, alternately add dry ingredients in thirds and sour cream and milk in halves. Fold in half of the cherries.

5. Turn batter into a buttered 9x9x2-inch baking pan, spreading evenly to edges. Arrange remaining cherries, cut side down, on batter; press gently.

6. Bake at 375°F about 35 minutes, or until a cake tester inserted in center of cake comes out clean. Set on a wire rack to cool slightly.

7. Meanwhile, whip ¾ *cup dairy sour cream* in a chilled bowl, using chilled beaters, until cream piles softly. If desired, blend in *confectioners' sugar* to taste.

8. Cut warm cottage pudding into serving-sized pieces and place on dessert plates. Put a dollop of whipped sour cream on top of each serving. Top generously with quartered *maraschino cherries*.

ABOUT 9 SERVINGS

WALNUT FUDGE BREAD PUDDING

This pudding, served in dainty soufflé dishes, is a sweet dessert for a family meal.

1½ cups milk	1 tablespoon butter or margarine
¾ cup sugar	
1 pkg. (6 oz.) semisweet chocolate pieces	1 egg
	⅛ teaspoon salt
1½ cups coarse dry bread crumbs*	½ cup chopped walnuts

1. Mix milk, sugar, chocolate pieces, and bread crumbs in the top of a double boiler. Cook and stir over hot water until chocolate is melted and mixture is thick.

2. Remove from heat; stir in the butter. Gradually add the egg (beaten with the salt) to the chocolate mixture, stirring constantly. Mix in the walnuts.

3. Spoon mixture into 6 greased individual soufflé dishes set in a shallow baking pan. Place pan on oven rack. Pour boiling water into pan to a depth of 1 inch.

4. Bake at 350°F about 50 minutes.

5. Remove puddings from water to a wire rack. Serve warm or chilled topped with *whipped dessert topping* or *sweetened whipped cream* and *walnut halves*. 6 SERVINGS

*Use crumbs torn by hand from bread several days old or bread left out to dry.

TORTE-STYLE CIDER PUDDING

This baked pudding is drenched with apple cider.

7 egg yolks
1½ cups sugar
2 teaspoons grated lemon peel
4 cups toasted coarse bread crumbs
1 teaspoon ground cinnamon
1 cup chopped toasted almonds
7 egg whites
1½ cups sweet apple cider

1. Beat egg yolks, sugar, and lemon peel together until very thick.
2. Combine the bread crumbs, cinnamon, and almonds; fold into the egg yolk mixture.
3. Beat egg whites until stiff, not dry, peaks are formed. Gently fold into bread crumb mixture. Turn into a well-greased 9-inch tubed pan.
4. Bake at 350°F about 1 hour, or until a cake tester inserted in center comes out clean and top is golden brown.
5. Loosen from sides of pan and then unmold immediately onto a warm serving plate.
6. Heat the cider and pour slowly over the pudding, using just enough to saturate it thoroughly. Serve immediately with *whipped cream.*

12 TO 16 SERVINGS

PEACHES 'N' CREAM KUCHEN

2 cups all-purpose flour
2 tablespoons sugar
½ teaspoon salt
¼ teaspoon baking powder
½ cup butter or margarine
9 fresh peach halves, peeled
¾ cup sugar
1 teaspoon ground cinnamon
2 egg yolks, slightly beaten
1 cup dairy sour cream

1. Combine the flour, 2 tablespoons sugar, salt, and baking powder in a bowl; mix well. Using a pastry blender or two knives, cut in butter until mixture resembles cornmeal.
2. Turn mixture into an 8x8x2-inch baking pan. Pat mixture evenly over bottom and halfway up sides of the pan.
3. Place peach halves, cut side up, in pan. Sprinkle a mixture of the ¾ cup sugar and cinnamon over the peaches.
4. Bake at 400°F 15 minutes. Combine the egg yolks and sour cream; mix thoroughly. Pour over peaches and bake 25 minutes longer. 6 SERVINGS

BAKED HOMINY DESSERT

1 qt. milk
½ cup butter or margarine, cut in pieces
1 cup long-cooking hominy grits
1 teaspoon salt

1. Heat the milk to boiling. Add the butter, then gradually add the hominy grits, stirring constantly. Bring to boiling and boil 3 minutes, or until mixture becomes thick, stirring constantly. Remove from heat.
2. Add the salt; beat at high speed of an electric mixer 5 minutes, or until grits have a creamy appearance.
3. Turn into a buttered 1½-quart casserole.
4. Bake at 350°F 1 hour or until lightly browned.
5. Serve hot with *light brown sugar, cream,* and *fresh blueberries.* 6 TO 8 SERVINGS

INDIAN PUDDING

One of many versions of an old New England pudding.

3 cups milk
½ cup yellow cornmeal
¼ cup sugar
1 teaspoon salt
1 teaspoon ground cinnamon
½ teaspoon ground ginger
1 egg, well beaten
½ cup molasses
2 tablespoons butter
1 cup cold milk

1. Scald the 3 cups milk in the top of a double boiler. Stirring constantly, slowly blend into milk a mixture of the cornmeal, sugar, salt, cinnamon, and ginger. Stir in a blend of the egg and molasses.
2. Cook and stir over boiling water 10 minutes, or until very thick. Beat in the butter.
3. Turn into a well-buttered 1½-quart casserole. Pour cold milk over top.
4. Bake at 300°F 2 hours, or until browned.

ABOUT 6 SERVINGS

QUICK INDIAN PUDDING

2 eggs, slightly beaten
¼ cup yellow cornmeal
¼ cup sugar
1 teaspoon salt
¾ teaspoon ground cinnamon
¼ teaspoon ground ginger
2 tablespoons cold milk
¼ cup light molasses
2 cups milk, scalded

1. Combine all ingredients except scalded milk in a bowl. Mix well and add the scalded milk gradual-

ly, stirring constantly. Turn mixture into a double-boiler top.

2.   Cook and stir over direct heat until mixture thickens. Place, covered, over simmering water and cook 15 minutes. Remove cover and cook 15 minutes longer.

3.   Serve hot with *ice cream, whipped cream,* or *fruit.*   4 TO 6 SERVINGS

CHANTILLY RAISIN RICE PUDDING

⅔ cup seedless raisins	⅛ teaspoon salt
1¼ cups milk	1 tablespoon vanilla
1¼ cups heavy cream	extract
2 eggs	1 cup cooked rice
3 tablespoons sugar	¼ cup chopped toasted
⅛ teaspoon ground	nuts (walnuts or
nutmeg	pecans)

1.   Combine raisins, milk, and cream in a saucepan; place over low heat.

2.   Beat the eggs with the sugar, nutmeg, salt, and extract until thoroughly blended. Mix with the cooked rice. Stir the hot liquid with raisins into the rice mixture and turn into a 1-quart deep baking dish or casserole.

3.   Set in a shallow pan of hot water in a 350°F oven. Bake 15 minutes, then sprinkle top with nuts and continue baking 15 to 20 minutes, or until custard is barely set in the center of pudding.

4.   Remove from oven and set in a pan with cold water to allow pudding to cool quickly and keep custard creamy.

5.   Serve pudding warm or cold. Top with *sweetened whipped cream* or *whipped dessert topping.*
                                                  8 SERVINGS

ORANGE NOODLE DESSERT

1 lb. wide egg noodles	1 cup coarsely chopped
5 or 6 navel oranges	walnuts
¼ to ⅓ cup lightly	½ cup dark seedless
packed brown sugar	raisins, plumped
5 eggs (about 1 cup)	½ teaspoon ground
1 cup sugar	cinnamon
2 teaspoons ground	⅓ cup butter or
cinnamon	margarine, melted
1½ tablespoons lemon	
juice	

1.   Cook noodles in boiling *salted water* as directed on package; drain.

2.   Meanwhile, grate enough peel from the oranges to make 1 tablespoon and set aside. Peel oranges and section them. Toss sections with brown sugar and set mixture aside.

3.   Put eggs, grated peel, sugar, 2 teaspoons cinnamon, and lemon juice into a large bowl; beat well. Mix in noodles, walnuts, and raisins.

4.   Turn one half of the mixture evenly into a well-greased 3-quart shallow baking dish. Spoon orange sections over first layer. Top with remaining noodle mixture. Sprinkle with ½ teaspoon cinnamon. Pour melted butter evenly over all.

5.   Bake at 350°F 45 minutes.

6.   Remove from oven and cool. Cut into squares and serve with *whipped dessert topping.*

                                                  8 to 10 SERVINGS

INDIVIDUAL STEAMED CHOCOLATE PUDDINGS

1⅓ cups all-purpose	2 eggs
flour	3 oz. (3 sq.) unsweet-
1½ teaspoons baking	ened chocolate, melted
powder	and cooled
½ teaspoon salt	¾ cup milk
⅔ cup butter or	1 cup unblanched
margarine	almonds, toasted and
2 teaspoons vanilla	coarsely chopped
extract	Vanilla Hard Sauce,
¾ cup plus 2 tablespoons	*page 555*
sugar	

1.   Combine the flour, baking powder, and salt; mix well.

2.   Cream the butter with extract until softened; add sugar gradually, beating constantly until blended. Beat in the eggs, one at a time, until mixture is fluffy. Blend in the chocolate.

3.   Beating just until blended after each addition, alternately add the dry ingredients in fourths and milk in thirds. Stir in the almonds.

4.   Turn batter into lightly buttered individual molds or small fruit juice concentrate cans, filling each one half to two-thirds full. Cover molds tightly with aluminum foil and set on rack in steamer. Add boiling water to no more than one half the height of the molds. Cover tightly and steam 30 minutes.

5.   Immediately loosen puddings from molds and unmold each onto an individual serving plate. Working quickly, pipe a swirl of Vanilla Hard Sauce on the top of each pudding. Serve immediately before hard sauce melts.   ABOUT 8 SERVINGS

How to Steam Puddings

1. Use, a mold or tin can large enough that the batter will fill mold one half to two thirds.
2. Grease the mold and the cover. If mold has no cover, use aluminum foil, parchment paper, or a double thickness of waxed paper tied on tightly.
3. Place filled mold on a trivet in a steamer or deep kettle with a tight-fitting cover.
4. Pour boiling water into the steamer to no more than one half the height of the mold. Add more boiling water during the steaming period, if necessary.
5. Tightly cover steamer.
6. Keep water boiling gently at all times.
7. If pudding is to be stored several days before serving, unmold onto wire rack. Let stand until cold. Wrap in foil and store in a cool place.
8. To resteam, heat pudding in a double boiler over simmering water or set foil-wrapped pudding on a trivet in steamer over a small amount of boiling water. Steam thoroughly.

MOLASSES STEAMED PUDDING

2 cups sifted all-purpose flour	1 cup buttermilk
1 teaspoon baking soda	¾ cup fine dry bread crumbs
1 teaspoon salt	6 oz. suet
1½ teaspoons ground cinnamon	½ cup sugar
¾ teaspoon ground nutmeg	1 egg, fork beaten
½ teaspoon ground ginger	1 cup light molasses
¼ teaspoon ground cloves	¼ cup water
	1 cup chopped nuts
	½ cup raisins
	Foamy Sauce, *page 556*

1. Generously grease a 2-quart mold (or two 1-quart molds). Grease tight-fitting cover. (If cover is not available, aluminum foil or baking parchment cut larger than mold may be substituted. Grease well before tying securely over mold.)
2. Sift the flour, baking soda, salt, and spices together and blend well; set aside.
3. Mix buttermilk and bread crumbs.
4. Pull suet apart, discarding membrane which coats it; put suet through fine blade of food chopper (about 2 cups lightly packed suet). Beat suet until

softened in a large mixing bowl; add the sugar and cream thoroughly. Beat in the egg, then the soaked bread crumbs, and a blend of molasses and water. Mix in nuts and raisins, and then the dry ingredients. Turn mixture into mold and cover tightly.
5. Steam about 3 hours (see *above*).
6. Remove pudding from steamer, unmold onto serving plate, and decorate as desired. Serve with Foamy Sauce.
7. If pudding is to be stored and served later, unmold onto wire rack and cool thoroughly. Wrap in foil or return to the mold and store in a cool place. Before serving, resteam in mold about 3 hours, or until thoroughly heated.

ABOUT 12 SERVINGS

STEAMED PUMPKIN PUDDING
Cinnamon apple rings wreathe this spicy pudding and a zesty lemon crème accompanies it. The result . . . a dessert of distinction.

1¼ cups fine dry crumbs	½ teaspoon ground cloves
½ cup sifted all-purpose flour	2 eggs, fork beaten
1 cup lightly packed brown sugar	1½ cups canned pumpkin
1 teaspoon baking powder	½ cup cooking or salad oil
½ teaspoon baking soda	½ cup undiluted evaporated milk
½ teaspoon salt	Lemon Zest Crème, *below*
½ teaspoon ground cinnamon	

1. Combine bread crumbs, flour, brown sugar, baking powder, baking soda, salt, cinnamon, and cloves in a large bowl. Set aside.
2. Beat eggs and remaining ingredients together. Add to dry ingredients; mix until blended.
3. Turn into a well greased 1½-quart mold. Cover tightly with a greased cover, or tie greased aluminum foil tightly over mold.
4. Steam about 3 hours (see *above*).
5. Remove pudding from steamer and unmold onto a serving plate. Decorate plate with drained *cinnamon-apple rings, whipped cream,* and *sugar cubes* soaked with *lemon extract.* Immediately ignite the sugar cubes. Accompany with a bowl of Lemon Zest Crème.   ONE 2¼-POUND PUDDING

LEMON ZEST CRÈME: Cream ½ *cup butter or margarine* with ½ *teaspoon ground ginger* and ¼ *teaspoon salt* in a bowl. Add 2 *cups confectioners' sugar* gradually, beating constantly. Add ¼ *cup lemon* *juice* gradually, continuing to beat until blended. Mix in *½ cup chopped nuts.*   ABOUT 2½ CUPS CRÈME

STEAMED RAISIN PUDDING

3 cups sifted all-purpose flour	¼ teaspoon cloves
1 teaspoon baking soda	4 oz. suet (about 1 cup, chopped)
1 teaspoon salt	1 cup molasses
½ teaspoon ground allspice	1 cup milk
½ teaspoon ground cinnamon	¼ cup water
½ teaspoon ground nutmeg	1 cup dark seedless raisins
	Brown Sugar Pudding Sauce, *below*

1.   Sift together the flour, baking soda, salt, and spices; set aside.
2.   Break apart the suet (discarding membrane which coats it) and finely chop. Combine suet with molasses, milk, and water. Mix in the raisins.
3.   Stir in the dry ingredients until well mixed.
4.   Turn into a well-greased 2-quart mold. Cover mold tightly and steam for 3 hours (see *page 510*).
5.   Serve with the sauce.   ABOUT 12 SERVINGS

BROWN SUGAR PUDDING SAUCE: Beat *1 egg*, well beaten, *1 cup packed brown sugar*, and *1 teaspoon vanilla extract* until creamy.   ABOUT 1 CUP SAUCE

ORANGE MARMALADE PUDDING

1 cup butter or margarine	1 cup orange marmalade
1 cup sugar	1 cup sifted all-purpose flour
4 eggs, well beaten	1 teaspoon baking soda

1.   Cream butter until softened. Add sugar gradually, beating until thoroughly blended. Add eggs in thirds, beating thoroughly after each addition, until mixture is light and fluffy. Beat in marmalade.

2.   Mix flour and baking soda thoroughly and add to butter mixture in fourths, beating only until blended after each addition.
3.   Turn into a greased 2-quart mold or 2-pound coffee can. Cover tightly with greased cover, or tie on greased aluminum foil, parchment, or waxed paper.
4.   Place mold on trivet or rack in a large kettle or steamer. Steam for 2 hours (see *page 510*).
5.   Remove from steamer and unmold onto warm serving dish. Serve with *Vanilla Sauce, page 550.*
ABOUT 8 SERVINGS

LIGHT PLUM PUDDING

2 cups sifted all-purpose flour	2 cups finely shredded raw carrot
2 cups sugar	2 cups finely shredded raw potato
2 teaspoons baking soda	1 tablespoon grated orange peel
1 teaspoon salt	
1 teaspoon ground cinnamon	¼ cup melted butter or margarine
½ teaspoon ground mace	1 cup pitted dates, cut in pieces
¼ teaspoon ground cloves	1 cup golden or dark seedless raisins, rinsed and drained
1 cup fine dry bread crumbs	

1.   Sift flour, sugar, baking soda, salt, and spices together into a large bowl. Add the bread crumbs, carrot, potato, orange peel, and melted butter; mix thoroughly. Blend in dates and raisins.
2.   Turn into a well-greased 2-quart mold. Cover tightly with greased cover, or tie on aluminum foil, parchment, or double thickness of waxed paper.
3.   Steam for 2 hours (see *page 510*).
4.   Remove pudding from steamer and uncover; let stand 10 minutes. Invert onto a warm serving platter.
5.   Serve hard sauce.   ABOUT 12 SERVINGS

DESSERT SOUFFLÉS—HOT & COLD

Collars for Soufflé Dishes
To make an aluminum foil collar: Fold a 2-foot length of foil lengthwise through the center. Wrap foil tightly around soufflé dish or casserole so that collar extends at least 2 inches above the rim. Bring the ends together with a double fold; tie securely.

To make a waxed paper collar: Cut a length of waxed paper long enough to encircle dish. Fold in fourths lengthwise. Bring ends together to form a circle and fasten together on outside of dish, allowing it to extend 2 inches above top of dish. Secure collar with cord wound around dish, if desired.

VANILLA SOUFFLÉ

1 tablespoon confectioners' sugar	4 egg yolks
¼ cup butter or margarine	½ cup sugar
¼ cup flour	2 teaspoons vanilla extract
1 cup milk	4 egg whites

1. Butter bottom of a 1½-quart soufflé dish (straight-sided casserole) and sift the confectioners' sugar over it; set aside.
2. Melt butter in a saucepan; stir in flour and cook until mixture bubbles. Gradually add milk, stirring until blended; return to heat, bring to boiling, and cook, stirring constantly, 1 to 2 minutes. Cool slightly.
3. Beat egg yolks, sugar, and extract together until mixture is thick. Stirring vigorously, pour sauce slowly into egg yolk mixture. Cool to lukewarm.
4. Beat egg whites until stiff, not dry, peaks are formed. Spread egg yolk mixture over egg whites and carefully fold together. Turn into soufflé dish. Set in a shallow pan with hot water.
5. Bake at 350°F 50 minutes, or until a metal knife comes out clean when inserted halfway between center and edge.
6. Serve immediately with an *apricot sauce* or a *purée of strawberries or raspberries*. **6 SERVINGS**

CHOCOLATE SOUFFLÉ

1 tablespoon confectioners' sugar	1½ cups milk
6 tablespoons butter or margarine	6 egg yolks
3 oz. (3 sq.) unsweetened chocolate	⅔ cup sugar
5 tablespoons flour	4 teaspoons vanilla extract
	6 egg whites

1. Butter bottom of a 1½-quart soufflé dish (straight-sided casserole) and sift the confectioners' sugar over it. Fold a length of aluminum foil lengthwise and tie around dish (see *page 511*).
2. Melt butter and chocolate together in a heavy saucepan over low heat. Blend in flour. Add milk gradually, blending thoroughly. Stirring constantly, bring to boiling over medium heat. Remove from heat and set aside.
3. Beat egg yolks, sugar, and extract together until very thick. Add sauce gradually, a spoonful at a time, beating until blended after each addition.

4. Beat egg whites until stiff, not dry, peaks are formed. Spread egg yolk mixture over egg whites and gently fold together. Turn into soufflé dish. Set in a shallow baking pan with hot water.
5. Bake at 375°F 70 minutes, or until a metal knife inserted halfway between center and edge comes out clean. Lightly sift *confectioners' sugar* over top. Carefully remove collar. Serve immediately.

6 TO 8 SERVINGS

CHOCOLATE FONDUE

4 oz. (4 sq.) unsweetened chocolate, cut in pieces	1 cup sugar
2 cups milk	½ teaspoon salt
1¼ cups fine soft bread crumbs	6 egg yolks, slightly beaten
2 tablespoons butter	4 to 6 teaspoons vanilla extract
	6 egg whites

1. Heat the chocolate and milk in large heavy saucepan, stirring until chocolate melts. Remove from heat. Stir in the bread crumbs, butter, sugar, and salt. Blend into the slightly beaten egg yolks in a large bowl. Cool. Stir in extract.
2. Beat the egg whites until stiff, not dry, peaks are formed. Fold into the cooled chocolate mixture.
3. Turn into a greased (bottom only) 2-quart shallow baking dish. Set in a shallow baking pan with hot water.
4. Bake at 350°F about 40 minutes, or until a knife inserted halfway between center and edge comes out clean.
5. Lightly sift *Dutch process cocoa* over top of fondue and serve warm. **8 SERVINGS**

VIENNESE CHOCOLATE SOUFFLÉ

6 egg yolks	3½ oz. (3½ sq.) unsweetened chocolate, grated
¾ cup sugar	
10 tablespoons sifted cake flour	1 tablespoon vanilla extract
2 cups milk	9 egg whites

1. Beat egg yolks and sugar until very thick in the top of a double boiler. Add the flour gradually, beating until smooth. Gradually add the milk, continuing to beat until blended.
2. Place over rapidly boiling water. Cook and stir 5 minutes, or until thickened. Remove from water; add the chocolate and stir until blended. Mix in the

Strawberry Shortcake

extract. Set on wire rack; allow to stand until mixture cools to lukewarm.

3. Meanwhile, butter a 2-quart soufflé dish (straight-sided casserole). Sprinkle lightly with *sugar* to coat bottom and sides. Fold a length of aluminum foil and tie around soufflé dish to give additional height (see *page 511*).

4. Beat the egg whites until stiff, not dry, peaks are formed and immediately fold with the chocolate mixture. Gently turn into the collared soufflé dish and immediately set in oven on rack (placed so top of product will be about at center of oven).

5. Bake at 375°F 45 to 50 minutes.

6. Remove from oven and carefully remove foil collar. Serve at once with a bowl of *Ice-Cream Sauce, below*. 8 TO 12 SERVINGS

ICE-CREAM SAUCE: Using equal parts of *vanilla ice cream* and *whipped cream*, fold the cream into softened ice cream just before serving.

DOUBLE-BOILER CHOCOLATE SOUFFLÉ

1 cup milk	4 egg yolks
2 oz. (2 sq.) unsweet-	1 teaspoon vanilla
ened chocolate	extract
3 tablespoons butter or	4 egg whites
margarine	¼ teaspoon cream of
3 tablespoons flour	tartar
½ cup sugar	

1. Combine milk and chocolate in a saucepan; cook over low heat, stirring occasionally, until chocolate is melted and mixture is blended.

2. Meanwhile, melt butter in a heavy saucepan; stir in the flour and cook until mixture is bubbly. Remove from heat and stir in the milk-chocolate mixture; blend in the sugar. Return to heat and bring the mixture to boiling, stirring constantly.

3. Beat egg yolks until very thick. Adding gradually, beat chocolate mixture into egg yolks until thoroughly blended. Mix in the extract. Cool to lukewarm.

4. Beat egg whites until frothy; add cream of tartar and continue beating until stiff, not dry, peaks are formed. Gently fold in the chocolate mixture until thoroughly blended.

5. Butter inside of top section of a 2-quart metal double boiler; turn mixture into it. Cover and set over boiling water (water should rise to no more than one half of the height of double-boiler top).

6. Keeping water gently boiling, cook 60 to 70 minutes, or until a metal knife inserted halfway between center and edge of soufflé comes out clean.

7. Run a spatula around edge of soufflé and invert onto a serving plate, or spoon into individual serving dishes. Serve immediately; garnish with *sweetened whipped cream*. ABOUT 6 SERVINGS

SOUFFLÉ VALTESSE
From the famous Tour d'Argent in Paris, France.

Praline Powder (use	3 egg yolks, well beaten
almonds), *page 501*	5 tablespoons sugar
Batter:	5 egg whites, beaten to
¼ cup butter	stiff, not dry, peaks
¼ cup flour	Vanilla Soufflé:
1⅓ cups hot milk	¼ cup sugar
½ teaspoon salt	3 egg yolks, well beaten
Chocolate Soufflé:	2 teaspoons vanilla
3 oz. (3 sq.) unsweet-	extract
ened chocolate,	5 egg whites, beaten to
melted	stiff, not dry, peaks

1. Prepare Praline Powder; reserve 2 teaspoons.

2. To prepare batter, melt butter in a saucepan; add flour and stir the "roux" until blended. Stir in the hot milk gradually and cook until smooth and thickened. Add salt and continue cooking over low heat about 3 minutes, stirring occasionally.

3. Divide batter in half; set one half aside.

4. For Chocolate Soufflé, add to one half the melted chocolate, 1 teaspoon of the praline powder, the egg yolks, and sugar; blend well.

5. For Vanilla Soufflé, add to second half the sugar, 1 teaspoon of the praline powder, the egg yolks, and extract; blend well.

6. Fold 5 stiffly beaten egg whites into each of the soufflé mixtures.

7. Lightly butter bottom and sides of a 2½-quart soufflé dish (straight-sided casserole) and coat with *sugar*.

8. Cut *6 ladyfingers* into pieces and soak in *maraschino liqueur*.

9. Turn half the vanilla soufflé mixture into dish. Arrange half of soaked ladyfingers over top. Cover with all the chocolate soufflé mixture and add a second layer of ladyfingers.

10. Cover with remaining vanilla mixture and sprinkle lightly with additional praline powder.

11. Bake at 375°F 35 to 40 minutes, or until soufflé is set. Serve at once. 8 TO 10 SERVINGS

Lemon Egg Fluff and Meringues with Custard Filling served with Cherry-Cinnamon Sauce

PETITE LEMON SOUFFLÉS

4 egg yolks	1¼ teaspoons grated
¼ cup butter or	lemon peel
margarine, softened	¼ cup lemon juice
¼ cup sugar	4 egg whites
Few grains salt	¼ cup sugar

1. Put the egg yolks, butter, ¼ cup sugar, salt, and lemon peel and juice into the top of a double boiler; mix well. Cook over simmering water, stirring constantly until thickened, 8 to 10 minutes. Remove double-boiler top from water and set aside to cool, stirring occasionally.

2. Beat the egg whites until frothy. Gradually add ¼ cup sugar, beating constantly until stiff peaks are formed. Using a wire whisk, gently blend the egg yolk mixture into egg whites.

3. Spoon mixture into six 6-ounce heat-resistant glass custard cups. Set in a shallow baking pan, place on oven rack, and pour hot water into pan to a ½-inch depth.

4. Bake at 350°F about 25 minutes, or until tops are lightly browned. Serve immediately.

6 INDIVIDUAL SOUFFLÉS

SOUFFLÉ AU GRAND MARNIER ET FRUITS

A recipe from Restaurant Lucien, Paris, France.

½ cup candied fruits	⅓ cup flour
2 tablespoons kirsch	⅛ teaspoon salt
2½ cups milk	4 egg yolks, slightly
1 piece (2 in.) vanilla	beaten
bean, split	¼ cup Grand Marnier
½ cup sugar	8 egg whites

1. Mix fruits and kirsch; set aside about 2 hours.

2. Scald milk with vanilla bean; cool and strain.

3. Blend sugar, flour, and salt; gradually mix in the scalded milk. Bring to boiling, stirring constantly; cook 3 minutes. Pour slowly into egg yolks, beating constantly until blended; mix in Grand Marnier. Cool to lukewarm.

4. Butter and coat with *sugar* the bottoms of six 8-ounce baking dishes or individual soufflé dishes.

5. Beat egg whites until stiff, not dry, peaks are formed. Spread egg yolk mixture over egg whites and carefully fold together.

6. Fill soufflé dishes about one half; distribute fruits over mixture; fill dishes to top with remaining soufflé mixture.

7. With a sharp knife make a small design from center to sides on tops of soufflés. Place in a shallow pan with hot water.

8. Bake at 350°F about 30 minutes, or until tops are lightly browned and a metal knife inserted into soufflés comes out clean.

9. Sprinkle each soufflé with *confectioners' sugar* and, if desired, drizzle with *1 teaspoon Grand Marnier*.

6 SERVINGS

CHILLED COFFEE SOUFFLÉ MOLD

2 env. unflavored	1 tablespoon vanilla
gelatin	extract
⅔ cup sugar	½ teaspoon salt
2¾ cups strong coffee,	2 egg yolks
cooled	2 cups heavy cream,
1½ cups creamed	whipped
cottage cheese	2 egg whites
	¼ cup sugar

1. Tie a foil collar (see *page 511*) around a 1½-quart soufflé dish so that collar extends at least 2 inches above the rim. Set aside.

2. Combine the gelatin and ⅔ cup sugar in a saucepan; mix well. Stir in 1 cup of the cooled coffee. Stir over low heat until gelatin and sugar are dissolved. Stir in remaining coffee.

3. Chill until mixture is slightly thickened, stirring occasionally.

4. Meanwhile, force cottage cheese through a food mill or sieve into a bowl. Blend in extract, salt, and egg yolks.

5. When coffee gelatin is of desired consistency, add gradually to the cottage cheese mixture, beating until well blended. Fold in whipped cream.

6. Beat egg whites until frothy; gradually add ¼ cup sugar, beating constantly until stiff peaks are formed. Spread egg whites over cottage cheese mixture and gently fold together until well blended.

7. Chill until mixture is very thick and piles softly when spooned out.

8. Spoon into soufflé dish and gently level with back of spoon. Garnish top with *grated unsweetened chocolate*. Chill until firm, about 6 hours.

9. When ready to serve, carefully remove foil collar.

8 TO 10 SERVINGS

RHUBARB SOUFFLÉ

1 env. unflavored gelatin	1½ cups rhubarb purée*
½ cup sugar	2 tablespoons grenadine
⅛ teaspoon salt	4 egg whites
4 egg yolks	½ cup sugar
½ cup cold water	1 cup heavy cream, whipped

1. Tie foil collar (see *page 511*) around a 1-quart soufflé dish so that collar extends 2 inches above the rim. Set aside.
2. Combine the gelatin, ½ cup sugar, and salt in the top of a double boiler. Beat egg yolks and water together until thoroughly blended. Stir into gelatin mixture.
3. Set over boiling water and cook about 5 minutes to cook egg yolks and dissolve gelatin, stirring constantly.
4. Remove from heat and stir in the rhubarb purée and grenadine; cool, then chill until mixture is slightly thickened, stirring occasionally.
5. Beat egg whites until frothy; add remaining ½ cup sugar, a little at a time, beating constantly until stiff peaks are formed.
6. Fold whipped cream and meringue together. Fold in chilled gelatin mixture until blended. Turn into prepared dish and chill until firm.
7. When ready to serve, carefully remove foil collar. ABOUT 8 SERVINGS
*To make rhubarb purée, cook about *3 cups cut-up rhubarb* with about *2 tablespoons water* in a heavy covered saucepan until rhubarb is tender. Force through a sieve or turn into an electric blender container and blend until smooth.

SUNNY CITRUS SOUFFLÉ
This lemon-lime gelatin dessert will add a dramatic flair to a buffet luncheon.

2 cups boiling water	1 teaspoon grated lemon peel
2 pkgs. (3 oz. each) lemon-flavored gelatin	¼ cup lemon juice
2 bottles (7 oz. each) lemon-lime carbonated beverage	2 cups heavy cream, whipped
	Few drops yellow food coloring

1. Tie foil collar (see *page 511*) around top of a 1½-quart soufflé dish so that collar extends about 2 inches above rim. Set aside.
2. Pour boiling water over gelatin in a bowl and stir until dissolved. Add carbonated beverage and lemon peel and juice; blend thoroughly. Chill until mixture is slightly thickened.
3. Beat gelatin until foamy. Fold in whipped cream and food coloring. Spoon mixture into prepared soufflé dish. Chill until firm, about 3 hours.
4. Carefully remove foil collar. Serve chilled with sweetened *fresh strawberries* or *Fresh Raspberry Sauce, page 554*. 8 SERVINGS

GELATIN DESSERTS

BLANCMANGE WITH ORANGE SAUCE
This glamorous dessert is one of Arlene Dahl's favorites.

1½ cups blanched almonds	½ cup water
2 cups water	1 cup heavy cream, whipped
1⅓ cups lump sugar	1 cup sugar
4 oranges	¾ cup water
4 teaspoons unflavored gelatin	4 teaspoons kirsch
	½ cup apricot preserves

1. Chop almonds in a food chopper; continue crushing almonds in a mortar, gradually adding the 2 cups water. When completely crushed, press through a cheesecloth and squeeze out the liquid, about 1¾ cups. Set aside. Discard the almonds.
2. Rub sugar lumps over the surface of the oranges so that the orange peel flavor will be absorbed. Add to almond liquid and stir occasionally to dissolve.
3. Soften gelatin in ½ cup water in a saucepan. Stir over low heat until gelatin is dissolved. Add to the almond liquid-sugar mixture. Chill in refrigerator until mixture is slightly thickened, stirring occasionally.
4. Fold in the whipped cream. Turn into a 1-quart mold. Chill until firm.
5. Combine 1 cup sugar and ¾ cup water in a saucepan. Bring to boiling and boil 10 minutes. Remove from heat and stir in the kirsch.
6. Meanwhile, remove the peel from oranges and cut into natural sections. (Be sure all peel and

membrane have been removed.) Soak sections in the syrup about 1½ hours.

7. Unmold blancmange onto a chilled plate and garnish with flavored orange sections.

8. Heat the apricot preserves and strain. Spoon over the orange sections just before serving.

6 SERVINGS

SNOW PUDDING

1 env. unflavored gelatin	1¼ cups water
½ cup plus 2 tablespoons sugar	¼ cup strained lemon juice
⅛ teaspoon salt	3 egg whites

1. Mix the gelatin, sugar, and salt in a saucepan. Stir in the water. Stir over low heat until gelatin and sugar are dissolved. Remove from heat and stir in the lemon juice.

2. Chill until mixture is slightly thickened, stirring occasionally.

3. When gelatin is of desired consistency, beat egg whites until stiff, not dry, peaks are formed.

4. Beat gelatin mixture until frothy. Fold into the beaten egg whites. Turn into a 1½-quart fancy mold. Chill until firm, about 3 hours.

5. Unmold onto a chilled serving plate and serve with *lingonberries* or *Raspberry Sauce, page 555.*

ABOUT 6 SERVINGS

SWEET CHERRY DELIGHT

1 pkg. (3 oz.) cherry-flavored gelatin	2 tablespoons confectioners' sugar
1 cup boiling water	¼ teaspoon almond extract
½ cup cold water	
1½ teaspoons lemon juice	1 cup heavy cream, whipped
3 tablespoons sugar	3 jelly roll slices (½ in. thick), cut in halves
1½ cups dark sweet cherries, halved and pitted	

1. Dissolve gelatin in the boiling water in a bowl; stir in the cold water and lemon juice. Chill until mixture is slightly thickened.

2. Mix the sugar with cherries in a bowl.

3. Blend confectioners' sugar and extract into whipped cream.

4. Beat thickened gelatin until light and frothy. Spread the whipped cream over gelatin; add the cherry halves and fold together.

5. Arrange jelly roll slices, rounded side up, around the inside of a 7-inch springform pan. Turn the gelatin mixture into the center and spread into an even layer, being careful to keep the jelly roll slices in place. Chill until firm.

6. To serve, remove rim from pan and set dessert on a serving plate.

ABOUT 8 SERVINGS

CREAMY CHERRY MOLD

1 can (29 oz.) pitted dark sweet cherries, drained (reserve syrup)	1 pkg. (3 oz.) cherry-flavored gelatin
	2 cups dairy sour cream

1. Add enough water to reserved cherry syrup to make 2 cups liquid. Heat 1 cup of the liquid to boiling and pour over the gelatin. Stir until dissolved. Stir in remaining liquid. Chill until mixture is slightly thickened, stirring occasionally.

2. Stir in the sour cream.

3. Halve the cherries and stir into gelatin mixture. Turn into a 1½-quart mold and chill until firm.

4. Unmold onto a chilled serving plate.

8 TO 10 SERVINGS

MOCHA-CARAMEL BAVARIAN

1 cup sugar	½ teaspoon vanilla extract
¾ cup boiling water	
1 env. unflavored gelatin	⅛ teaspoon salt
	1 cup undiluted evaporated milk, chilled and whipped
½ cup cold double-strength coffee	

1. Melt the sugar in a heavy light-colored skillet over low heat, gently moving it with wooden spoon toward center. Heat until golden brown.

2. Remove from heat and, stirring constantly, add the boiling water, a very small amount at a time. Return to low heat and continue stirring until bubbles are the size of dimes.

3. Meanwhile, soften gelatin in cold coffee. Gradually add the cooked syrup to the softened gelatin, stirring constantly; stir until gelatin is dissolved.

4. Stir the extract and salt into the gelatin mixture. Chill until mixture is slightly thickened, stirring occasionally.

5. Gently fold whipped evaporated milk into chilled gelatin mixture. Turn into a 1-quart mold. Chill until firm.

6. Unmold onto a chilled serving plate or spoon into chilled sherbet glasses.

6 SERVINGS

CRANBERRY JEWELED CROWN

4 cups (1 lb.) fresh cranberries, rinsed	1 pkg. (3 oz.) orange-flavored gelatin
1 cup cold water	¼ teaspoon salt
¾ to 1 cup sugar	1 cup heavy cream, whipped
¾ cup orange juice	1 cup walnuts, chopped

1. Combine cranberries in a saucepan with the cold water and sugar. Bring to boiling over medium heat and cook until skins of cranberries pop. Force through a sieve or food mill; set aside.
2. Heat orange juice. Combine gelatin and salt in a bowl; add orange juice and stir until gelatin is dissolved.
3. Stir in the sieved cranberries. Cool; chill until mixture is slightly thickened, stirring occasionally.
4. Fold whipped cream and walnuts into gelatin mixture. Turn into a 1½-quart fancy mold. Chill until firm. 6 TO 8 SERVINGS

LEMON EGG FLUFF

3 env. unflavored gelatin	1 can (6 oz.) frozen lemonade concentrate, thawed
½ cup sugar	10 egg whites
Few grains salt	½ cup sugar
1 cup water	Cherry-Cinnamon Sauce, below
10 egg yolks, beaten	

1. Thoroughly blend gelatin, sugar, and salt in a heavy saucepan. Mix in water. Stir over low heat until gelatin is dissolved.
2. Gradually add a small amount of hot gelatin mixture to egg yolks, stirring constantly. Blend into mixture in saucepan; cook and stir 2 minutes without boiling.
3. Remove from heat. Stir in lemonade concentrate. Chill until mixture is slightly thickened.
4. Beat egg whites until frothy. Gradually add sugar, continuing to beat until stiff peaks are formed; fold in gelatin mixture. Turn into a 2½-quart tower mold and chill until firm.
5. Unmold onto a chilled serving plate and serve with Cherry-Cinnamon Sauce. 12 SERVINGS

CHERRY-CINNAMON SAUCE: Combine ½ cup sugar and 2 tablespoons cornstarch in a saucepan; mix thoroughly. Drain 1 can (about 16 ounces) tart red cherries, reserving the liquid. Add cherry liquid and 3 tablespoons red cinnamon candies to sugar mixture. Bring to boiling, stirring constantly; continue cooking until mixture is thickened and clear. Remove from heat. Stir in 1 tablespoon lemon juice and the cherries. Cool. ABOUT 2¼ CUPS SAUCE

FIESTA MELON MOLD

5 teaspoons unflavored gelatin	1¾ cups watermelon juice (press pulp against sides of a fine sieve to extract juice)
1 cup orange juice	
½ cup water	
½ cup sugar	¼ teaspoon salt
¼ cup lime juice	¾ to 1 cup cantaloupe balls
	¾ to 1 cup honeydew melon balls

1. Soften gelatin in the orange juice; set aside.
2. Combine water and sugar in a small saucepan. Bring rapidly to boiling, stirring until sugar is dissolved. Boil 3 minutes. Remove from heat; add softened gelatin and stir until gelatin is dissolved. Blend in the remaining fruit juices and salt.
3. Chill until mixture is slightly thickened, stirring occasionally.
4. Stir in the melon balls. Turn mixture into a 1½-quart mold. Chill until firm.
5. To serve, unmold onto a chilled plate and, if desired, accompany with bowls of *sweetened whipped cream* and chopped *salted pecans*. Garnish plate with *Frosted Grapes, page 349.* ABOUT 8 SERVINGS

MELON-DUET MOLD

2 env. unflavored gelatin	3 cups sieved watermelon (6 cups, diced)
⅓ cup sugar	⅓ cup lemon juice
¼ teaspoon salt	2 cups cantaloupe balls
¾ cup chilled lemon-lime carbonated beverage	1 cup orange sections, cut in halves

1. Combine gelatin, sugar, and salt in a saucepan; mix in carbonated beverage. Stir over low heat until gelatin is dissolved.
2. Remove from heat and stir in sieved watermelon and lemon juice. Chill until mixture is slightly thickened, stirring often.
3. Stir in the cantaloupe balls and orange sections. Turn into a 5½-cup ring mold. Chill until firm.

4. Unmold onto a chilled serving plate. Fill center of mold with additional melon balls.

8 to 10 SERVINGS

COTTAGE CHEESE-MELON DESSERT ÉLÉGANT

2 pkgs. (16 oz. each) frozen melon balls, thawed and drained (reserve syrup)	2 cups heavy cream, whipped to soft peaks
2 pkgs. (3 oz. each) lemon-flavored gelatin	1 cup zwieback crumbs
	½ cup sugar
2 lbs. large-curd creamed cottage cheese, sieved	¼ cup finely chopped nuts
	¼ cup butter, melted
	½ teaspoon freshly grated nutmeg

1. Chop melon balls; set aside.
2. Bring reserved melon syrup to boiling; pour over gelatin in a bowl and stir until gelatin is dissolved. Cool.
3. Stir in 3 cups of the cottage cheese and then the melon balls; fold in whipped cream. Turn into a 9-inch tubed pan rinsed in cold water.
4. Mix crumbs, ¼ cup of the sugar, and nuts; blend in melted butter. Sprinkle evenly over top and press gently. Chill until firm, 6 to 8 hours.
5. Unmold (crumb side will be down).
6. Mix the remaining cottage cheese with a blend of the remaining sugar and nutmeg. Using a pastry bag and star tube, decorate as desired with the flavored cheese. 24 SERVINGS

CITRUS MOLD MARASCHINO

1 env. unflavored gelatin	3 env. unflavored gelatin
1¼ cups cold water	⅔ cup sugar
½ cup quartered maraschino cherries	1 cup maraschino cherry syrup
½ cup drained mandarin oranges	⅔ cup grapefruit juice
	⅔ cup lemon juice
½ cup small seedless green grapes	⅔ cup orange juice
	½ cup lime juice

1. Soften 1 envelope gelatin in ½ cup of the cold water in a small saucepan. Stir over low heat until gelatin is dissolved. Mix in remaining water and pour one half of the gelatin into a 2-quart charlotte mold or soufflé dish; chill until almost set, but not firm. Set remaining gelatin aside.
2. Lightly mark gelatin layer into quarters with a wooden pick. Arrange cherries in two opposite quarters, mandarin oranges in third, and grapes in fourth. Carefully pour remaining dissolved gelatin over fruits and chill until almost set, but not firm.
3. Meanwhile, combine 3 envelopes gelatin and the sugar in a saucepan. Mix well and stir in the remaining ingredients. Set over low heat until sugar and gelatin are dissolved, stirring constantly.
4. Turn into a bowl and set over ice and water, stirring frequently, until mixture is slightly thickened. Then beat with a hand rotary or electric beater until very light and fluffy.
5. Turn into mold, covering fruit layer. Chill until firm, about 3 hours.
6. Unmold onto a chilled serving plate. Garnish the plate with *stemmed maraschino cherries* and *green grapes*. If a glaze for cherries and grapes is desired, lightly brush each with *light corn syrup*.

8 TO 10 SERVINGS

SHERRY ELEGANCE

3 env. unflavored gelatin	¾ cup strained orange juice
1½ cups sugar	⅓ cup strained lemon juice
3 cups water	
1 cup plus 2 tablespoons sherry	9 drops red food coloring

1. Combine the gelatin and sugar in a large saucepan; mix well. Add water and stir over low heat until gelatin and sugar are dissolved.
2. Remove from heat and blend in remaining ingredients. Pour mixture into a 1½-quart fancy mold or a pretty china bowl. Chill until firm.
3. To serve, unmold gelatin onto chilled platter or serve in china bowl without unmolding. Serve with *whipped cream* or *whipped dessert topping*, if desired. 6 TO 8 SERVINGS

CREAMY PINEAPPLE MOLD

1 env. unflavored gelatin	⅓ cup mint-flavored apple jelly
1 can (20 oz.) crushed pineapple (reserve syrup)	1 cup heavy cream, whipped

1. Soften gelatin in ½ cup syrup in a saucepan. Stir over low heat until gelatin is dissolved. Remove from heat; add jelly and stir until melted.
2. Blend in the pineapple with remaining pineap-

ple syrup. Chill until mixture mounds slightly when dropped from a spoon, stirring occasionally.

3. Fold whipped cream into gelatin mixture. Turn into a 5-cup mold. Chill until firm.

4. Unmold on a chilled serving plate and garnish with *fresh mint.*   6 TO 8 SERVINGS

MOLDED PINEAPPLE-COCONUT CREAM

1 can (8½ oz.) crushed pineapple, drained (reserve syrup)	2 teaspoons grated lime peel
1 pkg. (3 oz.) lime-flavored gelatin	½ cup lime juice
	1 pt. vanilla ice cream
	¾ cup flaked coconut

1. Add enough water to reserved pineapple syrup to make 1 cup liquid. Heat to boiling.

2. Mix gelatin and a *few grains salt* in a bowl. Add boiling liquid and stir until completely dissolved. Mix in lime peel and juice. Add ice cream by spoonfuls; blend until smooth. Chill until mixture is slightly thickened, stirring occasionally.

3. Mix in pineapple and coconut. Turn into a 5-cup mold. Cover; chill until firm, about 2 hours.

4. To serve, unmold onto a chilled plate and garnish with half slices of *lime.*   ABOUT 8 SERVINGS

MOLDED RASPBERRY CRÈME

4 oz. (about 16) large marshmallows	1 cup boiling water
¼ cup grenadine	2 pkgs. (3 oz. each) raspberry-flavored gelatin
1⅓ cups dairy sour cream	1 cup cold water

1. Combine marshmallows and grenadine in the top of a double boiler. Heat over boiling water, stirring frequently, until marshmallows are melted. Remove from heat and blend in sour cream.

2. Pour boiling water over gelatin in a bowl, stirring until dissolved. Add the cold water.

3. Add gelatin slowly to sour cream mixture, stirring until well blended. Turn into a 1-quart mold or 6 individual tower molds. Chill until firm, about 3 hours.

4. To serve, unmold dessert and accompany with *a fresh red raspberry sauce*, if desired.   6 SERVINGS

CREAMY ALMOND-RICE RING
A creamy rich dessert to serve to a large group.

3 cups milk, scalded	½ cup cold water
3 cups boiling water	1 cup sugar
4 teaspoons vanilla extract	1 cup chopped toasted blanched almonds
1 teaspoon salt	3 cups heavy cream, whipped (whip one half at a time)
1 cup uncooked long grain rice	
4 teaspoons unflavored gelatin	1 tablespoon vanilla extract

1. Combine the scalded milk, boiling water, 4 teaspoons extract, and salt in a heavy saucepan. Bring to boiling; add the rice gradually, stirring with a fork. Continue to stir 1 minute. Cover and cook over low heat 45 to 60 minutes, until almost all of the liquid is absorbed and rice is tender. Stir occasionally.

2. Soften gelatin in cold water. Stir gelatin and sugar into hot rice until gelatin and sugar are completely dissolved. Cool.

3. Stir in the almonds. Fold in a mixture of the whipped cream and the 1 tablespoon extract until thoroughly blended.

4. Turn into a 3-quart ring mold which has been rinsed with cold water and, if desired, sprinkled lightly with *sugar.* Chill until firm, at least 3 hours.

5. Unmold on chilled serving plate. Stud crown and sides of mold with *pomegranate seeds* and serve with a colorful red *fruit sauce.*

16 TO 20 SERVINGS

SWEETHEART RICE MOLD
The name of this romantic strawberry-rice dessert and the heart-shaped mold both suggest Saint Valentine's Day.

1 pt. fresh strawberries	1 bottle (7 oz.) lemon-lime carbonated beverage
⅓ cup sugar	
1 env. unflavored gelatin	1 cup cooked rice
½ cup cold water	1 cup heavy cream, whipped

1. Rinse strawberries, drain, and reserve a few for garnish. Remove hulls from remaining berries and crush. Combine with the sugar and set aside in refrigerator.

2. Soften gelatin in cold water in a saucepan. Stir over low heat until gelatin is dissolved. Blend in the carbonated beverage. Combine with cooked rice and chill until mixture is slightly thickened.

3. Fold whipped cream into rice mixture until blended. Stir in the sugar-strawberry mixture. Turn into a 4½-cup heart-shaped mold. Chill until firm.

4. Using additional whipped cream and a pastry bag and decorating tube, decorate mold with a border; garnish with reserved strawberries.

ABOUT 8 SERVINGS

STRAWBERRY JEWEL DESSERT

2 cups boiling water	2 cups sliced
4 pkgs. (3 oz. each)	strawberries
strawberry-flavored	¼ cup sugar
gelatin	½ cup chopped pecans
3 cups cold water	1 cup dairy sour cream

1. Pour boiling water over gelatin in a bowl and stir until gelatin is dissolved. Mix in cold water. Chill until gelatin is slightly thickened, stirring often.

2. Toss berries with sugar, and fold with pecans into 2 cups of gelatin; turn into a 9-cup tubed mold. Chill until almost set, but not firm.

3. Add sour cream to remaining gelatin; whip until foamy. Spoon over layer in mold. Chill until firm, about 4 hours.

4. Unmold. Garnish with *whole strawberries*. Fill center with *dairy sour cream*.   12 TO 16 SERVINGS

ELEGANT STRAWBERRY CREAM

1½ tablespoons	½ teaspoon vanilla
unflavored gelatin	extract
¾ cup sugar	1 pkg. (16 oz.) frozen
¼ teaspoon salt	sliced strawberries,
1 cup cream	thawed
½ cup water	1 cup dairy sour cream

1. Mix the gelatin, sugar, and salt in a saucepan. Stir in the cream and water. Set over low heat and stir until sugar and gelatin are dissolved. Remove from heat and stir in the extract.

2. Cool slightly, then chill until mixture is slightly thickened, stirring occasionally.

3. Beat gelatin with hand rotary beater until light and fluffy. Add the strawberries and sour cream and stir lightly until blended. Turn into a 1-quart fancy mold and chill until firm.

4. Unmold dessert onto a chilled serving plate.

ABOUT 6 SERVINGS

NOTE: *Frozen raspberries* may be substituted for strawberries, if desired.

MOLDED STRAWBERRY CRÈME

2 pkgs. (3 oz. each)	½ cup cold water
strawberry-flavored	½ cup drained, frozen
gelatin	sliced strawberries
½ cup sugar	(reserve ½ cup syrup)
¼ teaspoon salt	1 cup heavy cream
2 cups boiling water	

1. Combine the gelatin, sugar, and salt in a bowl. Add boiling water and stir until gelatin is dissolved. Stir in the cold water and reserved strawberry syrup; cool. Chill until mixture is slightly thickened.

2. Add the cream and beat with a rotary beater until just blended. Mix in the strawberries.

3. Turn into a 5-cup fancy mold; chill until firm, about 4 hours.

4. Unmold and invert onto a chilled serving plate.   ABOUT 8 SERVINGS

STRAWBERRY-CHEESE FLUFF

1 env. unflavored	1 cup dairy sour cream
gelatin	¾ cup small-curd
¼ cup sugar	creamed cottage
⅛ teaspoon salt	cheese
¼ cup cold water	4 oz. cream cheese,
1 pkg. (10 oz.) frozen	softened
sliced strawberries,	
thawed and drained	
(reserve syrup)	

1. Combine the gelatin, sugar, and salt in a saucepan. Mix well and stir in the water and ¼ cup of the reserved strawberry syrup. Stir over low heat until gelatin and sugar are dissolved.

2. Combine in a bowl the strawberries, remaining syrup, and remaining ingredients. Beat until thoroughly blended. Stir in the dissolved gelatin. Pour into a bowl and chill until firm, 8 hours or overnight.

3. To serve, spoon dessert into chilled sherbet glasses. Accompany with a selection of toppings in small crystal bowls, such as *whipped cream*, *crushed strawberries*, and *flaked coconut*.

ABOUT 6 SERVINGS

MOLDED HOLIDAY PUDDING
A festive dessert for a large company dinner.

3 cups boiling water	1½ cups golden raisins, plumped
1¼ cups prunes	2¼ cups candied cherries
1 cup dried apricots	⅓ cup diced candied citron
1 cup sugar	⅓ cup diced candied lemon peel
1 teaspoon ground cinnamon	1½ cups walnuts, coarsely chopped
1 teaspoon ground nutmeg	3 env. (2 oz. each) dessert topping mix, or 3 cups heavy cream, whipped
1 teaspoon ground allspice	
1¼ cups orange juice	
3 env. unflavored gelatin	

1.   Pour boiling water over prunes and apricots in a saucepan. Return to boiling, cover, and simmer about 45 minutes, or until fruit is tender. Drain and reserve 1 cup liquid. Set liquid aside until cold. Remove and discard prune pits.

2.   Force prunes and apricots through a food mill or sieve into a large bowl. Stir in a mixture of the sugar, cinnamon, nutmeg, and allspice, mixing until sugar is dissolved. Blend in the orange juice and mix thoroughly.

3.   Soften gelatin in the 1 cup reserved liquid in a small saucepan. Stir over low heat until gelatin is dissolved. Stir into fruit-spice mixture. Chill until mixture is slightly thickened, stirring occasionally.

4.   Blend raisins, cherries, citron, lemon peel, and walnuts into gelatin mixture.

5.   Prepare the dessert topping according to package directions, or whip the cream. Gently fold into fruit mixture, blending thoroughly. Turn into 9- or 10-inch tubed pan. Chill until firm.

6.   Unmold onto chilled serving plate.

20 to 24 SERVINGS

NOTE: If a less sweet pudding is desired, decrease sugar to ½ cup. To develop flavor of dessert, prepare 2 to 4 days in advance of serving.

NEW ORLEANS HOLIDAY PUDDING: Follow directions for Molded Holiday Pudding. Reduce orange juice to 1 cup and add *3 tablespoons ruby red port wine* to the spice mixture. Blend in raisins, cherries, citron, and lemon peel; cover and set aside 1½ hours, stirring occasionally.

REFRIGERATOR DESSERTS

REGAL CHOCOLATE DESSERT

22 ladyfingers, split in halves	1½ teaspoons vanilla extract
3 oz. (3 sq.) unsweetened chocolate	2½ cups confectioners' sugar
⅓ cup sugar	6 egg whites
3 tablespoons water	⅓ cup sugar
6 egg yolks, well beaten	1 cup heavy cream, whipped
2 tablespoons light rum	1 cup almond macaroon crumbs*
1½ cups unsalted butter	

1.   Line the bottom of a 9-inch springform pan with about 18 ladyfinger halves; set aside.

2.   Combine the chocolate, ⅓ cup sugar, water, and a *few grains salt* in the top of a double boiler; heat over boiling water, stirring until smooth.

3.   Stir about 3 tablespoons of the chocolate mixture into egg yolks. Immediately blend into mixture in double boiler top and cook over boiling water, stirring constantly, about 5 minutes. Remove from water and set aside to cool. Stir in the rum.

4.   Cream the butter with the extract; add the confectioners' sugar, a small amount at a time, beating until light and fluffy after each addition. Blend in the chocolate mixture; set aside.

5.   Beat egg whites until frothy; gradually add the remaining ⅓ cup sugar, beating constantly until stiff peaks are formed.

6.   Fold whipped cream into chocolate mixture, then spread meringue over chocolate mixture; fold together. Fold in the macaroon crumbs.

7.   Pour one half of the mixture into the springform pan over the layer of ladyfingers. Arrange 18 ladyfinger halves over the chocolate mixture and cover with remaining one half of mixture.

8.   Chill until firm, 12 hours or overnight.

9.   Remove ring from springform pan and set cake on serving plate. Press remaining ladyfinger halves onto sides of mold. Garnish with *unsweetened whipped cream* and coarsely shredded *unsweetened chocolate.*

12 TO 16 SERVINGS

*If macaroons are moist, dry and toast them slightly in a 325°F oven before crushing.

ELEGANT CHOCOLATE DESSERT

2 oz. (2 sq.) unsweet-	1 cup unsalted butter
ened chocolate	1 cup confectioners'
½ cup sugar	sugar
¼ cup water	4 egg whites
4 egg yolks, fork beaten	36 graham crackers
1 teaspoon vanilla	
extract	

1. Combine the chocolate, sugar, and water in the top of a double boiler. Heat and stir over hot water until mixture is slightly thickened and smooth, about 12 minutes.
2. Blend about 3 tablespoons of the mixture into the egg yolks; immediately stir into mixture in double boiler. Cook and stir over boiling water 3 to 5 minutes. Remove from water and blend in the extract. Set aside to cool.
3. When mixture is cooled, cream the butter until softened. Gradually add confectioners' sugar, beating constantly until light and fluffy. Add the chocolate mixture, a small amount at a time, blending well after each addition.
4. Beat the egg whites until stiff, not dry, peaks are formed. Fold into chocolate mixture.
5. Use enough graham crackers to cover the bottom of a 8x8x2-inch pan. Spread one third of the chocolate mixture over crackers. Add a second layer of crackers and spread with remaining chocolate mixture. Repeat layering and top with graham crackers. Cover and chill about 48 hours.
6. Just before serving, swirl *whipped dessert topping* or *sweetened whipped cream* over top and sprinkle with shavings of *unsweetened chocolate* and chopped *salted pistachio nuts.* 8 OR 9 SERVINGS

CHARLOTTE PRIEURE
From Le Prieure, Villeneuve-les-Avignon, France.

½ cup water	¼ cup butter
½ cup sugar	4 egg yolks, well beaten
2 tablespoons rum	4 egg whites, beaten to
4 oz. semisweet	stiff, not dry, peaks
chocolate	Ladyfingers, halved
¾ cup coffee beverage	Whipped cream

1. Combine water, sugar, and rum in a saucepan; boil 5 minutes. Set syrup aside.
2. In another saucepan combine the chocolate with the coffee; cook and stir about 5 minutes. Remove from heat and stir in the butter. Add mix-

ture gradually to beaten egg yolks, beating until well blended. Fold in beaten egg whites.
3. Line small molds with ladyfingers which have been sprinkled with some of the rum syrup. Pour mixture into the molds, covering chocolate filling completely with more ladyfingers.
4. Chill until firm, 8 hours or overnight.
5. To serve, unmold and sprinkle remaining rum syrup over molds. Top with whipped cream.

ABOUT 8 SERVINGS

CHOCOLATE REFRIGERATOR CAKE

4 oz. (4 sq.) unsweet-	1½ cups butter or
ened chocolate	margarine
½ cup sugar	¾ lb. confectioners'
¼ cup water	sugar (about 3 cups)
6 egg yolks, well beaten	18 ladyfingers, split
1 tablespoon vanilla	6 egg whites
extract	6 tablespoons sugar

1. Combine the chocolate, ½ cup sugar, and water in the top of a double boiler over boiling water. Cook and stir until mixture is smooth.
2. Stir about 3 tablespoons hot mixture into well-beaten egg yolks. Return to mixture in a double-boiler top. Cook and stir over boiling water about 5 minutes. Remove from heat and set aside to cool slightly. Stir in the extract.
3. Cream the butter with the confectioners' sugar until light and creamy. Beat in the chocolate mixture until thoroughly blended. Set aside.
4. Line the sides and bottom of a 9-inch spring-form pan with the ladyfingers; set aside.
5. Beat the egg whites until frothy; gradually add the 6 tablespoons sugar, beating constantly until stiff peaks are formed. Fold into the cooled chocolate mixture until evenly blended. Spoon into ladyfinger-lined pan. Chill at least 24 hours.
6. Serve with *whipped cream.*

ONE 9-INCH CAKE

CHOCOLATE POMPADOUR
A favorite dessert served at Eastry House, Barbados, British West Indies.

1 lb. semisweet	1 cup heavy cream
chocolate	1 tablespoon Cointreau
6 egg yolks	6 egg whites

1. Melt the chocolate in the top of a double boiler over hot water.
2. Remove from heat and beat in the egg yolks,

one at a time, beating vigorously after each addition. Gradually add the cream, stirring constantly. Blend in the Cointreau; set aside.

3. Beat the egg whites until stiff, not dry, peaks are formed. Spread over chocolate mixture and fold together until blended. Turn into a shallow crystal serving bowl. Chill thoroughly, at least 4 hours.

4. Serve plain or with *whipped cream*.

10 to 12 SERVINGS

DESIR DE LA POMPADOUR WITH ENGLISH CREAM

A recipe from Lasserre Restaurant, Paris, France.

30 ladyfingers
2 egg yolks
2 tablespoons sugar
½ cup butter, softened
4 oz. (4 sq.) unsweetened chocolate, melted and cooled

½ cup sieved apricot jam
⅓ cup toasted chopped almonds
English Cream, *below*

1. Line the bottom of an 8-inch springform pan with 10 ladyfingers. Cut 10 ladyfingers in halves, crosswise, and arrange around side of pan; set aside.

2. Beat the egg yolks and sugar in a bowl until thick. Gradually blend in the butter, beating well. Blend in the melted chocolate.

3. Spread the chocolate mixture over the layer of ladyfingers. Arrange the remaining ladyfingers over the chocolate layer. Spread a thin layer of apricot jam over the top. Sprinkle with almonds. Chill 2 hours.

4. Serve in wedges topped with English Cream.

8 SERVINGS

ENGLISH CREAM

1⅓ cups milk
1 piece (2 in.) vanilla bean, split lengthwise

3 egg yolks, slightly beaten
6 tablespoons sugar
2 tablespoons kirsch

1. Heat the milk with vanilla bean in a heavy saucepan until scalded. Set aside.

2. Blend the egg yolks and sugar in the top of a double boiler. Remove vanilla bean from milk and gradually add the milk to egg yolk mixture, stirring constantly.

3. Cook and stir over boiling water until mixture coats a metal spoon; do not overcook. Remove from boiling water and cool to lukewarm over cold water. Blend in the kirsch.

4. Set in the refrigerator until ready to serve.

ABOUT 1½ CUPS SAUCE

MOCHA CORONET

2 env. unflavored gelatin
½ cup double-strength cold coffee
1½ cups double-strength hot coffee
1 cup sugar
2 doz. ladyfingers (about)

3 oz. (½ cup) semisweet chocolate pieces, melted
2 cups heavy cream
1 cup broken pecans
1 tablespoon vanilla extract or rum flavoring

1. Soften gelatin in cold coffee in a saucepan; stir over low heat until gelatin is dissolved. Add hot coffee and sugar; stir until sugar is dissolved. Chill until mixture is thickened, but not set.

2. Split 9 or 10 ladyfingers and dip one end of each in melted chocolate.

3. Whip chilled gelatin mixture until light and fluffy. Whip cream (one cup at a time) and fold into gelatin mixture along with pecans and extract.

4. Spoon mixture into a 9-inch springform pan to a depth of about ½ inch. Stand chocolate tipped ladyfingers upright around edge of pan, having chocolate tips upmost.

5. Spoon in about one third of the gelatin mixture and cover with a layer of plain split ladyfingers. Add another half of the gelatin mixture and a layer of split ladyfingers. Top with a layer of gelatin. Chill until firm.

6. To serve, remove side from pan. Sprinkle mold with a mixture of *1 tablespoon sugar* and *1 teaspoon instant coffee*. Garnish with additional whipped cream and the sugar-coffee mixture. 12 SERVINGS

CRANBERRY CLOUD DESSERT

1 env. unflavored gelatin
½ cup cold water
2 cups cranberries, finely chopped
1¼ cups sugar
1 teaspoon grated lemon peel

3 tablespoons lemon juice
15 ladyfingers, split in halves
1 can (14½ oz.) evaporated milk, chilled, *page 20*
1 tablespoon lemon juice

1. Soften gelatin in cold water in a saucepan. Stir over low heat until gelatin is dissolved.

2. Combine cranberries with the sugar, lemon peel, and 3 tablespoons lemon juice. Stir in the gelatin. Chill until mixture is thickened, but not set.

3. Meanwhile, arrange ladyfinger halves in bottom and around sides of a 9-inch springform pan.

4. Beat chilled evaporated milk until stiff; add 1 tablespoon lemon juice and beat until mixture is very stiff.

5. Blend cranberry-gelatin mixture into whipped evaporated milk, folding gently until blended. Turn filling into ladyfinger-lined pan.

6. Decorate top with green and red *maraschino cherry pieces* to form a wreath. Chill about 8 hours or overnight. ABOUT 12 SERVINGS

LEMON BISQUE

The term "bisque" commonly refers to thick French soups, however it sometimes refers to creamy refrigerator or frozen desserts.

1¼ cups boiling water	3 tablespoons lemon
1 pkg. (3 oz.) lemon-	juice
flavored gelatin	1 can (14½ oz.)
⅓ cup honey	evaporated milk,
⅛ teaspoon salt	chilled and whipped,
2 teaspoons grated	*page 20*
lemon peel	2 cups crushed vanilla
	wafers (about ½ lb.)

1. Pour boiling water over gelatin in a bowl; stir until dissolved. Add honey, salt, and lemon peel and juice; cool. Chill until mixture is slightly thickened, stirring occasionally.

2. Add thickened gelatin to whipped evaporated milk and blend thoroughly.

3. Spread half of the crushed vanilla wafers in bottom of a 13x9x2-inch pan. Pour lemon mixture over crumbs and spread evenly. Top with remaining half of crumbs. Chill overnight.

4. Cut and serve with *sweetened whipped cream.*
12 SERVINGS

MAPLE NUT MOLD

A recipe from Mrs. Hubert Humphrey.

¼ cup cornstarch	1½ cups lightly packed
¼ cup cold water	brown sugar
2 cups boiling water	3 egg whites
	½ cup walnuts, chopped

1. Thoroughly blend cornstarch and water until smooth in a heavy saucepan. Add boiling water gradually, stirring constantly. Mix in the brown sugar. Bring to boiling, continuing to stir. Reduce heat and cook 30 minutes, stirring occasionally.

2. Beat egg whites until stiff, not dry, peaks are formed. Pour hot cornstarch mixture gradually over egg whites, beating constantly until blended. Mix in walnuts.

3. Spoon into individual molds, cover, and chill. Unmold. Serve with *whipped cream.*
6 TO 8 SERVINGS

CHARLOTTE À L'ORANGE

Ladyfingers decorate the edge and form the base for this orange chiffon dessert.

22 single ladyfingers	½ cup water
Chocolate Glaze, *below*	1 can (6 oz.) frozen
1 env. unflavored	orange juice
gelatin	concentrate, thawed
⅔ cup sugar	1 cup undiluted
⅛ teaspoon salt	evaporated milk

1. Line the bottom of a 9-inch pie pan with 5 ladyfingers. Dip remaining ladyfingers into the Chocolate Glaze to coat about one-fourth of each. Arrange chocolate-tipped ladyfingers around edge of pie pan. Drizzle half of remaining glaze over ladyfingers in pan. (Reserve rest of glaze for topping.) Set aside.

2. Combine gelatin, sugar, and salt in a saucepan. Stir in water. Set over low heat, stirring constantly, until gelatin is dissolved.

3. Remove from heat and blend in undiluted orange juice concentrate. Chill until mixture is slightly thickened, stirring occasionally.

4. Pour evaporated milk into a refrigerator tray and place in freezer until ice crystals form around edge. Turn into a chilled bowl and beat until very stiff; fold into gelatin.

5. Turn filling into the pie pan. Drizzle top with remaining Chocolate Glaze. Chill until firm, about 3 hours. ONE 9-INCH PIE

CHOCOLATE GLAZE: Partially melt *2 ounces (2 squares) semisweet chocolate* and *2 tablespoons butter* over simmering water, being careful not to overheat. Remove from water and stir until chocolate is completely melted. Cool slightly.

PEPPERMINT STICK DELIGHT

1 cup vanilla wafer
  crumbs (about ¼ lb.)
2 tablespoons sugar
3 tablespoons butter or
  margarine, melted
5 small sticks (about 1½
  oz.) peppermint candy,
  coarsely crushed

½ cup walnuts, coarsely
  chopped
4 oz. marshmallows, cut
  in small pieces
1½ cups heavy cream,
  whipped

1. Mix crumbs with sugar in a bowl. Stir in the butter, using a fork. Using back of spoon, press crumb mixture firmly into an even layer on bottom of an 8-inch square pan.
2. Fold candy, walnuts, and marshmallows into the whipped cream. Turn into pan and chill about 12 hours.   8 SERVINGS

PINEAPPLE REFRIGERATOR DESSERT

1 env. unflavored
  gelatin
1 can (20 oz.) crushed
  pineapple, drained
  (reserve syrup)

2 cups heavy cream,
  whipped
40 graham crackers
¼ cup finely chopped
  crystallized ginger

1. Soften gelatin in ½ cup pineapple syrup in a saucepan. Stir over low heat until gelatin is dissolved. Blend into crushed pineapple. Chill until mixture is slightly thickened, stirring occasionally.
2. Fold half of the whipped cream into chilled gelatin mixture until evenly blended.
3. Spread a thin layer of the gelatin mixture on each graham cracker; turn crackers on end and press together to form a loaf.
4. Spread with remaining whipped cream; garnish with ginger. Chill about 3 hours.
5. To serve, cut into diagonal slices.
    ABOUT 10 SERVINGS

RASPBERRY FLUFF

30 marshmallows
  (about 8 oz.)
⅓ cup orange juice

1 pkg. (10 oz.) frozen
  raspberries, thawed
1 cup heavy cream,
  whipped

1. Heat marshmallows and orange juice in the top of a double boiler over boiling water until marshmallows are melted, stirring occasionally. Remove from heat and turn into a bowl; set aside to cool.
2. Stir thawed raspberries with their syrup into cooled marshmallow mixture. Gently fold in whipped cream. Cover and chill 3 to 4 hours.
3. To serve, spoon into parfait glasses.
    ABOUT 6 SERVINGS

DANISH RASPBERRY PUDDING

2 pkgs. (10 oz. each)
  frozen raspberries
3 cups water
1 piece (3 in.) stick
  cinnamon

Peel of ½ lemon, cut in
  pieces
½ cup sugar
6 tablespoons
  cornstarch

1. Combine in a saucepan the raspberries, water, stick cinnamon, and lemon peel. Bring rapidly to boiling; break up block of frozen raspberries with a fork. Boil 5 minutes. Remove from heat. Strain, pressing out liquid. Return liquid to saucepan.
2. Mix the sugar with cornstarch. Blend in ½ *cup water*. Stir into raspberry liquid. Bring to boiling, stirring constantly. Boil 1 minute.
3. Pour mixture into a serving dish. Set aside to cool. Cover; chill thoroughly 3 to 4 hours.
4. Spoon chilled dessert into individual serving dishes and serve with *sugar* and *cream*.
    ABOUT 10 SERVINGS

PASHKA

A traditional Russian Easter dessert.

2 pkgs. (8 oz. each)
  cream cheese,
  softened
1 cup large-curd
  creamed cottage
  cheese
½ cup butter, softened
½ cup sugar
1 tablespoon finely
  shredded lemon peel

1 tablespoon finely
  shredded orange peel
1 teaspoon vanilla
  extract
⅓ cup chopped candied
  red cherries
¼ cup golden raisins
2 tablespoons diced
  candied pineapple
¼ cup chopped toasted
  almonds

1. Combine cheeses, butter, sugar, lemon and orange peels, and extract; beat until smooth. Mix in remaining ingredients.
2. With a moistened piece of cheesecloth, line a thoroughly cleaned flowerpot (5½ inches across top and 5½ inches high) having a drainage hole.
3. Spoon cheese mixture into flowerpot. Place pot on a rack in a shallow pan. Cover and chill overnight or longer, to allow flavors to blend.
4. Unmold and garnish with whole *candied cherries*.
    10 TO 12 SERVINGS

FROZEN DESSERTS

AVOCADO MOUSSE

1½ cups mashed ripe avocado
1 teaspoon grated lemon peel
2 tablespoons lemon juice
2 tablespoons orange juice
¼ teaspoon salt
8 drops green food coloring
1 env. unflavored gelatin
½ cup milk
¼ cup confectioners' sugar
1½ cups heavy cream, whipped

1. Blend the avocado, lemon peel and juice, orange juice, salt, and food coloring; set aside.
2. Soften gelatin in milk in a small saucepan. Stir over low heat until dissolved. Blend into the avocado mixture. Chill about 45 minutes, or until mixture becomes slightly thicker.
3. Blend confectioners' sugar into whipped cream. Fold into the avocado mixture. Turn into a 5-cup fancy mold. Freeze until firm.
4. To serve, unmold on a chilled serving plate and allow to stand about 1 hour to soften slightly.

10 TO 12 SERVINGS

NOTE: Serve a wedge of the Avocado Mousse with a wedge of the *Molded Raspberry Sherbet, page 539.*

BEAU NASH DELIGHT

A recipe from the Pump Room of the Hotel Ambassador East, Chicago, Illinois.

6 oz. semisweet chocolate
1 cup egg yolks (about 12)
½ cup sugar
Pinch salt
2 cups heavy cream, whipped
½ cup hazelnuts (filberts)
1 tablespoon kirsch
1 teaspoon vanilla extract
Heavy cream, whipped (for decoration)

1. Melt the chocolate in the top of a double boiler. Cool slightly and use it to line 6 to 10 paper baking cups, swirling the chocolate with a teaspoon to coat them evenly. Chill the cups until the chocolate is hard, then peel off the paper.
2. Beat egg yolks, sugar, and salt in top of a double boiler over hot water. Stir mixture constantly with wire whip until it is warm and very light. Cool over crushed ice, beating constantly.

3. Fold in the whipped cream, nuts, kirsch, and extract. Spoon mixture into the chocolate baskets. Place in freezer for several hours or until firm. To serve, top with whipped cream.   6 TO 10 SERVINGS

FROZEN CHOCOLATE PUDDING PIE WITH CHERRY FLAIR

1 can (15½ to 18 oz.) ready-to-serve vanilla pudding, chilled
2 cups whipped dessert topping or thawed, frozen whipped topping
1 can (16 to 18 oz.) ready-to-serve chocolate pudding, chilled
Chocolate Cookie Crumb Crust, *below*
3 tablespoons chilled caramel topping sauce
½ cup salted almonds, coarsely chopped
Maraschino cherries with stems

1. Empty vanilla pudding into a large bowl and blend in 1 cup of the whipped dessert topping.
2. Empty chocolate pudding into the same bowl and draw a rubber spatula or spoon through the chocolate and vanilla puddings until partially streaked to give a marbled design.
3. Turn into the Chocolate Cookie Crumb Crust. Set in freezer to chill, about 15 minutes.
4. Remove from freezer and drizzle with the caramel topping sauce. Top with the chopped salted almonds.
5. To garnish, drop spoonfuls of the remaining dessert topping onto the nuts around outer edge of pie. Put a stemmed maraschino cherry onto each mound of topping. Set in freezer for several hours or until filling is firm.
6. If necessary, allow pie to remain at room temperature to soften slightly before cutting.

8 TO 10 SERVINGS

CHOCOLATE COOKIE CRUMB CRUST: Drizzle *5 tablespoons melted butter or margarine* over *2 cups finely crushed chocolate cookie crumbs* (from refrigerated baked cookie dough, commercial chocolate cookies or wafers), mixing thoroughly with a fork. Blend in *1 ounce (1 square) unsweetened chocolate,* grated. Gently, but firmly, press mixture over bottom and sides of a 10-inch pie plate. Chill in refrigerator until firm, or set in freezer about 15 minutes.

ONE 10-INCH PIE SHELL

CHOCOLATE-BANANA FROZEN POPS
A hearty pick-me-up snack for hungry small fry.

6 ripe bananas | 1 pkg. (6 oz.) semisweet chocolate pieces

1. Peel bananas and cut crosswise into halves. Insert a wooden stick into the end of each. Place in shallow pan; set in freezer for 2 to 3 hours.
2. Melt chocolate pieces over hot (not boiling) water. Using a spatula, spread chocolate over each banana, using lengthwise strokes and completely coating banana. Chocolate will become firm immediately as it is spread.
3. Wrap each banana in aluminum foil and store in freezer. Serve while still frozen.   12 FROZEN POPS

PASTEL PARFAITS

1 env. unflavored gelatin | 1 teaspoon vanilla extract
¼ cup sugar | 1 env. whipped dessert topping mix, prepared according to pkg. directions
2 cups milk |
1 cup instant nonfat dry milk |
¼ cup cinnamon candies |

1. Thoroughly mix gelatin and sugar in a saucepan. Stir in milk, then the instant nonfat dry milk and cinnamon candies. Stir over low heat until gelatin and candies are dissolved. Let cool.
2. Mix in the extract and pour into refrigerator tray; freeze.
3. Turn the frozen mixture into a bowl; allow it to soften slightly and whip until smooth, using an electric mixer.
4. To serve, alternate 2 layers of the cinnamon mixture with one layer of the dessert topping in parfait glasses. Top each serving with *2 or 3 cinnamon candies*.   ABOUT 8 SERVINGS

COCONUT-GREEN TEA MOUSSE

3 cups milk | 1 cup cookie coconut (packaged grated coconut)*
10 green tea bags (individual size) |
1 cup sugar | Few drops green and yellow food coloring
1 env. unflavored gelatin | 1 cup heavy cream, chilled

1. Heat milk to boiling in a saucepan. Add tea bags and allow to steep over medium heat 15 minutes, pressing the bags very gently with the back of a wooden spoon during steeping to avoid floating. Remove bags to a strainer and drain over saucepan several minutes. (Do not press or break bags; discard bags.)
2. Add a blend of the sugar and the gelatin; stir until gelatin is dissolved. Remove from heat, blend in coconut, and let stand 10 to 20 minutes before chilling for hot mixture to absorb the full coconut flavor. Stir in enough food coloring to tint a pale green.
3. Chill in refrigerator or over a bowl of ice and water until mixture is slightly thickened, stirring often. When thickened, beat well.
4. Whip the chilled cream until soft, not stiff, peaks are formed. Fold into gelatin.
5. Turn into a 1-quart fancy mold and freeze 6 to 8 hours. Or spoon into 8 individual molds.
6. When unmolded, garnish with chopped *salted pistachio nuts*.   ABOUT 1 QUART MOUSSE
*Or use flaked coconut, finely chopped in an electric blender.

MACAROON MOUSSE
This towering Christmas dessert stands as its own monument to delicate, delectable flavor.

½ cup butter or margarine | 1 teaspoon unflavored gelatin
1 teaspoon vanilla extract | ¼ cup cold water
¾ cup sugar | 1 cup icy cold water
4 eggs, well beaten | 1 cup instant nonfat dry milk
1¾ cups fine almond macaroon crumbs* | 2 tablespoons lemon juice

1. Cream butter with extract until softened. Gradually beat in the sugar until thoroughly blended. Add the eggs in thirds, beating thoroughly until light and fluffy.
2. Add the macaroon crumbs and beat at high speed with electric mixer about 5 minutes.
3. Soften gelatin in ¼ cup cold water. Stir over low heat until dissolved. Set aside to cool.
4. Mix the 1 cup cold water and dry milk in a bowl. Beat until soft peaks are formed, 3 to 4 minutes. Very gradually add the dissolved gelatin, beating constantly. Add the lemon juice and beat until stiff peaks are formed, 3 to 4 minutes.
5. Fold macaroon mixture into whipped milk and

turn into a 1½-quart mold which has been rinsed with cold water. Freeze overnight or until firm.

6.   Unmold onto a chilled serving plate and garnish plate as desired. Serve immediately.

8 TO 10 SERVINGS

*If macaroons are moist, dry and toast them slightly in a low oven before crushing. Crumbs may be prepared in an electric blender, crushing a portion at a time.

COFFEE MOUSSE

2 cups heavy cream	Few grains salt
½ cup ground coffee	1 teaspoon vanilla
½ cup sugar	extract
2 tablespoons Dutch process cocoa	

1.   Combine ½ cup of the cream and coffee in top of a double boiler. Set over boiling water 10 minutes. Strain mixture through a fine sieve or clean cheesecloth. Cool and chill.
2.   Beat the remaining 1½ cups cream until it piles softly. Beat in the sugar, cocoa, salt, extract, and coffee mixture. Pour into refrigerator tray and freeze until firm, without stirring.
3.   To serve, spoon into sherbet glasses and top with *shredded unsweetened chocolate.*

1½ PINTS MOUSSE

PARFAIT GRAND MARNIER

A recipe from Pavilion, Henry the Fourth, in Paris.

1½ cups sugar	2 tablespoons Grand Marnier
½ cup water	
6 egg yolks, beaten	1 cup heavy cream, whipped

1.   Bring sugar and water to boiling in a saucepan; cook rapidly 5 minutes.
2.   Gradually beat the syrup into egg yolks, using a hand rotary or electric beater. When thoroughly blended, return mixture to the saucepan. Simmer over low heat (do not boil), stirring constantly until thick and smooth.
3.   Strain mixture through a fine sieve into a bowl. Place over cracked ice and stir until cold.
4.   Blend in the Grand Marnier and fold in the whipped cream.
5.   Turn mixture into a parfait mold, seal tightly, and freeze in a mixture of ice and salt for 2 to 3 hours.

ABOUT 6 SERVINGS

PEACHES À LA MELBA WITH CHEESE FREEZE

1 cup creamed cottage cheese	1 cup dairy sour cream
1 tablespoon lemon juice	1 can (29 oz.) cling peach halves, drained
1 strip lemon peel (yellow portion only)	Raspberry Sauce, *page 555*
½ cup sugar	

1.   Put the cottage cheese, lemon juice and peel, sugar, and sour cream into a blender container and blend until smooth and creamy.
2.   Turn mixture into a refrigerator tray and freeze just until frozen around edges.
3.   Turn into a chilled bowl and beat until smooth. Return mixture to tray, cover tightly, and freeze until firm.
4.   About 20 minutes before serving, transfer from freezer to refrigerator to soften slightly.
5.   To serve, place a peach half, cut side up, in each chilled sherbet glass. Fill the center of each peach half with a scoop or square of the frozen cottage cheese mixture. Spoon Raspberry Sauce over all.

6 TO 8 SERVINGS

PEANUT BRITTLE MOUSSE

1 pkg. (10½ oz.) miniature marshmallows	¼ cup cold water
	1 egg white
1 cup milk	¾ cup crushed peanut brittle
½ cup strong coffee	
1 teaspoon unflavored gelatin	1 cup heavy cream, whipped

1.   Combine marshmallows, milk, and coffee in top of a double boiler. Heat over boiling water until marshmallows are melted; stir occasionally.
2.   Soften gelatin in water in a saucepan. Stir over low heat until gelatin is dissolved.
3.   Remove marshmallow mixture from heat and stir in gelatin. Cool slightly and chill until slightly thickened, stirring occasionally.
4.   Beat egg white until stiff, not dry, peaks are formed. Gently fold peanut brittle, beaten egg white, and whipped cream into marshmallow mixture. Turn into a 1½-quart mold rinsed with cold water.
5.   Freeze until firm, but not solid. Before serving time, place mold in refrigerator 45 to 60 minutes to soften slightly.

ABOUT 12 SERVINGS

PEPPERMINT-CHOCOLATE FROZEN DESSERT

1 cup chocolate wafer
   crumbs
1 tablespoon
   confectioners' sugar
¼ cup butter or
   margarine, softened

1 env. (2 oz.) whipped
   dessert topping mix
⅓ cup coarsely crushed
   peppermint-stick
   candy
1 cup miniature
   marshmallows

1.   Turn crumbs into a bowl. Blend in confectioners' sugar and butter. Using the back of a spoon, press crumb mixture firmly into an even layer on the bottom of an 8x8x2-inch pan.
2.   Prepare dessert topping mix according to package directions, using *1 teaspoon vanilla extract*. Fold in peppermint candy and marshmallows. Turn into prepared pan and spread evenly to corners. Freeze until firm, about 3 hours.
3.   Allow to thaw slightly before serving. Top with shaved *unsweetened chocolate* or *chopped nuts*.
ABOUT 8 SERVINGS

FROZEN PEPPERMINT DESSERT

1 can (20 oz.) crushed
   pineapple, undrained
1 pkg. (3 oz.) straw-
   berry-flavored gelatin
1 pkg. (10½ oz.) min-
   iature marshmallows

¼ cup (about 2 oz.)
   cinnamon candies
¼ lb. soft butter mints,
   crushed
2 cups heavy cream,
   whipped

1.   Combine the pineapple, gelatin, marshmallows, and cinnamon candies in a large bowl and mix well. Cover and refrigerate overnight.
2.   Add the butter mints and whipped cream to the chilled pineapple mixture and fold together until thoroughly blended. Turn mixture into a 10-inch tubed pan. Freeze until firm.
3.   Unmold the dessert onto a chilled serving plate and garnish with sprigs of *fresh mint*.
16 TO 20 SERVINGS

NESSELRODE PUDDING

2 egg yolks
½ cup sugar
⅓ cup confectioners'
   sugar
1¼ teaspoons vanilla
   extract

1¾ cups heavy cream,
   whipped
2 egg whites
⅛ teaspoon salt
1 jar (10 oz.)
   Nesselrode mixture

1.   Beat egg yolks with sugar until very thick.

2.   Blend confectioners' sugar and extract into whipped cream.
3.   Beat egg whites with salt until stiff, not dry, peaks are formed.
4.   Blend Nesselrode mixture into egg yolk mixture. Spread whipped cream and egg whites over egg yolk mixture; gently fold together. Spoon into a 1½-quart mold or refrigerator trays. Freeze until firm.
5.   If desired, garnish with *nut* and *maraschino cherry halves*.
8 SERVINGS

FROZEN DESSERT ROYALE

3 cups vanilla wafer
   crumbs (about 12 oz.)
6 tablespoons sugar
¾ cup butter, softened
2 tablespoons sugar
1 pt. fresh strawberries,
   rinsed, drained, and
   hulled
2 cups undiluted
   evaporated milk
1 pkg. (10½ oz.)
   miniature marshmallows

1 can (20 oz.) crushed
   pineapple, drained
2 cups small date pieces
2 cups chopped walnuts
1 can (6 oz.) frozen
   lemonade concen-
   trate, thawed
1 tablespoon finely
   chopped crystallized
   ginger

1.   Mix crumbs and 6 tablespoons sugar in a bowl. Blend in butter with a fork or pastry blender. Reserve ¾ cup crumb mixture for topping.
2.   Using back of spoon, press crumb mixture firmly into an even layer on bottom and sides of a 9-inch springform pan.
3.   Sprinkle 2 tablespoons sugar over strawberries in a bowl; set aside, stirring occasionally, until sugar is dissolved.
4.   Combine evaporated milk and marshmallows in the top of a double boiler. Heat over boiling water, stirring occasionally, until marshmallows are just melted. Remove from water and cool completely.
5.   Blend strawberries, drained pineapple, dates, walnuts, lemonade concentrate, and crystallized ginger into cooled marshmallow mixture.
6.   Turn into crumb-lined pan. Sprinkle reserved crumb mixture evenly over top.
7.   Freeze just until firm.
ABOUT 12 SERVINGS

CARNIVAL SNOW

8 oz. cream cheese, softened
½ teaspoon salt
¼ cup maraschino cherry syrup
½ teaspoon grated lemon peel
1 tablespoon lemon juice
2 teaspoons vanilla extract
½ teaspoon almond extract

1 cup dark or golden raisins, plumped
1 can (11 oz.) mandarin oranges, drained (reserve ¾ cup syrup)
1 can (8½ oz.) pineapple tidbits, drained (reserve ¼ cup syrup)
4 oz. miniature marshmallows
1 cup heavy cream, whipped

1. Combine the cream cheese, salt, cherry syrup, lemon peel and juice, and the extracts in a bowl; mix thoroughly. Blend in the raisins and the reserved orange and pineapple syrups.
2. Stir in the oranges, pineapple, and marshmallows until well mixed. Fold in the whipped cream.
3. Turn into a 1½-quart fancy mold. Cover; freeze at least 24 hours.
4. Unmold. Allow to stand at room temperature to soften slightly before serving. 8 TO 10 SERVINGS

FROZEN CHRISTMAS PUDDING

1½ cups macaroon crumbs (about 14 small macaroons, crushed)*
½ cup chopped pecans
½ cup chopped pitted dates
¼ cup chopped candied pineapple
¼ cup chopped candied orange peel

1¼ teaspoons grated lemon peel
¼ teaspoon ground cinnamon
¼ teaspoon ground nutmeg
8 marshmallows, quartered
¼ cup orange juice
¼ cup sugar
1 cup heavy cream, whipped

1. Combine crumbs, pecans, dates, pineapple, orange and lemon peels, cinnamon, and nutmeg in a bowl; set aside.
2. Heat marshmallows, orange juice, and sugar together in the top of a double boiler over boiling water until marshmallows are melted, stirring occasionally. Blend into fruit mixture. Fold in whipped cream.
3. Put 10 paper baking cups, 2¼x1¼ inches, into refrigerator trays or muffin-pan wells. Spoon mixture into cups; freeze until firm.

4. When ready to serve, garnish each with a holly spray formed with *red cinnamon candies* and pieces of *green gumdrops*. 10 SERVINGS
*If macaroons are moist, dry and toast them slightly in a 325°F oven before crushing.

Ice-Cream Desserts

BAKED ALASKA

1 qt. chocolate ice cream
1 qt. strawberry ice cream
Pound cake, sponge cake, or ladyfingers

5 egg whites
½ teaspoon vanilla extract
¼ teaspoon salt
¾ cup sugar

1. Line a chilled 2-quart melon mold with chocolate ice cream. Pack firmly against sides of mold. Fill center of mold with strawberry ice cream, packing firmly. Freeze until firm.
2. Cut a layer of cake about ¼ inch larger than mold and about 1¼ inches thick. Place on a wooden board or on a baking sheet lined with 2 sheets of heavy paper; set aside.
3. Beat egg whites with extract and salt until frothy; gradually add sugar, beating constantly until stiff peaks are formed.
4. Unmold ice cream onto center of cake. Working quickly, completely cover ice cream and cake with meringue, spreading evenly and being careful to completely seal bottom edge. With spatula, quickly swirl meringue into an attractive design and, if desired, garnish with *maraschino cherries*.
5. Set in a 450°F oven 4 to 5 minutes, or until meringue is lightly browned. Quickly slide onto a chilled serving plate, slice and serve immediately. (If not ready to serve immediately, place baked Alaska in freezer so ice cream does not melt.)
12 to 16 SERVINGS
NOTE: If desired, a layer of *fresh fruit* (orange, mandarin orange, or grapefruit sections, sliced peaches, etc.) may be arranged over cake slice before unmolding ice cream over it.
BAKED ALASKA LOAF: Follow recipe for Baked Alaska. Substitute *1-quart brick ice cream* for molded ice cream. Cut cake about ¼ inch larger than mold on all sides.
INDIVIDUAL BAKED ALASKAS: Follow recipe for

Baked Alaska. Decrease ice cream to 1½ pints chocolate, strawberry, or vanilla. Omit cake. Chill *8 canned pineapple slices*. Pat dry with absorbent paper and arrange on a thick wooden board. Quickly place 1 scoop of very firm ice cream in center of each slice. Completely cover ice cream with meringue, spreading evenly. Be careful to completely seal bottom edge to pineapple slice. Set in a 450°F oven about 4 minutes, or until meringue is lightly browned. Serve immediately. (Place in freezer if not ready to serve immediately.)   8 SERVINGS

ICE CREAM-CHERRY PYRAMID
Dramatic and elegant in its simplicity, you're bound to impress your guests with this handsome creation.

3 qts. vanilla ice cream	3 cans or jars (17 oz.
3 tablespoons cornstarch	each) pitted dark
1 tablespoon sugar	sweet cherries,
2 tablespoons grated	drained (reserve
lemon peel	syrup)

1.   Arrange scoops of ice cream, pyramid fashion, on a serving plate. Set in freezer until serving time.
2.   Meanwhile, combine cornstarch, sugar, and lemon peel in a heavy saucepan. Stir in the reserved cherry syrup. Bring rapidly to boiling; cook and stir 3 minutes. Mix in the cherries and heat, stirring occasionally.
3.   To serve, pour the cherry sauce over ice cream pyramid. Place a *sugar cube* soaked with *lemon extract* on top and ignite it. Pass additional sauce.
14 TO 16 SERVINGS

FROZEN CHERRY EASTER EGG
This attractive mold should rate "four stars" for glamor appeal.

3 pts. vanilla ice	3 tablespoons
cream, softened	maraschino cherry
1½ cups chopped	syrup
candied red	1 tablespoon vanilla
cherries	extract
¾ cup chopped toasted	1 env. (2 oz.) dessert
filberts	topping mix, prepared
¼ cup finely chopped	according to pkg.
flaked coconut	directions

1.   Mix into the softened ice cream the cherries, filberts, and coconut, then a blend of the syrup and extract. Pack mixture into a 1½-quart melon mold,

which has been rinsed with cold water and drained. Cover and freeze until firm, about 3 hours.
2.   Invert the mold on a chilled plate. Dip a clean towel in hot water, quickly wring it almost dry, and wrap it around the mold for a few seconds; lift off mold. If mold cannot be lifted off immediately, repeat. If necessary, set in freezer before frosting.
3.   Frost the egg with the whipped dessert topping. Decorate, using a cake decorating set (aerosol cans of tinted frosting with decorating tips) or your favorite decorating frosting and pastry bag with decorating tubes. Pipe frosting onto frozen egg in an attractive design. Garnish with whole *candied red cherries*. Set in freezer until ready to serve.
10 TO 12 SERVINGS

RHUBARB FREEZE
IN PASTRY TART SHELLS

1 lb. tender pink	3 or 4 drops red food
rhubarb, cut in 1-in.	coloring
pieces (about 4 cups)	1 pt. vanilla ice cream,
¾ to 1 cup sugar	slightly softened
½ teaspoon ground	8 tart shells (see
cinnamon	Pastry for Little Pies
1 teaspoon grated lemon	and Tarts, *page 454*),
peel	or individual meringue
2 teaspoons lemon juice	shells

1.   Toss rhubarb with sugar, cinnamon, and lemon peel in a 1-quart shallow baking dish having a cover. Drizzle with lemon juice.
2.   Bake, covered, at 350°F 20 to 25 minutes. Cool and chill.
3.   Using an electric blender, chop rhubarb with syrup. Tint with food coloring. Gradually blend with the softened ice cream. Turn into refrigerator trays, cover, and freeze.
4.   Before serving, set in refrigerator to soften slightly. Spoon into tart shells and serve. 8 SERVINGS

CANDLELIGHT PINEAPPLE BOMBE

1 can (20 oz.) crushed	1 teaspoon almond
pineapple, undrained	extract
⅛ teaspoon salt	½ cup chopped toasted
3 cups miniature	pecans
marshmallows	2 qts. vanilla ice cream,
2 teaspoons vanilla	softened slightly
extract	

1.   Combine pineapple, salt, marshmallows, and a

blend of extracts in a heavy saucepan. Set over low heat, stirring occasionally, until marshmallows are melted.

2.   Remove from heat and cool. Stir in the pecans. Turn mixture into a refrigerator tray and set in freezer until sufficiently set to spoon into lined bombe.

3.   Thoroughly chill a deep 7-cup mold by filling it with ice and water; set aside. When ready to use, pour out ice and water and quickly line the mold with two thirds of the ice cream. Turn thickened

pineapple mixture into center and spread remaining ice cream over the top. Cover with aluminum foil; freeze overnight.

4.   Shortly before ready to serve, wrap a hot towel around mold for a few seconds only, and run a knife around edge. Invert mold onto a chilled serving plate. If mold does not lift off, repeat the hot towel procedure.

5.   Decorate the bombe with rosettes of tinted *whipped cream*, stemmed *maraschino cherries*, and *canned pineapple chunks*.   8 TO 10 SERVINGS

ICE CREAMS, SHERBETS & ICES

PHILADELPHIA ICE CREAM

¾ cup sugar
⅛ teaspoon salt
2 cups light cream, scalded

1 teaspoon vanilla extract
2 cups heavy cream, whipped

1.   Stir the sugar and salt into the scalded cream; set aside to cool. Blend in the extract.

2.   Pour mixture into refrigerator trays and freeze until mushy.

3.   Remove from freezer and turn into a chilled large bowl. Beat with a rotary beater just until smooth. Fold in the whipped cream. Return to trays and freeze until firm, about 2 hours.

ABOUT 2 QUARTS ICE CREAM

STRAWBERRY ICE CREAM: Follow directions for Philadelphia Ice Cream through step 2, omitting vanilla extract. Force *3 cups fresh strawberries* through a food mill; add *¾ cup sugar* to pulp and let stand about 20 minutes. Stir into beaten mixture before final freezing.

CRIMSON-RIBBONED FRENCH ICE CREAM

2 cups sugar
1 cup water
¼ teaspoon cream of tartar
8 egg yolks

2 cups heavy cream, whipped
1 (6 oz.) can frozen raspberry-lemon punch concentrate, partially thawed

1.   Combine sugar, water, and cream of tartar in a saucepan. Stir over low heat until sugar is dissolved; increase heat and bring mixture to boiling.

Cover saucepan and boil mixture 5 minutes. Uncover and continue cooking to 232°F (spins a 2-inch thread when dropped from a spoon); remove syrup from heat.

2.   Beat egg yolks until very thick. Beating constantly, gradually pour syrup in a very fine stream into egg yolks. Cook mixture in top of double boiler over simmering water, stirring constantly, 8 to 10 minutes.

3.   Cool over ice and water, beating constantly until mixture is cold.

4.   Fold whipped cream into egg-yolk mixture. Turn into 9x9x2-inch pan. Freeze until partially frozen.

5.   Remove from freezer; stir mixture until it is of even consistency. Working quickly, drizzle partially thawed punch concentrate in small amounts onto ice cream; stir with a spoon or cut in with two knives to produce a rippled effect. Return to freezer and freeze until firm, 2 to 3 hours.

ABOUT 1½ QUARTS ICE CREAM

BANANA-PECAN ICE CREAM

3 medium-sized firm ripe bananas
1 tablespoon lemon juice
½ cup sugar
¼ teaspoon salt
⅓ cup milk
2 egg yolks

1 teaspoon vanilla extract
2 egg whites
1 cup heavy cream, whipped
½ cup chopped pecans

1.   Cut bananas into pieces and put into a blender container with lemon juice, sugar, salt, milk, egg yolks, and extract; blend until smooth.

2.   Beat egg whites until stiff, not dry, peaks are

formed. Fold whipped cream into egg whites and blend thoroughly. Stir in the banana mixture.

3. Turn into refrigerator trays; freeze until mixture begins to thicken, about 1½ hours (do not freeze solid).

4. Turn into a chilled bowl and beat until creamy and smooth. Stir in the pecans and return to trays. Freeze until firm, about 2 hours.

ABOUT 1 QUART ICE CREAM

  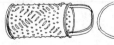

BANANA-PINEAPPLE ICE CREAM

This dasher-type ice cream is at its satiny smooth peak of perfection immediately after ripening.

2 cups mashed ripe bananas (about 5 medium-sized bananas)	3 tablespoons lemon juice
1 cup sugar	2 tablespoons lime juice
1 teaspoon grated orange peel	1½ cups unsweetened pineapple juice
1 teaspoon grated lemon peel	⅓ cup orange juice
	2 cans (14½ oz. each) evaporated milk

1. Wash and scald cover, container, and dasher of a 3- or 4-quart ice cream freezer. Chill well.

2. Combine bananas, sugar, orange and lemon peels, and lemon and lime juices; blend thoroughly. Set aside about 10 minutes.

3. Stir pineapple and orange juices into banana mixture. Gradually add evaporated milk, stirring until well blended.

4. Fill chilled freezer container no more than two thirds full with ice cream mixture. Cover tightly. Set into freezer tub. (For electric freezer, follow manufacturer's directions.)

5. Fill tub with alternate layers of crushed ice and rock salt, using 8 parts ice to 1 part salt. Turn handle slowly 5 minutes. Then turn rapidly until handle becomes difficult to turn, about 15 minutes. Add ice and salt as necessary.

6. Wipe cover and remove dasher. Pack down ice cream and cover with waxed paper or moisture-vaporproof material. Replace lid. (Plug dasher opening unless freezer has a solid cover.) Repack freezer container in ice, using 4 parts ice to 1 part salt. Cover with heavy paper or cloth. Let ripen 2 hours.

ABOUT 2 QUARTS ICE CREAM

CHERRY JUBILEE ICE CREAM

2 cups fresh dark sweet cherries, rinsed and stems and pits removed	½ teaspoon vanilla extract
1¼ cups sugar	¼ teaspoon lemon extract
1 teaspoon cornstarch	Red food coloring
1½ cups milk	1 cup heavy cream, whipped
2 eggs	

1. Finely chop or grind 1 cup cherries. Quarter remaining cherries; set in refrigerator.

2. Combine the sugar and cornstarch in the top of a double boiler; mix well. Add the milk and eggs; beat with hand rotary or electric beater until smooth. Set over boiling water about 10 minutes, stirring constantly. Remove from heat and cool.

3. Stir in the chopped cherries, extracts, and food coloring, a drop at a time, until desired color is obtained. Pour into refrigerator trays and freeze until partially frozen, stirring occasionally.

4. Using a chilled bowl and beater, beat the mixture just until smooth. Fold in the whipped cream and the quartered cherries. Return to trays. Freeze until firm, stirring occasionally.

ABOUT 1½ QUARTS ICE CREAM

HAITIAN ICE CREAM

2 cups milk	¼ teaspoon ground cloves
2 oz. (2 sq.) unsweetened chocolate	3 egg yolks, slightly beaten
1 cup sugar	2 cups cream
1 tablespoon flour	2 teaspoons vanilla extract
¼ teaspoon salt	

1. Combine milk and chocolate in top of a double boiler; heat over boiling water until milk is scalded and chocolate is melted.

2. Combine sugar, flour, salt, and cloves; add gradually to milk mixture, blending well. Cook and stir over direct heat 5 minutes.

3. Remove from heat and vigorously stir about 3 tablespoons of the hot mixture into the egg yolks; immediately stir into hot mixture. Cook over boiling water 10 minutes, stirring constantly, until mixture coats a metal spoon.

4. Remove from heat; cool. Stir in cream and extract. Pour into refrigerator trays and freeze until mushy.

5. Turn into a chilled bowl and beat with hand

rotary or electric beater until smooth and creamy. Return mixture to trays and freeze until firm.

ABOUT 1½ QUARTS ICE CREAM

COCONUT ICE CREAM

½ cup sugar
Few grains salt
1 cup milk, scalded
1 medium-sized coconut (about 2½ cups small pieces)

2 cups heavy cream
2 teaspoons vanilla extract
2 tablespoons confectioners' sugar

1. Stir the sugar and salt into the scalded milk until dissolved. Pour into an electric blender container; add a few pieces of the coconut and blend. Continue adding coconut while blending. Finally blend 5 minutes. Mix with 1 cup of the cream and the extract.
2. Pour into refrigerator trays; freeze until mixture is mushy.
3. Whip remaining cup of cream until of medium consistency (piles softly). Beat in confectioners' sugar with final few strokes.
4. Remove the partially frozen mixture from freezer and turn into a chilled bowl. Beat just until smooth. Fold in the whipped cream. Return to trays and freeze until firm.   ABOUT 1½ QUARTS ICE CREAM
NOTE: Substitute 2 cans (3½ ounces each) flaked coconut for the fresh coconut, if desired. Reduce sugar to 2 tablespoons.

CHOCO-COCONUT ICE CREAM

1 can (14 oz.) sweetened condensed milk
3 oz. (3 sq.) unsweetened chocolate
1 cup cold water

2 cups cream
1 teaspoon vanilla extract
1 cup flaked coconut, cut

1. Put sweetened condensed milk and chocolate into the top of a double boiler. Cook, stirring frequently, over boiling water until mixture begins to thicken, then stir constantly until thick and smooth.
2. Remove double-boiler top from water. Add the cold water gradually, beating constantly. Add cream and extract gradually, mixing constantly until thoroughly blended. Stir in coconut.
3. Turn mixture into refrigerator trays or spoon into colorful paper cups. Freeze until firm.

ABOUT 1½ QUARTS ICE CREAM

CHOCOLATE-MOCHA ICE CREAM

1 pkg. chocolate pudding and pie filling (instant or regular)
½ cup dark corn syrup
½ teaspoon vanilla extract

1 cup undiluted evaporated milk, chilled and whipped, page 20
½ cup chopped walnuts

1. Prepare pudding according to directions on package, substituting ½ cup double-strength coffee for ½ cup of the milk. Add the corn syrup and extract to pudding and blend well.
2. Pour into refrigerator trays and freeze until mushy, about 1 hour.
3. Turn into a chilled bowl and beat until smooth. Fold in the whipped evaporated milk and walnuts.
4. Return to trays and freeze until firm, 3 to 4 hours, stirring several times.

ABOUT 1½ QUARTS ICE CREAM

FROZEN CRANBERRY CREAM

2 cups fresh cranberries, rinsed
½ cup water
1 cup sugar
⅛ teaspoon ground cinnamon

Few grains ground cloves
Few grains ground nutmeg
1 cup heavy cream, whipped

1. Combine cranberries and water in a saucepan. Bring to boiling over medium heat and cook until skins pop. Force cranberries through a sieve or food mill.
2. Add the sugar, cinnamon, cloves, and nutmeg and stir until sugar is dissolved. Cool; chill about 1 hour.
3. Fold whipped cream into the cranberry mixture and turn into a refrigerator tray. Freeze until mixture is mushy.
4. Turn ice cream mixture into a chilled bowl and beat with a hand rotary or electric beater until smooth. Return to tray and freeze until firm.

ABOUT 1 QUART ICE CREAM

LEMON-CHEESE ICE CREAM

6 oz. cream cheese
⅔ cup sugar
2 cups cream
2 tablespoons lemon juice

1 teaspoon grated lemon peel
¼ teaspoon vanilla extract

1. Using an electric beater, beat the cream

cheese until softened. Gradually add the sugar, beating until fluffy.

2. Add cream slowly, mixing well. Beat in remaining ingredients until thoroughly mixed. Pour into a refrigerator tray and freeze until mushy.

3. Turn mixture into a chilled bowl and beat with a hand rotary or electric beater until smooth. Return to refrigerator tray and freeze until firm.

ABOUT 1 QUART ICE CREAM

MARSHMALLOW ICE CREAM

20 marshmallows
1 cup milk
1 tablespoon vanilla
  extract
2 tablespoons strawberry
  jam

7 drops red food
  coloring
1 cup heavy cream,
  whipped

1. Combine marshmallows and milk in the top of a double boiler; heat over boiling water until marshmallows are melted, stirring occasionally.

2. Cool; chill until mixture is slightly thickened, stirring frequently.

3. Blend in extract, jam, and food coloring. Fold in whipped cream. Turn into refrigerator tray and freeze until mushy, about 40 minutes.

4. Turn into a chilled bowl and beat until smooth. Return to tray and freeze until firm.

ABOUT 1½ PINTS ICE CREAM

MOCHA-BRAZIL NUT ICE CREAM

1 env. unflavored
  gelatin
¾ cup firmly packed
  light brown sugar
⅛ teaspoon salt
1 tablespoon instant
  coffee
1¼ cups water

1 oz. (1 sq.) unsweet-
  ened chocolate, cut
  in small pieces
2 teaspoons vanilla
  extract
1 can (14½-oz.)
  evaporated milk
1½ cups heavy cream
¾ cup chopped toasted
  Brazil nuts

1. Mix the gelatin, brown sugar, salt, and instant coffee thoroughly in a saucepan. Stir in water and chocolate pieces. Cook and stir over medium heat until gelatin and sugar are dissolved and chocolate is melted. Remove from heat; set aside to cool.

2. Stir extract, evaporated milk, and cream into the cooked chocolate mixture. Pour into refrigerator trays. Freeze until mushy.

3. Turn into a chilled bowl and beat with rotary

beater until smooth. Return to tray and freeze until partially frozen.

4. Stir in the nuts. Cover top with shaved *unsweetened chocolate* and freeze until firm.

ABOUT 1½ QUARTS ICE CREAM

CREAMY ORANGE VELVET

2 cups sugar
2 cups milk, scalded
2 cups heavy cream

2 tablespoons grated
  orange peel
¾ cup orange juice
½ cup lemon juice

1. Stir sugar into scalded milk; set aside to cool.

2. Stir cream, orange peel, and orange and lemon juices into milk mixture. Pour into refrigerator trays. Freeze until mushy.

3. Turn mixture into a chilled bowl and beat until smooth, but not melted. Return to trays and freeze until firm.

ABOUT 2 QUARTS ICE CREAM

PEACH ICE CREAM SUPERB

12 medium-sized (about
  3 lbs.) fully ripe
  peaches, peeled
  and pitted
2¾ cups sugar
1 tablespoon lemon juice

1½ qts. chilled heavy
  cream
¼ teaspoon salt
1 teaspoon vanilla
  extract
1 teaspoon almond
  extract

1. Wash and scald cover, container, and dasher of a 4-quart ice cream freezer. Chill thoroughly.

2. Force peaches through a sieve or food mill. Stir the sugar and lemon juice into peaches and set aside 20 minutes.

3. Combine the cream, salt, and extracts; mix with peaches until blended.

4. Fill freezer container two thirds full with ice cream mixture. Cover tightly. Set in freezer tub. (For electric freezer, follow manufacturer's directions.)

5. Fill tub with alternate layers of 8 parts crushed ice and 1 part rock salt. Turn handle slowly 5 minutes. Add crushed ice and rock salt as necessary.

6. Wipe cover free of ice and salt. Remove dasher and pack down ice cream. Cover with moisture-vaporproof material. Replace cover and plug opening for dasher. Repack freezer with alternate layers of ice and salt, using 4 parts ice and 1 part rock salt. Cover with heavy paper or cloth. Let stand 2 to 3 hours to ripen.

ABOUT 3 QUARTS ICE CREAM

MAPLE ICE CREAM SUPERB: Follow recipe for Peach Ice Cream Superb. Omit peaches, sugar, lemon juice, and almond extract. Pour *1½ cups maple syrup* into a medium-sized saucepan. Bring rapidly to boiling and boil to reduce to 1¼ cups, about 15 minutes. Remove from heat and cool. Increase vanilla extract to 1 tablespoon and blend with the cream and salt. Add maple syrup gradually, stirring constantly until thoroughly blended.

CHOCOLATE ICE CREAM SUPERB: Follow recipe for Peach Ice Cream Superb. Omit peaches and lemon juice. Decrease sugar to 1¾ cups. Combine cream with *3 ounces (3 squares) unsweetened chocolate* in a saucepan and heat until chocolate is melted. Omit extracts. Stir in the sugar and salt until dissolved. Cool, then chill.

APRICOT ICE CREAM SUPERB: Follow recipe for Peach Ice Cream Superb. Substitute *1 pound (about 3 cups) dried apricots* for peaches. Put apricots into a saucepan with *4 cups water.* Cover and simmer 40 minutes, or until tender. Force apricots through a sieve or food mill. Decrease sugar to 1¾ cups and stir sugar and lemon juice into apricot pulp. Cool, then chill. Blend into cream mixture.

VANILLA ICE CREAM SUPERB: Follow recipe for Peach Ice Cream Superb. Omit peaches, lemon juice, and almond extract. Decrease sugar to 1¼ cups. Increase vanilla extract to 3 tablespoons. Blend ingredients.

FRESH PURPLE PLUM ICE CREAM

This elegant ice cream will add a regal touch to many a commonplace luncheon or dinner.

24 fresh purple plums, pitted and quartered	⅓ cup cold water
1 cup sugar	2 tablespoons lemon juice
½ cup light corn syrup	
1½ cups water	2 teaspoons vanilla extract
2 teaspoons unflavored gelatin	2 cups heavy cream, whipped

1. Mix the plums, sugar, corn syrup, and water in a saucepan. Simmer, uncovered, over low heat until fruit is very tender, about 25 minutes. Force plum mixture through a sieve or food mill.
2. Soften gelatin in the cold water. Immediately add gelatin to hot sieved mixture, stirring until completely dissolved. Blend in lemon juice. Chill until mixture is thick and syrupy.
3. Blend extract into whipped cream and fold into

plum gelatin mixture. Pour into refrigerator trays and freeze until mushy.
4. Turn into a chilled bowl and beat until smooth; return to trays and freeze until firm.

ABOUT 2 QUARTS ICE CREAM

PUMPKIN ICE CREAM

1 cup canned pumpkin	2 tablespoons orange juice
⅓ to ½ cup sugar	
½ teaspoon ground cinnamon	2 teaspoons vanilla extract
¼ teaspoon ground ginger	1 cup heavy cream, whipped
¼ teaspoon ground nutmeg	

Mix pumpkin with sugar, spices, orange juice, and extract. Fold into whipped cream. Turn into a refrigerator tray; freeze until firm.

ABOUT 1½ PINTS ICE CREAM

STRAWBERRY GELATO

5 teaspoons unflavored gelatin	2 pkgs. (10 oz. each) frozen sliced strawberries, thawed
1½ cups sugar	
4 cups milk	¼ cup kirsch
2 cups instant nonfat dry milk	¼ teaspoon red food coloring

1. Thoroughly mix the gelatin and sugar in a large saucepan. Stir in the milk and then the nonfat dry milk. Stir over low heat until sugar and gelatin are dissolved. Set aside to cool.
2. Turn strawberries and kirsch into an electric blender container; add food coloring and blend until smooth. If necessary, strain through a fine sieve to remove seeds.
3. Pour into refrigerator trays and freeze until firm, 2 to 3 hours.
4. Spoon the amount of ice cream to be served into a bowl; allow it to soften slightly and whip until smooth, using an electric mixer. Spoon into chilled stemmed glasses and serve immediately.

ABOUT 2 QUARTS GELATO

STRAWBERRY-BANANA GELATO: Follow recipe for Strawberry Gelato. Omit the frozen strawberries and kirsch. Combine *2 pints ripe strawberries,* rinsed, hulled, and crushed, with *¾ to 1 cup sugar* in a bowl. Mix and let stand about 1 hour. Turn half of the sweetened strawberries and *1 ripe banana,* peeled and cut in pieces, into an electric blender container; blend. Add remaining berries and blend thoroughly. Strain if necessary. Stir into cooled milk. ABOUT 2½ QUARTS GELATO

MINT GELATO: Follow recipe for Strawberry Gelato. Reduce gelatin to 4 teaspoons and sugar to 1 cup. Omit strawberries, kirsch, and food coloring. Stir *2 teaspoons vanilla extract* and *½ teaspoon mint extract* into cooled milk.

ABOUT 1½ QUARTS GELATO

FROZEN STRAWBERRY CRÈME

1 cup sugar	2 cups heavy cream,
4 egg yolks, slightly	whipped to medium
beaten	consistency
1 cup milk, scalded	1 tablespoon lemon
2 cups crushed ripe	juice
strawberries, slightly	½ teaspoon almond
sweetened	extract
	Salted toasted almonds

1. Combine sugar with egg yolks and beat until thoroughly blended. Slowly add scalded milk, stirring constantly. Strain the mixture into a double-boiler. Place over simmering water; stirring frequently, cook until mixture coats a metal spoon.
2. Remove from heat and chill immediately in ice and water, stirring the custard occasionally.
3. Add crushed berries to custard and fold in a blend of whipped cream, lemon juice, and extract.
4. Pour into refrigerator trays and set in freezer until mixture is partially frozen. Top with almonds and freeze until firm. ABOUT 1½ QUARTS CRÈME

SPUMONE

½ cup sugar	2 drops green food
⅛ teaspoon salt	coloring
1 cup milk, scalded	½ cup heavy cream,
3 egg yolks, beaten	whipped
1 cup heavy cream	1 maraschino cherry
½ oz. (½ sq.) unsweet-	1 tablespoon sugar
ened chocolate, melted	6 unblanched almonds,
2 teaspoons rum extract	finely chopped
1 tablespoon sugar	¼ teaspoon almond
⅛ teaspoon pistachio	extract
extract	½ cup heavy cream,
	whipped

1. Stir ½ cup sugar and salt into the scalded milk in the top of a double boiler. Stir until sugar is dissolved.

2. Stir about 3 tablespoons of the hot milk into the egg yolks. Immediately return to double boiler top. Cook over boiling water, stirring constantly, about 5 minutes, or until mixture coats a metal spoon. Remove from heat and cool.
3. Stir in 1 cup heavy cream and divide mixture equally into two bowls.
4. Add melted chocolate to mixture in one bowl and mix thoroughly. Set in refrigerator.
5. Add rum extract to remaining mixture and pour into refrigerator tray. Freeze until mushy.
6. Turn into a chilled bowl and beat until mixture is smooth and creamy. Spoon into a chilled 1-quart mold and freeze until firm.
7. Fold 1 tablespoon sugar, pistachio extract, and food coloring into ½ cup heavy cream, whipped. Spoon over firm rum ice cream; freeze until firm.
8. When pistachio cream becomes firm, place the maraschino cherry in the center and return to freezer.
9. Fold 1 tablespoon sugar, chopped almonds, and almond extract into remaining ½ cup heavy cream, whipped. Spoon over firm pistachio cream. Freeze until firm.
10. When almond cream is firm, pour chocolate ice cream mixture into refrigerator tray and freeze until mushy.
11. Turn into a chilled bowl and beat until mixture is smooth and creamy. Spoon mixture over firm almond cream. Cover mold with aluminum foil or waxed paper. Return to freezer and freeze 6 to 8 hours, or until very firm.
12. To unmold, quickly dip mold into warm water. 6 TO 8 WEDGE-SHAPED SERVINGS

BISCUIT TORTONI

⅓ cup confectioners'	1 cup heavy cream,
sugar	whipped
1 tablespoon sherry	1 egg white
½ cup plus 2 tablespoons	
fine dry macaroon	
crumbs	

1. Fold sugar, sherry, and ½ cup macaroon crumbs into whipped cream until well blended.
2. Beat egg white until stiff, not dry, peaks are formed. Fold into whipped cream mixture.
3. Divide mixture equally into ten 2-inch heavy paper baking cups and sprinkle with the remaining crumbs. Freeze until firm. 10 SERVINGS

CHOCOLATE-CHIPPED TORTONI

2 tablespoons sugar	1 egg white
1½ teaspoons vanilla extract	2 tablespoons sugar
½ cup almond macaroon crumbs*	3 oz. (½ cup) semisweet chocolate pieces
1 cup heavy cream, whipped	1 tablespoon vegetable shortening

1. Fold 2 tablespoons sugar, extract, and macaroon crumbs into the whipped cream until blended.
2. Beat egg white until frothy; gradually add 2 tablespoons sugar, beating constantly until stiff peaks are formed. Fold into whipped cream mixture. Turn into refrigerator tray and set in freezer until mixture begins to freeze, about 1 hour.
3. Place six 2-inch paper baking cups in muffin-pan wells.
4. About 20 minutes before removing mixture from freezer, melt chocolate pieces in the top of a double boiler over hot (not steaming) water. When melted, blend in the shortening.
5. Turn partially frozen mixture into a chilled bowl. Quickly crush and stir with a spoon until smooth but not melted. Stir constantly while pouring in a thin stream of melted chocolate. (The chocolate forms thin, firm pieces or "chips" as it is blended into the cold mixture.) Immediately spoon mixture into paper cups. Return to freezer and freeze until firm, about 2 hours.
6. Decorate with *whipped cream rosettes* or a border of *whipped cream.* 6 SERVINGS

*If macaroons are moist, dry and toast them slightly in 325°F oven before crushing.

CREAMY CRANBERRY SHERBET

2½ cups cranberries, rinsed	¼ cup orange juice
1¼ cups water	1 tablespoon lemon juice
1½ cups sugar	1 cup heavy cream, whipped

1. Combine cranberries and water in a saucepan; cook until skins pop. Force through a sieve or food mill. Immediately add the sugar and fruit juices; stir until sugar is dissolved. Cool and chill.
2. Fold whipped cream into chilled cranberry mixture. Turn into refrigerator trays and freeze until mushy.
3. Turn into a chilled bowl and beat until smooth, but not melted. Return to trays and feeeze until firm. ABOUT 5 CUPS SHERBET

NOTE: Serve the sherbet in fancy punch cups as a poultry accompaniment at dinner.

LEMON SHERBET

Serve this versatile sherbet atop chilled fruit juice as a shrub, on individual fruit salads for a luncheon entrée, as an accompaniment for a main dish, or as a cooling dessert to end a warm weather meal.

2 cups sugar	⅓ cup lemon juice
1½ teaspoons grated lemon peel	1 qt. milk

1. Blend sugar and lemon peel and juice in a bowl. Add milk slowly, stirring until sugar is dissolved. Pour into two refrigerator trays, cover, and freeze until mixture becomes firm around edges.
2. Turn into a chilled bowl and beat until smooth. Return to trays and cover. Freeze until firm. ABOUT 2½ PINTS SHERBET

NOTE: If desired, add a few drops of *yellow food coloring* to mixture before freezing.

LEMON FREEZE

2 egg yolks, slightly beaten	¾ cup heavy cream, whipped
¼ cup sugar	2 egg whites
¼ cup lemon juice	¼ cup sugar
½ teaspoon grated lemon peel	

1. Combine egg yolks, ¼ cup sugar, *few grains salt,* and lemon juice in a double-boiler top. Cook over simmering water, stirring constantly, until slightly thickened; cool. Fold in lemon peel and whipped cream.
2. Beat egg whites until foamy; gradually add ¼ cup sugar and beat until stiff peaks are formed. Fold into lemon mixture. Turn into refrigerator tray and freeze until firm, about 4 hours.
3. To serve, allow to stand at room temperature 10 to 15 minutes. Spoon into sherbet glasses and top with chopped *salted pecans.* 6 TO 8 SERVINGS

LIME SHERBET DE LUXE

1 cup boiling water
1 pkg. (3 oz.) lime-flavored gelatin
½ cup sugar
2 cups milk
1 cup heavy cream
2 tablespoons lemon juice

1. Pour boiling water over gelatin and sugar in a bowl. Stir in milk, cream, and lemon juice. Pour into refrigerator trays and freeze until mushy.
2. Turn into a chilled bowl and beat until firm.

ABOUT 1 QUART SHERBET

PEACH-LIME SHERBET

1 can (29 oz.) cling peach slices
1½ to 2 cups sugar
1½ teaspoons grated lime peel
⅓ cup lime juice
1 qt. milk
Green food coloring (about 4 drops)
1 cup chopped salted almonds or pecans

1. Using an electric blender, chop peaches in syrup.
2. Mix sugar and lime peel and juice. Add milk gradually, stirring until sugar is dissolved. Blend in the desired amount of food coloring. Mix in peaches and syrup.
3. Turn into refrigerator trays and set in freezer, stirring occasionally until partially frozen.
4. Press nuts onto surface. Freeze until firm.

ABOUT 2 QUARTS SHERBET

SPRINGTIME SHERBET

2 cups diced rhubarb (about ¾ lb.)
½ cup sugar
⅛ teaspoon salt
1¼ cups water
3 tablespoons strawberry-flavored gelatin
1 cup crushed strawberries
2 egg whites

1. Combine rhubarb, sugar, salt, and ¾ cup of the water in a saucepan. Bring to boiling; reduce heat and simmer until rhubarb is soft.
2. Soften gelatin in remaining ½ cup water. Add to hot rhubarb mixture. Add strawberries and set aside to cool.
3. Pour mixture into refrigerator tray and freeze until mushy.
4. Turn into a chilled bowl and beat.
5. Beat egg whites until stiff, not dry, peaks are formed. Fold into frozen mixture and return to tray. Freeze until firm, stirring once.

1 QUART SHERBET

MOLDED RASPBERRY SHERBET

3 pkgs. (10 oz. each) frozen red raspberries, thawed and forced through a fine sieve
1½ tablespoons lemon juice
1½ cups confectioners' sugar
1½ teaspoons unflavored gelatin
⅓ cup milk

1. Combine raspberry syrup, lemon juice, and confectioners' sugar; beat with a hand rotary beater until smooth.
2. Soften gelatin in milk in a small saucepan. Stir over low heat until dissolved. Blend into raspberry mixture. Pour into refrigerator trays and freeze until mushy.
3. Turn into a bowl and beat until creamy. Turn into a 1-quart fancy mold. Freeze until firm.
4. Unmold onto a chilled serving plate.

10 TO 12 SERVINGS

TANGERINE SHERBET

1¼ cups sugar
2 teaspoons grated tangerine peel
½ cup tangerine juice
2 tablespoons lemon juice
⅛ teaspoon salt
2 cups cream
2 or 3 drops orange food coloring

1. Blend the ingredients in order in a bowl. Stir until sugar is dissolved. Pour into a refrigerator tray and freeze until mushy.
2. Turn mixture into a chilled bowl and beat with electric beater until smooth. Return mixture to tray and freeze until firm.

1½ PINTS SHERBET

CRANBERRY ICE

4 cups (1 lb.) cranberries
2 cups water
2 cups sugar
2 teaspoons unflavored gelatin
1¾ cups water
½ cup orange juice
2 teaspoons grated lemon peel
¼ cup lemon juice

1. Rinse the cranberries (discarding imperfect berries) and drain. Cook in 2 cups water until skins pop. Force cranberries through a sieve or food mill. Immediately stir a mixture of sugar and gelatin into hot pulp until sugar is dissolved.
2. Blend in remaining ingredients; pour into refrigerator tray. Freeze until mixture is firm, stirring several times.

1 QUART ICE

BOYSENBERRY ICE

2 cans (16 oz. each) boysenberries, drained (reserve syrup)
2 teaspoons unflavored gelatin
¼ cup sugar
¾ cup water
1 tablespoon lemon juice

1. Force drained boysenberries through a fine sieve; set aside.
2. Mix the gelatin and sugar in a saucepan. Stir in the water and set over low heat until gelatin and sugar are dissolved, stirring constantly.
3. Remove from heat and stir in 1½ cups of the reserved syrup, boysenberries, and lemon juice.
4. Pour into a 1-quart refrigerator tray and freeze until firm, stirring several times.
5. Serve in chilled sherbet glasses.

ABOUT 1 QUART ICE

LIME ICE

2 teaspoons unflavored gelatin
2 cups sugar
3¼ cups cold water
¾ cup lime juice
2 tablespoons lemon juice
2 teaspoons grated lemon peel
Green food coloring

1. Mix the gelatin and sugar in a saucepan. Stir in the water and set over low heat until gelatin and sugar are dissolved, stirring constantly.
2. Blend in the lime and lemon juices and lemon peel. Mix in the food coloring, a drop at a time, to tint the desired color. Cool.
3. Pour into a refrigerator tray and freeze until firm, stirring several times. 1 QUART ICE

APRICOT ICE: Follow recipe for Lime Ice. Decrease water to 1¾ cups and sugar to 1 cup. Substitute *2 cups apricot nectar* for lime juice and *orange juice* for lemon juice. Omit green food coloring.

MOCHA ICE: Follow recipe for Lime Ice. Increase water to 3¾ cups. Decrease sugar to 1 cup. Mix *2 tablespoons instant coffee* with sugar and gelatin. Omit lime and lemon juices, lemon peel, and food coloring. Top with *sweetened whipped cream*.

ORANGE ICE: Follow recipe for Lime Ice. Decrease water to 2¼ cups and sugar to 1¼ cups. Substitute *2 cups orange juice* for lime juice and *orange peel* for lemon peel. Use *orange food coloring*.

RASPBERRY ICE: Follow recipe for Lime Ice. Decrease water to 2¼ cups and sugar to ¾ to 1 cup. Omit lime juice, lemon peel, and food coloring. Force *1 pint rinsed, sorted, and drained raspberries*

through a fine sieve. Blend sieved raspberries into gelatin mixture with lemon juice.

GREENGAGE PLUM ICE

2 teaspoons unflavored gelatin
½ cup sugar
⅛ teaspoon salt
1 cup water
2½ cups (20 oz. can) greengage plums and syrup
1 cup orange juice
2 tablespoons lemon juice
1 or 2 drops green food coloring

1. Combine the gelatin, sugar, and salt in a saucepan. Stir in the water and set over low heat until gelatin and sugar are dissolved, stirring constantly. Set aside to cool.
2. Cut plums into halves, pit, and force through a sieve or food mill (about 2¼ cups purée). Combine with cooled gelatin and the orange and lemon juices. Stir in the food coloring.
3. Pour into an 8-inch square pan and freeze until firm, stirring several times. ABOUT 1 QUART ICE

ITALIAN STRAWBERRY WATER ICE
(Granita di Fragole)

2 cups sugar
1 cup water
4 pts. fresh ripe strawberries, rinsed and hulled
⅓ cup orange juice
¼ cup lemon juice

1. Combine sugar and water in a saucepan; stir and bring to boiling. Boil 5 minutes; let cool.
2. Purée the strawberries in an electric blender or force through a sieve or food mill. Add juices to a mixture of the cooked syrup and strawberries; mix well.
3. Turn into refrigerator trays, cover tightly, and freeze.
4. About 45 minutes before serving time, remove trays from freezer section to refrigerator to allow the ice to soften slightly. Spoon into sherbet glasses or other serving dishes. ABOUT 2 QUARTS WATER ICE

FRUIT DESSERTS

QUICK APPLESAUCE WHIP

2 cups applesauce	½ teaspoon ground
½ teaspoon grated lemon	cinnamon
peel	3 egg whites
2 teaspoons lemon juice	⅛ teaspoon salt
	6 tablespoons sugar

1. Combine applesauce, lemon peel and juice, and cinnamon; mix well and set aside.
2. Beat egg whites with salt until frothy; gradually add the sugar, beating constantly until stiff peaks are formed.
3. Fold egg whites into applesauce mixture and serve immediately. Sprinkle *ground nutmeg* over each serving.   6 SERVINGS

SWEDISH APPLECAKE WITH VANILLA SAUCE
(Äpplekaka med Vaniljsås)

13 rusks (4 oz.), finely	2½ cups thick
crushed (about 2 cups	applesauce
crumbs)	¼ cup butter or
¼ cup sugar	margarine
⅓ cup butter or	¼ cup confectioners'
margarine, melted	sugar
	Vanilla Sauce, *below*

1. Blend the crumbs and sugar in a bowl. Toss lightly with the melted butter until crumbs are evenly coated.
2. Generously grease a 1-quart casserole. Add one third of the crumbs and press them firmly into an even layer on bottom and sides of dish. Spoon one half of the applesauce into the dish. Dot with one half the remaining butter and sprinkle with one half the remaining crumbs. Repeat layering, ending with crumbs.
3. Bake at 350°F 30 to 40 minutes, or until crumbs are golden brown.
4. Cool completely and chill.
5. To form a design on top of cake, sift confectioners' sugar through a lacy paper doily placed on cake, then carefully lift off doily.   8 SERVINGS

VANILLA SAUCE: Cream *⅓ cup butter or margarine* until softened; add *½ cup sugar* gradually, beating thoroughly. Add *6 egg yolks* gradually, beating constantly until fluffy. Stir in *¾ cup boiling water*

very gradually. Pour mixture into the top of a double boiler. Cook over simmering water, stirring, until thickened. Blend in *1 teaspoon vanilla extract.* Cool; chill in refrigerator.   ABOUT 2 CUPS SAUCE

CRUSTLESS APPLE PIE
A recipe contributed by Mrs. Richard Nixon.

⅓ to ½ cup sugar	1 cup all-purpose flour
1 teaspoon ground	1 teaspoon baking
cinnamon	powder
1 cup water	Salt (optional)
6 medium-sized (about 2	6 tablespoons
lbs.) cooking apples,	shortening
washed, cut into	½ cup lightly packed
eighths, cored, and	brown sugar
pared	

1. Blend sugar and cinnamon in a large heavy saucepan. Stir in water and apples. Bring to boiling, reduce heat, and cook 10 minutes, stirring occasionally.
2. Meanwhile, sift flour and baking powder together; set aside.
3. Cream shortening with brown sugar until fluffy. Beat in the flour mixture, adding gradually.
4. Turn apples and syrup into a greased 9-inch pie pan. Cover apples completely with the topping.
5. Bake at 350°F about 35 minutes, until apples are tender and topping is browned. Cool on rack.
6. Serve hot or cold with *whipped cream.*
                    ONE 9-INCH PIE

APPLE CHARLOTTE

6 thin slices white bread	¼ cup sugar
½ cup butter, melted	2 tablespoons lemon
2 tablespoons butter	juice
6 large apples,	1 cup golden raisins
quartered, cored, and	½ cup coarsely chopped
pared	pecans

1. Remove crusts from bread slices; cut each into 3 strips. Dip into melted butter; line bottom of a 1½-quart deep glass casserole or ovenproof bowl with strips, then arrange remaining strips upright around sides.
2. Heat the 2 tablespoons butter in a skillet; add the apples and cook until apples are tender but not

mushy. Sprinkle with sugar and lemon juice. Lightly mix in raisins and pecans. Turn mixture into bread-lined casserole.

3.   Bake at 350°F about 40 minutes, or until bread is golden brown.

6.   Cool; unmold and serve with a choice of *Apricot Sauce, page 551,* or *whipped cream.*

6 TO 8 SERVINGS

APPLE BROWN BETTY

Long a favorite at historic Smithville Inn, Absecon, New Jersey.

4 cups diced apples	Grated peel and juice of
1 cup brown sugar	1 lemon
4 cups cubed day-old	½ cup water
coffee cake	½ cup coarse bread
1 cup sugar	crumbs
½ teaspoon ground	¼ cup butter, melted
cinnamon	

1.   Brush a 1½-quart deep round baking dish well with *butter.* Cover bottom with a layer of apples and sprinkle with about one third of the brown sugar. Cover with half of the cubed coffee cake.

2.   Combine sugar, cinnamon, and lemon peel; sprinkle half of mixture over coffee cake layer.

3.   Cover with a second layer of apples; sprinkle with ⅓ cup brown sugar; cover with remaining cubed cake, sugar-cinnamon mixture, and sprinkle with a blend of lemon juice and water.

4.   Cover with remaining apples, brown sugar, and bread crumbs tossed with melted butter.

5.   Cover and bake at 350°F 30 to 40 minutes. Uncover and bake 10 minutes longer, or until golden brown on top.

6.   Serve with your favorite *lemon sauce.*

6 TO 8 SERVINGS

BROWN BETTY PUDDING

4 cups thinly sliced	⅛ teaspoon ground
pared apples (4	cinnamon
medium-sized)	2 teaspoons butter
2 cups bread cubes	¼ cup hot water
¾ cup firmly packed	
brown sugar	

1.   Butter a 1¼-quart baking dish. Arrange a layer of apples on bottom. Top with half of the bread cubes and half of the brown sugar. Add a layer of apples, the remaining bread, and apples. Top with remaining brown sugar, sprinkle with cinnamon,

and dot with butter. Pour in the water.

2.   Cover and bake at 350°F about 30 minutes. Uncover and bake about 10 minutes, or until pudding is browned on top.

3.   Serve with *hard sauce* or *Lemon Sauce, page 550.*

4 TO 6 SERVINGS

FAVORITE APPLE PUDDING

5 slices white bread,	1 teaspoon ground
toasted, buttered on	cinnamon
both sides and cut in	¼ teaspoon ground
halves	nutmeg
6 to 7 medium-sized firm,	3 tablespoons butter or
tart cooking apples,	margarine
quartered, cored,	1 teaspoon grated
pared, and cut in	orange peel
⅛-in. slices	¾ cup finely shredded
¾ cup firmly packed	Cheddar cheese
brown sugar	¼ cup orange juice
3 tablespoons flour	½ cup buttered soft
½ teaspoon salt	bread cubes

1.   Butter a 2-quart casserole having a cover. Arrange one third of the sliced apples on bottom of the casserole.

2.   Thoroughly blend brown sugar, flour, salt, cinnamon, and nutmeg. Using a pastry blender or two knives, cut in butter and grated orange peel until mixture is in coarse crumbs. Mix in cheese.

3.   Sprinkle one third of the sugar-cheese mixture over apples and cover with one half of the toast. Repeat. Cover the top with remaining apples and sugar-cheese mixture.

4.   Pour orange juice over surface and top with the buttered bread cubes. Cover casserole.

5.   Bake at 425°F for 30 minutes. Uncover and bake 10 minutes longer.

6 TO 8 SERVINGS

DANISH APPLE CAKE

2 to 3 lbs. apples,	⅓ cup butter
cored, pared, and	2½ cups coarse dry
sliced	bread crumbs
¼ cup water	1 cup heavy cream,
½ cup sugar	whipped

1.   Cook apples in a covered heavy saucepan with the water and one half of the sugar until soft, about 20 minutes.

2.   Heat the butter in a heavy skillet. Add the

remaining sugar and bread crumbs. Stir over low heat about 5 minutes, or until crumbs are golden brown and crisp.

3. Turn one third of the crumbs into a 1½-quart glass serving dish. Cover with about half the applesauce; continue layering, ending with crumbs.

4. Spoon the whipped cream onto the cake to form a border and decorate with spoonfuls of *jelly* or *jam*. Serve while still warm. ABOUT 8 SERVINGS

APPLE PANDOWDY DE LUXE

A lemon and nutmeg sauce tops off this apple dessert with pastry crust.

6 to 8 (about 2 lbs.)
   tart cooking apples,
   pared and sliced
1 cup sugar
1 teaspoon ground
   cinnamon
⅛ teaspoon salt
1 teaspoon grated lemon
   peel

1 tablespoon lemon juice
3 tablespoons butter,
   melted
Pastry for 1-crust
   9-inch pie
Lemon-Nutmeg Sauce,
   below

1. Put apple slices into a 1½-quart baking dish. Sprinkle with a mixture of the sugar, cinnamon, salt, and lemon peel. Pour the lemon juice and melted butter evenly over the top.

2. Bake at 400°F 25 to 30 minutes, or until apples are almost tender. Remove baking dish from oven and increase oven temperature to 450°F.

3. Prepare pastry and roll out to fit over apple mixture. Slit pastry in several places to allow steam to escape during baking. Place on apple mixture.

4. Bake at 450°F 10 minutes, or until pastry is golden brown.

5. Serve hot with *Lemon-Nutmeg Sauce* or *cream*.
6 TO 8 SERVINGS

LEMON-NUTMEG SAUCE: Mix *½ cup sugar, 1 tablespoon cornstarch*, and *⅛ teaspoon salt* together in a saucepan. Add *1½ cups boiling water* gradually, stirring constantly. Continue to stir and bring mixture to boiling; simmer 5 minutes. Blend in *3 tablespoons butter, 1 teaspoon grated lemon peel, 2 tablespoons lemon juice*, and *½ teaspoon ground nutmeg*. Serve hot. ABOUT 1½ CUPS SAUCE

BANANAS FOSTER BRENNAN'S
A specialty of Brennan's in New Orleans.

1 tablespoon butter
2 teaspoons brown sugar
Dash ground cinnamon
1 firm ripe banana, cut
   crosswise in 4 pieces

2 tablespoons warm rum
1 teaspoon warm
   banana liqueur

1. Heat butter, brown sugar, and cinnamon in a chafing dish; add banana and sauté until tender.

2. Pour rum and banana liqueur over banana and flame the spirit. 1 SERVING

BANANAS WITH ROYAL PINEAPPLE SAUCE

3 tablespoons dark brown
   sugar
2 teaspoons cornstarch
1 can (8½ oz.) crushed
   pineapple, undrained
1 tablespoon butter or
   margarine
⅛ teaspoon almond
   extract

¼ teaspoon grated
   lemon peel
1 tablespoon lemon
   juice
¼ cup butter or
   margarine
4 firm bananas, peeled

1. Mix brown sugar and cornstarch and combine with pineapple, 1 tablespoon butter, and extract. Bring to boiling and cook 2 to 3 minutes, stirring constantly. Remove from heat and stir in lemon peel and juice. Set the sauce aside.

2. Heat the ¼ cup butter in a heavy skillet. Add bananas; turn them by rolling to cook evenly and brown lightly. (Do not overcook.)

3. Allowing one-half banana per person, serve at once, topped with the warm pineapple sauce. Sprinkle with *shredded coconut*. 8 SERVINGS

FRESH BLUEBERRY "COBBLER"

¾ cup firmly packed
   light brown sugar
3 tablespoons quick-
   cooking tapioca
¼ teaspoon salt
¼ teaspoon ground
   cinnamon
Few grains ground
   cloves

2 pts. fresh blueberries,
   rinsed and drained
1 tablespoon lemon
   juice
2 tablespoons butter or
   margarine
Pastry for 2-crust pie

1. Combine the brown sugar, tapioca, ¼ teaspoon

salt, cinnamon, and cloves; mix well. Toss with blueberries until thoroughly mixed. Drizzle lemon juice over berries. Turn into a 10-inch plate. Dot with butter; set aside.

2. Prepare pastry. Shape into a ball and flatten on a lightly floured surface. Roll into a rectangle about ⅛ inch thick. Cut pastry diagonally into strips with a pastry wheel or knife, cutting one long strip 2 inches wide to use around edge of plate; cut remaining strips ½ inch wide.

3. Form a lattice design over berries. Arrange wider strip around edge so that it extends about ½ inch beyond rim of plate. Fold edge of wide strip under and flute pastry.

4. Bake at 425°F about 30 minutes, or until golden brown.

5. Serve warm or cool. If desired, garnish cobbler with additional fresh berries placed between lattice strips.   6 TO 8 SERVINGS

BLUEBERRY DESSERT PIZZA

1 pkg. active dry yeast	1 teaspoon vanilla
¼ cup warm water	extract
½ cup scalded milk	3 to 3¼ cups all-
¼ cup sugar	purpose flour
1 teaspoon salt	Cream Cheese Filling,
2 tablespoons soft	*below*
butter or margarine	Blueberry Topping,
2 eggs	*below*

1. Soften yeast in warm water; set aside.
2. Combine scalded milk, sugar, salt, and butter in a large bowl; cool to lukewarm.
3. Stir eggs, extract, and softened yeast into lukewarm milk mixture. Beat in enough flour to form a dough, beating well after each addition. Cover. Let rise in a warm place until doubled, about 1 hour.
4. Divide dough in half. Roll out each half on a lightly floured surface to form a round 1 inch larger than an inverted 13-inch pizza pan. Place each in a well-greased pizza pan. Fold edges under to form a standing rim; flute.
5. Spread half of filling over each pie. Drop topping onto cheese mixture by the teaspoonful. Let pizzas rise again, uncovered, until doubled, 30 to 40 minutes.
6. Bake at 375°F 15 to 20 minutes, or until crust is brown. Sprinkle with *confectioners' sugar*, if desired.   TWO 13-INCH DESSERT PIZZAS

CREAM CHEESE FILLING: Beat *8 ounces cream cheese* until fluffy. Blend in *⅓ cup sugar, 1 tablespoon flour, 1 or 2 eggs, and 1 teaspoon vanilla extract.*

BLUEBERRY TOPPING: Combine *½ cup sugar* and *3 tablespoons cornstarch* in a heavy saucepan. Add *1 package (12 ounces) frozen blueberries.* Cook and stir until thick. Stir in *1 tablespoon lemon juice* and *1 tablespoon butter.* Set aside to cool.

MINTED CANTALOUPE BALLS

1 large ripe cantaloupe	1 tablespoon butter or
½ cup sugar	margarine
1½ teaspoons cornstarch	2 drops green food
Few grains salt	coloring
¾ cup water	Mint sprigs
12 mint leaves	

1. Using a melon-ball cutter, cut out balls (about 3 cups) from cantaloupe; cover and chill thoroughly.
2. Combine sugar, cornstarch, and salt in a saucepan. Blend in the water. Stir in mint leaves and bruise by pressing with back of a spoon. Stirring constantly, bring rapidly to boiling and cook until mixture is transparent and slightly thickened.
3. Remove from heat; cool slightly and strain. Mix in butter and then food coloring. Chill.
4. To serve, turn chilled melon balls into a chilled serving bowl and pour sauce over them. Garnish bowl with mint sprigs.   ABOUT 6 SERVINGS

GRECIAN GLAZED ORANGES

Using a shredder, remove the peel from *oranges* (allow one per serving). Pour freshly *boiling water* over peel to cover, let stand 10 minutes, and drain. Repeat twice, being sure that the water is boiling each time it is poured over peel. Meanwhile, cut off and discard all the white underskin from oranges. Prepare a sugar syrup allowing for each orange *⅓ cup water* and *⅓ cup sugar*; boil for 10 minutes. Tint with a *few drops yellow or orange food coloring*. Pour boiling syrup over oranges; let stand about 15 minutes. Stir in the peel and pour over oranges; cool. Stack oranges pyramid fashion in a serving dish and pour syrup over them to glaze.

PEACHES WITH LIME CREAM

1 can (29 oz.) peach halves, drained (reserve ½ cup syrup)	2 tablespoons confectioners' sugar
⅓ cup firmly packed brown sugar	Few drops vanilla extract
Few grains salt	1 tablespoon lime juice
⅓ cup orange juice	½ cup heavy cream, whipped
2 tablespoons lime juice	1 teaspoon grated lime peel

1. Combine reserved peach syrup, brown sugar, salt, orange juice, and 2 tablespoons lime juice in a heavy skillet. Stirring constantly, cook over low heat until sugar is dissolved.
2. Add peach halves and simmer 15 minutes, turning peaches several times.
3. Blend confectioners' sugar, extract, and 1 tablespoon lime juice into whipped cream.
4. Spoon warm peaches and syrup into individual serving dishes. Top with the whipped cream and sprinkle with lime peel. ABOUT 6 SERVINGS

SPICY PEACH COBBLER

1 can (29 oz.) peach slices, drained (reserve 1 cup syrup)	2 tablespoons cider vinegar
½ cup firmly packed brown sugar	1 tablespoon butter or margarine
2 tablespoons cornstarch	1 cup biscuit mix
⅛ teaspoon salt	½ cup shredded sharp Cheddar cheese
⅛ teaspoon ground cinnamon	2 tablespoons butter or margarine, melted
⅛ teaspoon ground cloves	¼ cup milk

1. Place drained peaches in a 1-quart shallow baking dish; set aside.
2. Combine brown sugar, cornstarch, salt, cinnamon, and cloves in a saucepan; stir in the reserved peach syrup, vinegar, and 1 tablespoon butter. Bring mixture to boiling, stirring frequently; cook until clear and thickened. Pour over peaches and set in a 400°F oven.
3. Combine biscuit mix and cheese and mix thoroughly. Stir in melted butter and milk to form a soft dough. Remove baking dish from oven and drop dough by heaping tablespoonfuls onto peaches.
4. Return to oven and bake 20 minutes, or until crust is golden brown. Serve warm. 6 SERVINGS

SPICED PEACHES IN CASSEROLE

1 can (29 oz.) cling peach halves, drained (reserve ¼ cup syrup)	¼ teaspoon ground nutmeg
¼ cup packed brown sugar	¼ cup butter or margarine, melted
½ teaspoon ground cinnamon	¼ cup coarsely crushed corn flakes
	¼ cup finely chopped pecans

1. Put peach halves, cut side up, in a 1½-quart shallow baking dish. Pour a mixture of the reserved syrup, sugar, spices, and 2 tablespoons of the butter over peaches.
2. Bake at 350°F 10 minutes. Spoon a mixture of the remaining ingredients over peaches. Increase oven temperature to 400°F and bake 10 minutes.
4 TO 6 SERVINGS

PEACHES À L'ORANGE

¼ cup firmly packed brown sugar	1 can (29 oz.) peach halves, drained (reserve ½ cup syrup)
1½ teaspoons cornstarch	½ cup orange juice
1 tablespoon grated orange peel	8 whole cloves
Few grains salt	6 whole allspice

1. Combine sugar, cornstarch, orange peel, and salt in a saucepan. Add the reserved peach syrup and orange juice gradually, stirring constantly; mix in the cloves and allspice.
2. Bring to boiling, stirring constantly. Add the peach halves and simmer 5 minutes; turning peaches several times.
3. Serve warm or chilled. ABOUT 6 SERVINGS

PEACHES 'N' CORNBREAD, SHORTCAKE STYLE

¾ cup plus 2 tablespoons all-purpose flour	1 egg, well beaten
½ teaspoon baking soda	½ cup buttermilk
¼ teaspoon salt	⅓ cup dairy sour cream
1 cup yellow cornmeal	Peach Butter Élégant, *page 497*
¾ cup firmly packed light brown sugar	Sweetened fresh peach slices

1. Combine the flour, baking soda, salt, cornmeal, and brown sugar in a bowl; set aside.
2. Beat the egg, buttermilk, and sour cream together until well blended. Make a well in center of

dry ingredients and add liquid all at one time. Stir until just smooth (do not overmix).

3. Turn into a greased (bottom only) 11x7x1½-inch pan and spread batter evenly to corners and sides of pan.

4. Bake at 425°F about 20 minutes, or until a cake tester or wooden pick inserted in center comes out clean.

5. While still warm, cut cornbread into serving-sized pieces, remove from pan, and split into two layers. Spread Peach Butter Élégant generously between layers. Top with peach slices.

9 TO 12 SERVINGS

PEAR PUDDING DE LUXE

2 cans (29 oz. each) pears, drained	½ cup quick-cooking rolled oats
½ cup sugar	½ cup all-purpose flour
2 tablespoons flour	½ cup packed brown sugar
½ teaspoon ground cinnamon	½ cup butter or margarine
¼ teaspoon ground mace	

1. Coarsely dice pears and put into a 1½-quart baking dish. Sprinkle evenly with a mixture of the sugar, flour, cinnamon, and mace; mix lightly. Set aside.

2. Combine in a bowl the rolled oats, flour, and brown sugar. Using a pastry blender or two knives, cut in the butter until mixture is crumbly. Spoon mixture evenly over pears.

3. Bake at 350°F 45 minutes, or until mixture is bubbly and topping is lightly browned.

4. Serve warm with *cream* or *whipped cream*.

ABOUT 8 SERVINGS

ORANGE BAKED PEARS

1 tablespoon butter or margarine, melted	Few grains mace
	Few grains salt
⅓ cup orange zwieback crumbs (about 4 slices)	1 can (29 oz.) pear halves, drained (reserve syrup)
3 tablespoons light brown sugar	
½ teaspoon grated orange peel	Plantation Orange Sauce, *below*

1. Combine melted butter, crumbs, brown sugar, orange peel, mace, and salt; mix well.

2. Arrange pears, cut side up, in a shallow baking dish; fill hollows of pears with crumb mixture.

3. Pour ½ cup of the reserved pear syrup around pears; cover with aluminum foil.

4. Bake at 350°F 15 minutes; uncover and bake 15 minutes longer, or until crumbs are browned.

5. Serve warm with Plantation Orange Sauce.

ABOUT 8 SERVINGS

PLANTATION ORANGE SAUCE: Blend *3 ounces cream cheese*, softened, with *2 tablespoons cream* in a bowl. Beat in *¾ teaspoon grated orange peel*, *1 tablespoon orange juice*, and *4 teaspoons confectioners' sugar* until thoroughly blended. Chill 30 minutes. ABOUT ½ CUP SAUCE

PEAR BACON CRISP

6 cups sliced firm ripe pears	1 teaspoon ground cinnamon
2 tablespoons lemon juice	½ teaspoon ground nutmeg
½ cup flaked coconut	6 slices bacon, diced and fried until crisp (reserve 2 tablespoons drippings)
½ cup all-purpose flour	
¼ cup sugar	
¼ cup packed brown sugar	2 tablespoons butter or margarine
¼ teaspoon salt	

1. Sprinkle pears with lemon juice. Toss with coconut. Put half of the pears into a greased 2-quart casserole.

2. Mix flour, sugars, salt, cinnamon, and nutmeg. Blend in reserved drippings and butter. Stir in bacon. Sprinkle half the mixture over pears, add remaining pears, and sprinkle with flour mixture.

3. Bake at 350°F 50 minutes, or until tender.

4. Garnish each serving with *flaked coconut*.

8 SERVINGS

PEARS FLAMBÉ

½ cup dried apricots	1 teaspoon vanilla extract
½ cup water	
2 cups water	6 firm ripe pears
1 cup sugar	

1. Set apricots with the ½ cup water over low heat; cover, and cook slowly about 25 minutes, or until tender. Purée through a sieve and set aside.

2. Combine the 2 cups water and sugar in a large saucepan. Bring to boiling and boil about 5 minutes, stirring until sugar is dissolved. Remove from heat and stir in the extract.

3. Rinse, halve, and carefully remove the core

from the pears. Poach them in the syrup over medium heat, simmering about 5 minutes, or until just tender. Carefully remove from syrup. Allowing 2 halves per serving, spoon into individual dishes.

4. Blend the apricot purée into the syrup. Simmer, stirring until sauce is of desired thickness. Spoon apricot sauce over pears.

5. Heat ¼ *to* ½ *cup brandy.* Ignite and pour while flaming over the pears. 6 SERVINGS

PINEAPPLE WITH RUM CARAMEL SAUCE

3 tablespoons butter or margarine
1 can (20 oz.) pineapple slices, drained (reserve 1 tablespoon syrup)

¼ cup firmly packed light brown sugar
1 teaspoon lemon juice
1 tablespoon rum

1. Heat 2 tablespoons of the butter until foamy in a small saucepan. Stir in reserved pineapple syrup, brown sugar, and lemon juice. Cook 3 to 4 minutes, stirring constantly; remove from heat. Stir in the rum.

2. Meanwhile, heat remaining 1 tablespoon butter in a large skillet. Brown pineapple slices lightly on both sides.

3. Transfer slices to serving plates. Spoon rum caramel sauce over each. 5 SERVINGS

PURPLE PLUM CRUNCH

Here's a delightful version of old-fashioned cobbler with the tangy sweetness of the plums accenting the flavor of the buttery spicy crunch topping.

5 cups pitted, quartered fresh purple plums
¼ cup packed brown sugar
3 tablespoons flour
½ teaspoon ground cinnamon
1 cup sifted all-purpose flour

1 cup sugar
1 teaspoon baking powder
¼ teaspoon salt
¼ teaspoon ground mace
1 egg, well beaten
½ cup butter, melted and cooled

1. Put plums into an ungreased 2-quart shallow baking dish. Sprinkle with a mixture of brown sugar, 3 tablespoons flour, and cinnamon; mix gently with a fork.

2. To prepare topping, sift together 1 cup flour, sugar, baking powder, salt, and mace. Add to the

beaten egg and stir with a fork until mixture is crumbly; sprinkle evenly over plums in baking dish. Pour the melted butter evenly over top.

3. Bake at 375°F 40 to 45 minutes, or until topping is lightly browned.

4. Serve warm with *cinnamon whipped cream.*

6 TO 8 SERVINGS

CHOCOLATE-PRUNE WHIP

1 pkg. (6 oz.) semisweet chocolate pieces, melted

1 cup sieved cooked prunes
1 cup heavy cream, whipped

Stir melted chocolate into sieved prunes until thoroughly blended. Fold into whipped cream and pile mixture into chilled parfait or sherbet glasses. Chill thoroughly. ABOUT 6 SERVINGS

CREAMY PRUNE WHIP

½ lb. dried prunes, cooked and pitted
2 tablespoons lemon juice
2 egg whites

⅛ teaspoon salt
½ cup sugar
1 cup heavy cream, whipped

1. Force prunes through a food mill or sieve into a bowl. Stir in lemon juice.

2. Beat egg whites with salt until frothy. Add sugar gradually, beating until stiff peaks are formed. Turn beaten egg whites and whipped cream onto prune purée and gently fold together until blended. Chill thoroughly before serving.

3. Spoon into dessert dishes and decorate with swirls of *sweetened whipped cream* and *candied cherries,* if desired. ABOUT 6 SERVINGS

BAKED RHUBARB WITH PASTRY TOPPING

1½ lbs. tender pink rhubarb, cut in 1-in. pieces (about 6 cups)
1¼ to 1½ cups sugar
¾ teaspoon ground cinnamon
1½ teaspoons grated lemon peel

1 tablespoon lemon juice
Pastry Topping, *page 454*
2 tablespoons sugar
½ teaspoon ground cinnamon

1. Toss rhubarb with 1¼ to 1½ cups sugar, cinna-

mon, and lemon peel in a 1½-quart shallow baking dish. Drizzle with lemon juice.

2. Moisten rim of dish with cold water. Carefully place Pastry Topping over rhubarb and trim edge, allowing ½ inch to hang over. Fold edge under and press gently to seal. Flute edge. Sprinkle entire surface with a mixture of remaining ingredients.

3. Bake at 450°F 10 minutes; reduce temperature to 325°F and bake 15 minutes.

4. Serve warm with *whipped dessert topping.*

6 TO 8 SERVINGS

SPRINGTIME RHUBARB AMBROSIA

1 lb. tender pink rhubarb, cut in 1-in. pieces (3 to 4 cups)	½ teaspoon ground cinnamon
¾ cup sugar	1 teaspoon grated lemon peel
	2 teaspoons lemon juice

1. Toss rhubarb with sugar, cinnamon, and lemon peel; turn into a 1-quart casserole. Drizzle with lemon juice.

2. Cover and cook in a 350°F oven 20 to 25 minutes, or until tender. Serve warm or cold.

4 OR 5 SERVINGS

TEA CREAM FOR STRAWBERRIES

Tea Cream is a traditional recipe dating back to our Early American period.

1 tablespoon black tea	3 tablespoons boiling water
1 slice orange peel (2 in.)	2 cups heavy cream
½ cinnamon stick	2 pts. fresh strawberries, sliced
1 whole nutmeg	¼ cup sugar

1. Put tea, orange peel, and spices into a bowl. Add the boiling water and allow brew to stand at room temperature 1 hour.

2. Strain brew through a fine sieve or a sieve lined with cheesecloth. Mix with cream. Allow to stand 30 minutes.

3. Meanwhile, put berries into a bowl and sprinkle with *brown or granulated sugar* to taste. Chill 15 to 30 minutes.

4. Stir the ¼ cup sugar into the tea cream (whip, if desired). Serve with the sugared berries. Accompany with *old-fashioned lemon or sugar cookies* or *gingerbread.*   6 SERVINGS

QUINCE OR CRAB APPLE CREAM FOR STRAWBERRIES: Beat together until blended *¼ cup quince jelly* and *1 tablespoon confectioners' sugar,* (or *¼ cup crab apple jelly* and *1 tablespoon honey*). Add *1 cup chilled heavy cream* and whip to soft peaks. Serve with *strawberries,* sweetened to taste, and *cookies* or *gingerbread.*

STRAWBERRIES ROMANOFF

This Mike Romanoff specialty is as delicious as it is easy to prepare.

Marinate fresh ripe *strawberries* in a little *orange juice* and *curaçao* and refrigerate several hours. Pile berries and juice in a glass serving dish and top generously with *sweetened whipped cream.*

GLAZED STRAWBERRY TART

A crown of glazed strawberries tops the creamy filling in this scrumptious tart.

Pastry for 1-crust 9-in. pie	½ teaspoon grated lemon peel
⅓ cup sugar	½ teaspoon vanilla extract
3 tablespoons cornstarch	¼ cup white grape juice
¼ teaspoon salt	2 pts. ripe strawberries, rinsed, hulled, and thoroughly dried
⅓ cup instant nonfat dry milk	
1½ cups milk	⅓ cup currant jelly
2 eggs, beaten	1 tablespoon sugar

1. Line tart or pie pan with pastry; bake and set aside on wire rack to cool completely.

2. Combine the ⅓ cup sugar with the cornstarch and salt in a heavy saucepan; mix well.

3. Blend the nonfat dry milk with the milk and stir into the cornstarch mixture until smooth. Bring mixture to boiling, stirring constantly; boil 2 to 3 minutes, continuing to stir.

4. Vigorously stir about 3 tablespoons of the hot mixture into the eggs; return to mixture in saucepan. Cook and stir over low heat about 3 minutes, or until very thick.

5. Remove from heat and stir in the lemon peel and extract. Cool slightly, then beat in the white grape juice with a hand rotary or electric beater until blended.

6. Spread the cooled filling in the baked shell and

refrigerate until thoroughly chilled. Top with the strawberries; set aside.

7. Heat jelly until melted and continue to cook about 5 minutes. Spoon over strawberries on the tart filling. Just before serving, sprinkle remaining 1 tablespoon sugar over the tart. ONE 9-INCH TART

GLAZED FRUIT TART

The artful arrangement of fruits in this tart appeals to both the eye and the appetite.

Pastry for a 2-crust 9-in. pie	¼ cup sugar
2 cups drained canned pineapple chunks (reserve ¾ cup syrup)	1 tablespoon cornstarch
	⅛ teaspoon salt
	1½ tablespoons cold water
2 cups drained canned sliced peaches	⅛ teaspoon grated lemon peel
1⅓ cups drained pitted syrup-packed tart red cherries	1½ teaspoons lemon juice
1¼ cups drained canned blueberries	1 teaspoon butter or margarine

1. Prepare pastry and shape into a ball. Roll dough into a rectangle 4 inches longer and wider than the overall size of an 11x7x1½-inch baking pan (do not stretch). Turn under the extra pastry around top of pan; flute edge.
2. Bake pastry at 450°F 10 to 15 minutes, or until light golden brown. Cool on wire rack.
3. Refrigerate the drained fruits until chilled.
4. To prepare glaze, combine sugar, cornstarch, and salt in a small heavy saucepan. Stir in the water and reserved pineapple syrup. Cook and stir over direct heat until boiling; boil 2 to 3 minutes. Remove from heat and blend in the lemon peel and juice and butter. Cool and refrigerate.
5. To complete the tart, spoon ¼ cup of the chilled glaze evenly over the cooled pastry. Remove chilled fruit from refrigerator. Arrange one half of the cherries across the narrow end of pastry shell, then half the peaches, blueberries, and pineapple chunks; repeat, covering entire pan with rows of fruits. Refrigerate until serving time.
6. To serve, cut the tart so each person is served some of each fruit. 6 TO 8 SERVINGS
NOTE: If desired, *fresh ripe fruits* in season (dark sweet cherries, sliced nectarines, peaches and apricots, whole strawberries, blueberries, and melon balls) may be substituted.

GLAZED MIXED FRUIT

1 pkg. (about 12 oz.) mixed dried fruits	½ cup light corn syrup
	½ cup dark corn syrup
3 cups water	¼ teaspoon ground cinnamon
½ cup orange juice	
⅓ cup quick-cooking tapioca	¼ teaspoon ground nutmeg
2 tablespoons sugar	⅛ teaspoon salt

1. Combine fruit and water in a saucepan; bring to boiling and cook, uncovered, until fruit is tender. Remove from heat.
2. Remove fruit with a slotted spoon and arrange on a serving platter. Set aside.
3. Add orange juice to the cooking liquid in saucepan. Stir in a blend of tapioca and sugar. Set over low heat and bring to boiling; cook until mixture thickens and tapioca becomes transparent.
4. Stir in corn syrups and a mixture of the remaining ingredients; blend thoroughly. Remove the saucepan from heat and pour glaze over fruit. Let stand until glaze is set.
5. Serve in sauce dishes either warm or chilled and garnish with *whipped cream*, if desired.
ABOUT 8 SERVINGS

COUPE ST. JACQUES

Lime, Orange, and Raspberry Ice, *page 540*	½ cup white seedless grapes, halved
	¼ cup fresh blueberries
2 cups fresh pineapple wedges	1 cup confectioners' or granulated sugar
1 cup orange pieces	⅓ cup kirsch
1 cup fresh peach pieces	¼ cup fresh raspberries

1. Have the fruit ices ready. (If desired, commercial ices may be used.)
2. Prepare the fresh fruits and combine all fruits (except raspberries) in a bowl; toss gently with the sugar and pour the kirsch over all. Refrigerate to chill thoroughly.
3. Before serving, gently mix in the raspberries. Spoon mixture into chilled serving dishes, spooning some of the juice over fruit.
4. Top each serving with one scoop of Lime, Orange, and Raspberry Ice. Serve at once.
12 TO 14 SERVINGS

DESSERT SAUCES

VANILLA SAUCE

1 cup sugar
2 tablespoons cornstarch
¼ teaspoon salt
2 cups boiling water

¼ cup butter or
  margarine
2 teaspoons vanilla
  extract

1. Combine the sugar, cornstarch, and salt in a saucepan. Mix well and add boiling water gradually, stirring constantly. Continue to stir, bring to boiling and simmer 5 minutes.
2. Remove from heat and blend in butter and extract. Serve warm. ABOUT 2 CUPS
LEMON SAUCE: Follow recipe for Vanilla Sauce. Substitute *3 tablespoons lemon juice* and *2 teaspoons grated lemon peel* for extract.
BRANDY SAUCE: Follow recipe for Lemon Sauce. Decrease lemon juice to 1 tablespoon and stir in *3 tablespoons brandy.*

GOLDEN SAUCE

This rich, delicately flavored sauce is delightful served over Snow Pudding, vanilla or chocolate pudding, steamed fruit pudding, or slices of cake.

3 tablespoons butter
¼ cup sugar
3 egg yolks, slightly
  beaten

⅓ cup boiling water
1 teaspoon vanilla
  extract

1. Cream the butter and beat in the sugar until fluffy. Gradually add the egg yolks, blending well. Very gradually add the boiling water while stirring. Turn mixture into the top of a double boiler; stir and cook over simmering water until thickened.
2. Remove from heat and blend in the extract. Cool; chill. ABOUT 1 CUP

SEA-FOAM SAUCE

½ cup firmly packed
  brown sugar
¼ cup sugar
6 tablespoons water
1½ teaspoons light corn
  syrup

½ teaspoon cider
  vinegar
⅛ teaspoon salt
1 egg white
½ cup heavy cream,
  whipped

1. Combine in a saucepan the sugars, water, corn syrup, vinegar, and salt. Stir over low heat until sugars are dissolved. Increase heat and bring mixture rapidly to boiling. Cover saucepan and boil mixture gently 5 minutes.
2. Uncover saucepan and set a candy thermometer in place. Continue cooking without stirring. During cooking, wash down crystals from sides of saucepan with a pastry brush dipped in water. Cook until thermometer registers 230°F (thread stage). Remove from heat.
3. Beat egg white until stiff, not dry, peaks are formed. Continue beating egg white while pouring the hot syrup over it in a thin steady stream (do not scrape bottom and sides of pan). Fold in the whipped cream.
4. Serve over steamed pudding. ABOUT 3 CUPS

ALMOND BUTTERSCOTCH SAUCE

1¼ cups firmly packed
  light brown sugar
⅔ cup heavy cream
⅔ cup light corn syrup

¼ cup butter or
  margarine
⅛ teaspoon salt
½ cup toasted blanched
  almonds, chopped

1. Combine all ingredients except almonds in a 2-quart heavy saucepan; stir over low heat until sugar is dissolved and butter is melted. Increase heat to medium and bring to boiling; stir occasionally.
2. Set a candy thermometer in place. Cook without stirring until thermometer registers 226°F.
3. Remove from heat and cool slightly. Stir in the almonds. Serve warm. ABOUT 2½ CUPS
NOTE: Sauce may be stored in a tightly covered container in the refrigerator and reheated before using.

LUSCIOUS BUTTERSCOTCH SAUCE

1 cup firmly packed
  light brown sugar
⅓ cup butter

⅓ cup cream
Few grains salt

1. Combine all ingredients in a small heavy saucepan; stir over low heat until sugar is dissolved.
2. Increase heat to medium and bring mixture to boiling, stirring occasionally. Boil 5 minutes without stirring. Serve warm. ABOUT 1¼ CUPS SAUCE

APRICOT SAUCE

1½ cups apricot jam
½ cup water
2 tablespoons sugar

1 tablespoon apricot
brandy

1. Combine the jam, water, and sugar in a saucepan. Bring to boiling and cook over low heat 5 to 10 minutes, stirring to prevent scorching.
2. Sieve mixture. Stir in apricot brandy. Serve hot or cold.   ABOUT 1¾ CUPS

CHERRY SAUCE

1 cup sugar
½ cup water
1 tablespoon light corn
   syrup

10 to 15 drops red food
   coloring
⅓ cup brandy
½ cup finely chopped
   candied cherries

1. Combine the sugar, water, and corn syrup in a saucepan. Bring to boiling, stirring constantly. Cover and cook 5 minutes. Set aside to cool.
2. Tint to desired color with food coloring. Stir in the brandy and then the cherries.
3. Serve over *plum pudding*.   ABOUT 1½ CUPS

SPICY CHERRY SAUCE
(Kirschsosse)

1 can (20 oz.) pitted
   tart red cherries
   (2½ cups)
2 whole cloves
1 piece (2 in.) stick
   cinnamon
4 teaspoons sugar
4 teaspoons cornstarch
¼ teaspoon salt
4 teaspoons cold water

3½ tablespoons corn
   syrup
4 teaspoons butter or
   margarine
1½ teaspoons lemon
   juice
¼ teaspoon almond
   extract
1 drop red food coloring

1. Combine cherries, cloves, and stick cinnamon in a covered saucepan. Cook 5 minutes. Remove from heat and discard spices. Force cherries through a sieve or food mill into a saucepan.
2. Combine the sugar, cornstarch, and salt in a small bowl. Blend in the water and corn syrup and stir into the hot cherry mixture. Bring rapidly to boiling; cook and stir about 3 minutes.
3. Remove from heat and stir in the remaining ingredients. Serve hot with steamed puddings.
                                    ABOUT 1¾ CUPS

REGAL CHOCOLATE SAUCE

1 cup sugar
1 cup hot water
½ cup light corn syrup
3 oz. (3 sq.) unsweet-
   ened chocolate, cut
   into very small pieces

1 cup undiluted
   evaporated milk
2 teaspoons vanilla
   extract

1. Combine sugar, water, and corn syrup in a saucepan. Set over low heat and stir until sugar is dissolved. Increase heat and cook rapidly.
2. Set candy thermometer in place and continue cooking syrup until temperature reaches 236°F (or until a small amount of syrup forms a soft ball in very cold water). Wash down crystals from sides of pan occasionally.
3. Remove syrup from heat and add chocolate pieces; stir gently until melted. Stir in the evaporated milk and extract.
4. Serve hot, or cool and store in covered jar in refrigerator.   ABOUT 2¼ CUPS

CHOCOLATE SAUCE

2 oz. (2 sq.) unsweet-
   ened chocolate
6 tablespoons water
½ cup sugar

Few grains salt
2 tablespoons butter
½ teaspoon vanilla
   extract

1. Combine chocolate and water in a saucepan. Stir over low heat until smooth and blended.
2. Add sugar and salt; stir constantly until sugar is dissolved and mixture thickens slightly, about 5 minutes. Remove from heat.
3. Blend in butter and extract. Cool slightly.
                                    ABOUT 1 CUP

SEMISWEET CHOCOLATE SAUCE

2 oz. semisweet
   chocolate
½ cup butter

2 eggs, beaten
½ cup sugar

1. Melt chocolate and butter together in a heavy saucepan over low heat; stir occasionally.
2. Meanwhile, combine eggs and sugar in the top of a double boiler and cook over simmering water, stirring constantly until mixture is amber colored, about 10 minutes.
3. Slowly add egg mixture to chocolate mixture, stirring constantly until blended.
4. Cool, stirring occasionally, and chill.

5. Serve over *ice cream*. ABOUT 1½ CUPS

NOTE: For a chocolate frosting or filling, blend *confectioners' sugar* into the sauce until of spreading consistency.

BITTERSWEET CHOCOLATE SAUCE DE LUXE

12 oz. semisweet chocolate pieces	1 cup heavy cream
2 oz. (2 sq.) unsweetened chocolate	1 teaspoon vanilla extract

1. Heat all ingredients together in the top of a double boiler set over hot (not steaming) water; stir frequently until smooth.
2. Sauce may be stored, covered, in refrigerator. Serve hot for ice cream sundaes or cool for ice cream sodas. 2 CUPS

NOTE: For a cake filling or topping, slowly add ½ *cup heavy cream* to *1 cup cooled Bittersweet Chocolate Sauce de Luxe*, beating constantly with an electric beater until light and fluffy.

CHOCOLATE-MARSHMALLOW SAUCE

16 marshmallows, cut in quarters	⅛ teaspoon salt
1 cup light corn syrup	1 tablespoon butter or margarine
2 oz. (2 sq.) unsweetened chocolate	1 teaspoon vanilla extract

1. Put marshmallows, corn syrup, chocolate, and salt into the top of a double boiler. Heat over boiling water, stirring occasionally, until marshmallows and chocolate are melted.
2. Remove from heat and blend in butter and extract. Serve hot over ice cream.

ABOUT 2 CUPS SAUCE

NOTE: Sauce may be stored in a covered jar in the refrigerator. Reheat sauce before serving.

FUDGE SAUCE

1⅓ cups undiluted evaporated milk	2 oz. (2 sq.) unsweetened chocolate
1 cup sugar	⅛ teaspoon salt
¼ cup butter or margarine	1 tablespoon vanilla extract

1. Combine evaporated milk, sugar, butter, choc-

olate, and salt in a heavy saucepan. Cook and stir over low heat until sugar is dissolved.
2. Cover and heat for 20 minutes, without stirring. Then stir until all ingredients are blended and cook over medium heat until thickened, stirring constantly. Remove from heat and stir in extract.
3. Serve hot or cool over *ice cream* or *other desserts*. ABOUT 1½ CUPS

NOTE: Sauce becomes very thick after storing in refrigerator. Before serving, reheat over simmering water to restore its original consistency.

HOT FUDGE SAUCE

¼ cup butter or margarine	½ cup undiluted evaporated milk
2 oz. (2 sq.) unsweetened chocolate	1 teaspoon vanilla extract
¾ cup sugar	Few grains salt
¼ cup cocoa	

1. Heat butter and chocolate together in a heavy saucepan or top of a double boiler over low heat until melted, stirring to blend.
2. Remove from heat and stir in a mixture of the sugar and cocoa.
3. Blend in the remaining ingredients and return saucepan to low heat (place double boiler top over boiling water) and cook until sauce is thickened; stir constantly. 1⅓ CUPS

MOCHA FUDGE SAUCE

½ cup sugar	⅛ teaspoon salt
½ cup strong coffee	2 tablespoons butter or margarine
2 oz. (2 sq.) unsweetened chocolate, broken in pieces	½ teaspoon vanilla extract
1 tablespoon cream	

1. Mix all ingredients, except butter and extract, in a small heavy saucepan. Cook over low heat, stirring constantly, until sauce is slightly thickened.
2. Remove from heat and blend in butter and extract. Serve warm or cool over *ice cream*.

ABOUT 1 CUP

COCONUT-PRALINE SAUCE

⅓ cup butter
1 cup flaked coconut
½ cup firmly packed
　brown sugar
2 tablespoons dark corn
　syrup

⅛ teaspoon salt
¾ cup undiluted
　evaporated milk
½ teaspoon vanilla
　extract

1.　Heat butter in a saucepan over low heat. Add coconut and stir frequently until golden brown. Remove coconut and set aside.
2.　Add brown sugar, corn syrup, and salt to butter in saucepan; mix well. Cook over low heat, stirring constantly, until mixture bubbles vigorously.
3.　Remove from heat. Gradually add evaporated milk, stirring until blended. Return to heat and stir constantly until thoroughly heated.
4.　Remove from heat; stir in coconut and extract. Serve warm or cold over *cake* or *ice cream*.

ABOUT 2 CUPS

CUSTARD SAUCE

⅓ cup sugar
1 teaspoon flour
⅛ teaspoon salt
2 eggs

1 egg yolk
1½ cups milk
1½ teaspoons vanilla
　extract

1.　Combine sugar, flour, and salt in the top of a double boiler. Add the eggs and egg yolk; mix thoroughly. Blend in ¼ cup of the milk.
2.　Heat remaining milk just until hot. Blend into mixture in double-boiler top. Stirring constantly, cook over simmering water until mixture coats a metal spoon, about 10 minutes.
3.　Remove from water; stir in extract. Cool; chill at least 3 hours.　ABOUT 2 CUPS

CREAMY ORANGE-CUSTARD SAUCE

4 egg yolks
⅓ cup sugar
⅛ teaspoon salt
2 cups milk or cream,
　scalded

¼ cup partially thawed
　frozen orange juice
　concentrate
2 tablespoons butter or
　margarine
⅛ teaspoon ground
　mace

1.　Slightly beat egg yolks, sugar, and salt in the top of a double boiler. Gradually add milk, stirring constantly. Cook over simmering water, stirring constantly, until mixture coats a metal spoon.

2.　Remove from heat. Cool slightly; blend in orange juice concentrate, butter, and mace. Cover and set aside to cool to lukewarm. Stir, then chill.
3.　Serve over *ice cream* or *cake*.　ABOUT 2½ CUPS

ZESTY LEMON SAUCE

½ cup butter
1 cup sugar
¼ cup water
1 egg, well beaten

3 tablespoons lemon
　juice
1 tablespoon grated
　lemon peel

Combine all ingredients in a saucepan. Cook over medium heat, stirring constantly, just until mixture comes to boiling. Remove from heat and serve warm.　ABOUT 1½ CUPS SAUCE

GRECIAN ORANGE SAUCE

6 oranges
Water

3 cups sugar
¼ cup currant jelly

1.　Wash oranges; remove thin orange-colored top of the peel in small pieces with vegetable parer. Put peel in saucepan with *2 cups water*; bring to boiling. Boil 15 minutes; drain.
2.　Cut oranges into eighths; reserve juice. Measure juice and add water, if necessary, to make 1 cup; combine in saucepan with sugar and jelly. Stir and bring to boiling; cook 25 minutes.
3.　Add cooked peel and continue cooking until a candy thermometer registers 230°F.
4.　Remove from heat and add orange sections. Cover and refrigerate at least 8 hours.

ABOUT 4 CUPS

SPICED ORANGE SAUCE

¼ cup firmly packed
　light brown sugar
2 teaspoons cornstarch
1 tablespoon grated
　orange peel

½ cup orange juice
½ cup canned peach
　syrup
8 whole cloves
6 whole allspice

1.　Mix brown sugar, cornstarch, orange peel, and a *few grains salt* together in a saucepan. Add the orange juice and peach syrup gradually, stirring constantly. Mix in the cloves and allspice.
2.　Bring mixture to boiling, stirring constantly. Reduce heat and simmer 5 minutes. Cool; chill.
3.　Remove and discard the cloves and allspice. Serve over *ice cream*.　1 CUP

PEACH SUNDAE SAUCE

½ cup sugar
1 tablespoon cornstarch
Few grains salt
1 can (29 oz.) peach
  slices, drained and
  coarsely crushed
  (reserve ½ cup syrup)

½ cup orange juice
1 tablespoon lemon
  juice
1 tablespoon lime juice
1 piece (1 in.)
  preserved ginger,
  finely chopped

1. Combine the sugar, cornstarch, and salt in a saucepan. Blend in peach syrup and fruit juices. Bring to boiling; stir and cook until slightly thickened and clear. Stir in peaches and ginger. Simmer about 5 minutes. Cool.
2. Serve over *ice cream*.   ABOUT 2¾ CUPS

PEANUT CRUNCH SAUCE

1 cup light corn syrup
½ cup crunchy peanut
  butter

¼ cup butter or
  margarine
1 teaspoon vanilla
  extract

Combine the corn syrup, peanut butter, and butter in a small heavy saucepan. Cook over low heat, stirring occasionally, until blended. Remove from heat and stir in extract. Serve hot.   ABOUT 1¾ CUPS

PEANUT BUTTER SUNDAE SAUCE SUPERB

½ cup firmly packed
  light brown sugar
¾ cup light corn syrup
¼ cup water
20 miniature
  marshmallows
½ cup peanut butter

¼ cup butter or
  margarine
½ cup undiluted
  evaporated milk
1 teaspoon vanilla
  extract

1. Combine the brown sugar, corn syrup, and water in a small heavy saucepan. Stir over low heat until sugar is dissolved.
2. Increase heat and bring mixture to boiling. Wash down crystals from sides of pan with a pastry brush dipped in warm water. Set candy thermometer in place. Cook, stirring occasionally to prevent scorching, until thermometer registers 234°F (softball stage), washing down crystals from sides of pan and changing water each time.
3. Remove from heat and stir in the remaining ingredients. Stir until smooth and creamy.

4. Serve warm as a topping for *ice cream*. Remaining sauce may be refrigerated; reheat before serving.   ABOUT 2 CUPS

ELEGANT PURPLE PLUM SAUCE

½ cup sugar
⅓ cup light corn syrup
⅔ cup water
12 fresh purple plums,
  rinsed, pitted, and
  quartered
1 tablespoon cold water

1 tablespoon cornstarch
1 teaspoon grated
  lemon peel
8 whole cloves
1 teaspoon lemon juice
½ teaspoon vanilla
  extract

1. Combine in a saucepan the sugar, corn syrup, and the ⅔ cup water. Place over medium heat and stir until sugar is dissolved. Bring to boiling. Add plums; reduce heat and simmer, uncovered, until fruit is tender but not mushy. Remove plums from syrup and set aside.
2. Stir the 1 tablespoon cold water into the cornstarch to form a smooth paste. Gradually add the cornstarch mixture to the hot syrup, stirring constantly.
3. Add lemon peel and cloves to sauce. Bring rapidly to boiling, stirring constantly. Cook until mixture is thick and clear. Return to sauce and heat thoroughly.
4. Remove from heat and blend in the lemon juice and extract. Remove cloves. Serve sauce hot or cold with *ice cream* or over *cake slices*.
                                    ABOUT 1¾ CUPS
NOTE: If desired, fold *1 cup heavy cream*, whipped, into cooled sauce.

FRESH RASPBERRY SAUCE

2 cups fresh raspberries,
  rinsed and thoroughly
  drained
½ cup sugar

1 tablespoon cold water
1½ teaspoons
  cornstarch

1. Force raspberries through a sieve into a small heavy saucepan. Blend in sugar.
2. Mix water into cornstarch to make a smooth paste. Thoroughly blend with berry mixture.
3. Stirring gently and constantly, bring rapidly to boiling. Continue to stir and boil about 3 minutes. Set aside to cool. Store in refrigerator. ABOUT 1 CUP
NOTE: For strawberry sauce, use rinsed and hulled *strawberries*.

RASPBERRY SAUCE

2 pkgs. (10 oz. each)
   frozen raspberries,
   thawed (do not drain)
¼ cup sugar
2 tablespoons light
   brown sugar

2 teaspoons cornstarch
Few grains salt
½ teaspoon lime juice
¼ teaspoon grated lime
   peel

1. Sieve raspberries into a saucepan; discard seeds. Combine sugars, cornstarch, and salt. Stir into raspberries.
2. Bring rapidly to boiling, stirring constantly; boil about 3 minutes. Remove from heat and stir in lime juice and peel. Cool; chill thoroughly.

ABOUT 1⅓ CUPS

RASPBERRY-STRAWBERRY SAUCE

2 pkgs. (10 oz. each)
   frozen raspberries,
   thawed and drained
   (reserve syrup)

1 teaspoon cornstarch
¼ cup strawberry
   preserves

1. Blend reserved raspberry syrup and cornstarch in a saucepan. Bring to boiling; cook and stir until mixture is clear and slightly thickened, 2 to 3 minutes.
2. Stir in the drained raspberries and strawberry preserves. Chill thoroughly.

ABOUT 1¾ CUPS

ROSY GINGER SAUCE

Enhance sponge cake or ice cream with this quick sauce for a sophisticated spring dessert.

1 lb. fresh rhubarb
1 pt. fresh strawberries
½ cup sugar
2 teaspoons cornstarch
½ teaspoon ground
   allspice

½ cup sugar
2 tablespoons finely
   chopped preserved
   ginger

1. Cut rhubarb into ¾-inch slices (do not peel, if tender). Rinse and slice strawberries.
2. Combine rhubarb and ½ cup sugar in a heavy saucepan; cover tightly and cook until rhubarb is tender, about 5 minutes.
3. Meanwhile, mix together cornstarch, allspice, and remaining ½ cup sugar. Stirring constantly, gradually add to rhubarb and cook until mixture boils and thickens slightly.
4. Add strawberries and ginger. Cook 2 to 3 minutes, stirring occasionally. Cool.

ABOUT 3 CUPS

STRAWBERRY SAUCE

2 cups water
1 cup sugar
Few grains salt
4 teaspoons lemon juice

1 tablespoon orange
   juice
2 pts. strawberries,
   washed and hulled

1. Combine water, sugar, and salt in a heavy saucepan. Stir in lemon and orange juices. Bring rapidly to boiling, stirring constantly until sugar is dissolved.
2. Skim off foam and boil for 5 minutes. Add strawberries and boil 1 minute longer.
3. Cool and chill. Serve over thick slices of *pound* or *angel food cake*.

ABOUT 1 QUART

NOTE: If desired, omit orange juice and substitute *1 teaspoon vanilla extract*. Add to the sauce before chilling.

FOAMY VANILLA SAUCE

¼ cup butter
1 teaspoon vanilla
   extract

1½ cups confectioners'
   sugar
2 egg whites

1. Cream butter with extract; add sugar gradually, beating until well blended.
2. Beat egg whites until stiff, not dry, peaks are formed; spread over butter-sugar mixture. Fold together until well blended.

ABOUT 1½ CUPS

VANILLA HARD SAUCE

⅔ cup butter or
   margarine
2 teaspoons vanilla
   extract

2 cups confectioners'
   sugar
Few grains salt
2 teaspoons cream

1. Cream butter with extract. Add confectioners' sugar with salt gradually, beating until fluffy after each addition. Beat in the cream.
2. Chill until mixture is stiff enough to force through a pastry bag and tube.

ABOUT 1⅓ CUPS

NOTE: If desired, press hard sauce evenly into an 8-inch square baking pan. Chill until firm and cut into fancy shapes.

ALMOND HARD SAUCE: Follow recipe for Vanilla Hard Sauce. Substitute ½ *teaspoon almond extract* for the vanilla extract and mix in ½ *cup finely chopped almonds.*

BRANDY HARD SAUCE: Follow recipe for Vanilla Hard Sauce. Substitute ¼ *cup brandy* for the vanilla extract. Increase confectioners' sugar if necessary and omit cream.

FOAMY SAUCE

2 tablespoons butter	1 egg yolk
¼ teaspoon vanilla extract	2 tablespoons milk
1½ cups confectioners' sugar	1 egg white
	1 cup heavy cream, whipped

1. Cream the butter with extract. Add ¼ cup of the confectioners' sugar and beat until fluffy. Add the egg yolk and beat thoroughly.
2. Beating until smooth after each addition, alternately add 1 cup of the sugar in thirds and the milk in halves to creamed mixture.
3. Beat the egg white until rounded peaks are formed. Add the remaining ¼ cup of sugar gradually, beating in with the final few strokes.
4. Fold the whipped cream and beaten egg white into creamed mixture. Chill until ready to serve. ABOUT 3 CUPS

WINE SAUCE

1 cup sugar	¼ cup butter or margarine
2 tablespoons cornstarch	2 teaspoons vanilla extract
¼ teaspoon salt	½ cup white wine
2 cups boiling water	
1 egg yolk, slightly beaten	

1. Combine sugar, cornstarch, and salt in the top of a double boiler. Stir in the boiling water and blend thoroughly. Stir and cook over direct heat until mixture comes to boiling; cook about 3 minutes longer.
2. Set over simmering water and cook, covered, about 10 minutes, stirring several times.
3. Stir about 3 tablespoons of the sauce into egg yolk and return to double-boiler mixture. Blend well and cook over simmering water 3 to 5 minutes; stir occasionally.
4. Remove from heat and stir in the remaining ingredients, blending thoroughly. ABOUT 2 CUPS

RUM SAUCE

⅓ cup sugar	1 egg, slightly beaten
2 tablespoons cornstarch	2 to 3 tablespoons rum
¼ cup cold milk	1 cup heavy cream, whipped
¾ cup milk, scalded	

1. Combine sugar and cornstarch in a saucepan. Mix in the cold milk. Gradually add the scalded milk, stirring to blend.
2. Bring to boiling, stirring constantly; stir and cook 5 minutes over low heat.
3. Stir about 3 tablespoons of the hot mixture into beaten egg. Immediately blend into mixture in saucepan. Cook 3 to 5 minutes, stirring constantly.
4. Remove from heat, cover and cool to lukewarm. Blend in the rum. Chill.
5. Shortly before serving, gently fold the whipped cream into chilled sauce. Serve cold. ABOUT 3 CUPS

CINNAMON-PLUM SAUCE

1 jar (29 oz.) purple plums, drained and pitted	⅛ teaspoon ground cinnamon
2 tablespoons sugar	¼ teaspoon grated lemon peel

Force plums through a sieve or food mill. Blend in a mixture of the remaining ingredients. Chill thoroughly. Serve over *ice cream.* 1⅓ CUPS

ROCKY ROAD SAUCE

½ cup butter or margarine	½ cup chocolate sauce
1 cup confectioners' sugar	3 egg whites
3 egg yolks, beaten until thick	1 cup pecans, coarsely chopped
	8 oz. marshmallows, cut in small pieces

1. Cream butter; gradually add confectioners' sugar, beating well. Add beaten egg yolks in thirds; beating thoroughly after each addition. Blend in chocolate sauce.
2. Beat egg whites until stiff, not dry, peaks are formed. Gently fold into the chocolate mixture. Fold in the pecans and marshmallows. Chill.
3. Serve over slices of *angel food cake.*
ABOUT 4½ CUPS

The unknown person who originated the first cookies probably was unaware of the importance of her (or his) creation. Throughout the years this food item has had special appeal to people all around the world. It continues to be the perfect treat not only for children, but for the child in all of us that never grows up. On these pages are treasured recipes for all types of cookies, including the everyday variety appropriate for filling the cookie jar and the special-occasion type used for entertaining and for gifts.

The perfect cookie should have good flavor, tender crumb unless the variety is a hard cookie, soft or crisp texture depending upon variety of cookie, uniform color, and uniform shape depending upon the type of cookie.

TYPES

Cookies are considered in many ways—by the texture of the baked cookie (soft or crisp), the consistency of the batter or dough (soft or stiff), the richness of cookie (plain or rich). They are classified by the method of shaping the cookie.

Bar—Dough is baked in a rectangular or square baking pan, often in layers, and cut into bars or squares after baking.

Drop—Batter or dough is dropped from a spoon onto a cookie sheet.

Molded—Dough is shaped by hand.

Pressed—Dough is soft enough to go through a cookie press or a pastry bag and tube.

Refrigerator (*icebox*)—Dough is pressed into a cookie mold or shaped into a thick roll or bar, then wrapped in moisture-vaporproof material and stored in the refrigerator until thoroughly chilled. When ready to use, the dough is thinly sliced, placed on cookie sheets, and baked.

Rolled—Dough is rolled to desired thickness on a lightly floured surface and cut into various shapes with a cookie cutter, pastry wheel, or knife for bak-

ing as well as for deep frying (see recipes, *pages 595* and *596*).

Packaged mixes and refrigerated and frozen doughs are also available for made-in-a-hurry cookies of many types.

INGREDIENTS

Each ingredient has its own role to play in the cookie batter or dough.

Fat increases tenderness, gives flavor, and aids in browning.

Sugar contributes sweetness and flavor. As sugar is increased in proportion to flour it tends to increase browning and crisping. Liquid forms of sweetening (honey, sugar syrup, maple syrup, and molasses) may supply liquid.

Eggs may or may not be used; they increase fineness of texture, add flavor and color, act to bind the ingredients together, and sometimes leaven the batter or dough, especially beaten egg whites. Too large a proportion of eggs can make the texture tough; when large number of eggs is used, amount of fat should be increased to counteract the toughening effect of eggs.

Flour—generally all-purpose—is the major ingredient in all batter and dough products; when combined with moisture flour gives structure to baked products.

Leavening agents may or may not be needed. Often both baking powder and baking soda are used together. *Air* may be the only leaven when beaten into egg whites, as in ladyfingers and meringue-type cookies. *Baking powder* may be the sole leavening agent. *Baking soda* is used to neutralize acid foods such as molasses, buttermilk, sour cream, fruit juices, and dried fruits. When baking soda is not used to neutralize the acid ingredient in cookies, it nevertheless tends to tenderize the cookies. Some cookies with no baking soda or an insufficient amount tend to have light-colored centers and browned edges.

Other ingredients include various flavoring extracts, spices, nuts, fruits in several forms, citrus peels, cereals, chocolate, cocoa, candies, mincemeat, and coconut, used alone or in suitable combinations for the various cookies. Wheat germ, when added, increases food value and imparts a pleasing nutlike flavor and crispness. Avoid chunky pieces in the cookie dough when using a cookie press.

TECHNIQUES FOR MAKING COOKIES

(Read also *Use Correct Techniques, page 10.*)
To measure dry ingredients, liquids, and shortening, see *page 10.*
To beat eggs, see *page 10.*
To cream shortening with sugar, see *page 14.*
To prepare cookie sheets or baking pans—grease lightly if so directed in recipe. (Avoid dull pans darkened in color from long usage, also pans with sides except when making bar cookies. If pans with sides are used for roll or drop cookies, turn upside-down and bake cookies on the bottom.) As a general rule, cookies containing considerable shortening are baked on ungreased sheets. When recipe calls for a cookie press, the dough is usually quite rich in fat and cookie sheets are not greased. When pans are greased, follow directions in each recipe—greasing lightly or generously as indicated. For bar cookies the bottom of the pan is usually greased and, if desired, it may be lined with waxed paper and the paper lightly greased. Macaroon- and meringue-type cookies are baked on unglazed paper or baking parchment.
To roll out dough (especially dough which is rich in shortening), use a lightly floured pastry canvas and stockinet-covered rolling pin. If dough tends to stick to canvas, try chilling dough thoroughly before rolling. If it still proves difficult, dust the canvas with a mixture of 1 part granulated sugar and 2 parts all-purpose flour.

To bake cookies, place them in a preheated oven. Do not let cookie sheets or pans touch sides or back of oven to allow proper air circulation. Avoid peeking. Frequent opening of oven door prevents browning of cookies. It is advisable to accurately check the first batch and peeking will be unnecessary for subsequent batches.
To test cookies for doneness—Thin crisp cookies are done when they are delicately and evenly browned. Drop cookies (thick and soft varieties) are done when almost no imprint remains when lightly touched with fingertips. Bar cookies sometimes test done when a wooden pick or cake tester inserted in center comes out clean. This test may not be used, however, for cookies such as brownies which are especially rich with chocolate and shortening. Follow timing directions in recipe for such cookies.
To remove cookies from cookie sheets or pans, use a metal spatula. Unless otherwise directed in recipe, remove cookies immediately to wire racks to cool. Cool cookie sheets and pans after removing baked cookies from them. A hot pan melts fat in the cookie dough and will spoil the shape of the next batch.
To store cookies, cool thoroughly before placing in cookie jar, canister, or casserole having a cover. Do not store crisp cookies with other types. If they have softened during storage, place them in a 300°F oven for a few minutes to restore crispness.
To soften cookies, store for several days with a piece of apple or orange.
To pack cookies for mailing, wrap (separately if possible) in moisture-vaporproof material in sturdy container lined with extra wrapping material. Use crumbled waxed paper, popcorn, or shredded packing material to fill extra space.

FLAVORED SUGARS

Vanilla Confectioners' Sugar: Cut a *vanilla bean* lengthwise, then crosswise, into pieces. Poke pieces into *1 to 2 pounds confectioners' sugar* at irregular intervals. Cover tightly and store. (The longer sugar stands, the richer the flavor.) When necessary, add more sugar. Replace vanilla bean when aroma is gone. Flavor *granulated sugar* this way, also.

Spiced Confectioners' Sugar: Blend ½ *cup confectioners' sugar* and *1 tablespoon ground mace* or *ground nutmeg.*

Cinnamon Sugar: Blend ¾ *cup sugar* and ¼ *cup ground cinnamon.*

BAR COOKIES

ALMOND AWARDS

Rich, crunchy, with melt-in-your-mouth goodness, call it cookie or candy it deserves an award, no matter what the classification.

1 cup butter	½ teaspoon salt
2 teaspoons grated lemon peel	1 cup almonds, finely chopped
1 cup sugar	½ cup heavy cream
1 cup sifted all-purpose flour	

1. Cream ½ cup of the butter with the lemon peel and ½ cup of the sugar. Blend flour and salt; add in halves, mixing until blended after each addition.
2. Turn into an 11x7x1½-inch baking pan and spread into an even layer.
3. Bake at 375°F 12 minutes.
4. Meanwhile, melt remaining ½ cup butter in a heavy saucepan; add almonds and remaining ½ cup sugar. Cook the mixture 3 minutes, stirring constantly.
5. Stir in cream and heat to boiling; cool slightly. Spoon topping over partially baked layer.
6. Return to oven and bake 20 minutes, or until light golden.
7. Cool completely; cut into squares or bars.

ABOUT 5 DOZEN COOKIES

DUTCH ALMOND COOKIES

2 cups sifted all-purpose flour	¼ teaspoon ground cinnamon
1 teaspoon baking powder	1 cup butter
¼ teaspoon salt	½ cup milk
1 cup firmly packed dark brown sugar	½ lb. blanched almonds, ground
½ teaspoon ground nutmeg	1 cup sugar
	1 tablespoon grated lemon peel
	1 egg, slightly beaten

1. Blend flour, baking powder, salt, brown sugar, nutmeg, and cinnamon; cut in butter until particles are the size of rice kernels. Add milk and stir until blended.
2. Spoon half of mixture into an ungreased 11x7x1½-inch baking pan and spread evenly; set aside.
3. Mix remaining ingredients well. Turn mixture

onto waxed paper and shape into an even layer the size of the pan. Invert over layer in pan and peel off paper. Spoon remaining mixture over almond layer and spread evenly.
4. Bake at 350°F 45 minutes.
5. Cut into bars while warm; cool completely before removing from pan. ABOUT 2 DOZEN COOKIES

BELGIAN CHRISTMAS COOKIES

⅔ cup butter	1½ teaspoons baking powder
1 teaspoon almond extract	½ teaspoon salt
1 cup firmly packed dark brown sugar	½ cup finely chopped unblanched almonds
2 eggs	½ teaspoon ground cinnamon
1⅔ cups sifted all purpose flour	2 teaspoons red sugar
	2 teaspoons green sugar

1. Cream butter with extract; add brown sugar gradually, creaming until fluffy. Add eggs, one at a time, beating thoroughly after each addition.
2. Sift flour, baking powder, and salt together; add in thirds to creamed mixture, mixing until blended after each addition. Turn into a greased 15x10x1-inch jelly roll pan and spread evenly to edges.
3. Sprinkle a mixture of almonds and cinnamon over batter, then sprinkle with a mixture of red and green sugars.
4. Bake at 375°F 10 to 12 minutes.
5. Cut into bars while still warm.

ABOUT 5 DOZEN COOKIES

ARISTOCRATS

A distinctive pecan topping is the praise-winning feature of these apricot cookies of French origin.

¾ cup butter	1 egg
1 teaspoon vanilla extract	2 cups sifted cake flour
⅔ cup sugar	⅔ cup apricot preserves
	Pecan Topping

1. Cream butter with extract; add sugar gradually, creaming until fluffy. Add egg and beat thoroughly.
2. Add flour in fourths, mixing until blended after each addition.

3. Turn dough into a lightly greased 11x7x1½-inch baking pan and spread evenly. Spread the apricot preserves over dough.

4. Bake at 350°F 20 to 25 minutes, or until edges are lightly browned. Remove pan to wire rack (do not remove cookie layer from pan).

5. Prepare Pecan Topping and spread evenly over cooled cookie layer. Chill 2 to 3 hours.

6. Cut into strips, about 2½x¾-inch. Place strips about ½ inch apart on cookie sheets.

7. Bake at 375°F 15 minutes, or until topping is delicately browned.   ABOUT 4 DOZEN COOKIES

PECAN TOPPING: Beat *1 egg white* with *⅛ teaspoon salt* until frothy. Add *⅔ cup sugar* and *2 teaspoons flour* gradually, beating thoroughly after each addition. Beat until stiff peaks are formed. Fold in *⅔ cup pecans*, finely chopped.

APRICOT SOURS

This cookie makes a delicious dessert when cut into large squares and topped with sweetened whipped cream.

⅔ cup butter, chilled	¼ teaspoon vanilla
1½ cups sifted	extract
all-purpose flour	½ cup finely snipped
1 egg	apricots, cooked*
½ cup firmly packed	½ cup pecans, chopped
light brown sugar	Lemon Glaze, *below*

1. Cut butter into flour until particles are the size of rice kernels. Press mixture evenly and firmly into a 13x9x2-inch baking pan.

2. Bake at 350°F 15 minutes.

3. Meanwhile, beat egg, brown sugar, and extract until thick; stir in a mixture of apricots and pecans.

4. Spread evenly over partially baked layer in pan.

5. Return to oven and bake about 20 minutes, or until lightly browned.

6. Remove from oven and immediately spread Lemon Glaze over top. When cool, cut into bars.   ABOUT 4 DOZEN COOKIES

*Put snipped apricots into a heavy saucepan with a small amount of water (3 to 4 tablespoons). Cover tightly and cook over low heat about 10 minutes, or until apricots are soft and liquid is absorbed. Cool.

NOTE: If packaged dried apricots are extremely soft, it may not be necessary to cook the apricots.

LEMON GLAZE: Blend ¾ *cup confectioners' sugar* with *2 tablespoons lemon juice.*

DREAM BARS DE LUXE

1 cup sifted all-purpose flour	1½ cups firmly packed light brown sugar
3 tablespoons confectioners' sugar	2 tablespoons flour
½ cup butter or margarine, softened	¼ teaspoon baking powder
2 eggs	⅛ teaspoon salt
1½ teaspoons vanilla extract	¾ cup walnuts, chopped
	½ cup flaked coconut

1. Blend 1 cup flour, confectioners' sugar, and butter. Press evenly into an 11x7x1½-inch baking pan.

2. Bake at 350°F 20 minutes; remove pan to wire rack.

3. Meanwhile, beat eggs with extract and brown sugar until thick.

4. Blend in a mixture of 2 tablespoons flour, baking powder, and salt; mix in ½ cup of the walnuts and ¼ cup coconut.

5. Spread evenly over partially baked layer in pan and sprinkle with a mixture of remaining nuts and coconut.

6. Return to oven and bake 25 minutes.

7. Cool completely; cut into bars.

ABOUT 3 DOZEN COOKIES

CHEWY BUTTERSCOTCH BARS

Topping, *page 561*	½ cup corn oil
1⅓ cups sifted cake flour	2 teaspoons vanilla
2 teaspoons baking powder	extract
1 teaspoon salt	2 eggs
2 cups firmly packed brown sugar	1 cup coarsely chopped pecans
	1 cup flaked coconut

1. Prepare Topping; set over simmering water.

2. Sift flour, baking powder, and salt together; set aside.

3. Beat brown sugar, corn oil, and extract; add eggs, one at a time, beating thoroughly after each addition.

4. Stir in flour mixture until blended. Mix in pecans and coconut.

5. Turn into a well-greased 15x10x1-inch jelly roll pan and spread into corners. Drizzle hot topping over entire surface.

6. Bake at 350°F 30 minutes.

7. Cool 30 minutes in pan, cut into bars, and remove from pan.   ABOUT 2½ DOZEN COOKIES

TOPPING: Blend *¾ cup firmly packed brown sugar, 2 tablespoons butter, 3 tablespoons cream or evaporated milk,* and *¼ cup dark corn syrup* in a saucepan. Cook over medium heat, stirring occasionally, to 234°F (soft-ball stage, *page 430*). Remove from heat; blend in *1 teaspoon vanilla extract.*

ABOUT ⅔ CUP

FUDGY BROWNIES

Fudge Sauce, *below*	¾ cup sifted all-purpose
½ cup butter	flour
1½ oz. (1½ sq.)	½ teaspoon baking
unsweetened chocolate	powder
2 eggs	⅛ teaspoon salt
1 cup sugar	¾ cup pecans, coarsely
	chopped

1. Prepare Fudge Sauce; set aside.
2. Melt butter and chocolate together; set aside to cool.
3. Beat eggs and sugar until thick and piled softly; add cooled chocolate mixture and beat until blended.
4. Sift together flour, baking powder, and salt; add in halves to chocolate mixture, mixing until blended after each addition.
5. Turn half of batter into a greased 9x9x2-inch baking pan and spread evenly.
6. Pour half of Fudge Sauce evenly over batter; remove remaining sauce from heat but allow to stand over hot water.
7. Spread remaining batter evenly over sauce.
8. Bake at 350°F 35 to 40 minutes.
9. Set on wire rack 5 minutes; top with remaining sauce; sprinkle with pecans.
10. Broil 4 inches from source of heat 1 to 2 minutes, or until entire top is bubbly; do not allow sauce to burn. Cool completely before cutting into squares.

3 DOZEN COOKIES

FUDGE SAUCE

⅓ cup undiluted	1½ teaspoons butter
evaporated milk	¼ teaspoon vanilla
⅓ cup sugar	extract
4 teaspoons water	⅛ teaspoon salt
½ oz. (½ sq.) unsweet-	
ened chocolate, grated	

1. Combine evaporated milk, sugar, and water in the top of a double boiler; stirring constantly, bring to boiling. Boil 3 minutes.

2. Remove from heat; blend in remaining ingredients.
3. Set over simmering water until needed.

ABOUT ½ CUP SAUCE

DOUBLE CHOCOLATE SQUARES: Follow recipe for Fudgy Brownies. Omit Fudge Sauce. Increase chocolate to 2 ounces (2 squares). After final addition of ingredients stir in pecans. Omit broiling; cool completely. If desired, spread with *Chocolate Glaze II, page 440*, decreasing butter to 1 tablespoon; arrange pecan halves on top. Leave in pan until glaze has become firm.

LUXURY MALLOW-NUT BROWNIES: Follow recipe for Double Chocolate Squares. Omit Chocolate Glaze and pecan halves. Melt *12 ounces semisweet chocolate pieces* and *2 tablespoons butter.* Cut *12 marshmallows* into quarters (or use 1⅓ cups miniature marshmallows) and stir into melted chocolate with *½ cup coarsely chopped salted nuts,* such as pecans, pistachios, filberts, or almonds. Immediately spread over the baked brownies; cool.

LAYERED CHOCOLATE CONFECTIONS

Chocolate Layer:	½ cup chopped salted
½ cup butter or	pecans
margarine	Cream Layer:
2 oz. (2 sq.) unsweet-	½ cup heavy cream
ened chocolate	⅓ cup butter or
2 eggs	margarine
1 cup sugar	1½ cups sugar
1 teaspoon vanilla	2 tablespoons brandy
extract	2 oz. (2 sq.) unsweet-
½ cup sifted all-purpose	ened chocolate,
flour	melted and cooled
	slightly

1. Chocolate Layer: Melt the butter and chocolate together; set aside to cool.
2. Beat eggs, sugar, and extract until thick and piled softly. Add cooled chocolate mixture and beat until blended. Stir in flour, then pecans. Turn into a greased 11x7x1½-inch baking pan and spread evenly.
3. Bake at 350°F about 25 minutes.
4. Cool in pan on wire rack.
5. Cream Layer: Combine cream, butter, and sugar in a heavy saucepan. Cook, stirring occasionally, over low heat until mixture reaches 236°F (soft-ball stage, *page 430*). Remove from heat; cool, undisturbed, to 110°F or just cool enough to hold pan

on palm of hand. Turn into small bowl, add brandy, and beat until mixture is smooth and creamy. Spread on cooled chocolate layer. Chill slightly until top is firm to the touch. Spread melted chocolate over creamy layer. Chill thoroughly.

6. Cut into 1-inch squares. Place in bonbon cups to serve or pack in a gift box.

ABOUT 6 DOZEN CONFECTIONS

NOTE: A drop or two of *food coloring* may be blended with cream mixture to harmonize with various party color schemes.

SOUTHERN BROWNIES

Mrs. Andy Griffith, wife of the well known TV star, contributed this recipe.

3 tablespoons shortening	1 teaspoon vanilla extract
2 oz. (2 sq.) unsweetened chocolate	1 cup sugar
2 egg yolks, well beaten	½ cup all-purpose flour
	½ cup chopped nuts
	2 egg whites

1. Melt shortening and chocolate together in a large saucepan; cool.
2. Stir in egg yolks, then extract, sugar, flour, and nuts.
3. Beat egg whites until stiff, not dry, peaks are formed. Blend into chocolate mixture.
4. Spread batter in a well-greased 8x8x2-inch pan.
5. Bake at 350°F 30 minutes, or until a wooden pick comes out clean.
6. Cool completely before cutting.

ABOUT 2 DOZEN COOKIES

DINAH SHORE BROWNIES

When the fragrance of chocolate wafts from the kitchen of Dinah Shore, charming singing star and television personality, her family knows it's time for a batch of her famous brownies.

¾ cup butter or margarine	1½ teaspoons vanilla extract
4 oz. (4 sq.) unsweetened chocolate	¾ cup sifted all-purpose flour
3 eggs	½ cup coarsely chopped pecans
1½ cups sugar	

1. Melt butter and chocolate together; cool.
2. Beat eggs, sugar, and extract until thick and piled softly. Add cooled chocolate mixture and beat until blended.

3. Mix in flour, then pecans. Turn into a greased 8x8x2-inch baking pan and spread evenly.
4. Bake at 350°F about 35 minutes.
5. Cut into squares.

ABOUT 2 DOZEN COOKIES

COCOA ALMOND BARS SUPREME

⅔ cup sifted all-purpose flour	½ teaspoon almond extract
⅓ cup Dutch process cocoa	¾ cup sugar
½ teaspoon baking powder	1 egg
¼ teaspoon salt	1 egg yolk
½ cup butter	1 cup toasted blanched almonds, coarsely chopped
¼ cup almond paste	1 egg white
1½ teaspoons vanilla extract	¼ teaspoon cream of tartar
	¼ cup sugar

1. Blend flour, cocoa, baking powder, and salt; set aside.
2. Cream butter with almond paste and extracts until thoroughly blended. Add ¾ cup sugar gradually, beating until fluffy. Add egg and egg yolk; beat vigorously.
3. Mixing until blended after each addition, add dry mixture in thirds, then ½ cup of the almonds. Turn into a lightly greased 8x8x2-inch baking pan.
4. Beat egg white and cream of tartar until frothy. Add ¼ cup sugar gradually, continuing to beat until stiff peaks are formed. Fold in remaining almonds. Spread over batter in pan.
5. Bake at 350°F 35 to 40 minutes, or until meringue is lightly browned.
6. When thoroughly cooled cut into 2x1-inch bars.

2½ DOZEN COOKIES

MANSION SQUARES

½ cup butter	½ teaspoon baking powder
1 teaspoon vanilla extract	⅛ teaspoon baking soda
¾ cup firmly packed brown sugar	⅛ teaspoon salt
1 egg	6 oz. semisweet chocolate pieces
1 cup sifted all-purpose flour	

1. Cream butter with extract; add brown sugar gradually, beating until fluffy. Add egg; beat well.

2. Sift flour, baking powder, baking soda, and salt together; add in thirds to creamed mixture, mixing until blended after each addition. Turn into greased 11x7x1½-inch baking pan. Top with chocolate pieces.
3. Bake at 350°F about 30 minutes.
4. While warm, cut into squares.

ABOUT 2 DOZEN COOKIES

NUT MANSION SQUARES: Follow recipe for Mansion Squares. Substitute *1 cup coarsely chopped filberts* for semisweet chocolate pieces.

CHOCOLATE-NUT MANSION SQUARES: Follow recipe for Mansion Squares. Top with chocolate pieces immediately after removing from oven rather than before baking. When chocolate is softened, spread evenly over surface. Sprinkle with *1 cup filberts*, coarsely chopped.

SURPRISE BARS

A crunchy, nutty-rich top layer disguises a delectable bottom layer . . . the surprise element of this cookie bar.

1 oz. (1 sq.) unsweetened chocolate	½ cup sugar
½ cup graham cracker crumbs	1 egg
2 tablespoons butter, melted	¾ cup sifted all-purpose flour
½ cup butter or margarine	⅛ teaspoon baking soda
½ teaspoon vanilla extract	⅛ teaspoon salt
	¼ cup dairy sour cream
	¾ cup walnuts, coarsely chopped

1. Melt chocolate and set aside to cool.
2. Blend crumbs and melted butter; set aside.
3. Cream the ½ cup butter with the extract; add sugar gradually, beating until fluffy. Add egg and beat thoroughly.
4. Sift flour, baking soda, and salt together; add alternately to creamed mixture with sour cream, mixing until blended after each addition.
5. Divide mixture in half; blend cooled chocolate into one portion.
6. Turn chocolate mixture into a greased 8x8x2-inch baking pan and spread evenly. Cover with the crumbs and press lightly.
7. Stir walnuts into remaining portion; drop by spoonfuls over crumbs and carefully spread evenly.
8. Bake at 375° 25 to 30 minutes.
9. While warm, cut into bars. 2½ DOZEN COOKIES

GRAHAM SENSATIONS

1¼ cups graham cracker crumbs	½ teaspoon grated lemon peel
¼ cup sifted all-purpose flour	½ cup flaked coconut
¼ teaspoon salt	¾ cup coarsely chopped pecans
1 can (14 oz.) sweetened condensed milk	½ cup semisweet chocolate pieces
¾ teaspoon vanilla extract	

1. Blend crumbs, flour, and salt. Add condensed milk, extract, and lemon peel; mix well. Stir in remaining ingredients. Turn into a greased 13x9x2-inch baking pan and spread evenly.
2. Bake at 325°F 30 minutes.
3. While warm, cut into bars.

ABOUT 4 DOZEN COOKIES

CROWN JEWELS

Toppings, *below* and *page 564*	½ cup sugar
1 cup butter or margarine	2 hard-cooked egg yolks, sieved
½ teaspoon grated orange peel	2 cups sifted all-purpose flour

1. Prepare Toppings.
2. Cream butter with orange peel. Gradually add sugar, beating until fluffy.
3. Blend in sieved hard-cooked egg yolks. Add flour in fourths, mixing well after each addition.
4. Press dough firmly onto bottom of ungreased 15x10x1-inch jelly roll pan.
5. Bake at 350°F 20 minutes.
6. While still warm, spread with Date Topping and then Candied Fruit Topping. Cool thoroughly and cut into fancy shapes. ABOUT 3 DOZEN COOKIES

CANDIED FRUIT TOPPING

½ lb. red and green candied pineapple, finely chopped (1⅔ cups)	2 oz. candied orange peel, finely chopped (⅓ cup)
¼ lb. candied red cherries, finely chopped (⅔ cup)	⅓ cup rum

Mix candied fruit with rum in the top of a double boiler. Heat, covered, over simmering water 30 minutes, stirring occasionally; cool slightly.

DATE TOPPING: Mix *1 cup (about 7 ounces) pitted dates*, finely chopped, with *¼ cup orange juice* in the top of a double boiler. Heat, covered, over simmering water 10 minutes, stirring occasionally; cool.

DATE PERFECTIONS

¾ cup sifted all-purpose flour	¾ cup sugar
¾ teaspoon baking powder	1½ cups dates, finely chopped
¼ teaspoon salt	1 cup pecans, finely chopped
2 eggs	Lemon Glaze, *page 560*

1. Sift flour, baking powder, and salt together; set aside.
2. Beat eggs and sugar together until mixture is thick and piled softly.
3. Fold in dry ingredients, dates, and pecans until blended. Turn into a greased 11x7x1½-inch baking pan and spread evenly into corners.
4. Bake at 325°F 30 to 35 minutes.
5. Immediately brush surface with Lemon Glaze. While warm, cut into squares.

ABOUT 2 DOZEN COOKIES

NOTE: Dried figs or apricots may be used instead of dates.

FRUITY POLISH MAZUREK

Delightful small colorful cookie squares—fruity, nutty, and chock-full of wonderful citrus flavor.

2 cups sifted all-purpose flour	1½ cups pitted dates, chopped
1 cup sugar	1¼ cups dried figs, chopped
½ teaspoon salt	1 cup chopped walnuts
½ cup butter or margarine	⅓ cup sugar
1 egg	2 eggs
¼ cup cream	½ cup orange juice
1⅔ cups seedless raisins, chopped	3 tablespoons lemon juice

1. Sift flour, 1 cup sugar, and salt together into a bowl. Cut in butter.
2. Beat egg and cream together and add to flour mixture. Mix lightly with a fork until mixture forms a ball.
3. Spread dough in a greased 15x10x1-inch jelly roll pan.

4. Bake at 350°F about 30 minutes, or until dough is lightly browned around edges.
5. Meanwhile, prepare fruit topping by combining the chopped fruits and walnuts with a mixture of the ⅓ cup sugar, 2 eggs, and fruit juices; mix thoroughly. Spread over partially baked dough in pan.
6. Return to oven and bake 20 minutes.
7. Remove to wire rack; cool. If desired, garnish with *candied fruit* such as candied cherries, candied pineapple, and/or candied orange peel. Cut in 2x1-inch pieces.

ABOUT 6 DOZEN COOKIES

HONEY CAKES
(Lebkuchen)

The glaze on this German cookie specialty adds lustre and complements the rich spicy flavor.

3 cups sifted all-purpose flour	2 eggs
¼ teaspoon baking soda	1 cup sugar
1 teaspoon ground cinnamon	½ cup honey
½ teaspoon ground allspice	¾ cup unblanched almonds, finely chopped
½ teaspoon ground cloves	2 oz. candied orange peel, finely chopped
½ teaspoon ground nutmeg	2 oz. candied lemon peel, finely chopped
	Glaze, *below*

1. Sift flour, baking soda, and spices together; set aside.
2. Beat eggs with sugar until very thick. Add honey gradually, beating well.
3. Add dry ingredients in fourths, folding until blended after each addition. Mix in almonds and candied peels. Turn into a greased 15x10x1-inch jelly roll pan and spread evenly.
4. Bake at 350°F 25 to 30 minutes.
5. Remove pan to wire rack and cool slightly. Spread Glaze evenly over warm surface. Cut into bars.

ABOUT 3 DOZEN COOKIES

GLAZE: Blend thoroughly *⅓ cup confectioners' sugar, 1 tablespoon water*, and *1 teaspoon lemon juice*.

NOTE: More traditionally Lebkuchen is a rolled cookie which is cut into bars before baking.

LUSCIOUS LEMON BARS

1 cup sifted all-purpose flour	2 tablespoons flour
¼ cup confectioners' sugar	½ teaspoon baking powder
½ cup butter, chilled	3 eggs, well beaten
1 cup sugar	½ cup unstrained lemon juice

1.   Blend the 1 cup flour and confectioners' sugar in a bowl. Cut in the butter until blended. Firmly and evenly press into an ungreased 9x9x2-inch baking pan.
2.   Bake at 350°F about 15 minutes.
3.   Meanwhile, combine sugar, 2 tablespoons flour, and baking powder; blend into beaten eggs along with the lemon juice.
4.   Pour mixture over crust in pan. Return to oven and bake 25 minutes.
5.   Remove to wire rack to cool. Spread with a thin *confectioners' sugar icing* and top with *toasted sliced almonds*. Cut into bars.

ABOUT 3 DOZEN COOKIES

LEMON-COCONUT SOURS

⅓ cup butter, chilled	1 cup firmly packed light brown sugar
¾ cup sifted all-purpose flour	¾ cup flaked coconut
2 eggs	½ cup pecans, coarsely chopped
1 teaspoon grated lemon peel	Lemon Glaze, *page 560*
½ teaspoon vanilla extract	

1.   Cut butter into flour until thoroughly blended. Press evenly and firmly into an ungreased 13x9x2-inch baking pan.
2.   Bake at 350°F 10 minutes.
3.   Meanwhile, beat eggs, lemon peel, extract, and brown sugar until thick. Stir in coconut and pecans. Spread evenly over partially baked layer in pan.
4.   Return to oven and bake about 20 minutes.
5.   Immediately spread Lemon Glaze evenly over top. When cool, cut into bars or squares.

ABOUT 4 DOZEN COOKIES

PINEAPPLE BARS: Follow recipe for Lemon Coconut Sours. Substitute *unblanched almonds*, toasted and chopped, for pecans. Omit lemon peel and Lemon Glaze. Fold in ⅓ *cup drained crushed pineapple* with coconut and almonds. Bake about 25 minutes.

PEANUT BUTTER DREAMS

¼ cup butter	1 cup firmly packed light brown sugar
½ cup peanut butter	⅓ cup sifted all-purpose flour
½ cup firmly packed light brown sugar	½ teaspoon baking powder
1 cup sifted all-purpose flour	¾ cup flaked coconut
2 eggs	6 oz. semisweet chocolate pieces
1 teaspoon vanilla extract	

1.   Cream butter with peanut butter thoroughly; add ½ cup brown sugar gradually, beating until fluffy.
2.   Add 1 cup flour in halves, mixing until blended after each addition. Press evenly into greased 9x9x2-inch baking pan.
3.   Bake at 350°F 10 to 15 minutes, or until lightly browned.
4.   Meanwhile, beat eggs, extract, and 1 cup brown sugar until thick. Add a mixture of ⅓ cup flour and the baking powder; beat until blended.
5.   Stir in coconut and chocolate pieces. Spread evenly over partially baked layer in pan.
6.   Return to oven and bake 30 minutes.
7.   Cool completely and cut into squares or bars.

ABOUT 2 DOZEN COOKIES

PEANUT BLONDE BROWNIES

½ cup chunk-style peanut butter	2 eggs
¼ cup butter or margarine	½ cup sifted all-purpose flour
1 teaspoon vanilla extract	1 cup chopped salted peanuts
1 cup firmly packed light brown sugar	Confectioners' sugar

1.   Cream peanut butter with butter and extract. Gradually add brown sugar, beating well. Add eggs, one at a time, beating until fluffy after each addition.
2.   Add flour in halves, mixing until blended after each addition. Stir in peanuts. Turn into a greased 8x8x2-inch baking pan and spread evenly.
3.   Bake at 350°F 30 to 35 minutes.
4.   Remove pan to wire rack to cool 5 minutes before cutting into 2-inch squares. Remove from pan and cool on rack. Sift confectioners' sugar over tops.

16 BROWNIES

GOLDEN NUT BARS

1 cup finely crushed round scalloped crackers	1 cup sugar
½ cup pecans, finely chopped	1 teaspoon baking powder
	3 egg whites
	¼ teaspoon salt

1. Blend crumbs, pecans, sugar, and baking powder.
2. Beat egg whites and salt until stiff, not dry, peaks are formed; fold in the crumb mixture, a small amount at a time.
3. Turn into an ungreased 11x7x1½-inch baking pan and spread evenly.
4. Bake at 350°F 25 minutes.
5. Cool completely before cutting into bars.

ABOUT 3 DOZEN COOKIES

CINNAMON PECAN BARS

½ cup butter	1¼ teaspoons ground cinnamon
1 cup sugar	
1 egg	¼ teaspoon salt
½ cup all-purpose flour	1 cup pecans, finely chopped

1. Cream butter; add sugar gradually, creaming thoroughly. Add egg and beat until fluffy.
2. Sift flour, cinnamon, and salt together. Add to creamed mixture and mix until blended. Stir in pecans. Turn into a greased 8x8x2-inch baking pan and spread evenly.
3. Bake at 350°F 40 minutes.
4. Cut into small bars while still warm; coat with *confectioners' sugar*.   ABOUT 2½ DOZEN COOKIES

ENGLISH TOFFEE BARS

1 cup butter	1 egg white, slightly beaten
1 cup sugar	
1 egg yolk	1 cup chopped pecans
2 cups sifted all-purpose flour	2 oz. (2 sq.) semisweet chocolate, melted
1 teaspoon ground cinnamon	

1. Cream butter; add sugar gradually, beating until fluffy. Beat in egg yolk.
2. Sift the flour and cinnamon together; gradually add to creamed mixture, beating until blended.
3. Turn into a greased 15x10x1-inch jelly roll pan and press evenly. Brush top with egg white. Sprinkle with pecans and press lightly into dough.
4. Bake at 275°F 1 hour.
5. While still hot, cut into 1½-inch squares. Drizzle with melted chocolate. Cool on wire rack.

5 TO 6 DOZEN COOKIES

DROP COOKIES

CRISP SUGAR COOKIES

2½ cups sifted all-purpose flour	1 cup butter
2 teaspoons cream of tartar	1 teaspoon vanilla extract
1 teaspoon baking soda	1 cup sugar
½ teaspoon salt	2 eggs

1. Sift flour, cream of tartar, baking soda, and salt together; set aside.
2. Cream butter with extract; add sugar gradually, beating until fluffy. Add eggs, one at a time, beating thoroughly after each addition.
3. Add dry ingredients in fourths, mixing until blended after each addition.
4. Chill dough in refrigerator 1 hour.
5. Shape small balls by dropping small amounts of dough from a teaspoon 2 inches apart onto lightly greased cookie sheets. For glaze (this glaze is very important) dip bottom of a glass in *water*; then dip in *sugar*. Flatten each ball with sugar-coated glass.
6. Bake at 375°F 10 minutes.

ABOUT 2 DOZEN COOKIES

IMPERIALS
A dream-of-a-cookie to please a sovereign's palate.

¾ cup unsalted butter	1 cup sifted all-purpose flour
¾ cup sugar	
4 egg yolks (about 5 tablespoons), well beaten	

1. Cream butter; add sugar gradually, beating until fluffy. Add egg yolks in thirds, beating thoroughly after each addition.
2. Add flour in halves, mixing until blended after

each addition. Chill thoroughly, about 2 hours.

3. Using 1½ teaspoons of dough for each cookie, drop dough about 2 inches apart onto ungreased cookie sheets; flatten with a glass dipped in *sugar*.

4. Bake at 350°F about 8 minutes.

5. If desired, dip cooled cookies into *Chocolate Glaze I, page 440*; place cookies on wire racks until glaze is set.   ABOUT 5 DOZEN COOKIES

COOKIE CIGARETTES

For these interesting delicacies (of French derivation), both cookies and filling may be prepared ahead and the cookies filled shortly before serving.

¼ cup egg whites	¾ teaspoon vanilla
½ cup confectioners'	extract
sugar	Rich Chocolate Filling,
⅓ cup sifted flour	*below*
3 tablespoons butter,	
melted and cooled	

1. Beat egg whites until frothy; add confectioners' sugar gradually, beating thoroughly after each addition; beat until stiff peaks are formed.

2. Fold in flour in halves. Blend in cooled butter and extract.

3. Quickly grease a preheated cookie sheet.*

4. Drop mixture by heaping teaspoonfuls 4 inches apart onto hot cookie sheet; spread very thinly without making holes; bake only a few cookies at one time (they are difficult to roll when cool).

5. Bake at 400°F 2 to 3 minutes, or until edges are lightly browned.

6. Immediately remove from cookie sheet. Quickly roll each cookie around a pencil-thin wooden rod; place on wire rack. Remove rods when cooled.

7. Store in a tightly covered container.

8. Shortly before serving, using a pastry bag and decorating tube, fill cookies from both ends with Rich Chocolate Filling.

9. Dip in chopped *pistachio nuts* or *chocolate shot*.   ABOUT 2 DOZEN COOKIES

*Bake a trial cookie; if it is too brittle to roll, the batter needs a little more flour; if the cookie is thick and difficult to roll, add a little more cooled melted butter.

NOTE: These cookies may also be made using a krumkake iron (see *Norwegian Cones, page 579*). Spoon 1 teaspoonful of mixture onto heated iron, close iron, and bake for 1 minute over medium heat, turning once. Roll as directed.

RICH CHOCOLATE FILLING

1½ oz. (1½ sq.)	2 egg yolks, slightly
unsweetened	beaten
chocolate	½ teaspoon vanilla
2 tablespoons sugar	extract
1 tablespoon water	½ cup butter
⅛ teaspoon salt	1 cup confectioners'
	sugar

1. Heat chocolate, sugar, water, and salt over boiling water, stirring until mixture is smooth.

2. Blend egg yolks into mixture in double-boiler top and cook 3 to 5 minutes, stirring constantly. Stir in extract; set aside to cool.

3. Cream butter; add confectioners' sugar gradually, beating until fluffy.

4. Add chocolate mixture gradually, beating well; cover and chill.

5. Before using, beat filling with a spoon to soften slightly.   ABOUT 1¼ CUPS

FLORENTINES
(Echte Florentiner)

An Austrian cookie despite its Italian sounding name.

¼ cup butter	¾ cup sifted cake flour
⅓ cup firmly packed	¼ teaspoon salt
light brown sugar	1 cup slivered blanched
2 tablespoons honey	almonds
2 tablespoons light corn	3 oz. candied orange
syrup	peel, finely chopped
1 tablespoon	Chocolate Glaze I, *page*
heavy cream	*440;* triple recipe

1. Cream butter; add brown sugar gradually, creaming until fluffy. Add honey, corn syrup, and cream gradually, beating well after each addition.

2. Sift flour and salt together; add in thirds to creamed mixture, mixing until blended after each addition. Mix in almonds and candied peel.

3. Drop by level tablespoonfuls 3 inches apart onto greased and lightly floured cookie sheets; spread into 2-inch rounds.

4. Bake at 350°F about 7 minutes. (Cookies should be delicately browned and about 3 inches in diameter with a slightly lacy appearance.)

5. Cool 2 to 3 minutes on cookie sheets. Carefully remove cookies to wire racks; turn flat side up and cool completely.

6. Evenly spread bottom of each cookie with

about 1½ teaspoons Chocolate Glaze I. When chocolate is almost set, draw wavy lines through glaze.   ABOUT 2 DOZEN COOKIES

LACY ALMOND CRISPS

⅓ cup blanched almonds, grated	3 tablespoons butter or margarine
¼ cup sugar	1 tablespoon milk
2 teaspoons flour	

1. Mix almonds, sugar, and flour in a bowl. Blend in butter and milk.
2. Drop batter by teaspoonfuls about 4 inches apart onto greased and lightly floured cookie sheets.
3. Bake at 350°F 6 to 7 minutes, or until golden brown.
4. Let set about 1 minute; carefully remove with a spatula to a wire rack. Cool completely. Store in an airtight container.   ABOUT 2 DOZEN 3-INCH COOKIES

LACY FILBERT CRISPS: Follow recipe for Lacy Almond Crisps. Substitute ⅓ cup filberts, grated, for the almonds. Add ¼ teaspoon ground mace.

CHOCOLATE ALMOND MACAROONS

1 oz. (1 sq.) unsweetened chocolate	¾ teaspoon vanilla extract
½ lb. almond paste	½ cup sugar
⅓ cup egg whites, unbeaten (slightly more or less egg white may be needed, depending on moisture in almond paste)	½ cup confectioners' sugar

1. Melt the chocolate; set aside to cool.
2. Force almond paste through a coarse sieve a little at a time. Gradually add egg whites, blending until smooth after each addition.
3. Blend in cooled chocolate and the extract.
4. Mix a blend of the sugars, a little at a time, into almond paste mixture; final mixture should be thick enough to hold its shape but must not be stiff.
5. Drop by teaspoonfuls 2 inches apart onto cookie sheets lined with unglazed paper. Flatten the top of each macaroon.
6. Bake at 300°F 25 to 30 minutes.
7. Remove cookies to wire racks. (If necessary, slightly moisten underside of paper directly under each macaroon to remove.)   ABOUT 3 DOZEN COOKIES

YELLOW ALMOND MACAROONS: Follow recipe for Chocolate Almond Macaroons. Omit chocolate. Mix ¼ cup sifted flour with the sugars. Blend ¼ teaspoon yellow food coloring with extract. Sift confectioners' sugar over tops before baking.

ANISE DROPS
(Anisscheiben)

During baking, these German cookies form a cake-like layer with a crisp "frosting" on the top.

2 extra-large eggs (½ cup)	1⅔ cups sifted all-purpose flour
1 cup sugar	¼ teaspoon baking powder
¼ teaspoon anise oil	

1. Beat the eggs, sugar, and anise oil until thick and piled softly.
2. Sift flour and baking powder together; add in fourths to egg-sugar mixture, blending thoroughly after each addition.
3. Drop by teaspoonfuls 2 inches apart onto greased cookie sheets.
4. Set cookie sheets aside in a cool place (not in refrigerator) 8 to 10 hours or overnight. *Do not cover and do not disturb!*
5. Bake at 350°F 5 to 7 minutes.
     ABOUT 4 DOZEN COOKIES

BANANA-BRAN COOKIES

¾ cup sifted all-purpose flour	⅛ teaspoon ground cloves
½ teaspoon baking powder	1 cup bran flakes
¼ teaspoon baking soda	½ cup mashed banana
¼ teaspoon salt	⅓ cup butter
½ teaspoon ground cinnamon	½ cup sugar
⅛ teaspoon ground allspice	1 egg
	¼ cup coarsely chopped pecans

1. Sift flour, baking powder, baking soda, salt, and spices together; set aside.
2. Combine bran flakes and the banana; set aside.
3. Cream butter; add sugar gradually, beating until fluffy. Add egg and beat thoroughly.
4. Add dry ingredients to creamed mixture alternately with the banana mixture, mixing until blended after each addition. Stir in pecans.

5. Drop by slightly rounded teaspoonfuls onto greased cookie sheets.
6. Bake at 375°F 10 to 12 minutes.

ABOUT 4 DOZEN COOKIES

CHOCOLATE-BANANA-BRAN COOKIES: Follow recipe for Banana Bran Cookies. Stir in ½ cup semi-sweet chocolate pieces with the nuts.

BANANA SPICE COOKIES: Follow recipe for Banana Bran Cookies. Increase flour to ¾ cup plus 2 tablespoons. Decrease cinnamon to ¼ teaspoon. Omit allspice and bran flakes. Substitute vegetable shortening for butter. Increase pecans to ½ cup. Drop by tablespoonfuls onto the cookie sheets. If desired, frost cooled cookies with a butter cream frosting flavored with a few drops banana extract.

BRAN FLAKE DROPS: Follow recipe for Banana Bran Cookies. Increase baking powder to 1 teaspoon; omit baking soda. Omit banana; combine bran flakes with ¼ cup milk.

CHOCOLATE MERINGUES

3 egg whites	¾ teaspoon vanilla
¾ cup sugar	extract
¾ teaspoon cider	3 tablespoons Dutch
vinegar	process cocoa

1. Beat egg whites until frothy, using medium speed of electric mixer.
2. Add half of sugar gradually, beating constantly; beat 5 minutes after last addition of sugar.
3. Beat in vinegar and extract. Add remaining sugar gradually, beating constantly. Increase speed to high; beat until very stiff peaks are formed, about 3 minutes. Do not overbeat.
4. Sift cocoa evenly over meringue; using a flexible spatula, carefully fold in the cocoa until almost blended. (Mixture will be streaked.)
5. Force meringue through a pastry bag and star decorating tube, or drop meringue by heaping teaspoonfuls onto cookie sheets covered with unglazed paper; swirl to form rosettes.
6. Bake at 250°F 1½ hours.

ABOUT 2 DOZEN COOKIES

MINT MERINGUES: Follow recipe for Chocolate Meringues. Beat 6 drops of red or green food coloring with egg whites. Omit vanilla extract and cocoa; add ¼ teaspoon peppermint extract. Bake at 200°F 1½ hours.

WHITE MERINGUES: Follow recipe for Chocolate Meringues. Omit cocoa. Bake at 200°F 1½ hours.

FROSTED CHOCOLATE NUT DROPS

4 oz. (4 sq.) unsweetened chocolate	½ teaspoon baking powder
1 cup butter	½ teaspoon baking soda
2 teaspoons vanilla extract	½ teaspoon salt
2 cups sugar	1 cup buttermilk
3 eggs	2 cups black walnuts or walnuts, chopped
2¾ cups sifted all-purpose flour	Rich Chocolate Frosting, page 438

1. Melt chocolate; set aside to cool.
2. Cream butter with extract; add sugar gradually, beating until fluffy.
3. Add eggs, one at a time, beating thoroughly after each addition. Blend in cooled chocolate.
4. Sift flour, baking powder, baking soda, and salt together; add to creamed mixture alternately with buttermilk, mixing until blended after each addition. Stir in walnuts.
5. Drop by tablespoonfuls about 3 inches apart onto lightly greased cookie sheets.
6. Bake at 350°F 12 to 15 minutes.
7. Spread frosting on cooled cookies.

ABOUT 4 DOZEN COOKIES

NOTE: If desired, for 1 cup of nuts substitute 1 cup raisins, 1 cup chopped dates, or ½ cup chopped maraschino cherries.

COCONUT MACAROONS DE LUXE

7 oz. flaked coconut, finely chopped (in blender, if desired); about 2½ cups, chopped	¾ cup (about 6) egg whites, unbeaten
	1 cup sugar
	1 tablespoon cornstarch
	¼ teaspoon almond extract

1. Put all ingredients into a 2-quart saucepan and mix thoroughly. Set over very low heat and stir until mixture is thickened and sugar is dissolved, about 20 minutes; keep temperature of mixture just below 150°F.
2. Remove from heat; cool 5 minutes.
3. Force through pastry bag and No. 7 star tube, which has been opened entirely, or drop by heaping teaspoonfuls directly onto cookie sheets lined with unglazed paper.
4. Press a candied cherry piece onto top of each.
5. Bake at 350°F 20 minutes.
6. Remove cookies to wire racks. (If necessary,

slightly moisten underside of paper directly under each macaroon to remove.) ABOUT 3 DOZEN COOKIES

CHOCOLATE MACAROONS: Follow recipe for Coconut Macaroons de Luxe. Add *2 ounces (2 squares) unsweetened chocolate*, grated, to saucepan with coconut. Heat mixture to 120°F about 5 minutes.

MOUNT SHASTA COOKIES

Each cookie is baked with a mounded topping of coconut meringue, reminding one of a Western mountain peak.

½ cup shortening	1½ cups sifted all-
1 teaspoon vanilla	purpose flour
extract	¾ teaspoon salt
½ cup sugar	3 tablespoons milk
½ cup firmly packed	1 cup walnuts, chopped
brown sugar	1 egg white
1 egg yolk	½ cup sugar
	1 cup flaked coconut

1. Cream shortening with extract; add ½ cup sugar and brown sugar gradually, beating until fluffy. Add egg yolk; beat thoroughly.
2. Blend flour and salt; add to creamed mixture alternately with milk, mixing until blended after each addition. Stir in walnuts.
3. Drop by rounded teaspoonfuls onto ungreased cookie sheets; flatten slightly. Set aside.
4. Beat egg white until frothy; add ½ cup sugar gradually, beating constantly until stiff peaks are formed. Blend in coconut.
5. Top each cookie round with a teaspoonful of coconut meringue, shaping into a peak.
6. Bake at 375°F 10 to 12 minutes.

ABOUT 4½ DOZEN COOKIES

TIPSY CURRANT CHASERS

It's the currants in these melt-in-your-mouth cookies that are tipsy.

½ cup unsalted butter	1 cup sifted all-purpose
½ cup sugar	flour
2 eggs	Currants in Rum, *below*

1. Cream butter; add sugar gradually, beating until fluffy. Add eggs, one at a time, beating thoroughly after each addition.
2. Add flour, ½ cup at a time, mixing until blended after each addition.
3. Stir in 1 cup of drained currants; let stand 10 to 15 minutes to allow flavors to blend.

4. Drop by teaspoonfuls 2 inches apart onto lightly greased cookie sheets.
5. Bake at 425°F 6 minutes.

ABOUT 4 DOZEN COOKIES

CURRANTS IN RUM: Combine *2 cups currants* and *1 cup rum* in a jar; cover tightly and store in refrigerator. Shake occasionally. The longer currants are stored, the more flavor will be absorbed. Remaining currants may be stored for use in other food preparation, adding more currants as needed.

CURRANT CAKES

A Pennsylvania Dutch Christmas cookie.

2 cups butter	6 eggs, well beaten
2 teaspoons grated	3¼ cups sifted all-
lemon peel	purpose flour
2 tablespoons lemon	¼ teaspoon salt
juice	½ lb. (1½ cups)
2¼ cups sugar	currants

1. Cream butter with lemon peel and juice; add sugar gradually, beating until fluffy. Add eggs in thirds, beating thoroughly after each addition.
2. Blend flour and salt; add to creamed mixture in thirds, mixing until blended after each addition. Mix in the currants.
3. Drop by teaspoonfuls onto large well-greased cookie sheets, spreading batter for each cookie very thinly.
4. Bake at 350°F 10 minutes.

ABOUT 7½ DOZEN COOKIES

PASSOVER COOKIES

¼ cup shortening	⅔ cup ground toasted
1 teaspoon grated lemon	filberts (to toast
peel	nuts, see *page 20*)
1 cup sugar	2 tablespoons potato
6 eggs	starch
1 cup matzo cake meal	⅛ teaspoon salt

1. Cream shortening with lemon peel. Add sugar gradually, beating constantly. Add eggs, one at a time, beating until light and fluffy after each addition.
2. Combine cake meal, ground filberts, potato starch, and salt; fold into creamed mixture, a little at a time.
3. Drop by tablespoonfuls onto ungreased cookie sheets. Sprinkle lightly with *sugar* and press a whole *filbert* into center of each cookie.

4. Bake at 400°F about 10 minutes, or until lightly browned.

5. Remove from cookie sheets immediately and cool on wire racks. ABOUT 3½ DOZEN COOKIES

SOFT GINGER CREAMS

2 cups sifted all-purpose flour
½ teaspoon baking soda
¼ teaspoon salt
2 teaspoons ground ginger
¼ teaspoon ground cinnamon
¾ cup butter or margarine
1 cup firmly packed light brown sugar
3 tablespoons light molasses
1 egg
½ cup dairy sour cream
Glossy Orange Frosting, *below*

1. Sift the flour, baking soda, salt, and spices together; set aside.
2. Cream butter with brown sugar; blend in molasses. Add egg and beat well.
3. Mixing until blended after each addition, add dry ingredients in thirds and sour cream in halves.
4. Drop by teaspoonfuls about 2 inches apart onto lightly greased cookie sheets.
5. Bake at 375°F 8 to 10 minutes.
6. Remove cookies to wire racks to cool. Frost with Glossy Orange Frosting. 7 DOZEN COOKIES

GLOSSY ORANGE FROSTING: Beat *1 egg white* slightly. Blend in *1½ cups confectioners' sugar.* Add *1 tablespoon butter*, melted, *⅛ teaspoon salt, 1 teaspoon vanilla extract*, and *1 teaspoon orange extract*; beat until smooth. ABOUT 1 CUP

GINGERSNAPS

3 cups sifted all-purpose flour
3 teaspoons baking soda
3 teaspoons ground ginger
½ teaspoon ground cinnamon
1 cup butter
1 cup sugar
½ cup molasses
1 egg

1. Sift flour, baking soda, ginger, and cinnamon together; set aside.
2. Cream butter; add sugar gradually, beating until fluffy. Blend in molasses. Add egg and beat thoroughly.
3. Add dry ingredients in thirds, mixing until blended after each addition.

4. Drop by teaspoonfuls about 3 inches apart onto ungreased cookie sheets; sprinkle generously with *sugar.*
5. Bake at 350°F 10 to 12 minutes.
ABOUT 6 DOZEN COOKIES

QUEEN BEES

½ cup butter
½ cup sugar
½ cup honey
1 egg
1¾ cups sifted all-purpose flour
1 teaspoon baking powder
½ teaspoon salt
¼ cup sherry
1 cup chopped toasted blanched almonds
½ cup finely chopped crystallized ginger

1. Cream butter; add sugar gradually, then honey, creaming until fluffy. Add egg and beat thoroughly.
2. Sift flour, baking powder, and salt together; add to creamed mixture alternately with sherry, mixing until blended after each addition. Stir in a mixture of almonds and ginger.
3. Chill dough thoroughly.
4. Drop by teaspoonfuls 2 inches apart onto lightly greased cookie sheets.
5. Bake at 400°F about 10 minutes.
ABOUT 4½ DOZEN COOKIES

CHOCOLATE BEES: Follow recipe for Queen Bees. Omit crystallized ginger; use *½ cup finely chopped chocolate-coated crystallized ginger.*

HAZELNUT BALLS
(Haselnuss Bällchen)
A German cookie.

2 egg whites
1 cup sugar
1½ cups (about 6 oz.) hazelnuts (filberts), grated

1. Beat egg whites until frothy; add sugar gradually, beating constantly until stiff peaks are formed.
2. Sprinkle hazelnuts over the egg whites and gently fold together just until blended.
3. Drop mixture by teaspoonfuls onto lightly greased cookie sheets. If necessary, work over each portion with the back of a spoon to round it.
4. Bake at 300°F about 25 minutes.
5. With a spatula, carefully remove cookies from cookie sheets to wire racks.
ABOUT 4 DOZEN COOKIES

VIRGINIA REBELS

The recipe for this cocoa-flavored oatmeal cookie was contributed by a young Southern belle.

1 cup sifted all-purpose flour	1 teaspoon vanilla extract
½ teaspoon baking soda	1½ cups sugar
½ teaspoon salt	1 egg
6 tablespoons cocoa	¼ cup water
1¼ cups butter	3 cups uncooked rolled oats

1. Sift flour, baking soda, salt, and cocoa together; set aside.
2. Cream butter with extract; add sugar gradually, beating until fluffy. Add the egg and beat well.
3. Alternately add dry ingredients with water, mixing until blended after each addition. Add rolled oats gradually, stirring well.
4. Drop by teaspoonfuls 2 inches apart onto ungreased cookie sheets.
5. Bake at 350°F about 12 minutes.

ABOUT 15 DOZEN COOKIES

NOTE: If desired, after addition of rolled oats, mix in any of the following: *1 cup chopped dark seedless raisins, 6 ounces semisweet chocolate pieces, 1 cup drained, chopped maraschino cherries, or ½ cup chopped candied cherries and ½ cup chopped candied pineapple.*

MOM'S SULTANAS

The delicious tang of lemon and golden raisins will make these oatmeal cookies a family favorite.

1 cup sifted all-purpose flour	½ cup sugar
¾ teaspoon baking powder	1 egg
⅛ teaspoon baking soda	2 tablespoons lemon juice
⅛ teaspoon salt	1 cup uncooked rolled oats
⅔ cup butter	½ cup golden raisins
2 teaspoons grated lemon peel	

1. Sift flour, baking powder, baking soda, and salt together; set aside.
2. Cream butter with lemon peel; add sugar gradually, creaming until fluffy. Add egg and beat thoroughly.
3. Alternately add dry ingredients with lemon juice, mixing until blended after each addition. Stir in rolled oats and raisins.

4. Drop by teaspoonfuls about 2 inches apart onto lightly greased cookie sheets.
5. Bake at 375°F 12 to 15 minutes.

ABOUT 4 DOZEN COOKIES

STOUFFER'S OATMEAL MACAROONS

From the famous Stouffer Restaurant chain.

½ cup butter	½ teaspoon baking powder
1 cup quick-cooking rolled oats	¼ teaspoon salt
½ cup plus 2 tablespoons sugar	1 egg, slightly beaten
¼ cup cake flour	½ teaspoon vanilla extract
	¼ cup chopped nuts

1. Melt butter in a 2-quart saucepan. Stir in rolled oats and brown lightly over medium heat (3 to 4 minutes), stirring constantly; set aside to cool.
2. Blend sugar, flour, baking powder, and salt; stir into cooled oats.
3. Blend in egg and extract; beat thoroughly. Stir in nuts.
4. Drop by rounded teaspoonfuls 3 inches apart onto lightly greased cookie sheets.
5. Bake at 360°F 10 to 12 minutes.
6. While still hot, transfer to wire rack.

ABOUT 2 DOZEN COOKIES

ORANGE CANDY CRISPS

⅔ cup sifted all-purpose flour	¾ cup butter or margarine
½ teaspoon baking powder	½ teaspoon vanilla extract
¼ teaspoon baking soda	½ cup sugar
⅛ teaspoon salt	½ cup firmly packed brown sugar
½ lb. (about 1¼ cups) jellied candy orange slices, cut in small pieces	1 egg
	¾ cup uncooked rolled oats
3 tablespoons flour	½ cup flaked coconut

1. Sift ⅔ cup flour, baking powder, baking soda, and salt together; set aside.
2. Mix candy orange pieces with the 3 tablespoons flour; set aside.
3. Cream butter with extract; add the sugars gradually, beating until fluffy. Add the egg and beat thoroughly.
4. Add dry ingredients in halves, mixing until blended after each addition. Stir in the candy orange pieces, rolled oats, and coconut.

5. Drop by teaspoonfuls 2 inches apart onto greased cookie sheets.
6. Bake at 375°F 10 to 12 minutes.
7. If necessary, cool cookies slightly before transferring to wire racks. ABOUT 7 DOZEN COOKIES

NUT COLONELS
These salted peanut cookies are sure to please all.

1 egg	1½ cups salted peanuts
½ cup sugar	or cashews, coarsely
¼ teaspoon vanilla	chopped
extract	2 teaspoons flour

1. Beat egg, sugar, and extract until thick. Add nuts and flour gradually, folding in after each addition.
2. Drop by teaspoonfuls 2 inches apart onto greased cookie sheets.
3. Bake at 350°F 10 to 12 minutes.
ABOUT 3 DOZEN COOKIES

PEANUT BOUNTIES
One recipe of these marvelous crispy cookies will easily fill several cookie jars.

1 cup butter	½ teaspoon baking soda
1 cup firmly packed	½ cup crushed corn
brown sugar	flakes
1 egg	1 cup uncooked rolled
1 cup sifted all-purpose	oats
flour	¾ cup to 1 cup salted
½ teaspoon baking	Spanish peanuts
powder	

1. Cream butter; add brown sugar gradually, beating until fluffy. Add the egg and beat thoroughly.
2. Sift flour, baking powder, and baking soda together; add to creamed mixture in halves, mixing until blended after each addition. Stir in the remaining ingredients.
3. Drop by half-teaspoonfuls 2 inches apart onto ungreased cookie sheets.
4. Bake at 375°F 5 to 7 minutes.
5. Remove cookie sheets to wire racks; cool about 3 minutes before removing cookies.
ABOUT 14 DOZEN COOKIES

PEANUT BUTTER BOUNTIES: Follow recipe for Peanut Bounties. Decrease butter to ¾ cup; cream with ¼ *cup peanut butter* and *1 teaspoon vanilla extract*. Substitute *granulated sugar* for brown sugar. Increase eggs to 2 and flour to 1⅔ cups; omit corn flakes and rolled oats.

AUSTRIAN PECAN COOKIES

2 tablespoons plus 2	2 eggs, well beaten
teaspoons butter	½ cup sifted cake flour
1½ teaspoons vanilla	1 teaspoon baking
extract	powder
2 cups firmly packed	½ teaspoon salt
light brown sugar	1½ cups chopped
	pecans

1. Cream butter with extract; add brown sugar gradually, blending well. Add beaten eggs in halves, beating thoroughly after each addition.
2. Sift cake flour, baking powder, and salt together; add to creamed mixture in halves, mixing until blended after each addition. (Batter will be thin.) Stir in pecans.
3. Drop by teaspoonfuls at least 2 inches apart onto cookie sheets lined with baking parchment.
4. Bake at 375°F about 6 minutes.
5. Cool completely, then remove from paper.
ABOUT 10 DOZEN COOKIES

PECAN DAINTIES

1 egg white	1¼ cups chopped
½ cup firmly packed	pecans
brown sugar, sifted	1½ tablespoons flour

1. Beat egg white until frothy. Add brown sugar gradually, beating until very stiff peaks are formed. Fold in pecans and flour.
2. Drop by teaspoonfuls 2 inches apart onto lightly greased cookie sheets; shape into balls with the back of a spoon.
3. Bake at 350°F about 10 minutes.
ABOUT 4 DOZEN COOKIES

PLANTATION CRISPS

¼ cup butter	½ cup sifted all-purpose
½ teaspoon vanilla	flour
extract	¼ teaspoon salt
1 cup firmly packed dark	1 cup pecans, coarsely
brown sugar	chopped
1 egg	

1. Cream butter with extract; add brown sugar gradually, beating until fluffy. Add egg and beat thoroughly.

2. Blend flour and salt; add to creamed mixture in halves, mixing until blended after each addition. Stir in the pecans.

3. Drop by teaspoonfuls 3 inches apart onto ungreased cookie sheets; bake about 6 cookies at one time (they are difficult to remove when cooled).

4. Bake at 350°F 10 to 12 minutes.

5. Immediately remove cookies to wire racks to cool. ABOUT 3½ DOZEN COOKIES

PUMPKIN JUMBOS

Raisin lovers take note . . . here's a big fat pumpkin-like cookie to please you.

2 cups dark seedless raisins	¼ teaspoon ground allspice
1½ cups water	¼ teaspoon ground nutmeg
4½ cups sifted all-purpose flour	1 teaspoon vanilla extract
1 teaspoon baking powder	2 cups sugar
1 teaspoon baking soda	3 eggs
1 teaspoon salt	1 cup chopped walnuts
1¼ cups butter or margarine	Creamy Orange Frosting, *below*
1 teaspoon ground cinnamon	

1. Combine raisins and water in a saucepan. Bring to boiling and simmer 5 minutes. Drain, reserving ½ cup liquid. Set raisins and liquid aside.

2. Sift flour, baking powder, baking soda, and salt together; set aside.

3. Cream butter with spices and extract; add sugar gradually, beating until fluffy. Add eggs, one at a time, beating thoroughly after each addition.

4. Add dry ingredients alternately with raisin liquid, mixing until blended after each addition. Mix in raisins and walnuts.

5. Drop by heaping tablespoonfuls 2 inches apart onto lightly greased cookie sheets.

6. Bake at 400°F about 10 minutes.

7. Remove to wire racks. When cool, frost with Creamy Orange Frosting. Decorate to resemble jack-o'-lantern faces. With a wooden pick or fine brush dipped in *melted chocolate*, draw lines to in-

dicate grooves in pumpkin and to make the face. Use a piece of *citron* or *angelica* for stem.

ABOUT 4 DOZEN COOKIES

CREAMY ORANGE FROSTING

¼ cup butter or margarine	1 egg yolk
1½ teaspoons vanilla extract	2 to 3 tablespoons orange juice
⅛ teaspoon salt	Red and yellow food coloring
1 lb. (about 3½ cups) confectioners' sugar	

1. Cream the butter with extract and salt. Add the confectioners' sugar gradually, creaming until blended. Add egg yolk and beat until smooth.

2. Add the orange juice gradually, beating until frosting is of desired consistency. Blend in food coloring, one drop at a time (approximately 3 drops of red and 6 drops of yellow), until frosting is tinted a light orange. ABOUT 1⅓ CUPS

HERMITS

These old-fashioned spicy raisin cookies are a part of our New England heritage.

1 cup dark seedless raisins	½ teaspoon ground nutmeg
2½ cups sifted all-purpose flour	⅛ teaspoon ground cloves
¾ teaspoon baking soda	¾ cup butter
½ teaspoon salt	1½ cups firmly packed brown sugar
1 teaspoon ground cinnamon	3 eggs
	1 cup walnuts, chopped

1. Pour *2 cups boiling water* over raisins in a saucepan and bring to boiling; pour off water and drain raisins on absorbent paper. Coarsely chop raisins and set aside.

2. Sift flour, baking soda, salt, and spices together and blend thoroughly; set aside.

3. Cream butter; add brown sugar gradually, beating until fluffy. Add eggs, one at a time, beating thoroughly after each addition.

4. Add dry ingredients in fourths, mixing until blended after each addition. Stir in raisins and walnuts.

5. Drop by teaspoonfuls 2 inches apart onto lightly greased cookie sheets.

6. Bake at 400°F about 7 minutes.

ABOUT 8 DOZEN COOKIES

MOLDED COOKIES

MOJI PEARLS

¾ cup butter
½ teaspoon vanilla
  extract
⅓ cup sugar

1½ cups sifted all-
  purpose flour
⅛ teaspoon salt

1. Cream butter with extract; add sugar gradually, beating until fluffy.
2. Blend flour and salt; add in thirds to creamed mixture, mixing until blended after each addition. Chill dough until easy to handle.
3. Shape into 1-inch balls or into crescents (if desired, roll in sesame seed). Place about 2 inches apart on ungreased cookie sheets.
4. Bake at 325°F 20 minutes.
5. If desired, while still warm, roll in *Vanilla Confectioners' Sugar, Spiced Confectioners' Sugar, or Cinnamon Sugar, page 558.*

ABOUT 3 DOZEN COOKIES

PECAN POOFS: Follow recipe for Moji Pearls. Substitute *¼ cup confectioners' sugar* for sugar. Decrease flour to 1 cup. Mix in *1 cup pecans,* finely chopped. Shape dough into balls or pyramids.

GREEK BUTTER BALL COOKIES
(Kourabiedes)

3 cups sifted cake flour
¼ teaspoon baking soda
¾ cup chopped blanched
  almonds, crushed with
  rolling pin
1 cup unsalted butter
1 tablespoon sugar

1½ teaspoons brandy
½ teaspoon lemon juice
Few drops almond
  extract
1 teaspoon olive oil
1 large egg yolk, fork
  beaten
Confectioners' sugar

1. Mix the flour, baking soda, and almonds; set aside.
2. Heat butter slowly in a small deep saucepan. Cool. Carefully spoon off into a large bowl the clarified butter from top of cloudy solids which have settled at bottom of pan.
3. Add sugar, brandy, lemon juice, extract, oil, and egg yolk to butter; beat well. Add the flour-nut mixture in fourths, mixing thoroughly after each addition.
4. Shape dough into ¾-inch balls and place on ungreased cookie sheets.

5. Bake at 350°F 15 minutes.
6. Meanwhile, line a jelly roll pan with absorbent paper and generously sift confectioners' sugar over paper. Remove cookies carefully to the sugar and roll gently to coat. Transfer to cookie jar when cool.

ABOUT 4 DOZEN COOKIES

SPANISH BUTTER WAFERS
(Mantecaditos)

½ cup butter
½ cup lard
1½ teaspoons grated
  lemon peel, or 1
  teaspoon anise seed
  (or both)

1 teaspoon vanilla
  extract
1¼ cups sugar
2 eggs
1¾ cups sifted all-
  purpose flour
½ teaspoon salt

1. Cream butter and lard with lemon peel and extract. Add sugar gradually, beating until fluffy. Add eggs, one at a time, beating thoroughly after each addition.
2. Blend flour and salt; add to creamed mixture in thirds, mixing until blended after each addition. Chill dough several hours, or until easy to handle.
3. Removing a small portion of dough at a time from refrigerator, shape into ¾- to 1-inch balls and place 1½ inches apart on an ungreased cookie sheet.
4. Bake at 350°F 8 to 10 minutes.

6 TO 7 DOZEN COOKIES

SNOWBALL MELTAWAYS
These melt-in-your-mouth morsels truly live up to their name.

1 cup butter
½ cup confectioners'
  sugar
1 teaspoon vanilla
  extract

2½ cups sifted all-
  purpose flour
½ cup finely chopped
  pecans

1. In a heavy saucepan over low heat, melt and heat butter until light brown in color. Pour into a small mixing bowl; chill until firm.
2. Cream browned butter with confectioners' sugar and extract until light and fluffy. Gradually add flour, mixing until blended. Stir in the pecans. Chill several hours for ease in handling.

3. Shape into 1-inch balls. Place on ungreased cookie sheets.
4. Bake at 350°F about 20 minutes.
5. Remove to wire racks. While still hot, dust with *confectioners' sugar*. ABOUT 4 DOZEN COOKIES

BERLIN WREATHS
(Berlinerkranser)
A Norwegian specialty.

1 cup butter	3 hard-cooked egg yolks, sieved
½ teaspoon vanilla extract	2 cups sifted all-purpose flour
½ cup sugar	
2 uncooked egg yolks	

1. Cream butter with extract; add sugar gradually, beating until fluffy.
2. Add uncooked egg yolks, one at a time, beating thoroughly after each addition; mix in hard-cooked egg yolks.
3. Add flour in fourths, mixing until blended after each addition. Chill dough thoroughly.
4. Shape small amounts of dough into strips 4 inches long and ¼ inch thick; the ends of strips should be slightly pointed. Form wreaths on ungreased cookie sheets, overlapping ends of strips about ¼ inch.
5. Brush wreaths with slightly beaten *egg white*; sprinkle lightly with crushed *loaf sugar*.
6. Bake at 350°F 10 to 12 minutes. ABOUT 5 DOZEN COOKIES

SWEDISH COFFEE FINGERS
(Mördegspinnar)

½ cup butter	Egg white, slightly beaten
1 teaspoon almond extract	½ cup finely chopped blanched almonds
2 tablespoons sugar	3 tablespoons sugar
1¼ cups sifted all-purpose flour	

1. Cream butter with extract; add 2 tablespoons sugar gradually, beating until fluffy.
2. Add flour in fourths, mixing until blended after each addition. Chill dough thoroughly.
3. Shape small amounts of dough into fingers 2½ inches long and ¼ inch thick.
4. Brush each finger of dough with the egg white, then roll in mixture of the almonds and the remaining sugar.

5. Bake on ungreased cookie sheets at 350°F 10 to 12 minutes.
6. Carefully remove cookies to wire racks. ABOUT 5 DOZEN COOKIES

ALMOND CAKES

½ cup unsalted butter	¼ teaspoon baking powder
1 tablespoon dry gin	
¼ teaspoon almond extract	2 tablespoons finely chopped toasted blanched almonds
¼ cup sugar	Blanched almond halves
1 cup sifted all-purpose flour	

1. Cream butter with gin and extract; add sugar gradually, beating until fluffy.
2. Sift flour and baking powder together; add, ½ cup at a time, to creamed mixture, mixing until blended after each addition. Mix in chopped almonds.
3. Using 1 teaspoon dough at a time, shape into balls and place on lightly floured cookie sheets. Flatten each until about ¼ inch thick and press an almond half onto each.
4. Bake at 350°F 12 to 15 minutes. ABOUT 3 DOZEN COOKIES

CHINESE ALMOND COOKIES
Typical of the well-known almond cookies served in Chinese restaurants.

2½ cups blanched almonds	1¼ cups butter
2¼ cups sifted all-purpose flour	1¼ cups sugar

1. Finely chop 1⅔ cups almonds; toast remaining almonds, if desired, and set aside for garnish.
2. Mix flour and chopped almonds; set aside.
3. Cream butter; add sugar gradually, beating thoroughly.
4. Add flour-nut mixture gradually, mixing until blended after each addition.
5. Divide dough into thirds, wrap in waxed paper, and chill until easy to handle.
6. Shape dough into 1-inch balls; place about 2 inches apart on ungreased cookie sheets and flat-

Cherry Jewels, Spicy Ginger Crunchies, and Snowball Meltaways

ten each until about ½ inch thick. Press a whole almond onto the top of each.

7. Bake at 325°F 10 to 15 minutes.

8. Immediately remove cookies to wire racks.

ABOUT 6 DOZEN COOKIES

NOTE: Firmly packed light brown sugar may be substituted for the granulated sugar.

SWEDISH SAND TARTS
(Sandbakelse)

These tender, buttery-rich dainties are especially popular in Sweden at Christmastime.

1 cup butter	2 cups sifted all-
¼ teaspoon almond	purpose flour
extract	⅓ cup blanched
¾ cup sugar	almonds, finely
1 egg	chopped

1. Cream butter with extract; add sugar gradually, beating until fluffy. Add egg and beat thoroughly.

2. Add flour in fourths, mixing until blended after each addition. Stir in almonds. Chill dough thoroughly.

3. Remove a small portion of dough at a time from refrigerator and, depending upon size of mold, place 1 or 2 teaspoonfuls in each sandbakelse mold (usually available in the housewares section of department stores); press firmly to cover bottom and sides of mold evenly. Set lined molds on cookie sheets.

4. Bake at 375°F 6 to 8 minutes.

5. Immediately invert molds onto a smooth surface; cool slightly.

6. To remove sand tart, hold mold and tap lightly but sharply with back of spoon. Remove molds and cool cookies. Invert and sift *Vanilla Confectioners' Sugar, page 558,* over cookies.

ABOUT 5 DOZEN COOKIES

ANISE COOKIE STICKS

½ cup butter	3 teaspoons baking
3 oz. cream cheese	powder
1 cup sugar	½ teaspoon salt
4 eggs	2 teaspoons anise seed
3¼ cups sifted all-	
purpose flour	

1. Cream butter and cream cheese together. Add sugar gradually, beating thoroughly after each addition. Beat in eggs one at a time; continue beating until light and fluffy.

2. Add a mixture of the remaining ingredients; mix well.

3. Divide dough in half, place on a lightly greased cookie sheet, and form into 2 rolls the length of baking sheet and 1½ inches wide.

4. Bake at 350°F 30 to 35 minutes, or until light brown.

5. Remove from oven and cut rolls crosswise into slices about ¾ inch thick. Place on cookie sheets cut side down. Return to oven. Bake 10 minutes, or until toasted and crisp. ABOUT 4 DOZEN COOKIES

CHERRY JEWELS

½ cup butter	1 tablespoon lemon
1 teaspoon vanilla	juice
extract	1¼ cups sifted all-
¼ cup sugar	purpose flour
1 egg	¾ cup finely chopped
1 teaspoon grated lemon	pecans
peel	18 candied cherries,
	halved

1. Cream butter with extract and sugar until light and fluffy. Add the egg and lemon peel and juice; beat thoroughly. Gradually add flour, mixing until blended. Chill.

2. Shape dough into 1-inch balls, roll in chopped pecans and place on greased cookie sheets. Press a cherry half onto center of each ball.

3. Bake at 350°F 10 to 12 minutes.

4. Cool on wire racks. 3 DOZEN COOKIES

COCOA BUTTER STICKS
(Chokladbröd)

This delectable cookie is a Swedish specialty.

1½ cups sifted all-	¾ cup sugar
purpose flour	1 egg, slightly beaten
2 tablespoons cocoa	1 tablespoon cold water
1 teaspoon baking powder	3 tablespoons finely
½ teaspoon salt	chopped blanched
¾ cup butter or	almonds
margarine	2 tablespoons sugar

1. Sift flour, cocoa, baking powder, and salt together; set aside.

2. Cream butter; add ¾ cup sugar gradually, beating until fluffy. Reserve 1 tablespoon egg;

English Toffee Bars, assorted Spritz, and Moji Pearls with Savory Miniature Croustades, Cheese Balls, and eggnog

blend remainder into butter mixture, beating thoroughly.

3.   Add dry ingredients in fourths, mixing until blended after each addition. Chill dough thoroughly.

4.   Divide dough into 4 portions; shape each into a roll ¾ inch in diameter.

5.   Place rolls 4 inches apart on ungreased cookie sheets; flatten each until ¼ inch thick with a fork dipped in flour; smooth dough at edges.

6.   Combine water with reserved egg; brush top of dough lightly.

7.   Sprinkle a mixture of almonds and 2 tablespoons sugar over dough.

8.   Bake at 400°F 8 to 10 minutes.

9.   Cool 1 minute; cut crosswise into 1-inch pieces and remove to wire racks.   5 TO 6 DOZEN COOKIES

NOTE: For additional chocolate flavor, increase cocoa to ¼ cup and decrease salt to ¼ teaspoon.

COCOA BUTTER BALLS: Follow recipe for Cocoa Butter Sticks. Shape dough into ¾-inch balls; place about 2 inches apart on cookie sheets and flatten each with a fork. Brush tops with egg; sprinkle with almond-sugar mixture.

FILBERT FORM COOKIES
A Czechoslovakian inspiration.

¾ cup sifted all-purpose flour	⅛ teaspoon ground cloves
⅛ teaspoon baking powder	⅛ teaspoon ground nutmeg
½ cup confectioners' sugar	½ cup filberts, grated
¼ teaspoon salt	1 teaspoon grated lemon peel
⅛ teaspoon ground cinnamon	6 tablespoons butter, chilled

1.   Sift flour, baking powder, confectioners' sugar, salt, and spices together; mix in the filberts and lemon peel.

2.   Cut in butter until mixture becomes a soft dough (requires working beyond the stage when particles are the size of rice kernels).

3.   Cut off small pieces of dough and press into lightly greased fancy 1¼x¼-inch cookie forms (usually available in housewares section of department stores), or half fill lightly greased sandbakelse molds with dough. Set molds on a cookie sheet.

4.   Bake at 375°F 10 minutes.

5.   Cool about 2 minutes on wire racks. With the point of a knife, loosen cookies from molds; invert onto the racks. Sift *Vanilla Confectioners' Sugar, page 558*, over cookies.   ABOUT 4 DOZEN COOKIES

PECAN FORM COOKIES: Follow recipe for Filbert Form cookies. Omit spices and lemon peel. Substitute ⅔ *cup pecans*, grated, for filberts. Mix in *1 teaspoon vanilla extract* with the butter.

GINGER COOKIES

2 cups sifted all-purpose flour	½ teaspoon ground cloves
1 teaspoon baking powder	½ teaspoon ground mace
½ teaspoon baking soda	1 cup butter
½ teaspoon salt	1 cup firmly packed brown sugar
1 teaspoon ground cinnamon	¼ cup dark molasses
1 teaspoon ground ginger	1 egg

1.   Sift flour, baking powder, baking soda, salt, and spices together; set aside.

2.   Cream butter; add brown sugar gradually, beating until fluffy. Blend in molasses. Add egg and beat thoroughly.

3.   Add dry ingredients in fourths, mixing until blended after each addition. Chill thoroughly.

4.   Shape dough into 1-inch balls and dip in *sugar*. Place 2 inches apart on ungreased cookie sheets.

5.   Bake at 350°F 10 to 15 minutes.
                          ABOUT 6 DOZEN COOKIES

LUMBERJACK COOKIES
Double the size for a veritable Paul Bunyan of a cookie.

2 cups sifted all-purpose flour	1 teaspoon ground ginger
	⅔ cup butter
½ teaspoon baking soda	½ cup sugar
½ teaspoon salt	½ cup dark molasses
1 teaspoon ground cinnamon	1 egg

1.   Sift flour, baking soda, salt, cinnamon, and ginger together; set aside.

2.   Cream butter; add sugar gradually, beating until fluffy. Add molasses gradually, blending well. Add egg and beat thoroughly.

3.   Add dry ingredients in fourths, mixing until blended. Chill the dough thoroughly.

4.   Shape dough into 1-inch balls; roll in *sugar*;

place 2 inches apart on ungreased cookie sheets.

5. Bake at 350°F 10 to 12 minutes.

ABOUT 4 DOZEN COOKIES

LUMBERJACK THINS: Follow recipe for Lumberjack Cookies. Increase butter to 1¼ cups. Use light for dark molasses. Shape into ¾-inch balls.

MOLASSES BUTTER BALLS

1 cup butter	2 cups sifted all-
½ teaspoon vanilla	purpose flour
extract	½ teaspoon salt
¼ cup molasses	2 cups pecans, finely
	chopped

1. Cream butter with extract; add molasses and beat well.
2. Blend flour and salt; add in fourths to creamed mixture, mixing until blended after each addition. Stir in the pecans.
3. Shape dough into 1-inch balls; place on lightly greased cookie sheets.
4. Bake at 350°F 12 to 15 minutes.
5. Cool slightly; roll in *confectioners' sugar.*

ABOUT 5 DOZEN COOKIES

THUMBPRINT COOKIES

1 cup butter	½ teaspoon baking
1½ teaspoons vanilla	powder
extract	½ cup finely chopped
½ cup sugar	pecans
1 egg yolk	1 egg white, slightly
1 tablespoon cream	beaten
2 cups sifted all-	Pecans, finely chopped
purpose flour	(about ¾ cup)

1. Cream butter with extract; add sugar gradually, beating until fluffy. Beat in egg yolk with cream.
2. Sift flour and baking powder together; add to creamed mixture in fourths, mixing until blended after each addition. Stir in the ½ cup pecans.
3. Shape dough into 1-inch balls; dip into egg white and roll in remaining pecans.
4. Place 1 inch apart on ungreased cookie sheets, then press thumb into center of each.
5. Fill with *jelly, a red or green maraschino cherry half, candied cherry half,* or, after baking, fill with *Tinted Butter Frosting, page 437.*
6. Bake at 350°F 15 to 18 minutes.

ABOUT 4½ DOZEN COOKIES

SPICY GINGER CRUNCHIES

2¼ cups sifted all-	½ teaspoon ground
purpose flour	cloves
2 teaspoons baking soda	¾ cup butter
1 teaspoon salt	1 teaspoon vanilla
1 teaspoon ground	extract
cinnamon	1 cup sugar
¾ teaspoon ground	1 egg
ginger	¼ cup molasses

1. Sift flour, baking soda, salt, and spices together; set aside.
2. Cream butter with extract; gradually add sugar, beating until light and fluffy. Add egg and molasses; beat thoroughly.
3. Gradually add dry ingredients to creamed mixture, mixing until blended. Chill several hours.
4. Shape dough into ¾-inch balls, roll in *sugar* and place 2 inches apart on greased cookie sheets.
5. Bake at 375°F 7 to 8 minutes.
6. Immediately remove to wire racks to cool.

6 TO 7 DOZEN COOKIES

NORWEGIAN CONES
(Krumkaker)

This traditional Christmas confection is extremely fragile, so handle and store it carefully.

1½ cups sifted all-	1 cup butter
purpose flour	1¼ cups sugar
½ cup cornstarch	3 egg yolks
1½ teaspoons ground	3 egg whites
cardamom	⅛ teaspoon salt

1. Blend flour, cornstarch, and cardamom.
2. Cream butter; add sugar gradually, beating until fluffy. Add egg yolks, one at a time, beating thoroughly after each addition.
3. Add dry ingredients in fourths, mixing until blended after each addition.
4. Beat egg whites and salt until stiff peaks are formed; gently fold into batter.
5. Heat krumkake iron (usually available in the housewares section of department stores) following manufacturer's instructions until a drop of water "sputters" on hot surface.
6. For each, spoon 1½ to 2 teaspoons batter onto hot iron; close the iron and bake on each side for a few minutes, or until lightly browned.
7. Using a spatula, immediately remove wafer and roll into cone. Cool completely.

ABOUT 4 DOZEN COOKIES

DANISH PEPPERNUTS
(Pebernødder)

The Danes have achieved an especially fine blend of flavors with sugar and spices and good Danish butter in this version of Pebernødder.

4 cups sifted all-purpose flour	1 teaspoon ground ginger
1 teaspoon crushed ammonium carbonate (available at your pharmacy)	¾ cup butter
	4 teaspoons finely shredded lemon peel
1½ teaspoons ground cinnamon	1¼ cups sugar
	2 eggs
1 teaspoon white pepper	¾ cup finely chopped almonds

1. Thoroughly blend flour, ammonium carbonate, cinnamon, white pepper, and ginger; set aside.
2. Cream butter with lemon peel. Add sugar gradually, beating until fluffy. Add eggs, one at a time, beating well after each addition. Stir in almonds.
3. Add dry ingredients in thirds, mixing until blended after each addition. Chill about 1 hour.
4. Shape dough into ¾- to 1-inch balls; place on ungreased cookie sheets.
5. Bake at 350°F 12 or 13 minutes.

ABOUT 12 DOZEN COOKIES

NORWEGIAN CHRISTMAS COOKIES
(Peppernötter)

1¾ cups sifted all-purpose flour	½ teaspoon ground cloves
½ cup cornstarch	1 cup butter or margarine
2 teaspoons baking powder	
½ teaspoon salt	¼ teaspoon vanilla extract
¼ to ½ teaspoon pepper	1 cup sugar
½ teaspoon ground cardamom	¼ cup cream
½ teaspoon ground cinnamon	⅔ cup finely chopped blanched almonds

1. Sift flour, cornstarch, baking powder, salt, and spices together; set aside.
2. Cream butter with extract. Add sugar gradually, beating until light and fluffy.
3. Add dry ingredients alternately with cream, mixing after each addition. Stir in almonds.
4. Shape dough into ¾-inch balls; place 1 inch apart on ungreased cookie sheets.
5. Bake at 350°F about 15 minutes.

ABOUT 6 DOZEN COOKIES

Pressed Cookies

BUTTER CRISPS

Here's a version of the universal favorite known as spritz you're sure to like. Enriched with cream cheese, this butter cookie is especially crisp and flavorsome.

1 cup butter	1 egg yolk
3 oz. cream cheese	2¼ cups sifted all-purpose flour
1 teaspoon vanilla extract	½ teaspoon salt
1 cup sugar	¼ teaspoon baking powder

1. Cream butter and cream cheese with extract; add sugar gradually, beating until fluffy. Add egg yolk and beat thoroughly.
2. Sift flour, salt, and baking powder together; add in fourths to creamed mixture, mixing until blended after each addition.
3. Following manufacturer's directions, fill a cookie press with dough and form cookies of varied shapes directly onto ungreased cookie sheets.
4. Bake at 350°F 12 to 15 minutes.
5. Cool on wire racks. ABOUT 8 DOZEN COOKIES
NOTE: Dough may be tinted different colors, and before baking, the shapes may be sprinkled with colored sugar or with cinnamon-sugar. Cooled cookies may be decorated with tinted frosting.

SPRITZ

1 cup butter	2 cups sifted all-purpose flour
1 teaspoon vanilla extract	½ teaspoon baking powder
½ cup sugar	
1 egg yolk	¼ teaspoon salt

1. Cream butter with extract; add sugar gradually, beating until fluffy. Add egg yolk and beat thoroughly.
2. Sift flour, baking powder, and salt together; add to creamed mixture in fourths, mixing until blended after each addition.
3. Following manufacturer's directions, fill a cookie press with dough and form cookies of varied shapes directly onto ungreased cookie sheets.
4. Bake at 350°F 12 minutes.

ABOUT 5 DOZEN COOKIES

CHOCOLATE SPRITZ: Follow recipe for Spritz.

Thoroughly blend ¼ *cup boiling water* and *6 tablespoons cocoa*; cool. Mix in after addition of egg yolk.

NUT SPRITZ: Follow recipe for Spritz. Stir in ½ *cup finely chopped nuts* (black walnuts or toasted blanched almonds) after the last addition of dry ingredients.

CHOCOLATE-TIPPED SPRITZ: Follow recipe for Spritz. Dip ends of cooled cookies into *Chocolate Glaze I, page 440*. If desired, dip into finely chopped *nuts*, crushed *peppermint stick candy*, or *chocolate shot*. Place on wire racks until glaze is set.

MARBLED SPRITZ: Follow recipe for Spritz. Thoroughly blend *2 tablespoons boiling water* and *3 tablespoons cocoa*; cool. After the addition of egg yolk, remove a half of the creamed mixture to another bowl and mix in a half of the dry ingredients. Into remaining half of creamed mixture, stir cocoa mixture; blend in remaining dry ingredients. Shape each half of dough into a roll and cut lengthwise into halves. Press cut surfaces of vanilla and chocolate flavored doughs together before filling cookie press.

SPRITZ SANDWICHES: Spread *chocolate frosting* or *jam* on bottom of some cookies. Cover with unfrosted cookies of same shape to form sandwiches.

JELLY-FILLED SPRITZ: Make slight impression at center of cookie rounds and fill with ¼ *teaspoon jelly or jam* before baking.

REFRIGERATOR COOKIES

OVERNIGHT COOKIES
(Hoide Kager)
A Danish cookie.

2¼ cups sifted all-purpose flour	¼ teaspoon vanilla extract
1 cup sugar	⅛ teaspoon lemon extract
1 cup butter	
½ cup cream	

1. Sift flour and sugar together; cut in butter until particles are the size of rice kernels.
2. Combine cream and extracts; add gradually to flour mixture, mixing with a fork until well blended.
3. Chill dough until easy to handle.
4. Shape into two 1½-inch rolls. Wrap and chill overnight.
5. Cut each roll into ⅛- or ¼-inch slices. Transfer slices to ungreased cookie sheets.
6. Bake at 350°F 9 to 12 minutes.

6 to 8 DOZEN COOKIES

COCONUT CLASSICS

1 cup butter or margarine	1 egg
½ teaspoon vanilla extract	2 cups grated coconut
1 cup sugar	1¾ cups sifted all-purpose flour
	½ teaspoon baking soda

1. Cream butter with extract; add sugar gradually, beating until fluffy. Add egg and beat well.
2. Thoroughly blend in 1¾ cups of the coconut.
3. Sift flour and baking soda together; add in fourths to creamed mixture, mixing well after each addition.
4. Knead lightly with fingertips 5 to 10 times until mixture holds together.
5. Shape into six 1-inch rolls; coat with remaining coconut; wrap and chill at least 3 hours.
6. Cut each roll into ¼-inch slices; place ¾ inch apart on lightly greased cookie sheets.
7. Bake at 325°F about 15 minutes.

ABOUT 18 DOZEN COOKIES

BROWN WAFERS
Spices and orange peel lend a pleasing flavor blend to this Danish cookie.

1 cup butter	½ teaspoon ground cloves
1¼ cups sugar	
½ cup light corn syrup	½ cup slivered almonds
2½ teaspoons crushed ammonium carbonate (available at your pharmacy)	½ cup finely shredded orange peel
	4 cups sifted all-purpose flour
3 tablespoons ground cinnamon	

1. Heat butter, sugar, and corn syrup to boiling in a heavy saucepan; stir to blend. Cool.
2. Stir a small amount of *cold water* (about 1 teaspoon) into the ammonium carbonate. Blend into cooled butter mixture.
3. Add the spices, almonds, and orange peel, stirring only enough to blend the ingredients.

4. Add the flour in thirds, stirring until blended after each addition; mix well.

5. Shape the dough into four 2¼-inch rolls. Wrap in moisture-vaporproof material; chill overnight or longer.

6. Cut each roll into thin slices. Transfer slices to greased cookie sheets.

7. Bake at 350°F 5 to 7 minutes.

8. Store cookies in a loosely covered container.

ABOUT 8 DOZEN COOKIES

MY FAVORITE COOKIE

This cookie, featuring pecans—native to the "Lone Star State"—is a favorite of Jean Houston Daniel, wife of a former governor of Texas. The recipe was given to Mrs. Daniel by her Great-Aunt Jennie, a granddaughter of General Sam Houston.

1 cup butter or margarine	1 teaspoon salt
1 cup sugar	1 teaspoon vanilla extract
1 cup firmly packed brown sugar	2 cups broken pecans
2 eggs, well beaten	4 cups sifted all-purpose flour
1 teaspoon baking soda	

1. Soften butter in a large bowl; add sugars gradually, beating until fluffy. Blend in eggs, baking soda, salt, and extract.

2. Stir in broken pecans and the flour until thoroughly mixed.

3. Tear off 6 pieces of waxed paper about 18 inches long. Divide the dough into 6 portions; put each portion onto a piece of waxed paper and shape into a 1½-inch roll. Wrap in waxed paper.

4. Chill until cold and firm.

5. Cut each roll into thin slices; place the waxed paper the dough was wrapped in on cookie sheets; transfer cookies to waxed paper-covered cookie sheets.

6. Bake at 350°F 5 to 7 minutes, or until light brown.

7. Remove cookies on waxed paper on which they were baked to a wire rack to cool. When cooled, remove cookies from paper.

3 TO 4 DOZEN COOKIES PER ROLL

BLACK WALNUT WAFERS

1 cup butter	¾ cup black walnuts, finely chopped
1 teaspoon vanilla extract	2½ cups sifted all-purpose flour
2 cups firmly packed brown sugar	1 teaspoon baking soda
2 eggs	1 teaspoon salt

1. Cream butter with extract; add brown sugar gradually, beating until fluffy. Add eggs, one at a time, beating thoroughly after each addition. Mix in black walnuts.

2. Sift flour, baking soda, and salt together. Add in fourths to creamed mixture, mixing until blended after each addition.

3. Shape dough into 1½-inch rolls. Wrap and chill several hours or overnight.

4. Remove one roll of dough at a time from refrigerator and cut into thin slices. Place slices 1½-inches apart on ungreased cookie sheets.

5. Bake at 350°F 8 minutes.

ABOUT 8 DOZEN COOKIES

WHEAT SCOTCHIES

1½ cups sifted all-purpose flour	¾ cup butter or margarine
1 teaspoon baking soda	½ teaspoon vanilla extract
½ teaspoon cream of tartar	1 cup firmly packed dark brown sugar
½ teaspoon salt	1 egg
½ cup finely crushed shredded wheat	½ cup raisins

1. Sift flour, baking soda, cream of tartar, and salt together; mix in crushed shredded wheat and set aside.

2. Cream butter with extract; add brown sugar gradually, beating until fluffy. Add egg and beat thoroughly.

3. Add the dry ingredients in fourths, mixing until well blended after each addition. Stir in the raisins.

4. Shape into 1½-inch rolls. Wrap each roll and chill several hours or overnight.

5. Cut each roll into ⅛-inch slices. Place about 1 inch apart on ungreased cookie sheets.

6. Bake at 375°F 6 to 8 minutes.

ABOUT 9 DOZEN COOKIES

NOTE: If desired, lightly brown the finely crushed shredded wheat in *1 tablespoon butter or margarine*; stir occasionally.

ROLLED COOKIES

HOLIDAY STRING-UPS

1 cup butter	3¼ cups sifted all-
2 teaspoons vanilla	purpose flour
extract	1 teaspoon baking
1½ cups sugar	powder
2 eggs	½ teaspoon salt
	Fluffy Frosting, *below*

1. Cream butter with extract; add sugar gradually, beating until fluffy. Add eggs, one at a time, beating thoroughly after each addition.
2. Sift flour, baking powder, and salt together; add to creamed mixture in fourths, mixing until blended after each addition. Chill dough thoroughly.
3. Roll a small amount of dough at a time ¼ inch thick on a floured surface; cut into a variety of shapes with cutters. Transfer to ungreased cookie sheets.
4. Insert 1-inch long pieces of paper straws or macaroni into top of each cutout, or press both ends of a piece of colored cord into the dough on the underside of each cutout.
5. Bake at 400°F 6 to 8 minutes.
6. Cool; gently twist out straws, leaving holes for ribbons or cord to be pulled through after decorating. Decorate baked cookies with Fluffy Frosting, *decorative sugars*, and tiny *colored candies*.

ABOUT 5 DOZEN COOKIES

NOTE: This versatile dough may be thinly rolled and baked cookies sandwiched together with a filling.

CHOCOLATE STRING-UPS: Follow recipe for Holiday String-Ups. Blend in *2 ounces (2 squares) unsweetened chocolate*, melted and cooled, after the eggs are added. Mix in *1 cup finely chopped pecans* after the last addition of dry ingredients.

FLUFFY FROSTING

1½ cups sugar	2 egg whites
⅓ cup water	1 teaspoon vanilla
1½ tablespoons light	extract
corn syrup	

1. Stir sugar, water, and corn syrup together in a saucepan over low heat until sugar is dissolved. Cook without stirring until mixture reaches 240°F.
2. Beat the egg whites until stiff, not dry, peaks are formed; continue beating while pouring the hot syrup over them in a steady thin stream. Continue beating until frosting is very thick and will form and retain swirls when beater is lifted. Blend in the extract.

ABOUT 2¼ CUPS

HUNGARIAN BUTTER COOKIES

2¾ cups sifted all-	4 egg yolks, slightly
purpose flour	beaten
3 teaspoons baking	1 cup dairy sour cream
powder	¼ cup sugar
¼ teaspoon salt	1 egg white, slightly
1½ cups unsalted butter,	beaten
chilled	

1. Sift flour, baking powder, and salt together into a bowl. Cut in butter until particles are the size of rice kernels.
2. Add a mixture of egg yolks, sour cream, and sugar, mixing until blended.
3. Knead until a smooth dough is formed.
4. Roll dough ¼ inch thick on a lightly floured surface; cut with a 2½-inch round cutter.
5. With a sharp knife make a crisscross pattern on top of each; brush with egg white and sprinkle lightly with *vanilla granulated sugar, page 558*. Place on ungreased cookie sheets.
6. Bake at 400°F 5 minutes. Reduce oven temperature to 350°F and bake about 14 minutes.

ABOUT 4 DOZEN COOKIES

SAND TARTS

This particular recipe is a Pennsylvania Dutch favorite. However, variations of the butter-rich cookie appear in several European countries, and in England and Scotland, where it is known as shortbread.

2 cups butter	4 cups sifted all-
2½ cups sugar	purpose flour
2 eggs	1 egg white, slightly
	beaten

1. Cream butter; add sugar gradually, beating until fluffy. Add eggs one at a time, beating thoroughly after each addition.
2. Add flour in fourths, mixing until well blended after each addition. Chill dough overnight.
3. Removing from refrigerator only amount needed for a single rolling, roll dough about 1/16 inch

thick on a floured surface; cut with 2-inch round or fancy cutter. Brush tops with egg white; sprinkle with a mixture of *½ cup sugar* and *2 teaspoons ground cinnamon*.

4. Transfer to ungreased cookie sheets; press a quarter of *pecan* onto center of each cookie.

5. Bake at 350°F about 9 minutes.

ABOUT 17½ DOZEN COOKIES

MORAVIAN SCOTCH CAKES

Bright colors in rich assortment are a feature of the famous bountiful tables of the Pennsylvania Dutch folk. These traditional cookies are as big as their hearts, as gayly colorful as Mom's aprons, and as tender as a maedle's (maiden's) blush!

4 cups sifted all-purpose flour	2 teaspoons caraway seed
½ cup sugar	1½ cups butter

1. Combine flour, sugar, and caraway seed in a bowl. Cut in butter until mixture becomes a soft dough (requires working beyond the stage when particles are the size of rice kernels); shape into a ball.

2. Roll a third of dough at a time ¼ inch thick on a floured surface. Cut into 2-inch squares. Transfer to lightly greased cookie sheets.

3. Bake at 325°F about 20 minutes.

4. Cool cookies; spread with *Snowy Icing, page 431,* and sprinkle with *colored sugar.*

ABOUT 3½ DOZEN COOKIES

SCOTTISH SHORTBREAD

2 cups sifted all-purpose flour	2 tablespoons cornstarch
6 tablespoons sugar	¾ cup butter

1. Sift flour, sugar, and cornstarch into a bowl. Cut in butter until mixture becomes a soft dough (requires working beyond the stage when particles are the size of rice kernels).

2. Shape dough into a ball; knead lightly with fingertips until mixture holds together.

3. Roll half of the dough at a time ¼ to ½ inch thick on a floured surface.

4. Cut into 1½x½-inch strips, or use fancy cutters. Place on ungreased cookie sheets.

5. Bake at 350°F 25 to 30 minutes; do not brown.

2½ TO 4 DOZEN COOKIES

PETTICOAT TAILS: Follow recipe for Scottish Shortbread. Roll dough about ¼ inch thick; cut out 5- or 6-inch rounds and cut a 2½-inch round from the center of each. (Bake centers for samplers.) Cut each ring into 8 pieces; crimp all edges of each piece and prick the surface with a fork; bake as directed.

GRASMERE SHORTBREAD: Follow recipe for Scottish Shortbread. Blend *½ teaspoon ground ginger* with dry ingredients. After addition of butter, stir in *½ cup finely chopped crystallized ginger.* Roll a fourth of dough at a time ⅛ inch thick on a floured surface; cut with a 2-inch fluted round cutter. Bake on ungreased cookie sheets at 350°F 12 minutes. Cool. Spread *Ginger Filling, below,* over bottoms of half the cooled cookies; cover with remaining cookies.

ABOUT 3 DOZEN COOKIES

Ginger Filling: Cream *¼ cup butter* and *1 teaspoon vanilla extract;* add *2 cups confectioners' sugar* gradually, beating until fluffy. Stir in *1 tablespoon milk* until of spreading consistency. Stir in *2 tablespoons grated crystallized ginger.* ABOUT ⅔ CUP

MEDALLION COOKIES
(Medaljakager)

This Danish cream-filled frosted cookie may be served in pairs on individual plates and eaten with a fork as dessert.

Cream Filling II, *page 585*	1 egg
2 cups butter	4¼ cups sifted all-purpose flour
1 cup confectioners' sugar	Confectioners' Sugar Icing III, *page 585*

1. Prepare filling and chill.

2. Cream butter; add confectioners' sugar gradually, beating until fluffy. Add egg; beat thoroughly.

3. Add flour in fourths, mixing until blended after each addition. Cover and set aside 20 minutes (do not refrigerate).

4. Roll a third of the dough at a time ¼ inch thick on a floured surface; cut with 2-inch round cutter. Transfer to ungreased cookie sheets.

5. Bake at 375°F about 10 minutes.

6. Spread about ¾ teaspoon filling over bottom of each of half the cooled cookies; top with remaining cookies; spread icing over tops.

ABOUT 5 DOZEN COOKIES

NOTE: The cookies should be filled shortly before serving time. Fill only as many cookies as will be needed. Refrigerate the filled cookies if they are to be held for any length of time.

CREAM FILLING II

⅓ cup sugar	2 egg yolks, slightly
2 tablespoons flour	beaten
⅛ teaspoon salt	1 tablespoon butter
1 cup milk	1 teaspoon vanilla
	extract

1. Mix sugar, flour, and salt in a double-boiler top. Add the milk gradually, stirring until blended. Stirring constantly, bring mixture rapidly to boiling; boil 3 minutes.
2. Vigorously stir about 3 tablespoons of the hot mixture into the egg yolks; immediately blend into mixture in the double boiler.
3. Cook over simmering water 3 to 5 minutes, stirring constantly.
4. Stir in the butter and extract. Cool slightly; chill. ABOUT 1 CUP

CONFECTIONERS' SUGAR ICING III: Combine *1 cup confectioners' sugar* and *½ teaspoon vanilla extract*. Blend in *milk or cream* (about 1 tablespoon) until icing is of spreading consistency. ABOUT 1 CUP

NOTE: To tint, blend in *1 or 2 drops food coloring.*

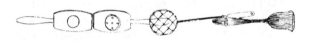

DANISH KNOTS
(Kringler)

2¼ cups sifted all-	½ cup firm butter
purpose flour	1 cup chilled heavy
1 tablespoon sugar	cream, whipped
1 teaspoon baking	Crushed loaf sugar
powder	

1. Sift flour, sugar, and baking powder together into a bowl. Cut in butter until particles are the size of rice kernels.
2. Mix in cream with a fork and knead lightly with fingertips until mixture makes a ball.
3. Roll a fourth of dough at a time into a 6x4-inch rectangle ¼-inch thick on a floured surface. Sprinkle crushed loaf sugar over the dough, pressing in lightly. Cut into 6x¼-inch strips. Form into figure eights or loose knots to resemble pretzels. Place on ungreased cookie sheets.
4. Bake at 400°F about 12 minutes.
ABOUT 5 DOZEN COOKIES

MELTING SNOWFLAKES

⅓ cup butter, chilled	½ teaspoon almond
1 cup sifted all-purpose	extract
flour	Egg white, slightly
2 egg yolks	beaten
1 teaspoon cream	

1. Cut butter into flour until particles are the size of rice kernels.
2. Beat egg yolks, cream, and extract until very thick. Using a fork, blend into flour mixture in halves, mixing well after each addition. Chill dough thoroughly.
3. Roll dough ¼ inch thick on a floured surface; fold lengthwise in half, then crosswise in half; chill 1 hour.
4. Again roll dough ¼ inch thick. Cut with 1¼-inch round cutter. Transfer to ungreased cookie sheets. Brush rounds with egg white.
5. Bake at 350°F about 20 minutes.
6. Remove cookies to wire racks and sift with *Vanilla Confectioners' Sugar, page 558.*
ABOUT 2 DOZEN COOKIES

ALMOND CRISSCROSSES

2 cups sifted all-	1 cup butter, chilled
purpose flour	and cut in pieces
1 teaspoon baking	1 egg yolk, slightly
powder	beaten
¾ cup sugar	Almond Filling, *below*

1. Sift flour, baking powder, and sugar together into a bowl. Cut in the butter until mixture becomes a soft dough (requires working beyond the stage when particles are the size of rice kernels). Blend in the egg yolk.
2. Shape dough into a ball, kneading lightly with fingertips until mixture holds together.
3. Spread two thirds of the dough evenly over bottom and up ¼ inch on the sides of a 13x9x2-inch baking pan. Spread Almond Filling over dough; set aside.
4. Roll remaining dough ⅛ inch thick on a floured surface. Using a pastry wheel, cut into strips ¾ inch wide. Arrange strips to make a lattice design over the filling.
5. Bake at 350°F 35 to 40 minutes.
6. While still warm, cut into bars.
ABOUT 4 DOZEN COOKIES

ALMOND FILLING: Blend *1 cup confectioners' sugar, ½ teaspoon ground cardamom,* and *½ teaspoon ground cinnamon.* Stir in ¾ *cup unblanched almonds,* grated. Add a mixture of *1 egg white* and *2 tablespoons water;* mix thoroughly.

SCANDINAVIAN SPRINGERLE

Unlike the firm anise-flavored German Springerle, this delicately spiced cookie is pleasingly tender.

2 cups sifted all-purpose flour	1 cup butter
½ teaspoon ground cardamom	1 cup confectioners' sugar
½ teaspoon ground cinnamon	¾ cup blanched almonds, finely chopped

1. Sift flour and spices together; set aside.
2. Cream butter; add confectioners' sugar gradually, beating until fluffy. Add flour mixture in fourths, mixing until well blended after each addition. Stir in almonds. Chill dough thoroughly.
3. Roll dough ¼ inch thick on a floured surface or between sheets of waxed paper. Press lightly floured springerle rolling pin firmly into dough, rolling carefully to make clear designs; or press individual springerle molds firmly into dough.
4. Brush surface of dough gently with a soft brush to remove excess flour; cut the frames apart. Transfer to ungreased cookie sheets.
5. Bake at 350°F 10 minutes.

ABOUT 2½ DOZEN COOKIES

AUSTRIAN NUT BUTTER COOKIES

Rich Chocolate Filling, *page 567*	¼ teaspoon ground cloves
2 cups sifted all-purpose flour	¾ cup unblanched almonds, grated
⅔ cup sugar	1¼ cups butter, chilled
½ teaspoon ground cinnamon	Glossy Chocolate Frosting, *below*

1. Prepare Rich Chocolate Filling.
2. Sift flour, sugar, and spices together; mix in almonds.
3. Cut in butter until mixture becomes a soft dough (requires working beyond the stage when particles are the size of rice kernels). Using fingertips, shape into a ball.
4. Roll a third of dough at a time ⅛ inch thick on a floured surface; cut with 2½-inch round cutter.
5. Bake on ungreased cookie sheets at 325°F 12 minutes; do not brown.

6. When cool, sandwich cookies together with filling. Lightly spread top of each double cookie with sieved *apricot jam,* then with Glossy Chocolate Frosting; top each with a *pecan half* or *slivered almond piece.* ABOUT 2½ DOZEN COOKIES

GLOSSY CHOCOLATE FROSTING

½ cup sugar	2 tablespoons butter or margarine
2 tablespoons cornstarch	1 teaspoon vanilla extract
¼ teaspoon salt	
½ cup boiling water	
1 oz. (1 sq.) unsweetened chocolate, cut in pieces	

1. Mix sugar, cornstarch, and salt in a saucepan; stir in the water and chocolate.
2. Cook over medium heat until mixture thickens, stirring frequently.
3. Remove from heat; stir in butter and extract. Spread while frosting is warm. ABOUT 1 CUP

ISCHL COOKIES

These regal Tyrolean cookies originated at Franz Josef's famous summer residence.

Follow recipe for Austrian Nut Butter Cookies. Omit filling, frosting, and nuts for garnish. After cutting out rounds, place half on cookie sheets and bake. From remainder, cut out from each round 3 small rounds ¼ to ½ inch in diameter; bake. When cookies are cool, spread each plain cookie with about ½ *teaspoon currant jelly.* Cover with cookies having holes.

ALMOND WREATHS
(Mandelkranzchen)

This rich German cookie is a favorite at Christmas time.

¾ cup butter	Egg yolk, slightly beaten
½ cup sugar	½ cup blanched almonds, finely chopped
1 egg	
2 cups sifted all-purpose flour	

1. Cream butter; add sugar gradually, beating until fluffy. Add egg and beat thoroughly.
2. Add flour in fourths, mixing until well blended after each addition. Chill dough thoroughly.
3. Roll one half of dough at a time ¼ inch thick on a floured surface; cut with 1¾-inch round cutter

and cut out centers with a ¾-inch round cutter. (Bake centers for samplers.)

4. Transfer rounds and rings to ungreased cookie sheets. Brush tops with egg yolk and sprinkle with almonds.

5. Bake at 350°F 10 to 15 minutes.

ABOUT 6 DOZEN COOKIES

ALMOND FLAKES NORMANDY

⅔ cup butter	Few grains salt
1¼ cups sifted all-purpose flour	1 egg white
½ cup toasted blanched almonds, grated or finely chopped	½ teaspoon almond extract
	1 egg yolk, slightly beaten
¾ cup confectioners' sugar	3 to 4 tablespoons sugar

1. Cut butter into flour until particles are the size of rice kernels.

2. Blend in almonds, confectioners' sugar, and salt.

3. Beat the egg white and extract until frothy; add to flour-sugar mixture, mixing until a soft dough is formed.

4. Shape dough into a ball; knead lightly with fingertips until mixture holds together. Chill dough thoroughly.

5. Roll a third of dough at a time ⅛ inch thick between sheets of waxed paper. Cut with a 2-inch round cutter.

6. Transfer to ungreased cookie sheets; brush tops with egg yolk and sprinkle each with ¼ teaspoon sugar.

7. Bake at 300°F 18 to 20 minutes.

ABOUT 3 DOZEN COOKIES

ANISE FORM COOKIES
(Springerle)

These cookies require a special decorative rolling pin or molds to prepare. They're popular at Christmastime in German-speaking countries.

2 eggs	2 cups sifted all-purpose flour
1 cup sugar	
½ teaspoon grated lemon peel	¼ teaspoon crushed ammonium carbonate (available at your pharmacy)
8 drops anise oil	

1. Beat eggs, sugar, lemon peel, and anise oil until very thick.

2. Blend flour and ammonium carbonate; add in fourths to egg-sugar mixture, mixing until blended after each addition.

3. Cover with a clean towel and let stand at room temperature 1 hour.

4. Shape dough into a ball and, on a floured surface, knead lightly with fingertips; roll ¼ inch thick.

5. Press lightly floured springerle rolling pin or mold firmly into dough to make clear designs.

6. Brush dough surface gently with soft brush to remove excess flour; cut the frames apart; cover and let stand 24 hours.

7. Lightly grease cookie sheets; sprinkle entire surface with *anise seed*.

8. Lightly brush back of each frame with water and set on anise seed.

9. Bake at 325°F 8 minutes.

10. When thoroughly cool, store in a tightly covered container 1 to 2 weeks before serving. To soften cookies, see *page 558*.

ABOUT 4 DOZEN COOKIES

BASLER BRUNSLI

As appropriate to Christmas as it is uniquely Swiss (Basler translates "from Basle"), this rich cookie will be one of your great joys of the season.

1 lb. unblanched almonds, grated* (5 cups)	2½ cups sugar
	1 teaspoon ground cinnamon
4 to 4½ oz. (4 to 4½ sq.) unsweetened chocolate, grated*	1 tablespoon kirsch
	4 egg whites (about ⅔ cup)

1. Thoroughly blend almonds and chocolate with a mixture of sugar and cinnamon. Drizzle with the kirsch.

2. Beat the egg whites until stiff, not dry, peaks are formed. Blend into nut mixture. Chill thoroughly.

3. Roll a fourth of the mixture at a time ½ inch thick on a lightly sugared surface. Cut with 1¼-inch round cutter. Place on lightly greased cookie sheets.

4. Bake at 300°F 15 minutes. Cool on wire racks.

ABOUT 10 DOZEN COOKIES

*Blender grating speeds the job.

CHOCOLATE-ALMOND CRESCENTS

2½ cups sifted all-
   purpose flour
¼ cup sugar
½ teaspoon salt
1 cup butter, chilled
   and cut in pieces
1 cup blanched, toasted
   almonds, finely
   chopped

⅓ cup semisweet
   chocolate pieces,
   grated
2 egg yolks, slightly
   beaten
Confectioners' sugar

1. Blend flour, sugar, and salt in a bowl. Cut in the butter with pastry blender or two knives until particles are the size of rice kernels.
2. Mix in the almonds and chocolate. Add the egg yolks gradually, mixing thoroughly with a fork. Gather dough into a ball, working with fingertips until mixture holds together. Chill dough thoroughly.
3. Sift confectioners' sugar lightly and evenly over a flat surface. Roll a third of the dough about ¼ inch thick on the sugared surface. Cut with a lightly floured crescent-shaped cookie cutter. Transfer to lightly greased cookie sheets. Repeat for remaining dough.
4. Bake at 350°F about 7 minutes.
5. Immediately remove cookies to wire racks.

ABOUT 7 DOZEN COOKIES

SPICY CINNAMON TOWERS

Let the smallfry assist in creating these "towers."

½ cup butter
¾ cup sugar
1 egg
1 tablespoon milk
2¼ cups sifted all-
   purpose flour

1½ teaspoons baking
   powder
1 teaspoon ground
   cinnamon
¼ teaspoon salt
¼ to ⅓ cup apple butter

1. Cream butter; add sugar gradually, beating until fluffy. Add egg and milk; beat well.
2. Sift flour, baking powder, cinnamon, and salt together. Add in fourths to creamed mixture, mixing until blended after each addition. Chill several hours, or until dough is firm enough to roll.
3. Remove amount of dough needed for single rolling and return remainder to refrigerator. Roll dough on a lightly floured surface to a thickness of not more than ¼ inch.
4. Using lightly floured scalloped cookie cutters that are 2 inches, 1¼ inches, and ¾ inch in diameter, cut out an equal number of cookies of the three

sizes. Place cookies on ungreased cookie sheets. (Keeping cookies of one size together on sheets speeds the job of assembling cookie towers.)
5. Bake at 425°F 5 to 7 minutes.
6. Immediately and carefully remove cookies to wire racks to cool.
7. Using large cookies for bases of cookie towers, spoon ¼ to ½ teaspoon apple butter onto centers. Top with smaller-sized cookies. Spoon apple butter onto centers and top with smallest cookies.
8. Set cookie towers on waxed paper. Sift *confectioners' sugar* lightly over cookies.

ABOUT 2½ DOZEN COOKIE TOWERS

ALMOND-STRAWBERRY TOWERS: Follow recipe for Spicy Cinnamon Towers. Cut an equal number of cookies with 2-inch scalloped cookie cutter and with 1¼-inch round cookie cutter; omit ¾ inch cookies. Sprinkle smaller, unbaked cookies with crushed *rock candy*. Bake as directed. Substitute *strawberry jelly* for apple butter. Place a dot of jelly on center of each candy-sprinkled cookie; top with one *whole blanched almond.*

CINNAMON STARS
(Zimtsterne)

The rich blend of almond and cinnamon flavor adds a touch of distinction to this star-shaped confection, a German-Swiss holiday favorite.

⅓ cup plus 1 tablespoon
   egg whites
1 cup confectioners'
   sugar
1 teaspoon grated lemon
   peel

¾ teaspoon ground
   cinnamon
2 cups unblanched
   almonds, grated

1. Lightly grease 2 cookie sheets, sprinkle with *flour*, and shake off excess; set aside.
2. Using an electric beater, beat egg whites until stiff, not dry, peaks are formed. Add confectioners' sugar gradually, beating 5 minutes at medium speed. Remove ⅓ cup of meringue and set aside.
3. Into remaining meringue, beat the lemon peel and cinnamon. Fold in the almonds.
4. Turn almond mixture onto a pastry canvas sprinkled with *confectioners'* or *granulated sugar*. Gently roll ¼ to ⅜ inch thick. Lightly sprinkle with sugar. Cut with a 2-inch star-shaped cookie cutter dipped in confectioners' sugar.
5. Transfer to cookie sheets; drop about ½ teaspoonful of reserved meringue onto each star and

spread out evenly onto points. Set aside in a warm place (about 80°F) 1½ hours.

6. Bake at 375°F 5 minutes.

ABOUT 3 DOZEN COOKIES

JAN HAGEL

These Dutch delicacies are popular throughout the holiday season and particularly on the feast day of Saint Nicholas.

1 cup butter	4 pieces loaf sugar,
1 cup sugar	finely crushed
1 egg yolk	½ teaspoon ground
2 cups sifted all-	cinnamon
purpose flour	½ cup finely chopped
¼ teaspoon salt	nuts
1 egg white	

1. Cream butter; add sugar gradually, beating until fluffy. Add egg yolk and beat well.
2. Blend flour and salt; add in fourths to creamed mixture, mixing until blended after each addition.
3. Divide dough into halves and roll each on an ungreased cookie sheet into a 12x10-inch rectangle.
4. Beat egg white slightly with a small amount of *water*; brush lightly over dough. Mix crushed sugar with cinnamon and nuts; sprinkle over each rectangle.
5. Bake at 375°F 15 minutes.
6. Trim the edges and cut into bars while warm.

ABOUT 4 DOZEN COOKIES

COFFEE-CHOCOLATE RINGLES

2 oz. (2 sq.) unsweet-	¼ teaspoon ground
ened chocolate	cinnamon
1¾ cups sifted all-	⅔ cup butter
purpose flour	½ teaspoon vanilla
2 teaspoons baking	extract
powder	1 cup sugar
⅛ teaspoon salt	1 egg
1 tablespoon instant	
coffee	

1. Melt chocolate; set aside to cool.
2. Sift flour, baking powder, salt, instant coffee, and cinnamon together; set aside.
3. Cream butter with extract; add sugar gradually, beating until fluffy. Add egg and beat thoroughly. Blend in cooled chocolate.
4. Add dry ingredients in fourths, mixing until blended after each addition. Chill thoroughly.

5. Roll one third of dough at a time ¼ inch thick on a floured surface or between two sheets of waxed paper; cut with 1½-inch scalloped cutter. Cut out centers, if desired.
6. Transfer to ungreased cookie sheets and sprinkle tops with *sugar*.
7. Bake at 350°F about 10 minutes.

ABOUT 6½ DOZEN COOKIES

KOLACKY COOKIES

1 cup butter	2¼ cups sifted all-
8 oz. cream cheese,	purpose flour
softened	½ teaspoon salt
¼ teaspoon vanilla	Cherry preserves,
extract	apricot preserves, or
	prune filling

1. Cream butter and cream cheese with extract until fluffy.
2. Blend flour and salt; add in fourths to creamed mixture, mixing until blended after each addition. Chill dough thoroughly.
3. Roll dough ¼ inch thick on a floured surface; cut with 2-inch round cutter or fancy-shaped cutters. Transfer to ungreased cookie sheets, make a small indentation in center of each round, and fill with ½ teaspoon preserves.
4. Bake at 350°F 10 to 15 minutes, or until delicately browned.

ABOUT 3½ DOZEN COOKIES

EDINBURGH SQUARES

A melt-in-your-mouth, nut-rich layer, covered with jelly topped with chocolate meringue, results in taste-tempting squares you'll make often.

1½ cups sifted all-	1½ tablespoons currant
purpose flour	jelly or apricot
¼ cup sugar	preserves
½ cup butter, chilled	1 egg white
¾ cup unblanched	⅛ teaspoon cream of
almonds, grated (2	tartar
cups)	¼ cup sugar
2 egg yolks, well beaten	1½ oz. sweet chocolate,
	melted and cooled

1. Blend flour and ¼ cup sugar. Cut in butter until pieces are the size of small peas. Blend in 1½ cups of the grated almonds. Add egg yolks and mix thoroughly.
2. Shape dough into a ball, kneading lightly with fingertips; put onto an ungreased cookie sheet; roll

into a 10½x7½-inch rectangle. Spread evenly with jelly; set aside.

3. Beat egg white and cream of tartar until frothy; gradually add ¼ cup sugar, continuing to beat until stiff peaks are formed.

4. Gently fold in cooled chocolate and remaining grated almonds; spread evenly over jelly-topped dough.

5. Bake at 300°F 25 to 30 minutes.

6. When cool, cut into squares.

ABOUT 3 DOZEN COOKIES

SHREWSBURY BISCUITS

Americans would call these tender, currant-flecked treats cookies, but being an English favorite, they're biscuits.

¾ cup butter	1 egg
2 teaspoons grated lemon peel	1¾ cups sifted all-purpose flour
2 tablespoons lemon juice	½ teaspoon baking powder
¾ cup sugar	¼ teaspoon salt
	1 cup currants

1. Cream butter with lemon peel and juice; add sugar gradually, beating until fluffy. Add egg and beat thoroughly.

2. Sift flour, baking powder, and salt together; add in fourths to creamed mixture, mixing until blended after each addition. Mix in currants. Chill dough thoroughly.

3. Roll a third of dough at a time ¼ inch thick on a floured surface. Cut with 2½-inch fluted cutter. Brush cutouts with *milk*; sprinkle with *sugar*. Transfer to ungreased cookie sheets.

4. Bake at 350°F 12 to 15 minutes.

ABOUT 2½ DOZEN COOKIES

BUTTER STICKS

¼ cup sugar	¼ teaspoon almond extract
3 hard-cooked egg yolks, sieved	2¼ cups sifted all-purpose flour
1 cup butter, softened	

1. Add sugar gradually to sieved egg yolks, mixing well after each addition.

2. Add butter, a small amount at a time, beating until fluffy after each addition. Mix in extract.

3. Add flour in fourths, mixing until blended after each addition. Knead lightly with fingertips and form into a ball.

4. Roll a fourth of dough at a time ¼ inch thick on a floured surface.

5. Brush dough with slightly beaten *egg white*; sprinkle with a mixture of *ground cinnamon* and crushed *loaf sugar*. Cut into 4x¼-inch strips. Transfer to ungreased cookie sheets.

6. Bake at 350°F 8 to 10 minutes.

ABOUT 10 DOZEN COOKIES

FILLED CRESCENTS

1 cup sifted all-purpose flour	⅓ cup sugar
¼ teaspoon salt	1 tablespoon dairy sour cream
½ cup butter, chilled	1 teaspoon vanilla extract
1 hard-cooked egg yolk, sieved	¼ cup apricot preserves

1. Blend flour and salt in a bowl. Cut in butter until mixture becomes a soft dough (requires working beyond the stage when particles are the size of rice kernels).

2. Blend in sieved egg yolk, sugar, sour cream, and extract. Knead lightly with fingertips and form into a ball.

3. Roll a half of the dough at a time into a 10-inch round on a floured surface; cut into 12 wedge-shaped pieces.

4. Spread ½ teaspoon preserves on wide part of each wedge; roll up, starting at outer edge. Place on ungreased cookie sheet with point underneath; curve into a crescent.

5. Bake at 375°F 10 to 12 minutes.

6. Remove to wire racks to cool slightly. While still warm, sift *Vanilla Confectioners' Sugar, page 558*, over cookies. 2 DOZEN COOKIES

GINGER SHORTBREAD

1½ cups sifted all-purpose flour	½ cup butter or margarine
1 teaspoon ground ginger	⅓ cup firmly packed brown sugar
¼ teaspoon salt	1 tablespoon heavy cream

1. Sift flour, ginger, and salt together; set aside.

2. Cream butter; add brown sugar gradually,

beating well. Add flour mixture gradually, mixing until well blended. Stir in cream.

3. Divide dough into halves. Place on an ungreased cookie sheet. Flatten into rounds about ½ inch thick. Mark into wedges. Flute the edges and prick centers with a fork.

4. Bake at 350°F about 20 minutes.

5. While still warm, cut into wedges.

2 SHORTBREAD ROUNDS

SWEDISH GINGERSNAPS
(Pepparkakor)

It is the pride of Swedish cooks to roll wafer-thin the rich, spicy dough of their traditional Christmas Pepparkakor.

1½ cups sifted all-purpose flour	½ cup butter
1 teaspoon baking soda	¾ cup sugar
1½ teaspoons ground ginger	1 egg
	1½ teaspoons dark corn syrup
1 teaspoon ground cinnamon	Whole blanched almonds, cut in small pieces
¼ teaspoon ground cloves	

1. Sift flour, baking soda, and spices together; set aside.

2. Cream butter; add sugar gradually, beating until fluffy. Add egg and corn syrup and beat thoroughly.

3. Blend in dry ingredients in fourths, mixing thoroughly after each addition. Refrigerate dough several hours.

4. Using a portion of the dough at a time, roll about ¹⁄₁₆ inch thick on a lightly floured surface. Cut with lightly floured cookie cutters into various shapes. Transfer to ungreased cookie sheets. Place one almond piece in the center of each.

5. Bake at 375°F 6 to 8 minutes.

ABOUT 7 DOZEN COOKIES

LEMON SUGAR COOKIES

¾ cup butter	2 cups sifted all-purpose flour
1 teaspoon grated lemon peel	1½ teaspoons baking powder
1 tablespoon lemon juice	½ teaspoon salt
1¼ cups sugar	
2 eggs	

1. Cream butter with lemon peel and juice; add the sugar gradually, creaming until fluffy. Add the

eggs, one at a time, beating thoroughly after each addition.

2. Sift flour, baking powder, and salt together; add in fourths to creamed mixture, mixing until blended after each addition. Chill dough thoroughly.

3. Roll a third of dough at a time ⅛ inch thick; cut with 2¼-inch round or fancy cutter. Transfer to ungreased cookie sheets.

4. Bake at 325°F 15 to 18 minutes.

ABOUT 4½ DOZEN COOKIES

NOTE: If desired, add sugar sparkle by evenly sprinkling *granulated sugar* over the rolled dough. Roll lightly to press sugar into dough. Or, add decorations by brushing rolled dough with slightly beaten *egg white* (or egg yolk beaten with 1 tablespoon water or milk); top with pieces of *angelica, citron,* or *candied cherries* or sprinkle with *colored sugar* or crushed *rock candy.*

BROWN SUGAR COOKIES: Follow recipe for Lemon Sugar Cookies. Omit lemon peel and juice; add *1 teaspoon vanilla extract.* Substitute *1 cup firmly packed brown sugar* for granulated sugar.

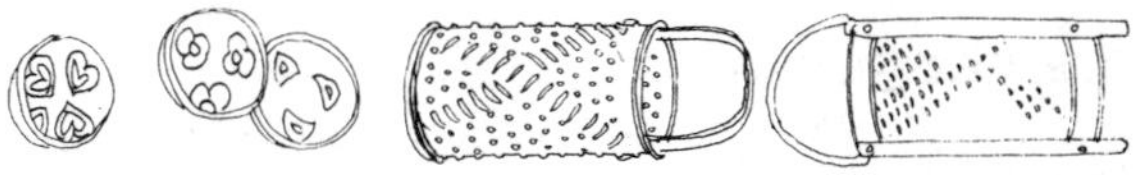

SWISS CHRISTMAS COOKIES
(Mailaenderli)

¾ cup butter	1 egg yolk
½ teaspoon grated lemon peel	2¾ cups sifted all-purpose flour
¼ teaspoon lemon juice	⅛ teaspoon salt
¾ cup sugar	1 egg yolk, beaten
1 egg	

1. Cream butter with lemon peel and juice; add sugar gradually, beating until fluffy. Add egg and 1 egg yolk, beating thoroughly after each addition.

2. Add a mixture of flour and salt in fourths, mixing until well blended after each addition. Chill dough thoroughly, at least 1 hour.

3. Roll a third of dough at a time about ¼ inch thick on a floured surface; cut with fancy cookie cutters. Transfer to lightly greased cookie sheets; brush tops with beaten egg yolk.

4. Bake at 375°F 10 to 12 minutes.

ABOUT 6 DOZEN COOKIES

TEXAS COOKIES

A recipe from Mrs. Lyndon B. Johnson, former First Lady of the United States.

½ cup butter	1 tablespoon cream
1 tablespoon grated lemon peel	1½ cups sifted all-purpose flour
½ teaspoon lemon extract	1 teaspoon baking powder
1 cup sugar	½ teaspoon salt
1 egg	

1. Cream butter with lemon peel and extract; add sugar gradually, beating until fluffy. Add egg and beat thoroughly. Mix in cream.
2. Sift remaining ingredients together; add in thirds to creamed mixture, mixing until blended after each addition.
3. Chill dough 2 to 3 hours, or overnight.
4. Roll a small portion of dough at a time very thin on a lightly floured surface. Cut with a state-of-Texas-shaped cutter or other large cookie cutter. Transfer to ungreased cookie sheets.
5. Bake at 375°F 8 to 10 minutes.
6. Cool cookies on wire racks.

ABOUT 5 DOZEN COOKIES

JOE FROGGERS

A big, soft, fat molasses cookie known in New England by that name.

4¾ cups sifted all-purpose flour	¼ teaspoon ground cloves
1½ teaspoons salt	¾ cup vegetable shortening
1 teaspoon baking powder	1 cup firmly packed brown sugar
1 teaspoon baking soda	1 cup molasses
1½ teaspoons ground ginger	½ cup water

1. Sift flour, salt, baking powder, baking soda, and spices together and blend thoroughly; set aside.
2. Beat shortening and gradually add brown sugar, beating until fluffy.
3. Mix the molasses and water.
4. Alternately add dry ingredients in fourths and molasses mixture in thirds to creamed mixture, blending well after each addition. Chill dough about 1½ hours, or until firm enough to roll.
5. Working with a small amount of dough at a time, roll ¼ inch thick on a lightly floured surface. Cut with a floured 3-inch round cookie cutter.

Place about 2 inches apart on lightly greased cookie sheets.
6. Bake at 375°F 10 to 12 minutes.
7. Carefully remove cookies to wire racks; cool completely. ABOUT 2 DOZEN COOKIES

GERMAN MOLASSES COOKIES

1 cup butter	1 teaspoon salt
1¼ cups light molasses	2 teaspoons ground ginger
¾ cup firmly packed light brown sugar	1 teaspoon ground cinnamon
4 cups sifted all-purpose flour	½ to ¾ teaspoon ground cloves
1 teaspoon baking soda	

1. Melt butter in a saucepan; add molasses and brown sugar and heat until sugar is dissolved, stirring occasionally. Pour into a bowl; cool.
2. Sift remaining ingredients together; add to cooled mixture in fourths, mixing until blended after each addition.
3. Turn dough onto a floured surface and knead until easy to handle, using additional flour if necessary.
4. Wrap in moisture-vaporproof material; refrigerate and allow dough to ripen one or two days.
5. Roll one fourth of dough at a time about ⅛ inch thick on a floured surface; cut with a 3-inch round cutter or fancy cutters. Transfer to ungreased cookie sheets.
6. Bake at 350°F about 7 minutes.

ABOUT 8 DOZEN COOKIES

NOTE: For gingerbread men, roll dough ¼ inch thick and cut with a gingerbread-man cutter. Bake about 13 minutes.

BROWN MORAVIAN COOKIES

A Pennsylvania Dutch cookie.

4 cups sifted all-purpose flour	¼ teaspoon ground ginger
¼ teaspoon baking soda	1 cup firmly packed light brown sugar
¼ teaspoon salt	½ cup butter
1 teaspoon ground cinnamon	½ cup lard*
½ teaspoon ground cloves	1½ cups light molasses
	½ teaspoon cider vinegar

1. Sift flour, baking soda, salt, and spices together

into a large bowl. Add brown sugar; mix well.

2. Cut in butter and lard. Add molasses and vinegar gradually, mixing well. Chill dough thoroughly.

3. Using a small amount of dough at a time, roll out about 1/8-inch thick on a lightly floured surface. Cut with fancy cookie cutters. Transfer to greased cookie sheets.

4. Bake at 350°F 8 to 10 minutes.

ABOUT 6 DOZEN COOKIES

*Use butter, if desired, but then cookie will not be authentic.

GERMAN PUFF PASTRY COOKIES
(Blätterteig Pastetchen)
Layer upon tender layer describes these jelly-filled flaky rounds, each with a small "cap."

2 cups sifted all-purpose flour	1 cup sieved cooked potato, chilled
1/4 cup confectioners' sugar	1 cup butter, chilled
	1 teaspoon vanilla extract

1. Blend flour and confectioners' sugar; chill.

2. Add potato and mix gently with a fork. Cut in butter until pieces are the size of small peas.

3. Sprinkle extract over mixture, a few drops at a time, mixing lightly with fork (dough should be crumbly). Shape dough into a ball; chill thoroughly.

4. Roll dough, a half at a time, 1/4 inch thick on a floured surface; cut with 1 3/4-inch round cutter and cut centers from half the rounds with a 3/4-inch round cutter. Place rounds, rings, and centers on separate ungreased cookie sheets.

5. Bake at 400°F 10 to 15 minutes.

6. When cool, spread rounds with *currant jelly* and top with rings; fill centers of rings with a small amount of jelly; top with centers.

ABOUT 2 DOZEN COOKIES

ITALIAN BUTTER COOKIES
(Canestrelli)

4 cups sifted all-purpose flour	4 egg yolks, beaten
1 cup sugar	1 cup firm unsalted butter, cut in pieces
2 1/2 teaspoons grated lemon peel	1 egg white, slightly beaten
1 tablespoon rum	

1. Combine flour, sugar, and lemon peel in a large bowl; mix thoroughly. Add rum and then egg yolks

in fourths, mixing thoroughly after each addition.

2. Cut butter into flour mixture with pastry blender until particles are fine. Work with fingertips until a dough is formed.

3. Roll one half of dough at a time about 1/4 inch thick on a lightly floured surface. Cut into desired shapes. Brush tops with egg white. Transfer to lightly greased cookie sheets.

4. Bake at 350°F about 15 minutes.

ABOUT 6 DOZEN COOKIES

LOVE LETTERS
(Szerelmes Levél)
Rich pastry squares folded like envelopes, with a nut-meringue filling inside, become Hungarian "love letters."

2 cups sifted all-purpose flour	1/2 cup coarsely chopped walnuts
2 tablespoons sugar	1 teaspoon grated lemon peel
1/4 teaspoon salt	2 egg whites
3/4 cup butter, chilled	1/4 cup sugar
4 egg yolks, slightly beaten	1/2 teaspoon ground cinnamon

1. Blend flour, sugar, and salt. Cut in butter until particles are the size of rice kernels.

2. Add egg yolks gradually, blending with a fork (mixture will be crumbly). Knead lightly with fingertips and shape into a ball.

3. Divide dough into halves; wrap in waxed paper and chill 1 hour.

4. Mix walnuts and lemon peel; set aside.

5. Fifteen minutes before chilling time is ended, beat egg whites until frothy. Add a mixture of sugar and cinnamon gradually, beating well after each addition; beat until stiff peaks are formed.

6. Gently fold in nut mixture; set aside.

7. Roll one half of dough at a time 1/8 inch thick on a floured surface; cut into 3-inch squares.

8. Put about 2 teaspoons of filling onto center of each square; bring opposite corners together, overlapping slightly at center; repeat with other two corners.

9. Transfer to ungreased cookie sheets. Brush tops with slightly beaten *egg*.

10. Bake at 350°F about 20 minutes.

11. Cool cookies on wire racks. Sift a mixture of *2 to 3 tablespoons confectioners' sugar* and *1/2 to 1 teaspoon ground cinnamon* over cooled cookies.

ABOUT 2 1/2 DOZEN COOKIES

PEPPERNUTS
(Pfeffernüsse)

In this recipe that famous spicy German favorite has been given a slightly different twist . . . the flavor of brandy permeates both cookie and frosting.

2 cups sifted all-purpose flour	⅛ teaspoon ground mace
⅛ teaspoon salt	¼ cup blanched almonds, grated
⅛ teaspoon black pepper	2 eggs
1 teaspoon ground cinnamon	1 cup sugar
¼ teaspoon ground allspice	¼ cup chopped candied citron
¼ teaspoon ground cloves	Brandy
¼ teaspoon ground nutmeg	Frosting, *below*

1. Sift flour, salt, and spices together and blend in the almonds; set aside.
2. Beat eggs and sugar until very thick.
3. Add dry ingredients in thirds, mixing until well blended after each addition. Stir in the citron.
4. Roll dough ½ inch thick on a floured surface; cut with 1-inch round cutter. Place on lightly greased cookie sheet; put a drop of brandy on the center of each cutout.
5. Bake at 350°F 12 to 15 minutes.
6. Frost cookies while still warm. Cool on racks before storing. To soften cookies, see *page 558*.

ABOUT 5½ DOZEN COOKIES

FROSTING: Mix *1 cup confectioners' sugar, 1 teaspoon brandy*, and *4 to 5 teaspoons water* until smooth.

ABOUT ⅓ CUP

APRICOT CRESCENTS

1 pkg. active dry yeast	2½ cups sifted all-purpose flour
¼ cup warm water	3 egg yolks
1 cup softened butter	Confectioners' sugar
2 tablespoons sugar	¾ cup Splendent Filling, *page 595*, or apricot preserves
1 teaspoon vanilla extract	
¼ teaspoon salt	
¼ cup cream, scalded	

1. Soften yeast in the warm water; set aside.
2. Mix in a large bowl the butter, sugar, extract, and salt. Add scalded cream and stir to blend. Thoroughly beat in ½ cup of the flour.

3. Add yeast to butter mixture; mix thoroughly. Add the egg yolks, one at a time, beating thoroughly after each addition. Add about half of the remaining flour and beat until very smooth. Beat in enough flour to make a soft dough.
4. Sift confectioners' sugar lightly and evenly over a flat surface. Roll a fourth of the dough at a time into a 12-inch round on the sugared surface. Cut into 16 wedge-shaped pieces. Spread wide end of each wedge with about ½ teaspoon filling. Roll up each wedge, beginning at the wide end; place with point down on an ungreased cookie sheet. Curve into crescents.
5. Cover with waxed paper and a clean towel; let stand 20 minutes (cookies will rise only slightly).
6. Bake at 350°F 15 to 20 minutes, or until lightly browned.
7. Remove cookies to wire racks and cool slightly. Sift *Vanilla Confectioners' Sugar, page 558*, over tops.

5 DOZEN COOKIES

CELESTIAL COOKIES

A heavenly walnut-filled sour cream cookie made from a very rich yeast dough.

1 pkg. active dry yeast	1 cup butter, chilled
¼ cup warm water	2 egg yolks
4 cups sifted all-purpose flour	⅛ teaspoon vanilla extract
2 tablespoons sugar	1 cup dairy sour cream
½ teaspoon salt	Nut Filling, *page 595*

1. Soften yeast in the warm water; set aside.
2. Blend flour, sugar, and salt in a bowl. Cut in butter with a pastry blender or two knives until particles are the size of rice kernels; set aside.
3. Beat egg yolks and extract until thick. Add yeast and sour cream gradually, beating well after each addition.
4. Add to the flour-butter mixture gradually, blending well after each addition. Cover and chill overnight.
5. The next day prepare Nut Filling; set aside.
6. Roll a half of dough at a time into a 16x12-inch rectangle on a floured surface. Spread surface of dough with filling.
7. Roll the other half of dough to the same size on waxed paper. Invert dough on waxed paper over filling; press down gently and evenly; peel off paper.
8. Cut into 2-inch squares or into bars or trian-

gles; press edges together to seal. Place on lightly greased cookie sheets.

9.   Bake at 350°F 15 minutes.

ABOUT 4 DOZEN COOKIES

NUT FILLING: Blend *1½ cups walnuts*, grated, with *1 cup plus 2 tablespoons sugar*. Gradually add *3 egg whites*, slightly beaten, and *¼ teaspoon vanilla extract*, blending well after each addition.

MINIATURE KOLACKY

A yeast-raised "sweet" considered a rich bun in some countries. Probably of Czech origin, there are many different versions and spellings of the name.

1 cake (⅝ or ³/₅ oz.) compressed yeast	1 cup butter, chilled
1 cup cream, scalded and cooled	4 egg yolks
½ teaspoon sugar	¼ cup sugar
3 cups sifted all-purpose flour	2 teaspoons grated lemon peel
⅛ teaspoon salt	California or Splendent Filling, *below*

1.   Soften yeast in lukewarm cream. Stir in ½ teaspoon sugar and let stand 15 minutes.
2.   Blend flour and salt. Cut in the butter with a pastry blender or two knives until particles are the size of rice kernels; set aside.
3.   Beat egg yolks and ¼ cup sugar together until very thick. Beat in cream mixture and lemon peel.
4.   Make a well in the center of the flour-butter mixture; add egg yolk mixture and blend well. Chill dough overnight.

5.   Put half of the chilled dough on a lightly floured surface; roll ¼ inch thick. Cut out rounds with a lightly floured 1½-inch cookie cutter; transfer to ungreased cookie sheets.
6.   Make a slight depression in the center of each round and fill with about 1 teaspoonful of filling. Repeat, using remaining dough.
7.   Cover and allow to stand in a warm place 10 to 15 minutes.
8.   Bake at 350°F 15 to 20 minutes, or until lightly browned. Remove cookies to wire racks.

ABOUT 7 DOZEN KOLACKY

CALIFORNIA FILLING

1¼ cups prunes (about 8 oz.), cooked, drained, and pitted	2 teaspoons grated lemon peel
¼ cup sugar	3 tablespoons lemon juice

Force prunes through a sieve or food mill. Blend in remaining ingredients; let cool.   1 CUP

SPLENDENT FILLING

1¼ cups dried apricots, rinsed (about 8 oz.)	¼ teaspoon ground cinnamon
¾ cup boiling water	2 tablespoons butter
½ cup sugar	

1.   Chop apricots and cover with boiling water; cover tightly; simmer 10 to 20 minutes, or until tender.
2.   Remove from heat; add remaining ingredients and stir until sugar is dissolved and butter is melted. Set aside to cool.   1½ CUPS

DEEP-FRIED COOKIES

FATTIGMANN

A traditional Norwegian Christmas favorite.

10 egg yolks	5 cups sifted all-purpose flour
2 egg whites	
¾ cup sugar	2 teaspoons ground cardamom
¼ cup brandy	
1 cup heavy cream	Lard for deep frying

1.   Beat egg yolks, egg whites, sugar, and brandy until very thick. Add cream slowly, stirring well.
2.   Sift flour and cardamom together; add about ½ cup at a time to egg mixture, mixing thoroughly after each addition. Wrap and chill overnight.

3.   Heat lard to 365° to 370°F in a deep saucepan.
4.   Roll dough, a small portion at a time, 1/16 inch thick on a floured surface.
5.   Using a floured knife or pastry wheel, cut into diamond shapes, 5x2 inches; make a lengthwise slit in the center of each diamond. Pull the tip of one end through each slit and tuck back under itself.
6.   Deep fry 1 to 2 minutes, or until golden brown, turning once. Drain and cool.
7.   Sprinkle cookies with *confectioners' sugar*. Store in tightly covered containers.

ABOUT 6 DOZEN COOKIES

TINY DOUGHNUT COOKIES
(Jortitog)

This is one of Norway's fine cookies—more like "fried cake" than cookie.

½ cup butter
1 cup sugar
4 eggs
3 cups sifted all-
    purpose flour

½ teaspoon crushed
    ammonium carbonate
    (available at your
    pharmacy)
½ teaspoon salt
Fat for deep frying
    heated to 375°F

1. Cream butter; add sugar gradually, beating until fluffy. Add eggs, one at a time, beating thoroughly after each addition.
2. Blend flour, ammonium carbonate, and salt; add in fourths to creamed mixture, mixing until blended after each addition. Chill dough at least 1 hour.
3. Roll a fourth of dough at a time ¼ inch thick on a floured surface; cut into 2x½-inch strips.
4. Roll each strip 3 inches long; bring ends together to form ring and press to seal; make 3 slanted cuts at equal intervals around each. Let dry about 1 minute.
5. Deep fry in hot fat 1 to 2 minutes, or until lightly browned; turn once.
6. Drain; serve while still warm.

ABOUT 16 DOZEN COOKIES

CARNIVAL PANCAKES
(Fastnacht Kuchlein)

The Swiss Mardi Gras, called Fasching, is celebrated for two weeks prior to the Lenten season. These traditional "little cakes" highlight the festivities. These inviting deep-fried "cakes" beckon from every pastry shop window to all passersby.

2 tablespoons butter,
    melted
¼ cup milk
¼ cup heavy cream
½ teaspoon salt
1 teaspoon kirsch

4 eggs
3⅓ cups sifted all-
    purpose flour
¼ cup cornstarch
Lard for deep frying

1. Combine butter, milk, cream, salt, kirsch, and eggs in a bowl and beat thoroughly.
2. Blend flour and cornstarch; add about ½ cup at

a time to egg mixture, mixing until well blended after each addition. Chill dough thoroughly.
3. Heat lard to 365° to 370°F.
4. Divide dough into 32 equal portions and cover until ready to use. Roll each into a "two-hand" size round.
5. Sprinkle one round liberally with *flour*, then place another on top and roll 1/16 inch thick. Separate carefully; brush off excess flour and place each round between pieces of waxed paper. Repeat with all portions of dough before starting to deep fry.
6. Deep fry each round in hot fat 1 to 2 minutes, or until golden brown, turning once. Drain over fat a few seconds, then remove to absorbent paper; cool.
7. Sprinkle with *confectioners' sugar.*

32 (8-INCH) PANCAKES

NOTE: If desired, roll out dough the day before, place between sheets of waxed paper, and refrigerate overnight. Deep fry the next day as needed.

SWEDISH DOUGHNUT MINIATURES

1½ cups sifted all-
    purpose flour
1 teaspoon baking powder
Few grains salt
1 egg
⅓ cup sugar
1 teaspoon vanilla
    extract

1½ teaspoons grated
    lemon peel, or ½ to
    ¾ teaspoon ground
    cardamom
⅓ cup cream
2 tablespoons butter or
    margarine, melted
Fat for deep frying
    heated to 375°F

1. Sift flour, baking powder, and salt together.
2. Beat egg, sugar, extract, and lemon peel together until thick and piled softly. (If using cardamom, blend with flour.)
3. Alternately add dry ingredients in halves with mixture of cream and butter, beating until just blended after each addition. Chill dough if necessary for easier handling.
4. Roll dough to ¼-inch thickness on a floured surface. Cut dough with a lightly floured 2¼-inch scalloped cutter and use a small round cutter (about ½ inch) to cut out center.
5. Fry in hot fat about 2 minutes, or until golden brown, turning immediately as doughnuts rise to surface and several times during cooking.
6. Remove from fat with a slotted spoon and drain on absorbent paper. Coat doughnuts with *sugar.* Serve while warm.

ABOUT 1½ DOZEN COOKIES

Chapter 19

CANDIES & CONFECTIONS

Candymaking is one of the most rewarding of the household arts. There is nothing quite like a box of beautifully made candy for telling someone that you love him — or her. At their best, candies represent a happy blend of art and science — or beauty and delectability.

The Role of Sugar in Candymaking — Sugar is a crystalline product with the inherent power of recrystallizing after it has been boiled in a solution. If we want to make candies that are noncrystalline (or that have small crystals), we must know what chemical or mechanical means to use to achieve our purpose. The sugar itself always reacts in the same way under the same conditions. Therefore, if we do not get the expected results, it is we who have acted differently, not the sugar. In candymaking, proper handling of sugar brings success; improper handling causes "failures." For perfect results there are some basic rules to follow for using sugar in solution.

Types of Candy Produced with Sugar — *Crystalline* — The outstanding characteristic of standard crystalline candy is that the sugar crystals are so small that the candy at all times feels creamy and velvety to the tongue. Fondant, fudge, panocha, bonbons, pralines, divinity, and kisses are common examples.

To produce great numbers of very tiny crystals and thereby ensure a creamy candy: 1) The sugar must be completely dissolved. 2) The sugar solution must be boiled to a certain temperature and then cooled to a much lower temperature before agitation or beating, thereby producing a highly supersaturated solution (a solution holding more dissolved sugar than it ordinarily would at this lower temperature). 3) The sugar crystals in the supersaturated solution must recrystallize in a great number of very tiny crystals. Therefore, when the mixture has cooled to the proper temperature, it must be agitated or beaten at this temperature so

many small crystals may form. 4) Ingredients known as interfering substances help to avoid the formation of large crystals. In fudge, these substances are butter, corn syrup, and the starch of chocolate or cocoa; in fondant, corn syrup and an acid such as lemon juice, vinegar, or cream of tartar is generally used; in divinity, egg protein is the substance.

Noncrystalline — Toffee, peanut brittle, lollipops, butterscotch, and caramels are examples of noncrystalline candies. As in making crystalline candies, completely dissolving the sugar crystals is important. The mixture must be cooked to a high enough temperature to produce a highly viscous (resistance of the solution to pouring) solution which, upon cooling quickly, immediately becomes thicker (as caramels) or solidifies (as lollipops).

Ingredients which help to produce viscous mixture in caramels are the large quantities of milk solids and fat. In caramels, the cream, with corn syrup, or milk solids are classified as interfering substances and help to prevent the formation of sugar crystals. If the total amount of cream or milk is added at the beginning of the cooking period of caramels, the milk or cream may curdle. Therefore, milk or cream should be added in more than one addition to avoid curdling.

During pulling of taffies, air bubbles become incorporated, causing taffies to become white or, if made with molasses, to become much lighter in color.

Baking soda is frequently added to brittles. It neutralizes the acidity; it also gives a porous texture to the brittle because of gas formation.

CANDYMAKING EQUIPMENT

Candy bars (steel) are useful and, for large-quantity candymaking, quite necessary. They are used on a marble slab or wood surface to form various-sized spaces into which are poured creamy candy mixtures such as caramel and fudge. These steel bars may be arranged to hold any quantity of candy and will regulate the size and thickness of the pieces. They may be purchased at confectioners' supply houses.

Candy gloves are used when working with caramel corn, brittles, etc.

Candy hook (taffy hook) is useful and inexpensive. Candy is usually lighter and fluffier when it has been pulled on a hook.

Candy paddle is useful for working fondants, fudge, and candy mixtures to a creamy consistency on a marble slab or large platter. Obtainable at a paint store, it is also used as a putty and paint scraper.

Candy thermometer is used to accurately test the temperature of candy syrups. Select one with the scale marks 2° apart and a reading of up to 320°F if you expect to make high-cooked candies; otherwise, a 300° to 310°F mercury column will be satisfactory. A thermometer for testing melted fondant or chocolate has a reading from 180° to 220°F and is much easier to use for this particular work than a regular candy thermometer.

Caramel cutter consists of a metal framework filled with transverse and longitudinal metal bars which, when pressed on the surface of a caramel or taffy-type candy mixture, mark it into a number of small squares. The squares are then cut apart.

Dipping fork is used for fondant and chocolate dipping. Made of wire with several prongs or a loop at the end, it is helpful in removing dipped candies from the coating mixture.

Funnel and stick are used in forming wafer-thin patties from melted fondant.

Marble slab is not absolutely necessary, but is used by professionals because of its smooth, cold surface. Candy mixtures poured on a marble slab will cool quickly. Also, it is much more convenient to work large quantities of fondant or fudge on marble than to beat them.

Platter (large and heavy) is useful for cooling and creaming when a marble slab is not available.

Medicine dropper is useful for adding small amounts of oil flavoring to candy mixture.

Saucepans used for cooking candy mixtures should be large enough to allow contents to cook freely without cooking over onto range. Medium-weight metal pans are satisfactory for most candies. However, a syrup which must be boiled to a high temperature should be cooked in a heavy saucepan to avoid scorching.

Electric mixer is convenient for beating many candy mixtures. Good divinity, for example, is much easier to produce when beating with an electric mixer than by hand.

Other equipment might include baking sheets or other large pans or trays; chocolate grater; cutting board; decorating tubes and bags; double boiler; food chopper; kitchen scales; kitchen shears; measuring cups and spoons; pastry brush; rolling pin; stirring paddles; wooden mixing spoons.

CANDYMAKING INGREDIENTS

Acids—Cream of tartar, vinegar, acetic acid (36 percent), and lemon juice are used in candymaking to help prevent crystallization. Since these vary in amount of acidity, cream of tartar is most commonly used, as it is uniform in its acid content and is inexpensive.

Chocolate and chocolate products—see *page 11*.

Dairy products—Milk (fresh, evaporated, nonfat), cream, (sweet and dairy sour), and butter, see *page 12*.

Fats—see *page 11*.

Flavoring extracts—These are necessary in candymaking and should be of high quality and purity. Oils are much stronger in flavor than extracts and are obtainable at a drugstore.

Food colorings—Available in pastes, powders, and liquids. Liquid colorings are the easiest to blend into candy mixtures.

Gelatin—Granulated, unflavored.

Nuts—Almonds, Brazil nuts, butternuts, cashews, chestnuts, filberts, hickory nuts, peanuts, pecans, pine nuts, pistachio nuts, and walnuts may be used in making candy. Be sure they are fresh as nuts become rancid quickly (especially in hot weather) due to their high fat content. Store shelled nuts in unopened bags or cans, tightly covered jars, or tightly sealed moisture-vaporproof bags in the central portion of refrigerator to assure freshness. They will remain fresh for months. When using nuts in candy, best results are obtained if the nuts are warmed in a 300°F oven before mixing with the cooked syrup.

Sugars and syrups—Classification, see *page 13*.

When using brown sugar in candies, light brown is usually preferred to dark brown because of its milder flavor. Brown sugar contains some acid; therefore, if milk or cream is used in the candy curdling might occur during cooking. If this condition does occur, stir the mixture gently during cooking. When using granulated brown sugar instead of regular, follow package directions for the substitution.

Measurements & Equivalents
(See page 10 for additional ingredients)

Almonds, blanched, whole	1 cup	5½ ounces
Almond paste	2 cups	1 pound
Apricots, dried	1 cup	5⅓ ounces
Cherries, candied, whole	1 cup	7 ounces
Chocolate, grated	3 cups	1 pound
Chocolate, melted	1½ cups	1 pound
Citron, candied, sliced	1 cup	7 ounces
Cocoa	1 cup	about 4 ounces
Corn syrup	1⅓ cups	1 pound
Dates, pitted, cut	1 cup	6⅓ ounces
Figs, cut fine	1 cup	6 ounces
Filberts, shelled	1 cup	4¾ ounces
Fondant (basic)	1 cup	12 ounces
Ginger, crystallized, diced	1 cup	6 ounces
Honey	1⅓ cups	1 pound
Molasses	1⅓ cups	1 pound
Peanuts, shelled	1 cup	5 ounces
Pecans, chopped	1 cup	4½ ounces
Pecan halves	1 cup	3¾ ounces
Raisins, seedless	1¼ cups	8 ounces
Walnuts, chopped	1 cup	4½ ounces
Walnut halves	1 cup	3½ ounces

TECHNIQUES FOR MAKING CANDY

Make candy on a cool, dry day for best results. If it is necessary to make it on a hot, humid day (air contains an excessive amount of moisture), cook the mixture 2 degrees higher than the temperature specified in the recipe.

Test candy thermometer for accuracy each time before using it since the boiling point of water varies from day to day depending upon barometric readings. Place the bulb of thermometer in 3 inches of water in saucepan and bring rapidly to boiling; boil 3 minutes and take a reading. Water boils at 212°F at sea level but it drops 1° for each 500 feet of increased altitude. Both humidity as well as mechanical discrepancies can affect the thermometer readings. If the reading is 210°F in the boiling water, you should cook the candy syrup 2° lower than specified since all degrees given in recipes are for 212°F boiling of water. At no time plunge a cold thermometer into boiling liquid and vice versa.

To test candy mixture, put thermometer into mixture after sugar has dissolved and candy starts boiling. Syrup depth should be at least 3 inches. Hang thermometer on pan so the bulb does not touch side or bottom of pan. To read thermometer hold it in an upright position with the mercury bulb completely under the syrup. The eye should be level with the top of mercury. Remove saucepan from heat as soon as correct reading is obtained and, when finished, place thermometer in a pan of hot water. If the mixture is to be cooled in the saucepan, set pan in cold water for about 1 minute to cool the pan quickly.

To test syrup in cold water (when no thermometer is available), remove the saucepan from heat each time a small amount of syrup is dropped into water. Do not use ice and water. Use a clean spoon each time a sample is tested. For the six stages in cooking sugar, see *When You Cook Syrups, page 430.*

To avoid graininess in candy, stir sugar mixture at the beginning of cooking period over low heat until sugar is completely dissolved and mixture begins to boil. Stir gently so sugar crystals do not adhere to sides of pan. Cover the saucepan for the first few minutes of cooking so that the steam formed will help wash down the crystals still clinging to sides of pan.

Wash down crystals formed during cooking with a pastry brush dipped in water. Move the thermometer to one side and wash down any crystals which might have formed under it.

Cook candy mixtures containing milk, cream, or molasses uncovered to avoid boiling over. Cook over medium heat until mixture thickens slightly, then reduce heat and cook slowly. Sugar and water mixtures may be cooked more rapidly.

Cool candy to lukewarm (100° to 110°F) before beating unless otherwise specified. Do not move or jar candy during cooling period because any agitation could cause the formation of coarse crystals with sugary, grainy candy the result.

Store candy in tightly covered containers in a cool place. Refrigerate during hot, humid weather.

CHOCOLATE DIPPING

For success in dipping, follow these directions:

1. Never dip on a warm, humid day and avoid all drafts. Room temperature should be about 65°F.

2. Shaped candy centers should be ready at room temperature. Cover wire racks with waxed paper. Have ready a chocolate thermometer, double boiler, and a fork for dipping.

3. Semisweet dipping chocolate is generally used (½ pound will cover about 1 pound of centers). Do not use ordinary cooking chocolate for dipping. It is advisable to melt 2 to 3 pounds because a small amount cools too quickly. What is left can be remelted if it has not been overheated.

4. Shave or chop chocolate, then melt in double-boiler top over hot (not boiling) water. Cover until chocolate begins to melt, then stir often until completely melted. Insert chocolate thermometer; do not let chocolate go above 110°F.

5. To keep chocolate at this temperature add hot water to bottom of double boiler until water is 85°F. Quickly replace chocolate.

6. Chocolate is now ready for dipping, but must always be stirred between each dip. Drop center into chocolate and cover well. Lift out with fork, tap on rim of saucer to remove excess chocolate, and draw fork carefully across rim. Invert piece on waxed paper, remove fork, and form a design across top with chocolate that is still on fork. Work fast. If necessary, repeat steps 4, 5, and 6.

CANDIES

CHOCOLATE FUDGE I

⅔ cup milk or cream
2 cups sugar
2 oz. (2 sq.) unsweetened chocolate, chopped

2 tablespoons light corn syrup
2 tablespoons butter
1 teaspoon vanilla extract

1. Combine milk, sugar, chocolate, corn syrup, and butter in a saucepan and heat slowly, stirring until sugar is dissolved. Wash down any sugar crystals. Set candy thermometer in place. Cook, stirring occasionally, until the temperature reaches 236°F (soft-ball stage).

2. Add a *few grains salt* and the extract; cool, without stirring, to lukewarm (about 110°F).

3. Beat until creamy and mixture starts to lose its shine. Pour into buttered square pan and mark into squares.   ABOUT 1¼ POUNDS

NOTE: If mixture becomes too stiff to pour, it may be kneaded, or a little *cream* may be added.

WHITE FUDGE: Follow recipe for Chocolate Fudge I. Omit chocolate. Cook to 238°F.

RIBBON FUDGE: Follow recipe for Chocolate Fudge I. Add *½ cup chopped nuts*; pour into deep square pan. Make a double recipe of White Fudge. When cooked (to 236°F), turn half into another pan. To one add *1 or 2 drops red food coloring* and *½ cup cut maraschino cherries*. When the White Fudge starts to set up, spread over Chocolate Fudge; when pink fudge is beaten, spread it over white layer.

CHOCOLATE FUDGE II

This creamy-soft fudge will keep well if stored in a tightly covered container.

3 pkgs. (6 oz. each) semisweet chocolate pieces, or 1 pkg. (8 oz.) unsweetened chocolate, broken in pieces
½ lb. butter or margarine

3 tablespoons vanilla extract
2 lbs. sugar
1⅔ cups heavy cream, or 1 can (14½ oz.) evaporated milk

1. Put chocolate pieces, butter, and extract into a large bowl; set aside.

2. Combine sugar and cream in a large heavy saucepan. Stir over medium heat until sugar is completely dissolved. Increase heat and bring mixture to boiling. Wash down crystals from sides of pan with a pastry brush dipped in water. Set candy thermometer in place.

3. Cook, stirring constantly, until thermometer registers 236°F, washing down crystals from sides of pan and changing water after each washing.

4. Remove from heat and pour over ingredients in bowl. Replace thermometer and let stand, without stirring or jarring, until lukewarm (about 110°F).

5. Remove thermometer and beat with a wooden spoon until mixture thickens. If desired, mix in *1 cup chopped nuts*. Immediately pour into two lightly buttered 8-inch square pans. Allow to stand 5 or 6 hours, then cut into squares.   ABOUT 4 POUNDS

FUDGE SUPREME

1 cup milk	½ oz. (½ sq.)
3 cups firmly packed	unsweetened
brown sugar	chocolate, grated
½ cup butter or	¼ cup heavy cream
margarine	1 teaspoon vanilla
Few grains salt	extract
	1 cup chopped walnuts

1. Combine the milk, brown sugar, butter, and salt in a heavy 3-quart saucepan. Stir over low heat until sugar is dissolved.
2. Increase heat and bring to boiling. Wash down crystals from sides of pan with a pastry brush dipped in water. Set candy thermometer in place. Cook and stir to 240°F, washing down crystals from sides of pan and changing water each time.
3. Remove from heat and remove thermometer. Add the chocolate and beat vigorously about 3 minutes. Add cream gradually while continuing to beat, then beat in the extract and walnuts until mixture has stiffened. Quickly turn into a buttered 7- or 9-inch square pan; spread evenly. Cool, then cut into squares. ABOUT 2 POUNDS

COCOA WALNUT FUDGE

2 cups sugar	1 teaspoon vanilla
6 tablespoons cocoa	extract
¾ cup cold water	1 cup walnut pieces
½ cup butter or	
margarine	

1. Combine sugar, cocoa, and water in a saucepan and stir until sugar is dissolved.
2. Add butter; set a candy thermometer in place and cook, without stirring, to 234° to 236°F (soft-ball stage).
3. Cool to 110°F. Add extract and beat until almost creamy. Stir in walnuts; drop from teaspoon onto waxed paper. Or, turn into a buttered pan and when cooled, cut as desired. ABOUT 1½ POUNDS

LOUISIANA CREAM FUDGE

3 cups sugar	¼ cup butter
1 cup light corn syrup	½ cup all-purpose flour
2 cups cream	2 cups pecans, chopped

1. Put sugar, corn syrup, and cream in a 3-quart saucepan; blend thoroughly. Bring to boiling over medium heat, stirring until sugar is dissolved. Set candy thermometer in place. Cook until mixture reaches 234°F (soft-ball stage).
2. Remove from heat and set aside to cool about 5 minutes. Blend in butter and beat until mixture begins to thicken, about 5 minutes. Blend in flour. Beat until creamy and thick, about 15 minutes.
3. Stir in chopped pecans. Turn fudge into a buttered 13x9-inch pan. Cool completely.
4. Cut into squares. ABOUT 2¾ POUNDS

PANOCHA

2 cups firmly packed	1 tablespoon butter
light brown sugar	1 teaspoon vanilla
⅔ cup heavy cream	extract
2 tablespoons corn syrup	

1. Combine brown sugar, cream, corn syrup, and butter in a saucepan and stir over low heat until sugar is dissolved. Set candy thermometer in place. Cook to 238°F (soft-ball stage), stirring occasionally to avoid scorching.
2. Remove from heat; add extract without stirring; cool to 110°F.
3. Beat until thick and creamy. If desired, add ½ cup chopped pecans. Turn into a buttered pan.
ABOUT 1 POUND

SEA FOAM
(White Divinity)

This soft creamy candy, sometimes called white divinity or divinity fudge, has various interpretations. An American favorite, it goes back to Colonial days.

3 cups sugar	1 teaspoon vanilla
⅔ cup water	extract
½ cup light corn syrup	1 cup (about 4 oz.)
2 egg whites	pecans, coarsely
Few grains salt	chopped

1. Mix the sugar and water in a heavy 2-quart saucepan. Stir over low heat until sugar is dissolved; stir in corn syrup.
2. Bring mixture to boiling; cover pan and boil gently 5 minutes. Uncover and set candy thermometer in place. Without stirring, cook to 252°F (hard-ball stage). During cooking, wash down any sugar crystals from sides of pan.
3. In a large heatproof mixing bowl, beat egg whites with salt to stiff peaks.

4. As soon as syrup reaches 252°F pour it in a steady stream over egg whites, beating constantly with electric beater at high speed. Continue beating until mixture begins to lose its gloss and is stiff enough to hold its shape when dropped. During the last few minutes use a long wooden spoon rather than the mixer.

5. Quickly stir in extract and pecans. Drop by teaspoonfuls onto buttered baking sheets. Cool thoroughly. Store in cool place in a tightly covered container. ABOUT 1½ POUNDS

BROWN SUGAR DIVINITY: Follow recipe for Sea Foam. Use *1½ cups granulated sugar* and *1½ cups firmly packed light brown sugar.*

CHOCOLATE DIVINITY

2 oz. (2 sq.) unsweetened chocolate	¼ teaspoon salt
2 cups sugar	3 egg whites
⅔ cup water	1 teaspoon vanilla
½ cup light corn syrup	extract

1. Melt chocolate and set aside to cool.

2. Combine sugar, water, corn syrup, and salt in a heavy 2-quart saucepan; set over medium heat and stir only until mixture begins to boil. Cover and cook 5 minutes. Remove cover and set candy thermometer in place. Cook, without stirring, until syrup reaches 252°F (hard-ball stage). During cooking, wash down any crystals from sides of pan with a pastry brush dipped in water.

3. Shortly before syrup reaches required temperature, beat egg whites in a large bowl at high speed of electric mixer until stiff peaks are formed.

4. When syrup reaches 252°F, immediately pour in a fine stream onto beaten egg whites, beating constantly at high speed. The mass will flow down from beater in a continuous ribbon. Continue beating until mixture begins to lose its gloss and no longer flows but holds its shape (about 35 minutes). Immediately blend in extract and chocolate.

5. Working quickly, drop by teaspoonfuls onto a lightly buttered baking sheet. Cool until set. Store in a cool place in a tightly covered container. ABOUT 1½ POUNDS

PECAN PRALINES

Originally a plantation favorite of the old South, these goodies are now appreciated throughout America.

1 cup firmly packed dark brown sugar	1½ cups (about 5½ oz.) pecan halves
1 cup sugar	1 teaspoon vanilla
½ cup cream	extract
2 tablespoons butter	

1. Mix sugars and cream in a heavy saucepan. Stir over low heat until sugar dissolves. Set candy thermometer in place.

2. Increase heat and cook rapidly without stirring until mixture reaches 230°F. During cooking, wash any sugar crystals from sides of pan with pastry brush dipped in water. When mixture reaches 230°F stir in butter and pecan halves.

3. Continue cooking, stirring occasionally, until syrup reaches 236°F (soft-ball stage). Remove thermometer; cool 2 to 3 minutes without stirring.

4. Add extract. Gently stir syrup for about 2 minutes, or until it becomes slightly thicker and pecans appear well coated with the syrup. Quickly drop by tablespoonfuls onto aluminum foil or greased waxed paper. (The candy will flatten.) Cool.

5. When completely cool, wrap each praline in moisture-vaporproof material. Store in a covered container in a cool dry place. ABOUT 1½ POUNDS

ALMOND-FILLED CARAMELS

1 cup sugar	1½ teaspoons vanilla
¾ cup light molasses	extract
½ cup cream	24 whole salted almonds
⅓ cup butter	

1. Butter a 15x10x1-inch jelly roll pan.

2. Combine sugar, molasses, cream, and butter in a heavy saucepan and stir over low heat until sugar is dissolved. Set candy thermometer in place. Increase heat; cook rapidly, stirring gently, until mixture reaches 248°F (hard-ball stage).

3. Remove from heat and stir in extract. Pour into jelly roll pan without scraping bottom or sides of saucepan. Cool until lukewarm.

4. Cut caramel mixture into 2½-inch squares. Place a whole almond in center of each square. Shape caramel around each almond. Wrap in transparent plastic film and then in colored foil.

ABOUT 1¼ POUNDS

CREAM CARAMELS

2 cups sugar
2 cups light corn syrup
½ cup butter (at room temperature)
1⅔ cups heavy cream, heated
1 teaspoon vanilla extract

1. Mix sugar and corn syrup in heavy saucepan. Set candy thermometer in place. Stir and cook to 244°F.
2. Add butter and warm cream slowly so mixture does not stop boiling. Cook again to 244°F, stirring gently.
3. Cool on wire rack to 220°F.
4. Carefully stir in extract, then turn into 2 buttered 8-inch square pans. Set aside until firm enough to cut and wrap.   ABOUT 2½ POUNDS

CHOCOLATE CARAMELS SUPREME

3 cups heavy cream, heated
2 cups sugar
1 cup light corn syrup
¼ teaspoon salt
2 tablespoons butter or margarine
4 oz. (4 sq.) unsweetened chocolate, melted
⅔ cup nuts, chopped
1 tablespoon vanilla extract

1. Combine 1 cup cream, the sugar, corn syrup, and salt in a heavy 3-quart saucepan. Blend well and set over low heat; stir until sugar is dissolved. Increase heat and bring mixture to boiling. Set candy thermometer in place.
2. Cook, stirring frequently, until thermometer registers 234°F (soft-ball stage); during cooking wash crystals from sides of pan.
3. Stirring constantly, gradually add another cup of cream so slowly that boiling does not stop. Continue cooking, stirring frequently, over low heat until thermometer registers 234°F.
4. Stirring constantly, gradually add remaining cream and the butter so slowly that boiling does not stop. Stirring frequently, cook to 244° to 246°F (firm-ball stage).
5. Remove from heat; remove thermometer. Immediately add the melted chocolate, nuts, and extract and stir just until blended. Immediately pour hot mixture into a buttered 8-inch square pan; do not scrape bottom or sides of saucepan. Set on wire rack.
6. When completely cool, turn out onto a cutting board and remove pan. Working in a cool place, mark candy into 1-inch squares; using a sharp, long-bladed knife, cut candy with a sawing motion.
7. Wrap each caramel tightly in waxed or glassine paper. Store in a covered container in a cool dry place.   ABOUT 2½ POUNDS

FRENCH HONEY NOUGAT

A special confection which "takes a bit of doing."

2 cups sugar
1 cup water
2 tablespoons light corn syrup
4 egg whites
1 cup honey
2 tablespoons light corn syrup
2 teaspoons vanilla extract
½ cup blanched pistachio nuts, chopped
1 cup blanched and toasted almonds, chopped

1. Combine the sugar, water, and 2 tablespoons corn syrup in a heavy saucepan. Set over low heat and stir until sugar is dissolved. Increase heat to medium and bring to boiling. Cover tightly; boil mixture gently 5 minutes. Uncover and set candy thermometer in place. Cook without stirring to 290°F (soft-crack stage). During cooking, wash down crystals from sides of pan.
2. Meanwhile, beat egg whites in a 4-quart bowl until stiff, not dry, peaks are formed.
3. Remove syrup from heat and remove thermometer. Immediately pour syrup in a fine stream onto stiffly beaten egg whites; using electric mixer, beat constantly at high speed until mixture is thick and bowl is warm to touch.
4. Meanwhile, mix in a small saucepan the honey and 2 tablespoons corn syrup. Set candy thermometer in place (mixture must cover bulb). Cook over medium heat until temperature reaches 270°F (soft-crack stage).
5. Immediately pour in a fine stream into egg white mixture, beating constantly at medium speed until mixture has lost some of its gloss. (The longer mixture is beaten, the shorter will be the drying period over boiling water.)
6. Transfer mixture to a double-boiler top and place over boiling water. Constantly stir and turn mixture with a wooden spoon until it no longer appears moist (at least 25 minutes).
7. Mix in extract and gradually add nuts while stirring. Turn into a thoroughly buttered 8-inch square pan. Set on a wire rack 10 minutes; press down firmly with hand. Cool; cover tightly.

8. Set candy aside to "ripen" at least 24 hours.
9. Loosen sides and shake to remove block of candy to cutting board. Cut into 1½-inch oblong pieces. Wrap each piece in waxed or glassine paper.   ABOUT 2 POUNDS

CHOCOLATE NOUGAT

2 cups sugar	2 oz. (2 sq.) unsweet-
⅔ cup light corn syrup	ened chocolate,
⅓ cup water	melted
⅓ cup (about 2) egg	½ cup candied cherries,
whites	chopped
⅛ teaspoon salt	¾ cup toasted blanched
½ teaspoon almond	almonds, chopped
extract	

1. Line an 11x7-inch pan with aluminum foil and butter it; set aside.
2. Combine the sugar, syrup, and water in a 1½-quart saucepan; stir until sugar is moistened. Wash down crystals from sides of pan with a pastry brush dipped in water. Cover and bring to boiling. Uncover, wash down any crystals, and set candy thermometer in place. Cook without stirring until the thermometer registers 270°F.
3. Meanwhile, beat egg whites with salt until stiff, not dry, peaks are formed. When syrup reaches required temperature, set aside to let bubbles subside. Wash crystals from pouring side and pour syrup over egg whites in a steady stream, beating constantly until all the syrup is added.
4. Using a wooden spoon, stir in extract, chocolate, cherries, and almonds. Beat by hand until mixture will fall in large chunks.
5. Turn into prepared pan and level mixture. Cover. Let stand overnight before cutting. Cut into pieces and wrap each.   ABOUT 1½ POUNDS

PECAN CRUNCH

2 cups (about 8 oz.)	½ cup water
pecans	1 tablespoon cider
1 teaspoon baking soda	vinegar
2¼ cups sugar	1 teaspoon salt
1½ cups butter or	4 oz. milk chocolate
margarine	

1. Very coarsely chop 1 cup pecans; finely chop remaining pecans and reserve ½ cup for topping. Mix coarsely chopped pecans and ½ cup finely chopped pecans with the baking soda; set aside.
2. In a heavy 2-quart saucepan, combine the sugar, butter, water, vinegar, and salt. Set over low heat and stir until sugar is dissolved. Set candy thermometer in place. Continue cooking, without stirring, until thermometer registers 290°F (soft-crack stage).
3. Remove from heat and remove thermometer; add pecan-soda mixture and stir until just blended. Pour into a buttered 10-inch square pan. Cool completely on wire rack.
4. When candy is cooled, melt chocolate over simmering water, cool slightly, and spread evenly over candy. Sprinkle remaining pecans over chocolate.
5. When chocolate is set, turn candy out of pan and break into pieces. Store between pieces of moisture-vaporproof material in a tightly covered container.   ABOUT 2 POUNDS

BROWN SUGAR TAFFY
A rollicking old-fashioned taffy pull is a great holiday party idea.

2¼ cups firmly packed	¼ teaspoon salt
dark brown sugar	½ cup undiluted
1½ cups light corn	evaporated milk
syrup	Butter
4 teaspoons cider	
vinegar	

1. Combine the brown sugar, corn syrup, vinegar, and salt in a heavy 3-quart saucepan. Set over low heat and stir until sugar is dissolved. Increase heat and bring to boiling, stirring constantly.
2. Add evaporated milk slowly, stirring constantly, so that boiling does not stop. Set candy thermometer in place. Cook, stirring constantly, until mixture reaches 248°F (firm-ball stage). During cooking, wash down crystals from sides of pan with a pastry brush dipped in water.
3. Remove from heat and remove thermometer. Immediately pour mixture into a buttered shallow pan or platter; do not scrape saucepan.
4. When mixture is just cool enough to handle, pull a small portion at a time with buttered hands. Work in a cool place. Pull until candy is ivory colored and no longer sticky to the touch.
5. Twist pulled strip slightly and place on waxed paper or a board. Cut with scissors or sharp knife into 1-inch pieces.

6. For storing, wrap pieces in moisture-vapor-proof material and store in a tightly covered container in a cool, dry place.   ABOUT 2 POUNDS

TOFFEE

2 cups butter	2 tablespoons light corn
2 cups sugar	syrup
2 cups salted almonds, coarsely chopped	1 teaspoon vanilla extract
6 tablespoons water	8 oz. milk chocolate

1. Start melting butter in a heavy 2-quart saucepan over low heat. Gradually add sugar, stirring constantly. Blend in 1 cup almonds, water, and corn syrup. Set candy thermometer in place. Cook over medium heat, stirring a few times, until temperature reaches 300°F (hard-crack stage).
2. Remove from heat and stir in extract. Quickly pour into buttered 15x10x1-inch jelly roll pan and spread to corners. Cool slightly; mark into squares with a sharp knife. Cool.
3. Meanwhile, melt chocolate over hot water. Cool. When candy is completely cool, spread melted chocolate evenly over top. Sprinkle remaining nuts over chocolate. When chocolate is set, break toffee into pieces. Store in a covered container.
                    ABOUT 3 POUNDS

CRACKLE PEANUT BRITTLE

2 cups sugar	2 teaspoons butter or
1 cup light corn syrup	margarine
1 cup water	2 teaspoons baking soda
2 cups shelled, unroasted peanuts	1 teaspoon vanilla extract

1. Combine sugar, corn syrup, and water in a heavy 3-quart saucepan. Set pan over low heat and stir until sugar is dissolved.
2. Increase heat and bring to boiling; cover tightly and boil mixture gently 5 minutes. Uncover and set candy thermometer in place. Cook, without stirring, until mixture reaches 234°F. During cooking, wash down crystals from sides of pan.
3. Mix in the peanuts and butter. Cook over medium heat, stirring frequently, until mixture reaches 306°F.
4. Remove from heat and remove thermometer. Add baking soda and extract and mix well. Pour onto two lightly buttered baking sheets, spreading as thinly as possible.

5. As soon as candy is cool enough to handle, wet hands with water and stretch candy as thin as desired. (Or wear canvas gloves.) Turn candy over and cool completely.
6. When cool and firm, break into medium-sized pieces. Store in a tightly covered container.
                    ABOUT 2 POUNDS

TRUFFLES

2 tablespoons double-strength coffee	2 egg yolks, slightly beaten
½ lb. semisweet chocolate, melted	½ cup butter
¼ cup heavy cream, scalded	1 teaspoon vanilla extract
	½ cup confectioners' sugar

1. Stir coffee into the chocolate; set aside to cool.
2. Blend hot cream into the egg yolks; immediately pour into the top of a double boiler. Cook over simmering water, stirring constantly, 3 to 5 minutes, or until mixture thickens. Cool.
3. Cream butter with extract and confectioners' sugar. Gradually add cooled chocolate and egg mixtures, beating well.
4. Place bowl over ice and water and continue beating until firm enough to shape into 1-inch balls. Keep mixture over ice and water while shaping.
5. Roll each ball in finely chopped *pecans* or salted *pistachio nuts, Dutch process cocoa*, or in a mixture of *2 tablespoons Dutch process cocoa* and *½ cup finely chopped pecans*. If desired, shape some of the balls around a *candied* or well-drained *maraschino cherry quarter*, or a small piece of *red or green candied pineapple* before rolling in nuts or cocoa. Chill thoroughly. Serve in bonbon cups.
                    ABOUT 1 POUND

FONDANT

As creamy, smooth confection, fondant's uses far surpass other candies because it not only forms the base of many delightful sweets, but is used for coating nuts, fruits, and other confections.

3 cups sugar	2 tablespoons light corn
1 cup water	syrup, or ⅛ teaspoon cream of tartar
	Flavoring, if desired

1. Mix sugar and water in large saucepan; stir over medium heat until sugar is dissolved. Add corn syrup; bring to boiling, cover, and boil gently

about 5 minutes. Uncover and wipe down crystals. Set candy thermometer in place. Continue cooking, without stirring, until thermometer registers 238° to 240°F (soft-ball stage).

2. Remove from heat at once. Pour syrup onto a large platter or marble slab which has been wiped with a cold, damp cloth. Do not scrape the pan. Set in a cool place and when lukewarm or when just cool enough to hold platter on hand, add the flavoring (if used).

3. With a wooden spoon or paddle or a wide spatula, scrape the fondant from edge of platter toward center. Work until smooth and the whole mass becomes white and creamy. Pile into a mound, cover with a bowl, and let rest 20 to 30 minutes.

4. With hands, work fondant in a kneading motion until free from lumps. Wrap in waxed paper or moisture-vaporproof material and place in a covered container. Let stand at room temperature at least 24 hours to allow candy to "ripen." Fondant may be stored, tightly covered, in refrigerator for weeks. ABOUT 1½ POUNDS

FONDANT BONBONS: Take any quantity of fondant; add any desired flavor and color and knead until blended. Do not overwork (fondant will become too soft). If too soft to shape, stiffen with finecut *nuts, macaroon coconut* (fine dry coconut—a special bakers' product). *confectioners' sugar, cocoa,* or *chocolate.* Minced *candied fruits* may be added for flavor. Break off small pieces of the fondant and shape or cut into balls, cubes, strips, patties, diamonds, or odd shapes. Place shapes on waxed paper-covered tray and let dry about 30 minutes to develop thin crust.

To Prepare Fondant for Dipping: Place fondant in the top of a double boiler or in a dish placed in a pan of water. Heat, keeping water just below the boiling point. Stir only enough to blend. If fondant is too thin when temperature reaches 135°F, let stand a few minutes; if too thick, add a few drops of boiling water. When melted, add coloring and flavoring desired; stir as little as possible.

To Dip Bonbons: Remove double boiler from heat. Lift top part and insert a silver knife between the upper and lower parts. This will give you a "well" for dipping, and help to keep the fondant fluid. Lower the centers, one at a time and upside down, into the fondant on a dipping fork. Lift out, gently scrape off excess fondant, then deposit the bonbon on waxed paper.

NOTE: Work quickly. If fondant becomes too thick, add a few drops boiling water.

CONFECTIONS

GLAZED SPICED NUTS

2 cups mixed whole nuts	2 to 3 teaspoons ground
1 cup sugar	cinnamon
⅓ cup water	Few grains salt

1. Spread nuts in a large shallow baking pan and heat in a 275°F oven 15 to 20 minutes, or until they are lightly browned; stir occasionally.

2. Combine the sugar, water, cinnamon, and salt in a heavy 1-quart saucepan. Stir over low heat until sugar is dissolved. Increase heat and bring to boiling. Wash down crystals from sides of pan with a pastry brush dipped in water. Set candy thermometer in place.

3. Cook, without stirring, until thermometer registers 296°F, washing down crystals from sides of pan as necessary and changing water after each washing.

4. Remove at once from heat and place pan of syrup over hot water. Remove thermometer. Dip 3 to 5 nuts into syrup at one time, evenly coating each nut. Do not stir syrup. Using a buttered fork, lift nuts to aluminum foil or a buttered baking sheet. Cool.

5. Slide nuts off foil or baking sheet and store in an airtight container. ABOUT 1 POUND

FILBERT GLACÉ

¾ cup sugar	1 teaspoon light corn
¼ cup water	syrup, or ⅛ teaspoon
½ teaspoon salt	cream of tartar
	¾ cup filberts

1. Coat 2 sheets of waxed paper heavily with *butter or margarine* and set aside.

2. In a small saucepan combine the sugar, water, salt, and corn syrup. Stir over medium heat until sugar is dissolved and mixture comes to boiling. Cover for 2 to 3 minutes, then uncover and stir in

the filberts. Continue cooking without stirring until mixture begins to turn a rich brown.

3. Immediately pour filbert mixture into a sieve held over one sheet of the buttered waxed paper. Quickly shake the sieve several times to drain excess syrup from nuts. Turn the nuts out onto remaining sheet of buttered paper. Quickly separate the filberts with a fork; set aside to cool.

4. Lift the cooled nuts from paper and store them in a covered container.

5. Use the glazed nuts as a garnish for meat platters or as a "nibble" food.　ABOUT ¾ POUND

NOTE: Leftover syrup may be cooled, then broken apart and served as a candy or crushed and used as a dessert topping.

COFFEE NUTS
(Kaffeenuss Guetzli)

This different nut confection is a Swiss favorite.

2 cups (about 7½ oz) ground walnuts	1½ teaspoons instant coffee
1¾ cups confectioners' sugar	1 tablespoon (about) hot water
1 tablespoon instant coffee	¾ cup confectioners' sugar
2 tablespoons (about) hot water	Walnut halves (about 12), quartered

1. Combine the ground walnuts and 1¾ cups confectioners' sugar in a bowl; mix thoroughly.

2. Dissolve the 1 tablespoon instant coffee in 2 tablespoons hot water; stir into nut mixture until "dough" begins to follow the spoon. (Add a little more hot water if mixture is too thick to shape into a smooth ball.) Chill the ball thoroughly.

3. Sift a small amount of *confectioners' sugar* over surface and roll out the chilled mixture 1 inch thick. Cut into 1-inch rounds using a cutter dipped in confectioners' sugar. Cover the cutouts with waxed paper or aluminum foil and set aside 8 hours, or overnight.

4. Dissolve the remaining instant coffee in 1 tablespoon hot water and stir into the ¾ cup confectioners' sugar until smooth. (Add a little more hot water, if needed, to make the glaze of spreading consistency.)

5. Coat each round with the glaze and top with a walnut piece. Set aside until "set."

6. Store in a cool place in a tightly covered container.　ABOUT 1 POUND

CARAMEL APPLES

An all-American snack popular with the small-fry.

16 small to medium apples, washed and dried	1 cup sugar
	⅔ cup firmly packed brown sugar
2 cans (14 oz. each) sweetened condensed milk	2 tablespoons butter or margarine
1 cup light corn syrup	1 tablespoon vanilla extract

1. Remove stems and blossoms from apples; insert 4- to 6-inch wooden skewers in stem ends of apples; set aside.

2. Mix condensed milk, corn syrup, sugar, and brown sugar together in a large heavy saucepan. Set candy thermometer in place.

3. Stirring constantly, cook to 234°F (soft-ball stage), about 35 minutes. During cooking, occasionally remove thermometer and stir completely around bottom and sides of pan.

4. Remove from heat and stir in butter and extract. Set pan over very hot water and quickly dip and twirl apples in caramel mixture to coat evenly. Cool on a well-greased baking sheet, skewers upright.　16 CARAMEL APPLES

CARAMEL-COATED MARSHMALLOWS

1 can (14 oz.) sweetened condensed milk	¼ cup butter or margarine
½ cup sugar	1½ teaspoons vanilla extract
⅓ cup firmly packed light brown sugar	1 lb. marshmallows
¾ cup light corn syrup	Cream (about 3 tablespoons)

1. Mix the condensed milk, sugars, and corn syrup together in a heavy 2-quart saucepan. Set candy thermometer in place. Cook until mixture reaches 234°F (soft-ball stage), stirring constantly.

2. Remove from heat and stir in the butter and extract.

3. Set saucepan in a pan of hot water while dipping marshmallows. Thin the coating mixture with a little cream as necessary to maintain dipping consistency.

4. Using a buttered two-tined fork to spear marshmallows, quickly dip and twirl each in caramel mixture to coat evenly, removing as much excess coating as possible. For ease in handling, push marshmallows from fork with a buttered spatula onto a

well-buttered baking sheet. Allow to cool 4 to 6 hours.

5. Wrap each marshmallow in moisture-vapor-proof material. ABOUT 2½ POUNDS

CANDIED ORANGE PEEL

3 large oranges (thick peel is preferred)	5 cups water
1½ cups water	1 cup sugar
¼ teaspoon salt	Sugar for coating (about ½ cup)

1. Remove the peel in 4 lengthwise sections. Put into a 2-quart saucepan and add 1½ cups water and salt. Bring to boiling and cook until orange peel is almost tender, about 15 minutes. Remove from heat and drain well.

2. Return orange peel to saucepan and add 1½ cups water. Bring to boiling; drain immediately. Repeat procedure two more times. After last draining, scrape the white part from the peel. Cut peel into ¼-inch strips.

3. Combine the 1 cup sugar and the remaining ½ cup water in the saucepan. Stir over low heat until sugar is dissolved. Cover saucepan and boil gently 5 minutes. Uncover and set candy thermometer in place.

4. Continue cooking mixture, without stirring, until thermometer registers 230° to 234°F, washing down crystals from sides of pan as necessary and changing water after each washing. Remove thermometer. Add strips of peel and cook very slowly, stirring frequently until most of the syrup is absorbed and peel begins to look transparent.

5. Remove peel to cooling rack. When peel has cooled slightly, roll, a few pieces at a time, in sugar. Cool completely. Store in tightly covered container. ABOUT 1 POUND

MARZIPAN

½ lb. almond paste, cut in small pieces	⅔ cup marshmallow cream
3 tablespoons light corn syrup	3 cups confectioners' sugar
½ teaspoon vanilla extract	Food coloring

1. Mix together the almond paste, corn syrup, extract, and marshmallow cream in a large bowl. Add the confectioners' sugar, ½ cup at a time, kneading thoroughly until smooth after each addition.

2. Divide into as many portions as colors desired. Blend food coloring into each portion. Knead in enough confectioners' sugar to form a stiff paste. Form rolls about 1 inch in diameter and cut crosswise into pieces.

3. Shape each piece between the fingers to resemble fruits or vegetables. Among the simplest shapes to make are carrots, pumpkins, apples, pears, peaches, oranges, bananas and strawberries. Affix appropriate marzipan leaves where needed.

Tinting Completed Shapes: Allow shapes to stand, uncovered, at least 2 hours before tinting. Use paste coloring and a tiny brush to paint the "blush" on fruits such as apples, pears, and peaches.

Glazing Syrup: Blend together *¼ cup light corn syrup* and *1 tablespoon hot water.* Apply to completed shapes with a brush. If marzipan candies are glazed, allow shapes to stand several hours before glazing. After glaze has been applied, allow to stand several hours for glaze to set. Place each finished piece in a glassine candy case.

ABOUT 1½ POUNDS

POPCORN PUMPKIN
Captivate the moppets with this creation at a Halloween party.

4 qts. popped corn	9 drops yellow food coloring
1 cup sugar	
1 cup light corn syrup	1 drop red food coloring
½ cup water	A thick citron stem
2 tablespoons butter or margarine	Seedless raisins for "face"

1. Put popped corn into large bowl or pan; place in a 250°F oven to keep it warm.

2. Combine sugar, corn syrup, water, and butter in a deep saucepan. Stir over low heat until sugar is dissolved.

3. Cover and bring to boiling; uncover and set candy thermometer in place; continue cooking to 245°F (firm-ball stage).

4. Remove from heat and stir in food colorings. Pour syrup slowly over the corn, turning until all is coated.

5. When corn is cool enough to handle, shape into a pumpkin, using buttered hands. Press firmly into shape. Put a citron stem at center top, then make a face using dark seedless raisins for the features. Secure them in place with some of the syrup.

1 LARGE PUMPKIN

Chapter 20

BEVERAGES—Hot & Cold

All over the world people have their favorite beverages. Here in the United States we are inclined to have many favorites and seem to have no truly national beverage. Americans usually judge the rightness of a drink by the occasion for which it is intended. But there is almost universal agreement among Americans that the day properly starts with coffee—coffee brewed the regular way from finely or coarsely ground coffee beans or coffee made the quick way by dissolving instant-type coffee in water.

For those who prefer starting the day with tea, there is the brew made from dried tea leaves, or the faster way—dissolving the "instant" product in water.

Milk drinks such as chocolate and cocoa are favorite beverages, too, especially in some foreign countries, and are served either hot or cold. Other milk drinks include shakes and eggnogs.

The variety of fruit-beverage concoctions is almost endless, both for everyday and special occasions.

Coffee—To prepare perfect coffee, follow these important rules:

Select a blend of coffee that suits your taste and continue to use it.

Buy the grind of coffee that is suitable to the coffee maker used. Regular grind is recommended for a percolator, drip (all-purpose) grind for a drip pot, and fine grind for a vacuum pot.

Keep coffee maker sparkling clean and rinse with boiling water before using.

Use fresh coffee and once the container is opened, use in about a week. Keep it tightly covered at all times, storing it in the refrigerator or other cool, dry place.

Start with freshly drawn cold water.

Use the correct measurements of coffee to water: 2 level measuring tablespoons (1 Approved Coffee Measure) coffee to each ¾ standard measuring cup water.

Use a coffee maker to at least ¾ of its capacity.

Time the brewing of coffee consistently to have properly brewed coffee.

Serve coffee as soon after brewing as possible. To retain its original flavor, coffee should not be held at serving temperature more than 1 hour. Avoid reheating coffee.

"Instant coffee" is made following label directions with either hot or cold water.

Tea—Selecting one that satisfies your taste can be a pleasant experience. The flavor depends upon the size of the leaf (small leaves being more desirable) and its treatment, whether fermented or unfermented, pan-fired or basket-fired. Also, one can make a selection of teas and blend them at home. There are three general classifications for tea: *Green tea*, from unfermented leaves; *Black tea*, from fermented leaves; *Oolong tea*, from semifermented leaves. Scented tea is oolong tea with dried flowers or bits of fruit (such as orange peel) added. *To steep tea*, pour briskly boiling freshly drawn water over tea in a heated teapot. Cover pot and allow to steep 3 to 5 minutes. Strength of brew depends upon amount of tea used and time steeped.

"Instant tea" is made following label directions with either hot or cold water.

Milk—Store fresh milk and milk products, covered, in coldest part of refrigerator. Wipe off container before storing. Always keep milk covered as it quickly absorbs the odors of other foods. Return it immediately to refrigerator after using.

Instant nonfat dry milk spells convenience to the homemaker. Reconstitute and use as fluid milk. Store package in a cool, dry place.

Chocolate and Cocoa Beverage—The starch content of chocolate and cocoa is high so be sure that this starch is cooked properly (at a high temperature) when preparing the beverages. To precook the starch, combine the cocoa or chocolate with sugar and water in a saucepan and cook to boiling. Boil several minutes before mixing with hot milk. This precooking not only cooks the starch, but also delays separation of the starch particles, improves the flavor, and gives more body to the beverage.

Beating the hot beverage with a hand rotary beater or French whisk before serving forms a pleasant froth on the surface and also prevents a film from forming on the top.

Fruit Drinks—Among these are the frozen fruit juice concentrates to which water is usually added when they are used as beverages. Then there are the orange-flavored instant granular-type breakfast drinks and packaged soft drink mixes which are also blended with water before serving. The electric blender is very useful for reconstituting any of these beverages.

Available also are the endless varieties of fruit drink mixtures—fresh, frozen, and canned—which may be served alone or in combination with other beverages such as brewed tea and carbonated beverages. Add carbonated beverages to drinks just before serving.

Fresh, frozen, and canned fruits are sometimes puréed in an electric blender or forced through a sieve and used in drinks.

SERVING TIPS FOR BEVERAGES

Sugar Syrup—Sometimes called "simple syrup" and is useful to have on hand to sweeten beverages. To prepare, mix in a saucepan 2 cups sugar and 2 cups water; stir over low heat until sugar is dissolved. Cover, bring to boiling and boil 5 minutes. Cool and store covered in refrigerator. This makes about 2½ cups syrup.

Frosted Glasses—Rub the edge of each glass with cut surface of lemon, lime, or orange. Or brush rim with citrus juice. Dip the rim of each glass in fine granulated or confectioners' sugar. Place glasses in refrigerator to chill. Carefully pour beverage into glasses without touching frosted edges.

Pink Sugar for Pink-Frosted Glasses—Measure ½ cup sugar into a shallow pan. Tint sugar the desired pink color by thoroughly mixing in, one drop at a time, a mixture of red food coloring and water (equal amounts of each). To obtain a more even-colored sugar, put through a fine sieve.

Decorative Ice Cubes—Fill ice cube tray one third full with water. Place in freezing compartment of refrigerator; remove ice cube tray when water is partially frozen. Place well-drained maraschino cherry, mint sprig, pineapple chunk, orange wedge, berry, or small piece of fruit, and a mint leaf in each cube section. Fill tray with water and freeze.

Flavored Ice Cubes—For lemonades, punches, and other cool drinks, freeze reconstituted soft drink mixes in ice cube trays. Blend complimentary flavors and colors.

Decorative Ice Blocks—Fill a loaf pan or fancy mold one third full with water. Place in freezing compartment of refrigerator; remove pan or mold when water is partially frozen. Arrange flowers, such as roses or gardenias, or fruits (small whole, pieces, or slices) in interesting designs and combinations suitable for the occasion. Fill pan or mold, covering flowers or fruit, with water and freeze. Boiling water before freezing or stirring water as it freezes helps to make the ice clear.

Decorative Punch Bowl—Trim stems of daisies, sweetheart roses, or other small flowers to 1 inch. Secure flowers around edge of punch bowl with pieces of cellulose tape. Secure two flowers to ladle handle and one flower to each punch cup handle.

Beverage Syrups

COCOA SYRUP

2 cups sugar	1 cup hot water
1 cup cocoa	2 teaspoons vanilla
½ teaspoon salt	extract
1 cup cold water	

Combine the sugar, cocoa, and salt in a saucepan. Stir in cold water to make a paste. Blend in hot water. Simmer 4 to 6 minutes, stirring until thick and smooth. Cool and stir in the extract. Store in a tightly covered container in refrigerator.

ABOUT 3 CUPS

NOTE: For a chocolate eggnog, allow 3 tablespoons of the syrup per serving.

CHOCOLATE SYRUP

5 oz. (5 sq.) unsweet- ened chocolate	½ teaspoon salt
2 cups sugar syrup, *page* *610*	2 cups hot water
	2 teaspoons vanilla extract

Combine the chocolate, sugar syrup, and salt in a saucepan. Stir in the hot water. Simmer 4 to 6 minutes, stirring until thick and smooth. Cool. Stir in extract. Store, tightly covered, in refrigerator.

ABOUT 4 CUPS

NOTE: For each serving of chocolate milk shake, allow 2 to 3 tablespoons of the syrup.

CARAMEL SYRUP

1 cup sugar	1 cup boiling water

Melt the sugar in a heavy light-colored skillet over low heat, stirring constantly. When sugar becomes a golden brown syrup, remove from heat. Add the boiling water carefully and very gradually, stirring constantly. (Be careful so steam does not burn hand.) Return to low heat and continue to stir about 10 minutes, or until of syrup consistency. Cool and store, tightly covered, in refrigerator. ABOUT 1 CUP

NOTE: To flavor an 8-oz. serving of milk, stir in 2 tablespoons or more of the syrup.

LEMON SYRUP

1½ cups sugar	1 tablespoon grated
1 cup water	lemon peel
	½ cup lemon juice

1. Combine sugar, water, and lemon peel in a saucepan. Set over low heat and stir until sugar is dissolved. Cover, bring to boiling, and boil 5 minutes.

2. Remove from heat and stir in lemon juice. Set aside to cool. Chill thoroughly. Store covered in refrigerator. Use to sweeten iced tea. ABOUT 1½ CUPS

LIME SYRUP: Follow recipe for Lemon Syrup. Substitute *lime peel and juice* for the lemon.

MINT SYRUP: Follow recipe for Lemon Syrup. Decrease sugar to 1 cup. Omit lemon peel and juice. Stir ¼ *teaspoon mint extract* into syrup when removed from heat.

HOT BEVERAGES

DRIP COFFEE

Preheat a drip coffee maker by filling it with boiling water. Drain. For each standard measuring cup of water, using standard measuring spoon, measure *2 tablespoons drip grind coffee.* Put into filter section of drip coffee maker or in cone with filter paper. Pour measured freshly *boiling water* into upper container or cone. Cover, depending on type of pot used. Allow all of water to drip through coffee, keeping coffee maker over low heat 5 to 8 minutes, or as long as coffee is dripping. Do not let coffee boil at any time. Remove coffee compartment; stir and cover the brew. Place coffee maker over low heat. Stir before serving.

PERCOLATED COFFEE

Use *regular grind coffee.* Follow Drip Coffee recipe for amount to use. Put into strainer basket of coffee maker. Measure freshly drawn *cold water* into bottom of percolator. Place basket in coffee maker. Cover. Place over heat. When percolating begins, reduce heat to low so that percolating will be gentle and slow. Timing varies from 5 to 10 minutes after percolation starts. It's wise to experiment to determine exact timing for the amount of coffee generally made in your percolator. Larger amounts of coffee require the longer timing. Remove coffee basket, cover coffee maker, and keep coffee hot over low heat. Do not let coffee boil.

STEEPED COFFEE

Use *regular grind coffee.* Follow Drip Coffee recipe for amount to use. Put into coffee maker. To clarify coffee, mix in *1 teaspoon slightly beaten egg* for each 2 tablespoons coffee used. Measure and add freshly drawn *cold water.* Bring very slowly to boiling, stirring occasionally. Remove from heat at once. Pour ¼ *cup cold water* down spout to settle grounds. Let stand 3 to 5 minutes without heat. Strain through a fine strainer into a server which has been preheated with boiling water. Let coffee stand over low heat.

VACUUM-DRIP COFFEE

Use *drip or vacuum grind coffee*. Follow Drip Coffee recipe for amount to use. Specific directions for making vary according to the type of coffee maker used. Usually, freshly drawn *cold water* is measured and poured into the decanter or lower bowl. Coffee is measured into upper bowl. Cover. Place coffee maker over moderate to low heat. When all but a small amount of water has risen to upper bowl, remove coffee maker from heat. Remove top bowl when the brew has run into decanter. Cover. Serve immediately or keep hot over very low heat. Do not boil at any time.

DEMITASSE
(After-Dinner Coffee)

Using ½ measuring cup water per serving, prepare Drip Coffee or any variation. Serve hot in demitasse or after-dinner cups.

COFFEE FOR TWENTY
(Steeped)

Mix *½ pound regular grind coffee* with *1 egg and crushed egg shell*. Tie loosely in fine cheesecloth or put into a lightweight muslin bag. Put into a large kettle with *1 gallon freshly drawn cold water*. Cover tightly. Set over low heat and bring very slowly to boiling. Boil 3 to 5 minutes. Taste to test strength. Remove bag when coffee is desired strength. Cover kettle and let stand 10 to 15 minutes over low heat without boiling.

CAFÉ L'ORANGE

2 medium-sized oranges, sliced
Whole cloves
8 cups (coffee-cup size) hot coffee
Sweetened whipped cream
Brown sugar
Ground cinnamon

1. Stud each orange slice with 4 cloves; pour hot coffee over them and allow to steep for 30 minutes. Discard orange slices and cloves.
2. Reheat coffee. Pour coffee into a handsome coffeepot or carafe.
3. Accompany with bowls of the whipped cream and brown sugar and a shaker of cinnamon so that guests may flavor their coffee as desired.

8 SERVINGS

CAFÉ AU LAIT

For each cup of freshly brewed *coffee*, scald an equal measure of rich *milk*. Simultaneously pour hot coffee and hot milk into each cup. Sweeten if desired.

BOSTON COFFEE: Serve *coffee* and *cream* in equal proportions.

VIENNA COFFEE: Serve *coffee* with *whipped cream*.

HOT TEA

Heat teapot thoroughly by filling with boiling water. Pour off water; put into pot *1 rounded teaspoon loose black tea* or *1 tea bag* for each cup of tea to be brewed, or use 1 large tea bag for about 4 cups tea. For each cup of tea, pour *1 cup briskly boiling freshly drawn water* into the teapot. Cover pot and allow tea to steep 3 to 5 minutes. Stir the brew and strain the tea into each teacup as it is poured or remove tea bag or bags before pouring.

HOT GINGER TEA

4 tea bags
2 pieces (3 in. each) stick cinnamon
8 whole cloves
2 large pieces crystallized ginger, cut in very thin slices
3 to 4 tablespoons sugar
6 cups boiling water

1. Put the tea bags, cinnamon sticks, cloves, crystallized ginger, and sugar into a large teapot. Pour on boiling water; allow to steep 3 minutes. Remove tea bags and steep for 5 minutes.
2. To serve, pour tea into cups and float a quarter slice of *orange* in each cup. ABOUT 8 SERVINGS

DRESSY TEA

1 qt. freshly drawn water
½ cup sugar
4 whole cloves
1 stick cinnamon
2 rounded teaspoons tea or 2 prepared tea bags
1 cup orange juice

1. Combine water, sugar, cloves, and cinnamon in a 2-quart saucepan. Set over medium heat and stir

until sugar is dissolved. Increase heat and bring mixture to boiling.

2. Put tea into preheated teapot. Pour in the spice mixture. Cover and let tea steep 3 to 5 minutes.

3. Heat orange juice until hot. Strain tea and return to teapot. Mix in the hot orange juice. Serve with *lemon slices*.   ABOUT 6 SERVINGS

HOT COCOA

5 to 6 tablespoons cocoa, sieved	1 cup water
	3 cups milk
5 to 6 tablespoons sugar	½ teaspoon vanilla
¼ teaspoon salt	extract

1. Mix cocoa, sugar, and salt in a heavy saucepan. Blend in the water. Boil gently 2 minutes over direct heat, stirring until slightly thickened.

2. Stir in the milk, heating slowly until scalding hot. Remove from heat. Cover and keep hot, if necessary, over hot water.

3. Just before serving, mix in the extract. Beat with hand rotary or electric beater until foamy. Serve steaming hot, plain or with *whipped cream*, *marshmallow cream*, or *marshmallows*.   6 SERVINGS

HOT CHOCOLATE

2½ cups milk, scalded	¼ cup sugar
2 oz. (2 sq.) unsweet- ened chocolate, quartered	1 teaspoon vanilla extract
	Dash salt

1. Rinse an electric blender container with hot water.

2. Put into container about ½ cup scalded milk, chocolate, sugar, extract, and salt. Cover and blend about 1 minute, or until smooth and color is even throughout.

3. Add remaining scalded milk and blend until thoroughly mixed. Serve immediately.   4 SERVINGS

MEXICAN CHOCOLATE I

4 oz. sweet chocolate	1 teaspoon ground
4 cups milk	cinnamon

1. Combine all ingredients in a heavy saucepan. Cook over medium heat, stirring frequently, until chocolate is melted and mixture is heated.

2. Beat with a hand rotary beater or mix in an electric blender until frothy, about 1 minute. Serve steaming hot.   6 TO 8 SERVINGS

MEXICAN CHOCOLATE II

2 oz. (2 sq.) unsweet- ened chocolate	1/16 teaspoon ground allspice
½ cup strong coffee	Few grains salt
½ cup sugar	3 cups milk
1 teaspoon ground cinnamon	1½ teaspoons vanilla extract
	Whipped cream

1. Heat chocolate and coffee together in a heavy saucepan, stirring until chocolate is melted and mixture is smooth. Cook 2 minutes, stirring constantly.

2. Mix in the sugar, cinnamon, allspice, and salt. Gradually add the milk, stirring until blended; heat thoroughly.

3. Remove from heat; blend in extract. Top each serving with whipped cream.   ABOUT 4 SERVINGS

HOT APRICOT NIP

2 tablespoons sugar	1½ cups (12 oz. can)
4 whole cloves	apricot nectar
1 piece (3 in.) stick cinnamon	2 tablespoons lemon juice
1 cup water	

1. Combine sugar, cloves, cinnamon stick, and water in a small saucepan. Cook and stir over low heat until sugar is dissolved. Increase heat to boiling and cook gently 5 minutes.

2. Add apricot nectar and continue to heat until very hot. Remove spices; stir in lemon juice and serve at once.   ABOUT 4 SERVINGS

HOT SPICED CIDER

2 qts. apple cider	2 pieces (3 in. each)
1 teaspoon whole cloves	stick cinnamon
1 teaspoon whole allspice	½ cup firmly packed light brown sugar
	Few grains salt

Bring all ingredients to boiling in a large saucepan; simmer, covered, 30 minutes. Remove spices. Serve hot, garnished with slices of unpared *red apples*.   ABOUT 2 QUARTS

COLD BEVERAGES

ICED COFFEE

For stronger flavor pour over coffee ice cubes. Using ½ measuring cup water per standard measure of coffee, prepare *Drip Coffee, page 611*, or any variation. Fill tall glasses to brim with ice cubes. Pour the hot coffee over the ice. Serve with *granulated* or *confectioners' sugar, sugar syrup, cream,* or *whipped cream* sprinkled with *ground cinnamon.*

CHOCOLATE JAVA

3 oz. (3 sq.) unsweet- ened chocolate	4 egg yolks ¼ cup sugar
3 cups strong coffee	4 egg whites
½ cup sugar	¼ cup sugar
2 cups milk	

1. Combine chocolate, coffee, and ½ cup sugar in a saucepan. Set over low heat and stir constantly until chocolate is melted. Bring rapidly to boiling, stirring constantly. Reduce heat; cook and stir 3 minutes.
2. Remove from heat. Stir in the milk; chill thoroughly.
3. Beat egg yolks and ¼ cup sugar together until very thick. Gradually blend in the chilled chocolate mixture.
4. Beat egg whites until frothy; gradually add ¼ cup sugar, beating until rounded peaks are formed. Turn onto the chocolate mixture and slowly beat together until just blended. Chill. Serve topped with *Mocha Whipped Cream, page 441.*

ABOUT 10 SERVINGS

ICED CINNAMON COFFEE

4 cups strong coffee (use 2 to 4 teaspoons instant coffee to 1 cup boiling water)	1 piece (3 in.) stick cinnamon, broken in pieces ½ cup heavy cream Coffee Syrup, *below*

1. Pour hot coffee over cinnamon pieces; cover and let stand about 1 hour.
2. Remove cinnamon and stir in the cream. Chill thoroughly.
3. To serve, pour into ice-filled glasses. Stir in desired amount of Coffee Syrup. If desired, top

with *sweetened whipped cream* and sprinkle with *ground cinnamon.* Use *cinnamon sticks* as stirrers.

ABOUT 4 SERVINGS

COFFEE SYRUP

1 cup sugar ¾ cup water	1 teaspoon instant coffee ¼ cup boiling water

1. Combine sugar and the ¾ cup water in a saucepan. Stir over low heat until sugar is dissolved. Cover, bring to boiling, and boil 5 minutes. Remove from heat.
2. Dissolve instant coffee in boiling water. Stir into syrup. Cool; store covered in refrigerator.

ABOUT 1 CUP

ICED ORANGE MOCHA

4 cups strong coffee (use 4 tablespoons instant coffee to 4 cups hot water)	6 tablespoons sugar 3 tablespoons Dutch process cocoa 2 cups cold milk
2 medium-sized oranges, sliced	

1. Pour coffee over orange slices. Let stand 30 minutes.
2. Remove orange slices; thoroughly chill the coffee.
3. Combine the sugar and cocoa. Add ¼ cup of the milk; stir until smooth. Bring to boiling over direct heat and cook 1 to 2 minutes. Remove from heat. Add remaining milk gradually, blending well. Cover and chill until ready to use.
4. To serve, mix the chilled coffee and cocoa. Top each serving with *sweetened whipped cream*, sprinkled with a mixture of shaved *unsweetened chocolate* and grated *orange peel.*

6 TO 8 SERVINGS

ICED TEA

Fruit kabobs — lime quarters, pineapple chunks, and whole strawberries threaded onto skewers — make attractive stirrers for tall iced drinks.

COLD-WATER METHOD: For each ¾ cup (6 ounces) *cold water use 3 teaspoons tea or 3 tea bags.* Measure tea into quart jar or other glass or china container; add measured cold water. Cover; set in refrigerator for 12 to 24 hours. Strain; pour over ice.

HOT METHOD I: Use *6 teaspoons (2 tablespoons) tea* or *6 tea bags* for each *1 pint (16 ounces) water*. Measure tea into quart jar or other glass or china container. Pour measured boiling water on top; let stand in warm place 5 minutes, strain, pour over ice.

HOT METHOD II: Use *3 teaspoons tea* or *3 tea bags* for each *1½ cups boiling water*. Make as directed under Hot Method I, let stand 5 minutes, strain, cover, and let cool for 2 to 3 hours without refrigeration before pouring over ice.

To serve with tea—Lemon wedges, crosswise slices of orange with whole cloves stuck in edges, fresh mint leaves, preserved ginger, or brandied cherries.

LEMONADE

1 cup sugar	4 cups cold water
1 cup water	¾ cup lemon juice

1. Mix the sugar and 1 cup water in a saucepan. Stir over low heat until sugar is dissolved. Increase heat, cover, and boil 5 minutes. Remove from heat; cool.
2. Mix the cold water and lemon juice with the cooled syrup. Pour over chipped ice or ice cubes in tall glasses.   ABOUT 1½ QUARTS

LIMEADE: Follow recipe for Lemonade. Substitute *¾ cup lime juice* for lemon juice.

ORANGEADE: Follow recipe for Lemonade. Decrease lemon juice to ¼ cup (or substitute ¼ cup lime juice for lemon juice), decrease cold water to 1 cup, and mix *3 cups orange juice*.

FROTHY LEMONADE

1 cup water	2 egg whites
¼ cup lemon juice	Few grains salt
¼ cup honey	4 ice cubes

1. Put all ingredients except ice cubes into an electric blender container. Cover and blend until thoroughly mixed.
2. Add the ice cubes, one at a time, blending until mixed. Pour into glasses and spoon froth over top of each.   3 SERVINGS

GINGER ICE COOLER

1 can (6 oz.) frozen lemonade concentrate, partially thawed	⅔ cup light corn syrup 1 qt. ginger ale, chilled

1. Blend lemonade concentrate with corn syrup, then ginger ale.
2. Pour into individual glasses over ginger ice (freeze additional ginger ale in ice cube trays and finely crush the ice).   1½ QUARTS

RASPBERRY DELIGHT: Purée partially thawed *frozen red raspberries*. Blend with desired amount of Ginger Ice Cooler mixture. Strain if necessary. Serve thoroughly chilled in 4-ounce stemmed glasses. Omit ginger ice.

LEMON-CHERRY COOLER

4 cups water	1 can (6 oz.) frozen
½ cup sugar	pineapple juice
1 pkg. lemon-flavored	concentrate, thawed
soft drink mix	1 bottle (12 oz.)
1 pkg. cherry-flavored	sparkling water,
soft drink mix	chilled
1 can (6 oz.) frozen	
orange juice	
concentrate, thawed	

1. Combine water and sugar in a saucepan. Set over low heat and stir until sugar is dissolved. Bring to boiling and boil 2 minutes. Cool; chill.
2. Combine soft drink mixes and juice concentrates; beat with a rotary beater or mix in a blender. Stir in the chilled syrup. Pour over ice in a large pitcher. Add the sparkling water.
3. Mix well and pour into glasses. If desired, top each with a scoop of *vanilla ice cream*.

ABOUT 2 QUARTS

LEMON-CRANBERRY NECTAR

1 cup chilled cranberry juice cocktail	1 can (6 oz.) frozen lemonade concentrate
¾ cup chilled apricot nectar	(not reconstituted) Fresh ripe strawberries
¾ cup water	

1. Blend thoroughly the cranberry juice, apricot nectar, and water. Stir in lemonade concentrate until melted.
2. Pour into tall glasses over ice cubes or crushed ice.   ABOUT 3¼ CUPS

LIME-ROSEMARY ZING

1½ tablespoons crushed rosemary leaves
2½ tablespoons sugar
⅛ teaspoon salt
⅓ cup water
1½ cups apricot nectar
¾ cup lime juice
3 cups ginger ale, chilled

1. Combine rosemary, sugar, salt, and water in a small saucepan; simmer 2 minutes. Cool; strain. Blend with apricot nectar and lime juice; chill.
2. Blend ginger ale with chilled fruit juice mixture. Pour over crushed ice in tall glasses. Garnish each serving with spiral strips of *lime peel*.

ABOUT 5 CUPS

BANANA-LIME EXOTICA

Refreshing . . . a variation of a banana specialty served in beautiful Charlotte Amalie in the Virgin Islands.

⅓ cup lime juice
3 tablespoons confectioners' sugar
½ large ripe banana
2 ice cubes

Put all ingredients into a chilled electric blender container. Cover and blend on high speed about 1 minute. Pour into an ice-filled glass.   1 SERVING
NOTE: For a sweeter drink increase sugar.

PURPLE PLUM COOLER

2 cups purple plum juice*
2 cups sugar
1½ teaspoons cider vinegar
2⅔ cups sparkling water, chilled

1. Combine plum juice and sugar in a saucepan. Set over low heat and stir until sugar is dissolved; increase heat and simmer 10 minutes. Remove from heat and stir in vinegar. Cool; chill thoroughly.
2. Just before serving, pour sparkling water into chilled mixture.   ABOUT 5¼ CUPS
*Plum Juice: Rinse fresh *purple plums*. Cut into halves and remove pits. Put in kettle with *cold water*, allowing ¼ cup cold water to 1 quart firmly packed plums. Cover. Bring to boiling. Simmer at least 10 minutes, or until plums are soft. Strain through a jelly bag. Allow to hang several hours. Reserve the pulp for preparing purée. This juice may be frozen and used for jellymaking or may be sweetened for beverage use, such as the shrub.

ICY NECTARINE-PLUM WHIRL

1 or 2 medium-sized firm ripe nectarines
2 or 3 medium-sized fresh red plums
½ cup sugar
½ cup cold milk
3 tablespoons lemon juice
1 cup crushed ice

1. Rinse, cut into halves, remove pits, and cut the nectarines and plums into pieces (enough to yield ½ cup each).
2. Put fruit into an electric blender container with the remaining ingredients. Cover and blend until thoroughly mixed. Serve immediately.

ABOUT 3 CUPS

PEACH JULEP

½ cup sugar
1 tablespoon light brown sugar
2 tablespoons honey
1 cup water
2 whole cloves
1 piece (3 in.) stick cinnamon
1 cup coarsely chopped peaches, puréed in an electric blender or forced through food mill or sieve
½ cup lemon juice
2 cups orange juice

1. Combine the sugars, honey, water, cloves, and cinnamon stick in a saucepan; heat, stirring constantly, until sugar is completely dissolved. Cool; remove cloves and cinnamon.
2. Blend peach purée, lemon juice, and orange juice into the cooled sugar syrup. Chill.
3. Serve in stemmed glasses.   ABOUT 12 SERVINGS

CANTALOUPE-PINEAPPLE-GRAPEFRUIT DRINK

2 cups diced ripe cantaloupe
¼ cup sugar
2 tablespoons lime juice
1 tablespoon lemon juice
Few grains salt
1 can (12 oz.) pineapple-grapefruit drink, chilled

1. Put the cantaloupe, sugar, lime and lemon juices, and salt into an electric blender container. Cover and blend thoroughly; chill.
2. Stir the blended mixture into the chilled fruit drink. To serve, pour over ice cubes or crushed ice in chilled glasses.   ABOUT 3 CUPS

RASPBERRY AND LIME SWIZZLE

1 cup sugar
2 cups ripe red
  raspberries
1 cup lime juice

Lemon-lime carbonated
  beverage, chilled
Watermelon Sherbet,
  below
Thin lime slices

1. Sprinkle sugar over berries in an electric blender container; let stand 1 hour. Blend thoroughly.
2. Add lime juice and chill at least 2 hours. Strain through a sieve.
3. Pour ¼ cup of the raspberry syrup into each glass; add ½ cup lemon-lime carbonated beverage and stir. Top with a small scoop of Watermelon Sherbet. Garnish each glass with a thin slice of lime. ABOUT 10 SERVINGS

WATERMELON SHERBET: Mix *4 cups diced watermelon, ¼ cup lemon juice, 1 cup sugar,* and *⅛ teaspoon salt* together; chill 30 minutes; force through a sieve into a bowl. Soften *1 envelop unflavored gelatin* in *½ cup cold water* in a small saucepan. Set over low heat until dissolved, stirring constantly. Stir into watermelon mixture. Turn into refrigerator trays and freeze until firm, stirring once.
ABOUT 3 CUPS SHERBET

MILK AND HONEY

4 eggs
½ cup honey
1 cup instant nonfat dry
  milk
3 cups apricot nectar,
  chilled

1⅓ cups orange juice,
  chilled
2 to 4 tablespoons
  lemon juice

1. Beat eggs until thick and piled softly; add honey gradually, beating constantly until blended.
2. Stir the dry milk into a mixture of apricot nectar and juices until dissolved. Add gradually to egg-honey mixture; beat until foamy. Chill and beat again before serving. ABOUT 1½ QUARTS

MINTED CHOCOLATE REFRESHER

3 oz. (3 sq.) unsweet-
  ened chocolate
1 cup boiling water
¾ cup sugar
16 large marshmallows

½ teaspoon peppermint
  extract
1 quart milk
Mint sprigs

1. Melt chocolate in boiling water. Add sugar and stir until dissolved; pour into an electric blender container. Add marshmallows and extract; cover and blend until smooth.
2. Mix into milk; chill thoroughly.
3. Mix well before pouring over ice cubes in tall chilled glasses. Garnish each serving with a mint sprig. ABOUT 6 CUPS

PEANUT BUTTER MILK DRINK

¾ cup water
⅓ cup instant nonfat
  dry milk
1 tablespoon sugar
Few grains salt

2 tablespoons smooth
  peanut butter
⅛ teaspoon vanilla
  extract

Combine all ingredients in an electric blender container. Blend thoroughly. Serve chilled. 1 SERVING

CHOCOLATE-BANANA SHAKE

8 ripe bananas
6 cups cold milk
1 cup instant chocolate-
  flavored drink mix

1 teaspoon vanilla
  extract
1½ pts. vanilla ice
  cream

1. Cut about one third of bananas into large pieces and put into an electric blender container. Add one third of each of the remaining ingredients; blend thoroughly. Pour into a chilled large pitcher. Repeat twice with remaining ingredients.
2. Pour into glasses and, if desired, top each with scoop of *vanilla ice cream.* 10 TO 12 SERVINGS

WEST INDIAN CHOCOLATE FROST

2 cups milk
½ cup heavy cream
1 cup chocolate sauce or
  topping
4 teaspoons sugar
1 teaspoon vanilla
  extract

1 tablespoon instant
  coffee
½ teaspoon ground
  cinnamon
½ teaspoon ground
  cloves
1 pint vanilla ice cream

1. Combine all ingredients in an electric blender container; cover and blend. Chill thoroughly.
2. Beat slightly before pouring into tall glasses. Garnish with *chocolate curls.* 6 CUPS

FROSTED COFFEE SHAKE

2 cups cold milk
2 tablespoons sugar
1 tablespoon instant
   coffee
½ pt. vanilla or
   chocolate ice cream

Put milk, sugar, and instant coffee into an electric blender container. Cover and blend thoroughly. Add ice cream by spoonfuls and blend until mixed.

ABOUT 3 CUPS

SPANISH LEMON AND LIME

1 cup instant nonfat dry
   milk
1 qt. icy cold milk
⅓ cup sugar
⅔ cup lime juice
1 pt. lemon sherbet
1 qt. crushed ice

1. Stir the dry milk into the cold milk until blended. Stir in the sugar until dissolved. Add the lime juice and sherbet and beat with hand rotary or electric beater until foamy.
2. Pour foamy beverage into a pitcher or individual glasses over part of the crushed ice. Garnish with *lemon and/or lime slices* and fresh *mint leaves*, along with the remaining ice. Serve with straws.

ABOUT 2 QUARTS

STRAWBERRY SHAKE

1 pt. strawberries,
   rinsed
1⅓ cups cold milk
¼ cup sugar
2 scoops vanilla or
   strawberry ice cream

Combine strawberries with the milk and sugar in an electric blender container. Cover and blend thoroughly. Add the ice cream and blend a few seconds.

3 SERVINGS

STRAWBERRY FROST

1 pt. ripe strawberries
½ cup sugar
2 cups cold milk
¼ cup cream
2 tablespoons lemon
   juice
1 teaspoon vanilla
   extract
⅛ teaspoon salt
Vanilla ice cream

1. Crush strawberries; add sugar and 1 cup of milk; beat with hand rotary or electric beater until of a creamy consistency.
2. Gradually add remaining ingredients except ice cream, beating well.

3. Put 1 or 2 scoops ice cream into each chilled glass. Fill with strawberry mixture. If desired, garnish with *strawberries*.

ABOUT 5½ CUPS

APRICOT WHIRL

1 can (12 oz.) apricot
   nectar
1 pt. vanilla ice cream
¼ cup instant natural-
   flavored malted milk
   powder
2 tablespoons lemon
   juice

1. Pour apricot nectar into refrigerator tray; freeze until mushy.
2. Spoon apricot nectar and ice cream into an electric blender container; add malted milk powder and lemon juice. Cover and blend until smooth and creamy.
3. Pour into chilled glasses and serve immediately with straws.

ABOUT 3¾ CUPS

CHOCOLATE MALTED MILK

2 cups cold milk
¼ cup Chocolate Syrup,
   page 611
¼ cup malted milk
   powder
4 scoops chocolate or
   vanilla ice cream

Pour milk, Chocolate Syrup, and malted milk powder into an electric blender container. Cover and blend until frothy. Add the ice cream while motor is running. Blend only until mixed.

ABOUT 3 CUPS

To vary: Add a few round *peppermint hard candies* with milk for a minty chocolate malted. Use a different flavored syrup, ice cream, or *sweetened fruit* to create the malted of your choice.

HOMEMADE CHOCOLATE SODA

1 small scoop chocolate
   or vanilla ice cream
2 to 4 tablespoons
   sweetened chocolate
   syrup
½ cup cold milk
½ cup sparkling water
   or ginger ale
1 or 2 scoops softened
   ice cream

1. For each soda, blend a small scoop of ice cream and the chocolate syrup in a tall glass.
2. Add milk and sparkling water; mix thoroughly.
3. Float scoops of ice cream on top. Serve with straws and long-handled spoon.

1 SERVING

HOMEMADE LEMON SODA: Follow recipe for Home-made Chocolate Soda. Use *vanilla ice cream* and substitute *2 tablespoons thawed frozen lemonade concentrate* for the chocolate syrup.

HOMEMADE PEACH SODA: Follow recipe for Homemade Chocolate Soda. Use *vanilla ice cream* and substitute *⅓ cup mashed, sweetened ripe fresh peaches* for the chocolate syrup.

HOMEMADE PINEAPPLE SODA: Follow recipe for Homemade Chocolate Soda. Use *vanilla ice cream* and substitute *¼ cup canned or frozen crushed pineapple* for the chocolate syrup.

HOMEMADE RASPBERRY OR STRAWBERRY SODA: Follow recipe for Homemade Chocolate Soda. Use *vanilla ice cream* and substitute *¼ cup crushed, sweetened red raspberries or strawberries* for the chocolate syrup.

SNAPPY CHOCOLATE SODA

1 cup chocolate syrup	1 bottle (28 oz.)
⅓ to ½ cup lemon juice	sparkling water,
6 scoops vanilla ice cream	chilled

Combine the chocolate syrup and lemon juice. Divide evenly into six tall chilled soda glasses. Add a scoop of vanilla ice cream to each glass and fill with the chilled sparkling water, stirring to blend. Serve immediately. 6 SERVINGS

CHERRY-COLA SODA, BLENDER STYLE

This is a summer-time treat with fresh cherries.

¾ cup cold cola beverage or milk	4 large scoops vanilla ice cream
½ cup sugar	Cola beverage
1 pt. pitted dark sweet cherries	

1. Put the cola beverage and sugar into an electric blender container. Cover and turn on motor. Add cherries and then ice cream. Blend until thick and smooth.
2. Divide mixture among 8 tall glasses. Fill with cola beverage. Give a quick stir and top each with a scoop of *ice cream.* 8 TALL SERVINGS

PUNCHES

SPARKLING PUNCH

Here's an easy-to-make punch for a Halloween party, a fine go-along with cake—refreshments to please guests of all ages.

2 qts. apple cider	4 bottles (12 oz. each)
8 whole cloves	lemon-lime
2 pieces stick cinnamon	carbonated
6 whole allspice	beverage, chilled
1 can (6 oz.) frozen pineapple-orange juice concentrate	

1. Refrigerate 1 quart of the cider and pour remaining 1 quart into a saucepan with the spices. Cook 15 minutes and strain to remove spices.
2. Combine the spiced and chilled cider and fruit juice concentrate in a chilled punch bowl; blend well. Slowly pour in the carbonated beverage.
3. Add ice cubes or a fancy ice mold (see *page 610*). ABOUT 3 QUARTS PUNCH

FROSTY COLA APRIC-ADE

¾ cup sugar	1½ cups lime juice
1½ cups water	¾ cup orange juice
3 cans (12. oz. each) apricot nectar	Cola Sherbet, *below*

1. Mix sugar and water; stir over low heat until sugar is dissolved. Cover, bring to boiling, and boil 5 minutes. Cool.
2. Blend the apricot nectar, lime juice, orange juice, and the cooled syrup. Chill thoroughly.
3. When ready to serve, pour fruit juice mixture into a chilled bowl. Serve in punch cups or mugs and top each serving with a scoop of Cola Sherbet. ABOUT 2 QUARTS PUNCH

COLA SHERBET: Blend in a large bowl *¾ cup sugar, 1 cup carbonated cola beverage, 1 teaspoon grated lime peel, few grains salt,* and *1½ cups cream.* Stir until sugar is dissolved. Pour into a 1-quart refrigerator tray. Freeze until mixture is mushy.

When mushy, turn into a chilled bowl and beat with a chilled beater until smooth. Immediately return mixture to refrigerator tray and freeze until firm, about 3 hours.　　　ABOUT 1½ PINTS SHERBET

ICED CARDAMOM COFFEE IN PUNCH BOWL

½ cup instant coffee	2½ teaspoons ground
⅓ cup sugar	cardamom
	2 qts. boiling water

1.　Mix the instant coffee, sugar, and cardamom in a heat-resistant bowl. Pour in boiling water and stir until sugar is dissolved. Cool or chill.
2.　When ready to serve, pour coffee over an ice mold in a punch bowl. Ladle into punch cups and serve with a bowl of *sweetened whipped cream* and a crystal shaker of *ground cardamom* for guests to help themselves.　　　2½ QUARTS COFFEE
NOTE: This punch is also delicious served hot.

FOUR-FRUIT REFRESHER

4 cups apple juice	2 teaspoons vanilla
2 cups cranberry juice	extract
cocktail	¼ cup sugar
2 cups orange juice	2 cups ginger ale,
¼ cup lemon juice	chilled

1.　Combine all ingredients except ginger ale; stir until sugar is completely dissolved. Chill thoroughly.
2.　When ready to serve, pour fruit juice mixture into a chilled punch bowl, add ginger ale, and stir gently to blend.　　　ABOUT 2½ QUARTS PUNCH

CRANBERRY PUNCH

4 cups firm cranberries,	4 cups pineapple juice,
rinsed	chilled
4 cups water	1 cup orange juice,
1½ cups sugar	chilled
2 tablespoons lemon	
juice	

1.　Combine cranberries and water in a saucepan. Cook over medium heat until cranberry skins pop.
2.　Sieve cooked cranberries. Stir in sugar and lemon juice. Return to saucepan; bring to boiling and cook 2 minutes, stirring constantly. Immedi-

ately remove from heat; cool and chill thoroughly in refrigerator.
3.　To serve, pour over ice cubes in a large pitcher or punch bowl. Stir in pineapple and orange juices. Serve in punch cups.　　　ABOUT 1½ QUARTS PUNCH
NOTE: For a refreshing start to a luncheon or dinner, fill small glasses with Cranberry Punch and top each glass with a small scoop of *lemon sherbet.*

SPICY CRANBERRY PUNCH

4 pieces (3 in. each)	3 qts. cranberry juice
stick cinnamon, broken	cocktail
in pieces	1 orange, sliced
8 whole allspice	6 bottles (7 oz. each)
18 whole cloves	lemon-lime carbonated
	beverage, chilled

1.　Tie spices together in cheesecloth bag.
2.　In a large saucepan, combine the cranberry juice cocktail, orange slices, and spice bag. Bring to boiling, reduce heat, and simmer about 20 minutes. Set aside to cool; discard spice bag and orange; chill cranberry juice.
3.　Just before serving, pour into chilled punch bowl; add lemon-lime carbonated beverage and stir to blend. If desired, garnish with additional *orange slices.*　　　ABOUT 17 CUPS

WHITE GRAPE JUICE-CRANBERRY PUNCH

1 qt. cranberry juice	3 tablespoons lemon
cocktail	juice
1 cup sugar	1 large bottle (about 3½
½ cup orange juice	cups) sparkling white
	grape juice, chilled

1.　Combine the cranberry juice cocktail and sugar; stir until sugar is dissolved. Add orange and lemon juice and chill fruit juice mixture until ready to use.
2.　Just before serving, pour mixture into a punch bowl over ice cubes and blend in the sparkling white grape juice. Float *Sugar-Frosted Candied Cranberries, page 42,* in punch, if desired.
　　　ABOUT 2 QUARTS PUNCH

LOGANBERRY-LEMONADE PUNCH

4 cans (6 oz. each)
    frozen lemonade
    concentrate
2 cups loganberry,
    blackberry, or
    raspberry juice

3 cups cold water
3½ cups sparkling water,
    chilled
3½ cups ginger ale,
    chilled

1.   Mix thoroughly the lemonade concentrate, berry juice, and water. Set in refrigerator to chill thoroughly.
2.   When ready to serve, pour mixture into a chilled punch bowl. Add the sparkling water and ginger ale; stir to blend. If desired, a decorative ice block may be floated in the punch bowl.

ABOUT 3¾ QUARTS

PUNCH À LA CHAMPAGNE

The flavor of this punch rivals that of champagne.

1 cup orange juice
¾ cup lime juice
½ cup sugar

1 large bottle (about
    3½ cups) sparkling
    white grape juice,
    chilled

1.   Combine the fruit juices and sugar; stir until sugar is dissolved. Chill thoroughly.
2.   When ready to serve, pour the fruit juice mixture into a chilled small punch bowl; add the sparkling white grape juice and stir gently.

ABOUT 5 CUPS PUNCH

SPARKLING GOLDEN COOLER

1 cup sugar
1½ cups water
2 medium-sized oranges
1 lemon
1 lime
2 medium-sized bananas,
    cut in pieces

1 can (12 oz.) pineapple
    juice
2 qts. ginger ale,
    chilled
Fresh strawberries

1.   Combine sugar and water in a saucepan; stir over low heat until sugar is dissolved. Increase heat and bring to boiling; boil 3 minutes. Cool.
2.   Meanwhile, extract the juice from oranges, lemon, and lime. Put juice into an electric blender container with the bananas; blend until smooth. Mix with syrup and pineapple juice. Freeze in refrigerator trays until firm, about 3 hours.
3.   To serve, scoop frozen crush into a large bowl; stir in ginger ale. Serve at once, garnished with fresh strawberries.   20 SERVINGS

GREEN SHUTTERS INN PUNCH

A Nova Scotia specialty from Lunenburg County.

1 cup red currant jelly
2 cups boiling water
2 cups fresh orange
    juice

½ cup fresh lemon juice
½ cup sugar
1 qt. ginger ale,
    chilled

1.   Beat jelly with hand rotary or electric beater until frothy. Stir in boiling water, fruit juices, and sugar; cool. Chill.
2.   Just before serving, pour punch into a pitcher and stir in ginger ale; add ice if desired.

ABOUT 2½ QUARTS PUNCH

SPARKLING FRUIT REFRESHER

1 can (6 oz.) frozen
    orange juice concentrate, thawed
1 can (6 oz.) frozen
    lemonade concentrate,
    thawed
3 cups cold water

2 drops red food
    coloring
1 bottle (12 oz.) ginger
    ale, chilled
1 pkg. (16 oz.) frozen
    whole strawberries,
    just thawed
1 pt. orange sherbet

Combine concentrates and water in a punch bowl; stir until well blended. Mix in food coloring and ginger ale. Add strawberries (including syrup). Float scoops of sherbet on punch. Serve immediately.   ABOUT 12 SERVINGS

IMPERIAL PUNCH

1½ cups orange juice
¾ cup unsweetened
    pineapple juice
¾ cup lemon juice
¼ cup lime juice
¾ cup grenadine

½ cup sugar
3 cups ginger ale,
    chilled
1 cup sparkling water,
    chilled

1.   Combine the fruit juices, grenadine, and sugar; stir until sugar is completely dissolved. Chill thoroughly.
2.   When ready to serve, pour fruit juice mixture into a chilled punch bowl. Add the chilled ginger ale and sparkling water; stir gently to blend. Float a tinted ice block or ring mold, if desired. Or garnish with slices of *strawberries* and *orange*.

ABOUT 2 QUARTS

NOTE: If desired, prepare a Grenadine Ice Ring Mold for the punch bowl—freeze 4½ *cups boiling water* and ½ *cup grenadine* in a 1½-quart ring mold.

PINK CLOUD PUNCH

1 cup unsweetened
pineapple juice,
chilled
¼ cup lemon juice
4 teaspoons grenadine

2 egg whites
2 tablespoons sugar
1 qt. ginger ale,
chilled

1. Blend thoroughly the pineapple juice, lemon juice, and grenadine.
2. Beat egg whites until frothy. Add sugar and beat until stiff peaks are formed. Gradually add juice mixture, beating constantly until blended.
3. Add the ginger ale; stir gently to mix. Pour over ice block in a punch bowl. ABOUT 2 QUARTS PUNCH

SPARKLING RASPBERRY PUNCH

3 pkgs. (10 oz. each)
frozen raspberries,
thawed
½ cup orange juice

2 bottles (28 oz. each)
raspberry or black-
cherry-flavored
carbonated beverage,
chilled
1 bottle (28 oz.) lemon-
flavored carbonated
beverage, chilled

1. Several hours before serving prepare an ice mold for the punch bowl, if desired.
2. Force contents of 1½ packages thawed berries through a sieve or food mill. Mix in the orange juice.
3. Pour over the ice mold or ice cubes in a punch bowl. Add the carbonated beverages and remaining thawed berries; stir gently. If desired, garnish with *orange slices.* Ladle punch into cups and serve. ABOUT 4 QUARTS PUNCH

RASPBERRY FRUIT PUNCH

3 env. raspberry-
flavored instant soft
drink mix
3 env. grape-flavored
instant soft drink mix
2¼ cups sugar
3 cans (6 oz. each)
frozen pineapple-
orange juice concen-
trate, thawed

1½ teaspoons red food
coloring
½ teaspoon almond
extract
12 bottles (7 oz. each)
lemon-lime carbo-
nated beverage,
chilled

1. Mix thoroughly in a large bowl the soft drink

mixes and sugar. Add *6 quarts water* gradually, stirring constantly until soft drink mixes and sugar are dissolved. Stir in the pineapple-orange juice concentrate, food coloring, and extract; stir until well blended.
2. Chill thoroughly.
3. Just before serving, stir in the chilled lemon-lime beverage. ABOUT 8 QUARTS PUNCH

GOLDEN PUNCH

1½ cups sugar
3 cups water
3 cups freshly prepared
tea (cool at room
temperature)
3 cups unsweetened
pineapple juice

1½ cups lime juice
1 can (6 oz.) frozen
orange juice
concentrate, thawed
3 cups ginger ale,
chilled

1. Combine sugar and water in a saucepan. Set over low heat and stir until sugar is dissolved. Increase heat, cover, and boil 5 minutes. Remove from heat; set aside to cool.
2. Combine in a large bowl the tea, pineapple juice, lime ice, and orange juice concentrate. Stir to blend ingredients. Chill in refrigerator.
3. When ready to serve, pour chilled fruit juice mixture into a chilled punch bowl. Pour in the sugar syrup and chilled ginger ale; stir to blend thoroughly. If desired, a decorative ice block may be floated in the punch. ABOUT 3 QUARTS PUNCH

WATERMELON PUNCH

2½ cups water
¼ cup lemon juice
1 cup sugar
3 cups watermelon juice*
2 cups orange juice

6 tablespoons lemon
juice
Lemon, lime, and
orange slices

1. Combine one half of the water, lemon juice, and sugar in a saucepan; mix well. Bring to boiling and boil 3 minutes; cool.
2. Mix in remaining water and fruit juices. Chill thoroughly.
3. Pour over decorative ice block in a punch bowl. Garnish with fruit slices. ABOUT 2 QUARTS PUNCH
*To prepare watermelon juice, extract juice from diced watermelon (about 5½ cups) by pressing it against the sides of a fine sieve. If desired, strain juice through cheesecloth.

FLUFFY LIME PUNCH

1 qt. unsweetened
  pineapple juice,
  chilled

1 qt. ginger ale,
  chilled
1 qt. lime sherbet
1 qt. vanilla ice cream

1.   Combine ingredients in a large bowl. Using a hand rotary or electric beater, beat until just smooth. Pour mixture into a chilled punch bowl.
2.   Decorate punch bowl with clusters of *Frosted Grapes, page 350.* Float *lime slices* garnished with small sprigs of *mint* in center of each slice.

ABOUT 4 QUARTS PUNCH

SUMMER STRAWBERRY BOWL

4 pts. fresh straw-
  berries, rinsed and
  hulled
2 cups icy cold water
½ cup lemon juice,
  strained

2 cups instant nonfat
  dry milk
¾ cup sugar
1 qt. vanilla ice cream,
  softened
2 qts. crushed ice

1.   Purée some of the strawberries in an electric blender; turn into a large bowl. Repeat with the remaining strawberries.
2.   Mix the water and lemon juice into the purée. Stir in dry milk and sugar until thoroughly blended.
3.   Pour half of the strawberry mixture into a bowl. Using an electric mixer, beat in half of the ice cream until well blended. Pour into a chilled large punch bowl.
4.   Repeat the mixing of remaining strawberries and ice cream. Pour into punch bowl. Blend in part of the ice, then add remaining ice and serve.

ABOUT 3 QUARTS PUNCH

CHAMPAGNE STRAWBERRY BOWL: Follow recipe for Summer Strawberry Bowl. Blend *3 cups chilled champagne* into the cream strawberry mixture. Float *2 cups fresh strawberry halves* in the punch.
ROSÉ STRAWBERRY BOWL: Follow recipe for Summer Strawberry Bowl. Blend *3 cups chilled rosé wine* into the creamy strawberry mixture. Float *2 cups fresh strawberry halves* in the punch.
NOTE: Some tastes may prefer champagne or rosé wine added in equal amounts with the creamy strawberry mixture.

CREAMY PINK PUNCH
The deep pink color and flavor of maraschino cherries in this punch are complemented by a pale pink peppermint-flavored frost.

¼ cup (2 oz.) crushed
  striped peppermint
  candy
¾ cup marshmallow
  cream
½ cup boiling water
½ cup very cold
  water
½ cup instant nonfat
  dry milk

2 tablespoons lemon
  juice
¾ cup maraschino
  cherry syrup
⅓ cup chopped mara-
  schino cherries
1 large bottle (about 3½
  cups) sparkling
  white grape juice,
  chilled

1.   To make peppermint frost, combine candy, marshmallow cream, and boiling water. Stir until candy is dissolved; chill.
2.   Pour the cold water into a bowl; add the dry milk and whip until soft peaks are formed, 3 to 4 minutes. Add lemon juice and continue whipping until stiff, 3 to 4 minutes.
3.   Fold peppermint mixture into whipped dry milk. Turn into a refrigerator tray and freeze until firm.
4.   To serve, mix cherry syrup and cherries in a chilled punch bowl. Blend in sparkling white grape juice and float scoops of peppermint frost on the punch. If desired, garnish each serving with a whole *maraschino cherry.*   ABOUT 12 SERVINGS
NOTE: The amount of peppermint frost is sufficient for a double recipe of the punch.

WITCH-DRAUGHT WITH ORANGE FLOATS

3 medium-sized oranges
Whole cloves
2 qts. apple cider
2 cups water
1 cup packed brown
  sugar
1 cup orange juice

6 tablespoons lemon
  juice
½ teaspoon ground
  nutmeg
2 pieces (3 in. each)
  stick cinnamon

1.   Stud oranges with whole cloves, inserting them about 1 inch apart. Place in shallow baking dish and bake at 325°F about 1 hour, or until juice begins to form. Remove from oven; prick peel thoroughly with a fork.

2. Mix remaining ingredients in a saucepan. Set over medium heat and stir until sugar is dissolved. Bring to boiling, add oranges, and simmer 15 minutes.

3. Transfer oranges to heat-resistant punch bowl; strain punch through fine sieve into the bowl. Serve hot.　　　　ABOUT 2 QUARTS PUNCH

HOT AROMATIC PUNCH

4½ cups boiling water	¼ cup sugar
5 tea bags	2 to 3 tablespoons
1 qt. apple cider	rubbed sage

1. Pour boiling water over tea bags in a heated teapot. Let steep about 5 minutes; remove the tea bags.

2. Meanwhile, combine apple cider, sugar, and sage in a saucepan. Cover, bring to boiling, and simmer 5 minutes.

3. Add the tea to apple cider mixture and simmer 10 minutes longer. Strain.

4. Serve hot in mugs. Garnish each with a twist of *lemon*.　　　　ABOUT 7½ CUPS PUNCH

SAGE CIDER PUNCH

"Sage brew"*	1 cup sugar
"Tea brew"**	2 tablespoons lime juice
1 qt. apple cider	(1 small lime)

1. Prepare the sage and tea brews; set aside.

2. Meanwhile, combine cider and sugar in a saucepan; set over low heat and stir until sugar is dissolved. Cover saucepan and heat the cider to simmering.

3. Add the strained sage and tea brews and the lime juice; blend thoroughly. Cover and keep hot over low heat until ready to serve. (Do not boil.)

4. Serve in small glasses or mugs. If desired, float several *sage leaves* on each serving.

ABOUT 5½ CUPS PUNCH
*To prepare "sage brew," pour *1 cup boiling water* over *2 tablespoons leaf sage* in a small saucepan. Bring to simmering; cover tightly and remove from heat. Let stand about 10 minutes to brew. Strain through cheesecloth or a fine sieve.　ABOUT ⅔ CUP
**To prepare "tea brew," pour *1 cup boiling water* over *1 tea bag* in a small saucepan; cover tightly and let stand about 10 minutes. Remove tea bag.　　　　　　　　　ABOUT 1 CUP

HOT BUTTERED CRANBERRY PUNCH
Fresh cranberries, pineapple juice, and spices contribute to the happy blend of flavors in this tangy-sweet punch.

2 cups water	¼ teaspoon ground
4 cups fresh cranberries, rinsed	cloves
1½ cups water	⅛ teaspoon ground nutmeg
⅔ cup lightly packed brown sugar	⅛ teaspoon salt
½ teaspoon ground cinnamon	1 can (18 oz.) unsweetened pineapple juice
¼ teaspoon ground allspice	Butter or margarine

1. Combine the 2 cups water and cranberries in a saucepan. Bring to boiling and cook until skins pop. Force cranberries through a food or sieve to make a purée.

2. Meanwhile, bring to boiling in a saucepan the 1½ cups water, brown sugar, spices, and salt. Add the cranberry purée and pineapple juice. Return to heat and simmer 5 minutes. Keep hot over simmering water until serving time.

3. Ladle punch into serving cups or mugs and add dots of butter to each cup. Serve with *cinnamon stick* stirrers, if desired.　ABOUT 1½ QUARTS PUNCH

SPICED LEMON TEA PUNCH
Accented with crystallized ginger and a generous amount of lemon juice, you'll agree . . . this tea drink is something extra-special.

3 cups freshly boiling water	1 cup sugar
6 tea bags or 6 rounded teaspoons black tea	¼ to 1 cup lemon juice
2 pieces (2 in. each) stick cinnamon	6 cups freshly boiling water
12 to 16 whole cloves	2 pieces (2 in. each) crystallized ginger, cut lengthwise in halves
2 to 3 teaspoons grated lemon peel	

1. Pour 3 cups boiling water over tea. Add cinnamon sticks, cloves, and lemon peel. Allow to steep for 5 minutes.

2. Remove tea bags; add sugar and stir until dissolved. Strain. Return cinnamon sticks to the tea. Add lemon juice, 6 cups boiling water, and ginger pieces; stir to blend. Ladle hot punch into serving cups.　　　　ABOUT 2½ QUARTS PUNCH

Bonus Chapter

PRESERVING, PICKLING & FREEZING

Included in this chapter are the following methods of home food preservation—home canning; preserving, *i.e.* making jellies, jams, marmalades, preserves, conserves, and fruit butters; pickling; and also home freezing.

HOME CANNING OF FRUITS & VEGETABLES

To preserve foods by canning we must do two things—first, provide sufficient heat to destroy all microscopic life that will cause spoilage in food; second, provide a perfect seal which will prevent re-entrance of the micro-organisms.

The problems of preventing spoilage have been practically solved by improved methods of canning which are explained here. It must be remembered, however, that the process of canning never improves the product; it only preserves it for future use. Only the freshest produce should be canned.

METHODS OF CANNING

These methods refer to the manner in which food is prepared and packed into jars and must not be confused with methods of processing foods.

Open-Kettle—This method involves cooking the food completely and ladling it into hot sterilized jars (filling and sealing one jar at a time). Sterilized equipment and utensils should be used throughout.

With the open-kettle method there is always a possibility of spoilage through contamination of the food or jars since there is no period of sterilization after the jars have been sealed. Foods which are cooked in a thick syrup (jams, preserves, fruit butters, pickles, etc.) may be safely canned by this method. However, it is not recommended for canning fruits, juices, and tomatoes. Spoilage can re-

sult because the organisms (bacteria, yeast, and molds) which cause it are either not destroyed during cooking or they enter the jar before it is sealed.

Never use this method for canning vegetables or meat.

Cold (raw) Pack—This method involves packing the food firmly into clean hot jars and adding boiling liquid (syrup, water, or fruit juice), leaving some space between the packed food and the jar lid. Most raw fruits and vegetables shrink during processing so ½ inch space is usually sufficient. Exceptions are corn, lima beans, and peas which expand during processing. These should be packed loosely and about 1 inch of space allowed at top of jar. Enough boiling liquid should be added to completely cover the food.

Air bubbles are released from filled jars before adjusting lids. (Follow manufacturer's directions for the type of jars and lids being used.) The food is then cooked and sterilized simultaneously by processing in boiling water or in steam.

Fruits (except apples, pears, and pineapples) and tomatoes may be canned using the cold-pack method. Vegetables are packed raw into cans only if they are to be processed in a pressure canner.

Hot Pack—This method involves precooking the product a short time before packing it very hot into clean hot jars, then adding hot cooking liquid (or hot syrup or water), releasing air bubbles, sealing jars, and processing them.

Precooking food before packing causes it to shrink, thus allowing for slightly more to be packed into jars than when food is packed raw. Pack precooked foods loosely and allow about ½ inch headspace.

"Floating" (the rising of food to the top of jar during processing) can often be prevented by precooking before packing.

The hot-pack method is used for both vegetables and fruits.

EQUIPMENT

Glass Jars—Glass jars are sold with several types of caps or closures. Always use the correct size of closure (widemouth or regular) to fit your jars. When using a two-piece closure consisting of a metal screwband and flat metal lid with sealing compound, use the metal lid one time only. The band may be used again if it is in good condition. For a closure consisting of a porcelain-lined zinc cap with a rubber shoulder ring, always use clean, new rings of the right size for the jars. Do not test rings by stretching them.

Check jars and closures for nicks, dents, chips, or other defects. Use only perfect jars and closures.

Tin Cans—Tin cans may be purchased plain or with enamel linings of two types. *R-enamel type* cans have a bright gold lining and are recommended for certain fruits and vegetables to prevent discoloration of the food. Beets, red berries, red and black cherries, plums, pumpkin, rhubarb, and winter squash are canned in the R-enamel type. The *C-enamel type* has a dull gold lining and is used for corn and hominy.

The plain tin can is used for other fruits and vegetables and meat.

A mechanical sealer is necessary if tin cans are used. The sealer should be tested and adjusted each time before using it following manufacturer's directions.

Processing Equipment

Pressure Canner or Cooker—Vegetables (except tomatoes), meats, and other low-acid foods should be processed in steam in a pressure canner in order to destroy the spore-forming bacteria.

The pressure canner must be fitted with a rack in the bottom, a steam-tight cover, petcock, safety valve, and an accurate gauge or weight which measures definite pressures. The food processed in a canner reaches temperatures many degrees above the boiling temperature of water. Therefore, follow manufacturer's directions carefully for operating the canner.

Water-Bath Canner—Fruits and acid vegetables may be processed in a water-bath canner. This is available on the market but any large metal container with a tight-fitting cover may be used. It must be deep enough to allow 2 to 4 inches space above the jars for brisk boiling of the water. It must also have a wire or wooden rack in the bottom.

If a pressure canner is deep enough it may be used for a water-bath canner. When used for this purpose, cover the canner, but do not fasten, and leave the petcock open so that pressure does not build up inside.

Miscellaneous Equipment

Include several large kettles and pans, widemouthed funnel, colander, vegetable brushes, long-handled tongs and forks, a 1-quart measure, food chopper, jar lifter for lifting hot jars in and out of the canner, and cheesecloth.

CANNING PROCEDURE

Inspect and test equipment before beginning to prepare the product for canning.

Wash glass jars in hot soapy water and rinse thoroughly. Wash and rinse metal rings and bands and rubber rings (if used).

Sterilize jars if the open-kettle method of canning is used. To sterilize, put clean jars on a rack or folded dish cloth placed in bottom of a large kettle. Include a knife, spoon, and widemouthed funnel. Cover jars with boiling water and boil 15 minutes. Keep jars covered with water the entire time and leave in water until ready to use. Sterilization is unnecessary when food is cold- or hot-packed and processed in a water bath or pressure canner. Just wash and rinse the jars and leave in the hot rinsing water until ready to fill. Drain jars just before filling.

Follow manufacturer's directions for sterilizing jar closures. In some instances the jar caps are boiled 15 minutes along with the jars. Metal lids with sealing compounds may need to be submerged in boiling water for several minutes before using.

Prepare the product for canning—Use young, tender vegetables; use fresh, firm, not overripe fruits. Sort fruits and vegetables for size and ripeness or maturity so that the contents of each jar will be as nearly uniform as possible. Can the food before it loses its freshness. This is especially necessary with asparagus, peas, beans, and corn.

Wash the product thoroughly whether or not it is to be pared. Dirt contains some of the bacteria hardest to kill (spore forming) so wash foods under cold, running water or through several changes of water. Handle fruits and vegetables gently to avoid bruising. Do not let them soak in water before packing in jars.

Fill and seal jars—Pack the food to not more than ½ inch of top of jars. Exceptions are fruit juices, preserves, relishes, and some other foods which are not processed in the water bath or pressure canner. Only ¼ inch headspace is necessary for these.

Add salt to vegetables, if desired—1 teaspoon per quart; ½ teaspoon per pint.

Add liquid to jars—boiling syrup, water, or extracted fruit juice for fruits; hot cooking liquid or water for vegetables.

Air bubbles will rise as the liquid is poured into jar. Assist the bubbles to come to the top and break them by running a knife or spatula down the side of jar. Add more hot liquid, if needed, to entirely cover the food in jar and leave the recommended amount of headspace at top of jar.

Wipe the rim of jar free of any food particles before adjusting lid. If the food is hot and processing is to be done in a water-bath canner, seal jar completely for any type of closure. Self-sealing lids are always sealed completely before processing the food in either the water-bath or pressure canner. If using rubber rings and the food is to be processed in a pressure canner, screw tops on tightly, then turn back ¼ inch. After processing, immediately tighten the tops (do not force them).

Process jars in pressure canner or water-bath as directed for specific foods. When processing in boiling-water bath, start counting the time after water has reached a full boil and keep it boiling for the entire time. Add more boiling water, if needed, to keep jars covered. Remove jars from water as soon as processing is completed.

When processing in pressure canner, have enough water in the canner to come up to the bottom of the rack (1 to 2 inches). Place filled jars or cans on rack, adjust cover of canner, and clamp down securely. Make sure that the petcock is open. Place canner over heat and when steam escapes from the petcock the specified number of minutes (follow manufacturer's directions), close petcock.

When the indicator on the canner registers the specific pressure start counting the processing time. Remove canner from heat as soon as processing is completed and allow to cool until pressure reaches zero. Then open petcock slowly; do not open canner until pressure is entirely released. Complete the seal if jars are only partially sealed.

Cool jars by placing them upright on folded towels or wire racks away from drafts. Inspect completely cooled jars for a perfect seal. Leakage or bubbles rising in jars means that the contents must be used or recanned at once.

Store jars in a cool, dry place after wiping with a damp cloth and labeling them. Boil home-canned vegetables (except tomatoes) 10 to 15 minutes before tasting or serving them.

SWEETENING FRUITS

Sugar helps canned fruit hold its shape, color, and flavor. Most fruits call for sweetening to be added in the form of a sugar syrup. For very juicy fruit packed hot, use sugar with no liquid added.

To prepare a sugar syrup—Boil sugar and water (or juice extracted from some of the fruit) together 5 minutes. Use a thin, medium, or heavy syrup depending on the sweetness of the fruit and individual tastes. To make syrup, combine water and sugar and boil 5 minutes.

PROPORTIONS

Cups Water (or juice)	Cups Sugar	Cups Syrup	Result
4	2	5	thin
4	3	5½	medium
4	4¾	6½	heavy

Keep syrup hot until needed but do not continue boiling after 5 minutes. A 1-quart jar of fruit requires 1 to 1½ cups syrup.

CANNING FRUITS USING BOILING-WATER BATH

Apples—Wash, pare, core, and cut into slices, quarters, or halves. To keep apples from darkening, immerse pieces in water containing 2 tablespoons each salt and vinegar per gallon of water. Drain fruit and boil 5 minutes in thin syrup (or water). Pack into jars and cover with the hot syrup (or water), leaving headspace; adjust lids. Process—pints 15 minutes; quarts 20 minutes.

Applesauce—Prepare applesauce and ladle hot into jars to within ¼ inch of top. Adjust lids and process—pints and quarts 10 minutes.

Apricots—Follow directions for Peaches except peel apricots or not, as desired.

Berries (except Strawberries)—Wash and sort berries. Can perfect berries and use imperfect ones in making the syrup. If packed into jars cold (uncooked), shake the jars to pack berries closely without crushing them. Fill jars to within 1 inch of top with hot thin or medium syrup. If berries are firm, the hot pack may be used, bringing berries to boiling in a medium or heavy syrup before packing. Cover berries in jars with hot syrup, leaving headspace; adjust lids. Process—pints 10 minutes; quarts 15 minutes for hot or cold pack.

Cherries, sweet—Wash, remove stems and pits. For hot pack, bring cherries to boiling in hot thin or medium syrup, then pack fruit into jars and fill jars with hot syrup, leaving headspace. Adjust lids. Process pints 10 minutes; quarts 15 minutes. For cold pack, pack cherries into jars and shake them down while filling jars to make a full pack. Pour medium or heavy syrup over fruit and proceed as for Cherries (sweet). Process—pints 20 minutes; quarts 25 minutes.

Cherries, tart—Follow directions for Cherries (sweet) using a heavy syrup.

Peaches—Immerse in boiling water until skins slip, then plunge into cold water and drain. Peel, halve, and pit the peaches. For cold pack, arrange peaches in jars, cut side down, packing firmly. Cover with medium syrup, leaving headspace at top of jar. For hot pack, bring fruit to boiling in medium syrup, then pack into jars and cover with syrup, leaving headspace. Adjust lids. (To prevent darkening of fruit during preparation, see Apples.) Process—pints 25 minutes; quarts 30 minutes for cold pack. Reduce processing time 5 minutes for hot pack.

Pears—Wash, pare, halve, and core fruit. Cook in medium syrup 3 to 5 minutes depending upon hardness of fruit. Pack hot into jars; cover with syrup, leaving headspace; adjust lids. Process—pints 20 minutes; quarts 25 minutes.

Plums—Wash fruit and prick several times with a needle to prevent bursting when heated. For cold pack, pack fruit firmly into jars and add hot medium syrup, leaving headspace. For hot pack, bring plums to boiling in medium or heavy syrup before packing into jars and adding the syrup. Process—pints 25 minutes; quarts 30 minutes for cold pack. Reduce processing time 5 minutes for hot pack.

Rhubarb—Wash and cut into ½ inch pieces. Add ½ cup sugar for each quart rhubarb and let stand several hours to draw out the juice. Then bring to boiling and pack hot into jars. Adjust lids. Process—pints and quarts 10 minutes.

Strawberries—Use firm, red-ripe strawberries. Strawberries tend to fade and lose color when canned. Hull, rinse, drain, and measure berries. Halve large strawberries, if desired. Use ½ to ¾ cup sugar for each quart strawberries. Gently toss with the sugar and let stand about 5 hours in a cool place. Heat slowly until sugar dissolves and strawberries are hot. Pack into hot jars and seal. Process—pints and quarts 20 minutes.

Tomatoes—Use firm, ripe, unblemished tomatoes. Scald them, plunge into cold water, drain, and peel. Pack closely into jars, pressing tomatoes down gently to fill all spaces. Add salt—½ teaspoon per pint, 1 teaspoon per quart. (Do not add water to tomatoes.) Adjust lids. Process—pints 35 minutes; quarts 45 minutes.

The hot-pack method of canning tomatoes is preferred by many. Quarter the peeled tomatoes and bring them to boiling in a kettle. Fill jars, leaving headspace. Add salt and adjust lids. Process—pints and quarts 10 minutes.

Tomato Juice—Cut peeled tomatoes into pieces and cook slowly in a kettle until soft. Put through a food mill or strainer. Add 1 teaspoon salt for each quart and bring to boiling in a kettle. Quickly ladle into jars, leaving headspace. Process—pints and quarts 10 minutes.

CANNING VEGETABLES USING PRESSURE CANNER

Vegetables are processed at 10 pounds pressure.

Asparagus—Wash, trim off scales and tough ends, and wash asparagus again. Cut into 1 inch pieces. For cold (raw) pack, pack asparagus firmly into jars to within ½ inch of top; add ½ teaspoon salt to pints; 1 teaspoon to quarts. Add boiling water, leaving headspace. Adjust lids. For hot pack, precook asparagus 2 to 3 minutes in boiling water before packing into jars. If the cooking liquid is free of grit use it to fill jars instead of boiling water. Adjust jar lids. Process—pints 25 minutes; quarts 30 minutes.

Beans, lima—Shell and wash beans, preferably

young, tender ones. For raw pack, follow directions for asparagus except increase headspace to 1 inch. For hot pack, cover shelled beans with boiling water and bring to boiling. Pack hot beans loosely into jar. Add salt and boiling water, leaving headspace. Adjust lids. Process—pints 40 minutes; quarts 50 minutes.

Beans, snap—Wash, remove ends and cut beans into even lengths. Proceed as for Asparagus. Process—pints 20 minutes; quarts 25 minutes.

Beets—Wash and sort beets for size; cut off tops, leaving about 1 inch of stem. Cook beets in boiling water 15 to 25 minutes, or until skins slip easily. Remove skins; leave small beets whole. Cube, slice, or quarter medium or large beets. Pack hot into jars and proceed as for Asparagus. Process— pints 30 minutes; quarts 35 minutes.

Carrots—Wash and scrape carrots; slice, dice, or leave whole if young and tender. For cold (raw) pack, see Asparagus. For hot pack, cook washed carrots in boiling water until skins slip off. Remove skins, slice, dice, or leave whole. Fill jars and process (see Asparagus).

Corn, cream style—Remove corn from cobs by cutting at about the center of kernel and scraping cobs using the dull edge of knife. Pack corn into jars (pints only) to within 1½ inches of top. Add salt and fill jars with boiling water to within ½ inch of top. Adjust lids and process 95 minutes. For hot pack, remove kernels from cobs (scraping cobs). To each quart of corn add 1 pint boiling water. (If desired, add a small amount of sugar.) Heat to boiling. Pack hot into jars (pints only) to 1 inch of top. Add salt; adjust lids. Process—85 minutes.

Corn, whole kernel—Husk corn and remove silk. Cut from cob at about ⅔ the depth of kernel. For cold (raw) pack, pack kernels into jars (do not press or shake down). Proceed as for Asparagus. Process—pints 55 minutes; quarts 85 minutes. For hot pack, cut kernels from cobs and for each quart of corn add 1 pint boiling water. Heat to boiling in a

kettle and pack hot corn into jars. Cover with boiling hot cooking liquid, leaving 1 inch headspace. Add salt and adjust lids. Processing time (see cold-pack).

Peas, fresh green—Use tender, young peas. Shell, discarding blemished ones. Wash, cover with boiling water, and bring to boiling. Pack hot peas into jars and proceed as for Asparagus. Process—pints and quarts 40 minutes.

Spinach and other greens—Can only freshly picked, tender spinach. Remove tough stems and blemished leaves. Wash thoroughly (see *page 626*). Place about 2½ pounds spinach in a cheesecloth bag and steam 10 minutes or until leaves are wilted. Pack hot spinach loosely into jars; add ¼ teaspoon salt to pints; ½ teaspoon to quarts. Cover with boiling water, leaving headspace. Adjust lids. Process—pints 70 minutes; quarts 90 minutes.

Pumpkin (cubed)—Wash, remove seeds, and pare pumpkin. Cut into 1 inch cubes. Add just enough boiling water to cover and bring to boiling. Pack hot into jars. Add salt—½ teaspoon to pints; 1 teaspoon to quarts. Cover with hot cooking liquid, leaving headspace. Adjust jar lids. Process—pints 55 minutes; quarts 90 minutes.

Pumpkin (strained)—Steam the cubed pumpkin until tender, about 25 minutes. Put through a strainer or food mill. Cook slowly in a heavy saucepan until thoroughly heated, stirring to prevent sticking to bottom of pan. Ladle hot pumpkin into jars, allowing headspace. Add no salt or liquid. Adjust lids. Process—pints 65 minutes; quarts 80 minutes.

Squash, summer and zucchini—Wash thoroughly; do not pare. Cut into slices, halves, or quarters to make pieces of uniform size. Add just enough boiling water to cover and bring squash to boiling. Pack loosely into jars and proceed as for Asparagus. Process—pints 30 minutes; quarts 40 minutes.

Squash, winter, crookneck, Hubbard and banana—See Pumpkin, *above*.

PRESERVING

JELLIES

Jelly is made by combining fruit juice and sugar in the correct proportions and cooking until the mixture will "gel" when cool. A good jelly is clear and sparkling and free from sediment or crystals. It has

the natural color and flavor of the fresh fruit. When turned from the glass it will hold its shape, but will quiver slightly. When cut, the edges are sharp and the jelly will cling to the knife.

Fruits Suitable for Jelly—To make a good jelly,

fruit must be rich in both pectin and acid or it must be combined with another fruit which will supply whichever substance is lacking. Fruits which contain both pectin and acid in sufficient amounts are: apples (tart), blackberries, crab apples, currants, gooseberries, grapes, loganberries, plums, quinces, and raspberries.

Fruits lacking sufficient pectin are: cherries, peaches, pineapple, rhubarb, and strawberries.

Fruits lacking sufficient acid are: apples (sweet), blueberries, huckleberries, and pears.

Slightly underripe fruit usually contains more acid and pectin than fully ripe fruit but the flavor is not as good. A proportion frequently used is ¼ underripe fruit and ¾ ripe fruit. Fruits lacking in either pectin or acid are often combined with tart apples since apple juice affects color and flavor the least.

Use of Commercial Pectin — Juice from practically any fruit (overripe included) can be made into jelly by the addition of commercial pectin (liquid or powdered) and a large amount of sugar. Other advantages of this procedure are that less time is required to cook the jelly and, for the inexperienced, at least success is more certain.

If a commercial pectin is used, the directions provided with the product must be followed exactly.

Extracting Fruit Juice — Look over the fruit, removing stems and any signs of decay.

Cut up large fruit such as apples. Remove cores from quinces.

Crush juicy fruits and add no water or only a small amount. To less juicy fruits add only enough water to be seen through the pieces of fruit. If more water than necessary is added it must be evaporated from the juice later, which causes a dark color and loss of flavor. Cook the fruit, covered, until tender and the juice runs freely. (Avoid overcooking.) Pour into a jelly bag or through cheesecloth (see note) and set aside until the juice ceases to drip through into the bowl. For a clear jelly, do not squeeze the bag. More juice is obtained by squeezing, but the resulting jelly will be cloudy. If the bag is not squeezed the pulp in the bag may be forced through a food mill or sieve and made into jam or fruit butter.

NOTE: Purchase a jelly bag or prepare one in this manner: cut a double thickness of cheesecloth about 36 inches long; fold in half. Dip into hot water and wring as dry as possible. To strain the juice from pulp, put a large strainer or colander lined with the folded cheesecloth over a large bowl. Pour in the hot cooked fruit, gather up corners of cheesecloth and tie firmly.

Test for Pectin — To determine the proportion of pectin present in a fruit juice, combine 1 tablespoon extracted juice and 1 tablespoon grain alcohol; shake gently. If a large quantity of pectin is present it will appear in a single clot when poured from the glass. If pectin does not form into a clot, less sugar will be needed for the jelly. If pectin slips from glass in several clots, the quantity present is in good proportion and the usual amount of sugar will be needed.

Addition of Sugar — In general, ⅔ to ¾ as much sugar as fruit juice is sufficient. (Cane and beet sugar are equally suitable.) Too little sugar will cause the jelly to be firm; too much sugar will produce a syrupy jelly. The optimum amount of sugar needed will vary with the amount of pectin, acid, and water present and cannot be given exactly. When in doubt, it is better to use less sugar then more.

Cooking the Jelly — Use no more than 4 cups juice at a time to retain the best color, flavor, and texture in the jelly. Heat juice to boiling and add sugar gradually, stirring constantly. Boil rapidly until jellying stage is reached.

To make a jelly test — Dip a small amount of boiling liquid from saucepan with a spoon and slowly pour it back into saucepan from edge of spoon. If jelly is insufficiently cooked the liquid will run off in parallel drops. When jelly is sufficiently cooked, the drops will run together and fall from spoon in a sheet, leaving edge of spoon clean. Remove jelly from heat while testing. Avoid long cooking after the jelly test is obtained as mixture will become syrupy.

Skim jelly and pour into hot sterilized glasses to within ⅜ inch of top.

Pour melted paraffin over the surface of jelly at once, making a layer about ⅛ inch thick. Let this layer cool completely, then repeat with a second layer, tilting glass to distribute paraffin evenly over top and seal to edge of glass. When paraffin has cooled, place metal covers on the jelly glasses or cover securely with aluminum foil. (*Paraffin is unnecessary when glass jars with self-sealing lids are used.*)

Wipe glasses or jars with a damp cloth, label, and store in a cool, dry, dark place.

JAMS

Jams are made from whole small fruits which are either mashed or cooked to a pulp with sugar. Good jam is soft, tender, and jellylike in texture, bright and sparkling in color, and of the same consistency throughout the mixture.

HELPFUL HINTS FOR SUCCESSFUL JAMS

• Use some underripe fruit. Portions of fruit left-over from canning or broken fruit may be used for jam but at least a portion of the fruit should be underripe. Overripe fruit lacks pectin, the jellying substance so necessary for good jam.

• In order to develop the pectin substance, the fruit should be cooked a few minutes before the sugar is added. If fruit does not have sufficient juice, add just enough water to keep it from sticking to bottom of kettle. Cover the kettle. Avoid too much sugar. The best jam is made by using not more than ¾ pound sugar for each pound of fruit.

• Cook jam quickly and not too long. After the sugar is added to fruit, continue the cooking rapidly until jam has a jellylike appearance. It should hang in sheets from the spoon or set quickly if a portion is dropped onto a cold plate. It should be tender, not thick and tough. Jam thickens on cooling and an allowance must be made for this. Overcooking darkens the product. Cooking a small amount at a time is recommended, using enamel or porcelain cooking utensils if possible. Stir jam to prevent burning. It is a highly concentrated mass and will scorch easily unless the mass is lifted from bottom of kettle with a wooden spoon.

MARMALADES

Marmalade is made from fruits which have some jellymaking properties (both pectin and acid are present). Thin slices of fruit are used and the product shows a clear jelly or jellylike syrup in which the sliced or cut fruit is suspended. If a fruit is used lacking these jellying properties, they are often supplied by adding sliced orange or lemon, tart apple juice, or commercial pectin.

Marmalades are prepared in the same way as jams, except that the fruit remains in slices or cut portions and is not mashed. Marmalades should be clear and sparkling in color.

PRESERVES

Preserves are fruits in which the tissues have absorbed enough heavy syrup to replace the water in the tissues. Good preserved fruit is plump and tender in texture, bright in color, and filled with sweetness.

HELPFUL HINTS FOR SUCCESSFUL PRESERVES

• Precook hard fruits before combining with heavy syrup. Hard pears, underripe peaches, pineapples, apples, quinces, watermelon rind, and citron must be cooked in a small amount of water until fruit is just tender or soft enough so that the heavy syrup enters the cells of fruit. Hard fruit added to the syrup will result in preserves which are hard and tough instead of plump and tender.

Tender fruits (ripe peaches, plums, cherries, and berries) are added to the syrup immediately. Drain precooked fruits thoroughly before adding to the syrup.

Bring fruits to boiling rapidly in the syrup and continue the rapid cooking until fruit has a bright, clear, sparkling appearance, indicating that the syrup has permeated the fruit completely. Avoid overcooking as this results in a dark, stiff product. Plump the fruit for an extra fine quality of preserve. For plumping, add fruit to syrup and heat it only until mixture is bubbly. Then let stand overnight in a covered bowl or enamel preserving kettle. The next day continue the cooking. In this way more syrup is absorbed by the fruit. If desired, the heating and cooling processes may be repeated several times. Pears, peaches, green tomatoes, whole tomatoes, crab apples, citron, and melon rind are especially adapted to plumping. Fruit to be candied should be plumped.

• Seal preserves in clean hot jars (see *Open-Kettle method, page 625*). Jelly glasses may be used but melted paraffin must be poured over top of preserves before covering glasses with lids or with aluminum foil.

• If trouble has been experienced with molds appearing on preserves, it may be desirable to process the sealed jars (not glasses) in a boiling-water bath, *page 625*, about 5 minutes as an extra precaution. If filled jars are not to be processed, it is necessary to sterilize jars, closures, spoons, and any other utensil used.

CONSERVES

Conserves, like marmalades, may be made of large or small fruits. They differ in that several fruits are often combined and nuts are usually added. In this way it is possible to develop pleasing combinations of flavors and to combine fruits that have good acid and pectin content with fruits that lack these qualities. Add nuts, if used, at the end of cooking time.

FRUIT BUTTERS

Fruit Butters are among the most wholesome of fruit sweets and are easy to prepare. The whole fruit is cooked until tender, then put through a food mill or sieve. Sugar is added (also spice if desired) and the mixture is cooked until smooth and thick. Like jams, fruit butters must be watched carefully and not overcooked.

HELPFUL HINTS ABOUT PRESERVING

• To remove odors from jars and bottles, pour a solution of water and dry mustard into them and let stand several hours. Or use a dilute chlorine solution and rinse jars in hot water.
• When covering jelly with melted paraffin, pour a thin layer over top; place a strong piece of string on paraffin with end over edge of glass. Pour another layer of paraffin over string. Set aside until paraffin is firm. When jelly is to be used, lift off the paraffin layer by using the string.
• To open glass jars containing fruit easily, set them upside down in hot water for a few minutes.

Jellies

APPLE JELLY

| 4 lbs. tart apples | Sugar |
| 4 cups water | Paraffin |

1. Rinse, remove stem ends, and quarter apples. (Do not core or pare fruit.) Add the water to apples in a preserving kettle. Cover and cook gently until fruit is soft, stirring occasionally.
2. Strain fruit through a jelly bag, *page 630.* The pulp remaining in bag may be used to make apple butter, if desired.
3. To prepare jelly, measure not more than 4 cups of apple juice into saucepan. Measure ¾ cup sugar for each cup of juice. Heat the juice to boiling and stir in the sugar. Return to boiling and cook rapidly until mixture responds to jelly test, *page 630.*
4. Remove from heat; skim off foam. Ladle into hot sterilized glasses. Cover with melted paraffin, *page 630.*　　　　FIVE 8-OUNCE GLASSES JELLY

QUICK SPARKLING JELLY

1 qt. bottled apple juice	1 box powdered fruit
½ env. (about 1	pectin
tablespoon) strawberry-	4¼ cups sugar
flavored soft drink	Paraffin
mix	

1. Blend apple juice, drink mix, and pectin in a large heavy saucepot; stir over high heat until mixture comes to a full boil.
2. Add the sugar all at one time and blend thoroughly. Bring to a full rolling boil; boil 1 minute, stirring constantly.
3. Remove jelly from heat; let stand several minutes and skim off foam.
4. Pour jelly into hot sterilized glasses and seal with melted paraffin, *page 630.*
　　　　SEVEN 8-OUNCE GLASSES JELLY

BLUEBERRY JELLY

1 large lemon, sliced	Sugar (about 4½ cups)
3 qts. blueberries	Paraffin
3 lbs. tart apples	

1. Add enough water to lemon slices to just cover (about 1 cup). Cover and set aside 12 hours, or overnight.
2. Pick over blueberries, discarding blemished berries. Rinse and drain. Turn into a saucepot.
3. Wash apples; remove stems, blossom ends, and blemished portions. Quarter the apples and put into a kettle; cover with water (about 2½ cups). Cook, covered, over medium heat until apples are soft.
4. Drain the liquid from lemon slices and mix with blueberries (discard lemon peel). Cook gently until blueberries are soft and juice flows freely.
5. Pour both fruit mixtures into a jelly bag, *page 630;* let drain 6 to 12 hours. (There should be about 6 cups juice.)
6. To make jelly, measure half the juice into a 2-quart saucepan and bring rapidly to boiling. For

each cup of juice add ¾ cup sugar and stir until sugar is dissolved. Continue cooking rapidly until mixture responds to jelly test, *page 630*.

7. Remove from heat; skim off any foam. Pour jelly into hot sterilized glasses. Repeat step 6 using remaining juice.

8. Immediately cover jelly in glasses with melted paraffin, *page 630*.

ABOUT SEVEN 8-OUNCE GLASSES JELLY

CURRANT JELLY

| 4 lbs. (about 4 qts.) ripe red currants | 4 cups sugar |
| 1 cup water | Paraffin |

1. Rinse, remove leaves (not the stems), drain, and put currants into a kettle. Crush them thoroughly and stir in the water.

2. Bring rapidly to boiling; reduce heat and simmer, covered, 10 minutes. Strain through a jelly bag, *page 630*.

3. Measure 4 cups juice into a saucepan and bring rapidly to boiling. Add sugar and stir until dissolved; continue cooking rapidly until mixture responds to jelly test, *page 630*.

4. Remove from heat; skim off any foam. Pour jelly into hot sterilized glasses and seal with melted paraffin, *page 630*.

ABOUT SIX 8-OUNCE GLASSES JELLY

CRAB APPLE JELLY: Follow recipe for Currant Jelly. Omit currants. Rinse, remove stem ends, and cut into quarters enough *crab apples* to yield 3 quarts. (Do not core or pare the fruit.) Increase water to 3 cups and cook 20 minutes, or until apples are very tender. Decrease sugar to 3 cups.

BASIL GRAPE JELLY

½ cup boiling water	3½ cups sugar
1 tablespoon basil	½ bottle liquid fruit pectin
1½ cups bottled grape juice	Paraffin

1. Pour boiling water over basil in a small saucepan; cover tightly and set aside 10 to 15 minutes. Strain "herb brew" through fine strainer or cheesecloth into a 4-quart kettle or saucepan. Discard herb.

2. Add grape juice and sugar to the kettle; stir over medium heat until sugar is dissolved. Increase heat and bring mixture to boiling.

3. Stir in the pectin and return to boiling; boil rapidly 1 minute, stirring constantly. Remove from heat and skim off foam.

4. Pour into hot sterilized glasses and seal immediately with melted paraffin, *page 630*.

ABOUT FOUR 8-OUNCE GLASSES JELLY

SPICED GRAPE JELLY

3 lbs. Concord grapes	7 cups sugar
½ cup cider vinegar	½ bottle liquid fruit pectin
2 teaspoons ground cinnamon	Paraffin
1 teaspoon ground cloves	

1. Rinse grapes, discard stems and blemished grapes. Drain and put into a large kettle. Crush grapes thoroughly.

2. Mix vinegar and spices and blend with grapes. Bring rapidly to boiling; reduce heat, cover kettle, and simmer mixture 10 minutes. Strain through a jelly bag, *page 630*.

3. Measure 4 cups of the strained juice into a large saucepan; cook over high heat until very hot. Add the sugar and stir until dissolved. Bring rapidly to boiling and stir in the pectin. Boil vigorously 1 minute, stirring constantly.

4. Remove from heat; skim off foam. Pour into hot sterilized jelly glasses and cover with melted paraffin, *page 630*. EIGHT 8-OUNCE GLASSES JELLY

SPICED PORT-GRAPE JELLY

1 cup boiling water	½ cup bottled grape juice
1 piece (3 in.) stick cinnamon, broken	1½ cups port wine
5 whole cloves	1 tablespoon lemon juice
3 cups sugar	Paraffin
1 box powdered fruit pectin	

1. Pour boiling water over cinnamon and cloves in a small saucepan; cover and place over low heat 5 minutes. Set aside 5 minutes. Strain (discard spices) and add more water, if needed, to make 1 cup liquid.

2. Measure the sugar into a bowl; set aside.

3. Blend the pectin with grape juice, wine, "spice brew," and lemon juice in a large saucepan; stir until pectin is dissolved.

4. Cook over high heat until mixture comes to a full rolling boil, stirring constantly. Add the sugar

all at one time. Cook and stir over high heat until mixture returns to a full boil; boil, stirring constantly, 1 minute.

5. Remove from heat; skim off any foam. Ladle into hot sterilized jelly glasses. Seal with melted paraffin, *page 630*.

ABOUT FIVE 8-OUNCE GLASSES JELLY

SAVORY GRAPEFRUIT JELLY

½ cup boiling water	Few drops green food
2 tablespoons savory	coloring
1 cup unsweetened	½ bottle liquid fruit
grapefruit juice	pectin
3¼ cups sugar	Paraffin

1. Pour boiling water over savory in a small saucepan; cover tightly and set aside 10 to 15 minutes. Strain "herb brew" through fine strainer or cheesecloth into a measuring cup; add enough water to make ½ cup. Discard savory.
2. Pour liquid into a 4-quart kettle or saucepan. Add grapefruit juice and sugar; stir over medium heat until sugar is dissolved. Increase heat and bring mixture to boiling. Stir in food coloring and then pectin. Return to boiling; boil rapidly 1 minute, stirring constantly. Remove from heat and skim off foam.
3. Pour into hot sterilized glasses and seal immediately with melted paraffin, *page 630*.

ABOUT FOUR 6-OUNCE GLASSES JELLY

MINT-HONEY JELLY

For those who appreciate the distinctive flavor of honey this mint jelly, served with a lamb roast, will be sheer ambrosia.

¾ cup boiling water	Few drops green food
2 tablespoons dried mint	coloring
leaves	½ bottle liquid fruit
2½ cups strained honey	pectin
	Paraffin

1. Pour boiling water over mint in a saucepan; cover tightly and let stand 15 minutes. Strain and add enough water to make ¾ cup.
2. Add honey and heat to boiling. Stir in coloring to tint a light green. Add pectin, stirring constantly. Bring to full rolling boil. Remove from heat and skim off foam.
3. Pour jelly into hot sterilized glasses. Seal with melted paraffin, *page 630*.

FIVE 6-OUNCE GLASSES JELLY

GOLDEN JELLY

4 cups sugar	2 tablespoons lime juice
2 cups orange juice	½ bottle liquid fruit
3 tablespoons lemon	pectin
juice	Paraffin

1. Mix sugar and juices in a heavy 3-quart saucepan. Stir over medium heat until sugar is dissolved; bring to boiling.
2. Immediately stir in pectin and return to boiling; stir and boil rapidly 1 minute. Remove from heat; skim off any foam.
3. Ladle into hot sterilized glasses and seal with melted paraffin, *page 630*.

FOUR 8-OUNCE GLASSES JELLY

PINEAPPLE JELLY

2¼ cups unsweetened	4½ cups sugar
pineapple juice	1 bottle liquid fruit
¼ cup lemon juice	pectin

1. Measure pineapple juice and lemon juice into a large kettle; add sugar and mix well.
2. Bring to boiling rapidly, stirring constantly. Stir in pectin and bring to a full rolling boil; boil vigorously 1 minute, continuing to stir.
3. Remove from heat; skim off any foam. Pour into hot sterilized jelly glasses; seal with melted paraffin, *page 630*. (If jelly is to be used within 2 months, omit the paraffin.)
4. Cover glasses with lids, waxed paper, or aluminum foil, and store in refrigerator.

SEVEN 6-OUNCE GLASSES JELLY

PINEAPPLE-STRAWBERRY JELLY-JAM

2½ cups whole	3 tablespoons lemon
strawberries	juice
1 can (12 oz.) unsweet-	1 box powdered fruit
ened pineapple juice	pectin
	4 cups sugar

1. Wash, hull, and quarter berries; measure 2 cups.
2. Mix berries, juices, and pectin in a flat bottomed preserving kettle. Place over high heat and stir until mixture comes to a full boil. Stir in the sugar and return to rolling boil; boil vigorously 1 minute, stirring constantly.
3. Skim foam from surface and ladle into hot sterilized jars or glasses. Seal, *page 626*.

ABOUT SIX 8-OUNCE JARS JELLY-JAM

SPICED PLUM JELLY

4 lbs. fully ripe tart
   clingstone plums*
1 cup water
6½ cups sugar
½ teaspoon ground
   cinnamon
⅛ teaspoon ground
   allspice
½ bottle liquid fruit
   pectin
Paraffin

1. Rinse, halve, pit, and crush plums (do not peel). Place in a large saucepan; add the water. Bring to boiling; reduce heat and simmer, covered, 10 minutes.
2. Ladle mixture into a jelly bag, *page 630*, and squeeze out juice. Measure 4 cups of the juice into a very large saucepan. Mix in a blend of sugar and spices.
3. Stir over high heat until mixture comes to a full boil. Immediately stir in fruit pectin and bring to a full rolling boil; boil rapidly 1 minute, stirring constantly.
4. Remove from heat and skim off foam. Pour at once into hot sterilized jelly glasses to within ½ inch of top. Immediately seal with melted paraffin, *page 630*. ABOUT TEN 8-OUNCE GLASSES JELLY
*If using sweet plums or freestone purple plums, use 3½ cups prepared juice and add ¼ cup lemon juice.

ROSEMARY JELLY

1½ cups boiling water
2 teaspoons dried
   rosemary
3½ cups sugar
2 tablespoons cider
   vinegar
4 drops red food
   coloring
½ bottle liquid fruit
   pectin
Paraffin

1. Pour boiling water over rosemary in a small saucepan; cover tightly and set aside about 15 minutes.
2. Strain "herb brew" through a fine sieve or cheesecloth into a large saucepan. Add the sugar, vinegar, and food coloring.
3. Stir over medium heat until sugar is dissolved; increase heat and bring mixture to boiling. Add pectin, bring to boiling, and boil rapidly 1 minute, stirring constantly. Remove from heat; skim off foam.
4. Pour into hot sterilized glasses; seal with melted paraffin, *page 630*.
THREE 8-OUNCE GLASSES JELLY

TANGERINE JELLY

1 box powdered fruit
   pectin
2 cups water
¾ cup (6 oz.) undiluted
   frozen tangerine juice
   concentrate
½ teaspoon grated
   lemon peel
2 tablespoons lemon
   juice
3½ cups sugar
Paraffin

1. Combine the pectin and water in a large saucepan; mix well. Bring to full rolling boil and boil 1 minute, stirring constantly.
2. Reduce heat; add the undiluted tangerine juice concentrate, lemon peel and juice, and sugar. Stir and cook until sugar is completely dissolved. Do not boil.
3. Remove from heat and skim off foam. Ladle into hot sterilized jelly glasses and immediately seal with melted paraffin, *page 630*.
FOUR 8-OUNCE GLASSES JELLY

WINE JELLY I
Topped with snowy-white whipped paraffin, this jelly becomes an attractive gift item.

4 cups sugar
1 box powdered fruit
   pectin
¾ cup water
3 cups wine*
Snow Topping, *below*

1. Measure sugar; set aside.
2. Thoroughly mix pectin and water in a large saucepan. Bring rapidly to boiling over high heat and boil 1 minute, stirring constantly.
3. Reduce heat to medium and immediately add wine and all the sugar; keep mixture just below the boiling point and stir until the sugar is dissolved, about 5 minutes. Remove from heat.
4. If necessary, skim off foam with a metal spoon. Pour jelly mixture quickly into hot sterilized jelly glasses and cover at once with Snow Topping.
SIX 6-OUNCE GLASSES JELLY
*Use Madeira, Rosé, or champagne.
NOTE: If using champagne, the recipe will make 5 glasses jelly. (Yield is less because of the bubbling quality of champagne which results in a great deal of foam loss.)

SNOW TOPPING: Melt *2 bars paraffin* over boiling water. Pour a thin layer over hot jelly, using about 1 tablespoon melted paraffin for each glass. Cool remaining paraffin until it becomes cloudy and starts to solidify. Quickly whip with rotary beater or a fork until paraffin is foamy and starts to harden. Work quickly. (If paraffin becomes too hard, melt and start again.) Spoon over thin layer of paraffin on the jelly. Makes enough for about 6 jelly glasses. NOTE: A 1 pound package of paraffin contains 5 bars. It is called household wax on package.

WINE JELLY II

3 cups sugar
2 cups wine*

½ bottle liquid fruit pectin
Snow Topping, *page 635*

1. Measure sugar and wine into the top of a double boiler; mix well. Place over rapidly boiling water and stir until sugar is dissolved, about 2 minutes. Remove from heat.
2. At once stir in pectin and mix well. Skim off foam, if necessary.
3. Quickly pour jelly mixture into hot sterilized glasses. Cover at once with Snow Topping.

FIVE 6-OUNCE GLASSES JELLY

*Use sherry, Burgundy, sauterne, port, muscatel, claret, Tokay, or fruit wines—loganberry, currant, blackberry.
NOTE: This recipe may be doubled, if desired.

SPICED SAUTERNE JELLY

¾ cup boiling water
Strips of peel from ½ lemon
Strips of peel from ½ orange
2 pieces (1 in. each) stick cinnamon

5 whole cloves
1½ cups sauterne
1 tablespoon lemon juice
3 cups sugar
½ bottle liquid fruit pectin

1. Pour boiling water over citrus peel, stick cinnamon, and cloves in a small saucepan. Cover and place over very low heat 5 minutes; set aside 5 minutes. Strain (discard spices) and add water, if needed, to make ¾ cup "citrus brew."
2. Combine "citrus brew" in a large saucepan with the wine and lemon juice. Place over low heat and bring to simmering. Add the sugar and stir until dissolved.
3. Increase heat and quickly bring to a full rolling boil; stir in pectin and return to boiling. Boil rapidly 1 minute, stirring constantly.
4. Remove from heat and skim off any foam. Ladle into hot sterilized jelly glasses and seal with melted paraffin, *page 630*.

FIVE 8-OUNCE GLASSES JELLY

Jams

BLUEBERRY-LEMON JAM

1 qt. fresh blueberries, rinsed and drained
1½ tablespoons grated lemon peel
⅔ cup lemon juice
7 cups sugar

¼ teaspoon salt
¼ teaspoon ground cloves
½ bottle liquid fruit pectin

1. Put blueberries into a kettle and crush thoroughly. Add the lemon peel and juice, sugar, salt, and cloves and blend thoroughly.
2. Stir over medium heat until sugar is dissolved; bring to boiling; boil 1 minute without stirring.
3. Remove from heat and stir in the pectin; skim off any foam.
4. Ladle jam into hot sterilized jars and seal.

EIGHT ½-PINT JARS JAM

SPIRITED CHERRY JAM

2 lbs. fresh sweet cherries
¼ cup lemon juice
1 box powdered fruit pectin

¼ teaspoon ground allspice
5 cups sugar
1 cup Burgundy or port wine

1. Rinse, stem, pit, and chop cherries (3 cups, chopped). Mix in a heavy kettle with the lemon juice, pectin, and allspice. Blend thoroughly.
2. Bring to a rolling boil and stir in the sugar and wine; return to rolling boil and boil rapidly 1 minute, stirring constantly.
3. Remove from heat; skim off the foam. Ladle into hot sterilized jars and seal, *page 626*.
4. Let stand 25 minutes, then shake gently to prevent fruit from floating.   SEVEN ½-PINT JARS JAM

CHERRY-PLUM JAM

2 lbs. dark sweet cherries
10 medium-sized red plums
1 cup water

1 tablespoon lemon juice
Sugar
1 box powdered fruit pectin

1. Rinse, stem, halve, and pit the cherries. (There should be about 1 quart.)
2. Rinse, halve, and pit the plums. (There should be about 3½ cups.)

3. Mix fruits, water, and lemon juice in a kettle. Bring to boiling, stirring occasionally; reduce heat and cook gently 3 minutes.

4. Remove from heat; measure mixture and return to kettle. For each cup of cooked fruit, add an equal amount of sugar. Stir until thoroughly blended.

5. Stir in the pectin and return to heat. Bring rapidly to full rolling boil, stirring constantly; boil and stir 2 minutes.

6. Remove from heat; skim off any foam. Ladle into hot sterilized jars and seal, *page 626*.

TEN ½-PINT JARS JAM

ROSY BANANA PEACH JAM

1 cup mashed fully ripe bananas (about 3 medium-sized)	½ cup drained chopped maraschino cherries
3¼ cups mashed fully ripe peaches (about 2 lbs. peaches, peeled)	2 tablespoons lemon juice
	6 cups sugar
	1 box powdered fruit pectin

1. Put prepared fruit and lemon juice into a large saucepan; mix.

2. Measure sugar into a bowl; set aside.

3. Mix pectin into fruit in saucepan. Stir and cook over high heat until mixture comes to a full rolling boil. Immediately add and stir in the sugar. Bring to a full rolling boil; stirring constantly, boil rapidly 1 minute.

4. Remove from heat; skim foam with metal spoon and then stir and skim for 5 minutes, to cool slightly and prevent floating fruit.

5. Immediately ladle into sterilized jars, filling to within ½ inch of top. Seal immediately following manufacturer's directions.

ABOUT EIGHT ½-PINT JARS JAM

PINEAPPLE-RHUBARB JAM

1 pkg. (16 oz.) frozen rhubarb, thawed	2 tablespoons lemon juice
1 can (20½ oz.) crushed pineapple	6 cups sugar
1 teaspoon grated orange peel	½ bottle liquid fruit pectin
½ teaspoon grated lemon peel	Few drops red food coloring

1. Combine rhubarb, pineapple, orange and lemon peels, and lemon juice in a large heavy saucepan. Add sugar and mix thoroughly. Bring to full rolling boil over high heat and boil rapidly 1 minute, stirring constantly.

2. Remove from heat; stir in pectin and food coloring. Skim foam, then stir about 10 minutes to cool jam slightly and keep fruit in suspension.

3. Ladle jam into hot sterilized jars and seal, *page 626*.

SEVEN ½-PINT JARS JAM

MIXED FRUIT JAM

You'll love the delicate harmony of color and flavors in this attractive jam.

½ orange juice	½ cup drained maraschino cherries, chopped
¼ cup lemon juice	
1 cup coarsely chopped peaches	5 cups sugar
1 cup coarsely chopped pears	½ bottle liquid fruit pectin
1 can (8¾ oz.) crushed pineapple	

1. Mix the juices, fruits, and sugar in a large heavy saucepan; let stand 1 hour. Bring to a full rolling boil and boil 1 minute.

2. Remove from heat and immediately blend in the pectin. Stir for 5 minutes.

3. Ladle into hot sterilized jars and seal, *page 626*.

SIX ½-PINT JARS JAM

BLACKBERRY JAM
(Refrigerator-Freezer Type)

3 cups mashed or sieved blackberries	1 box powdered fruit pectin
5½ cups sugar	1 cup water

1. Mix the berries and sugar in a bowl; let stand 20 minutes, stirring occasionally.

2. Blend the pectin and water in a large saucepan; bring to boiling and boil rapidly 1 minute, stirring constantly. Remove from heat; add the berry-sugar mixture and stir about 2 minutes.

3. Ladle into clean hot jars, cover, and let stand 24 to 48 hours, or until the jam is "set". Store, tightly covered, in freezer. (Jam will keep several weeks in refrigerator.)

SEVEN ½-PINT JARS JAM

PEACH-ROSEMARY JAM
(Refrigerator-Freezer Type)

¾ cup boiling water	4¼ cups sugar
2 tablespoons dried rosemary	1 box powdered fruit pectin
1½ lbs. ripe peaches, peeled and pitted	Few drops yellow food coloring (optional)
Juice of ½ lemon (1½ to 2 tablespoons)	

1. Pour boiling water over rosemary in a small saucepan; cover tightly and set aside 10 minutes. Strain through cheesecloth and add water to make ¾ cup. Set aside.
2. Put peaches through food chopper, using medium blade. (There should be about 1¾ cups.)
3. In a large bowl, mix peaches and lemon juice; stir in the sugar; set aside about 20 minutes.
4. Meanwhile, combine the "herb brew" with the pectin in a small saucepan; bring to a rolling boil and boil 1 minute, stirring constantly.
5. Pour pectin mixture into fruit, stirring about 3 minutes, or until thoroughly blended. Stir in food coloring, if used.
6. Ladle jam into clean hot jars; seal immediately and set aside until jam is "set."
7. Store in refrigerator if used within 2 or 3 weeks. Store in freezer if kept longer.

FIVE ½-PINT JARS JAM

PEACH AND NUT JAM: Follow recipe for Peach-Rosemary Jam. Omit rosemary and use ¾ *cup cold water* with the pectin. Add *1 teaspoon almond extract* and *⅓ cup slivered blanched almonds* to peach-sugar mixture. SIX ½-PINT JARS JAM

SPICED PEACH JAM: Follow directions for Peach-Rosemary Jam. Omit rosemary and use ¾ *cup cold water* with the pectin. Add ¼ *teaspoon ground nutmeg* to peach-sugar mixture. SIX ½-PINT JARS JAM

STRAWBERRY JAM
(Refrigerator-Freezer Type)

4 cups sugar	¾ cup water
2 cups crushed ripe strawberries (about 2 pts.)	1 box powdered fruit pectin

1. Add sugar to crushed strawberries in a large bowl; mix well and set aside.
2. Combine the water and pectin in a small saucepan; blend well. Bring to boiling and boil 1 minute,

stirring constantly. Stir into sweetened strawberries. Continue stirring about 3 minutes. (There will be some sugar crystals remaining.)
3. Quickly ladle jam into jars and cover with tight-fitting lids. Let stand until "set."
4. If used within 2 or 3 weeks store in refrigerator; if kept longer store in freezer.

FIVE ½-PINT JARS JAM

STRAWBERRY-MINT JAM: Follow recipe for Strawberry Jam. Add *1 or 2 drops mint extract* to each jar before filling. Stir quickly to blend. Cover immediately.

STRAWBERRY-CARDAMOM JAM: Follow recipe for Strawberry Jam. Mix *2 teaspoons ground cardamom* with the sugar and add to strawberries; blend well.

Marmalades

PEACH MARMALADE

3 lbs. firm ripe peaches (about 12 medium-sized)	1 orange 3 cups sugar

1. Plunge peaches into boiling water to loosen skins; plunge into cold water and gently slip off skins.
2. Halve and pit the peaches; coarsely chop enough to yield 4 cups.
3. Wash the orange; cut off ends and thinly slice; discard seeds.
4. Combine peaches, orange, and sugar in a large saucepot; stir over medium heat until sugar is dissolved. Increase heat and cook rapidly until clear and thick, stirring frequently to prevent sticking. (Cooking time will vary with degree of ripeness and type of peach.)
5. Remove marmalade from heat and skim off any foam. Immediately fill hot sterilized jars and seal, *page 626*. THREE ½-PINT JARS MARMALADE

CITRUS MARMALADE

1 large grapefruit	Sugar
2 medium-sized oranges	¼ cup fresh lemon juice
1 medium-sized lemon	

1. Wash the fruit. Slice into thin cartwheel slices. Cut grapefruit cartwheels into thirds, orange and lemon into halves.

2. Measure the fruit into a large kettle and add 1 cup water for each cup fruit. Bring to boiling; boil 20 minutes.

3. Remove from heat and measure the hot mixture; return to kettle and bring to boiling.

4. Remove from heat· and add ¾ cup sugar for each cup of fruit and juice. Stir with a wooden spoon until thoroughly blended.

5. Return to heat and return to boiling. Boil 20 to 25 minutes, or until jellying stage is reached. (To test, remove marmalade from heat and spoon a small amount onto a cold saucer; chill quickly. If marmalade does not "set" to the proper consistency, cook a few minutes longer.)

6. Just before removing from heat, stir in lemon juice.

7. Ladle into hot sterilized glasses and cover marmalade with melted paraffin, *page 630*.

EIGHT 6-OUNCE GLASSES MARMALADE

LIME MARMALADE

Lime lovers take note . . . the robust, tangy flavor of the fruit permeates this marmalade.

4 medium-sized limes   Sugar
2 medium-sized lemons

1. Wash and dry the fruit. Cut through peel and pulp into very thin slivers; discard seeds.

2. Measure the fruit and juice into a large bowl. (There will be about 2½ cups.) Add 3 times the amount of water. Cover and set aside overnight.

3. The next day, turn the mixture into a large kettle and bring rapidly to boiling; reduce heat and simmer about 30 minutes. Return to the bowl, cover, and set aside overnight.

4. The third day measure the mixture into a heavy saucepan or kettle. (There will be about 6 cups.) For each cup add ¾ cup sugar; mix well.

5. Cook gently over low heat until the mixture thickens. (To test, drop a teaspoon of marmalade onto a chilled saucer and chill quickly in refrigerator. If it is of marmalade consistency, remove from heat.)

6. Ladle into hot sterilized jars and seal, *page 626*.

FIVE ½-PINT JARS MARMALADE

Preserves

CANTALOUPE PRESERVES

1 large unripe cantaloupe	½ lemon, thinly sliced
1 qt. water	2 tablespoons thinly sliced crystallized ginger
2 cups sugar	

1. Cut cantaloupe into wedges, discarding seedy portion. Pare wedges and cut pink portion into 1-inch pieces. (There should be 3½ to 4 cups cantaloupe pieces.)

2. Cover cantaloupe in a bowl with a *salt solution* (dissolve 1 tablespoon salt in 2 quarts cold water). Cover and let stand 8 hours, or overnight.

3. Drain cantaloupe in a colander and rinse with cold water. Put into a large saucepan and cover with boiling water; cook 8 to 10 minutes, or until cantaloupe is tender. (Do not cook until soft.) Drain thoroughly.

4. Meanwhile, mix the water and sugar in a saucepan. Bring to boiling, stirring until sugar is dissolved; boil, uncovered, about 5 minutes. Add the cantaloupe, lemon, and ginger. Cook rapidly until cantaloupe is translucent, 30 to 40 minutes. Remove from heat and let stand overnight.

5. The next day, reheat the preserves to boiling and ladle into hot sterilized jars. Seal immediately, *page 626*.   FOUR ½-PINT JARS PRESERVES

CHERRY BERRY PRESERVES

1 lb. dark sweet cherries, rinsed, stemmed, pitted, and halved (about 2½ cups)	3 cups sugar
	¼ cup water
	½ cup lemon juice
	¼ teaspoon almond extract
1 pt. strawberries, sliced (about 2 cups)	

1. Mix fruits, sugar, and water in a large saucepan. Cook and stir over low heat until sugar is dissolved.

2. Increase heat and bring to boiling, stirring occasionally. Stir in lemon juice and extract and boil 1 minute longer.

3. Remove from heat; skim off foam. Ladle preserves into hot sterilized glasses or jars. Cover preserves in glasses with melted paraffin; adjust lids on jars, *page 630*.

SEVEN 4-OUNCE GLASSES PRESERVES

FRESH PINEAPPLE PRESERVES

2 medium-sized fresh pineapples (about 2 lbs. each)	Sugar

1. Cut off spiny tops and rinse the pineapples. Cut into ½-inch crosswise slices. With a sharp knife, cut away and discard the rind and "eyes" from each slice. Cut out the core and cut slice into small wedges.
2. Measure 4 cups of the pineapple wedges and 3 cups sugar. Place half the fruit into a bowl and cover with half the sugar. Repeat with remaining fruit and sugar. Cover bowl tightly and set aside overnight.
3. The following day, drain the pineapple; reserve the syrup. Bring syrup to boiling in a saucepan and boil 1 minute. Remove from heat and add drained pineapple. Turn the mixture into a shallow heat-resistant dish and set aside to cool.
4. Ladle cooled preserves into hot sterilized jars and seal, *page 626.*   THREE ½-PINT JARS PRESERVES

LEBANON COUNTY RHUBARB PRESERVES

One of "seven sweets and seven sours" which comprise a typical Pennsylvania Dutch dinner menu.

2½ lbs. rhubarb	2 to 2½ tablespoons grated orange peel
1½ lbs. sugar	¾ cup orange juice

1. Wash rhubarb and cut into small pieces. (Peel stalks only if skin is tough.) Combine in a saucepan with the sugar and orange peel and juice.
2. Stir over low heat until sugar is dissolved, then bring to boiling over medium heat. Reduce heat and cook slowly until mixture thickens, about 30 minutes, stirring occasionally.
3. Ladle into hot sterilized jars and seal, *page 626.*   ABOUT 3 PINTS PRESERVES

PRIZE STRAWBERRY PRESERVES

3 cups fresh firm ripe strawberries	3 cups sugar

1. Rinse, hull, and drain berries thoroughly on absorbent paper. Halve the very large berries. Put into a heavy saucepan.
2. Add 1 cup sugar; stirring gently, bring to boiling. Boil 5 minutes, stirring constantly.

3. Repeat step 2 twice more, using remaining 2 cups sugar and boiling 5 minutes after each addition.
4. Turn into shallow glass dish, cover, and let stand 24 hours. Stir occasionally while cooling.
5. Ladle into hot sterilized jars and seal, *page 626.*   THREE ½-PINT JARS PRESERVES

HOLIDAY TREAT PRESERVES

4 cups (1 lb.) cranberries	1 can (14 oz.) pineapple tidbits, drained (reserve ¼ cup syrup)
2 cups diced pears (about 3 small)	½ cup water
	2 cups sugar

1. Wash, drain, and sort cranberries.
2. Rinse, halve, core, pare, and dice enough pears to yield 2 cups. Sprinkle reserved pineapple syrup over pears.
3. Mix water and sugar in a saucepan; stir over medium heat until boiling; cover and boil gently 5 minutes. Add the cranberries and cook, uncovered, until all the skins burst.
4. Add the pears with syrup and drained pineapple. Continue cooking until thick, about 20 minutes. Remove from heat; skim off any foam.
5. Ladle into hot sterilized jars and seal, *page 626.*   FIVE ½-PINT JARS PRESERVES

GINGER TOMATOES

Call these tomatoes a preserve, marmalade, or relish, whatever the name, they are irresistible as an accompaniment for meat or poultry or with toast for breakfast.

6 lbs. green tomatoes	3 lemons, thinly sliced
2 lbs. firm ripe tomatoes	1 teaspoon whole cloves
5 lbs. sugar	3 pieces (½ in. each) ginger root

1. Rinse tomatoes and cover with boiling water to loosen skins; plunge into cold water and remove skins and stem ends; quarter the small tomatoes and cut larger ones into eighths.
2. Combine tomatoes with sugar, lemon slices, cloves (tied in a spice bag), and ginger root in a large kettle; bring to boiling over medium heat. Reduce heat and cook slowly until mixture thickens, stirring occasionally to prevent sticking.
3. Ladle into hot sterilized jars (remove cloves and ginger root) and seal, *page 626.*   ABOUT 8 PINTS PRESERVES

BEST-EVER TOMATO PRESERVES

1 lb. tart green apples	2 lemon slices, ¼-in.
4 lbs. firm, ripe	thick
tomatoes	4 cups sugar

1. Wash, pare, quarter, core, and cut apples into small cubes. (There should be about 3 cups.)
2. Rinse, scald, peel, and cut tomatoes into small pieces. (There should be about 2 quarts.)
3. Mix apples, tomatoes, and lemon in a large preserving kettle. Bring to simmering over medium heat and stir in the sugar. Cook gently, uncovered, until of desired consistency, about 1½ hours. Stir occasionally as the mixture begins to thicken.
4. If desired, stir in several drops of *red food coloring* before ladling preserves into hot sterilized jars. Seal, *page 626.* FOUR ½-PINT JARS PRESERVES

Conserves

GINGER-APRICOT CONSERVE

1 lb. dried apricots	½ cup thinly sliced
2½ cups water	crystallized ginger
7 cups sugar	1 cup thinly sliced
	Brazil nuts

1. Cover apricots with the water in a heavy saucepan; set aside 1 hour. Stir in sugar and ginger.
2. Bring to a rolling boil over medium heat; reduce heat and cook gently 15 to 20 minutes, or until of desired consistency. Stir occasionally to prevent sticking.
3. Stir in the nuts and remove from heat; skim off any foam. Pour into hot sterilized jars; seal immediately, *page 626.* EIGHT ½-PINT JARS CONSERVE

CRANBERRY CONSERVE

4 cups (1 lb.) fresh	1 tablespoon grated
cranberries	orange peel
1 cup water	⅓ cup orange juice
1 cup dark seedless	1 cup coarsely chopped
raisins, chopped	walnuts (or other
2½ cups sugar	nuts)

1. Wash and drain cranberries.
2. Put cranberries into a saucepan and add water; bring to boiling and cook, uncovered, 5 minutes, or until all the skins burst.

3. Force cranberries through a sieve or food mill. Combine purée in a saucepan with the raisins, sugar, and orange peel and juice; mix well. Stir over medium heat until sugar is dissolved, then continue cooking about 15 minutes, or until thick.
4. Remove from heat; stir in walnuts. Ladle into hot sterilized jars and seal, *page 626.*
THREE ½-PINT JARS CONSERVE

ORANGE CONSERVE

2 cups cold water	1 teaspoon vanilla
4½ cups thinly sliced	extract
oranges	½ cup pecans or
1 lemon, thinly sliced	walnuts, chopped
3 cups sugar	¼ cup maraschino
	cherries

1. Pour cold water over oranges and lemon in a bowl. Let stand, covered, 8 hours or overnight.
2. Turn into a large kettle and cook gently, uncovered, 1½ hours, or until peel is tender.
3. Measure the mixture into a saucepan. (There should be about 3 cups.) Stir in 3 cups sugar (or use equal parts sugar and fruit). Cook gently until thickened, 1 to 1½ hours.
4. Add extract, nuts, and cherries several minutes before cooking time is ended.
5. Ladle into hot sterilized jars and seal, *page 626.*
THREE ½-PINT JARS CONSERVE

BEST-EVER PURPLE PLUM CONSERVE

5 to 6 lbs. firm purple	½ cup orange juice
plums, rinsed, pitted,	¼ cup lemon juice
and quartered cross-	1 lb. dark seedless
wise (3 qts. cut-up	raisins (use half
plums)	golden raisins, if
8 cups sugar	desired)
1 tablespoon grated	1 cup walnuts, broken in
orange peel	coarse pieces (do not
1 tablespoon grated	chop)
lemon peel	

1. Mix plums with 4 cups of the sugar in a large bowl; set aside in a cool place several hours or overnight. Pour off the syrup which has formed into a heavy 3-quart saucepot.
2. Add the remaining sugar to syrup and bring to boiling; boil 5 minutes, stirring constantly.
3. Add plums and fruit peels and juices; cook gently about 30 minutes, reducing heat as the mixture thickens. Stir frequently with a wooden spoon.

4.   Add raisins and continue cooking about 25 minutes, stirring gently from time to time (do not overcook).

5.   Stir in the walnuts several minutes before cooking time is ended. (To test conserve, quickly chill a spoonful on a chilled saucer. It should be of spreading consistency.)

6.   Ladle into hot sterilized jars and seal, *page 626.*

TWELVE ½-PINT JARS CONSERVE

RHUBARB CONSERVE

2 pkgs. (16 oz. each) frozen sweetened rhubarb, thawed	2 tablespoons white vinegar
1 large orange	5½ cups sugar
1 cup water	¼ teaspoon salt
½ cup golden raisins	1 bottle liquid fruit pectin
3 tablespoons Ginger Brew, *below*	½ cup chopped pecans

1.   Put rhubarb with syrup into a large kettle.

2.   Wash and halve the orange; remove seeds; cut through peel and pulp into fine slivers about ¾ inch long. Mix with the water in a saucepan and simmer until peel is almost tender, about 4 minutes; add to the rhubarb.

3.   Stir in raisins, Ginger Brew, vinegar, sugar, and salt; blend well. Bring rapidly to boiling; boil vigorously 1 minute, stirring constantly.

4.   Remove from heat; immediately stir in pectin. Skim off any foam. Add pecans; continue stirring 5 minutes to keep fruit and nuts in suspension.

5.   Ladle into hot sterilized jars and seal, *page 626.*

NINE ½-PINT JARS CONSERVE

GINGER BREW: Combine *2 teaspoons crushed ginger root* with *½ cup water* in a small saucepan. Cover and bring to boiling; simmer over low heat 2 minutes. Remove from heat; let stand 5 minutes and strain.

CHERRY-TOMATO CONSERVE

4 large tomatoes, peeled and chopped	1 lemon, thinly sliced
1½ cups sugar	1 teaspoon ground ginger
1 medium-sized onion, chopped	1 jar (8 oz.) red maraschino cherries, drained and chopped
1 green pepper, chopped	½ cup nuts, chopped

1.   Mix tomatoes and sugar together in a sauce-

pan. Let stand 3 hours, or until sugar is dissolved; stir occasionally.

2.   Add onion, pepper, lemon slices, and ginger; mix well. Bring to boiling. Reduce heat and simmer until thick, 1½ to 2 hours, stirring occasionally.

3.   Remove from heat and mix in cherries and nuts. Ladle mixture into hot sterilized jars and seal immediately, *page 626.*

THREE ½-PINT JARS CONSERVE

Fruit Butters

MOSELEM SPRINGS APPLE BUTTER
A favorite Pennsylvania Dutch recipe.

16 medium-sized tart apples (about 6 lbs.)	1 teaspoon ground cinnamon
2 qts. water	1 teaspoon ground allspice
1½ qts. apple cider	1 teaspoon ground cloves
1½ lbs. sugar	

1.   Wash and cut the apples into small pieces. (There should be about 4 quarts.) Cover with the water in a large kettle and cook, covered, until apples are soft, stirring occasionally.

2.   Press through a coarse sieve or food mill to remove skins and seeds.

3.   Bring cider to boiling in a heavy saucepot; stir in the apple pulp and sugar. Cook and stir over medium heat until sugar is dissolved. Reduce heat and cook slowly until mixture thickens, stirring occasionally to prevent sticking.

4.   Blend in a mixture of the spices and continue cooking until apple butter is of spreading consistency.

5.   Ladle into hot sterilized jars and seal, *page 626.*

ABOUT 4 PINTS APPLE BUTTER

BANANA-PECAN BUTTER

3 cups crushed ripe bananas (6 to 7 medium sized)	6½ cups sugar
	½ teaspoon butter or margarine
1 teaspoon grated lemon peel	1 bottle liquid fruit pectin
¼ cup lemon juice	1 cup pecans, chopped

1.   Combine the bananas, lemon peel and juice, sugar, and butter in a large heavy saucepan; blend thoroughly.

2. Bring to boiling and boil 2 minutes, stirring constantly to prevent sticking on bottom.

3. Remove from heat; stir in pectin and chopped pecans. Ladle into hot sterilized jars and seal, *page 626*.　　EIGHT ½-PINT JARS FRUIT BUTTER

GRAPE BUTTER

2 lbs. Concord grapes　　4½ cups sugar

1. Rinse the grapes; discard stems and blemished grapes. Drain and put into a large heavy saucepot.

Add sugar and mix thoroughly. Stir over medium heat until sugar is dissolved. Increase heat and cook rapidly 20 minutes, stirring frequently to prevent sticking.

2. Remove the grape mixture from heat and force through a coarse sieve or food mill.

3. Return the pulp to saucepot and bring to boiling over high heat, stirring constantly. Boil rapidly 1 minute.

4. Remove from heat and skim off any foam. Ladle into hot sterilized jars and seal, *page 626*.

ABOUT FIVE ½-PINT JARS BUTTER

PICKLING

Pickling is the process of preserving foods in a salt brine (a solution of salt and water) or in vinegar.

Pickles and relishes have little food value but their crispness, tangy flavor, and color add interest to meals and stimulate the appetite.

Both vegetables and fruits may be pickled whole, halved, quartered, or sliced. Cucumbers, tomatoes, onions, beets, red and green peppers, carrots, cauliflower and cabbage, also peaches, pears, and crab apples, are commonly used for pickles and relishes. To make good pickles at home one must use the proper equipment, the right ingredients, and reliable recipes.

Cooking Utensils—Enamel, aluminum, stainless steel, and glass are the best types of kettles to use for cooking the pickle liquid or the pickles. Wooden, aluminum, or stainless steel spoons are preferred for stirring or lifting pickles. (Avoid brass, copper, iron, and galvanized kettles. These metals may cause undesirable color changes or chemical reactions with acid and salt.)

Containers for Storage—Best results are obtained if homemade pickles are stored in sterilized glass jars with tight-fitting lids. To insure a perfect seal the filled jars may be processed in a boiling-water bath, *page 626*, 5 to 10 minutes.

Ingredients—Select firm, fresh, unblemished vegetables and fruits. Scrub vegetables in clear water and thoroughly wash fruits. Use small or medium cucumbers with ¼ to ⅛-inch stems. If cucumbers are not pickled within 24 hours, cover them with a salt solution (2 to 4 tablespoons salt per quart water) and let stand several hours or overnight.

Use fresh whole spices when possible as they keep their flavor longer than ground spices. Tie them loosely in a spice bag or square of cheesecloth. Remove spice bag before packing pickles into jars.

Use pickling (or dairy) salt for best results. Free-flowing table salt is undesirable as the substance added to keep salt from caking interferes with pickling.

Avoid too much salt as it toughens and shrivels the vegetable to be pickled.

Use a good, clear vinegar free of sediment. Cider vinegar is preferred but white (distilled) vinegar will help to retain the natural color of light-colored fruits and vegetables. Use vinegar of 4% to 6% acidity. A vinegar solution which is too strong may bleach the vegetables or fruits or cause them to soften after pickling.

Granulated white sugar (cane or beet) is generally used for pickling, but brown sugar is called for in some recipes.

Alum is sometimes added to give pickles crispness. If good pickling methods are used alum should not be necessary.

Soft water is best for use in preparing a salt brine. Hard water may interfere with the curing (fermenting) of cucumbers. If hard water must be used, boil it and let stand 24 hours; remove scum and strain water through several thicknesses of cheesecloth.

Limewater (available at most pharmacies) is sometimes called for in recipes. It adds crispness to pickles such as those using watermelon rind and green tomatoes.

Vegetable Pickles

PICKLED CARROTS

3 lbs. young carrots
2 teaspoons whole cloves
2 teaspoons whole allspice
1 teaspoon whole mace
1 piece (3 in.) stick cinnamon
3 cups white vinegar
½ cup water
2 cups sugar

1. Cook washed carrots in boiling *salted water* until skins slip easily (carrots are only partially cooked). Drain and remove skins. If carrots are very small, leave whole; if large, cut lengthwise into halves or quarters.
2. Tie spices loosely in spice bag and put into a saucepan with remaining ingredients. Bring to boiling and boil gently 10 minutes.
3. Pour the hot syrup over carrots in a saucepan; set aside several hours.
4. Place over medium heat and bring to boiling; cover and boil gently 5 minutes. Remove spices.
5. Pack carrots into hot sterilized jars; pour the boiling syrup over them and remove air bubbles from jars, *page 626*. Add more syrup if needed to fill jars to within ½ inch of top. Seal, *page 626*.
6. Process jars 10 minutes in boiling water bath, *page 626*. 3 PINTS PICKLED CARROTS

BREAD AND BUTTER PICKLES
(Midwestern Style)

2 qts. ¼-in. cucumber slices (about 16 cucumbers, 4 to 5 in. each)
½ cup coarse salt
1 qt. boiling water
2 cups chopped onion
2 cups chopped green pepper
¾ cup chopped red pepper
2 cups cider vinegar
2 cups sugar
1 teaspoon celery seed
1 teaspoon mustard seed
¾ teaspoon ground turmeric

1. Prepare the cucumber slices and toss with salt in a large bowl. Pour boiling water over cucumbers, cover, and let stand overnight.
2. The next day prepare the chopped vegetables.
3. Combine remaining ingredients in a large saucepot and stir over medium heat until sugar is dissolved. Increase heat and bring to boiling. Add the chopped vegetables and cucumbers and cook gently about 5 minutes.

4. Immediately pack the pickles into hot sterilized jars and seal, *page 626*.

ABOUT 4 PINTS PICKLES

BREAD AND BUTTER PICKLES
(New England Style)

2 qts. ¼-in. cucumber slices (about 16 cucumbers, 4 to 5 in. each)
2 medium-sized onions, thinly sliced
½ cup coarse salt
Ice cubes
Cold water
2 cups cider vinegar
2 cups sugar
2 tablespoons cassia buds
1 tablespoon white mustard seed
½ teaspoon ground turmeric
¼ teaspoon celery seed

1. Toss cucumbers, onions, and salt in a bowl.
2. Fill a 1-quart measuring cup for liquid with ice cubes. Add cold water to bring water level to the 1-quart mark. Pour over the vegetables; cover and set aside 3 hours.
3. Drain vegetables thoroughly; discard liquid.
4. Measure remaining ingredients into a large kettle. Cook and stir over medium heat until the sugar is dissolved. Increase heat and bring to boiling. Add the drained vegetables and cook gently until thoroughly heated.
5. Immediately pack the pickles into hot sterilized jars. Add hot liquid, remove air bubbles, and seal jars, *page 626*. ABOUT 3 PINTS PICKLES

YELLOW CUCUMBER PICKLES
(Senfgurken)

12 large ripe cucumbers
½ cup coarse salt
4½ cups water
1 qt. cider vinegar
6 cups sugar
2 tablespoons yellow mustard seed
1 tablespoon whole cloves
1 piece (3 in.) stick cinnamon

1. Wash, pare, and halve the cucumbers lengthwise; remove seeds. Cut each half through center, crosswise, then cut each quarter into lengthwise pieces of desired thickness. Let stand 12 hours, or overnight, in a brine made of the salt and water. Drain cucumbers thoroughly.
2. Bring vinegar, sugar, and spices (tied in a spice bag) to boiling in a large kettle; add cucumbers. Cook gently until pieces begin to look transparent but are still crisp.

3. Fill hot sterilized jars with pickles, then pour the hot syrup over them, leaving headspace. Seal, *page 626*. ABOUT 3 QUARTS PICKLES

SLICED CUCUMBER PICKLES

6 lbs. cucumbers (about 4 in. long), thinly sliced; do not pare	5 cups cider vinegar
	5 cups sugar
	1½ teaspoons ground turmeric
4 large onions, shredded (about 1 quart)	
2 green peppers, shredded (about 2 cups)	2 tablespoons mustard seed
	2 tablespoons plus 2 teaspoons celery seed
½ cup salt	16 whole cloves
Small ice cubes	

1. Mix the vegetables and salt in a large bowl or earthenware crock. Cover with ice cubes and top with a weighted plate; set aside about 3 hours. Drain.
2. Meanwhile, blend vinegar and remaining ingredients together in a large kettle. Add drained vegetables and set over medium heat. Heat thoroughly (do not boil), stirring occasionally with a wooden spoon.
3. Pack into sterilized jars and seal, *page 626*. 8 PINTS PICKLES

CURRY PICKLES

3 lbs. cucumbers (5 in. each)	2 tablespoons mustard seed
1¾ cups cider vinegar	2 tablespoons salt
1¼ cups water	1½ teaspoons curry powder
1 cup sugar	1½ teaspoons celery salt

1. Wash cucumbers and cut into 1-inch chunks.
2. Mix remaining ingredients in a saucepot and heat to boiling.
3. Add the cucumbers; return to boiling; reduce the heat to simmer while quickly packing cucumbers into hot sterilized jars to within ⅛ inch of top. (Be sure the pickling solution covers cucumbers.) Seal immediately, *page 626*. ABOUT 5 PINTS PICKLES

EASY HOMEMADE SWEET PICKLES

1 jar (1 qt.) whole dill pickles	1 tablespoon crushed stick cinnamon
½ clove garlic	1 tablespoon celery seed
2 cups sugar	1½ teaspoons mustard seed
1 cup cider vinegar	

1. Drain liquid from the jar of pickles. Cut pickles diagonally into ½-inch slices. Wash, rinse, and drain the jar; fill with the pickle slices. Add garlic.
2. Mix in a saucepan sugar, vinegar, cinnamon, celery seed, and mustard seed. Bring to boiling, stirring until sugar is dissolved.
3. Pour the hot mixture over pickles; seal jar and set aside to cool, then refrigerate at least 1 week. 1 QUART PICKLES

CHERRY-PICKLE CHUNKS

1 jar (qt.) whole dill pickles, drained (about 12)	2 cups sugar
	1 piece (3 in.) stick cinnamon, crushed
Maraschino cherries, well drained (about 36 small)	1 teaspoon whole cloves
	1 teaspoon mixed pickling spices
½ cup white vinegar	2 bay leaves
¼ cup water	

1. Cut pickles crosswise into 1-inch thick slices. Using a corer, remove center from each pickle chunk and insert a cherry into each cavity. Put into a shallow dish; set aside.
2. Mix remaining ingredients in a saucepan; blend well and bring to boiling. Reduce heat and simmer 5 minutes.
3. Strain the spice mixture through a sieve over the pickles. Cover dish and refrigerate at least 1 week before serving. 1 QUART PICKLES

DILL PICKLES, KOSHER STYLE

4 lbs. 4 in. cucumbers	14 cloves garlic, halved
3 cups cider vinegar	Dill seed
3 cups water	Peppercorns
6 tablespoons pure granulated salt	

1. Scrub cucumbers and halve lengthwise.
2. Mix vinegar, water, salt, and garlic in a saucepan; bring to boiling.
3. Pack cucumbers into clean, hot 1-pint jars. Add 2 tablespoons dill seed, 3 peppercorns, and 4

garlic halves (from the pickling liquid) to each jar.
4. Fill jars with hot pickling liquid, leaving ½ inch
headspace. Adjust lids, *page 626*, and process jars
in boiling water bath 10 minutes, *page 626*.

7 PINTS PICKLES

DILL PICKLES, FRESH PACK

17 to 18 lbs. cucumbers (3 to 5 in. long)	9 cups water
About 2 gallons 5% brine (¾ cup pure granulated salt per gallon of water)	2 tablespoons whole mixed pickling spices
	Mustard seed
	Garlic cloves (optional)
6 cups cider vinegar	Dill plant (fresh or dried), 3 heads per
¾ cup pure granulated salt	qt. jar (or dill seed, 1 tablespoon per qt.
¼ cup sugar	jar)

1. Scrub cucumbers thoroughly with a vegetable
brush; rinse and drain. Cover with the salt brine
and set aside overnight. Drain.
2. Mix the vinegar, salt, sugar, water, and spices
(tied loosely in cheesecloth); bring mixture to boiling.
3. Pack cucumbers into clean hot 1-quart jars. To
each jar, add 2 teaspoons mustard seed, 2 cloves
garlic (if used), and the dill plant (or dill seed).
Cover with boiling vinegar mixture to within ½ inch
of top of jar. Adjust jar lids, *page 626*.
4. Process jars in boiling water bath 20 minutes,
page 626.
5. Remove jars and complete seal, if necessary.
Cool jars upright on a wire rack.

7 QUARTS PICKLES (PACKED 7 TO 10 PER JAR)

PICKLED ONIONS

Boiling water	1 qt. white vinegar
2 qts. small white onions	1 cup sugar
½ cup salt	2 tablespoons whole mixed pickling spices

1. Pour boiling water over onions; let stand 2
minutes. Drain and cover with cold water.
2. Peel onions and put into a bowl or crock. Add
enough cold water to cover, sprinkle with the salt,
and set aside overnight.
3. The following day, drain onions; rinse with cold
water and drain thoroughly.
4. Mix white vinegar and sugar in a saucepan;
add spices (tied in a spice bag) and bring to boiling.
5. Remove from heat; pack onions into hot sterilized jars. Remove spices and pour hot syrup over
onions, leaving headspace. Seal immediately, *page 626*.

ABOUT 5 PINTS PICKLED ONIONS

DELICIOUS RED PEPPER PICKLES

12 large sweet red peppers (about 3½ lbs.)	1¼ cups sugar
	1 piece (3 in.) stick cinnamon
2½ cups cider vinegar	12 whole cloves

1. Wash peppers, quarter lengthwise, remove
seeds and white membrane, and cut quarters into
¾-inch strips.
2. Pour boiling water over peppers in a bowl;
cover and set aside about 3 minutes. Drain off the
water and immediately cover peppers with icy cold
water. Set aside about 10 minutes.
3. Meanwhile, combine vinegar with the remaining ingredients (cloves tied in cheesecloth) in a
saucepan; bring to boiling, stirring until sugar is
dissolved. Boil 2 to 3 minutes.
4. Drain peppers in a colander. Pack into hot sterilized jars. Quickly cover with the hot pickling liquid, leaving headspace. Remove air bubbles and
adjust lids. Seal, *page 626*.

3 PINTS PICKLES

GARLIC-FLAVORED GREEN TOMATO PICKLES

4 lbs. green tomatoes, thinly sliced	1½ cups packed brown sugar
3 medium-sized onions, thinly sliced	¾ teaspoon dry mustard
¼ cup salt	1 teaspoon ground ginger
3 medium-sized green peppers, chopped	1 teaspoon celery seed
1 large or 2 small sweet red peppers, chopped	9 whole cloves
2 cups cider vinegar	1 piece (1 in.) stick cinnamon, broken in smaller pieces
1 large or 2 small cloves garlic, minced	

1. Arrange tomatoes and onions in layers in a
large bowl, sprinkling salt between the layers.
Cover and let stand overnight.
2. Drain the vegetables in a colander and rinse
them thoroughly under cold running water to remove excess salt.
3. While vegetables are draining, wash and prepare the peppers. Mix peppers with vinegar, garlic,

and brown sugar in a kettle. Bring to boiling, stirring occasionally. Add drained vegetables and spices. (Tie cloves and cinnamon in a spice bag, if desired.)

4. Bring to boiling, stirring to mix well. Cook gently, covered, until green tomatoes are translucent, 35 to 45 minutes. Quickly pack pickles into hot sterilized jars and seal, *page 626.*   4 PINTS PICKLES

GREEN TOMATO-CUCUMBER PICKLES

5 cucumbers (5 in. each), thinly sliced (about 2 cups)	1 medium-sized sweet red pepper, chopped (about ¾ cup)
1½ lbs. green tomatoes, thinly sliced (about 4 cups)	3 cups cider vinegar
	3 cups sugar
	1 tablespoon salt
4 medium-sized green peppers, chopped (about 3 cups)	1 tablespoon celery seed
	1 tablespoon mustard seed

1. Prepare the vegetables and set aside.
2. Combine vinegar with remaining ingredients in a heavy saucepot. Cook over medium heat, stirring occasionally, until sugar is dissolved and mixture comes to boiling. Add vegetables, reduce heat, and simmer about 10 minutes.
3. Continue simmering while ladling the pickles into hot sterilized jars to within ⅛ inch of top. Fill and complete one jar at a time. (Be sure the vinegar solution covers the vegetables.)

ABOUT 5 PINTS PICKLES

GREEN TOMATO PICKLES

8 lbs. green tomatoes, thinly sliced	2 tablespoons mustard seed
6 large onions, thinly sliced	2 teaspoons pickling spices
Salt	3½ cups cider vinegar
2 tablespoons whole cloves	2 cups sugar
2 tablespoons whole allspice	2 teaspoons dry mustard
	2 large red peppers, coarsely chopped

1. Put tomatoes and onions into separate bowls; sprinkle tomatoes with ¼ cup salt and onions with 2 tablespoons salt. Cover and let stand 12 hours.
2. Drain vegetables thoroughly; discard liquid.
3. Tie whole spices in a spice bag and put into a large kettle; add vinegar and a mixture of sugar and dry mustard. Heat to boiling, stirring until sugar is dissolved.
4. Add tomatoes, onions, and red peppers; cook slowly, uncovered, until tomatoes are just tender, about 20 minutes.
5. Pack into sterilized jars and seal, *page 626.*

4 PINTS PICKLES

MUSTARD PICKLES
(Chowchow)

1 large head cauliflower, rinsed and separated in florets (about 1½ qts.)	2 large green peppers, cleaned and chopped (about 2 cups)
1 qt. small white pickling onions, peeled	2 large sweet red peppers, cleaned and chopped (about 2 cups)
1 qt. gherkin or small cucumbers, scrubbed	2 qts. cider vinegar
	6 tablespoons prepared mustard
1 qt. small green tomatoes, washed and blossom ends removed	1½ cups packed light brown sugar
	⅔ cup all-purpose flour
	2 tablespoons ground turmeric

1. Prepare the vegetables and combine in a large bowl. Cover with a salt solution made by dissolving *½ cup salt* in *3 quarts cold water.* Cover and set aside 24 hours.
2. Drain the salt solution from vegetables through a colander into a saucepan. Bring solution to boiling and immediately pour over vegetables in the colander. Set aside to drain.
3. Meanwhile, in a large heavy saucepan, combine the vinegar, mustard, and a mixture of the brown sugar, flour, and turmeric; blend thoroughly. Cook and stir with a wooden spoon over medium heat until thickened and smooth.
4. Add the drained vegetables and cook gently until they are tender but not soft. Stir frequently to prevent scorching. (Mixture is quite thick.)
5. Working quickly, pack pickles into hot sterilized jars to with ½ inch of top. Seal, *page 626.*

11 PINTS PICKLES

ZUCCHINI PICKLE SLICES

2½ lbs. zucchini, scrubbed, rinsed, and cut in ¼-in. slices (2½ cups)	2 cups cider vinegar
	1 cup sugar
	4 to 5 tablespoons salt
¾ lb. onions, thinly sliced (2½ cups)	1½ teaspoons celery seed
	¼ to ½ teaspoon ground turmeric

1.   Prepare vegetables and set aside.
2.   Mix remaining ingredients in a heavy saucepan. Cook and stir over medium heat until sugar is dissolved and mixture comes to boiling. Remove from heat. Immediately add the vegetables; cover and let stand about 1 hour.
3.   Meanwhile, sterilize 1-pint jars, *page 626*. Leave them in the hot water until ready to fill.
4.   Bring the vegetable mixture to boiling rapidly; reduce heat and cook gently, uncovered, about 3 minutes. Remove from heat.
5.   Pack vegetables into hot jars; add hot pickling liquid to within ½ inch of top, being sure that vegetables are completely covered. Release air bubbles and adjust lids, *page 626*. Work quickly, completing one jar at a time.   ABOUT 4 PINTS PICKLES

Fruit Pickles

SPICED CANTALOUPE

2 very firm underripe cantaloupe	½ cup sugar
	10 whole cloves
1 cup cider vinegar	1 piece (3 in.) stick cinnamon, broken in small pieces
1 cup water	
½ lb. brown sugar (about 1⅓ cups packed)	½ teaspoon whole mace

1.   Remove rind and seeds and cut cantaloupe into 1-inch cubes. (There should be about 2 quarts cubes.)
2.   Put cubes into a bowl; cover with a *salt solution* (2 tablespoons salt dissolved in 1 quart icy cold water). Invert a plate over fruit to keep cubes submerged in solution. Set aside 2 hours, then drain thoroughly.
3.   Combine the vinegar, water, sugars, and the spices in a large heavy saucepan. Bring to boiling and add the drained melon. Cook, uncovered, over medium heat until cubes are almost transparent, stirring occasionally.

4.   Using a slotted spoon, remove cantaloupe to hot sterilized jars and pour the hot syrup over them. Remove air bubbles and add more syrup, if needed, to fill jars to within ½ inch of top; seal, *page 626*.   3 PINTS PICKLES

PICKLED CRAB APPLES

2½ lbs. firm crab apples with stems	1½ tablespoons whole allspice
1½ tablespoons whole cloves	3 cups vinegar
	6 cups sugar
2 pieces (3 in. each) stick cinnamon	3 cups water

1.   Wash crab apples and remove the blossom ends. Do not peel. Run a large needle through crab apples to keep them from bursting during cooking.
2.   Tie the spices loosely in a cheesecloth bag.
3.   Combine vinegar, sugar, and water in a kettle; add the spices and bring mixture to boiling; boil 5 minutes.
4.   Add crab apples, a layer at a time, and cook gently until tender, about 10 minutes.
5.   Using a slotted spoon, remove crab apples to a large bowl or crock. Repeat until all crab apples are cooked.
6.   Pour the boiling syrup over crab apples; cover and let stand in a cool place 12 to 18 hours.
7.   Using a slotted spoon, remove crab apples from syrup and pack into hot sterilized jars; remove spice bag from syrup.
8.   Heat the syrup to boiling and quickly pour over crab apples. Remove air bubbles from jars and add more syrup if needed to fill jars to within ½ inch of top. Seal immediately, *page 626*.
9.   Process jars in boiling water bath, *page 626*.
          ABOUT 4 PINTS PICKLES

BRANDIED PEACHES

5 lbs. small firm ripe peaches (about 30)	2 cups water
	3 cups sugar
Lemon juice or salt	½ to 1 cup brandy

1.   Plunge peaches into boiling water to loosen skins, then into cold water and gently remove skins. Keep peaches in salted water or lemon water (1 tablespoon lemon juice or salt to 2 quarts water) to prevent discoloration. Let stand no longer than 15 minutes.
2.   Combine water and sugar in a 4-quart kettle.

Stir over medium heat until sugar is dissolved and syrup comes to boiling.

3. Add about one fourth of the peaches (drained) at one time. Boil gently 10 minutes, or until peaches are just tender but not soft.

4. Using a slotted spoon, remove peaches from syrup and pack into hot sterilized jars to within ½ inch of top. Cover jars with their lids to keep peaches hot.

5. When all the peaches are cooked and in the jars, spoon 2 to 4 tablespoons brandy into each jar. Quickly bring the syrup to boiling and pour over peaches, leaving headspace. Seal, *page 626.*

ABOUT 2 QUARTS PICKLES

NOTE: Add more brandy or rum to any leftover syrup for a delicious topping for ice cream. Or pour brandied syrup over slices of pound cake or sponge cake, then top with scoops of ice cream for a quick Baba au Rum or Baba au Brandy. Top the ice cream with sliced fresh thawed or frozen peaches.

SPICED FRESH PEACHES

25 firm ripe peaches (about 6 lbs.)	3 pieces (3 in. each) stick cinnamon
Whole cloves	1 teaspoon whole allspice
2 cups sugar	
2 cups cider vinegar	2½ cups packed light brown sugar

1. Rinse and plunge peaches into boiling water to loosen skins. Plunge into cold water and gently slip off skins.

2. Insert 2 or 3 cloves into each peach and put into large kettle. Cover with boiling water and cook 5 minutes, or until almost tender. Drain, reserving ½ cup liquid for syrup.

3. Mix sugar, reserved peach liquid, vinegar, and cinnamon in a 4-quart kettle. Tie allspice in a spice bag and add to mixture. Boil 5 minutes.

4. Add one layer of peaches at a time to syrup, lower heat and simmer until peaches are thoroughly heated, 2 to 3 minutes. Remove to a large bowl. Repeat until all peaches have been heated.

5. Remove spice bag from syrup and pour syrup over peaches. Cover and let stand overnight.

6. The next morning, drain syrup from peaches into a 4-quart kettle; add brown sugar and bring to boiling, stirring until sugar is dissolved. Add peaches and bring syrup to full rolling boil. Remove from heat.

7. Pack hot peaches into hot sterilized jars; add hot syrup, leaving headspace. Seal, *page 626.*

3 QUARTS SPICED PEACHES

NOTE: Allowing peaches to stand in syrup overnight prevents shriveling and "floating."

SPICED PEARS

8 lbs. firm, ripe pears	2 pieces (3 in. each) stick cinnamon
2 cups cider vinegar	
4 cups packed brown sugar	2 tablespoons whole cloves

1. Wash pears. Pare them and leave whole if they are small. If large, halve and core them.

2. Combine remaining ingredients (spices tied in spice bag, if desired) in a saucepan. Bring to boiling; reduce heat and simmer 20 minutes.

3. Add pears to syrup, a few at a time, and cook gently until just tender (but not soft).

4. Pack pears into hot sterilized jars; add syrup, leaving headspace. Seal immediately, *page 626.*

ABOUT 3 QUARTS SPICED PEARS

SPICED PICKLED PURPLE PLUMS

4 to 5 lbs. fresh, very firm purple plums	1 teaspoon whole allspice
2 cups cider vinegar	1 tablespoon whole cloves
1 cup water	
4 cups sugar (or 2 cups sugar and 2 cups packed brown sugar)	Stick cinnamon, broken in pieces

1. Wash plums; insert a large needle several times into each plum to prevent bursting during cooking.

2. Combine vinegar, water, and sugar in a kettle.

3. Put allspice and cloves into a ¼ cup measure and add enough broken cinnamon stick to levelly fill the measure. Tie spices loosely in a piece of cheesecloth and add to kettle. Bring mixture to boiling and boil 10 minutes.

4. Add the plums to syrup; cover and return to boiling. Cook about 5 minutes. Let stand in syrup overnight.

5. The next morning, pack plums in hot sterilized jars. Bring the syrup to a brisk boil and pour at once over plums. Remove air bubbles from jars, *page 626,* and add more syrup if needed to fill jars to within ½ inch of top. Seal, *page 626.*

ABOUT 5 PINTS SPICED PLUMS

NOTE: Store leftover syrup in refrigerator to use for basting ham during baking . . . delicious!

WATERMELON PICKLES

2 lbs. prepared watermelon rind	¼ teaspoon mustard seed
½ cup salt	5 pieces (2 in. each) stick cinnamon
2 qts. water	
1 teaspoon whole allspice	3 cups vinegar
	2 cups water
1 teaspoon whole cloves	2 lbs. sugar

1. Pare the watermelon rind, removing all green and pink portions. Cut the rind into 2x1x½-inch pieces.
2. Prepare a brine of the salt and 2 quarts water; pour over rind. Cover and let stand overnight.
3. Drain rind; cover with fresh water and cook until tender when pierced with a fork. Remove from heat and let stand several hours; drain.
4. Tie the spices loosely in a spice bag or cheesecloth. Put into a large saucepot with the remaining ingredients. Bring to boiling and cook 5 minutes. Add the drained watermelon rind and cook gently until rind is clear and transparent. If desired, several minutes before end of cooking time, add enough *green or red food coloring* to the syrup to delicately tint the pickles. Remove and discard the spice bag.
5. Pack pickles into hot sterilized jars; cover with boiling syrup, leaving headspace. Remove air bubbles and seal, *page 626.* ABOUT 3 PINTS PICKLES

CHERRY-WATERMELON PICKLES

3 qts. water	6 cups sugar
6 tablespoons salt	2 pieces (3 in. each) stick cinnamon
2 qts. prepared watermelon rind* (rind of ½ a large melon)	1 teaspoon whole cloves
	1 jar (8 oz.) red maraschino cherries, drained
2 cups white or cider vinegar	

1. Combine water and salt in a 5- or 6-quart Dutch oven. Stir until salt is dissolved. Mix in rind. Set aside for 4 hours; drain, rinse, and drain again. Cover with water and bring to boiling; boil 10 minutes. Remove from heat; drain and reserve rind.
2. Put vinegar and sugar into a saucepan and stir until sugar is dissolved. Add spices tied in a cheese-cloth bag. Bring to boiling and boil 10 minutes. Remove from heat and add rind. Cool and refrigerate, covered, overnight.
3. Remove rind from syrup with slotted spoon. Bring syrup to boiling; add rind and cherries and boil 5 minutes. Discard spice bag.
4. Ladle rind and cherries into sterilized jars and pour syrup over rind, leaving headspace; release air bubbles and seal immediately, *page 626.*

ABOUT 3 PINTS PICKLES

*To prepare rind, remove green and pink portions of watermelon. Cut into 1-inch squares about ½ inch thick.

MINTED WATERMELON PICKLES

Rind of 1 large watermelon (about 12 cups cut rind)	3 pieces (3 in. each) stick cinnamon
	2 teaspoons whole cloves
¼ cup salt	
7 pts. water (14 cups)	2 teaspoons whole allspice
8 cups sugar	
2 cups cider vinegar	2 teaspoons mint extract
2 lemons, thinly sliced	Green food coloring

1. Pare the watermelon rind; remove green and pink portions. Cut rind into 1- to 1¼-inch squares. Add the salt to 8 cups water; stir until salt is dissolved. Pour over watermelon rind and let stand overnight. Drain.
2. Cover rind with fresh water and cook, covered, about 1 hour, or until tender. Drain thoroughly.
3. Combine remaining 6 cups water with sugar and vinegar in a 4-quart saucepan; cook gently about 8 minutes.
4. Tie lemon slices and the spices in a spice bag; add with the drained rind to syrup. Cook, uncovered, until rind is clear and transparent, about 1 hour.
5. Stir in mint extract and several drops food coloring; blend well. Remove rind from syrup with a slotted spoon and pack into hot sterilized jars. Pour syrup over rind, leaving headspace; release air bubbles and seal immediately, *page 626.*

ABOUT 6 PINTS PICKLES

Pickle Relishes

CUCUMBER-PEPPER RELISH

1 qt. coarsely chopped pared cucumber	2 tablespoons salt
2 cups coarsely chopped green pepper	1 tablespoon celery seed
1 cup coarsely chopped red pepper	1 teaspoon ground turmeric
1 cup coarsely chopped onion	1 tablespoon whole allspice
1 cup chopped ripe tomatoes	1 tablespoon whole cloves
1½ cups cider vinegar	3 pieces (3 in. each) stick cinnamon, broken in pieces
¾ cup sugar	

1. Put vegetables into a large heavy saucepot. Stir in the vinegar, sugar, salt, celery seed, and turmeric.
2. Tie spices in a spice bag and add to saucepot. Stir over medium heat until sugar is dissolved.
3. Bring to boiling; reduce heat and simmer, uncovered, 30 minutes, stirring occasionally. Remove spice bag.
4. Ladle relish into hot sterilized jars and seal, *page 626.* ABOUT 3 PINTS RELISH

CORN RELISH

Another long-popular preparation made from products of the farms of the Pennsylvania Dutch and served with the dinner medley known as "seven sweets and seven sours."

6 cups prepared fresh corn or vacuum-packed canned corn	1 clove garlic, minced
1 cup chopped mild white onion	1 teaspoon celery seed
	½ teaspoon ground ginger
1 cup chopped celery	3 cups white vinegar
1 green pepper, chopped	1 to 1½ tablespoons dry mustard
¼ cup chopped pimiento	
½ to 1 cup sugar	1 teaspoon ground turmeric
1 to 1½ tablespoons salt	3 tablespoons flour
1 teaspoon crushed red pepper	¼ cup water

1. If using fresh corn-on-the-cob, cook 5 minutes; plunge into cold water to cool thoroughly. Cut kernels from cobs (do not scrape cobs). If using canned corn, drain before measuring; set aside.

Combine onion, celery, green pepper, pimiento, sugar, salt, red pepper, garlic, celery seed, and ginger in a large kettle; add 2½ cups vinegar and blend well. Bring mixture to boiling; boil 5 minutes.
3. Blend thoroughly the dry mustard, turmeric, and flour; stir in the water until smooth, then the remaining ½ cup vinegar. Stir into the hot mixture and cook about 6 minutes. Continue stirring until liquid is thickened and smooth.
4. Add the corn; cook and stir 5 minutes longer.
5. Ladle the hot relish into hot sterilized jars and seal, *page 626.* FOUR ½-PINT JARS RELISH

WATERMELON-CORN RELISH

1 qt. fresh whole-kernel corn (about 5 large ears corn)	1½ cups packed light brown sugar
	1½ teaspoons mustard seed
1 qt. diced, pared watermelon rind, cooked (see *below*)	1½ teaspoons dry mustard
1 cup coarsely chopped celery	1 teaspoon salt
	1 teaspoon celery seed
1 cup finely diced red pepper	¼ teaspoon ground turmeric
½ cup finely diced green pepper	⅛ teaspoon cayenne pepper
½ cup coarsely chopped onion	2 cups cider vinegar
	½ cup water
	¼ cup cornstarch

1. Cut corn kernels from cobs (do not scrape cobs). Combine corn with the watermelon rind, celery, peppers, onion, and brown sugar in a large kettle. Stir in a mixture of the mustard seed, dry mustard, salt, celery seed, turmeric, and cayenne pepper.
2. Stir in the vinegar and a blend of the water and cornstarch. Bring to boiling, stirring constantly until slightly thickened.
3. Reduce heat and simmer, uncovered, about 25 minutes, stirring occasionally.
4. Ladle relish into hot sterilized jars and seal, *page 626.* ABOUT 4 PINTS RELISH
To prepare and cook watermelon rind, put diced, pared watermelon rind into a bowl; cover with *2 cups water* mixed with *2 teaspoons salt.* Let stand, covered, about 4 hours. Drain rind well and put into a saucepan with *2 cups water.* Cover, bring to boiling and boil 5 minutes, or until tender (but not soft). Drain.

FAVORITE CORN RELISH

1 qt. whole-kernel corn (about 8 medium-sized fresh corn ears), or 3 pkgs. (10 oz. each) thawed frozen corn
½ small head young green cabbage, finely chopped (about 2 cups)
2 medium-sized sweet red peppers, cut in cubes (about 1¼ cups)
½ bunch celery including heart, root, and leaves, finely chopped (about 1 qt.)

1 large onion, finely chopped (about 1 cup)
1 small clove garlic, minced
1½ teaspoons celery seed
1 cup sugar
1 tablespoon salt
1 tablespoon dry mustard
1 teaspoon ground turmeric
¼ teaspoon cayenne pepper
2 cups cider vinegar

1. If using fresh corn, cut kernels from cobs.
2. Combine corn, cabbage, red peppers, celery, onion, garlic, celery seed, and a mixture of the sugar, salt, dry mustard, turmeric, and cayenne pepper in a large kettle. Stir in the vinegar.
3. Bring mixture to boiling over medium heat; reduce heat and simmer, uncovered, 15 to 20 minutes (do not overcook).
4. If the consistency of relish is too thin, mix 2 to 3 tablespoons flour with ½ cup cold water and blend into the relish. Bring to boiling and continue cooking until the liquid portion is thickened and smooth, stirring constantly.
5. Ladle into hot sterilized jars and seal, *page 626*.

4 PINTS RELISH

AUNT VINNIE'S PICCALILLI

1 qt. chopped cabbage
1 qt. chopped green tomatoes (about 8 medium-sized)
1 cup chopped green pepper
½ cup chopped sweet red pepper
1 cup chopped onion
3 cups cider vinegar
1¾ cups sugar
1 tablespoon dry mustard

1½ teaspoons ground ginger
¼ teaspoon ground cinnamon
¼ teaspoon ground cloves
¼ teaspoon ground mace
1 tablespoon mustard seed
¼ teaspoon dried hot red pepper

1. Prepare the vegetables. Chop finely or put through coarse blade of food chopper.

2. Put vegetables into large kettle; add vinegar, sugar, dry mustard, ginger, cinnamon, cloves, mace, and mustard seed, and red pepper (tied in cheesecloth).
3. Stir over medium heat until sugar is dissolved; increase heat and cook rapidly about 20 minutes, or until vegetables are tender. Stir frequently.
4. Remove hot red pepper and immediately ladle into hot sterilized jars and seal, *page 626*.

ABOUT 4 PINTS RELISH

BRANDIED MINCEMEAT

1 lb. lean beef, cut in 2-in. cubes
5 lbs. tart apples
½ lb. suet
½ lb. seedless raisins, chopped
1 lb. currants
¼ lb. candied citron, chopped
¼ lb. candied orange peel, chopped
2 tablespoons grated orange peel
1 tablespoon grated lemon peel
¼ cup orange juice
2 tablespoons lemon juice
2 cups sugar

1 teaspoon salt
½ teaspoon pepper
1 teaspoon ground cinnamon
½ teaspoon ground cloves
½ teaspoon powdered coiander seed
½ teaspoon ground mace
½ teaspoon ground nutmeg
2 cups apple cider
1 can (16 oz.) tart red cherries with juice
½ lb. walnuts, coarsely chopped
1 cup brandy

1. Put beef cubes into a small heavy saucepan with *½ to 1 cup boiling water;* cover tightly and cook slowly until almost tender, about 1 hour. (Water should all be absorbed.) Cool.
2. Meanwhile, wash, quarter, core, and pare the apples; coarsely chop or put through coarse blade of a food chopper (about 6 cups, chopped).
3. Finely chop the cooled meat and suet, or put through coarse blade of food chopper. Combine in a heavy saucepot with all the ingredients except walnuts and brandy.
4. Cook slowly, uncovered, for 2 hours or until thickened, stirring frequently to prevent sticking.
5. Stir in the walnuts and cook several minutes longer; add the brandy and blend well.
6. Remove from heat and quickly ladle the mincemeat into hot sterilized jars; seal, *page 626*.

ABOUT 7 PINTS MINCEMEAT

NOTE: A double-crust pie requires about 4 cups.

MINCEMEAT, HOMESTYLE

½ cup (about 4 oz.) ground suet	1 teaspoon salt
1½ cups ground cooked beef	1 teaspoon ground cinnamon
4 medium-sized apples	½ teaspoon ground cloves
1 cup packed brown sugar	½ teaspoon ground nutmeg
1 cup apple cider	¼ teaspoon ground mace
½ cup fruit jelly	1 tablespoon grated lemon peel
½ cup seedless raisins, chopped	1 tablespoon lemon juice
½ cup currants	
2 tablespoons molasses	

1.   Mix suet and beef in a large heavy skillet and set aside.
2.   Wash, core, pare, and chop apples (about 3 cups, chopped).
3.   Combine apples with meat in skillet with the brown sugar, cider, jelly, raisins, currants, and molasses. Stir in a mixture of the salt and spices.
4.   Cook slowly, uncovered, about 1 hour, or until most of the liquid has been absorbed; stir occasionally to prevent sticking to bottom of skillet.
5.   Stir in lemon peel and juice.
6.   If not used immediately, pack hot mincemeat into hot sterilized jars and seal, *page 626*.

ABOUT 3½ CUPS MINCEMEAT

Chutney

PEACH CHUTNEY

1 large apple	¾ cup cider vinegar
⅓ cup seedless raisins	½ cup sugar
1 can (29 oz.) cling peach slices	½ teaspoon salt
1 cup chopped celery	¼ teaspoon ground ginger
¼ cup chopped green pepper	Few grains cayenne pepper
1 tablespoon instant minced onion	

1.   Wash, quarter, core, and chop the apple. (Do not pare.) Combine in a kettle with raisins, peaches, and remaining ingredients; stir until blended.
2.   Cook, uncovered, over low heat about 1 hour, or until syrup is thickened and chutney is of desired consistency. Stir occasionally to prevent sticking.

3.   Ladle into clean hot jars, cover tightly, and, when cool, store in refrigerator.

TWO 1-PINT JARS CHUTNEY

PEACH 'N' APPLE CHUTNEY

Serve this chutney as an accompaniment for meat or poultry, blend it with mayonnaise and serve on greens, or combine it with dairy sour cream and serve as a cocktail dip.

3 cups chopped peeled ripe peaches (6 to 7 medium-sized)	1 can (16 oz.) tomatoes plus enough water to yield 3½ cups
3 cups chopped, pared, and cored tart apples (6 to 7 medium-sized)	1 teaspoon salt
	½ teaspoon ground ginger
1 cup chopped green pepper	½ teaspoon dry mustard
	½ cup red wine vinegar
¼ cup chopped onion	¾ cup honey

1.   Put all ingredients except honey into a 6-quart kettle; mix well. Bring to full rolling boil over medium heat, stirring frequently. Reduce heat and cook slowly 30 minutes, stirring occasionally to prevent sticking.
2.   Blend in the honey and continue cooking slowly 30 minutes, stirring often.
3.   Ladle into clean hot jars and seal immediately, *page 626*. Process jars 5 minutes in boiling water bath, *page 626*.
4.   Store in cool, dry place. After jar is opened, store in refrigerator.   SIX ½-PINT JARS CHUTNEY

Catsup & Chili Sauce

TOMATO CATSUP

7 lbs. ripe tomatoes (about 21 medium-sized)	1 clove garlic
	½ cup coarsely chopped hot red pepper
1 cup cider vinegar	1 piece (3 in.) stick cinnamon, broken in pieces
1 cup sugar	
1½ teaspoons paprika	
1 teaspoon salt	½ teaspoon whole cloves
½ teaspoon garlic salt	
2 medium-sized onions, sliced	

1.   Rinse tomatoes, plunge into boiling water, then into cold water. Peel and quarter tomatoes; remove as many seeds as possible.

2. Force tomatoes through a sieve or food mill. (There should be about 2 quarts pulp.)

3. Combine pulp in a large saucepot with the vinegar, sugar, paprika, salt, garlic salt, onion, and garlic.

4. Tie remaining ingredients loosely in a cheesecloth bag and add to tomato mixture. Bring to boiling over medium heat; reduce heat and simmer 1 hour, or until catsup is of desired consistency. Stir occasionally to prevent sticking to bottom. Remove cheesecloth bag.

6. Ladle into hot sterilized jars and seal, *page 626*.

ABOUT 3½ PINTS CATSUP

PENNSYLVANIA DUTCH CATSUP

When the tomatoes ripened, an early Pennsylvania Dutch hausfrau usually made enough catsup to have it on the table all the year long.

7 lbs. firm, ripe tomatoes, rinsed and quartered	1 piece (3 in.) stick cinnamon
2 cups chopped celery	2 bay leaves
1½ cups chopped onion	12 whole cloves
1 cup cider vinegar	2 teaspoons paprika
1 cup sugar	½ teaspoon ground ginger
1 teaspoon salt	½ teaspoon garlic salt
1 teaspoon mustard seed	2 cups unsweetened applesauce

1. Mix tomatoes, celery, onion, vinegar, sugar, and salt in a large saucepot.

2. Tie mustard seed, cinnamon, bay leaves, and cloves in a cheesecloth bag. Add to tomatoes with a mixture of the paprika, ginger, and garlic salt.

3. Cover and bring mixture to boiling; cook quite vigorously, stirring occasionally, about 1 hour. Discard spice bag.

4. Force the mixture through a sieve or food mill. Return the purée to saucepot, cover, and cook gently about 1 hour, or until quite thick, stirring frequently as mixture begins to thicken.

5. Stir in the applesauce and cook to boiling.

6. Quickly ladle into hot sterilized jars and seal, *page 626*.   3 PINTS CATSUP

CHILI SAUCE

5 lbs. ripe tomatoes, peeled (about 15 medium-sized)	1⅓ cups cider vinegar
	1⅓ cups sugar
4 medium-sized green peppers, membrane and seeds removed	4 teaspoons salt
	½ teaspoon black pepper
4 medium-sized onions, peeled	½ teaspoon ground cloves
2 stalks celery	¼ teaspoon ground cinnamon

1. Finely chop the vegetables; combine in a large saucepot with the vinegar and a mixture of the remaining ingredients.

2. Bring to boiling and cook slowly, uncovered, 1½ to 2 hours, or until sauce is of desired thickness. Stir occasionally.

3. Ladle immediately into hot, sterilized jars and seal, *page 626*. Store in a cool place.

ABOUT 4 PINTS CHILI SAUCE

FREEZING

Freezing as a way of preserving food is recognized by most modern homemakers as not only a simple, economical, and safe method, but one whereby the food undergoes remarkably little, if any, change in flavor, color, and texture. Research also seems to show that freezing retains vitamins and minerals in foods better than most other preserving methods. Frozen foods such as fruits and vegetables, which are frozen promptly after harvesting, often rate higher in nutritive values than the so-called fresh product purchased in the market hours, even days, after harvesting.

However, to insure perfect results and to help you get the most from your food freezer some basic rules pertaining to its operation and the preparation of the food to be stored are given here. Other sources of information are the freezer manufacturer's instruction booklet (usually supplied with the purchase of a freezer), bulletins from U.S. Department of Agriculture, Washington, D.C., your state university extension service, and manufacturers of freezer containers and wrapping materials.

PLAN YOUR FREEZER SPACE

Keep your freezer filled with food. The more food

stored each year the less cost per pound. Keep in mind the foods which are perennial family favorites and freeze these in season when they are top quality. Don't overstock commercially-frozen foods which are always available. Watch for special bargains and reduced prices on these items and save on the food budget. But even at bargain prices, avoid overstocking any one item. This applies to home-frozen foods as well. You don't want to find yourself short of space when other desirable foods come into season.

Unless you have a very large freezer, don't freeze such foods as carrots, beets, etc., which are usually available all year around.

Allow freezer space for short-time storage of prepared dishes, baked goods, leftovers, lunch box meals, complete meals, and special party food. To accomplish this, use your freezer space for preserving seasonal foods such as fruits and vegetables when the supply is abundant and the price is moderate. When these foods (along with the meats and poultry) are consumed, use the space for cooked, baked, and ready-to-eat items.

When freezing seasonal foods, freeze only the amounts you will consume before they are in season again.

FOLLOW APPROVED FREEZING METHODS

Select varieties of fruits and vegetables which freeze best. Your state agricultural extension service is a good source for that information.

Freeze only high-quality foods. Remember that freezing retains quality but cannot improve it.

Freeze foods promptly. Garden products, especially vegetables, rapidly lose quality at room temperature. If it is impossible to freeze at once, refrigerate them.

Freeze foods in small amounts. Buy or prepare only the amounts that can be frozen at one time. Your own freezer instruction bulletin should be the best source of information for recommended amounts. Overloading your freezer should be avoided as it results in unduly raising the temperature of the foods already stored. Overloading also keeps the new items from freezing as rapidly as is necessary for optimum quality. A general rule is to add not more than 3 pounds of food per cubic foot of freezer space during any 24 hour period. If you have more than recommended amounts to freeze, have the food frozen at a locker plant, if one is available, then store it in your home freezer.

Process foods carefully. Before freezing, blanch or scald vegetables in boiling water, or steam to stop the chemical action caused by enzymes. If the enzymes remain active, the vegetable will develop undesirable flavors and become lower in quality during the freezer storage.

Package foods properly. Use moisture-vaporproof materials which will protect the food from the air and also against loss of moisture. Make sure the packages and containers you use can be sealed tightly. When air reaches food during storage, the result is loss of moisture accompanied by a change in flavor. This condition is called "freezer burn."

Allow some headspace in containers and jars for expansion during freezing. For dry pack, allow about ½ inch; for liquids or semi-liquids, allow from ½ to 1½ inches, depending upon the width of the neck opening of container.

Some foods can be frozen loose on baking sheets or in shallow pans. Immediately after they are frozen they must be packed in moisture-vaporproof containers or bags. After packaging, freeze foods at once. If there must be delay, keep packages in refrigerator.

Label foods accurately. Write on label the date, name of product, weight (meat), and number of servings. It is helpful to add the "maximum-storage date" so food will be used before that time.

Freeze and store foods at 0°F or lower. Put unfrozen foods in the fastest freezing area of your freezer or in direct contact with freezer walls or shelves and away from already frozen foods. Leave some space between packages to permit circulation of air.

Keep a thermometer in the storage compartment and make sure the temperature remains at zero or below. Ice or snow inside the packages usually indicates fluctuations of temperatures above zero.

Foods frozen first should be used first. Always remember that freezing retards bacterial and enzymatic action but it cannot stop it entirely.

To help you with a normal turnover of foods in the freezer, set up a record or "checking account." Use a wall chart or book and as food is put into the freezer, record it. Then as packages are removed, check them off the record.

Refreezing completely thawed food is not recommended. Uncooked fruits and vegetables suffer loss of color, flavor, and texture even if thawed for a short time. Refreezing causes further loss of quality. However, if ice crystals remain in partially thawed fruits and vegetables it is probably safe to refreeze them. Completely thawed fruit and fruit juice concentrates which have reached room temperature may still be safe unless fermentation has already started making them inedible.

If prepared foods containing milk, eggs, fish, and meat have not thawed completely, they may be safe to use if they are thoroughly heated before serving. Meats, poultry, and fish which have a normal odor are usually safe to use. When in doubt, discard.

The final decision on whether or not to refreeze should be based on the temperature of the thawed food as measured with a reliable thermometer. If the temperature of the food has risen about 40°F, discard it. According to the United States Department of Agriculture, "No health hazard is involved if the temperature of the food has not risen above ordinary refrigerator temperatures."

Maximum Time Limits

General time limits (in months except as noted) for storing frozen foods at 0°F or lower.

Baked and Cooked Foods

Breads, yeast, baked	2 to 3
bakery (in original wrap)	less than 1
quick, baked	1 to 3
unbaked	2 weeks
rolls, baked	2 to 3
brown and serve	2 to 3
unbaked	less than 1
Cakes, frosted	1 to 2
unfrosted	2 to 3
batters	less than 1
cupcakes	2 to 3
fruitcakes	12
Cookies, baked	9
dough	9
Pies, baked	2 to 3
unbaked	3 to 4
chiffon	1
pastry shells	2
Sandwiches	less than 1
Stews, soups, prepared main dishes	2 to 3
Leftover cooked foods	1

Fruits and Vegetables	8 to 12

Dairy Products

Creamery butter, Cheddar cheese	4 to 5
Cottage cheese (not creamed)	4 to 6
Cream (40%)	3 to 4
whipped	1
Eggs, whole and yolks	12
whites	9
Ice cream	1 to 2
Milk (homogenized)	1

Fish and Shellfish

Fish, lean	6 to 8
fatty	3 to 4
salmon	2 to 3
Shellfish	4 to 6
shrimp, cooked, peeled	2 to 3
cooked, unpeeled	4 to 6
Game	8 to 18
Game Birds	8 to 12

Poultry

Chicken, whole	6 to 8
cut up	4 to 6
giblets	1 to 3
Duckling, turkey	6 to 8
Goose	3 to 4

Meats

Fresh, beef	6 to 12
veal	6 to 9
lamb	6 to 9
pork	3 to 6
ground beef, veal, lamb	3 to 4
ground pork	1 to 3
variety meats	3 to 4
Smoked ham, whole	2
Corned beef	2 weeks
Cooked, leftover	2 to 3
meat pies	3
Swiss steak	3
stews	3 to 4
Prepared meat dinners	2 to 6

Nuts

Salted	3
Unsalted	9 to 12

FREEZING FRUITS

Fruits including berries are prepared for freezing in one of three ways—packed dry with no sugar; with dry sugar; or with a sugar syrup (or a combination of sugar syrup and corn syrup).

Generally, the natural color and flavor are better retained if fruits are sweetened before freezing. However, there are a few fruits that freeze satisfactorily without sweetening and are used for pies, jam and jelly-making, and for special diets. Among them are blueberries, cranberries, pineapple, raspberries, and rhubarb. To freeze them, rinse and drain off excess water by spreading them on absorbent paper so they will not freeze in a solid mass. Then pack in moisture-vaporproof containers.

Dry-sugar pack—Sprinkle sugar over the fruit as it is put into the freezer container, coating the fruit well. Or mix the fruit and sugar together lightly in a bowl before filling containers.

The most commonly used ratio is 4 cups fruit to 1 cup sugar. For a sweeter product, use 3 cups fruit to 1 cup sugar. For a less sweet product, use 5 cups fruit to 1 cup sugar.

Syrup-pack—This method of sweetening is good from the standpoint of completely covering the fruit.

To prepare the syrup, combine sugar with water and stir until sugar is dissolved. Chill syrup thoroughly before using. About 1 cup syrup is needed for a 1 pound package of fruit.

Amounts of Sugar and Water Needed for Syrups

Syrup	Cups Sugar	Cups Water
Light (30%)	2	4
Medium (40%)	3-3½	4
Heavy (50%)	4-5	4

If you wish to substitute a dry-sugar pack for a sugar syrup, the following ratios of fruit and sugar, which closely correspond to the above syrup concentration, will be a helpful guide:

30% syrup—5 cups fruit to 1 cup sugar
40% syrup—4 cups fruit to 1 cup sugar
50% syrup—3 cups fruit to 1 cup sugar

If you wish to use corn syrup in combination with a sugar syrup, substitute ⅓ of the sugar in the above amounts with light corn syrup.

Preventing Discoloration of Fruits

There are several ways to prevent discoloration of apples, apricots, peaches, pears, and other fruits. The use of ascorbic acid is the recommended method. It is available in powdered or crystalline form and may be purchased at drugstores and locker plants. Use 1½ to 2 teaspoons for each gallon of chilled syrup and add just before using the syrup.

Commercially prepared mixtures containing some ascorbic acid are also available. They usually cost less than pure ascorbic acid, but a greater amount is needed to prevent discoloration. Follow package directions for their use.

Citric acid (or lemon juice) alone or in combination with ascorbic acid may be used for treating some fruits, but it is not as effective as ascorbic acid. Citric acid is available in powdered or crystalline form. Use ¼ teaspoonful per quart of water.

If using lemon juice, use 1 teaspoon per quart of water. Let the fruit stand in the acidified water for 2 minutes, then drain thoroughly before packaging with the syrup.

Preparing Fruits

Apples (sliced)—Wash, pare, core, and slice about ½ inch thick. To prevent discoloration during preparation, slice apples into a salt solution (1½ tablespoons salt for each quart water). When all the apples are sliced, rinse in cold water and drain thoroughly. To prevent discoloration during freezing, scald the apples in live steam for about 2 minutes. If apples are quite soft, add calcium chloride to water used for scalding (1 tablespoon for each 2 quarts water). Cool immediately in cold running water and drain. If apples are to be used for pies, the amount of dry sugar needed may be added before packaging.

A second method of preventing discoloration is to submerge the slices in a sodium bisulfite-water solution (1½ teaspoons per gallon cold water) for 5 minutes. Mix the solution in an earthenware, glass, stainless steel, or enameled container. Drain slices thoroughly and pack with or without sugar. For the sugar pack, sprinkle ½ cup sugar over each quart (1¼ pounds) of apple slices. For the syrup pack, use a 40% syrup with ½ teaspoon ascorbic acid added for each quart of syrup.

Apples (baked whole), Applesauce—Prepare as for serving; cool thoroughly. Put into containers and freeze immediately.

Apricots—Wash, peel, halve, and pit. Add dry sugar or 40% syrup which contains ascorbic acid.

Blackberries, boysenberries, raspberries, loganberries, dewberries, youngberries—Wash, discarding soft, mushy, and underripe fruit. Drain in a colander or on absorbent towels. For use in desserts, put berries into freezer containers and cover with 40% or 50% syrup. Or mix gently with dry sugar in a flat pan (¾ cup sugar per quart berries). For use in pies and other cooked products, sweeten with sugar or freeze unsweetened.

Blueberries, elderberries, huckleberries—Wash, sort, and drain, discarding stems and underripe berries. For use in fruit cups and other desserts, cover with cold 40% syrup. For use in pies, muffins, and other cooked products, freeze unsweetened.

Cherries—Wash, sort, stem, drain, and pit cherries. (If cherries are sweet, pitting is unnecessary.) Sweeten tart cherries for fruit pies with ¾ to 1 cup sugar per quart of pitted fruit. Pack sweet cherries directly into containers and cover with 40% syrup which contains 1 teaspoon ascorbic acid for each 4 quarts of syrup.

Cranberries—Wash, sort, and stem, discarding imperfect berries. Drain. Pack dry; no sugar is needed.

Cranberries purchased in sealed moisture-vaporproof bags may be frozen immediately. When ready to use, rinse the frozen berries in cold water and drain. Use as you would fresh berries. Thawing is unnecessary before chopping or grinding for preparations such as cranberry relish.

Citrus fruits (grapefruit, oranges)—Freeze firm, tree-ripened fruit. Wash and peel; divide into sections; remove all membrane and seeds (see *page 356*). Or slice oranges, if desired. Drain off the juice and sweeten it with dry sugar. Pack fruit into containers and pour sweetened juice over it. Or mix the juice with a 50% syrup, to which has been added ½ teaspoon ascorbic acid for each quart syrup, just before pouring over fruit in containers.

Grapes—Wash, sort, stem, and drain. If used for fruit cups, remove seeds and pack whole in 40% syrup. If grapes are to be used for jelly-making or jam, pack unsweetened.

Melons—Wash, halve, and remove seeds; cut into slices, cubes, or balls of uniform size. Pack into containers and cover with 30% syrup. If desired, pack cantaloupe balls with whole seedless grapes and cover with orange juice.

Peaches—Freeze only peaches ripe enough for immediate eating. To remove peel, plunge fruit into boiling water, then into cold running water. If fruit is ripe, the peel will slip off easily. Halve the fruit, remove pit with a spoon, and slice halves directly into containers which contain a 40% syrup. (Start with ½ cup syrup for a 1-pint container.) When container is filled, press fruit down and add more syrup if needed to cover fruit. To prevent darkening of the peaches, add ascorbic acid to syrup (½ teaspoon per quart) just before pouring over fruit. To keep fruit submerged in the syrup, place crumpled waxed paper on top of it. If desired, peaches may be sugar-packed, mixing dry sugar with ascorbic acid powder. Follow directions on package. Mix ⅔ cup sugar with each quart (1½ pounds) prepared peaches.

Pineapple—Freeze ripe pineapple of good flavor. Pare, remove "eyes," and core. Slice, dice, crush, or cut into wedges. Pack without sugar or cover with 30% or 40% syrup.

Plums, Prunes—Sort, wash, halve, and remove pits. Pack into containers and cover with 40% syrup containing ¾ to 1 teaspoon ascorbic acid for each 2 quarts syrup. Or sweeten fruit with sugar and pack.

Rhubarb—Wash, remove leaves, and cut stalks into 1-inch pieces. Pack unsweetened for pies, or sweeten with dry sugar, mixing 1 pound sugar with each 4 pounds of cut rhubarb. To help retain color and flavor, heat rhubarb in boiling water for 1 minute, cool quickly in icy cold water, drain thoroughly, and package with or without sugar. To freeze rhubarb sauce, prepare as you would for immediate use, package, and freeze.

Strawberries—Rinse in water with ice, then sort, hull, and halve the large berries. Small berries may be frozen whole, but cutting them helps preserve color and flavor. Gently mix with sugar, using ½ to ¾ cup with each quart berries. Medium-sized whole berries may be covered with a 40% or 50% syrup. For special diets, place whole berries in freezer containers and cover with water containing 1 teaspoon ascorbic acid for each quart water.

Juices (apple, berry, cherry, grape, plum, rhubarb)—Simmer fruits for 5 minutes in just enough water to prevent sticking. Drain through a sieve or a jelly bag, if clear juice is desired. Sweeten to taste, or, if juices are to be used later for making jelly, freeze without sugar. When freezing fruit juices, work quckly to save vitamin C. Exposure to air destroys this valuable nutrient.

To freeze citrus juices (orange, grapefruit, lemon, or lime), extract juices, strain, and sweeten to taste, or freeze without sugar.

Thawing Fruits

Thaw fruits in their containers in refrigerator, at room temperature, or under cold running water until pieces can be separated, but are still icy cold.

FREEZING VEGETABLES

Use young, barely mature vegetables. Overmature vegetables become starchy and do not freeze well.

Wash thoroughly in cold running water. Sort, trim, and cut vegetables into uniform pieces.

Blanch or scald in boiling water or live steam. For home freezing, the boiling water method is generally used. However, blanching in steam is recommended by some authorities. (For directions, see U.S. Department of Agriculture bulletins.)

Leafy vegetables should always be scalded in boiling water so that leaves heat uniformly and do not mat. On the other hand, steam-blanching is considered slightly better for broccoli.

To blanch in boiling water, use about 4 quarts boiling water for each 1 pound batch of vegetables. Put vegetables into a wire basket or cheesecloth bag and immerse in rapidly boiling water. Cover kettle and immediately start counting the blanching time. If water takes more than 60 to 75 seconds to return to boiling, reduce the amount of vegetables being blanched at one time.

Chill thoroughly in water with ice. Add ice cubes to keep water very cold. Chill vegetables about as long as they have been blanched. Drain thoroughly and package. Seal packages, label, and freeze at once.

Preparing Vegetables

The scalding or blanching times given below are for the boiling water method unless otherwise designated.

Asparagus — Freeze only the tender portion. Thoroughly wash the stalks. Dirt tends to lodge under scales. If asparagus is very gritty, snip off the scales or lift them to clean thoroughly. Sort stalks according to thickness and freeze them whole (cut to the size of the container) or cut in 1-inch pieces. Scald 2 to 3 minutes. Chill in icy cold water, drain, and package.

Beans, lima — Shell, wash, and discard discolored, split, white beans. Sort into large and small sizes. Scald 2 minutes for large beans, 1 minute for small. Chill in icy cold water, drain, and package.

Beans, snap — Wash, snip off ends, and sort into two or three sizes. Small beans may be packed whole, medium-sized beans sliced lengthwise (French style), and large ones cut in 1-inch lengths. Scald 1½ minutes for whole and French style, 2½ minutes for cut beans. Chill in icy cold water; package.

Broccoli — Trim off large leaves, wilted parts, and woody stem ends. Wash thoroughly. If there is evidence of insect damage, cover stalks with salted water (4 teaspoons salt to 4 cups water); let stand 30 minutes. Rinse in running cold water. Separate the heads into suitable pieces for serving. Slice very large stalks lengthwise into uniform pieces about 1½ inches in diameter. Scald in steam about 5 minutes, in boiling water about 3 minutes. Chill in icy cold water, drain, and package.

Brussels sprouts — Wash thoroughly; trim coarse leaves. If there is evidence of insect damage, let stand in salted water (see *Broccoli*). If sprouts are not uniform in size, sort as to size. Scald small sprouts 3 minutes, large ones 4 minutes. Chill, drain, and package.

Cauliflower — Trim off leaves. To remove foreign matter from heads of cauliflower, let stand in salted water (see *Broccoli*). Separate heads into florets and scald as for broccoli. Chill in icy cold water, drain, and package.

Corn-on-cob — Use freshly picked, young, tender ears. Husk, remove silk, wash, trim tips, and sort ears according to size. Scald 7 minutes for small ears, 9 minutes for medium, and 11 minutes for large. Chill in icy cold water. Pack in cartons or wrap ears individually in aluminum foil.

Corn, whole kernel — Prepare as for corn-on-cob, scalding ears 3 to 7 minutes, depending on size. After chilling, drain and cut kernels from cob. Avoid cutting into cob. Package and freeze.

Eggplant — Pare and slice or dice. Scald 4 minutes in boiling water containing 4½ teaspoons citric acid (or ½ cup lemon juice) per gallon of water. Chill in icy cold water, drain, and package.

Greens (spinach, kale, beet tops, mustard greens, etc.) — Use only tender, young leaves free from woody or fibrous stems. Wash thoroughly to remove all dirt and sand. Scald 3 minutes in 170°F water. Stir occasionally during scalding to keep leaves from matting. Chill in icy cold water, drain thoroughly, chop, if desired, and package.

Mushrooms — Sort for size. Wash; cut off stem ends. Slice mushrooms larger than 1 inch in diameter. To prevent darkening, before scalding mushrooms immerse them in a solution of 1 teaspoon lemon juice (or 1½ teaspoons citric acid) and 2 cups cold water for 5 minutes. Scalding by live steam is recommended — 3½ minutes for small, whole mushrooms, and 3 minutes for sliced mushrooms. Chill in icy cold water, drain, and package.

If desired, mushrooms may be cooked in hot butter or margarine about 5 minutes, then cooled quickly and packaged.

Peppers, green or red — Wash, cut out stems, cut peppers into halves, and remove seeds and fiber. If desired, cut into strips or rings. Scald 2 to 3 minutes. Chill in icy cold water, drain, and package.

Peppers to be used in uncooked foods are best frozen without scalding. No headspace is necessary when packaging.

If peppers are to be stuffed, freeze them whole without scalding.

Peas, green, blackeyed — Shell peas and discard

overmature ones. Scald 1 minute for tender, immature peas, 2½ minutes for mature ones. Chill in icy cold water, drain, and package.

Squash, summer—Wash and cut into ½ inch slices. Scald 3 minutes. Chill in icy cold water, drain, and package.

Squash, winter, and pumpkin—Wash, cut into pieces, remove seeds and fiber. Cook until tender in pressure cooker or in 350°F oven. Scoop out pulp from rind and mash it or put through a food mill. Chill by setting the pan in water with ice. Package.

When freezing pumpkin to be used later for pie filling, the spices may be added before freezing.

Cooking Frozen Vegetables

Do not thaw vegetables before cooking (corn-on-cob is an exception). Cook covered in a small amount of boiling, salted water until just tender. They will cook in about one half the time required for the garden-fresh product since the scalding or blanching treatment previous to packaging them was a short precooking process.

Vegetables such as squash and pumpkin which have been entirely cooked before freezing should be reheated for serving in the top of a double boiler over boiling water or heated in the oven.

FREEZING MEATS

Freezing is the simplest and safest method of preserving meat and a highly satisfactory one, provided the basic rules of freezing are carefully observed.

Freeze only high quality meats. Meat from young beef which has been aged is recommended. Lamb and game are also improved in flavor and texture if allowed to age.

Package meat in portions to fit family needs. Be sure it is cut according to the way you plan to cook it. Remove the butcher's paper from meat purchased from the market. Also remove any moisture-absorbing labels or backing boards. These may give an off-flavor to frozen meat. Trim off excess fat and remove bones, when possible, to avoid wasting storage space. (Make soup stock from the bones and freeze it for future use.) Trim sharp edges from bones which cannot be removed from meat. (Sharp edges could puncture the outer wrap.) Wrap meat tightly in moisture-vaporproof material—waxed locker paper (use double thickness), freezer foil, or plastic film. When wrapping steaks, chops, and meat patties, place a layer of the wrap between individual pieces of meat to make separation easy without completely thawing out the meat when ready to use it.

Use enough wrapping material to allow for folding the edges down at least three times. Place the meat in center of the wrap, bring the two edges together above the meat, and fold down in ½ to 1 inch folds until the paper is tight against the meat. Fold the ends in the same manner. Press the wrap firmly against meat to squeeze out as much air in package as possible. Seal securely with freezer tape and label with the date, kind of meat, cut, and number of servings (or the weight). Freeze meat quickly and store at zero degrees or lower.

Thawing Frozen Meats

To completely thaw a large roast at room tempera-

DRUGSTORE WRAP FOR MEATS

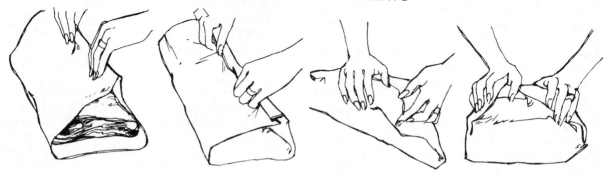

1. Place meat near center of sheet of freezer paper. Bring edges of paper together over meat.

2. Fold the paper over once; then fold again so that the second fold is tight against the meat.

3. Make top folds evenly. Smooth ends close to meat and fold into triangles. Invert package.

4. Fold ends under package away from top fold. Seal with freezer tape. Label and date.

ture allow 2 to 3 hours per pound; in refrigerator allow 4 to 7 hours per pound.

Thawing meat in water is recommended only if it is to be cooked in liquid.

To thaw a 1-inch steak at room temperature allow 2 to 4 hours; in refrigerator allow 12 hours.

Cooking Frozen Meats

Frozen meat which has been completely thawed may be cooked in the same way as meat not frozen. This is also true of meat cooked without thawing, except that a longer time is required.

Frozen roasts require a third to a half again as long for cooking as roasts which have been thawed.

The additional time for cooking steaks and chops will vary according to surface area and thickness of meat as well as the broiling temperature.

Broil thick frozen steaks, chops, and ground meat patties further from the heat than thawed ones so that the meat will be cooked to the desired degree of doneness without browning too much on the surface. If pieces of meat are dipped in egg and coated with crumbs or dipped in a batter before cooking, thaw the meat partially so that the coating will adhere to meat.

Panbroil frozen steaks and chops in a very hot skillet so that the meat has a chance to brown well before thawing on surface. (Thawing retards browning.) When sufficiently browned, reduce heat and continue cooking, turning meat occasionally so that it will cook in the center without becoming too brown on the outside.

FREEZING POULTRY

All poultry for freezing must be thoroughly cleaned and prepared so that they are ready for cooking when removed from freezer. Freeze whole or disjointed (cut in pieces).

To prepare whole birds, lock the wings and fold neck skin neatly over wings. If leg ends are sharp, wrap them to prevent puncturing the outer wrap. Then push the legs down and forward and tie them compactly against body of bird. Wrap the bird in moisture-vaporproof sheet wrapping, or use a plastic bag. Press out as much air as possible and seal tightly with freezer tape.

To prepare disjointed poultry, flatten the pieces and place double thicknesses of wrapping material between them so they can be easily separated while poultry is still frozen. If leg ends are sharp, wrap them. Then wrap and seal the pieces the same as for whole birds.

Package giblets (except livers) separately and use within three months. Package livers and use within one month.

Turkeys usually are packaged whole. However, halves and quarters of very large birds are often more convenient than a whole bird and freeze well.

Do not stuff poultry before it is frozen. A stuffed bird makes an excellent place for harmful bacteria to grow either while thawing at room temperature or in the oven before the internal temperature of the bird reaches cooking temperature. The stuffing is best if put into the bird just before it is put into the oven for roasting. This does not apply to commercially stuffed frozen birds however. They are perfectly safe to use as they are frozen under carefully controlled conditions which cannot be duplicated in the home.

To freeze leftover cooked poultry, cut meat from the bones and package in slices or pieces. Freezing slices in leftover gravy or cream sauce keeps air away from the meat and helps to retain its flavor.

Thawing Frozen Poultry

Thaw poultry in wrappings in the refrigerator or, if package is airtight, under running cold water. For a turkey, allow two to three days for a large (18 pounds or over) bird to thaw in refrigerator: allow several hours in running cold water.

Cook all poultry as soon as thawed and while extremely cold. Do not refreeze the uncooked poultry.

FREEZING GAME

When freezing game of any kind, be sure to check regulations in your state concerning length of time game may legally be stored and amount of each kind you may store.

In general, freeze game birds and animals just as you would either poultry or meat.

FREEZING FISH

Most fish freeze satisfactorily provided it is handled quickly and kept cold until frozen. (Fish is a highly perishable food.) If possible, freeze it on the day it is caught. Clean fish as you would for immediate serving. Freeze small ones whole, large ones in steaks and fillets.

To prepare lean fish (such as perch and halibut), a salt brine dip is recommended (½ cup salt dissolved in 1 quart cold water). Dip fish in brine 20 seconds. This firms the fish and reduces leakage or drip when fish is thawed.

To prepare fat fish such as lake trout, pink salmon,

and mackerel, an ascorbic dip is recommended (2 teaspoons ascorbic acid to 1 quart cold water). Dip fish in the solution 1 minute.

To package fish, place double thicknesses of freezer wrap between each whole fish, fillet, or steak so they will separate easily before they are completely thawed. Put only enough fish for one meal in a package; wrap tightly in freezer wrap, seal with freezer tape, and label.

FREEZING SHELLFISH

To freeze oysters, clams, and scallops, rinse the sand from them before removing from shells; save the liquor. Wash shellfish in a salt brine (dissolve 1 cup salt in 1 quart cold water). Pack shellfish in their own liquor and freeze promptly.

To freeze crabs, remove the back shell (use only live crabs); eviscerate and wash them. Be sure to remove newly forming shell, a jelly-like substance which might discolor the body meat. Break the crabs in halves and cook them in boiling water for 15 minutes. Cool slightly and remove the meat, keeping the body meat and leg meat separate for packing. Pack the meat in freezer containers and cover with a salt brine (dissolve 1 tablespoon salt in 1 quart water). Seal and freeze promptly.

To freeze lobsters, drop them live in boiling salted water and cook 20 minutes. Lay them on their backs to cool. When cooled, remove edible meat from the shells. Package and freeze immediately.

To freeze shrimp, peel, clean and package. Or, if desired, freeze in the shell. (Cooking before freezing is not recommended as cooked shrimp has a tendency to toughen during storage.)

Thawing Frozen Fish and Shellfish

Thaw in wrappings in refrigerator and allow to thaw slowly. Fish may also be thawed at room temperature, but less leakage occurs with slow thawing. Once thawed, do not refreeze. Cook while still very cold.

Thaw seafood only long enough to separate it, then cook promptly.

FREEZING EGGS

Whole eggs—Gently mix whites and yolks (do not beat air into eggs). If used for desserts such as cake and custard, stir in 1 tablespoon sugar per cup eggs. If used for scrambling, omelets, or other kinds of cooking, stir in 1 teaspoon salt per cup eggs.

Yolks—Follow directions for whole eggs, increasing sugar or syrup to 2 tablespoons per cup. (Amount of salt remains the same.)

Whites—No special treatment is needed.

Thawing Frozen Eggs

Thaw in their container in refrigerator or at room temperature. Thawing can be hastened by placing watertight containers of frozen eggs in a pan of cold water. Thawed whole eggs and yolks should be used at once. Whites alone will remain fresh in refrigerator two or three days.

Using Frozen Eggs in Cooking

Frozen eggs may be substituted in any recipe requiring fresh eggs.

The thawed whites, beaten when they have reached room temperature, give just as good volume as fresh egg whites, making them suitable for angel cakes, meringues, and fluffy icings.

To estimate the amount of thawed yolks, whites, or whole eggs to use for fresh eggs, use the following measurements:

1 to 1½ tablespoons yolk—1 egg yolk
1½ to 2 tablespoon white—1 egg white
2½ to 3 tablespoons yolks and whites—1 egg

FREEZING DAIRY PRODUCTS

Butter—Overwrap the original waxed carton with aluminum foil or other freezer material. Butter is extremely sensitive to odors or flavors picked up from other foods, so be sure to use an odorproof wrap.

Cheese—Cottage cheese does not freeze very well. Cheddar-type cheeses may be frozen, but they have a tendency to crumble when thawed. Wrapped properly, they may be kept in the refrigerator for reasonable lengths of time so not much is gained by freezing them. Leftover grated or shredded cheese may be frozen, if desired.

Cream—Pasteurized cream with at least 40% butterfat may be frozen satisfactorily. For best results, add ⅓ cup sugar to 1 quart of cream before freezing. Cream may be frozen in the original carton if tightly sealed.

Mounds of whipped cream sweetened with confectioners' sugar may be frozen on a baking sheet, then wrapped and stored for as long as one month, to be used later for dessert topping. Mounds thaw quickly so place them on desserts just before serving.

Ice cream—One-half or one gallon cartons of ice cream are favorite items among store "specials." Freeze in original carton. When once opened, overwrap the carton with freezer wrap or put it into a plastic bag for extra protection. When purchased in gallon containers, it is advisable to repack the ice cream in several smaller containers before storing.

FREEZING BAKED PRODUCTS

Yeast breads, rolls, and coffee cakes—Use your favorite recipes. Prepare and bake yeast breads for freezing just as you would for immediate consumption. If preparing rolls for freezing, for best results use a generous amount of fat and sugar in recipe.

Cool baked products quickly, then wrap in aluminum foil or other moisture-vaporproof material. Overwrap commerically baked goods even though they are already packaged.

To prepare bread for serving, thaw the loaf in original wrap at room temperature, allowing 1 to 2 hours. If loaf is foil-wrapped, it may be heated in a 300°F oven, allowing 20 to 30 minutes.

Sliced bread may be toasted without thawing.

To prepare rolls for serving, thaw in original wrap at room temperature, allowing about 30 minutes; or place, unthawed and wrapped in foil, on baking sheet and heat in 250° to 300°F oven about 15 minutes.

To prepare coffee cake for serving, thaw at room temperature, allowing 1 to 2 hours depending upon size; or heat in oven (see rolls). If coffee cake is to be frosted, spread on frosting just before serving.

Quick breads—Biscuits, muffins, corn bread. doughnuts, nut breads, waffles, and popovers freeze well. When baked, cool product and wrap in moisture-vaporproof material. Use freezer foil if product is to be reheated in oven before serving.

Some quick breads, such as baking powder biscuits and muffins, are more satisfactorily frozen unbaked. They may be baked unthawed or thawed, allowing more time when baked in the frozen state.

Cakes—All kinds, including those made from mixes, may be frozen. If cakes are frosted, freeze the cake until frosting is set before wrapping. Butter frostings are best for freezing. Icings made with egg whites become frothy and spongy.

To prepare cakes for serving, thaw at room temperature. Unwrap frosted cakes; leave unfrosted cakes in wrapper. Cupcakes thaw in about 30 minutes, cake layers in 1 hour, loaf cakes in 2 to 3 hours.

Cookies (baked)—Cool, then package in sturdy containers (coffee or shortening cans are good). Pack in layers, separating each layer with sheet freezer wrap. Freeze fragile cookies; then wrap.

Thaw bar or crisp cookies in containers; unwrap others.

Cookie dough—For rolled cookies, cut out shapes from rolled dough and stack cutouts in layers, separating with sheet freezer wrap. When ready to use, place on cookie sheets and bake without thawing.

Shape refrigerator cookie dough into rolls and wrap in freezer foil. When ready to use, thaw the wrapped rolls of dough in refrigerator just enough to slice easily.

For drop cookies, drop the dough in mounds of desired size about ¼ inch apart on cookie sheets. Freeze until firm. Transfer mounds to containers, separating layers with sheet freezer wrap. Bake, unthawed, on cookie sheets.

If desired, cookie dough may be wrapped in a mass and frozen. When ready to use, thaw the dough until it can be handled easily, then prepare and bake as directed in the recipe.

Pies—In general, pies may be frozen baked or unbaked, whichever is more convenient. However, pies with fruit and berry fillings tend to have a crisper crust if frozen before baking.

Freezing custard-type and cream filled pies is not recommended. Meringue toppings should also be avoided as they toughen during freezing.

Fruit and mince pies—Prepare in the usual manner. If pie is to be frozen before baking, do not cut slits in top crust. (Do this before pie is put into oven.) To prevent soggy undercrust, brush it with melted fat, egg white, or spread inside of pie plate with a coating of 2 parts shortening creamed with 1 part flour. If using fresh fruit for pie filling, add lemon juice or ascorbic acid to the fruit to prevent darkening during freezing. If using frozen fruit, thaw it just enough to break apart. Thicken juice for filling with cornstarch or flour.

Chiffon pies—Prepare in the usual manner. Chill until filling is set before wrapping for freezing.

Pumpkin pie—Prepare and bake in usual manner; cool and wrap for freezing. If desired, filling may be prepared and frozen in containers. When ready to use, thaw filling, pour into unbaked pastry shell, and bake pie as usual.

To package pies, cool thoroughly (if they have been baked) and wrap in foil or other freezer material; slip pie into a plastic freezer bag, seal, and place in a flat carton for extra protection.

Pies that are too tender to wrap easily may be frozen until firm, then packaged immediately.

Covering a pie with an inverted paper plate before wrapping will help protect the top crust.

To prepare an unbaked pie for serving, remove the wrapping and bake, unthawed, in a 425° to 450°F oven 15 to 20 minutes; reduce oven temperature to 350° to 375°F and complete the baking.

To prepare a baked pie for serving, thaw, wrapped, at room temperature 1 to 1½ hours if it is to be served cold. Remove wrapping and place pie in a 375°F oven 35 to 50 minutes if served warm.

To freeze pastry, prepare as usual and shape into a ball; freeze in plastic freezer bag. Or roll out pastry into rounds 2 to 3 inches larger than pie plates or pans. Stack the rounds on a stiff cardboard circle with layers of waxed paper between the rounds. Overwrap with freezer wrap or slip pastry rounds into freezer bags and seal.

To freeze pie shells, prepare in the usual manner in pie plates or pans. Then freeze, whether baked or unbaked, before wrapping. Frozen unbaked pie shells may be removed from pie pans and stacked before wrapping, putting several layers of crumpled waxed paper between each frozen shell.

To use a frozen baked pie shell, remove the wrap and place shell in 375°F oven 10 minutes. Or thaw the shell in the wrap at room temperature.

To use an unbaked pie shell, unwrap and bake at 450°F 5 minutes, then prick pastry with tines of a fork and bake about 15 minutes.

To use frozen unrolled pie dough, thaw overnight in refrigerator, or thaw at room temperature, then roll out as desired.

FREEZING SANDWICHES

Making sandwiches in quantities when it is convenient or whenever you have filling ingredients on hand, is a wonderful timesaver for homemakers with lunchbox toters in the family. But keep in mind the fact that although all kinds of fresh bread freeze well, not all fillings do. The following are some filling ingredients which do freeze well: peanut butter; finely chopped nut meats; cooked egg yolk; sliced or ground cooked or canned chicken, turkey, and fish; sliced or ground cooked meat; dried chopped fruit; chopped or sliced olives; crushed pineapple. Suitable ingredients which may be used to hold filling mixture together are lemon, orange, or pineapple juice, milk, dairy sour cream, and applesauce. Use mayonnaise and salad dressings sparingly as they tend to separate when frozen. Avoid very moist fillings such as egg salad.

Also avoid raw chopped, grated, or sliced vegetables, as they lose their crispness when frozen. Such ingredients as tomato slices, lettuce, celery, and carrots should be added to sandwiches just before eating.

Spread each slice of bread for sandwiches generaously with softened butter or margarine. This will keep the filling from soaking into bread. For variety, season the butter with prepared horseradish or mustard, or chili sauce.

Wrap the filled sandwiches with moisture-vapor-proof material, each in its own individual wrap.

Freeze sandwiches no longer than two weeks. Thaw at room temperature in their wrappings.

FREEZING COOKED FOODS

Prepare your favorite recipes in double or triple amounts so there will be enough food to freeze after a family meal. Undercook rather than overcook foods that must be heated before serving. Meat should be tender but still firm and vegetables crisptender.

Cool foods quickly after cooking by placing the utensil in water with ice. Then package and freeze. Omit potatoes from stews and meat pies as they become mushy; add them before serving.

Avoid hard-cooked egg whites in frozen dishes as they change in texture and develop an off flavor. Use as little fat as possible in gravies and sauces. Fats have a tendency to separate, but if used in smaller quantities they will recombine with the sauce when stirred while reheating. Fried foods are apt to become rancid after one or two months storage. Use seasonings sparingly as some of them change in flavor during storage (pepper, especially, gets stronger). Add most of the seasoning when reheating the food for serving.

Pack foods to be baked or reheated in oven in heat-resistant casseroles or baking dishes or foil freezer boxes so they may go directly from freezer to the oven.

Package in amounts suitable for family servings. Cooked foods, once reheated, should not be refrozen.

Pack cooked food which is to be reheated on surface of the range in straight-sided containers. To remove the food before thawing completely, dip container into warm water a few seconds and the food will slip out into saucepan or double boiler. Some containers may be peeled off and the contents removed.

OUTDOOR COOKING

Grilling outdoors is a very ancient way of cooking food. It's a relatively easy way to entertain a large group, and besides, it's lots of fun for everyone. Outdoor cooking is a man's art and one distaff job that women are quite willing to relinquish to the men.

The essentials for grilling are few — a grill (of which there are many types), the fuel, the fire-starter, the tools, the food for the feast, and, if possible, an imaginative chef.

Fuel — Charcoal lumps or briquets are preferred by most experts. At times you may want to use fruit wood or hardwood such as apple or hickory chips. Dampened hickory chips tossed on a charcoal fire just before the meat is placed on the grill add an interesting flavor. Soft woods like pine are undesirable as they give food a tarry, sooty coating and also produce an unsatisfactory bed of coals.

To build a fire — Start with a bed of charcoal 2 to 3 inches deep. (It should last the entire cooking period.) Apply a liquid or solid-type lighter and ignite it. Start grilling when the coals have burned to a gray color with a ruddy glow underneath. (This requires about 30 minutes.) Another way to start the fire is by beginning the bed with a little paper and kindling, then adding a small amount of charcoal. When it is burning, build the entire bed as directed.

To control heat — The distance from the top of the coals to the food helps determine the degree of heat. More distance makes less heat and slower cooking. Many grills have adjustable fireboxes that can raise or lower the bed of coals. Hoods built on the back of some grills intensify the heat. Using this type of grill shortens cooking times slightly.

Length of cooking periods will vary with the size of firebox, degree of heat, amount and direction of the wind, and the type of grill used.

During cooking, when flare-ups occur (caused by fat dripping onto the coals), douse flames with a basting tube filled with water, or a water pistol.

Grill equipment — Besides the grill, there are many items available — some necessary, some useful, and others merely colorful gadgets. Useful additions are items such as: long-handled tools with heat-resistant handles (forks, spoons, turners, tongs), asbestos or well-padded mitts, a baster (which doubles as a douser if fat flares in the fire), a wooden cutting board, a sharp knife, a pot for a marinade or basting sauce, a basting brush, and paper towels. Long metal skewers, a steak broiler, and a spit attachment for the grill all aid in developing one's outdoor culinary skills.

The chef who wants to grill out-of-doors, but demands all the conveniences which are associated with indoor broiling, might find that preparing a fire of glowing charcoal is too much of a challenge to his patience. For him there is available the gas-fired grill with its easily controllable flame and special ceramic briquets which provide perfect radiant heat in a hurry and can be used again and again.

Marinades & Sauces

CAPER MARINADE: Mix *½ cup cider vinegar, ½ cup sweet pickle liquid, ⅓ cup olive oil, 1 tablespoon dry mustard, 1 teaspoon salt, ½ teaspoon pepper, and 2 tablespoons capers.* Marinate lamb cubes for kabobs 6 hours.

CLARET MARINADE: Mix *¾ cup olive oil, ¾ cup claret, 3 large cloves garlic, crushed, 4 drops Tabasco, ½ teaspoon dry mustard, 1 teaspoon ground nutmeg, and ¼ cup finely chopped pimiento-stuffed* *olives.* Marinate steaks or beef cubes for kabobs 6 hours or overnight, turning occasionally.

HERB MARINADE: Blend *⅔ cup cooking or salad oil, ¾ cup lemon juice, 1 tablespoon prepared horseradish, 1 teaspoon seasoned salt, ⅛ teaspoon cayenne pepper, ½ teaspoon crushed savory, ½ teaspoon crushed tarragon leaves,* and *1 large clove garlic,* crushed. Mix well. Marinate raw shrimp several hours or overnight.

PINEAPPLE MARINADE: Blend *1 cup honey, 1 cup unsweetened pineapple juice, 2 cans (8½ ounces each) crushed pineapple, ⅔ cup red wine vinegar, 2 tablespoons soy sauce, 6 large cloves garlic,* crushed, *2 tablespoons ground ginger, 1 tablespoon ground coriander, 1 teaspoon salt,* and *½ cup chopped onion* in a large skillet. Cook over medium heat, stirring occasionally, about 40 minutes, or until thickened. Reserve 1 cup to heat and serve with ribs. Marinate ribs (4 pounds) 24 hours.

BUTTER SAUCE: Heat *1 cup butter, 2 tablespoons lemon juice, ¼ teaspoon salt, ¼ teaspoon paprika, ⅛ teaspoon black pepper,* and *¼ cup chopped parsley* until butter is melted. Brush lobster tails with sauce. Serve remaining sauce hot with lobster.

MINT SAUCE: Stir together *½ cup water, ¼ cup lemon juice, 12 fresh mint leaves,* crushed, *2 split cloves garlic, 2 tablespoons chopped onion,* and *1*

teaspoon rosemary. Let stand overnight. Brush lamb chops with sauce.

ORANGE BASTING SAUCE: In a small saucepan mix *2 tablespoons light corn syrup, 1 teaspoon garlic salt, 1 teaspoon dry mustard, ½ teaspoon monosodium glutamate, ½ cup orange juice, few drops Tabasco,* and *2 tablespoons butter or margarine.* Heat until butter melts; stir to blend and brush chicken or pork while sauce is still warm. (If using chicken, coat pieces with cooking oil and let stand about 30 minutes.)

TOMATO BASTING SAUCE: Lightly brown *½ cup chopped onion* in *1 tablespoon melted butter.* Blend in *1 cup ketchup, ¾ cup cider vinegar, ½ cup water, ½ cup light molasses, 1 envelope garlic salad dressing mix,* and *2 beef bouillon cubes;* bring to boiling. Simmer 15 minutes. Brush chicken or scored frankfurters with sauce.

NOTE: *Sake* may be substituted for vinegar and *French salad dressing mix* for garlic dressing mix.

PIQUANT TOMATO SAUCE: Mix *1 cup ketchup, ¼ cup lemon juice, 1 tablespoon soy sauce, 2 tablespoons brown sugar, 1 tablespoon prepared horseradish mustard, 1 tablespoon grated onion, 1½ teaspoons salt, ½ teaspoon black pepper, ¼ teaspoon oregano, ¼ teaspoon Tabasco,* and *1 split clove garlic.* Simmer 10 minutes. Brush on ribs.

MEATS ON THE GRILL

How to Grill Meats

STEAKS (Porterhouse, sirloin, T-bone, or rib): Have steaks cut 1½ inches thick. Marinate in *Claret Marinade, page 665,* if desired. Grill 3 inches from coals (brushing frequently with marinade, if used). When well browned, turn and season or continue brushing. Total grilling time: 12 minutes for rare. For medium or well done, increase distance from coals and grilling time.

KABOBS (beef or lamb): Marinate meat cubes, 1 to 1½ inches, in *Claret Marinade* (for beef) or *Caper Marinade* (for lamb), *page 665.* Thread marinated meat cubes onto skewers. Place rather close together for rare meat or separate slightly for well done. Grill about 3 inches from coals 15 to 20 minutes, or until tender and browned, turning and brushing frequently with marinade.

SPARERIBS AND BACK RIBS: Marinate in *Pineapple Marinade, above,* if desired. Place on a rack in a large shallow pan. Cover with aluminum foil; partially cook in a 350°F oven 30 minutes. (If done in advance and refrigerated, return to room temperature.) To grill, place 6 to 8 inches from coals and brush with marinade or sauce. Grill 40 to 50 minutes, or until meat is done, turning and brushing frequently. (To grill ribs without precooking, grill over a drip pan about 2 hours, turning occasionally. Turn and brush frequently with marinade or sauce last 40 minutes.)

SINGLE RIBS FOR APPETIZERS: Have meat dealer saw spareribs (unnecessary for back ribs) across rib bones, if desired. Precook as directed above. Cut into individual ribs. Arrange in a broiler basket and brush with marinade or sauce. Grill 6 inches from coals 40 to 50 minutes, turning and brushing frequently.

LAMB CHOPS: Have chops cut 1½ inches thick. Grill 4 inches from coals (brushing often with *Mint Sauce, page 666,* if desired). When well browned, turn and season or continue brushing. Total grilling time: 16 minutes for medium done.

FRANKFURTERS: Score frankfurters and grill 3 inches from coals 5 to 6 minutes, or until browned, turning frequently (and brushing with *Tomato Basting Sauce, page 666,* or bottled barbecue sauce, if desired).

GRILLED BEEF TENDERLOIN

2 env. cheese-garlic salad dressing mix	1 beef tenderloin (3 to 4 lbs.)
¼ cup salad oil	

1. Blend salad dressing mix with oil.
2. Brush tenderloin generously with dressing mixture. Place the meat on a greased grill 4 to 6 inches from the coals.
3. Grill 25 to 35 minutes, or until the tenderloin reaches the desired degree of doneness, turning frequently so that the meat cooks and browns evenly on all sides.
4. To serve, cut into thin slices.   6 TO 8 SERVINGS

MARINATED BLACK PEPPER STEAK
The amount of crushed peppercorns used depends entirely on personal taste. As a guide, try two teaspoonfuls for each side of a large steak.

Purchase a *sirloin steak,* cut 1½ to 2 inches thick. (Allow ¾ to 1 pound per person.) Put steak in a large shallow pan and cover with *Steak Marinade, below;* allow to marinate several hours or overnight, turning occasionally. Before grilling, remove steak from marinade and press coarsely crushed *peppercorns* liberally into both sides of steak. Grill 3 to 4 inches from coals, allowing about 15 minutes for total grilling time; turn once. (Test doneness by slit-

ting meat near bone and noting color of meat.) To serve, cut steak diagonally into thin slices.

STEAK MARINADE

1 cup red wine vinegar	¼ teaspoon salt
½ cup salad oil	¼ teaspoon marjoram
⅓ cup firmly packed brown sugar	¼ teaspoon rosemary
	¾ cup chopped onion
Few drops Tabasco	1 clove garlic, minced

Combine all ingredients in a screw-top jar. Shake well to blend.   ABOUT 2 CUPS

GRILLED STEAK WITH GARDEN BUTTER SAUCE

Place *4 pounds beef steak,* such as sirloin, porterhouse, T-bone, or rib, cut 1½ inches thick, on a lightly greased grill about 3 inches from coals. Grill about 6 minutes, or until first side is browned. Turn with tongs and season with *salt* and *black pepper.* Grill second side about 6 minutes, or until done. (To test doneness, slit meat near bone and note color of meat.) Season second side of steak. Remove from grill to serving plate and slice. Serve with *Garden Butter Sauce, below.*   ABOUT 4 SERVINGS

GARDEN BUTTER SAUCE: Melt ¼ *cup butter* in a skillet or saucepan. Add ¼ *cup finely chopped parsley, 2 tablespoons finely chopped watercress, 2 tablespoons finely chopped celery tops, ¼ teaspoon crushed tarragon,* and *1 cup beef bouillon* (dissolve 1 beef bouillon cube in 1 cup boiling water); mix well. Add *10 sliced pimiento-stuffed olives* and stir gently. Set skillet on edge of grill to keep warm.   ABOUT 1½ CUPS

HERBED BEEF STEAK

Sprinkle *steak* generously on both sides with *garlic salt.* Pour ¼ *cup cooking or salad oil* into a shallow pan or dish. Put steak into pan and turn to coat with oil. Allow to stand 1 hour, turning occasionally. Grill to desired degree of doneness, brushing frequently with *Herbed Vinegar, below.*

HERBED VINEGAR: Combine ½ *cup tarragon vinegar,* ½ *teaspoon dill weed,* crushed, ¼ *teaspoon thyme,* crushed, and *1 tablespoon finely chopped parsley.*

FULL-FLAVORED STEAK

To marinate is to glamorize the flavor of the king of American meats . . . steak.

2½ tablespoons brown sugar
1½ tablespoons sugar
1 tablespoon ground ginger
1 clove garlic, crushed
½ cup soy sauce
1 tablespoon tarragon vinegar
3 lbs. beef steak (sirloin, porterhouse, T-bone, or rib), cut 1½ inches thick

1. Combine the sugars, ginger, garlic, soy sauce, and vinegar.
2. Put meat into a large shallow dish and pour soy sauce mixture over meat. Allow to marinate at least 30 minutes, basting frequently and turning once or twice.
3. When ready to grill, remove meat from marinade, reserving marinade.
4. Place steak on grill about 3 inches from coals. Brushing frequently with marinade, grill about 6 minutes, or until one side is browned. Turn and grill other side about 6 minutes, or until done. (To test doneness, slit meat near bone and note color of meat.) Serve immediately.   4 TO 6 SERVINGS

RIB STEAKS, WESTERN STYLE

1 cup hot bacon drippings
3 tablespoons butter or margarine
⅓ cup lemon juice
3 tablespoons Worcestershire sauce
2 tablespoons ketchup
1 tablespoon paprika
½ cup finely chopped onion
½ clove garlic, crushed
1½ bay leaves
2 teaspoons prepared horseradish
½ teaspoon salt
⅛ teaspoon pepper
4 rib steaks, cut about 1-in. thick (each steak about 1 lb.)

1. Mix all ingredients except steaks thoroughly. Pour over steaks and allow to stand about 30 minutes at room temperature for flavors to blend. Remove bay leaves.
2. Lightly grease grill with cooking oil. Place steaks on grill about 3 inches from coals. Grill about 4 minutes, or until first side is browned. Turn with tongs; grill second side about 4 minutes, or until done. (To test doneness, slit meat near bone and note color of meat.) During grilling, baste frequently with the sauce. Serve at once.   4 SERVINGS

GRILLED SIRLOIN STEAK JULIANA

1 cup tomato juice
1 cup orange juice
½ cup minced onion
½ cup finely chopped pimiento-stuffed olives
2 cloves garlic, crushed
1 tablespoon soy sauce
1 teaspoon salt
1 teaspoon paprika
¼ teaspoon cayenne pepper
Sirloin steak, cut about 2 in. thick (allow ½ to ¾ lb. per person)

1. Combine the juices, onion, olives, garlic, and soy sauce; stir in a mixture of the salt, paprika, and cayenne pepper.
2. Pour sauce over steak in a shallow dish; allow to stand about 1 hour at room temperature, turning occasionally.
3. Transfer steak from sauce to grill and brown quickly on both sides close to hot coals. Continue grilling about 4 inches from coals, basting occasionally with sauce. Allow about 30 minutes total grilling time, depending upon desired doneness of meat. (Test doneness by slitting meat near bone and noting color of meat.) To serve, cut steak diagonally into thin slices and serve with remaining heated sauce.   1 STEAK

GRILLED BURGERS WITH CHEESE SAUCE

2 lbs. ground beef
2 teaspoons salt
¼ teaspoon pepper
½ teaspoon monosodium glutamate

1. Lightly mix all ingredients and shape into 8 patties. Place in a greased broiler basket or on a greased grill. Grill about 3 inches from coals 10 to 15 minutes, turning once.
2. Serve on toasted *hamburger buns* with *Lightning Cheese Sauce, below.*   8 BURGERS

NOTE: For variety, mix in one or more of the following: *½ cup chopped onion, 1 cup chopped green onion, ¼ cup chopped green pepper, ¼ cup chopped pimiento-stuffed olives, or 1 teaspoon dill weed.*

BLACK PEPPER BURGERS: Mix in *1 tablespoon Worcestershire sauce* with the seasonings and press about *¾ teaspoon coarsely crushed peppercorns* onto top and bottom of each patty before grilling.

LIGHTNING CHEESE SAUCE: Blend *1 can (10¾ ounces) condensed Cheddar cheese soup, 1 tablespoon lemon juice, ½ teaspoon prepared mustard,* and a *few grains cayenne pepper* in a saucepan. Heat thoroughly.   ABOUT 1⅓ CUPS

SAUCY ROQUEFORT BURGERS

Make a large depression in the center of each 1-inch thick *hamburger.* Fill with *2 teaspoons crumbled Roquefort cheese* and *½ teaspoon olive oil.* Reshape burgers to seal in filling. Grill in broiler basket or on a greased grill 4 to 5 inches from coals, brushing frequently with *bottled barbecue sauce.* When browned, turn and season or continue brushing. Total grilling time: 10 minutes for medium done.

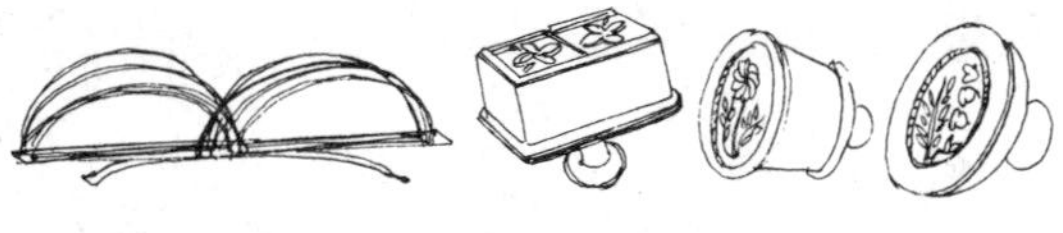

GRILLED GROUND BEEF "FRANKS" IN BUNS

1 lb. ground beef	¼ teaspoon crushed thyme
1 egg, fork beaten	¼ cup chopped onion
3 tablespoons fine dry bread crumbs	2 tablespoons chopped green pepper
½ teaspoon salt	¼ cup snipped parsley
⅛ teaspoon pepper	½ cup finely diced sharp Cheddar cheese
¼ teaspoon ground nutmeg	

1. Combine ground beef and a mixture of egg, crumbs, salt, pepper, nutmeg, and thyme. Add onion, green pepper, parsley, and cheese; mix lightly but thoroughly.
2. Divide meat mixture into 6 equal portions and shape each into a 6-inch long "frankfurter." Wrap each with *bacon* to cover completely; fasten ends of bacon with wooden picks.
3. Thread each "frankfurter" lengthwise onto a skewer. Grill about 4 inches from coals until meat is of desired doneness, about 20 minutes, turning occasionally.
4. Serve in hot toasted buttered *frankfurter buns.*

6 SERVINGS

APPETIZER SPARERIBS

These ribs not only awaken the appetite—they tantalize the nose, delight the eye, and reward the palate.

Put *4 pounds spareribs,* meaty side up, in a shallow roasting pan. Rub with *1 cut clove garlic* and sprinkle with *salt.* Roast in a 350° oven 1½ hours or until done, draining off excess fat as it accumulates. Cut ribs apart. Dip in either *Tangy Plum Sauce* or *Sweet-Sour Apricot Sauce, below;* grill about 3 inches from coals until well browned, turning frequently.

APPETIZERS FOR 10 TO 12

TANGY PLUM SAUCE: Drain *1 can (16 ounces) purple plums,* reserving ¼ cup syrup. Pit plums and force through a sieve or food mill into a bowl. Blend in the reserved syrup, *½ cup thawed frozen orange juice concentrate,* and *½ teaspoon Worcestershire sauce.* Store, covered, in refrigerator until ready to use.

ABOUT 1½ CUPS

SWEET-SOUR APRICOT SAUCE

2 cans (30 oz. each) apricot halves, drained	½ teaspoon salt
½ cup drained crushed pineapple	Few grains white pepper
½ cup honey	2 tablespoons cider vinegar
½ cup brown sugar	2 large cloves garlic, quartered

1. Force apricots through a sieve or food mill into a saucepan. Stir in a mixture of pineapple, honey, brown sugar, salt, white pepper, and vinegar, then garlic.
2. Bring mixture to boiling, reduce heat to medium, and cook 10 minutes, stirring occasionally. Remove garlic. Cool and store, covered, in refrigerator until readv to use.

ABOUT 2½ CUPS

BARBECUED RIBS

4 lbs. back ribs	¼ cup lemon juice
3 cloves garlic, crushed	3 tablespoons Worcestershire sauce
¼ cup cooking or salad oil	¼ cup firmly packed brown sugar
1 cup chopped onion	1 teaspoon salt
1 can (8 oz.) tomato sauce	¼ teaspoon pepper
½ cup water	

1. Rub ribs with crushed garlic; cut into serving-sized pieces. Place the ribs in a large shallow pan; set aside.
2. Heat oil in a skillet; add onion and cook until tender, stirring occasionally. Blend in tomato sauce, water, lemon juice, Worcestershire sauce, brown sugar, salt, and pepper; bring to boiling, reduce heat, and simmer 5 minutes.
3. Pour sauce over ribs and marinate 2 hours at room temperature, or overnight in refrigerator.
4. Remove ribs from marinade (reserve for brush-

ing) and put on grill or in a broiler basket 5 inches from coals. Grill 1 hour or until done, turning and brushing frequently with the marinade.

ABOUT 6 SERVINGS

SAUCE-PAINTED SPARERIBS

4 lbs. meaty spareribs or back ribs, cut in serving portions	1 tablespoon grated onion
1 cup ketchup	1½ teaspoons salt
¼ cup lemon juice	½ teaspoon pepper
2 tablespoons brown sugar	¼ teaspoon oregano, marjoram, or thyme
1 tablespoon soy sauce	¼ teaspoon Tabasco
1 tablespoon prepared horseradish mustard	1 clove garlic

1. Partially cook ribs in a 350°F oven about 30 minutes.
2. Meanwhile, combine remaining ingredients in a saucepan. Simmer over low heat at least 10 minutes. Remove garlic.
3. To grill, place ribs, meaty side down, on grill. Slowly grill about 3 inches from coals. Turn about every 5 minutes, brushing with sauce. Grill until ribs are deep brown and crisp, about 25 minutes.

8 SERVINGS

BARBECUED RIBS HAWAIIAN: Pour over ribs in a roasting pan a mixture of ½ *cup soy sauce*, ¼ *cup cornstarch*, and *3 tablespoons chopped preserved or crystallized ginger*. Let stand about 30 minutes, turning frequently. Roast and grill as directed in recipe for Sauce-Painted Spareribs. During grilling, brush frequently with a mixture of ¾ *cup sugar*, ½ *cup unsweetened pineapple juice*, and *3 tablespoons cider vinegar*.

STUFFED PORK TENDERLOIN PATTIES

8 pork tenderloin patties	¼ cup chopped onion
4 slices bacon	2 tablespoons ketchup
16 medium-sized mushrooms, chopped (about 1⅓ cups)	¼ teaspoon salt
	Orange Basting Sauce, *page 666*

1. Remove excess fat from patties and flatten to about ¼ inch thickness. Set patties aside.
2. To make stuffing, cook bacon in a skillet until crisp; drain on absorbent paper, crumble, and set aside. Pour off all but 3 tablespoons bacon fat and

add mushrooms and onion to skillet. Cook until mushrooms are lightly browned and onion is soft, stirring frequently. Remove from heat and mix in bacon, ketchup, and salt.
3. Sprinkle meat lightly with *salt*. Spoon stuffing equally onto half of the patties. Top with remaining flattened patties.
4. Brush outside surfaces of meat with *cooking or salad oil*.
5. Grill in a broiler basket or on grill about 6 inches from coals 25 to 30 minutes, turning frequently and brushing with Orange Basting Sauce.

4 GENEROUS SERVINGS

GINGER-GLAZED LAMB CHOPS

Season double *loin lamb chops* with *salt, monosodium glutamate,* and *pepper.* Brush with *Ginger Glaze, below,* and grill 5 to 6 inches from coals 12 to 15 minutes on each side; brush frequently with glaze. Meanwhile, put *canned yams* into small aluminum foil pans and spoon some of glaze over them. Set on grill; turn and baste with glaze until thoroughly heated.

GINGER GLAZE: Mix thoroughly *1 cup ginger marmalade, ¼ cup butter or margarine, 2 tablespoons lemon juice,* and *1 teaspoon soy sauce.*

LAMB CHOPS BURGUNDY

8 loin or rib lamb chops, cut 1½ to 2 in. thick	3 peppercorns, crushed
¼ cup olive oil	½ teaspoon cumin seed, crushed
½ cup Burgundy	⅔ cup chopped red onion
½ clove garlic, crushed	
¼ teaspoon salt	

1. Put chops into a shallow dish; combine remaining ingredients in a screw-top jar; shake to blend.
2. Pour marinade over meat. Cover and set in refrigerator to marinate about 2 hours, turning chops occasionally.
3. Grill chops about 4 inches from coals 16 to 20 minutes, or until meat is browned, turning occasionally and brushing with remaining marinade. (To test doneness, slit meat near bone and note color of meat.)

8 SERVINGS

MINTED LAMB CHOPS

¼ cup finely chopped mushrooms, lightly browned in butter or margarine	¼ cup firmly packed brown sugar
2 tablespoons crushed fresh mint leaves, or 1 tablespoon dry mint leaves	1 teaspoon dry mustard
	½ teaspoon salt
	2 tablespoons wine vinegar
	8 loin or rib lamb chops, cut 1½ to 2 in. thick

1. Combine mushrooms, mint, brown sugar, dry mustard, salt, and vinegar; toss gently to mix.
2. Grill chops about 4 inches from coals 8 to 10 minutes on one side. Turn chops and spoon mushroom mixture over surface of each; grill second side 8 to 10 minutes, or until done.   8 SERVINGS

BARBECUED BOLOGNA ROLL

4 lb. bologna roll	1 teaspoon prepared horseradish
1½ tablespoons prepared mustard	1 cup chili sauce
1½ teaspoons brown sugar	3 tablespoons cider vinegar

1. Score bologna roll on one side, making cuts ½- to 1-inch deep and 1 inch apart. Secure roll on a long skewer.
2. Mix mustard, brown sugar, and horseradish. Spread into cuts.
3. Place roll directly on grill about 3 inches from coals. Baste well with a mixture of chili sauce and vinegar. Turning frequently, grill 15 to 20 minutes or until roll is thoroughly heated and browned.
4. Remove skewer and slice meat.   16 SERVINGS

CRUNCHY BOLOGNA IN A BUN

1 lb. bologna, about 2½ in. in diameter (in one piece)	1 cup finely crushed potato chips
⅓ cup bottled barbecue sauce	Buttered hot dog buns

1. Cut bologna lengthwise into 6 pieces. Coat each piece with the barbecue sauce, then with the potato chips. Allow to stand about 30 minutes to set coating.
2. Grill about 4 inches from coals about 2 minutes on each side, or until coating is browned and the bologna is hot; turn carefully with two forks.

3. Serve in the hot dog buns and accompany with crisp *carrot and celery sticks*, *pickles*, bowls of *potato chips*, and an assortment of chilled *carbonated beverages*.   6 SERVINGS

BACON-WRAPPED FRANKS

Slit *frankfurters* almost through lengthwise. Spread cut surfaces with about *1 teaspoon process blue cheese spread*. Starting at one end, wrap *1 slice bacon* around each frankfurter; secure ends with *whole cloves*. Put in a hot-dog roaster or on the grill. Grill about 3 inches from coals, turning often, until bacon and frankfurters are lightly browned. (If desired, partially cook bacon before wrapping around franks.)

MARINATED FRANKS

For 1¼ cups marinade, in a shallow dish mix *½ cup soy sauce, ⅓ cup ketchup, ¼ cup salad oil, ¼ cup cider vinegar, 1 teaspoon prepared horseradish, ½ teaspoon dry mustard,* and *¼ teaspoon thyme.* Cut gashes in *frankfurters.* Put the frankfurters into marinade and let stand about 3 hours, turning frequently to coat well. Drain and reserve marinade. Put frankfurters in roaster or on grill. Grill about 10 minutes, turning often and basting with reserved marinade.

DOUBLE TREAT FRANK-BURGERS

2 lbs. ground beef	6 strips (½ in. each) Cheddar cheese
2 teaspoons salt	3 dill pickles, cut in quarters lengthwise
2 tablespoons ketchup	Bottled barbecue sauce
6 frankfurters, cut in halves lengthwise	

1. Lightly toss the ground beef, salt, *pepper*, and ketchup together. Form into twelve flat patties.
2. Place 2 frankfurter halves, cut side down, on each of 6 patties; place a strip of cheese and two pickle strips between the frankfurter halves. Brush lightly with barbecue sauce. Top with remaining patties and brush with sauce.
3. Place frank-burgers, sauce side down, in a broiler basket. Brush tops with sauce and close broiler basket. Grill about 3 inches from coals 10 to 15 minutes, frequently turning and brushing with barbecue sauce.   6 SERVINGS

GLAZED BEEF-FRUIT KABOB DUO

3 lbs. boneless beef (sirloin, rib or tenderloin), cut in 1½-in. cubes	Spicy Apricot-Lime Sauce, *below* Glazed Fruit Kabobs, *below*

1. Thread beef cubes onto eight 5-inch skewers, separating pieces slightly. Brush with Spicy Apricot-Lime Sauce. Place on a greased grill and cook 4 to 5 inches from coals, turning and brushing frequently with the sauce until meat is the desired degree of doneness, 12 to 15 minutes.

2. Arrange beef and fruit kabobs on fluffy cooked rice, if desired. Serve immediately with the remaining hot sauce.   8 SERVINGS

GLAZED FRUIT KABOBS: Thread alternately onto eight 4-inch skewers, 16 large orange wedges (4 large oranges, peeled), 16 lime slices (2 large limes cut in ¼-inch slices), and 16 honeydew melon slices, 2¾ inches each. Brush with Spicy Apricot-Lime Sauce, below; and grill or broil 4 to 5 inches from source of heat about 10 minutes, turning and brushing frequently with the sauce until fruit is heated and well glazed.

SPICY APRICOT-LIME SAUCE

1 cup apricot preserves	1 teaspoon ground
½ cup light corn syrup	cinnamon
½ cup butter	¼ teaspoon ground
¼ cup lime juice	cloves

Combine all ingredients in a saucepan. Stirring occasionally, bring slowly to simmering and cook until slightly thicker, about 10 minutes.   2 CUPS

BEEF KABOBS WITH ORIENTAL SAUCE

¾ cup cooking or salad oil	1½ teaspoons garlic powder
¼ cup soy sauce	1½ teaspoons finely
3 tablespoons honey	chopped green onion
2 tablespoons cider vinegar	1½ lbs. boneless sirloin steak, cut in 1½-in.
1½ teaspoons ground ginger	cubes

1. Combine oil, soy sauce, honey, vinegar, ground ginger, garlic powder, and chopped green onion in a large shallow dish. Add the meat cubes; turn until pieces are coated. Set in refrigerator to marinate for at least 4 hours, turning several times.

2. Remove meat from marinade with a slotted spoon and drain. Reserve marinade for basting.

3. Thread three meat cubes onto each 6-inch skewer. Place meat close together for rare; separate cubes slightly for well done.

4. Grill kabobs on a greased grill about 3 inches from coals, turning often for even browning. Baste frequently with marinade. Grilling period ranges from 10 to 20 minutes, or until meat is done to the desired stage. (Test for doneness by cutting a slit in meat and noting internal color.)   ABOUT 4 SERVINGS

MARINATED LAMB KABOBS

½ cup soy sauce	1½ lbs. boneless lamb
1 clove garlic, crushed	(leg or shoulder), cut
1 teaspoon chopped candied ginger	in 1½-in. cubes Mushroom caps
3 tablespoons sugar	1-in. green pepper squares
	Pimiento-stuffed olives

1. Combine the soy sauce, garlic, ginger, and sugar in a shallow dish. Add the meat cubes and turn until pieces are coated. Refrigerate at least 6 hours, turning several times.

2. Remove meat from marinade with a slotted spoon and drain; reserve marinade for basting.

3. Alternately thread onto four 16-inch skewers mushrooms, lamb, green pepper, and olives, ending each skewer with a mushroom and olive.

4. Basting generously and frequently, grill kabobs on a greased grill about 3 inches from coals about 20 minutes, or until meat is tender and rich brown.   ABOUT 4 SERVINGS

LAMB KABOBS

1½ lbs. boneless lamb (loin, leg, or shoulder), cut in 1½-in. cubes	2 tablespoons piccalilli 1 tablespoon dry mustard
½ cup cider vinegar	1 teaspoon salt
⅓ cup olive oil	½ teaspoon pepper
¼ cup corn syrup	2 tablespoons capers

1. Put lamb cubes into a shallow dish. Pour a mixture of vinegar and remaining ingredients over them. Marinate at least 6 hours, turning pieces occasionally. Drain the meat, reserving marinade.

2. Thread meat cubes onto skewers. Place rather close together for rare meat, or separate slightly for well done.
3. Place on grill about 3 inches from coals and cook 15 to 20 minutes, or until tender and browned, frequently turning and brushing the meat with marinade. ABOUT 4 SERVINGS

HAM 'N' PICKLE KABOBS

1 jar (10 oz., about 1 cup) currant jelly	Leftover cooked ham (about 1½ lbs.), cut in 1-in. cubes
⅓ cup prepared mustard	8 to 10 canned peach halves, each cut in 3 wedges
2 tablespoons light corn syrup	Pickle slices

1. Melt jelly in a saucepan. Blend in mustard and corn syrup until well blended; boil 2 minutes.
2. Stir in ham cubes; reduce heat and simmer, covered, 20 minutes. Gently stir in peaches and pickle slices; cover and heat 10 minutes. Drain sauce from ham, peaches, and pickles and reserve for brushing on kabobs.
3. Alternately thread ham cubes, pairs of pickle slices, and peach wedges onto skewers, starting and ending with ham. Brush kabobs with sauce.
4. Grill about 4 inches from coals until ham is thoroughly browned, turning and brushing frequently with sauce; allow about 30 minutes grilling time. ABOUT 8 KABOBS

HELP-YOURSELF APPETIZER KABOBS

Arrange a Lazy Susan or tray with individual bowls of *canned Vienna sausage*, cut in halves, thick slices of *banana* (having green-tipped peel), *pineapple chunks*, pitted large *ripe olives*, *canned green chilies*, cut in large pieces, and *bottled sweet and sour sauce*. Spear morsels (your choice) on a 6-inch skewer, coat generously with the sauce, and grill 2 to 3 inches from coals until sauce is bubbly and tidbits begin to brown.

QUICKIE KABOBS

Allowing ¼ pound meat per serving, cut *canned luncheon meat or bologna* into 1- to 1½-inch cubes; cut *green pepper* and *bacon* into 1- to 1½-inch pieces. Alternately thread onto skewers along with *pitted olives*. Grill on greased grill about 3 inches from coals about 5 minutes, turning and brushing constantly with your favorite *salad dressing* (bottled or prepared from a mix) or a *bottled barbecue sauce*.

CHICKEN ON THE GRILL

LEMON-DIPPED CHICKEN
Pick up your chicken and eat it out of hand.

1 cup lemon juice	1 teaspoon Tabasco
½ cup cooking or salad oil	2 broiler-fryers (1 to 1½ lbs. each), split lengthwise
2 tablespoons molasses	
2 teaspoons salt	

1. Mix together in a large shallow dish the lemon juice, oil, molasses, salt, and Tabasco. Add chicken halves; turn until pieces are coated. Set in refrigerator to marinate for at least 4 hours, turning several times.
2. Drain and reserve marinade for basting. Place chicken halves on greased grill or in a greased steak broiler; brush with marinade. Grill, cut side down, about 3 inches from coals. Turn every 5 minutes to brown and cook evenly. Brush frequently with the reserved marinade.
3. Grill about 20 minutes, or until chickens test done. (Chicken is done when meat on thickest part of drumstick cuts easily.) ABOUT 4 SERVINGS

CHICKEN ORIENTAL

2 broiler-fryers (1 to 1½ lbs. each)	½ teaspoon monosodium glutamate
½ cup soy sauce	Few grains paprika
¼ cup sugar	1 clove garlic, crushed
3 drops Tabasco	Melted butter or margarine
1½ teaspoons ground ginger	

1. Clean, rinse, and dry chickens. Split each

chicken in half lengthwise. (If chickens are frozen, thaw according to directions on package.) Crack joints of drumsticks, thighs, and wings so chicken can be kept flat during grilling.

2. Combine in a large shallow dish the soy sauce, sugar, Tabasco, ginger, monosodium glutamate, paprika, and garlic. Add chicken to soy sauce marinade; cover and marinate about 3 hours, turning occasionally.

3. Drain and reserve marinade for basting. Place chicken halves on greased grill or in a greased steak broiler. Brush with melted butter. Grill, cut side down, about 3 inches from coals. Turn every 5 minutes to brown and cook evenly. Brush frequently with reserved marinade.

4. Grill about 20 minutes, or until chickens test done. (Meat on thickest part of drumstick should cut easily and show no pink.)   4 SERVINGS

SAUCY CINNAMON CHICKEN

¾ cup lemon juice	1 tablespoon ground
¾ cup cooking or salad	cinnamon
oil	1½ teaspoons curry
6 tablespoons light corn	powder
syrup	1½ teaspoons salt
1 small clove garlic,	2 broiler-fryers (1½ to
crushed	2 lbs. each), split
	lengthwise

1. Combine the lemon juice, oil, corn syrup, and garlic; stir in a mixture of the cinnamon, curry powder, and salt.

2. Pour mixture over chickens in a shallow pan. Cover and refrigerate several hours or overnight to marinate, turning and basting chickens occasionally.

3. Drain chickens, reserving marinade for basting sauce. Grill about 4 inches from coals, basting frequently with marinade and turning occasionally to brown evenly. Grill about 35 minutes, or until breast meat near wing joint is fork-tender.

4 SERVINGS

GLAZED GRILLED CHICKEN

Split *2 broiler-fryers* (1½ to 2 pounds each) into halves lengthwise. Put chicken halves, cut side down, on a greased grill 3 to 5 inches from coals. Turn and brush with *Barbecue Sauce* or *Currant-Mustard Glaze, page 677,* every 5 minutes for even cooking and browning. Grill about 20 minutes, or until chicken tests done. (Chicken is done when meat on thickest part of drumstick cuts easily.)   4 SERVINGS

NOTE: Chicken halves, quarters, or pieces may also be brushed with *Tomato Basting Sauce, page 666, Tangy Plum Sauce, page 669, Pineapple Marinade, page 666,* or a *lemon-flavored butter* and placed in a greased steak broiler. Brush frequently with sauce and turn every 5 minutes until chicken tests done.

FISH & SHELLFISH ON THE GRILL

GRILLED TROUT

A sportsman's contribution to outdoor cooking.

6 cleaned fresh trout	2 tablespoons minced
(about 5 to 6 oz. each)	parsley
⅔ cup olive oil	2 teaspoons salt
¼ cup lemon juice	½ teaspoon black
2 tablespoons water	pepper
2 tablespoons grated	1 teaspoon curry powder
onion	½ teaspoon celery flakes
	½ teaspoon tarragon

1. Remove heads and fins from trout, if desired; rinse trout under cold running water and pat dry

with absorbent paper. Put in a shallow dish.

2. Combine remaining ingredients in a screw-top jar. Shake well to blend. Pour over trout, cover, and set in refrigerator to marinate at least 2 hours, turning occasionally.

3. Drain and reserve marinade. Put trout on greased grill or in a greased broiler basket; brush with marinade. Grill 3 inches from coals about 4 minutes; turn, brush with marinade, and grill second side about 4 minutes, or until fish flakes easily. Serve immediately.   6 SERVINGS

NOTE: Other fresh-water fish may be prepared this way.

GRILLED ROCK LOBSTER TAILS

6 frozen South African rock lobster tails, thawed
¾ cup pineapple juice
½ cup packed brown sugar
¼ cup cider vinegar
2½ teaspoons dry mustard

1. Cut underside membrane of lobster tails around edges and remove. Insert skewers lengthwise through meat to keep tails flat during cooking.
2. Place on grill about 4 inches from coals, flesh side down, 3 to 5 minutes. Turn, brush meat with a mixture of pineapple juice and remaining ingredients, and continue grilling until meat is opaque and tender. Brush meat several times during cooking and just before serving. Serve with remaining sauce and *lemon wedges*.   6 SERVINGS
NOTE: *Butter Sauce, page 666*, may be substituted for the pineapple mixture.

GRILLED LOBSTER TAILS ITALIANO
Cooking with garlic presents no olfactory problems when it's done outdoors.

4 South African rock lobster tails (about 6 oz. each)
⅓ cup butter or margarine, melted
1 tablespoon grated onion
1 clove garlic, crushed
2 tablespoons snipped parsley
½ teaspoon basil, crushed
¼ teaspoon oregano, crushed
¼ cup shredded Parmesan cheese

1. Thaw rock lobster tails according to package directions. Cut underside membrane around edges and remove. To prevent curling, hold tail in hands and bend it toward shell side to crack in three places; or insert skewer lengthwise through meat to keep tail flat.
2. Blend butter with onion, garlic, and a mixture of the parsley and herbs. Brush flesh side of lobster tails with the seasoned butter.
3. Grill lobster tails, shell side down, about 4 inches from coals 5 minutes, brushing flesh side generously with seasoned butter. Turn and continue broiling until meat is opaque and tender when tested with a fork. Turn flesh side up and sprinkle each lobster tail with about 1 tablespoon cheese; heat until cheese is melted. Transfer lobster tails to heated serving platter and serve with remaining butter sauce.   4 SERVINGS

ROCK LOBSTER TAILS SUPERB

4 frozen South African rock lobster tails (8 oz. each)
½ cup cooking or salad oil
2 tablespoons soy sauce
1 tablespoon minced onion
1 teaspoon salt
½ teaspoon pepper
1 teaspoon dry mustard
1 teaspoon ground ginger
1 clove garlic, crushed

1. Drop lobster tails into boiling *salted water* to cover. Bring to boiling, lower heat, and simmer about 5 minutes, or until just tender and opaque. Drain and cool.
2. Using scissors, cut through center of bony membrane and remove meat from shell in one piece.
3. Combine remaining ingredients for marinade; pour over lobster tails in a shallow dish; cover and refrigerate about 3 hours, turning occasionally.
4. Remove lobster tails from marinade and thread each one on an 8-inch skewer. Grill about 3 inches from coals until light golden in color and thoroughly heated, brushing frequently with marinade.
          4 SERVINGS

ROCK LOBSTER TAILS WITH ORANGE-BUTTER SAUCE

1 can (6 oz.) frozen orange juice concentrate, undiluted
¼ cup lemon juice
½ teaspoon dry mustard
¼ teaspoon rosemary
½ teaspoon celery salt
½ teaspoon onion powder
½ teaspoon salt
¼ teaspoon Angostura bitters
½ cup butter or margarine
12 frozen South African rock lobster tails (2 pkgs., 1½ lbs. each)

1. For sauce, combine all ingredients except butter and lobster in a saucepan; heat slowly, stirring constantly, until mixture comes to a boil; boil 1 minute.
2. When ready to grill, melt butter in a small saucepan over fire; add sauce, stirring to blend thoroughly; use to brush rock lobster tails during grilling and serve remaining sauce for dipping.
3. Let frozen rock lobster tails thaw gradually; when ready to cook, slit thin underside membrane down center and peel open; insert tails on long skewers. (If tails are cooked flat on grill, prevent curling by bending tails backward to crack sharply in several places.)

4. Grill tails, shell side down, about 4 inches from coals 5 minutes, brushing occasionally with butter sauce; turn tails and grill 5 minutes longer, or until meat is opaque and creamy white.

5. Serve with remaining sauce.   8 SERVINGS

GRILLED SHRIMP APPETIZERS

Shell fresh *shrimp*, leaving tails; devein and rinse under running cold water; put into a large bowl. Partially cover with *bottled Italian salad dressing*; cover bowl and refrigerate at least 2 hours, turning shrimp several times. Drain shrimp, reserving marinade. Allow guests to thread onto metal or bamboo skewers (soak bamboo skewers in water before using): *shrimp, cherry tomatoes, green pepper squares*, and *avocado pieces*. Grill 3 inches from coals about 3 minutes, or until shrimp are done, turning and brushing with marinade.

MARINATED GRILLED SHRIMP

Cut each *raw shrimp* through shell along back; remove black vein. Carefully spread shell open; rinse and drain well. Marinate in *Herb Marinade, page 666*, several hours or overnight. Put shrimp, one layer deep, in a broiler basket. Turning occasionally, grill 3 inches from coals 15 minutes, or until shrimp are done.

GRILLED SHRIMP IN SHELLS

Serve this exotic shrimp piping hot as an appetizer. Plenty of paper napkins are a necessity as well as a convenience.

2 lbs. jumbo-sized shrimp or prawns, fresh or thawed frozen (about 24)	2 tablespoons chopped parsley
1 cup olive oil	½ teaspoon thyme, crushed
½ cup lemon juice	½ teaspoon marjoram, crushed
2 tablespoons soy sauce	½ teaspoon celery seed
½ teaspoon salt	
1 large clove garlic, crushed	

1. Using scissors, cut through shell at the back of each raw shrimp; remove the black vein. Wash shrimp with shells thoroughly; drain on absorbent paper. Put the shrimp into a large bowl.

2. Combine remaining ingredients; mix well and pour over shrimp. Cover and refrigerate at least 2 hours, turning shrimp several times.

3. Arrange the shrimp in a hinged steak broiler or broiler basket. Grill about 3 inches from coals until shells are slightly charred. Turn broiler and grill shrimp several minutes longer. Serve immediately.   ABOUT 6 SERVINGS

NOTE: If desired, substitute *1 tablespoon chopped onion* for garlic. Omit thyme, marjoram, and celery seed. Add *4 teaspoons crushed tarragon, ½ teaspoon chervil*, and *¼ teaspoon basil*.

SPIT COOKERY

ROAST LOIN OF PORK
(Schweinebraten)

For a traditional German dinner, serve this succulent pork roast with sauerkraut and apples.

3½-lb. (8 ribs) pork loin roast	½ teaspoon marjoram, crushed
1½ teaspoons onion salt	¼ teaspoon pepper

1. Rub roast with a mixture of the salt, marjoram, and pepper. Secure roast on spit. Insert meat thermometer. Adjust spit about 8 inches above prepared coals, placing aluminum foil pan under pork to catch drippings. If using a gas-fired grill, adjust flame size following manufacturer's directions.

2. Roast until meat thermometer registers 170°F. or until meat is tender. About 30 minutes before roast is done, score surface.

3. Place roast on a warm serving platter. Garnish with *parsley*.   8 SERVINGS

NOTE: To roast in the oven, place pork loin, fat side up, on a rack in a shallow roasting pan. Roast, uncovered, at 325°F about 2½ hours.

HAM ON A SPIT

Center a *canned ham* on a motor-driven spit following grill manufacturer's directions. Roast until thoroughly heated and browned, brushing with a blend of *apricot preserves* and *fruit juices*, or with one of *Glazes for Ham, page 187*.

LAMB BARBACOA

6-lb. boned leg or
  shoulder of lamb,
  rolled and tied
1 cup water
1 cup port wine
½ cup olive oil
1 tablespoon salt
1 teaspoon freshly
  ground black pepper
⅛ teaspoon marjoram
⅛ teaspoon dry mustard

8 to 10 drops Tabasco
2 medium-sized
  tomatoes, diced
1 medium-sized green
  pepper, diced
1 medium-sized onion,
  sliced
½ cup coarsely chopped
  parsley
3 cloves garlic, minced

1. Insert a skewer at intervals to make small holes all over lamb. Set lamb in a large shallow pan.
2. Combine and thoroughly blend the remaining ingredients and pour over the lamb. Cover and marinate about 24 hours in refrigerator; baste frequently, turning the lamb occasionally.
3. When ready to grill, remove the lamb from the marinade (reserve) and secure roast on spit, making sure it is evenly balanced. Insert meat thermometer so tip does not touch the spit or rest in fat; put drip pan in place and start motor.
4. Basting frequently with the liquid from the marinade, rotate on spit 2½ to 3 hours, or until meat thermometer registers 175°F for medium done or 180°F for well done.
5. Serve hot with the cold vegetable marinade as a relish.   8 TO 12 SERVINGS

BARBECUED CHICKEN ON A SPIT

2 broilers-fryers (1½ to
  2 lbs. each)
2 teaspoons salt

Barbecue Sauce or
  Currant-Mustard
  Glaze, *below*

1. Remove spit from grill before building fire.
2. Clean chickens; rinse and pat dry with absorbent paper. Rub cavities of birds with salt. Skewer neck skin to back; tuck wings under. Carefully insert spit lengthwise through both birds. Be sure they are well balanced on spit for even turning. Tie drumsticks to spit. Brush chickens with Barbecue Sauce or glaze.
3. Grill 8 inches from coals, turning frequently. Baste often with the sauce. (Hold a pan under the chickens while basting to catch any drippings.) Grill until a drumstick twists out of joint easily, about 1 hour. Serve with remaining sauce.
    4 SERVINGS

BARBECUE SAUCE

1 can (8 oz.) tomato
  sauce
1 can (6 oz.) tomato
  paste
⅓ cup chopped onion
1 clove garlic, crushed
¼ cup firmly packed
  brown sugar
¼ cup cider vinegar

1 tablespoon Worces-
  tershire sauce
⅛ teaspoon Tabasco
1 teaspoon salt
⅛ teaspoon pepper
½ teaspoon celery salt
½ teaspoon dry mustard
½ teaspoon chili
  powder

Combine all ingredients in a heavy saucepan. Bring to boiling, stirring until brown sugar is dissolved. Reduce heat, cover, and simmer about 20 minutes.   ABOUT 1½ CUPS

NOTE: This sauce keeps well and may be stored in the refrigerator for days before using. Heat before serving.

CURRANT-MUSTARD GLAZE: Combine *1 jar (8 ounces) red currant jelly, ⅓ cup prepared mustard,* and *½ teaspoon Tabasco* in a small saucepan. Set over low heat until well blended and jelly is melted, stirring occasionally.   ABOUT 1 CUP

BARBECUED TURKEY ROAST

1 frozen boneless turkey
  roast (5 to 7 lbs.)

Savory Sweet-Tart
  Sauce, *below*, or
  barbecue sauce

1. If not preseasoned, rub surface of turkey roast with *salt* and *pepper*. Center roast on a motor-driven spit, following manufacturer's directions for roasts. Insert meat thermometer, being sure it does not touch spit. Brush roast with *melted butter or margarine.*
2. Roast turkey until done, 2½ to 3 hours (meat thermometer should register 170° to 175°F). During last 20 to 30 minutes, brush roast occasionally with Savory Sweet-Tart Sauce.
3. Remove roast from spit; let stand 15 minutes before slicing. Serve with additional sauce.

SAVORY SWEET-TART SAUCE: Cook *¼ cup chopped onion* in *1 tablespoon hot cooking or salad oil* in a saucepan until soft. Add *1 cup commercial barbecue sauce, 1 cup unsweetened pineapple juice, 3 to 4 tablespoons dark corn syrup, ½ teaspoon grated lemon peel, 1 to 2 tablespoons lemon juice, 1 chicken bouillon cube,* and *a few grains ground ginger.* Simmer until sauce is thickened, stirring occasionally.   ABOUT 1¾ CUPS

COOKING IN ALUMINUM FOIL

Cooking in aluminum foil over an open fire of hot coals becomes increasingly more popular—and no wonder. The method is convenient, quick and easy, and a marvelous way of retaining the natural flavors and juices in the food. And best of all, foil packets take relatively little space on an outdoor grill.

Individual packets—Cut 8- to 12-inch squares of heavy-duty aluminum foil. Spoon equal amounts of a suggested vegetable mixture onto each square. Wrap loosely and seal securely, using the drugstore wrap. Place on grill 5 inches from coals. Turning packets occasionally, cook 15 to 20 minutes, or until vegetables are tender.

Large packets—Using 18-inch squares of foil, wrap, seal, and cook vegetables as for individual packets, allowing 20 to 35 minutes. Mix gently before serving.

NOTE: Try to combine foods in packets which require approximately the same cooking time.

FISH DINNER DE LUXE IN FOIL

½ cup butter or margarine	2 cups coarsely crumbled saltines
½ cup chopped celery	¼ cup finely snipped parsley
½ cup chopped onion	6 fish fillets (sole or flounder)
½ lb. fresh mushrooms, sliced	6 tomatoes
½ teaspoon salt	6 ears sweet corn, husked and brushed with melted butter
¼ teaspoon pepper	
2 teaspoons Worcestershire sauce	

1. Heat the butter or margarine in a skillet. Add celery, onion, and mushrooms; cook 5 minutes or until mushrooms are lightly browned, stirring occasionally.
2. Mix in the salt, pepper, and Worcestershire sauce, then the crumbled saltines and parsley; blend thoroughly.
3. Form a ring with each fish fillet, overlapping ends and fastening with wooden picks. Place each rolled fillet on an 18-inch square of heavy-duty aluminum foil.
4. Fill each fillet with stuffing, reserving 6 tablespoons. Cut out stem end from each tomato and fill with 1 tablespoon of the stuffing. Add a tomato and

an ear of corn to each packet. Sprinkle each ear of corn lightly with *salt*.
5. Wrap packets securely, using drugstore wrap. Place on grill 3 inches from coals and cook 10 minutes. Turn packet and cook 10 minutes longer, or until fish and vegetables are done.   6 PACKETS

SHRIMP-GREEN PEPPER PACKETS

1 lb. shrimp, peeled, deveined, and rinsed	1 teaspoon salt
½ cup bottled barbecue sauce	⅛ teaspoon pepper
	½ teaspoon ground ginger
1 large green pepper, cut in long ¼-in. strips	½ teaspoon dry mustard
	¼ cup lime juice
1 clove garlic, minced	1 tablespoon honey
1 teaspoon grated onion	8 drops Tabasco
½ cup butter	

1. Combine shrimp and barbecue sauce; turn shrimp to coat well with sauce. Set aside.
2. Divide green pepper equally on center of 4 large pieces of heavy-duty aluminum foil. Bring edges of foil up slightly to hold sauce.
3. Stir garlic and onion into hot butter in a skillet; cook 2 minutes. Remove from heat and blend in a mixture of salt, pepper, ginger, and dry mustard, then the remaining ingredients. Pour the seasoned butter over green pepper.
4. Divide the shrimp and sauce equally among the 4 packets. Bring edges of foil up over mixture and seal tightly, using drugstore wrap.
5. Place on grill 3 to 4 inches from coals and cook about 20 minutes; turn packets over once to cook shrimp evenly.   4 PACKETS

MACE-FLAVORED GREEN BEANS IN PACKET

2 pkgs. (9 oz. each) frozen cut green beans, partially thawed	1 teaspoon salt
	⅛ teaspoon pepper
	¼ teaspoon ground mace
½ lb. sliced fresh mushrooms	¼ cup butter or margarine
¼ cup chopped onion	

1. Put beans, mushrooms, and onion onto center

of a large square of heavy-duty aluminum foil. Break beans apart, if necessary.

2. Sprinkle a mixture of seasonings over vegetables and dot with butter. Bring foil up over contents and seal tightly, using drugstore wrap.

3. Place packet on grill about 5 inches from coals and cook about 35 minutes, or until beans are just tender; turn packet over once during the cooking period.

4. If desired, before serving, top with or blend in chopped *salted almonds*.   ABOUT 8 SERVINGS

MIXED BEAN PACKET

1 pkg. (9 oz.) frozen cut green beans	⅛ teaspoon pepper
1 pkg. (9 oz.) frozen cut wax beans	¼ teaspoon ground mace
1 pkg. (10 oz.) frozen lima beans	¼ cup chopped onion
1 teaspoon salt	¼ cup butter or margarine, cut in pieces

1. Partially thaw frozen vegetables; toss lightly with remaining ingredients. Put in center of a large square of heavy-duty aluminum foil; wrap and seal.

2. Cook on grill until tender.   ABOUT 8 SERVINGS

WAX BEAN PACKET

1 pkg. (9 oz.) frozen wax beans, partially thawed	½ teaspoon salt
½ medium-sized green pepper, cut in strips	⅛ teaspoon freshly ground black pepper
¼ cup sliced green onions with tops	¼ teaspoon paprika
¼ lb. fresh mushrooms, sliced	½ clove garlic, minced
	3 tablespoons butter or margarine, cut in pieces

1. Put the beans, green pepper, onion, and mushrooms in center of a large square of heavy-duty aluminum foil. Sprinkle with a mixture of salt, pepper, and paprika. Mix in garlic. Top with butter. Wrap and seal.

2. Cook on grill until tender.   ABOUT 4 SERVINGS

CARROT-CELERY-GREEN PEPPER PACKET

2 cups raw carrot slices (¼ in.)	¼ cup cooking or salad oil
2 cups diagonally cut celery slices (½ in.)	2 teaspoons salt
2 cups green pepper pieces (½ in.)	⅛ teaspoon black pepper
	1 teaspoon dill weed

1. Measure all ingredients onto a large square of heavy-duty aluminum foil; wrap and seal.

2. Cook on grill 35 minutes.   8 SERVINGS

CORN IN FOIL

Remove husks, silk, and blemishes from ears of *corn*. Place each ear on a piece of heavy-duty aluminum foil. Brush generously with *Golden Glow Butter, below*. Wrap foil around ears, sealing edges with double folds. Cook on grill about 15 minutes, turning frequently. Partially unwrap and serve corn in foil with a bowl of Golden Glow Butter and a shaker of *salt*.

CORN ON THE GRILL: Loosen husks only enough to remove silks and blemishes from ears of *corn*. Dip ears in *water*. Shake well. Rewrap husks around corn. Plunge into water again and let stand until husks are soaked, about 1 hour. Place ears over coals and roast, turning frequently, until tender, about 15 minutes. Immediately husk the corn, brush with *Golden Glow Butter* or *Perky Butter Sauce, below*, and sprinkle with *salt*.

GOLDEN GLOW BUTTER: Heat together ½ *cup butter or margarine, 2 tablespoons sieved pimiento, ½ teaspoon onion juice, ¼ teaspoon paprika, ⅛ teaspoon salt, and a few grains black pepper.*

PERKY BUTTER SAUCE: Heat together ½ *cup butter or margarine, ½ teaspoon dry Italian salad dressing mix, ½ teaspoon paprika, and ¼ teaspoon chili powder.* Serve hot.

DILLED ONION PACKET

1 large Bermuda onion	½ teaspoon dill weed
1 teaspoon butter or margarine	Seasoned salt

1. Peel and partially core the onion (allow 1 for each serving). Put the butter and dill weed into cav-

ity; sprinkle generously with the seasoned salt. Wrap in a square of heavy-duty aluminum foil.

2. Cook on grill 1 to 1½ hours. Serve topped with *dairy sour cream.*   1 SERVING

GRILLED WHOLE ONIONS: Leave dry outer skins on *Spanish or Bermuda onions.* Wet thoroughly and place on grill about 50 minutes, or until onions are black outside and soft and creamy inside. Roll occasionally to cook evenly.

PEAS IN FOIL PACKETS

2 pkgs. (10 oz. each) frozen green peas, slightly thawed	2 teaspoons celery seed
	1 teaspoon sugar
	1 teaspoon salt
1 cup sliced green onion with tops	¼ teaspoon freshly ground black pepper
½ lb. fresh mushrooms, sliced lengthwise	6 tablespoons butter or margarine

1. Put peas, onion, and mushrooms onto center of a large square of heavy-duty aluminum foil.

2. Sprinkle a mixture of celery seed, sugar, salt, and pepper over peas and dot with butter. Bring corners of foil up over peas and seal tightly.

3. Place packet on grill about 5 inches from coals and cook about 35 minutes, or until peas are just tender; turn packet over once during cooking.

ABOUT 10 SERVINGS

ROASTED POTATOES IN FOIL

Scrub, dry, and rub *potatoes* with *fat.* Wrap in aluminum foil, sealing edges with double folds. Place on grill about 1 hour, or until potatoes are soft when pressed with glove-protected fingers. Turn several times. Loosen foil, cut a cross in top each potato, and pinch open. Spoon *Herb Butter, below,* into each potato. Rewrap; grill to melt cheese.

HERB BUTTER: Blend ½ *cup softened butter* with *2 teaspoons minced parsley, 1 teaspoon crushed sweet basil,* and *1 teaspoon crushed tarragon.* Top with *grated cheese.*

POTATOES BAKED IN COALS: Wash and scrub large baking potatoes and bury in the coals for 45 minutes to 1 hour. Potatoes are done when they can be easily pierced with a fork.

DILLED POTATOES IN PACKETS

6 medium-sized potatoes, pared	2 tablespoons snipped parsley
½ cup butter or margarine, softened	1 tablespoon dill weed

1. Cut each potato crosswise into 1-inch slices and place on an individual square of heavy-duty aluminum foil. Sprinkle slices generously with *salt* and spread with butter. Sprinkle evenly with snipped parsley and dill weed.

2. Put slices together to reassemble each potato; wrap in foil, sealing tightly.

3. Place on grill 3 inches from coals and cook about 35 minutes, or until potatoes are tender. Turn packets occasionally to cook evenly.

6 SERVINGS

RICE AND PEAS IN A POUCH

6 cups cooked rice	2 medium-sized tomatoes, cut in thin wedges
1 pkg. (10 oz.) frozen green peas, partially thawed	
	¾ cup butter or margarine
1 can (5 oz.) water chestnuts, drained and sliced	1½ teaspoons seasoned salt
	Freshly ground black pepper
½ cup chopped green onion with tops	1½ teaspoons basil, crushed

1. Make 8 pouches from 18x12-inch pieces of heavy-duty aluminum foil by pressing each sheet of foil into a small bowl; remove from bowl.

2. Divide all ingredients equally among the 8 pouches. Seal each pouch securely. Place on grill over hot coals until mixture is thoroughly heated, 15 to 20 minutes.

4. Open foil and fluff with a fork before serving.

8 SERVINGS

TOMATOES IN FOIL

4 large tomatoes	⅓ cup chopped green onion with tops
Salt	
Freshly ground black pepper	1 teaspoon basil, crushed
8 teaspoons butter or margarine	1 teaspoon tarragon, crushed
¼ cup chopped parsley	1 clove garlic, crushed

1. Halve tomatoes crosswise. Sprinkle cut sur-

faces generously with salt and pepper; top each with 1 teaspoon butter.

2. Mix remaining ingredients and mound equally on each tomato half. Set four tomato halves on each of 2 large pieces of heavy-duty aluminum foil; wrap and seal tightly. Grill 3 inches from coals about 10 minutes, or until just tender (not mushy). 8 SERVINGS

CHEESE-TOPPED TOMATOES IN PACKETS

Large ripe tomatoes, cut crosswise into halves	Chopped chives
Seasoned salt	Creamy Roquefort or blue cheese salad dressing

1. Place each tomato half in the center of a 6-inch square of heavy-duty aluminum foil. Sprinkle cut surfaces of tomatoes with salt and chives. Top with dressing. Bring corners of foil up over tomatoes.
2. Cook on grill 3 to 5 minutes.

1 TOMATO HALF PER SERVING

ZUCCHINI PACKET

6 small zucchini, cut crosswise in ¼-in. slices	1 tablespoon brown sugar
1 medium-sized onion, halved and thinly sliced	1 beef bouillon cube, crushed
½ teaspoon salt	¼ teaspoon crushed fennel seed
¼ teaspoon pepper	3 tablespoons butter or margarine, cut in pieces

1. Put zucchini and onion onto center of a large square of heavy-duty aluminum foil. Sprinkle with salt, pepper, brown sugar, bouillon cube, and fennel seed, then dot with butter. Wrap and seal.
2. Cook 20 minutes, or until tender.

4 TO 6 SERVINGS

FENNEL-FLAVORED VEGETABLE PACKET

2 tomatoes, cut in wedges	1 beef bouillon cube, crushed
1 cup finger-sized pieces eggplant	½ teaspoon salt
1 medium-sized onion, sliced	⅛ teaspoon pepper
2 zucchini, sliced	¼ teaspoon crushed fennel seed
1 tablespoon brown sugar	3 tablespoons butter, cut in pieces

1. Toss all ingredients lightly in a bowl. Put onto center of a large square of heavy-duty aluminum foil. Seal packet securely, using drugstore wrap.
2. Place on grill 5 inches from coals and cook about 30 minutes, turning packet over once.

ABOUT 4 SERVINGS

HERBED VEGETABLE MEDLEY

4 medium-sized zucchini, cut crosswise into ½-in. slices	¼ teaspoon marjoram
	½ teaspoon salt
1 or 2 large tomatoes, cut in pieces	Few grains freshly ground black pepper
1 medium-sized onion, thinly sliced	¼ cup highly-seasoned French dressing (preferably with wine vinegar)
½ teaspoon basil	
¼ teaspoon thyme	

1. Put the zucchini, tomatoes, onion, and a mixture of remaining ingredients in the center of a large square of heavy-duty aluminum foil. Bring corners of foil up over vegetables; seal tightly.
2. Cook on grill about 20 minutes, or until zucchini is tender but not mushy. Sprinkle with *seasoned salt* before serving. 6 TO 8 SERVINGS

VEGETABLE MEDLEY IN FOIL

3 medium-sized zucchini, cut in ½-in. slices	8 large pimiento-stuffed green olives, sliced
7 large mushrooms, sliced lengthwise through caps and stems	3 tablespoons olive oil
	1 clove garlic, crushed
1 large tomato, cut in pieces	1 teaspoon parsley flakes
3 medium-sized onions, thinly sliced	½ teaspoon sweet basil
	1 teaspoon salt
	Freshly ground black pepper

1. Toss the vegetables and olives together in the center of a large square of heavy-duty aluminum foil; gently mix in remaining ingredients. Bring edges of foil up over mixture and seal tightly to avoid leakage when packet is turned.
2. Place on grill about 3 inches from coals and cook 15 to 20 minutes, or until zucchini is tender. Turn packet over occasionally to cook vegetables evenly. 4 TO 6 SERVINGS

ZUCCHINI-TOMATO PACKET

6 small zucchini, cut
  crosswise in ¼-in.
  slices
1 medium-sized onion,
  halved and thinly
  sliced
2 tomatoes, cut in small
  pieces

¼ cup shredded
  Cheddar cheese
1 teaspoon salt
Few grains black pepper
3 tablespoons butter or
  margarine, cut in
  pieces
2 tablespoons soy sauce

1. Mix all ingredients and put onto center of a large square of heavy-duty aluminum foil; wrap and seal.
2. Cook on grill 20 minutes, or until tender.

4 TO 6 SERVINGS

CHEESY ENGLISH MUFFIN SPLITS

¼ cup butter or
  margarine
2 tablespoons snipped
  chives
¼ teaspoon garlic salt
¼ teaspoon oregano
1 teaspoon Worcester-
  shire sauce

2 drops Tabasco
15 oz. (3 jars)
  pasteurized process
  cheese spread
14 grilled, buttered,
  large English muffin
  halves

1. Cream the butter with chives, salt, oregano, Worcestershire sauce, and Tabasco; beat in the cheese. Spread on the grilled English muffins.
2. Heat on aluminum foil on grill.

14 MUFFIN HALVES

SKILLET COOKING

CHILI-ETTI

1 can (about 16 oz.)
  chili with beans
1 can (15¼ oz.)
  spaghetti in tomato
  sauce with cheese

1 tablespoon instant
  minced onion
2 tablespoons grated
  Parmesan cheese

1. Turn chili and spaghetti into a heavy skillet. Mix in the onion.
2. Put skillet on back of grill and cook slowly 8 to 10 minutes, stirring occasionally until mixture is thoroughly heated. When ready to serve, sprinkle with the Parmesan cheese.   4 SERVINGS

CRAZY DOGS

1 teaspoon fat
¼ cup chopped onion
1½ lbs. lean ground beef
1 can (about 16 oz.) chili
  with beans

8 frankfurters, cut
  diagonally in ½-in.
  pieces
⅔ cup condensed
  tomato soup
½ cup ketchup
½ teaspoon salt

1. Heat fat in a skillet on the grill. Add onion and cook until transparent, occasionally moving and turning with a spoon. Add the ground beef and cook until lightly browned, breaking into small pieces with a spoon.
2. When meat is browned, mix in the remaining ingredients.

3. Put skillet on back of grill and cook slowly about 45 minutes, stirring occasionally. Spoon bean mixture onto *Toasted Buns, below.*

ABOUT 12 SERVINGS

TOASTED BUNS: Cut *buns* into halves and brush the cut side with *melted butter.* Place on grill and toast buttered side. Serve hot.

PORK AND BEANS ON THE GRILL

4 slices bacon
½ cup finely chopped
  onion
¼ cup chopped green
  pepper
2 cans (14 to 17 oz.
  each) pork and beans
  with tomato sauce

1 tablespoon dark
  molasses
2 teaspoons Worcester-
  shire sauce
3 tablespoons dark
  brown sugar
½ teaspoon salt
⅛ teaspoon pepper
¼ teaspoon oregano

1. Fry bacon in a skillet; reserve 2 tablespoons drippings. Crumble bacon and set aside.
2. Heat the reserved drippings in skillet. Add onion and green pepper and cook about 5 minutes, stirring occasionally.
3. Turn beans into a 1½-quart heat-resistant casserole. Mix in onion, green pepper, bacon, molasses, Worcestershire sauce, and a mixture of remaining ingredients.
4. Cover and set on top of grill until thoroughly heated.   ABOUT 6 SERVINGS

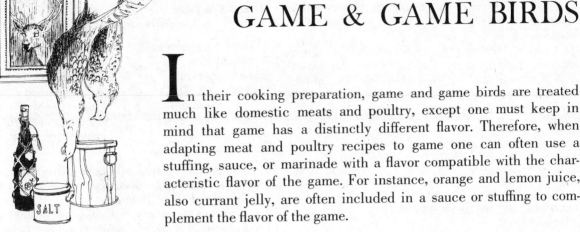

Bonus Chapter

GAME & GAME BIRDS

In their cooking preparation, game and game birds are treated much like domestic meats and poultry, except one must keep in mind that game has a distinctly different flavor. Therefore, when adapting meat and poultry recipes to game one can often use a stuffing, sauce, or marinade with a flavor compatible with the characteristic flavor of the game. For instance, orange and lemon juice, also currant jelly, are often included in a sauce or stuffing to complement the flavor of the game.

Game is a dry meat and a cooking method should be selected to make the meat as tasty and moist as possible. Large game, such as venison and reindeer, may be tough or tender depending upon the maturity of the animal. Tough venison may be tenderized somewhat by marinating the meat in a mixture of vinegar and water up to 48 hours. Or a commercial tenderizer may be used, following manufacturer's directions for its use. When roasting, generously "larding" the game is also recommended and cooking the meat at a low temperature.

The proper care of game after killing is important. Game birds should be eviscerated immediately and cooled as soon as possible. When birds are transported before evisceration and arrive home with no chance for the body heat to escape, the meat deteriorates rapidly and develops a strong flavor.

Dress rabbits and squirrels and other small game properly and keep in a cool, ventilated place while bringing them home. Venison should be bled promptly after killing. After dressing it the body cavity should be wiped thoroughly with a dry cloth. Avoid water as moist meat deteriorates more rapidly than dry. Store venison in a cool, well-ventilated place while transporting it.

The feathers of birds need not be plucked, as both feathers and skin can be removed with one process. To accomplish this, use the paraffin method suggested on *page 685*, or use the following: With a sharp knife, scrape a few feathers off the breast and insert knife under skin at this spot. Then cut the skin down the breast and pull the skin (along with feathers) away from the bird. Wash and clean the bird the same as for poultry. To add flavor, stuff celery tops (with green leaves) into the cleaned cavity of the bird until time for cooking.

GAME

Rabbit & Squirrel

To prepare a rabbit for cooking — Have the skin removed and rabbit opened and drawn. If you must do this yourself, tie the hind legs together with a strong cord and hang rabbit on a nail or hook. Cut around feet and cut a slit with a sharp knife. Then proceed to pull skin down. (It comes off easily.) Open rabbit at breast and remove the organs. Remove gall bladder and liver carefully, using only the liver. Remove head and feet and wash rabbit under cold running water. Dry with absorbent paper. Disjoint rabbit as you would a frying chicken.

If the characteristic "wild" flavor is undesirable, remove it in this manner: Cover rabbit with *cold water* in a saucepan, add *green celery tops, 1 onion, 3 whole cloves* and *3 whole allspice.* Cover and cook slowly 10 minutes. Drain at once and dry thoroughly. Then proceed with desired method of cooking.

To prepare squirrels for cooking—Follow above method. Young squirrels opened down the breast and flattened may be cooked much like rabbit. Stewing (see *Rabbit Stew, below*) is the best method for cooking older squirrels.

MARINATED RABBIT STEW
(Hasenpfeffer)

1 rabbit (2½ to 3 lbs.), cut in pieces	1 tablespoon salt
3 cups red wine vinegar	1 teaspoon mixed pickling spices
3 cups water	¼ teaspoon pepper
½ cup sugar	⅓ cup flour
1 onion, sliced	1 teaspoon salt
2 carrots, pared and cut in pieces	¼ teaspoon pepper
	3 tablespoons fat
	¼ cup flour

1. Put rabbit into a deep bowl and cover with a mixture of the vinegar, water, sugar, onion, carrots, 1 tablespoon salt, pickling spices, and pepper. Cover and refrigerate 2 to 3 days to marinate; turn pieces frequently.
2. Drain the rabbit; strain and reserve the marinade. Dry rabbit with absorbent paper. Coat pieces with a mixture of ⅓ cup flour, 1 teaspoon salt, and pepper.
3. Heat the fat in a Dutch oven or saucepot. Add the rabbit and brown slowly on all sides. Add 2 cups of the marinade. Cover and cook slowly about 45 minutes, or until meat is tender.
4. Thoroughly blend ½ cup of the reserved marinade and ¼ cup flour. Slowly pour one half of the mixture into cooking liquid, stirring constantly. Bring to boiling. Gradually add only what is needed of remaining mixture for consistency desired. Bring to boiling after each addition. Finally, cook 3 to 5 minutes.
5. Arrange rabbit on a serving platter. Pour some

of the gravy over the rabbit and serve remaining gravy in a gravy boat.   6 SERVINGS

RABBIT STEW
Squirrels are equally delicious cooked this way.

1 rabbit, cleaned and disjointed	1 medium-sized onion, quartered
3 cups beef broth (dissolve 2 beef bouillon cubes in 3 cups boiling water)	½ cup tomato sauce, or ½ cup strained stewed tomatoes
1 carrot, cut up	1 to 2 teaspoons Worcestershire sauce
2 stalks celery, cut up	

1. Cover rabbit pieces with cold *salted water* in a saucepan (2 to 3 tablespoons salt to 6 to 8 cups water). Let stand about 1 hour.
2. Drain off the water in saucepan and add the broth, carrot, celery, and onion to rabbit. Bring to boiling; reduce heat and cook slowly, covered, 1 hour. Strain the liquid and return to saucepan with the rabbit. Add tomato sauce and Worcestershire sauce and continue cooking slowly about 30 minutes, or until rabbit is tender.
3. Remove rabbit to heated serving dish. Combine *2 to 3 tablespoons flour* with ¼ *cup cold water* and stir into the cooking liquid; cook and stir until boiling and thickened. Season to taste with *salt* and *pepper* and cook several minutes longer. Pour over the rabbit or serve in a bowl.   3 OR 4 SERVINGS

FILET OF VENISON

6 venison filets, cut 2 in. thick	1 tablespoon olive oil
Instant meat tenderizer (seasoned)	3 tablespoons Madeira
Olive oil	1 tablespoon lemon juice
1 clove garlic, split	1 firm banana with all-yellow peel, cut diagonally in slices
1 tablespoon butter or margarine	

1. Prepare the meat as follows: Moisten each side of meat with *water* and sprinkle evenly with the instant meat tenderizer on all sides, using about ½ teaspoon per pound. Pierce meat deeply with a fork at approximately ½-inch intervals.
2. Heat the olive oil with garlic in a heavy skillet. Remove garlic before adding meat to the hot oil. Fry filets until they are brown outside but rare in-

side, about 20 minutes. Transfer to a hot platter and keep hot while preparing the sauce.

3. Add the butter and the 1 tablespoon olive oil to the skillet with the Madeira. Simmer about 2 minutes, stirring constantly. Pour over the filets just before serving.

4. Drizzle the lemon juice evenly over the banana slices and fry slices in hot butter or margarine until thoroughly heated.

5. Garnish each filet with a banana slice and serve with *Hot Brandied Cranberries* or *Chestnut Purée, below.*   6 SERVINGS

NOTE: Pieces of round steak the same size as the venison filets can be treated with the seasoned instant meat tenderizer and prepared in the same manner.

HOT BRANDIED CRANBERRIES: Combine *1 cup sugar, 1 cup water*, and *⅛ teaspoon salt* in a saucepan. Heat to boiling and boil, uncovered, 5 minutes. Add *2 cups (about ½ pound) washed and sorted cranberries.* Continue to boil, uncovered, without stirring, about 5 minutes, or until the skins pop. Remove from heat and stir in *3 to 4 tablespoons brandy.* Serve hot with the venison.   ABOUT 2 CUPS

CHESTNUT PURÉE: Shell about *2 pounds chestnuts* by making a small slit in the shell of each chestnut. Put in a saucepan and cover with *boiling water.* Boil about 20 minutes; drain. Remove shells and inner skin from chestnuts immediately. Return nuts to saucepan, cover with water, and bring to boiling. Boil, covered, about 5 minutes, or until tender; drain. Force chestnuts through a sieve or food mill. Season with *salt* and *pepper* and beat in a small amount of *butter or margarine* and *hot cream.*

ROAST VENISON

A marinade to tenderize and moisturize is needed for all venison roasts except those from very young animals. An uncooked or cooked marinade may be used. For a *venison roast* (leg) from a very young animal, sprinkle the roast with *salt* and *pepper* and dredge with *flour.* Cover with strips of *salt pork* unless meat is fat. Put into a shallow roasting pan and roast, uncovered, at 300°F, allowing 20 to 22 minutes per pound.

GAME BIRDS

TIMETABLE FOR ROASTING GAME BIRDS

Bird	Oven Temperature	Approx. Total Roasting Time
Grouse	425°F	20 to 25 minutes
Guinea hen	350°F	1½ to 2 hours
Partridge	350°F	30 to 40 minutes
Pheasant	325°F	1½ to 2 hours
Squab	400°F	35 to 45 minutes
Wild duck	450°F	15 minutes (rare) 25 minutes (medium)
Wild goose	325°F	20 to 25 minutes per pound

ROAST WILD GOOSE

1 wild goose	1 peeled onion, or 1
Salt	cored and quartered
Pepper	apple and 1 orange
1 tablespoon vinegar	

1. Clean goose, cutting out any visible fat. Singe, rinse, and pat dry. Sprinkle cavities with salt and pepper; sprinkle with the vinegar. Skewer neck skin to back. Put onion or fruits into body cavity.

2. Place on rack in shallow roasting pan. Roast goose at 325°F 20 to 25 minutes per pound, basting frequently with drippings. Allow about 1 pound per person.

Wild Duck

Canvasback, mallard, pintail, teal, and the others of the wild duck family should hang in a cool place at least 24 hours, and are better after 48 hours. Bleed the bird soon after shooting and allow it to hang by the head. To pluck wild duck remove large feathers dry. Then prepare the following mixture: Melt *⅜ pound paraffin* in *7 quarts boiling water.* Dip duck in and out of mixture 4 or 5 times or until paraffin has coated the feathers. Cool duck to let paraffin harden, then strip off feathers and paraffin at the same time. Singe and remove any remaining pin-feathers with a pointed knife. Cut head and feet from birds; remove entrails. Wipe ducks with a damp cloth; dry well. Some wild ducks develop a fishy taste because of their eating habits or the region in which they live. To help reduce a fishy flavor rub duck thoroughly, inside and out, with *lemon*, or put a whole peeled lemon, *sliced celery*, *parsley*, *a small onion*, or *apple slices* into the cavity of a bird that is not to be stuffed. Remove "stuffing" before serving. Marinating birds in a *red wine* with *onion* or *garlic* will also help eliminate fishy taste. Do not overcook as the meat will become dry and crumbly.

ROAST WILD DUCKS

3 wild ducks, (about 2 lbs. each)	Raisin-Orange Stuffing, *below*
Salt	6 slices bacon, halved
	1 cup orange juice

1.   Singe and clean ducks. Cut out oil sac at base of tail; cut off neck at body, leaving on neck skin. Wash ducks under cold running water; dry with absorbent paper. Rub cavities with *salt*.
2.   Spoon Raisin-Orange Stuffing lightly into body and neck cavities. If desired, leave cavity open while roasting and as dressing expands it will add to the attractiveness of the duck when served.
3.   Place ducks, breast up, on rack in shallow roasting pan. Lay four bacon pieces over breast of each bird. Roast, uncovered, at 450°F 15 minutes for very rare, 20 minutes for medium rare, and 25 minutes for medium well. Baste ducks occasionally with orange juice during roasting.
4.   When ducks are roasted to the desired degree of doneness, place on heated platter. (Reserve drippings from roasting pan for use in Orange Sauce preparation.) Garnish with *watercress, orange slices*, and whole *cooked prunes*. Serve with *Orange Sauce, below*.
6 SERVINGS

RAISIN-ORANGE STUFFING

6 cups ½-in. bread cubes (slightly dry)	1 cup thinly sliced celery
1 cup dark seedless raisins, rinsed and drained	1 tablespoon grated orange peel
½ cup butter or margarine	1 teaspoon salt
½ cup chopped onion	Few grains pepper
	½ teaspoon ground thyme

1.   Combine bread cubes and raisins in a large bowl.

2.   Heat butter in a skillet. Add onion and celery and cook over low heat about 5 minutes. Mix in orange peel and a mixture of salt, pepper and thyme. Pour over bread and raisins; toss gently until well mixed. Spoon lightly into birds.
STUFFING FOR THREE 2 POUND DUCKS

ORANGE SAUCE: Drain off all but 2 tablespoons fat from roasting pan, leaving brown residue in pan. Add *3 tablespoons flour* and stir until smooth. Add ½ *cup water* gradually, stirring constantly. Continue to stir until boiling; cook 1 to 2 minutes longer. Blend in ⅔ *cup orange juice* and heat to boiling. Pour into a gravy boat and sprinkle with ½ *teaspoon grated orange peel* and ½ *teaspoon grated lemon peel*. Serve over roast duck.
ABOUT 1¼ CUPS

ROAST WILD DUCK WITH WILD RICE STUFFING

2 wild ducks, singed and cleaned	4 slices bacon or salt pork
1 to 2 teaspoons salt	1 cup orange juice, cider, or dry red wine (optional)
1 to 2 teaspoons monosodium glutamate	
Wild Rice Stuffing (½ recipe, *page 260*)	

1.   Remove oil sac at base of tail of each duck; cut off neck at body, leaving on the neck skin. Wash birds in cold running water; dry on absorbent paper. Rub cavities with salt and monosodium glutamate.
2.   Prepare the stuffing and spoon lightly into the body and neck cavities of the ducks. Using skewers, close the body cavities and fasten neck skin to back of birds and wings to bodies.
3.   Put ducks, breast up, on a rack in roasting pan. Arrange bacon or salt pork over breasts.
4.   Roast, uncovered, at 400°F to 450°F 20 to 25 minutes for medium-rare. (Wild duck is traditionally served rare.) If orange juice is used, baste the birds occasionally during roasting.
5.   To serve ducks, remove skewers and place birds on heated platter. Keep warm.
6.   Scrape pan drippings into a small saucepan. Combine ½ *cup water* and *1 tablespoon flour*. Gradually stir mixture into drippings and bring rapidly to boiling, stirring constantly until gravy is thickened. Cook about 3 minutes longer. Serve with ducks.
ABOUT 4 SERVINGS

STUFFED ROAST WILD GOOSE: Follow recipe for

Roast Wild Duck with Wild Rice Stuffing. Use *1 goose* for the ducks. Use a full recipe for stuffing. Roast at 325°F about 3 hours, basting frequently with the orange juice.

WILD DUCK WITH PECAN STUFFING

4 cups soft bread crumbs	2 eggs, beaten
1 cup finely chopped celery	2 wild ducks (about 2½ lbs. each), dressed
1 cup finely chopped onion	6 slices bacon
1 cup seedless raisins	1 cup ketchup
1 cup pecans, chopped	¼ cup Worcestershire sauce
½ teaspoon salt	¼ cup steak sauce
½ cup milk, heated	½ cup chili sauce

1. Mix the bread crumbs, celery, onion, raisins, pecans, and salt thoroughly. Add hot milk to the beaten eggs and toss with crumb mixture.
2. Rub cavities of birds with *salt*. Fill with stuffing (leave cavity open).
3. Place, breast up, on rack in shallow roasting pan. Lay 3 strips bacon over breast of each bird.
4. Roast, uncovered, at 450°F 15 minutes for very rare, 20 minutes for medium rare, and 25 minutes for medium well. Baste ducks with a mixture of the remaining ingredients while roasting.
5. To serve, place ducks on heated platter and garnish with *parsley* and slices of *orange* with a few *candied cranberries* in center of each slice.
6. Skim the fat from the liquid left in roasting pan and serve liquid with ducks.   4 OR 5 SERVINGS

Pheasant, Partridge & Grouse

A distinction must be made between light and dark meat in cooking these birds.

Pheasant is perhaps the most popular of the game birds, with a young bird weighing about 2½ pounds or 1½ pounds after dressing and drawing. It serves 3 or 4. Pheasant is usually roasted and, because of its delicate flavor, need not be stuffed.

Partridge, like quail, is light meat and should be well cooked but not dry (cook as for chicken.)

Grouse (prairie chicken) and pheasant (also wild duck, snipe, plover, and woodcock) are dark meat and may be served rare. These birds may be cooked using the same methods, varying them only as to the degree of doneness desired.

ROAST PHEASANT

2 young pheasant, about 2 lbs. each	1½ teaspoons monosodium glutamate
Wild Rice with Mushrooms, *page 298*	¼ cup unsalted butter, melted
1½ teaspoons salt	Brown Gravy, *page 348*

1. Cut off necks close to bodies, leaving neck skin on to help hold the stuffing. Remove any pin feathers; singe if necessary. Rinse inside and out in warm water; drain; pat dry with absorbent paper.
2. Cover giblets (except liver) and neck with water; bring to boiling, then simmer until tender, about 1 hour. During last 15 minutes, add some *salt* and the livers.
3. Prepare Wild Rice with Mushrooms for stuffing. Rub pheasant cavities with the salt and monosodium glutamate. Lightly fill neck and body cavities with stuffing. Close cavities with skewers and lace with cord.
4. Place birds, breast up, on rack in roasting pan. Brush with melted butter. Roast at 325°F 1½ to 2 hours, or until pheasant test done; baste frequently.
5. Reserve liquid from giblets for gravy; finely chop the hearts, gizzards and livers.
6. Transfer birds to platter and keep warm while making Brown Gravy, adding *2 tablespoons red wine* along with giblets.   4 SERVINGS

PHEASANT WITH SPAETZLE

Some historians give George Washington credit for the introduction of pheasant to the United States.

2 pheasant, cleaned and quartered	1 cup butter or margarine
2 qts. boiling water	1 teaspoon paprika
4 chicken bouillon cubes	7 tablespoons flour
½ cup all-purpose flour	1 cup Chablis
	1 cup dairy sour cream

1. Take necks, backs, giblets, etc., from pheasant and simmer in water, strengthened with chicken bouillon cubes. Cook until stock is reduced to 1½ quarts.
2. Flour remaining pieces of pheasant; sauté in ½ cup butter until brown; set aside.
3. Melt remaining ½ cup butter in a large frying pan and add paprika.
4. Strain pheasant stock and add all but 1 cup to butter and paprika; bring to boiling. Adding gradu-

ally, stir a blend of 1 cup cooled stock and the flour into boiling stock. Cook and stir to 2 minutes. Stir in the wine and cook gently 30 minutes.

5. Add browned pheasant; cover and cook until tender 1 to 1½ hours.

6. Remove pheasant. Stir in sour cream, about a spoonful at a time. Heat but do not boil. Place pheasant in chafing or serving dish and spoon over some of the wine sauce. Serve with *Spaetzle II, below,* also with wine sauce spooned over them.

ABOUT 6 SERVINGS

SPAETZLE II: Combine *3 beaten eggs, ½ teaspoon salt,* and *1 cup heavy cream.* Stir in enough *flour* (about 2 cups) to make a thick batter which breaks from spoon. (Batter is too thin if it pours in a steady stream.) Drop from end of a teaspoon into boiling *chicken stock.* Keep spaetzle no larger than a twenty-five cent piece by dripping enough to cover just end of spoon. Cook 5 minutes and then drain. Sauté in *¼ cup butter* until light brown.

STUFFED PARTRIDGES

3 partridges	Salt pork
Stuffing (bread or wild rice)	¼ cup water
	½ cup sherry

1. Clean, stuff, and truss birds.
2. Place in a greased casserole; top with slices of salt pork and add water.
3. Roast at 350°F 15 minutes. Add sherry, cover and continue roasting about 25 minutes, or until tender. Serve with a *grapefruit sauce,* if desired.

4 TO 6 SERVINGS

Squabs & Pigeons

Domestic and wild pigeons are both eaten, the latter being quite tough and requiring longer cooking with moist heat. Squabs are the nestlings of pigeons and are usually marketed at about 4 weeks of age when they weigh between 12 ounces and 1¼ pounds. At this age the meat is tender, milky, and delicately flavored. The breast flesh is light and the legs are full and moist. One squab will serve one or two persons. They are on the market all year. Squabs may be prepared using recipes calling for Rock Cornish game hens.

BROILED MARINATED SQUAB

Cut ready-to-cook *squabs* into halves lengthwise. Marinate in a *melted butter* and *dry white wine* mixture 30 minutes. Sprinkle squabs with *salt* and *pepper.* Place, skin side down, in broiler pan. Broil 5 to 7 inches from source of heat 15 minutes. Turn and continue broiling until tender, about 10 minutes, basting frequently.

BROILED DEVILED SQUAB: Cut slashes in *4 dressed squabs;* rub in a mixture of *dry mustard* and *cayenne pepper.* Broil as directed in recipe for Broiled Marinated Squab. Meanwhile, cream together *½ cup butter or margarine, 2 teaspoons dry mustard, 2 teaspoons Worcestershire sauce, ¼ teaspoon black pepper, few grains cayenne pepper,* and *¼ teaspoon salt.* Spread over squabs just before serving.

Quail

Quail, like chicken, may be left whole or split down the back and roasted, broiled, panbroiled, or braised. To roast quail, put in a shallow roasting pan with strips of *bacon* or *salt pork* placed on birds. Roast at 325°F about 1 hour, or until tender. Allow 1 bird per serving and serve on *toast squares.* Accompany with a *currant or pineapple sauce* or spoon sauce over birds before serving. To broil, panbroil, or braise quail, follow recipes for chicken.

QUAIL COOKED IN WINE

½ cup fat	½ teaspoon salt
2 small onions, minced	⅛ teaspoon black
2 whole cloves	pepper
1 teaspoon peppercorns	Few grains cayenne
2 cloves garlic, minced	pepper
½ bay leaf	1 teaspoon minced
6 quail, cleaned and trussed	chives
	2 cups cream or
2 cups dry white wine	evaporated milk

1. Melt fat in a large deep skillet; add onion, cloves, peppercorns, garlic, and bay leaf; heat for several minutes.

2. Add quail and brown on all sides. Add wine, salt, peppers, and chives. Cover and cook slowly until tender, about 30 minutes.

3. Remove quail to hot serving dish.

4. Strain liquid into a saucepan; add cream and heat to boiling.

6 SERVINGS

Bonus Chapter

ENTERTAINING IS EASY!

The secret of successful entertaining is to enjoy your own parties. Entertaining should be as much fun for the hostess as it is for the guests. If you plan carefully, adapting your plans to the special conditions of your home, everything is bound to run along smoothly with everyone having a wonderful time, including you.

Some people seem to be born with a knack for entertaining. Good food appears at their parties as if by magic, the guests are relaxed and conversation flourishes. You may be sure, however, that none of this just "happens." The food appears because someone has prepared it; the guests are relaxed because their hostess feels no strain; conversation flows because their hostess is on hand to help it along instead of coping with a crisis in the kitchen. And all of this means that she has planned carefully. She has planned a menu that requires a minimum of attention after the guests arrive, planned and arranged the flowers and other accessories, and set out all the little appurtenances of comfort. She probably has planned her guest list, too, inviting only persons who will be congenial. And if she is the completely thoughtful hostess, her menu has been planned with due regard for the food likes and dislikes of her guests.

In planning a company menu it is wise to follow the same principles that guide all menu-making. Avoid repetition of foods in the same meal—if fish is the appetizer do not use it for the main dish. Maintain a balance between firm and soft foods. Do not serve too many starches (rice, potatoes, and bread at the same meal are not good planning) or too much of any other single food stuff. Avoid too many strong flavors—flavors should harmonize or contrast but not compete. Plan meals with an eye to the over-all arrangement, varying the foods in color, texture and flavor. Include something sweet and something tart, something hot and something cold in every meal. Delight guests with an occasion-al surprise, but try out the new recipe on the family first.

Starred recipes (*) are in the book; see index for page numbers. Increase recipes where necessary for the desired number of servings.

BRUNCH & MORNING COFFEE

Brunch, a delightful meal combining both breakfast and lunch, may be served any time before one o'clock in the afternoon. When served early, brunch usually means simple breakfast foods. Served later, the menu may be an expanded and more elaborate breakfast, possibly served buffet style. Or it may more closely resemble a luncheon except for soup and salad which seldom are included in a brunch menu. If dessert is served it is a light fruit in season and/or cookies.

A mid-morning social gathering often called simply "morning coffee" is sometimes used by hostesses as an easy, informal, and friendly means of entertaining a few friends. It is almost certain to be a feminine affair with the menfolks safely out of the house. It is a gracious way to entertain an out-of-town friend when time is limited.

Most informal of all is the impromptu coffee (the *kaffeeklatsch*) to which neighbors drift in and are welcomed by plenty of hot coffee accompanied by coffee cake, sweet rolls, or doughnuts. No specific service is required; a bright sunny kitchen is usually a pleasant place for a gathering of a few neighbors or good friends.

When guest have been invited for a real morning coffee "party," usually about 10 or 11 o'clock, more elaborate preparations are in order.

Coffee, coffee breads, and one or more trays of bite-size relishes of contrasting color and flavor (sweet and sour, bland and savory), may all be arranged on a prettily spread buffet table in living or dining room. The hostess herself will want to pour the coffee for her guests—a hospitable as well as a practical gesture; but a stack of plates on the table, with napkins and teaspoons arranged beside them, will permit each guest to serve herself to whatever she wants of the other foods provided. The "main course" will be bread and a good plan is to allow one big, beautiful coffee cake of the good-without-butter kind, already cut for the convenience of the guests, when the party is small; when the group is larger, a selection of delicious sweet rolls should be added.

The relish tray may hold tangy cheese bits, crisp radish roses or celery curls, ripe or green olives, along with fruits such as small clusters of grapes, whole strawberries washed but with hulls intact for finger eating, pineapple chunks, melon balls, or hulled berries impaled on picks. An attractive fresh fruit relish bowl can be made by cutting into halves and scooping out a chilled honeydew melon or a fresh pineapple with its spiny crown intact, and heaping with balls or chunks cut from the fruit bowl itself and other fruits, all on wooden picks.

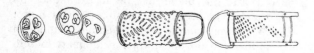

KICK-OFF BRUNCH FOR TEEN-AGE ATHLETES
Orange Juice
Ready-to-Eat Cereal with Fruit Topping and Cream
Scrambled Eggs*   Pork Sausage Links
Toasted Buttered English Muffins
Milk   Hot Cocoa*

BOUNTIFUL COLD-WEATHER BREAKFAST OR BRUNCH
Fruit Cup
Hominy Grits   Butter or Margarine
Shirred Eggs with Sausage and Cheese*
Buttered Toast   Pineapple-Coconut Bread*
Coffee   Hot Cocoa*

LUNCHEONS

All parties are fun, but luncheons are in a class by themselves. They are usually given by women and for women, and so the light and even "fancy" touches which are special fun for the hostess are quite appropriate.

Whether you invite one guest or a dozen, you will summon all the artistry at your command to make the setting of your party beautiful and appropriate. Almost any kind of cloth, table mat, or runner is suitable if it harmonizes with the dishes and other accessories, the flowers, and to some extent with the season.

Table decorations, as at any meal, should be kept low, pretty but unobtrusive. Flowers are always appropriate, and so are attractive arrangements of fruits, foliage, handsome vegetables, vines, shells, quaint or beautiful figurines, and low-growing plants. Since luncheons are mid-day affairs, candles are not suitable. Flatware and crystal are placed as for a dinner party.

Luncheon for a group may be introduced by cocktails and appetizers in the living room. The luncheon menu itself may include two to four courses, the wise hostess planning it according to what she can handle easily and gracefully. The main dish is often a creamed mixture served in croustades, patty shells, or over split baking powder biscuits. It may be accompanied by salad or not. Particularly if salad is omitted, a nice touch is to garnish the plates with spiced fruit such as spiced crab apples or peaches, watermelon pickles or the like, or with crisp bread-and-butter pickles or preserved kumquats. The dessert should be keyed to the rest of the meal: If the main dish is a rich creamed mixture, serve a light dessert—fruit or a fruit mold or sherbet; if a salad bowl is the main course, an elaborate dessert is in order.

The manner of service depends upon your home, your facilities and your guests. Keep it simple and informal, and be your most gracious self.

GREET-THE-SPRING LUNCHEON
Sunshine Cocktail*
Shrimp and Avocado Salad
Cheesy Sesame-Stuffed Celery
Cloverleaf Rolls   Butter or Margarine
Strawberry Shortcake*
Tea

SUNNY BRIGHT LUNCHEON
Greek Lemon Soup*   Sesame Seed Twists*
Deviled Crab in Shells*
Buttered French-Style Green Beans with
Sieved Hard-Cooked Egg Topping
Sparkling Fresh Peach Mold*
Gold Cake with Orange Seven-Minute Frosting*
Iced Tea

INFORMAL LUNCHEON FOR EIGHT
Vichyssoise*   Crisp Crackers
Tomato-Bacon Soufflé*   Peas Distinctive*
Biscuit Surprises*
Chantilly Raisin-Rice Pudding*
Tea   Coffee

WARM-WEATHER LUNCHEON ON THE TERRACE
Chilled Tomato Soup   Wafers
Ham Mousse with Stuffed Eggs*
Asparagus Vinaigrette Platter*
Mace 'n' Cheese Biscuits*
Chocolate-Mocha Cream Pudding*
Coconut Macaroons*
Iced Tea with Lemon or Lime Syrup*

TEAS

A pleasant and flexible way of entertaining friends or acquaintances is the afternoon tea. There is not very much difference between a formal and informal tea, except the difference involved in serving a larger or a smaller number of guests. The usual hour for tea is between four and five, but it may be extended if many of the guests are career women, and may start earlier if a large number is expected.

The Informal Tea
Invitations to informal teas are usually extended in person, by telephone, or by an informal note, with the time stated. The number invited may vary from five or six to a large number, depending upon the occasion. If a hostess has asked a few friends to drop in for tea, she may serve it in the living room. The tea service should be arranged on an uncovered tray and placed on a low table, spread with a cloth which may barely cover the table or may hang as much as eighteen inches over the sides.

If the hostess has a silver tea service with an alcohol lamp, the tray will contain a kettle of water kept boiling over the flame (which should be lighted only after the tray is safely placed on the table), an empty tea pot, creamer, sugar bowl, a plate of lemon slices with a lemon fork, a tea caddy, and an empty bowl for tea leaves and for dregs poured from the guests' cups before refilling. In this case the hostess makes the tea in the presence of the guests and serves it with or without additional hot water, according to preference, and with or without cream, sugar, or lemon. If the hostess prefers, or if she does not have a tea service with a means of keeping water boiling, the tea may be brewed and strained in the kitchen into a heated tea pot, and boiling water poured into a second heated pot to dilute the strong tea as guests request. In this case water should be kept boiling on the range so the supply may be frequently replenished and always hot.

Cups and saucers with teaspoons laid on the saucers to the right of the cups may be placed on the tea tray if it will hold them all, or some may be on the table beside it. Tea plates (7 to 8 inches in diameter), in a stack, and 12-inch tea napkins are also on the table near the tray. If possible little tables or some other convenient surface should be provided near the chair of each guest to hold plate, cup, and saucer. Many hostesses omit saucers entirely, in which case tea cup and food are both placed on the tea plate.

The food provided may consist only of strips of cinnamon toast, finger sandwiches spread with whipped butter, cucumber or watercress sandwiches, or tiny hot biscuits with jam. Small crisp cookies or thinly sliced fruit cake, mints, and salted nuts may be served too. Only at small intimate teas will hot crumpets or buttered toasted English muffins be offered in the fashion of a hearty English tea. The serving of these, or of jam, requires spreaders. At formal teas or for a larger group, serve only finger foods.

For a large group, or even in a small group if the hostess knows that some guests prefer it, coffee may be offered as well as tea; and in warm weather there may be some who will like the strong, hot tea or coffee poured over cracked ice in tall glasses. On very hot days a bowl of fruit punch with plenty of ice may replace the tea service altogether.

If the group, even at an informal tea, is quite large, the hostess may ask one close friend to pour the tea for her, another to pour the coffee, and perhaps a third to assist by keeping the serving plates replenished with food, so that she herself may be free to greet her guests. Constant replenishing of the serving plates is necessary to keep the arrangement of the tea table attractive.

The Formal Tea

These large teas are seldom given except for a special occasion—perhaps to introduce a visiting celebrity, or for a club meeting or other official event. Invitations (on a correspondence card or on the hostess' visiting card, with "To meet _____" across the top and the date and hour in a lower corner) are issued about two weeks before the event.

A long table is used for a formal tea, with flowers and tall, white, formal candles (which if present should be lighted, but should not be present unless needed). The cloth, of formal damask or lace, usually hangs over the table edge from one-quarter to one-half yard. The tea tray, arranged just as for an informal tea, will be at one end of the table. At the other end will be a coffee or chocolate service, or on a warm day, a bowl of ice fruit punch. Only finger foods should be served. Cucumber and watercress sandwiches are traditional at a formal tea, as are little cakes such as petits fours, thinly sliced fruitcake, mints, and salted nuts.

Tea cups and saucers with teaspoons laid on the saucer at the right of the cup are usually arranged near each beverage service; additional plates for sandwiches and cakes may be stacked (not more than six or eight high) on the table with napkins. The foods and the cups, saucers, plates, and napkins should be replenished as they are used.

Two intimate friends of the hostess, preferably ladies who are acquainted with most of the guests, should be asked to pour the beverages. They may be replaced by two others at the end of an hour, if the tea is large. Their assistance, and that of a third person to replenish the serving plates and remove the guests' cups and plates as they are emptied, will permit the hostess, together with the guest of honor, to receive her guests.

WARM-WEATHER TEA
Assorted Glazed Canapés*
Bonnet Sandwiches*
Ripe Olives   Anchovy-Stuffed Olives
Imperials*   Coffee Nuts*
Watermelon Punch Bowl*   Iced Tea

COLD-WEATHER TEA
Broiled Bacon-Cheese Canapés*
Cheddar Puffs*
Sardine Finger Canapés*
Small Fancy Cakes (Petits Fours)*
Glazed Spiced Nuts*
Coffee   Tea

DINNERS

"Company" dinners are classified according to their formality. Most of the dinners an average hostess will give are informal and the rest are semiformal. The formal dinner is characterized by written or engraved invitations in the third person (also answered in the same manner), by full-evening dress, by a menu written in French (sometimes accompanied by an English translation), and consisting of no fewer than seven courses, but often as many as twelve with six or more wines. Preparation and serving of a seven course formal dinner consisting of appetizer, soup, fish, meat with vegetables, salad, dessert, and fruit (also nuts), followed by coffee or liqueurs in the drawing room, demands skilled help provided by a trained service staff. The style of service used is known as *Russian* or *Continental*, with host and hostess taking no part in it. The average family would find little occasion to use this formal style of service.

For the family with no outside kitchen help the *English* or *family style* of service is more practical. All the food is served at the table by the host and hostess instead of being served from the kitchen in individual servings.

A third type, usually called "*compromise*" service, is also used especially for semiformal meals and is described below.

The Semiformal Dinner

This is the most formal meal most homemakers are likely to give. Invitations may be partially engraved, with names, dates, and hours filled in by hand; or they may be extended in an informal letter or by telephone. The time is usually eight or eight-thirty. Men are usually expected to wear dinner jackets, black or, in warm weather, white, rather than business suits; and women usually wear informal evening dress or dinner dresses. The considerate hostess will include a hint of the degree of formality in her invitation.

The dinner itself consists of only four or five courses—soup, fish (usually in the form of a cocktail), meat and vegetables, salad, and dessert, and of these either the fish course or the salad is often omitted. After-dinner coffee is usually served in the living room.

Service of a semiformal dinner is known as "compromise" service and is a combination of English and Russian style, sometimes called American. It is suited to the home with one maid or with a part-time waitress, and means that while the first course, salad, and dessert are served by the maid, the host or the host and hostess participate in serving the main course. The host generally carves the meat and places it on plates, which may be passed by the maid or handed down the table by the guests. The hostess sometimes serves the potatoes and vegetables; or the serving dishes may be offered to the guests by the maid. When there is no man of the house, the carving may be done by a close friend; or the hostess may do all the serving.

The Informal Dinner

Invitations to the most frequent and most intimate form of dinner may be issued personally, by telephone, or by informal letter. The guests will seldom number more than ten, especially if there is no maid. The guests' dress is dictated by custom; it is perfectly proper for the men to come in business suits and the women to dress accordingly. If the meal is a real "party" on a non-business day, dinner jackets and dinner dresses are quite in order.

The menu may consist of only two or three courses—either soup or fish, meat and vegetables, and dessert; or casserole, salad, and dessert. After-dinner coffee in the living room is still a pleasant custom, but coffee may be served at the table. The "family-style" service may be assisted by a maid, or by a member of the family or a guest, but the hostess will probably do most of the serving. And the hour may be any time from six to eight-thirty.

Table Setting

The hostess's common sense as well as her knowledge of tradition will be called upon in setting the table for dinner. Everything should be correctly planned in an orderly manner.

The first step is to lay the cloth. For a really formal dinner a pure white or pale cream-colored cloth of linen damask is traditional, though a handsome lace cloth may be used. At least 9 inches of overhang should be allowed at each end. For less formal dinners, pastel damask, lace, linen edged with lace, or place mats may be used. A silence cloth or felt is always used under damask or linen.

Next, the dinner plates are placed. These should be spaced equidistant from each other, and one inch from the edge of the table. To allow the guests elbow room, a minimum of twenty inches must be allowed for each place—twenty-five or thirty inches is better.

The flat silver is arranged next. Only pieces actually needed for the food to be served should be put on the table, and these should be arranged in the order in which they will be used, starting from the outside. Forks (except cocktail forks) are placed to the left of the plate; knives, spoons, and cocktail forks to the right. All should be parallel to each other and at right angles to the edge of the table, with the handles an inch from the edge. Butter knives are placed on the butter plates, either parallel or at right angles to the table edge. Dessert forks or spoons are usually brought in with the dessert, though at an informal dinner they may be placed on the table.

The water glass is set at the tip of the dinner knife. Other glasses (for wines) are placed to the right and slightly in front of the water glass. The butter plate occupies the position at the tip of the dinner fork. Folded napkins are placed on the dinner plate if it is empty when the guests come to the table, or at the left of the forks; the folding should display the monogram, if there is one, and the open edges should be parallel with the fork and edge of the table and next to the fork. Individual ashtrays with matches and a few cigarettes should be supplied at each place. Iced water should be poured at the last moment; there should be no ice in the glasses.

Any centerpiece should be low enough to permit conversation across the table. Candles should be tall enough to burn above eye level.

Seating of Guests

When dinner is announced, at a semiformal dinner, the hostess leads the way in to the dining room, followed by the ladies and then by the gentlemen, with the host. Only at very formal dinners does the host enter first with the lady guest of honor on his arm; then the hostess goes in last with the gentleman guest of honor. The host is always seated at one end of the table with the lady of honor at his right, and the hostess at the opposite end with the gentleman guest of honor at her right. If there is no difference in age, rank, or distinction among the guests, the lady at the host's right and the gentlemen at the hostess' right have the positions of honor. Ladies and gentlemen alternate along the sides of the table, with husbands and wives usually not seated side by side.

A thoughtful hostess will make her seating plan with her guests' interests and tastes in mind, and try to place together those who will find one another interesting and congenial. In a large party, place cards will be helpful, but at a smaller dinner she may indicate to each guest where he or she is to sit.

Serving Procedure

Whatever the degree of formality, the lady seated at the host's right is always the first to be served. The hostess is never served first, unless she is the only lady present. Nor should the hostess ever be the first to help herself from an untouched serving dish. The classic sequence of serving goes clockwise around the table, starting with the lady guest of honor, but other sequences are also possible and correct; *i.e.*, one course clockwise, the next counter-clockwise, so that a different gentleman is last to be served in each case. When several have been served, guests may begin eating without waiting for the hostess, but the considerate hostess will lay her fork on her plate as a signal if she sees that the guests are waiting for her to begin. She should always be the last to finish.

All plates are placed and removed and all serving dishes offered to guests from the left. Ideally, the dishes offered should be held in the waitress's left hand, but in the interest of saving time, she may bring in two dishes at once, or present two dishes on a tray. Water and wine should both be poured from the right, by the waitress's right hand.

Dishes are always removed singly, never "stacked" on the table. When the main course is finished, serving dishes are removed first; then each place is cleared; then the maid takes away the pepper and salt shakers and the breadbasket on a tray, and crumbs the table, using a folded napkin and a clean plate. Dessert plates and silver are then put on the table.

Serving after-dinner coffee in the living room is a practical as well as a pleasant custom. It may be done in three ways, according to the size and character of the group, the formality of the occasion, and the service available. One way is to pour the coffee in the kitchen and have it brought in to the living room on a tray by the maid. Another way is to carry in to the living room a tray containing the silver coffee pot, creamer, sugar bowl, and the cups; the hostess then pours and hands the cups to guests who are nearby, or the the host or other member of the family, who will hand them to more distant guests. The hostess may ask each guest for his cream and sugar preference, or they may help themselves. And the third way, perfectly acceptable at informal gatherings, is for the hostess to make the coffee freshly in the presence of the guests, using an electric coffee maker on a tray.

Some Factors in a Successful Dinner

Formal or informal, any dinner party will be more successful if it has been planned in detail. Whether the hostess expects to have a regular or part-time maid for part of the service or to handle it all herself, writing down the work schedule will help to prevent last-minute confusion. A maid brought in for the occasion will work more smoothly if time can be given to rehearsal beforehand.

Since the food is still the most important part of the dinner party, its quality should be safeguarded. Hot foods must be piping hot when they are brought from the kitchen, and cold foods should be served very cold. Serving platters and dishes for hot meats and vegetables should be warmed and plates for salads and for refrigerator or frozen desserts chilled.

More important than the observance of every rule of etiquette is that the dinner party should be enjoyed by everyone, guests and hostess alike. This happy result is most easily attained if the hostess has invited no more guests than she can comfortably seat and serve, and if her planning has been such that everything goes smoothly without visible effort. A dinner is a challenge for any hostess, and it can be fun too.

The Cocktail Hour

The hour before dinner is, in many homes, the cocktail hour—a pleasant interlude during which guests may relax from the cares of the day and become better acquainted before they dine.

The appetizers that are served with the cocktails should be both delicious and attractive. One or two kinds are enough—perhaps a piquant dip served with crisp crackers or potato chips, and a tiny hot appetizer such as cheese balls. Hot appetizers are better served with before-dinner cocktails than at a cocktail party, because the hostess can be reasonably sure they will be eaten before they cool.

As always, when cocktails are served, a nonalcoholic beverage should be provided for guests who prefer it. It may be a well-seasoned tomato juice, a fruit juice or tart fruit punch.

FEMININE V.I.P. DINNER
Shrimp with Peppy Cocktail Sauce*
Consommé   Miniatures Florentine*
Roast Lamb with Sour Cream Sauce au Claret*
Corn with Mushrooms*
Molded Avocado-Grapefruit Salad*   Relishes
Hot Rolls   Butter
Grasshopper Chiffon Pie*
Coffee

GERMAN FAMILY DINNER
Apple Cider
Roast Loin of Pork*
Kraut with Apples*   German Potato Salad*
Crusty Rye Bread
Hazelnut Torte with Strawberry Whipped Cream*
Coffee

PENNSYLVANIA DUTCH DINNER
Flash un Kas*
Schnitz un Knepp*
Paprika Cream Schnitzel and Shupp Noodles*
Pennsylvania Dutch Roast Chicken*
with Potato Balls
German Noodle Ring*
Lancaster County Lima Beans*   Squash
Tossed Salad   Pepper Cabbage*
Assorted breads: Moravian Sugar Cake*
Rye Cakes* Soft Gingerbread*
Molded Butter
Assorted Relishes
Frau Moyer's Cheese Custard Pie*
Lemon Sponge*
Blitzkuchen*   Moravian Scotch Cakes*
Milk   Coffee

ITALIAN-STYLE DINNER
Antipasto-Relish Tray*   Crisp Crackers
Chicken Cacciatore with Spaghetti*
Broccoli Sicilian Style*
Bread Sticks*
Biscuit Tortoni*   Italian Butter Cookies*
Coffee Espresso

FRENCH DINNER
Liver Pâté on Toast Squares
Filet of Venison with Hot Brandied Cranberries*
Chestnut Purée*   Ratatouille*
Tossed Salad with French Dressing
Croissants*   Butter Curls
Pears Flambé*
Demitasse*

BUFFETS

Buffet service fits perfectly into the relaxed, informal pattern of contemporary living. If you have limited dining space, or if you are a do-it-yourself hostess, buffet service permits you to entertain with more ease than any other type of service, and just as graciously and pleasantly.

Your buffet table may be set against a wall, or in the center of the room. For only six or eight guests, it is often placed with the long side against a wall; a larger number may need both long sides for sufficient elbow room when serving themselves. Because it presents all the food to the guests at one time and is thus the center of interest, the table should be arranged with care and artistry—and with common sense too, for the buffet table is functional and its arrangement is as important as its beauty.

The table itself should be dressed as attractively as possible, in lace, linen, or pretty place mats. And this is the time for bringing out your beautiful serving trays and plates. Flowers have an important role to play on the buffet table. If the table is against the wall, the flower arrangement may be a background for the foods; if in the center of the room, it will probably be a centerpiece. Since guests will all be standing, there is no need to keep it low. If candles are used for lighting the table, be sure to use plenty of them, placed so they really illuminate.

For the convenience of your guests, plan the arrangement of the table carefully. Confusing traffic plans should be avoided in order to help the serving line progress with ease and speed. Place a stack of large dinner plates at the point where guests are to start—probably at one end of the table. Napkins and silverware should be where they will be picked up last, after the plates are filled. Unless the guests are to eat at small tables, it is customary to serve only foods that can be eaten with a fork, since use of a knife is difficult. Rolls are usually buttered before they are put on the buffet. If you serve a tossed salad, tongs are far more easily handled than the conventional salad fork and spoon, when one hand is occupied by a plate. Since seasoning is so largely a matter of individual preference, individual salt and pepper shakers should be provided on snack tables or other convenient surfaces near the guests' chairs rather than on the buffet. A side table may hold a tray with goblets or glasses and a pitcher of iced water.

When guests have served themselves, partially emptied serving dishes should be refilled and empty ones removed from the buffet. Second servings may be passed by the hostess, or she may ask the guests to return to the buffet to serve themselves. When the first course is eaten, the buffet table is cleared, and dessert and the dishes in which it is to be served are then brought out.

The basic pattern of buffet service is varied in many ways. For the most informal type of service, guests may serve themselves with everything, even pouring their own coffee. At a semiformal buffet party, the hostess or a friend may pour the coffee at one end of the table; sometimes another friend may be asked to serve the main hot dish, if it is a casserole. Ornamental trays large enough to hold the plate and coffee cup, napkin and silverware, and water glass may be provided for the guests; the trays may be held on the guests' laps, or they may be mounted on folding legs; if trays are not provided, snack tables or card tables should be provided to set things on while guests deal with their plates on their laps. Plates and silver used in the first course may be returned by the guests (either to the kitchen, if the party is very informal, or to a table set up near the kitchen), or cleared away by the hostess or the host, or a friend. On some occasions, when space allows, a partial buffet may be preferred. Under this arrangement, guests select their food and seat themselves at smaller tables, such as card tables, where a place is set for each one.

Courses for a buffet meal are usually limited to just two—a main course with salad and rolls, and a dessert. Dishes should be chosen that are easy to serve and that stand up well. Casserole dishes are better than delicate soufflés which need to be served immediately. A chafing dish is a great convenience on a buffet table; heat-retaining casseroles are also an aid in keeping hot food hot. Mixtures should not be too thin and runny, salads not too juicy. Tossed or molded salads are always good; fruit salad mixtures may be served in lettuce cups which can be transferred to plates.

Remember to consider eye appeal of foods as well as their taste appeal. The colors of the foods themselves as well as their arrangement on serving dishes and their garnishings are important, for a buffet meal provides almost the only opportunity for guests to see the whole menu at once. In planning for your party, be sure to estimate quantities generously, for there is something about a buffet which is irresistible to the appetite!

Larger, heartier buffet meals are sometimes served. For one such, a roast turkey may be placed at one end, and a handsomely garnished baked tender ham at at the other; both of these may be set out either hot or cold, and sliced or partly sliced beforehand, or else sliced and served by the hostess's helpers. To complete this particular meal, little hot Southern biscuits are delicious, with a big relish tray of carrot sticks, celery curls, olives, cranberry jelly to go with the turkey and spiced crab apples or peaches for the ham, a platter of sliced tomatoes drizzled with French dressing, cauliflower polonaise, and lemon meringue tarts. Sumptuous!

The Cocktail Party

The cocktail party is a special kind of buffet party. The purpose of hor d'oeuvres at this party is a little different from the before-dinner cocktail hour, since no other food is ordinarily to be provided. A variety should be served, allowing at least five or six "pieces" for each guest. Hot hors d'oeuvres should not be attempted unless they can be served piping hot. Tiny and attractively garnished canapés are very much in order. One non-alcoholic beverage should be provided.

In keeping with the delicate and fine quality of cocktail glasses, other serving equipment and the service itself will tend to be formal rather than informal. A beautiful tablecloth, flowers, and candles form an attractive background for the hors d'oeuvres trays. Small plates may or may not be provided, but plenty of cocktail napkins should be placed at both ends of the table.

Smörgåsbord

Best-known of all Scandinavian dining customs is the smörgåsbord—usually the prelude to the feast, but on some occasions the whole feast itself. In Sweden, where the custom is believed to have originated in the festivities of country people, the smörgåsbord is served as a first course. A small number of appetizers, which invariably include herring, are presented buffet-style to guests who relax and nibble, exchange toasts and conversation, and then assemble around the dining table with appetites pleasantly stimulated but unimpaired. In other countries, and especially in America, the character and function of the smörgåsbord have altered and it may comprise the principal part of a meal. A munificent variety of fish, meat, cheese, egg, and vegetable dishes is arranged on a necessarily commodious buffet or table and guests visit it as often as they please. A dessert (by recommendation, simple) and good strong coffee bring the feast to a close.

A time-tried ritual is prescribed for the proper enjoyment of either a small smörgåsbord or the full-scale, panoramic affair. First, and always first if one is to observe the Scandinavian spirit of the occasion, the herring! Then one adventures (with clean plate in hand) through dishes in which fish is combined with other ingredients, then cold meats, the delicious hot dishes, the salads and aspics, and finally, for digestion's sake and to soothe a possibly jaded palate, a bit of cheese.

In Norway, the smörgåsbord is also called *koldt bord*. It usually consists of a few appetizers—fish, meat, and cheese—but on special occasions may be elaborate and bountiful, including roasts of meat and several kinds of fish. Roast beef tenderloin, for example, and loin of pork served with prunes and apple slices; boiled lobster with mayonnaise, whole baked or boiled salmon with sour cream; and a whole cold ham. Include parsley potatoes in the more elaborate type of smörgåsbord. Rum pudding usually rounds out these heroic collations.

A Swedish adaptation of the smörgåsbord is the gracious *supé*—a late supper served after the theater or an evening of dancing. The supé too is governed to some extent by tradition. Hot dishes are always served. They may be croustades with creamed filling, an omelet or soufflé, new potatoes with fresh dill. Breads, especially the fragrant limpa, accompany the dishes. Fish and a relish, such as sliced tomatoes, are included as a matter of course. Amounts served are not lavish. The dishes are kept small, but always garnished with the flair for beauty that characterizes Scandinavian cuisine. Cookies are sometimes included in supé and coffee is always served. To precede a Swedish dinner, a plate of three (it must be three) canapés is placed before each individual. Canapés would not be served with a smörgåsbord.

The American homemaker can make a respectable gesture toward a smörgåsbord with herring, sardines, anchovies or other small canned fish, a platter of ready-to-serve meats and cheese, and a relish or two—all of which may also be included in a much more elaborate buffet.

A word about bread and cheeses: Custom dictates that only the dark breads belong to the smörgåsbord and that knackebrod (hardtack in American parlance) should be among them. Cheese may be Swiss, Danish Bleu, Edam, goat cheese, or bond ost, but it is never proffered in slices. Guests cut it to individual preference.

BUFFET DINNER
Caviar with Egg*
Fresh Leg of Pork with Exotic Stuffing*
Whipped Potatoes   Gravy
Broccoli with Buttery Lemon Crunch*
Artichoke Salad with Gourmet Salad Dressing*
Sour Cream Crescents*   Butter
Celery Sticks   Radish Roses
Dobos Torte*
Coffee

SPRING BUFFET SUPPER
Punch à la Champagne*   Assorted Canapés
Cucumber-Salmon Ring*   Cold Turkey and Ham
Festive Creamy Carrots*
Whole Wheat Popovers*   Butter or Margarine
Baked Rhubarb with Pastry*
Coffee   Tea

AFTER-THE-GAME BUFFET SUPPER
Herb-Buttered Hot Tomato Juice*
Parmesan-Nut Sticks*
Chili-Turkey Pie*
Crisp Relishes
Caramel-Fudge-Frosted Cake
Milk   Coffee

DESSERT PARTIES

Most feminine of all forms of entertaining is probably the dessert party. There are a dozen excuses for it: a club meeting in the home, an afternoon of bridge, a shower for bride- or baby-to-be, the introduction of a newcomer in the neighborhood to your friends. It's a gay sort of affair, usually given in the afternoon when the men-folk are away, but occasionally late of an evening when they may possibly be persuaded to participate. And it calls for your most special magic to produce a really breath-taking pièce de résistance.

The dessert's the thing—for a dessert party is not and should not be a meal, but merely a gesture of dainty, delectable hospitality. The whole menu served at the dessert party need consist of no more than the dessert itself—eye-appealing, taste tempting, and irresistibly delicious—with, of course, a beverage of distinction. Include salted nuts and mints if you wish.

Service for the dessert party should be of the simplest. You may have your card table or tables spread with dainty cloths and set with silver and napkins when your guests arrive; this permits your guests to finish eating and you to clear the tables before the business or pleasure of the meeting gets under way. Or finish the business first, and then set the tables, so guests may relax over your dessert masterpiece. The dessert itself may either be served and prettily garnished in the kitchen; or if the dessert is particularly beautiful, by all means display the attractively garnished platter before you serve it with a flourish.

Some dessert suggestions in addition to the recipes given here (all recipes are in the book):
Ambrosia Cakes
Charlotte à l'Orange
Peppermint-Chocolate Frozen Dessert
Banana Cake Royale
Venetian Crème Torte
Pineapple Volcano Chiffon Pie

Beverages to consider other than coffee or tea:
Café l'Orange
Hot Buttered Cranberry Punch
Iced Orange Mocha
Iced Cinnamon Coffee
Ginger Ice Cooler

CHOCOLATE DESSERT SUPERBE À LA BELGIQUE

This exquisite dessert—both "cake" and filling—is a modern version of a sensational chocolate specialty a tourist might be served at one of the charming countryside inns of Belgium.

½ lb. sweet chocolate
7 tablespoons double-strength coffee
½ cup (about 7) egg yolks
¾ cup sugar
1 teaspoon vanilla extract
1 cup (about 8) egg whites
¼ teaspoon salt

¼ cup sugar
2 tablespoons Dutch process cocoa
Mocha Butter Cream Filling, *page 699*
1 cup chilled heavy cream
3 tablespoons confectioners' sugar
1 teaspoon vanilla extract

1. Grease bottom of a 15x10x1-inch jelly roll pan; line bottom with waxed paper, allowing paper to extend about 1 inch beyond ends of pan; grease waxed paper. Set aside.
2. Put chocolate and coffee in the top of a double boiler. Set over simmering water until chocolate is melted. Set aside to cool.
3. Combine egg yolks, ¾ cup sugar, and 1 teaspoon extract in a large bowl; beat until very thick.
4. Using a clean beater, beat egg whites and salt until frothy. Add ¼ cup sugar gradually, beating well after each addition. Beat until stiff peaks are formed.
5. Blend cooled chocolate into egg yolk mixture. Gently stir in egg whites. Turn into the pan and spread evenly.
6. Bake at 350°F 15 minutes. Turn off oven. Remove pan after 5 minutes. Set on wire rack until cool.
7. Sift Dutch process cocoa over clean towel. Turn dessert onto towel. Carefully remove paper. If desired, let stand about 30 minutes to absorb cocoa flavor. Cover with waxed paper until ready to serve.
8. Prepare Mocha Butter Cream Filling; spread generously over dessert. Cut into 16 equal portions

and transfer 8 portions to dessert plates. Top with remaining squares, cocoa side up.

9.   Beat cream until soft peaks are formed. Beat in confectioners' sugar and 1 teaspoon extract with final few strokes until blended. Spoon generous amounts over each serving. If desired, the mocha filling may be omitted and additional sweetened whipped cream substituted for the filling.

8 SERVINGS

MOCHA BUTTER CREAM FILLING

1 cup unsalted butter	3 egg yolks
2 tablespoons rum	2 teaspoons instant
1 to 2 teaspoons almond	coffee
extract	1½ teaspoons Dutch
1 teaspoon vanilla	process cocoa
extract	2 teaspoons boiling
2 cups confectioners'	water
sugar, sifted	

1.   Beat butter, rum, and extracts in a bowl until blended. Gradually add about 1½ cups of the confectioners' sugar, continuing to beat until fluffy. Beat in egg yolks, one at a time.
2.   Blend instant coffee and cocoa in a small cup; add the boiling water and stir until thoroughly mixed; cool. Beat into the butter mixture with the remaining ½ cup confectioners' sugar. Chill until ready to use. Allow to come to room temperature; beat, if necessary, to spreading consistency.

PEPPERMINT ICE-CREAM CAKE

1 qt. chocolate ice	⅔ cup sugar
cream	⅔ cup milk
1 qt. vanilla ice cream	⅓ cup crushed
1½ cups sifted cake	peppermint-stick
flour	candy
1½ teaspoons baking	2 egg whites
powder	Filling, *below*
¼ teaspoon salt	½ cup sugar
½ cup butter	1 cup heavy cream,
½ teaspoon peppermint	whipped
extract	

1.   Firmly pack scoops of chocolate and vanilla ice cream alternately into a 9-inch layer cake pan. Cover and freeze until firm.
2.   Blend flour, baking powder, and salt; set aside.
3.   Cream butter with extract until softened. Gradually add ⅔ cup sugar, beating until fluffy. Beating only until blended after each addition, alternately

add dry ingredients in thirds, milk in halves. Blend in about ¼ cup of the peppermint candy.
4.   Beat egg whites until stiff, not dry, peaks are formed. Fold into batter. Turn into a prepared 9-inch layer cake pan.
5.   Bake at 350°F about 30 minutes, or until cake tests done. Cool. Wrap and refrigerate or freeze.
6.   To assemble cake, remove ice cream from pan, dipping bottom of pan quickly into hot water and inverting onto serving plate. Return to freezer about 15 minutes to firm. Spread ice cream with one half of the Filling. Top with cake layer. Spread top of cake with remaining filling. Freeze 3 hours.
7.   Beat ½ cup sugar into whipped cream; spread over sides and top edge of cake. Sprinkle remaining peppermint candy over top. Freeze.
8.   Set out to soften slightly before serving.

16 SERVINGS

FILLING

1 egg	1 teaspoon vanilla
2 egg yolks	extract
¼ cup sugar	3 oz. semisweet
½ cup butter	chocolate, melted

1.   Blend the egg, egg yolks, and sugar in the top of a double boiler. Heat over boiling water until mixture is amber colored.
2.   Cream the butter with extract until softened. Gradually add egg mixture and chocolate, beating until smooth. Chill.
3.   Before using, beat to soften slightly.

ABOUT 1¼ CUPS FILLING

CALYPSO PIE

Chocolate Crumb Crust,	3 tablespoons
page 700	confectioners' sugar
Chocolate Fudge Sauce,	1 cup heavy cream,
page 700	whipped
2 pints coffee ice cream	1 cup nuts, chopped

1.   Prepare Chocolate Crumb Crust and chill thoroughly in freezer.
2.   Prepare Chocolate Fudge Sauce and chill.
3.   To complete pie, set out ice cream to soften slightly. Blend confectioners' sugar into whipped cream during final few strokes of beating.
4.   Spoon softened ice cream into chilled pie shell; spread evenly. Spread chilled Chocolate Fudge Sauce over ice cream. Top with whipped cream and sprinkle with nuts. Freeze until firm, about 4 hours. Wrap pie if storing overnight.

5. Before serving, allow pie to stand at room temperature for a few minutes to soften very slightly.

ONE 10-INCH PIE

CHOCOLATE CRUMB CRUST: Crush *18 cream filled chocolate sandwich-style cookies* (about 2 cups crumbs). Using a fork or pastry blender, blend in *¼ cup softened butter.* Turn into a 10-inch pie pan. Using back of spoon, press crumb mixture firmly into an even layer on bottom and sides of pie pan. Set in freezer.   ONE 10-INCH PIE SHELL

CHOCOLATE FUDGE SAUCE: Melt *3 squares (3 ounces) unsweetened chocolate* and *¼ cup butter* in top of a double boiler over boiling water. Remove from heat; stir in *⅔ cup sugar* and *⅛ teaspoon salt* until blended. Gradually add *⅔ cup (6-ounce can) evaporated milk*, blending well. Cook over boiling water, stirring constantly, about 4 minutes. Remove from water and stir in *1 teaspoon vanilla extract* and a few drops *almond extract.* Chill thoroughly.   ABOUT 1½ CUPS

SWISS APPLE PIE

Travelers who have dined at Schloss Herblingen, the ancient castle near the Rhinefall on the Swiss-German border, should find this pie familiar.

6 tablespoons butter	1½ lbs. tart apples,
1½ cups all-purpose	pared and thinly
flour	sliced
3 to 4 tablespoons cold	2 eggs
water	2 egg yolks
1 tablespoon ground	2 cups heavy cream
toasted almonds	½ cup sugar
1 tablespoon fine dry	2 tablespoons butter,
bread crumbs	melted
	¼ cup sugar

1. Cut butter into flour with a pastry blender or two knives until the pieces are size of small peas. Add water gradually, mixing with a fork until pastry holds together. Shape into a ball.
2. Roll pastry about ⅛ inch thick on a lightly floured surface. Line a 10-inch pie pan with pastry; flute edge. Sprinkle a mixture of almonds and crumbs over bottom; cover with apples.
3. Bake at 350°F 5 minutes.
4. Meanwhile, beat eggs and egg yolks slightly; add cream and ½ cup sugar; blend well. Pour half of the mixture over the apples.
5. Bake until firm, about 30 minutes. Pour remaining mixture over apples and continue baking

about 45 minutes, or until a metal knife inserted halfway between center and edge of pie comes out clean.
6. Remove pie from oven and pour melted butter evenly over the top. Sprinkle with remaining sugar and return to oven for 5 minutes. Cool before serving.   ONE 10-INCH PIE

ELEGANT DATE FINGERS

¾ lb. (about 2 cups)	⅔ cup firmly packed
pitted dates, cut in	brown sugar
pieces	1½ cups sifted
1 cup hot water	all-purpose flour
½ cup orange juice	¾ teaspoon baking soda
½ cup pecans, chopped	¼ teaspoon salt
¾ cup butter	1¼ cups uncooked
1 teaspoon grated orange	rolled oats
peel	2 tablespoons
⅛ teaspoon almond	confectioners' sugar
extract	

1. Invert a 9x9x2-inch pan onto piece of waxed paper; using a knife, mark around pan to form outline without cutting through paper and set aside; turn pan right side up and grease bottom.
2. Combine dates, water, and orange juice in a saucepan and cook over medium heat, stirring occasionally, about 15 minutes, or until mixture is blended and thick. Stir in pecans; set aside.
3. Cream butter with orange peel and extract; add brown sugar gradually, beating until fluffy.
4. Sift flour, baking soda, and salt together; add in thirds to creamed mixture, mixing until blended after each addition. Stir in rolled oats.
5. Press half of the mixture into an even layer on bottom of pan.
6. Spread filling over dough to within ¼ inch of sides of pan; pat remaining dough over the marked-off square of waxed paper; invert waxed paper onto top of filling and press down gently; carefully peel off waxed paper.
7. Bake at 400°F 20 to 25 minutes, or until golden brown.
8. Cool completely; cut into bars and remove from pan. Sift the confectioners' sugar over cookies.   ABOUT 3 DOZEN COOKIES

NOTE: For a tea table, cut into diamond shapes and decorate with pink butter frosting rosettes and green butter frosting leaves. For a dessert, cut into large squares and top with whipped cream.

SPICY ICED TEA

1 cup water	4 whole allspice
1 cup sugar	4 pieces (2 in. each)
⅛ teaspoon ground	stick cinnamon
nutmeg	3 tablespoons tea or 3
6 whole cloves	to 5 tea bags

1. Combine all ingredients except tea in a saucepan. Stir over low heat until sugar is dissolved. Cover tightly and simmer 20 minutes. Strain, cool, and chill thoroughly.
2. Bring *2 cups freshly drawn cold water* to a full rolling boil in a saucepan. Remove from heat and immediately add the tea; stir. Let tea steep 5 minutes. Stir and strain into a pitcher containing *2 cups cold water.* (Remove tea bags, if used, and omit straining.) Blend in the spiced syrup.
3. Pour into ice-filled glasses. Serve with thin slices of *lime or lemon.*　　　ABOUT 1 QUART

ORANGE TEA JULEP

4 teaspoons instant tea	4 cups orange juice
½ cup boiling water	½ cup lime juice
1½ cups cold water	¾ to 1 cup sugar
1 teaspoon grated orange	⅓ cup chopped mint
peel	leaves

1. Dissolve tea in the boiling water. Add the remaining ingredients and stir until sugar is dissolved. Chill thoroughly.
2. Stir well and strain the mixture into a pitcher. Serve over crushed ice in tall glasses. If desired, garnish with sprigs of *mint.*　　ABOUT 8 SERVINGS

LEMONADE DELIGHT

1½ cups sugar	½ cup orange juice
1 cup water	(about 2 oranges)
2 cups lemon juice	Cold water
(about 12 lemons)	Lemon wedges

1. Combine the sugar and water in a small saucepan. Stir over low heat until sugar is dissolved. Cover, bring to boiling, and boil 5 minutes. Remove from heat and set aside to cool.
2. Combine the lemon and orange juice and refrigerate.
3. When syrup is cooled, blend with fruit juices. Cover and refrigerate until ready to use.
4. To serve, put ice cubes into tall glasses and add about ½ cup of the lemon syrup to each glass. Fill glasses with cold water. Stir until blended. Garnish with lemon wedges.　　8 SERVINGS

PIÑA COLADA

This is a version of a drink reminiscent of old San Juan.

¾ cup unsweetened pineapple juice	3 tablespoons grenadine
	3 ice cubes
2¼ cups fresh ripe pineapple pieces	

Combine all ingredients except ice cubes in a chilled electric blender container. Cover; blend on high speed, adding the ice cubes one at a time. Strain into ice-filled glasses. Garnish as desired.　　ABOUT 4 SERVINGS

SPARKLING SHOWER PUNCH

2½ cups sugar	2 tablespoons chopped fresh mint leaves
1 qt. water	
1 cup strong tea (¼ cup black tea or 4 to 6 tea bags and 1⅓ cups boiling water; follow pkg. directions for brewing)	2 tablespoons chopped cucumber peel
	Few grains cayenne pepper
	1 qt. ginger ale, chilled
2 cups lemon juice, chilled	Hulled ripe whole strawberries
½ cup orange juice, chilled	Sweetened fresh pineapple chunks (or drained canned)
⅓ cup grape juice, chilled	

1. Combine sugar and water in a saucepan. Set over low heat and stir until sugar is dissolved. Cover and boil 5 minutes. Cool and chill.
2. When ready to serve, stir tea and juices, mint, cucumber peel, and cayenne pepper into syrup. Pour over ice block, *page 610,* or ring in a punch bowl. Add ginger ale and stir gently to blend. Garnish with strawberries and pineapple.
　　ABOUT 4 QUARTS PUNCH

PARTY FRUIT PUNCH

1 cup water	1 cup orange juice
1 cup sugar	⅔ cup lemon juice
4 cups unsweetened pineapple juice	½ cup lime juice
1 cup cranberry juice cocktail	1½ qts. ginger ale, chilled

1.   Combine the water and sugar in a small saucepan. Stir over low heat until sugar is dissolved. Cover, bring to boiling, and boil 5 minutes. Remove from heat; set aside to cool.

2.   Put the fruit juices into a large pitcher or bowl. Add the cooled syrup and stir until well blended. Cover and chill.

3.   When ready to serve, pour mixture over a decorative ice ring, *page 610*, in a punch bowl. Add the ginger ale and stir to blend.

ABOUT 3½ QUARTS PUNCH

GALA PINEAPPLE WEDDING PUNCH

2 cans (46 oz. each) pineapple juice	½ cup grenadine
2 cups strained orange juice	1 cup sugar
	6 cups sparkling white grape juice, chilled
1 cup strained lime juice	

1.   Combine the pineapple, orange, and lime juices, grenadine, and sugar; stir until sugar is completely dissolved. Chill thoroughly.

2.   When ready to serve, stir chilled fruit-juice mixture to blend and pour it into a punch bowl. Add the white grape juice; stir gently to blend. Float *Heart-Shaped Ice Mold, below,* in the punch.

ABOUT 5½ QUARTS PUNCH

HEART-SHAPED ICE MOLD: Arrange *pineapple slices* and *fresh strawberry halves* in water to a depth of about ½ inch in a heart-shaped mold. Freeze until firm so fruits are securely held in place. Fill mold with water; freeze. For ease in unmolding, quickly dip the mold into hot water and invert.

HOLIDAY EGGNOG

Here's a blending of "spirits" with super-rich eggnog to create a New Year's drink to truly dazzle your guests.

6 egg yolks	1 cup brandy
2 cups sugar	3 pts. heavy cream
1 pt. bourbon	2 cups milk
1 cup Jamaica rum	6 egg whites

1.   Beat the egg yolks with sugar until very thick. Gradually add the liquors, stirring constantly. Blend in the cream and milk.

2.   Beat egg whites until stiff, not dry, peaks are formed. Gently fold into eggnog. Turn into a punch bowl; cover and chill.

3.   To serve, ladle eggnog into punch cups; sprinkle with *ground nutmeg.*   ABOUT 25 SERVINGS

MENUS FOR HOLIDAYS & SPECIAL OCCASIONS

EASTER BRUNCH
Orange Juice   Fresh Strawberries
Roast Canadian-Style Bacon   Mustard Sauce*
Eggs Farci*
Assorted Sweet Rolls   Butter
Coffee

EASTER DINNER
Broiled Date Appetizers*
Roast Leg of Lamb
Franconia Potatoes*   Gravy
Green Beans with Garlic*
Tossed Green Salad   Hot Rolls
Frozen Cherry Easter Egg*   Coffee

HALLOWEEN HOSPITALITY
Hot Aromatic Punch*
Multi-Cheese Blendip*   Crackers and Potato Chips
Hot Dog-It's Beans*
Double Ginger-Pumpkin Muffins*
Ripe Olives   Carrot Sticks
Fudge Cake*   Orange Sherbet

TRICK-OR-TREAT PARTY
Hot Spiced Cider*
Witches' Hat Casserole*
Apricot Salad Squares*   Celery Sticks
Pumpkin Cake*   Pumpkin Jumbos*
Coffee   Milk

FAMILY-REUNION HOLIDAY DINNER
Hot Madriléne*
Stuffed Butter-Roasted Turkey*   Gravy
Molded Cranberry Sauce
Butter-Pecan Squash Casserole*
Asparagus-Cauliflower Platter*
Tossed Green Salad   Sour Cream Mayonnaise*
Molasses Steamed Pudding*   Foamy Sauce*
Coffee

HOLIDAY DINNER FOR TWELVE
Spicy Cranberry Punch*
Homemade Pot Cheese*   Crisp Crackers
Roast Turkey with Filbert Stuffing*
Tangy Plum Sauce*
Vegetable Trio in Casserole*
Party-Perfect Salad Molds*
Watermelon Pickles*
Assorted Rolls   Butter or Margarine
Vanilla Ice Cream   Luscious Lemon Bars*
Coffee

HEARTY CHRISTMAS DINNER
Borsch*   Crisp Crackers
Roast Duckling à l'Orange*   Orange Gravy*
Whipped Potatoes*
Candied Yams
Brussels Sprouts in Herb Butter*
Hot Rolls   Butter
Mince Pie*
Coffee

CHRISTMAS SEASON BUFFET WITH OLD-WORLD OVERTONES
Fruit Punch
Finnish Meatballs*
Norwegian Christmas Bread*   Butter Balls
Cream Puff Christmas Tree*   Cheese Tray
Coffee

DANISH CHRISTMAS EVE DINNER
Rice Porridge*
Danish Beer
Roast Goose*   Roast Fresh Leg of Pork*
Sugar-Browned Potatoes*
Parsley-Buttered Potatoes   Red Cabbage*
Danish Apple Cake*   Coffee

INFORMAL PARTY FOR THE BRIDE-TO-BE
Party Fruit Punch*
Chicken Salad*
Parslied-Parmesan Loaf*
Philadelphia Ice Cream*   Angel Food Cake*
Mints   Nuts
Coffee

AFTERNOON BRIDAL SHOWER BUFFET
Sparkling Shower Punch*
Crab-Avocado Canapés*
Cucumber-Chicken Canapés*
Cottage Cheese-Melon Dessert Élégant*
Mixed Nuts   Mints

WEDDING RECEPTION BUFFET
Gala Pineapple Wedding Punch*
Piquant Pecans*
Creamed Ham and Sweetbreads*   Patty Shells
French-Style Green Beans with Water Chestnuts*
Ice Cream
Wedding Cake

LUAU

The luau is a traditional Hawaiian celebration feast probably of Polynesian origin. For an island luau, Kalua Pig is the pièce de résistance of the feast. If the roast pig is omitted, the feast is then usually referred to as a poi supper. To serve, the foods are set out buffet style on leaf- or fern-covered ground or table.

MENU
Fruit Punch
Lomi Lomi Salmon*
Kalua Pig, *page 704*   Poi
Baked Fish
Baked or Boiled Sweet Potatoes
Baked or Steamed Bananas
Coconut Pudding (Haupia)*   Fresh Pineapple

NOTE: For a mainland-style luau, *Barbecued Ribs with Pineapple, page 185,* and *Teriyaki, page 26,* may be substituted for the Kalua Pig. For dessert, *Pineapple with Rum Caramel Sauce, page 547,* or *Bananas with Royal Pineapple Sauce, page 543,* may be served.

KALUA PIG
(Pit-Roasted Whole Pig)

Dig the pit (imu) according to the size of pig purchased and prepare as for a closed-pit barbecue: Line the bottom of pit with round smooth stones, build and start a wood fire, and add some extra stones (for cavity of pig). Add more wood as the fire burns to ashes (allow 4 to 5 hours). *To prepare the cleaned and drawn pig:* Rub well inside and out with *soy sauce, lemon, garlic,* and *white wine.* Place the extra heated stones in the cavity of the pig and tie legs together. Rake the ashes from the fire and reserve in a large can or tub. Cover surface thoroughly with banana leaves. Lower the pig into the pit (in a wire basket, if desired) and surround it with heavy-duty aluminum foil-wrapped *bananas, yams* and, if desired, serving portions of *fish,* allowing one of each per person. Cover with additional leaves or layers of aluminum foil, then with a layer of hot ashes and with some burlap bags or a sheet of metal. Cover completely with earth. Roast pig about 5 hours. When ready to serve, uncover the pig and remove packets of cooked food. Remove the pig to a board or table for carving. Serve with *poi* (a paste of cooked and fermented taro root).

NEW ENGLAND CLAMBAKE

The oldest eating tradition along New England's rocky shore line is the clambake, a legacy from the Indian tribes who greeted the white man. In the three centuries that the tradition has been honored by New Englanders, the form and method of the bake have remained essentially unchanged. Basically it consists of green corn, clams, and fish closely covered and steamed in seaweed over white-hot stones to a medley of goodness.

The modern clambake is apt to include foods not known to the Indians—sweet potatoes, chicken, sausages, butter for the clams, coffee for the follow-up—and such latterday trappings as cheesecloth, paper bags, or wire baskets to confine the separate foods, but fundamentally the clambake has withstood the advances of civilization and mechanization.

Every bakemaster has his own opinion on how to conduct the preliminary stages of a clambake, but the general working procedure shapes up to something like this: A fire of wood is burned in a shallow pit over layers of stones about the size of cabbages. When the stones are crackling hot (after about an hour of exposure to intense heat), embers and ashes are swept away and a layer of wet seaweed or rockweed is laid atop the stones to a depth of several inches.

Ingredients follow in this approximate order—well-scrubbed *clams* (a dozen or two per serving) followed by a second layer of seaweed; unpared *white* or *sweet potatoes* or both; ears of *corn* stripped to the inner husks and cleaned of silk; *fish,* preferably bluefish, in paper bags; sausages similarly encased; vivacious *lobsters* (one per serving) arranged side by side in a large square of cheesecloth securely tied; *broiler chickens,* if you must, also tied in cheesecloth. Four to six inches of seaweed are now laid snugly over the food and the imposing heap is closely shrouded with a clean wet canvas. The edges of the canvas are weighted down with stones and the tiniest apertures are plugged with seaweed. For an hour (some experts allege a longer time is allowable) the pungent steam of seaweed and clam penetrate the edibles.

The tantalizing aroma slowly seeps through the containing canvas with stimulating effect on the taste buds of the waiting company. Appetites may be appeased with *relishes*—sliced cucumbers, tomatoes and onions—*bread,* and cups of *clam broth.* Then with the ceremonial lifting of the canvas the banquet is ready. Tin plates are piled high. *Melted butter* daubs unheeding chins. The feast is on!

For small family-sized clambakes variations on the standard procedure are permitted, and a barrel or a washboiler is an acceptable container for the bake. A wooden-hooped barrel is recommended and a lining of sheet-metal scraps will prevent the hot stones from igniting its sides. For best results the barrel must be sunk in sand, the deeper the better. The washboiler clambake is an admittedly weak facsimile of the genuine article. The traditional foods are layered atop a rack placed in the bottom of the boiler over an inch or so of water. The lid must fit tightly. Cooking is over an open fire. And to be certain that everyone will have as many steamed clams as he wants, it is best to prepare an auxiliary supply.

Bonus Chapter

CARVING MEATS & POULTRY

Skill in carving depends upon two things: first, a knowledge of the anatomy of that which is to be carved, and second, good tools with which to work. Carving done at the table by a skillful carver adds to the charm and graciousness of dining. Proper carving of meat also contributes to its tenderness and appetite appeal. Then too, a good knowledge of carving usually encourages the use of a wider variety of the unfamiliar cuts of meat.

EQUIPMENT FOR CARVING

For the average family, two carving knives are desirable, one with a long blade for large roasts, and a smaller, lighter one for steaks, cutlets, and poultry. The smaller knife will be adequate for the small family where large roasts are not served. One two-pronged fork can be used with both knives.

The carving knife should be sharp when it is brought to the table. The carver may sit or stand while carving, depending upon which is more convenient and comfortable.

The platter should be large enough not only for the meat that is to be carved, but also for the carved portions.

Kinds of Knives

The *standard set* includes a knife with a curved blade from 8 to 9 inches long, a matching fork, and a steel. This set is especially desirable for medium-sized pieces of meat, but it may be used for other cuts when necessary

The *steak set* is a junior edition of the standard set. The blade is from 6 to 7 inches long and the fork is not equipped with a guard. This set is most useful for steaks, chops, and game and poultry.

The *roast slicer and carver's helper* work well together, but they are seldom sold as a set. They come in various sizes and shapes and are designed for use with standing rib roasts, whole or half hams, and other large cuts of meat. A good roast slicer has a long flexible blade especially suited for carv-

ing across large surfaces of meat. The blade should be a minimum of 11 inches in length. The widely spread tines in the carver's helper will help to hold a large roast steady.

How to Steel a Knife

1. Hold steel firmly in left hand, thumb along top of handle. Place heel of blade against far side of steel, with steel and blade of knife making a 25-degree angle.

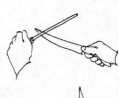

2. Bring blade down along steel to left with a swinging motion of right wrist. Entire length of blade should pass lightly over steel.

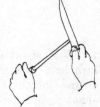

3. Bring knife back into starting position, but this time with blade on near side of steel making the 25-degree angle. Repeat stroking motion. Continue alternating strokes until edge is trued.

HOW TO CARVE MEATS

Beef Standing Rib Roast

  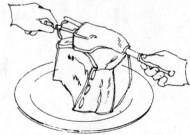

1. Insert fork below top rib. Carve across the "face" of roast to rib bone.

2. With fork still inserted, cut along rib bone with knife to release slice.

3. Slide knife back under slice and, steadying it with fork, lift to side of platter.

Beef Blade Pot Roast

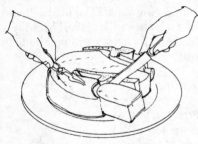 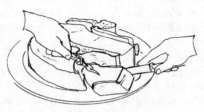 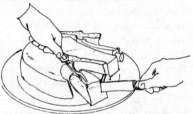

1. Cut between muscles and around bones to remove one solid section of pot roast.

2. Turn section so meat fibers are parallel to platter in order to carve across grain of meat.

3. Holding meat with fork, carve removed section into slices about ¼ inch thick. Repeat.

Shank Half of Ham

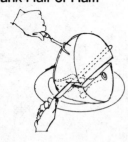  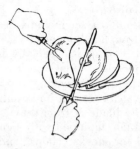

1. With shank at carver's left, turn ham so thick cushion side is up. Cut along top of leg and shank bones and under fork to lift off boneless cushion.

2. Place cushion meat on carving board and make perpendicular slices as illustrated.

3. Cut around leg bone with tip of knife to remove meat from this bone. Turn meat so that thickest side is down. Slice in same manner as cushion piece.

Beef Porterhouse Steak

1. Hold steak steady with fork. Use tip of knife to cut closely around bone. Lift bone to one side of platter.

2. Carve across full width of steak, cutting through both top loin and tenderloin. Diagonal slicing (instead of perpendicular) is recommended for thick steaks. (See *Corned Beef, page 708*, for description of diagonal slices.)

Pork Loin Roast

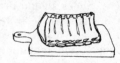

1. Before roast is brought to table, remove back bone leaving as little meat on it as possible. Place roast on platter with rib side facing carver so he can see angle of ribs and can make his slices accordingly.

2. Insert fork in top of roast. Make slices by cutting closely along each side of rib bone. One slice will contain the rib; the next will be boneless.

Whole Ham

1. Ham is placed on platter with decorated or fat side up and shank to carver's right. Location of bones in right and left hams may be confusing so double-check location of knee cap which may be on near or far side of ham. Remove two or three lengthwise slices from thin side of ham which contains knee cap.

2. Make perpendicular slices down to leg bone or lift off boneless cushion similar to method illustrated for Picnic Shoulder.

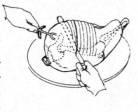

3. Release slices by cutting along leg bone.

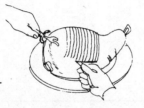

Picnic Shoulder

Carving is the same for both a roasted (baked) smoked picnic and a roasted (baked) fresh picnic.

1. Remove a lengthwise slice as shown here. Turn picnic so that it rests on surface just cut. Cut down to arm bone at a point near elbow bone. Turn knife and cut along arm bone to remove boneless arm meat.

2. Carve boneless arm meat by making perpendicular slices from top of meat down to cutting board.

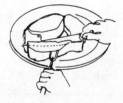

3. Remove the meat from each side of the arm bone. Then carve the two boneless pieces.

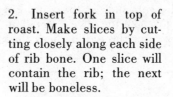

Corned Beef

The brisket is usually three "faces," as shown here. Slices should be thin and they should be cut at a slight angle (referred to as diagonal slices). Slices are made in rotation so that the different "faces" will remain equal to each other in size. The meat fibers in the brisket are relatively long, but when thin slices are carved across the grain, the meat is very tender. Other cuts of corned beef are carved like the rolled rump. Keep in mind when carving the less tender cuts such as those used in making corned beef to make the slices very thin. It is better to serve two or three thin slices than one thick slice.

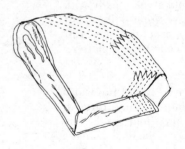

Lamb Leg Roast

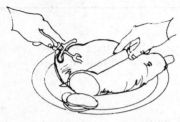 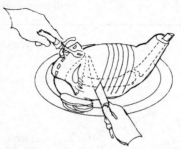 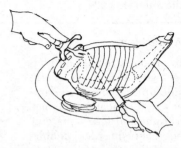

1. With lower leg bone to right, remove two or three lengthwise slices from thin side of leg. This side has the knee cap.

2. Turn roast up on its base and, starting where shank joins the leg, make slices perpendicular to leg bone or lift off cushion similar to method shown for picnic shoulder.

3. Loosen slices by cutting under them, following closely along top of leg bone. Lift slices to an auxiliary platter for serving.

Crown Roasts

1. The usual crown roast of lamb, pork, or veal contains about 14 ribs, but crowns with 40 or 50 ribs can be made. To facilitate carving and serving, the backbone should be completely removed in the market. Crown roasts may be garnished so elaborately that at first glance they may appear difficult to carve, but such is not the case. Remove from the center of the crown any garnish that might interfere with carving.

2. Slice down between the ribs, removing one rib chop at a time. Stuffing in the center of the crown, depending upon its consistency, may be either carved or removed with a spoon and served with the meat.

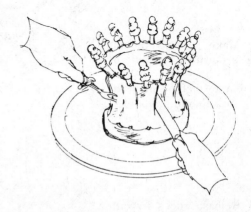

Courtesy National Live Stock and Meat Board

HOW TO CARVE POULTRY

Standard Style

1. To remove leg (drumstick and thigh), hold the drumstick firmly with fingers, pulling gently away from body of bird. At the same time cut through skin between leg and body.

2. Press leg away from body with flat side of knife. Then cut through joint joining leg to backbone and skin on the back. Hold leg on service plate with drumstick at a convenient angle to plate. Separate drumstick and thigh by cutting down through the joint to the plate.

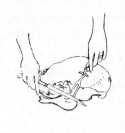

3. Slice drumstick meat. Hold drumstick upright at a convenient angle to plate and cut down, turning drumstick to get uniform slices. Drumsticks and thighs from smaller birds are usually served whole.

4. Slice thigh meat. Hold thigh firmly on plate with a fork. Cut slices of meat parallel to the bone.

5. Cut into white meat parallel to wing. Make a cut deep into the breast to the body frame parallel to and close to the wing.

6. Slice white meat. Beginning at front, starting halfway up the breast, cut thin slices of white meat down to the cut made parallel to the wing. The slices will fall away from the bird as they are cut to this line. Continue carving until enough meat has been carved for first servings. Carve more as needed.

Side Style

1. Remove wing tip and first joint. Grasp wing tip firmly with fingers, lift up, and cut between first and second joint. Place wing tip and first joint portion on side of platter. Leave second joint attached to bird.

2. Remove the drumstick. Grasp end of drumstick and lift it up and away from the body, disjointing it from the thigh. Thigh is left attached to the bird. Place drumstick on service plate for slicing. Hold drumstick upright at an angle and cut down toward plate, parallel with bone, turning to make even slices.

3. Anchoring the fork where it is most convenient to steady the bird, cut slices of thigh meat parallel to the body until the bone is reached. Run the point of the knife around the thigh bone, lift up with fork, and remove bone. Slice the remaining thigh meat.

4. Begin at front end of bird and slice white meat until the wing socket is exposed. Remove second joint of wing. Continue slicing until enough slices have been provided, or until the breastbone is reached.

5. Remove stuffing from hole cut into cavity under thigh. Slit the thin tissue in the thigh region with tip of knife and make an opening large enough for a serving spoon. Stuffing in breast cavity may be served by laying the skin back.

Courtesy Poultry & Egg National Board

Bonus Chapter

WHEN YOU SERVE WINE

Wine through the years has meant many things to many people around the world. To the average Frenchman or Italian, wine, along with bread, is almost as important as life itself and is a daily requisite at family meals. To the true connoisseur, especially one living in France from whence come some of the finest wines, it is a miracle of color and bouquet to be enjoyed by one's family and friends.

Probably due to increased travel to foreign countries where wine is a familiar commodity, large numbers of Americans have been added to the list of wine-lovers who have known for centuries what an enjoyable experience wine drinking can be.

For those people who are quite earnest in their desire to learn more about this fascinating subject, here are a few suggestions which can be helpful. There is one basic fact, however, which one should keep in mind—that choosing a wine is a matter of personal taste plus a consideration of the money available for purchasing it.

WINE-SERVING TIPS

• Wine-serving etiquette requires that the host be served first for a very practical reason—to sniff or taste the wine to check on its quality before offering it to guests.

• Wine is appreciated most when served with food, so make it easily available by placing it on the dining table, allowing guests to serve themselves. If served in its own bottle, place it in a wine basket in which the bottle lies on its side. The slanting position of the bottle keeps any sediment in the bottom.

Covering the bottle with a napkin is unnecessary as many people like to see the label to know what they are drinking. The purpose of the napkin is to keep the bottle, if iced, from slipping in your hand, also to absorb drops of wine that might fall. If a napkin is used, hold a small one in your left hand while pouring with your right. For an elaborate table setting one might stand the bottle in an antique

silver holder designed for serving wine at the table.

• The familiar rule of serving white wine with white meat and red wine with red meat should not be considered a binding one. It often needs modification, and it is the individual who must decide which wine gives him the most enjoyment with certain foods. For instance, there are wine connoisseurs who find the full red wines of Bordeaux perfect with roast chicken or some of the red wines of Burgundy good with roast turkey. A not-too-dry white wine is delightful with roast ham or a vin rosé with roast pork. A rather light red Bordeaux or a Beaujolais is a perfect foil for veal or sweetbreads. A red Bordeaux also goes well with roast leg of lamb and a full-flavored red Burgundy adds to the enjoyment of a good lamb stew.

• Vins rosé are in a class by themselves and are pink in color and rather light-bodied. They are usually considered to be compatible with all types of food, but this, too, is just a generalization.

• There is an old saying that no aged wine should ever be served over 72°F. Today, it is customary to serve red wines at room temperature (meaning 65° to 75°F), dry wines and vins rosé cooled, and sweet wines and champagne cooler still. It is said that no wine should be icy-cold as it deadens the taste. Here again one must add that many wine drinkers find white wines and rosés much more refreshing when thoroughly chilled.

• Wine left in the bottle after a meal should not be served again as a beverage wine. However, if there is no sediment in the bottom of the bottle the wine may be used for cooking. The bottle should be tightly corked, refrigerated, and the wine used within a few days.

• The so-called cooking wines obtainable at the market should be avoided unless their quality is comparable to a good table wine. As wine users know, the alcohol in the wine, also the water, evaporates during the cooking process and all that remains in the food is the flavor. Since that is the reason for adding the wine in the first place one must be sure the flavor is a pleasant one.

It should be added here that wine labeled "cooking wine" indicates that salt has been added. Therefore, if this type is used in recipes, it is often necessary to adjust the amount of salt called for in the recipe. Wine with salt added is unpalatable for drinking, and it is said that the practice developed in restaurants to discourage the employees from drinking wine intended for cooking.

• When serving more than one wine at a meal a dryer wine should precede a sweeter one and a lighter wine come before a heavier one.

WINE GLASSES

To play up the beautiful color and the delightful bouquet of good wine to best advantage, use a stemmed glass made of clear crystal with the bowl about the size of an orange (at least 6-ounce capacity) and tulip-shaped. A large bowl enables the taster to swirl the wine around in the glass which should not be filled more than half. The tapering of the glass at the top serves as a sort of chimney allowing the wine bouquet to rise up to the nose as one sniffs the wine. If your budget and storage space is limited, select one wine glass appropriate for most types of wine. Champagne, however, requires a special type of glass. Be sure that wine glasses are always sparkling clean and free of any detergent odors.

GLOSSARY

Abbaccato — Means sweet or semisweet when used with Italian wines. The opposite would be *secco*, meaning the wine is dry.

*Acidity — The quality of tartness, or sharpness, in a wine — not to be confused with sourness, dryness, or astringency. The presence of agreeable fruit acids.

Amelioration — A term used by winemakers covering certain practices (some necessary and some illegal) such as adding sugar to the grape juice, "correcting" the acidity of juice, etc.

Apéritif — The French word for appetizer and when used in connection with wine it usually refers to wines taken before meals (sherry, Madeira, etc.). In the United States the term "apéritif wine" usually refers to vermouths and other wines of the appetizer class which are especially flavored with herbs and other aromatic substances.

Aroma — The aroma of a wine and its bouquet are quite different (see Bouquet). The aroma is related to the odor of the fresh grape and is more pronounced in the young wine. Some varieties of grapes are easily identifiable by their characteristic odors alone. As the fruit juice ferments the scent of the grape gradually disappears. Extremely dry wine loses its aroma almost entirely and as the aging process continues the bouquet replaces the aroma. The term "aromatic" is often used on the labels of apéritif-type wines which indicates that herbs, spices, sugar, etc., have been added to the fruit juice.

*Astringency — The "puckeriness" of wines, usually derived from tannin from the skins and seeds. Moderate astringency is considered desirable in most red table wines.

Beaujolais — A very popular French wine, usually red (a small amount of rosé and white are also given the name) and probably among the finest red table wines found anywhere.

Bishop (also called Farmer's Bishop) — A mulled red wine concoction consisting of a whole unpeeled orange liberally studded with whole cloves, a bottle of wine (usually port), and several tablespoonfuls of sugar, all heated together until the flavors are blended, then served warm.

Bouquet — The bouquet of a fine wine is almost too complex to define and is probably its greatest attraction. As distinguished from "aroma" which is the fragrance of the grape, "bouquet" is that fragrance which originates from fermentation and aging. Young wines give off aroma, odor, perfume, or what-have-you, while a freshly opened bottle of fine vintage wine exudes "something" which could be a combination of all those plus much more. Many wine-lovers inhaling the bouquet of a fine wine can determine everything about the wine from its origin to its age. Wines with high acid content usually have more bouquet than those with lower acid.

One need not be an expert to appreciate the delightful bouquet of a good wine.

Brandy — A spirit produced from the wine of fresh grapes. Any brandy produced from other fruits must be so labeled (*i.e.* apricot brandy).

Brut — The name is given to extra-dry champagne and other sparkling wines. When used it should indicate that no sweetening agent (called dosage) has been added. Actually, all champagnes contain a small amount of dosage, yet they carry the brut label. So that alone is no guarantee of quality champagne.

Burgundy — A French province (Bourgogne) from whence comes some of the world's best wine — red, white, and small amounts of rosé. All wines from that province cannot be called Burgundy wine, however. The name is reserved for only the fine wines coming from certain regions of Bourgogne. In addition to these rare Burgundy wines, the province produces other well known wines — Chablis, Gamay, Pinot, Chardonnay, Beaujolais, and many more. Today the word *Burgundy* has become a generic term and is used by winemakers around the world wherever red wine is produced. American winemakers in California, New York State, Ohio, Michigan, and other states even use the name for sweet wine made from Concord grapes.

California wines — California produces about 80 percent of all wine consumed in the United States, the remaining coming from other states which often use California-grown grapes crushed and fermented elsewhere. In most wine-producing countries, table wines predominate. The reverse is true in the state of California where most of the wines produced are fortified (sherry, port, muscatel, etc.). Up to a few years ago most of these wines were inferior in quality, cheap, and sold before they were a year old. Today this is untrue as California has made great strides in its production of better-quality table wines. Some of its output of red and white table wines, both cheap and more expensive, are equal in quality to their counterparts in Spain and France.

Chablis — A white wine, probably the most famous of all white Burgundy wines. It is made only from the Chardonnay grapes which are grown in the little French town of Chablis and its surrounding areas. The best quality Chablis is pale golden in color, dry, with a delicate bouquet. The name Chablis, too, has become a generic term outside of France and any white table wine may be called "Chablis."

Champagne — The word originally meant a specific French sparkling wine made from certain varieties of grapes grown in a specific area of France near Rheims, east of Paris. But since the best Champagnes are made using a blend of more than one wine (with dosages added usually consisting of sugar syrups and brandy) other countries have now produced some excellent blends of sparkling wines, calling them Champagne also. Some countries recognize France as the originator of champagne and so give their sparkling wines other names such as *Sekt* in Germany, *Spumante* in Italy, and *Xampán* in Spain. With a number of wines being used to make a good champagne, many people judge its quality by the brand name rather than the vineyard or district from which it originated.

Chianti — A ruby red, dry Italian table wine made in Tuscany and considered quite inexpensive and common throughout Italy, it enjoys world-wide fame probably because of the fiasco or straw-covered bottle in which it is usually shipped. Served with Italian food, including pasta dishes, it is refreshing and enjoyable. Italy also produces a more expensive Chianti made from the San Gioveto and Cannaiola grapes along with several varieties of white grapes. It is considered one of Italy's best wines, improving as it ages in the bottle. Many wines of the Chianti label are produced outside of Italy. The state of California and parts of Argentina are two such areas.

Cradle — A wicker or straw basket made to hold a bottle of wine in nearly the same horizontal position it has in the wine celler. Keeping the bottle in that position permits serving the wine without disturbing any sediment in the bottle.

Claret — Wines with this label can mean almost any red table wine. This is especially true in the United States where the word is used quite loosely. In England it usually refers to red Bordeaux, but in France and Spain the word has no legal standing.

Decanting — This word is used for pouring wine from its original bottle to another container (a carafe or decanter) in order to separate the wine from any sediment in the bottom of the bottle. Old red wines such as clarets and Burgundies often "throw" some sediment and therefore need decanting. This does not mean the wine is bad — it is only the result of a natural aging in the bottle. Decanting is usually done several hours before serving. The bottle is carefully placed in the cradle, the cork removed, and the wine slowly poured into a carafe or decanter until the sediment begins to appear. A light behind the bottle while pouring helps to detect the line of sediment as it appears. The sediment in red wine contains pigment and tannin which can give the wine a disagreeable flavor. The colorless deposit sometimes formed in white wine is usually tartaric acid crystals and is tasteless and harmless.

Dosage—This is the term used for the syrup added to champagne which is always extremely dry before the dosage is added. The dosage consists of a blend of cane sugar or rock candy and old wine with a little brandy added sometimes. The amount of syrup added to the dry champagne determines the classification of the product, whether it will be sold as *brut, extra-dry, sec*, or *demi-sec* champagne.

Dry—When referring to wine the term dry means the opposite of sweet, but it never means sour. Almost all table wines are classified as dry except in the case of California wines which are called dry when they are unfortified. California sherry is called a sweet wine not because of its flavor but because it is a fortified wine (see Fortified).

Dubonnet—This is an apéritif wine usually consisting of a sweet fortified wine with quinine and herbs added. It is often an ingredient used in mixed cocktails, but it can also be chilled and served as it comes from the bottle.

Fortified—This is a term, probably originating in England, indicating that brandy (or other spirits) has been added to wines before bottling for the purpose of increasing alcoholic content. Sherry, port, muscatel, Madeira, etc., are all examples of fortified wines. In the United States the word fortified (or unfortified) does not appear on the bottle labels. Instead, wines which have been fortified are designated as "dessert wines" or "apéritif wines."

*Fruity—Having the fragrance and flavor of the grape, a freshness, sometimes called "grapey."

Gamay—A red wine produced in the Beaujolais area of France. This particular wine is of superfine quality not to be confused with an inferior wine produced in Burgundy from Gamay grapes. California also produces an excellent Gamay wine sold as Gamay du Beaujolais which should not be confused with a lower quality called simply Gamay.

German wines—The Rhine wines and Moselles of Germany are world famous, yet Germany is not considered a great wine-producing country. Its unfavorable northern climate makes the cost of producing wine very high. So it follows that good German wines are never cheap. Much of Germany's white wine is sent to the United States and it is of surprisingly good quality. During poor years sugar is added to the grapes during the fermentation process, but this is not done for the best tasting wines. Wines with no sugar added are designated as *natur, naturwein, rein* (genuine and natural). On the bottle label will appear such terms as *Wachstum, Kreszenz, Gewächs* (growth), and the vineyard owner's name; *Kellerabfüllung, Schlossabzug* (estate bottled); *Kabinett* (special reserve); *Spätlese* (late picking); *Auslese* (special selection). The last two terms may indicate sweeter, more expensive wine. Names such as *Liebfraumilch* and *Moselblümchen* are meaningless and German wines from the poorest to the best may bear that label. The word Liebfraumilch means "Milk of the Blessed Mother" and was originally given to the wine produced around the Liebfraun Kirche (church) in Worms on the Rhine. Since the word is used today for almost any Rhine wine, one must look for words such as *Spätlese* and *Auslese* on the label for indications of good quality.

Madeira—This term is used for not one, but a whole class of fortified wines which originally came from Madeira, a Portuguese island located in the Atlantic Ocean. Madeiras range in flavor from very dry to very sweet and in color from pale straw to deep gold. Rainwater Madeira, an extremely pale wine, was created by an American wine-lover. That name is used quite loosely among Madeira producers today.

Marsala—A popular Italian fortified wine, amber in color, either dry or sweet, and somewhat like sherry. It originated in Marsala, a city in Sicily.

*Mature—A wine that has developed all of its characteristic qualities.

*Mellow—A "soft" wine, often with some sweetness. Used in reference to some red table wines.

Neuchâtel—This is perhaps the best known white wine of Switzerland, but not the best in quality. It is produced near the French border around the northern shore of Lake Neuchâtel. It is pale in color, refreshing, and inexpensive, and is usually bottled when less than six months old. A small amount of red Neuchâtel is also produced. For Swiss consumption the Neuchâtel is sometimes a sparkling wine.

*Nose—Term for the total fragrance, aroma and bouquet, of a wine.

Port—This is no doubt the most famous of all dessert wines. It originally was a sweet, heavily fortified wine from northern Portugal. Port produced in the United States must be called American or New York or California port, the latter state producing much more than does Portugal.

Rhine wine—This term should mean any wine from the Rhine valley. However, in the United States any white wine with less than 14 percent alcohol may have that label no matter what kind of grapes were used. The California wines comparable in quality to German Rhine wines are Johannisberg Riesling and Sylvaner. Some of the better wines made in the Finger Lake region of New York State also equal the Rhine wines of Germany although the flavor is not similar.

Rosé—The word means *pink* in French, but wines given that name come from all over the world. A true vin rosé is usually made from black grapes and owes its color to the fact that it was neither fermented entirely with the grape skins (as is done for red wines) nor entirely without the skins (as is done for white wines). Excellent varieties of rosé come from France and the state of California, also some from Italy. It is a young wine and is served chilled.

Sauternes—Originally these golden white, full-bodied, fragrant wines all came from an area around Sauternes, a French village located south of Bordeaux. In France and many other countries the name cannot be used for wines not produced from the grapes grown in that area. The United States is an exception and uses the term for almost any dry white wine. In California where much of the Sauterne is produced the wine is labeled Sauterne, dropping the final *s*. These wines have little resemblance to their French counterpart.

Sherry—This gold or amber-colored wine originated in a district around a little Spanish city near Seville called Jerez, the word *sherry* being an English pronunciation of the name. Sherry is probably the finest and most famous apéritif wine anywhere. Other countries besides Spain have been producing it for a long time and the state of California today produces far more sherry than Spain. It is a sweet wine fortified with high-proof brandy and is sold before it is a year old. Its popularity is due to its cheapness and the fact that it contains a minimum of 20 percent alcohol. Sherry is served often as a "dessert wine" and is usually well chilled.

Sound—A wine which is pleasant to look at, good smelling and tasting.

Table wine (also called dinner wine)—Includes all still wines not over 14 percent alcohol content by volume. Most table wines are dry, but not all of them as was formerly true. Today many dinner wines like sweet sauterne are actually semisweet or sweet, while some wines of the dessert or appetizer class are nearly dry (*i.e.* sherry). Wines appropriate for serving with meals are sometimes referred to as "light wines," "dry wines," or "natural wines."

*Tart—Possessing agreeable acidity (as a touch of lemon makes food tart).

*Courtesy Wine Advisory Board

WINE & FOOD CHART

Wine Class	Best-Known Types	Wine and Food Combinations
Appetizer Wines	Sherry Vermouth Flavored wines	Serve at cocktail time, chilled, without food, or with hors d'oeuvres, nuts, cheeses
White Table Wines	Sauterne Chablis Rhine wine	Serve well chilled with lighter dishes such as chicken, fish, shellfish, omelets, any white meat
Red Table Wines	Burgundy Chianti Claret Rosé "Vino" types	Serve at cool room temperature with hearty dishes such as steaks, chops, roasts, game, cheese dishes, spaghetti (Rosé with all foods)
Dessert Wines	Muscatel Angelica Cream (sweet) Sherry Port Tokay	Serve at dessert, chilled or at cool room temperature, with fruits, cookies, nuts, cheese, fruit cake, poundcake
Sparkling Wines	Champagne Pink Champagne Sparkling Burgundy Cold Duck	Serve well chilled with any food—appetizers, the main course, or dessert (especially good in party punches)

Courtesy Wine Advisory Board

Bonus Chapter

FOOD SHOPPING GUIDE

First and foremost, give careful thought to the amount of money you allot to your food budget. Since a balanced diet is so necessary, the health of your family depends upon the wise apportionment of this allowance.

Do your own marketing so that you choose the best possible quality foods. Buy food supplies for the most part in quantities which will be consumed in the week ahead. Avoid stocking up on huge amounts of food which will deteriorate in quality when stored for any reasonable length of time. Even canned goods will deteriorate after being kept beyond their "shelf life."

Owning a refrigerator with a generous freezing compartment enables one to keep foods safely longer than one week. However, even a refrigerator-freezer unit has its storage limitations and food should be stored no longer than the time recommended by the manufacturer of the equipment.

Supermarkets regularly offer food bargains. Consult your local newspaper for these bargains, but do not buy just because of low price. It seldom pays to buy perishable foods merely because of low price. Foods which are in plentiful supply each week—fresh vegetables, fruits, meats, eggs, and poultry—are usually good choices and the best buys.

After checking supplies on hand in your refrigerator, freezer, and on pantry shelves, prepare your shopping list. Be at the market early when it is uncrowded and the fresh produce is at its best. Avoid buying withered and bruised vegetables and fruit. After purchasing get foods home promptly so that fresh products can be refrigerated as soon as possible.

PURCHASING "SHELF" SUPPLIES

Stock the cupboard or pantry shelves with only the quantity of foods you will be using within the next few months. Exceptions to this rule are the so-called staples which will keep longer. Even these must be checked occasionally for freshness. Spices and herbs lose considerable flavor after overlong storage. Vegetable oils, once opened and stored in the refrigerator too long, become rancid. Baking powder is another item to check. Here is a suggested list of staples to keep on hand:

Baking powder
Baking soda
Cereals
Cocoa, coffee, tea
Cornstarch
Extracts
Flour—all-purpose
Gelatin—flavored, un-
  flavored
Herbs
Ketchup
Molasses
Paprika

Pastas—spaghetti,
  macaroni, noodles
Pepper—black,
  seasoned, cayenne
Rice
Salt—plain, seasoned,
  onion, garlic, celery
Spices
Sugar—granulated,
  confectioners', cube,
  brown
Syrup—corn, maple
Vinegar

Here are canned and packaged items with limited "shelf life:"

Bouillon cubes
Canned goods
  baked beans
  corned beef hash
  fish, shellfish
  fruits
  juices—fruit, vegetable
  soups
  tomato paste, sauce
  vegetables
Crackers
Garlic cloves
Jams, jellies, spreads

Milk—evaporated,
  instant nonfat dry
Nuts
Oil—cooking, salad,
  olive
Onion—instant minced
  or flaked
Packaged mixes
Potatoes—packaged
  instant
Salad dressings
Sauces—chili, Tabasco,
  Worcestershire

HELP FOR THE SHOPPER

Here is a list of equivalents (some in cups, others in servings) of many everyday foods.

Beverages

Cocoa, unsweetened	8 oz.	2 cups
Coffee, regular grind	1 lb. (5 cups)	about 45 cups
instant	2 oz. (1 cup)	about 25 cups
Tea, regular	4 oz. (about 1½ cups)	about 250 cups

Cereals and Cereal Products

Corn flakes	1-lb. 2-oz. pkg.	about 16 cups
Cornmeal, white and yellow	1-lb. 8-oz. pkg.	4½ cups
uncooked	1 cup	about 4 cups cooked
Cracked wheat	1 lb.	about 2¼ cups
Farina	1-lb. 12-oz. pkg.	about 4⅓ cups
Hominy grits	1-lb. 8-oz. pkg.	about 3¾ cups
uncooked	1 cup	about 4 cups cooked
Macaroni, elbow or shell	8-oz. pkg.	2 to 2¼ cups
uncooked	1 cup	about 2 cups cooked
Noodles	8-oz. pkg.	3 to 3½ cups
uncooked	1 cup	1 to 1¼ cups cooked
Oats, rolled	1-lb. 2-oz. pkg.	5⅔ cups
quick-cooking, uncooked	1 cup	about 2 cups cooked
Rice, white polished	1 lb.	2¼ to 2⅓ cups
uncooked	1 cup	about 3 cups cooked
Spaghetti	1-lb. pkg.	about 4 cups
uncooked	1 cup	2 cups cooked

Dairy Products

Butter	1 lb.	2 cups, 48 squares
Cheese		
Cheddar, shredded	1 lb.	4 cups
cream	8-oz. pkg.	1 cup
	3-oz. pkg.	6 tablespoons
cottage	8-oz. carton	1 cup
Eggs (with shells), large	1 lb.	7 or 8 eggs
medium	1 lb.	9 or 10 eggs
small	1 lb.	11 or 12 eggs
Milk, sweetened condensed	14-oz. can	1¼ cups
evaporated	14½-oz. can	1⅔ cups
	6-oz. can	⅔ cup
fresh	1 pt.	2 cups
instant nonfat dry	9½-oz. pkg.	3 quarts fluid
	1⅓ cups	1 quart fluid

Flour

All-purpose, sifted	1 lb.	4 to 4¼ cups
Cake, sifted	1 lb.	4¾ to 5 cups
Rye, sifted	1 lb.	about 5 cups
Soy, sifted	1 lb.	about 7½ cups
Whole wheat, unsifted	1 lb.	about 3½ cups

Fats

Margarine	1 lb.	2 cups
Suet, chopped	1 lb.	about 3¾ cups
Vegetable shortening	1 lb.	2½ cups

Fruits and Peels, Candied

Cherries, whole	1 lb.	2¼ cups
Citron, chopped	4-oz. jar	½ cup
Lemon or orange peel, chopped	4 oz.	½ cup
Mixed candied fruits, chopped	1 lb.	2½ cups

Fruits, Dried

Apples, cooked	8-oz. pkg.	about 5 cups
uncooked	8-oz. pkg.	2 cups
Apricots, cooked	1 lb.	about 5 cups
uncooked	1 lb.	3 cups
Currants	11-oz. pkg.	about 2 cups
Dates, whole, unpitted, cut up	1 lb.	3 cups
whole, pitted	8-oz. pkg.	1½ cups
Figs, whole, cooked	1 lb.	about 5½ cups
uncooked	1 lb.	2¾ cups
Peaches, halved, cooked	1 lb.	6 cups
uncooked	1 lb.	3 cups
Prunes, medium, cooked	1 lb.	4 cups
uncooked	1 lb.	2½ cups
Raisins, seedless	15-oz. pkg.	3 cups

Fruits, Fresh

Apples, pared, sliced	1 lb. (3 or 4 medium)	3 cups
Apricots, cooked	1 lb. (8 to 14)	about 2½ cups
Bananas, mashed	1 lb. (3 or 4 medium)	about 2 cups
sliced	1 lb. (3 or 4 medium)	about 2½ cups
Blueberries	1 pt.	2 cups
Cherries, pitted	1 lb.	2 to 2½ cups
Cranberries	1 lb.	4 to 4½ cups
Grapefruit	1 lb. (1 medium)	¾ to 1 cup juice
Lemons	3 lbs. (12 medium)	about 2 cups juice
	1 medium	2 to 3 tablespoons juice
Oranges	6 lbs. (12 medium)	about 1 quart juice
	1 medium	⅓ to ½ cup juice
Peaches, peeled, sliced	1 lb. (3 or 4 medium)	2 to 2½ cups
Pears, pared, sliced	1 lb. (3 or 4 medium)	about 2½ cups
Pineapple, cubed	2 lbs. (1 medium)	about 2½ cups
Plums	1 lb.	10 to 20 plums
Rhubarb, cut in ½-in. pieces	1 lb. (4 to 8 stalks)	2 to 2½ cups
Strawberries, hulled	1 pt.	about 1½ cups

Nuts in the Shell

Almonds	2 lbs.	2½ to 3 cups nutmeats
Brazil nuts	2 lbs.	about 3 cups nutmeats
Filberts	2 lbs.	about 3 cups nutmeats
Peanuts	2 lbs.	3½ to 4 cups nutmeats
Pecans	2 lbs.	4 to 4½ cups nutmeats
Walnuts, black	2 lbs.	1 to 1¼ cups nutmeats
English	2 lbs.	3 to 3¼ cups nutmeats

Nuts, Shelled

Almonds, blanched, whole	1 lb.	about 3¼ cups
Brazil nuts, whole	1 lb.	3 to 3⅓ cups
Filberts, whole	1 lb.	3 to 3¼ cups

Peanuts, halves	1 lb.	about 3¼ cups
Pecans, halves	1 lb.	about 4¼ cups
chopped	1 lb.	about 3¾ cups
Walnuts, halves	1 lb.	4¼ to 4½ cups
chopped	1 lb.	3⅔ cups
Sugar		
Brown, light and dark	1- and 2-lb. pkgs.	about 2¼ cups (packed) per pound
granulated brown	1-lb. pkg.	about 3 cups
Confectioners'	1- and 2-lb. pkgs.	3 to 4 cups (unsifted) per pound
Cube, lump, tablet	1-, 1½-, 2-lb. pkgs.	198 cubes per pound
Granulated	1-, 2-, 5-, 10-lb. pkgs.	about 2¼ cups per pound
Vegetables, Dried		
Kidney beans	1 lb. (2½ cups)	6½ to 7 cups cooked
Lima beans	1 lb. (2½ cups)	6¼ to 6½ cups cooked
Navy beans	1 lb. (2⅓ cups)	6 cups cooked
Split peas	1 lb. (2¼ cups)	5 cups cooked
Vegetables, Fresh		
Asparagus	1 lb. (16 to 20 spears)	about 4 servings
Beans, green or wax,		
cut in pieces	1 lb. (3 cups)	4 or 5 servings
lima (in pods)	1 lb. (⅔ cup shelled)	2 servings
shelled	1 lb. (2 cups)	4 to 6 servings
Beets	1 lb. (1 bunch, 3 or 4 beets)	about 4 servings
Broccoli	1½ to 2 lbs. (1 bunch)	4 to 6 servings
Brussels sprouts	1 lb. (3 to 4 cups)	4 or 5 servings
Cabbage, raw	1 lb. (½ small head, 4 cups shredded)	7 or 8 servings
cooked	1 lb. (2½ cups)	3 servings
Carrots, cooked	1 lb. (2½ cups sliced)	4 servings
Cauliflower, cooked	2-lb. head (3 cups flowerets)	4 or 5 servings
Celery, cooked	1¼-lb. bunch (3 cups diced)	4 or 5 servings
Corn, ears	12 medium	about 6 servings
kernels cut from ears	3 cups	6 servings
Eggplant, cooked	1 lb. (2½ cups diced)	5 servings
Mushrooms	1 lb. (35 to 45 medium)	about 6 servings
Onions, dry	1 lb. (3 large)	4 servings
Parsnips, turnips	1 lb. (4 medium)	4 or 5 servings
Potatoes, white	1 lb. (3 medium)	3 servings
diced, cooked	2½ cups	4 servings
Potatoes, sweet	1 lb. (3 medium)	3 servings
cooked, mashed	2¾ cups	4 servings
Rutabagas, cooked, diced		
or mashed	2¾ cups	3 or 4 servings
Spinach and other greens	1 lb. (1½ to 2 cups cooked)	3 or 4 servings
Squash, summer, cooked	2 lbs. (2 cups mashed)	3 or 4 servings
winter, cooked	5 lbs. (5 cups mashed)	8 to 10 servings
Tomatoes, sliced	1 lb. (4 small)	4 servings
Miscellaneous		
Coconut, flaked	3½-oz. can	1⅓ cups
shredded	4-oz. can	1½ cups
Gelatin, flavored	3-oz. pkg.	7 tablespoons
unflavored	1 env.	about 1 tablespoon

PURCHASING FRUITS

Apples—Choose firm fruit of good color and flavor. Immature apples are poor in color and shrivel after storage. Overripe apples are mealy and poor in flavor. A brown-tinted irregular area on the surface is called "scald." It is caused by gases given off during the storage. If "scald" is slight, it affects the quality of fruit very little. The many varieties differ in appearance, flesh characteristics, and suitability for different uses. Eating apples include: *Delicious, McIntosh, Staymen, Golden Delicious, Jonathan,* and *Winesap.* Apples best for pie-making and sauce are tart (slightly acid) varieties: *Gravenstein, Grimes Golden, Jonathan,* and *Newton.* Apples best for baking include: *Rome Beauty, Northern Spy, Rhode Island Greenings, Winesap,* and *York Imperial.*

Apricots—Most apricots are marketed in June and July with a limited supply available in December and January. Apricots are usually picked slightly underripe (ripe fruit is very perishable and cannot be shipped well). The best quality is tree-ripened and can be purchased near the growing area. Choose plump, firm, uniformly-colored fruit. Immature apricots are greenish-yellow, hard, slightly shriveled, and lack flavor.

Avocados—They may vary from spherical to pear shaped, in size 5 ounces to 3 pounds, thin skin to thick rough skin, green in color to almost black. The shape, size, and skin do not indicate quality. Select bright fresh-looking fruit just beginning to soften; avoid bruised fruit. Light brown irregular marking does not affect quality. Decay is indicated by dark sunken spots.

Bananas—They are harvested green and develop their best eating quality after harvesting. Look for a full yellow or reddish color flecked with brown. Avoid soft, mushy bananas with blackened areas. When subjected to a temperature below 50°F they do not ripen properly and have poor flavor. Ideal ripening temperature is 60°F and 70°F.

Blueberries—They are on the market from May through September. Select plump, fresh looking, clean, dry berries. Deep full color indicates good quality; mold indicates decay; moisture indicates breakdown of fruit. Overripe fruit is dull and lifeless. Berries held long after picking are dull and shriveled.

Cantaloupe—Available from May through September. A ripe cantaloupe has a yellowish rind with the netting coarse, corky and greyish. It has a pleasant cantaloupe odor when held to the nose, and will yield slightly to light thumb pressure on the stem end of the melon. Do not depend entirely on this softening as a test. Repeated pressure will produce the same softening on an immature melon. When first displayed at the market most melons are quite firm and require two to four days at room temperature to allow for complete ripening. Before serving melon, chill in refrigerator several hours.

Casaba melon—Available from July to November. Select melon with a yellow-colored rind, softening at blossom end. Immaturity is shown by firmness and greenish-white color, decay by dark sunken areas.

Cherries—Select sweet cherries for eating and tart cherries for cooking. Sweet cherries are available from May through August. Red tart cherries are usually shipped to processing plants and are canned or frozen. Bright fresh appearance, plumpness, and good color indicate good quality. Unripe cherries are small, hard, poor in color, usually very acid. Overripe fruit is soft, dull in color, shriveled, and leaky. Avoid fruit with small brown circular spots.

Cranberries—They are usually available in large volume from September through January. Look for plump, firm berries with a lustrous color. Duller varieties should at least have some red color.

Figs (fresh)—Choose soft, fully ripe figs without bruises. Color and size depend upon variety. Ripe figs are very perishable and will sour and ferment quickly; this is indicated by the odor.

Grapefruit—Available all year with most abundant supplies from January through May. The russet on fruit does not affect the flavor. Grapefruit should be firm and springy to the touch, not soft and flabby. They should be heavy for their size. Decay is indicated by a soft, discolored area at bottom end of fruit. Fruit should be picked "tree ripe" and be ready to eat when purchased.

Grapes—To be served on the stem they should be firm and highly colored and the grape should adhere to the stem. To be used for juice ripeness is essential, but compactness or shattering from the stem is not important. Frozen grapes have poor flavor indicated by dullness, stickiness, and shattering from stems. Decay is indicated by mold, wet grapes, and stained containers.

Honey ball or Honeydew melon—Available to some extent all year long with the most abundant supply from July through October. Choose a melon with a light yellow rind which yields slightly to pressure. Dark sunken spots indicate decay. The flavor will be unaffected if the decay has not penetrated the rind. Greenish-white color and hardness indicate immaturity.

Lemons—Select heavy fruit with smooth-textured peel, rich yellow in color with a slight gloss. Avoid decay at stem end or soft, spongy lemons.

Limes—Select green, heavy fruit with a glossy peel. Surface blemishes do not indicate poor fruit. Yellow fruit indicates insufficient acid.

Oranges—Select firm, heavy fruit. Surface blemishes do not affect the quality of fruit. Avoid light, puffy fruit with badly creased peel.

Peaches—The "blush" (red color) on fruit varies according to the variety. Soft, creamy-to-gold undercolor of the yellow portion is a sign of ripeness. Firm-ripe, medium-to-large peaches are generally best and should be kept at room temperature several days until fully ripe, then refrigerated until eaten.

Pears—The most popular variety is the *Bartlett* available from August through November. Fall and winter varieties include: *Anjou, Bosc, Winter Nelis,* and *Comice.* These keep well in cold storage and are available from November through May. Choose firm, but not hard fruit, free from blemish, clean not misshapen, and for immediate consumption, fruit which is soft at base of stem. Wilted or shriveled pears indicates too-early picking and they will not ripen or have good flavor. Avoid fruit with a water soaked appearance.

Persian melon—Available in August and September. Resembles cantaloupe but is more nearly round and has finer netting. Look for indications of ripeness as described for cantaloupe.

Pineapple—Fruit is at peak supply in April and May, but also available during the year. Pineapple should be picked when hard (but mature) and allowed to ripen at room temperature before eating. A ripe pineapple has a dark orange-yellow color and fragrant odor and the eyes are flat. Select fruit relatively heavy for its size. If picked when too immature the fruit will not ripen. Immature fruit is dull and lifeless, often yellow in color with eyes poorly developed. Avoid bruised fruit. Pineapple looses moisture and shrinks in size if held too long. The color darkens and fruit decays rapidly. Decayed fruit looks dark at base or around eyes, has a sour odor, and mold. Light-colored area on side of

fruit indicates sunburn; such fruit will be hard, dry, and pithy.

Plums and prunes—Ripe fruit is plump and yields to slight pressure. Immature fruit is hard, shriveled, poor in color and flavor. Overmature fruit is soft, leaky, and insipid. Brownish color on side of fruit indicates sunburn resulting in poor flavor.

Quinces—Good fruit is hard, free from blemish and has a greenish-yellow color. Immature fruit is green and lacks flavor.

Raspberries, blackberries, dewberries, loganberries, boysenberries, etc.—Look for a bright clean appearance and a uniform good color for the species. Berries should be plump and tender, but not mushy, with no stems attached. Avoid leaky, moldy berries, also stained or wet spots on the container which are signs of poor quality.

Rhubarb—Choose bright, crisp, tender, thick red or pink stalks.

Strawberries—Available in limited supply in January with the supply increasing until fall. Strawberries are in best supply in May and June. Look for berries with bright red color and bright luster, firm flesh, and the cap stem still attached. Berries should be dry and clean. The medium-to-small berries have better eating qualities than larger ones. Avoid berries with large uncolored areas or with seedy areas, a dull shrunken appearance or softness. Avoid mold which spreads rapidly from one berry to another.

Tangerines—Available from late November to early March with the peak supply in December and January. Look for deep yellow or orange color and a bright luster as the best indication of fresh, flavorful fruit. Avoid pale yellow or greenish fruit and fruit with punctured and very soft spots.

Watermelon—Available from early May through September with peak supply in June, July, and August. Melon should be firm, symmetrical, have good color, a bloom on surface, lower side yellowish in color. Immature melon is hard, unripe in appearance, underside is white or pale green. Overmature melons are dull, lifeless, and feel springy to the touch. Misshapen melons are often of poor quality. Worm injury is shown as healed punctures or burrows. Decay occurs at the stem and spreads rapidly. Fresh-cut stems are often painted with copper sulphate paste to prevent decay. Decay at blossom end is shown by a flat, dry, leathery spot. Dark, sunken, watery spots on body of melon do not affect the quality if flesh is not penetrated.

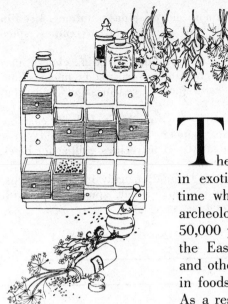

SPICES AND HERBS

The word "spice" to many persons conjures scenes of romance in exotic tropical places. It is, perhaps, difficult to imagine a time when spices and herbs were not so available as now, yet archeologists have determined that spices were known at least 50,000 years ago. In general, the more important spices come from the East—Ceylon, India, the Spice Islands (Bali, Java, Sumatra, and others). With the popularity of international travel, the interest in foods containing spices and herbs has increased tremendously. As a result many spices and herbs from all over the world are now readily obtainable.

Along with spices and herbs, seeds are also included in the chart on the following pages. Parts of plants which usually grow in the tropics are known as *spices*. The "parts" are in these forms: barks, dried leaves, seeds, berries, stigma, coverings. Red peppers, since they are grown in almost every country of the world, would be an exception to the grown-in-the-tropics rule. *Herbs* are leaves of plants grown in the temperate zone. *Seeds* come from either spice or herb plants. *Blends*, described below, often include both spices and herbs.

Spices and herbs should be marked with the purchase date before storing in a cool dry place and will remain fresh for a few months if kept in tightly closed containers. Test for freshness by sniffing the ground or crushed herb or spice. Since ground herbs tend to loose flavor and aroma faster than ground spices, many times it is advisable to buy herbs in leaf or whole form.

In adding spices or herbs to a recipe, if possible start with a tested recipe in order to become familiar with the flavors. Or, begin with ¼ teaspoon in 4 servings and then taste before adding more. When substituting dried herbs for fresh, use about ½ teaspoon dried leaf herb in place of 2 teaspoons finely chopped fresh herb. Crush or grind leaf herbs before adding, preferably to liquid called for in a recipe. Whole spices added to liquid should be tied in a small piece of cheesecloth or put into an aluminum tea ball for easy removal.

The chart is merely a guide for experimenting with spices and herbs.

BLENDS

Chili powder—Ground; usually including caraway seed, chili peppers, cumin, garlic powder, onion powder, oregano, black and cayenne peppers. Used in seafood cocktail sauces, cheese spreads, egg recipes, beef stews, ground meat dishes.

Curry powder—Ground; usually including cinnamon, cloves, cumin, fenugreek seed, black and red peppers, turmeric. Used in clam chowder, potato soup, egg recipes, lamb patties, curried dishes, scalloped tomatoes, butter for corn, French dressing, glazed apples, pickles.

Italian seasoning—Ground; usually including basil, marjoram, rosemary, sage, savory, thyme; sometimes cayenne pepper and garlic powder. Used in seasoning pizza, spaghetti sauces, Italian-style zucchini and eggplant, Italian salad dressing.

Mixed pickling spices—Whole; usually including allspice berries, bay leaves, stick cinnamon pieces, coriander seed, ginger root pieces, mace blades, mustard seed, black and white peppercorns, red peppers. Used in meat soups and stews, vegetables, sauces, pickling and preserving, relishes.

Poultry seasoning—Ground; often including all-spice, coriander, marjoram, black pepper, sage, savory, thyme, and sometimes rosemary. Used in fish, pork, poultry, and veal stuffings; biscuits to serve with poultry.

Barbecue spice—Ground; usually including chili peppers, cloves and other spices, cumin, garlic, paprika, salt, sugar. Used in barbecue sauces, meat, poultry, and fish recipes, salad dressings.

Lemon pepper marinade—Ground; usually including coarsely ground black pepper, garlic, dried lemon peel, monosodium glutamate, salt, sugar. Used especially with meats, fish, and shellfish.

Pumpkin pie spice—Ground; usually including all-spice, cinnamon, cloves, ginger, nutmeg. Used in pumpkin pie and other pumpkin recipes, spice cookies, gingerbread.

Salad seasoning—Ground; including cheese, garlic, celery, poppy and sesame seeds, monosodium glutamate, salt, spices. Used in salads and salad dressings.

Seasoned pepper—Ground; including coarsely ground black pepper, other spices, dried sweet peppers, sugar. Used in recipes calling for black pepper.

Seasoned salt—Ground; usually including herbs, monosodium glutamate, salt, spices. Used with meats, vegetables, sauces.

SPICES & HERBS CHART

Name	Form	Flavor and Aroma	Some Uses	Origin
Allspice	whole, ground	suggests cloves, cinnamon, and nutmeg	meat broths; stewed tomatoes; fruitcakes; pies; pickling recipes	Jamaica, Mexico, Central America, South America
Anise seed	whole, ground	sweet aromatic, licorice-like	cottage cheese; baked products: sweet breads, cookies, cakes; fruit cups and compotes	Spain, Mexico
Basil	whole	mild anise with slight mint aftertaste	vegetable soups; meat pies and stews; fish and shellfish recipes; vegetables: broccoli, green peas; grape jelly	United States, Northern Mediteranean area
Bay leaf	whole	pungent, aromatic	soups; beef stew; fish recipes; potatoes	Turkey, Greece, Yugoslavia, Portugal
Caraway seed	whole	tangy	cheese spreads; beef broth; baked products: rye bread, cake; beef stew; pork dishes; sauerkraut	Netherlands
Cardamom seed	whole, ground	aromatic; related to ginger	baked products: Danish pastry, coffee cakes, cookies; pies: apple, pumpkin; chilled melon; coffee	Guatemala, India, Ceylon

Cayenne pepper, see *Red pepper or cayenne*

Name	Form	Flavor and Aroma	Some Uses	Origin
Celery seed	whole	warm, slightly bitter taste	clam juice; tomato juice; oyster stew; rolls; fish recipes; potato salad; salad dressings	India, France
Chervil	whole	resembles tarragon and licorice	cream soups; omelets; salads	United States, France
Chives	fresh, freeze dried	in the onion family	egg and cheese dishes; green vegetables; green salads	United States
Cinnamon	whole (stick), ground	pungent and sweet	baked products: breads, cakes, cookies, pies; chocolate desserts; cooked apples and bananas; coffee and hot chocolate	Indonesia, South Vietnam
Cloves	whole, ground	very hot and aromatic	studding roast ham and pork; vegetables: beets, boiled onions, winter squash; desserts, especially chocolate; pickled fruit	Malagasy Republic (Madagascar). Tanzania (Zanzibar)
Coriander seed	whole, ground	wild, delicately fragrant; in the parsley family	baked products: banana bread, cakes, cookies; lemon meringue pie	Morocco, Romania, Yugoslavia, Argentina, France
Cumin seed	whole, ground	somewhat like caraway, strong	stuffed eggs; cheese recipes; pork and sauerkraut	Egypt, Morocco, Lebanon, Syria, Iran
Dill seed and weed	whole	aromatic, caraway-like	cucumber soup; stuffed eggs; veal and lamb recipes; fish sauces; cole slaw; macaroni; vegetables: potatoes, sauerkraut, squash; dill pickles	India, United States
Fennel seed	whole, ground	anise-like, aromatic	breads and rolls: fish, shellfish, pork, and poultry recipes; vegetables: tomatoes, zucchini; apple pie	India, Argentina, Romania
Fenugreek seed	whole, pepper	pleasantly bitter, curry powder-like aroma	custard; whipped cream; chutney	India, France, Lebanon, Argentina

Name	Form	Flavor and Aroma	Some Uses	Origin
Ginger	whole, ground	spicy sweet	soups; baked products: breads, cakes, cookies; meat, poultry, and fish recipes; beets; fruits: pears, rhubarb	Nigeria, Sierra Leone, Jamaica, India
Mace (outer covering of nutmeg)	whole, ground	nutmeg-like aroma but less sweet	fish sauces; pound cake; cherry pie	Indonesia, West Indies (Grenada)
Marjoram	whole, ground	sweet and spicy with slight mint aftertaste; may be substituted for sage	egg, lamb, and chicken recipes; green vegetables: lima beans, Brussels sprouts, peas	France, Portugal, Greece, Romania, United States
Mint	whole	strong, sweet aroma with cool aftertaste	lamb; vegetables: carrots, peas; green salads; frozen desserts; chocolate recipes	Belgium, France, Germany, United States (West Coast)
Mustard	whole, ground	sharp, hot, and pungent	egg and cheese dishes; meat, fish, and poultry sauces; salad dressings; pickles	Canada, Denmark, Netherlands, United States
Nutmeg	whole, ground	sweet, delicate aroma	chicken soup; vegetables: spinach, sweet potatoes; lemon sauce for desserts; eggnog	Indonesia, West Indies (Grenada)
Oregano (wild marjoram)	whole, ground	strong clove, slightly bitter	pizza; egg and cheese dishes; meat, fish, and pheasant recipes; vegetables: green beans, tomatoes, zucchini	Greece, Mexico, Dominican Republic, Turkey
Paprika	ground	sweet to hot	soups; eggs; fish, meat, and chicken recipes; vegetables; salads and salad dressings	Spain, Hungary, Yugoslavia, Morocco, Bulgaria, United States
Parsley	fresh, dried	sweet, spicy flavor	dips; soups; omelets; creamed dishes; sandwiches; salads; salad dressings	United States (Texas, California)
Pepper, black and white	whole, ground	black pepper is more pungent than white pepper, which is the core of a peppercorn	soups; meat, fish, poultry, and game recipes; vegetables; salad dressings; Christmas cookies	Indonesia, India, Brazil, Ceylon, Maylaysia

Name	Form	Flavor and Aroma	Some Uses	Origin
Poppy seed	whole	nut-like flavor	baked products: breads, rolls, cakes, cookies; broiled fish; noodle and rice dishes; vegetables: green beans, boiled onions, potatoes; salad dressings	Netherlands, Poland, Denmark, Sweden, Balkan countries, Turkey, Argentina
Red pepper or cayenne	whole, ground	very hot and pungent	eggs; meat; fish; vegetables; sauces	Japan, Turkey, Africa, Mexico, United States
Rosemary	whole	sweet, aromatic, piney	lamb, chicken, and shrimp recipes; vegetables: green beans, beets, cauliflower, eggplant, mushrooms, summer squash, turnips; fruit cups	France, Spain, Portugal, Yugoslavia, United States (California)
Saffron	whole	pleasantly bitter	breads; rice recipes	Spain, Portugal
Sage	whole, ground	fragrant, aromatic, slightly bitter	cheese spreads; tomato juice; pork and poultry stuffings; baked fish; salad dressings	Yugoslavia, United States
Savory	whole	warm, aromatic, and pungent	cheese spreads; soups; stuffed eggs; meat loaf; creamed sweetbreads; fried chicken; sauces; salads	France, Spain
Sesame seed	whole	nut-like when toasted	cream soups; baked products; chicken recipes; vegetables: asparagus, green beans, tomatoes; salad dressings	Nicaragua, Ethiopia, Egypt, Mexico, Guatemala, Brazil, Salvador, United States
Tarragon	whole	aromatic, bittersweet, anise-like	veal, chicken, fish, and shellfish recipes; celery root recipes; sauces; egg salad	United States, France, Yugoslavia
Thyme	whole, ground	strong, warm, clove-like	clam chowder; meat loaf; scallops; Creole fish, shellfish, and vegetable dishes; asparagus; salad dressings	Spain, France, United States
Turmeric	ground	warm and sweet; may be substituted for saffron	egg, chicken, fish, and shellfish recipes; rice and macaroni dishes; potatoes	India, Haiti, Jamaica, Peru

Bonus Chapter

MEAL PLANNING

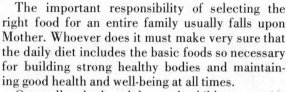

Good food and plenty of it—that describes briefly the food situation in these United States. We could boast and add that no country in the world has a better or safer food supply.

Physical growth depends upon many conditions, among them, fresh air, sunshine, adequate sleep, a happy home, and most important of all—the right food. Therefore, from the vast supply of foods available it behooves us to make the right choice.

The important responsibility of selecting the right food for an entire family usually falls upon Mother. Whoever does it must make very sure that the daily diet includes the basic foods so necessary for building strong healthy bodies and maintaining good health and well-being at all times.

Generally, both adults and children require the same kinds of food, which means that the homemaker can plan her menus for the family as a whole. The wise homemaker makes weekly rather than daily plans, always making sure the four basic food groups are well represented.

Fortunately, most of the everyday foods we eat have one or more of the necessary nutrients, but no one food will have them all in the right amounts. Therefore, to maintain a well-balanced diet, variety is of paramount importance. This can best be checked by putting your weekly meal plans in writing. A written menu plan also helps you make decisions more easily and to organize your grocery-shopping time and meal-planning time to greater advantage.

Individual food items which the homemaker includes in her daily menus depend to some extent on seasonal supplies available and how much money the family budget allows for food. Personal likes and dislikes as well as special dietary needs for certain members of the family are often considered, too. But for most families the most important consideration is a nutritious

and well-balanced diet. This is where *A Guide to Good Eating, page 727*, will be a helpful reminder to include the basic food in each day's menus.

Many families have a collection of favorite recipes for dishes which the menu-planner may want to serve rather frequently. If those dishes contain the essential nutrients this is permissible providing there is a wide variety in the other foods which accompany the favorite dish.

HELPFUL HINTS FOR MEAL PLANNING

• Keeping in mind the amount of money available for food in the family budget, make your meals as different as possible each week.

• Vary the methods you use for preparing foods. For example, since chicken is usually considered one of the most economical sources of protein, it is served often in most homes. So to avoid monotony, serve it broiled for one meal, fricasseed (with dumplings) for another, and roasted (with a flavorful stuffing) for still another.

• Introduce new foods with unusual flavors occasionally. Serve a new exotic dish to your family in small amounts. If it isn't well accepted the first time, try it again when everyone is very hungry.

• Use both tart- and sweet-flavored foods, hot and cold dishes, and soft- and crisp-textured foods in the same meal. With smooth-textured food (creamed fish, chicken, sweetbreads, etc.) serve something crunchy (tossed crisp green salad, fruit salad containing crisp apple, celery, and nuts, or

deep-fried corn fritters prepared with a crisp coating of crushed ready-to-eat cereal).
• Make use of the in-season foods when they are in plentiful supply and usually good "buys."
• Avoid serving too many foods at one meal. The most successful meals often consist of a few well-chosen dishes carefully prepared.
• Balancing the food budget usually involves using low-cost food items along with the more expensive. Use your imagination with low-budget foods and combine them with other foods in such a manner as to add an element of surprise to the meal.
• Add your own special touch to the dishes you prepare, but always encourage suggestions from other members of the family.
• Well-planned and well-cooked meals can be further enhanced with attractive, yet simple table settings. Add touches of brightness to the table with colored napkins, place mats, and centerpieces. (A potted plant can be used for a colorful centerpiece.)

A GUIDE TO GOOD EATING

MILK GROUP

Use daily: 3 or more glasses* milk — children and pregnant women; *4 or more glasses milk* — teen-agers and nursing women; *2 or more glasses milk* — adults.

These quantities of milk provide about three fourths of the day's calcium recommended for good nutrition. Milk is our main source of calcium in foods. For calcium:

1 slice (1 oz.) American cheese = ¾ glass milk
½ cup creamed cottage cheese = ⅓ glass milk
½ cup (¼ pt.) ice cream = ¼ glass milk

Milk also contributes fine quality protein, vitamins — especially riboflavin and vitamin A — and many other nutrients. For children, three glasses of milk supply two thirds to all the protein recommended daily and all the riboflavin. For adults, two glasses supply about one fourth the protein, about one half the riboflavin.

Skim milk lacks whole milk's fat and vitamin A (unless fortified); other food values are the same, calories less. One glass of skim milk plus 1 scant tablespoon of butter equals the food values of whole milk. Butter supplies milk's flavorful and easily digested fat along with its vitamin A.

Use milk as a beverage and in cooking — in hot cereals, milk soups, white sauces, puddings, and custards. Pour on fruit, cereal, and puddings. The combination of milk with cereal or bread is excellent, especially in meals where little or no meat or eggs are served. The proteins in milk make those in cereals and bread more useful in the body.

*A glass equals 8 ounces or ¼ quart of milk. Needs of some younger children may be met by a 6-ounce glass instead of an 8-ounce.

MEAT GROUP

Use 2 or more servings daily: Meat, fish, poultry, eggs, or *cheese* — with *dry beans, peas, nuts,* or *peanut butter* as alternates*

Use amounts of these foods to supply at least as much protein as that in 4 ounces of cooked meat (about ⅓ pound raw meat). Good practices to follow: An egg a day or at least 3 to 5 a week; liver, heart, kidney, or sweetbreads about once a week; other kinds of meat, fish, poultry, or cheese 4 to 5 or more times a week.

Foods in the meat group are counted on to supply about one half the protein recommended daily for good nutrition. Two servings for an adult might be, for example, one medium serving of meat (3 ounces, cooked) plus one egg. Choose combinations from the following which are about equal in amount of protein:

1 oz. cooked lean meat, poultry, or fish
1 egg
1 slice (1 oz.) American or Swiss cheese
2 tablespoons (1 oz.) creamed cottage cheese
½ cup cooked dried beans or peas

Eggs and meat, especially liver, are important for iron; also for B-vitamins. Pork supplies large amounts of the B-vitamin, thiamine. The legumes — dried beans, peas, nuts — are good sources of iron and thiamine, but their protein should be supplemented with an animal protein. *With dried beans, peas, nuts, or peanut butter, serve milk or cheese. The animal protein makes the vegetable protein more useful in the body.

VEGETABLES AND FRUITS GROUP

Use 4 or more servings* daily: Include a *dark green leafy* or *deep yellow vegetable* or *yellow fruit* at least 3 to 4 times a week for vitamin

A; a *citrus fruit, tomatoes*, or *other good source* of vitamin C every day.

Use fresh, canned, or frozen vegetables and fruits for variety as well as for their minerals, vitamins, and roughage. (Dried fruits are valuable for iron.) Serve potatoes frequently for all these food values plus food energy. Save food values and flavors of vegetables by cooking quickly in a small amount of water.

Foods in this group should supply over half the vitamin A and all of the vitamin C recommended daily for good nutrition.

Vegetables and fruits high in vitamin A:

apricots	all "greens"
broccoli	kale
cantaloupe	spinach
carrots	sweet potatoes
chard	tomatoes

Vegetables and fruits about equal in vitamin C:

¾ cup broccoli	½ grapefruit (¾ cup
1½ cups raw cabbage,	juice)
shredded	1 cup strawberries
½ large cantaloupe	2 medium tomatoes
1 medium orange (¾	(2 cups juice)
cup juice)	

*A serving is ½ cup or more.

BREADS AND CEREALS GROUP

Use 4 or more servings daily: Use *enriched* or *whole grain products*. Check labels!

Choose from breads, cooked and ready-to-eat cereals, cornmeal, crackers, grits, spaghetti and macaroni, noodles, rice, quick breads, and other baked goods if made with whole grain or enriched flour.

Foods in this group supply valuable amounts of protein, iron, several B-vitamins, and food energy. Cereals cooked and/or served with milk and breads made with milk are improved in quality of protein as well as quantity of protein, minerals, vitamins.

*A serving is 1 slice bread; ½ to ¾ cup cereal.

Additional Foods

The foods recommended form the foundation of a good diet. In general, use smaller servings for young children; larger servings may be needed by teenagers and pregnant and nursing women.

Most nutrient needs are met by the amounts of food suggested. Special attention must be given to food sources of iron for young children, teenagers, and women. Liver, eggs, meat,

legumes, dried fruit, dark green leafy vegetables, enriched or whole grain breads and cereals are good iron sources.

More food for energy—calories—is usually required. The amount varies with age, size, and activity. Food from the four groups helps to achieve an adequate diet. Calorie restricted diets can be pleasing and satisfying when energy comes mostly from foods in these groups.

Some source of vitamin D should be included for infants and children, pregnant and nursing women, and adults getting little sunshine. Good sources are milk, fish liver oils, and sunshine.

Courtesy National Dairy Council

SPECIAL-DIET NOTES

When a member of the family is ill at home or is convalescing after a period in the hospital, the doctor may prescribe a special diet for the patient. He will often suggest the menus and foods to be prepared. However, if he suggests a particular diet, such as a liquid diet, soft diet, etc., without supplying a list of foods to be prepared, the following diet classification will be helpful. But remember to consult with the doctor as much as possible about the foods you are feeding the patient. During the recovery period he may want to suggest changes from day to day, adding or omitting certain foods.

Liquid diets are usually prescribed at the beginning of an illness or when the patient is very weak or when there are digestive upsets. There are two degrees of liquid diets:

Clear liquid diet, which has little nutritive value, hence is a very temporary diet. Foods included are clear liquids (no food particles), fat-free broths (chicken, beef), tea or coffee with or without sugar but no milk or cream, occasionally clear fruit or vegetable juice or clear fruit-flavored gelatin dessert, or ginger ale as the doctor allows.

Full liquid diet is also temporary, supplying more nutritive elements than a clear liquid diet. Foods allowed may include strained fruit or vegetable juice, strained cooked cereal (oatmeal gruel), milk, buttermilk, eggnog, tea or coffee with or without sugar, cocoa, clear broths or strained cream soups, ginger ale, clear fruit-flavored gelatin dessert, vanilla cornstarch pudding, and frozen desserts.

Soft diet usually follows a liquid diet. It includes all foods on liquid diets plus cooked or canned fruits (no skins or seeds), bananas, applesauce, stewed apple slices (no skins), cooked or ready-to-eat cereals, enriched white bread, soda crackers, cooked macaroni or spaghetti (lightly seasoned), ground beef or lamb broiled, minced chicken or meat, occasionally tender chicken or fish, sweetbreads, soft-cooked or poached eggs, milk, light cream, butter, cottage or cream cheese, Cheddar cheese used in cooking, cooked vegetables, potatoes baked (no skin), boiled, mashed, and scalloped, fruit-flavored gelatins, plain or with cooked fruits, plain cookies, milk beverages, honey, jelly, and cornstarch pudding.

Light diet usually follows a soft diet. Foods allowed include any foods on the liquid or soft diet plus fresh citrus fruits, enriched whole-wheat bread, broths and milk soups strained or unstrained, tender beef, lamb, veal steaks or chops, bacon, tender chicken, sweetbreads, liver broiled, soft-cooked or poached eggs, tomato and lettuce salad, canned fruit and lettuce salad.

Serving Suggestions

Appealing meals served attractively in pleasant surroundings tell the patient that somebody cares and is giving him special attention. Meals with eye- and appetite-appeal may even aid in good digestion. Here are a few ways to show him you care:
• Understand fully just what foods the patient can and cannot have and the reason why. If you do not know, ask your doctor or a local hospital dietitian.
• Be pleasant but very strict about food gifts from well-meaning friends and relatives.
• Serve small portions to encourage eating.
• If the tap water in your community is distasteful to the patient because of heavy chlorination or other reasons, serve him bottled spring water and also use it in preparing his tea or coffee.
• Prepare or serve foods in bite-size pieces so that the patient has no difficulty in cutting.
• Serve foods, including liquids, in dishes that will not tip easily.

CHOLESTEROL IN FOODS

Dietary planning makes it desirable to know the foods which have the highest content of cholesterol and to avoid their frequent or regular use when low-fat, low-cholesterol diets have been prescribed.

Much research has and is still being done on fat and its use by the body. On the basis of our present knowledge, the cholesterol levels seem to have little relationship to the cholesterol content of foods. Apparently the body can make cholesterol from fat in the forms in which it is found in food.

Foods Lowest in Cholesterol

• All fruits are low in cholesterol; so are most vegetables. These foods should be prepared and served without butter, cream, lard, or suet. Usually small amounts of margarine, most vegetable oils, and mayonnaise may be used for flavoring.
• Breads and cereals are low in cholesterol.
• Skim or nonfat milk, buttermilk, and cottage cheese can replace whole milk and cheese.
• Use lean meats and fish.
• Marmalade, jelly, jam, syrup, and sugar (largely carbohydrate) may be used in place of fats unless calories and carbohydrates should be kept low.

Foods Highest in Cholesterol

Food	Mg. per 100 Gms.
Egg yolk, dried	2800-3900
Brain, beef	2235
Egg, whole, dried	2140
Egg yolk, fresh	2000
Liver, lamb	610
Egg, whole, fresh	495
Liver, pork	420
Kidney, beef	405
Liver, calf	360
Butter	280
Sweetbreads, beef	235-280
Liver, beef	260
Oysters	230-470
Cheese, American	160
Cheese, process American	155
Shrimp	150
Crab meat	145
Cheese, process Swiss	145
Heart, beef	145
Cheese, pimiento, cream	140
Cheese, Limburger	135
Beef, round, medium fat	125
Pork, spareribs	105
Beef, round, lean	95
Chicken, light meat	90
Sardines	70
Duck	70
Lamb	70
Veal	65-140
Pork	60
Chicken, dark meat	60
Salmon	60
Cod	50

Courtesy, in part, FOOD VALUES OF PORTIONS COMMONLY USED, *9th ed., publ. by J. B. Lippincott Co., Philadelphia, Pa.*

Bonus Chapter

LOW-CALORIE COOKING

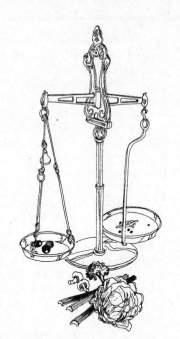

Y ou can be slim—and you can become slim without giving up the foods that are especially dear to your palate! In fact, if you *do* become slim without giving up the foods that you enjoy, without punishing yourself every day by going without what you like by sheer will-power, the pounds you lose are far less likely to come back once you have achieved your goal—because there is then no reason for you to heave a sigh of relief, relax, and go back to your old ways of eating just a little too much.

Over a period of years, it is quite possible for anyone to put on ten, twenty, thirty pounds by eating as few as one or two hundred calories too much each day—those extra calories may be accounted for by a bowl of rich cream soup, a Manhattan cocktail, or even by a serving of buttered young "non-fattening" carrots! In short, there's really a very small difference between the amount and kind of food that will reduce your weight, the food that will maintain it, and the food that will slowly but surely increase it.

These pages are not designed to set a pattern for your reducing—that is a highly personal problem that should be dealt with by you and your physician, who can tell you how many calories you personally need to achieve the weight that is right for you, and to maintain it, once achieved.

If you can cut out just fifty calories here, fifty calories there, a hundred calories somewhere else, and one drink-before-dinner, you have taken the first step toward losing those unwanted pounds. Remember, when more calories are taken in than the body needs, the extra energy is stored in the tissues as fat. When less food is eaten that is required for energy, stored fat is oxidized by the body and weight is lost.

Remember, too, weight lost gradually, a pound or two each week, is likely to stay lost because the dieting required to lose it need not be painful—and slow weight loss is usually more becoming, too.

HOW MANY CALORIES DO YOU NEED?

Calories are a measure of the units of energy which any food or beverage supplies when it is taken into the body. From the foods it consumes, the body takes enough calories to make the energy it needs for the day's activities—and that includes breathing and the beating of the heart, as well as work and play and exercise. The calories that are not converted into energy are stored in the body's tissues as fat. The theory behind every reducing diet is to supply the body with fewer calories than are needed for its daily energy output, thereby forcing it to spend each day some of its stored calories—its fat. It is safe to take about 500 calories a day from this stored supply. This means that, in general, a safe reducing diet will provide about 500 fewer calories than the body needs for energy.

How many calories is that? The answer is different for each individual. It depends on body weight, body frame, and activity. In general, you can calculate your calorie needs very simply. If you are a moderately active person, you need about fifteen calories a day to maintain each pound of body weight (slightly more or less depending on activity). Determine (from the charts on *page 731*) what your own ideal body weight is, for your height and your frame. Multiply that, the weight you want to achieve and maintain, by fifteen. Then subtract 500, the number of calories you want your body to draw from your stored fat reserve every day. The result is the number of calories which should enable you to lose your excess weight at a safe and reasonable rate of one pound per week.

Here's an example: You are a moderately active homemaker, age 30 to 35. You are five feet four inches tall. You have a medium frame—not very small- nor very large-boned. Ordinarily dressed, your best weight is about 135 pounds. So—

$$135 \times 15 = 2025 \text{ calories}$$
$$\text{less} \quad 500 \text{ calories}$$
$$1525 \text{ calories per day}—$$

is the number of calories which should enable you to bring your weight down to normal at the rate of one pound a week.

But—remember that losing weight is not the only consideration in planning a reducing diet. You also want to maintain your basic health, and you want to feel well while you lose weight. That means that you must choose wisely the foods for your reducing diet—foods which will furnish the building and regulating materials (proteins, vitamins, and minerals) that your body needs for health, without providing more than your requirement of calories.

Non-Caloric Sweetening Agents

These are available in solution (liquid), tablet, or granular form. The sweetening power of these products varies greatly, so follow manufacturer's directions for sugar equivalents and substitutions.

DESIRABLE WEIGHTS
(Weight in pounds according to frame in indoor clothing.)

HEIGHT (without shoes)	Small Frame	WEIGHT Medium Frame	Large Frame
WOMEN AGES 25 AND OVER (For girls between 18 and 25, subtract 1 pound for each year under 25.)			
4 ft. 10 in.	96-104	101-113	109-125
4 ft. 11 in.	99-107	104-116	112-128
5 ft.	102-110	107-119	115-131
5 ft. 1 in.	105-113	110-122	118-134
5 ft. 2 in.	108-116	113-126	121-138
5 ft. 3 in.	111-119	116-130	125-142
5 ft. 4 in.	114-123	120-135	129-146
5 ft. 5 in.	118-127	124-139	133-150
5 ft. 6 in.	122-131	128-143	137-154
5 ft. 7 in.	126-135	132-147	141-158
5 ft. 8 in.	130-140	136-151	145-163
5 ft. 9 in.	134-144	140-155	149-168
MEN AGES 25 AND OVER			
5 ft. 2 in.	115-123	121-133	129-144
5 ft. 3 in.	118-126	124-136	132-148
5 ft. 4 in.	121-129	127-139	135-152
5 ft. 5 in.	124-133	130-143	138-156
5 ft. 6 in.	128-137	134-147	142-161
5 ft. 7 in.	132-141	138-152	147-166
5 ft. 8 in.	136-145	142-156	151-170
5 ft. 9 in.	140-150	146-160	155-174
5 ft. 10 in.	144-154	150-165	159-179
5 ft. 11 in.	148-158	154-170	164-184
6 ft.	152-162	158-175	168-189
6 ft. 1 in.	156-167	162-180	173-194
6 ft. 2 in.	160-171	167-185	178-199
6 ft. 3 in.	164-175	172-190	182-204

Courtesy Metropolitan Life Insurance Company

COUNT YOUR CALORIES

FOOD	SERVING	CALORIES
Beverages		
Beer	12 fl. oz.	150
Cocoa, homemade	1 cup	245
Coffee (*no cream or sugar added*)	1 cup	0
Cola beverage	12 fl. oz.	145
Gin, Rum, vodka, whiskey (*86-proof*)	1½ fl. oz. (jigger)	105
Ginger ale	12 fl. oz.	115
Root beer	12 fl. oz.	150
Tea (*no cream or sugar added*)	1 cup	0
Tomato juice, canned	1 cup	45
Wine, table	3½ fl. oz. (glass)	85
Breads and Cereals		
Biscuits, baking powder	1, 2-in. diam.	105
Bran flakes (*40% bran*)	1 cup	105
Breads, rye	1 slice, ½ in.	60
white	1 slice, ½ in.	70
whole wheat	1 slice, ½ in.	60
Corn flakes	1 cup	100
Crackers, graham	4, 2½-in. sq.	110
saltines	4 crackers	50
Farina, cooked	1 cup	105
Macaroni, cooked	1 cup	190
Muffins	1, 3-in. diam.	120
Noodles, cooked	1 cup	200
Oatmeal, cooked	1 cup	130
Pancakes, griddlecakes	1, 4-in. diam.	60
Rice, cooked	1 cup	225
puffed	1 cup	60
Rolls, yeast, plain	1 roll	85
sweet	1 roll	180
Spaghetti, cooked	1 cup	155
Waffles	1, 7-in. diam.	210
Wheat, puffed	1 cup	55
shredded	1 biscuit	90
Confections and Sweets		
Chocolate, milk, plain	1 oz.	145
semisweet pieces	1 cup	860
unsweetened	1 oz. (1 sq.)	145
Coconut, shredded	1 cup	450
Corn syrup	1 tablespoon	60
Fudge (*without nuts*)	1 oz.	115
Honey, strained	1 tablespoon	65
Marshmallows	1 oz.	90
Molasses, light	1 tablespoon	50

FOOD	SERVING	CALORIES
Sugar, brown	1 tablespoon	51
granulated	1 tablespoon	40
confectioners'	1 tablespoon	29
Dairy Products		
Butter or margarine	1 tablespoon	100
Buttermilk, cultured	1 cup	90
Cheese, Cheddar	1 oz.	115
cottage	12-oz. pkg.	360
cream	3-oz. pkg.	320
Cream, half-and-half	1 cup	325
heavy	1 tablespoon	55
light	1 tablespoon	30
sour	1 tablespoon	25
Eggs, whole	1 medium	80
white	1 white	15
yolk	1 yolk	60
Milk, chocolate-flavored	1 cup	190
condensed, sweetened	1 cup	980
evaporated, undiluted	1 cup	345
nonfat dry (*solids*)	1 tablespoon	28
skim	1 cup	90
whole	1 cup	160
Desserts		
Cakes, angel food	1/12 of 10-in. cake	135
cupcakes	1, 2½-in. diam.	90
fruitcake	1 slice, ⅜ in.	55
pound	1 slice, ½ in.	140
sponge	1/12 of 10-in. cake	195
yellow, 2-layer (*without icing*)	1/16 of 9-in. cake	200
Cookies, nut brownies	1 brownie	95
butter	1, 3-in. diam.	110
chocolate chip	1 cookie	50
fig bars	1 cookie	50
vanilla wafers	2 cookies	45
Custard, baked	1 cup	305
Ice cream	1 cup	255
Pie, apple	⅛ of 9-in. pie	305
custard	⅛ of 9-in. pie	250
lemon meringue	⅛ of 9-in. pie	265
mince	⅛ of 9-in. pie	320
pecan	⅛ of 9-in. pie	430
pumpkin	⅛ of 9-in. pie	240
Pudding, vanilla	1 cup	285
Sherbet	1 cup	260
Fish and Shellfish		
Crab meat, canned	3 oz.	85

FOOD	SERVING	CALORIES
Flounder, cooked	1 piece, 4x3x¾ in.	80
Halibut, broiled	1 steak, 4x3x½ in.	230
Lobster, canned	3 oz.	80
Oysters, raw	1 cup	160
Salmon, canned	3 oz.	120
fresh, cooked	1 steak, 4x3x½ in.	205
Sardines, canned in oil	3 oz.	175
Shrimp, canned	3 oz.	100
Tuna, canned in oil	3 oz.	170

Fruits and Fruit Juices

FOOD	SERVING	CALORIES
Apples	1 medium	70
Apple juice, canned or bottled	1 cup	120
Applesauce, sweetened	1 cup	230
unsweetened	1 cup	100
Apricots, canned in syrup	1 cup	220
dried	1 cup (40 halves)	390
fresh	3 medium	55
Avocados	1, 3⅛-in. diam.	370
Bananas	1 medium	100
Blackberries, canned in syrup	½ cup	110
water pack	⅓ cup	45
fresh	1 cup	85
Blueberries, canned in syrup	½ cup	125
water pack	½ cup	45
fresh	1 cup	85
Cantaloupe	1, 5-in. diam.	120
Cherries, canned, tart red	1 cup	125
fresh	1 cup	95
Cranberry juice cocktail	1 cup	165
Cranberry sauce, sweetened	1 cup	405
Dates, pitted, cut	1 cup	490
Grapefruit, canned in syrup	1 cup	180
fresh	1, 3¾-in. diam.	90
Grapefruit juice, canned, unsweetened	1 cup	100
Grapes	1 cup (40 grapes)	95
Lemon juice	1 tablespoon	4
Lemons	1 medium	20
Lime juice	1 tablespoon	4
Orange juice, fresh	1 cup	110
Oranges	1 medium	65
Peaches, canned in syrup	1 cup	200
water pack	1 cup	75
fresh	1 medium	35

FOOD	SERVING	CALORIES
Pears, canned in syrup	1 cup	195
water pack	1 cup	75
fresh	1 medium	100
Pineapple, canned, crushed	1 cup	195
sliced (*and juice*)	2 small or 1 large	90
fresh, diced	1 cup	75
Pineapple juice, canned	1 cup	135
Plums	1, 2-in. diam.	25
Prune juice	1 cup	200
Prunes, cooked	1 cup	295
Raisins, seedless	½-oz. pkg.	40
Raspberries, black	1 cup	100
red	1 cup	70
Rhubarb, cooked (*sugar added*)	1 cup	385
Strawberries	1 cup	55
Tangerines	1, 2⅜-in. diam.	40
Watermelon	1 wedge, 4x8 in.	115

Meats and Poultry

FOOD	SERVING	CALORIES
Bacon, broiled or fried	2 slices	90
Beef, ground, broiled	3 oz.	245
rib roast	3 oz.	375
round, broiled	3 oz.	220
sirloin, broiled	3 oz.	330
Corned beef	3 oz.	185
Dried or chipped beef	2 oz.	115
Chicken, breast, fried	½ breast	155
drumstick, fried	2 oz.	85
canned, boneless	3 oz.	170
Frankfurters	1 frankfurter	170
Ham, smoked, roasted	3 oz.	245
Heart, braised	3 oz.	160
Lamb, chops, broiled	1 thick chop	400
leg, roasted	3 oz.	235
Liver, beef, fried	2 oz.	130
Pork, chops, cooked	1 thick chop	260
roast, oven-cooked	3 oz.	310
Sausage, bologna	2 slices, 3-in. diam.	80
Braunschweiger	2 slices, 2-in. diam.	65
pork links, cooked	2 links	125
Veal, cooked, cutlet	3 oz.	185
roast	3 oz.	230

Nuts

FOOD	SERVING	CALORIES
Almonds, shelled, whole	1 cup	850
Brazil nuts	5 nuts	140
Cashew nuts, roasted	1 cup	785
Peanuts, roasted, salted	1 cup	840
peanut butter	1 tablespoon	95

FOOD	SERVING	CALORIES
Pecans, halves	1 cup	740
Walnuts, chopped	1 cup	790
Preserves, Pickles, Relishes, and Condiments		
Chili sauce	1 tablespoon	15
Jams and preserves	1 tablespoon	55
Jellies	1 tablespoon	50
Ketchup	1 tablespoon	15
Olives, green	4 medium	15
ripe	2 large	15
Pickle relish	1 tablespoon	20
Pickles, dill	1 medium	10
sweet	1 small	20
Soups		
Beef broth	1 cup	30
Clam chowder		
(*Manhattan*)	1 cup	80
Cream of chicken	1 cup	180
Cream of mushroom	1 cup	215
Split pea	1 cup	145
Tomato	1 cup	175
Vegetable beef	1 cup	80
Vegetables		
Asparagus, canned	1 cup	45
fresh, cooked	4 spears	10
Baked beans, pork		
and molasses sauce	1 cup	385
pork and tomato sauce	1 cup	310
Beans, green or wax,		
canned	1 cup	45
green or wax, fresh,		
cooked	1 cup	30
kidney, canned	1 cup	230
lima, fresh, cooked	1 cup	190
Beets, canned	1 cup	85
cooked, diced or		
sliced	1 cup	55
Broccoli, cooked,		
whole spears	1 medium	45
spears cut in ½-in.		
pieces	1 cup	40
Brussels sprouts,		
cooked	1 cup (7 to 8 sprouts)	55
Cabbage, cooked	1 cup	30
raw, coarsely shredded	1 cup	15
Carrots, cooked, diced	1 cup	45
raw, whole	1, 5½x1 in.	20
Cauliflower, cooked	1 cup	25
Celery, raw	1 stalk, 8 in.	5
pieces, diced	1 cup	15

FOOD	SERVING	CALORIES
Corn, canned	1 cup	170
fresh, cooked	1 ear, 5x1¾ in.	70
Cucumbers, raw, sliced	6 slices, ⅛ in.	5
Lettuce, Iceberg	1 head, 4¾-in. diam.	60
Mushrooms, canned	1 cup	40
Onions, cooked	1 cup	60
raw	1, 2½-in. diam.	40
young green		
(*without tops*)	6 onions	20
Peas, canned	1 cup	165
fresh, cooked	1 cup	115
Peppers, green, raw or		
cooked	1 medium	15
Potatoes, baked	1 medium	90
boiled	1 medium	80
French-fried	10 pieces, 2x½x½ in.	155
mashed (*milk and butter added*)	1 cup	185
Radishes (*without tops*)	4 small	5
Sauerkraut, canned	1 cup	45
Spinach, canned	1 cup	45
fresh, cooked	1 cup	40
Squash, summer,		
cooked, diced	1 cup	30
winter, baked, mashed	1 cup	130
Sweet potatoes, baked	1, 5x2 in.	155
boiled	1, 5x2 in.	170
candied	1, 3½x2¼ in.	295
Tomatoes, canned	1 cup	50
raw	1, 3-in. diam.	40
Miscellaneous		
Barbecue sauce	1 cup	230
Cooking or salad oil	1 tablespoon	125
Gelatin, flavored	3-oz. pkg.	315
unflavored	1 env.	25
Malted milk powder	1 oz.	115
Pizza, cheese	⅛ of 14-in. pie	185
Popcorn, large kernel,		
popped (*with oil and salt*)	1 cup	40
caramel corn	1 cup	135
Potato chips	10, 2-in. diam.	115
Pretzels, twisted	1 thin	25
Salad dressing, French	1 tablespoon	65
mayonnaise	1 tablespoon	100
thousand island	1 tablespoon	80
Tartar sauce	1 tablespoon	75
White sauce, medium	1 cup	405

Courtesy, in part, U.S. Department of Agriculture

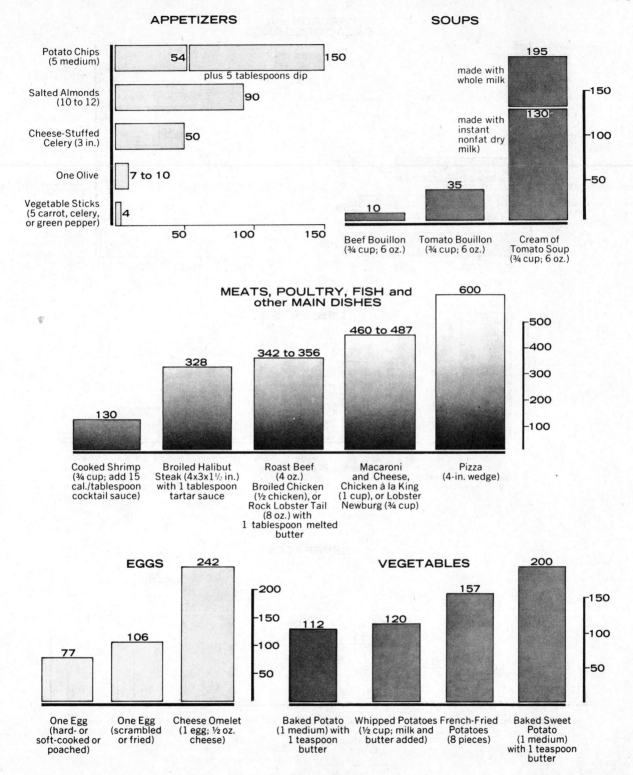

APPETIZERS

Potato Chips (5 medium) — 54 | 150
plus 5 tablespoons dip

Salted Almonds (10 to 12) — 90

Cheese-Stuffed Celery (3 in.) — 50

One Olive — 7 to 10

Vegetable Sticks (5 carrot, celery, or green pepper) — 4

50   100   150

SOUPS

195 — made with whole milk

130 — made with instant nonfat dry milk)

35

10

Beef Bouillon (¾ cup; 6 oz.)
Tomato Bouillon (¾ cup; 6 oz.)
Cream of Tomato Soup (¾ cup; 6 oz.)

MEATS, POULTRY, FISH and other MAIN DISHES

130 — Cooked Shrimp (¾ cup; add 15 cal./tablespoon cocktail sauce)

328 — Broiled Halibut Steak (4x3x1½ in.) with 1 tablespoon tartar sauce

342 to 356 — Roast Beef (4 oz.) Broiled Chicken (½ chicken), or Rock Lobster Tail (8 oz.) with 1 tablespoon melted butter

460 to 487 — Macaroni and Cheese, Chicken à la King (1 cup), or Lobster Newburg (¾ cup)

600 — Pizza (4-in. wedge)

EGGS

77 — One Egg (hard- or soft-cooked or poached)

106 — One Egg (scrambled or fried)

242 — Cheese Omelet (1 egg; ½ oz. cheese)

VEGETABLES

112 — Baked Potato (1 medium) with 1 teaspoon butter

120 — Whipped Potatoes (½ cup; milk and butter added)

157 — French-Fried Potatoes (8 pieces)

200 — Baked Sweet Potato (1 medium) with 1 teaspoon butter

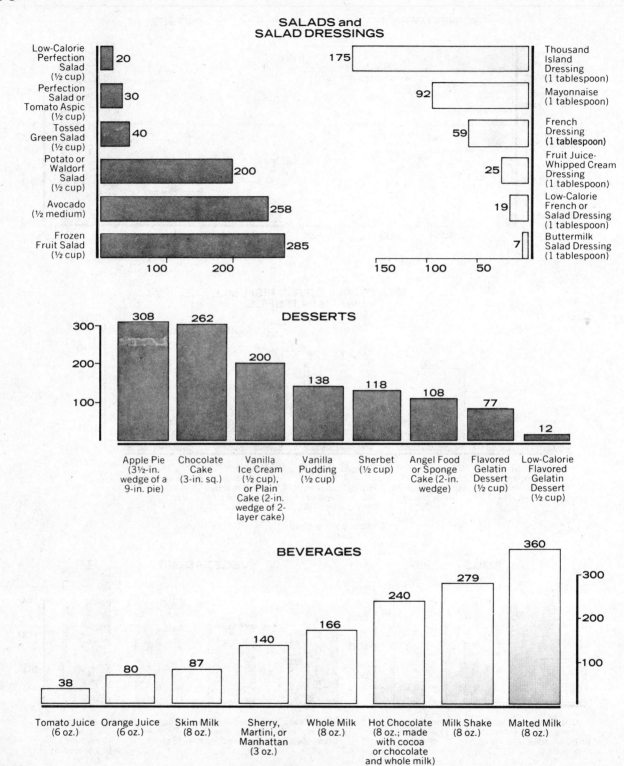

SALADS and SALAD DRESSINGS

Low-Calorie Perfection Salad (½ cup) — 20
Perfection Salad or Tomato Aspic (½ cup) — 30
Tossed Green Salad (½ cup) — 40
Potato or Waldorf Salad (½ cup) — 200
Avocado (½ medium) — 258
Frozen Fruit Salad (½ cup) — 285

100   200

Thousand Island Dressing (1 tablespoon) — 175
Mayonnaise (1 tablespoon) — 92
French Dressing (1 tablespoon) — 59
Fruit Juice-Whipped Cream Dressing (1 tablespoon) — 25
Low-Calorie French or Salad Dressing (1 tablespoon) — 19
Buttermilk Salad Dressing (1 tablespoon) — 7

150   100   50

DESSERTS

300   200   100

Apple Pie (3½-in. wedge of a 9-in. pie) — 308
Chocolate Cake (3-in. sq.) — 262
Vanilla Ice Cream (½ cup), or Plain Cake (2-in. wedge of 2-layer cake) — 200
Vanilla Pudding (½ cup) — 138
Sherbet (½ cup) — 118
Angel Food or Sponge Cake (2-in. wedge) — 108
Flavored Gelatin Dessert (½ cup) — 77
Low-Calorie Flavored Gelatin Dessert (½ cup) — 12

BEVERAGES

300   200   100

Tomato Juice (6 oz.) — 38
Orange Juice (6 oz.) — 80
Skim Milk (8 oz.) — 87
Sherry, Martini, or Manhattan (3 oz.) — 140
Whole Milk (8 oz.) — 166
Hot Chocolate (8 oz.; made with cocoa or chocolate and whole milk) — 240
Milk Shake (8 oz.) — 279
Malted Milk (8 oz.) — 360

LOW-CALORIE APPETIZERS & SOUPS

COTTAGE CHEESE DIP
(253 cal./cup; 6 cal./tablespoon)

1 cup (8 oz.) cottage cheese

2 tablespoons Low-Calorie Salad Dressing, *page 742*

3 tablespoons minced parsley

2 tablespoons finely chopped onion

2 tablespoons finely chopped chives

1 tablespoon prepared mustard

2 teaspoons crushed mint leaves

2 teaspoons dill seed

1 to 2 teaspoons prepared horseradish

Few drops Tabasco

1. Put the cottage cheese and salad dressing into a bowl. Add any *one* of the remaining ingredients. Beat together until light and fluffy.
2. Accompany with crisp *vegetables sticks or strips, cauliflowerets,* and *radish roses.*

ABOUT 1 CUP DIP

NOTE: Dip may be served in *Green Pepper Shells* or *Tomato Shells, below.*

GREEN PEPPER SHELLS: Rinse and cut a thin slice from stem end of chilled *green peppers.* Remove white fiber and seeds.

TOMATO SHELLS: Rinse and chill *tomatoes.* Cut a slice from tops, remove pulp from tomatoes with a spoon and invert shells to drain.

LOBSTER GUMBO
(106 cal./serving)

1 tablespoon butter or margarine

½ cup chopped onion

¼ cup chopped green pepper

1 clove garlic, minced

¼ lb. okra, washed, stems removed, and sliced (about 1 cup)

1 can (28 oz.) tomatoes, drained and cut in pieces

½ bay leaf, crushed

½ teaspoon salt

¼ teaspoon monosodium glutamate

¼ teaspoon pepper

¼ teaspoon chili powder

1 can (6 oz.) lobster meat, drained and separated

1 teaspoon filé powder

1. Heat the butter in a large heavy skillet. Add onion, green pepper, and garlic; cook, stirring occasionally, until onion is tender. Add okra, tomatoes, bay leaf, and a blend of salt, monosodium gluta-

mate, pepper, and chili powder. Cover; simmer 20 minutes, or until okra is almost tender.
2. Mix lobster meat into tomato mixture and cook, covered, 10 minutes, or until okra is tender and lobster is heated.
3. Remove skillet from heat. Measure about ⅓ cup liquid and mix thoroughly with the filé powder in a small bowl. Return mixture to skillet and blend thoroughly. Ladle gumbo into soup plates.

4 SERVINGS

NOTE: Filé powder should always be added after the mixture has been removed from the heat. If cooked, it will make the gumbo stringy and unpalatable.

ONION SOUP
(20 cal./serving)

3 cups beef broth (dissolve 4 beef bouillon cubes in 3 cups boiling water)

3 medium-sized onions, quartered and thinly sliced

⅛ teaspoon Worcestershire sauce

1. Prepare beef broth in a saucepan. Add the onions and Worcestershire sauce. Cover and simmer until onions are tender.
2. If desired, top each serving with *1 tablespoon shredded Parmesan or sharp Cheddar cheese.* (Add 28 calories to each serving when using cheese.)

4 SERVINGS

BOSTON CLAM CHOWDER
(61 cal./serving)
Potatoes and salt pork have been banished but the really important part of a fish chowder is the fish, which is fine low-calorie fare.

1 cup drained canned clams, cut in halves (reserve liquid)

½ cup chopped onion

½ cup diced carrot

½ cup water

¼ teaspoon salt

¼ teaspoon pepper

¼ teaspoon crushed thyme

2 cups skim milk

Chopped parsley

1. Pour ½ cup clam liquid into a saucepan. Add onion, carrot, water, and a blend of salt, pepper, and thyme; mix well. Cook, covered, over low heat about 20 minutes, or until vegetables are tender.

2. Add the clams. Gradually add the skim milk, stirring constantly. Simmer 5 minutes.

3. Garnish each serving with parsley. 6 SERVINGS

OYSTER CHOWDER (77 cal./serving): Follow recipe for Boston Clam Chowder. Substitute *oysters* for clams. Drain and pick over oysters to remove any shell particles. Use *oyster liquor* instead of clam liquid.

SQUARE-MEAL VEGETABLE-BEEF SOUP
(121 cal./serving)

1 tablespoon fat	1 cup fresh green beans,
1 lb. lean beef (chuck	cut in 1-in. pieces
or plate), cut in	¾ cup diced raw turnip
1-in. pieces	2 teaspoons salt
1 large soup bone,	¼ teaspoon celery salt
cracked	¼ teaspoon pepper
¾ cup chopped onion	¼ teaspoon mono-
2 qts. boiling water	sodium glutamate
1 cup sliced raw	4 cups canned tomatoes
carrots	with liquid, sieved
1 cup sliced celery	¼ cup chopped parsley

1. Heat the fat in a 6-quart saucepot or kettle. Add meat and brown on all sides.

2. Add the soup bone, onion, and water to the saucepot. Cover tightly and bring to boiling over high heat. Remove foam. Reduce heat and simmer 2 to 3 hours, or until meat is almost tender. Skim off any foam. Remove soup bone.

3. Add the remaining raw vegetables, salt, celery salt, pepper, and monosodium glutamate to the saucepot. Cover and simmer 30 minutes.

4. Remove from heat; set aside to cool. Skim fat.

5. Stir sieved tomatoes into soup along with parsley. Reheat soup and serve hot. 12 SERVINGS

CHILLED CUCUMBER-CHIVE SOUP
(77 cal./serving)

2 medium-sized	1 teaspoon salt
cucumbers	⅛ teaspoon pepper
2½ cups reconstituted	½ teaspoon paprika
instant nonfat dry	2 bouillon cubes
milk	3 tablespoons chopped
2 tablespoons flour	chives

1. Cut twelve ⅛-inch slices from one cucumber for a garnish. Place slices in a small bowl of ice and water and set in refrigerator. Shred enough of the remaining cucumber to yield 2 cups shredded cucumber.

2. Pour the milk into the top of a double boiler. Evenly sprinkle a blend of flour, salt, pepper, and paprika over milk. Beat with hand rotary or electric beater until just blended. Add the shredded cucumber, bouillon cubes, and chives.

3. Cook over boiling water, stirring constantly, about 15 minutes, or until bouillon cubes are dissolved and mixture is slightly thickened.

4. Cool; chill about 3 hours.

5. Garnish servings with the cucumber slices. 6 SERVINGS

CHILLED TOMATO BOUILLON
(36 cal./serving)

1 cup double-strength	1 teaspoon Worcester-
beef broth (dissolve	shire sauce
2 beef bouillon cubes	1 teaspoon sugar
in 1 cup boiling	½ teaspoon salt
water)	½ teaspoon monoso-
3 cups tomato juice	dium glutamate
½ cup chopped green	⅛ teaspoon ground
pepper	cloves
2 teaspoons lemon	Few grains pepper
juice	½ clove garlic

1. Combine all ingredients except garlic in a saucepan. Cover; simmer 6 to 8 minutes and strain. Add the garlic.

2. Cool; chill about 3 hours. Remove garlic before serving. 5 SERVINGS

JELLIED TOMATO BOUILLON (43 cal./serving): Follow recipe for Chilled Tomato Bouillon. While bouillon is simmering, soften *1 envelope unflavored gelatin* in ½ *cup cold water.* Stir into hot bouillon until gelatin is dissolved. Cool; chill until set, about 5 hours. Lightly beat with a fork before serving.

JELLIED CONSOMMÉ MADRILÈNE (50 cal./serving): Follow recipe for Jellied Tomato Bouillon. Substitute *chicken bouillon cubes* for beef bouillon cubes and increase water to ¾ cup and gelatin to 2 tablespoons. Omit Worcestershire sauce, salt, monosodium glutamate, cloves, pepper, and garlic. Add the lemon juice and *2 teaspoons Angostura bitters* after straining. Garnish servings with *lemon slices.*

HOT TOMATO BOUILLON (36 cal./serving): Follow recipe for Chilled Tomato Bouillon. Add the ½ clove garlic to the tomato juice mixture before cooking (do not add garlic after straining). Cover, simmer, and strain. Serve immediately.

LOW-CALORIE MAIN DISHES

BEEF RAGOUT
(206 cal./serving)

2 teaspoons butter or margarine	⅛ teaspoon ground thyme
1 lb. beef round steak, cut in 1-in. pieces	2 medium-sized carrots, cut in ½-in. pieces
1 onion, sliced	
1½ cups hot water	¼ lb. green beans, cut in 1-in. pieces (about ¾ cup)
½ teaspoon salt	
½ teaspoon monosodium glutamate	
⅛ teaspoon pepper	2 onions, quartered
¼ teaspoon basil, crushed	2 tablespoons tomato paste

1. Heat the butter in a large skillet or saucepot. Add meat and brown over medium heat on all sides. Add onion the last few minutes of cooking.
2. Add the water and a blend of the salt, monosodium glutamate, pepper, basil, and thyme. Cover and simmer 1½ hours. If necessary, add more hot water as meat cooks.
3. Add the carrots, beans, and onion to skillet; cover and cook 15 to 25 minutes, or until vegetables are tender. Blend in tomato paste.
4. Garnish ragout with chopped *parsley*. Serve immediately. 5 SERVINGS

VEAL RAGOUT (208 cal./serving): Follow recipe for Beef Ragout. Substitute *boneless veal shoulder* for round steak. Substitute ½ *teaspoon rosemary, crushed,* and ⅛ *teaspoon cayenne pepper* for basil and thyme. Add *3 tablespoons lemon juice* with the seasonings. Omit green beans. Add *1 medium-sized green pepper,* cut in strips, to vegetables with *1 cup drained canned sliced mushrooms.*

SAVORY PANFRIED LIVER
(187 cal./serving)

4 slices (about 1 lb.) veal or calf's liver, cut about ½-in. thick	½ teaspoon dry mustard
	¼ teaspoon pepper
	¼ teaspoon chili powder
¼ cup flour	
1 teaspoon monosodium glutamate	2 tablespoons butter or margarine
¾ teaspoon salt	

1. If necessary, remove tubes and outer membrane from liver. Coat slices with a blend of flour and seasonings.
2. Heat the butter in a large heavy skillet. Add liver slices and brown on both sides. Do not overcook. Place on a warm serving platter. Garnish with sprigs of *celery leaves* (from inner stalks).
4 SERVINGS

SUKIYAKI
(249 cal./serving)

1 tablespoon butter or margarine	1 medium-sized onion, quartered and thinly sliced
1 lb. beef round steak, cut in very thin strips about 2-in. long	
	5 green onions, cut in ¼-in. pieces
1 cup drained canned sliced mushrooms	1 cup chicken broth
	¼ cup soy sauce
1 can (5 oz.) bamboo shoots, drained and thinly sliced	½ teaspoon salt
	Non-caloric sweetener equal to 2 teaspoons sugar, see *page 731*
2 stalks celery, cut in 1-in. pieces	¼ lb. fresh spinach, washed and cut in large shreds

1. Heat the butter in a large heavy skillet. Add the meat and brown on all sides. Add mushrooms, bamboo shoots, celery, onions, broth, soy sauce, salt, and sweetener. Cover, bring to boiling and simmer, moving and turning mixture occasionally with a spoon, about 20 minutes, or until vegetables are partially tender.
2. Add spinach to the meat-vegetable mixture, partially cover skillet and cook, moving and turning pieces occasionally with a spoon, 5 to 10 minutes, or until spinach is just tender.
4 SERVINGS

LOW-CAL EGG FOO YONG
(52 cal./cake)

6 eggs	2 cups drained canned bean sprouts
¾ teaspoon salt	
⅛ teaspoon pepper	½ cup finely chopped onion
2 teaspoons butter or margarine	

1. Beat eggs, salt, and pepper together only until well blended.

2. Heat a large heavy skillet until just hot enough to sizzle a drop of water. Heat the butter in the skillet.

3. Mix vegetables with the beaten eggs. Spoon about ½ cup of the mixture into hot fat in the skillet and spread to form a round about 4 inches in diameter. Repeat using remaining mixture. Sauté until cakes are lightly browned on both sides, turning once. Drain thoroughly on absorbent paper. Serve with *soy sauce*.   ABOUT 14 CAKES

SALMON EGG FOO YONG (86 cal./cake): Follow recipe for Egg Foo Yong. Beat eggs with *¼ cup water*; sprinkle *6 tablespoons instant nonfat dry milk* over egg mixture and beat only until well blended. Mix *1 cup drained canned salmon*, flaked, with vegetables.

CRAB MEAT EGG FOO YONG (65 cal./cake): Follow recipe for Egg Foo Yong. Mix *1½ cups drained canned crab meat*, separated, with vegetables.

BEEF EGG FOO YONG (90 cal./cake): Follow recipe for Egg Foo Yong. Mix *1 cup cooked lean beef strips* with vegetables.

JELLIED VEAL LOAF
(109 cal./serving)

A cool, refreshing answer to the hot-weather meal problem, and one that gives calorie-counters lots of flavor satisfaction at low-calorie cost.

1¾ cups beef broth (dissolve 2 beef bouillon cubes in 1¾ cups boiling water)	1 tablespoon prepared horseradish
½ cup chopped onion	1 teaspoon salt
½ teaspoon celery seed	½ teaspoon monosodium glutamate
3 or 4 peppercorns	1 hard-cooked egg, chilled
4 teaspoons low-calorie lemon-flavored gelatin	2 cups ground cooked veal
	¼ cup finely chopped parsley

1. Prepare the broth in a saucepan. Add onion, celery seed, and peppercorns. Simmer over low heat about 5 minutes.

2. Strain hot broth over gelatin in a bowl and stir until gelatin is dissolved. Stir in horseradish, salt, and monosodium glutamate.

3. Chill until gelatin mixture is slightly thickened.

4. Meanwhile, cut 3 slices from the hard-cooked egg and arrange in bottom of a 9x5x3-inch loaf pan or 1½-quart ring mold.

5. Spoon a small amount of the slightly thickened gelatin mixture (enough to make a thin layer covering egg slices) over bottom of pan or mold. Chill until just beginning to set.

6. Blend the veal and parsley into remaining gelatin mixture. Chill if mixture has not thickened slightly. Spoon veal mixture evenly over first layer. Chill until firm.

7. Unmold loaf onto a chilled platter and garnish with parsley and *notched carrot slices*, or as desired.   ABOUT 8 SERVINGS

SHRIMP-STUFFED BAKED TOMATOES
(139 cal./serving)

4 large tomato shells	¾ teaspoon Worcestershire sauce
1 tablespoon butter or margarine	½ teaspoon salt
⅓ cup chopped onion	Few grains pepper
¼ cup chopped celery	¼ teaspoon thyme, crushed
2 tablespoons chopped green pepper	1½ tablespoons finely shredded Cheddar cheese
1 cup drained canned shrimp, chopped	
¼ cup soft bread crumbs	

1. Prepare the tomato shells, reserving the pulp. Do not chill the shells.

2. Heat the butter in a skillet. Add the onion, celery, and green pepper and cook until onion is soft. Remove from heat.

3. Combine the reserved tomato pulp, shrimp, cooked vegetables, bread crumbs, Worcestershire sauce, and a blend of salt, pepper, and thyme.

4. Spoon mixture into tomato shells, heaping slightly. Place in a 1-quart shallow baking dish. Sprinkle top of each stuffed tomato with shredded cheese.

5. Bake at 375°F 15 to 20 minutes, or until cheese is melted.   4 SERVINGS

SHRIMP-STUFFED EGGPLANT (125 cal./serving): Follow recipe for Shrimp-Stuffed Baked Tomatoes. Substitute *1 medium-sized (about 1 pound) eggplant* for tomatoes. Rinse and cut eggplant into halves lengthwise; cook, covered, in a small amount of boiling *salted water* about 10 minutes, or until just tender. Remove from water. Scoop out pulp, leaving a ½ inch thick shell. Finely chop pulp and mix with chopped shrimp mixture. Bake at 375°F 20 to 25 minutes.

SPECIAL STUFFED FISH
(177 cal./serving fish; 91 cal./serving stuffing)

3 lb. dressed fish
(striped bass or trout)
Pickle Bread Stuffing,
below

2 tablespoons butter
or margarine, melted
½ teaspoon salt
¼ teaspoon pepper

1. Rinse body cavity of fish with cold water, drain well, and pat dry with absorbent paper.
2. Rub the fish cavity with *salt* (about 2 teaspoons). Lightly spoon (do not pack) stuffing into fish. To close cavity, fasten with skewers and lace with cord. Put fish into a shallow baking dish and brush with a mixture of butter, salt, and pepper.
3. Bake at 350°F about 45 minutes, or until fish flakes easily when tested with a fork.
4. Remove the skewers and cord from the fish. Using two wide spatulas, carefully remove the fish to a warm serving platter.   6 SERVINGS

PICKLE BREAD STUFFING: Toss *2 cups soft bread crumbs, ½ cup minced sweet pickle,* and *1 tablespoon chopped onion.* Drizzle with a mixture of *3 tablespoons melted butter or margarine, 1 tablespoon lemon juice, ½ teaspoon salt, ½ teaspoon celery seed,* and *⅛ teaspoon thyme.* Toss until crumbs are coated.   STUFFING FOR A 3-POUND FISH

LOW-CALORIE SALADS & SALAD DRESSINGS

APPLE SLAW
(61 cal./serving)

3 cups (about ¾ lb.)
shredded cabbage
2 medium-sized red
apples, washed,
quartered, cored,
and thinly sliced
¼ cup undiluted
evaporated milk

2 tablespoons lemon
juice
1 teaspoon grated onion
1 tablespoon sugar
1 tablespoon celery seed
1 teaspoon salt
¼ teaspoon monoso-
dium glutamate
⅛ teaspoon pepper

1. Toss cabbage and apple in a large bowl.
2. Pour evaporated milk into a bowl. Gradually add lemon juice, stirring constantly. Stir in onion and remaining ingredients. Pour dressing over cabbage mixture and toss to coat well. Chill.
          6 SERVINGS

CABBAGE SLAW (39 cal./serving): Follow recipe for Apple Slaw. Omit apples. Toss with *green pepper strips.*

SUNSHINE SLAW (45 cal./serving): Follow recipe for Apple Slaw. Omit apples and celery seed. Toss *1¼ cups shredded carrots* with the cabbage.

RED 'N' GREEN SLAW (65 cal./serving): Follow recipe for Apple Slaw. Substitute *1 cup shredded red cabbage* for apples. Toss *⅔ cup drained canned unsweetened pineapple tidbits* with cabbage. Omit *celery seed.*

RED CABBAGE-PINEAPPLE SLAW (70 cal./serving): Follow recipe for Apple Slaw. Use *red cabbage.* Omit celery seed. Toss *⅔ cup drained canned unsweetened pineapple tidbits* with cabbage.

CRANBERRY-ORANGE RELISH
(254 calories; 8 cal./tablespoon)

2 cups (about ½ lb.)
fresh cranberries,
rinsed
1 orange, rinsed, cut
in eighths, and seeds
removed

1 apple washed,
quartered, cored,
and cut in eighths
Non-caloric sweetener
equal to 48 teaspoons
sugar (see *page 731*)

1. Force cranberries, orange, and apple through medium blade of food chopper. Lightly mix with the sweetener.
2. Spoon relish into a bowl. Chill, covered, at least 1 hour to allow flavors to blend.
          ABOUT 2 CUPS RELISH

TOMATO ASPIC
(53 cal./serving)

3½ cups tomato juice
⅓ cup chopped celery
leaves
⅓ cup chopped onion
1 tablespoon sugar
1¼ teaspoons salt
½ teaspoon monosodium
glutamate

½ bay leaf
2 env. unflavored
gelatin
½ cup cold water
½ cup cold tomato
juice
2½ tablespoons cider
vinegar

1. Pour the 3½ cups tomato juice into a saucepan. Add celery leaves, onion, sugar, salt, monosodium glutamate, and bay leaf; mix well. Simmer, uncovered, 10 minutes.
2. Meanwhile, soften gelatin in the cold water and tomato juice. Set aside.

3. Strain the hot tomato juice mixture into a large bowl and stir in gelatin. Continue stirring until gelatin is dissolved; blend in the vinegar.

4. Pour ⅔ cup of the mixture into each individual mold. Cool; chill until firm.

5. Unmold onto chilled individual salad plates lined with *lettuce*, if desired.   6 SERVINGS

PERFECTION SALAD
(12 cal./serving)

1 env. unflavored gelatin	Non-caloric sweetener
½ cup cold water	equal to 6 teaspoons
1 cup water	sugar (see *page 731*)
3 to 4 tablespoons	½ teaspoon salt
cider vinegar	1 cup diced celery
1 tablespoon lemon	¾ cup finely cut
juice	cabbage
	4 teaspoons chopped
	pimiento

1. Soften gelatin in cold water in a small saucepan. Stir over low heat until gelatin is dissolved. Remove from heat. Stir in 1 cup water, vinegar, lemon juice, sweetener, and salt. Chill until mixture is slightly thickened.

2. Stir in the vegetables. Turn mixture into a 1-quart mold. Chill until firm.

3. To serve, unmold onto a chilled platter.
          8 SERVINGS

LOW-CALORIE SALAD DRESSING
(306 cal.; 19 cal./tablespoon)

2 eggs	1 teaspoon monosodium
½ cup reconstituted	glutamate
instant nonfat dry	½ teaspoon paprika
milk (use double	½ teaspoon dry mustard
amount of dry milk)	¼ cup cider vinegar
2 drops Tabasco	

1. Slightly beat the eggs in the top of a double boiler. Blend in the milk, Tabasco, and a blend of dry seasonings.

2. Set over boiling water. Gradually add vinegar, stirring constantly. Cook and stir over boiling water until mixture thickens, about 10 minutes.

3. Remove from heat and cool. Store in a tightly covered jar in refrigerator.   ABOUT 1 CUP DRESSING
NOTE: For a less sharp dressing, decrease vinegar to 2 tablespoons and increase milk to ½ cup plus 2 tablespoons.

BUTTERMILK SALAD DRESSING
(59 cal.; 7 cal./tablespoon)

A light, zestful dressing, particularly good for tossed greens, citrus fruit salad, or slaw.

½ cup buttermilk	⅛ teaspoon dry mustard
4 teaspoons prepared	⅛ teaspoon salt
horseradish	Few grains pepper
1 teaspoon sugar	

Mix all ingredients thoroughly and chill.
          ABOUT ½ CUP DRESSING

CELERY SEED DRESSING
(53 calories; 3 cal./tablespoon)

1 tablespoon cornstarch	½ to ¾ teaspoon onion
1 teaspoon sugar	salt
1 teaspoon paprika	1 cup water
1 teaspoon celery seed	¼ cup wine vinegar
½ teaspoon dry mustard	

Mix in a saucepan. Bring to boiling; stir constantly until thickened. Chill; shake before using.
          1 CUP DRESSING

LOW-CALORIE FRENCH DRESSING
(350 cal.; 18 cal./tablespoon)

2 teaspoons cornstarch	Non-caloric sweetener
¾ cup water	equal to 2 teaspoons
¼ cup lemon juice	sugar (see *page 731*)
¼ cup ketchup	¾ teaspoon salt
2 tablespoons salad oil	½ teaspoon mono-
1 teaspoon Worcester-	sodium glutamate
shire sauce	¼ teaspoon pepper
	¼ teaspoon paprika
	¼ teaspoon dry mustard

1. Combine the cornstarch and water in a saucepan. Bring to boiling over high heat. Reduce heat and cook 5 minutes, or until mixture is thick and clear. Remove from heat and set aside to cool.

2. Add to cooled mixture the lemon juice, ketchup, oil, Worcestershire sauce, sweetener, and a blend of remaining ingredients. Beat with a rotary beater until smooth and well blended. Store, covered, in refrigerator. Shake well before using.
          ABOUT 1¼ CUPS DRESSING

GARLIC FRENCH DRESSING (18 cal./tablespoon): Follow recipe for Low-Calorie French Dressing. Cut *1 clove garlic* into halves, and add to completed dressing. Chill dressing about 12 hours to blend flavors. Remove garlic before serving.

LOW-CALORIE DESSERTS

LOW-CAL SOFT CUSTARD
(55 cal./serving)

2 eggs	⅛ teaspoon salt
Non-caloric sweetener equal to 8 teaspoons sugar (see *page 731*)	2 cups skim milk, scalded
	2 teaspoons vanilla extract

1. Slightly beat eggs with the sweetener and salt in a bowl. Gradually add the scalded milk, stirring constantly.
2. Strain mixture into the top of a double boiler. Cook over simmering water, stirring constantly, until mixture coats a metal spoon. Remove from water and cool to lukewarm over cold water.
3. Blend in the extract. Pour custard into 6 sherbet glasses and chill immediately. Or, chill and use as a sauce. 6 SERVINGS

BAKED CUSTARD (55 cal./serving): Follow recipe for Low-Cal Soft Custard. Strain egg-milk mixture, blend in extract and pour into six heat-resistant custard cups. Sprinkle tops with *ground nutmeg.* Bake at 325°F in a pan of hot water 30 to 45 minutes, or until a knife comes out clean when inserted halfway between center and edge of custard. Remove from water immediately. Serve warm or cold.

GRAPE SHERBET
(52 cal./serving)

1 env. unflavored gelatin	1 tablespoon grated lemon peel
½ cup cold water	Non-caloric sweetener equal to 24 teaspoons sugar (see *page 731*)
1¾ cups water	
2 cups unsweetened grape juice	2 egg whites
¼ cup lemon juice	¼ teaspoon salt

1. Soften gelatin in cold water in a small saucepan. Stir over low heat until gelatin is dissolved.
2. Meanwhile, combine the 1¾ cups water, grape juice, lemon juice and peel, and sweetener. Stir in the dissolved gelatin.
3. Pour into a refrigerator tray and freeze until of mushy consistency, stirring 2 or 3 times.
4. Beat egg whites and salt until rounded peaks are formed.
5. Turn mushy grape mixture into a chilled bowl

and beat until just smooth but not melted. Add beaten egg whites and beat until smooth. Return to refrigerator tray and freeze until firm. 8 SERVINGS

ORANGE SHERBET (37 cal./serving): Follow recipe for Grape Sherbet. Substitute *orange juice* for grape juice and *orange peel* for lemon peel.

PEACH SHERBET (29 cal./serving): Follow recipe for Grape Sherbet. Omit grape juice. Force *2 cups undrained canned low-calorie sliced peaches* through a coarse sieve or food mill. Mix the sieved peaches with water-lemon juice mixture.

CHERRY DESSERT MOLD
(66 cal./serving)

1 cup drained canned low-calorie light, sweet cherries (reserve liquid)	¾ cup water
	¼ cup lemon juice
	Non-caloric sweetener equal to 8 teaspoons sugar (see *page 731*)
4 teaspoons low-calorie cherry-flavored gelatin	

1. Add water, if necessary, to cherry liquid to make 1 cup. Heat to boiling. Pour over gelatin in a bowl and stir until gelatin is dissolved. Blend in the water, lemon juice, and sweetener.
2. Chill until gelatin is slightly thickened.
3. Halve and pit the drained cherries; set aside.
4. Blend cherries into slightly thickened gelatin. Turn mixture into a 1 quart mold. Chill until firm.
5. Unmold onto a chilled serving plate.
4 SERVINGS

RASPBERRY FOAM
(30 cal./serving)

¾ cup boiling water	1½ tablespoons lemon juice
4 teaspoons low-calorie raspberry-flavored gelatin	
	1 egg white
1¼ cups ginger ale	⅛ teaspoon salt

1. Pour boiling water over gelatin in a bowl and stir until dissolved. Blend in the ginger ale and lemon juice. Chill until slightly thickened.
2. Beat egg white and salt until rounded peaks are formed. Fold into the gelatin.
3. Spoon mixture into sherbet glasses. Chill until firm. 5 SERVINGS

Bonus Chapter

COOKING FOR ONE OR TWO

A career girl or another individual living alone and perhaps cooking her own meals for the first time in her life, or the newly-married working wife with little culinary experience, must both resist the temptation of planning everyday meals and putting them together in the quickest way possible, giving little thought to the nutritional value or the appetite- or eye-appeal of the food. Such haphazard planning can easily lead to poor eating habits with too much repetition and monotony in everyday diets.

Preparing meals for just one or two need never be an excuse for serving meals which are poorly balanced and lack variety. With all the fresh, frozen, and canned items available in today's markets one can purchase foods in almost any desired quantity. And besides, the freezer compartments of most modern refrigerators offer the lone individual every opportunity to prepare both normal and large quantities of wholesome, delectable dishes, some of which may be used immediately and the remainder divided into serving portions, wrapped for freezing, then frozen for future meals.

To help you plan well-balanced meals, here briefly are the basic foods to be included at least once a day in your menus.

Milk — a pint or more served as a beverage or used in preparing other foods.

Citrus fruits or tomatoes — both important for providing vitamin C in the diet. Also serve one or more of the other fruits — fresh, canned, or frozen.

A dark-green or deep-yellow vegetable — important as a source of vitamin A (serve not less than every other day). Also add other vegetables, including potatoes.

Protein foods — meat, fish or shellfish, poultry, eggs, cheese, etc.

Whole-grain cereal (enriched or restored) or some form of bread.

Fats — butter, margarine, cooking oil, or olive oil.

Desserts or a sweet.

The beginning cook, or for that matter anyone responsible for planning household menus, will find it a good idea to plan meals for an entire week rather than just one day at a time. As much as possible one should follow those plans regularly, although a few changes sometimes have to be made before the week is ended.

For the beginner, the following are basic meals included in the everyday diet with the essential foods to be included in each:

Basic Breakfast

Citrus fruit juice (orange or grapefruit), *tomato juice*, or a *fruit* in season (strawberries, cantaloupe, peaches, pears, etc.)

Cereal — cooked or ready-to-eat

Toast

Egg (3 to 5 times a week)

Beverage — milk, cocoa, coffee, or tea

The basic breakfast becomes a hearty breakfast or a Sunday or special occasion brunch with several additions and substitutions:

• Substitute for the plain toast — French toast, waffles, pancakes with maple syrup, or popovers with jam or jelly.

• Omit the cereal and, instead, serve panfried bacon or ham with eggs — scrambled or in a plain or fancy omelet.

Basic Lunch

Soup — hearty creamed vegetable type, served hot or cold

Sandwich — meat, cheese, or peanut butter
Fruit — banana, pear, peach, or other fruit in season
Beverage — milk, coffee, or tea

The basic lunch becomes a heartier meal with several changes such as:

• Add to the menu a fish, vegetable, or fruit salad on crisp greens.

• Omit the sandwich and substitute a hot dish such as baked beans with frankfurters, baked macaroni and cheese, or a hot meat, fish, or vegetable and rice casserole.

• Add crisp nibblers such as celery, carrot, or cucumber sticks.

• For dessert, serve cake or cookies with fresh, canned or frozen fruit, applesauce, or a fruit gelatin dessert.

Basic Dinner

Broiled or fried ground meat patties, *chops*, *fish fillets*, or *chicken*
Potatoes — mashed, baked, scalloped, etc.
Green or yellow vegetable, buttered
Dessert — ice cream with cupcakes or cookies
Beverage — coffee or tea

The basic dinner becomes a hearty family or special occasion dinner with the following substitutions or additions:

• Substitute for the plain meat patties a festive meatloaf (or ring) topped with tomato sauce.

• Serve broiled fish fillets topped with amandine sauce (slivered almonds lightly browned in butter) or lemon-flavored butter. Accompany the dish with broiled tomato halves topped with shredded cheese and buttered crumbs.

• Serve broiled lamb chops with broiled mushroom caps.

• Brush chicken while broiling with a flavorful marinade or barbecue sauce.

• Toss cooked green vegetables with herb-flavored butter or margarine or with almonds browned in butter.

• Substitute for plain ice cream a meringue-topped cream pie, a double-crust fruit pie, or a fancy refrigerator or frozen dessert.

Snacks

For many families a four-meal-a-day routine is a must. Active fathers and growing children require some snacks and pick-me-ups in addition to three basic meals. Here are a few between-meal and before-bedtime suggestions:

Cereal and nut mixtures such as *Crunchy Nibblers, page 40*
Cheese-stuffed celery, celery or carrot sticks
Pizza, hamburgers, cheeseburgers
Cookies, cupcakes
Assorted cheese and crackers
Popcorn, caramel corn, cereal balls
Milk, soft drinks

MENUS & RECIPES

The beginning meal planner (or any other meal planner, for that matter) might want to use several or all of the menus which appear here in her weekly plans. Recipes for particular dishes included in the menus follow with step-by-step directions for preparing each menu. Recipes in menus followed by a star (*) indicate that these are elsewhere in the book. Look them up by title in the index.

Many of the larger recipes in this book can be easily adjusted to serve one or two. For example, if the recipe is for 6 servings, use only ⅓ of the amount of each ingredient. However, try to avoid using recipes which call for hard-to-divide ingredients such as 1 egg white or 1 egg yolk. (To divide a whole egg into halves or thirds, beat the whole egg slightly before measuring.)

BREAKFAST
Broiled Grapefruit
Sausage Pancakes with Hot Maple Butter
Creamy Scrambled Eggs
Milk   Coffee

The How-To-Do-It Plan (*Follow steps in order*)
1. Prepare coffee (if percolated or filtered).
2. Prepare grapefruit halves for broiling.
3. Prepare maple butter and cook sausage for pancakes.
4. Mix ingredients for scrambled eggs.
5. Prepare pancake batter.
6. Start broiling grapefruit.
7. Bake pancakes and scramble eggs. Keep pancakes warm in oven and scrambled eggs warm over hot water while eating grapefruit.
8. Pour milk when ready to serve.

BROILED GRAPEFRUIT

Rinse *1 grapefruit* and cut into halves. With a grapefruit knife or sharp paring knife loosen sections; do not remove fibrous center. Spoon over each half *1 tablespoon sugar* (brown, maple, or granulated), *2 tablespoons crushed peppermint stick candy*, or *1 tablespoon honey or maple syrup*. Sprinkle a few grains of *salt* over each. Dot each half with *½ teaspoon butter or margarine*. Place grapefruit halves under broiler with tops about 4 inches from source of heat. Broil 8 to 10 minutes, or until very lightly browned around edges. (Overcooking may cause a bitter taste.) Garnish the centers with *fresh strawberries, cherries, berries,* or *mint sprigs.* Serve at once. 2 SERVINGS

SAUSAGE PANCAKES

¼ lb. bulk pork	¼ teaspoon baking soda
sausage	1 cup buttermilk
1 cup pancake mix	1 egg

1. Brown sausage in skillet; drain off fat.
2. Combine pancake mix and baking soda in a bowl, mix well. Add buttermilk, egg, and sausage; stir only until dry ingredients are moistened.
3. Bake on a hot, lightly greased griddle. Serve with *Hot Maple Butter, below.* ABOUT 6 PANCAKES

HOT MAPLE BUTTER: Combine *½ cup butter* and *¾ cup maple syrup* in a small saucepan. Heat and stir until butter is melted. Serve hot. ABOUT 1 CUP

CREAMY SCRAMBLED EGGS

3 eggs	¼ cup dairy sour
¼ teaspoon salt	cream
Few grains pepper	1 tablespoon butter or
¼ teaspoon prepared	margarine
mustard	

1. Combine eggs in a bowl with salt, pepper, mustard, and sour cream, mixing with a fork only until blended.
2. Heat butter in a skillet until melted and hot enough to sizzle when a drop of water is added. Pour in egg mixture; cook over low heat, lifting eggs from sides and bottom as mixture thickens; do not stir. Cook to desired doneness and serve immediately. 2 SERVINGS

COTTAGE CHEESE SCRAMBLED EGGS: Follow recipe for Creamy Scrambled Eggs. Add *⅓ to ½ cup creamed cottage cheese* and *¾ teaspoon minced chives* to eggs as they begin to thicken.

MUSHROOM SCRAMBLED EGGS: Follow recipe for Creamy Scrambled Eggs. Mix in desired amount of drained *canned broiled-in-butter mushrooms.*

LUNCH
Turkey à la King
Hot Baking Powder Biscuits*
Crisp Vegetable Relishes
Frozen Fruit Harmony*
Sherry Elegance* Imperials* Coffee

The How-To-Do-It Plan (*Follow steps in order*)

1. Prepare frozen salad and cookies several days ahead; prepare gelatin dessert a day ahead.
2. Prepare ahead and chill vegetable relishes such as carrot and celery curls, green pepper strips, and radish roses. Chill salad plates.
3. Prepare biscuits, using ½ recipe; cut out, arrange on baking sheet, and refrigerate until 20 minutes before serving time.
4. Assemble ingredients for Turkey à la King.
5. Start coffee (percolated or filtered), if serving with main course.
6. Prepare Turkey à la King and bake biscuits.
7. Put salad on plates shortly before serving.

TURKEY À LA KING

2 tablespoons finely	1 can (4 oz.) sliced
chopped green pepper	mushrooms, drained
1½ tablespoons butter	(reserve liquid)
or margarine	1 teaspoon grated
2 tablespoons flour	onion
¼ teaspoon salt	1 cup diced cooked
Few grains pepper	turkey
½ cup turkey or	1 tablespoon chopped
chicken broth	pimiento
½ cup milk	1 to 2 tablespoons dry
	sherry (optional)

1. Cook green pepper in heated butter in a skillet about 3 minutes. Stir in flour, salt, and pepper; cook until bubbly. Mix in broth, milk, and mushroom liquid. Bring to boiling; stir and cook 1 to 2

minutes. Mix in the onion, turkey, mushrooms, and pimiento; heat thoroughly. Blend in sherry.

2. Serve over *hot biscuits, cornbread, cooked noodles,* or *waffles,* or in hot *patty shells.*   2 SERVINGS

DINNER
Twosome Meat Loaf
Dilled New Potatoes
Zucchini and Tomatoes au Gratin
Tossed Green Salad   Tarragon French Dressing*
Hot Rolls
Vanilla Ice Cream   Almond Butterscotch Sauce*
Coffee

The How-To-Do-It Plan (*Follow steps in order*)

1. Rinse and chill salad greens well ahead of serving time. Prepare French dressing (or use a commercial dressing).
2. Prepare Almond Butterscotch Sauce ahead of time; heat just before serving.
3. Prepare individual meat loaves; place in preheated oven about 35 minutes before serving time.
4. Prepare potatoes for cooking; start cooking about 25 minutes before serving time.
5. Prepare Zucchini and Tomatoes au Gratin. Heat in oven with meat loaf about the last 10 minutes of baking.
6. Prepare coffee (if percolated or filtered).
7. Heat rolls.

TWOSOME MEAT LOAF

½ lb. lean ground beef	2 tablespoons sweet
½ teaspoon salt	pickle liquid (or
Few grains pepper	water)
⅛ teaspoon dry	1 tablespoon ketchup
mustard	1 tablespoon sweet
¼ teaspoon onion	pickle liquid (or
powder	water)
1 egg, beaten	1 teaspoon brown sugar
¼ cup uncooked rolled	
oats	

1. In a bowl lightly mix the ground beef with a blend of salt, pepper, dry mustard, and onion powder, the beaten egg, rolled oats, and 2 tablespoons pickle liquid.
2. Shape into two loaves and put into a shallow baking pan. Spoon a mixture of remaining ingredients over loaves.
3. Bake at 350°F 30 to 35 minutes.   2 SERVINGS

DILLED NEW POTATOES

½ lb. new potatoes	1 teaspoon dill weed
½ teaspoon salt	Few grains pepper
2 teaspoons butter or	
margarine	

1. Wash and scrape potatoes. Put into a saucepan with enough boiling water to make 1 inch in bottom of pan. Add salt, cover tightly, and cook about 15 minutes, or until tender. Remove cover and keep over low heat until all moisture is evaporated.
2. Add remaining ingredients and toss lightly.

2 SERVINGS

ZUCCHINI AND TOMATOES AU GRATIN

¼ lb. zucchini	½ cup cooked or canned
1 tablespoon chopped	tomatoes
onion	¼ teaspoon salt
1 tablespoon butter or	¼ cup shredded
margarine	Cheddar cheese

1. Wash zucchini and cut into ½-inch pieces.
2. Cook onion in butter in a saucepan until soft. Add zucchini and cook slowly 5 minutes, stirring frequently. Mix in tomatoes, salt, and a *few grains pepper;* cover and cook about 5 minutes.
3. Turn mixture into a greased baking dish and sprinkle cheese over top.
4. Heat in a 350°F oven until cheese is melted.

2 SERVINGS

COMPANY BRUNCH FOR SIXTEEN
Fruit Juices and Coffee
Glazed Smoked Ham
Skillet Roast Beef Hash with Eggs
Hot Bread Duo   Frosted Nut Bread Ring

NOTE: If a simpler menu is desired, omit the ham and rolls and accompany the hash and eggs with the nut bread ring or muffins.

The How-To-Do-It Plan (*Follow steps in order*)

1. A day in advance, bake and store the nut bread.
2. The morning of the brunch, put the ham in the oven *early* enough (about 3 hours in advance of serving) to allow for thoroughly heating and glazing.
3. Reconstitute frozen orange juice concentrate or orange drink and refrigerate it in pitchers. Empty cans of tomato juice or cocktail vegetable juice into a pitcher and refrigerate. Cut orange slices into quarters and lemons or limes into wedges for garnishing juice glasses; wrap and chill.
4. Prepare the hash and put it into a large skillet.

5. Prepare muffin batter and get crescent rolls ready for baking. Remove ham, reset oven control for muffins; after baking, reset for rolls.

6. Spread glaze over ham; set aside.

7. Put nut bread ring on a plate; frost.

8. After baking rolls, reduce oven temperature and return ham to oven; heat until glazed, about 45 minutes.

9. While hash is heating, prepare toast points; tuck in around hash. Fry eggs for topping and additional eggs to be kept hot in an electric skillet on table with hash.

10. Have freshly brewed hot coffee available throughout the morning.

FRUIT JUICES AND COFFEE

Set up a side table with a tray of garnished juice glasses and the pitchers of chilled *juices*, a shaker of *seasoned salt* and a bottle of *Worcestershire sauce* so guests can easily serve themselves. For those who like coffee before breakfast, keep a carafe of *water* boiling at this table. Accompany with a jar of *instant coffee*, teaspoons, cups, and saucers.

GLAZED SMOKED HAM

Place a 5- to 7-pound butt half of a fully cooked *smoked ham*, fat side up, on rack in a shallow roasting pan; insert meat thermometer. Heat uncovered at 325°F until thermometer registers 130°F (allowing 18 to 24 minutes per pound). About 45 minutes before end of heating period, trim and score fat surface of ham to make a diamond pattern. Spread with a glazing mixture of ½ cup firmly packed brown sugar, 2 teaspoons flour, ½ teaspoon dry mustard, and 1 tablespoon cider vinegar. Return to oven for about 45 minutes.

SKILLET ROAST BEEF HASH WITH EGGS

4 cans (15 oz. each) roast beef hash	½ cup chili sauce
1 cup sweet pickle relish	1 tablespoon prepared horseradish

1. Mix hash with a blend of pickle relish, chili sauce, and horseradish in a large bowl.

2. Turn into a hot skillet over medium heat, tossing gently until thoroughly heated, about 30 minutes. Spread lightly and evenly to sides of skillet.

3. Before serving, top hash with fried or poached *eggs* sprinkled with *paprika*. Surround hash with buttered *toast points*. Serve from skillet.

12 SERVINGS

HOT BREAD DUO

Team *muffins*, prepared from a mix and topped with finely chopped *nuts* before baking, with *crescent yeast rolls*, prepared from packages of refrigerated fresh dough. Before baking, brush crescents with *egg white* and *caraway seed*.

FROSTED NUT BREAD RING LOAF

1 pkg. (13¾ oz.) hot roll mix	2 cups water
1 pkg. (about 16 oz.) yellow cake mix	1 cup pecans, coarsely chopped
3 eggs	Mocha Frosting, *below*

1. Empty package of hot roll mix and its packet of yeast into a large bowl; mix. Add cake mix and blend thoroughly.

2. Add eggs and water. Using an electric mixer at medium speed beat 2 minutes. Stir in the pecans.

3. Turn batter into a well-greased 10-inch tubed pan. Using a spoon or spatula, gently pull batter from tube toward edge of pan.

4. Bake at 375°F 10 minutes. Reduce oven temperature to 350°F and bake 45 minutes, or until a cake tester comes out clean.

5. Remove from oven to a wire rack and allow to stand about 10 minutes before removing from pan to rack. Cool completely and store. Next day, frost top. If desired, garnish with chopped *candied fruit*.

ONE 10-INCH TUBED BREAD

MOCHA FROSTING: Following package directions, prepare about *½ package (13½- or 14-ounce) creamy white frosting mix or vanilla butter cream frosting mix*. Stir in *1 teaspoon instant coffee* until blended. For a thinner spreading consistency, mix in *2 or 3 teaspoons of water*.

The How-To-Do-It Plan (*Follow steps in order*)

1. Prepare bread pudding the day before serving; cool and refrigerate.
2. Prepare lamb for roasting; place in oven 3 to 3½ hours before serving time.
3. Meanwhile, prepare Orange Yam Cups and heat in oven with the roast about the last 40 minutes of roasting.
4. Prepare coffee.
5. About 25 minutes before serving time, start cooking the boil-in-a-bag vegetables for the All Green Vegetable Skillet. When vegetables are tender, continue with the preparation.
6. Meanwhile, prepare rolls using refrigerated fresh dough. After lamb and Orange Yam Cups have been removed from oven, increase oven heat to desired temperature and bake rolls. Keep Orange Yam Cups warm and allow roast to stand 15 minutes for easier carving.

DOUBLE BOILER
CHOCOLATE BREAD PUDDING

Refrigerating this pudding 1 or 2 days before serving permits flavors to fully mellow.

3 oz. (3 sq.) unsweet-ened chocolate	1 tablespoon vanilla extract
3 cups milk	2 eggs, beaten
¾ cup sugar	6 slices white bread, cut in small cubes
⅔ cup firmly packed brown sugar	2 oz. marshmallows (8)
½ teaspoon salt	

1. Combine chocolate and milk in a double-boiler top over simmering water. Stir occasionally until chocolate is melted. Mix in the sugar.
2. Meanwhile, beat the brown sugar, salt, and extract into the eggs until thoroughly blended. Add bread cubes and toss until thoroughly mixed.
3. Stir into chocolate mixture in the double boiler top and add marshmallows.
4. Cover and continue to cook over simmering water about 30 minutes. Stir until well mixed; cook, covered, an additional 15 or 20 minutes.

5. Remove from heat, stir, and transfer to a serving dish. Cool and serve warm or thoroughly chilled. Accompany with a pitcher of *cream* or a bowl of *unsweetened whipped cream*.

6 TO 8 SERVINGS

ROAST LAMB SHOULDER, COLORADO STYLE

1 boned shoulder of lamb (about 5 lbs.), rolled and tied	1 teaspoon salt
	1 teaspoon ground ginger
⅓ cup honey	½ teaspoon ground cloves
2 tablespoons lime juice	

1. Put lamb on a rack in a shallow roasting pan. Insert meat thermometer. Roast at 325°F about 2½ hours.
2. Remove from oven and drain off excess fat. Mix honey, lime juice, and a blend of salt, ginger, and cloves. Spread over roast lamb.
3. Return meat to oven and roast ½ to 1 hour, or until thermometer registers 175° to 180°F, basting frequently with pan drippings.
4. Remove from oven, and allow to stand 15 or 20 minutes before carving. 6 SERVINGS
NOTE: If desired, add a small amount of *water* to roasting pan over direct heat and stir until drippings are loosened. Blend in *1 to 2 tablespoons mint-flavored apple jelly*. Heat thoroughly; pour into a gravy boat and serve with the meat.

ALL GREEN VEGETABLE SKILLET

1 boil-in-a-bag pkg. (about 9 oz.) diagonally sliced green beans in butter sauce	¼ cup finely chopped onion
	¼ cup butter or margarine
1 boil-in-a-bag pkg. (about 10 oz.) lima beans in butter sauce	1 lb. (about 4 cups) sliced zucchini
	½ cup snipped parsley

1. Cook the green and lima beans following package directions. Do not overcook.
2. Meanwhile, cook onion about 2 minutes in heated butter in a large skillet. Add zucchini and toss until slices are well coated. Cover, and cook about 15 minutes, stirring occasionally.
3. Mix in parsley, and then the cooked green beans and limas with their sauces. Season to taste with *seasoned salt or pepper*. Spoon into a warm serving dish. 6 TO 8 SERVINGS

ORANGE YAM CUPS

3 medium-sized navel oranges	1 tablespoon dark brown sugar
2 tablespoons butter or margarine, melted	¼ teaspoon salt
3 tablespoons orange juice	1⅔ cups mashed cooked yams
	½ cup coarsely chopped pecans

1. Cut oranges into halves. Using a sharp paring knife, run it along the membranes of each orange section and remove pieces to a sieve set over a small bowl. Empty collecting juice into the bowl. Using scissors, snip membrane as close to peel as possible and discard. Set the orange cups aside.

2. Combine butter, orange juice, brown sugar, salt, and mashed yams in a bowl; blend thoroughly. Mix in orange pieces and pecans. Pile into orange cups.

3. Set close together in a baking dish or pan. Put into a 325°F oven and heat thoroughly, about 40 minutes. Serve with the roast lamb.   6 SERVINGS

QUICK-TRICK IDEAS

Here are suggestions for quick-and-easy dishes with flair and taste-appeal especially useful for career girls and working wives who wish to serve an occasional company meal after a "working" day when time for preparing the meal is of the essence.

electric blender container with ½ *pint dairy sour cream* and *salt* and *pepper* to taste. Blend until puréed and add *1¾ cups chicken stock* (or *broth*). Blend thoroughly. Heat in saucepan; do not boil. Serve hot, garnished with sprigs of *parsley or watercress*.   6 SERVINGS

SOUPS FOR TWO

TOMATO-VEGETABLE SOUP: Using *1 can (10¾ ounces) condensed vegetarian vegetable soup*, add *1 soup can water, ½ cup chopped fresh or canned tomato, 1 small clove garlic, crushed, ⅛ teaspoon oregano, 1 tablespoon butter or margarine*, and about *½ cup cooked elbow macaroni*. Heat thoroughly, stirring occasionally.

SPLIT PEA-TOMATO SOUP: Using *1 can (11¼ ounces) condensed split pea with ham soup*, add *1 soup can water, ½ cup chopped fresh or canned tomato*, and *2 tablespoons chopped green onion* cooked until tender in *1 tablespoon butter or margarine*.

BLENDER CREAM OF VEGETABLE SOUP: Put *leftover cooked vegetables*—carrots, peas, asparagus, spinach, etc. (about ½ cup)—into an electric blender container with *1 tablespoon flour, 1 cup milk or cream, 1 thin slice onion*, and *1 or 2 sprigs parsley*. Blend until smooth. Cook in a saucepan over medium heat until mixture comes to boiling. Add *1 tablespoon butter or margarine* and cook several minutes longer, stirring occasionally. Serve hot.

COMPANY CREAMY BRUSSELS SPROUTS SOUP: Using *1 package (10 ounces) frozen Brussels sprouts* (thawed and halved), combine in an

MAIN DISHES

JIFFY LAMB CURRY: Cook *1 medium-sized onion*, chopped, in *2 tablespoons hot butter or margarine* in a large heavy skillet. Stir in *2 cups cooked cubed lamb, 1 cup prepared mincemeat, 2½ cups water or chicken broth*, and *3 tablespoons lemon juice*. Bring rapidly to boiling. Add *1 package (6 ounces) curry-seasoned rice*; stir thoroughly. Cover tightly, reduce heat and cook 25 to 30 minutes, or until rice is tender and liquid is absorbed. Turn rice mixture into a bowl. Serve with bowls of chopped *filberts, green pepper*, and *coconut*.   4 TO 6 SERVINGS

INDIVIDUAL HAM LOAVES: Put *1 pound cooked ham*, ground, and *1 pound bulk pork sausage* into a bowl. Add *1 cup raisin bran flakes, 1 egg*, slightly beaten, *½ cup milk, 2 tablespoons chopped onion*, and *2 tablespoons chopped parsley*; mix lightly with a fork until blended. Divide into six portions and shape into individual loaves. Place in a shallow baking pan. Bake at 350°F 25 to 30 minutes; brush with *dark corn syrup* during baking.   6 SERVINGS

HURRY-UP HUNGARIAN DINNER: Combine *2 cans (24 ounces each) beef stew, 1 can (16 ounce) sauerkraut, 1 tablespoon paprika*, and *½ teaspoon caraway seed* in a large saucepan.

Bring to boiling; simmer, covered, 15 to 20 minutes. Blend in ⅓ *cup dairy sour cream* and heat mixture thoroughly. Meanwhile, heat *canned apple pie filling* to serving temperature. Arrange stew mixture on a large deep serving plate. Garnish with *parsley*. Accompany with a bowl of the warm apples to which *grated lemon peel* and *ground nutmeg* have been added.

ABOUT 6 SERVINGS

CRANBERRY-GLAZED CANADIAN-STYLE BACON: Arrange *10 slices (about 1 pound) Canadian-style bacon*, cut about ¼ inch thick, in a baking dish. Sprinkle slices with a mixture of *1 tablespoon grated orange peel*, ½ *teaspoon sugar*, ⅛ *teaspoon ground cloves*, and *few grains ground nutmeg*. Spoon *1 cup canned whole cranberry sauce* over bacon slices. Heat in a 350°F oven about 25 minutes; baste with sauce. 5 SERVINGS

TUNA-ZUCCHINI ITALIENNE: Combine *2 cans (16 ounces each) cut zucchini in Italian-style sauce* and *2 teaspoons cornstarch* in a saucepan, stirring until well blended. Cook over medium heat until mixture thickens, stirring occasionally. Mix in *1 can (6½ or 7 ounces) chunk-style tuna*, drained and separated; heat thoroughly. To serve, spoon mixture into the center of *Saffron Rice Ring, page 297*. ABOUT 6 SERVINGS

FLAVOR-RICH BAKED BEANS: Mix together *1 can (14 to 17 ounces) baked beans in tomato sauce*, ½ *cup gingersnap crumbs*, *2 tablespoons molasses*, *2 tablespoons ketchup*, 1½ *teaspoons instant minced onion*, and ¼ *teaspoon seasoned salt*. Turn into a small baking dish and top with *3 strips bacon*. Set in a 375°F oven 15 to 20 minutes, or until thoroughly heated. Set under broiler to crisp bacon. 4 SERVINGS

PANFRIED FISH: Thoroughly blend ½ *cup pancake mix*, ¼ *teaspoon pepper*, ½ *teaspoon onion salt*, and ¼ *teaspoon garlic salt*; evenly coat *8 cleaned small whole fish (3 to 4 pounds)*. Fry in hot *fat* in a heavy skillet until fish are golden brown on both sides and tender. Drain on absorbent paper. 4 SERVINGS

ADD FLAIR TO COOKED VEGETABLES
Plain old vegetables! Does that sound familiar? Don't let anyone say that about your vegetable dishes. Here are a few suggestions for adding variety to the vegetables you serve:

• Toss cooked green vegetables with *lemon butter* (melted butter mixed with lemon juice.

• Serve vegetables with this quick hollandaise sauce: Combine *3 egg yolks* with *2 tablespoons lemon juice* in a small saucepan; add ¼ *cup butter or margarine* and stir with a wooden spoon over low heat until butter is melted. Add a second ¼ *cup butter or margarine* and continue cooking and stirring until sauce is thickened. (Sauce also enhances fish, chicken, or eggs.)

• Hollandaise sauce becomes Sauce Béarnaise by adding the following: *1 tablespoon minced fresh parsley*, ½ *teaspoon dried tarragon*, and *1 teaspoon vinegar*. (Plain broiled hamburgers become something special, too, topped with this sauce.)

• Enhance cooked green, yellow, and white vegetables with a sprinkling of this crunchy topping: Toss blanched slivered *almonds*, small *bread cubes*, and coarsely crushed *corn flakes* (or crushed sesame seed crackers) with enough melted *butter or margarine* to coat the mixture well. This topping also adds enhancement to casserole dishes and broiled or baked fish fillets and steaks.

SALADS FOR TWO
ONE-TWO-THREE SALAD: Heat to boiling *1 can (12 ounces) cocktail vegetable juice*. Pour over *1 package (3 ounces) lemon-flavored gelatin* in a bowl; stir until dissolved. Stir in *1 can (10¾ ounces) condensed vegetable soup*. Pour mixture into individual molds or a fancy 3-cup mold. Chill until firm. Unmold on crisp *greens*.

MEAL-IN-ONE SALAD: Arrange *1 to 1½ cups cooked elbow macaroni*, ½ *cup diced cooked ham*, *1 cup diced cooked chicken*, and *1 or 2 ripe tomatoes*, quartered, on a bed of *lettuce* in a small salad bowl. Garnish with sprigs of *parsley* and, if desired, thin slices of *Spanish onion*. Season with *salt* and *pepper* and serve with *French dressing*.

WILTED LETTUCE-MEAT SALAD: Panbroil *4 slices bacon* in a skillet until crisp. Remove bacon from skillet and crumble; return *3 to 4 tablespoons fat* to skillet and set aside. Cut *3 ounces sliced salami* into julienne strips and put into a bowl. Add ½ *small head lettuce*, shredded, *1 tablespoon chopped onion*, *2 tablespoons crumbled blue cheese*, and the crumbled bacon; toss well. Mix *2 tablespoons cider vinegar*, *1 teaspoon sugar*, and ¼ *teaspoon Worcestershire* *sauce* into drippings in skillet. Heat thoroughly and pour over salad ingredients; toss until well coated. Spoon into two salad bowls and garnish with *thin onion rings*.

EMPRESS SALAD: Thoroughly chill salad ingredients before preparing salad. Toss *watermelon chunks*, *pear cubes* (unpared), *cucumber cubes*, and *escarole*, torn in pieces, with slightly sweetened *French dressing* (made with lemon juice, not vinegar) to coat evenly. Serve immediately.

TOSSED SALAD WITH COMICE PEARS: Fill a salad bowl with assorted crisp *salad greens* and short *green pepper strips*. Empty *1 jar chilled oil-vinegar-marinated artichoke hearts* over the greens. Just before serving, add chilled *avocado* and fresh *pear wedges*. Drizzle with an *oil-and-vinegar salad dressing* delicately sweetened with *light corn syrup*.

SPICED PEACH SALAD: Drain syrup from *1 jar (about 16 ounces) spiced peaches*; remove pits from peaches. Add *water* to syrup to make 1 cup. Pour *1 cup boiling water* over *1 package (3 ounces) cherry-flavored gelatin* in a bowl; stir until dissolved. Stir in the peach syrup and chill until slightly thickened. Spoon about 2 tablespoons into each of five ¾-cup molds. Place a peach in each mold and cover the fruit with remaining gelatin mixture. Chill until firm. Serve in *lettuce cups*.

COMPANY DESSERTS

SPARKLING STRAWBERRIES: Sprinkle *sugar* over whole fresh *strawberries;* chill thoroughly. To serve, spoon berries, including syrup, into sherbet glasses. Pour over berries a mixture of *4 parts chilled sparkling white grape juice* and *1 part grenadine*.

CREAMY CHEESE PERFECTION: Prepare *1 package vanilla pudding* according to package directions, using *2 cups milk*. Remove from heat and stir in *1 package (3 ounces) raspberry-flavored gelatin*. Slowly add ½ *cup milk* to *1 package (8 ounces) cream cheese*, beating until smooth. Add to gelatin mixture, beating until thoroughly blended. Chill.

CHERRY-CHOCOLATE ANGEL PIE: Prepare *Meringue Shell, page 459;* set aside to cool. Melt *4 ounces sweet chocolate;* cool, then blend in *3 tablespoons rum* and *1 teaspoon vanilla extract*. Whip *1 cup heavy cream* to soft peaks in a

bowl. Spread chocolate mixture over whipped cream and gently fold together. Turn filling into the cooled meringue shell. With back of a spoon, gently form swirls over entire surface of pie. Refrigerate just until thoroughly chilled. (Filled meringue shells tend to become soggy if chilled too long.) Garnish edge of filling with *maraschino cherries* having stems.   ONE 9-INCH PIE

CREAMY CHOCOLATE PUDDING: Prepare *1 package chocolate pudding* according to directions, using 1½ *cups milk*. Beat ½ *pint dairy sour cream* until it piles softly, beating in *2 tablespoons confectioners' sugar* and ½ *teaspoon vanilla extract* with final strokes. Fold into hot pudding and chill thoroughly. If desired, fold in ¼ *cup coarsely chopped walnuts* and ¼ *cup well-drained sliced maraschino cherries*.

ANGEL FOOD PARTY DESSERT: Prepare an *angel food cake mix* according to package directions. Beat *heavy cream* until soft peaks are formed, blending in *brown sugar* and *vanilla extract* with final few strokes. Fold in drained *crushed pineapple* and grated *unsweetened chocolate*. Split cooled cake into several layers and spread each layer with additional *sweetened whipped cream* and garnish the top with *unsweetened chocolate curls*, if desired.

Whipped dessert topping is used in these recipes:

SHORTCAKE: Buy or bake a *one-layer cake*. Divide layer in half, crosswise, and place one half on a serving plate. Spoon *fresh or well-drained canned fruit* (peaches, apricots, strawberries, raspberries, etc.) over top and cover with second half of cake. Spoon more fruit over all and cover with *whipped dessert topping* flavored with *almond extract*.

RICE PUDDING WITH PURPLE PLUMS: Blend *2 cans rice pudding* with *1 cup whipped dessert topping*. Spoon *canned purple plums* over individual servings of pudding. Garnish each with additional whipped dessert topping and a sprinkling of *ground cinnamon*.   8 SERVINGS

STRAWBERRY BAVARIAN CREAM: Whip *1 envelope dessert topping mix*, following package directions. Dissolve *1 package (3 ounces) strawberry-flavored gelatin* in 1¾ *cups hot water* in a bowl. Chill until mixture begins to gel. Fold in the whipped dessert topping. Turn into a 1-quart fancy mold. Chill until firm. Unmold on serving plate and garnish with additional *whipped dessert topping* and fresh whole *strawberries*.   4 TO 6 SERVINGS

Index

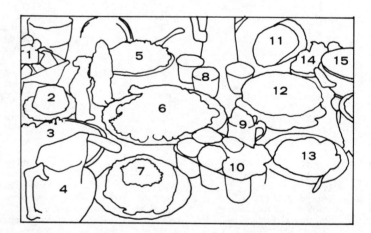

On the endpapers—A typical Pennsylvania Dutch Dinner might include these foods: 1) Rye Cakes and Norwegian Sugar Cake, 2) molded butter, 3) salad, 4) milk, 5) Paprika Cream Schnitzel and Shupp Noodles, 6) Pennsylvania Dutch Roast Chicken with potato balls, 7) German Noodle Ring, 8) Lemon Sponge, 9) Flash un Kas, 10) assorted relishes, 11) Moravian Scotch Cakes, 12) Frau Moyer's Cheese Custard Pie, 13) squash, 14) Blitzkuchen, and 15) Brown Flour Soup.